Contemporary Authors®

ISSN 0010-7468

Contemporary Authors®

**A Bio-Bibliographical Guide to
Current Writers in Fiction, General Nonfiction,
Poetry, Journalism, Drama, Motion Pictures,
Television, and Other Fields**

volume 209

GALE®

THOMSON

™

GALE

Detroit • New York • San Diego • San Francisco • Cleveland • New Haven, Conn. • Waterville, Maine • London • Munich

THOMSON
GALE

Contemporary Authors, Vol. 209

Project Editor
Scot Peacock

Editorial
Katy Balcer, Sara Constantakis, Anna Marie Dahn, Alana Joli Foster, Natalie Fulkerson, Arlene M. Johnson, Michelle Kazensky, Julie Keppen, Jennifer Kilian, Joshua Kondek, Lisa Kumar, Thomas McMahon, Jenai A. Mynatt, Judith L. Pyko, Mary Ruby, Lemma Shomali, Susan Strickland, Anita Sundaresan, Maikue Vang, Tracey Watson, Denay L. Wilding, Thomas Wiloch, Emiene Shija Wright

Research
Tamara C. Nott, Sarah Genik, Nicodemus Ford, Michelle Campbell

Permissions
Lori Hines

Imaging and Multimedia
Dean Dauphinais, Robert Duncan, Leitha Etheridge-Sims, Mary K. Grimes, Lezlie Light, Dan Newell, David G. Oblender, Christine O'Bryan, Kelly A. Quin, Luke Rademacher

Composition and Electronic Capture
Carolyn A. Roney

Manufacturing
Stacy L. Melson

LIBRARY OF CONGRESS CATALOG CARD NUMBER 62-52046

ISBN 0-7876-5202-4
ISSN 0010-7468

Printed in the United States of America
10 9 8 7 6 5 4 3 2 1

Contents

Indexing note: All *Contemporary Authors* entries are indexed in the *Contemporary Authors* cumulative index, which is published separately and distributed twice a year.

As always, the most recent Contemporary Authors cumulative index continues to be the user's guide to the location of an individual author's listing.

Preface

Contemporary Authors (*CA*) provides information on approximately 115,000 writers in a wide range of media, including:

- Current writers of fiction, nonfiction, poetry, and drama whose works have been issued by commercial publishers, risk publishers, or university presses (authors whose books have been published only by known vanity or author-subsidized firms are ordinarily not included)

- Prominent print and broadcast journalists, editors, photojournalists, syndicated cartoonists, graphic novelists, screenwriters, television scriptwriters, and other media people

- Notable international authors

- Literary greats of the early twentieth century whose works are popular in today's high school and college curriculums and continue to elicit critical attention

A *CA* listing entails no charge or obligation. Authors are included on the basis of the above criteria and their interest to *CA* users. Sources of potential listees include trade periodicals, publishers' catalogs, librarians, and other users of the series.

How to Get the Most out of *CA*: Use the Index

The key to locating an author's most recent entry is the *CA* cumulative index, which is published separately and distributed twice a year. It provides access to *all* entries in *CA* and *Contemporary Authors New Revision Series* (*CANR*). Always consult the latest index to find an author's most recent entry.

For the convenience of users, the *CA* cumulative index also includes references to all entries in these Gale literary series: *Authors and Artists for Young Adults, Authors in the News, Bestsellers, Black Literature Criticism, Black Literature Criticism Supplement, Black Writers, Children's Literature Review, Concise Dictionary of American Literary Biography, Concise Dictionary of British Literary Biography, Contemporary Authors Autobiography Series, Contemporary Authors Bibliographical Series, Contemporary Dramatists, Contemporary Literary Criticism, Contemporary Novelists, Contemporary Poets, Contemporary Popular Writers, Contemporary Southern Writers, Contemporary Women Poets, Dictionary of Literary Biography, Dictionary of Literary Biography Documentary Series, Dictionary of Literary Biography Yearbook, DISCovering Authors, DISCovering Authors: British, DISCovering Authors: Canadian, DISCovering Authors: Modules* (including modules for Dramatists, Most-Studied Authors, Multicultural Authors, Novelists, Poets, and Popular/Genre Authors), *DISCovering Authors 3.0, Drama Criticism, Drama for Students, Feminist Writers, Hispanic Literature Criticism, Hispanic Writers, Junior DISCovering Authors, Major Authors and Illustrators for Children and Young Adults, Major 20th-Century Writers, Native North American Literature, Novels for Students, Poetry Criticism, Poetry for Students, Short Stories for Students, Short Story Criticism, Something about the Author, Something about the Author Autobiography Series, St. James Guide to Children's Writers, St. James Guide to Crime & Mystery Writers, St. James Guide to Fantasy Writers, St. James Guide to Horror, Ghost & Gothic Writers, St. James Guide to Science Fiction Writers, St. James Guide to Young Adult Writers, Twentieth-Century Literary Criticism, 20th Century Romance and Historical Writers, World Literature Criticism,* and *Yesterday's Authors of Books for Children.*

A Sample Index Entry:

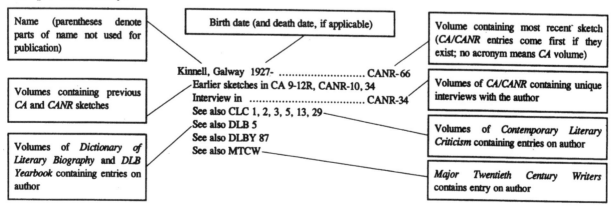

Name (parentheses denote parts of name not used for publication)

Birth date (and death date, if applicable)

Volume containing most recent sketch (*CA/CANR* entries come first if they exist; no acronym means *CA* volume)

Volumes containing previous *CA* and *CANR* sketches

Volumes of *Dictionary of Literary Biography* and *DLB Yearbook* containing entries on author

Kinnell, Galway 1927- CANR-66
Earlier sketches in CA 9-12R, CANR-10, 34
Interview in CANR-34
See also CLC 1, 2, 3, 5, 13, 29
See also DLB 5
See also DLBY 87
See also MTCW

Volumes of *CA/CANR* containing unique interviews with the author

Volumes of *Contemporary Literary Criticism* containing entries on author

Major Twentieth Century Writers contains entry on author

How Are Entries Compiled?

The editors make every effort to secure new information directly from the authors; listees' responses to our questionnaires and query letters provide most of the information featured in *CA*. For deceased writers, or those who fail to reply to requests for data, we consult other reliable biographical sources, such as those indexed in Gale's *Biography and Genealogy Master Index*, and bibliographical sources, including *National Union Catalog, LC MARC,* and *British National Bibliography.* Further details come from published interviews, feature stories, and book reviews, as well as information supplied by the authors' publishers and agents.

An asterisk (*) at the end of a sketch indicates that the listing has been compiled from secondary sources believed to be reliable but has not been personally verified for this edition by the author sketched.

What Kinds of Information Does An Entry Provide?

Sketches in *CA* contain the following biographical and bibliographical information:

- **Entry heading:** the most complete form of author's name, plus any pseudonyms or name variations used for writing

- **Personal information:** author's date and place of birth, family data, ethnicity, educational background, political and religious affiliations, and hobbies and leisure interests

- **Addresses:** author's home, office, or agent's addresses, plus e-mail and fax numbers, as available

- **Career summary:** name of employer, position, and dates held for each career post; resume of other vocational achievements; military service

- **Membership information:** professional, civic, and other association memberships and any official posts held

- **Awards and honors:** military and civic citations, major prizes and nominations, fellowships, grants, and honorary degrees

- **Writings:** a comprehensive, chronological list of titles, publishers, dates of original publication and revised editions, and production information for plays, television scripts, and screenplays

- **Adaptations:** a list of films, plays, and other media which have been adapted from the author's work

- **Work in progress:** current or planned projects, with dates of completion and/or publication, and expected publisher, when known

- **Sidelights:** a biographical portrait of the author's development; information about the critical reception of the author's works; revealing comments, often by the author, on personal interests, aspirations, motivations, and thoughts on writing

- **Interview:** a one-on-one discussion with authors conducted especially for *CA*, offering insight into authors' thoughts about their craft

- **Autobiographical essay:** an original essay written by noted authors for *CA*, a forum in which writers may present themselves, on their own terms, to their audience

- **Photographs:** portraits and personal photographs of notable authors

- **Biographical and critical sources:** a list of books and periodicals in which additional information on an author's life and/or writings appears

- **Obituary Notices** in *CA* provide date and place of birth as well as death information about authors whose full-length sketches appeared in the series before their deaths. The entries also summarize the authors' careers and writings and list other sources of biographical and death information.

Related Titles in the *CA* Series

Contemporary Authors Autobiography Series complements *CA* original and revised volumes with specially commissioned autobiographical essays by important current authors, illustrated with personal photographs they provide. Common topics include their motivations for writing, the people and experiences that shaped their careers, the rewards they derive from their work, and their impressions of the current literary scene.

Contemporary Authors Bibliographical Series surveys writings by and about important American authors since World War II. Each volume concentrates on a specific genre and features approximately ten writers; entries list works written by and about the author and contain a bibliographical essay discussing the merits and deficiencies of major critical and scholarly studies in detail.

Available in Electronic Formats

GaleNet. *CA* is available on a subscription basis through GaleNet, an online information resource that features an easy-to-use end-user interface, powerful search capabilities, and ease of access through the World-Wide Web. For more information, call 1-800-877-GALE.

Licensing. *CA* is available for licensing. The complete database is provided in a fielded format and is deliverable on such media as disk, CD-ROM, or tape. For more information, contact Gale's Business Development Group at 1-800-877-GALE, or visit us on our website at www.galegroup.com/bizdev.

Suggestions Are Welcome

The editors welcome comments and suggestions from users on any aspect of the *CA* series. If readers would like to recommend authors for inclusion in future volumes of the series, they are cordially invited to write the Editors at *Contemporary Authors*, Gale Group, 27500 Drake Rd., Farmington Hills, MI 48331-3535; or call at 1-248-699-4253; or fax at 1-248-699-8054.

Contemporary Authors Product Advisory Board

The editors of *Contemporary Authors* are dedicated to maintaining a high standard of excellence by publishing comprehensive, accurate, and highly readable entries on a wide array of writers. In addition to the quality of the content, the editors take pride in the graphic design of the series, which is intended to be orderly yet inviting, allowing readers to utilize the pages of *CA* easily and with efficiency. Despite the longevity of the *CA* print series, and the success of its format, we are mindful that the vitality of a literary reference product is dependent on its ability to serve its users over time. As literature, and attitudes about literature, constantly evolve, so do the reference needs of students, teachers, scholars, journalists, researchers, and book club members. To be certain that we continue to keep pace with the expectations of our customers, the editors of *CA* listen carefully to their comments regarding the value, utility, and quality of the series. Librarians, who have firsthand knowledge of the needs of library users, are a valuable resource for us. The *Contemporary Authors* Product Advisory Board, made up of school, public, and academic librarians, is a forum to promote focused feedback about *CA* on a regular basis. The seven-member advisory board includes the following individuals, whom the editors wish to thank for sharing their expertise:

- **Anne M. Christensen,** Librarian II, Phoenix Public Library, Phoenix, Arizona.

- **Barbara C. Chumard,** Reference/Adult Services Librarian, Middletown Thrall Library, Middletown, New York.

- **Eva M. Davis,** Youth Department Manager, Ann Arbor District Library, Ann Arbor, Michigan.

- **Adam Janowski, Jr.,** Library Media Specialist, Naples High School Library Media Center, Naples, Florida.

- **Robert Reginald,** Head of Technical Services and Collection Development, California State University, San Bernadino, California.

- **Katharine E. Rubin,** Head of Information and Reference Division, New Orleans Public Library, New Orleans, Louisiana.

- **Barbara A. Wencl,** Media Specialist, Como Park High School, St. Paul, Minnesota.

International Advisory Board

Well-represented among the 115,000 author entries published in *Contemporary Authors* are sketches on notable writers from many non-English-speaking countries. The primary criteria for inclusion of such authors has traditionally been the publication of at least one title in English, either as an original work or as a translation. However, the editors of *Contemporary Authors* came to observe that many important international writers were being overlooked due to a strict adherence to our inclusion criteria. In addition, writers who were publishing in languages other than English were not being covered in the traditional sources we used for identifying new listees. Intent on increasing our coverage of international authors, including those who write only in their native language and have not been translated into English, the editors enlisted the aid of a board of advisors, each of whom is an expert on the literature of a particular country or region. Among the countries we focused attention on are Mexico, Puerto Rico, Germany, Luxembourg, Belgium, the Netherlands, Norway, Sweden, Denmark, Finland, Taiwan, Singapore, Spain, Italy, South Africa, Israel, and Japan, as well as England, Scotland, Wales, Ireland, Australia, and New Zealand. The sixteen-member advisory board includes the following individuals, whom the editors wish to thank for sharing their expertise:

- **Lowell A. Bangerter,** Professor of German, University of Wyoming, Laramie, Wyoming.

- **Nancy E. Berg,** Associate Professor of Hebrew and Comparative Literature, Washington University, St. Louis, Missouri.

- **Frances Devlin-Glass,** Associate Professor, School of Literary and Communication Studies, Deakin University, Burwood, Victoria, Australia.

- **David William Foster,** Regent's Professor of Spanish, Interdisciplinary Humanities, and Women's Studies, Arizona State University, Tempe, Arizona.

- **Hosea Hirata,** Director of the Japanese Program, Associate Professor of Japanese, Tufts University, Medford, Massachusetts.

- **Jack Kolbert,** Professor Emeritus of French Literature, Susquehanna University, Selinsgrove, Pennsylvania.

- **Mark Libin,** Professor, University of Manitoba, Winnipeg, Manitoba, Canada.

- **C. S. Lim,** Professor, University of Malaya, Kuala Lumpur, Malaysia.

- **Eloy E. Merino,** Assistant Professor of Spanish, Northern Illinois University, DeKalb, Illinois.

- **Linda M. Rodríguez Guglielmoni,** Associate Professor, University of Puerto Rico—Mayagüez, Puerto Rico.

- **Sven Hakon Rossel,** Professor and Chair of Scandinavian Studies, University of Vienna, Vienna, Austria.

- **Steven R. Serafin,** Director, Writing Center, Hunter College of the City University of New York, New York City.

- **David Smyth,** Lecturer in Thai, School of Oriental and African Studies, University of London, England.

- **Ismail S. Talib,** Senior Lecturer, Department of English Language and Literature, National University of Singapore, Singapore.

- **Dionisio Viscarri,** Assistant Professor, Ohio State University, Columbus, Ohio.

- **Mark Williams,** Associate Professor, English Department, University of Canterbury, Christchurch, New Zealand.

CA Numbering System and Volume Update Chart

Occasionally questions arise about the *CA* numbering system and which volumes, if any, can be discarded. Despite numbers like " 29-32R," " 97-100" and "208," the entire *CA* print series consists of only 253 physical volumes with the publication of *CA* Volume 209. The following charts note changes in the numbering system and cover design, and indicate which volumes are essential for the most complete, up-to-date coverage.

CA First Revision	• 1-4R through 41-44R (11 books) *Cover:* Brown with black and gold trim. There will be no further First Revision volumes because revised entries are now being handled exclusively through the more efficient *New Revision Series* mentioned below.
CA Original Volumes	• 45-48 through 97-100 (14 books) *Cover:* Brown with black and gold trim. 101 through 209 (109 books) *Cover:* Blue and black with orange bands. The same as previous *CA* original volumes but with a new, simplified numbering system and new cover design.
CA Permanent Series	• *CAP*-1 and *CAP*-2 (2 books) *Cover:* Brown with red and gold trim. There will be no further Permanent Series volumes because revised entries are now being handled exclusively through the more efficient *New Revision Series* mentioned below.
CA New Revision Series	• CANR-1 through CANR-117 (117 books) *Cover:* Blue and black with green bands. Includes only sketches requiring significant changes; **sketches are taken from any previously published CA, CAP, or CANR volume.**

If You Have:	You May Discard:
CA First Revision Volumes 1-4R through 41-44R and *CA Permanent Series* Volumes 1 and 2	*CA* Original Volumes 1, 2, 3, 4 Volumes 5-6 through 41-44
CA Original Volumes 45-48 through 97-100 and 101 through 209	**NONE:** These volumes will not be superseded by corresponding revised volumes. Individual entries from these and all other volumes appearing in the left column of this chart may be revised and included in the various volumes of the *New Revision Series*.
CA New Revision Series Volumes *CANR*-1 through *CANR*-117	**NONE:** The *New Revision Series* does not replace any single volume of *CA*. Instead, volumes of *CANR* include entries from many previous *CA* series volumes. All *New Revision Series* volumes must be retained for full coverage.

A Sampling of Authors and Media People
Featured in This Volume

Nicholas A. Basbanes

Basbanes's first book, *A Gentle Madness: Bibliophiles, Bibliomanes, and the Eternal Passion for Books,* published in 1995, examines the world of book collecting. The volume profiles such historical bibliophiles as the Italian poet Petrarch as well as modern enthusiasts like Ruth Baldwin, a woman who collected children's books despite the fact that she disliked children. Basbanes is also the author of *Among the Gently Mad: Perspectives and Strategies for the Book-Hunter in the Twenty-first Century,* published in 2002.

Kelly Cherry

Award-winning poet and novelist Cherry is concerned with conveying abstract notions of morality in her work. "My novels deal with moral dilemmas and the shapes they create as they reveal themselves in time," she once told *CA*. "My poems seek out the most suitable temporal or kinetic structure for a given emotion." Her collections of poetry include *Lovers and Agnostics* and *Death and Transfiguration,* and she is also the author of *The Society of Friends,* a book of stories, and the novel *Augusta Played.* An autobiographical essay by Cherry is included in this volume of *CA*.

Michelle de Kretser

De Kretser is an Australia-based writer whose works include the novel *The Rose Grower,* in which an American balloonist finds love and danger with a pair of sisters in Gascony, during the French Revolution, and the editorship of the volume *Brief Encounters: Stories of Love, Sex, and Travel,* an anthology which consists of stories that reveal the romantic, and sometimes erotic, nature of travel. Contributors to *Brief Encounters* include Pico Iyer, Lisa St. Aubin de Teran, Mona Simpson, and Paul Theroux.

Paul Heyse

Heyse was an enormously popular German writer in his day, best known for his "novellen," or short stories, a form he helped establish during the last half of the nineteenth century. His tales most often feature exotic locales, fanciful, romantic plots, and beautiful, strong-willed heroines. His first novel, *Kinder der Welt* (*Children of the World*), was typical of his novels, in that it was long, complex, very popular, and received generally good reviews. Awarded the Nobel Prize for literature in 1910, Heyse's reputation fell into sharp decline soon after his death.

John Maddox

Maddox is a theoretical physicist, writer, and long-time *Nature* magazine editor who is known for his general expertise in the various sciences. He is a compelling advocate of greater scientific awareness for political leaders, government officials, and the general public. In *What Remains to Be Discovered: Mapping the Secrets of the Universe, the Origins of Life, and the Future of the Human Race,* he writes on the nature of science throughout history, addressing such subjects as quantum mechanics, genetics, and cosmology.

Greg Rucka

Rucka is a novelist and a writer of comic books and graphic novels. Most of his novels, including *Keeper,* feature the protagonist Atticus Kodiak, a tough, smart bodyguard who follows his heart rather than his pocketbook when it comes to taking on assignments. Rucker is also the author of numerous graphic novels, including *Whiteout,* which won the Eisner Award for Best Limited Series in 2000, and *Queen & Country: Operation Broken Ground,* which was nominated for an Eisner Award.

Jon Stewart

Comedian and actor Stewart has been the host of Comedy Central's *The Daily Show* since 1999. He is also the author of the book *Naked Pictures of Famous People,* which consists of eighteen original humor pieces on a par with Woody Allen's *Without Feathers* and Steve Martin's *Cruel Shoes.* Stewart's prose retains the same smart, irreverent humor the comedian is known for on television, such as the piece which describes a visit to a room where the Kennedys keep their unsuccessful children.

Ronald Sukenick

Writer and theorist Sukenick, one of the leaders in the meta-fiction trend of the 1960s, recognized that conventional literary tradition—a standardized way of looking at an art form—had become one of fiction's strongest enemies. He posited that a new tradition could be built to replace the old without rejecting the works upon which the old was built. Among Sukenick's works are *Wallace Stevens: Musing the Obscure,* a study of a poet concerned with the complex relation between language, imagination, and reality, and the novel *Out.* An autobiographical essay by Sukenick is included in this volume of *CA*.

Acknowledgments

Grateful acknowledgment is made to those publishers, photographers, and artists whose work appear with these authors' essays. Following is a list of the copyright holders who have granted us permission to reproduce material in this volume of *CA*. Every effort has been made to trace copyright, but if omissions have been made, please let us know.

Photographs/Art

Kelly Cherry: All photos reproduced by permission of the author, except as noted: opening portrait by Daaave Summers. Reproduced by permission.

David Mura: All photos reproduced by permission of the author, except as noted: opening portrait by M. C. O'Leary. Reproduced by permission.

Ronald Sukenick: All photos reproduced by permission of the author, except as noted: portrait of Sukenick at Grand Army Plaza by Richard Brown; portrait of Sukenick (at San Diego Zoo) and portrait of Sukenick (holding cat) by Lynn Luria-Sukenick. All reproduced by permission.

A

ABMA, G(erben) Willem 1942-
(Daniël Daen)

PERSONAL: Born July 12,1942, in Folsgeare, Netherlands. *Education:* Attended school in Leeuwarden, Netherlands.

ADDRESSES: Office—c/o Utjouwerij Frysk en Frij, Spoarstrkitte 132/B, 8933 CG Ljouwert, Netherlands.

CAREER: Poet, author, and editor.

AWARDS, HONORS: Gysbert Japicxpriis for poetry, 1973, for *De âlde en de leave hear as lead om âld izer, Op libben en dea,* and *Mosken en Goaden;* Rely Jorritsmapriis, 1983, for "Ôfskie."

WRITINGS:

De utfanhuzer, Osinga (Boalsert, Netherlands), 1962.
De gersidders, Osinga (Boalsert, Netherlands), 1969.
De nacht fan in leechrinner, Butenpost, 1973.
Leafde op Bitter-Lemon, Koperative Utjowerij (Bolsward, Netherlands), 1973.
Prosit, 1973.
En it barde, 1980.
In Satansbern, De Tille (Leeuwarden, Netherlands), 1981.
De Klinyk, De Tille (Leeuwarden, Netherlands), 1982.
De Onantaasting, De Tille (Leeuwarden, Netherlands), 1983.

De sprong, 1985.
Dieden, 1986.
(Editor, with Y. Kuiper and J. Rypkema) *Tussen Goed en Fout. Nieuwe Gezichtspunten in de Geschiedschrijiving 1940-1945,* T. Wever (Franeker, Netherlands), 1986.
Bist noait wa'st wieste, 1987.
Dea fan de moskefrou, 1987.
Freonen âder elkoar, 1993.
In nacht yn de Andes (thriller), illustrated by Willem Mook, Frysk en Frij (Leeuwarden, Netherlands), 1993.
De mafiaman (thriller), illustrated by Willem Mook, Frysk en Frij (Leeuwarden, Netherlands), 1994.
Moeting, Frysk en Frij (Leeuwarden, Netherlands), 1994.
Te fûnling, Frysk en Frij (Leeuwarden, Netherlands), 1999.
Kuiers of definysjes fian in ik. Proazagedichten, Frysk en Frij (Leeuwarden, Netherlands), 2000.

"HEERD HISSEMA" SERIES

De oantaasting, 1983.
De Roekkat, 1986.
It Byldsje mei brieven oan Priscilla, 1988.
It Orakel, 1990.

POETRY; AS DANIËL DAEN

De âlde en de leave hear as lead om âld izer, 1970.
Op libben en dea, Miedema (Leeuwarden, Netherlands), 1970.
Mosken en Goaden, 1972.

Bûen it skûiif, 1973.
Fitraazjewrâld, 1975.
De iken fan Dodona, 1976.
Rûnen fan forjitnis, 1977.
Hjerstreach, 1979.
Nachtfeest, 1982.

WORK IN PROGRESS: Another book of poetry.

SIDELIGHTS: Dutch poet, author, and editor G. Willem Abma, who often writes verse under the pseudonym Daniël Daen, has garnered much critical success in the Netherlands for his work. Abma has published over twenty books, which include collections of poetry and a number of novels. Born July 12, 1942, in the Dutch town of Folsgeare, Abma published his first work in 1970. In 1973 he earned the prestigious Gysbert Japiexpriis for his first three collections of poetry: *De âlde en de leave hear as lead om âld izer, Op libben en dea,* and *Mosken en Goaden,* all published under the Daniël Daen pseudonym. In addition, he received the Rely Jorritsma Prize in 1983.

Abma's novels include several thrillers, one of which is 1995's *De mafiaman.* His literary credits also include *Tussen Goed en Fout: Nieuwe Gezichtspunten in de Geschiedschrijiving 1940-1945,* which he coedited. The book contains a number of articles about the Nazi occupation of the Dutch province of Friesland during World War II. Louis de Jong and Hans Blom, the latter a history professor at the University of Amsterdam, are among the contributors to the work.

BIOGRAPHICAL AND CRITICAL SOURCES:

PERIODICALS

European History Quarterly, January, 1991, pp. 109-118.

OTHER

Frysk en Frij Web site, http://frys-en-frij.nl/ (June 6, 2001), "G. Willem Abma."
Frysk Letterkundich Museum en Dokumintaasjesintrum, http://www.flmd.nl/ (March 15, 2001).*

AHLES, Carol Laflin 1948-

PERSONAL: Born January 13, 1948; daughter of William L., Sr. and Margaret (Elias) Laflin; married Ronald F. Ahles, May 23, 1970; children: Daniel R., Emily Ahles Dickey. *Education:* Loyola University, New Orleans, LA, B.A., 1970.

ADDRESSES: Home—3110 Ashlock Dr., Houston, TX 77082. *E-mail*—cahles@hia.net.

CAREER: Buttons 'n' Bows Fabrics, Houston, TX, co-owner and teacher of sewing classes, 1981-88; seamstress, pattern designer, and writer. Teacher of sewing classes; speaker at festivals and conventions; guest on media programs, including *America Sews with Sue Hausmann,* Public Broadcasting Service, 2001.

MEMBER: Smocking Arts Guild of America, American Sewing Guild.

WRITINGS:

Fine Machine Sewing: Easy Ways to Get the Look of Hand Finishing and Embellishing, Taunton Press (Newtown, CT), 1996, revised edition, 2001.

Author of operator manuals for various sewing machines, including (with Jackie Dodson) *Know Your Elna,* Chilton Book Co. Contributor to books, including *Notions: Fifty Great Gadgets You Can't Live Without,* Taunton Press (Newtown, CT), 2000. Author of "Carol Ahles Answers," a column in *Creative Needle.* Contributor to sewing magazines, including *Threads* and *Creative Machine Newsletter.*

*   *   *

AINSLIE, Peter III 1867-1934

PERSONAL: Born June 3, 1867, in Dunnsville, VA; died February 23, 1934, in Baltimore, MD; son of Peter (a minister) and Rebecca Etta (Sizer) Ainslie; married Mary Elizabeth Weisel, 1925. *Education:* Attended Transylvania College, 1886-89.

CAREER: Minister of Christian Church (Disciples of Christ); worked as supply minister at a Christian church in Newport News, VA, 1889-91; Calhoun Street Christian Church (later Christian Temple), Baltimore, MD, pastor, 1891-1933. International Convention of Christian Churches, president, 1910; Council on Christian Union of the Disciples of Christ (also known as Association for the Promotion of Christian Unity and Council on Christian Unity), founder and president; Christian Unity League for Equality and Brotherhood, member, beginning 1927; Church Peace Union, member of board of trustees; conference organizer and participant in the United States and abroad; lecturer at educational institutions. Local advocate for religious, racial, and ethnic unity; founder of nondenominational club for working girls, 1899.

WRITINGS:

Plain Talks to Young Men on Vital Issues, Christian Publishing (St. Louis, MO), 1897.
Religion in Daily Doings, 1903.
Studies in the Old Testament, 1907.
God and Me, Temple Seminary Press (Baltimore, MD), 1908, published as God and Me: Being a Brief Manual of the Principles That Make for a Closer Relationship of the Believer with God, Fleming H. Revell (New York, NY), 1909.
Among the Gospels and the Acts: Being Notes and Comments Covering the Life of Christ in the Flesh, and the First Thirty Years' History of His Church, Temple Seminary Press (Baltimore, MD), 1908.
The Unfinished Task of the Reformation, 1910.
Introduction to the Study of the Bible, 1910.
My Brother and I: A Brief Manual of the Principles That Make for a Wider Brotherhood with All Mankind, Fleming H. Revell (New York, NY), 1911.
The Message of the Disciples for the Union of the Church, Including Their Origin and History, Fleming H. Revell (New York, NY), 1913.
Christ or Napoleon—Which?, Fleming H. Revell (New York, NY), 1915.
Working with God; or, The Story of a Twenty-five-Year Pastorate in Baltimore, Christian Board of Publication (St. Louis, MO), 1917.
Towards Christian Unity, Association for the Promotion of Christian Unity (Baltimore, MD), 1918.
If Not a United Church—What?, Fleming H. Revell (New York, NY), 1920.
(With H. C. Armstrong) A Book of Christian Worship for Voluntary Use among Disciples of Christ and Other Christians, Seminary House Press (Baltimore, MD), 1923.
The Way of Prayer, Fleming H. Revell (New York, NY), 1924.
(With H. C. Armstrong) The Scandal of Christianity, Willett, Clark & Colby (Chicago, IL), 1929.
Some Experiments in Living, Association Press (New York, NY), 1933.
Cultivating the Fruit of the Spirit, Bethany Press (St. Louis, MO), 1968.

Contributor to books, including Week-day Sermons in King's Chapel: Sermons Preached to Week-day Congregations in King's Chapel, Boston, edited by Harold Edwin Balme Speight, Macmillan (New York, NY), 1925; and Recollections and Reflections, by Newman Smyth, Scribner (New York, NY), 1926. Christian Union Quarterly, cofounder, 1911, editor, 1911-34.

OBITUARIES:

PERIODICALS

Baltimore Sun, February 24, 1934; February 27, 1934.
Christian Century, March 7, 1934.
Christian-Evangelist, March 1, 1934; March 8, 1934.*

*   *   *

AKE, David (Andrew) 1961-

PERSONAL: Born May 11, 1961, in New Haven, CT; son of Theodor and Beatrice Ake; married Hillary Case, June 23, 2001. Education: University of Miami, Coral Cables, FL, B.Mus., 1983; California Institute of the Arts, M.F.A., 1987; University of California—Los Angeles, M.A., 1996, Ph.D., 1998.

ADDRESSES: Home—3150 Wedgewood Ct., Reno, NV 89509. Office—Department of Music, University of Nevada, Reno, NV. E-mail—dake@unr.nevada.edu.

CAREER: El Camino College, Torrance, CA, lecturer in music, 1996-97; California State University—Fullerton, lecturer in music, 1997; University of Nevada,

Reno, assistant professor of music, 1999—, director of jazz studies, 2001—. Dartmouth College, visiting faculty, 1997; guest lecturer at other institutions, including Arizona State University, 1995, and Consumnes River College and University of California—Los Angeles, 2001. Pianist, with concert performances in the United States, Canada, and Armenia, and on television programs; performer with such groups as Ravi Coltrane Quintet, Charlie Haden's Liberation Music Orchestra, Reno Philharmonic Orchestra, and Hal Singer Quartet; recordings include *Double Faces* with the Harald Ruschenbaum Big Band, Swingtime, 1985; *Sun Sound* with the Phil Farris Quartet, Posi-tone, 1996; *Sound and Time* with the David Ake Group, Posi-tone, 1998; *With and Against* with the David Borgo Quartet, Resurgent Music, 1999; *North* with the Collective, 2000; and *Brian Landrus Project,* 2001.

MEMBER: International Association for the Study of Popular Music, International Association of Jazz Educators, American Musicological Society, Society for American Music, Society for Ethnomusicology, American Studies Association, Broadcast Music Inc., For the Love of Jazz Society (member of board of directors, 2002—).

AWARDS, HONORS: Outstanding Small Ensemble Award and Outstanding Piano Soloist award, Notre Dame Jazz Festival, 1986; first prize, Cognac Hennessey Jazz Search, 1990; first prize, John Coltrane Festival Competition, 1994; Outstanding Small Ensemble award, Reno Jazz Festival, 1996; grants for Paris, France, from University of Nevada, 2000—.

WRITINGS:

Jazz Cultures, University of California Press (Berkeley, CA), 2002.

Contributor to books, including *The Cambridge Companion to Jazz,* edited by David Horn and Mervyn Cooke, Cambridge University Press (New York, NY), 2002; and *Playing Changes: New Jazz Studies,* edited by Robert Walser, Duke University Press (Durham, NC), 2003. Contributor of articles and reviews to periodicals, including *Echo.* Member of editorial advisory board, *American Music,* 2001-02.

ALBERY, Nicholas 1948-2001

PERSONAL: Born July 28, 1948, in St. Albans, England; died from injuries suffered in a car accident June 3, 2001, in Prices Risborough, Buckinghamshire, England; son of Sir Donald and Heather (Boys) Albery; married Josefine Speyer May 19, 1991; children: Merlyn. *Education:* Attended St. John's College, Oxford University; Institute of Psychotherapy and Social Studies, diploma, 1986.

CAREER: Poet, social activist, and nonfiction author. Formerly worked for BIT. Institute for Social Inventions, founder and principal officer; Natural Death Center, London, England, director, beginning 1991; Council for Posterity, general secretary, beginning 1993; Global Ideas Bank, Internet editor, 1994; Poetry Marathon, England, director, beginning 1995; Social Inventors, London, England, chair, beginning 1985; *Social Inventions Journal,* editor.

AWARDS, HONORS: Schumacher Society Award, 1994.

WRITINGS:

AS EDITOR

(With Mark Kinzley) *How to Save the World: A Fourth World Guide to the Politics of Scale,* Turnstone Press (Wellingborough, Northamptonshire, England), 1984.

The Book of Visions: An Encyclopaedia of Social Innovations, 1993.

Poem for the Day: 366 Poems Worth Learning by Heart, Steerforth Press (South Royalton, VT), 1996.

World's Best Ideas, Institute of Social Inventions, (London, England), 1998.

Time out Book of Country Walks, Penguin Books (London, England), 1997.

SIDELIGHTS: Nicholas Albery was born into a life of riches, as his father, Sir Donald, was head of what has been referred to as a dynasty of British theaters. Albery himself won a scholarship at age sixteen to the prestigious St. John's College, Oxford. However, after two years at St. John's and under the influence of the counter-culture of the 1960s, Albery dropped out of school and traveled to the United States, eventually settling in the Haight-Ashbury district of San Francisco and taking on the hippie culture of the day.

In 1968 Albery returned to Great Britain and went to work for BIT, the alternative information arm of the newspaper *International Times,* which dealt with issues important to the counter-culture movement of that time. It was through his association with BIT that Albery met Nicholas Saunders, who would become, according to Albery's obituary in the London *Times,* his "mentor and closest friend," eventually helping Albery to funnel his ideas into practical applications, as they shared "ideas of how communities could take control of their own lives."

Albery met his wife, Josefine, an art student from Berlin, in 1972. Several years into their relationship, they took over a row of townhouses that they shared with a group of international artists. The homes were scheduled to be demolished and then replaced with new commercial buildings; but Albery and his group fought to keep the row houses intact. They refused to be evicted and renamed this section of Notting Hill the Free Republic of Frestonia, declaring themselves independent of the United Kingdom. They won their fight against the bulldozers, and Albery, the following year in 1978, ran as a candidate in the Ecology Party, winning a total of eight hundred votes.

"The collaboration of the two Nicholases, Saunders and Albery," as stated in Albery's obituary in the London *Independent,* "became the pivot for a series of social innovations for the next quarter-century; Albery the socially involved ideas man who stayed up all hours with the computer . . . Saunders, the entrepreneur risk-taker with the Midas touch." One of the main innovations Albery and Saunders were involved with was the Institute for Social Inventions, founded in 1985. It was through the Institute that Albery established several other organizations, including the Natural Death Centre (through which inexpensive family-based funerals could be arranged), the Global Ideas Bank (an Internet site open to suggestions that could positively affect society), the International Poetry Challenge Day (challenging students to memorize a poem in order to earn money for charitable organizations), and the Apprentice-Master Alliance (which links students with small businesses). In summing up Albery, the *Independent* writer stated, "The

breadth of his thinking and the scope of his output was extraordinary."

Albery was also involved in editing and writing several books during his lifetime. The first was *The Encyclopaedia of Social Inventions,* which contains ideas that Arnold Evans, in the *Times Educational Supplement,* described as ranging "from the eminently sensible to the screwball." Evans further commented that some of the suggestions are "destined to change the way we live," while others "(let's hope)" are "doomed never to get off the back of the envelope."

Albery's 1994 *Poem for the Day: 366 Poems Worth Learning by Heart* is set up as a diary might be, with notes on the selected poem of the day as well as notes about the poet, listings of literary birthdays, and the poem itself, which might be written by Blake, Tennyson, Yeats, Shakespeare, Wordsworth, or lesser-known poets such as Adam Thorpe, Vikram Seth, Michael Young, or Sasha Moorsom. Tony O'Sullivan, writing for the *School Librarian,* called it "a versatile book for sure—at home equally on a teacher's desk or on a bedside table."

The final book published before Albery's death was *World's Best Ideas,* for which he acted as coeditor. This book is not "Utopian," wrote Brian Eno in a review for *Whole Earth,* but rather "it offers much more pragmatic, much more incrementalist strategy." Eno added, "It's a work of research—scanning the world for signs of more successful and human ways of doing things."

In the London *Times* obituary, Albery was described as "one of the few luminaries of the 1960s counter-culture whose sense of mission to improve the world carried over into the ensuing decades." The *Times* writer also stated that the way in which Albery died was ironic. "It is an unhappy irony that, having so long campaigned for walking, cycling and more society-friendly alternatives to the car, and never having learnt to drive," that he should end up being "killed in a car accident." Albery died on June 3, 2001.

BIOGRAPHICAL AND CRITICAL SOURCES:

PERIODICALS

New Scientist, July 5, 1997, review of *The Time out Book of Country Walks,* p. 45.

School Librarian, May, 1995, Tony O'Sullivan, review of *Poem for the Day,* p. 73.

Times Educational Supplement, June 28, 1991, Arnold Evans, review of *The Encyclopaedia of Social Inventions,* p. 31.

Whole Earth, spring, 1999, Brian Eno, review of *World's Best Ideas,* p. 58.

OBITUARIES:

PERIODICALS

Independent (London, England), June 18, 2002, "Nicholas Albery."

Times (London, England), June 7, 2001, "Nicholas Albery, Leading Light of Alternative London in the Sixties, Who Spent the Next Three Decades Trying to Make Life—and Death—Better for Everyone."*

*   *   *

ALEXANDER, Will 1948-

PERSONAL: Born 1948, in Los Angeles, CA. *Ethnicity:* African-American. *Education:* University of California, B.A. (English and creative writing).

ADDRESSES: Home—Los Angeles, CA. *Agent*—c/o Author Mail, Pavement Saw Press, 349 East Morrill Ave., Columbus, OH 43207.

CAREER: Poet, teacher, painter. Writer in residence at University of California, San Diego, New College (San Francisco, CA), and Hofstra University. Taught at Jack Kerouac School of Disembodied Poetics, Boulder, CO.

WRITINGS:

POETRY

Vertical Rainbow Climber, Jazz Press (Aptos, CA), 1987.

Arcane Lavender Morals, Leave Books (Buffalo, NY), 1994.

The Stratospheric Canticles, Pantograph Press (Berkeley, CA), 1995.

Asia & Haiti, Sun & Moon Press (Los Angeles, CA), 1995.

Above the Human Nerve Domain, Pavement Saw Press (Columbus, OH), 1998.

Towards the Primeval Lightning Field, (essays), O Books (Oakland, CA), 1998.

Contributor to various small press publications, including *Callaloo, Conjunctions, apex of the M, Orpheus Grid,* and *Gem.*

SIDELIGHTS: Will Alexander is a poet whom critics have not been able to categorize easily. An African-American child of the post-World War II baby boom who grew up in south central Los Angeles, he also does not fit any clichéd image of that generation's avant-garde poets. The son of a World War II veteran, Alexander was influenced by the revolutionary struggles of the Third World that first inspired his father during a military tour of the Caribbean. The elder Alexander found there was a sharp contrast in how black Americans lived in the United States as compared to other Third World countries. According to Harryette Mullen, writing in *Callalloo.* "There, the elder Alexander was impressed to see black people in positions of power, and his story of that experience left a distinct impression on his son, who counts among his culture heroes Césaire of Martinique and Wifredo Lam of Cuba," Mullen noted.

Born in Los Angeles, Alexander has remained a lifetime resident of the city. Although he received a B.A. degree in English and creative writing, he has followed his own direction in his writing and painting. According to Clayton Eshleman, writing in *American Poet,* Alexander was probably first published in 1981 in the small press literary journal *Sulfur.* Until the mid-1990s, he made his living in an assortment of low-paying jobs. He has since given readings of his work and held artist-in-residence posts at various colleges.

Alexander's first work to attract critical attention was *Asia & Haiti.* Writing on the collection for *Sulfur,* John Olson commented: "Poetry and politics make peculiar bedfellows. One is private experience made public, the other public experience made private. In Will Alexander's *Asia & Haiti . . .* poetry writhes like a wounded snake in a miasma of brutality and oppression." He added, "Shelley called poets legislators and prophets, visionaries who drew their authority from 'that partial apprehension of the agencies of the invisible world which is called religion.' This is what gives *Asia* such tremendous pathos, taking China's invasion of Tibet as point of departure. It is a poem with a surrealistic aperture, oracular lens and Delphic tripod."

In discussing a passage from *Towards the Primeval Lightning Field,* Eshleman wrote, "The desire in such writing is for a paradise of language, for the creation, in language, of a reality that uses particles from the observational world to foment interlocking nonsequitor constellations that ignite new constellations as they burst." As Alexander wrote in the first paragraph of the work, "It is not with the steepness of vultures that I seek to procure an arcane stability in the void, but by the blending of halts and motions, like the vertical equilibria of fire, brought to an incandescent pitch of value." In his introduction to *Towards the Primeval Lightning Field,* Andrew Joron pointed out that Alexander's imagination is embued with the pre-Romantic idea of imagination as "the link of links": "Here, the energy of the imagination has not yet been harnessed (as it would be in Romanticism) to the goals of bourgeois subjectivization. It can never be a matter of 'possessing' this imagination, but only (as in the communalistic spirit of *voudou*) of being possessed by it. Imagination is the conductor of primeval lightning, the fiery trickster leaping between frozen and fragmented *realia,* the universal translator of the multitude of tongues (both human and inhuman) emitted by the Signal of signals."

In *American Book Review,* Mark Scroggins stated that Alexander is "acutely conscious of the issue of poetic voice, and is unwilling to let poetry's potential for ventriloquizing or exploring the voices of others be subsumed in an impersonal *écriture* or ultimately homogenous montage. He seems as well interested in the spiritual dimension of poetry, especially in the degrees to which poetry can give us access to spiritual or emotional states beyond those we normally experience."

Critics have observed that Alexander reaches for almost a whole new language, while making use of the inferences of the language he has at his disposal. Mullen explained: "Although Alexander resists discussions of the technical aspects of writing, it would be useful to have a fuller account of his process of lexical selection and combination; to understand how his reading habits and writing practices overlap in the intertextuality and diverse vocabularies incorporated into his poetry; to appreciate how certain rare, unusual, specialized, foreign, or archaic words are used in the poem for their precise denotative meaning, connotative meaning, metaphorical resonance, aural or phonemic qualities, or all of the above." As is common with surrealists, Alexander works through automatic writing, trying to achieve a state of trance, as Mullen pointed out. His preference for the British spelling of English words adds a whole dimension to his use of language, which becomes more than simply American and certainly differs from the "black" language of many modern African-American writers. Mullen concluded: "His literary influences connect him to an international avant-garde, just as his experience as an African American connects him to a black diaspora, and to the political struggles of Third World people."

In her explanation of the book *Above the Human Nerve Domain,* Mullen wrote: "The domain of poet Will Alexander's nervy curiosity ranges from the icy Himalayas, to African savannahs, from physics, astronomy, and music, to alchemy, philosophy, and painting. Orishas, angels and ghosts all sing to this poet, instructing him in their art of verbal flight. This is a poet whose lexicon, a 'glossary of vertigo,' might be culled from the complete holdings of a reconstituted Alexandrian library endowed for the next millennium."

BIOGRAPHICAL AND CRITICAL SOURCES:

BOOKS

Alexander, Will, *Towards the Primeval Lightning Field,* O Books (Oakland, CA), 1998, p. 7.

PERIODICALS

American Book Review, February, 1996, Mark Scroggins, "Logolatry," review of *Asia & Haiti,* p. 7.
American Poet, winter, 2000-2001, Clayton Eshleman, "A Note on Will Alexander," p. 15.

Callaloo, spring, 1999, Harryette Mullen, "'A Collective Force of Burning Ink': Will Alexander's *Asia & Haiti,*" p. 417.

Fessenden Review, 1989, review of *Vertical Rainbow Climber,* p. 88.

Hambone, fall, 1998, Barbara Barrigan, "'Hewing the Void': Linguistic Rebellion in Will Alexander's *Asia & Haiti,*" p. 201.

Lingo, 1997, Garrett Caples, "Is the Analysis Impure?," p. 74.

Sulfur, spring, 1996, John Olson, review of *Asia & Haiti,* p. 165.

OTHER

Electronic Poetry Center http://www.epc.buffalo.edu/ (February, 1998), profile of *apex of the M.*

O Books, http://www.obooks.com/ (March 1, 2002), review of *Towards the Primeval Lightning Field.*

Pavement Saw Press, http://www.pavementsaw.org/ (March 1, 2002).*

*   *   *

ALUMIT, Noel 1968-

PERSONAL: Born 1968, in the Philippines. *Education:* University of Southern California, B.F.A.; studied playwriting at the David Henry Hwang Writers Institute at East West Players.

ADDRESSES: Agent—c/o Author Mail, MacAdam/Cage Publishing, 155 Sansome Street, Suite 550, San Francisco, CA 94104.

CAREER: Actor, writer, and performance artist. Has played parts on the television shows *Beverly Hills 90210* and *The Young and the Restless.* Also appeared in the 1990 movie *Red Surf* starring George Clooney.

MEMBER: Asian Pacific AIDS Intervention Team.

AWARDS, HONORS: Los Angeles *Weekly* Award for ensemble work in Chay Yew's play *A Language of Their Own;* Pen Center USA West's Emerging Voices fellowship; University of California, Los Angeles Community Access scholarship to UCLA's Writer's Extension.

WRITINGS:

Letters to Montgomery Clift: A Novel, MacAdam/Cage Publishers (San Francisco, CA), 2002.

Author of plays, including one-man shows *The Rice Room: Scenes from a Bar,* and *Master of the (Miss) Universe,* and one-act play *Mr. & Mrs. La Questa Go Dancing*

SIDELIGHTS: In 1986, while Noel Alumit was a freshman at the University of Southern California, his father left his family to return to his birthplace in the Philippines. His father eventually returned to the States and to his family twelve years later, but his absence deeply affected Alumit and influenced the topic of his first novel, *Letters to Montgomery Clift.*

Alumit was born in the Philippines, but his family immigrated to the United States and created a home for themselves in Los Angeles. Alumit suspects that his father's departure, as he stated in a commentary about his novel for the online publication *Our Own Voice,* had something to do with his father's need to "recapture a bit of himself that had vanished. That bit of himself secured somewhere on an island in the ocean." Due to this ever-present theme in Alumit's life, he thought that the writing of his novel would help him explore various "forms of disappearing." He explained that in the novel, he tried to look "at people and things that managed to slip away: friends, family, and ideals that vanished over time. More importantly, I illustrated the desperate attempts to retrieve some of those people or things."

Letters to Montgomery Clift is told through the eyes of the protagonist Bong Bong Luwad, who becomes fascinated with a 1950s movie starring Montgomery Clift. Bong Bong had been sent from the Philippines to the United States to live with his aunt after his mother had been beaten by government officials loyal to the Marcos regime and his father had been taken away. Bong Bong's aunt, in an attempt to help the young boy come to terms with his longing for his parents, tells him to write letters to saints or to dead relatives to ask for favors, such as returning his parents to him.

Bong Bong had, early on, learned to escape his sorrows by watching old black-and-white movies on television. His favorite movie was *The Search* (1948) in which Montgomery Clift helps a young boy find his mother. Due to his fascination with this movie, Bong Bong eventually convinces himself that the deceased movie star is the perfect person to whom to write letters and plead for his parent's safe return.

It is through his evolving admiration for Clift that Bong Bong begins to create an image of himself. As he approaches adolescence, his fantasy world deepens. He escapes, in his mind, with Clift to exotic locations like Hawaii, the Nevada desert, Europe, and small cabins in the woods—places he visits through other Clift movies. Any place is better than his present-day Los Angeles, which reminds him that his parents are not with him. Bong Bong thus grows up using Clift as a sort of surrogate parent.

"This occasionally radiant coming-of-age tale," wrote a *Publishers Weekly* reviewer, "crams human rights violations, the cultural and emotional turmoil of immigrant life, self-mutilation, family ties, abortion, coming out and the ubiquitous search for self all into a brisk, sometimes jarring read."

Although Alumit's story is compelling for his revelation of human drama, he does not forget his sense of humor. As an example, Ghalib Shiraz Dhalla, in a review for the online publication *Asian Week,* relates one of the humorous parts of the story, in which Bong Bong becomes extremely curious about the sounds of lovemaking that are emitted from his neighbor's apartment below. Bong Bong's aunt warns him that the neighbor is evil and that he should completely ignore him. Contrary to his aunt's wishes, Bong Bong, one day, hides in the laundry room, waiting for the neighbor to appear. After Bong Bong sees the young man, he returns to his own apartment and writes his own conclusions in his next letter to Clift. If that young neighbor is evil, Bong Bong writes, "Evil is real good-looking."

Alumit has also written and performed in two one-man shows, *The Rice Room: Scenes from a Bar,* which explores the lives of gay Asian men, and *Master of the (Miss) Universe.* After a very successful tour with these two shows, he wrote a one-act play, *Mr. & Mrs. LaQuesta Go Dancing,* which was produced by Teatro Ng Tanan in San Francisco. All of his works have been critically acclaimed, especially by the California press.

BIOGRAPHICAL AND CRITICAL SOURCES:

PERIODICALS

Publishers Weekly, January 28, 2002, review of *Letters to Montgomery Clift,* p. 270.

OTHER

Asian Week, http://www.asianweek.com (March 30, 2003), Ghalib Shiraz Dhalla, "For Saints and Sinners."
Our Own Voice, http://www.oovrag.com/ (June 17, 2002), Noel Alumit, commentary about *Letters to Montgomery Clift.**

*　　　*　　　*

ALVAREZ, Alex 1963-

PERSONAL: Born April 21, 1963, in Biloxi, MS; son of Leroy C. (an air force career soldier and high school teacher) and Marianne (Graber) Alvarez; married Donna Engleson; children: Ingrid, Joseph, Astrid. *Ethnicity:* "Latino." *Education:* Northland College, Ashland, WI, B.S., 1985; University of New Hampshire, M.A., 1987, Ph.D., 1991. *Hobbies and other interests:* Climbing, running, reading.

ADDRESSES: Home—2451 East Elder, Flagstaff, AZ 86004. *Office*—Box 15005, College of Arts and Sciences, Northern Arizona University, Flagstaff, 86011; fax: 928-523-8011. *E-mail*—alex.alvarez@nau.edu.

CAREER: Northern Arizona University, Flagstaff, AZ, fellow, 1990-91, assistant professor, 1991-97, associate professor of criminal justice, 1997—, director of Martin-Springer Institute for Teaching the Holocaust, Tolerance, and Humanitarian Values, 2001—. Coconino County Victim Compensation Board, member, 1993—; Justice Services, Inc., speaker, 1997-98.

AWARDS, HONORS: Certificate of appreciation, Disability Support Services, Northern Arizona University, 1998.

WRITINGS:

Governments, Citizens, and Genocide: A Comparative and Interdisciplinary Approach, Indiana University Press (Bloomington, IN), 2001.
(With Ronet Bachman) *Murder American Style,* Wadsworth Publishing (Belmont, CA), 2002.

Contributor to books, including *Native Americans, Crime, Law, and Criminal Justice,* edited by M. Nielsen and R. Silverman, Westview Press (Boulder, CO), 1996; *Popular Culture, Crime, and Justice,* edited by D. Hale and F. Bailey, Wadsworth Publishing (Belmont, CA), 1998; and *Investigating Difference: Human and Cultural Relations in Criminal Justice,* Allyn & Bacon, 1999. Contributor to academic journals, including *Idea: Journal of Social Issues, International Journal of Comparative and Applied Criminal Justice, Sociological Imagination, Social Science History,* and *Journal of Criminal Justice.* Associate editor, *Violence and Victims,* 1997-99; member of editorial board, *War Crimes, Genocide, and Crimes against Humanity,* 2000-02.

WORK IN PROGRESS: Genocide, War Crimes, and Law Enforcement: The Intersection of Human Rights and Policing; Cruelty in the Camps; Institutional Scapegoating: Ethnicity and the Illusion of Self-Defense, with M. Beeman; research on genocide and the Holocaust, patterns of violence, homicide and justifiable homicide, media portrayals of violence, criminological theory, sentencing of minorities, and fear of crime.

*   *   *

AMBROSE, Stephen E(dward) 1936-2002

OBITUARY NOTICE—See index for *CA* sketch: Born January 10, 1936, in Decatur, IL; died of lung cancer October 13, 2002, in Bay St. Louis, MS. Historian, educator, and author. Ambrose was a popular author of history who was especially acclaimed for his writings about World War II. He earned his master's degree from Louisiana State University (now the University of New Orleans) in 1958 and his doctorate from the University of Wisconsin in 1963. Except for the five-year period from 1964 to 1969 when he was an associate professor of history at Johns Hopkins University, Ambrose spent most of his academic career at the University of New Orleans, where he was Boyd Professor of History from 1989 until his 1995 retirement as professor emeritus. Ambrose's writing career began in 1962 when he published *Halleck: Lincoln's Chief of Staff.* The book so impressed former President Dwight D. Eisenhower that he asked the historian to write his two-volume biography. Ambrose eventually went on to write six books about Eisenhower, including one for children. Ambrose was also the founder of the Eisenhower Center, and was Dwight D. Eisenhower Professor of War and Peace at Kansas State University from 1970 to 1971. In addition to Eisenhower, Ambrose was fascinated by Richard M. Nixon, writing a three-volume set on the more recent former U.S. president. Despite being a prolific writer, however, the historian remained known largely within academic circles until he published the bestseller *D-Day, June 6, 1944: The Climactic Battle of World War II* (1994). The popularity of this work encouraged Ambrose to write many more military histories, including *Citizen Soldiers: The U.S. Army from the Normandy Beaches to the Bulge to the Surrender of Germany* (1997) and *The Good Fight: How World War II Was Won* (2001). He also wrote acclaimed books about explorers Lewis and Clark, the construction of the Transcontinental Railroad, and the western expansion of the United States. By the late 1990s Ambrose had become well-known to the general reading public, but his success was somewhat eclipsed by accusations of plagiarism in his 2001 book *The Wild Blue: The Men and Boys Who Flew the B-24s over Germany.* Although he survived the scandal by saying he had properly footnoted the passages, Ambrose did not escape being grouped with several other academics accused of plagiarism in a rash of scandals in academia during that same time. Nevertheless, he continued to be praised for his role in helping to popularize the study of World War II in America. In addition to his writing accomplishments, Ambrose was the founder and director, beginning in 2000, of the National D-Day Museum in New Orleans and the president of his own company, Stephen Ambrose Historical Tours. He was a consultant to the 1998 film *Saving Private Ryan* and the Ken Burns-directed documentary *Lewis & Clark.* His book *Band of Brothers: E Company, 506th Regiment, 101st Airborne, from Normandy to Hitler's Eagle's Nest* was adapted as a television miniseries in 2001.

OBITUARIES AND OTHER SOURCES:

BOOKS

Contemporary Literary Criticism, Volume 145, Gale (Detroit, MI), 2001.
Who's Who in America, 56th edition, Marquis (New Providence, NJ), 2001.

PERIODICALS

Chicago Tribune, October 14, 2002, section 2, p. 7.
New York Times, October 14, 2002, p. A19.
Times (London, England), October 14, 2002.
Washington Post, October 14, 2002, p. B7.

*   *   *

ANCTIL, Pierre 1952-

PERSONAL: Born July 27, 1952, in Quebec City, Quebec, Canada; son of Jean-Louis and Constance (Barry) Anctil; children: Gabriel, Liliane, Philippe. *Ethnicity:* "French-Canadian." *Education:* Laval University, B.A., 1973, M.A., 1975; New School for Social Research, Ph.D., 1980; École Nationale d'Administration Publique, Montreal, Quebec, Canada, graduated, 2000. *Religion:* Roman Catholic. *Hobbies and other interests:* Philately.

ADDRESSES: Office—Conseil des relations interculturelles, Government of Quebec, 500 boulevard René-Lévesque W., Bureau 10.04, Montreal, Quebec, Canada H2Z 1W7. *E-mail*—pierre.anctil@conseil interculturel.gouv.qc.ca.

CAREER: Quebec Institute for Research on Culture, Montreal, Quebec, Canada, researcher, 1980-88; McGill University, director of French-Canadian studies program and postdoctoral fellow in Jewish studies, 1988-91; Government of Quebec, Montreal, specialist in education, 1991-93, counselor in Strategic Planning Division, Department of Relations with Citizens and Immigration, 1993-98, director of Department of Relations with Citizens and Immigration, 2001-02, president of Conseil des relations interculturelles, 2002—; Miriam Foundation, Montreal, director general, 1998-

99. University of Quebec, associate professor of history, 1996—. Museum of Civilization, member of scientific committee for an exhibition on immigrants and their stories, 1995-96; Museum of French America, member of scientific committee for a permanent exhibition on French America, 1996; Montreal Museum of Archaeology and History, researcher and guest curator, 2002-03.

AWARDS, HONORS: Ezekiel Hart Prize, Canadian Jewish Congress, 1998, for contributions to intercultural relations; J. I. Segal Award, Montreal Jewish Public Library, 2002, for *L'empire de Kalman l'infirme.*

WRITINGS:

(With Gary Caldwell) *Juifs et réalités juives au Quebec,* Institut Québécois de Recherche sur la Culture (Quebec, Canada), 1984.
Le rendez-vous manqué: Les juifs de Montreal face au Quebec de l'entre-deux-guerres, Institut Québécois de Recherche sur la Culture (Quebec, Canada), 1988.
(With Ira Robinson and Mervin Butovsky) *An Everyday Miracle: Yiddish Culture in Montreal,* Véhicule Press (Montreal, Quebec, Canada), 1990.
(With Ira Robinson and Gérard Bouchard) *Juifs et Canadiens français dans la société québécoise,* Éditions du Septentrion (Sillery, Quebec, Canada), 2000.
(Editor and author of introduction) *Through the Eyes of the Eagle: The Early Montreal Yiddish Press, 1907-1916,* translated from Yiddish by David Rome, Véhicule Press (Montreal, Quebec, Canada), 2001.
Saint-Laurent, Montreal's Main, Éditions du Septentrion (Sillery, Quebec, Canada), 2002.

Contributor to books. Contributor to periodicals, including *Relations.*

TRANSLATOR

(And author of introduction) Jacob Isaac Segal, *Poèmes yiddish* (poetry), Noroît (Montreal, Quebec, Canada), 1992.
(And author of introduction and annotations) Israel Medresh, *Le Montreal juif d'autrefois* (title means "Jewish Life in Montreal"), Éditions du Septentrion (Sillery, Quebec, Canada), 1997.

Tur Malka, *Flâneries sur les cimes de l'histoire juive montrealaise,* Éditions du Septentrion (Sillery, Quebec, Canada), 1997.

Shulamis Yelin, *Une enfance juive à Montreal* (title means "Stories from a Montreal Childhood"), Humanitas (Montreal, Quebec, Canada), 1998.

(And author of introduction and annotations) Simon Belkin, *Le mouvement ouvrier juif au Canada, 1904-1920* (title means "The Jewish Labor Movement in Canada, 1904-1920"), Éditions du Septentrion (Sillery Quebec, Canada), 1999.

(And author of introduction and annotations) Hirsch Wolofsky, *Un demi-siècle de vie yiddish à Montreal* (title means "A Half-Century of Yiddish Life in Montreal"), Éditions du Septentrion (Sillery, Quebec, Canada), 2000.

Yehuda Elberg, *L'empire de Kalman l'infirme* (title means "The Empire of Kalman the Cripple"), Leméac (Montreal, Quebec, Canada), 2001.

Israel Medresh, *Le Montreal juif entre les deux guerres* (title means "The Montreal Jew between Two Wars"), Éditions du Septentrion (Sillery, Quebec, Canada), 2001.

WORK IN PROGRESS: Translations; research on the "Jewish history of Quebec."

*   *   *

ANDERSON, (Tom) Scoular

PERSONAL: Male. *Education:* Attended art school in Glasgow, Scotland. *Hobbies and other interests:* Gardening, playing the guitar, cooking, walking.

ADDRESSES: Home—Dunoon, Argyll, Scotland. *Agent*—c/o Author Mail, A. and C. Black, Inc., 37 Soho Sq., London W1D 3QZ, England.

CAREER: Writer and illustrator. Appeared in *Storybook TV: A Video Collection of Eight Well-loved Children's Picture Books, Introduced and Read by Their Authors,* Scottish Council for Educational Technology, 1999.

WRITINGS:

AND ILLUSTRATOR

My First Joke Book, Young Corgi (London, England), 1986. (With Chris Powling) *The Phantom Carwash,* 1986, Barn Owl (London, England), 2001.

A-Z of Animal Jokes, Young Corgi (London, England), 1987.

The Enormous Chocolate Pudding, Dent (London, England), 1987.

(With Chris Powling) *Hiccup Harry,* A. and C. Black (London, England), 1988, Dutton Children's Books (New York, NY), 1990.

The Daring Dot-to-Dot Dinosaur, Young Corgi (London, England), 1989.

The Knock Knock Joke Book, Hippo (London, England), 1989.

A Journey down the Clyde, Drew (England), 1989.

A Plunder of Pirates, Puffin (London, England), 1989, published as *Project Pirates: Amazing Facts! Amazing Fun!,* Viking (London, England), 1994.

The Spider and Chips Joke Book, Young Corgi (London, England), 1989.

(With Chris Powling) *Harry's Party,* A. and C. Black (London, England), 1989.

Never Keep a Python as a Pet, Dent (London, England), 1990.

The Really Revolting Puzzle Book, Piccolo (England), 1990.

Wendy's Wheels, Ginn (England), 1990.

(With Chris Powling) *Harry with Spots On,* A. and C. Black (London, England), 1990.

Why Did the Chicken Cross the Road?, Hippo (London, England), 1991.

The Magic Boomerang; The Magic Present, Macmillan Children's (London, England), 1991.

School Jokes for Aliens, Young Corgi (London, England), 1991.

The Puffin Book of Royal London, Puffin (London, England), 1991.

Dreamy Daniel, Brainy Bert, Simon & Schuster Young Books (Hemel Hempstead, England), 1992.

The Curse of Hackjaw Island, Puffin (London, England), 1992.

Changing Charlie, A. and C. Black (London, England), 1992.

Land Ahoy! The Story of Christopher Columbus, Puffin (London, England), 1992.

Puzzling People, Puffin (London, England), 1992.

The Elephant Joke Book, Scholastic (London, England), 1993.

The Haunted Dot-to-Dot Hotel, Young Corgi (London, England), 1993.

The Puffin Factfile of Kings and Queens, Puffin (London, England), 1993.

(With Chris Powling) *Harry Moves House,* A. and C. Black (London, England), 1993.

Clogpots in Space, A. and C. Black (London, England), 1994.

A Puzzling Day at Castle MacPelican, Walker Books (London, England), 1994, Candlewick Press (Cambridge, MA), 1995.

The Survival Guide to Parents, Lions (London, England), 1994.

The Amazing Mark in Creepstone Castle, Viking (London, England), 1994.

The Survival Guide to Pets, Lions (London, England), 1995.

Finlay MacTrebble and the Fantastic Fertiliser, A. and C. Black (London, England), 1995.

Plotting and Chopping: Tudors and Stuarts with a Few Gory Bits, Puffin (London, England), 1995.

(With Chris Powling) *Harry the Superhero,* A. and C. Black (London, England), 1995.

Backseat's Special Day, Hippo (London, England), 1996.

A Puzzling Day in the Land of the Pharaohs, Candlewick Press (Cambridge, MA), 1996.

The Survival Guide to Food, Collins (London, England), 1996.

(With Chris Powling) *Harry on Holiday,* A. and C. Black (London, England), 1997.

1314 and All That, Canongate Books (Edinburgh, Scotland), 1998.

MacPelican's American Adventure, Candlewick Press (Cambridge, MA), 1998.

Ghost Docs on Patrol, Collins Children's (London, England), 1998.

Images of Dunoon and the Cowal Peninsula (for adults), Argyll Publishing (Glendaruel, Argyll, Scotland), 1998.

Raiding and Trading: Vikings with a Few Gory Bits, Puffin (London, England), 1998.

Fun: The Awful Truth, Hodder Children's (London, England), 1999.

Grown-ups: The Awful Truth, Hodder Children's (London, England), 1999.

School: The Awful Truth, Hodder Children's (London, England), 1999.

Ghost Docs at School, Collins Children's (London, England), 1999.

(With Chris Powling) *Rover Goes to School,* A. and C. Black (London, England), 1999.

(With Chris Powling) *Rover Shows Off,* A. and C. Black (London, England), 1999.

(With Chris Powling) *Rover the Champion,* A. and C. Black (London, England), 1999.

(With Chris Powling) *Rover's Birthday,* A. and C. Black (London, England), 1999.

(With Chris Powling) *The Book about Books,* A. and C. Black (London, England), 2000.

1745 and All That: The Story of the Highlands, Berlinn (Edinburgh, Scotland), 2001.

The Bin Bears, Corgi Pups (London, England), 2001.

My First Knock Knock Joke Book, Young Corgi (London, England), 2001.

Rob the Roman Gets Eaten by a Lion (Nearly), Hippo (London, England), 2001.

Trev the Tudor Gets the Chop (Nearly), Scholastic (London, England), 2001.

Some of Anderson's books have been translated into Spanish.

"WIZARD BOY" SERIES; AND ILLUSTRATOR

The Perfect Pizza, A. and C. Black (London, England), 2000.

The Posh Party, A. and C. Black (London, England), 2000.

The Potty Panto, A. and C. Black (London, England), 2000.

The Muddled Monsters, A. and C. Black (London, England), 2000.

ILLUSTRATOR

Sybil Marshall, *Polly at the Window,* Puffin (Harmondsworth, England), 1975.

Charles Dickens, *Oliver Twist,* adapted by Norman Wymer, Collins (London, England), 1979.

Charles Dickens, *Hard Times,* adapted by Viola Huggins, Collins (London, England), 1979.

Viola Huggins, *Five Ghost Stories,* Collins (London, England), 1980.

WAC Ghosts, Monsters, and Legends, Corgi (London, England), 1986.

WAC Jokes, Corgi (London, England), 1986.

David Pugh, editor, *The Grisly Joke Book,* Armada (London, England), 1986.

Jennifer Kavanagh, editor, *The Methuen Book of Humorous Stories,* Methuen (London, England), 1987.

Brian Ball, *The Quest for Queenie,* Macdonald (England), 1988.

Corley Byrne, *Kipper & Co.,* Dent (London, England), 1988.

Dick Cate, *Alexander and the Star Part,* Macmillan Children's (London, England), 1988.

Ruth Manning-Sanders, editor, *A Cauldron of Witches* (short stories), Methuen (London, England), 1988.

Jennifer Curry and Graeme Curry, *Down Our Street,* Methuen (London, England), 1988.

Victor Osborne, *Rex, the Most Special Car in the World,* Dent (London, England), 1988, Carolrhoda Books (Minneapolis, MN), 1989.

Phillip Schofield, *The Philip Schofield for File,* Bantam (England), 1988.

Miranda Seymour, *Pierre and the Pamplemousse,* Hodder & Stoughton (London, England), 1989.

Dick Cate, *Alexander and the Tooth of Zaza,* Macmillan Children's (London, England), 1989.

Dick Cate, *Scared!,* Macdonald (England), 1989.

Carol Vorderman, *Dirty, Loud, and Brilliant Too,* Knight (England), 1989.

Paul Jackson, *Flying Mobiles,* [England], 1989, Watermill Press (Mahwah, NJ), 1990.

Mary Danby, *How to Halt a Hiccup,* Knight (England), 1990.

Corley Byrne, *Kipper & Co. Strike Again!,* Dent (London, England), 1990.

Robert Swindells, *Tim Kipper,* Macmillan Children's (London, England), 1990, new edition, 1992.

John Dinneen, *Super-Challenge 2,* HarperCollins, 1991.

Saviour Pirotta, *Pineapple Crush,* Hodder & Stoughton (London, England), 1991.

Peter Hayward, *Nature File,* Puffin (London, England), 1992.

Christina Noble, *The Story of Loch Fyne Oysters,* Oyster Ideas (Cairndow, Scotland), 1993.

Robert Swindells, *The Siege of Frimly Prim,* Methuen Children's (London, England), 1993.

Theresa Breslin, *Bullies at School,* Canongate Books (Edinburgh, Scotland), 1994.

Roy Apps, *Nigel the Pirate,* Simon & Schuster Young Books (Hemel Hempstead, England), 1994.

Sam McBratney, *The Stranger from Somewhere in Time,* Heinemann (London, England), 1994.

Hazel Townson, *The Armband Band,* Collins Educational (London, England), 1995.

Wes Magee, *The Scumbagg School Scorpion,* Orchard (London, England), 1995.

Sam McBratney, *The Firetail Cat,* Macdonald Young Books (Hemel Hempstead, England), 1995.

Wes Magee, *The Spook Spotters of Scumbagg School,* Orchard (London, England), 1996.

Wes Magee, *Sports Day at Scumbagg School,* Orchard (London, England), 1996.

Elisabeth Jane McNair, *Robert Burns: Maker of Rhymes,* Viking (London, England), 1996.

Dick Cate, *Bernard's Prize,* Walker Books (London, England), 1996.

Sally Grindley, *Jimjams and the Ratnappers,* Macdonald Young Books (Hove, England), 1997.

Judy Allen, *The Most Brilliant Trick Ever,* Walker Books (London, England), 1997.

Jack Marlowe, *Explorers,* Hodder Children's (London, England), 1997.

Jack Marlowe, *Inventors,* Hodder Children's (London, England), 1997.

Jack Marlowe, *Scientists,* Hodder Children's (London, England), 1997.

Jack Marlowe, *Writers: Truly Terrible Tales,* Hodder Children's (London, England), 1997.

Dick Cate, *Bernard's Magic,* Walker Books (London, England), 1997.

Dick Cate, *Bernard's Gang,* Walker Books (London, England), 1998.

Hazel Richardson, *How to Split the Atom: The Hands-on Guide to Being a Science Superstar,* Oxford University Press (Oxford, England), 1999, Franklin Watts (New York, NY), 2001.

Clive Gifford, *How to Meet Aliens,* Franklin Watts (New York, NY), 2001.

Hazel Richardson, *How to Build a Rocket,* 1999, Franklin Watts (New York, NY), 2001.

Jeremy Strong, *Problems with a Python,* Barrington Stoke (Edinburgh, Scotland), 1999.

Dyan Sheldon, *Leon Loves Bugs,* Walker Books (London, England), 2000.

Margaret McAllister, *Doughnut Dilemma,* Oxford University Press (Oxford, England), 2000.

Margaret McAllister, *The Worst of the Vikings,* Oxford University Press (Oxford, England), 2000.

Timothy de Jongh Scott, *History Hoaxes,* Hodder Children's (London, England), 2000.

Clive Gifford, *How to Live on Mars,* 2000, Franklin Watts (New York, NY), 2001.

Barbara Taylor, *How to Save the Planet,* Franklin Watts (New York, NY), 2001.

David Shenton, *A Day in the Life of a Roman Charioteer,* Pearson Education (Harlow, England), 2001.

Jeremy Strong, *Living with Vampires,* Barrington Stoke (Edinburgh, Scotland), 2001.

Pat Thomson, *Pirates, Gold, and Custard,* Oxford University Press (Oxford, England), 2001.

Garry Kilworth, *Monster School,* A. and C. Black (London, England), 2002.

K. M. Briggs, *Hobberdy Dick,* Barrington Stoke (Edinburgh, Scotland), 2002.

Illustrator of numerous other children's books.

Contributor of short stories to journals, including *Puffin Post.*

SIDELIGHTS: Scoular Anderson is the author and illustrator of more than sixty books and the illustrator of at least a hundred more. His internet web site informs the viewer that he likes to write about unusual facts or events, and he enjoys writing history books because it allows him to read widely and search for "interesting facts." Many of Anderson's titles are history books, illustrated with his own cartoons, and some couch their history lessons in puzzle series that readers can solve along the way. Anderson's books are popular among young readers, even as young as age six or seven, and it is said that the humorous cartoon illustrations make them appealing to older, reluctant readers as well.

One of Anderson's early successes was *A Plunder of Pirates,* in which he relates the stories of several famous pirates, both male and female. From their stories the reader learns interesting background information about how people came to be pirates, how they dressed and talked, what daily life was like aboard a pirate ship, and about the ships and their armaments as well. The book proved popular enough to merit a redesign and reprint titled *Project Pirates,* which Stuart Hannabuss referred to in *School Librarian* as a witty and "light-hearted" presentation for young readers. A *Junior Bookshelf* reviewer cautioned, however, that *Project Pirates* does "include some chilling details." Yet Kevin Steinberger praised the reprint in *Magpies* as full of facts so "engaging" and "comically presented" that children would be inspired "to read it [from] cover to cover."

In *Land Ahoy! The Story of Christopher Columbus,* Anderson introduces young readers to the self-styled "admiral of the ocean sea." In humorous narrative, punctuated by lively cartoons, maps, and other line drawings, the author/illustrator presents a great deal of biographical and historical detail and even offers his views on what might have compelled the explorer to risk his life and the lives of his crew, not once, but four times in his futile quest to reach the East Indies. Though Barbara Roberts reported "some minor discrepancies" in her *Science Books & Films* review, Ingrid Broomfield, writing for *School Librarian,* commended Anderson for an account that is "factually accurate without being . . . boring." In *Books for Keeps,* Veronica Holliday noted a "carefully balanced . . . blend of humour and factual information." Holliday also recommended *Land Ahoy!* for its "refreshingly lively, anecdotal style."

Anderson has penned and illustrated two popular children's histories of his native Scotland, *1314 and All That*—1314 being the year the Scots won their independence from England at the Battle of Bannockburn—and *1745 and All That: The Story of the Highlands.* He described daily life in other times in *Trev the Tudor Gets the Chop (Nearly)* and *Rob the Roman Gets Eaten by a Lion (Nearly).* Each of these books contains facts about historical events, humorous anecdotes and obscure trivia about the people and the times in which they lived and, of course, Anderson's trademark cartoon illustrations.

Sometimes Anderson disguises his histories in puzzle books. He introduces inventor Hector MacPelican in *A Puzzling Day at Castle MacPelican,* which takes readers on a treasure hunt full of puzzles to solve, mazes to explore, and tiny details of evidence to spot in the illustrations. In her *School Librarian* review, Elizabeth J. King noted an "amazing amount of detail" in the art work and the "sheer fun" of pursuing the hidden treasure. In *MacPelican's American Adventure* the inventor leads readers, along with the whole MacPelican family, on a tour of the United States as it appeared in 1898, the year of the "Grand Louisiana Exhibition." Readers with the "patience, fortitude, and great vision" required to solve the puzzles in this book, observed Susan Pine in *School Library Journal,* will also be treated to a scenic tour of America at the end of the nineteenth century. In *A Puzzling Day in the Land of the Pharaohs* the adventurous reader travels backward in time with Mrs. Pudget and her students to ancient Egypt. In what *School Library Journal* critic Jane Claes called a "lighthearted romp around an ancient world," readers can't help but learn something about Egyptian history as they search for the clues they need to solve puzzles that will return them to their own world and time.

Anderson is also a fiction writer. In his "Wizard Boy" series, he introduces Eric and his father, a somewhat bumbling wizard whose attempts at magic often stray far afield. In *The Perfect Pizza* Dad attempts to spruce up dinner with a magic spell that ends up turning pizza dough into snow and transforming the family's pets beyond recognition, not to mention creating a mess in the kitchen. Therefore, in *The Posh Party,* when Dad offers to substitute for a birthday-party magician, Eric has some anxious reservations. In *The Potty Panto* Dad is assigned to provide special effects for a children's play, and in *The Muddled Monsters* he tries to repair one of the rides at the Mighty Monster Theme Park. Margaret Mallett, in a *School Librarian* review of *The Perfect Pizza,* described the combination of page layout, narrative, and cartoon-style illustrations as "cleverly matched" to "add energy and interest." The series is meant for beginning readers, and Mallett predicted that the books will encourage children toward the joy of reading and the joy of learning as well.

Also for the beginning reader is *Dreamy Daniel, Brainy Bert.* Daniel is a daydreamer, not much interested in reading or learning. During idle moments in class he begins to notice a little mouse who lives in the classroom. Sherbert the mouse is no daydreamer; he can read and write. The boy and the mouse become friends, and "Bert" offers a series of tips to help Daniel with his studies, including a trip to the school library. The book is intended to motivate reluctant readers, but Frances Ball pointed out in *School Librarian* that Bert is a well-rounded, engaging little fellow, "and the advice about reading is nicely disguised."

For the very young Anderson has written and illustrated *The Enormous Chocolate Pudding,* about a king with an incongruous problem. Somehow the palace garden sprouted a chocolate pudding so huge that it is blocking the king's view from his window. What to do? The king tries everything, to no avail. The court jester finds an answer, but he must somehow get the king to think it was his own royal idea. The solution unfolds in a colorful two-page spread that requires no narrative explanation. A *Books for Keeps* contributor remarked that the story, with its detailed illustrations, provides "plenty to laugh about." Critic Elizabeth J. King enthusiastically recommended *The Enormous Chocolate Pudding* in the *British Book News,* citing a "good story line" with "funny, expressive illustrations" that demonstrate the author's sense of "visual and verbal humour."

Anderson is also noted for the sense of humor he demonstrates in numerous joke books for young readers and his "awful truth" books, in which he offers fun facts and quasi-facts about school, grownups, and other aspects of childhood that sometimes puzzle and frustrate young readers everywhere.

BIOGRAPHICAL AND CRITICAL SOURCES:

PERIODICALS

Books, October, 1989, review of *The Knock Knock Joke Book,* p. 22; July, 1991, Tony Bradman, review of *The Puffin Book of Royal London,* p. 8.

Books for Keeps, May, 1989, review of *The Enormous Chocolate Pudding,* p. 8; March, 1992, review of *The Magic Boomerang; The Magic Present,* p. 9; May, 1992, Veronica Halliday, review of *Land Ahoy! The Story of Christopher Columbus,* p. 22; July, 1992, review of *Dreamy Daniel, Brainy Bert,* p. 11; May, 1995, review of *The Amazing Mark in Creepstone Castle,* p. 11; November, 1999, review of *MacPelican's American Adventure,* p. 24.

British Book News, December, 1987, review of *The Enormous Chocolate Pudding,* p. 11.

Horn Book Guide, spring, 1997, Kelly A. Ault, review of *A Puzzling Day in the Land of the Pharaohs,* p. 142; fall, 1998, Patricia Riley, review of *MacPelican's American Adventure,* p. 399.

Junior Bookshelf, June, 1995, review of *Project Pirates: Amazing Facts! Amazing Fun!,* p. 98.

Magpies, May, 1995, Kevin Steinberger, review of *A Plunder of Pirates* and *Project Pirates,* p. 36.

Publishers Weekly, August 5, 1996, review of *A Puzzling Day in the Land of the Pharaohs,* p. 442.

School Librarian, August, 1992, review of *Dreamy Daniel, Brainy Bert,* p. 99; August, 1992, review of *Land Ahoy!,* p. 105; May, 1995, Elizabeth J. King, review of *A Puzzling Day at Castle MacPelican,* p. 62; May, 1995, Stuart Hannabuss, review of *Project Pirates,* p. 68.

School Library Journal, May, 1990, Carolyn Jenks, review of *Hiccup Harry,* p. 90; June, 1995, JoAnn Rees, review of *A Puzzling Day at Castle MacPelican,* p. 76; October, 1996, Jane Claes, review of *A Puzzling Day in the Land of the Pharaohs,* p. 120; August, 1998, Susan Pine, review of *MacPelican's American Adventure,* p. 132; spring, 2001, Margaret Mallett, review of *The Perfect Pizza,* p. 17; summer, 2001, Carol Woolley, review of *The Bin Bears,* p. 73.

Science Books & Films, November, 1992, Barbara Roberts, review of Land Ahoy!, p. 244.

OTHER

Scoular Anderson, http://www.scoularanderson.co.uk (March 8, 2002).*

*   *   *

ANDRIĆ, Stanko 1967-

PERSONAL: Born January 27, 1967, in Strizivojna, Croatia; son of a farmer, and a homemaker. *Ethnicity:* "Croatian". *Education:* University of Zagreb, B.A., 1993; Central European University, Budapest, Hungary, Ph.D., 1998.

ADDRESSES: Home—B. Radića 344, Strizivojna, Croatia 31410. *Office*—Croatian Institute of History, Starčevićeva 8, HR-35000, Slavonski Brod, Croatia; fax: 385-447-243. *E-mail*—stankoa@yahoo.com.

CAREER: Croatian Institute of History, Slavonski Brod, Croatia, research fellow in medieval history, 1996—.

MEMBER: PEN Croatia, Croatian Writers' Association.

AWARDS, HONORS: Vladimir Nazor Award, Croatian Ministry of Culture, 2001.

WRITINGS:

The Miracles of St. John Capistran, Central European University Press (Budapest, Hungary), 2000.
Povijest Slavonije u Sedam Požara: Enciklopedija Nijtavila; Dnevnik iz Jna, Volume 1, Durieux (Zagreb, Croatia), 2001.
(Editor) *Scrinia Slavonica,* [Slavonski Brod, Croatia], 2001.

WORK IN PROGRESS: Simurg, a novel; research on medieval monasteries of Slavonia, in northeastern Croatia.

SIDELIGHTS: Stanko Andrić told *CA:* "Most of my prose writing is influenced by literary and historical erudition. My favorite major writers include Bruno Schulz, Isak Babel, Boris Pilnyak, André Gide, Quevedo, and many others. I first wrote three books of prose texts that somehow combine essay and fiction (they are collected in my second book), then I also started writing scholarly works in medieval history (which is the basis of my present-day profession). Along with this, I am slowly writing a novel titled *Simurg* (the name of a mythological bird), which is a blend of fiction and autobiography."

*   *   *

ANGOLD, Michael

PERSONAL: Male. *Education:* Oxford University, B.A., D. Phil.

ADDRESSES: Agent—c/o Author Mail, St. Martin's Press, 175 Fifth Ave., New York, NY 10010. *E-mail*—Michael.Angold@ed.ac.uk.

CAREER: University of Edinburgh, professor of Byzantine history, 1970—.

WRITINGS:

A Byzantine Government in Exile: Government and Society under the Laskarids of Nicaea, 1204-1261, Oxford University Press (London, England), 1975.
The Byzantine Empire 1025-1204: A Political History, Longman (London, England), 1984.
(Editor) *The Byzantine Aristocracy, IX to XIII Centuries,* B.A.R. (Oxford, England), 1984.
Church and Society in Byzantium under the Comneni, 1081-1261, Cambridge University Press (Cambridge, England), 1995.
Byzantium: The Bridge from Antiquity to the Middle Ages, St. Martin's Press (New York, NY), 2001.

SIDELIGHTS: Michael Angold is a professor of history and an accomplished scholar who focuses his studies on the Byzantine Empire. From his first book to his most recent, critics and colleagues have praised his scholarship and extensive research. For instance, *History Today*'s Alan Haymes wrote in his review of Angold's first book, *A Byzantine Government in Exile: Government and Society under the Lascarids of Nicaea*

1204-1261, "On the evidence of this book Michael Angold can be admitted to the select ranks of first-rate Byzantinists writing in English."

More than twenty years later, in a review of Angold's *Church and Society in Byzantium under the Comneni 1081-1261* for the *Journal of Theological Studies,* Andrew Louth wrote: "Angold's book is a major achievement; it draws together a mass of scholarship and has an even-handedness that is based on a sure knowledge of the sources."

In his *A Byzantine Government in Exile,* Angold explores the fall and attempted resurrection of Constantinople, at one time the capital of the Byzantine government. He focuses on the fifty-seven-year span when Theodore Lascaris retreated to Nicaea after the crusaders toppled his power base in Constantinople. It was during this time that Lascaris created a very tight and less-complex form of rule than the previous government in Constantinople. The new Nicaean government fought its enemies successfully and gained considerable wealth and stability. With this kind of success, as John L. Teall put it in *American Historical Review,* "Was not the reconquest [of Constantinople] . . . a mistake rather than an achievement?" Teall went on to suggest that this question is "implicitly posed in Michael Angold's substantial survey of the institutions of the empire of Nicaea."

Anthony Bryer, writing for the *Times Literary Supplement,* came away from reading *A Byzantine Government in Exile* with another suggestion as to Angold's underlying theme. Bryer concluded that Angold's thesis is "how the Nicaean aristocracy definitively concluded . . . a process in Byzantine government which had begun a century before: a shift from the old Byzantine Whitehall departments to a 'household' government, and the confirmation that kinship, rather than office, now led to power."

Despite the difference of opinions, most reviewers praised Angold's first book, which was a revision of his doctoral dissertation. As Robert Browning stated in the *English Historical Review,* "Angold's book will take its place . . . among the most authoritative and valuable studies of the strange Babylonian exile of the East Roman Empire, when so many of the features which determined its subsequent development first emerged."

For his second book, Angold dropped back a couple of centuries in order to cover, as J. D. Howard-Johnston noted in the *Times Literary Supplement,* the "high drama" of the history of Byzantium. Angold's *The Byzantine Empire 1025-1204: A Political History* relates the events that took place during a period of initial peace. The Empire, which stretched out over a wide section of the Near East and the Balkans, was shortly afterward shattered by an invasion of Turks and then one by the Normans, with the final blow arriving in the form of Western crusaders who took control of Constantinople in 1204.

"Michael Angold," Howard-Johnston explained in his review, "places these political events, which form the main subject of his book, in their cultural, economic and social context." Two of the most notable characteristics of this economic and social context were the development and revival of town life, which Angold believes, as stated by Howard-Johnston, were "the motors of economic growth and social differentiation." Another important factor was the development of elite clans, "which could rival the official imperial authority itself," wrote Howard-Johnston.

Angold's writing style invites non-scholars into his work. As Patrick Leigh Fermor of the *Spectator* wrote, "The story will fascinate not only historians but all those interested in politics. Let them draw parallels between then and now as they please. The book is well-written."

In 1995 Angold focused his writing on the relationship between the Byzantine church and its society. *Church and Society in Byzantium under the Comneni, 1081-1261* roughly covers the same period as his first and second books combined, but in this third book Angold takes a different angle. "Most books on Byzantium tend to discuss its history in terms of state and church to the neglect of 'society,'" wrote *Choice* critic F. Ahmad. However, Angold "rectifies this major shortcoming" with his "thorough analysis" of the period contained in this book.

The relationship between church and state in the Byzantine Empire was tightly knit and, for many historians, difficult to decipher. The patriarchs of the church wielded power unlike any other church elites, including even the Roman church. Angold, fortunately for the modern reader, had access to newly discovered texts, which provided him with a clearer understanding of the complexities and conflicts of power between those two powers that eventually led to the fall of the ancient empire. Louth, in his review for the *Journal of Theological Studies,* wrote that because of this new research, Angold is able to scrutinize "the genuine complicities that characterized Byzantine society," which allow him to argue "that they produced a society in which power and leadership failed to mesh, thus making the fall of Constantinople perhaps more inevitable than it has sometimes been regarded."

Angold's *Church and Society,* like his previous books, received much critical praise. Rosemary Morris, writing for the *English Historical Review,* stated, "It is a mark of the achievement of Michael Angold's monumental new study that the two fundamental questions that underlie it: 'What was the Byzantine Church?' and 'What was Byzantine Society?' are so forcibly confronted. The exemplary clarity of the writing and the logical structure of the work make it always possible to see the wood for the trees." Finding Angold's work comprehensive, although a bit complex, Dion C. Smythe, of the *Journal of Ecclesiastical History,* concluded: "The book is not an easy introduction, but for anyone wishing a serious treatment of this complex yet engrossing subject, a reading of this work . . . will prove most edifying."

In his most recent book, *Byzantium: The Bridge from Antiquity to the Middle Ages,* Angold relates the transition of the Mediterranean world from the vastly powerful Roman Empire to the birth of the Catholic, Byzantine, and Islamic civilizations. "Of these," wrote critic Robert J. Andrews for the *Library Journal,* "Angold believes that Byzantium played a pivotal role by being the entity by and against which the emerging civilizations of the Catholic West and Islam defined themselves."

Angold begins *Byzantium* in this book with Constantine, who was responsible for decreeing that Christianity would be the official religion of the Roman Empire. He then moved to Constantinople, which competed with Rome as the center of power for the Roman Empire. Christianity in Rome differed in practice from that in Constantinople, thus increasing tensions already existing between the two large centers. When Islamic forces invaded Constantinople in the seventh century, the unity of the city began to crumble. A reviewer for

Publishers Weekly referred to Angold's book as a "richly layered narrative" that "brings to life the many faceted cultures of Byzantium, crown jewel of the East from the fourth century to the Middle Ages."

BIOGRAPHICAL AND CRITICAL SOURCES:

PERIODICALS

American History Review, April, 1978, John L. Teall, review of *A Byzantine Government in Exile: Government and Society under the Laskarids of Nicaea, 1204-1261,* p. 413.

Choice, March, 1996, F. Ahmad, review of *Church and Society in Byzantium under the Comneni, 1081-1261,* p. 1192.

English Historical Review, April, 1976, Robert Browning, review of *A Byzantine Government in Exile,* pp. 356-358; January, 1988, Simon Franklin, review of *The Byzantine Empire, 1025-1204: A Political History,* pp. 173-134; June 1997, Rosemary Morris, review of *Church and Society in Byzantium under the Comneni, 1081-1261,* pp. 679-681.

History Today, September, 1975, review of *A Byzantine Government in Exile,* pp. 652-653; December, 2001, Paul Stephenson, review of *Byzantium: The Bridge from Antiquity to the Middle Ages,* p. 60.

Journal of Ecclesiastical History, July, 1997, Dion C. Smythe, review of *Church and Society in Byzantium under the Comneni, 1081-1261,* pp. 544-545.

Journal of Theological Studies, October, 1996, Andrew Louth, review of *Church and Society in Byzantium under the Comneni, 1081-1261,* pp. 737-739.

Library Journal, February 15, 2002, Robert J. Andrews, review of *Byzantium,* pp. 156-157.

Publishers Weekly, October 29, 2001, review of *Byzantium,* p. 47.

Spectator, August 17, 1985, Eric Christiansen, "Were the Logothetes in Control?" pp. 21, 24.

Times Educational Supplement, January 3, 1986, review of *The Byzantine Empire, 1025-1204,* p. 16.

Times Literary Supplement, September 5, 1975, Anthony Bryer, "Doing without Constantinople," p. 1005; May 31, 1985, J. D. Howard-Johnston, "The Gathering Clans," p. 616; November 23, 2001, Averil Cameron, "A Mobile Empire," p. 21.*

ANGUELOV, Zlatko 1946-

PERSONAL: Born June 18, 1946, in Varna, Bulgaria; immigrated to Canada, 1992; naturalized Canadian citizen; son of Radoslav and Velika Anguelov; married; wife's name, Lyudmila (deceased); married May 15, 1965; wife's name, Tatyana (marriage ended); married Roumyana Slabarova (a professor of linguistics), August 7, 1984; children: (second marriage) Radoslava, Vela, Aglika, Zlatko, Kamen; (third marriage) Bistra. *Ethnicity:* "Bulgarian." *Education:* Medical Academy of Bulgaria, M.D., 1972; McGill University, M.A., 1995, and doctoral study. *Politics:* Liberal. *Religion:* Greek Orthodox. *Hobbies and other interests:* Movies, car racing, travel, photography, gardening.

ADDRESSES: Home—207 Golfview Ave., Iowa City, IA 52246-1909. *Office*—Joint Office for Planning, Marketing, and Communications, University of Iowa Health Care, 200 Hawkins Dr., Suite 8762 JPP, Iowa City, IA 52242-1009; fax: 319-384-7099. *E-mail*—zlatko-anguelov@uiowa.edu.

CAREER: Medical Academy, Varna, Bulgaria, began as assistant professor, became associate professor of anatomy, 1974-83; District Hospital, Sofia, Bulgaria, general practitioner of family medicine, 1983-86; freelance medical and political journalist, 1986-90; Medical Academy, Sofia, Bulgaria, public relations officer and spokesperson, 1990-92; McGill University, Montreal, Quebec, Canada, research and teaching assistant, 1993-96; Benefit Canada, Montreal, Quebec, Canada, international health consultant, 1995-96; LBJ*FRB Communications, Montreal, Quebec, Canada, medical writer, 1996-99; University of Iowa Health Care, Iowa City, editor and senior communications specialist in Joint Office for Planning, Marketing, and Communications, 1999—. Barry and Associates, legal secretary, 1993.

AWARDS, HONORS: AAMC/GIA awards of distinction, 2001, and award for excellence, 2002, all for *Currents.*

WRITINGS:

Communism and the Remorse of an Innocent Victimizer (memoir), Texas A & M University Press (College Station, TX), 2000.

Contributor to periodicals in Bulgaria and elsewhere, including *Financial Times* newsletters in England. Founder and editor of Bulgarian newspaper *Rights and Liberties; Currents,* editor; *East European Reporter,* coeditor. Anguelov's memoir has been published in Bulgarian translation.

WORK IN PROGRESS: Conversations with My Daughter, a "non-fictional novel," completion expected in 2005.

SIDELIGHTS: Zlatko Anguelov told *CA:* "I began my career as a professor of anatomy in a medical school, but interrupted it after nine years because of irreconcilable disagreements with the communist-oriented educational and biomedical research environment in my native Bulgaria. I freelanced as a medical journalist for six years, then became a political commentator involved in the first years of democratization after changes in the East European communist regimes were unleashed in 1989. In August, 1992, my family and I immigrated to Canada.

"It was only too natural that, from the Canadian vantage point, I embarked on reflections about my life under communism—a life blemished by failures, frustrations, and inevitable compromises with the communist authorities. As a result, I drafted my memoir in 1995 while studying for a doctorate in political sociology at McGill University. English not being my native language, the manuscript needed to brew for several years, a time that also helped me better shape my own memories, ideas, and the entire message of my book. It also was a time when I contacted literary agents and acquainted myself with the publishing world in the United States and Canada. In 1999, I moved to an editorial position with the University of Iowa Health Care and reworked my manuscript before sending it out to five university presses and two small commercial publishers. In February, 2001, I got word from Texas A & M University Press that my manuscript was accepted for publication.

"The effect of this memoir upon myself was the realization that my large extended family has a rich history rooted in the Balkans and now, after most of my children moved to live in a freer world, that can be a great resource for my writing. My first book was, for obvious reasons, nonfiction. However, I entertain the conviction that I have life-material interesting enough to create stories or novels that would be called 'non-fictional' short stories or novels. Thus, I'm now focused on this genre merger and am working on my next book. It draws mainly from a rich correspondence and phone conversations that I have had with one of my daughters for more than a decade and keep having almost every day. We started our relationship back in Bulgaria, she suffered from my divorce from her mother, and then we both moved to the United States (although via different routes). The building of our relationship contains tons of messages, implications, stories, and so forth related to the father-daughter relationship, the formation of a child into an adult, and the integration of an immigrant family into the United States.

"It is not so often that a writer has his or her first book published at the age of fifty-six, but the circumstances of my life—and chiefly, the lack of fundamental freedom—delayed this event. I have always considered myself a writer, however, and behaved as such. My style is mostly shaped by journalism. Journalism has been my real school of writing, and I still earn my bread and butter through it, but writing is my vocation. I'm happy that now I have the freedom to embark, no matter how late, on the life project of writing books that will, no matter what, have some historic value. Communism was a political deviation that changed the fortunes of so many people. The story of communism, unlike that of the Holocaust, has not yet been publicized in its wholeness, and awareness of its universal meaning is still lacking. In my opinion, the best way to raise awareness about communism is to tell the stories of those of us ordinary citizens who were both victims and victimizers of our peers."

*   *   *

ANREUS, Alejandro 1960-

PERSONAL: Born September 11, 1960, in Havana, Cuba; naturalized U.S. citizen; son of Margarita Rodriguez (a factory worker); married Debra Bleharr, October 12, 1985; children: David Rentkiewicz, Isabel. *Ethnicity:* "Latino." *Education:* Kean College of New Jersey, B.A., 1984; City University of New York, M.A., 1995, Ph.D., 1997. *Politics:* "Democratic Socialist." *Religion:* Roman Catholic. *Hobbies and other interests:* Fellini films, Don DeLillo novels, walking.

ADDRESSES: Office—Department of Art, William Paterson University of New Jersey, 300 Pompton Rd., Wayne, NJ 07470. *E-mail*—anreusa@wpunj.edu.

CAREER: Montclair Art Museum, Montclair, NJ, began as assistant curator, became curator, 1986-93; Jersey City Museum, Jersey City, NJ, curator, 1993-2001; William Paterson University of New Jersey, Wayne, NJ, associate professor of art history, 2001—.

MEMBER: College Art Association of America.

AWARDS, HONORS: Nancy Hanks Award, American Association of Museums, 1993.

WRITINGS:

Ben Shahn and the Passion of Sacco and Vanzetti, Rutgers University Press (Piscataway, NJ), 2001.
Orozco in Gringoland, University of New Mexico Press (Albuquerque, NJ), 2001.

WORK IN PROGRESS: Editing *The Social and the Real,* with others, for Princeton University Press (Princeton, NJ), completion expected in 2003; a manuscript on exile and Cuban-American artists.

SIDELIGHTS: Alejandro Anreus told *CA:* "I am an art historian. I write to elucidate the meaning(s) of art and its social context. My thinking and writing about art history are influenced by the social historians of art: Arnold Hauser, Meyer Schapiro, John Berger, Marta Traba, and Alan Wallach.

"Writing is quite an ordeal. My mother tongue is very baroque (Spanish), so I am always struggling for clarity. Models of clear prose include Orwell and Camus. I write first in pencil, longhand. Then I type a first draft, edit it, then make a final draft.

"I am inspired by the crossroads of art and politics, particularly during the 1920s and 1930s in the Americas. Here are the subjects for the rest of my writing career."

*   *   *

AQUINO, Michael A. 1946-

PERSONAL: Born October 16, 1946, in San Francisco, CA; married Lilith Sinclair (a Satanic cult leader). *Education:* University of California, Santa Barbara, B.A., 1968, M.A., 1976, Ph.D., 1980.

ADDRESSES: Home—P. O. Box 470307, San Francisco, CA 94147. *E-mail*—Xeper@aol.com.

CAREER: U.S. Army, career officer specializing in psychological warfare, began 1968, became Lieutenant colonel in military intelligence, retired; served in Vietnam. Ordained Satanic priest, c. 1971-72; Temple of Set, founder and leader, 1975-96.

MEMBER: Eagle Scouts Honor Society (past national commander).

WRITINGS:

The Church of Satan, privately printed, 1989.

Contributor to periodicals, including *Cloven Hoof.*

SIDELIGHTS: In 1969, one year after Michael A. Aquino both graduated from University of California Santa Barbara with a B.A. in political science and joined the army as a psychological warfare specialist, he joined the Church of Satan, headed by Anton LaVey; Aquino then served a tour of duty in Vietnam. When he returned, the army stationed him in Kentucky and he became a priest within the Church of Satan, forming a grotto—a group of believers—that met in his home there. Aquino soon became disenchanted with the Church, however, under LaVey's leadership, and in 1972, he, along with Lilith Sinclair—a Church of Satan leader who eventually married Aquino—split from it. This split appears to stem, in large part, from the two men's conflicting ideologies: LaVey, an atheist, believed that Satan did not exist but rather represented, as a symbol, strength and defiance; Aquino, on the other hand, believed in the literal existence of Satan, and in 1975, he established a church of his own, known as the Temple of Set.

Set, an ancient Egyptian god who evolved into the Judeo-Christian figure of Satan, reportedly appeared before Aquino and gave him a document called *The Book of Coming Forth by Night,* the founding text of the Temple. According to a contributor to *Religious Leaders of America,* Aquino defined the Temple's ambition as "awakening the divine power of the individual through the deliberate exercise of will and intelligence," referring to the process by which this

happens as "Xeper." Two reasons why so little is known about the group, including the size of its following, stems from its secretive atmosphere, as well as its emphasis on the individual over unity.

While in the position of high priest of the Temple of Set, Aquino wrote and self-published *The Church of Satan.* In 1996, Aquino stepped down from his position, leaving the group in the hands of Don Webb.

BIOGRAPHICAL AND CRITICAL SOURCES:

BOOKS

Encyclopedia of Occultism and Parapsychology, 5th edition, Gale (Detroit, MI), 2001.
Religious Leaders of America, 2nd edition, Gale (Detroit, MI) 1999.

ONLINE

Temple of Set Official Web site, http://www.xeper.org/ (April 1, 2003), biography of Aquino.
University of Virginia Religious Movements Web site, http://religiousmovements.lib.virginia.edu/ (December 8, 2000), Joe Abrams, Temple of Set profile.*

*   *   *

ARCHER, Richard 1941-

PERSONAL: Born November 22, 1941, in Whittier, CA; married; children: one daughter, one son. *Education:* University of California—Santa Barbara, B.A., 1964, M.A., 1966, Ph.D., 1968.

ADDRESSES: Office—Department of History, Whittier College, Whittier, CA 90608.

CAREER: Central Michigan University, Mount Pleasant, MI, assistant professor, 1968-72, associate professor of history, 1972-75, director of honors program, 1972-74; Whittier College, Whittier, CA, began as assistant dean, became associate dean for academic affairs, 1975-92, director of Whittier scholars program, 1977-92, professor of history, 1982—, dean of college life, 1989-90, faculty master, 1990-94.

AWARDS, HONORS: Fellow of Haynes Foundation, 1984; Whittier College, Harry Nerhood Teaching Excellence Award, 1986, Marilyn Veich Award, 1993; named outstanding academic advisor for Pacific region, American College Testing Program and National Academic Advising Association, 1989.

WRITINGS:

Fissures in the Rock: New England in the Seventeenth Century, University Press of New England (Hanover, NH), 2001.

Coauthor of booklet *From Commonwealth to Commerce: The Pre-industrial City in America,* Forum Press, 1978. Contributor of articles and reviews to periodicals, including *American Studies* and *William and Mary Quarterly.*

WORK IN PROGRESS: Editing *Pen, Ink, and Paper: Letters of a Nineteenth-Century American Family,* with Virginia Archer; *New England in a Revolutionary Era.*

SIDELIGHTS: Richard Archer told *CA:* "*Fissures in the Rock: New England in the Seventeenth Century* is the product of a long and circuitous journey. When I left graduate school for my first job in 1968, I was a historian of the early national period. My dissertation was on the Hartford Convention, and it reflected my interests in the question of how governments function after a revolution and in anti-war movements.

"1968 turned out to be a threshold year for me. Not only was I finally finished with being a student and was beginning my first full-time position, but by the time my wife and I left California for Michigan that summer she was pregnant with our first child. In a larger context, of course, were the assassination of Martin Luther King, Jr., and the election of [president] Richard Nixon. As a new teacher, I questioned how I could justify taking up some of the allotted hours of my students' time. As a father-to-be, I began to read books on child development and child-rearing—books like *Summerhill, How Children Learn,* and *Growing*

up Absurd. As a citizen, I began to question whether the American system worked. All told, I was becoming disillusioned with many American institutions and started a search for alternatives.

"Four years later I was director of the honors program at Central Michigan University. In many ways, that was a surprise. A son of teachers, I generally had a low opinion of administrators (I must confess to a certain extent I still hold that view), and now I was one. That was not the way I had envisioned my career, but the honors program provided a rare opportunity. It had died, and the president of the university wanted it resuscitated. He offered a small group of us pretty close to *carte blanche,* and we leapt at the chance. We transformed it into a residential program in one of the residence halls where alternative educational options were offered to students, and it became an honors program in name only. Quickly it grew to 500 students. Although I was teaching only part-time, I introduced some topics that had not been available in the history department, such as a course on intentional communities and communes.

"The course sparked my interest in the topic so much that I began a research project on the history of American intentional communities. Here is where seventeenth-century New England comes in. What better place to begin the study? Several of the path-breaking New England town studies that were just being published suggested that these were utopian villages. Several years later I came to the conclusion that they were not early communes, and I abandoned the project; but my interest in early New England remained.

"In 1975 I returned to California. Whittier College attracted me with its long tradition of innovative education and the social ethic of its Quaker founders. Here was an opportunity to create a full-fledged, degree-granting, individualized program, and it also would bring our two children closer to their California grandparents. For the next half-dozen years, most of my energy was devoted to developing a program and helping to rear our children. Occasionally I produced an article or a review, and I taught one course a year in the history department, but I had no large-scale research project.

"Gradually the seed that became *Fissures in the Rock* began to sprout and tentatively grow. I had noticed that all of the marvelous books that were coming out on early New England focused only on a local subject (such as towns) or an idea (such as aspects of Puritanism and other forms of Reformed Protestantism) or on specific issues (such as gender). There were no studies that examined all of New England comprehensively. I decided I wanted to do a study that looked at the early history of New England from the bottom up, from the top down, and from all possible angles—a total history, if possible. I wanted to see how the pieces fit together. I wanted to examine diversity and culture. And, believing that professional history had become too incestuous, I wanted to write a history accessible to a general audience as well as to scholars.

"The work started by compiling a broad database of as many of the early residents as possible. That was necessary to find patterns that transcended the parts, and also it was manageable in short time-spans that I would work between administrative and family responsibilities. By 1987 the database had grown to 22,000 New England souls, all captured in my computer. Most of this was a slow, tedious examination of records, but it also included research trips/ family vacations, such as a three-week trip where the four of us primarily visited seventeenth-century New England houses. Some of us were more enthused about the venture than others. This first stage of research culminated in an article on the demographic history of seventeenth-century New England that was published in the *William and Mary Quarterly* in 1990.

"In 1992 I left administration but, along with my wife, served as a faculty master. When we left I was treated to an uninterrupted fifteen months of sabbatical leave before at long last returning to my original career choice of being a faculty member. Then I was able to flesh out the research and eventually begin writing."

*   *   *

ARNOLD, Edwin 1832-1904

PERSONAL: Born June 10, 1832, in Gravesend, England; died March 24, 1904, in London, England; son of Robert Coles Arnold (a Sussex magistrate); married Katharine Elizabeth Biddulph, 1854 (died 1864); married Fannie Maria Adelaide Channing, 1864 (died 1889); married Tama Kura Kawa, 1897. *Education:* University College, Oxford, B.A. (with honors), 1854, M.A., 1856.

CAREER: Poet, journalist, and translator. King Edward's School, Birmingham, England, master, 1854-56; Deccan College at Poona, Bombay, India, principal, 1856-61; *Daily Telegraph,* London, England, writer, subeditor, then editor, 1861-88.

MEMBER: Order of the White Elephant of Siam (officer), Third Class of the Imperial Order of the Medjidie, Royal Asiatic and Royal Geographical Societies (fellow), Société de Géographie (Marseilles, France).

AWARDS, HONORS: Newdigate Prize, 1852, for *The Feast of Belshazzar;* Companion of the Star of India, 1877; Knight Commander of the Order of the Indian Empire, 1888.

WRITINGS:

The Feast of Belshazzar: A Prize Poem, Macpherson (Oxford, England), 1852, [New York, NY], 1868.

Poems, Narrative and Lyrical, Macpherson (Oxford, England), 1853.

Griselda, a Tragedy, and Other Poems, Bogue (London, England), 1856.

The Wreck of the Northern Belle: A Poem, Bacon (Hastings, England), 1857.

Education in India, Bell & Daldy (London, England), 1860.

The Marquis of Dalhousie's Administration of British India, two volumes, Saunders, Otley (London, England), 1862-65.

The Poets of Greece, Cassell, Peter & Galpin (New York, NY), 1869.

A Simple Transliteral Grammar of the Turkish Language with Dialogues and Vocabulary, Trübner (London, England), 1877.

The Light of Asia; or, The Great Renunciation— Mahâbhinishkramana; Being the Life and Teaching of Gautama, Prince of India and Founder of Buddhism (as Told in Verse by an Indian Buddhist), Trübner (London, England), 1879, Roberts Brothers (Boston, MA), 1880.

Poems, Roberts Brothers (Boston, MA), 1880.

Indian Poetry, Dutton (New York, NY), 1881.

Pearls of the Faith; or, Islam's Rosary; Being the Ninety-nine Beautiful Names of Allah (Asmâ-el-husmâ) with Comments in Verse from Various Oriental Sources as Made by an Indian Mussulman, Roberts Brothers (Boston, MA), 1883.

The Secret of Death, with Some Collected Poems, Roberts Brothers (Boston, MA), 1885.

Edwin Arnold Birthday Book, Compiled from the Works of Edwin Arnold, with New and Additional Poems Written Expressly Therefor, edited by Katherine Lilian Arnold and Constance Arnold, D. Lothrop (Boston, MA), 1885.

India Revisited, Roberts Brothers (Boston, MA), 1886.

Death—and Afterwards, Trübner (London, England), 1887.

Lotus and Jewel, Containing "In an Indian Temple," "A Casket of Gems," with Other Poems, Trübner (London, England), 1887.

Poems, National and Non-Oriental, with Some New Pieces, Trübner (London, England), 1888.

With Sa'di in the Garden; or, The Book of Love; Being the "Ishk" or Third Chapter of the "Bostân" of the Persian Poet Sa'di—Embodied in a Dialogue Held in the Garden of the Taj Mahal, at Agra, Roberts Brothers (Boston, MA), 1888.

In My Lady's Praise; Being Poems, Old and New, Written to the Honour of Fanny, Lady Arnold, and New Collected for Her Memory, Trübner (London, England), 1889.

The Light of the World; or, The Great Consummation, Funk & Wagnalls (New York, NY), 1891.

Japonica, Scribners (New York, NY), 1891.

Seas and Lands, Longmans, Green (New York, NY), 1891.

Sir Edwin Arnold's Poetical Works, eight volumes, Kegan Paul, Trench, Trübner (London, England), 1891-1909.

Potiphar's Wife and Other Poems, Scribners (New York, NY), 1892.

Adzuma; or, The Japanese Wife: A Play in Four Acts, Longmans, Green (New York, NY), 1893.

Wandering Words, Longmans, Green (New York, NY), 1894.

The Tenth Muse and Other Poems, Longmans, Green (London, England), 1895.

Victoria, Queen and Empress: The Sixty Years, Longmans, Green (New York, NY), 1896.

The Queen's Justice: A True Story of Indian Village Life, Burleigh (London, England), 1899.

(Translator) *The Gulistan; Being the Rose-Garden of Shaikh Sa'di. The First Four "Babs," or "Gateways,"* Harper (New York, NY), 1899.

The Voyage of Ithobal: A Poem, Dillingham (New York, NY), 1901.

SIDELIGHTS: Edwin Arnold was a well-known British journalist and poet of the late nineteenth century.

Although much of his work did not endure into the twentieth century, Arnold enjoyed tremendous public and critical popularity throughout his lifetime.

Early in his career, Arnold lived in India and studied several languages of the Eastern world: Arabic, Persian, Sanskrit, and Turkish. As a result of his studies, he gained an appreciation for the culture, literature, and philosophy of the East, and he strove to bring Western readers into contact with these exotic worlds through his writings and translations. In particular, Arnold had a great love and respect for India, which is evidenced by his most popular work, *The Light of Asia: or, The Great Renunciation—Mahâbhinishkramana; Being the Life and Teaching of Gautama, Prince of India and Founder of Buddhism (as Told in Verse by an Indian Buddhist).* In the introduction to this book, Arnold wrote: "[It] is inspired by an abiding desire to aid in the better mutual knowledge of East and West." He further stated: "I hope . . . [that] this book . . . will preserve the memory of one who loved India and the Indian peoples."

During his undergraduate studies, Arnold was awarded the Newdigate Prize in 1852 for his poem *The Feast of Belshazzar.* This piece, which was based upon the Old Testament story of the prophet Daniel and King Belshazzar, was later published in Arnold's first collection of poetry, *Poems, Narrative and Lyrical.*

After his graduation from Oxford, Arnold married Katharine Elizabeth Biddulph. He then began to work as an educator, teaching for two years at King Edward's School in Birmingham, England. In 1856 he received a job offer from Deccan College in Bombay, India. Shortly thereafter, he and his wife moved to India, where Arnold worked as the principal of the government school. They lived in India for six years, during which time Arnold studied Eastern languages, customs, and culture.

Arnold returned to England in 1861. This move was precipitated by his wife's illness (she subsequently died in 1862) and the death of their only child. Upon his return to his homeland, Arnold embarked upon a new and different career. He began to write for the *London Daily Telegraph,* and continued employment with that newspaper until 1888. His journalistic skills were highly regarded and Arnold graduated from writing articles and editorials to a position as the newspaper's editor. Despite his highly demanding career, Arnold found time to pursue his other writing interests.

In 1879 he published his most well-known work, *The Light of Asia*. This poetic rendering of the life of Siddhartha Gautama (who would later become the Buddha) was an immediate success. Sixty editions of the book were published in England, while eighty editions appeared in the United States. The book's popularity was so great that it was also translated into other languages. These stories proved fascinating to European readers, for the life and teachings of Buddha were nearly unheard of in Europe before the publication of Arnold's work.

The Light of Asia relates the life of Prince Siddhartha from his birth and youth to his enlightenment under the Bodhi tree and subsequent ascendance to the status of Buddha. The eight books, written in blank verse, are told in the voice of an Indian Buddhist. According to Arnold in the book's introduction, he employed that technique "because, to appreciate the spirit of Asiatic thoughts, they should be regarded from the Oriental point of view." Oliver Wendell Holmes, as quoted by Bernard R. Kogan in the *Dictionary of Literary Biography*, described *The Light of Asia* as: "a work of great beauty. It tells a story of intense interest, which never flags for a moment; its descriptions are drawn by the hand of a master with the eye of a poet." Holmes also wrote: "its tone is so lofty that there is nothing with which to compare it but the New Testament." A writer for the London *Times*, also quoted by Kogan, noted: "The verse flows easily and is rich and luscious with oriental imagery; the thought never rises into heights where it is hard to follow."

Although *The Light of Asia* was widely received and highly acclaimed, there was a group of critics who "attacked the poem on both literary and moral-religious grounds," observed Kogan. Kogan noted that these writers, who embraced the Christian philosophy, denounced Arnold's work as "a pernicious book." William Cleaver Wilkinson was one of the strongest critics. In his book, *Edwin Arnold as Poetizer and as Paganizer*, he wrote: "Those who admire Mr. Edwin Arnold's poetry, admire unwisely." Wilkinson considered *The Light of Asia* to be "a broad joke from beginning to end." Kogan commented that Wilkinson was offended by Arnold's poem, feeling it "ensnared vast numbers of Christian readers" and forced them "from their ancient faith into the arms of a not altogether wholesome pagan one."

For the next twelve years, Arnold wrote various books; some dealt with Asian themes and others did not. His *Poems, National and Non-Oriental, with Some New Pieces* appeared as a "response to the reiterated charge that he wrote only Oriental poems," remarked Kogan. After the death of his second wife in 1889, Arnold published the work *In My Lady's Praise; Being Poems, Old and New, Written to the Honour of Fanny, Lady Arnold, and New Collected for Her Memory*.

Arnold may have felt compelled to write *The Light of the World; or, The Great Consummation* in order to appease critics of *The Light of Asia*. This poetic work paraphrases selected New Testament writings as the life of Jesus is conveyed to an Indian follower. By the end of the work, the disciple compares the teachings of Jesus to those of Buddha. According to Kogan: "Arnold failed to mitigate the negative feelings generated by the earlier *Light of Asia*, and the Christian epic achieved only a moderate success."

Despite various physical infirmities, Arnold continued to write until a few years before his death. He published several volumes of poetry, a biography of Queen Victoria, and a play titled *Adzuma; or, The Japanese Wife*. However, none of these works ever achieved the popularity of *The Light of Asia*.

An obituary in the London *Times*, quoted by Kogan, praised Arnold for his "astonishing fertility of language [and] luxuriant wealth of imagery." The writer felt that Arnold was an author who pursued "a subject of his own on which most of his countrymen and countrywomen were sadly ignorant, and of which they were quite willing to learn so much as could be presented to them in an attractive form."

BIOGRAPHICAL AND CRITICAL SOURCES:

BOOKS

Bell, Mackenzie, *The Poets and the Poetry of the Nineteenth Century,* Volume 5: *Sir Edwin Arnold,* Routledge (London, England), 1905.

Dictionary of Literary Biography, Volume 35: *Victorian Poets after 1850,* Gale (Detroit, MI), 1985, pp. 9-13.

Wilkinson, William Cleaver, *Edwin Arnold as Poetizer and as Paganizer,* Funk & Wagnalls (New York, NY), 1884.

OTHER

Light of Asia, http://www.triplegem.org/ (March 22, 2002).*

*   *   *

ARQUILLA, John

PERSONAL: Born in Oak Park, IL. *Education:* Rosary College, B.A., 1975; Stanford University, M.A., 1989, Ph.D., 1991. *Politics:* "Progressive." *Hobbies and other interests:* Chess.

ADDRESSES: Office—U.S. Naval Postgraduate School, Monterey, CA 93943.

CAREER: RAND Corp., Santa Monica, CA, consulting analyst, 1990—. U.S. Naval Postgraduate School, Monterey, CA, professor of defense analysis, 1993—. *Military service:* U.S. Coast Guard Reserve, 1981-87.

WRITINGS:

Dubious Battles, Crane Russak, 1992.
From Troy to Entebbe, University Press of America (Lanham, MD), 1996.
(Editor, with David Ronfeldt) *In Athena's Camp: Preparing for Conflict in the Information Age,* RAND Corp. (Santa Monica, CA), 1997.
Networks and Netwars: The Future of Terror, Crime, and Militancy, RAND Corp. (Santa Monica, CA), 2001.

Contributor to periodicals, including *Christian Science Monitor* and *San Francisco Chronicle.*

WORK IN PROGRESS: Ronald Reagan and the Making of the Twenty-First Century World.

BIOGRAPHICAL AND CRITICAL SOURCES:

PERIODICALS

Choice, May, 2002, E. Lewis, review of *Networks and Netwars: The Future of Terror, Crime, and Militancy,* p. 1661.

International Affairs, July, 1998, Andrew Rathmell, review of *In Athena's Camp: Preparing for Conflict in the Information Age,* p. 39.
Library Quarterly, January, 2000, Howard Besser, review of *In Athena's Camp,* p. 133.
Perspectives on Political Science, winter, 1999, Dennis Pirages, review of *In Athena's Camp,* p. 44.
SAIS Review, summer-fall, 1998, Belkis Leong-Hong, review of *In Athena's Camp,* p. 232.
Studies in Conflict and Terrorism, July-September, 1999, Philip L. Ritcheson, review of *In Athena's Camp,* p. 273.

*   *   *

ASHBEE, C(harles) R(obert) 1863-1942

PERSONAL: Born 1863, in Isleworth, England; died, 1942, in Sevenoaks, England; son of Henry Spencer Ashbee (a merchant and author). *Education:* Attended Wellington College and King's College.

CAREER: Bodley & Gerner, apprentice; architect. Founder, Guild and School of Handicraft, London, 1888, and Essex House Press.

WRITINGS:

From Whitechapel to Camelot, Guild and School of Handicraft (London, England), 1892.
A Few Chapters in Workshop Reconstruction and Citizenship, Essex House Press (London, England), 1894.
The Trinity Hospital in Mile End: An Object Lesson in National History, Guild and School of Handicraft (London, England), 1896.
The Treatises of Benvenuto Cellini on Goldsmithing and Sculpture, E. Arnold (London, England), 1898.
An Endeavor towards the Teaching of John Ruskin and William Morris, E. Arnold (London, England), 1901.
American Sheaves and English Seed Corn: Being a Series of Addresses Mainly Delivered in the United States, E. Arnold (London, England), 1901.
A Bibliography of the Essex House Press, with Notes on the Designs, Blocks, Cuts, Bindings, etc., from the Year 1898 to 1904, Essex House Press (Campden, Gloucestershire, England), 1904.

Conradin: A Philosophical Ballad, Essex House Press, (Campden, Gloucestershire, England), 1908.

Craftmanship in Competitive Industry, Essex House Press (Campden, Gloucestershire, England), 1908.

Modern English Silverwork: An Essay, Essex House Press (Campden, Gloucestershire, England), 1909, reprinted by B. Wienreb (London, England), 1974.

The Private Press: A Study in Idealism, Essex House Press (Campden, Gloucestershire, England), 1909.

Should We Stop Teaching Art, B. T. Batsford (London, England), 1911.

Where the Great City Stands: A Study in the New Civics, Essex House Press (London, England), 1917.

Caricature, Chapman and Hall (London, England), 1928.

Kingfisher out of Egypt: A Dialogue in an English Garden, H. Milford Oxford University Press (London, England), 1934.

Lyrics of the Nile, H. Milford Oxford University Press (London, England), 1938.

EDITOR

The Manual of the Guild and School of Handicraft, Cassell (London, England), 1892.

The Survey of London: Being the First Volume of the Register of the Committee for the Survey of the Memorials of Great London, containing the Parish of Bromley-by-Bow, P. S. King (London, England), 1900.

A Book of Cottages and Little Houses, Essex House Press (Campden, Gloucestershire, England), 1906.

Jerusalem, 1918-1920, Being the Records of the Pro-Jerusalem Council during the Period of the British Military Administration, J. Murray, for the Council of the Pro-Jerusalem Society (London, England), 1921.

Jerusalem, 1920-1922; Being the Records of the Pro-Jerusalem Council during the First Two Years of the Civil Administration, Council of the Pro-Jerusalem Society (London, England), 1924.

Peckover, the Abbotscourt Papers, 1904-1931, Astolat Press (London, England), 1932.

SIDELIGHTS: Although trained as an architect, C. R. Ashbee was better known as a designer of furniture, cabinetry, and metalwork which included jewelry and silverware. He also created leatherwork and was founder of the Essex House Press, for which he bound and printed books. Ashbee's name is strongly connected with the English Arts and Crafts movement due to having founded the Guild and the School of Handicraft.

Ashbee took advantage of his college training and designed several buildings, most of them private homes including a cluster located in Cheyne Walk, Chelsea, on the riverfront in London. Another group of homes designed by Ashbee are located in Chipping Campden in Gloucestershire.

In Chelsea, Ashbee took pains to create a village atmosphere in the city by, for one, varying the heights of adjoining buildings. He also made sure that the windows in one building were not duplicated in the next. The rooflines and dormer windows from one house to the next never matched one another, giving the illusions that the houses had been built at different times.

Ashbee took an interest in historical architecture and in 1900 became involved in the founding of the British preservation movement. He was disturbed by the demolition of the Old Palace of James I at Bromley-by-Bow, and shortly afterward he created a watch committee whose purpose it was to list all the historical buildings in London. His work with this committee led to the publication of *The Survey of London: Being the First Volume of the Register of the Committee for the Survey of the Memorials of Great London, containing the Parish of Bromley-by-Bow.*

In 1901 Ashbee wrote *An Endeavor towards the Teaching of John Ruskin and William Morris.* The book concerns the philosophy of two men who were equally involved in art, literature, and politics and who would greatly influence the Arts and Crafts movement in Britain. In an attempt to sum up the philosophy of the Arts and Crafts movement, Oscar Wilde, as printed in his *Essays and Lectures,* wrote "People often talk as if there was an opposition between what is beautiful and what is useful. There is no opposition to beauty except ugliness: all things are either beautiful or ugly, and utility will be always on the side of the beautiful thing." Ruskin and Morris were proponents of this philosophy, and while in college Ashbee was influenced by their philosophy and found a way to express it in his work.

Ruskin and Morris were also proponents of socialism, another philosophy that affected Ashbee, influencing his decision to apprentice with George Frederick Bodley, who was known as a Ruskinian Gothic revivalist. While an apprentice, Ashbee lived in London's East End, home of several settlements of working-class people. It was here that Ashbee gave lectures on Ruskin's social philosophy and began the Guild and School of Handicrafts.

In 1902, when Ashbee moved the Guild and his publishing company to Chipping Campden in Gloucestershire, his involvement in architecture consisted mostly of restoring old buildings and homes, creating additions, and building new structures to match the historical setting. According to Alan Crawford in the *Macmillan Encyclopedia of Architects,* Ashbee's "conservative aim was to fit in with Campden's stone-built vernacular; the old work was carefully repaired, and the new was kept modest and unpretentious."

In 1974 Ashbee's 1909 work*Modern English Silverwork: An Essay* was reissued with introductory essays by Shirley Bury and Alan Crawford. When Ashbee first wrote the book he was embittered by the financial collapse of his Guild and School of Handicraft and wrote the book mostly as a justification of his work. In reviewing the new edition of the book, Charles Oman, writing for *Burlington Magazine,* found that these additional essays "add greatly to the value of the work since the one provided by Ashbee is a mere diatribe very deficient in facts." Crawford's essay provides a brief biography of Ashbee, while Bury's offers "an intimate account of the working of the Guild of Handicraft."

BIOGRAPHICAL AND CRITICAL SOURCES:

BOOKS

Macmillan Encyclopedia of Architecture, edited by Adolf K. Placzek, Macmillan Publishing Co. (New York, NY), 1982, pp. 108-109.
McCarthy, Fiona, *The Simple Life: C. R. Ashbee in the Cotswolds,* University of California Press (Berkeley, CA), 1981.
Stansky, Peter, and William Morris, *C. R. Ashbee and the Arts and Crafts,* Nine Elms Press (London, England), 1984.

PERIODICALS

Books & Bookmen, May, 1975, John Betjeman, "A Complete Craftsman," p. 54.

New Statesman, April 4, 1975, Robert Melville, "Hand-made," pp. 455-456.
Burlington Magazine, May, 1975, Charles Oman, review of *Modern English Silverwork: An Essay,* pp. 308, 311.

OTHER

Art and the Handicraftsman, http://www.burrows.com/founders/art.html (June 19, 2002), Oscar Wilde, excerpt from *Essays and Lectures by Oscar Wilde.**

*   *   *

ASKEW, Rilla 1951-

PERSONAL: Born 1951, in OK; married Paul Austin (a playwright and actor). *Education:* University of Tulsa, B.F.A (theater performance), 1980; Brooklyn College, M.F.A. (creative writing), 1989.

ADDRESSES: Home—P.O. Box 324, Kauneonga Lake, NY 12749.

CAREER: Novelist and author of short stories. Teacher of fiction writing at Brooklyn College, Syracuse University, University of Central Oklahoma, and at various literary conferences.

AWARDS, HONORS: Oklahoma Book Award, 1993, for *Strange Business; The Mercy Seat* was nominated for the PEN-Faulkner Award, the Dublin AMPAC Prize, and the Mountains and Plains Booksellers Award, and received the Oklahoma Book Award and the Western Heritage Award for Best Novel, both 1997.

WRITINGS:

Strange Business, Viking (New York, NY), 1992.
The Mercy Seat, Viking (New York, NY), 1997.
Fire in Beulah, Viking (New York, NY), 2001.

Short stories published in *Prize Stories 1993: O. Henry Awards Anthology* (Doubleday, 1993). Contributor to *Nimrod, Puerto del Sol,* and *Carolina Quarterly.*

SIDELIGHTS: The descendent of a number of interesting Oklahomans—coal miners, sharecroppers, bootleggers, school teachers, Baptist deacons, pioneer women, a county deputy sheriff, Choctaws, and Cherokees—writer Rilla Askew grew up in Bartlesville, Oklahoma surrounded by reminders of American history and images of the Old West. Her ancestors appear in her work often, and although she has lived in California and Arkansas, her three novels attest to Oklahoma as her true home.

Askew's first book, the short story collection *Strange Business,* focuses on the lives of a shrinking Oklahoma town's residents. Askew explores a broad range of life experiences, from childhood anxieties and teenage epiphanies to adult traumas. Michael Upchurch of *Book World* called *Strange Business* "a knockout story collection which, with its lyrical precision, tart humor, and profound compassion for its characters, called to mind the young Eudora Welty." Another *Washington Post Book World* reviewer also praised the collection, writing: "Although the author's technical skill will take your breath away, it's ultimately her warm heart that makes *Strange Business* a small masterpiece."

Many critics also praised Askew's first novel, *The Mercy Seat,* a variation on the Cain and Abel story as told by eleven-year-old Mattie Lodi. Set in late nineteenth-century Oklahoma, the story focuses on two brothers: John (Mattie's father) and Fayette. John, a reputable gunsmith, flees Kentucky with his family and his brother, a man whose dishonesty as a bootlegger and mule thief triggers their exodus. Tragedies abound on the journey westward, however: Mattie's mother and sister die, her brother suffers brain-damage, and her taciturn father starts to feud with Fayette. Mattie tries to diffuse the tension between the brothers, but instead, she inadvertently fuels the fire. A *Publishers Weekly* reviewer gave *The Mercy Seat* a starred rating and praised Askew's prose as "mesmerizing, saturated with the rhythms of the prophets and patriarchs (as heard by Faulkner rather than Steinbeck)." Upchurch, however, labeled the work as ambitious but flawed. "It's a novel that contains many moments of perfection—and a few miscalculations. Askew occasionally succumbs to grandiloquent overkill, especially in her chapter openings." Nonetheless, *Booklist* reviewer Emily Melton highly recommended the book, calling it, "Bleak, dark, and moving, peopled with vivid characters and filled with compelling details and poetically rendered narrative."

The Mercy Seat was nominated for three awards and won two others, including the 1997 Oklahoma Book Award.

Askew's next novel is also set in Oklahoma, during the oil rush years of the 1920s. *Fire in Beulah* explores the Tulsa Race Riot of 1921, one of the bloodiest and least publicized outbreaks of racial violence in U.S. history. Combining historical fact with fiction, Askew tells the story using two protagonists: pampered socialite Althea Whiteside and her young black maid, Graceful. Althea, hiding her impoverished, abusive past from her oil-baron husband, finds herself both fascinated and repulsed by her maid. Both their lives are changed forever, however, when Althea's younger brother, Japheth, unexpectedly appears. John Gregory Brown, in the *Chicago Tribune,* described Japheth as "a character so convincingly contemptuous and downright evil that his every word seems to spew forth like fire from his mouth." Japheth's sudden appearance, along with a mysterious letter and a double lynching, force Althea and Graceful to acknowledge their responsibility to one another, even as the fire and riot draw near.

In both history and in Askew's novel, a black shoeshine boy's arrest for allegedly assaulting a white elevator girl provokes the riot. Richard Lloyd Jones, a well-known journalist and publisher of the *Tulsa Tribune,* sensationalizes the story with a front-page headline that reads "To Lynch Negro Tonight." Incensed by the editorial, whites form a mob outside the courthouse, and local blacks, attempting to avert the lynching, gather there, too. The white mob burns more than 3,000 African-American homes to the ground, razes thirty-six square blocks, and kill as many as 300 people. Tulsa's black community—concentrated in an area called Greenwood, and known for its cultural and financial achievements—is thus destroyed.

Adam Nossiter, critic for the *New York Times Book Review,* critiqued Askew's writing style in *Fire in Beulah.* "She is not well served by prose that can be overwrought, and by a tendency to spell out internal states that the reader should merely sense." Doug Jones of *Black Issues Book Review,* however, heralded the novel: "Askew adeptly shows the hardships and heroicism of her characters' lives. There are no pat machinations here, and *Fire in Beulah* is unflinchingly brutal." A *Publishers Weekly* critic also praised the novel as "an arresting examination of race and heritage. . . . Her prose—rich, leisurely, graceful—engages all the senses and encloses the reader in a bell jar of heat, hate, and budding violence."

BIOGRAPHICAL AND CRITICAL SOURCES:

BOOKS

Directory of American Poets and Fiction Writers, 1999-2000 edition, Poets & Writers, Inc. (New York, NY), 1998.

PERIODICALS

Belles Lettres, winter 1992, Yvonne Fraticelli, review of *Strange Business,* p. 59.
Black Issues Book Review, March, 2001, Doug Jones, review of *Fire in Beulah,* p. 21.
Booklist, July, 1992, Mary Carroll, review of *Strange Business,* p. 1916; August, 1997, Emily Melton, review of *The Mercy Seat,* pp. 1874-1875.
Chicago Tribune, February 11, 2001, John Gregory Brown, "Separate and Unequal," p. 1, 5.
Christian Science Monitor, September 15, 1997, Merle Rubin, review of *The Mercy Seat,* p. 13.
Library Journal, July, 1997, Editha Ann Wilberton, review of *The Mercy Seat,* p. 122; April 1, 1998, review of *The Mercy Seat,* p. 152; February 1, 2001, Barbara L. Roberts, review of *Fire in Beulah,* p. 124; April 15, 2001, Nancy Pearl, "The Moral of the Story," p. 164.
New York Times Book Review, August 9, 1992, Mark Childress, review of *Strange Business,* p. 6; October 12, 1997, James Polk, review of *The Mercy Seat,* p. 21; November 11, 2001, Adam Nossiter, "Something Tulsa Forgot: In 1921, White People in Tulsa Made War on Black People," p. 33.
Publishers Weekly, May 11, 1992, review of *Strange Business,* pp. 52-53; June 23, 1997, review of *The Mercy Seat,* p. 69; November 13, 2000, review of *Fire in Beulah,* p. 83.
Washington Post Book World, January 3, 1993, review of *Strange Business,* p. 6; August 17, 1997, Michael Upchurch, "Lighting out for Indian Territory," p. 5.
Yale Review, January, 1999, Diana Postlethwaite, review of *The Mercy Seat,* pp. 144-146.

OTHER

Oklahoma State Department of Education Web site, http://www.title3.sde.state.ok.us/ (March 16, 2002).
PreviewPort, http://www.previewport.com/ (May 28, 2002), profile of Rilla Askew.
University of Tulsa Web site, http://www.utulsa.edu/ (March 12, 2002), profile of Rilla Askew.*

*   *   *

ATKINSON, Jay 1957-

PERSONAL: Born 1957. *Education:* Methuen High School, Methuen, MA, 1975; University of Florida, M.F.A., 1982.

ADDRESSES: Home—7 Cochrane Street, Methuen, MA 01844-3142. *Office*—Salem State College, 352 Lafayette Street, Salem, MA 01970.

CAREER: Salem State College, Salem, MA, professor of creative writing.

AWARDS, HONORS: Fiction award, *Boston* magazine; Pushcart Prize nominee; Notable Book of the Year, *Publishers Weekly,* 2001, for *Ice Time: A Tale of Fathers, Sons, and Hometown Heroes.*

WRITINGS:

Caveman Politics, Breakaway Books (Halcottsville, NY), 1997.
Ice Time: A Tale of Fathers, Sons, and Hometown Heroes, Crown Publishing Group (New York, NY), 2001.

Also writes for various magazines and newspapers, including *Men's Health, Boston Globe, Boston Herald,* and the *New York Times.*

WORK IN PROGRESS: A historical novel set in a mill in Lawrence, Massachusetts; *Private Investigator: A Year on the Street* about the life of a private eye at Boston's McCain Investigations, for Crown (New York, NY).

SIDELIGHTS: Jay Atkinson, whose work has been syndicated in many national magazines and newspapers, has published two vastly different books. His first, the novel *Caveman Politics,* explores issues of race, justice, and self-examination. *Ice Time: A Tale of Fathers, Sons, and Hometown Heroes,* however, is Atkinson's memoir about the season he spent coaching his old high school's hockey team.

Caveman Politics is narrated by Joe Dolan, a Florida newspaper reporter, rugby player, and self-described Peter Pan, who spends most of his time playing rugby, chasing women, and partying with teammates. When Mike Melendez, a black teammate, is falsely accused of raping a white woman, Dolan uses his reporter's position, and his investigative skills, to vindicate his friend while confronting his own demons, including bigotry. While working to clear Melendez's name, Dolan gets involved with a corrupt district attorney and inadvertently discovers another innocent ensnared in a legal system trap—a singer who is convinced he is Elvis. Through it all, Dolan struggles to leave his childhood behind him and pursue a potentially fulfilling life as a gifted writer.

A *Booklist* reviewer gave Atkinson's novel high marks, describing his characters as "heroically deranged people." *Library Journal* called *Caveman Politics* a "jauntily unpretentious, solidly plotted book that displays good insights into character." Regarding this last point, Keith Dixon of the *New York Times* critiqued Atkinson's tendency toward stereotypes— "particularly the woefully named accuser, Sherri Hogg, and her abusive boyfriend, T-Bone"—but he also noted Atkinson's abilities and identified the novel's key ingredients. "It is the humor and insight of his characters that make the novel work."

Ice Time, on the other hand, recounts Atkinson's year as assistant coach of his former high school hockey team, the Methuen Rangers. Methuen is a small, working-class town composed of Italians and French-Canadians who eat, drink, and sleep hockey. Atkinson's return to his alma mater, where he played twenty-five years before, combines elements of nostalgia, wisdom, and wit. *Ice Time* also examines Atkinson's time as a hockey-obsessed adolescent. In an interview with Bill Reynolds of the *Providence Journal,* Atkinson said, "I have often fantasized about going back to high school, to take one shot at that defining period in my life. This book details my return to Methuen High . . . to

discover what it was about my experience there and on the ice that shaped me and my future." The book relates friendly conversations, locker-room banter, and Atkinson's recollections of his hockey-playing days. Readers see not only the fun of hockey life, but the rough, gut-wrenching low points as well.

In 1975, when Methuen first began its hockey program, Atkinson was the team's backup goalie. He was scheduled to play in an exhibition game after the regular season ended, but the opposing team broke the agreement. In *Ice Time,* Atkinson explains that "I couldn't help feeling as I drove away . . . that I'd been shortchanged one game in my career." After playing that imaginary game in his head for a quarter century, Atkinson, in his early forties, decided to something about it.

"It is a celebration of family life, 1950s values, that seemed out of fashion until September 11 and then came back into fashion," Atkinson is quoted as saying on the Marlboro, Massachusetts *Community Advocate* Web site "However, they were never out of fashion in small Massachusetts towns." Larry Little, in *Library Journal,* described the book as a story "of personal triumphs, both on and off the ice, of friendship, loyalty, perseverance, and dedicated parents." Stephan Talty wrote in the *New York Times Book Review* that while the profiled high school students never really seemed to accept Atkinson into their world, the author nonetheless "offers affecting elegies to small-town life. Admirably modest, blue-collar and Northern to the core." *Capital Times* columnist Adam Mertz judged Atkinson's sentiment as overwhelming, however. "There are only so many adjectives to describe a glossy pond primed for a pickup game—and if you stuck a spigot in Atkinson's side, you'd draw more sap than from a Vermont sugar maple." Reynolds, in contrast, simply called *Ice Time* "a book about why sports matter."

BIOGRAPHICAL AND CRITICAL SOURCES:

PERIODICALS

Booklist, March 1, 1997, Thomas Gaughan, review of *Caveman Politics,* p. 1108; September 1, 2001, Wes Lukowsky, review of *Ice Time: A Tale of Fathers, Sons, and Hometown Heroes,* p. 33.

Boston Magazine, January, 1998, Sarah Wright, review of *Caveman Politics,* p. 89.

Library Journal, March 15, 1997, David Keymer, review of *Caveman Politics,* p. 87; August, 2001, Larry R. Little, review of *Ice Time,* p. 118.

New York Times Book Review, June 15, 1997, Keith Dixon, review of *Caveman Politics,* p. 22; September 11, 2001, Stephan Talty, review of *Ice Time,* p. 28.

Publishers Weekly, February 17, 1997, review of *Caveman Politics,* p. 210; August 6, 2001, review of *Ice Time,* p. 80.

OTHER

Captimes.com, http://www.captimes.com/ (December 7, 2001), Adam Mertz, "Hockey Staves off Midlife Crisis."

Community Advocate Web site, http://www.communityadvocate.com/ (April 26, 2002), Cindy R. Dorsey, "Author Celebrity Series Features Regional Author."

Lawrence Eagle-Tribune Web site, http://www.eagletribune.com/ (December 23, 2001), John Tomase, "Chronicling a Season at the Rink."

Projo.com, http://www.projo.com/ (March 20, 2002), Bill Reynolds, "These Sports Booksa about More than Wins."

Salem State College Web site, http://www.salemstate.edu/ (May 20, 2002), "Salem State Professors Reflect on Basketball, Hockey in Latest Books."*

*   *   *

AWKWARD, Michael

PERSONAL: Male. *Education:* University of Pennsylvania, Ph.D., 1986.

ADDRESSES: Office—Department of English, 3808 Walnut-Bennett 320, University of Pennsylvania, Philadelphia, PA 19104. *E-mail*—michawk@dept.english.upenn.edu.

CAREER: University of Michigan, Ann Arbor, associate professor of Afro-American and African studies, director of English; University of Pennsylvania—Philadelphia, professor of English, 2000—. Cultural critic, writer and scholar.

WRITINGS:

Inspiriting Influences: Tradition, Revision, and Afro-American Women's Novels, Columbia University Press (New York, NY), 1989.

(Editor) *New Essays on Their Eyes Were Watching God,* Cambridge University Press (New York, NY), 1990.

Negotiating Difference: Race, Gender, and the Politics of Positionality, University of Chicago Press (Chicago, IL), 1995.

Scenes of Instruction: A Memoir, Duke University Press (Durham, NC), 1999.

SIDELIGHTS: Michael Awkward describes in *Scenes of Instruction: A Memoir* what it was like to be raised in extreme poverty in Philadelphia. His father left the family after years of abuse. His mother was an alcoholic who struggled with and eventually overcame her addiction. Awkward's problems worsened when, as a young child, he pulled a red-hot cast-iron skillet down onto his head, causing serious physical and emotional trauma. In his formative years Awkward struggled with issues of race, class, gender, and sexuality. After earning a Ph.D. from the University of Pennsylvania in 1986, Awkward devoted his energy to the study and teaching of contemporary Afro-American literature and culture. His interests also encompass autobiography, gender studies, film studies, and popular culture.

In *Inspiriting Influences: Tradition, Revision, and Afro-American Women's Novels* Awkward surveys the works of four important black authors and the ways in which their work interplay. Concentrating on Zora Neale Hurston's *Their Eyes Were Watching God,* Toni Morrison's *The Bluest Eye,* Gloria Naylor's *The Women of Brewster Place,* and Alice Walker's *The Color Purple,* Awkward views Hurston as a literary forerunner and mentor to contemporary black authors such as Morrison, Naylor, and Walker. According to A. Deck in *Choice,* "He presents a convincing argument that Zora Neale Hurston, Toni Morrison, Gloria Naylor, and Alice Walker each infuse the western genre of the novel with the specific expressive elements of Afro-American culture. . . . This is a brilliant study of a specific Afro-American cultural trait that links these novels into a discernible tradition."

Edna L. Steeves in *Modern Fiction Studies* commented that "Michael Awkward describes his book as one black male's contribution to what Mary Helen Washington has pointed out as an important project, that is, the knitting together of the continuities of the African-American woman's literary tradition."

Awkward's second book, *New Essays on Their Eyes Were Watching God,* presents five essays written by recognized scholars on the importance of Hurston's *Their Eyes Were Watching God.* The essays are authored by Hurston biographer Robert Hemenway and critics Nellie McKay, Hazel V. Carby, and Rachel Blau DuPlessis, all of whom are well known for their work on African American literature and, more specifically, on Hurston as an author. Awkward serves as editor of the book and also provides an introduction, outlining key points made in prior critical reviews. According to Missy Dehn Kubitschek in *African American Review,* "Awkward, Hemenway, and Carby address the history of the novel's reception by critics and the academy; McKay delineates the novel's relationship to traditions of autobiography; and DuPlessis explores the work's implications for feminist cultural studies. The theses of the essays are often explicitly identified, and although all present engaged, complicated analyses, their clarity and minimal jargon will make the volume particularly accessible to its principal audience."

In *Negotiating Difference: Race, Gender, and the Politics of Positionality* Awkward explores the dynamics of "positionality," or how one's work reflects one's racial, sexual or other unique characteristics. One of the key elements of the book involves debates among black and feminist scholars over who has jurisdiction to interpret various texts. The book is divided into two parts, the first titled "Surveying the Critical Terrain." According to Shanna Green Benjamin of *African American Review,* "In part one, Awkward explicates critical texts to chart his sense of Black male feminism and examines 'the differences race can make in the interpretation of black texts.' The second section, 'Interpretation of the Borders,' questions the 'relationship between race and reading' in selected texts. In part two, close readings take center stage against a backdrop of other relevant theories." According to Benjamin, "There can be little doubt that Awkward's questions move Afro-Americanist literary and cultural thought to a new level of interpretive rigor."

In *Scenes of Instruction: A Memoir,* Awkward presents his "autocritography," or "an account of individual, social, and institutional conditions that help produce a scholar." As an academic, critic and writer, Awkward has spent his career studying those issues that confused and bewildered him as a youth. He talks about the poverty in which he lived, as well as the impact of a significant childhood burn incident that left physical and emotional scars. According to a reviewer in *Publishers Weekly,* "Wisely, Awkward confronts his demons head-on with clarity and candor. However, he occasionally retreats from his gutsy revelations with verbose investigations of classic works of African-American fiction such as *The Bluest Eye* and *Black Boy,* which he uses to expand his musings on his life. . . . Awkward acknowledges that many will resist his antipatriarchal stance, but he continues to press for 'the dismantling of the phallocentric rule by which black females and . . . countless other African American sons have been injuriously 'touched.'"

BIOGRAPHICAL AND CRITICAL SOURCES:

PERIODICALS

African American Review, summer, 1994, Missy Dehn Kubitschek, review of *New Essays on Their Eyes Were Watching God,* p. 305; fall, 1999, Shanna Greene Benjamin, review of *Negotiating Difference: Race, Gender, and the Politics of Positionality,* p. 533; fall, 2001, Robert B. Stepto, review of *Scenes of Instruction: A Memoir,* p. 493.

American Literature, December, 2000, Kenneth W. Warren, review of *Scenes of Instruction: A Memoir,* p. 893.

Belles Letres, spring, 1991, review of *New Essays on Their Eyes Were Watching God.*

Booklist, December 1, 1999, Vernon Ford, review of *Scenes of Instruction: A Memoir,* p. 680.

Callaloo, fall, 1990, review of *Inspiriting Influences: Tradition, Revision, and Afro-American Women's Novels,* p. 928.

Choice, December, 1989, A. Deck, review of *Inspiriting Influences: Tradition, Revision, and Afro-American Women's Novels,* p. 628; December 1991, review of *New Essays on Their Eyes Were Watching God,* p. 594; June, 2000, T. Bonner, Jr., review of *Scenes of Instruction: A Memoir,* p. 1808.

Chronicle of Higher Education, April 28, 1995, review of *Negotiating Difference: Race, Gender, and the Politics of Positionality,* p. A38.

Modern Fiction Studies, winter, 1991, Edna L. Steeves, review of *Inspiriting Influences,* p. 737.

Publishers Weekly, November 15, 1999, review of *Scenes of Instruction: A Memoir,* p. 47.*

B

BACHELOR GIRL
See CURTISS, Harriette Augusta

* * *

BAKER ROSHI, Richard 1936-
(Zentatsu Myomu)

PERSONAL: Born 1936, in ME; assumed the Buddhist name Zentatsu Myomu, 1966; married; children: a daughter. *Education:* Attended Harvard University.

ADDRESSES: Agent—c/o Author's Mail, Riverside Press, Penguin Putnam, 375 Hudson St., New York, NY 10014.

CAREER: Ordained Buddhist priest, 1966; Tassajara Center, cofounder and leader, beginning 1966; Buddhist teacher at a Rinzai Zen monastery, Daitokuji, and at Soto monasteries, Enheji and Antaiji, all in Japan, 1968-70; Zen Center of San Francisco, San Francisco, CA, abbot, 1971-c. 83; Zen teacher at Dharma Sangha, in New Mexico, c. 1983, and in Crestone, CO, beginning 1984. Also teacher in Germany. Founder of Green Gulch Farm, Green Gulch Grocery, Tassajara Bakery, Shunryu Suzuki Study Center, Neighborhood Foundation, Alaya Storehouse, and Greens (vegetarian restaurant), all in Marin County, CA.

WRITINGS:

UNDER NAME ZENTATSU MYOMU

Original Mind: The Practice of Zen in the West,
Riverside Press (New York, NY), 1997.*

BANKS, Margaret A(melia) 1928-

PERSONAL: Born July 3, 1928, in Quebec City, Quebec, Canada; daughter of Thomas Herbert and Bessey (Collins) Banks. *Ethnicity:* "Anglo-Scottish." *Education:* Bishop's University, Lennoxville, Quebec, Canada, B.A. (with honors), 1949; University of Toronto, M.A., 1950, Ph.D., 1953. *Religion:* Anglican.

ADDRESSES: Agent—c/o Author's Mail, McGill-Queen's University Press, 3430 McTavish St., Montreal, Quebec, Canada H3A 1X9. *E-mail*—mabanks@ uwo.ca.

CAREER: Ontario Archives, Toronto, Ontario, Canada, archivist, 1953-61; University of Western Ontario, London, Ontario, Canada, law librarian, 1961-89, assistant professor, 1967-74, associate professor, 1974-86, professor of law and history, 1986-89, professor emeritus, 1989—.

MEMBER: Canadian Association of Law Libraries, Canadian Historical Association, American Institute of Parliamentarians, National Association of Parliamentarians (United States), Osgoode Society for Canadian Legal History, Arts and Letters Club of Toronto.

WRITINGS:

Edward Blake, Irish Nationalist: A Canadian Statesman in Irish Politics, 1892-1907, University of Toronto Press (Toronto, Ontario, Canada), 1957.

Using a Law Library: A Guide for Students in the Common-Law Provinces of Canada, School of Library and Information Science, University of Western Ontario (London, Ontario, Canada), 1971, 2nd edition published as *Using a Law Library: A Guide for Students and Lawyers in the Common-Law Provinces of Canada,* Carswell Co. (Toronto, Ontario, Canada), 1974, 5th edition published as *Banks on Using a Law Library: A Canadian Guide to Legal Research,* 1991, 6th edition (with Karen E. H. Foti), 1994.

The Libraries at Western, 1970 to 1987, with Summaries of Their Earlier History and a 1988 Postscript, University Library System, University of Western Ontario (London, Ontario, Canada), 1989.

Understanding Canada's Constitution, Including Summaries of Some Reports Recommending Changes, privately printed (London, Ontario, Canada), 1991.

(With Virginia Schlotzhauer, Floyd M. Riddick, and John R. Stipp) *Parliamentary Opinions II: Solutions to Problems of Organizations,* Kendall/Hunt Publishing (Dubuque, IA), 1992.

Sir John George Bourinot, Victorian Canadian: His Life, Times, and Legacy, McGill-Queen's University Press (Montreal, Quebec, Canada), 2001.

Contributor to periodicals, including *Parliamentary Journal,* 1990—.

WORK IN PROGRESS: An autobiography; continuing research on parliamentary procedure and constitutional law and history.

SIDELIGHTS: Margaret A. Banks told *CA:* "From the age of eight I wanted to be a writer. As a child I wrote a few little poems and plays; they have not survived. In high school I had a short story published in a yearbook. Since then I have concentrated on nonfiction, writing mainly for scholarly journals, though I have also had several books published. I believe (and I have also been told) that I write in plain English; it isn't necessary to be a scholar to understand what I write.

"My most recent book is *Sir John George Bourinot, Victorian Canadian: His Life, Times, and Legacy.* People often ask me what led to my interest in Bourinot. To qualify as a professional parliamentarian, I had studied and been examined on books on parliamentary procedure written by Henry M. Robert,

George Demeter, Alice Sturgis, and other American authors. Being a Canadian, I thought I should also learn something about Bourinot, long regarded as the leading Canadian authority on the subject. I quickly discovered that Bourinot had many other interests in addition to parliamentary procedure, and all of them were of interest to me. No book-length biography of him had been published, and I decided that I would like to write one. It was a major project which took several years to complete and several more to get published.

"I am now in the very early stages of writing what I hope will be an autobiography. My childhood was spent mainly in Quebec City, where life was very different from what it is today. I was a graduate history student at the University of Toronto when several prominent historians were teaching there. My impressions of them may be of some interest. It was a time when women were simply not appointed to academic positions (unless they had influential relatives) and because of the current popularity of women's history, my experiences in trying to obtain a university teaching position may be of interest. For me, things turned out for the best—I believe that I have had a more interesting life as a law librarian (my principal occupation) than I would have had as a history professor."

*   *   *

BARATTA, Don 1932-

PERSONAL: Born March 2, 1932; son of Peter Baron (a machinist) and Laura (a homemaker; maiden name, McGonnell) Baratta; married, June 24, 1956; wife's name, Joan (died, June 23, 1989); children: Michael James, David Donald (deceased). *Education:* Pasadena Community College, A.A., 1958; Louisiana State University, B.A., 1959; Claremont Graduate School, teaching credential, 1960. *Religion:* Roman Catholic. *Hobbies and other interests:* Reading history.

ADDRESSES: Agent—c/o Author Mail, Firefly Books Ltd., 3680 Victoria Park Ave., Toronto, Ontario, Canada M2H 3K1. *E-mail*—dbaratta@coastaccess. com.

CAREER: Farmers Insurance Group, Los Angeles, CA, worked as insurance adjuster for more than thirty years; writer. *Military service:* U.S. Air Force, aerial gunner, 1951-55; served in Korea; received Air Medal with battle star and United Nations Service Medal.

WRITINGS:

The Sicilian Gentleman's Cookbook, Prima Publications, 1987, reprinted, Firefly Books, 2002.

WORK IN PROGRESS: Tales of the Sacramento Kid, the "mostly-comic adventures of a California street cop."

SIDELIGHTS: Don Baratta told *CA:* "*The Sicilian Gentleman's Cookbook* was written because my father had died and I did not want to let it go at that. So, I wrote about him and disguised the work by including a bookful of his recipes. I never expected it to be published and am even more surprised that it has been on the market for nearly twenty years. Well, so much for my expert opinion.

"I like to write about things that offer hope and to write with humor whenever possible, My inclinations can probably be labeled shallow and inconsequential, but I have never thought my talent was much more than mediocre, and this is the best I can do. Anyway, I generally find works of hopeless tragedy to be tedious, which again reflects my unfortunate taste."

BIOGRAPHICAL AND CRITICAL SOURCES:

PERIODICALS

Publishers Weekly, December 18, 1987, John Mutter, review of *The Sicilian Gentleman's Cookbook,* p. 60.
Winston-Salem Journal, May 22, 2002, Michael Hastings, review of *The Sicilian Gentleman's Cookbook,* p. E2.

*　　*　　*

BÀRBERI SQUAROTTI, Giorgio 1929-

PERSONAL: Born 1929, in Turin, Italy. *Education:* University of Turin, doctorate degree, 1953.

ADDRESSES: Office—Departemento di Scienze Letterarie e Filologiche, Universiti Torino, via S. Ottavio 20, 1-10124 Torino, Italy.

CAREER: Unione tipografico-editrice torinese (UTET), Turin, Italy, chief editor, 1958-67; University of Turin, Turin, Italy, teacher of modern Italian literature.

WRITINGS:

Astrazione e realità (title means "Abstraction and Reality"), Rusconi e Paolazzi (Milan, Italy), 1960.
La voce roca (title means "The Raucuous Voice"), All'insegna del Pesce d'Oro (Milan, Italy), 1960.
Poesia e narrativa del secondo Novecento, U. Mursia (Milan, Italy), 1961, reprinted, 1978.
Grande dizionario della lingua italiana, UTET (Turin, Italy), 1961.
Metodo, stile, storia, Fratelli Fabbri (Milan, Italy), 1962.
Nel tempo delle metamorfosi, Linar (Florence, Italy), 1962.
(Joint editor) *La poesia italiana contemporanea dal Carducci ai giorni nostri, con appendice di poeti stranieri,* D'Anna (Messina-Florence, Italy), 1963.
Candelaio, Einaudi (Turin, Italy), 1964, reprinted, 1981.
Teoria e prove dello stile del Manzoni, Silva (Milan, Italy), 1965.
La narrativa italiana del dopoguerra, Cappelli (Bologna, Italy), 1965.
(With Stefano Jacomuzzi) *La poesia italiana contemporanea dal Carducci ai giorni nostri,* D'Anna (Messina, Italy), 1965.
Vita nuova: Rime, Fogola (Turin, Italy), 1965.
La decamazione onesta (title means "The Honest Declamation"), Rizzoli (Milan, Italy), 1965.
Pagine di teatro, Società editrice internazionale (Turin, Italy), 1965.
La forma tragica del 'Principe' e altri saggi sul Machiavilli, Olschki (Florence, Italy), 1966.
(With Angelo Jacomuzzi) *Letteratura e critica: antologia della critica letteraria,* D'Anna (Messina-Florence, Italy), 1967.
La bottega del caffè, Petrini (Turin, Italy), 1967.
Simboli e strutture della poesia del Pascoli, D'Anna (Messina-Florence, Italy), 1966.
(With Angelo Jacomuzzi) *Letteratura e critica: antologia della critica letteraria,* D'Anna (Messina-Florence, Italy), 1968.

La cultura e la poesia italiana del dopoguerra, Cappelli (Bologna, Italy), 1968.

(Editor) Torquato Tasso, *Aminta,* R.A.D.A.R. (Padua, Italy), 1968.

Manzoni, R.A.D.A.R. (Padua, Italy), 1968.

Canzoniere, Fògola (Turin, Italy), 1968.

Rime, Einaudi (Turin, Italy), 1969.

Critica dantesca: Antologia di studi e letture del Novecento, Società editrice internazionale (Turin, Italy), 1970.

(With Maria Grazia Amadori) *La casa in stile antico,* (Novara, Italy), 1970.

Camillo Sbarbaro, U. Mursia (Milan, Italy), 1971.

Poesia e narrative del secondo novecento, U. Mursia (Milan, Italy), 1971.

Il gesto improbabile, Flaccovio (Palermo, Italy), 1971.

L'artificio dell'eternità, Fiorini (Verona, Italy), 1972.

Il codice di Babele, Rizzoli (Milan, Italy), 1972.

Laberinto d'amore (title means "Labyrinth of Love"), Il centro (Naples, Italy), 1972.

Natura e storia nella litteratura italiana fra Otto e Novecento, Giappichelli (Turin, Italy), 1973.

(Compiler) *Manzoni: testimonianze di critica e di polemica,* D'Anna (Messina-Florence, Italy), 1973.

Gli inferi e il libirinto: da Pascoli a Montale, Capelli (Bologna, Italy), 1974.

Il tragico nel mondo boghese, Giappichelli (Turin, Italy), 1974.

(With Jusuè Antonio Capo) *Via del tascapane,* Rebellato (Padua, Italy), 1975.

Poesia e ideologia borghese, Liguori (Naples, Italy), 1976.

(With Uiuseppe Bonaviri) *Follia,* Società di storia patria per la Siciila orientale (Catania, Italy), 1976.

(With others) *Nove poesie e nove disegni,* Edizioni 32 (Milan, Italy), 1976.

Simboli e strutture della poesia del Pascoli, D'Anna (Messina-Florence, Italy), 1976.

(With Mario Ricciardi) *Società e cultura: proposte di lettura per il biennio delle scuole medie superiori e per la prima classe dell'istituto magistrale,* Mursia (Milan, Italy), 1977.

Notizie dalla vita (title means "News from Life"), Bastogi (Livorno, Italy), 1977.

(Author of introduction) Guido Gozzano, *Poesie,* Biblioteca Universale Rizzoli (Milan, Italy), 1977.

Le sorti del tragico: il Novecento italiano, romanzo e teatro, Longo (Ravenna, Italy), 1978.

Fine dell'idillio: da Dante a Marino, Il Melangolo (Genova, Italy), 1978.

(Coauthor) *Poesie,* Garzanti (Milan, Italy), 1978.

Il romanzo contro la storia: studi sui "Promessi sposi," Vita e pensiero (Milan, Italy), 1980.

Il marinaio del Mar Nero e altre poesie (title means "The Sailor of the Black Sea and Other Poetry"), Reballato (Padua, Italy), 1980.

Ritratto di intellettuale (title means "Portrait of an Intellectual"), Lacaita (Manduria, Italy), 1980.

(With others) *La poesia in Toscana dagli anni Quaranta agli anni Settanta,* D'Anna (Messina-Florence, Italy), 1981.

La narrativa dal '45 ad oggi: elementi di coninuità; risultati caratterizzanti il nostro momento, Centro Pitrè (Palermo, Italy), 1981.

Invito alla lettura de Gabriele D'Annunzio, Mursia (Milan, Italy), 1982.

Belfagor arcidiavolo, Melangolo (Genoa, Italy), 1982.

Dall'anima al sottosuolo: problemi della letteratura dell'Ottocento da Leopardi a Lucini, Longo (Ravenna, Italy), 1982.

Giovanni Verga: le finzioni dietro il verismo, Flaccovio (Palermo, Italy), 1982.

Canto V dell'Inferno, Loffredo (Naples, Italy), 1982.

(With Emma Giammattei) *Gli amici del poeta,* Forum/Quinta generazione (Forli, Italy), 1982.

Del principe e delle lettere, Serra e Riva (Milan, Italy), 1983.

(Editor) Giosuè Carducci, *Poesie,* Garzanti (Milan, Italy), 1983, ninth edition, 1996.

Opere minori di Dante Alighieri, UTET (Turin, Italy), 1983.

Il potere della parola: studi sul "Decameron," Federico & Ardia (Naples, Italy), 1983.

Da Gerico, Guida (Naples, Italy), 1983.

(With Salvatore Agati) *Gli eredi di Verga: atti del Convegno nazionale di studi e ricerche patrocinato dal comune di Randazzo e organizzato dalla Sezione italiana di "Letteratura Amica," Randazzo, 11, 12 e 13 dicembre 1983,* Letteratura Amica (Catania, Italy), 1984.

(With Anna Maria Golfieri) *Dal tramonto dell'ermetismo alla neoavanguardia,* La Scuola (Brescia, Italy), 1984.

La poesia del Novecento: morte e trasfigurazione del soggetto, Sciascia (Caltanissetta, Italy), 1985.

Metamorfosi della novella, Bastogi (Foggia, Italy), 1985.

La letteratura in scena: il teatro del Novecento, Tirrenia stampatori (Turin, Italy), 1985.

L'onore in corte: dal Castiglione al Tasso, Angeli (Milan, Italy), 1986.

Dalla bocca della balena (title means "From the Mouth of the Whale"), Genesi (Turin, Italy), 1986.

Machiavelli, o, La scelta della letteratura, Bulzoni (Rome, Italy), 1987.

La forma e lat vita: il romanzo del Novecento, Mursia (Milan, Italy), 1987.

D'Annunzio Notturno: atti dell VIII Convegno di studi dannunziani, Pescara, 8-10 ottobre 1986, Centro nazionale di studi dannunziani (Pescara, Italy), 1987.

(With Rinaldo Rinaldi) *I Bersagli della satira,* Tirrenia stampatori (Turin, Italy), 1987.

Prospettive sul furioso, Tirrenia stampatori (Turin, Italy), 1988.

(With Giusi Baldissone) *Lo specchio che deforma: le immagini della parodia,* Tirrenia stampatori (Turin, Italy), 1988.

L'ombra di Argo: studi sulla "Commedia," Genesi (Turin, Italy), 1988.

Il sogno della letteratura, Angeli (Milan, Italy), 1988.

Manzoni: le delusioni della letteratura, Marra Editore (Rome, Italy), 1988.

In nome di Beatrice e altre voci, Genesi (Turin, Italy), 1989.

(With Giusi Baldissone) *Prospettive sul Decameron,* Tirrenia stampatori (Turin, Italy), 1989.

(With others) *La cene,* Rizzoli (Milan, Italy), 1989.

Inivto alla lettura di Gabriele d'Annunzio, Mursia (Milan, Italy), 1990.

In un altro regno, Genesi (Turin, Italy), 1990.

Storia dell civiltà letteraria italiana, UTET (Turin, Italy), 1990.

I Mondi impossibili: l'utopia, Tirrenia stampatori (Turin, Italy), 1990.

Le maschere dell'eroe: dall'Alfieri a Pasolini, Milella (Lecce, Italy), 1990.

La simologia di Giovanni Pascoli, Mucchi (Modena, Italy), 1990.

Almanacco del poeta, Genesi (Turin, Italy), 1990.

(With others) *Storia dell civiltà letteraria italiana,* six volumes, UTET (Turin, Italy), 1990-1996.

(With Sandro Gros-Pietro) *Rime burlesche,* Rizzoli (Milan, Italy), 1991.

(With others) *Opere,* Rusconi (Milan, Italy), 1991.

(With Maria Gabriella Stassi) *Prospettive sui Promessi sposi,* Tirrenia stampatori (Turin, Italy), 1991.

(With others) *Mario Soldati: la scrittura e lo sguardo,* Museo nazionale del cinema (Turin, Italy), 1991.

(With Giusi Baldissone) *Cronaca e letteratura,* Tirrenia stampatori (Turin, Italy), 1991.

(With Paola Mastrocola) *La fucina di quale dio,* Genesi (Turin, Italy), 1991.

L'Editoria torinese del secondo Ottocento, la narrativa, Tirrenia stampatori (Turin, Italy), 1991.

La scrittura verso il nulla: D'Annunzio, Genesi (Turin, Italy), 1992.

Le colline, i maestri gli dei, Santi Quaranta (Treviso, Italy), 1992.

(With Gian Paolo Porreca) *Una atagione fiamminga,* Guida (Naples, Italy), 1992.

(With Gian Paolo Porreca) *Tre sogni della letteratura,* Guida (Naples, Italy), 1992.

L'italianistica: introduzione allo studio della letertura e dilla lingua italiana, UTET (Turin, Italy), 1992.

(With others) *Ghandelier,* Belles Lettres (Paris, France), 1993.

(With Roberto Cicala) *Scrittori e città: l'immagine di Novara negli sguardi letterari de sei scrittori sell'ultimo secolo,* Centro Novarese di Studi Letterari, 1993.

Il sogno e l'epica, Genesi (Turin, Italy), 1993.

I Classici italiani tra mercato e accedemia: un anno di discussioni, Edizioni RES (Turin, Italy), 1993.

(With others) *Oeuvres complètes,* Belles Lettres (Paris, France), 1993.

(With others) *Poesia e spiritualità in Clemente Rebora,* Sodalitas (Stresa, Italy), 1993.

(With others) *Commedie,* Edizioni Res (San Mauro Torinese, Italy), 1994.

La scena del mondo, Genesi (Turin, Italy), 1994.

Ascesa e decadenza del romanzo moderno, Tirrenia stampatori (Turin, Italy), 1994.

(With Eugenio Corsini) *Voce di molte acque: miscellanea di studi offerti a Eugenio Corsini,* Zamorani (Turin, Italy), 1994.

(With others) *Notturno,* Mursia (Milan, Italy), 1995.

(With others) *Sonnetti e poemi,* Longanesi (Milan, Italy), 1995.

(With others*) La coscienza de Zeno,* Fabbri (Milan, Italy), 1995.

(With Giusi Baldissone) *Luoghi e forme della lirica,* Tirrenia stampatori (Turin, Italy), 1996.

(With Luciano Fusi) *Il corpo del luogo,* P. Manni (Lecce, Italy), 1996.

(With Marco Marchi) *La zona dolente: studi su Arturo Loria,* Giunti (Florence, Italy), 1996.

(With Daniela Rota) *Tasso e l'Europa: con documentazione inedita; atti del vonvegno internazionale (IV centenario della morte del poeta: Universita di Bergamo, 24-25-26 magio 1995,* M. Baroni (Viareggio, Italy), 1996.

(With Carlo Ossola) *Litteratura e industrial: atti del XV Congresso A.I.S.L.L.I., Torinao, 15-19 maggio 1994,* L. S. Olschki (Florence, Italy), 1997.

La novella del buon vecchio e della bella fanciulla, Marco (Lungro, Italy), 1997.

Romanzi, UTET (Turin, Italy), 1997.

With Riccardo Verzini: Il canone della letteratura: antolgia degli autori da Dante a Marino, Tirrenia stampatori (Turin, Italy), 1997.

In vista del poerto, Maramanica (Marina di Munturno, Italy), 1997.

Le capricciose ambaga della letteratura, Tirrenia stampatori (Turin, Italy), 1998.

Parodia e pensiero: Giordano Bruno, Greco & Greco (Milan, Italy), 1998.

Dal fondo del tempio, Genesi (Turin, Italy), 1999.

Il terzo giorno, T. Pironti (Naples, Italy), 1999.

(With others) *Favole,* Edizioni RES (Turin, Italy), 1999.

(With others) *La quatra triade,* Spirali (Milan, Italy), 2000.

(With others) *Ludovico Ariosota/Giorgio Bàrberi Squarotti/Torquato Tasso/Sergio Zatti,* Editalia (Rome, Italy), 2000.

Contributor to *Io non sono un poeta: Sergo Corazzini (1886-1907): atti del convegno internazionale di studi, Roma, 11-13 marzo 1987,* Presses universitaires de Nancy (Rome, Italy), 1989.

SIDELIGHTS: Giorgio Bàrberi Squarotti's poetry "ought to be measured against the literary parameters of the 1960s," maintained Gaetana Marrone in the *Dictionary of Literary Biography.* "His formation is that of the . . . generation of Italian poets concerned with departing from the confining boundaries of the hermetic tradition and with creating new linguistic codes."

Born in 1929, Bàrberi Squarotti grew up in Turin, Italy, where he earned his doctorate in Italian literature in 1953. After serving as instructor at the University of Turin, Bàrberi Squarotti took his first professional position, as editor at the Italian publishing house UTET, in 1958. As the 1960s dawned, he began publishing his own works, beginning with the theoretical volume *Astrazione e realtà* and the poetry collection *La voce roca.* He returned to the University of Turin in 1967, where he remained as an instructor of contemporary Italian literature.

According to Marrone, Bàrberi Squarotti's early poems "portray the existence of a defenseless man who grieves over his desolate loneliness. Paradigmatic of this mode of being are the themes of *errore* (error) and *inganno* (deceit), often represented by a rich heraldic bestiary: lion, hawk, dog, and unicorn; and by symbols of terror and threat: lightning, floods, and storms." In 1972 the author published *Laberinto d'amore,* containing poems written between 1966 and 1971. The lyrics in this volume, in Marrone's view, reflect "imaginary experiences with the oppression of governments: those of Vietnam, Chile, Greece, and Italy, as affected by obscure conspiracies. More openly political than any of Bàrberi Squarotti's preceding works, *Laberinto d'amore* concentrates on a personal search for [salvation] in a world of inexhaustible allegories."

By 1980 Bàrberi Squarotti had produced two major collections: *Ritratto di intelletuale* and *Il marinaio del Mar Nero e altre poesie.* Noted Marrone, "The 'intellectual' of the first book refers both to the recurring figure of a self-centered poet, . . . and to the *intellettuale organco* (organic intellectual)" of one particular poem, "XXV." Of the latter work, Marrone commented that *Il marinaio del Mar Nero e altre poesie* "ostensibly reinforces the programmatic acceptance of the poetic langue as the only reality within the unreality of the world."

Bàrberi Squarotti's poetry, Marrone concluded, "does not draw on private history alone. The past to which the poems allude is also the collective past of literary and cultural tradition, including language itself, the common linguistic codes from which he forms his ecriture. Poetry must find its space between tradition and innovation . . . Bàrberi Squarotti succeeds in being an alternative voice in an ideological normative climate and achieves a perilous balance between the negativity of his message and the positivity of poetry as 'Other.'"

As an essayist, Bàrberi Squarotti carries on the tradition of the noted Italian author Alessandro Manzoni. His reflections are collected in a series of critical volumes that attempts to capture "Manzoni's disenchantment with literature as a vehicle for truth and his consequent turning to historiography as to the ultimate route of a moral inquiry into the perversity of a human and historical system based on oppression and victimization of the innocent," as A. Illiano noted in *Forum Italicum.* The "extremely subjective" viewpoint of Anna Maria Golfieri and Bàrberi Squarotti's 1984 volume, *Dal tramonto dell'ermetismo all aneoavanguardia,* covers the Italian avant-garde movement between 1950 and 1970. This book, Vivienne Hand remarked in *Modern Language Review,* "traces the decline of Hermeticism following postwar demands for a new realism based upon social and political commitment in literature." To Hand, "the authors' polemical orientation, evident particularly in their choice of 'testimoniaze,' gives energy and thrust to the content of their discourse."

BIOGRAPHICAL AND CRITICAL SOURCES:

BOOKS

Dictionary of Literary Biography, Volume 128: *Twentieth-Century Italian Poets,* Gale (Detroit, MI), 1993.

PERIODICALS

Classical Review, January, 1997, pp. 196-197.
Forum Italicum, spring, 1990, A. Illiano, "On Manzoni's Disillusionment with Literature," pp. 111-115.
Modern Language Review, January, 1988, Vivienne Hand, review of *Dal tramonto dell'ermetismo alla noavanguardia,* p. 212.
Times Literary Supplement, October 31, 1975, "Annessi e connessi," p. 1310.*

*   *   *

BARGUM, Johan 1943-

PERSONAL: Born May 13, 1943, in Helsinki, Finland; son of Viveca Hollmerus Bargum (a writer).

ADDRESSES: Agent—c/o Editions Esprit Ouvert, 3 chemin de Mornex, 1003 Lausanne, Switzerland.

CAREER: Novelist, short story writer, and playwright.

WRITINGS:

Svartvitt (collection; title means "Black and White"), Söderström (Stockholm, Sweden), 1965.
Femte advent (title means "Fifth Advent"), Bonnier (Borga, Finland), 1967.

Tra två ett (title means "Three, Two, One"), Söderström (Stockholm, Sweden), 1968.
Finsk rulett (title means "Finnish Roulette"), Söderström (Tammerfors, Finland), 1971.
Tre skådespel, Söderström (Helsinki, Finland), 1974.
Mörkrum (title means "Darkroom"), Söderström, (Helsinki, Finland), 1977.
Den privata detektiven (title means "The Private Detective"), Norstedts & Söners (Stockholm, Sweden), 1980.
Pimeä huone, Tammi (Helsinki, Finland), 1977.
Pappas flicka (title means "Daddy's Girl"), Söderström (Borga, Finland), 1982.
Sommarpojken, (title means "The Summer Boy"), Söderström (Helsinki, Finland), 1984.
Husdjur (collection), Norstedts & Söners (Stockholm, Sweden), 1986.
Resor (collection; includes "Architekten," "Förläggaren," and "Regissören"), Söderström (Helsinki, Finland), 1988.
Matkoja, Tammi (Helsinki, Finland), 1988.
Den svarta portföljen, Söderström (Helsinki, Finland), 1991.
Sensommar, Söderström (Helsinki, Finland), 1993.
Charlie Boy, Tammi (Helsinki, Finland), 1995.
(With Phillippe Bouquet) *La Mallette noire,* Esprit Ouvert (Lausanne, Switzerland), 1996.

Also author of plays, including *Som snort* (title means "A Cinch"), *Bygga bastu* (title means "Building a Sauna"), and *Virke och verkan* (title means "Material and the Making"). Has written works for television, radio, and cabaret.

ADAPTATIONS: Mörkrum was the basis for Swedish director Lars Lennart Forsberg's 1979 film *Kristoffers hus.*

SIDELIGHTS: The novels and stories of Finnish writer Johan Bargum consistently explore themes related to family relationships of multiple generations, whether between parent and child, sibling and sibling, or in-laws. Early books and stories bear what George C. Schoolfield, writing in *Encyclopedia of World Literature in the Twentieth Century,* called Bargum's "hallmark" of the "interjection of sudden violence into normal and even humdrum circumstances." Throughout his career, Bargum has remained interested in the "psychological interplay of his characters," Schoolfield said. "He specializes in laconic but vivid descriptions of a series of events," wrote Gustaf Widén in *Books from Finland,* "and he fashions each episode with unusual skill."

Born in Helsinki, Finland in 1943, Bargum writes in Swedish, and is one of the few Finland-Swedish authors who has consistently been able to make his living solely by writing, said Widen. The writing life appears to be something of a family tradition for Bargum. His mother, Viveca Hollmerus, wrote a number of well-received novellas in the 1950s, and his maternal grandmother, Margaret von Weillebrand-Hollmerus, was a prolific novelist.

Bargum's first book, *Svartvitt,* consists of six novellas. His second, *Femte advent,* is a novel that "might better be called a collection of portraits, from the Christmas season, of lonely and unhappy people," Schoolfield remarked. Characters include a suicidal nymphomaniac, an intoxicated Santa Claus, and, more mundanely, a father ignored by his son. Bargum's third novel, *Tre två ett,* returns to themes of violence, and is the author's "closest approach to the aggressive social criticism so often practiced by other writers from the minority during the revolutionary 1960s," Schoolfield said. Bargum's 1971 novel *Finsk rulett* "demonstrates how the weak are inevitably abused by the relatively stronger," Schoolfield wrote.

Many of Bargum's works have displayed elements of the more sophisticated detective novel, as exemplified by Raymond Chandler or Dashiell Hammett. "Bargum likes to turn his audience into detectives," Schoolfield wrote in a review of Bargum's *Sensommar* in *World Literature Today.* "He creates mysteries, but, because of his lucid way of telling about events and memories of events, he is never a mystificator." Bargum began refining his own form of detective novel with *Mörkrum* in 1977. A freelance photographer discovers the body of a retired farmer, abandoned and dead in his apartment for many days. The photographer becomes obsessed with the man's death and embarks on an investigation to determine the cause of death, why the dead man was neglected by his children, and how someone could be left to rot in a modern, affluent city. Bargum's conclusion, Widén noted, is that "no one hears that someone is alive. No one hears when someone dies." For Widén, "a novel like *Mörkrum* is impressive for its sophisticated structure and the unswerving sense of composition informing it."

Sometimes Bargum's characters themselves become detectives, subtly or more blatantly, as in *Den privata*

detektiven. The book follows an ex-police inspector Arnold Stroemburg as he attempts to learn a sordid secret held by his daughter, Eva. As Arnold searches for answers, Eva turns to prostitution to help finance her plans to leave for the United States with young drop-out and petty thief Skaedi.

In both *Mörkrum* and *Den privata detektiven,* Bargum returns to the theme of inter-generation family conflict. *Mörkrum* concerns the relationship between a middle-aged man and his ten-year-old daughter, while *Den privata detektiven* centers on a fifty-year old man and his twenty-year-old daughter. "All attempts to communicate, at least between the generations, seemed doomed to failure," Widen observed.

The father-daughter theme becomes even more pervasive in *Pappas flicka,* as thirty-seven-year-old Sissy attempts to come to terms with the death of her beloved father. Structured as a series of long conversations between Sissy and her psychiatrist, the book examines the relationship between Sissy and her pragmatist husband, in contrast with that between her and her father. In the process, a twist on the father-child relationship is revealed through Sissy's illegitimate half-brother.

In *Sommarpojken,* a story of father-son conflict, the narrator decides, after his mother's funeral, to locate his long-absent father. This effort, Schoolfield wrote, "makes him relive the summers he spent as the poor-boy companion of rich children at a seaside cottage."

Husdjur, a collection of four stories, has an entirely different type of human relationship at its core: that between humans and their pets. In this collection, according to Schoolfield, Bargum reveals a new talent: "an ability to slide over into the credibly fantastic." Elements of the fantastic recur in *Resor,* a collection of three novella-length stories. In the first story, "Arkitekten," which Schoolfield deemed a "masterpiece," a young woman explores her father's diary after his sudden death by heart attack. To her surprise, the diary describes her father's mysterious bond with a giant elk. This animal, he writes, will one day lie down atop his chest and crush him. Sure enough, an autopsy reveals ribs that are slightly caved in. Less reliant on the fantastic are the collection's other two stories, "Förläggaren," which Schoolfield considered a "painfully comic account of a lazy poet, a phrase maker who cuckolds his long-suffering protector," and "Regissören" about "a flashback to a nasty childhood that has led to a severe disorder of personality."

Bargum returns to the structure of the mystery novel with *Den svarta portföljen,* in which a jaded reporter, hindered by his interfering mother and her dog, searches for clues to a mystery amid the dangers of the international drug trade.

In *Sensommar,* a Swedish matriarch returns to the family summer place to die. This she accomplishes with the help of her two sons, Olof, described by Schoolfield as "a faintly unsuccessful musicologist and journalist," and Carl, Olof's younger brother, "a businessman in San Francisco, as aggressive and vigorous as his artistic sibling is aimless and unathletic." Also present are Carl's wife, Klara, and two children, Sam and Sebastian, one of whom may be an illegitimate child of Olof's; their sister, Heidi; and Uncle Tom, a doctor and family friend who served, for a time, as Olof and Carl's surrogate father. During the novel, Carl's bullying of his brother persists, scandalous family sexual secrets are discovered, and family dynamics continue to seethe. "As is usual in Bargum's novels and stories," Schoolfield commented, "the reader is left to make up his mind about a great many suggestions and ellipses" in the story.

Bargum's 1995 collection of nine stories, *Charlie Boy,* finds the author returning to familiar ground with pieces that revolve around mysteries. Schoolfield said in a *World Literature Today* review that, "to date, *Charlie Boy* is his masterpiece in compressed prose." Schoolfield also cautions the reader that "the nine stories must not be read swiftly; doing so reduces them to entertainment literature." Another familiar Bargum theme surfaces, as "all the stories depict young people, often confronted by parental or quasi-parental figures" and almost all contain a "strong sense of place," Schoolfield wrote. The stories include "The Man from Manhattan," in which "innocent Nordic travelers" explore the sometimes menacing and often thrilling New York City; "Prince Valiant," an emotionally wrenching story of a shy young man infatuated with a female barber; "Sun Path," an equally strong emotional story about a father driving his daughter to the Helsinki depot and symbolically releasing her for her first trip on her own; and "The Spy," in which a cuckolded father, jailed for financial wrongdoing, convinces the titular Charlie Boy to undertake some sleuthing work on his behalf.

Also a playwright, Bargum has written for the stage, television, and cabaret. His plays include *Tre skådespel,* a collection of dramas about the difficulties of small businessmen, and *Finns det Tigrar i Congo,* a play about AIDS written with director Bengt Ahlfors in 1990. Bargum's "dramas are less intricately wrought than his narratives," Schoolfield remarked, "perhaps because they are often topical." But of Bargum's prose work, Schoolfield stated that "all of Bargum's narratives are compact," with the "deft suggestion of emotional nuances," and "deliberate craftsmanship."

BIOGRAPHICAL AND CRITICAL SOURCES:

BOOKS

Encyclopedia of World Literature in the Twentieth Century, Volume 1, St. James Press (Detroit, MI), 1999.

PERIODICALS

Books from Finland, Volume 16, 1982, Gustaf Widén, "Johan Bargum's Analyses," pp. 66-76.
World Literature Today, fall, 1996, George C. Schoolfield, review of *Charlie Boy,* pp. 977-978; winter, 1995, George C. Schoolfield, review of *Sensommar,* p. 165; winter, 1990, George C. Schoolfield, review of *Resor,* pp. 132-133.*

* * *

BARRINGER GORDON, Sarah 1955-

PERSONAL: Born 1955, in Princeton, NJ; married; husband's name Daniel; children: Patrick, Sophia. *Education:* Vassar College, B.A., 1982; Yale University, J.D., M.A.R.; Princeton University, Ph.D. (history), 1995. *Religion:* "Episcopalian." *Hobbies and other interests:* Marathon running.

ADDRESSES: Home—Mount Airy, PA. *Office*—University of Pennsylvania Law School, 3400 Chestnut St., Room 107, Philadelphia, PA 19104. *E-mail*—sgordon@law.upenn.edu.

CAREER: University of Pennsylvania, professor of law; Vassar College, member of board of trustees.

MEMBER: Historical Society of Pennsylvania councilor, Library Company of Philadelphia board member, University of Pennsylvania chair of Sesquicentennial Committee.

AWARDS, HONORS: Pew Program in Religion and American History, Yale University; Laurence S. Rockefeller scholarship, Princeton University Center for Human Values; Fletcher Foundation fellow for the Huntington, all 1997-98, for work on legal history of religion, property, and marriage.

WRITINGS:

The Mormon Question: Polygamy and Constitutional Conflict in Nineteenth-Century America, University of North Carolina Press (Chapel Hill, NC), 2002.

Wrote introduction for *Women and the Unstable State in Nineteenth-Century America,* edited by Alison M. Parker and Stephanie Cole, Texas A & M Press (College Station, TX), 2000. Also publishes articles for academic journals, including *Yale Journal of Law & the Humanities, New York University Law Review* and *DePaul Law Review.*

SIDELIGHTS: University of Pennsylvania law professor Sarah Barringer Gordon has published countless papers and articles about constitutional law, the relationship between church and state, and gender. Her first published treatise concerns how plural marriage has transformed the American legal system. Although many books have been written about polygamy, *The Mormon Question: Polygamy and Constitutional Conflict in Nineteenth-Century America* is one of the only works to explore the practice from a legal and historical standpoint.

As the title suggests, the book specifically examines the controversy that plural marriage sparked in the nineteenth century. Barringer Gordon, in a *Chronicle of Higher Education* interview with Scott McLemee, explained, "We just can't understand American history without understanding the vital role this faith, and debates over it, have played."

When Mormons fled to Utah in the 1840s, they felt persecuted and unprotected by their federal government. Once established in Utah, however, the Church of Jesus Christ of Latter-Day Saints, under Brigham Young's direction, publicly declared its sanction of polygamy in 1852. Victorian-era society was outraged, and the controversy began. In 1890, in the interest of Utah's admission to the Union, the church formally announced it would no longer encourage its members to disobey "the laws of man" by practicing polygamy, a declaration that mostly satisfied anti-polygamists.

Barringer Gordon's book explores the moral and legal conflicts that arose during those four decades between declarations. In McLemee's interview, Barringer Gordon said, "The claim of anti-Mormons was that polygamy was a form of tyranny that could not coexist with democracy. . . . This was a genuine conflict that played itself out on the political and legal as well as the religious and cultural stages. It made a huge difference in our understanding of the Constitution and in determining what kind of society was fit to take its place among 'the sisterhood of states' as people referred to it."

The controversy boiled down to this: How could anti-polygamists legally prohibit Mormons from their practice of plural marriage without damaging rights guaranteed by the U.S. Constitution? Some of the documents' most powerful tenets, in fact, safeguarded the Mormons. According to Barringer Gordon, though modern society may assume the Mormons could not possibly have won the conflict, they did, in fact, have legal precedent on their side and they won many key victories along the way. In a *Publishers Weekly* profile by Jana Riess, Barringer Gordon explained, "We misunderstand the course of the conflict unless we realize that it was a real conflict, right up until the end."

The basis for *The Mormon Question* was the two-volume dissertation on polygamy in the nineteenth century that Barringer Gordon wrote to fulfill her doctoral requirements at Princeton University. In Riess's article, Barringer Gordon said, "I'm very interested in the kinds of conflicts that lead believers to question the commands of their governments, and vice versa—the conflict of sovereign authority."

A *Publishers Weekly* reviewer praised Barringer Gordon as "a fine scholar whose penetrating research and interdisciplinary approach break new ground in the fields of Mormon studies and legal history."

BIOGRAPHICAL AND CRITICAL SOURCES:

PERIODICALS

Publishers Weekly, November 12, 2001, Jana Riess, "Sarah Barringer Gordon: Focus on Religious Freedom," pp. 18-19; November 26, 2001, review of *The Mormon Question: Polygamy and Constitutional Conflict in Nineteenth-Century America,* p. 56.

OTHER

History Department Web site, University of Pennsylvania, http://www.history.upenn.edu/ (April 16, 2002), faculty profiles.
Penn Law Journal Web site, http://www.law.upenn.edu/alumnijournal/ (fall 2000).
University of Pennsylvania Almanac, http://www.upenn.edu/almanac/ (April 29, 1997), "Honors and Other Things."
World Religious News Service, http://www.wrns.org/ (May 28, 2002), Scott McLemee, "Scholars of Mormonism Confront the History of What Some 'The Next World Religion.'"*

* * *

BARRON, Francis (Xavier) 1922-2002
　(Frank Barron)

OBITUARY NOTICE—See index for *CA* sketch: Born June 17, 1922, in Lansford, PA; died from complications from a fall October 6, 2002, in Santa Cruz, CA. Psychologist, educator, and author. Barron was a groundbreaking psychologist who was interested in human creativity and how creative personalities differ from other people. He graduated in 1942 with a bachelor's degree from La Salle University before serving as a medic during World War II. Following the war he returned to college to earn a master's degree from the University of Minnesota in 1948 and a Ph.D. from the University of California at Berkeley in 1950. During the 1950s and 1960s he became well known for his research into creativity at the Institute for Personality Assessment and Research at Berkeley where, among other accomplishments, he created the Barron Ego-Strength Scale and other tests to measure human creativity. He also conducted research using hallucinatory drugs such as LSD and psilocybin, something he later regretted doing given the adverse effects the drugs had on people's health. He remained at Berkeley until 1974, when he moved to the University of California at Santa Cruz, retiring in 1992. Under the name Frank Barron, he wrote or edited over a dozen books during his career, including the acclaimed works *Creativity and Psychological Health* (1963) and *Creativity and Personal Freedom* (1968), both of which are considered groundbreaking works in psychology. Among Barron's last published works were *No Rootless Flower: An Ecology of Creativity* (1995) and the coedited *Creators on Creating: Awakening and Cultivating the Imaginative Mind* (1997). Barron, who freely integrated ideas from religion, philosophy, and literature into his theories, also enjoyed writing poetry; a collection of his verses titled *Ghosts*, was planned for posthumous publication. He was a recipient of several awards, including the Richardson Creativity Award in 1969 and the Rudolf Arnheim Award for outstanding contribution to psychology and the arts in 1995, both from the American Psychological Association.

OBITUARIES AND OTHER SOURCES:

BOOKS

Sheehy, Noel, Antony J. Chapman, and Wendy A. Conroy, editors, *Biographical Dictionary of Psychology,* Routledge (London, England), 1997.

PERIODICALS

Los Angeles Times, October 15, 2002, p. B13.
New York Times, October 13, 2002, p. A29.

* * *

BARRON, Frank
　See BARRON, Francis (Xavier)

* * *

BASBANES, Nicholas A. 1943-

PERSONAL: Born 1943, in Lowell, MA; married; wife's name, Constance; children: two daughters. *Education:* Bates College, 1965; Pennsylvania State University, M.A., 1969,

ADDRESSES: Home—North Grafton, MA. *Agent*—c/o Author Mail, Henry Holt & Co., 115 West 18th Street, New York, NY 10011. *E-mail*—nabasbanes@aol.com.

CAREER: Worcester *Sunday Telegram,* literary editor, 1978-91; national syndicated columnist, 1991-99; author. *Military service:* U.S. Navy, public information officer.

AWARDS, HONORS: National Book Critics Circle Award finalist and New York Times Notable Book of the Year both for *A Gentle Madness.*

WRITINGS:

A Gentle Madness: Bibliophiles, Bibliomanes, and the Eternal Passion for Books, Henry Holt and Co. (New York, NY), 1995.

Patience and Fortitude: A Roving Chronicle of Book People, Book Places, and Book Culture, Harper-Collins (New York, NY), 2001.

Among the Gently Mad: Perspectives and Strategies for the Book-Hunter in the Twenty-first Century, Henry Holt and Co. (New York, NY), 2002.

WORK IN PROGRESS: Life beyond Life: The Permanence of Books in an Impermanent World for Harper-Collins;

SIDELIGHTS: Nicholas A. Basbanes had worked as a reporter for many years when the management at the Worcester *Sunday Telegram* decided to cut costs by eliminating the newspaper's book section, Basbanes lost his long-standing job as book review editor. He was forty-seven years old at the time, married, and had two children. Both he and his wife, Constance, had faith in his ability to write, so instead of looking for another fulltime job, Basbanes decided to become a part time freelance writer and devote the majority of his time and energy to writing a book.

Although confident of his skills in telling a good story, he had trouble selling his book concept to a publisher. No one thought that a book about books would ever sell, not even to an academic audience. To everyone's surprise, once Basbanes's first book, *A Gentle Madness: Bibliophiles, Bibliomanes, and the Eternal Passion for Books,* was published in 1995, it turned out to be a bestseller.

A Gentle Madness is more than a book about books. It is a book about the people who have collected books and the significance of their collections. Basbanes uses his skills as a journalist to keep his readers involved in a story about other people's love of books. He incorporates interesting details of such ancient figures as Alexander the Great and the Italian poet Petrarch and then he moves into contemporary times with stories about characters such as Ruth Baldwin, a woman who collected children's books despite the fact that she disliked children, and Charles L. Blockson, who left his career as a professional football player to collect books on the cultural history of African Americans. One of Basbanes's most interesting stories involves the trial of Stephen C. Blumberg, a man who stole rare books from almost three hundred different libraries from all over the United States. Blumberg pleaded not guilty at his trial for reasons of insanity. He eventually lost his case.

Writing for the *New York Times Book Review,* Philip Kopper praised Basbanes' collection of stories about people who collect books. "It is a brave writer who attempts a comprehensive study that's fit to read. Nicholas A. Basbanes succeeds on several counts, for *A Gentle Madness* is an impressive achievement in its compilation of vast information, as well as instructive and interesting." Kopper then recommended the book for anyone "seriously interested in books or curious about the manic nature of collecting." Donna Seaman, writing for *Booklist,* also noted the manic nature of book collectors as she wrote: "A surprising number of these stories involve nefarious dealings and vicious rivalries, proving that even in our digitized age, books arouse intense emotions, from worship to greed."

In 2001, Basbanes published his second book, *Patience and Fortitude: A Roving Chronicle of Book People, Book Places, and Book Culture,* a sort of sequel to his first book. In this volume, Basbanes looks at the great libraries and their librarians through the ages. He also relates stories of bookmakers, booksellers, antiquarians, great authors, as well as book collectors. He tackles the current controversy over print media versus digital media, the problems of storing old books that few people want to read any more, and the ever-rising cost of paper in the production of books and journals. To illustrate some of the problems, he points out the volume of books that large libraries receive each day, such as the Library of Congress's load of twenty-five thousand new books each day.

In a review of *Patience and Fortitude,* a writer for *Publishers Weekly* concluded: "Basbanes's fund of stories will delight readers who value books for more than just a good story, have a yen for second-hand books plucked from dusty shops or like to look at catalogs for suspense and excitement."

Basbanes, an admitted bibliophile himself, lives in a small house in rural Massachusetts with his wife, two daughters, and over ten thousand books. In an article written for the online *I Read Pages,* Basbanes told Laurie Mason, "I fall over them, they fall down. Upstairs, we've added a library on to the house. All of the bedrooms are full. The bathroom downstairs, if you open the closet looking for towels, you're going to see books."

In 2002, Basbanes' third book, *Among the Gently Mad: Strategies for the Book-Hunter in the Twenty-first Century* was published.

BIOGRAPHICAL AND CRITICAL SOURCES:

PERIODICALS

Booklist, August, 1995, Donna Seaman, review of *A Gentle Madness: Bibliophiles, Bibliomanes, and the Eternal Passion for Books,* p. 1913; September 15, 2001, Donna Seaman, review of *Patience and Fortitude: A Roving Chronicle of Book People, Book Places, and Book Culture,* p. 166.
Houston Chronicle, November 9, 2001, Earl L. Dachslager, "He Digs the Bookworms,"
Kirkus Reviews, August 1, 2001, review of *Patience and Fortitude,* p. 1079.
Library Journal, September 1, 2001, Paul D'Alessandro, review of *Patience and Fortitude,* p. 176.
Los Angeles Times Book Review, December 3, 1995, David Kipen, "Collecting Myself," p. 18.
New York Review, December 20, 2001, Larry McMurtry, "Mad about the Book," pp. 57-59.
New York Times Book Review, August 20, 1995, Philip Kopper, "Crazy about Books," p. 25; October 14, 2001, Diane Cole, review of *Patience and Fortitude,* p. 28.
Publishers Weekly, July 3, 1995, review of *A Gentle Madness,* p. 45; August 13, 2001, review of *Patience and Fortitude,* p. 296.
Washington Post Book World, December 9, 2001, Henry Wessells, "The Tomes of Their Lives," p. 12.*

BAUER, Cat

PERSONAL: Born in SC. *Education:* Studied at Stella Adler Conservatory of Acting, New York, NY, and at University of California, Los Angeles extension. *Hobbies and other interests:* Reading, traveling, gardening, snorkeling.

ADDRESSES: Home—Venice, Italy. *Agent*—c/o Brandt & Hochman, 1501 Broadway, Suite 2310, New York, NY 10036. *E-mail*—cat@catbauer.com.

CAREER: Actress, playwright, and writer. Appears in television commercials and daytime dramas.

AWARDS, HONORS: Sue Alexander Award for Most Promising New Work, Society of Children's Book Writers and Illustrators, 2000; and Best Books for Young Adults, American Library Association, Top-Ten Youth First Novel, *Booklist,* Top-Ten Teen First Novel, *Bookreporter,* and Book of the Year, Young Adult Fiction, *ForeWord,* all 2001, all for *Harley, like a Person.*

WRITINGS:

Harley, like a Person, Winslow Press (Delray Beach, FL), 2000.

Also writes newspaper articles for *International Herald Tribune Italy Daily.* Contributor to *Sassy.*

SIDELIGHTS: Cat Bauer's first novel began as a short story, published in the teen magazine *Sassy.* A strong response from the magazine's readers compelled Bauer to tell the rest of story in a full-length novel, titled *Harley, like a Person.* Harley, a teenage girl in a dysfunctional family, has an alcoholic, abusive father and an unsupportive mother. When Harley makes an unexpected discovery, she learns she is adopted, leading her on a search for one of her "real" parents. However, her obsession with her birth father nearly derails her.

On *Authors on the Web,* Bauer described how she submitted her manuscript of *Harley, like a Person* for review at the Society of Children's Book Writers and Illustrators conference. She recalled, "I was fortunate enough to have [young adult author] Walter Dean My-ers read my manuscript. . . . He reinforced everything I felt instinctively." After this professional evaluation, Bauer left her publisher and her agent, feeling that their vision for *Harley* and her own were not compatible. She soon found a new agent and a small publisher, and although they called for "radical changes" in the manuscript, Bauer wrote that "in this case, they felt right."

Readers and reviewers often found the strength of Bauer's novel in the authentic voice of its heroine, Harley. Patricia Morrow, for example, in *Voice of Youth Advocates,* remarked that "Harley's voice is true to the experience of many young people," and that "Although the outcomes are not unexpected, they do not follow any formulas." Similarly, writing for *Booklist,* Frances Bradburn said, "Harley's strength of character, her humor, and her vulnerability will resonate with teen readers." A critic for *Horn Book* wrote that although the novel could have used "more structure and focus," it "offers a compelling read and a close-up look at adolescent emotional life." Francisca Goldsmith, in *School Library Journal,* found some problems in the construction of the novel, remarking that some characters have "disappointingly flat walk-on roles," and noted that Harley's quest to find her father is "flawed but credible in method." Goldsmith nonethe-less concluded, however, that Bauer's "well-felt story" would resonate with young adult readers.

BIOGRAPHICAL AND CRITICAL SOURCES:

PERIODICALS

Booklist, June 1, 2000, Frances Bradburn, review of *Harley, like a Person,* p. 1880; November 15, 2000, Hazel Rochman, review of *Harley, like a Person,* p. 631.

Bulletin of the Center for Children's Books, May, 2000, Kate McDowell, review of *Harley, like a Person,* pp. 306-07.

Horn Book, May, 2000, review of *Harley, like a Person,* p. 307.

School Library Journal, May, 2000, Francisca Gold-smith, review of *Harley, like a Person,* p. 166.

Voice of Youth Advocates, October, 2000, Patricia Mor-row, review of *Harley, like a Person,* p. 260.

OTHER

Authors on the Web, http://www.authorsontheweb.com/ (October 6, 2001), "Cat Bauer."*

*   *   *

BAYLEY, Edwin (Richard) 1918-2002

OBITUARY NOTICE—See index for *CA* sketch: Born August 24, 1918, in Chicago, IL; died October 27, 2002, in Green Bay, WI. Journalist, educator, adminis-trator, and author. Bayley will be best remembered as the founding dean of the University of California at Berkeley's School of Journalism, as well as for his ardent criticism of the activities of U.S. Senator Joseph McCarthy during the mid-twentieth century. He was a graduate of Lawrence College (now Lawrence University), where he earned his B.A. in English with honors, and he attended graduate courses at Yale University from 1940 to 1941. Bayley left school for his first reporting job with the Green Bay *Press-Gazette,* but with U.S. entry into World War II he joined the Navy as an ensign and fought in the Mediterranean and North Atlantic. After the war he returned to journalism as a reporter for the *Milwaukee Journal,* where he remained through the 1950s. His interest in politics as a reporter led to his being hired as chief of staff and executive secretary to Wisconsin Governor Gaylord Nelson and then as special assistant to President John F. Kennedy during the early 1960s. Bayley took on several administrative positions during the mid- to late 1960s, including director of informa-tion for the U.S. Agency for International Develop-ment and vice president of administration for National Educational Television, which was the precursor of the Public Broadcasting Service. In 1969 he was hired by the University of California at Berkeley to set up the university's School of Journalism, and it was there that he remained until his retirement in 1985, although he continued to give lectures and write. During his tenure as dean at Berkeley, Bayley was credited for making the journalism school one of the best in the country. Besides writing numerous articles for newspa-pers and journals, he was also notable for his book *Joe McCarthy and the Press* (1981) in which he criticized the media for the way they failed to fully investigate McCarthy's claims about alleged communists infiltrating the U.S. government. The book was nominated for a Pulitzer Prize and a National Book Award, and it won the George Polk Award. Bayley was honored in 1985 with the Berkeley Citation and the 1986 Alumni Distinguished Service award from Lawrence University. His alma mater also gave him an honorary doctorate degree.

OBITUARIES AND OTHER SOURCES:

PERIODICALS

Los Angeles Times, October 30, 2002, p. B10.
New York Times, October 29, 2002, p. C20.
Washington Post, November 2, 2002, p. B7.

*   *   *

BEALE, Howard K(ennedy) 1899-1959

PERSONAL: Born April 8, 1899, in Chicago, IL; died following a heart attack December 27, 1959; son of Frank A. and Nellie Kennedy Beale; married Georgia Robinson, 1942; children: three sons. *Education:* University of Chicago, B.A., 1921; Harvard University, M.A., 1922, Ph.D., 1927.

CAREER: Author and educator. Grinnell College, Grinnell, IA, instructor, 1925-26; Bowdoin College, Brunswick, ME, instructor, 1926-30; University of Chicago, Chicago, IL, visiting associate professor of history, 1934; New York University, New York, NY, lecturer, 1934-35; University of North Carolina, Chapel Hill, professor, director of graduate studies, 1935-48; University of Wisconsin, professor, 1948-59; University of Munich, Munich, Germany, Fulbright professor, 1955-56.

MEMBER: Phi Beta Kappa, American Association of University Professors, National Education Association, American Federation of Teachers, American Civil Liberties Union, National Association for the Advancement of Colored People.

WRITINGS:

The Critical Year: A Study of Andrew Johnson and Reconstruction, Harcourt, Brace (New York, NY), 1930.

(Editor) *The Diary of Edward Bates, 1859-1866,* U.S. Government Printing Office (Washington, DC), 1933.
Are American Teachers Free? An Analysis of Restraints upon the Freedom of Teaching in American Schools, Scribners (New York, NY), 1936.
A History of Freedom of Teaching in American Schools, Scribners (New York, NY), 1941.
(Editor) *Charles A Beard: An Appraisal,* University of Kentucky Press (Lexington, KY), 1954.
Theodore Roosevelt and the Rise of America to World Power, Johns Hopkins University (Baltimore, MD), 1956.
(Editor) *The Diary of Gideon Welles, Secretary of the Navy under Lincoln and Johnson,* Norton (New York, NY), 1960.

Contributor to periodicals, including *American Historical Review, Harper's, Independent Woman, Annals of the American Academy of Political and Social Science, Nation,* and *Pacific Historical Review.*

SIDELIGHTS: Howard K. Beale was a historian who published works on topics ranging from the presidencies of Andrew Jackson and Theodore Roosevelt to the restraints found within America's educational system. Beale also worked untiringly as an educator, social crusader, and political activist. After graduating from the University of Chicago, he moved to New England where he completed his master's and doctoral degrees at Harvard University. *Dictionary of Literary Biography* contributor Allan D. Charles reported how Beale's mentor at Harvard, Edward Channing, challenged him to research the "extensive and thorny historical problem of Andrew Johnson's presidency." At first, Beale felt himself incapable of tackling such a complicated subject, but under his mentor's guidance, Beale accomplished the task. A revised version of this dissertation, *The Critical Year: A Study of Andrew Johnson and Reconstruction,* was published in 1930.

The Critical Year was radical because it stood in direct opposition to prevailing, post-Civil War views, but after its publication Beale was regarded by many as a leader in the movement to revise popular notions of the Reconstruction Era, and his ideas becoming known as the "Beale Thesis." In *The Critical Year,* Beale describes how a Radical Republican faction dominated the U.S. Congress of 1867. Instead of working toward reconciliation between the North and South, said

Charles, this group of Northern congressmen sought to "chasten the defeated South." Beale concludes that the anti-Southern sentiment was fueled by economic motives, and not by any idealistic goals of helping the freed slaves, because the North lost interest in them once "the new economic order was firmly entrenched in power." According to Charles, Beale discusses how these northern Republicans feared the diminishing tariffs of peaceful times, and how they were also convinced that if the Southerners were readmitted to Congress, they would not support such Republican measures as "federal support for transportation and central banking." Congressmen Charles Sumner of Massachusetts and Thaddeus Stevens of Pennsylvania were considered the leaders of the Radical Republicans, who championed the cause of the industrial North against the agrarian Southern states. According to Robert David Ward in the *Encyclopedia of Southern History,* Beale "influenced a generation of students to regard the Radicals as manipulative politicians." Furthermore, Ward noted that although Beale's revisionist ideas of Reconstruction had fallen out of favor by the late twentieth century, "his work remains a major step in the efforts to understand our past."

In 1932 Beale published *The Diary of Edward Bates, 1859-1866.* Bates, a vocal opponent of slavery, served as U.S. attorney general from 1861 to 1863, during the Lincoln administration. The man left behind five voluminous diaries, which Beale transcribed and edited, resulting in a 685-page work. Beale noted that Bates had been a contender for the 1860 presidential nomination, and—regarding Lincoln's quick rise from obscurity—Bates' first mention of Lincoln as a possible presidential nominee appeared in a journal entry, only three weeks before the Republican convention.

For his next books, Beale pursued a totally different subject: academic freedom. He based his first book, *Are American Teachers Free? An Analysis of Restraints upon the Freedom of Teaching in American Schools,* upon interviews with teachers, and upon the results of questionnaires that were anonymously answered. In regard to the questionnaires, Beale soon observed something quite remarkable: despite a strict promise of their anonymity, many teachers would not permit their answers to be published. That fact, in itself, led Beale to conclude that there was a serious lack of freedom in the educational world. He reexamined these questions in *A History of Freedom of Teaching in American Schools,* in which he discovered that emotionally or politically charged issues were forbidden topics for teachers to pursue in the classroom.

Beale's *Theodore Roosevelt and the Rise of America to World Power,* was based upon lectures that Beale originally gave at Johns Hopkins University. Beale thoroughly researched this work by interviewing Roosevelt's friends, family, and various government representatives. He also studied diplomatic records, said Charles, in order to understand "how Roosevelt was viewed in foreign capitals as well as how foreign diplomatic efforts were seen in Washington." Charles also commented that Beale's work "married intellectual history and biography in a context of diplomatic history."

Beale's final book, *The Diary of Gideon Welles, Secretary of the Navy under Lincoln and Johnson,* was published posthumously. The idea for this book originated during Beale's years as a graduate student at Harvard, when he questioned the reliability of Welles' diary. Many critics, Charles concluded, "praised the Beale edition as an excellent achievement and a useful aid to scholarship."

BIOGRAPHICAL AND CRITICAL SOURCES:

BOOKS

Dictionary of Literary Biography, Volume 17: *Twentieth-Century American Historians,* Gale (Detroit, MI), 1983, pp. 32-38.
Encyclopedia of Southern History, Louisiana State University Press (Baton Rouge, LA), 1979, p. 111.*

*   *   *

BECKER, Deborah Zimmett 1955-
(Debbie Zimmett)

PERSONAL: Born July 7, 1955, in Waukegon, IL; divorced; children: Neil, Isaac, Noah. *Education:* University of Pennsylvania, B.S.N., 1977. *Politics:* "Liberal/Democrat." *Religion:* Jewish.

ADDRESSES: Home—4740 Barcelona Ct., Calabasas, CA 91302. *E-mail*—dzimmett@aol.com.

CAREER: Buttercup Preschool, discrete trial therapist. Also works as registered nurse at a residential summer camp.

WRITINGS:

AS DEBBIE ZIMMETT

Eddie Enough!, illustrated by Charlotte Murray, Woodbine House (Bethesda, MD), 2001.

WORK IN PROGRESS: Children's books "whose themes help kids make sense of confusing situations"; screenplays.

SIDELIGHTS: Deborah Zimmett Becker told *CA:* "I always loved to read! Books were my favorite companions. When I was in fourth grade, we lived within walking distance of the local library. My special treat was to walk there by myself and choose books to check out. I was never a great student, and I certainly didn't like to write! My background in nursing and education are the motivating factors in my decision to write children's books because I like to explain things to kids. When kids understand what is happening to them or around them, they are happier and there is no limit to what they can achieve.*"

*   *   *

BECKMAN, Linda Hunt

PERSONAL: Female. *Education:* Hunter College, City University of New York, B.A. (English); University of California at Berkeley, M.A. (English), Ph.D. (English).

ADDRESSES: Office—333 Ellis Hall, Ohio University, Athens, OH 45701. *E-mail*—huntli@ohio.edu.

CAREER: Author and educator. Ohio University, Athens, associate professor of English.

WRITINGS:

A Woman's Portion: Ideology, Culture, and the Female Novel Tradition, Garland (New York, NY), 1988.
Amy Levy: Her Life and Letters, Ohio University Press (Athens, OH), 2000.

Contributor of numerous articles to various periodicals, including *Victorian Literature and Culture, Studies in the Novel,* and *The Feminist Teacher.*

SIDELIGHTS: American scholar Linda Hunt Beckman published a biography of Amy Levy, a British author who wrote during the late nineteenth century. A number of literary critics lauded Beckman's book, titled *Amy Levy: Her Life and Letters,* because it sheds light on many elements of Levy's tragic life, which came to an end when she committed suicide in 1889. Critic R. T. Van Arsdel, for example, in a *Choice* review, called Beckman's book a "well-researched and insightful biography."

Beckman is an associate professor at Ohio University, where she primarily teaches nineteenth-century literature. She published her first book, *A Woman's Portion: Ideology, Culture, and the Female Novel Tradition,* in 1988, and she published articles and essays in numerous publications. For Levy's biography, Beckman relied heavily on archival material, including Levy's letters, which were recently collected and made available by the Jewish Museum of London. Indeed, Beckman's book marks the first publication of a large number of Levy's letters, more than thirty-five of which are printed in the book's appendix. "My book examines Levy's life, work, and times," Beckman writes in her introductory prologue. "I examine Levy's writings as works of art, and scrutinize them, along with letters (her own and those of people who knew her), scrapbooks, sketches, and other personal artifacts, and cultural documents of various kinds, for insight into her intense emotional and intellectual life."

Levy, who was born in 1861, made her mark in London literary circles during the 1880s. She was just the second Jewish woman to be admitted to prestigious Cambridge University, and she was a close friend of a number of British luminaries, including Oscar Wilde, George Bernard Shaw, Karl Pearson, and Vernon Lee. Levy published her first book of poetry before the age of twenty and went on to publish three short novels, numerous essays, and two more volumes of poetry. However, as Beckman explains, Levy was haunted by several internal demons, including her homosexuality and her ambivalence regarding her Jewishness, which alienated her from many of her contemporaries. Her emotional struggle ultimately led Levy to take her own life at the age of twenty-seven, just eight years after publishing her first work.

According to Beckman's introduction, one of her motivations in writing the book was to correct misinformation that has appeared about Levy over the years in various articles and reference books, especially about her background, education, physical appearance, and politics. In particular, Beckman refutes the idea that Levy was a "radical, a socialist, or social reformer." Instead, Beckman describes Levy as a "witty, troubled, gifted, ironic, and singular young woman negotiating the troubled waters of her time." In an interview for Ohio University's *Perspectives,* Beckman explained to Andrea Gibson that she hoped her book would create new interest in Levy's life and work: "I hope she gets the niche in the literary canon that she deserves."

Beckman's book was well received by critics, including a contributor for *Nineteenth-Century Literature,* who called the work a "lucid study" and an "impressive volume." Similarly, Diane Gardner Premo, reviewing the book for *Library Journal,* felt that it is an "important biography." In addition, Talia Schaffer, a critic for the *Women's Review of Books,* felt that Beckman has "gone to remarkable lengths to flesh out her subject's brief life," and that she has "restored Levy's 'life' and voice to our consciousness, and has given us a new appreciation of this 'woman of letters.'" However, Schaffer did criticize a number of "small errors and misjudgments about the Victorian era" on Beckman's part, which she believed tend to "undermine the reader's confidence." Critic Ruth Bernard Yeazell, however, wrote in the *London Review of Books,* "Despite some inclination to special pleading, *Amy Levy: Her Life and Letters* is a valuable guide to its subject. The thinness of the record necessarily makes it a more speculative biography than most, but Beckman is always careful to make clear on what grounds she has constructed her hypotheses. She is especially good at sorting out the different voices in which Levy speaks."

BIOGRAPHICAL AND CRITICAL SOURCES:

PERIODICALS

Choice, January, 2001, R. T. Van Arsdel, review of *Amy Levy: Her Life and Letters,* p. 900.
Library Journal, May 15, 2000, Diane Gardner Premo, review of *Amy Levy,* p. 93.
London Review of Books, November 16, 2000, Ruth Bernard Yeazell, "Is Everybody's Life like This?," p. 14.
Nineteenth-Century Literature, March, 2001, review of *Amy Levy,* p. 561.
Women's Review of Books, May, 2001, Talia Schaffer, "Brief Life," p. 20.

OTHER

Perspectives: Research, Scholarship, and Creative Activity at Ohio University, http://www.ohiou.edu/perspectives (February 21, 2002), Andrea Gibson, "A Woman's Words," spring-summer, 2000.*

*   *   *

BEERS, Henry A(ugustin) 1847-1926

PERSONAL: Born July 2, 1847, in Buffalo, NY; died September 7, 1926, in New Haven, CT; son of George Webster and Elizabeth Victoria (Clerc) Beers; married Mary Heaton, July 7, 1873; children: Thomas, Elizabeth, Katherine, Frederick, Dorothy, Mary, Henry, Donald. *Education:* Yale University, B.A., 1869; studied law in New York, NY, 1869; attended University of Heidelberg, 1876; attended Bronson Alcott's School of Philosophy, 1877.

CAREER: Author and educator. Yale University, New Haven, CT, tutor of English literature, 1871-74; assistant professor, 1875-80; professor of English, 1880-1916; professor emeritus, 1916-26. Admitted to the Bar of New York state, 1870.

MEMBER: Phi Beta Kappa, Kappa Sigma Epsilon, Alpha Delta Phi, Skull and Bones, Elizabethan Club of New Haven, CT, Author's Club of New York City.

AWARDS, HONORS: Honorary M.A., Yale University, 1887.

WRITINGS:

Odds and Ends: Verses Humorous, Occasional, and Miscellaneous, Houghton, Osgood (Boston, MA), 1878.

(Editor) *A Century of American Literature 1776-1876,* Holt (New York, NY), 1878.

Nathaniel Parker Willis, Houghton, Mifflin (Boston, MA and New York, NY), 1885.

The Thankless Muse, Houghton, Mifflin (Boston, MA and New York, NY), 1885.

An Outline Sketch of English Literature, Chautauqua Press (New York, NY), 1886, published as *From Chaucer to Tennyson: English Literature in Eight Chapters, with Selections from Thirty Authors,* Chautauqua Press (New York, NY), 1890.

An Outline Sketch of American Literature, Chautauqua Press (New York, NY), 1887, published as *Initial Studies in American Letters,* Chautauqua Press (New York, NY), 1891, published as *Studies in American Letters,* Jacobs (Philadelphia, PA), 1895, published as *A Short History of American Literature,* Unwin (London, England), 1906.

(Editor and author of introduction) *Selections from the Prose Writings of Samuel Taylor Coleridge,* Holt (New York, NY), 1893.

A Suburban Pastoral, and Other Tales, Holt (New York, NY), 1894.

The Ways of Yale in the Consulship of Plancus, Holt (New York, NY), 1895.

Brief History of English and American Literature, Eaton & Mains (New York, NY), 1897.

A History of English Romanticism in the Eighteenth Century, Holt (New York, NY), 1899.

A History of English Romanticism in the Nineteenth Century, Holt (New York, NY), 1901.

Points at Issue and Some Other Points, Macmillan (New York, NY), 1904.

Milton's Tercentenary: An Address Delivered before the Modern Language Club at Yale University on Milton's Three Hundredth Birthday, Yale University Press (New Haven, CT), 1910.

The Two Twilights, Badger (Boston, MA), 1917.

(Editor and author of foreword) *Afterglow,* Yale University Press (New Haven, CT), 1918.

Four Americans: Roosevelt, Hawthorne, Emerson, Whitman, Yale University Press (New Haven, CT), 1919.

The Connecticut Wits, and Other Essays, Yale University Press (New Haven, CT), 1920.

Poems, Yale University Press (New Haven, CT), 1921.

Bumblebee, Bernhardt Wall (New Preston, CT), 1925.

Wrote introduction to *Readings from Ruskin: Italy,* Chautauqua Press (Boston, MA), 1885. Contributor to several anthologies and periodicals, including *Stories by American Authors, The Memorial History of Hartford County, Connecticut 1633-1884, Yale Literary Magazine, Chautauquan,* and *Century.*

SIDELIGHTS: Henry A. Beers was well known for his contributions to literary scholarship at the end of the nineteenth century and at the beginning of the twentieth. For more than forty years, Beers taught the subject of English literature at Yale University. He was a devoted teacher whose "intimate knowledge of all kinds of literature," according to *Dictionary of Literary Biography* contributor Philip B. Eppard, "was legendary." Prior to Beers' career in the English literature department, the Yale curriculum focused exclusively upon grammar. Beers, however, quickly redirected the program toward "a more historically based study of literature itself."

Although Beers lived nearly his entire life in Connecticut, he was actually born on July 2, 1847, in Buffalo, New York, while his parents were traveling. His childhood years were spent in Hartford, Connecticut, where he attended school, and after his high school graduation Beers began his studies at Yale University. In 1869, he received his bachelor's degree, then moved to New York City in order to study law; he successfully passed the bar exam and practiced as a lawyer for one year. This career did not suit him, however, and he returned to Yale as an English tutor in 1871 and remained there until 1916, when he retired as professor emeritus.

In 1885, Beers published a scholarly biography titled *Nathaniel Parker Willis,* which Eppard considered "one of Beers's most substantial works." Beers carefully investigates the life of this nineteenth-century essayist and poet, and Eppard noted that Beers's book is important, "particularly for its use of original source material, some of which has been lost." In the book, Beers also praises much of Willis's work, lamenting the fact that literary critics had ceased to favor him.

Beers followed his biography with two introductory histories of literature: *An Outline Sketch of English Literature* (1886) and *An Outline Sketch of American Literature* (1887). These works were tremendously popular and were re-published in several editions. Eppard reported that a student of Beers, Francis Parsons, felt that the book contained a "vividness of statement and portrayal of character coupled with a wise conciseness which . . . generate a kind of electric sparkle."

In 1899 and 1901, Beers wrote the books which would confirm and assure his reputation as a literary scholar. *A History of English Romanticism in the Eighteenth Century* and *A History of English Romanticism in the Nineteenth Century* were based upon lectures Beers had prepared for his literature classes at Yale. In these works Beers demonstrates his comprehensive knowledge of both English and European literature. He also attempts to illustrate how the Romantic Movement manifested itself in various cultures. Although these books were considered somewhat controversial due to Beers's definition of romanticism, Henry Barrett Hinckley, a reviewer for *Bookman,* stated that the author "is admirably free from that dullness of the specialist which prevents so much excellent scholarship from appealing to the people."

Although most of Beers's books were scholarly literary studies, he also had a penchant and a talent for writing verse. At the beginning of his writing career, Beers published *Odds and Ends: Verses Humorous, Occasional, and Miscellaneous.* His final works were also collections of poetry. Eppard noted that William Lyon Phelps once described Beers by saying: "Had he had any ambition he would have been one of the best known of contemporary creative writers."

BIOGRAPHICAL AND CRITICAL SOURCES:

BOOKS

Bacon, Leonard, *Semi-Centennial: Some of the Life and Part of the Opinions of Leonard Bacon,* Harper (New York, NY), 1939.
Canby, Henry S., *Alma Mater: The Gothic Age of the American College,* Farrar & Rinehart (New York, NY), 1936.
Cross, Wilbur, *Connecticut Yankee: An Autobiography,* Yale University Press (New Haven, CT), 1943.
Dictionary of Literary Biography, Volume 71: *American Literary Critics and Scholars, 1880-1900,* Gale (Detroit, MI), 1988.
National Cyclopedia of American Biography, Volume 44, James T. White & Co. (New York, NY), 1962.
Parsons, Francis, *Six Men of Yale,* Yale University Press (New Haven, CT), 1939.
Phelps, William Lyon, *Autobiography with Letters,* Oxford University Press (New York, NY), 1939.
Pierson, George Wilson, *Yale College: An Educational History 1871-1921,* Yale University Press (New Haven, CT), 1952.

PERIODICALS

Bookman, June, 1899, Henry Barrett Hinckley, review of *A History of English Romanticism in the Eighteenth Century.**

*   *   *

BELGRAD, Daniel 1964-

PERSONAL: Born January 15, 1964. *Education:* Attended Princeton University; Yale University, Ph.D.

ADDRESSES: Office—Humanities and American Studies, College of Arts and Sciences, University of South Florida, 4202 East Fowler Ave., CPR 107, Tampa, FL 33620. *E-mail*—belgrad@chumal.cas.usf.edu.

CAREER: University of South Florida, Tampa, College of Arts and Sciences, assistant professor of humanities and American studies.

WRITINGS:

The Culture of Spontaneity: Improvisation and the Arts in Postwar America, University of Chicago Press (Chicago, IL), 1998.

SIDELIGHTS: In *The Culture of Spontaneity: Improvisation in the Arts in Postwar America,* Daniel Belgrad attempts to account for the unprecedented rise of spontaneous artistic expression in a variety of arts, including painting, dance, literature, and music in the decades immediately following World War II. According to the author, many postwar artists reacted negatively to the increasing pressure of corporate culture and set about creating ways of expressing themselves in art characterized by spontaneity. These artists "produced abstract expressionism and bebop jazz, beat poetry and Zen pottery, pop art," and other "antitraditional movements," reviewer K. Marantz observed in *Choice.* Belgrad's artists include the painter Jackson Pollock, poets Charles Olson and Allen Ginsberg, writer Jack Kerouac, ceramicist Peter Voulkos, philosopher Alfred North Whitehead, musician Charlie Parker, and others. *Times Literary Supplement* contributor Roger Kimball complained that Belgrad's theory fails to consider the work of numerous significant figures in the arts he examines, among them George Balanchine in dance, Wallace Stevens in poetry, and Edmund Wilson in criticism, and others. Kimball implies that the aforementioned were not advocates of spontaneous artistic expression although they remain pivotal figures in the era studied.

"Belgrad is not wrong to understand his artists, writers and musicians as expressing antagonism toward the destructiveness, spiritual and material, of modern society," asserted *Art in America* reviewer Paul Mattick, Jr. Where the author goes wrong, Mattick continued, is in his tendency "to oversimplify the avant-garde's purported antagonist." Mattick asserted that the unprecedented success of American corporate culture in the 1950s not only brought with it the repressive social conformity for which the decade is remembered, but greatly expanded consumer buying-power and leisure time and enriched the nation's educational system, thereby not only supporting artistic expression but, through universities, giving artists "spaces for 'spontaneity' to flourish." While Belgrad's insights may have more limited applicability than his title implies, a contributor to *Boston Review* said that the author writes "a compelling narrative, putting living flesh on shorthand intuitions that connect North Beach to Black Mountain College, Fenollosa to Pollock, Jackson Lears's *No Place of Grace* to Todd Gitlin's *The Sixties.*"

BIOGRAPHICAL AND CRITICAL SOURCES:

PERIODICALS

American Historical Review, December, 1999, George H. Roeder Jr., review of *The Culture of Spontaneity: Improvisation and the Arts in Postwar America,* p. 1708.

American Literature, December, 1999, Wendy Martin, review of *The Culture of Spontaneity,* p. 812.

American Studies, fall, 1998, Karal Ann Marling, review of *The Culture of Spontaneity,* p. 200.

American Studies International, June, 1999, Sandy Zipp, review of *The Culture of Spontaneity,* p. 109.

Art in America, March, 1999, p. 37.

Boston Review, 1996.

Choice, November, 1998, p. 506.

Contemporary Sociology, May, 1999, Eugene Halton, review of *The Culture of Spontaneity,* p. 323.

Journal of Aesthetics and Art Criticism, summer, 1999, Tobyn Demarco, review of *The Culture of Spontaneity,* p. 384.

Journal of American History, June, 1999, Michael Leja, review of *The Culture of Spontaneity,* p. 306.

Times Literary Supplement, December 18, 1998, p. 22.

* * *

BELL, Frank
See BENSON, Mildred (Augustine Wirt)

* * *

BELLEZZA, Dario 1944-1995

PERSONAL: Born September 5, 1944, in Rome, Italy; died of an AIDS-related disease, March 31, 1995, in Rome, Italy.

CAREER: Novelist and poet. Worked as secretary for Pier Paolo Pasolini.

WRITINGS:

L'Innocenza (novel; title means "Innocence"), De Donato (Bari, Italy), 1970.

Invettive e licenze (poetry; title means "Invectives and Lasciviousness"), Garzanti (Milan, Italy), 1971.

Lettere de Sodoma (novel), Garzanti (Milan, Italy), 1972.

Il carnefice (novel; title means "The Executioner"), Garzanti (Milan, Italy), 1973.

Morte segreta (poetry; title means "Secret Death"), Garzanti (Milan, Italy), 1976.

Angelo (novel), Garzanti (Milan, Italy), 1979.

Morte di Pasolini (biography; title means "Pasolini's Death"), Mondadori (Milan, Italy), 1981.

Libro d'amore (poetry; title means "Book of Love"), Guanda (Milan, Italy), 1982.

Storia de Nino, Mondadori (Milan, Italy), 1982.

Io (poetry), Mondadori (Milan, Italy), 1983.

Turbamento (novel), Mondadori (Milan, Italy), 1984.

Colesso: Apolegia de teatro (poetry and drama; title means "Colosseum: Apologia for the Theatre"), Pellicanolibri (Catania, Italy), 1985.

Piccolo canzoniere per E. M. (poetry; title means "Little Songbook for E. M."), Giano (Rome, Italy), 1986.

L'amore felice, Rusconi (Milan, Italy), 1986.

Serpenta (poetry; title means "Serpents"), Mondadori (Milan, Italy), 1987.

Libro di poesia (title means "Book of Poetry"), Garzanti (Milan, Italy), 1990.

Contributor to periodicals, including *Bimestre, Carte Segrete, Paragone, Paese Sera,* and *Nuovi argomenti.*

Work represented in translation in anthology *Italian Poetry Today: Currents and Trends,* edited by Ruth Feldman and Brian Swann, New Rivers (New York, NY), 1979.

SIDELIGHTS: Dario Bellezza was an Italian writer known for various poetry collections and novels reflecting his homosexuality. He first came to prominence in the mid-1960s as a contributor to the periodical *Nuovi argomenti,* where he proved himself to be what a *Times Literary Supplement* critic called "a very young and very daring poet who unashamedly describes his homosexual exploits." Bellezza's first published book, *L'Innocenza,* is a novel in which a young man comes to realize his homosexuality. The protagonist, Nino, is a teenaged orphan who finds himself alone in Rome. He eventually obtains shelter at a monastery, where the friars initiate him in homosexual practices, after which he returns to Rome and supports himself as a prostitute before reuniting with his long-lost relatives, who have been living in an asylum for the insane. A *Times Literary Supplement* reviewer summarized *L'Innocenza* as "a very promising first novel," and a *Booklist* reviewer described it as "gripping."

Bellezza followed *L'Innocenza* with his first poetry collection, *Invettive e licenze,* which was notable for its frank, uncluttered verse. In the book, Bellezza uses homosexuality as a platform from which he examines subjects ranging from masturbation and incest to spirituality and friendship. Corrado Federici, writing in the *Dictionary of Literary Biography,* contended that Bellezza "transcends the parameters of his homosexuality by focusing on sentiments that pertain to relationships in general," and proclaimed *Invettive e licenze* "one of the most piercing expressions of spiritual affliction and personal isolation in the modern Italian lyric." A *Times Literary Supplement* reviewer affirmed that Bellezza "uses the living language of ordinary people to describe the most painful and tragic situations . . . , but always without compromise or conformity."

In the novel *Il carnefice,* Bellezza presents a chaotic environment described by a *Times Literary Supplement* reviewer as "the city within a city that is drug-ridden, homosexual Rome." The reviewer, who noted that the novel's title refers to "a butcher in the sense of executioner, torturer," explained that the book deals with Rome's "torturers and tortured, its saints and its damned." A subsquent novel, *Angelo,* concerns the relationship between two emotionally troubled individuals, a man and a woman. A *Booklist* critic deemed this tale "highly interesting." Another novel, *Turbamento,* relates the sexual exploits of a woman who fails as a poet and then begins operating a brothel that caters to both sexes. Peter Hainsworth, writing in the *Times Literary Supplement,* stated that *Turbamento* "confronts large issues."

While producing such novels as *Il carnefice, Angelo,* and *Turbamento,* Bellezza also continued to generate poetry. *Morte segreta* constitutes what Federici, writing in the *Dictionary of Literary Biography,* called Bellezza's "furious, rage-filled analysis of himself." Federici added that the various poems "are mostly laments of unsuccessful relationships," and he described *Morte segreta* as "a dirge over misplaced opportunities for ennobling encounters." In another collection, *Libro d'amore,* Bellezza expresses what Federici called "a profound regard for his countrymen," while in *Io* the poet considers what Federici acknowledged as "his loss of desire to pursue the dream of innocence." Other collections include *Serpenta,* a relatively reserved volume that Federici consequently rated as Bellezza's "most impressive product," and *Libro di poesia,* a more typically explicit and self-lacerating volume that Peter Hainsworth, writing in the *Times Literary Supplement,* regarded as "either . . . a parody of poetry or its ultimate book."

In addition to writing fiction and poetry, Bellezza published *Morte di Pasolini,* an account of the controversial writer and filmmaker who was killed in 1975. N. S. Thompson, in a *Times Literary Supplement* review, acknowledged Bellezza as "Pasolini's one-time literary secretary and friend" and summarized *Morte di Pasolini* as "a very convincing portrait."

Bellezza died in 1996 after contracting an AIDS-related illness.

BIOGRAPHICAL AND CRITICAL SOURCES:

BOOKS

Dictionary of Literary Biography, Volume 128: *Twentieth-Century Italian Poets, Second Series,* Gale (Detroit, MI), 1993.

PERIODICALS

Booklist, February 1, 1974, review of *L'Innocenza,* p. 574; June 15, 1980, review of *Angelo,* p. 1499.
Times Literary Supplement, December 18, 1970, review of *L'Innocenza,* p. 1483; February 11, 1972, review *of Invettive e licenze,* p. 146; December 7, 1973, review of *Il carnefice,* p. 1512; October 8, 1982, N. S. Thompson, "Poet into Man," p. 1105; May 11, 1984, Isabel Quigley, "Scarf-Love," p. 529; October 4, 1991, Peter Hainsworth, "Montale and After," p. 32.

OBITUARIES:

PERIODICALS

Times (London, England), April 13, 1996, p. 23.*

*   *   *

BENARD, Cheryl 1953-

PERSONAL: Born 1953, in New Orleans, LA; married Dr. Zalmay Khalilzad (U.S. envoy to Afghanistan); children: Alexander, Max.

ADDRESSES: Agent—c/o Publicity Director, Farrar, Straus & Giroux, 19 Union Square W., New York, NY 10001.

CAREER: Writer, consultant, and sociologist. Bltzmann Institute, Vienna, Austria, research director; consultant on Middle Eastern affairs for RAND Corporation.

WRITINGS:

FICTION

The Moghul Buffet, Farrar, Straus & Giroux (New York, NY), 1998.
Turning on the Girls, Farrar, Straus & Giroux (New York, NY), 2001.

NONFICTION

(With Zalmay Khalilzad) *"The Government of God": Iran's Islamic Republic,* Columbia University Press (New York, NY), 1984.
(With Daniel Byman and others) *Strengthening the Partnership: Improving Military Coordination with Relief Agencies and Allies in Humanitarian Operations,* RAND Corporation (Washington, DC), 2000.
Veiled Courage: Inside the Afghan Women's Resistance, Broadway Books (New York, NY), 2002.

Contributor to periodicals and author of nonfiction books, primarily on women's issues, published in German. Benard's work has been translated into several languages, indlucing Spanish and Turkish.

SIDELIGHTS: Scholar and author Cheryl Benard lives on two continents, speaks two languages, and, as a sociologist, works as the research director for the Boltzmann Institute in Vienna, Austria. Additionally, she works as a consultant for the RAND Corporation think tank—specifically, the Center for Middle East Public Policy in Washington, D.C. Interestingly, Benard's nonfiction books written in German, have also appeared in Spanish, Turkish, French, Hungarian, and Russian; the one language in which she has never published books about women's issues is English.

Benard met her husband, Dr. Zalmay Khalilzad, the U.S. envoy to Afghanistan, at the University of Chicago when he was working on his doctorate. They have two children and live in North Potomac, Maryland, but Benard also maintains a home in Austria. Talking to an *Amazon.com* interviewer about how she went from writing scholarly articles as an assistant professor to writing fiction, Benard said, "it didn't seem right to take interesting material, lively interviews, and absorbing case histories and then publish them only in dry professional journals, so I wrote a popular version of my first research project, it was well received and I just kept going on that path."

Benard's first novel published in the United States, *Moghul Buffet,* is set in the border frontier town of Peshwar, Pakistan. The story focuses on several characters: Mara Blake, an American who works in a refugee camp and struggles to recover from her broken marriage to a Pakistani aristocrat; the Maulana, an Islamic fundamentalist televangelist; Fatima, the Maulana's young mistress and housemaid; and his nephew and chauffeur, Mushahed, an economics student who has fallen in love with Fatima. A *Kirkus Reviews* contributor remarked that although Benard's novel had great potential, "the author's deft blend of humor and suspense lapses into a confusing tangle of subplots." Jo Manning, however, reviewing the novel for *Library Journal,* noted that "Benard debuts with a surprisingly successful black comedy/mystery reminiscent in its droll narrative style of the works of Australian author Peter Carey." In addition, a *Publishers Weekly* reviewer noted that "Benard nimbly swings from farce to social satire."

Benard's second novel, *Turning on the Girls,* is part science fiction, part feminist comedy. The story takes place in the middle of the twenty-first century, ten years after women have taken over the world. In this new world order, aromatherapy is used in the workplace, and an entire bureaucracy is devoted to de-programming men and women of patriarchal thought patterns. Lisa, the protagonist, is an operative of the Ministry of Thought, whose task is to find an acceptable sexual fantasy for women. In the process, she infiltrates Harmony, a counterrevolutionary men's movement, with Justin, her administrative assistant. A *Booklist* reviewer commented, "If Dorothy Parker had written *Brave New World,* it might have resembled Benard's satiric vision of a utopia designed and run by women." Janelle Brown, in *Salon.com,* found the novel, at times, "laugh-out-loud funny," particularly when it mocks gender theory; however, Brown also remarked that Benard's "plot gets so convoluted that it's impossible to follow, and even more difficult to care." A *Publishers Weekly* contributor, meanwhile, remarked, "this contra-Atwoodesque social fiction may satirize political correctness, but it also manages to salute present and future feminist triumphs, albeit in a roundabout fashion."

In a *Borders Books Web site* online interview, Benard told Jessica Jernigan: "I wanted to write a realistic utopian novel. So I took what I know about feminism and about women's ways of approaching things, including the annoying and exasperating parts, and extrapolated. They tend to be meddlesome, to micromanage, to know what's best for everybody, to be on the hypersensitive alert at all times, to lack a sense of humor, and to be competitive and back-stabbing while pretending they're not. There's a politburo aspect to organized feminism."

BIOGRAPHICAL AND CRITICAL SOURCES:

PERIODICALS

Booklist, April 15, 1998, Bill Ott, review of *Moghul Buffet;* February 15, 2001, Bonnie Johnston, review of *Turning on the Girls.*
Kirkus Reviews, February 15, 1998, review of *Moghul Buffet.*
Library Journal, March 1, 1998, Jo Manning, review of *Moghul Buffet.*
People, April 27, 1998, review of *Moghul Buffet.*
Publishers Weekly, February 23, 1998, review of *Moghul Buffet;* 2001, review of *Turning on the Girls.*

OTHER

Amazon.com, http://www.amazon.com/ (March 7, 2001), interview with Cheryl Benard.
Borders Books Web site, www.bordersstores.com/ (February 2, 2002), Jessica Jernigan, "Grrrl Talk Interview: Women on Top."
Salon.com, www.salon.com/ (April 23, 2001), Janelle Brown, review of *Turning on the Girls.**

*   *   *

BENOIT, Jacques 1941-

PERSONAL: Born November 28, 1941, in Saint-Jean, Quebec, Canada; son of Jean-Marie (an immigration official) and Yvette (Deneault) Benoit; married Michelle Gelinas; children: Elisabeth, Frederique. *Education:* Degrees in literature from University of Montreal and McGill University.

ADDRESSES: Home—4139, av. Old Orchard, Montreal, Quebec, Canada H4A 3B3.

CAREER: Journalist and author.

MEMBER: Union Écrivaines; Quebec writers group.

AWARDS, HONORS: Province of Quebec award, 1968, for *Jos Carbone;* Judith-Jasmin Award, 1976; Canada Heritage Award, 1977.

WRITINGS:

Jos Carbone, Editions du Jour (Montreal, Quebec), 1967, translated by Sheila Fischman, Harvest House (Montreal, Quebec), 1974.
Les Voleurs, Editions du Jour (Montreal, Quebec), 1969.
Patience et Firlipon, Editions du Jour (Montreal, Quebec), 1970.
La Maudite Galette (screenplay), CINAK Cie Cinématographie, 1972.
(With Denys Arcand) *Réjeanne Padovani* (screenplay), CINAK Cie Cinématographie, 1973.
Les Princes, Editions du Jour (Montreal, Quebec), 1973, translated by David Lobell as *The Princes* Oberon (Montreal, Quebec), 1977.
L'Extréme Gauche, La Presse (Montreal, Quebec), 1978.
L'Affaire Coffin (screenplay), Films Cine Scene/ Productions Videofilms, 1979.
Gisèle el le serpent, Libre Expression (Montreal, Quebec), 1981.
Les Plaisirs du vin, Libre Expression (Montreal, Quebec), 1985.

SIDELIGHTS: Jacques Benoit is a native of Quebec, and though his primary occupation is journalism, he has written several novels. However, as Jacqueline Viswanathan noted in the *Dictionary of Literary Biography,* "It is not easy to situate Jacques Benoit in the context of contemporary Quebec literature."

Benoit's first novel, *Jos Carbone,* won the Province of Canada Award in 1974 and impressed readers with its originality. Jos and his girlfriend, Myrtie, live in a forest cottage surrounded by only the wilderness and their intense love for each other. Their peaceful lives are disrupted when a stranger arrives and threatens to take over Jos's home and Myrtie. The story involves a manhunt through the forest, which ends in murder, after which Jos and Myrtie return to their wilderness utopia. The story is, in many ways, similar to a fairy tale, but there are modern elements and vivid descriptions of the real world. The characters seem to be pushed by a sort of primitive instinct, which inevitably erupts in violence.

This instinctual violence can be found in all of Benoit's novels. For example, in the political satire *Les Voleurs,* three convicts are released from jail by their victim, a bishop. Later, he attempts to enlist their help to rig a political election, and they brutally beat him. In contrast, *Les Princes* is a novel about a haunting world inhabited by Blue Men, Monsters (half man, half animal), and Dogs. These creatures live in an oppressive world and are driven by instinct. Starvation forces a Blue Man to kill and eat a Dog, which leads to a vicious fight, and eventually, both groups are exterminated in the mutual slaughter. The world Benoit creates in this novel could be viewed as social commentary: man is basically an animal, motivated only by instincts and a drive for power.

In addition to writing fiction, Benoit has compiled a series of his award-winning articles on the radical Left into a book titled *L'Extréme Gauche.*

BIOGRAPHICAL AND CRITICAL SOURCES:

BOOKS

Dictionary of Literary Biography, Volume 60: *Canadian Writers since 1960,* Gale (Detroit, MI), 1987, pp. 6-10.*

*   *   *

BENSON, Mildred (Augustine Wirt) 1905-2002 (Millie Benson; Frank Bell, Joan Clark, Julia K. Duncan, Alice B. Emerson, Frances K. Judd, Don Palmer, Helen Louise Thorndyke, Dorothy West, pseudonyms; Carolyn Keene, house pseudonym)

OBITUARY NOTICE—See index for *CA* sketch: Born July 10, 1905, in Ladora, IA; died May 28, 2002, in Toledo, OH. Journalist and author. As the author of twenty-three of the first "Nancy Drew" novels, as well as over one hundred other books for young readers, Benson has a secure place in literary history. She had early aspirations to become a writer, publishing her first story at the age of twelve in the children's magazine *St. Nicholas.* She pursued her interest professionally by studying journalism at the University of Iowa, where she earned a master's degree in 1927. While still in school, she earned money to fund her education by writing short stories and working as a reporter and society editor for the *Clinton Herald.* She became associated with Edward Stratemeyer, owner of the Stratemeyer syndicate that published children's book series, by responding to a call for writers in a newspaper ad. Her first books for Stratemeyer were in the "Ruth Fielding" series, and her first contribution, *Ruth Fielding and Her Great Scenario,* under the Alice B. Emerson pseudonym, was published in 1927. After receiving her master's degree, Benson accepted the assignment to write a book in the new "Nancy Drew" series. The teenaged amateur sleuth made her debut in *The Secret of the Old Clock* in 1930, and Benson wrote many more books in the series after that, all under the house pseudonym Carolyn Keene. However, by contractual agreement she was forbidden to tell anyone that she was the author. The truth was finally revealed in 1980 when a court case proved that Benson, and not Harriet Adam, was the original author of the first "Nancy Drew" books. Benson gained a great deal of attention after that, although she did not always enjoy her fame and once complained that she was sick of Nancy Drew. For decades she had been happily working as a reporter and columnist for the *Toledo Times,* where she worked from 1944 to 1975. When the *Times* closed its doors, she moved to the *Toledo Blade,* where she reported on court cases and local government, and wrote the weekly columns "Millie Benson's Notebook" and "On the Go with Millie Benson" until her death. She also wrote many more children's books under a wide array of pseudonyms, including those featuring such series characters as Penny Parker and Dot and Dash. Her young characters were always notable for their fierce independence and ability to operate on an equal footing with adults. Some of those who knew Benson felt that her characters' independent spirits reflected those of the author, who among other exploits, became a pilot at the age of sixty, liked to swim, golf, and canoe, and was an amateur archaeologist who studied the Mayan civilization. Her literary accomplishments earned her the Agatha Award for Lifetime Achievement in 2000 and the Edgar Allan Poe Special Award in 2001, as well as several journalism awards.

OBITUARIES AND OTHER SOURCES:

BOOKS

Writers Directory, 16th edition, St. James Press (Detroit, MI), 2001.

PERIODICALS

Los Angeles Times, May 30, 2002, p. B12.
New York Times, May 30, 2002, p. A23.
Times (London, England), May 31, 2002, p. 40.
Washington Post, May 30, 2002, p. B7.

*   *   *

BENSON, Millie
    See BENSON, Mildred (Augustine Wirt)

*   *   *

BERGESEN, Albert J. 1942-

PERSONAL: Born October 4, 1942, in Rockville Center, NY; son of Albert G. (a regional commissioner of U.S. Customs) and Dorothy Bergesen; married Susie; children: Jay M. *Education:* University of California, Santa Barbara, B.A., 1964; Stanford University, Ph.D., 1974.

ADDRESSES: Office—Department of Sociology, University of Arizona, Tucson, AZ 85721. *E-mail*—albert@email.arizona.edu.

CAREER: University of Arizona, Tucson, professor of sociology, 1973—.

MEMBER: American Sociological Association, American Political Science Association, Pacific Sociological Association, International Studies Association.

WRITINGS:

(Editor) *Studies of the Modern World-System,* Academic Press (New York, NY), 1980.
(Editor) *Crises in the World System,* Sage (Beverly Hills, CA), 1983.

(With R. Wuthnow, J. Hunter, and E. Kurtzweil) *Cultural Analysis: The Work of Peter Berger, Mary Douglas, Michel Foucault, and Jurgen Habermas,* Routledge (London, England), 1984.

The Sacred and the Subversive: Political Witch-Hunts as National Rituals, "Study of the Scientific Study of Religion" monograph series
, 1984.

(With Andrew M. Greeley) *God in the Movies,* Transaction Press (Piscataway, NJ), 2000.

WORK IN PROGRESS: Grammar of Art.

SIDELIGHTS: Albert J. Bergesen is an avid movie buff and, with fellow faculty member and Catholic priest Andrew M. Greeley, is the author of *God in the Movies.* Together, the two men taught a class on religion and film, and the book evolved from this course. Although some movies, such as *The Ten Commandments* and *The Robe,* deal directly with religious images and themes, Bergesen and Greeley contend that God "makes cameo appearance in genres ranging from action western to quirky comedy," according to a contributor in *Newswise.* The book discusses these images, as well as the cultural parables they present. Bergesen told Angela Orlando, in the *Arizona Daily Wildcat Online,* "We are like urban anthropologists reporting on the personality of today's culture. Not every movie is religious, but the theme certainly shows up." For example, the book notes that "The Force" in the *Star Wars* saga is a science-fiction metaphor for God or the divine spirit; in *Field of Dreams* God is manifested as a voice giving instructions to the main character, and as the tight bond between father and son. In *Flatliners* God is shown as pure white light. Bergesen told Orlando, "These movies aren't made by fanatics. . . . They're about people believing in something else, wanting redemption and forgiveness."

BIOGRAPHICAL AND CRITICAL SOURCES:

PERIODICALS

Contemporary Sociology, January, 1988, p. 27.
International Organization, winter, 1982, p. 135; spring, 1996, p. 325.
Social Forces, September, 1989, p. 323.

OTHER

Newswise, http://www.newswise.com/ (December 8, 2000), "God in Cinema: New Book Explores the Imagery."
Arizona Daily Wildcat Online, http://www.wildcat. Arizona.edu/ (February 12, 2001), Angela Orlando, "Redemption at the Movies."*

*   *   *

BERGMANN, Peter G(abriel) 1915-2002

OBITUARY NOTICE—See index for *CA* sketch: Born March 24, 1915, in Berlin, Germany; died October 19, 2002, in Seattle, WA. Physicist, educator, and author. Bergmann was an assistant to physicist Albert Einstein and was at the forefront of teaching and promoting Einstein's theory of relativity. After graduating from the University of Prague in 1936 he went to work for Einstein at the Institute for Advanced Study in Princeton, New Jersey. He remained there for five years, helping the famous scientist with his development of a unified field theory. Most famously, it was Bergmann who proposed that an explanation for all the forces in nature might be tied together if there were a fifth dimension that existed in addition to the other four known dimensions. Although Einstein himself did not pursue this theory, it has in more recent times become a central concern to physicists working on a grand unified theory. Bergmann left Einstein in 1941 to take on several university and scientific institute posts, including at Black Mountain College, Lehigh University, and the Woods Hole Oceanographic Institution. In 1947 he joined the faculty at Syracuse University, where he remained until 1982, retiring as professor emeritus. It was here that he became well known as a teacher of Einstein's theories; indeed, for some time Syracuse was the only place students could attend if they were interested in studying relativity. The book he used for his courses was his own 1942 work, *Introduction to the Theory of Relativity,* which was the standard text at universities for decades. Bergmann was also the author of *Basic Theories of Physics* (1949), *The Riddle of Gravitation* (1968; third edition, 1992), and *Gravitation and Modern Cosmology: The Cosmological Constant Problem* (1991), as well as an editor and contributor to several other books. After retiring from Syracuse, Bergmann took a post as a research professor at New York University until 1999, when his health began to decline and he moved to Seattle to be with his son.

OBITUARIES AND OTHER SOURCES:

BOOKS

American Men and Women of Science, 20th edition, Bowker (New Providence, NJ), 1998.
Who's Who in Technology, seventh edition, Gale (Detroit, MI), 1995.

PERIODICALS

New York Times, October 23, 2002, p. A23.

*   *   *

BERLE, Milton 1908-2002

OBITUARY NOTICE—See index for *CA* sketch: Born Milton Berlinger, July 12, 1908, in New York, NY; died of colon cancer March 27, 2002, in Los Angeles, CA. Comedian, actor, and author. Berle was a renowned comedian who was known to many as "Mr. Television" for his role in making television programming popular when the medium was in its infancy. He spent his entire life in show business, beginning at the age of five by entering Charlie Chaplin look-alike contests and becoming a child performer in vaudeville before moving on to silent movies. In addition to this early experience, Berle gained some formal training at New York's Professional Children's School and took dance lessons in Harlem. His debut film was 1914's *The Perils of Pauline*, and he also appeared with such stars as Douglas Fairbanks Sr. in *The Mark of Zorro*. Berle first took to the stage in New York City in 1920 before returning to vaudeville, where in 1931 he became the youngest master of ceremonies at the Palace Theater on Broadway. During the 1930s he continued work on the stage in such productions as *Ziegfeld Follies*, made his radio debut in 1934, and starred in more movies, including *Margin for Error*, *Over My Dead Body*, and *Tall, Dark, and Handsome*. In the 1940s Berle turned to the night-club circuit and

continued to appear on radio programs before becoming the host of the early television comedy-variety program *Texaco Star Theatre* in 1948. It was here that Berle became an instant smash and gained his claim to fame. The show, which aired at eight o'clock on Tuesday nights, was so popular that businesses would shut down across the country just so people could watch the cigar-smoking comic with the wide, toothy grin. Berle was consequently given the nickname "Mr. Tuesday Night," and he also became known to many Americans as "Uncle Miltie" after the comic used the name while advising children it was time to go to bed.

From the time *Texaco Star Theatre* aired in 1948 through the 1951-52 season, television ownership in the United States increased from about 400,000 sets to over ten million, and many believe that much of the credit for this expansion belongs to Berle. By the end of the third season, however, the comic cut back his hectic schedule, hosting the program only three weeks out of every four. Ratings consequently declined and the NBC network canceled the program in 1953. However, NBC had given Berle an unprecedented lifetime contract that secured his career. After *Texaco Star Theatre* was over he hosted *The Milton Berle Show* for one season in 1955, and starred in such television shows as *The Kraft Music Hall, Jackpot Bowling Starring Milton Berle*, and 1966's *The Milton Berle Show*. The 1960s and 1970s saw Berle appearing as a guest star in various television shows and in nightclubs in Las Vegas, Chicago, and Miami Beach. He also starred in more films, including *It's a Mad, Mad, Mad, Mad World, Who's Minding the Mint, The Muppet Movie, Broadway Danny Rose, Driving Me Crazy*, and *Storybook*. During his lifetime Berle penned several books, including the autobiographies *Out of My Trunk* and *Milton Berle: An Autobiography*, the joke books *Milton Berle's Private Joke File* and *More of the Best of Milton Berle's Private Joke File*, and the novel *Earthquake*. For his work, Berle was awarded many honors, including a 1979 Emmy Award.

OBITUARIES AND OTHER SOURCES:

BOOKS

International Motion Picture Almanac, Quigley Publishing (New York, NY), 1996.
Slide, Anthony, *Encyclopedia of Vaudeville*, Greenwood Press (Westport, CT), 1994.
Who's Who in America, 54th edition, Marquis (Providence, NJ), 2000.

PERIODICALS

Los Angeles Times, March 28, 2002, pp. A1, A24.
New York Times, March 28, 2002, pp. A1, C13.
Times (London, England), March 29, 2002, p. 39.
Washington Post, March 28, 2002, pp. A1, A10.

*　　*　　*

BERNSTEIN, Peter L. 1919-

PERSONAL: Born 1919, in New York, NY. *Education:* Harvard University, B.S., 1940.

ADDRESSES: Home—205 East 63rd St., New York, NY 10021.

CAREER: Business analyst. Economist, Modern Industrial Bank, 1949-51; president and chair, Bernstein-Macaulay, Inc., 1951-73; chair, Investment Policy Committee, Hayden Stone, 1970-73; president, Peter L. Bernstein, Inc., 1973—.

WRITINGS:

The Price of Prosperity: A Realistic Appraisal of the Future of Our National Economy, Doubleday (Garden City, NY), 1962.
(With Robert L. Heilbroner) *A Primer on Government Spending,* Random House (New York, NY), 1963.
A Primer on Money, Banking, and Gold, Random House (New York, NY), 1965.
Economist on Wall Street: Notes on the Sanctity of Gold, the Value of Money, the Security of Investments, and Other Delusions, Macmillan (New York, NY), 1970.
(Editor) *The Theory and Practice of Bond Portfolio Management,* Institutional Investor Books (New York, NY), 1977.
(Editor) *International Investing,* International Investor Books (New York, NY), 1983.
(With Robert Heilbroner) *The Debt and the Deficit: False Alarms/Real Possibilities,* Norton (New York, NY), 1989.
(Moderator) *Improving the Investment Decision Process: Better Economic Inputs in Securities Analysis and Management: March 31, 1991,*

Washington, DC, edited by H. Kent Baker, CFA/ Association for Investment Management and Research (Charlottesville, VA), 1992.
Capital Ideas: The Improbable Origins of Modern Wall Street, Free Press (New York, NY), 1992.
(Editor) *The Portable MBA in Investment,* Wiley (New York, NY), 1995.
(With Christopher M.) *The Practical Guide to Practically Everything,* Random House (New York, NY), 1995.
Against the Gods: The Remarkable Story of Risk, Wiley (New York, NY), 1996.
(Editor, with Frank J. Fabozzi) *Streetwise: The Best of the Journal of Portfolio Management,* Princeton University Press (Princeton, NJ), 1997.
(Editor, with Aswath Damodaran) *Investment Management,* Wiley (New York, NY), 1998.
The Power of Gold: The History of an Obsession, Wiley (New York, NY), 2000.

Contributor to *Risk Management: Proceedings of the AIMR Seminar "Effective Risk Management in the Investment Firm": October 10, 1999, Boston, Massachusetts,* Association for Investment Management and Research (Charlottesville, VA), 1996. Founding editor of *Journal of Portfolio Management* and publisher of the biweekly publication *Economics and Portfolio Strategy.*

ADAPTATIONS: The Power of Gold: The History of an Obsession was adapted as an audiobook, Random House, 2000.

SIDELIGHTS: For more than fifty years, business economist Peter L. Bernstein has closely scrutinized the American economy. In the early 1970s, Bernstein reported on such matters as the stock market, investment, inflation, gold, and money. The monthly briefs he wrote over a period of years at his investment firm Bernstein-Macaulay, Incorporated, are collected in *Economist on Wall Street: Notes on the Sanctity of Gold, the Value of Money, the Security of Investments, and Other Delusions.* Morton R. Brown, writing in *Library Journal,* called the book "good reading for students of the market and the economy." Robert Lekachman, reviewing the book in *New York Times Book Review,* called Bernstein "among the shrewdest and most humane of the operators on the street of blasted dreams." By the end of that decade Bernstein had edited the book *The Theory and Practice of Bond*

Portfolio Management. Paul S. Nadler, a reviewer in the *Journal of Finance,* commented that, "to those without any idea of how active bond management can be, it remains a readable eye-opener."

Two decades later Bernstein published *Capital Ideas: The Improbable Origins of Modern Wall Street.* David Morton, reviewing the book for *Management Today,* noted, "Bernstein's book is a fascinating case for the defence of a score of quiet academics who had devised the new systems . . . who had followed their statistical findings as far as they could logically go, and discovered that they had walked right up Wall Street." Edmund A. Mennis, a reviewer in *Business Economics,* stated that "Bernstein has done an outstanding job in making this [economic] revolution understandable and interesting. . . . And in no other book is modern portfolio theory presented with such remarkable clarity." Books recommended for college libraries are *The Portable MBA in Investment and Investment Management.* Both are edited by Bernstein, and the latter is co-edited with Aswath Damodoran.

Adopting a more philosophical tone in his writing, Bernstein published *Against the Gods: The Remarkable Story of Risk.* A reviewer in *Parameters* noted, "Bernstein brilliantly presents the history of mankind's encounter with uncertainty and risk, phenomena that pervade every aspect of the military experience." The reviewer observed, "Bernstein's final chapters include a comprehensive survey of the leading thinkers of risk management, a field that is so young that most of these individuals are still alive." Brian J. Glenn, writing in the *Journal of Risk and Insurance,* stated, "Bernstein presents the reader with an easy to read and often entertaining introduction to the history and theory behind financial risk analysis." Robin Pearson, a reviewer in *Business History,* observed, "For those interested in such fundamental questions about coping with change, Bernstein's book will provide an excellent primer."

Perhaps Bernstein's best-received book was *The Power of Gold: The History of an Obsession.* Norm Hutcherson, reviewing it in *Library Journal,* said, "A master historian at the peak of his art here recounts the timeless story of our obsession with gold." A reviewer in *Publishers Weekly* stated, "Bernstein does deliver a page-turning history of the not-so-heavy metal and its influence on people through the ages." David Pitt, reviewing the book in *Booklist,* commented, "Never

has there been a more enlightening, instructive, and entertaining look at the power of this most precious of metals."

BIOGRAPHICAL AND CRITICAL SOURCES:

PERIODICALS

African Business, December, 2000, Derek Parker, review of *The Power of Gold: The History of an Obsession,* p. 21.

American Economic Review, Volume 64, 1974.

Barron's, November 27, 1995, Robert L. Friedman, "Mastering Markets on the Cheap," p. 43.

Bond Buyer, January 20, 1992, Brad Miner, review of *Capital Ideas,* p. 321.

Booklist, January 1, 1971, review of *Economist on Wall Street: Notes on the Sanctity of Gold, the Value of Money, the Security of Investments, and Other Delusions,* p. 346; December 15, 1995, David Rouse, review of *The Portable MBA in Investment,* p. 674; September 15, 1996, Gilbert Taylor, review of *Against the Gods: The Remarkable Story of Risk,* p. 185; August, 2000, David Pitt, review of *The Power of Gold,* p. 2083.

Business Economics, April, 1992, Edmund A. Mennis, review of *Capital Ideas: The Improbable Origins of Modern Wall Street,* p. 67; January, 1997, Edmund A. Mennis, review of *Against the Gods,* p. 70; April, 2001, Edmund A. Mennis, review of *The Power of Gold,* p. 60.

Business History, January, 1999, Robin Pearson, review of *Against the Gods,* p. 178.

Business Week, November 6, 2000, "Glory, Greed, and All That Glitters," p. 21.

Choice, March, 1996, W. S. Curran, review of *The Portable MBA in Investment,* p. 1181; July-August, 1998, H. Mayo, review of *Investment Management,* p. 1899.

Economist, October 14, 2000, "History of Gold: It Defileth Not," p. 103.

Industry Standard, September 25, 2000, Daniel Akst, "Hard Currency," p. 202.

Journal of Economic Literature, September, 1998, review of *Streetwise: The Best of the Journal of Portfolio Management,* p. 1580.

Journal of Finance, December, 1978, Paul S. Nadler, review of *The Theory and Practice of Bond Portfolio Management,* p. 1477.

Journal of Risk and Insurance, September, 1999, Brian J. Glenn, review of *Against the Gods,* p. 517.

Library Journal, September 1, 1970, Morton R. Brown, review of *Economist on Wall Street,* p. 2795; September 1, 2000, Norm Hutcherson, review of *The Power of Gold,* p. 233.

Management Today, September, 1992, David Morton, review of *Capital Ideas,* p. 111.

National Underwriter Property and Casualty-Risk and Benefits Management, January 6, 1997, David M. Katz, review of *Against the Gods,* p. 9; February 10, 1997, Peter W. Rice, review of *Against the Gods,* p. 13.

New Leader, March 23, 1992, Harvey H. Segal, review of *Capital Ideas,* p. 17.

New York Times, November 27, 1995, review of *The Practical Guide to Practically Everything,* p. C15.

New York Times Book Review, November 15, 1970, Robert Lekachman, review of *Economist on Wall Street,* p. 46.

Parameters, autumn, 2000, review of *Against the Gods,* p. 162.

Publishers Weekly, September 9, 1996, review of *Against the Gods,* p. 72; August 21, 2000, review of *The Power of Gold,* p. 57.

Social Studies, March, 1970, review of *A Primer on Money, Banking and Gold,* p. 140.

Washington Post Book World, September 20, 1998, review of *Against the Gods.**

*   *   *

BERTELLI, Sergio

PERSONAL: Born in Italy.

ADDRESSES: Office—University of Florence, via S. Gallo 10, 50129 Firenze, Italy. *E-mail*—sergio. bertelli@unifi.it.

CAREER: University of Florence, Florence, Italy, professor of history.

WRITINGS:

Ribelli, libertini e ortodossi nella storiografia barocca (title means "Rebels, Libertini and Orthodox in the Baroque Historiograophy"), La Nuova Italia (Florence, Italy), 1973.

(Editor with Piero Innocenti) *Bibliografia Machiavelli-ana* (title means "Machiavellian Bibliography"), Edizioni Valdonega (Verona, Italy), 1979.

(With others) *Italian Renaissance Courts,* Sidgwick & Jackson (London, England), 1986.

(With Francesco Bigazzi) *PCI: La storia dimenticata* (title means "PCI: The Forgotten History"), Mondadori (Milan, Italy), 2001.

The King's Body: Sacred Rituals of Power in Medieval and Early Modern Europe, translated by R. Burr Litchfield, Pennsylvania State University Press (University Park, PA), 2001.

SIDELIGHTS: Sergio Bertelli, professor of history at the University of Florence in Italy, is a well-known expert on Renaissance and post-Renaissance studies. One of his many published works of scholarship has been translated into English as *The King's Body: Sacred Rituals of Power in Medieval and Early Modern Europe.* In this book, Bertelli addresses sovereign rule, and he emphasizes the importance of the sovereign in maintaining the order of medieval society rather than focusing on the making of the state. Bertelli explores the cult of kingship in an analysis spanning the Vandal kings of Spain through Charles I and Louis XVI of England.

Bertelli's first book, *Ribelli, libertini e ortodossi nella storiografia barocca,* concerns the evolution of historiography during the Baroque period—from the third decade of the sixteenth century until the end of the seventeenth.

Bibliografia Machiavelliana was a joint effort with coeditor Piero Innocenti. The editors assembled a bibliography of 1,080 titles from across the world containing philosopher Niccolò Machiavelli's writings. In this work, Bertelli also proposes several corrections to common notions about Machiavelli's importance, and proves that Machiavelli's theories were considered most seriously throughout Florence. Eric Cochrane praised the bibliography in *Journal of Modern History,* commenting "If the other volumes [in the series] maintain the high editorial standards set in this one, the texts contained therein will certainly be recognized as authoritative, and all editions and translations will have to be based on them."

The Courts of the Italian Renaissance is a heavily illustrated book that reproduces frescoes, sculpture, costumes and scenes common to court life in the Italian Renaissance. David Ekserdjian, in the *Spectator,* called it "a splendid introduction to an absorbing and eccentric world of banquets, festivities, triumphal entries and state funerals." Although the only name on the cover of the book is Bertelli's, the title page reveals it is actually involves six contributing authors. Werner Gundersheimer of *Renaissance Quarterly* found the lack of attribution a problem. "The extraordinary frustrations posed by this book as a physical object are compounded by the text itself. Idiosyncratically organized and frequently repetitious, it subjects the reader to dizzying shifts of place and time, often telescoping centuries into a single sentence."

PCI: La Storia Dimenticata, which Bertelli penned with journalist Francesco Bigazzi, concentrates on the history of the Italian Communist Party. A reviewer in the *Economist* said, "It contains no stunning revelations, but it has succeeded in upsetting many older party members with its suggestion that the massacre at the Ardeatine caves. . . . actually helped the underground communist leaders of the time by disposing of some of their more undependable comrades." In the 1944 massacre, 355 prisoners of occupied Italy were executed as punishment for a partisan attack on Nazi soldiers.

BIOGRAPHICAL AND CRITICAL SOURCES:

PERIODICALS

American Historical Review, February, 1975, Grazia Avitabile, review of *Ribelli, libertini e ortodossi nella storiografia barocca,* pp. 99-100.
Economist, April 28, 2001, review of *PCI: La storia dimenticata,* pp. 89-90.
History Today, November, 2001, Anne Pointer, review of *The King's Body: Sacred Rituals of Power in Medieval and Early Modern Europe,* p. 54.
Library Journal, September 15, 1986, review of *The Courts of the Italian Renaissance,* p. 53.
Journal of Modern History, December, 1975, Donald R. Kelley, "Faces in Clio's Mirror: Mistress, Muse, Missionary," pp. 679-690; September, 1980, Eric Cochrane, review of *Bibliografia Machiavelliana,* pp. 534-536.
Modern Language Review, April, 1982, H. K. Moss, review of *Biblografia Machiavelliana,* pp. 470-471.

Publishers Weekly, December 3, 2001, review of *The King's Body,* p. 52.
Renaissance Quarterly, winter, 1980, Fredi Chiappelli, review of *Bibliografia Machiavelliana,* pp. 747-750; spring, 1988, Werner Gundersheimer, review of *The Courts of the Italian Renaissance,* pp. 114-116.
Spectator, December 13, 1986, David Ekserdjian, "My Coffee-table Is Full of Plates," pp. 36-37.*

*   *   *

BETHEA, David M. 1948-

PERSONAL: Born 1948.

ADDRESSES: Agent—c/o Author Mail, University of Washington Press, P.O. Box 50096, Seattle, WA 98145-5096.

CAREER: Writer and editor.

WRITINGS:

Khodasevich: His Life and Art, Princeton University Press (Princeton, NJ), 1983.
The Shape of Apocalypse in Modern Russian Fiction, Princeton University Press (Princeton, NJ), 1989.
(Editor) *Pushkin Today,* Indiana University Press (Bloomington, IN), 1993.
Joseph Brodsky and the Creation of Exile, Princeton University Press (Princeton, NJ), 1994.
Realizing Metaphors: Alexander Pushkin and the Life of the Poet, University of Washington Press (Seattle, WA), 1998.

SIDELIGHTS: Author and editor David M. Bethea describes the life and times of twentieth-century Russian poet Vladislav Felitsianovich Khodosevich in his book *Khodosevich: His Life and Art.* Victor Terras, a reviewer in *World Literature Today,* commented that Bethea "provides a wealth of biographical information." Considering Bethea's translations of Khodosevich's poetry "competent" and his comments "useful," Terras called the book "a valuable contribution to scholarship." *New Republic* reviewer Clarence

Brown stated that Bethea "is that rarity amongst American specialists in Russian literature," and noted that Bethea "writes with clarity and grace."

Maintaining his avid interest in Russian literature, Bethea develops his "new" study of the apocalyptic myth in his book *The Shape of Apocalypse in Modern Russian Fiction*. Maria Carlson, a reviewer in *Modern Language Review*, claimed Bethea "writes with wit and the manner of his presentation makes his book a pleasure to read." Carlson insisted that *The Shape of the Apocalypse* "pushes the reader to keep up with the author, and thereby explore our assumptions not only about [the] classics of modern Russian literature but about 'the Russian Idea' as well."

Bethea continued his study of Russian literature with his editing of *Pushkin Today*, a collection of twenty-four papers from fourteen North American scholars examining Pushkin's work. Barbara Heldt, a reviewer for *Slavic Review*, called the "Pushkin Symposium" perhaps "the only work in the collection that will make indigenous Russian scholars wonder why they themselves hadn't written it."

In *Joseph Brodsky and the Creation of Exile*, Bethea attempts to define Brodsky's theories in metaphysical terms. According to Victor Terras in *World Literature Today*, the book "is an immensely stimulating and very carefully crafted study." Peter France, a reviewer in *Times Literary Supplement*, claimed that Bethea seeks "to explain the absolutism in Brodsky's view of poetry, the prophetic tone which sounds so strange . . . to postmodern Western ears." France insisted that the book "is a sympathetic, inward account of its subject, showing the grandeur . . . of Brodsky's stance, and finishing with a suggestive afterword on the future for a bardic view of poetry in an unpoetic world."

Investigating the difficulties of poetic biography occupies Bethea's interest in his book *Realizing Metaphors: Alexander Pushkin and the Life of the Poet*. Andrew Kahn, a reviewer in the *Times Literary Supplement*, called Bethea's work "a combination of practical criticism and sophisticated intertextual analysis." Gene Shaw, a reviewer in *Library Journal*, praised Beathea for doing a "good job" and recommended it for Russian studies collections.

BIOGRAPHICAL AND CRITICAL SOURCES:

PERIODICALS

Insight on the News, May 23, 1994, p. 29.
Library Journal, October 15, 1998, pp. 69-70.

Modern Fiction Studies, winter, 1989, pp. 836-839.
Modern Language Review, July, 1991, pp. 808-810; January, 2001, Gerald E. Mikkelson, review of *Realizing Metaphors: Alexander Pushkin and the Life of the Poet,* p. 284.
New Republic, February 13, 1984, pp. 38-39.
Russian Review, January, 1995, pp. 116-117; January, 2000, Gene Fitzgerald, review of *Realizing Metaphors,* p. 118.
Sewanee Review, October, 1990, pp. 699-705.
Slavic and East European Journal, summer, 2000, Paul Debreczeny, review of *Realizing Metaphors,* p. 305.
Slavic Review, summer, 1994, pp. 566-567.
Times Literary Supplement, July 8, 1994, p. 21; May 28, 1999, p. 25.
World Literature Today, spring, 1984, p. 286; autumn, 1994, pp. 845-846.*

*   *   *

BIRAN, Michal 1965-

PERSONAL: Born 1965. *Education:* Hebrew University of Jerusalem, B.A., 1989, M.A., 1993, Ph.D., 1999.

ADDRESSES: Office—Institute for Asian and African Studies, Hebrew University of Jerusalem, Mt. Scopus, 91905, 74/9 Ben Zion Dinur St., Jerusalem, 93716 Israel. *E-mail*—biranm@h2.hum.huji.ac.il.

CAREER: Hebrew University of Jerusalem, Jerusalem, Israel, instructor in history.

MEMBER: AAS, Mongolia Society, Middle East Mediavalists, American Society for Central Asian Studies.

WRITINGS:

Qaidu and the Rise of the Independent Mongol State in Central Asia, Curzon (Surrey, England), 1997.

SIDELIGHTS: Michal Biran is a scholar who specializes in the Mongol Empire, the largest empire in the history of the world, that stretched from China to Persia (modern Iran) under the leadership of Genghis

Khan. In her 1997 book *Qaidu and the Rise of the Independent Mongol State in Central Asia,* Biran focuses on the short-lived Mongol state established in Central Asia by Qaidu, a grandson of the Great Khan's successor. *Times Literary Supplement* reviewer David Morgan noted that little has been written about this state because of the lack of primary sources and the relative scarcity of scholars proficient in Persian, Arabic, and Chinese; all of these languages are necessary to evaluate the secondary sources on this subject, comprised of contemporary documents written in neighboring, usually hostile, states. In writing about Qaidu's rise to power in central Mongolia, the relationship maintained between his state and neighboring states, the management of the state, and its collapse after his death in 1301, Biran "has done an excellent job," Morgan noted. "She has the necessary languages as well as a willingness to apply the equally essential critical judgment of her sources." The importance of *Qaidu and the Rise of the Independent Mongol State in Central Asia* is that it offers the most comprehensive portrait so far available of a state that became "the foundation of the remarkably enduring Chaghatai khanate of Central Asia," Morgan concluded.

BIOGRAPHICAL AND CRITICAL SOURCES:

PERIODICALS

Journal of the American Oriental Society, January-March, 2000, Gyorgy Kara, review of *Qaidu and the Rise of the Independent Mongol State in Central Asia,* p. 139.
Times Literary Supplement, January 22, 1999, p. 33.

*   *   *

BLOOMFIELD, B(arry) C(ambray) 1931-2002

OBITUARY NOTICE—See index for *CA* sketch: Born June 1, 1931, in London, England; died February 26, 2002, in Wye, Kent, England. Librarian and bibliographer. Bloomfield is best known for his meticulous bibliographies of work by authors such as W. H. Auden and Philip Larkin, the latter of whom offered high praise for the quality of Bloomfield's work, the comprehensive scope of his collection, and the speed with he was able to gather obscure information.

Much of his librarianship was dedicated to collections from the Asian world, where military service had taken him in the 1950s. Bloomfield worked as a librarian from 1956, spending several years at the London School of Oriental and African Studies and at the India Office Library and Records. It was he who successfully managed the diplomatically sensitive transfer of the India Office Library from the British Foreign and Commonwealth Office to the British Library, from which he retired in 1990. Bloomfield remained active after retirement; he was selected centenary president of the Bibliographical Society in 1990 and was appointed president of the Association of Independent Libraries in 2000. He was particularly respected for his skill at fund raising and his persistence at promoting the library collections he deemed most valuable.

OBITUARIES AND OTHER SOURCES:

PERIODICALS

Independent, March 2, 2002, obituary by Nicolas Barker, p. 6.
Times (London, England), February 26, 2002, p. 37.

*   *   *

BLOSSOM, Laurel 1943-

PERSONAL: Born June 9, 1943, in Washington, DC; daughter of Dudley (a business executive) and Jean Vilas (a homemaker) Blossom; married John L. Thomas, 1963 (divorced 1969); married Leonard Todd (a graphic designer), May 12, 1996; children: Rebecca Bingham Kovacik. *Education:* Vassar College, 1961-63; Radcliffe College, B.A. (English), 1966. *Politics:* Democrat. *Religion:* Unitarian Universalist. *Hobbies and other interests:* Swimming, reading, travel.

ADDRESSES: Home—920 Park Ave., New York, NY 10028. *E-mail*—lbaines920@aol.com.

CAREER: Poet, editor, and writer. Poets & Writers, New York, NY, development director, 1977-81; Writers Community, cofounder and director, 1976-86; Writers Community Committee, chair, YMCA National Writer's Voice, 1986—; Laura (Riding) Jackson Home

Preservation Foundation, 1995—. Member, board of trustees, William Bingham Foundation, 1963-2001; member, board of regents, Harris Manchester College, Oxford, 2000—.

MEMBER: Explorers Club, Academy of American Poets.

AWARDS, HONORS: Ohio Arts Council fellowship, 1980 and 1988; New York Foundations for the Arts fellowship, 1989; Harris Manchester College, Oxford, visiting fellow, 1996.

WRITINGS:

POETRY

Any Minute, Greenhouse Review Press (Santa Cruz, CA), 1979.
What's Wrong, Cobham & Hatherton Press (Cleveland, OH), 1987.
The Papers Said, Greenhouse Review Press (Santa Cruz, CA), 1993.

OTHER

(Editor) *Splash!: Great Writing about Swimming* (poetry, fiction, and nonfiction), Ecco Press (Hopewell, NJ), 1996.
(Editor) *Many Lights in Many Windows: Twenty Years of Great Fiction and Poetry from the Writers Community,* Milkweed Editions (Minneapolis, MN), 1997.

Contributor to *Night Errands: How Poets Use Dreams,* University of Pittsburgh Press (Pittsburgh, PA), 1998. Also regular contributor of reviews and articles to *"things,"* a British cultural journal; regular book reviewer for *American Book Review, Publishers Weekly,* and others.

WORK IN PROGRESS: Degrees of Latitude, a book-length poem depicting "the geography of a woman's life"; "The Longitude Problem," a book-length poem and companion to "Degrees of Latitude,"; "Sky High," an anthology of literature about flying; "The Book of Drafts," a book detailing the development of a single

poem; ongoing research into the lives of poets Edna St. Vincent Millay, Laura Riding Jackson, Jorie Graham, Louise Glück, Carolyn Forché, and Sharon Olds.

SIDELIGHTS: Laurel Blossom wrote, in her introduction to *Splash!: Great Writing about Swimming,* "The literature of swimming is rich and varied, and like all good literature it does not confine itself to its primary subject, but delves deep into human experience." Accordingly, Blossom did not limit the writings included in *Splash!* to just the athletic side of the sport. Instead, as a reviewer for the *Economist* noted, she "has wisely chosen to focus on imaginative writing." This includes stories from authors like John Updike, John Cheever, and Ray Bradbury; poems by A. E. Housman and James Dickey, among others; and reminiscences from top competitors like Dawn Fraser, "whose account of winning the gold medal . . . at the 1956 Olympic Games in Melbourne is riveting," wrote Kirsten Conover, in the *Christian Science Monitor.* A *Publishers Weekly* contributor wrote regarding *Splash!:* "With a leisurely crawl, not a speed-stroke, readers will want to explore nearly every selection here."

BIOGRAPHICAL AND CRITICAL SOURCES:

PERIODICALS

Christian Science Monitor, July 25, 1996, Kirsten Conover, "Swimming in Literature: From Shallows to Depths," p. B3.
Economist, July 20, 1996, review of *Splash!: Great Writing about Swimming,* p. 7975.
Publishers Weekly, April 8, 1996, review of *Splash!,* p. 56.

*   *   *

BODANIS, David

PERSONAL: Born in Chicago, IL. *Education:* University of Chicago.

ADDRESSES: Home—London, England. *Agent*—c/o Publicity Director, Berkley Books, 375 Hudson St., New York, NY 10014. *E-mail*—DavidBodanis@compuserve.com.

CAREER: Science writer, consultant, and teacher. *International Herald Tribune,* Paris, France, reporter, beginning 1977; freelance writer, beginning 1982; St. Antony's College, Oxford, Oxford, England, senior associate member, beginning 1990; consultant to major firms in "mini-scenarios," beginning mid-1990s; speaker at major corporations and other organizations on global trends in science and research; Talent Foundation, London, England, strategy director.

WRITINGS:

The Body Book: A Fantastic Voyage to the World Within, Little, Brown (Boston, MA), 1984.

The Secret House: Twenty-four Hours in the Strange and Unexpected World in Which We Spend Our Nights and Days, Simon & Schuster (New York, NY), 1986.

Web of Words: The Ideas behind Politics, Macmillan Press (Houndmills, Basingstoke, Hampshire, England), 1988.

The Secret Garden: Dawn to Dusk in the Astonishing Hidden World of the Garden, Simon & Schuster (New York, NY), 1992.

The Secret Family: Twenty-four Hours inside the Mysterious World of Our Minds and Bodies, Simon & Schuster (New York, NY), 1997.

(With others; and presenter) *The Secret Family* (television documentary), Discovery Channel/CBC, 1997.

E=mc2: A Biography of the World's Most Famous Equation, Berkley Books (New York, NY), 2001.

Also contributor of reviews, essays, and other articles in *Guardian, London Times, Reader's Digest, New Scientist, Times Literary Supplement, Smithsonian Magazine,* and *Observer.*

SIDELIGHTS: An education in mathematics, physics, and economics was just the prelude to the varied and multifaceted career of David Bodanis. Consultant to global corporations, educator, and lecturer are just a few of the roles and occupations Bodanis has filled during his life. He is perhaps best known, however, for his best-selling books on the science of everyday life. Bodanis debuted with *The Body Book: A Fantastic Voyage to the World Within,* which S. E. Gunstream, writing in *Choice,* called "an imaginative description of the physiological processes involved in certain emo-

tions, activities, and states commonly experienced." Carol Krucoff, reviewing the book in the *Washington Post Book World,* claimed that "Bodanis packs the book with remarkable physical trivia." Commenting on Bodanis's writing style, Carla La Croix, reviewing *The Body Book* in *Library Journal,* stated that he "writes in a clear, lively, nontechnical style" that "includes cultural and historical references." This same style invited Alan Brien, writing in *New Statesman and Society,* to describe Bodanis's *Web of Words: The Ideas behind Politics,* as a book "where language about language is brilliantly and wittily used."

The book responsible for launching Bodanis's career as a science writer is *The Secret House.* As *Appraisal* reviewer Lavinia C. Demos discovered, "David Bodanis has highlighted a world that escapes observation." Through microphotography, the book focuses on the "hidden world" around us—dust mites, water vapor, the vibrations in the very floorboards upon which we walk. Another reviewer in *Appraisal* called the book "fanciful and fantastic" and "worth reading and revisiting." J. Baldwin, writing in *Whole Earth Review,* described the book's explanations and photographs as "bright, witty, and appealing to kids and adults alike." A *People Weekly* contributor remarked that *The Secret House* "is a bug-eyed look at the squiggly, squirmy life-forms that go unseen in the ordinary home."

Employing more photomicrographics, Bodanis's next book, *The Secret Garden: Dawn to Dusk in the Astonishing Hidden World of the Garden,* was called an "intriguing text" by contributor Charles Solomon in the *Los Angeles Times Book Review.* This time the topic involves the garden of the "everyman." David W. Kramer, writing in *Science Books and Films,* stated that Bodanis "skillfully infuses the facts with a dynamic tension that adds excitement to the interactions among plants, soil, fungi, insects, and people." Karen Van Epen, writing in *Whole Earth Review,* noted that Bodanis "uncovers how members of the microscopic world coexist, communicate and sometimes cooperate with each other."

Bodanis follows *The Secret Garden* with *The Secret Family: Twenty-four Hours inside the Mysterious Worlds of Our Minds and Bodies.* Donna Seaman, writing in *Booklist,* called the book "readable, informative, and lively." Mark L. Shelton, reviewing it in *Library Journal,* remarked that "this is the sort of book that turns grade schoolers into science lovers." A reviewer in *Kirkus Reviews* called *The Secret Family* "possible the perfect gift for a science-minded teenager." A. M. Daniels, writing in the *Times Literary Supplement,* described the book as a "cheerful, discursive and highly amusing account of a typical middle-class American family's Saturday." Sarah Richardson, reviewing *The Secret Family* in *Discover,* found that "a skim through the book offers rewards."

Bodanis published *E=mc2: A Biography of the World's Most Famous Equation* in 2002. Steve King, writing in the *Spectator,* commented, "Bodanis's engaging 'biographical' approach highlights Einstein's debt to earlier scientists." King noted that Bodanis tells the story of the famous equation "in the manner of a conventional biography, with chapters on the equation's 'ancestors, childhood, adolescence and adulthood.'" A reviewer in *Astronomy* found that Bodanis "brings to life a mathematical formula that enjoys a ubiquitous presence in our daily lives," and a *Publishers Weekly* reviewer described the book as "very approachable." James Olson, writing in *Library Journal,* called the work "surely one of the best books of the year." Jay Tolson, a reviewer in *U.S. News & World Report,* commended Bodanis for attempting "to ground the concept by means of historical vignettes." Writing in *School Library Journal,* Barbara A. Genco described the work as a "brilliant suite of essays" and concluded, "This book is engaging, accessible, and filled with vividly drawn characters."

BIOGRAPHICAL AND CRITICAL SOURCES:

PERIODICALS

Appraisal, summer, 1987, Lavinia C. Demos, review of *The Secret House: Twenty-four Hours in the Strange and Unexpected World in Which We Spend Our Nights and Days,* p. 21.

Astronomy, January, 2001, review of *E=mc2: A Biography of the World's Most Famous Equation,* p. 112.

Book, November, 2000, Tim LeClair, review of *E=mc2,* p. 71.

Booklist, August, 1997, Donna Seaman, review of *The Secret Family: Twenty-four Hours inside the Mysterious World of Our Minds and Bodies,* p. 1864; August, 2000, Gilbert Taylor, review of *E=mc2,* p. 2088; August 2000, Gilbert Taylor, review of *E=mc2,* p. 209.

Choice, December, 1984, S. E. Gunstream, review of *The Body Book: A Fantastic Voyage to the World Within,* p. 580.

Discover, February, 1998, Sarah Richardson, review of *The Secret Family,* p. 88; October 2000, Eric Powell, review of *E=mc2,* p. 104.

Encounter, March 1989, review of *Web of Words: The Ideas behind Politics,* p. 55.

Entertainment Weekly, August 22, 1997, Alexandra Jacobs, review of *The Secret Garden,* p. 128.

Kirkus Reviews, June 15, 1997, review of *The Secret Family,* p. 922.

Library Journal, September 15, 1984, Carla La Croix, review of *The Body Book,* p. 1764; July, 1997, Mark L. Shelton, review of *The Secret Family,* p. 118; November 1, 2000, James Olson, review of *E=mc2,* p. 124.

Los Angeles Times Book Review, December 26, 1993, Charles Solomon, review of *The Secret Garden: Dawn to Dusk in the Astonishing Hidden World of the Garden,* p. 11.

New Scientist, March 4, 1989, Roy Herbert, review of *The Secret House,* p. 60.

New Statesman and Society, February 3, 1989, Alan Brien, "Word Hunting," p. 45.

People Weekly, April 20, 1987, "They Say a Man's Home Is His Castle, but David Bodanis' *Secret House* Reveals the Creepy Truth," p. 133.

Publishers Weekly, June 8, 1984, review of *The Body Book,,* p. 59; September 18, 2000, review of *E=mc2,* p. 98.

School Library Journal, December, 2000, Barbara A. Genco, review of *E=mc2,* p. 63.

Science Books and Films, March, 1993, David W. Kramer, review of *The Secret Garden,* p. 46.

Spectator, November 4, 2000, Steve King, review of *E=mc2,* p. 53.

Times Literary Supplement, January 30, 1998, A. M. Daniels, "The Last Explorers," p. 36.

U.S. News and World Report, December 18, 2000, Jay Tolson, review of *E=mc2,* p. 54.

Washington Post Book World, December 2, 1984, Carol Kurcoff, review of *The Body Book,* p. 14.

Whole Earth Review, summer, 1987, J. Baldwin, review of *The Secret House,* p. 110; winter, 1994, Karen Van Epen, review of *The Secret Garden,* p. 104.

OTHER

CollegeClub.com, http://www.collegeclub.com/ (September 13, 2001), "David Bodanis biography."

BOËTIUS, Henning 1939-

PERSONAL: Born 1939, in Germany; son of Eduard (a zeppelin elevator operator) Boëtius.

ADDRESSES: Home—Lives near Frankfurt, Germany. *Agent*—c/o Nan A. Talese/Doubleday, 1540 Broadway, 18th Floor, New York, NY 10036.

CAREER: Novelist.

WRITINGS:

Utopie und Verwesung: zur Struktur von Hans Henny Jahnns Roman "Fluss ohne Ufer," Lang (Bern, Switzerland), 1967.

(Editor) *Dichtungstheorien der Aufklärung,* Niemeyer (Tübingen, Germany), 1971.

Der andere Brentano: 130 Jahre Literatur-Skandal, Eichborn (Frankfurt am Main, Germany), 1985.

Der verlorene Lenz: Auf der Suche nach dem inneren Kontinent, Eichborn (Frankfurt am Main, Germany), 1985.

Selbstgedichte, Eichborn (Frankfurt am Main, Germany), 1986.

Der Gnom (novel), Eichborn (Frankfurt am Main, Germany), 1989.

Blendwerk (novel), Eichborn (Frankfurt am Main, Germany), 1994.

Ich ist ein anderer: Das Leben des Arthur Rimbaud (novel), Eichborn-Verlag (Frankfurt am Main, Germany), 1995.

Der Walmann (novel), Eichborn (Frankfurt am Main, Germany), 1996.

(With others) *Henning Larson: The Architect's Studio,* Louisiana Museum of Modern Art (Denmark), 1996.

Undines Tod (novel), Btb (Munich, Germany), 1997.

Das Rubinhalsband: Ein Piet-Hieronymus (novel), Wilhelm Goldmann (Munich, Germany), 1998.

Tod in Weimar: Eine Novelle, Merlin (Gifkendorf, Germany), 1999.

Phönix aus Asche (novel) Wilhelm Goldmann (Munich, Germany), 2000, translated by John Cullen as *The Phoenix: A Novel about the Hindenburg,* Doubleday (New York, NY), 2001.

Schönheit der Verwilderung (novel), Wilhelm Goldmann (Munich, Germany), 2002.

ADAPTATIONS: Phönix aus Asche, read by Philipp Schepmann, was released by Random House Audio in CD and cassette formats in 2000.

SIDELIGHTS: Henning Boëtius is a German novelist who gained international attention when his novel *The Phoenix,* a fictional account of the *Hindenburg* zeppelin disaster, was translated into English in 2001. The author of numerous books in German since the 1970s, Boëtius has worked primarily in the mystery and suspense genres.

Boëtius began his literary career with academic studies, including analysis of works by Hans Henny Jahnns and Jakob Michael Reinhold Lenz. His 1971 volume *Dichtungstheorien der Aufklärung,* a collection of essays on critical theory written by Germans between the years 1720 and 1760, received compliments from Ida M. Kimber in *Modern Language Review.* The pieces in Boëtius's collection discuss such topics as taste and the imitation of nature. Kimber stated that "besides rendering us a service by making these inaccessible texts accessible, the editor provides very useful notes."

While Boëtius is the author of several volumes of fiction, he is best known for *The Phoenix: A Novel about the Hindenburg.* He is the son of one of the survivors; his father, Eduard Boëtius, served as the elevator operator on the famous airship. In an interview with publisher Nan A. Talese, Boëtius noted, "I grew up with stories of the *Hindenburg* and the catastrophe, and drank from *Hindenburg* teacups all my life." In the novel he does not merely retell his father's story. Boëtius uses the protagonist Birger Lund, a Swedish journalist who survives the crash but is presumed dead when the remains of a stowaway are identified as his, to explore what might have actually caused the zeppelin's destruction. Lund's face, burned in the crash, is reconstructed. He never returns to his wife and family. In the course of his investigations, he meets Edmund Boysen, a fictional character based on Boëtius's father. Although the destruction of the *Hindenburg* was ruled an accident, Boëtius speculates about ominous plots as possible reasons for the tragedy.

The Phoenix received several favorable reviews from critics. Although Ron Charles in the *Christian Science Monitor* had some reservations about the novel, he praised the plot thread in which "Lund travels to a North Sea island" and "enters a strange world as isolated from time as he is from humanity." Charles added, "It's the perfect setting for his brooding personality. He's befriended by a hunchback dwarf, an amorous barmaid, and a group of thugs who eventually try to kill him." Anthony Day in *Los Angeles Times* noted that *The Phoenix* "is also a delicately erotic love story." He called the novel "a meditation on appearance and reality" and "a subtle and convincing picture of the Germany from which Hitler sprang and the country he left in ashes." A *Publishers Weekly* reviewer remarked that "Boëtius has created an original plot peopled with intensely realized characters," while Gavin Quinn in *Booklist* predicted that "the mystery surrounding the infamous disaster will compel readers to keep turning the pages."

BIOGRAPHICAL AND CRITICAL SOURCES:

BOOKS

Boëtius, Henning, *The Phoenix: A Novel about the Hindenburg,* translated by John Cullen, Doubleday, 2001.

PERIODICALS

Booklist, November 15, 2001, Gavin Quinn, review of *The Phoenix,* p. 550.
Christian Science Monitor, December 27, 2001, Ron Charles, "A Zeppelin Story Full of Hot Air: A Popular German Author Brings the *Hindenburg* to America, Again," p. 15.
Library Journal, November 1, 2001, Ronnie H. Terpening, review of *The Phoenix,* p. 131.
Los Angeles Times, January 4, 2002, Anthony Day, "Novel Offers a Bird's-Eye View of History from the *Hindenburg,*" p. E3.
Modern Language Review, April, 1973, Ida M. Kimber, review of *Dichtungstheorien der Aufklärung,* p. 455.
New Yorker, April 22, 2002, Mark Rozzo, review of *The Phoenix,* p. 42.
New York Times Book Review, Tom Ferrell, review of *The Phoenix,* p. 24.
Publishers Weekly, October 8, 2001, review of *The Phoenix,* p. 40.

San Francisco Chronicle, December 2, 2001, David Lazarus, "Spies' Romance Echoes Rick and Ilsa," p. 5.

OTHER

Nan A. Talese Web site, http://www.randomhouse.com/nanatalese/ (June 11, 2002), interview with Henning Boëtius.*

* * *

BOILEAU, Pierre 1906-1989

PERSONAL: Born April 28, 1906, in Paris, France; died January 16, 1989; son of a shipping-firm manager and a homemaker. *Education:* Studied at a Parisian school of commerce.

CAREER: Worked as an architect, advertising copywriter, textile worker, and waiter. Served in French Welfare Department, 1939-42; writer.

AWARDS, HONORS: Prix du Roman d'Aventures, 1938, for *Le Repos de Bacchus.*

WRITINGS:

WITH THOMAS NARCEJAC; MYSTERY NOVELS; IN ENGLISH TRANSLATION

Celle qui n'était plus, 1952, translation by Geoffrey Sainsbury published as *The Woman Who Was No More,* Rinehart, 1954.
Les visages de l'ombre, 1953, translation published as *Faces in the Dark,* 1954.
D'entre les morts, 1954, translation by Geoffrey Sainsbury published as *The Living and the Dead,* Washburn, 1956.
Les louves, 1955, translation published as *The Prisoner,* 1957.
Le mauvais oeil, 1956, translation published as *The Evil Eye,* 1959.
Au bois dormant, 1956, translation published as *Sleeping Beauty,* 1959.

A couer perdu, 1959, translation published as *Heart to Heart,* 1959.

L'ingénieur qui aimait trop les chiffres, 1959, translation published as *The Tube,* 1960.

Maléfices, 1961, translation published as *Spells of Evil,* 1961.

Les victims, 1964, translation published as *Who Was Clare Jallu?,* 1965.

Et mon tout est un homme, 1965, translation by Brian Rawson published as *Choice Cuts,* Dutton (New York, NY), 1966.

UNTRANSLATED MYSTERY NOVELS; WITH THOMAS NARCEJAC

Les magiciennes, 1957.

La mort a dit, peut-être, 1967.

Delirium, 1969.

Maldonne, 1970.

La vie en miettes, 1972.

Opération primevère, 1973.

Frère Judas, 1974.

Le second visage d'Arsène Lupin, 1975.

La tenaille, 1975.

La lèpre, 1976.

Les veufs, 1977.

L'age bête, 1978.

Carte vermeille, 1979.

Le serment d'Arsène Lupin, 1979.

Terminus, 1980.

Box Office, 1981.

OTHER

Le Pierre qui tremble (novel), 1934.

André Brunel, policier (novel), 1934.

La promenade de minuit (novel), 1934.

Le repos de Bacchus (novel), 1938.

(With Thomas Narcejac) *Le foman policier* (nonfiction), 1975.

(With Thomas Narcejac) *Tandem: ou, Trente-cinq ans de suspence* (nonfiction), 1986.

ADAPTATIONS: The Woman Who Was No More was filmed by director Henri-Georges Clouzot as *Diabolique* in 1954; *D'entre les morts* was filmed as *Vertigo* by director Alfred Hitchcock in 1958.

SIDELIGHTS: Pierre Boileau was a French novelist best known, at least among English-language readers, for his mystery novels written in collaboration with Thomas Narcejac. Boileau began his literary career in the 1930s with such novels as *Le Repos de Bacchus,* for which he received the Prix du Roman d'Aventures. In that same decade, after the French government capitulated to the invading German forces, Boileau was named an enemy of the state, and he was thereupon conscripted into the French Welfare Department, which sent him on tours of prisons. During the course of this endeavor, which lasted until 1942, Boileau met numerous criminals. These acquaintances, in turn, led Boileau to consider writing mystery novels. His enthusiasm intensified after he read *Esthétique du roman policier,* Narcejac's analysis of crime fiction. Towards the end of the 1940s, after Boileau initiated correspondence, the two writers formed a writing partnership.

In the ensuing four decades, Boileau and Narcejac produced more than twenty novels together and distinguished themselves as masters of a strain of storytelling that juxtaposes the dull and the abnormal to horrific effect. Their first collaborative venture, *Celle qui n'était plus,* concerns a murder plot in which a salesman conspires with his lover to drown his wife. After committing the crime, though, the salesman becomes haunted by his wife's image. His anxiety intensifies after he fails to retrieve her corpse, which he had dumped in a pond, and he begins receiving ominous notes. A surprise ending reveals the salesman's perceptions to be justifiably alarming. Rose Feld, reviewing the novel in its English translation, *The Woman Who Was No More,* wrote in the *New York Herald Tribune* that the finale constitutes "an astounding turn that holds validity both for plot and characterization," and a *Time* reviewer observed that "Boileau and Narcejac keep the reader guessing." Another reviewer, Martin Levin, appraised *The Woman Who Was No More* in *Saturday Review* as "en entirely new variation on the double-indemnity theme."

Among Boileau and Narcejac's other novels in English translation is *D'entre les morts,* which was translated as *The Living and the Dead.* In this tale, a man agrees to secretly follow the wife of an old friend, who expresses concern over his spouse's apparent instability. The hero soon becomes preoccupied with his subject, especially after he rescues her during a suicide attempt. After the woman finally succeeds in killing herself, the distraught hero—like the salesman in *The Woman Who Was No More*—finds himself haunted by the deceased's image. When he finally apprehends a lookalike, he learns of a bizarre murder plot involving a body double. This knowledge compels him to commit his own criminal act. *New York Times* reviewer Anthony Boucher was less impressed with this novel, contending that Boileau and Narcejac attempted to duplicate the tricky plotting of the earlier *Woman Who Was No More* but met with "unfortunate results." L. G. Offord, however, wrote in the *San Francisco Chronicle* that this novel fares "very well on the scary side."

Boileau and Narcejac were also the authors of *Et Mon tout est un homme,* which appeared in English translation as *Choice Cuts.* Here, the corpse of a guillotined criminal is dismembered, and the various body parts are incorporated in surgical procedures to save maimed accident victims. These individuals, however, soon grow increasingly disturbed as a consequence of the transplants, and they ultimately resort to suicide. In his *New York Times Book Review* assessment, Anthony Boucher claimed that *Choice Cuts* "fails to attain any suspension of disbelief." A *Times Literary Supplement* critic, while conceding that the story "sounds preposterous," nonetheless called *Choice Cuts* "a first-rate entertainment."

Narcejac died in 1998, surviving coauthor Boileau by less than a decade.

BIOGRAPHICAL AND CRITICAL SOURCES:

PERIODICALS

Library Journal, March 15, 1954, Harold Lancour, review of *The Woman Who Was No More;* December 1, 1966, M. K. Grant, review of *Choice Cuts.*

New York Herald Tribune Book Review, April 11, 1954, Rose Feld, review of *The Woman Who Was No More,* p. 6.

New York Times, May 9, 1954, Anthony Boucher, review of *The Woman Who Was No More,* p. 21; May 5, 1957, Anthony Boucher, review of *The Living and the Dead,* p. 26.

New York Times Book Review, November 6, 1966, Anthony Boucher, review of *Choice Cuts,* p. 56.

San Francisco Chronicle, June 13, 1954, L. G. Offord, review of *The Woman Who Was No More,* p. 21.

Saturday Review, May 22, 1954, Martin Levin, review of *The Woman Who Was No More.*

Spectator, July 2, 1954, Penelope Houston, review of *The Woman Who Was No More,* p. 40; May 4, 1956, Christopher Pym, review of *The Living and the Dead,* p. 631.

Time, April 26, 1954, review of *The Woman Who Was No More.*

Times Literary Supplement, May 4, 1956, review of *The Living and the Dead,* p. 272; August 18, 1966, review of *Choice Cuts,* p. 737.*

* * *

BONANNO, Joseph 1905-2002

OBITUARY NOTICE—See index for *CA* sketch: Born January 18, 1905, in Castellammare del Golfo, Sicily, Italy; died of a heart ailment May 11, 2002, in Tucson, AZ. Mafia boss and author. Although he did not like the term "Mafia," Bonanno headed one of the original five family crime syndicates operating in New York City from the 1930s to the 1960s. His parents first brought him to the United States when Bonanno was three years old; the family returned to Sicily ten years later, but Bonanno came back to America illegally in 1924, quickly establishing himself as a mob leader. Although known to the police and FBI for his illegal activities, Bonanno escaped serious charges throughout his life and became a leader in "the Commission," a loose association of organized crime bosses in New York. His career in crime fell apart in the 1960s, however, when he led a power struggle that became known as "the Banana War" after his much-disliked nickname, "Joe Bananas." The result of his grab for power was thirteen murders, and Bonanno fled to Arizona, where he went into hiding. He wrote about his exploits in the 1983 autobiography *A Man of Honor: The Autobiography of Joseph Bonanno,* which many reviewers criticized as a self-serving book that reveals little about the Mafia. However, Rudolph Giuliani, the former New York mayor who in the 1980s was a federal prosecutor, found enough information in the book to bring its author to trial. Even so, Bonanno served little time in prison. From 1983 to 1984 he served an eight-month sentence for obstruction of justice, and then spent fourteen months in prison for contempt of court before going free again in 1986.

OBITUARIES AND OTHER SOURCES:

BOOKS

Sifakis, Carl, *The Mafia Encyclopedia,* second edition, Facts on File, 1999.

PERIODICALS

Los Angeles Times, May 12, 2002, p. B16.
New York Times, May 13, 2002, p. A15.
Washington Post, May 13, 2002, p. B4.

*   *   *

BOOTH, LaVaughn Vanchael
See BOOTH, L(aVaughn) Venchael

*   *   *

BOOTH, L(aVaughn) Venchael 1919-2002

PERSONAL: Some sources spell middle name "Vanchael"; born January 7, 1919, in Collins, MS; died November 16, 2002, in Memphis, TN; son of Frederick Douglas and Mamie (Powell) Booth; married Georgia Anna Morris, 1943 (deceased); married Yvette Livers; children: (first marriage) LaVaughn Venchael, Jr., William D., Anna M. Booth Metwally, Georgia A. Booth Leeper, Paul. *Education:* Alcorn Agricultural and Mechanical College (now Alcorn State University), B.A., 1940; Howard University, B.D., 1943; University of Chicago, M.A., 1945.

CAREER: Ordained minister of National Baptist Convention; pastor of Baptist churches in Warrenton, VA, 1943, and Gary, IN, 1944-52; Zion Baptist Church, Cincinnati, OH, pastor, 1952-84; Olivet Baptist Church, Silverton, OH, founder and pastor, beginning 1984. Progressive National Baptist Convention, founding member, 1961, vice president, 1961-71, president, 1971-84; Baptist World Alliance, vice president, 1970-75. University of Cincinnati, member of board of trustees, 1968—; Martin Luther King, Jr. Center, member of board of directors. Cincinnati Black Bank, organizer and chair, 1974; Hamilton County State Bank, founder and chair, 1980.

MEMBER: American Bible Society (member of board of management).

AWARDS, HONORS: Certificate of Merit, Cincinnati chapter, National Association for the Advancement of Colored People, 1963; L.H.D., Wilberforce University, 1964; D.D., Morehouse College, 1967; Distinguished Service Award, Churches of Detroit, 1968; Founders Award, Progressive National Baptist Convention, 1971; Award of Excellence, Operation PUSH, 1974; named to *Ebony* magazine Success Library, 1974; L.H.D., University of Cincinnati, 1989; named outstanding educator, *Applause,* 1991.

WRITINGS:

(Editor) Lillian B. Horace, *"Crowned with Glory and Honor": The Life of Rev. Lacey Williams,* Exposition Press (Hicksville, NY), 1978.*

*   *   *

BORGESE, Elisabeth Mann 1918-2002

OBITUARY NOTICE—See index for *CA* sketch: Born April 24, 1918, in Munich, Germany; died of complications from a respiratory infection February 8, 2002, in Samedan, near St. Moritz, Switzerland. Political scientist, environmentalist, educator, and author. Borgese devoted her life to the preservation of the seas and the responsible management of ocean resources. She was an organizer of the first Peace in the Oceans Conference in 1970 and a founder of the International Oceans Institute, which she headed until 1992. Her unflagging efforts contributed to the creation of the United Nations Law of the Seas Treaty in 1982. Borgese, the daughter of German novelist Thomas Mann, was born in Germany but fled that country in 1933. As a U.S. citizen from 1941 to 1983, her work included several years as a senior fellow at the Center for the Study of Democratic Institutions in Santa Barbara, California; she was also a founding member of the Club of Rome. Adopting Canadian citizenship in 1983, Borgese taught political science and law at Dalhousie University in Halifax, Nova Scotia. Her ongoing mission, however, was to protect the sea. She wrote several books, including *The Drama of the Oceans,* which was widely translated, *Ocean Gover-*

nance and the United Nations, and *The Oceanic Circle: Governing the Seas as a Global Resource.* She also promoted the development of the sea as a resource, in books like *Seafarm* and *The Mines of Neptune: Minerals and Metals of the Sea.* Borgese's accomplishments were honored worldwide. Her awards include the Order of Canada in 1987, a German Federal Order of Merit, and a Lifetime Achievement Award from the Nuclear Age Peace Foundation.

OBITUARIES AND OTHER SOURCES:

PERIODICALS

Los Angeles Times, February 24, 2002, p. B16.
New York Times, February 16, 2002, obituary by Wolfgang Saxon, p. B16.
Times (London, England), March 2, 2002.
Washington Post, February 10, 2002, p. C6.

*   *   *

BOSSE, Malcolm (Joseph, Jr.) 1926-2002

OBITUARY NOTICE—See index for *CA* sketch: Born May 6, 1926, in Detroit, MI; died of esophageal cancer June 14, 2002, in New York, NY. Educator and author. Bosse was an author of books for both children and adults and was well known for his stories set in Asia, including *The Warlord* (1983). He got his first exposure to Asia after high school when he worked as a merchant marine, and then later, after earning his bachelor's degree at Yale University and working in New York City for two years as an editorial writer for *Barron's Financial Weekly,* he served in the U.S. Navy during the Vietnam War. Vietnam became the setting for his first novel, *Journey of Tao Kim Nam* (1959). Returning home, Bosse earned his master's degree from the University of Michigan in 1960 and worked as a freelance writer. He continued his studies at New York University, where he received a Ph.D. in 1969. That same year, he began teaching English at the City College of the City University of New York, where he became a professor and eventually retired in 1992. Bosse began writing murder mysteries with his second novel, *The Incident at Naha,* and stories for young adults with 1979's *The Seventy-nine Squares.* Other young-adult books by Bosse include *The Barracuda*

Gang (1982) and *The Examination* (1994). He also continued to write books for adults, such as the historical novels *The Warlord* (1983) and its sequel, *Fire in Heaven* (1986), and was coeditor of *Foundations of the Novel* (1974) and *The Flowering of the Novel* (1975). During his career, Bosse received considerable praise for both his adult and young-adult fiction, including Edgar Allan Poe Award nominations in 1974 and 1975 for *The Incident at Naha* and *The Man Who Loved Zoos* respectively, a Dorothy Canfield Fisher Award in 1981, several honorable- and notable-book listings from the American Library Association, the Deutscher Jugendliteraturpreis, and the Prix Lecture-Jeunesse.

OBITUARIES AND OTHER SOURCES:

BOOKS

St. James Guide to Young Adult Writers, second edition, St. James Press (Detroit, MI), 1999.
Writers Directory, sixteenth edition, St. James Press, 2001.

PERIODICALS

New York Times, June 14, 2002, p. C11.

*   *   *

BOUREAU, Alain

PERSONAL: Male.

ADDRESSES: Office—Johns Hopkins University, Department of Romance Languages and Literatures, 328 Gilman Hall, 3400 North Charles St., Baltimore, MD 21218. *E-mail*—boureau@atacama.ehess.fr.

CAREER: Historian. Centre de Recherches Historiques, École des Hautes Etudes en Science Sociales, Paris, France, director; Johns Hopkins University, visiting professor of medieval and intellectual history.

WRITINGS:

La légende dorée: le systeme narratif de Jacques de Voragine (1298), Editions du Cerf (Paris, France), 1984.

L'aigle: chronique politique d'un emblème, Editions du Cerf (Paris, France), 1985.

La Papesse Jeanne, Aubier (Paris, France), 1988, translated by Lydia G. Cochrane as *The Myth of Pope Joan,* University of Chicago Press (Chicago, IL), 2001.

Le simple corps du roi: l'impossible sacralité des souverains français, XVe-XVIIIe siècle, Editions de Siècle (Paris, France), 1988.

Histoires d'un historien: Kantorowicz, Gallimard (Paris, France), 1990, translated by Stephen G. Nichols and Gabrielle M. Spiegel as *Kantorowicz: Stories of a Historian,* Johns Hopkins University Press (Baltimore, MD), 2001.

(Editor, with Claudio Sergio Ingerflom) *La Royauté sacrée dans le monde chretien: colloque de Royaumont, mars 1989,* Editions de l'École des Hautes Etudes en Sciences Sociales (Paris, France), 1992.

L'événement sans fin: récit et christianisme au Moyen âge, Belles Lettres (Paris, France), 1993.

(With Roger Chartier, Cecile Dauphin, and others) *La correspondence: les usages de la letter au XIXe siècle,* translated by Christopher Woodall as *Correspondence: Models of Letter-writing from the Middle Ages to the Nineteenth Century,* Princeton University Press (Princeton, NJ) 1997.

Le droit de cuissage: la fabrication d'un mythe (XIIIe-XXe siècle), Albin Michel (Paris, France), 1995, translated by Lydia G. Cochrane as *The Lord's First Night: The Myth of the Droit de Cuissage,* University of Chicago Press (Chicago, IL), 1998.

Théologie, science et censure au XIIIe siècle: le cas de Jean Peckham, Belles Lettres (Paris, France), 1999.

La loi du royaume: Les moines, le droit et la construction de la nation anglaise, XIe-XIIIe siècles, Belles Lettres (Paris, France), 2001.

Also contributor to *The Culture of Print: Power and the Uses of Print in Early Modern Europe,* edited by Roger Chartier, translated by Lydia G. Cochrane, Polity (Cambridge, England), 1989.

SIDELIGHTS: Alain Boureau, the director of the École des Hautes Etudes en Sciences Sociales in Paris, France, is the author of several books that focus on his speciality of medieval and intellectual history. His *La Papesse Jeanne,* translated as *The Myth of Pope Joan,* examines the legend of the mythical female pope. Boureau draws from many sources in his discussion of the legend, including Dominican preaching, the writ-ing of Giovanni Boccaccio, and the sermons of John Hus and Martin Luther. Unlike Peter Stanford, who concluded in his *The Legend of Pope Joan: In Search of the Truth* that there may in fact have been a female pope, Boureau concludes in *The Myth of Pope Joan* that there was no actual historical Joan.

Histoires d'un historien: Kantorowicz explores the life and work of German author Ernst Hartwig Kantorowicz (1893-1963), the biographer of Frederick II (1712-1786), who was king of Prussia from 1740. Kantorowicz, born in Germany in 1893, entered the army in 1914 and participated in many battles; he was wounded while fighting and decorated many times. After receiving wounds from combat with Soviet forces in Munich in 1919, he left the army and took up teaching at the university. He became a professor at a university in Frankfurt, Germany, but in 1934 the takeover of Germany by the Nazis pushed him into early retirement. In 1939 Kantorowicz left Germany for New York and consequently joined the faculties at the University of California at Berkeley, and the Princeton Institute for Advanced Study, until his death in 1963. John Hine Mundy, reviewing *Histoires d'un historien* in the *Journal of Modern History,* wrote, "Boureau gives a rich, if mildly Gallicized, genealogy of Kantorowicz's thought. What intrigues him about this German's work . . . is not only its basic conservatism, but also its enrichment of conventional history by the addition of the history of art, law, and literature." Mundy also noted that "Boureau does not shirk difficult questions" about Kantorowicz's life and work. Although faulting a few "slips" in the text, Mundy declared "this little book is a fine tribute to the master."

La Royaute sacrée dans le monde chretien: colloque de Royaumont, mars 1989 is a collection of fifteen essays, edited by Boureau in collaboration with Claudio Sergio Ingerflom, that discuss the medieval notion that kings were divinely appointed. *Catholic Historical Review* contributor Richard A. Jackson remarked that the book is "a contribution to the subject, full of interesting ideas, suggestive of further research, but hardly a definitive treatment."

The Lord's First Night: The Myth of the Droit de Cuissage looks at the notion that in the Middle Ages the lord of a manor had the right to bed his vassal's bride on her wedding night. According to Boureau, this custom, which was first written about in 1247 and has been believed in for seven hundred years, is actually a myth. Peter Linehan noted in the *Times Literary Supplement* that the book is "a richly informative study of attitudes to the past and the manipulation of history down the ages." In *Speculum*, Paul Freedman commented, "Few works cross with such confidence from the medieval to the contemporary. . . . [*The Lord's First Night*] shows us an intriguing and volatile aspect of the medieval imagination and the imagined Middle Ages."

BIOGRAPHICAL AND CRITICAL SOURCES:

PERIODICALS

Catholic Historical Review, July, 1993, Richard A. Jackson, review of *La Royaute sacrée dans le monde chretien*, pp. 498-499; April, 1987, p. 326.

English Historical Review, April, 2001, Richard Cross, review of *Théologie, science et censure au XIIIe siècle: le cas de Jean Peckham*, p. 458.

Journal of Modern History, June, 1993, John Hine Mundy, review of *Histoires d'un historien: Kantorowicz*, pp. 378-379.

Journal of Social History, winter, 1999, Konstantin Dierks, review of *Correspondence: Models of Letter-writing from the Middle Ages to the Nineteenth Century*, p. 466.

Library Journal, May 1, 2001, Carolyn M. Craft, review of *The Myth of Pope Joan*, p. 91.

Publishers Weekly, March 26, 2001, review of *The Myth of Pope Joan*, p. 87.

Speculum, July, 1996, Paul Freedman, review of *Le droit de cuissage: La fabrication d'un mythe (XIIIe-XXe siècle)*, pp. 696-698.

Times Literary Supplement, October 6, 1995, Peter Linehan, "Leg-over Legend," p. 44.*

*　　*　　*

BOYATZIS, Richard E(leftherios) 1946-

PERSONAL: Born October 1, 1946, in New York, NY; son of Kyriakos Eleftherios and Sophia (Glacous) Boyatzis; married Sandra Scott, September 17, 1977. *Education:* Massachusetts Institute of Technology, B.S., 1968; Harvard University, M.A., 1970, Ph.D., 1973.

ADDRESSES: Office—Department of Organizational Behavior, Weatherhead School of Management, Case Western Reserve University, 10900 Euclid Ave., Cleveland, OH 44106-7235. *E-mail*—Richard. Boyatzis@weatherhead.cwru.edu.

CAREER: Northrop/Norair, Los Angeles, CA, engineer, 1966-67; private consultant, 1967-72; Veterans Administration Hospital, Brockton, MA, consulting psychologist, 1970-72; McBer and Co., Boston, MA, director of research, 1972-76, president/CEO, 1976-87; Case Western Reserve University, Cleveland, OH, began as associate professor, professor, then dean, 1987—; Council for Adult Experimental Learning, Chicago, 1989-95; author. Member, Consortium on Research on Emotional Intelligence; *Journal of Management Education*, member of editorial board.

MEMBER: Academy of Management Learning and Education (founding member), American Psychology Association.

AWARDS, HONORS: Case Western Reserve University, Weatherhead School of Management, Theodore M. Alfred Distinguished Service Award, 1996, and Research Recognition Award, 2000.

WRITINGS:

The Competent Manager: A Model for Effective Performance, Wiley (New York, NY), 1982.

(With Scott S. Cowen, David A. Kolb, and others) *Innovation in Professional Education: Steps on a Journey from Teaching to Learning: The Story of Change and Invention at the Weatherhead School of Management*, Jossey-Bass Publishers (San Francisco, CA), 1995.

Transforming Qualitative Information: Thematic Analysis and Code Development, Sage Publications (Thousand Oaks, CA), 1998.

(With Daniel Goleman and Annie McKee) *Primal Leadership: Realizing the Power of Emotional Intelligence*, Harvard Business School Press (Boston, MA), 2002.

SIDELIGHTS: Richard E. Boyatzis, a psychologist, professor of organizational behavior, and former management consultant to several major U.S. corporations, has been hailed as highly influential, both nationally and internationally, in the field of human resource management. In fact, his 1982 publication, *The Competent Manager: A Model for Effective Performance,* is often referred to as a seminal work in the emerging industry of competency consultants, researchers, and academics. It was in *The Competent Manager* that Boyatzis first outlined several ways of assessing the characteristics of managers that best enable them to be most effective on the job. His continuing work as professor, lecturer, and author has led Boyatzis to refine and enhance his initial findings. He now concludes that the most important task for top executives is not maintaining budgets, establishing business strategies, or hiring staff but rather that managers should, most importantly, assess their own behaviors in order to understand the impact of their moods on the development of their companies. Employing his theories, Boyatzis has created innovative college business classes during which students must go through extensive self-assessments. He has also coauthored *Primal Leadership: Realizing the Power of Emotional Intelligence* (2002).

In an interview with Arthur K. Yeung for *Human Resource Management,* Boyatzis stated several characteristics that a successful manager, especially a human resource manager, must have. Among them are such things as the ability to be efficient, to pay attention to detail, to be flexible, to maintain self-control, to be persuasive, to exhibit empathy, to have self-confidence, and to communicate well, both orally and in written communications. However, Boyatzis believes that overall, the most important underlying characteristic of any manager is genuineness, which he defines as "being congruent with one's self and being open to others." Boyatzis also makes it clear that the characteristics of successful managers have not changed over the years. "As a matter of fact," he continued in his interview, "I would venture to guess that they haven't changed much in the past twenty years, nor do I think they will change a lot in the next twenty years." The business environments might change, Boyatzis admitted, but successful managers will always be those who are most efficient, empathetic, and confident.

In order to find out if a person has these characteristics, Boyatzis has created an assessment program. It is through such a program, Boyatzis pointed out in his interview with Yeung, that you can "figure out where

your strengths are. You have to use your strengths for your leverage. A second issue is you really have to spend some time developing your personal vision. If you don't know what it is you really want . . . you are going to be wasting a lot of time."

In his first book, *The Competent Manger,* Boyatzis lists what effective managers do that make them stand out from less-successful managers. As stated by Howard S. Schwartz for *Contemporary Psychology,* "the factors that determine effective managerial performance [are]: the 'competencies' of the manager, the demands of the job, and the organizational environment." Boyatzis's focus is on "competencies," which he "measures with a critical-incident interview technique and with which he attempts to predict effectiveness." As noted by Donald L. Grant, writing for *Personnel Psychology,* "psychologists and others interested in the topic" of competencies are offered "much to ponder" in Boyatzis's first book. "The modeling is especially provocative, and the lengthy list of references provides much material for further study."

In 1995 Boyatzis worked with several colleagues from Case Western Reserve University, where he is a professor in the Weatherhead School of Management. Together they wrote and published *Innovation in Professional Education: Steps on a Journey from Teaching to Learning.* This book chronicles the changes made to the MBA program at Case Western at a time when degrees in business were declining as students began questioning the value of an MBA. As reflected in the book, change was slow to come. Although suggestions for change were first made in 1981, it would not be until 1990 that any modifications would be implemented. Much of the material in the first chapter of this book, "Introduction: Taking the Path toward Learning," deals with the slow process of change as well as the necessity of the MBA faculty at Case Western to meet the needs of their students. As stated by Daniel J. Gallagher for *Personnel Psychology,* "the ideas in this chapter are quite thought provoking." The chapter covers the difficulties the faculty had in seeing their own shortcomings and transitioning to a place where they were giving students skills they would require in a business setting rather than information that would help them pass tests at the university.

Other topics in *Innovation in Professional Education* include the process of strategic planning to initiate the changes necessary. Part of this process involved linking the faculty to businesses outside the university, thus "prompting them," according to Gallagher, "to promote a curriculum aligned with changes in the external environment."

An element of Boyatzis's book that Gallagher found most interesting is a conclusion the authors came to: that in many college settings, teaching is more important than learning. As Gallagher wrote: "Observations of the current state of education would suggest that education is about everything but learning—about research, about teaching, about budgets and taxes, about drugs and discipline, about religion and values, about political correctness and political connections."

Although Gallagher stated that *Innovation in Professional Education* does not provide all the answers required to make the necessary changes on many college campuses, it does "ask all the right questions." Gallagher added: "This book deserves a wide audience, not only among our academic community . . . but for those stakeholders of the system or any party interested in how our educational system might be reoriented."

With his next book, *Primal Leadership: Realizing the Power of Emotional Intelligence,* a cooperative venture with Daniel Goleman and Annie McKee, Boyatzis focuses almost entirely on the ability to create business success through a positive emotional climate. In a review of the book for *T & D,* Deanne Bryce stated: "The first chapter explains . . . how leaders tap into our emotions." Bryce added: "The authors describe the ability to drive emotions in a positive direction as 'creating resonance' in an organization." If a leader maintains a positive emotional level, it appeals to the emotions of the employees and makes them "feel in sync. And true to the original meaning of resonance, that synchrony resounds, prolonging the positive emotional pitch."

This book also delves into how the brain works in regard to emotions. The authors explain that, according to current theories, the emotional centers in the human brain function in a so-called open-loop system, as contrasted to the closed-loop system of a body's blood circulation. "What's happening in the circulatory system of others around us does not impact our own," explained Bryce. Whereas, "an open-loop

system depends largely on external sources to manage itself." Thus, the positive emotions of one person will affect those around her or him. In conclusion, Bryce stated that *Primal Leadership* offers "sound advice worth understanding and promoting."

BIOGRAPHICAL AND CRITICAL SOURCES:

PERIODICALS

Academy of Management Executives, May, 1995, H. William H. Vroman, review of *Innovation in Professional Education: Steps on a Journey from Teaching to Learning,* p. 80.
Contemporary Psychology, January,1983, Howard S. Schwartz, "Tautology in Action," pp. 53-54.
Human Resource Management, spring, 1996, Arthur K. Yeung, "Competencies for HR Professionals: An Interview with Richard E. Boyatzis," pp. 119-131.
Personnel Psychology, winter, 1982, Donald L. Grant, review of *The Competent Manager: A Model for Effective Performance,* pp. 894-897; autumn, 1996, Daniel J. Gallagher, review of *Innovation in Professional Education,* pp. 749-752.
Publishers Weekly, January 28, 2002, review of *Primal Leadership: Realizing the Power of Emotional Intelligence,* p. 279.
Reference & Research Book News, August, 1998, review of *Transforming Qualitative Information: Thematic Analysis and Code Development,* p. 59.
T & D, March, 2002, Deanne Bryce, review of *Primal Leadership,* pp. 81-83.*

*   *   *

BRADFORD, Arthur 1969-

PERSONAL: Born 1969, in ME. *Education:* Yale University, B.A. (American studies); University of Texas at Austin, M.F.A., 1998.

ADDRESSES: Agent—c/o Publicity Director, Random House, 1540 Broadway, New York, NY 10036.

CAREER: Writer and filmmaker. Has worked at the Texas School for the Blind and at Camp Jabberwocky, MA, offering a video production class for disabled adults. Produced *How's Your News?* (a documentary film featuring five Camp Jabberwocky participants as news reporters), HBO/Cinemax, 2002.

AWARDS, HONORS: O'Henry Award, for "Catface," 1997; Stanford University, creative writing program, fellowship.

WRITINGS:

Dogwalker (short story collection), Knopf/Random House (New York, NY), 2001.

Contributor to magazines, including *Esquire* and *McSweeney's,* and to the *O. Henry Awards Anthology.*

SIDELIGHTS: Although he had been writing for years, Arthur Bradford did not call himself a writer until his first collection of short stories, *Dogwalker,* was published by Knopf in 2001 and greeted with rave reviews.

Born in Maine, Bradford moved to New York City after his parents were divorced. When he was mugged there, he was sent off to boarding school in Massachusetts and eventually graduated from Yale University. The summer after he graduated, Bradford took a job at Camp Jabberwocky, a camp for adults with disabilities, in Massachusetts. He would return there for nine summers, and many of the people he met there would become key players in his first major documentary film, *How's Your News?* Broadcast by HBO in the spring of 2002, the film follows several adults whom Bradford met at Camp Jabberwocky as they become news reporters, interviewing people all across America.

Owing to his fondness for Richard Linklatter's film *Slacker,* set in Austin, Texas, Bradford decided to move to Austin. While living there, he applied to Stanford University's creative writing program and received a fellowship. When his fellowship ended, he returned to Austin, where he pursued an M.F.A. in creative writing from the University of Texas. By 1999 Bradford had started moving north, living temporarily in Charlottesville, Virginia, before ending up in Vermont. In an interview with Robert Birnbaum for *Identity Theory,* Bradford noted, "I have lived in a lot of places, and

sometimes I'm sort of embarrassed about it. I do like to change scenery a lot." Bradford has also spent time in New York, a city he loves but would not want to live in. He is well known for his readings at McSweeney's, where hundreds of people often turn out to watch him perform.

Dogwalker is a collection of twelve humorous short stories, all told in the first person, including an O'Henry Award-winning story from 1997 titled "Catface." In his review of the book for *New York Times Book Review,* Rob Walker said that "Strange, freakish and flat-out impossible things happen all the time . . . but the protagonist usually remains resolutely poker-faced." The characters in Bradford's stories are those often referred to as "marginal," young men who live in cheap apartments and work as dishwashers. In "South for the Winter" the narrator steals the car of a blind man. When he runs out of gas and gets arrested, the blind man bails him out. "Chainsaw Apple" focuses on the narrator's practice of using a chainsaw to carve a friend's initials on an apple, while the friend holds the apple in his mouth. When performing the stunt in public, the narrator accepts a woman's offer to hold the apple and ends up injuring her face, which somehow leads to romance. In a review for *Library Journal,* Mary Szczesiul noted that even if Bradford's bizarre stories are plausible and seem upsetting, "he reserves a place for innocence, and the stories have an upbeat ending."

In an interview for *BookBrowser.com,* Bradford commented: "When I think about the narrator of these stories, I think of someone a little bit (or maybe a lot) like myself who is strangely fascinated by weird people and animals, and is also not very judgmental about it all. He is very open to these situations. Personally, I've found that I seek out oddballs; I like strange and eccentric people a lot. The narrator is a little different in each story, but he's always a basic variation of the same form, which is in a lot of ways based on me and probably also some of my other favorite narrators in fiction and nonfiction (William Burroughs's *Junky,* Hemingway's narrator in *The Sun Also Rises*). Sometimes the autobiographical link in each story is very literal, like I did work at the Texas School for the Blind, and I did once lose a mattress out of the back of a friend's truck. Other times it's more of just a feeling—like with 'Dogs' I was living in a house with eleven dogs and all I thought about was dogs. I never had sex with any of them, though. I chose the title

Dogwalker because that describes me pretty well. I spend a lot of time walking around with my dogs. I'd say the narrator is me in an alternate universe."

In addition to more filmmaking, Bradford intends to write a novel. "I would be happy to have one more book and one more movie. If they were good," Bradford told Birnbaum. "I don't think I'll have a prolific twenty-book output. If I only wrote one more book I would be okay with that and okay with one more movie, although I think that I'll do more than that. I'd like to teach. I think teaching is really cool. I think it's an honorable thing to do. I'd like to start a camp like Camp Jabberwocky with an artistic bent to it."

Douglas Wolk wrote in the *Village Voice* that Bradford is "careful not to make it explicit, but the subtext of both [his] movie and his fiction is tender to the point of sentimentality—several of *Dogwalker*'s stories end with couples walking off hand in hand or arm in arm, and one closes with, no kidding, six puppies parading in from the cold on Christmas Day. The repetitive obsessions, twisted bodies, and flatly disengaged voice of his work cover for the softheartedness at its center." In advance publicity for *Dogwalker*, Bradford's publisher noted that Bradford's "perfect, perfect stories remain in your head, much like, say, a severed torso might remain under the tracks of a train."

BIOGRAPHICAL AND CRITICAL SOURCES:

PERIODICALS

Book, July, 2001, Ken Greenberg, review of *Dogwalker,* p. 75.
Booklist, July, 2001, Brendan Dowling, review of *Dogwalker,* p. 1977.
Entertainment Weekly, September 7, 2001, Rebecca Ascher-Walsh, review of *Dogwalker,* p. 158.
Esquire, August, 2001, Adrienne Miller, review of *Dogwalker,* p. 38.
Knight-Ridder/Tribune News Service, August 8, 2001, Margaria Fichtner, review of *Dogwalker,* p. K2851.
Library Journal, August, 2001, Mary Szczesiul, review of *Dogwalker,* p. 168.
Los Angeles Times, September 11, 2001, Michael Harris, "Stories with a Charming Weirdness," p. E3.
New York Times, August 26, 2001, Rob Walker, review of *Dogwalker,* p. 20.

Publishers Weekly, July 23, 2001, review of *Dogwalker,* p. 48.
Review of Contemporary Fiction, summer, 2002, D. Quentin Miller, review of *Dogwalker,* p. 240.
Times (London, England), September 8, 2001, review of *Dogwalker,* p. 10.
Village Voice, August 15-21, 2001, Douglas Wolk, "Rebel without Paws," p. 133.

OTHER

BookBrowser.com, http://www.bookbrowser.com/ (October 6, 2001), interview with Arthur Bradford.
Identity Theory, http://www.identitytheory.com/ (March 5, 2002), Robert Birnbaum, "Interview: Arthur Bradford.*"

*   *   *

BRADFORD, Richard (Roark) 1932-2002

OBITUARY NOTICE—See index for *CA* sketch: Born May 1, 1932, in Chicago, IL; died of lung cancer March 23, 2002, in Santa Fe, NM. Editor, screenwriter, and author. Bradford is remembered primarily as the author of the novel *Red Sky at Morning,* a coming-of-age story that was compared by some reviewers to J. D. Salinger's *The Catcher in the Rye.* A graduate of Tulane University where he received his B.A. in 1952, Bradford spent the 1950s as a staff writer for the New Mexico State Tourist Bureau and then as an editor for the New Orleans Chamber of Commerce. In the early 1960s he continued working as an editor for Zia Co. in Los Alamos, New Mexico before becoming a research analyst in Santa Fe at the New Mexico Department of Development. Bradford completed *Red Sky at Morning* while working as a screenwriter for Universal Pictures, a job he left in 1970. His first novel was followed in 1973 with the less-critically successful *So Far from Heaven.* Suffering from writers block, Bradford never penned another novel, instead making his living as a medical transcriber and as a freelance book reviewer and contributor of humorous articles to various periodicals.

OBITUARIES AND OTHER SOURCES:

BOOKS

Writers Directory, 16th edition, St. James Press (Detroit, MI), 2001.

PERIODICALS

Los Angeles Times, March 29, 2002, p. B12.
New York Times, March 30, 2002, p. A15.
Washington Post, March 28, 2002, p. B7.

*   *   *

BRASSLOFF, Audrey 1934-

PERSONAL: Born 1934. *Education:* Earned B.A.,
Ph.D.

ADDRESSES: Agent—c/o St. Martin's Press, 175 Fifth
Ave., New York, NY 10010.

CAREER: University of Salford, Department of
Modern Languages, senior lecturer in Portuguese.

WRITINGS:

(Editor, with Wolfgang Brassloff) *European Insights:
    Postwar Politics, Society, Culture,* Elsevier Sci-
    ence (New York, NY), 1991.
*Religion and Politics in Spain: The Spanish Church in
    Transition, 1962-96,* St. Martin's (New York, NY),
    1998.

SIDELIGHTS: Audrey Brassloff, a scholar of Iberian
linguistics and religion, published two books in the
1990s. In 1991Brassloff teamed with Wolfgang Brassloff to edit *European Insights: Postwar Politics,
Society, Culture,* an examination of the various issues
that have affected the European continent since the
end of World War II. The book is a comprehensive
analysis, not focused on a single issue or nation, and
deals with political and economic issues, literature,
social changes, and the effects of the media. Brassloff
begins the book with an introductory chapter on the
various European economic developments since the
war. The editors further dissect these themes based on
the specific national or regional effects on France,
Italy, Spain, and the German-speaking regions of
Europe. Although they discuss historical issues, the
editors claim to do so only to illustrate the present
condition of Europe, and, in certain circumstances, to

predict what lies ahead. Richard Jurasek, a critic for
the *Modern Language Journal,* offered a mixed review
of *European Insights.* Although he called the effort
"ambitious and wide-ranging," Jurasek felt that "the
final effect is scattered and diffuse" and that it would
not provide much new material for experts on the
covered themes and nations.

In 1998 Brassloff published *Religion and Politics in
Spain: The Spanish Church in Transition, 1962-96.*

BIOGRAPHICAL AND CRITICAL SOURCES:

PERIODICALS

Catholic Historical Review, April, 1999, Jose M.
    Sanchez, review of *Religion and Politics in Spain:
    The Spanish Church in Transition, 1962-96,*
    p. 317.
Journal of Church and State, autumn, 2000, Paul Lar-
    son, review of *Religion and Politics in Spain,*
    p. 862.
Modern Language Journal, summer, 1994, pp. 246-
    247.
Times Literary Supplement, April 2, 1999, William J.
    Callahan, review of *Religion and Politics in Spain,*
    p. 8.*

*   *   *

BRAUN, Matt 1932-
(Warren Burke, Tom Lord)

PERSONAL: Born November 15, 1932, near Elk City,
OK; married Bettiane Shumska, 1969. *Education:* Attended military academies at Bartlesville and Clar-
emore, OK; Florida State University, B.A.
(journalism), 1955.

ADDRESSES: Agent—Richard Curtis, 171 East
Seventy-Fourth St., New York, NY 10021.

CAREER: Journalist and writer. *Military service:* U.S.
Army, 1955-57, ranger, taught survival training at Fort
Benning, GA and Fort Stewart, GA; attained rank of
first lieutenant.

MEMBER: Western Writers of America (member of board of directors).

AWARDS, HONORS: Spur Award for Best Historical Novel, Western Writers of America, for *The Kincaids,* 1977; Stirrup Award, for best articles in *Roundup,* 1987, 1988; Festival of the West Cowboy Spirit Award; lifetime appointment as Oklahoma Territorial Marshal.

WRITINGS:

Black Fox, Fawcett (New York NY), 1972.

Mattie Silks, Popular Library (New York, NY), 1972, republished as *The Gamblers,* St. Martin's Press (New York, NY), 1997.

The Savage Land, Popular Library (New York, NY), 1973.

El Paso, Fawcett (New York, NY), 1973.

Noble Outlaw, Popular Library (New York, NY), 1975.

Bloody Hand, Popular Library (New York, NY), 1975.

Cimarron Jordan, Fawcett (New York, NY), 1975.

Kinch, Doubleday (Garden City, NY), 1975.

Buck Colter, Dell (New York, NY), 1976.

The Kincaids, Putnam (New York, NY), 1976.

The Second Coming of Lucas Brokaw, Dell (New York, NY), 1977.

Hangman's Creek, Pocket Books (New York, NY), 1979.

Lords of the Land, Dell (New York, NY), 1979.

The Stuart Women, Putnam (New York, NY), 1980, published as *This Loving Promise,* Zebra Books (New York, NY), 1984.

Jury of Six, Pocket Books (New York, NY), 1980.

Tombstone, Pocket Books (New York, NY), 1981.

The Spoilers, Pocket Books (New York, NY), 1981.

The Manhunter, Pocket Books (New York, NY), 1981.

Deadwood, Pocket Books (New York, NY), 1981.

The Judas Tree, Pocket Books (New York, NY), 1982.

(Under pseudonym Warren Burke) *The Killing Touch,* Charter Books (New York, NY), 1983.

Santa Fe, Sphere (London, England), 1983, published as *Bloodstorm,* Pinnacle (New York, NY), 1985.

(Under pseudonym Tom Lord) *Highbinders,* Avon (New York, NY), 1984.

(Under pseudonym Tom Lord) *Crossfire,* Avon (New York, NY), 1984.

(Under pseudonym Tom Lord) *The Wages of Sin,* Avon (New York, NY), 1984.

Indian Territory, Pinnacle (New York, NY), 1985.

The Brannocks, New American Library (New York, NY), 1986.

(Under pseudonym Warren Burke) *A Time of Innocence,* Walker (New York, NY), 1986.

Windward West, New American Library (New York, NY), 1987.

Rio Hondo, New American Library (New York, NY), 1987.

A Distant Land, New American Library (New York, NY), 1988.

Tenbow, New American Library (New York, NY), 1991.

Wyatt Earp, St. Martin's Press (New York, NY), 1994.

Outlaw Kingdom, St. Martin's Press (New York, NY), 1995.

Texas Empire, St. Martin's Press (New York, NY), 1996.

Doc Holliday: The Gunfighter, St. Martin's Press (New York, NY), 1997.

One Last Town, St. Martin's Press (New York, NY), 1997.

The Last Stand, St. Martin's Press (New York, NY), 1998.

Rio Grande, St. Martin's Press (New York, NY), 1998.

Gentleman Rogue, St. Martin's Press (New York, NY), 1999.

Indian Territory, St. Martin's Press (New York, NY), 1999.

You Know My Name, St. Martin's Press (New York, NY), 1999.

Bloodsport, St. Martin's Press (New York, NY), 1999.

Shadow Killers, St Martin's Press (New York, NY), 2000.

Deathwalk, St. Martin's Press (New York, NY), 2000.

Kinch Riley, St. Martin's Press (New York, NY), 2000.

Hickok and Cody, St. Martin's Press (New York, NY), 2001.

The Wild Ones, St. Martin's Press (New York, NY), 2002.

NONFICTION

The Save-Your-Life Defense Handbook, Devin-Adair (Old Greenwich, CT), 1977.

Matt Braun's Western Cooking, Contemporary Books (Chicago, IL), 1988, Caxton Printers (Caldwell, ID), 1996.

How to Write Western Novels, Writer's Digest Books (Cincinnati, OH), 1988.

Also author of the novel *Westward of the Law,* written as promotion for a major cigarette manufacturer, 1991.

ADAPTATIONS: CBS six-hour miniseries adapted from the novel *Black Fox;* TNT movie, *You Know My Name,* adapted from Braun's novel, *One Last Town.*

SIDELIGHTS: Matt Braun, author of more than forty books, is a fourth-generation westerner born near Elk City, Oklahoma. Counting pioneers, ranchers, hunters, and land barons among his ancestors, Braun, not surprisingly, was pulled in the direction of writing about the land and the history he knows so well. Braun mixes fact and fiction when writing about many of his characters, including Wyatt Earp, Jesse James, and John Wesley Hardin.

After attending college and serving in the U.S. Army, Braun met and married Bettiane Shumska. Shortly thereafter, he and his wife moved to a mountain cabin where Braun was determined to give himself a year in which to write a novel that would sell. According to Carmen Faymonville, in *Twentieth-Century American Western Writers,* Braun's first published novel, *Black Fox,* is "generally considered his best." The novel recounts the adventures of Britt Johnson, a freed slave who settles near Fort Belknap, Texas, just before the U.S. Civil War, in the hopes of rescuing his family—as well as neighbors—who have been abducted by Comanche and Kiowa Indians.

Comparing Braun's characters to those of American novelist Theodore Dreiser's, Faymonville remarked, "though determined by their environment, seek to control their destinies but finally must discover that they are always 'in bondage to something or someone.'" By the mid-1970s Braun had already published nine novels, including *Noble Outlaw, Bloody Hand, The Second Coming of Lucas Brokaw,* and *Cimarron Jordan.* Regarding *Cimarron Jordan,* reviewer Genevieve Stuttaford wrote in *Publishers Weekly,* "Braun doesn't depart from a convention." Connie Fletcher, however, in *Booklist,* called *The Second Coming of Lucas Brokaw*—a speculative novel, published the same year as *Cimarron Jordan,* in which the protagonist discovers through dream analysis and hypnosis that he has lived before—"a well-plotted, amusing novel."

Braun's tenth novel, *The Kincaids,* is set between 1871 and 1924, and tells of a family's struggles during the settlement of Oklahoma and Kansas. At this time, the advent of the railroad and the land rush displaced many Native Americans. Using pioneer diaries, maps, and newspaper reprints, Braun re-creates the town of Guthrie, Oklahoma at this turbulent time. A contributor to *Kirkus Reviews* remarked on the novel's "Believable characters and . . . swift hard plot," while a reviewer for *Booklist* commented, "There's a ring of familiarity . . . yet skill infuses new life in old plots."

In 1979 Budd Arthur, in *Booklist,* called Braun's *Hangman's Creek*—in which the character Starbuck first appears—"a fast-moving adventure yarn." *Jury of Six,* the sequel to *Hangman's Creek,* continues Starbuck's adventures and features appearances by Billy the Kid and Pat Garrett. According to Frank A. Lydic, who reviewed the novel in *Booklist,* "the tale fairly well parallels historical accounts of the era." Starbuck next returns in *Tombstone,* wherein he befriends Wyatt Earp to gain his confidence. In *Publishers Weekly,* Barbara A. Bannon noted, "the resolution isn't quite what the reader expects . . . much to Braun's credit."

A *West Coast Review of Books* reviewer described Braun's *Bloodstorm* as "a savage saga of corruption and deceit in 1880s Denver" that struck the reviewer as "less a western novel than a terrific detective yarn." In addition, after publishing three novels in 1984 under the pseudonym Tom Lord, Braun published *Indian Territory,* a post-Civil War story in which the hero, John Ryan, clashes with the management of the Texas Railroad. Paul T. Clark, reviewing the book in *Booklist,* described the story as "entertaining" and "action-filled."

Braun's novel, *The Brannocks,* is the first part of a historical series that includes *Windward West, Rio Hondo,* and *A Distant Land.* Paul T. Clark, writing in *Booklist,* stated that the novel provided "an acceptable amount of action for western fans," while a *Publishers Weekly* reviewer called the novel "well plotted" and "entertaining." *Tenbow,* however, is another Braun murder mystery that features western detective Jack Stillman. Pat Costello, writing in *Voice of Youth Advocates,* commented that Braun's evocation of detail "plays out in the reader's mind as if on a movie screen," but that the novel's pacing was "slow and deliberate."

Recent interest in the western genre inspired Braun to write a guide to the western novel. According to Martin A. Brady, in *Booklist,* Braun "is eminently qualified to opine on the many different aspects of crafting a salable book." Michael T. Marsden, in *Western American Literature,* noted: "It is downright refreshing to read a straightforward, no-nonsense account of how a successful storyteller goes about his craft." Marsden concluded, "While Braun's focus is on the Western genre, his lessons are for all popular writers."

BIOGRAPHICAL AND CRITICAL SOURCES:

BOOKS

Dictionary of Literary Biography, Volume 212: *Twentieth-Century American Western Writers,* St. James Press (Detroit, MI), 1999.
Twentieth-Century Western Writers, St. James Press (Chicago, IL), 1991.

PERIODICALS

Booklist, July 15, 1976, review of *The Kincaids,* p. 1569; January 15, 1978, review of *The Second Coming of Lucas Brokaw,* p. 796; September 1, 1979, Budd Arthur, review of *Hangman's Creek,* p. 29; June 1, 1980, Frank A. Lydic, review of *Jury of Six,* p. 1413; November 1, 1985, Paul T. Clark, review of *Indian Territory,* p. 374; May 1, 1986, Paul T. Clark, review of *The Brannocks,* p. 1281; August, 1988, Martin A. Brady, review of *How to Write Western Novels,* p. 1883.
Kirkus Reviews, April 15, 1976, review of *The Kincaids,* p. 489; January 1, 1980, review of *The Stuart Women,* p. 16.
Library Journal, September 1, 1976, Mark Neyman, review of *The Kincaids,* p. 1795.
Publishers Weekly, February 3, 1975, Genevieve Stuttaford, review of *Cimarron Jordan,* p. 76; October 10, 1977, Genevieve Stuttaford, review of *The Second Coming of Lucas Brokaw,* p. 67; January 18, 1980, Barbara A. Bannon, review of *The Stuart Women,* p. 130; February 27, 1981, Barbara A. Bannon, review of *Tombstone,* p. 148; April 18, 1986, review of *The Brannocks,* p. 64; September 16, 1988, review of *Matt Braun's Western Cooking,* p. 77.
Voice of Youth Advocates, August, 1991, Pat Costello, review of *Tenbow,* p. 168.

West Coast Review of Books, May, 1985, review of *Bloodstorm,* p. 54.
Western American Literature, summer, 1989, Michael T. Marsden, review of *How to Write Western Novels,* p. 172.

OTHER

Matt Braun Web site, http://www.mattbraun.com (September 13, 2001).*

*   *   *

BRAY, Alan 1948-2001

PERSONAL: Born October 13, 1948, in Hunslet, Leeds, England; died of heart failure, November 25, 2001. *Education:* Bangor University, B.A.

CAREER: Inland Revenue, civil servant, 1970-97; historian, author.

MEMBER: Gay Liberation Front, Gay Christian Movement (founding member), Gay History Group (founding member), Gay News Defense Committee, Gay Activists Alliance.

AWARDS, HONORS: Honorary fellow, Birkbeck College, London, 1997; *History Workshop Journal,* member of editorial collective, 1994-97.

WRITINGS:

Homosexuality in Renaissance England, Gay Men's Press (London, England), 1982, Columbia University Press (New York, NY), 1995.

Also author of "The Friend."

SIDELIGHTS: Alan Bray, as stated in his London *Times* obituary, "was a remarkable historian, whose work was characterised by great clarity of thought and language, a quiet iconoclasm and a delight in paradox." His one published book, *Homosexuality in Renaissance England,* has never been out of print, and due to its popularity was reprinted in 1995. His book, again as stated in his *Times* obituary, "revolutionised the study of sexuality by challenging the then almost universal orthodoxy in which homosexuality was seen as a timeless human condition." Through his book Bray was able to demonstrate the contradictions in the social/sexual practices of Renaissance society that, on one hand, allowed homosexuality but, on the other hand, condemned those who performed homosexual acts if and when there was a need to find scapegoats for disruptions in social standards. Bray was not only interested in homosexual issues in the early modern era of England, but was also very active—sometimes even referred to as a radical—in fighting for gay rights in his own time.

Bray was born in Hunslet, Leeds, located in the heart of Yorkshire, Britain. His family was very poor, and his mother died when Bray was only twelve. Both the poverty and his mother's death were said to influence Bray for the rest of his life. While attending college at Bangor University (in Wales), Bray became intrigued by the Anglican Catholic religion, and upon graduation he trained to become a priest. His studies at the seminary lasted only one year, however, after which he joined the Inland Revenue, the Department of the Treasury Ministry, Britain's government agency that is responsible for taxes and national insurance matters.

During his employment at the Inland Revenue, Bray quickly developed a reputation for his ability to grasp complex issues and for his shrewd management skills. He was responsible for the case involving the giant insurance company Lloyd's of London, which almost everyone predicted would end in failure. Bray beat the odds and, according to the *Times* obituary "brilliantly reached a satisfactory settlement that many had thought impossible." Bray stayed with the Inland Revenue until his early retirement in 1997.

While working at the Inland Revenue during the day, Bray spent many of his evening hours researching and writing what would become the book reviewer Jean E. Howard, writing for *Shakespeare Studies,* called Bray's "discussion of the gap between the almost hysterical condemnation of sodomy in some polemical and religious writings and evidence that sexual acts between men were, in some social circumstances, quite widespread." Bray's work would also become "the first powerful expression," according to Howard, of the contemporary idea that "at least for men, while

homoerotic activity appears to have been significant and not necessarily incompatible with marriage, it was also always dangerously shadowed by the potential charge of sodomy." In other words, while the practice of homosexuality has been widespread and quite common throughout history, the social aspects of homosexuality have fluctuated from being accepted, or at least tolerated, to being conceived as something so horrific that even Satan was unable to think of it.

Bray begins his book, explained Anne Barton for the *London Review of Books* "by trying to understand how homosexuality fitted into the mental university of the 16th and 17th centuries, approaching the past as nearly as possible in its own terms." It was during these two centuries that homosexuality was often associated with sorcery and werewolves; and as a crime, it was linked with incest, adultery, heresy, and treason. However, Bray then questions, according to Barton, "if the case against homosexuality in the Renaissance was so cataclysmically black, and the penalties so dire, how did it manage to flourish as it did, quietly but often openly, among all social classes, and not just in the wicked metropolis of London, but in rural communities and small towns?"

Bray points out that the practice of homosexuality was common between teachers and students, masters and apprentices, as well as between King James I and his favored companions. It appeared to Bray that there were seemingly two ways of looking at homosexuality. One was the practice of it, the other was the crime of it. King James himself, quoting from Barton's review, "assured his son . . . that homosexuality was one of those 'horrible crimes' that a king was 'bound in all conscience never to forgive.'" Bray points out that the king was not really a hypocrite but rather had made some "extraordinary psychological separation between sodomy," (which was unlawful) and what he himself practiced.

Howard stated, "It is hard to overestimate the importance of Bray's work. It has been crucial in establishing the difference between the hysterical discourse concerning sodomy . . . and the evidence of widespread homoerotic practice."

Bray died of heart failure at the age of fifty-three. At that time, he was living in the Notting Hill section of London with his life-long friend Graham Wilson. Before his death, he completed a manuscript on friendship, tentatively titled "The Friend."

BIOGRAPHICAL AND CRITICAL SOURCES:

PERIODICALS

Choice, April, 1983, review of *Homosexuality in Renaissance England,* p. 1206.
London Review of Books, August 18, 1983, Anne Barton, "That Night at Farnham," p. 18.
New Statesman, December 16, 1983, Christopher Hill, review of *Homosexuality in Renaissance England,* p. 39.
Shakespeare Studies, 1998, Jean E. Howard, "The Early Modern and the Homocrotic Turn in Political Criticism," p. 105.
Times Literary Supplement, October 29, 1982, Imre Salusinsky, "Disorderly Behaviour," p. 1187.

OBITUARIES:

PERIODICALS

Times (London, England), November 30, 2001, "Alan Bray, Historian of Homosexuality," p. 25.*

*   *   *

BREDSDORFF, Elias Lunn 1912-2002

OBITUARY NOTICE—See index for *CA* sketch: Born January 15, 1912, in Roskilde, Denmark; died August 8, 2002, in Copenhagen, Denmark. Educator and author. Bredsdorff is best remembered for his efforts to make more readers aware that Hans Christian Andersen's works should be read by adults as well as by children. Educated at University College, London and Copenhagen University, where he studied English, Bredsdorff opposed the Nazis and was an avid communist until Russia invaded Finland in 1939, whereupon he renounced communism. From 1939 until 1943 he taught English and literature at Vordingborg Training College in Denmark, leaving to join the underground resistance movement and to publish anti-Nazi leaflets during World War II. When the war was over, he returned to academia, lecturing in Danish at University College during the late 1940s and then joining Cambridge University in 1949. He remained at Cambridge, where he became head of the Scandinavian

department, until his retirement in 1979. During his career and after, Bredsdorff published numerous books that covered subjects ranging from literary studies and grammar textbooks to biography, and autobiography. The most well known of these is his highly influential biography *Hans Christian Andersen: The Story of His Life and Work, 1805-1975.* Bredsdorff also published other works on Andersen, including *Hans Christian Andersen: An Introduction to His Life and Works* (1987), and penned biographies of other Danish authors and on Oscar Wilde, Charles Dickens, and John Steinbeck. He also wrote the autobiographical *Min egen kurs: erindringer, 1912-1946* and *Mit engelske liv: erindringer, 1946-1979.* Bredsdorff's respected textbook *Danish: An Elementary Grammar and Reader* (1956) continued to be available in print in 2000.

OBITUARIES AND OTHER SOURCES:

BOOKS

Writers Directory, 16th edition, St. James Press (Detroit, MI), 2001.

PERIODICALS

Chicago Tribune, August 20, 2002, section 2, p. 9.
Los Angeles Times, August 20, 2002, p. B11.
New York Times, August 19, 2002, p. A5.
Times (London, England), August 16, 2002.
Washington Post, August 21, 2002, p. B6.

*   *   *

BRIDGES, Kate

PERSONAL: Born in Ontario, Canada; married: children: one.

ADDRESSES: Home—Toronto, Ontario, Canada. *Agent*—c/o Author Mail, Harlequin Books, 225 Duncan Mill Road, Don Mills, Ontario, Toronto M3B 3K9, Canada. *E-mail*—kate@kbridges.com.

CAREER: Nurse in neonatal intensive care; researcher and writer for a television design program; author.

WRITINGS:

The Doctor's Homecoming, Harlequin (Toronto, Ontario, Canada), 2002.

Luke's Runaway Bride, Harlequin (Toronto, Ontario, Canada), 2002.

The Midwife's Secret, Harlequin (Toronto, Ontario, Canada), 2003.

SIDELIGHTS: Kate Bridges grew up on a fifty-acre farm in Ontario where she learned to appreciate nature. One of her favorite pastimes during her teenage years was to immerse herself in romantic novels. Her current profession as a fulltime novelist combines those early loves of the outdoors and romance to create historic western romances filled with adventures of the men and women who ventured forth into the wild open frontiers of pre-twentieth-century North America.

Bridges, although praised by a ninth-grade English teacher for her writing, did not always want to be a writer. She first worked for several years as a Toronto hospital nurse in the neonatal intensive care unit, where she tended critically ill newborn babies. Later, after going back to college for a second degree in interior design and architecture, she went to work for a local television station where she worked as a researcher and a writer for a home-and-garden program. At the television station she worked with a team of writers and after a while became discontented with the final results of her efforts. In an interview posted on the Harlequin Web site, Bridges stated: "When I worked in television, brainstorming was always done as a group effort and creativity got diluted; no one's voice stood out." It was at this time that she decided to take the plunge: leave her job and try her hand as a freelance writer. In the Harlequin interview, Bridges said: "As a novelist I create the characters and conjure the juicy plots. It's risky for this reason, but that's part of the thrill."

Bridges focuses her stories on people living before the 1900s in frontier settings in North America. She is attracted to the locale because of her own background of living in very rural settings such as in the Rocky Mountains. As for the time period, she reported in her Harlequin interview: "I like this era because of the hardworking pioneer spirit of the men and women who tamed the West. . . . It's fascinating to research because of the handful of people who sparked the changes, and because there was a lot more freedom in the West than in the Eastern cities."

Bridges's early experiences as a nurse provided her with material for her first novel, *The Doctor's Homecoming.* The story centers on Emma Sinclair, a young woman who falls in love with Wyatt Barlow, but is driven away by the history of feuds between their two respective families. Emma goes away to school after Wyatt lies to her about his feelings for her. She returns home after a sixteen-year absence, planning a short visit before setting up her medical practice somewhere else. Wyatt has, in the meantime, married another woman, believing that Emma would never return. His wife has since died, and now his daughter has fallen in love with Emma's younger brother.

It is through the struggling teenage love of her brother and Wyatt's daughter that Emma and Wyatt renew their relationship. A *Publishers Weekly* reviewer called Bridges's first novel "a delightful read . . . that is likely to satisfy most fans of western romances."

Bridges has also written two romances. *Luke's Runaway Bride* focuses on two young lovers who run away from high society to a small, rundown town in Wyoming where their romance blossoms. *The Midwife's Secret* is set in the mountains in Alberta. The protagonist of this 2003 novel moves to a tourist town to start a new life and brings with her a secret past which is soon matched by that of the man she ultimately falls in love with.

Bridges lives in Toronto with her husband—her college sweetheart—their child, and a menagerie of pets.

BIOGRAPHICAL AND CRITICAL SOURCES:

PERIODICALS

Publishers Weekly, January 28, 2002, review of *The Doctor's Homecoming,* p. 277.

OTHER

eharlequin.com, http://www.eharlequin.com/ (July 6, 2002), "An Interview with Kate Bridges."*

BRISTOL, Michael D. 1940-

PERSONAL: Born 1940. *Education:* Yale University, A.B.; Princeton University, Ph.D.

ADDRESSES: Office—McGill University, 845 Sherbrooke St., West Montreal, Quebec, Canada H3A 2T5.

CAREER: McGill University, professor of renaissance literature. Also taught at Princeton University and University of Illinois.

AWARDS, HONORS: David Thomson Award for Excellence in Graduate Supervision and Teaching; Charles Scribner fellowship; George McLean Harper fellowship; SSHRC research grant/research time stipend; National Endowment for the Humanities/Folger Library long-term fellowship.

WRITINGS:

Carnival and Theater: Plebeian Culture and the Structure of Authority in Renaissance England, Methuen (New York, NY), 1985.
Shakespeare's America: America's Shakespeare: Literature, Institution, Ideology in the United States, Routledge (New York, NY), 1990.
Big-Time Shakespeare, Routledge (New York, NY), 1996.
(Editor, with Arthur F. Marotti) *Print, Manuscript, and Performance: The Changing Relations of the Media in Early Modern England,* Ohio State University Press (Columbus, OH), c. 2000.
(Essayist) *Shakespeare in Performance,* St. Martin's Press (New York, NY), 2000.
(Editor, with Kathleen McLuskie) *Shakespeare and Modern Theatre: The Performance of Modernity,* Routledge (New York, NY), 2001.

SIDELIGHTS: Writer, essayist, and editor Michael D. Bristol embraced the challenge of explaining the sociology of theater in English Renaissance in his book *Carnival and Theater: Plebeian Culture and the Structure of Authority in Renaissance England.* *Choice*'s R. P. Griffin, "highly recommended" the work "for scholars, critics, and advanced students." John Wilders, a reviewer in *History and Theatre,* commended Bristol for his treatment of *Dr. Faustus* stating that Bristol "makes better sense than anyone of the clowning." Wilders insisted that Bristol's true skill is best illustrated "when he is dealing with relatively simple plays such as *Locrine,* and *The Merry Devil of Edmonton.*" *Encounter* reviewer Richard Maine called the book "too lively to be dull."

According to Bryan N. S. Gooch, a reviewer in *Canadian Literature,* Bristol's book *Shakespeare's America, America's Shakespeare: Literature, Institution, Ideology in the United States,* "looks at Shakespeare as a cultural 'given' in the United States, and takes account of the dramatist's place in the socio-economic-artistic-critical milieu." *Library Journal*'s Bryan Aubrey called *Shakespeare's America, America's Shakespeare* "a learned book about the relationship between Shakespeare and American political culture." In the *London Review of Books* Terence Hawkes commended Bristol for presenting a work that has "a much harder-hitting and more consciously stressed political dimension" than similar works, and noted that Bristol's "concrete detail enlivens the story."

Bristol addresses Shakespeare's "celebrity" in his book *Big-Time Shakespeare.* London *Observer*'s William Montgomery commented that Bristol "reminds us that Shakespeare's plays are survivors of a fiercely competitive marketplace." Jonathan Bate, a reviewer in *New Statesman,* applauded Bristol for his "brave attempt to go into new territory" with treatments of Shakespeare's plays. Grace Ioppolo, in the *Times Literary Supplement,* called Bristol's satire "sharp and funny." Ioppolo stated that Bristol "takes readers on an intellectually thrilling ride through Shakespearean reception, as practiced by literary theorists and . . . showbiz producers."

BIOGRAPHICAL AND CRITICAL SOURCES:

PERIODICALS

Canadian Literature, spring, 1992, Bryan N. S. Gooch, "Production and Interpretation," pp. 192-193.
Choice, April, 1986, R. P. Griffin, review of *Carnival and Theater: Plebeian Culture and the Structure of Authority in Renaissance England,* p. 1210.
Encounter, July, 1986, Richard Maine, review of *Carnival and Theater,* pp. 49-50.

Libraries & Culture, summer, 2002, Dolora Chapelle Wojciehowski, review of *Print, Manuscript, and Performance: The Changing Relations of the Media in Early Modern England,* p. 277.

Library Journal, January, 1990, Bevan Aubrey, review of *Shakespeare's America: America's Shakespeare: Literature, Institution, Ideology in the United States,* p. 108.

Observer (London, England), October 13, 1996, William Montgomery, review of *Big-Time Shakespeare,* p. 18.

London Review of Books, February 22, 1990, Terence Hawkes, "Bardbiz," pp. 11-13.

New Statesman, October 11, 1996, Jonathan Bate, review of *Big-time Shakespeare,* p. 46.

Notes & Queries, June, 2001, Scott Nixon, review of *Print, Manuscript, and Performance,* p. 177.

Review of English Studies, November, 2001, H. R. Woudhuysen, review of *Print, Manuscript, and Performance,* p. 562.

Sixteenth Century Journal, summer, 2001, Gregory Bak, review of *Print, Manuscript, and Performance,* p. 552.

Times Literary Supplement, July 18, 1986, John Wilders, "The People and The Play," p. 790; June 19, 1998, Grace Ioppolo, "More Cannon Fire Against the Canon," p. 32.*

*   *   *

BROCK, Rita Nakashima 1950-

PERSONAL: Born April 29, 1950, in Fukuoka, Japan; moved to United States, 1956; daughter of Clemente Morales Torres and Ayako Nakashima; stepdaughter of Roy Grady Brock; married Tommy Charles Douglas, April 15, 1980 (divorced May, 1982). *Education:* Chapman University (Orange, CA), B.A., 1972; Claremont Graduate School of Theology, M.A., 1981, Ph. D., 1988; attended graduate study at University of Basel and Ecumenical Studies Center of the World Council of Churches. *Politics:* Democrat. *Religion:* Christian Church (Disciples of Christ). *Hobbies and other interests:* Downhill skiing, painting, reading.

ADDRESSES: Office—Bunting Fellowship Program, 34 Concord Avenue, Cambridge, MA 02138.

CAREER: Instructor, Claremont College, Claremont, CA, 1977-80; instructor, Scripps College, Claremont, CA, 1980-81; instructor, Valparaiso University, Val-

paraiso, IN, 1983-84; director of women's studies, Stephen's College, Columbia, MO, 1984-89; assistant professor, Pacific Lutheran University, Tacoma, WA, 1989, 1990; professor, Hamline University, St. Paul, MN, 1990-97; director, Bunting Fellowship Program, Radcliffe Institute, Cambridge, MA, 1997—. Member, board of directors, Starr King School, Berkeley, CA, 1991—; Division of Overseas Ministries, Indianapolis, IN, 1996-97, Common Global Ministries, Cleveland, OH.

MEMBER: American Academy of Religion.

AWARDS, HONORS: Publisher's Award, 1988, for *Journeys by Heart: A Christology of Erotic Power;* Press Award, 1997, for *Casting Stones: Prostitution and Liberation in Asia and the United States.*

WRITINGS:

(With Rebecca Ann Parker) *Proverbs of Ashes: Violence, Redemptive Suffering, and the Search for What Saves Us,* Beacon Press (Boston, MA), 2001.

(With Susan Thistlethwaite) *Casting Stones: Prostitution and Liberation in Asia and the United States,* Fortress Press (Minneapolis, MN), 1996.

Journeys by Heart: A Christology of Erotic Power, Crossroads Press (New York, NY), 1988.

Setting the Table: Women in Theological Conversation, Chalice Press (St. Louis, MO), 1995.

SIDELIGHTS: A leading scholar of feminist theology and women's studies, Rita Nakashima Brock began questioning the theology of the cross early in her theological studies, when she worked with high-school students who told her of violence in their lives.

Brock became increasingly convinced that "Christianity could not promise healing for victims of intimate violence as long as its central image was a divine parent who required the death of his child." She maintains that the orthodox doctrine of God so loving the world that he gave his only begotten son and God's calling for Jesus' obedience and sacrificial death on the cross to atone for the world's sins is actually a theology that sanctions violence. In her first book, *Journeys by Heart: A Christology of Erotic Power,* Brock argues that sacrifice theology essentially makes God a child abuser.

Brock acknowledges that her work is troubling, even heretical, to many; fundamentalists have called her the anti-Christ. Mary Ellen Ross, writing in *Theology Today,* generally agreed with the author's premises: "I found this work strongest when it was most concrete and concentrated on family dynamics and the many ways the divine family of Father, Son, and Holy Ghost both reflects and reinforces abusive human family relationships. . . . Analyzing the problems of patriarchy is easier than creating solutions, for our immersion in patriarchal structures make imagining alternatives difficult. . . . This book will have broad appeal. Brock presents her ideas in an accessible way, and her theology of child abuse should interest anyone—lay person, cleric, or academic—who wants to know more about the relationship of religion to feminism."

In *Casting Stones: Prostitution and Liberation in Asia and the United States,* Brock and coauthor Susan Thistlethwaite examine the Asian sex trade and the responsibility of both the Buddhist and Christian hierarchies that permit it. "Evil," they write, "should be reconceived as whatever increases human helplessness, reinforces or inflicts pain without a healing purpose, and/or creates separation from relationships of love and nurture. Those three things—helplessness, pain, and separation—define evil as it is experienced by those exploited by the sex industry."

In a review for *Women's Review of Books,* Lillian Robinson noted that "*Casting Stones* is particularly strong in making connections between the military as masculine mindset and as economic force. The book underscores causal relationships between local and transnational economies—national planning mechanisms, multinational corporations, international lending agencies—and the sex trade. Its authors observe that, lacking restrictions on unfair competition and any kind of protective labor laws, 'the sex industry is one of the last bastions of pure capitalism.'" "The temptations of market economic theory," the authors conclude, "are to reduce every aspect of human life to its value in the marketplace. . . . The way in which certain economic systems contribute to human sin is to institutionalize the lack of care in a society and to make the consequences of this lack of care invisible."

In *Proverbs of Ashes: Violence, Redemptive Suffering, and the Search for What Saves Us,* Brock and co-author Rebecca Parker write alternate chapters to show how emphasizing Christ's obedience to God and

sacrifice on the cross sanctions violence and exacerbates its effects, condones silence about the abuse of human beings, and hinders any process of recovery. Their own experiences also led to questioning. Parker was sexually abused as a child but repressed the memory, trying to be the self-sacrificing Christian her Methodist family valued. Brock, part Japanese, faced racism and a sometimes violent father and could not find in church anything to support her conviction that she was not bad. In neither of their cases was there a place in the church for a child who was experiencing violence.

The authors do, however, still believe that there is a saving message in Christianity, involving the building of community, working to change unjust systems, being and having steady witnesses (people who are capable of facing violence straight on and supporting those who do), and actively thinking through theology.

Steven Schroeder praised *Proverbs of Ashes* in *Booklist,* noting, "The three sections of their book correspond to Lent, Pentecost, and Epiphany; this organization carries the text from suffering to presence, thereby presenting the argument in the order of the liturgical year. Within that continuum, which sustains theological reflection, Brock and Parker also tell the book's many particular stories beautifully. Furthermore, they report that their friendship made the book possible. Indeed, that friendship breathes in its pages as it pronounces good news for readers of all faiths who are seeking resources for resisting violence."

In "What is 'Religion?': Definitional Disruptions and Eruptions," a paper presented by Brock and Jace G. Weaver at the 1998 annual meeting of the American Academy of Religion, Brock concluded, "These days . . . I find my own sense of religion more in line with my Japanese pragmatic roots. I am more interested in the kinds of community and ritual that come from my religious affiliation than in the ideological power of particular beliefs. I am more interested in how religious communities participate in and work for justice, both within their communities and in the larger society, than in their doctrines. I have found that committing myself to religious communities of disparate people teaches me more about my world than seeking those too much like me. While I consider myself loosely Protestant, I have found there is much to be learned from the interaction of faiths—for religions are not fixed entities, but fluid processes by which human beings create meaning and live with one another."

BIOGRAPHICAL AND CRITICAL SOURCES:

PERIODICALS

America, January, 1995, p. 30.
Booklist, October 1, 2001, Steven Schroeder, review of *Proverbs of Ashes: Violence, Redemptive Suffering, and the Search for What Saves Us,* p. 280.
Canadian Women's Studies, summer, 2000, review of *Casting Stones: Prostitution and Liberation in Asia and the United States,* p. 158.
Christianity and Crisis, December 11, 1989, Carter Heywood, review of *Journeys by Heart: A Christology of Erotic Power,* p. 381.
Journal of the American Academy of Religion, fall, 1998, review of *Casting Stones,* p. 654; summer, 1992, review of *Journeys by Heart,* p. 328.
Library Journal, November 15, 2001, Stephen Joseph, review of *Proverbs of Ashes,* p. 71.
Publishers Weekly, March 17, 1989, William Griffin, review of *Journeys by Heart,* p. 73.
Theology Today, October, 1997, review of *Casting Stones,* p. 414; July, 1989, review of *Journeys by Heart,* p. 206.
Women's Review of Books, October, 1997, Lillian Robinson, review of *Casting Stones,* p. 19.

OTHER

Harvard University Gazette Online, http://www. news. harvard.edu/gazette/ (April 16, 2002), article on Rita Brock.*

* * *

BROCKMANN, R. John 1951-

PERSONAL: Born May 25, 1951, in New York, NY; son of Robert J. (in business) and Marilyn F. (a teacher) Brockmann; married, August 28, 1994; wife's name, Sarah J. (an Episcopal priest); children: Van John, Robert John III. *Ethnicity:* "German/Irish." *Education:* Georgetown University, B.A., 1973; University of Chicago, M.A., 1974; University of Michigan, D.Arts, 1980.

ADDRESSES: Office—Department of English, University of Delaware, Newark, DE 19716.

CAREER: Clarkson University, Potsdam, NY, assistant professor, 1979-80; Arizona State University, Tempe, AZ, assistant professor, 1980-84; University of Delaware, Newark, DE, professor of English, 1985—, Episcopal chaplain, 1999-2001. Ordained Episcopal priest; Bear-Glasgow Church without Walls, priest in charge, 1997-99.

MEMBER: Society for Technical Communication (fellow), National Maritime Historical Society, Association of Computing Machinery, Society of St. Francis (member of Third Order).

AWARDS, HONORS: Award from National Council of Teachers of English, 1984; Rigo Award, Association of Computing Machinery, for a collection of essays.

WRITINGS:

Writing Better Computer Documentation: From Paper to Hypertext, John Wiley (New York, NY), 1990.
From Millwrights to Shipwrights to the Twenty-first Century: Historical Considerations of American Technical Writing, Hampton Press (Creskill, NJ), 1998.
Exploding Steamboats, Senate Debates, and Technical Reports: The Convergence of Technology, Politics, and Rhetoric in the Steamboat Bill of 1838, Baywood Publishing (Amityville, NY), 2002.

WORK IN PROGRESS: The Rhetorical Dance of Nineteenth-Century Steamboat and Railroad Accident Investigations; research for *The Antebellum Colossus of New Jersey: Commodore Robert F. Stockton.*

BIOGRAPHICAL AND CRITICAL SOURCES:

PERIODICALS

Technical Communication, August, 1999, Charles R. Crawley, review of *From Millwrights to Shipwrights to the Twenty-first Century: Historical Considerations of American Technical Writing,* p. 396.

BROUGHTON, Trev Lynn 1959-

PERSONAL: Born 1959.

ADDRESSES: Agent—c/o Author Mail, Routledge, 29 West 35th St., New York, NY 10001.

CAREER: University of York, York, England, instructor in women's studies.

WRITINGS:

(Editor, with Linda Anderson) *Women's Lives/Women's Times: New Essays on Auto/Biography,* State University of New York Press (Albany, NY), 1997.

(Editor and author of introduction, with Joseph Bristow) *The Infernal Desires of Angela Carter: Fiction, Femininity, Feminism,* Addison-Wesley (Reading, MA), 1997.

(Editor with Ruth Symes) *The Governess: An Anthology,* St. Martin's (New York, NY), 1998.

Men of Letters, Writing Lives: Masculinity and Literary Auto/Biography in the Late-Victorian Period, Routledge (New York, NY), 1999.

SIDELIGHTS: Trev Lynn Broughton teaches women's studies at the University of York in England, and her studies focus on on "life writing" and on "Victorian masculinities." *Women's Lives/Women's Times: New Essays on Auto/Biography* reveals how autobiographies can be used in women's studies; *The Infernal Desires of Angela Carter: Fiction, Femininity, Feminism* examines the work of the polemical fiction writer who burst upon the British literary scene in the 1960s. Carter explores erotic fantasy, sexual fetishism, and women's desires in stories that contain elements of myth, fairy tale, and Gothic horror. She was renowned for her style, her subversive wit, and her commitment to feminist themes. *Desires of Angela Carter* gives an overview of Carter's career and illuminates the development of her feminist philosophy. *The Governess: An Anthology* looks at the figure of the governess in fact and fiction. Topics covered include "Becoming a Governess," "A Working Life," "The Problems of the Governess Life," "Benevolence," "The Governess and National Identities," and "Fantasies of the Governess." A critic for the *Nineteenth-Century Literature* journal called *The Governess* a "splendid anthology" that is "well illustrated and thoughtfully edited." The reviewer further noted that *The Governess* would be an aid to anyone studying Victorian literature.

In *Men of Letters, Writing Lives: Masculinity and Literary Auto/Biography in the Late-Victorian Period,* Broughton studies the life-writing of men at the end of the nineteenth century. Broughton points out the men of that age were obsessed with sexual performance, as well as with professional success. *Biography*'s Herbert Sussman wrote that "Broughton's perception of Victorian masculine sexual issues is always acute, especially in noting why certain male troubles were problemized at the end of the century." Sussman also noted that "Broughton's work enlarges our awareness of auto/biography and of the construction of masculinity." Martin A. Danahay, in *Victorian Studies,* called *Men of Letters, Writing Lives* "incredibly rich."

BIOGRAPHICAL AND CRITICAL SOURCES:

PERIODICALS

Biography, fall, 1998, p. 491; winter, 2000, Herbert Sussman, review of *Men of Letters, Writing Lives: Masculinity and Literary Auto/Biography in the Late-Victorian Period,* p. 254.

Choice, September, 1999, N. Allen, review of *Men of Letters, Writing Lives,* p. 140.

Journal of Men's Studies, fall, 2001, Clinton Machann, review of *Men of Letters, Writing Lives,* p. 102.

Nineteenth-Century Literature, September, 1998, p. 265.

Times Literary Supplement, June 4, 1999, Stefan Collini, review of *Men of Letters, Writing Lives,* p. 6.

Victorian Studies, winter, 2002, Martin A. Danahay, review of *Men of Letters, Writing Lives,* p. 318.

Women's History Review, winter, 2001, Laura Marcus, review of *Men of Letters, Writing Lives,* p. 729.

*   *   *

BROUWER, J(elle) H(indriks) 1900-1981

PERSONAL: Born August 8, 1900, in Beetsterswreach, Friesland, Netherlands; died January 22, 1981, in Leeuwarden, Friesland, Netherlands. *Education:* University of Gröningen, earned doctorate.

CAREER: Writer and professor of Frisian studies. Former director, Fryske Academy, Friesland, Netherlands.

WRITINGS:

(Editor with Alistar Campbell) *The Early Frisian Studies of Jan van Vliet,* Van Gorcum (Assen, Netherlands), 1939.

(Editor with P. Sipma) *De sprekwirden fen Burmania (1614),* Van Gorcum (Assen, Netherlands), 1940.

Jan Janszoon Starter, Van Gorcum (Assen, Netherlands), 1940.

Thet autentica riocht: Met inleiding, glossen, commentaár en woordenlijst, Van Gorcum (Assen, Netherlands), 1941.

(Editor with K. Fokkema) *Specimina linguae frisiae veteris,* E. J. Brill (Leiden, Netherlands), 1950.

Fryske styl: Ynleiding to it genietsjen fan literaire moaijens oan é hân fan R. P. Sybesma ayn Boerke Thae, Van Gorcum (Assen, Netherlands), 1952.

Hedendaagse aspecten van de Friese literatuur, Laverman, 1954.

(Editor with A. Feitsma and Pieter Gerbenzon) *Waatze Gribberts bruyloft: Synoptysk mei Teweschen Hochttydt en Tewesken Kindelbehr,* Fryst Ynstitüt oan de R.U. to Grins, 1955.

(With Pieter Gerbenzon and B. H. Slicher van Bath) *Rekenboack off memoriael,* Fryst Ynstitüt oan de R.U. to Grins, 1956.

De Friese Brief, Van Gorcum (Assen, Netherlands), 1957.

Encyclopedie van Friesland, Elsevier (Amsterdam, Netherlands), 1958.

Dramás yn duodecimo: Kriich en kreauwerij yn Fryslan, Van Gorcum (Assen, Netherlands), 1959.

De Fryske fersen fan Durk Lenige en oare Makkumers (poems), Osinga, 1959.

(Collaborator) Johannes Hansen, *Frucht fan toarre groun: Fersen,* Laverman, 1960.

Dunsan: Fersen, Laverman, 1962.

(Editor with H. Schmidt) Jäns Mungard, *Dit leewent en broket kraans: Söl'ring steken üp riimen Ütssaacht en ütdön,* Laverman, 1962.

It alderhillichst gebet yn Fryske lûden, Van Gorcum (Assen, Netherlands), 1964.

(With H. T. J. Miedema) *Studies over Friese en Groningse familienamen,* Institut voor Naamkunde (Louvain, Belgium), 1965.

(With P. Sipma and Jacob Haantjes) *Oantekeningen op Gysbert Japicx wurken,* Osinga, 1966.

(Editor) Jan Janzoon Starter, *Friesche lust-hof* (Dutch folk songs), Volume I: *Teksten: Uitg naar de eerste druk,* W. E. J. Tjeenk Willink (Zwolle, Netherlands), 1966.

(Editor) Gysbert Japicx, *Fries dichter,* Stichting IVO (Amsterdam, Netherlands), 1966.

(Editor) Gysbert Japicx, *Wurken,* two volumes, Osinga, 1966.

Erling Stensgård: Freon ta Fryslân (1876-1966), Fryske Akademy, 1968.

Dalarna of Dalecarlië: Bisjoen mei Fryske eagen, Van Gorcum (Assen, Netherlands), 1970.

(With P. Sipma) *Fryske nammekunde,* Volume II: *Haedstikken ût de Fryske toponymy,* Laverman, 1972.

Contributor to *Boerke Thae* by R. P. Sybesma, Fryske Akademy, 1978.*

*　　*　　*

BROWN, Norman O(liver) 1913-2002

OBITUARY NOTICE—See index for *CA* sketch: Born September 25, 1913, in El Oro, Mexico; died October 2, 2002, in Santa Cruz, CA. Philosopher, educator, and author. During the counterculture movement of the 1960s, Brown gained a following as a philosopher who blended New Age mysticism with Freudian psychoanalysis, Marxism, and religion, often questioning the ways of Western civilization. After graduating from Balliol College, Oxford in 1936, he completed his doctoral work in the classics at the University of Wisconsin in 1942. During World War II he was assigned to the Office of Strategic Services as a research analyst. When the war was over he returned to America to teach at Wesleyan University in Connecticut and at the University of Rochester. In 1968 he joined the faculty at the University of California, Berkeley, the year that institution opened, and was eventually made professor of humanities there, retiring in 1981. Brown's books were nearly as popular with college students during the 1960s and 1970s as the works of such authors as J. R. R. Tolkien and Herman Hesse. Notable among these are *Life against Death: The Psychological Meaning of History* (1959) and *Love's Body* (1966). Though he gained a large following of people who associated themselves with the counterculture, Brown resented being associated with the sexual and drug revolution, leading instead a quiet life of introspection. While in the beginning of his career he was a Marxist, he later abandoned Marx for Freud. He was often criticized by his colleagues for favoring individual freedom and eroticism over civilization, which he found oppressive, yet he also gained many admirers in academia for his iconoclastic ideas. After his retirement, he continued to write, publishing *Apocalypse and/or Metamorphosis* in 1991.

OBITUARIES AND OTHER SOURCES:

PERIODICALS

Los Angeles Times, October 5, 2002, p. B20.
New York Times, October 4, 2002, p. C20.
Times (London, England), October 8, 2002.
Washington Post, October 6, 2002, p. C10.

* * *

BROWN, Rosemary Eleanor 1916-2001

OBITUARY NOTICE—See index for *CA* sketch: Born July 27, 1916, in Sidmouth, Devon, England; died November 16, 2001, in London, England. Musical medium and author. Brown claimed to have been contacted by some of the world's most famous composers, who channeled their works from beyond the grave through her. Brown was not well educated in music, and only had a few years of piano instruction as a girl. She had her first "vision" when she was age seven from a man she later identified as Liszt, but as a teenager took a regular job with the post office. She married in 1952 and had two children, but was widowed nine years later. In 1964 Liszt, the first of the dead composers who would spend time with her, revisited her, so Brown claimed. Other composers who came to Brown included Bach, Beethoven, Chopin and Schubert, each of whom gave her melodies to play on the piano. Contemporary composers were split on whether they believed Brown could channel the dead. Richard Rodney Bennett, a British composer, was in her corner, having received help on his own composition from Debussy via Brown. Other admirers included former Scottish Arts Council member George

Firth who, with his wife, Mary, created a charitable trust that provided enough financial support that Brown could quit her day job and concentrate on music full time. Not all the musical work she turned out was viewed as stellar, but Brown was popular in both the United Kingdom and the United States. She wrote three books detailing her meetings with the dead composers: *Unfinished Symphonies, Immortals at My Elbow* and *Look beyond Today.*

OBITUARIES AND OTHER SOURCES:

PERIODICALS

New York Times, December 2, 2001, p. A31.
Times (London, England), November 29, 2001, p. 25.

* * *

BUFALINO, Gesaulado 1920-1996

PERSONAL: Born November 15, 1920, in Comiso, Sicily, Italy; died June 14, 1996; married Giovanna Leggio, 1982. *Education:* Attended universities of Catania and Palermo.

CAREER: Istituto Magistrale di Vittoria, professor of Italian and history, 1949-75; fiction writer and translator. *Military service:* Partisan solider in World War II.

AWARDS, HONORS: Campiello Prize, 1981, for *Diceria dell'untore;* Scanno Prize, 1986; Castiglione di Sicilia, 1987; Premio Strega, 1988, for *Le memzongne delle notte.*

WRITINGS:

Diceria dell'untore, Sellerio (Palmero, Italy), 1981, translation by Stephen Satarellie published as *The Plauge-Sower,* Il Poligrafico Piemontese (Hygiene, CO), 1988.
Mueseo d'ombre (short stories; title means "Museum of Shadows"), Sellerio (Palmero, Italy), 1982.
L'amaro miele, Einaudi (Turin, Italy), 1982.

Dizionario dei personnagi di romanzo da Don Chisciotte all'Innominabile, Il Saggiatore (Milan, Italy), 1982.

Argo il cieco, ovvero i sogni della memoria, Sellerio (Palmero, Italy), 1984, translation by Patrick Creagh published as *Blind Argus; or, The Fables of the Memory,* Collins Harvill (London, England), 1988.

Cere perse (short stories; title means "Lost Faces"), Sellerio (Palmero, Italy), 1985.

(With Mario Monteverdi and Enzo Papa) *Incontro con Pietro Palma: itinerario tra le isole,* Ediprint (Siracusa, Italy), 1986.

L'uomo invaso e altre invenzione (title means, "The Possessed Man and Other Stories"), Bompiani (Milan, Italy), 1986.

Il malpensante: Lunairo dell'anno che fu, Bompiani (Milan, Italy), 1987.

(With Nunzio Zago) *Gesualdo Bufalino: la figura e l'opera,* Pungitopo (Marina di Patti, Italy), 1987.

La luce e il lutto, Sellerio (Palmero, Italy), 1988.

Le memzongne della notte, Bompiani (Milan, Italy), 1988, translation by Patrick Creagh published as *Night's Lies* (also known as *Lies of the Night*), Collins Harvill (London, England), 1990.

Saline di Sicilia, Sellerio (Palmero, Italy), 1988.

Invito alle Fêtes galantes di Verlaine, Sciardelli (Milan, Italy), 1989.

(With Giovanna Bufalino) *Il matrimonio illustrato: testi d'ogni tempo e paese scelti per norma dei celibi e memoria dei coniugati,* Bompiani (Milan, Italy), 1989.

(Coauthor) *Trittico,* Sanfilippo (Catania, Italy), 1989.

Saldi d'autunno, Bompiani (Milan, Italy), 1990.

Il guerrin meschino: frammento di un'opera di pupi, Girasole (Cantania, Italy), 1991.

L'inchiostro del diavolo, Sciardelli (Milan, Italy), 1991.

Qui pro quo, Bompiani (Milan, Italy), 1991.

Calende greche: ricordi d'una vita immaginaria (novel; title means "Greek Kalends: Memories of an Imaginary Life"), Bompiani (Milan, Italy), 1992.

Il tempo in posa: immagini di una Sicilia perduta, Sellerio (Palmero, Italy), 1992.

Lamento del vecchio puparo, Edizioni dell'Elefante (Rome, Italy), 1992.

(With Nunzio Zago) *Cento Sicilie: testimonianze per un ritratto: antologia di testi,* Nuova Italia (Florence, Italy), 1993.

Bluff di parole, Sellerio (Palmero, Italy), 1994.

Carteggio di gioventù: 1943-1950, Il Girasole (Valverde, Italy), 1994.

Il fiele ibleo, Avagliano (Cava dei Tirreni, Italy), 1995.

L'enfant du pardis: cinefilie, Salarchi immagini (Cosimo, Italy), 1996.

Tommaso e il fotografo cieco, ovvero Il patatrac (novel; title means "Tommaso and the Blind Photographer"), Bompiani (Milan, Italy), 1996.

In corpore vili: autoritratto letterario: opera postuma, Gattopardo (Massa e Cozzile, Italy), 1997.

(With others) *Conversazione con Gesaulado Bufalino: essere o riessere,* Nuova Omnicron (Rome, Italy), 1997.

Contributor to *Names and Tears and Other Stories: Forty Years of Italian Fiction,* Graywolf Press (St. Paul, MN), 1990; and *The New Italian Novel,* Edinburgh University Press (Edinburgh, Scotland), 1993.

OTHER

(Editor) Gioacchino Iacono and Francesco Meli, *Comiso ieri: immagini di vita signorile e rurale,* Sellerio (Palermo, Italy), 1978.

(Translator) Jean Giradoux, *Susanne e il pacifico,* Sellerio (Palmero, Italy), 1980.

(Translator) Madame de la Fayette, *L'amor geloso,* Sellerio (Palmero, Italy), 1981.

(Editor and translator) Ernest Renan and Jean Gieradaux, *Due preghiere,* Sellerio (Palermo, Italy), 1981.

(Author of introduction) Gustave Flaubert, *Memorie di un pazzo,* Passigli (Florence, Italy), 1983.

(Translator) Charles Baudelaire, *I fiori del male,* Mondadori (Milan, Italy), 1983.

(Translator) Terence, *I due fratelli,* Istituo nazioniale del dramma antico (Siracusa, Italy), 1983.

(Translator) Victor Hugo, *Le orientali,* Sellerio (Palmero, Italy), 1985.

(Author of text) Giuseppe Leone, *L'isola nuda: aspetti del paesaggio,* Bompiani (Milan, Italy), 1988.

(Translator) Charles Baudelaire, *Per Poe,* Sellerio (Palmero, Italy), 1988.

(Author of preface) Bruno Caruso, *Mitologia,* Lombardi (Siracusa, Italy), 1989.

(Author of text with Adriano Baccilieri) *Clemente Fava: Opere 1975-1990: Palazzo dei Diamanti, centro Attivtà Visive 10 marzo-14 aprile,* Grafis Industrie Frafiche (Bologna, Italy), 1991.

(Author of preface) Enzo Leopardi, *Il signore delle isole,* Prova d'Autore (Catania, Italy), 1991.

(Author of text, with others) *Il colore della fede: la religiosità in Salvatore Fiume,* Paoline (Cinisello Ballsamo, Italy), 1992.

(Author of preface) *La Sicilia e il cinema,* Maimone (Catania, Italy), 1993.

(Editor and author of introduction) *Matteo Maria Boiardo,* Istituto Poligrafico e Zecca dello Stato (Rome, Italy), 1995.

(Author of text) *Verga e il cinema,* Maimone (Catania, Italy), 1996.

(Author of text, with others) Maria Teresa Serafini, *Come si scrive un romanzo,* Bompiani (Milan, Italy), 1996.

(Translator) Ramon Gomez de la Serna, *Sghiribizzi,* Bompiani (Milan, Italy), 1997.

SIDELIGHTS: Gesaulado Bufalino's story "is a remarkable case of late flowering," according to Peter Hainsworth. Writing in *The New Italian Novel,* Hainsworth explained: "Whilst, on his own account, he has written stories and poems since his youth, [Bufalino] had turned sixty when he published his first novel." The book was *Diceria dell'untore,* an autobiographical work that the Sicilian schoolteacher had begun just after World War II. He left the work unfinished for decades until a Palermo editor saw the manuscript in 1971 and persuaded Bufalino to finish the draft. The resulting book, completed ten years later, was a great critical and popular success, paving the way for further Bufalino novels and stories.

Diceria dell'untore is the first-person story of a young man who, having just escaped slaughter as a World War II soldier, finds himself virtually sentenced to death when he returns home diagnosed with tuberculosis. Committed to a sanitarium, the narrator awaits his fate along with other condemned characters, including a young dancer, Marta, with whom he engages in a gallows romance. In a plot twist, the young man learns he alone will survive the disease, twisting his relationship with Marta, whose death marks the climax of the story. The author, according to *Dictionary of Literary Biography* contributor Rosetta di Pace, "Is able to capture the whole personality of his characters through their gestures. With Marta it is her gait, which still shows a trace of the trained ballerina, and which exerted a great sexual allure on the narrator."

Key to the mood of the book, as well as a theme in much of Bufalino's writing, is the interpretation of death. Typical of his style is the depiction of Marta's demise from tuberculosis. As di Pace noted, that event "is described strictly from a naturalistic perspective in all its concrete and physical horror, a presentation that underscores Bufalino's belief that physical death is the final end. He makes no allowances for the mysteries of the cosmic energy that fuels the universe as well as the human body or for that possible survival of the spirit because he equates death with eternity." As *New York Times Book Review* writer Julia Markus stated, for the soldier who invested his emotions in Marta, "his last outing [with her] and the graphic and moving scene of her death, are extraordinary. . . . The secret he keeps, that he's going to live, creates, according to the narrator, a further distance between him and his doomed lover. But to this reader, it is exactly that distancing that opens up a compassion and humanity in the young hero." Daphne Day in *Southern Humanities Review* acknowledged Marta's death scene as a "tour de force."

Diceria dell'untore claimed the Campiello Prize, and a second Bufalino novel, *Le menzongne delle notte,* took Premio Strega honors. This book recalls such models as *Thousand and One Arabian Nights* and *Canterbury Tales* in its setup of several nineteenth-century political prisoners who tell stories to pass time the night before their scheduled execution. The main characters—a student, a baron, a soldier and a poet—receive an unusual offer from their jailer: their lives will be spared if one of the prisoners reveals the name of their mysterious leader during the long night. Will one of them bend to the offer and betray "[not] an idea, but only a man," as the jailer puts it? But can they trust the jailer to honor his word after receiving the leader's name?

In a *Listener* article, Harriett Gilbert praised *Le menzonge delle notte* as "a skeptical survey of human (or, more precisely, male) beliefs, aspirations and values, a survey conducted throughout with integrity and wit. But what is revealed in the final chapter, while true to all that's preceded it, washes back to life everything up to a higher and more exciting position: one in which it is suddenly clear that scepticism may also have faith, self-knowledge, courage, and honour a sense of humour." According to Patrick McGrath, writing in *Washington Post Book World,* "the truly distinctive aspect of this dense and tantalizing short novel is that it combines political and philosophical discourse of a deeply skeptical, self-reflexive tenor . . . with a narrative zest and drive of the most traditional kind."

Tommaso e il fotografo cieco, a novel published following Bufalino's death, also won critical notice. This novel, "about the entanglement of truth and invention," in the words of *New Statesman* reviewer Lucy Roeber, centers on a man who abandons family and career to live the life of a reclusive would-be novelist. Scorning those who would draw Tommaso out, the protagonist is drawn only to Bartolomeo, the blind photographer, whose murder sends Tommaso on a search for answers. With Bufalino "[weaving] plots within plots, and [painting] characters so strange and elusive that they too are never quite real," noted Carolyn Moorehead in *Times Literary Supplement*, "the result is a book which is at the same time comic and unsettling."

BIOGRAPHICAL AND CRITICAL SOURCES:

BOOKS

Dictionary of Literary Biography, Volume 196: *Italian Novelists since World War II, 1965-1995,* Gale (Detroit, MI), 1999.
The New Italian Novel, Edinburgh University Press (Edinburgh, Scotland), 1993.

PERIODICALS

American Book Review, May-June, 1990, Lois Nesbitt, "Double Ordeal," p. 25.
Choice, December, 1991, C. Fantazzi, review of *Lies of the Night,* p. 598.
Independent, June 22, 1996, p. 12.
Kirkus Reviews, February 1, 1991, review of *Lies of the Night,* p. 119; May 1, 1993, review of *Blind Argus,* p. 544.
Listener, June 21, 1990, Harriett Gilbert, "Midnight Feasts," p. 35.
New Statesman, April 10, 2000, Lucy Roeber, "Hall of Mirrors," p. 63.
New York Times Book Review, October 30, 1988, Julia Markus, "Brothers in Fraud," p. 24; May 19, 1991, M. J. Fitzgerald, "The Scaffold Awaits," p. 12.
Observer, May 7, 2000, Scott Bradfield, "Absolutely Fabulist," p. 15.
Quill & Quire, November, 1989, Paul Stuewe, "Of Some Import," p. 25.
Southern Humanities Review, summer, 1990, Daphne Day, review *of The Plaugue-Sower,* p. 289.
Times Literary Supplement, October 9, 1981, Masolino d'Amico, "Consumptive Communities," p. 1172; October 7, 1988, Peter Hainsworth, "Sicilian Myth and Reality," p. 1096; October 12, 1991, Hains-

worth, "Consoling Paradoxes," p. 1088; July 19, 1996, Lilian Pizzichini, "Between the Cracks," p. 13; May 12, 2000, Caroline Moorehead, "Worm's-eye View," p. 22.
Washington Post Book World, April 24, 1994, Patrick McGrath, "Prisoners' Dilemma," p. 5.
World Literature Today, autumn, 1982, Joseph Siracusa, review *of Diceria dell'untore,* p. 667; summer, 1983, Siracusa, review of *Museo d'ombre,* p. 441; winter, 1987, Michela Montante, review of *Cere perse,* p. 84; summer, 1992, Montante, review of *Qui Pro Quo,* p. 492; spring, 1993, Charles Klopp, review of *Calende greche,* p. 350; winter, 1995, Charles Klopp, review of *Il Guerrin Meschino,* p. 115.

OBITUARIES:

PERIODICALS

Times (London, England), June 19, 1996, p. 23.*

* * *

BURKE, Warren
See BRAUN, Matt

* * *

BURT, Guy 1972-

PERSONAL: Born 1972; son of a science teacher and an English teacher. *Education:* Graduated from Balliol College, Oxford. *Hobbies and other interests:* Cooking.

ADDRESSES: Agent—c/o Author Mail, Ballantine Books, 201 East 50th St., New York, NY 10022.

CAREER: Teacher and writer.

AWARDS, HONORS: W. H. Smith Young Writers Award.

WRITINGS:

After the Hole (novel), Transworld (London, England), 1993, published as *The Hole,* Ballantine (New York, NY), 2001.

Sophie (novel), Transworld (London, England), 1994, Ballantine (New York, NY), 2000.

The Visitor (teleplay), Channel Four, 1999.

Dandelion Clock (novel), Transworld (London, England), 2000.

ADAPTATIONS: *The Hole* was adapted for film in 2001.

SIDELIGHTS: Guy Burt is a novelist who won acclaim with his first publication, *After the Hole,* which he published in England when he was only twenty years old. The novel features five young characters who conduct a bizarre experiment, locking themselves into an abandoned school cellar for three days. Another student, assigned to release them after the third day, fails to arrive at the appointed hour, and the trapped students soon resort to what Harriet Klausner, in *BookBrowser.com,* described as "ugly things." Klausner—in a review of the American edition of the work, published as *The Hole*—called Burt's novel "a strong psychological thriller" and recommended it to "readers who enjoy dark . . . tales of human failure." King Kaufman, in the *New York Times Book Review,* noted that although the novel falls short of William Golding's classic *Lord of the Flies,* Burt's work is still "chilling," while a critic in *Publishers Weekly* deemed the novel "intriguing." Similarly, in *Books,* a reviewer called Burt's novel "compulsive and claustrophobic."

While still a student at Balliol College, Oxford Burt followed *The Hole* with a second novel, *Sophie,* in which a young man holds a female friend captive in an abandoned house. Writing in the London *Times,* Rachel Kelly described *Sophie* as "scary" and added that Burt's prose is "tense, moody, and difficult."

Burt's third novel, *The Dandelion Clock,* tells the story of three English children in Italy who, one summer, find a wounded man in a church. The secret they share from this summer shapes their lives and their relationships with each other, haunting them long after they grow up.

BIOGRAPHICAL AND CRITICAL SOURCES:

PERIODICALS

Books, January, 1993, review of *After the Hole,* p. 19.

New York Times Book Review, December 9, 2001, King Kaufman, "Dear Diary: I'm Locked in a Basement."

Publishers Weekly, August 27, 2001, review of *The Hole,* p. 48.

Times (London, England), August 18, 1994, Rachel Kelly, "A Student of Menace," p. 13.

OTHER

BookBrowser.com, http://www.bookbrowser.com/ (February 7, 2002), Harriet Klausner, review of *The Hole.**

* * *

BUYSSE, Cyriël 1859-1932

PERSONAL: Born September 20, 1859, in Nevele, Belgium; died August 25, 1932, in Afsnee, Belgium; married Nelly Dyserinck-Tromp, 1896. *Education:* Educated in Ghent.

CAREER: Writer. Worked as a businessman in United States, 1890-93.

MEMBER: Belgian Royal Academy.

WRITINGS:

IN ENGLISH

(With Maurice Maeterlinck and Louis Dumont-Wilden) *Belgium at War,* Van Hammée (Brussels, Belgium), 1918.

OTHER

De biezenstekker (short stories), 1890.

Het recht van de sterkste (novel; title means "The Law of the Strongest"), Versluys (Amsterdam, Netherlands), 1893.

Sursum corda, 1894.

Mea culpa, 1896.

Op 't Blauwhuis, Loman & Funke (The Hague, Netherlands), 1897.

Schoppenboer, 1898.

Uit Vlaanderen (title means "From Flanders"), 1899.

'n Leeuw van Vlaanderen, Van Kampen & Zoon (Amsterdam, Netherlands), 1900.

Van arme mensen (title means "About Poor People"), Van Kampen (Amsterdam, Netherlands), 1901.

Het gezin Van Paemel (play; title means "The Van Paemel Family"), 1903.

In de natuur, Van Dishoeck (Bussum, Netherlands), 1905.

(With W. G. van Riemsdÿk) *Se non evero . . . Tooneelspel in vier bedrÿven,* F. Bohn (Harlem, Netherlands), 1905.

t'Bolleken (novel; title means "The Little Ball"), Van Dishoeck (Bussum, Netherlands), 1906.

Het leven van Roseke van Dalen (novel; title means "The Life of Rosy van Dalen"), 1906.

Lente, Van Dishoeck (Bussum, Netherlands), 1907.

Het volle leven, Van Dishoeck (Bussum, Netherlands), 1908.

Het gezin van Paemel (play), Volksdrukkerij, Hoogpoort (Ghent, Belgium), 1908.

(With Herman Teirlinck) *'K kerinner Mij,* Van Dishoeck (Bussum, Netherlands), 1909.

Het Ezelken (novel; title means "The Little Ass"), 1910.

Stemmingen (short stories), Van Dishoeck (Bussum, Netherlands), 1911.

De nachtelijke aanranding (novel; title means "The Nocturnal Aggression"), Van Dishoeck (Bussum, Netherlands), 1912.

Oorlogsvisioenen (title means "Vision of the War"), Van Dishoeck (Bussum, Netherlands), 1915.

Zomerleven (title means "Summer Life"), Van Dishoeck (Bussum, Netherlands), 1915.

De vroolijke tocht, Van Dishoeck (Bussum, Netherlands), 1915.

De roman van den schaatsenrijder, Maatschappij voor Goede en Goedkoope Lectuur (Amsterdam, Netherlands), 1918.

De twee pony's, Meulenhoff (Amsterdam, Netherlands), 1919.

Zoals het was (novel; title means "Such as It Was"), 1921.

Sususususut (play), 1921.

Det laatste ronde, Van Dishoeck (Bussum, Netherlands), 1923.

Tantes (novel; title means "Aunts"), 1924.

Uleken (novel), Van Rysberghe & Rombaut (Ghent, Belgium), 1926.

Kerels, Van Dishoeck (Bussum, Netherlands), 1927.

De schandpaal (novel; title means "The Pillory"), 1928.

De plaatsvervangende vrederechter (play), 1930.

Twee werelden (novel; title means "Two Worlds"), 1931.

Verzameld werk (collected works), seven volumes, 1974-1982.

De beste verhalen van Cyriël Buysse, Manteau (Amsterdam, Netherlands), 1987.

Contributor to periodicals, including *De Nieuwe Gids* and *Le Réveil.* Co-founder and co-editor, *Van Nu en Straks* (title means "Now and Later"), 1893.

SIDELIGHTS: Cyriël Buysse was a distinguished Belgian writer who produced both fiction and drama in Flemish. Buysse was born in 1859 in Nevele, Belgium. He received his education in Ghent, then returned home to work in his father's factory. In 1886 he left Belgium and traveled to the United States, where he remained for four months. By this time, Buysse had already commenced his literary career. In 1890, while working in the United States, he produced *Het recht van de sterkste,* a naturalistic novel relating a farmer's struggles, and upon his return to Belgium in 1903 he completed *Het leven van Roseke van Dalen,* a play about rural hardships. In subsequent works, Buysse tempered his naturalism with romanticism and a measure of humor. Country life, however, continued to be a preferred theme, particularly in novels such as *Het Ezelken* and *De nachtelijke aanranding,* both of which were published before World War I erupted across continental Europe.

After the end of World War I in 1918, Buysse continued to produce notable works, including *Tantes, Uleken,* and *De Schandpaal,* a trio of novels reflecting the schism between Belgium's older and younger generations. Buysse's other works from this period include *Zoals het was,* an autobiographical novel that recalls his experiences in his father's factory, and *Twee Werelden,* a novel that derives, at least partially, from his earlier travels in the United States. In 1932, the year after he issued *Twee Werelden,* Buysse died in Afsnee, Belgium. His various publications were collected beginning in the mid-1970s and published in seven volumes as *Verzameld werk.*

BIOGRAPHICAL AND CRITICAL SOURCES:

PERIODICALS

Ons Erfdeel, September-October, 1972, Rik Lanckrock, "'Driekoningenavond'en hulde aan Staf Bruggen," pp. 121-122; September-October, 1982, Raymond Vervliet, "Cyriël Buysse tussen historiciteit en acctualiteit," pp. 538-548; November-December, 1988, Luc Van Doorslaer, "Cyriël Buysse in Duitsland," pp. 739-748.*

C

CABAÑERO, Eladio 1930-2000

PERSONAL: Born December 6, 1930, in Tomelloso, Spain; missing and presumed dead, 2000; son of Felix Cabañero Jareño (a teacher and lawyer) and Justa López de Cabañero; married Eduarda Moro (a writer), 1992.

CAREER: Writer. Worked as a mason until 1955; worked in National Library, Madrid, Spain, 1956-68; member of staff at Editorial Taurus, Madrid, Spain, 1968-78, and Publications Division, Ministry of Culture, Madrid, Spain. Member of editorial staff, then editor-in-chief, Estafeta Literaria.

AWARDS, HONORS: Juventud prize, 1955, for "El pan"; Adonais poetry prize honorable mention, 1958, for *Una señal de amor;* Premio Nacional de Poesía, 1963, for *Marisa Sabia y otros poemas;* Premio de la Crítica for *Poesía (1956-1970).*

WRITINGS:

POETRY

Desde el sol y la anchura (title means "From the Sun and the Open Space"), Sánchez (Madrid, Spain), 1956.
Una señal de amor (title means "A Signal of Love"), Rialp (Madrid, Spain), 1958.
Recordatorio (title means "Reminder"), Taurus (Madrid, Spain), 1961.
Marisa sabia y otros poemas (title means "Wise Maria, and Other Poems"), [Madrid, Spain], 1963.
Poesía (1956-1970), Plaza y Janés (Barcelona, Spain), 1970.
Señal de amor: Antología poética 1956-1991, Libertarias (Madrid, Spain), 1992.

SIDELIGHTS: Eladio Cabañero was a notable Spanish poet who came to prominence in the 1950s. Cabañero was born in 1930 in Tomelloso, where his father worked as a teacher and lawyer and served as secretary of the local socialist party. The elder Cabañero served in the Republican Army during the final months of the Spanish Civil War; when that conflict ended he was imprisoned, tried, and executed. Cabañero's mother also received a lengthy prison sentence, and she ultimately endured three years of incarceration. During his mother's imprisonment, Cabañero lived with various relatives, including his maternal grandfather, who gave him a volume of evangelical hymns that proved immensely appealing. Despite a lack of formal schooling, Cabañero became a proficient writer and an enthusiastic reader, and in his teens, while he trained as a mason, he consumed the works of Spanish masters such as Francisco Queveda and Miguel de Cervantes. By the mid-1950s he had read works by Felix Grande, a poet who also hailed from Tomelloso. Grande's writings sufficiently inspired Cabañero to begin producing his own verses.

Upon the death of his mother in 1956, Cabañero relocated to Madrid, where he found work in the National Library and subsequently befriended various literary figures, including Jorge Camos and Luis Rosales. That same year Cabañero published his first poetry collection, *Desde el sol y la anchura,* which reveals the influence of writers ranging from Queveda to Antonio Machado. Cabañero's debut volume shows him to be a master of poetic structure and a sympathetic delineator of the human condition. "He demonstrates an exceptional mastery of form and linguistic creativity," declared Susan Rivera in the *Dictionary of Literary Biography.* "Pain, poverty, ignorance and the ability to work hard are some of the human traits that Cabañero describes." Rivera added, however, that Cabañero's poetry scarcely qualifies as social criticism. "As opposed to writing social protest poems," wrote Rivera, "Cabañero almost always tends to justify or rationalize the situation of the peasants." Rivera called *Desde el sol y la anchura* "an example of profoundly religious poetry, the result of a sincere and emotional sentiment, not of rebellion or protest but rather of pity and understanding."

In *Una señal de amor* Cabañero abandoned the formal poetics of his first collection and assumed the realistic speech and freer verse that marked his later work. "The poetic meter is liberated from the rigidity of classical forms, and it tends toward a freer, more open form that gives Cabañero's diction an air of spontaneity," wrote Rivera. "This structure reinforces the realism that . . . characterizes his writing from 1958 on." Notable poems in *Una señal de amor* include a five-part sequence in which Cabañero contemplates lost love and perseverance in the wake of that disappointment. Other key poems disclose Cabañero's Christian sensibility, which he expresses in naturalistic language and nostalgic reflection. "The settings, situations, and characters are no longer presented in archetypal or idealized versions," Rivera explained. "This book is an example of 'poetry of experience,' in which the retelling of what was experienced surpasses any sentimental evocation and results in a meditative evaluation . . . of the meaning of human existence."

Cabañero followed *Una señal de amor* with *Recordatorio,* in which he demonstrates a greater range of expression and perspective. "The title of the book seems to indicate that it is a prolongation of the nostalgic attitude that characterized his previous poetry," observed Rivera, "and such is the case in the most intense, beautiful, and lucid parts of the book." But *Recordatorio* also shows indications of Cabañero responding to life's hardships with emotions other than reluctant acceptance. Rivera conceded that "religious allusions are not lacking in this book," but she added that "Cabañero no longer reacts precisely with Christian resignation in view of the injustices of this world." Rivera was especially impressed with "Desde esta habitación," a poem wherein Cabañero proclaims that he is producing verse that he describes—in Rivera's translation—as poetry "of profound protest and pain."

Cabañero's fourth collection, *Marisa sabia y otros poemas,* constitutes an extended consideration of love. "Although the topic is present in his previous writings, it is never as relevant as it is in *Marisa sabia,*" Rivera declared. "Love replaces all Cabañero's old obsessions, and he is engrossed in personal reactions toward his feelings and in the constant elaboration of the image of the beloved." The volume includes a sequence of poems in which Cabañero revels in the joys of a romantic relationship, and it continues with a selection of verses in which the poet laments the decline of that same affair. The collection ends with more characteristically nostalgic verses in which the poet longs for his childhood.

After completing *Marisa sabia y otros poemas* in 1963, Cabañero drastically reduced his poetic output. Both *Poesía (1956-1970)* and the anthology *Señal de amor: Antología poética 1956-1991* are largely comprised of poems from his first four collections. Missing for several years, Cabañero was declared dead in 2000.

BIOGRAPHICAL AND CRITICAL SOURCES:

BOOKS

Debicki, Andrew P., *Poetry of Discovery: The Spanish Generation of 1956-1971,* University Press of Kentucky (Lexington, KY), 1982.
Dictionary of Literary Biography, Volume 134: *Twentieth-Century Spanish Poets,* Gale (Detroit, MI), 1994.

PERIODICALS

Cuadernos Hispanoamericanos, April, 1972, Manuel Ríos Ruiz, "La poesía de Eladio Cabañero," pp. 151-167; March, 1982, Lalia Adib Abdul Wahed, "Eladio Cabañero: Poeta de la realidad," pp. 660-666.*

CALDWELL, Joseph 1938-

PERSONAL: Born October 2, 1938, in Milwaukee, WI. *Education:* Attended Marquette University, Columbia University, and graduate program, Yale University School of Drama.

ADDRESSES: Agent—Sarabande Books, 2234 Dundee Road, Suite 200, Louisville, KY 40205.

CAREER: Novelist, playwright, and television actor; instructor in fiction writing at Columbia University, New York University, Hofstra University, and 92nd Street YM-YWHA, New York, NY.

MEMBER: Yaddo Artists' Colony (elected 1993).

AWARDS, HONORS: John Golden fellowships in playwriting, Yale University School of Drama (1956, 1957); American Broadcasting Company fellowship in playwriting; Rome Prize in Literature from American Academy of Arts and Letters.

WRITINGS:

In Such Dark Places, Farrar, Straus & Giroux (New York, NY), 1984.
The Deer at the River, Little, Brown (Boston, MA), 1984.
Under the Dog Star, Viking Press (New York, NY), 1987.
The Uncle from Rome, Viking Press (New York, NY), 1992.
Bread for the Baker's Child, Sarabande Books (Louisville, KY), 2001.

SIDELIGHTS: Joseph Caldwell's talent and promise as a writer were first recognized when he received two Yale University John Golden fellowships in playwriting and an American Broadcasting Company fellowship in playwriting. His plays have been produced off-Broadway and adapted into television scripts, but he is primarily known for his novels.

Caldwell's first novel, 1978's *In Such Dark Places,* received mixed reviews, although critics agreed that the book was the work of a gifted young writer. Peter S. Prescott commented in *Newsweek,* "This is a talented first novel, an honorable attempt at a significant work of fiction that I found hard to like," and went on to note that "the book offers some good characterizations, some unexpected wit, and is written in an admirably cool style."

The story follows Eugene McNiven, a gay, faltering photographer and lapsed Catholic from the Midwest, as he films a street pageant in New York City's Little Italy. As he is taking pictures of a Roman soldier he hopes to seduce, the procession dissolves into a riot that ends with the murder of the young soldier and the theft of Eugene's camera. Eugene is convinced that if he finds the young street kid who committed the theft, the film in the camera will show the murderer. Barbara A. Bannon wrote in *Publishers Weekly,* "Caldwell captures the gritty nuances of urban desolation and the accommodation people make with despair, but overburdens a frail story line."

In his next novel, *The Deer at the River,* Caldwell recreates the Biblical story of Job in a poor, rural New Hampshire setting. Noah Dubbins is a simple New England carpenter whose life is shattered when his wife goes insane. He attempts to keep his family together and remain faithful to her as crushing money problems take away all hope and almost cost him his children. A reviewer in *Kliatt Young Adult Paperback Book Guide* wrote, "The allegorical nature adds to the power of its impact, yet it is complex and often confusing. Perhaps the greatest strength of the novel is the marvelously realistic picture of rural New Hampshire upon which Caldwell stages Noah's tragedy." Paul E. Hutchison praised the novel in a review for *Library Journal,* noting, "Caldwell's writing draws its strength from imaginative similes and strongly drawn characters, rapidly creating a moving portrait of one man's family ordeal and one man's triumph."

With *Under the Dog Star* Caldwell returns to the desperate American rural life examined in *The Deer at the River.* A reviewer for the *New Yorker* called the book a "novel about greed and guilt" that follows Grady Durant's return to her family's failed dairy farm after her husband is killed while robbing a gas station. With her are her children Peter and Anne, both teenagers, and five-year-old Martha. The novel begins to revolve around a seventeen-year-old orphan, Royal Provo, whom she hires as a handyman. He is idolized by Peter and despised by Anne, who sleeps with him anyway, while Grady juggles two half-heated affairs of her own. The *New Yorker* reviewer noted that "Caldwell is good at conveying the menace implicit in his characters' misreading of their own and others' motives, and at describing creatures that manifest the changing state of the family's combustion: an old bull blocking the road, a puppy galumphing about a milking, a beheaded chicken taking one last turn around the yard." Ultimately, the money stolen by Grady's dead husband turns up, casting blame in improbable places. A contributor to *Publishers Weekly* wrote, "Despite lackluster passages, Caldwell strikes a consistently ominous tone, and his resolution is at once sharp and bittersweet."

In *The Uncle from Rome,* Michael Ruane, an undistinguished opera singer from Indiana, has come to Naples to play a minor role in an important production of *Tosca.* A request from a diva on the set gives him an offstage role as well: that of "the uncle from Rome," a fictitious character Neapolitans engage to lend status to weddings. By agreeing, Michael entangles himself in the overheated and dysfunctional life of contemporary Naples. A reviewer for *Publishers Weekly* commented, "Caldwell balances the theatrics of his plot with an understated narration, and weights his themes—the interplay of life and art—with careful, colorful observations. (Of laundry hung out to dry, for example, he writes: 'The bold emblems or the tattered banners sent out their jubilant or melancholy news, and one could tell at a glance who was favored and who was scorned by the local gods.')"

Caldwell's *Bread for the Baker's Child,* published in 2001, received strong reviews. A *Kirkus Reviews* contributor considered the book a successful work of serious literature, "As luminous and elegiac as it is probing and disquieting—and sublimely steeped in its Catholic milieu." The plot allows Caldwell ample room to explore the recurring themes of faith, sexuality, and violence that have marked his novelistic career. The story revolves around Sister Rachel, a nun who receives word that her brother Phillip has been jailed for embezzlement. She tends to her ailing mother superior in the donated mansion belonging to her order, which is soon to be disbanded due to declining numbers. A former elementary school principal, Rachel has recovered somewhat from the trauma of a fire that killed dozens of her students and their teacher, although the electroshock treatment (which Phillip paid for) that brought her out of disabling grief did so

by robbing her of her memory of the victims' names. Phillip learns a key fact of prison life when he is persuaded to feign being the lover of a younger inmate to protect the man from their cellblock's predatory leaders. Although he is himself gay and landed in jail in the first place because he stole company money to help a co-worker with AIDS who had lost his health insurance, Phillip stays aloof from his "partner" until a sadistic guard pushes him too far. Now a convicted murderer, he is moved from medium security to death row. Rachel visits him only after the death of her elderly charge, when, with her dead students' names miraculously restored to memory, she brings him solace in the form of details of a family tragedy long ago. Margaret Flanagan praised the book in *Booklist,* noting that "A disturbing undercurrent of unresolved passions ripples through this elegiac tale of tragedy and redemption," and calling it an "emotionally compelling glimpse into two shattered spirits [that] celebrates the triumph of the soul over disaster and despair."

Since the mid-1980s Caldwell has been associated with the artists' colony of Yaddo in Saratoga Springs, New York, first as a guest and more recently as an assistant to the president. In 1993 he was elected to membership in the Corporation of Yaddo, following which the frequency and length of his stays at the colony increased.

BIOGRAPHICAL AND CRITICAL SOURCES:

PERIODICALS

Advocate, January 14, 1992, Felice Picano, review of *The Uncle from Rome,* p. 87.

Kirkus Reviews, November 1, 2001, review of *Bread for the Baker's Child,* p. 1502.

Kliatt Young Adult Paperback Book Guide, January, 1986, review of *The Deer at the River,* p. 5.

Lambda Book Report, March, 1992, Michael Klein, review of *The Uncle from Rome,* p. 22.

Library Journal, November 15, 2001, Patrick Sullivan, review of *Bread for the Baker's Child,* p. 96; December, 1991, Joanna M. Buckhardt, review of *The Uncle from Rome,* p. 193; May 1, 1987, Mary K. Prokop, review of *Under the Dog Star,* p. 80.

New York Times, March 13, 1992, Herbert Mitgang, review of *The Uncle from Rome,* p. B4; June 6, 1987, Michiko Katukani, review of *Under the Dog Star,* p. N13; May 4, 1984, Christopher Lehmann-Haupt, review of *The Deer at the River,* p. C29.

New York Times Book Review, May 17, 1987, Linda Hamalian, review of *Under the Dog Star,* p. 51.

New Yorker, July 6, 1987, review of *Under the Dog Star,* p. 80; June 4, 1984, review of *The Deer at the River,* p. 133.

Newsweek, February 6, 1978, Paul Prescott, review of *In Such Dark Places,* p. 84.

Publishers Weekly, November 12, 2001, review of *Bread for the Baker's Child,* p. 96; October 25, 1991, review of *The Uncle from Rome,* p. 44; March 27, 1987, Sybil Steinberg, review of *Under the Dog Star,* p. 37; March 9, 1984, review of *The Deer at the River,* p. 100.

OTHER

Sarabande Books Online, http://sarabandebooks.org/ (April 3, 2002), article on Joseph Caldwell.

University of Delaware Library Online, http://www. lib.udel.edu/ (April 3, 2002), article on Joseph Caldwell.*

*   *   *

CAMERON, Theresa 1954-

PERSONAL: Born January 29, 1954, in Buffalo, NY. *Ethnicity:* "African American." *Education:* State University of New York—Buffalo, B.S., 1976; University of Michigan, M.U.P., 1977; Harvard University, D.Des., 1991. *Hobbies and other interests:* Housing, fundraising, sports.

ADDRESSES: Home—3301 South Terrace Rd., Tempe, AZ 85282. *Office*—School of Planning and Landscape Architecture, Arizona State University, P.O. Box 872005, Tempe, AZ 85287-2005. *Agent*—George Thompson, Box 836, 80 South Main St., Harrisonburg, VA 22801. *E-mail*—tcameron@asu.edu.

CAREER: Philip Thompson and Associates, Portland, OR, project developer, 1978-79; City and County of San Francisco, CA, planner, 1979-82; community development consultant, San Francisco, CA, 1983-85; Boston Redevelopment Authority, Boston, MA, housing analyst, 1986-89; University of Colorado—Denver, visiting assistant professor of architecture and planning and member of Diversity Task Force, 1991-

92; Neighborhood Reinvestment Corp., Boston, MA, planner, 1992-93; Cornell University, Ithaca, NY, visiting assistant professor of city and regional planning, 1993-96; University of Florida, Gainesville, assistant professor of urban and regional planning, 1996-97; Arizona State University, Tempe, assistant professor, 1997-2000, associate professor of planning and landscape architecture, 2000—. Sea Port Business Development Center, research advisor, 1978-79; Bedford Stuyvesant Restoration Corp., community development consultant, 1988-89. Canine Companions for Independence, fund-raising organizer in Colorado, 1992-93; Southside Community Center, Ithaca, NY, fund-raising organizer, 1993-95; Interagency Case Management Project, board member, 2000—; Gabriel's Angels (pet therapy organization), fund-raiser and volunteer pet therapist with abused and at-risk children, 2001—.

MEMBER: American Association of University Women, Urban Affairs Association.

AWARDS, HONORS: Fellow of Urban League, 1975-76.

WRITINGS:

Foster Care Odyssey: A Black Girl's Story (memoir), University Press of Mississippi (Jackson, MS), 2002.

Contributor to books, including *Shelter, Women, and Development: First and Third World Perspectives,* edited by H. Dandekar, George Wahr Publishing (Ann Arbor, MI), 1993. Contributor of articles and reviews to periodicals, including *Policy Studies Journal, Urban Geography, AIDS and Public Policy Journal,* and *Journal of Health and Social Policy.*

WORK IN PROGRESS: A sequel to her memoir of life in foster care; research on single-room-occupancy hotel housing for single adults and welfare reform; research on the history of housing associations in England, Canada, and the United States; research on community-based housing in the United States and England; research on environmental justice and the siting of hazardous waste materials.

SIDELIGHTS: Theresa Cameron told *CA:* "I wrote *Foster Care Odyssey: A Black Girl's Story* to deal with the shame I felt about my out-of-wedlock birth.

For much of my life, I felt like nobody's little girl. I was abandoned at birth and spent the next eighteen years as a ward of New York State. A lifetime of hollow emotions nearly eroded my soul until one day I started writing about foster care and how it shaped my life. Initially I thought I'd have very little to say, but a friend convinced me my story was worth telling. Dredging up long-dormant memories about a painful childhood was emotionally wrenching, but it helped me to overcome the shame of foster care. I wrote *Foster Care Odyssey* not only to help myself, but also to inspire others. Thousands of men, women, and children of all races and backgrounds are scarred by foster care. Through my own strong will and indomitable spirit I found the courage to persevere. I hope readers who've endured sorrow can draw strength from my book.

"To write *Foster Care Odyssey,* I forced myself to write for at least one hour every day. The State of New York long ago destroyed all records pertaining to my tenure in foster care. Furthermore, I lost contact with everyone from my youth. Thus, I had to rely on my memory, and that was a very arduous process, one that tired me physically and emotionally. For inspiration I focused on the kindness of a few thoughtful people in my youth. These included teachers, classmates, and friends who believed I would someday rise above the despair that buried me most of my life."

BIOGRAPHICAL AND CRITICAL SOURCES:

PERIODICALS

Publishers Weekly, April 8, 2002, review of *Foster Care Odyssey: A Black Girl's Story,* p. 224.

*   *   *

CAMILLE, Michael 1958-2002

OBITUARY NOTICE—See index for *CA* sketch: Born March 6, 1958, in Keighley, Yorkshire, England; died of a brain tumor April 29, 2002, in Chicago, IL. Medieval art historian and author. Camille was an influential scholar at the University of Chicago, where he studied marginalized groups like pagans and homosexuals and how they fit into medieval art. He

grew up in England, and received a scholarship to Peterhouse College, Cambridge, from which he graduated with first class honors in art history and English in 1980. He followed with his doctorate in art history from Clare Hall, Cambridge in 1985. After leaving Cambridge he moved to the University of Chicago, where he was the Mary L. Block professor of art history. Camille's first book, *The Gothic Idol: Ideology and Image-making in Medieval Art,* was published in 1989, and several others followed: *Image on the Edge: The Margins of Medieval Art; Glorious Visions: Gothic Art; Master of Death: The Lifeless Art of Pierre Remiet, Illuminator,* which received a Governor's Award from Yale University Press; *Mirror in Parchment: The Luttrell Psalter and the Making of Medieval England;* and *Monsters of Modernity: The Gargoyles of Notre Dame.* Camille was a Guggenheim fellow in 2000.

OBITUARIES AND OTHER SOURCES:

PERIODICALS

Guardian, May 16, 2002, p. 20.
New York Times, May 27, 2002, p. A15.
Times (London, England), June 5, 2002.

*   *   *

CANTALUPO, Barbara 1947-

PERSONAL: Born December 7, 1947, in Rochester, NY; daughter of Anna Dorosh; married Charles Cantalupo (a professor of English), October 29, 1988; children: Elizabeth Claire, Christopher (stepson), Alicia, Alexandra. *Ethnicity:* "Ukrainian/Sicilian heritage." *Education:* University of Rochester, A.B., 1969; State University of New York—Buffalo, M.S.W., 1973, M.A.H., 1984, Ph.D., 1988.

ADDRESSES: Office—Pennsylvania State University—Lehigh Valley, 8380 Mohr Lane, Fogelsville, PA 18051-9999; fax: 610-285-5220. *E-mail*—bax7@psu.edu.

CAREER: Pennsylvania State University—Lehigh Valley, Fogelsville, associate professor of English.

AWARDS, HONORS: Fulbright teaching fellow in Morocco, c. 1990; fellow of National Endowment for the Humanities at City University of New York Graduate Center, 1991.

WRITINGS:

(Editor) Emma Wolf, *Other Things Being Equal,* Wayne State University Press (Detroit, MI), 2002.

Contributor to books, including *Poe Studies: Dark Romanticism* and *A Companion to Poe Studies.* Contributor to periodicals, including *Journal of Contemporary Thought.* Editor, *Edgar Allan Poe Review;* past associate editor, *Bestia.*

*   *   *

CAPRON, William M(osher) 1920-2002

OBITUARY NOTICE—See index for *CA* sketch: Born July 30, 1920, in New York, NY; died October 5, 2002, in Palo Alto, CA. Economist, educator, and author. Capron was a respected economist who was an advisor for both the Kennedy and Johnson administrations. A 1942 graduate of Swarthmore College, he served in the U.S. Army's Fifth Armored Division during World War II, fighting at the Battle of the Bulge and earning a Purple Heart and Distinguished Service Cross. After the war, he went back to school and completed his master's degree in economics at Harvard University in 1948. He then joined the faculty at the University of Illinois at Urbana-Champaign, resigning in protest when the chair of the economics department was dismissed under pressure by U.S. Senator Joseph McCarthy's Un-American Activities Committee. Capron worked for the RAND Corporation during the early 1950s and then returned to teaching as an assistant professor at Stanford University. In 1962 he became a senior economist for President John F. Kennedy's Council of Economic Advisers and helped to establish the Office of Economic Opportunity; he continued working for the government under the Johnson administration until his feelings about the Vietnam War caused him to leave his post for a position at the Brookings Institution. From 1969 until his retirement in 1990, Capron taught at the John F. Kennedy School of Government at Harvard; he also served as associate dean there and in 1971 edited the book *Technological Change in the Regulated Industries.* After his retirement Capron kept busy by advising governments all over the world on their economic policies.

OBITUARIES AND OTHER SOURCES:

BOOKS

Who's Who in America, 41st edition, Marquis (Wilmette, IL), 1980.

PERIODICALS

San Francisco Chronicle, October 12, 2002, p. A19.
Washington Post, October 14, 2002, p. B6.

*   *   *

CARR, Alice
See MYERS, Amy

*   *   *

CATLING, Patrick Skene 1925-

PERSONAL: Born February 14, 1925, in London, England; immigrated to United States; naturalized U.S. citizen, 1956.

ADDRESSES: Agent—Gillan Aitken, 17 Belgrave Place, London SW1, England.

CAREER: Writer. Worked on editorial staff of *Baltimore Sun,* Baltimore, MD, beginning 1947; journalist for *Manchester Guardian, Punch,* and *Newsweek.*

WRITINGS:

The Chocolate Touch (children's novel), illustrations by Mildred Coughlin McNutt, Morrow (New York, NY), 1952, new edition, illustrated by Margot Apple, 1979.

Better than Working (memoir), Macmillan (New York, NY), 1960.

The Right End of the Stick, Faber (London, England), 1963.

Tourist Attraction (novel), Macmillan (New York, NY), 1963.

The Experiment (novel), Trident Press (New York, NY), 1967.

The Exterminator (novel), Trident Press (New York, NY), 1969.

Freddy Hill: The Life and Loves of a Modern Man of Pleasure, Simon & Schuster (New York, NY), 1969.

The Catalogue, Simon & Schuster (New York, NY), 1970.

The Surrogate, 1972.

Best Summer Job, Simon & Schuster (New York, NY), 1974.

Secret Ingredients, Hart-Davis McGibbon (London, England), 1976.

Bliss Incorporated, Weidenfeld & Nicolson (London, England), 1976.

Jazz, Jazz, Jazz, Blond & Briggs (London, England), 1980, St. Martin's (New York, NY), 1981.

John Midas in the Dreamtime, illustrations by Jean Jenkins Lower, Morrow (New York, NY), 1986.

Contributor to periodicals.

SIDELIGHTS: Patrick Skene Catling is a writer whose works include novels, memoirs, and stories for children and who has written for various periodicals, including the *Manchester Guardian* and *Punch.* He began his career as a reporter with the *Baltimore Sun* in the late 1940s. In 1952 he published his first book, *Chocolate Touch,* a children's tale about a boy named John Midas whose desire for chocolate results in astonishing adventures, especially after he spends a magic coin and finds that all his food turns into chocolate. A *Kirkus Reviews* critic noted Catling's "tricks with alliteration," and Jeanne Massey wrote in the *New York Times* that Catling "has deftly given a modern twist" to the King Midas legend. A *New York Herald Tribune Book Review* critic, meanwhile, proclaimed *Chocolate Touch* "a hilarious success with children."

Catling followed *Chocolate Touch* with *Better than Working,* a memoir about his experiences as a writer at the *Baltimore Sun* and other periodicals. *Guardian*

reviewer Richard West wrote that Catling's recollections "are often hilarious," and J. F. Fixx commented in *Saturday Review* that Catling possesses "a keen eye for the absurd."

In 1963 Catling published *Tourist Attraction,* a comic novel about commercialism and romance in England and America. Prominent characters in the tale include a libidinous public-relations expert and a wealthy American widow determined to make a fresh start in England. The novel's more outrageous jibes at capitalist enterprise, meanwhile, include exploitative and misleading appeals aimed at curious, and gullible, tourists. Martin Levin, writing in the *New York Times Book Review,* affirmed that "the funny part of [*Tourist Attraction*] details the grosser commercial aspects of Britain and America," while a *Times Literary Supplement* critic declared that Catling produces "savage and . . . effective comedy."

Catling's next novel, *The Experiment,* relates the unlikely activities that ensue when a small college establishes a sex institute. Prostitutes, teachers, and local citizenry are soon performing sex acts on behalf of the institute, and some of those acts are even filmed. A *Times Literary Supplement* critic found the 1967 novel "unsubtle," and Martin Levy wrote in the *New York Times Book Review* that Catling's "mixture of perspectives . . . negate one another." A *Best Sellers* reviewer was even more vehement in expressing disapproval, dismissing *The Experiment* as "ephemeral trash." But R. H. Donahugh wrote in *Library Journal* that the novel is "often terribly funny" and concluded that it is "great fun."

In his novel *The Exterminator* Catling depicts a pest-control worker who must contend with his pregnant wife, who is quickly succumbing to the midsummer; a manic supervisor who is convinced that rats are undertaking world domination; and the rats themselves, who exhibit considerable cunning and resourcefulness. *Library Journal* reviewer P. F. Micciche dismissed *The Exterminator* as "a mediocre novel," but a *Times Literary Supplement* critic described it as "diverting . . . and horrifying" and added that Catling explores various themes "to admirable effect." Phyllis Meras wrote in *Book World* that *The Exterminator* "haunts the imagination" and affirmed that it is "skillfully told."

BIOGRAPHICAL AND CRITICAL SOURCES:

PERIODICALS

Book World, September 7, 1969.
Guardian, April 14, 1961.
Kirkus Reviews, July 1, 1952.
Library Journal, October 15, 1960; July, 1969.
New York Herald Tribune Book Review, September 14, 1952.
New York Times, October 19, 1952.
New York Times Book Review, January 5, 1964; August 24, 1969; March 14, 1971; June 30, 1974.
Punch, April 30, 1969; November 12, 1969; November 25, 1970; January 9, 1980.
Saturday Review, September 20, 1952; December 10, 1960; October 11, 1969.
Springfield Republican, November 6, 1960.
Times Literary Supplement, February 11, 1965; May 22, 1969; May 19, 1972; April 2, 1976; August 20, 1976; February 29, 1980.*

*   *   *

CA'ZORCI, Giacomo 1898-1960
(Giacomo Noventa, Emilio Sarpi)

PERSONAL: Born March 31, 1898, in Noventa di Piave, Italy; died of a brain tumor, July 4, 1960; son of Antonio and Emilia Ceresa Ca'Zorci; married Franca Reynaud, April 16, 1933; children: Alberto, Antonio, Emilia. *Education:* University of Turin, earned law degree, 1923. *Religion:* Roman Catholic.

CAREER: Poet and journalist. Worked briefly as an attorney. *La riforma letteraria* (journal), coeditor, 1936-38. Founder of *La Gazetta del Nord* (newspaper), 1946-47, *Il Socialista Moderno* (periodical), 1949-50, and *Il Giornale dei Socialisti* (periodical), 1951.

AWARDS, HONORS: Viareggio prize, 1956, for *Versi e poesie.*

WRITINGS:

UNDER NAME GIACOMO NOVENTA

Versi e poesie (poems; title means "Verse and Poems"), Edizioni di Comunità (Milan, Italy), 1956, revised and enlarged, Mondadori (Milan, Italy), 1975.

Il vescovo di Prato (selected journalism; title means "The Bishop of Prato"), Saggiatore (Milan, Italy), 1958.
Nulla di nuovo (selected journalism; title means "Nothing New"), Saggiatore (Milan, Italy), 1960.
Il re e il poeta, Scheiwiller (Milan, Italy), 1960.
Il grande amore in "uomini e no" di Elio Vittorini e in altri uomini e libri (journalism), All'Insegna del Pesce d'Oro (Milan, Italy), 1960.
(With Antonello Trombadori) *Renato Guttuso, Gott mit Uns,* Saggiatore (Milan, Italy), 1960.
Versi e poesie di Emilio Sarpi (poems; title means "Verse and Poems of Emilio Sarpi"), edited by Vanni Scheiwiller, Scheiwiller (Milan, Italy), 1963.
I calzoni di Beethoven (journalism; title means "Beethoven's Trousers"), Saggiatore (Milan, Italy), 1965.
Tre parole sulla Resistenza, All'Insegna del Pesce d'Oro (Milan, Italy), 1965, enlarged edition, Vallecchi (Florence, Italy), 1973.
C'era una volta, edited by Vanni Scheiwiller, Scheiwiller (Milan, Italy), 1966.
Portème via . . . , All'Insegna del Pesce d'Oro (Milan, Italy), 1968.
Caffè Greco, edited by Franca Noventa, Vallecchi (Florence, Italy), 1969.
Storia di una eresia, edited by Franca Noventa, Rusconi (Milan, Italy), 1971.
Hyde Park, All'Insegna del Pesce d'Oro (Milan, Italy), 1972.
Opere complete, four volumes, edited by Franco Manfriani, Marsilio (Venice, Italy), 1986-1989.
"Dio è con noi" e altri scritti, 1947-1960, edited by Franco Manfriani, Marsilio (Venice, Italy), 1989.

Also author of a play, *La fiala* (title means "The Vial"), published in *Situazione,* February, 1961. Contributor of essays to periodicals under the pen name Emilio Sarpi.

SIDELIGHTS: Italian poet, philosopher, and journalist Giacomo Ca'Zorci wrote under the pen name Giacomo Noventa. As a writer, Ca'Zorci stood throughout his life in a unique position outside the predominating trends of the age, including fascism, communism, socialism, and even the liberal Catholicism with which he was most in sympathy. Above all, he was anticonformist, criticizing the status quo in whatever form it took. Thus, though he was at heart a traditionalist who felt that no liberal political or cultural reforms should be so far-reaching that they alienated the Italian people and the true Catholic religion, he never aligned himself for long with any single political party or stance. "However," stated Erlena Urgnani in the *Dictionary of Literary Biography,* "it is precisely his refusal of ideologies and his battle against all kinds of dogmatism that place him among the moderns."

Ca'Zorci was born into an aristocratic family in Venice. He was educated in the law at the University of Turin and spent a short time practicing law in Rome before giving up his practice to spend the next decade traveling through Europe. He began writing poems and songs in the Venetian dialect that was his mother tongue and his language of choice throughout his career, and he adopted his pseudonym Noventa. During this time he published occasionally in the journals *La Libra* and *Cultura.* Ca'Zorci's affiliation with these journals brought him into conflict with Italian fascists in the 1930s, and he was jailed for a month in 1935; upon his release he was forbidden to travel abroad. The bulk of the poetry he published at this time appeared in the journal he started, *Riforma Letteraria,* under the pseudonym Emilio Sarpi, a poet Ca'Zorci claimed had died in London in 1933. *Riforma Letteraria* also gave Ca'Zorci a forum for his political and religious views, collected later in the volumes *Nulla di nuovo* and *I calzoni di Beethoven* (both 1965). Ca'Zorci's poems take up themes of love as well as politics and religion. As Urgnani wrote: "There is in the background of [Ca'Zaorci's] poetry a polemic revolt against hermetic solitude, which, he felt, built between people and the world a space populated by obscure and artificial forms. His values were friendship, loyalty, poetry, and love."

Ca'Zorci published his first book of poems, *Versi e poesie,* in 1956, for which he received the prestigious Viareggio Prize. He then published *Il vescovo di Prato,* a fictitious dialogue on Catholicism that resurrected Ca'Zorci's alter ego, Sarpi. Shortly before his death in July of 1960 of a brain tumor, Ca'Zorci published a collection of his philosophical essays in *Nulla di nuovo.* The remainder of his work was published at the behest of others after his death. Ca'Zorci's choice to write in the Venetian dialect instead of standard Italian, and his nuanced polemical stance, alternately anticlerical-Catholic and socialist-Catholic, found resonance with few others of his generation. John L. Brown, in a review of *"Dio è con noi" e altri scritti, 1947-1960* in *World Literature Today,* concluded: "[Ca'Zorci], isolated and controversial as he was,

remains . . . for a minority of followers 'an indispensable alternative' to the dominant Italian culture of his time." On the other hand, Thomas G. Bergin, writing in *World Literature Today,* described Ca'Zorci as honorably rising above his self-contradictions: "Patrician yet socialist, Catholic yet anticlerical, conservative yet radical, he was throughout his lifetime consistently anti-*comformista,* supporting his position with ironic eloquence and notable integrity."

BIOGRAPHICAL AND CRITICAL SOURCES:

BOOKS

Astengo, Domenico, *La poesia dialettale,* Marietti (Turin, Italy), 1976.
Dictionary of Literary Biography, Volume 114: *Twentieth-Century Italian Poets,* Gale (Detroit, MI), 1992.
Fortini, Franco, *I poeti del novecento,* Laterza (Bari, Italy), 1977.
Grana, Gianni, editor, *Novecento, I contemporanei,* Marzorati (Milan, Italy), 1979.
Pasolini, Pier Paolo, *Passione e ideologia,* Garzanti (Milan, Italy), 1960.

PERIODICALS

Comunita, December, 1986, "Giacomo Noventa," pp. 170-187, "Scrittura letteraria e intenzione," pp. 188-198, and "Noventa e Olivetti," pp. 199-220.
Diverse lingue, February, 1986, "Giacomo Noventa," pp. 19-26.
Italianist, Volume 4, 1986, "Introduzione ala lirica venta del Novecento," pp. 35-53.
Letteratura italiana: i contemporanei, Volume 3, 1975, G. Pampaloni, pp. 281-298.
Nuova Antologia, Volume 1, 1957, Claudio Varese, "Giacomo Noventa," pp. 273-275.
Ponte, Volumes 8-9, 1956, Franco Fortini, "Giacomo Noventa e la poesia," pp. 1393-1404.
Quaderni d'Italianistica, autumn, 1997, "The Dialect Poetry of Giacomo Noventa," pp. 261-271.
Vita e Pensiero, Volume 51, 1968, "Noventa Debenedetti," pp. 888-900.
World Literature Today, spring, 1987, Thomas G. Bergin, review of *Versi e poesie,* pp. 266-267; summer, 1990, John L. Brown, "'Dio è con noi' e altri scritti: 1947-1960," pp. 449-450.*

CHADWICK, Bruce (V.)

PERSONAL: Male; married. *Education:* Rutgers University, Ph.D.

ADDRESSES: Office—Department of History, Rutgers University, 16 Seminary Place, New Brunswick, NJ 08901-1108.

CAREER: Rutgers University, New Brunswick, NJ, lecturer on history and film; New Jersey City University, writing instructor; also worked as a journalist and a *New York Daily News,* editor.

WRITINGS:

(Editor) *Brother against Brother: The Lost Civil War Diary of Lt. Edmund Halsey,* Birch Lane Press/ Carol Publishing Group (Secaucus, NJ), 1997.
The Two American Presidents: A Dual Biography of Abraham Lincoln and Jefferson Davis, Carol Publishing Group (Secaucus, NJ), 1998.
Traveling the Underground Railroad: A Visitor's Guide to More than 300 Sites, Carol Publishing Group (Secaucus, NJ), 1999.
The Reel Civil War: Mythmaking in American Film, Knopf (New York, NY), 2001.

Various newspaper articles on arts and entertainment; columns on sports and trends in American culture.

SIDELIGHTS: Lecturer and journalist Bruce Chadwick has, through his scholarly work, pursued his interest in the U. S. Civil War in great depth. For example, he edited the diary and correspondence of a Union army soldier as *Brother against Brother: The Lost Civil War Diary of Lt. Edmund Halsey,* providing background information on the family, as well as historical annotations. Halsey, hailing from a prominent family in Rockaway, New Jersey, joined the Union army in 1862 and became an officer in the 15th New Jersey, though his father strongly opposed his enlistment. Fighting for principles, such as preserving the Union and freeing the slaves, Halsey saw combat in Chancellorsville, the Wilderness, and the Shenandoah Valley. Meanwhile, Halsey's older brother, Joseph, a proslavery landowner in Virginia, was equally committed to the Confederate cause. Nonethe-

less, the brothers overcame their differences not long after the end of the war. Though a reviewer for *Kirkus Reviews* found Chadwick's "annotations . . . too often misplaced" and Halsey's writing "listless and general," a *Publishers Weekly* reviewer noted that Halsey is "most eloquent in describing war's commonplace miseries," such as lice, illness, and homesickness. This reviewer also concluded that Chadwick's book "will be welcomed by readers interested in the Civil War's human dimension."

In *The Two American Presidents: A Dual Biography of Abraham Lincoln and Jefferson Davis,* Chadwick examines the personalities and private lives of the two leaders in order to explain the outcome of the Civil War. James I. Robertson, Jr., in *Historian,* wrote that in this book, "Chadwick has done a solid job of portraying the two antagonists in the nation's darkest hour." Using memoirs, correspondence, speeches, and congressional reports for his research, Chadwick pieces together the personalities of the Union and Confederate leaders, drawing the conclusion that the war was won by the North because Lincoln possessed better personal skills, which, ultimately, made him a more effective leader. *Civil War History* critic Michael Naragon felt that Chadwick should have drawn more ideas from current scholarship, but Naragon nonetheless noted that "The use of biography to explain the Union victory is provocative and serves as a welcome corrective to those who stress structure at the expense of agency."

In *Traveling the Underground Railroad: A Visitor's Guide to More than 300 Sites* Chadwick offers the history of the network that helped runaway slaves escape to free states in the North. For each site listed in the book, Chadwick provides a brief history and, if the site is open to the public, contact information for tourists who wish to visit. Although *Library Journal* contributor Julia Stump found the book unsuccessful as a guidebook, because there are "no maps or directions," she concluded that the book is nonetheless "interesting as history."

Chadwick discusses how Hollywood has portrayed the Civil War in *The Reel Civil War: Mythmaking in American Film.* Chadwick examines the myths films have propagated about Southerners, slaves, and Northerners, particularly in *Birth of a Nation* and *Gone with the Wind.* James M. McPherson noted, in the *New York Times,* that "Chadwick's dissection of the myths [these two films] helped to foster is superb. His chapters on the early silent films and on movies about Abraham Lincoln are also outstanding." Although McPherson did not agree with the author's premise that there is a "subtle pro-Southern bias" to movies about Abraham Lincoln, the critic concluded that overall, Chadwick's book is an "enlightening volume."

BIOGRAPHICAL AND CRITICAL SOURCES:

PERIODICALS

Booklist, March 15, 1998, Brad Hooper, review of *The Two American Presidents: A Dual Biography of Abraham Lincoln and Jefferson Davis,* p. 1197; January 1, 2000, Brad Hooper, review of *The Two American Presidents,* p. 869.

Book Report, January-February, 1998, James Gross, review of *Brother against Brother: The Lost Civil War Diary of Lt. Edmund Halsey,* p. 44.

Civil War History, March, 2000, Michael Naragon, review of *The Two American Presidents,* p. 63.

Economist, September 8, 2001, "Extra Special: Hollywood's Civil War."

Historian, summer, 2000, James I. Robertson, Jr., review of *The Two American Presidents,* p. 864.

Kirkus Reviews, 1997, review of *Brother against Brother.*

Library Journal, March 1, 1998, Brooks D. Simpson, review of *The Two American Presidents,* p. 100; September 1, 1999, Julia Stump, review of *Traveling the Underground Railroad: A Visitor's Guide to More than 300 Sites,* p. 221; August, 2001, Neal Baker, review of *The Reel Civil War: Mythmaking in American Film,* p. 110.

New York Times, September 30, 2001, James M. McPherson, "Klieg Lights and Magnolias: Civil War Movies May Be Ubiquitous, but They're Not Very Accurate," p. 19.

Publishers Weekly, July 30, 2001, review of *The Reel Civil War,* p. 73; March 23, 1998, review of *The Two American Presidents,* p. 83; April 21, 1997, review of *Brother against Brother,* p. 56.

OTHER

H-South, http://www2.h-net.msu.edu/ (September 1, 2000), Brian Dirck, review of *The Two American Presidents.**

CHEETHAM, Nicholas (John Alexander) 1910-2002

OBITUARY NOTICE—See index for *CA* sketch: Born October 8, 1910, in London, England; died January 14, 2002. Diplomat and author. Cheetham was a noted foreign diplomat who served Britain during the difficult and tense cold war years. After attending Christ Church, Oxford he joined the British Diplomatic Service, serving in posts in Athens, Buenos Aires, Mexico City, and Vienna. In the 1950s he also worked for the North Atlantic Council, becoming minister to Hungary from 1959 to 1961 and assistant undersecretary of the British Foreign Office in the early 1960s; he concluded his career as British ambassador to Mexico from 1964 to 1968. Throughout his years as a diplomat, Cheetham was largely praised as a shrewd negotiator. After he retired from public service, he decided to become a writer, producing such well-received works as *History of Mexico* (1970), *New Spain: The Birth of Modern Mexico* (1974), *Medieval Greece* (1981), and *Keeper of the Keys: A History of the Popes from St. Peter to John Paul II* (1983). For his loyal service to his country, Cheetham was made a knight commander of the Order of St. Michael and St. George.

OBITUARIES AND OTHER SOURCES:

BOOKS

Who's Who, St. Martin's Press (New York, NY), 2000.

PERIODICALS

Daily Telegraph (London, England), January 23, 2002.
Times (London, England), January 13, 2002, p. 37.

*   *   *

CHENEY, Ednah Dow (Littlehale) 1824-1904

PERSONAL: Born June 27, 1824, in Boston, MA; died November 19, 1904, in Boston, MA; daughter of Sargent Smith (a businessman) and Ednah Parker (Dow) Littlehale; married Seth Wells Cheney (a painter), 1853 (died 1856); children: Daisy. *Politics:* Abolitionist and social reformer.

CAREER: Writer, social reformer. Lecturer at the Concord School of Philosophy; secretary, New England Freedmen's Aid Society.

WRITINGS:

Handbook for American Citizens, 1860.

(Compiler) *Patience: A Series of Thirty Games with Cards,* Lee & Shepard (Boston, MA), 1970, third edition, 1895.

Social Games: A Collection of 31 Games with Cards, Lee & Shepard (Boston, MA)/Lee, Shepard & Dillingham (New York, NY), 1871.

Sally Williams, The Mountain Girl, illustrated by L. B. Humphrey, Lee & Shepard (Boston, MA)/Lee, Shepard & Dillingham (New York, NY), 1873.

The Child of the Tide, Lee & Shepard (Boston, MA), 1875.

Life of Susan Dimock, 1875.

Gleanings in the Fields of Art, Lee & Shepard (Boston, MA)/Lee, Shepard & Dillingham (New York, NY), 1881.

Memoir of Seth W. Cheney, Artist, Lee & Shepard (Boston, MA), 1881.

Faithful to the Light, and Other Tales, American Unitarian Association (Boston, MA), 1884.

(Editor) *Selected Poems from Michelangelo Buonarroti,* 1885.

Louisa May Alcott, the Children's Friend, L. Prang (Boston, MA), 1888.

Louisa May Alcott, Her Life, Letters, and Journals, Roberts (Boston, MA), 1889.

Memoir of Margaret Swan Cheney, Lee & Shepard (Boston, MA), 1889.

Nora's Return: A Sequel to "The Doll's House," Lee & Shepard (Boston, MA)/Lee, Shepard & Dillingham (New York, NY), 1890.

Memoirs of Lucretia Crocker and Abby W. May, [Boston, MA], 1893.

Life of Christian Daniel Rauch of Berlin, Germany, Lee & Shepard (Boston, MA), 1893.

Reminiscences of Ednah Dow Cheney, Lee & Shepard (Boston, MA), 1902.

SIDELIGHTS: Ednah Dow Cheney is little known today, but in Boston's intellectual and activist circles of the nineteenth century she was an important figure. As a writer, her output was limited, but her most famous work, a biography of Louisa May Alcott, remains an important resource for literary scholars even today.

Cheney was born in Boston in 1824. Her family was comfortably well-off, and although there are few specific details available about her upbringing, it is clear that she enjoyed a greater access to education than was the norm for women of her time. Between her family connections and her literary aspirations, she became active in Boston's intellectual circles, making the acquaintance of the leading literary and philosophical lights of the day, from Ralph Waldo Emerson to Louisa May Alcott.

Perhaps the single most important person in the development of young Cheney's intellectual development was Margaret Fuller, a prominent Boston-based journalist, feminist, and transcendentalist philosopher. In the early and mid-1800s it was not uncommon for women of Cheney's social station to attend salons and public lectures, but it was illegal for women to take to the public lectern. Thus, in 1839, Fuller began to hold private gatherings at her home, her so-called "conversations," to which were invited the leading thinkers and writers of the day. Among Fuller's many guests were Emerson and the Alcotts, with whom she had long been associated, having taught at Bronson Alcott's Temple School in Boston. It was through her attendance at Fuller's conversations that Cheney made the acquaintances that would strongly influence her own personal and intellectual development, as well as provide her with her first introduction to the woman whose biography she would ultimately write—Louisa May Alcott.

In the 1850s there were three powerful influences on the intellectual life of Boston. First was transcendentalism, the philosophical movement founded by Ralph Waldo Emerson; second was the anti-slavery movement, which found particular support in liberal northern cities like Boston and Cambridge; third was the early feminist movement, as educated women chafed against the legal restraints that hindered their full participation in the political and intellectual life of the time. These three influences, encouraged in conversation in Fuller's drawing room, had a profound influence on Cheney and colored the remainder of her life's work.

At about the same time that Cheney was enjoying the heady intellectual life offered through Fuller's conversations, she met and married painter Seth Cheney in 1853, when she was twenty-nine years old. During her brief marriage—it would last only three years—she continued to attend lectures and otherwise remain involved in Boston's intellectual life. It was not until 1856, when her husband died, that she threw herself full-force into a career of her own. When she did, it was with complete commitment. She became active in the abolitionist movement, making the acquaintance of Harriet Jacobs, former slave and author of the classic *Incidents in the Life of a Slave Girl* (1858), which shocked the nation with its revelations of sexual abuse within slavery. She joined the New England Freedman's Aid Society, an influential movement that devoted much of its efforts to purchasing the freedom of slaves in the pre-Civil War years and after the war gave assistance to the newly freed slaves to help them establish independent lives. At this time, she also began lecturing in her own right, speaking out on a variety of subjects from women's suffrage to art and transcendentalism.

As a writer, Cheney left behind few traces of her work. She is best remembered for writing the first, and still strongly authoritative, biography *Louisa May Alcott, Her Life, Letters, and Journals.* In writing this volume, she enjoyed the benefit of access to family archives, for by this time she had become a close family friend of the Alcotts. In 1902 she published *Reminiscences of Ednah Dow Cheney,* wherein she recounts the story of her long association with the intellectual elite of Boston and Cambridge. Her other writings, which include minor biographies, reflections on art, and books on card games, have all fallen out of print.

It may well be that Cheney's activism in social causes drew her attention away from writing. It is known that her friendship with Harriet Jacobs was a close one. When, in 1867, Jacobs returned to her North Carolina birthplace after the Civil War to help the family she had left behind in her flight from slavery, she corresponded with Cheney about the difficulties and successes she encountered. By this time, Cheney had attained the position of secretary to the New England Freedman's Aid Association, and had begun a career as a lecturer at the Concord School of Philosophy. She died in Boston in 1904.

BIOGRAPHICAL AND CRITICAL SOURCES:

BOOKS

Childhood in Poet, Gale (Detroit, MI), 1972.
Dictionary of Literary Biography, Volume 1: *The American Renaissance in New England,* Gale (Detroit, MI), 1978.*

CHERRY, Kelly 1940-

PERSONAL: Born 1940, in Baton Rouge, LA; daughter of J. Milton (a violinist and professor of music theory) and Mary (a violinist and writer; maiden name, Spooner) Cherry; married Jonathan Silver, December 23, 1966 (divorced, 1969); married Burke Davis III (a fiction writer), September 17, 2000. *Education:* Mary Washington College, B.A., 1961; attended University of Virginia; University of North Carolina at Greensboro, M.F.A., 1967.

ADDRESSES: Home—Halifax, VA. *Agent*—Elizabeth Sheinkman, c/o The Elaine Markson Literary Agency, 44 Greenwich Avenue, New York, NY 1001. *E-mail*—kcherry@facstaff.wisc.edu.

CAREER: University of Wisconsin—Madison, visiting lecturer, 1977-78, assistant professor, 1978-79, associate professor, 1979-82, professor of English and writer-in-residence, beginning 1982, Romnes Professor of English, 1983-88, Evjue-Bascom Professor in the Humanities, 1993-1999, Eudora Welty Professor of English, 1997-1999, Eudora Welty Professor Emerita of English and Evjue-Bascom Professor Emerita in the Humanities, 1999—. Southwest Minnesota State College, Marshall, writer-in-residence, 1974-75; Western Washington University, Bellingham, distinguished writer-in-residence, 1981; Rhodes College, Memphis, TN, distinguished visiting professor, 1985; University of Alabama—Huntsville, Eminent Scholar at the Humanities Center, 1999-2002; Hollins University, Wyndham Robertson Writer-in-Residence, 2000. Has taught at writers' conference workshops and presented numerous readings of her works at colleges and universities in both the United States and abroad, including Duke University, Bennington Writing Workshops, and Mount Holyoke Writers Conference.

MEMBER: Associated Writing Programs (member of board of directors, 1990-93), Phi Beta Kappa.

AWARDS, HONORS: University of Virginia Dupont Fellow in philosophy, 1962-63; Canaras Award for fiction, St. Lawrence University Writers Conference, 1974; Bread Loaf fellow, 1975; Pushcart Prize, 1977; Yaddo fellow, 1979 and 1989; National Endowment for the Arts fellowship, 1980; first prize for book-length fiction, Wisconsin Council of Writers, 1980, for

Kelly Cherry

Augusta Played, and 1991, for *My Life and Dr. Joyce Brothers;* PEN/Syndicated Fiction Award, 1983, for "Life at the Equator," 1987, for "Acts of Unfathomable Compassion," and 1990, for "About Grace"; Romnes fellowship, University of Wisconsin, 1983; fellowship, Wisconsin Arts Board, 1984, 1989, and 1994; Chancellor's Award, 1984; James G. Hanes Poetry Prize, Fellowship of Southern Writers, 1989, for distinguished body of work; Arts America Speaker Award (Republic of the Philippines), U.S. Information Agency, 1992; Hawthornden fellowship, 1994; Leidig lectureship in poetry, 1999; *Dictionary of Literary Biography* Award for distinguished volume of short stories, 2000; Bradley Major Achievement Award, 2000; Distinguished Alumnus award, Mary Washington College, 2000.

WRITINGS:

FICTION

Sick and Full of Burning, Viking (New York, NY), 1974.

Augusta Played, Houghton (Boston, MA), 1979, reprinted, Louisiana State Press (Baton Rouge, LA), 1998.

Conversion (chapbook), Treacle Press (New Paltz, NY), 1979.

In the Wink of an Eye, Harcourt (San Diego, CA), 1983.

The Lost Traveller's Dream, Harcourt (San Diego, CA), 1984.

My Life and Dr. Joyce Brothers: A Novel in Stories, Algonquin Books (Chapel Hill, NC), 1990, reissued, University of Alabama Press (Tuscaloosa, AL), 2002.

The Society of Friends: Stories, University of Missouri Press (Columbia, MO), 1999.

We Can Still Be Friends, Soho Press (New York, NY), 2003.

POETRY

Lovers and Agnostics, Red Clay Books (Charlotte, NC), 1975, revised edition, Carnegie Mellon University Press (Pittsburgh, PA), 1995.

Relativity: A Point of View, Louisiana State University Press (Baton Rouge, LA), 1977, reprinted, Carnegie Mellon University Press (Pittsburgh, PA), 2000.

Songs for a Soviet Composer (chapbook), Singing Wind Press (St. Louis, MO), 1980.

Natural Theology, Louisiana State University Press (Baton Rouge, LA), 1988.

God's Loud Hand, Louisiana State University Press (Baton Rouge, LA), 1993.

Benjamin John (chapbook), March Street Press (Greensboro, NC), 1993.

Time out of Mind (chapbook), March Street Press (Greensboro, NC), 1994.

Death and Transfiguration, Louisiana State University Press (Baton Rouge, LA), 1997.

An Other Woman (chapbook), Somers Rocks Press (Brooklyn, NY), 2000.

Rising Venus, Louisiana State University Press (Baton Rouge, LA), 2002.

NONFICTION

(Co-author and associate editor) *Lessons from Our Living Past* (textbook), Behrman House (New York, NY), 1972.

Teacher's Guide for Lessons from Our Living Past (textbook), Behrman House (New York, NY), 1972.

The Exiled Heart: A Meditative Autobiography, Louisiana State University Press (Baton Rouge, LA), 1991.

Writing the World (essays), University of Missouri Press (Columbia, MO), 1995.

The Poem: An Essay (chapbook), Sandhills Press (Grand Island, NE) 1999.

OTHER

Where the Winged Horses Take off into the Wild Blue Yonder (recording), American Audio Prose Library (Columbia, MO), 1981.

Also author of text ("A Lyric Cycle") for Symphony No. 4 ("Rock Symphony") by Imants Kalnins (world premiere by Detroit Symphony Orchestra, conducted by Neeme Järvi, 1997), recording by Latvian Symphony Orchestra, conducted by Imants Resnis, 1999, and Singapore Philharmonic Orchestra, conducted by Lan Shui, BIS, 2000. Contributor of translation to *Seneca: The Tragedies,* Volume 2, Johns Hopkins University Press (Baltimore, MD), 1994 and *Sophocles, 2,* University of Pennsylvania Press (Philadelphia, PA), 1999. Contributor to more than one hundred anthologies, including *The Girl in the Black Raincoat,* edited by George Garrett, Duell, Sloan & Pearce, 1966; *Best American Short Stories,* 1972; *Pushcart Prize II,* edited by Bill Henderson, Avon, 1977; *Strong Measures: Recent American Poems in Traditional Forms,* edited by Philip Dacey and David Jauss, Harper, 1985; *Prize Stories 1994: The O. Henry Awards,* Doubleday, 1994; *The Bedford Introduction to Literature,* 2001; and *The Norton Introduction to Literature,* 2001.

Contributor of stories, poems, essays, and book reviews to periodicals, including *American Scholar, Anglican Theological Review, Atlantic Monthly, Commentary, Esquire, Fiction, Georgia Review, Gettysburg Review, Independent, Los Angeles Times Book Review, Ms., Mademoiselle, New Literary History, New York Times Book Review, North American Review, Parnassus, Poetry, Red Clay Reader, Southern Poetry Review, Southern Review, Story Quarterly,* and *Virginia Quarterly Review. Book Forum,* contributing editor, 1984-88; *Anglican Theological Review,* consultant to poetry editor, 1986—; *Shenandoah,* advising editor, 1988-92; *The Hollins Critic,* contributing editor.

Cherry's works have been translated into numerous foreign languages, including Chinese, Czech, Dutch, German, Latvian, Lithuanian, Polish, Russian, Swedish, and Ukrainian.

SIDELIGHTS: Award-winning poet and novelist Kelly Cherry is concerned with philosophy; with, as she explains it, "the becoming-aware of abstraction in real life—since, in order to abstract, you must have something to abstract from." Within her novels, the abstract notions of morality become her focus: "My novels deal with moral dilemmas and the shapes they create as they reveal themselves in time," she once told *CA.* "My poems seek out the most suitable temporal or kinetic structure for a given emotion." Writing in the *Dictionary of Literary Biography Yearbook: 1983* on Cherry's fiction, Mark Harris concluded that "she manages to capture, in very readable stories, the indecisiveness and mute desperation of life in the twentieth century."

From the beginning of her career, Cherry has written both formal verse and free verse. Cherry's collections of poetry, including *Lovers and Agnostics, Relativity: A Point of View, God's Loud Hand,* and *Death and Transfiguration,* have been widely praised by critics. According to the citation preceding her receipt of the James G. Hanes Poetry Prize in 1989, "Her poetry is marked by a firm intellectual passion, a reverent desire to possess the genuine thought of our century, historical, philosophical, and scientific, and a species of powerful ironic wit which is allied to rare good humor." Reviewing *Relativity,* Patricia Goedicke noted in *Three Rivers Poetry Journal* that "her familiarity with the demands and pressures of traditional patterns has resulted . . . in an expansion and deepening of her poetic resources, a carefully textured over- and underlay of image, meaning and diction." Harris felt that Cherry's "ability to sustain a narrative by clustering and repeating images [lends] itself to longer forms, and 'A Bird's Eye View of Einstein,' the longest poem in [*Relativity*], is an example of Cherry at her poetic best." Reviewing Cherry's collection, *Death and Transfiguration,* Patricia Gabilondo wrote in *The Anglican Theological Review* that "'Requiem,' the abstract prose poem that closes this book . . . translates personal loss into the historical and universal, providing an occasion for philosophical meditation on the mystery of suffering and the need for transcendence in a post-Holocaust world that seems to offer none. Moving through the terrors of nihilism and doubt, Cherry, in a poem that deftly alternates between the philosophically abstract and the image's graphic force, gives us an intellectually honest and deeply moving vision of our relation to each other's suffering and of God's relation to humanity's 'memory of pain.'"

In her novels, Cherry has sometimes centered on female protagonists who cope with personal crises while searching for love, sexual fulfillment, and self-knowledge. Her first novel, *Sick and Full of Burning,* depicts the life and relationships of Mary "Tennessee" Settleworth, a newly divorced medical student facing her thirtieth birthday. "Like many of Cherry's other heroines, Tennessee Settleworth is unable to enjoy more than a casual friendship with the men she meets," Harris wrote. Tennessee's best male friend wants to live with her but refuses to make love to her; another male friend is eager to make love, but he has been impotent since his divorce. "The essential pessimism of the novel," said Harris, "finds a certain anodyne in the protagonist's humorous attempts to relieve her sexual frustrations." At another level, the novel attempts to "settle" the "worth" of Tennessee's own life as measured against her ethical obligation to others, especially other women. A reviewer for *Kirkus Reviews* described *Sick and Full of Burning* as "a just about perfect first novel"; a critic in the *Chicago Tribune Book World* called it "flawless."

Augusta Played, Cherry's second novel, published five years after *Sick and Full of Burning,* explores the dynamics of marriage and money through the tempestuous relationship between a young flutist and her musicologist husband, giving equal weight to both male and female points of view. Harris noted that *Augusta Played* "relies on improbable events and a series of misapprehensions much as the eighteenth-century comedy of manners did. . . . The mixture of realistic detail and improbable coincidence allows Cherry to explore a commonplace in our time—the breakdown of a marriage—in a refreshing and interesting manner." "Cherry's characters begin, as in high comedy, with stock types who gradually grow more and more complex," wrote Robert Taylor in a review for the *Boston Globe.* "Behind them is the sad music of mortality . . . proclaiming that even our vanities possess absurd dignity and the absurd lies on the borderline of heartbreak."

In the Wink of an Eye fused satire and fantasy to draw a political cartoon. Treating absurdities from the far right to the far left—and using "God's eye," or the aspect of eternity, as both a metaphor and a device for transitioning from place to place and point of view to point of view—the book deals with whether and how a just society can be established. *The Lost Traveller's Dream,* intended as a book of interlinked stories but published as a novel, likewise questions the nature of love and justice but where *In the Wink of an Eye* is gentle comedy, *The Lost Traveller's Dream* is lamentation. Cherry once told *CA* that she hopes someday to have the opportunity to restore *The Lost Traveller's Dream* to her original vision of it as a book of short stories, stripping away material she added to "make it a novel."

The unique structure of Cherry's *My Life and Dr. Joyce Brothers* was also favorably received by critics. Subtitled "A Novel in Stories," the book relates, in the words of *Los Angeles Times Book Review* contributor Judith Freeman, "the plight of a middle-aged, unmarried woman named Nina who understands how the numbing jargon of self-help, so prevalent in our culture and epitomized by the philosophy of Dr. Joyce Brothers, can do nothing to alleviate a sense of deep-rooted alienation and loneliness." Freeman observed that the novel is "far too witty, too savvy, too lyrical and compassionate to resort to bitterness." She praised Cherry for performing "the admirable feat of taking hackneyed fates and infusing them with tremendous freshness." A contributor to *Kirkus Reviews* called the book "richly satisfying," saying it "begins as light as Ephron's *Heartburn* and makes a quantum leap along the way into a kind of prayer." A writer for the *New York Times Book Review* called attention to the book's "prose of outstanding lyrical strength."

Cherry's book of stories, *The Society of Friends,* is a sequel to *My Life and Dr. Joyce Brothers.* There are thirteen stories here, six of which feature Nina Bryant, a writer and professor at the University of Wisconsin. Nina struggles with a number of troubles and challenges in her life, including her relationship with her adopted daughter and the emotional stress of her parents' deaths and memories of the time she was abused as a child. Other stories feature the lives of her neighbors. In the *New York Times Book Review,* a writer praised the stories' "emotional complexity and perceptive humor," concluding, "Cherry traces the shifts in her characters' emotional lives with an observant, elegiac precision, as if she were detailing the visceral effects of the changing seasons." A *Publishers Weekly* critic commented, "Cherry speaks to the heart of a particular privileged and yet angst-ridden contemporary subspecies, settled in university towns across the country." Joann Verica, writing in *Blooms-bury Review,* described the stories as "humorous, heartbreaking, and thought-provoking" and commended Cherry's "skillful, smart, and beautiful writing," calling the book "a must read for both writers and readers who are in love with the art of the word." *Society of Friends* was awarded the *Dictionary of Literary Biography* Award for a Distinguished Volume of Short Stories published in 1999; in his comments about the award in *Dictionary of Literary Biography Yearbook: 1999,* George Garrett noted that "With this work Kelly Cherry takes her place among our finest living story writers." Cherry told *CA* that she expects to write a third book in this series to complete what she thinks of as "a single extended story cycle."

The concerns Cherry addresses in her fiction are also reflected in *The Exiled Heart: A Meditative Autobiography.* Having met and fallen in love with a Latvian musician named Imant Kalnin during the cold war, Cherry was separated from him, and the couple was prevented from marrying by the Soviet government. She contemplated the nature and meaning of both love and justice while living in England and waiting for a visa to visit Kalnin. *The Exiled Heart* was the result: "One of the richest and most thoughtful books I have ever read," noted Fred Chappell in a review in *Louisiana Literature.* "The integrity of thought and courage of vision it portrays are qualities that abide in the memory, steadfast as fixed stars. One day this book will come into its own and will be recognized, along with some other works by Kelly Cherry, for the masterwork that it is."

"I'm concerned with the shape of ideas in time," Cherry told *CA* in a discussion of her writing, "the dynamic configuration a moral dilemma makes, cutting through a novel like a river through rock; the way a philosophical statement bounces against the walls of a poem, like an echo in a canyon. A writer, poet or novelist, wants to create a contained, complete landscape in which time flows freely and naturally. The *poems* are where I live. It's in poetry that thought and time most musically counterpoint each other, and I like a world in which the elements sing."

"I think that the crucial unit of the poem is the line; in the story, it's sentence, or voice; and in the novel, it's scene," the novelist explained to *CA,* going on to add

some thoughts on the inspiration for her works of fiction. "The hidden model for *Augusta Played* is *The Tempest;* the hidden model for *In the Wink of an Eye* is *A Midsummer Night's Dream.* Shakespeare and Beethoven, they're the main ones; the idea of an extended developmental passage—that's the root impetus for everything I write. I grew up on those two."

In an article for *Poets and Writers,* Nancy Bunge gave an overview of Cherry's work, explaining that for Cherry, "enriching her philosophic perspective always remains her primary goal. This fascination with exploring and exposing meaning gives her work depth as well as range. . . . [S]he creates work at once down-to-earth and transcendent, personal and universal, realistic and hopeful in multiple genres."

AUTOBIOGRAPHICAL ESSAY:

Kelly Cherry contributed the following autobiographical essay to *CA:*

When I start to talk about my parents and their lives as string quartet violinists—which I do whenever I'm asked about my own life, because music and my parents' devotion to it were there from the beginning for me, were what I was born into—listeners are apt to say, "Now we understand why you are so driven." They will sometimes offer up the thought that I see my work as a way to earn my parents' approval, that I hope, by meeting the standards for art set by my parents, to earn their love. This is why I am a perfectionist, they will—they have—told me. I don't argue with them, in part because people rarely want to know more about you than they already do; and in part because the truth involves feelings I have wanted to protect, out of guilt or a fear of embarrassing myself or maybe simply a fear of being wrong. I *could* be wrong, but I do not believe that I am driven. I do not believe I write hoping to win my (now-deceased) parents' love, attention, praise, approval. I believe that if I had wanted to win my late parents' love, attention, praise, approval, I would have said yes to the boy who asked me to the senior prom (and I wish I had). I would have gone through sorority rush (and I wish I had). I would have learned to dance (and I wish, wish, wish I had). I would have learned to cook and garden and play poker. I would have done those things and others like them, because although my parents would not tolerate the almost, the cheap, the untested, the unnecessary in their art, they were not ogres, and when they said that all they wanted from us, the children, was for us to be happy, they meant it. But, you see, I had already given my heart to that music I heard while I was still in the womb. I would have heard it anyway—it was what their days were made of—but my mother had read that babies in the womb are influenced by what they hear, and, as if rehearsals and practice sessions and concerts were not enough, she played recordings all through the Louisiana spring and summer and autumn to make *damn* sure that I heard it, the most beautiful music there is, a music made equally of logic and feeling. Thus, long before Siegfried Othmer stopped me just as I was getting on the school bus to go home and asked me if I would be his date for the prom, and I said no, but only because—I was too stupid, and too groggy, to tell him this—I had been up all night the night before reading or studying or writing or doing something, drawing a time line that showed the different geological eras or working on my history of the world, something like that, I had promised myself to another life. I had come into the world pinned, pledged, and preoccupied. Preoccupied by a revelation I felt had been vouchsafed me and by a corollary recognition that my task was to help others see what had been revealed to me. I was born a lover and evangelist. Like all disciples, I did not feel driven; I felt called.

The author, age eight months

*

I used to think I was special, even weird, in this regard, but now I suspect many, if not most, writers feel the same way. Writers' art is by the nature of its medium an art that both shows and tells, creates and seeks to understand. When I was young, I thought of myself as having been given a "mission"—that is the word I used, but only silently, to myself, because it would have been presumptuous, if not just plain foolhardy, to say it aloud.

Some kids believe they must have been stolen from their real parents and will someday be restored to their rightful inheritance, acknowledged at last as special. Maybe my mission was nothing more than a fantasy. There wasn't a lot of evidence that I would ever fulfill it. I wasn't, at least not often, one of those children who write stories at the age of eight or publish sonnets at twelve, and for years I simply listened to music, read, daydreamed, and tried to copy Kim Novak's haircut.

We'd left Baton Rouge when I was four, spending the summer on a lake outside Toronto, where my younger sister and I took turns rolling sideways in the washtub and we heard loons and had leeches pulled off of us and our big brother shot up and turned golden brown and dived off a cliff. In the fall we joined our father in Ithaca, New York, moving into the tenement apartment that would be our home for five years. Our parents were desperately busy, but my mother still found time to sew sequins onto my sister's and my cardboard cut-out crowns for our Halloween costumes. One year my mother dressed me as a "medieval lady," but the judges—she said—were looking the other way when I walked by. She made a stubborn point about not forgiving those judges in the grandstand, though the point quickly became a joke. She was not interested in what we now call "parenting"—I don't believe it ever occurred to her that children might require "raising"; she simply assumed that we were smart enough to figure things out on our own and, besides, needed us to do that, because she was profoundly dedicated to music and wanted to play the violin as well as possible and side by side with our father—but she was young and lively and full of fun, at least until war-time poverty in a cold, gray town populated by humorless Yankees wore her down. Finally my parents were able to escape what to them had proved a depressing, exhausting, bare-bones existence. They escaped to Richmond, Virginia.

All that time, nobody bothered me much. A little: there were a couple of brouhahas involving conflicts with parents about vocational goals. First, I announced I was quitting the piano in order to become a writer. I was twelve. My mother said that she would rather kill me than have me turn out like my big brother, a beatnik. She ran to the kitchen to get the butcher knife. My father grabbed her by the arms and made her drop the knife.

Next I wrote a long poem in rhyming quatrains. (It was Shakespeare who had caused me to do this; I was in love with the singing line, the felt idea, a rampaging world controlled by structure, the fantastic as a mirror of reality.) The teacher gave my poem a C. When she handed it back to me, I cried in spite of trying hard not to, but my grade stayed a C. She said she was grading "in relation to what you are capable of." But I had done the best I could do—pages and pages of quatrains titled "The Winter's Tale." I knew I couldn't write any better than that.

The following year I submitted a story to my high-school literary magazine; it was a story about a man, a failed writer, who was thinking of killing himself, quite likely with a butcher knife. As he walked along the street, deep in despair, he passed a conservatory. From one of the windows came the sounds of a pianist practicing the "Waldstein" Sonata. Hearing this music, beautiful beyond words, the man resolved to live. The editors of the literary magazine declined to publish my story, on the grounds that it was too depressing.

I told my guidance counselor, who asked me what my vocational goals were, that I was interested in writing, science, and drama. "Well," she said, "why don't you write science-fiction shows for television?"

When I was writing, late at night, my attic room cool at last briefly before dawn, I was possibly the happiest person on earth. I copied the final paragraph of *Moby-Dick* into a spiral notebook, feeling the long line of the words play itself out under my hands like the line attached to a harpoon. I pored over the battle scenes in *War and Peace,* reckoning them essential to the music of the whole.

This was the first room I had to myself, and it was magical. There was a wooden seat under the dormer window. My brother did some complicated wiring that allowed me to turn the downstairs dining-room radio on and off from upstairs, so I could listen to the all-night classical station; I could also stack records on the downstairs player and listen to them on speakers he'd put in my room. I had a closet with a small dresser and mirror at one end and no door, so I could primp in my babydoll (that meant short and filmy, very Tennessee Williams) pajamas while working on that Kim Novak hair style. My parents' room was in the attic at the other end, and they'd built in some privacy for themselves by putting in floor-to-ceiling bookshelves that formed a hallway from the stairs to my room. They did much of the carpentry and painting, thrilled to own a house at last. It was a tiny white stucco house, but when I was at my end of the attic, I might as well have been alone on an island.

My mother tried to make peace with me. She asked to see some of my poetry. I showed my mother a poem in which I used the word "nipple." She had a mock heart attack. None of us knew it was "mock," of course—not even she did—and when the doctor came to our house, black bag in hand, I thought I had killed my mother with my shameless poem.

"You must be careful," she said to me, on another occasion, "not to have more success than your big brother. He decided to be a writer first. And he's a boy."

My father took some of my work to one of his colleagues at Richmond Professional Institute. The colleague wrote me a letter in which he said I had a "flare" [*sic*] for words but that girls grew out of this kind of thing.

Even though I hadn't yet grown out of my wish to write, I had to quit writing at least for the foreseeable future in order to study science and mathematics. This was another of the many schemes that were launched on behalf of my future: I would be a pianist, a

Age two; with her mother, Mary, in Mobile, Alabama

housewife, an actress, a secretary, a scientist. An Indian chief, a candle maker. Science was now in the ascendence, and at seventeen I was transferring to the New Mexico Institute of Science and Technology for my sophomore year. (I was never allowed to apply to any of the undergraduate schools I wanted to attend; I suspect my mother was unconsciously reenacting *her* mother's refusal to let her go to her college of choice—where, they worried, she might follow in her sister's flapper footsteps. Around we go.) I made a note to myself about my academic obligation. "For the next several years," I wrote, "I must not write." But when I was kicked out of college for the second time and no college anywhere would enroll me, I wrote a novella, to show everyone I was serious about writing. It was called "The Silver Crow."

Luckily, a dean whose own daughter had been kicked out of school was fond of me because I reminded him of her, and he took me under his wing and got me reinstated. Back in school, thanks to the good offices of this compassionate man, I continued to write. The next youthful effort was an allegory about a man named Dev (short for Devil).

In my last summer of college—I was making up missed courses—I took on a non-credit course that a sociology professor and I had devised. We just sat down together and made it up, and didn't even ask whether it could be for credit. We called this course "Creative Symbolism," and we read Freud, Durkheim, Benjamin Whorf, Cassirer, and on and on. Every day we'd meet in the campus soda shop for three, four, five hours at a time; reading for the course kept me up until three, four, or five in the morning. One day near the end of summer I worked up the courage to show him my allegory. For four hours, he told me how I had no talent for writing and should stick with analytic studies. He was diligent and kindly and concerned about me and had, after all, given his entire summer to me, and he tried to couch his criticism in gentle terms. When he was finished, I said thank you and left the table. At the top of the high staircase, I fainted. When I came to, the sociology professor and the school nurse were bending over me. "Is it that time of month, dear?" asked the nurse, in a whisper that the sociology professor was not supposed to hear.

And this was how it went, for quite a long time. It would be nice to be able to say that I persevered, but sometimes I think the opposite is truer: I quit. I quit again and again, the way a thoroughly addicted smoker will keep quitting. Of course, like the smoker I returned each time to my addiction. I think perhaps I renounced all ability to choose whether I would write or not the first time I tried it. No, I think I renounced my right to choose before I was born, when I first heard a late Beethoven quartet.

I quit writing when I got married. I quit again when I got divorced. Every day I would tell myself that I had no business writing, it was not what I deserved to be doing; this was indeed a little lecture I honed and delivered to myself in the morning before going to work—out loud. Writing was never anything I could just say no to. I had better luck quitting smoking—I haven't smoked since the second draft of my first novel.

When I write, I am still in my attic room. I am not worried about whether I will have too much success or too little. It does not matter if no one approves of what I am doing. It does not even matter if my mother, reading it, would want to kill herself. I was shameless then, and I am shameless now—the way addicts are. My mother never stood a chance (and eventually, she gave in and even supported my habit).

Writing is a state of being in which the hope of beauty and the quest for truth combine, like a mirage, like a dream of natural power, but the place you are trying to get to can never quite be gotten to because it is a place that, like great music, is beyond words. Shakespeare, Melville, and Tolstoy are like directions on a map, but not even they are the place itself, which, as Socrates suggested, is where your soul first resided and where you have so inarticulately longed to return ever since you unwittingly left it. Call it the city of all-consciousness, the New Jerusalem (which, interestingly, is where Angel Cake, also known as Pieface, was headed, in a story you *did* write when you were a child). It is a place of pure harmony. The thought of reaching it will keep you alive, though also in thrall. It will fill you with a desire to write and write and write—stories like sonatas, novels like symphonies, poems like string quartets, the words spilling out of the window into the street for any despairing passerby to hear and be saved by. If your work does not do this, if no one is rescued, the impulse is still there. This is the intention: to create art that is irresistible, art that possesses the power to make us human beings—we paradoxical beings who are born haunted by our own skepticism—*want* to live. (And so it did matter about my mother, whether she wanted to kill herself or live—but I had to write, whether she resisted my work or not. Whether she had a real heart attack or only a mock one.)

Nonetheless, at my mother's suggestion I took typing in summer school and on my own elected to spend the savings from my first summer job, at sixteen, on private tutelage in algebra. So maybe she wasn't trying to rule my future; maybe, as she said, she was only trying to keep up with my exuberantly inclusive interests. "One day you want to be a chemist," she said. "The next day you want to be a drummer." Everybody knew that if I was going to write I had to be trained to do something else, because writers don't earn any money. I can't imagine how I got it into my head that drummers did.

*

I was twenty when I entered the University of Virginia as a graduate student in philosophy. There I met my cherished friends Henry Taylor, a sophomore, and R. H. W. (Richard) Dillard, a graduate student, both in the English department and both determined to be writers. Henry invited me to a small "bootleg" seminar, run by Fred Bornhauser, a professor of literature, which was, in effect, a non-credit poetry workshop. We met at night in a classroom in Cabell Hall. The next fall, George Garrett, young, acclaimed, energetic—and prolific, various, and published—and generous, empathetic, and prankish—arrived to teach an official writing class, the first such class at the University of Virginia—and quickly became the charismatic center of our literary activities. Nor did his example mislead: he would disappear from public view now and again, and we knew well that it was because he was writing, and we all deduced that the practical jokes and shaggy dog stories were supported by a writer's willingness to withdraw from the world to isolation and hard work.

Although I grew up in the South and at a time when women were not generally granted credibility as artists—or as doctors or scientists or scholars or corporate executives—I was incredibly lucky in my literary friendships. George, Henry, and Richard took my ambition seriously; if any one of them ever questioned it, he didn't let me know. At the time I took for granted that they were my good friends and writing buddies; now I look back and think how amazingly fortunate I was to find them. The women's movement hadn't even started, yet here and there were men who never thought to delimit a young woman's world but, on the contrary, helped to open the world to her. In her essay for the *Contemporary Authors Autobiography Series,* Rita Dove wrote that when she arrived in Charlottesville in 1989 to teach at the University of Virginia she found it "[h]ard to imagine that a mere twenty-five to thirty years ago this university was a fortress of racism and male chauvinism!" It had been, but there were those within who were working, deliberately or not, self-consciously or not, to open the gates, let down the drawbridge. Every revolution is heralded quietly, by individuals who choose to think or act in a new way.

I needed to cross over that bridge, walk into the world. Toward that end, I returned to Richmond to look for work. I worked three jobs at once, a day job, a night job, and a weekend job, to save money for a trip to Europe (I guess it took that many jobs because women earned so little; typing addresses on envelopes, we were paid by the envelope). Then I boarded a freighter to Amsterdam.

People frequently say that when they look back over their lives they can hardly recognize their earlier selves. Who was the young woman who, excessively shy though she was, nevertheless found herself in the Hotel Metropol in Moscow, in January, 1965, communicating in makeshift sign language with the young Latvian composer Imants Kalnins, already well known in the Soviet Union both for his music and independence? (The KGB, I would learn, was busily asking this same question. They asked it while they sat in their white Volvo, watching us from their parking place behind the trees at the edge of the cemetery outside Riga, at midnight, when we said good-bye.) I have no trouble recognizing her as myself. Someone else might—I no longer look like that young woman. But something in her eyes, the mere fact that she is in Moscow and is having a conversation with a composer whose language she doesn't know, seems, *feels,* true to form. I was always shy; I was always cautious; and I was always too curious about the world to stay home.

*

There were not many creative writing programs at that time. I sent for information from the University of Iowa, Stanford University, and the University of North Carolina at Greensboro. Catalogues in hand, I realized that Stanford was too far away—I could visualize the other side of the moon, but not California. Iowa required transcripts from every school I had attended, and I assumed they would not be overjoyed to learn that I had transferred six times to five schools, two of which had expelled me. A friend had lent me a copy of a book of poems by Robert Watson, who was on the faculty at UNC—G. Here was poetry that dared to rhyme, that dared the dramatic monologue, that, in short, ignored what seemed to have become the conventions of then-current verse and went its own, quite jaunty, way. I enrolled at UNC—G.

It was the perfect place. It was sleepy, out of the mainstream; the teachers were not in the celebrity game, and Fred Chappell, Robert Watson, Allen Tate, Guy Owen, and Peter Taylor conveyed their love of the highest standards. (Randall Jarrell was also on the faculty—I audited his class in Modern American Poetry for three months before his sudden death.) Visiting writers included Eudora Welty and Carolyn Kizer.

At University of Virginia I had been too scared to submit my work to the usual competitions—the

Academy of American Poets contests, for example (how could I survive the shame of an Honorable Mention?); and now, when our work was to be discussed by a festival of visiting writers, I hid out in an empty classroom. I wanted very much to listen to Stanley Kunitz and X. J. Kennedy, but, again, what if what they had to say was defeating? And earlier, as soon as Stanley Kunitz arrived on campus and was introduced to a few of us students, in somebody's living room, he had begun to exclaim about his protegée, Louise Glück. I didn't know how he was going to find room in his attention span for another young poet.

All this exquisite agony was no doubt silliness, a waste of time and energy, not to mention the waste of good contacts (I knew my teachers were trying to help me meet writers—they tried to help all the students meet writers), but perhaps it had its uses, too. It allowed me the solitude to read as unstoppingly as I always had, but having previously focused on philosophers, playwrights, and classical literature in translation, I felt especially eager to shore up the gaps created by not having taken literature classes in college. I bought survey texts for American and British literature and read them through; I collected syllabi and worked my way through them; and of course, I wandered the aisles of UNC—G's Jackson Library, sitting on the floor whenever I found a book that called to me to open it.

My lack of social skills gave me leeway to follow my own literary instincts, which I did, writing a long sequential poem, "Benjamin John," that told the story of a man's life—Mr. John was an imagined economics professor—through lyrical or dramatic moments.

A few weeks ago, my old classmate William Pitt (Bill) Root reminded me that he and I met with Allen Tate at a Greensboro diner to discuss our work. Mr. Tate decided to begin with me. "Tell me," he began, "why a woman who looks like you would want to write from a male point of view?" Bill said we were both stunned; he assured me that I recovered from my surprise immediately and answered Mr. Tate clearly and "firmly." I hope so. But the women's movement *still* hadn't started, and a girl's responses to male chauvinism could be hit or miss.

Besides, the girl I was wanted to be loved as much as she wanted to be published. Having been told by Soviet authorities that I would not be permitted to marry Imants, and having mourned the loss of him for nearly two years, I fell in love with and married Jonathan Silver, a sculptor, who had arrived at UNC—G in the capacity of visiting art historian.

That fall marked the publication of *The Girl in the Black Raincoat,* an anthology of fiction and poetry edited by George Garrett and inspired by my black raincoat. After I'd moved from Charlottesville back to Richmond, Henry wrote a story for George's class about "the girl in the black raincoat." When he read it to the class, many of the students were disturbed, thinking it was patently immoral of him to have written about someone they knew, someone who was not completely made up. To help them understand the complex relationship between reality and fiction, George directed the whole class to write stories about a girl in a black raincoat. But—why stop there? he wondered, and conceived the anthology. Contributors included Annie Dillard, Henry Taylor (with the story that started the whole thing), Leslie Fiedler, Mary Lee Settle, Carolyn Kizer, others. Donald Justice and Mark Strand produced a co-authored poem. They'd all had described to them—or some of them knew—a girl who used to wear a black raincoat even on sunny days. (I meant merely to use it as a sweater; my mother had bought it for me in downtown Richmond.)

It was the publication parties thrown for *The Girl in the Black Raincoat,* at Hollins College and in Charlottesville, that persuaded me I ought to be married: Everyone else—it seemed to me—was; everyone else had a real life as a real person and not just as a fantasy; everyone else knew enough not to go to a publication party without a poem stuck in her coat pocket. It hadn't even occurred to me that we would be giving readings! I knew Jonathan would ask me to marry him if I let him know I was available for marriage; he did, and I said yes.

(If I'd been smarter I might have known that I had also met the man I should have—and now have—married, but I wouldn't find this out for another three decades.)

My mother liked Jonathan. She and my father picked us up at the bus station the weekend we went to Richmond for a blood test. Jonathan and I got in the back seat. "Would you like a Life Saver?" my mother asked him, turning around to offer him the opened roll. "Too late," he said, and she was his.

Age eight; with her father, J. Milton, at Cascadilla Gorge in Ithaca, NY

Or would have been, if he had not been so determined to go at everything as if it were an obstacle. My mother gave me a handful of recipes, taught me how to make a white sauce, cautioned me that men's egos need bolstering. She and my father did their best to help us out, but Jonathan was suspicious of every gesture, every offer. It's no wonder: his own father asked him what it would cost to convince me I should break off the engagement ("go away" was how he put it, or "get lost"), told him he was disowned, and forbade Jonathan's mother to see her son, a commandment she broke once or twice but not comfortably. They did not come to the wedding in Richmond.

In the end, Jonathan decided he did not want children. (Before I accepted his proposal I had asked him if he did, and he said yes.) He now wanted a divorce, and though I had been the one less in love, that had changed while we were together; and it took me years, after the divorce, to recover a sense of self. I stayed in New York to do this, working in children's books, teaching at a private school for emotionally disturbed kids, and tutoring a teenager who had cerebral palsy. One day Con Edison turned off my electricity because a previous, extremely previous, tenant had not paid his bill. The representative on the telephone refused to believe that I was not that tenant. I said I had a sick child. Whether she believed me or not, the representative was required by law to turn the electricity back on after that. I was ashamed of myself, but pleased, too, and I figured that if I could holler at Con Ed and get them to do what I wanted, I had learned to be a New Yorker and my sense of self was back in working order.

*

Even so, it was a difficult time. Young women writers were not usually taken seriously, and there was not the same career ladder for writers, male or female, then that there is now. I wasn't close friends with established writers or magazine editors; I earned a pittance (and soon I had a day job, a night job, a weekend job); every morning I delivered my you-are-not-a-writer lecture to myself with my first cup of coffee, hoping I could teach myself to want less, to settle for what I had.

I was starting a new job on Monday. I had been asked, on the basis of some freelance copy editing I had done, to write a teacher's guide to Jewish morality tales. I spent the weekend smoking hash with a male friend. On Monday morning, I called my new boss to tell him I would not be coming in after all because I was thinking of killing myself and would therefore probably not be available for employment. "Let's have lunch first," he said. At lunch, he suggested that I write down what had happened. I no longer believed I could write a story and so I wrote him a long letter, even though I had only just met him. He showed the letter to the writer Abraham Rothberg, who nudged, coaxed, challenged, and persuaded me to make a story of it, by plastering the margins with X's, each indicating a scene in want of development, and by paying no attention at all to my reluctance. *Commentary* published the story, and my dry cleaner and his wife read it and recognized my name, as they told me when I handed him the ticket for the clothes I had dropped off, and I started writing again. Abe became a dear friend, one who has never pulled any punches, always telling me frankly what he liked and didn't like about my work. He is a distinguished journalist and novelist, with

particular expertise in the history of WWII, and anyone who has not read his books has something to look forward to. We have kept up a correspondence for years now; I save his letters.

*

I started work on my first novel, *Sick and Full of Burning,* and by the time I left New York City, passing up a raise and promotion and leave time to move back, broke, to Richmond, because I didn't think I could maintain the faith in New York, I had a rough draft.

*

Sick and Full of Burning recounts the adventures of a medical student, Mary (Tennessee) Settleworth, living in New York City, who earns her tuition by working as a live-in tutor to a handicapped teenager. The book poses this question: Am I my sister's keeper, even if that entails martyrdom? My protagonist answers the question with a *no* and yet, contrarily, acts out the answer *yes,* risking her life for her student's. This is how I put it to a newspaper interviewer: "The fire is the apocalypse. It is that extreme event at the point of which one comes to terms with whether or not one wants to live. Tennessee is unclear about her affection for life and she takes this question right down to the wire, which in this instance is the fire." It is in the consideration of questions that seem to permit, or even require, absolute and contradictory answers that I find the real subjects of my novels. I am not interested in writing novels that either supply easy solutions to philosophical questions or ignore the existence of such questions. Invited by *Library Journal* to say something about my first novel, I explained, "I took as my starting point Deuteronomy 30:19,' . . . I have set before you life and death . . . therefore choose life . . . ,' surely the wildest non sequitur in Western civilization, and set out to see what steps might be supplied which would establish a logical progression from the possibility of suicide, real or moral, to the injunction to reject it as an alternative. That's why the structure of the book is a spiral, like one of those slinky coils which walk down stairs to the delight of children, and why the book circles its own center on successive levels before it reaches the bottom" (October, 1974). I wanted what appeared to be a comedy about three women to turn itself inside out, like a Moebius strip, halfway through, revealing its tragic dimension.

While I was working on *Sick and Full of Burning* in Richmond, my mother decided to write a book about moving to England—as she and my father planned to do in retirement—and as it happened, my brother joined us to work on a nonfiction manuscript that would become *On High Steel,* about life as an ironworker. All three books were published in 1974— probably the first time three first books in one family appeared in one year. My mother was awarded a medal from the English-speaking Union. *Kirkus Reviews* called *Sick and Full of Burning* "a just about perfect first novel—bright, sassy, sad and with talent, well, to burn" (starred review, March 15, 1974). *The Chicago Tribune Book World* exclaimed, "A flawless first novel? You gotta be kidding! No kidding" (June 30, 1974). *People* magazine singled me out for a "Look-out" article in July of 1974. Mass paperback rights sold to Ballantine Books. In short, the successes of my mother's and my books were satisfying, no matter how modest. My brother's success was greater: NBC featured his book in five five-minute segments on the national *Evening News* one week. We were happy campers. My father took to saying he was going to write a book called *The Old Man and the C Scale.* None of us had an inkling about how rough things were going to turn. Nor did I yet care—I thought I would write my books, get them published, and someday—this was how the fantasy went—deliver an acceptance speech in Sweden. (The speech was going to be a barn-burner; hey, it would put Faulkner's in the shade!) I didn't expect money, but I did expect serious and smart reviewers.

*

I had always thought of myself as a poet first and foremost, but I had not been able to publish much poetry after leaving UNC—G (even though I had published a fair amount of it while I was a student, including "Benjamin John" in *Carolina Quarterly,* and three of my poems had been set by my father and performed in concert). It wasn't until later that I realized that my interest in form, meter, and rhyme was out of sync with the poetry of that period. When a small press in North Carolina called to ask me about my manuscript—Fred Chappell had referred the press to me; as I said, I would have been *lost* without my friends—I gladly seized the opportunity. *Lovers and Agnostics,* my first collection, of poems, which included "Benjamin John" appeared in 1975.

At that point I figured I had forfeited five years to being married and then to being divorced, and I didn't want to lose more time. I tried to sort out what books I wanted to write. (Perhaps I should have thought instead about the business of becoming a writer— sales, agents, networking for free-lance pieces—but I concentrated on the books themselves—my subjects, characters, imagery, the forms and structures.) I visualized a bookshelf holding the books I wished to write. This time I say "visualized" because I guess it *was* something like a vision, although making out the titles on the spines, or even just knowing which volume was poetry and which fiction, occupied my evenings for some weeks. I have never been rigid about what I would write, but a number of my books derive from that period of thinking about how I would fill the shelf. I also revised the lecture I delivered to myself daily from "You are not a writer" to "If you don't write your books, no one else will."

It was a gratification to see *Lovers and Agnostics* published. After all, in my mind I was a poet first, even if the first *book* I'd published was a *novel.* I turned to my poems-in-progress, which were already adding up. The publication of my second collection, *Relativity: A Point of View,* in 1977 marked the beginning of my very happy relationship with Louisiana State University Press, a relationship that has been, for me, both sustaining and guiding.

The final poem in *Relativity,* "A Bird's-eye View of Einstein," is an examination of the idea of the Trinity from a woman's point of view. In blank verse, the poem's three sections pursue various trinities: Son, Ghost, Father; husband, brother, father; Freud's three universal taboos of cannibalism, incest, murder; the three major prophets of the Old Testament (each presented in a "sermon"), Jeremiah, Ezekiel, Isaiah; the ideas of covenant, honesty, judgment; the tree of good and evil, the tree of community, the tree of faith in Revelation; future, past, present; sex, politics, creative knowledge; city, ocean, desert; Richmond, Ithaca, Baton Rouge; taste, light, sound. But because the poem is using the idea of relativity to look at the idea of trinity, it is not a simple scheme of threes: After a prologue introduces "the point of view," a bird's-eye point of view, which seems to be outside the trinities, the body of the poem rings changes on the point of view, finally returning to a bird's point of view, only now it is a different bird, or the bird itself seen from a different point of view; the bird is *time that flies*: "Time / Sings in the tree." Thus the Trinity, which is three-in-one, is one and one and one—and one.

Some reviewers have found the imagery overwhelming—overwrought, they sometimes say—not recognizing that much of it comes from the Book of Revelation and the three major prophets of the Old Testament, Isaiah, Ezekiel, and Jeremiah, nor that the tripartite structure of the poem is built on a number of levels, all of them sliced through by a point-of-view that shifts. I might wonder if what I thought I'd put into the poem had really got into the poem were it not that Fred Chappell, having already sent me a short, nice note about the book upon publication, wrote me back three months later, single-spaced, front and back, several pages, explaining with some excitement how my poem was put together. His analysis reflected precisely what I had thought I was doing. (A couple of years ago, Fred asked me who I think of as my audience. "You," I said. He seemed surprised. "I would have thought it was your parents," he said. My parents are sometimes my subjects—with their permission, I might add—but not my audience, even emotionally. The audience I think of myself as writing for is made up of readers I admire, whose serious regard and respect I want to earn. Some are writers, some not.)

In a *credo* on the jacket flap of *Relativity,* I gave my view of what I was up to: "I'm concerned with the shape of ideas in time: the dynamic configuration a moral dilemma makes, cutting through a novel like a river through rock; the way a philosophical statement bounces against the walls of a poem, like an echo in a canyon. A writer, poet or novelist, wants to create a contained, complete landscape in which time flows freely and naturally. The *poems* are where I live. It's in poetry that thought and time most musically counterpoint each other, and I like a world in which the elements sing."

*

Imants Kalnins would sometimes call me up from Moscow or Riga. In the summer of 1975, right after the Helsinki Accords were signed, I went back to Riga, and we tried again to get married. This time the KGB threatened us, made anonymous phone calls in the middle of the night, took photographs. After I left—my visa had expired—they frequently intercepted our mail, and we had to smuggle letters back and forth.

I no longer had a home base in the States. My parents had moved to England for their retirement—they wanted to listen to music, and they wanted to be near

c. 1960; in the woods near Richmond, Virginia

my sister, a solo flutist specializing in contemporary music and a professor at London School of Music and Trinity School of Music—so I joined them there, thinking I'd soon be allowed back in to the Soviet Union. I didn't know that I would not see Imants again until 1988, when he was invited to the States to attend the premiere of his fifth symphony. . . . I was to spend the next two years in England, studying Latvian with a BBC translator, and writing, among other things, my second novel, a modern-day restoration comedy about marriage and music. (I made the heroine a flutist.)

In a paperback of George Crabbe's poetry I'd found an epigraph that seemed to fit the young married couple I was writing about. I happened to mail the epigraph to my brother, who wrote back suggesting that two words in it, "Augusta played," would make a great title. Suddenly the book took off. I had a great time writing this book—my "golden" book, as I thought of it, for Augusta was herself a golden beauty, and her flute with its gold mouthpiece was a metaphor for how I wanted my prose to sing.

Augusta Played addresses the question I saw as being the logical next stop among the fiction entries on my bookshelf: Assuming that one *has* chosen to live, are one's other choices determined or free? Again, it seemed that this was a question to which both answers, contradictory though they are, could be supported. This time I supplied the contradictory answers by opposing two main characters, a husband and wife, the one representing a deterministic world view, the other free will. The wife, Augusta, is a flutist studying at Juilliard; her husband, Norman, is the first known "cultural musicologist," a field he has invented for himself, and a doctoral candidate at Columbia University. The two characters are presented with equal sympathy, as are a large cast of minor characters encompassing, among others, a stripper, a judge, an orchestra conductor, a blackmailer, two little boys (one of whom talked like Aldo Ray), and a synthesizer. How could I not have had a great time?

But in the real, unfictional world, I was a citizen of one country, living in a second country, seeking permission to live in a third country, and I was by now completely broke. When one day I got a call from the University of Wisconsin at Madison asking me if I'd like to come be a visiting lecturer for a year, I said yes.

At UW I had a killing load. Many, many professors do, in contrast to the popular notion of the professorial life. At least I had a novel in hand: *Augusta Played* was published in my second year of teaching at UW. It would be a while before I came out with another. Sans tweed jacket with leather elbow patches, sans pipe, sans evenings before the fire in the fireplace, glass of cognac in hand, with, in fact, approximately four thousand five hundred pages of student manuscript to read and mark up each semester, not counting work submitted by tutorial students, I wrote a long unpublished novel—but only by dint of giving up any hope of a personal life. Unfortunately, the novel, "Paula," an examination of rage and frustration, bore the marks of depression and exhaustion and is unpublishable as it stands. I like to think that somewhere in what became an incohesive, rambling mutter ("I will write no matter what," "I will write no matter what") a short, tight novel waits to be found, but I am reluctant to look for it, for fear it might not, after all, be there.

I put "Paula" away and began work on *In the Wink of an Eye,* which remains one of my favorite books. The question posed here was, Is revolution ever a just way of creating a just state? The novel is a political cartoon.

The contradiction suggested by the question (*yes* and *no*) is sustained via a *reductio ad absurdum* in which a small revolution that begins in the infamous Green Hell of the Santa Cruz State in Bolivia succeeds beyond its most extravagant dreams—succeeds, that is to say, *as* its most extravagant dreams, spreading first to other parts of the world and then *beyond* the world, into outer space and the realm of the imagination, for it is a part of my political program, as I say in the book, that "it is the inalienable right of the imagination to rejoice in itself."

To cover the ground I needed to cover—several continents and then no ground at all!—I converted the idea of an omniscient "I" into "God's eye." The action could take place wherever God's eye happened to glance in a given chapter. A further motive behind this novel was Northrop Frye's caveat against conjoining romance and satire; had I not already intended to write the book, that alone would probably have caused me to think of it. From the beginning I have enjoyed taking as challenges any advice about or analysis of writing that has seemed to me to limit, politically or aesthetically, the domain of the creative spirit.

I wish that *Wink* might have found more readers or at least had a chance to look for them, but it was an orphan book. *Sick and Full of Burning* had also been an orphan book, meaning the editor who had accepted it was gone from the publishing house before the book was published. *Augusta Played* wound up with a different house—Houghton Mifflin. In a two-book contract, *Wink* and my fourth book of fiction, *The Lost Traveller's Dream,* would also be orphan books, so that I had no continuity with a house or editor and none of the books received much in the way of promotion. *Wink* and *Traveller* were given a sandwich and an apple and abandoned by the side of the road.

The Lost Traveller's Dream was intended as a story collection, not a novel; I added material to make it such at the publisher's direction. I don't like the added material, and for years I thought I would like to restore the book to its original composition. Now, though, I am no longer interested in restoration so much as revision, and I hope that someday I may have a chance to publish a revision, a pretty drastic one at that.

Whether novel or story collection, *The Lost Traveller's Dream* continued the exploration of the theme of the imagination that I had begun in *In the Wink of an Eye,* but in a non-comic mode. With an epigraph taken from the poem by William Blake in which he says (speaking to Satan), "Every Harlot was a Virgin once, / Nor can'st thou ever change Kate into Nan," the book proceeds to change Kate into Nan. Kate, who is the narrator of the three stories of the first part, is the editor and writer who has created Lindy, the photographer and poet of the second part. Only in the third and final section do we learn that Kate was herself a created character, devised by Nan who reveals her working method in a series of stories in which Kate is one among many characters. In other words, Lindy has represented a dead-end of self-involvement that leads only to a loss of faith—embodied as a friend named Faith—while Nan turns the creative attention outward to embrace the world in which she lives. This is, ultimately, a work that argues process is product, and imagination, reality. "We were ourselves only part of a larger story," the book concludes, having brought the three narrators together in an editorial *we,* "whose ending we could not know, a dénouement that would find us whether or not we could find it. . . . The conclusion, lost to us in mystery, reveals itself in the act of self-knowledge, God's mind learning its own power."

*

At about this time I came across an article by David R. Slavitt and wrote to him about it. I had met David years before, at the *Girl in the Black Raincoat* party at Charlottesville, but we didn't know each other. He answered my letter, and out of that grew a fine friendship with another tremendously smart and learned man. He's an e-mailer, and that's primarily how we communicate these days. There have been times when e-mails from David were what kept me going.

I knew I was going to have trouble finding a publisher for another novel, and one Saturday night, as I worked on a story titled "War and Peace," I realized that by excerpting a few pages from a novella I had thrown aside a few years earlier, and two pages from an unpublished piece of ten years earlier, and adding stories about this, this, and that, I would have a group of stories that I would be able to publish individually, in magazines and journals, and that could also be put together to form a book-length narrative.

The Monday morning after my Saturday night epiphany I knocked on my friend and colleague Ronald Wallace's office door to tell him about it. From my first days at UW, Ron and I had always been mutually supportive, cheering each other on, interested in each other's ideas. He was encouraging and enthusiastic that day, and four years later offered helpful feedback as I worked toward the right ending to *My Life and Dr. Joyce Brothers.*

My Life and Dr. Joyce Brothers was billed by the publisher as a novel in stories. The overarching narrative does justify, I believe, the term "novel in stories"—a description I would have been happy to apply to *The Lost Traveller's Dream*—but eventually this book is to be seen as Book One of a story cycle; my next published book, *The Society of Friends* (1999), is Book Two; and there will be a third book. I don't think uncommercial writers are often able to publish long works of fiction, especially when they've been previously published by different houses, but that is my dream: to see the three in one volume, so that the shape of the whole will be clear.

My Life and Dr. Joyce Brothers was my first published fiction to refer to Madison, Wisconsin. In these stories about a woman, Nina Bryant, moving away from her own family and creating for herself a nontraditional family of friends, Madison becomes the nexus of comment about contemporary American society. *The Society of Friends* expands the fictional territory to the lives of some of Nina's neighbors. Among them are a high-school Latin teacher, a nurse, a commodities broker, a gallery owner, a medical librarian, a performance artist. They are decent people trying to live decent lives.

*

Eleven years elapsed between my second and third poetry collections. This was not because I was not writing poems or not submitting a poetry manuscript to publishers. *Natural Theology* was rescued by Henry Taylor, who looked at the manuscript when he was in Madison to give a reading and advised me to shorten it and switch the opening poems to later in the book. I asked him why they shouldn't stay at the beginning. "Because they are too peculiar," Henry said. "Nobody will know how to read them." He was right, and I did what he said and the manuscript was accepted for publication, though I wouldn't be surprised if Henry also wrote a letter of support.

For writers who believe in the language must also believe in one another. I doubt that I would ever have

c. 1969

succeeded in publishing anything, and I know I would not have published everything I have published, without the help and encouragement of such good friends. From them, I have learned to extend a similar hand wherever I can.

Natural Theology provided the occasion for the Fellowship of Southern Writers Poetry Award, the Hanes Poetry Prize, though the prize is awarded for a body of work rather than a single book. The presentation, in Chattanooga, was one of the most exciting events of my professional life. I, and the winners of other prizes, stood on a stage in front of an audience of fifteen hundred, many of whom were members of the literary establishment. I thought I would be speechless with stage fright, but as soon as I gripped the podium and looked out into the auditorium, I felt right at home up there. Perhaps a writer should not be moved by appeals to her vanity, but I was, I admit I was, and in the photographs taken after the ceremony, I couldn't stop smiling.

The title of my fourth book of poems, *God's Loud Hand,* comes from one of the poems, "Song for the Second Creation," in which "love" is "the sung word flung into the world by God's loud hand." The "sung word" referred to is Christ; the "loud hand" refers to the sound of one hand clapping, as in the well-known zen koan. After the book appeared, some readers assumed that I am a devout Christian. But—I tell them, when I have an opportunity—although I believe in the *idea* of Christ, I don't believe in God.

Death and Transfiguration, which arose out of a time of loss—the illnesses and deaths of my parents, my ex-husband, and others—closes with a long poem titled "Requiem," wherein I endeavor to deal directly and systematically with the question posed by Theodor Adorno: Can art be made, in good conscience, after the horror of the Holocaust? The poem is an argument and adheres to its line(s) of thought, deriving in conclusion a crucial distinction between experience, which is personal and subjective, and memory, which can be articulated and shared. At the same time, it sweeps up and holds together the losses tallied in the book's first, and only other, section.

I agree with W. H. Auden that the minor artist is the one who adheres to a competency instead of risking failure; a necessary condition, whether sufficient or not, for the artist aspiring to major achievement is that she avoid self-parody or a mannerist version of herself, and that means she has to keep pushing in unfamiliar directions, tackling the new. Perhaps, therefore, it is *better* not to be noticed, since notice tends to make writers hunger for more of it, which they are apt to go after by repeating whatever has brought them notice.

Rising Venus, which came out in 2002, looks at the experience of being female. I am at work on two poetry manuscripts, one a "new and selected," the other a book-length sonnet sequence, but I can't say when they will be ready to present to my publisher.

*

When it became clear that I was going to be a writer whether or no, my mother became as supportive and helpful as any daughter could hope. She read reams of works-in-progress; responded to my compulsively anxious queries about whether to use this word or that, this punctuation or that; told me to keep going when I imagined I should quit; and typed the entire handwritten draft of *The Exiled Heart.*

She typed it on her old manual, with the keys that had to be hammered half a mile down. I left the draft pages on the dining room table when I went to bed, and when I got up, I found them side by side with the typed pages.

I first wrote *The Exiled Heart* while I was still living in England, still trying to get a visa to return to Latvia in order to marry Imants. The book details that quest: the struggle of a man and a woman against arbitrary obstacles placed in their path by politicos and bureaucrats. It is a love story with a sad ending. It is also an autobiographical inquiry into meaning, making essayistic excursions into the kinds of things one thinks about in a situation like that: What is justice? Is forgiveness possible? What does the artist owe to art? And of course, What is love? As I explained in the opening chapter, "I didn't know, in 1965, where [the] train was taking me: to Moscow, I thought, but equally to my heart and my conscience. This book is a kind of log, a moral travelogue if you will, of a course that was set then and there, deep into heartland." The central question of the book is, What can love mean in a corrupt world? As has often been the case for me, there was a long lapse between the first writing and publication—fifteen or sixteen years, a revised draft every year or year and a half—and the Soviet Union fell six months after the book came out. A brief uncollected essay, "What Is Poetry? What Is Music?" published in *Agni,* functions as a coda to the book, telling the story of my meeting with Imants in 1997, when the Detroit Symphony Orchestra, with Maestro Neeme Järvi, offered the world premiere of the original version of Imants's Fourth Symphony, whose last movement is set to poems I had written for Imants. The Soviet authorities had insisted that the English text be omitted; now, post-Soviet tyranny, it had been returned to the music, and changes made in the score to accommodate the revision were also returned to the original. I included the poems in my first collection; the symphony has been made available on a BIS compact disc, played by the Singapore Symphony Orchestra.

My book of essays, *Writing the World,* includes other pieces about my time behind the Iron Curtain, along with essays on writing and the writer's life. The writer's life . . . ah, well, it is what I wanted and what I love, for better or worse.

I love when, writing, I lose track of myself, my self works free of the constraint of time. It's time that al-

In Latvia, c. 1975

lows us to recognize ourselves as selves, and when we forget ourselves, we live, however briefly, outside time. We know eternity, if only for a moment.

*

In 1999 I retired from UW—Madison. Burke Davis III, a fiction writer, and I were married September 17, 2000, in the small farmhouse we bought in southside Virginia. As I mentioned earlier in this essay, we had first met in Greensboro, in the sixties. We occasionally try to imagine how our lives might have gone had we dated and married back then, but mostly we are just very glad to be married now.

I sometimes teach as a visitor: a semester at Hollins University, in Roanoke, was a wonderful reunion with my old pal Richard Dillard, and several terms at the University of Alabama in Huntsville, where I have served as the Humanities Center's Visiting Eminent Scholar, have brought me new friendships and new experiences, both of which I treasure. In fact, teaching at UA—H has been one of the very special pleasures of my life.

Marriage and our small farm are, of course, others. It is my husband who deserves all the credit here—he makes our country life possible, by being good at all the things I haven't a clue how to do. We have forty-four acres, including an orchard, woods, a pond, and a vegetable patch. It's because of Burke that I can look out my window (the glass is from 1874) at the small rain falling on loblolly pines. Intermittently the pianissimo mizzle strengthens to a hard shower loud on the tin roof.

Intermittently, Burke gets the tractor stuck in mud, and Junior comes over from next door to tow him out.

I wish my parents could have known Burke, and that I am married to him. "You're so pretty," my mother said, after my father had died (I was forty-six, but she was my *mother*); "I wish you'd get a job somewhere else, find a good man, and get married." By then, we both knew I wasn't going to be a literary celebrity, that no grandstand judge was ever going to look my way, and although she didn't want me to quit writing, she did want me to have a happier life. And I do.

Part of what makes my life now happy is my knowledge that I've written at least some of the books I planned to write (I hope to write all the books on my "mental bookshelf"). If Burke and I had rediscovered each other earlier, maybe I could have been married *and* had kids *and* written my books—especially if I hadn't had to hold certain jobs—but if a choice was necessary, I think I made the right choice. I have had an enduring relationship with writing, with the dream of creating something lasting, something memorable, some poem or novel or story that would do what I think art should do—bring beauty and truth together in a way that will help others to know what the late Beethoven string quartets taught me; namely, that artists make meaning, and meaning is celebration, triumph, the most miraculous of miracles. Meaning is *logos,* and without it there never was a beginning, not to anything, not to us, not to the greatest story ever told and not even to the least.

In an unpublished memoir, my mother wrote about the sleeping porch that was the first apartment she and my father rented after they were married. They used to sleep in until the heat of the day caught up with them, and lying in bed, they'd hear the milkman setting his bottles on the front steps. My mother was twenty, a grad-school drop-out; my father was twenty-four. My mother was probably already pregnant, but she wouldn't have known it yet. I just love them to death, thinking of them like this: young and sexy and full of energy and laughter, and wildly smitten with each other. I'm glad my mother had that in her life. But me, I was always going to be in thrall to my work, and it's never not been, for me, a matter of love.

BIOGRAPHICAL AND CRITICAL SOURCES:

BOOKS

Authors in the News, Volume 1, Gale (Detroit, MI), 1976.
Cherry, Kelly, *The Exiled Heart: A Meditative Autobiography,* Louisiana State University Press (Baton Rouge, LA), 1991.
Dictionary of Literary Biography Yearbook: 1983, Gale (Detroit, MI), 1984, . . . *1999,* 2000.
Finding the Words: Conversations with Writers Who Teach, Swallow Press, 1985.

PERIODICALS

Anglican Theological Review, Volume 82, 2000, Patricia Gabilondo, review of *Death and Transfiguration,* pp. 242-245.
Bloomsbury Review, September-October, 2000, Joann Verica, review of *The Society of Friends,* p. 23.
Booklist, March 1, 2002, Donna Seaman, review of *Rising Venus,* p. 1086.
Boston Globe, March 17, 1979, Robert Taylor, review of *Augusta Played.*
Chicago Tribune, April 1, 1979; May 20, 1984; April 17, 1990.
Chicago Tribune Book World, June 30, 1974, review of *Sick and Full of Burning.*
Choice, November, 1995, p. 461.
Kirkus Reviews, March 15, 1974, review of *Sick and Full of Burning;* February 1, 1990, review of *My Life and Dr. Joyce Brothers: A Novel in Stories,* p. 119.
Library Journal, October 1, 1974.
Los Angeles Times Book Review, June 24, 1990, Judith Freeman, review of *My Life and Dr. Joyce Brothers;* August 20, 1995, p. 3.

Louisiana Literature, April, 1991, Fred Chappell, review of *The Exiled Heart: A Meditative Autobiography.*

New York Times Book Review, April 22, 1984; May 27, 1990; October 6, 1991; October 24, 1999, Megan Harlan, "Cozy but Not Comfy," p. 37.

Poets and Writers, November-December, 1999, pp. 28-37.

Publishers Weekly, February 15, 1993, p. 232; April 24, 1995, p. 57; August 9, 1999, review of *The Society of Friends,* p. 345.

Three Rivers Poetry Journal, March, 1977, Patricia Goedicke, review of *Relativity: A Point of View.*

Washington Post, April 9, 1991.

Washington Post Book World, April 7, 1991.

Writer's Digest, July, 1996, p. 12.

*   *   *

CHORLEY, Richard J(ohn) 1927-2002

OBITUARY NOTICE—See index for *CA* sketch: Born September 4, 1927, in Minehead, Somerset, England; died after a heart attack May 12, 2002, in Cambridge, England. Geographer, geologist, educator, and author. Chorley made significant contributions to geomorphology, the study of the Earth's surface and how it changes over time. He received his M.A. at Exeter College, Oxford in 1954, but it was during his studies at Columbia University under the influence of A. N. Strahler that his innovative ideas about geomorphology began to take root. While in the United States Chorley taught at Columbia and Brown universities during the 1950s; family reasons caused him to return to England, where he was a lecturer at Cambridge from 1962 to 1970 and a reader from 1970 to 1974. In 1974 he received his Sc.D. from Cambridge, becoming a professor in geography that same year. He remained at Cambridge until his retirement in 1994. Chorley caused waves in the field of geology with his theories about the evolution of the structure of the Earth's surface that were counter to the then-popularly held ideas of Davisian cycles of erosion expressed by W. M. Davis. Chorley convincingly argued his case for a General Systems Theory that used model-based paradigms to explain how surface structures evolved. Working with Antony J. Dunn and Robert P. Beckinsale, he published the landmark series "The History of the Study of Landforms; or, The Development of Geomorphology," with volumes released in 1964, 1973,

1991, and posthumously. These books form an important record covering the development of the science of geomorphology. Chorley was also interested in hydrology and meteorology and edited *Water, Earth, and Man: A Synthesis of Hydrology, Geomorphology, and Socio-Economic Geography* in 1969. In addition to many other edited books on geography and geomorphology, he wrote *Atmosphere, Weather, and Climate* with Roger Graham Barry in 1968, with the fourth edition being released in 1982, and, with S. A. Schumm and D. Sugdem penned *Geomorphology* (1985). An influential scholar, Chorley was also beloved by his students as an inspiring lecturer, mentor, and friend who supported and encouraged them even long after graduation.

OBITUARIES AND OTHER SOURCES:

BOOKS

Writers Directory, 16th edition, St. James Press (Detroit, MI), 2001.

PERIODICALS

Independent (London, England), May 18, 2002, p. 20.
Times (London, England), June 24, 2002.

*   *   *

CHYET, Stanley F. 1931-2002

OBITUARY NOTICE—See index for *CA* sketch: Born April 2, 1931, in Boston, MA; died of cancer October 19, 2002, in Sherman Oaks, CA. Historian, educator, and author. Rabbi Chyet was an expert on American Jewish history and helped establish and run the Skirball Cultural Center. He earned his bachelor's degree from Brandeis University in 1952 before attending Hebrew Union College—Jewish Institute of Religion, where he earned his master's degree and was ordained a rabbi in 1957, going on to receive his Ph.D. in 1960. From 1962 until 1976 he taught American Jewish history at Hebrew Union College in Cincinnati, Ohio while also working for the American Jewish Archives, where he was associate director from 1966 to 1976. In 1976 he moved to the Los Angeles campus of Hebrew

Union College, where he eventually became director of the Edgar F. Magnin School of Graduate Studies at the College Institute of Religion. In 1996, one year before retiring from Hebrew Union College, Chyet helped found the Skirball Cultural Center with Rabbi Uri D. Herscher. The center's goal is to educate the public about the history of Judaism and modern American Jewry. In addition to his teaching and administrative work, Chyet was acclaimed for his efforts as a translator and editor of Jewish literature, including two works with Warren Bargad: *Israeli Poetry: A Contemporary Anthology* (1986) and *No Sign of Ceasefire: An Anthology of Contemporary Israeli Poetry* (2002); he also wrote poetry, including his collection *The Lord Has a Taste for Clowning* (2003).

OBITUARIES AND OTHER SOURCES:

BOOKS

Directory of American Scholars, 10th edition, Gale (Detroit, MI), 2001.

PERIODICALS

Los Angeles Times, October 22, 2002, p. B10.

*   *   *

CLARK, Joan
    See BENSON, Mildred (Augustine Wirt)

*   *   *

CLARKE, Julia 1950-

PERSONAL: Born September 15, 1950, in Surrey, England; daughter of Pauline Margaret (Rutherford) Reay; married Michael Clarke (a journalist), August 8, 1979; children: Matthew, Bethany. *Education:* Goldsmiths' College, London, certificate in education, 1974; University of Leeds, M.A. (with distinction), 1999. *Religion:* Church of England.

ADDRESSES: Home and office—Harlow Grange Farm, Otley Rd., Harrogate, North Yorkshire, England. *Agent*—Rosemary Canter, Peters Fraser & Dunlop, Drury House, 34-43 Russell St., London WC2B 5HA, England.

CAREER: Writer.

WRITINGS:

YOUNG-ADULT NOVELS

Summertime Blues, Oxford University Press (Oxford, England), 2001.
The Starling Tree, Collins Flamingo (London, England), 2001.
Breakers, Collins Flamingo (London, England), 2002.
Between You and Me: Secrets, Lies, Love, Kisses, Tears, Oxford University Press (Oxford, England), 2002.

Author's work has been translated into Catalan, German, and Swedish.

OTHER

Author of six novels for adults. Also author of articles and short stories.

WORK IN PROGRESS: Fountains Earth (tentative title), a teen novel set on a farm after a contemporary crisis of foot-and-mouth disease.

SIDELIGHTS: In novels such as *Summertime Blues* and *The Starling Tree,* British novelist Julia Clarke writes about the emotional traumas and heartaches of the teenage years as many adolescents perceive them. Her characters often have parents who don't seem to care about them, who seem less mature than the teenagers themselves, and whose family decisions leave the young people with few choices of their own. Her characters see themselves stuck in unbearable circumstances from which they are desperate to break free. Clarke portrays them with sympathy, some critics claim, but also with a benign sense of humor.

Summertime Blues is the story of Alex, a teenager who sees himself as unwanted, uncomfortable, and perhaps unable to change his fate. When his parents divorce, Alex learns that neither really wants him around. His father in London is far too preoccupied with his pregnant girlfriend. His mother has remarried and moved to rural Yorkshire, reluctantly taking Alex with her to spend the summer. The boy feels miserable and out of place in the countryside, especially when he meets his new stepsister, Faye, a young woman of his own age so beautiful and perfect that Alex seems completely intimidated in her presence. In a *School Librarian* review, Linda Saunders described poor Alex as a boy "who is his own worst enemy." The situation changes when Alex meets a companion who distracts him from his own glum mood by teaching him to work with homeless animals. He gains enough self-confidence to believe that the admiration of his beautiful stepsister might not be so unattainable after all. Finally his father needs his help, and Alex returns to London to assist in welcoming his fragile, premature stepbrother into the world. The critical response to *Summertime Blues* was mixed. Saunders suggested that, while the protagonist is a teenage boy, the story might appeal more to girls, but she and other reviewers pointed to the realistic issues raised in the story and the authentic teenage voice of Alex as narrator. *Books for Keeps* contributor George Hunt called *Summertime Blues* a "moving and compelling" portrayal of the anguish of growing up.

The Starling Tree is a similar growing-up novel about a girl. Clarke presents Fawn through the girl's own eyes as the most normal component in a troubled family. Fawn studies hard at school and strives in general to be the best person she can be. She lives with her musician father, whose dissipated past has left him too paranoid and damaged to leave the house and earn a living, and a mother who spends all her energy working to raise the family out of poverty. Fawn's twin brother Ginna has become involved with a rowdy gang and is neglecting his education. On top of that, her soul-mate, a longtime boyfriend, has moved away. When it seems the situation couldn't be much worse, a new music teacher comes to town, and Fawn falls tumultuously and hopelessly in love. The music teacher encourages Fawn to pursue her gift for music, and she begins to emerge from the gloomy confines of her family and all of its problems. A *Guardian* reviewer called *The Starling Tree* "a real find" that portrays with "freshness and truth" how it

really feels to be a teenager in love for the first time. In *Magpies* critic Anne Briggs reflected an opposite view, that the "melodramatic" plot, unrealistic dialogue, and unbelievable characters would deter the typical teenage reader. A *Books for Keeps* contributor, on the other hand, recommended *The Starling Tree* as "a novel of alienation and loss: but one of hope and regeneration, too."

Clarke's third novel, *Breakers,* is the story of a teenage girl thrust into the role of mother. "Cat" mothers her mother who, it seems, has never been and never will be a grownup. She also mothers her little sister, who might otherwise never have a real mother. At the same time, Cat is growing up herself and struggling to build a life of her own. Kate Kellaway described *Breakers* in the London *Observer* as a token "of how dark—and distorted—being a teenager can be."

Clarke told *CA:* "I started writing when my children were very small and I was at home with them. I wrote six novels for adults, articles, and short stories.

"I started writing stories for teenagers when my children were teenagers. My son was ill and at home for two years, and we studied the English exam syllabus together (and read teenage books). I believe that reading for pleasure is vitally important for education, and I try to write stories that are accessible and emotionally satisfying.

"I have been influenced (and inspired) by *To Kill a Mockingbird* and *The Catcher in the Rye.* Writing through the eyes of a child or young adult is a constant challenge and joy to me."

BIOGRAPHICAL AND CRITICAL SOURCES:

PERIODICALS

Books for Keeps, July, 2001, review of *The Starling Tree,* p. 28.
Guardian, July 25, 2001, review of *The Starling Tree,* Arts section, p. 16.
Magpies, May, 2001, Anne Briggs, review of *The Starling Tree,* p. 38.

Observer (London, England), June, 2002, Kate Kellaway, review of *Breakers.*

School Librarian, September, 2001, George Hunt, review of *Summertime Blues,* p. 27; winter, 2001, Linda Saunders, review of *Summertime Blues,* p. 210.

Times (London, England), July 11, 2001, review of *Summertime Blues.*

Times Educational Supplement, August 17, 2001, Adéle Geras, review of *Summertime Blues,* p. 19.

*   *   *

CLEMENS, Will 1970-

PERSONAL: Born December 26, 1970, in Bloomington, IN; son of Jerome and Faye (Adolph) Clemens. *Ethnicity:* "White." *Education:* Indiana University, B.A., 1993; University of Dayton, M.A., 1995; University of Cincinnati, Ph.D., 2002.

ADDRESSES: Home—3635 Herschel Ave., Cincinnati, OH 45208.

CAREER: University of Cincinnati, Cincinnati, OH, adjunct instructor, 1997-98; Xavier University, Cincinnati, OH, adjunct professor, 2002—. *Antioch Review,* assistant fiction editor.

AWARDS, HONORS: Lily Peter fellow in creative writing, University of Arkansas, 1997; Ricking fellowship for Excellence in Doctoral Studies and Research, University of Cincinnati, 2001-2002.

WRITINGS:

(Editor) *All Shook Up: Collected Poems about Elvis,* photographs by Jon Hughes, University of Arkansas Press (Fayetteville, AR), 2001.

WORK IN PROGRESS: Snapshots: 100 Poems about Photography, 1907-2002.

BIOGRAPHICAL AND CRITICAL SOURCES:

PERIODICALS

Notes, June, 2002, Michael Adams, review of *All Shook Up: Collected Poems about Elvis,* p. 836.

COLE, G(eorge) D(ouglas) H(oward) 1889-1959

PERSONAL: Born September 25, 1889, in Cambridge, England; died January 14, 1959; son of George Cole; married Margaret Isabel Postgate (a lecturer and writer), 1918; children: one son, two daughters. *Education:* Attended Balliol College, Oxford.

CAREER: Head of Research Department, Amalgamated Society of Engineers, 1914-18; trade union adviser during World War I; head of Nuffield College Social Reconstruction Survey during World War II; fellow, Magdalene College; fellow, All Souls College, Oxford, England, 1944-57; Chichele professor of social and political theory, Oxford University, 1944-57; sub-warden, later fellow, Nuffield College, Oxford, England, 1957-59; staff member, *New Statesman,* London, England.

MEMBER: Fabian Society (chair of executive committee, 1939-46, 1948-50), University Socialist Federation, Independent Labour Party, Guild Socialist Movement, British Labour Party (director of research department), Association of Tutors in Adult Education (founder and president), Board of International Institute of Social History, Library at Oxford University.

AWARDS, HONORS: Honorary fellow, University College and Balliol College, Oxford University.

WRITINGS:

CRIME NOVELS

The Brooklyn Murders, Seltzer Publishing (New York, NY), 1924.

The Death of a Millionaire, Macmillan (New York, NY), 1925.

The Blatchington Tangle, Macmillan (New York, NY), 1926.

The Murder at Crowe House, Macmillan (New York, NY), 1927.

The Man from the River, Macmillan (New York, NY), 1928.

Poison in the Garden Suburb, Payson and Clark (New York, NY), 1929.

Burglars in Bucks, Brewer and Warren (New York, NY), 1930.

Corpse in Canoncials, Morrow (New York, NY), 1931.

The Great Southern Mystery, Morrow (New York, NY), 1931.

The Floating Admiral, Doubleday (New York, NY), 1932.

Dead Man's Watch, Doubleday (New York, NY), 1932.

Death of a Star, Doubleday (New York, NY), 1933.

The Affair at Aliquid, Collins (London, England), 1933.

End of an Ancient Mariner, Doubleday (New York, NY), 1936.

Death in the Quarry, Doubleday (New York, NY), 1935.

Big Business Murder, Doubleday (New York, NY), 1935.

Dr. Tandexter Begins; or, The Pendexter Saga, First Canto, Doubleday (New York, NY), 1935.

Scandal at School, Doubleday (New York, NY), 1936.

Last Will and Testament; or, The Pendexter Saga, Second Canto, Doubleday (New York, NY), 1936.

The Brothers Sackville, Macmillan (New York, NY), 1937.

Disgrace to the College, Hodder and Stoughton (London, England), 1937.

The Missing Aunt, Macmillan (New York, NY), 1938.

Off with Her Head!, Macmillan (New York, NY), 1939.

Double Blackmail, Macmillan (New York, NY), 1939.

Greek Tragedy, Macmillan (New York, NY), 1940.

Murder at the Munitions Works, Macmillan (New York, NY), 1940.

Counterpoint Murder, Macmillan (New York, NY), 1941.

Knife in the Dark, Macmillan (New York, NY), 1942.

Toper's End, Macmillan (New York, NY), 1942.

SHORT STORY COLLECTIONS

Superintendent Wilson's Holiday, Payson and Clark (New York, NY), 1929.

A Lesson in Crime and Other Stories, Collins (London, England), 1933.

Mrs. Warrender's Profession, Macmillan (New York, NY), 1939.

Wilson and Some Others, Collins (London, England), 1940.

Death in the Tankard, Todd (London, England), 1940.

Strychnine Tonic, Todd (London, England), 1940.

Birthday Gifts and Other Stories, Todd (London, England), 1946.

POETRY

The Record (privately printed), 1912.

New Beginnings, and The Record, Blackwell (Oxford, England), 1914.

The Crooked World, Gollancz (London, England), 1933.

NONFICTION

(With William Mellor) *The Greater Unionism,* National Labor Press (Manchester, England), 1913.

The World of Labor: A Discussion of the Present and Future of Trade Unionism, Bell Publishers (London, England), 1915.

(With William Mellor) *Trade Unionism in Wartime,* Limit (London, England), 1915.

The Principles of Socialism: A Syllabus, University of Socialist Federation (London, England), 1917.

Self Government in Industry, Bell (London, England), 1917, Books for Libraries Press (Freeport, NY), 1971.

The British Labor Movement: A Syllabus for Study Circles, University of Socialist Federation (London, England), 1917.

An Introduction to Trade Unionism, Allen and Unwin (London, England), 1917.

Trade Unionism on the Railroads, Allen and Unwin (London, England), 1917.

Labour in the Commonwealth; A Book for the Younger Generation, Hubesch (New York, NY), 1920.

Chaos and Order in Industry, Stokes Publishing (New York, NY), 1920.

Guild Socialism, Stokes Publishing (New York, NY), 1921.

English Economic History, Labour Research Department (London, England), 1922.

Unemployment: A Short Syllabus, Labour Research Department (London, England), 1923.

Out of Work: An Introduction to the Study of Unemployment, Labour Research Department (London, England), 1923.

Trade Unions and Munitions, Clarendon Press (Oxford, England), 1923.

Rents, Rings, and Houses, Labour Research Department (London, England), 1923.

The Life of William Cobbett, Harcourt Brace (New York, NY), 1924.

The Place of the Workers' Educational Association in Working Class Education, Blackfriars Press (London, England), c. 1924.

Robert Owen, Little, Brown (Boston, MA), 1925.

A Short History of the British Working Class Movement, Macmillan (New York, NY), 1938.

The Next Ten Years of British Social and Economic Policy, Macmillan (New York, NY), 1939.

The Bank of England, Society for Socialist Inquiry and Propaganda (London, England), 1931.

How Capitalism Works, Society for Socialist Inquiry and Propaganda (London, England), 1931.

The Crisis: What It Is, How It Arose, What to Do, New Statesman and Nation (London, England), 1931.

British Trade and Industry, Past and Future, Macmillan (New York), 1932.

Banks and Credit, Society for Socialist Inquiry and Propaganda (London, England), 1932.

The Essentials of Socialisation, New Fabian Research Bureau (London, England), 1932.

War Debts and Reparations; What They Are, Why They Must Be Cancelled, New Statesman and Nation (London, England), 1932.

The Intelligent Man's Guide through World Chaos, Gollancz (London, England), 1932.

Some Essentials of Socialist Propaganda, Fabian Society (London, England), 1932.

Modern Theories and Forms of Industrial Organisation, Gollancz (London, England), 1932.

The Gold Standard, Society for Socialist Inquiry and Propaganda (London, England), 1932.

The Intelligent Man's Guide to Europe Today, Knopf (New York, NY), 1933.

What Is Socialism? Letters to a Young Inquirer, Gollancz (London, England), 1933.

A Guide to Modern Politics, Gollancz (London, England), 1934.

Some Relations between Political and Economic Theory, Gollancz (London, England), 1934.

What Marx Really Meant, Knopf (New York, NY), 1934.

The Simple Case for Socialism, Gollancz (London, England), 1935.

The Condition of Britain, Gollancz (London, England), 1935.

The People's Front, Gollancz (London, England), 1937.

Practical Economics; or, Studies in Economic Planning, Penguin Books (London, England), 1937.

(With Raymond Postgate) *The Common People 1746-1936*, Knopf (New York, NY), 1947.

Living Wages: A Case for a New Minimum Wage, Gollancz (London, England), 1938.

Persons and Periods: Studies, Macmillan (New York, NY), 1938.

Socialism in Evolution, Penguin Books (London, England), 1938.

British Trade Unionism Today: A Survey, with the Collaboration of Thirty Trade Union Leaders, Barnes and Noble (New York, NY), 1955.

British Working Class Politics: 1834-1914, Routledge (London, England), 1941.

James Kier Hardie, Gollancz (London, England), 1941.

Chartist Portraits, Macmillan (New York, NY), 1965.

Europe, Russia and the Future, Gollancz (London, England), 1941.

The War on the Home Front, Fabian Society (London, England), 1941.

Victory of Vested Interest?, Routledge (London, England), 1942.

The Fabian Society, Past and Present, Fabian Society (London, England), 1942.

Richard Carlile, 1790-1843, Gollancz (London, England), 1943.

John Burns, Gollancz (London, England), 1943.

The Means to Full Employment, Gollancz (London, England), 1943.

Reparations and the Future of German Industry, Fabian Society (London, England), 1945.

The Intelligent Man's Guide to the Post-War World, Gollancz (London, England), 1947.

Samuel Butler and The Way of All Flesh, Swallow Books (Denver, CO), 1948.

A History of the Labour Party from 1914, Routledge (London, England), 1948.

The Meaning of Marxism, Gollancz (London, England), 1948.

Introduction to Economic History 1750-1950, St. Martin's Press (New York, NY), 1960.

A History of Socialist Thought, St. Martin's Press (New York, NY), 1960.

EDITOR

(With G. P. Dennis and Sherard Vines) *Oxford Poetry 1910-1913*, Blackwell (Oxford, England), 1913.

(With Sherard Vines) *Oxford Poetry 1914*, Blackwell (Oxford, England), 1914.

(With T. W. Earp) *Oxford Poetry 1915*, Blackwell (Oxford, England), 1915.

The Library of Social Studies, Methuen (London, England), 1920.

(With Margaret Cole) *The Bolo Book* (political songs), Allen and Unwin (London, England), 1921.

(With Margaret Cole) *The Ormond Poets,* Noel Douglas (London, England), 1927-28.

William Cobbett, *The Life and Adventures of Peter Porcupine,* Nonesuch Press (London, England), 1927.

What Everybody Wants to Know about Money, Gollancz (London, England), 1935.

William Morris, *Stories in Verse, Stories in Prose, Shorter Poems, Lectures and Essays,* Random House (New York, NY), 1934.

Studies in Capital and Investment, Gollancz (London, England), 1935.

Thomas Paine, *The Rights of Man,* Gollancz (London, England), 1937.

Letters to Edward Thorton, Written in the Years 1792 to 1800 by William Cobbett, Oxford University Press (Oxford, England), 1937.

The Essential Samuel Butler, Dutton (New York, NY), 1950.

(With A. W. Filson) *British Working Class Movements,* St. Martin's Press (New York, NY), 1965.

General editor, "Oxford Studies in Economics and Hutchinson's University Library."

TRANSLATOR

The Social Contract and Discourse of Rousseau, Dutton (New York, NY), 1935.

Henri de Man, *Planned Socialism,* Gollancz (London, England), 1935.

SIDELIGHTS: G. D. H. Cole was a prolific and renowned Socialist political theorist, economist, and journalist of the early twentieth century. According to *Critical Survey of Mystery and Detective Fiction,* Cole came to mystery-writing solely "as a cure for the boredom which attended a long recuperation from a mild case of pneumonia." Detective stories were in fashion with the English intelligentsia in the years between the two world wars, and Cole, who was an avid reader of mystery stories, decided to try his hand at writing one.

Cole came to public prominence in 1913, with the publication of his first book, *The World of Labor,* and quickly followed up with a number of other books on economics, socialism, and social history. Thus established by the 1920s as an eminent author of nonfiction, he had no trouble finding a publisher for his first novel. The plot of *The Brooklyn Murders* is straightforward—two nephews of Sir Vernon Brooklyn, who are also his heirs, have been murdered—but it is Cole's exploration of greed as a motivation for crime that is of most importance to the book. Throughout his years of writing mysteries the author, a longtime member of the Fabian Society, often delved into the miseries and behavioral changes that money could induce in human beings.

A second novel, *The Death of a Millionaire,* marked the beginning of the partnership between Cole and his wife Margaret, also a social historian, who became known as a biographer of Beatrice Webb. A contributor to *Critical Survey of Mystery and Detective Fiction* wrote, "More radical than her husband, and more often more intense in her espousal of Socialist economic principles, Margaret Cole nevertheless possessed a finely honed sense of humour which somewhat softened her criticism of capitalism in the mysteries she would co-author." While *The Death of a Millionaire* concerns the financial world, depicted with a suitably socialist eye as corrupt and sordid, the book includes a touch of humor, and the lessons in socialist economic theory that the authors impart do not detract from the mystery.

Many of the Coles' stories exhibit the charm and wit often associated with the British upper class. "The repartee of the gentleman's club and college senior common room," noted *Twentieth Century Crime and Mystery Writers,* "is often echoed in the remarks of the men and women who people their books."

With succeeding books the authors became known for creating ongoing characters that were alive and memorable to their readers. In *The Blatchington Tangle,* Detective Henry Wilson encounters amateur sleuth Everard Blatchington. Among the protagonists is an obnoxious American who immediately becomes a suspect when the body of a crooked financier is found in Lord Blatchington's library.

The Coles used humor and interesting settings to give depth to their characterizations. "*Scandal at School,*" noted a writer for *Critical Survey of Mystery and Detective Fiction,* "contains an air of authenticity born of long association with the academic world." *End of an Ancient Mariner* is less a mystery—the culprit is identified early in the story—than a psychological novel of crime, punishment, and motivation.

Dr. Tancred Begins; or, The Pendexter Saga, First Canto introduces a new character and a well-described Cornwall as a setting for the mysteries to unfold. The Coles wrote only two books featuring Dr. Tancred, the other being *Last Will and Testament; or, The Pendexter Saga, Second Canto,* but both were well received.

One of the Coles' last works, *Murder at the Munitions Works,* published in 1940 when the turmoil caused by Oswald Mosley's British Union of Fascists was still sweeping England, became popular not only as a mystery but as a primer of British socialist economic theory. After World War II, the couple gave up writing mysteries to focus on nonfiction and on the more important work of stabilizing and rebuilding their country. While some of his radical views kept him out of the Labour party government of Clement Attlee, Cole continued to publish his ideas and give lectures until his death in 1959.

Jeanne F. Bedell, writing in *Twentieth-Century Crime and Mystery Writers,* notes that Margaret Cole, in *The Life of G. D. H. Cole,* "dismisses in two pages the detective fiction she and her husband coauthored. Both viewed the detective stories as a pleasant, undemanding sideline, and Dame Margaret's view [was] that the books are 'competent but no more." Bedell concludes, "G. D. H. Cole's reputation will, of course, rest on his studies of social and economic history, especially the classic five-volume *History of Socialist Thought.*"

Cole's life's work can be seen as an definitive guide to all British socialist concerns. He was an invaluable historian of the Labor movement and contributed to the development of British labor policy. "Almost half a century later," wrote Bedell, "he remained influential as an inspirational force behind the nascent New Left, and he lived to see an official Parliamentary Labour party established as a major governing party."

BIOGRAPHICAL AND CRITICAL SOURCES:

BOOKS

Critical Survey of Mystery and Detective Fiction, edited by Frank N. Magill, Salem Press (Pasadena, CA), 1998.
Twentieth-Century Crime and Mystery Writers, Gale (Detroit, MI), 1991.*

COMER, Krista 1958-

PERSONAL: Born October 1, 1958, in Pueblo, CO; married José F. Aranda, Jr., 1992; children: Beinto Aranda-Comer, Jesse Arand-Comer. *Ethnicity:* "Caucasian." *Education:* Wellesley College, B.A., 1988; Brown University, Ph.D., 1996.

ADDRESSES: Office—Rice University, English Department, Box 1892, 6100 South Main St., Houston, TX 77005. *E-mail*—kcomer@rice.edu.

CAREER: Rice University, Houston, TX, instructor in English and women's studies, 1995—.

MEMBER: American Studies Association, Western Literature Association.

AWARDS, HONORS: Walker Prize for Best Essay, Western Literature Association, 1999.

WRITINGS:

Landscapes of the New West: Gender & Geography in Contemporary Women's Writing, University of North Carolina Press (Chapel Hill, NC), 1999.

Also author of essays on the culture of American West.

WORK IN PROGRESS: After California, a novel, expected 2003; *Cultural History, from Gidget to Surfergirls, 1960-Present,* 2005; Virtual Museum Web site, Women Surfer's Project, under construction.

*   *   *

CONOLLY-SMITH, Peter 1964-

PERSONAL: Born September 3, 1964, in Munich, Germany; son of David (a book dealer and sports journalist/writer) and Elizabeth (a teacher). *Ethnicity:* "White/Caucasian." *Education:* Free University (Berlin, Germany), B.A., 1988; Yale University, M.A.,

1992, Ph.D., 1996. *Politics:* "Decidedly liberal." *Religion:* "Thinking Christian." *Hobbies and other interests:* Collecting rare books, films, and videos.

ADDRESSES: Home—730 Riverside Dr., #10B, New York, NY 10031. *Office*—DeVry Institute, 630 U.S. Highway One, North Brunswick, NJ 08902-3362; fax: 732-435-4861. *E-mail*—pcs@admin.nj.devry.edu.

CAREER: Stefan Loose Travel Publications, Berlin, Germany, translator and travel writer, 1983-88; Doane Productions, New Haven, CT, producer of *The Nature of the Beast,* 1994; Paradise Productions, New York, NY, research coordinator/writer, 1995-96; Vanguard Films, New York, NY, researcher/script consultant/script doctor, 1996-97; Harvard University, Cambridge, MA, Longfellow Institute, postdoctorate fellow, 1997; Columbia University, New York, NY, visiting adjunct assistant professor, 1997; DeVry Institute, New Brunswick, NJ, associate professor of humanities, 1996—.

MEMBER: American Studies Association, American Historical Association, Modern Language Association, New York Council for the Humanities.

AWARDS, HONORS: German Academic Exchange Service fellowship, 1988-89; AAA Commendation, National Association for Visual Anthropology, 1995 and Grand Jury Prize and first prize in *Student Film* category, Bettina Russell Film Festival, 1996, both for *The Nature of the Beast*; John D. Sawyer fellowship, Longfellow Institute, Harvard University, 1997; "Best Keeper" first prize, DeVry National Faculty Symposia, 1998, 2000; Bambi (German Emmy Award) for Best Series Character, 1999, for "Nie wieder Oper" installment of *Tatort*; National President's Award, Devry, 2001.

WRITINGS:

(And research coordinator) *American Families* (five-part television screenplay), PBS, 1996-1997.

Also author of scripts for *Tatort* Austrian television series, including (with Robert Pejo) "Nie wieder Oper," 1999, and "Feine Herrschaften," 2001; and *Next of Kin,* a three-part series for PBS. Contributor to books, including *Multilingual America,* edited by Werner Sollors, New York University Press, 1998; *New York: Kultur und Geschichte,* edited by Stefan Loose, Loose Travel Publications (Berlin, Germany), 1998; *Young Americanists,* edited by Werner Sollors, New York University Press, 2000.

WORK IN PROGRESS: "The Translated Community: An Ethnic Press Looks at Popular American Culture, 1890-1920," for "Smithsonian Institution Press series on American Studies," edited by Mark Hirsch; a screenplay based on the life and times of Felipe Carillo Puerto, socialist governor of the Yucatan, Mexico, who was assassinated in 1924; *Cocaine,* a screenplay adaptation of *Romanza Cocaina* by Pittigrilli.

SIDELIGHTS: Peter Conolly-Smith told CA: "I have been writing since earliest childhood. The son of a bookshop owner, I was (and remain) driven by the desire of seeing my name on the spine of a book—a good book. Though I wrote throughout grammar and high school and even completed three dismal novels upon graduation, nothing was published for years. Indeed, the second of my unpublished novels elicited what may be the unkindest rejection ever: a New York agent's hand-written note attached to a form letter, suggesting that I might want to learn to write English before submitting other works in the future.

"I took the advice to heart, enrolling in the English and Comparative Literature Departments (I later added American Studies as a third major) at the Free University of Berlin, Germany, my childhood home, in hopes of learning the craft of great writing through the study of literature. The creative result of this period was the last (and worst) of my three unpublished novels. My years of study did, however, yield the fortunate byproduct of a B.A., which, in turn, led to a one-year fellowship at Yale University.

"Falling in love with the academic environment of Yale, I remained there and earned my Ph.D. in American studies from 1988-96, a period during which the iron discipline internalized during my fruitless years as a would-be novelist stood me in good stead: my dissertation, on New York's German-American immigrant community during World War I, was over 600 pages in length and passed with distinction.

"The Yale Ph.D. opened many doors, including those that led to my current, modest but fulfilling academic career, as well as several doors into the world of film and television writing. Even as a graduate student, I and some of my undergraduate protégés had produced a PBS-documentary on the life and case of a victim of domestic abuse now serving a life-sentence for first-degree murder (the multiple, international award-winning *The Nature of the Beast* on the case of Bonnie Foreshaw, 1994). With my Ph.D. under my belt as of '96, I soon found ample employment as a writer, researcher, and script doctor in the New York documentary film scene.

"This career, in turn, led to opportunities in fiction film and TV, and with a newfound collaborator and fellow New York émigré, the Austrian-Romanian director Robert Pejo, I have written and developed a number of successful fiction projects for European TV. I have found that I have a particular knack for dialogue (in multiple languages; I write in English and German and also have a good ear for French and languages in general). Most of my published work is academic in nature, and for my creative efforts I have recently focused exclusively on screen and teleplays, as well as documentary work.

"I am currently completing a version of my dissertation for publication with the Smithsonian Institution Press, and plan to tackle a feature script on the Mexican revolution thereafter, which, I hope, will pay for my future children's college tuition. My companion, Ms. Fiona Lin, whom I met at Yale in 1993, is like myself a teacher with a social conscience, currently studying for her Ph.D. at the University of Michigan in Ann Arbor. A tireless reader and editor and an excellent writer herself, she is most supportive of my creative efforts, though she finds my sentence structure cumbersome and Germanic, and worries about whether my writing will ever suffice to pay the bills.

"When writing, I have, since childhood, devoted endless hours (as many as twelve a day and more) to the task. I like word processors but still feel that work written in longhand is best. I prefer to write at home, at my desk, or in silent company of strangers in the New York Public Library or research libraries such as those of Columbia University and NYU. I hope to eventually give up my day job as a history and humanities professor and devote myself entirely to pen and paper, at which point I will also return to my original ambition of becoming a novelist."

COX, Jeffrey N.

PERSONAL: Male. *Education:* Wesleyan University, B.A., 1975; University of Virginia, Ph.D., 1981.

ADDRESSES: Office—Center for Humanities and the Arts, Macky 201, University of Colorado at Boulder, Boulder, CO 80309.

CAREER: Center for Humanities and the Arts, University of Colorado at Boulder, CO, professor of English and comparative literature.

WRITINGS:

In the Shadows of Romance: Romantic Tragic Drama in Germany, England, and France, Ohio University Press (Athens, OH), 1987.
(Editor) *Seven Gothic Dramas, 1789-1825,* Ohio University Press (Athens, OH), 1992.
(Editor, with Larry J. Reynolds) *New Historical Literary Study: Essays on Reproducing Texts,* Princeton University Press (Princeton, NJ), 1993.
Poetry and Politics in the Cockney School: Keats, Shelley, Hunt, and Their Circle, Cambridge University Press (New York, NY), 1998.
(Editor, with others) *Selected Writings of Leigh Hunt,* Pickering & Chatto (Brookfield, VT), 2002.

SIDELIGHTS: Jeffrey N. Cox is best known for his scholarly studies of Romantic drama, a relatively unmapped area of literary history. Through several studies and essay collections, Cox has attempted to make the dramatic world of the Romantics accessible to students.

Cox's first book, *In the Shadow of Romance: Romantic Tragic Drama in Germany, England, and France,* opens the field of Romantic drama to scholars and students. John Ehrstine, in an article for *Comparative Drama,* explained: "The central impulse for Jeffrey Cox's study is the simple fact that we know so little about Romantic drama and take so little pleasure in reading it. . . . Thus there has been a failure in criticism, especially in our understanding of Romantic tragedy. . . . 'I hope to steer a middle course,' Cox states, between the strictures of George Steiner's *The Death of Tragedy* (London, 1961), which imposes too narrow a norm for tragedy to include the Romantics, and Morris Weitz's *Hamlet and the Philosophy of Literary Criticism* (Chicago, 1964) whose relativist argument claims that 'The concept of tragedy is perennially debatable.'" This argument won much attention for its exploration of the forgotten literature; even George Steiner, in a reply to Cox's assertions, called Cox's work "a generous and stimulating brief." W. W. Waring, in a review for *Choice*, commented that "*In the Shadows of Romance* is valuable for its analyses of individual works and for its comprehensive view of romantic tragedy."

Cox edited *Seven Gothic Dramas, 1789-1825,* a collection of little-known plays from the period. By producing a new version of these plays, complete with explanatory notes, Cox enables students access to the difficult field of Romantic drama. B. F. Fisher, in an article for *Choice,* wrote: "Cox's command of the bibliography relevant to his subject is impressive, and his book will stand as a milestone of content, good scholarship, and clear style." John Mullan of the *Times Literary Supplement* called the book an "intriguing anthology" and commented: "*Seven Gothic Dramas, 1789-1825* gives us a chance to see how the London stage provided its equivalent of the thrills on offer at the circulating library, and its excellent introduction recreates the contemporary appetite for drama of apprehension and terror." David W. Lindsay, in *Review of English Studies,* felt that "Cox's scholarship and theoretical sophistication are [most] suitably employed in his analysis of the feminist dimension of *De Montfort* and in his exposition of the complex textual history of *Bertram.*" Lindsay added, moreover: "This substantial and well-produced volume is therefore to be welcomed, not only for its thoughtfully edited texts of seven representative plays but also for its ambitious and wide-ranging introduction."

In *Poetry and Politics in the Cockney School: Keats, Shelley, Hunt, and Their Circle,* Cox focuses on the group of writers and intellectuals in England that became known as the "Cockney School."

BIOGRAPHICAL AND CRITICAL SOURCES:

PERIODICALS

Choice, June 1988, W. W. Waring, review of *In the Shadows of Romance,* p. 1549; January 1993, B. F. Fisher, review of *Seven Gothic Dramas 1789-* *1825,* p. 797; September, 1999, G. A. Cevasco, review of *Poetry and Politics in the Cockney School: Keats, Shelley, Hunt, and Their Circle,* p. 141.

Comparative Drama, Summer 1988, John Ehrstine, review of *In the Shadows of Romance,* p. 187.

Keats-Shelley Journal, 2001, Grant Scott, review of *Poetry and Politics in the Cockney School,* p. 173.

Nineteenth-Century Literature, June, 2000, Scott McEathron, review of *Poetry and Politics in the Cockney School,* p. 118.

Notes & Queries, June, 2000, Richard Cronin, review of *Poetry and Politics in the Cockney School,* p. 267.

Review of English Studies, May 1995, David W. Lindsay, review of *Seven Gothic Dramas 1789-1825,* p. 281; May, 2000, Jon Mee, review of *Poetry and Politics in the Cockney School,* p. 311.

Studies in Romanticism, spring, 2001, Jack Stillinger, review of *Poetry and Politics in the Cockney School,* p. 165.

Times Literary Supplement, February 12, 1988, George Steiner, "Tragic and Counter-tragic," p. 168; December 24, 1993, "Ha, Reginald!," p. 7; October 8, 1999, Michael O'Neill, review of *Poetry and Politics in the Cockney School,* p. 32.*

* * *

CULBERTSON, Philip Leroy 1944-

PERSONAL: Born October 10, 1944, in Bartlesville, OK; son of Walter Leroy and Wanda Miriam (Atkins) Culbertson. *Education:* Washington University (St. Louis, MO), Mus.B., 1966; General Theological Seminary (New York, NY), M.Div., 1970; doctoral research at Hebrew University, 1974-76; New York University, Ph.D., 1977. *Politics:* Democrat. *Religion:* Episcopalian.

ADDRESSES: Office—University of Auckland, Auckland, New Zealand.

CAREER: Associate rector, Church of the Holy Trinity, New York, NY, 1970-74; rector, Christ Episcopal Church, Oberlin, OH, 1976-85; Episcopal Bishop's advisory commission on Christian-Jewish relations, member, 1986; Christ Episcopal Church, Tracy City,

TN, interim rector, 1986-87; University of the South, Sewanee, TN, professor of pastoral theology, 1985—; Auckland University, Auckland, New Zealand, lecturer.

MEMBER: Congress of Anglican Theologians, Guild of Clergy Counselors, Christian Study Group on Judaism and the Jewish People.

WRITINGS:

(Editor, with Arthur Shippee) *The Pastor: Readings from the Patristic Period,* Fortress Press (Minneapolis, MN), 1990.
New Adam: The Future of Male Spirituality, Fortress Press (Minneapolis, MN), 1992.
Counseling Men, Fortress Press (Minneapolis, MN), 1994.
A Word Fitly Spoken: Context, Transmission, and Adoption of the Parables of Jesus, State University of New York Press (Albany, NY), 1995.
Counselling Issues & South Pacific Communities, Accent Publications (Auckland, New Zealand), 1997.
Caring for God's People, Fortress Press (Minneapolis, MN), 2000.
(Editor) *The Spirituality of Men: Sixteen Christians Write about Their Faith,* Fortress Press (Minneapolis, MN), 2002.

SIDELIGHTS: In addition to a thirty-year career as an Episcopal priest, Philip Leroy Culbertson has been an integral part of a liberalization of pastoral counseling as well as a leader in important theological discussions in Christian-Jewish relations.

In *The Pastor: Readings from the Patristic Period,* Culbertson and co-editor Arthur Shippee present a collection of essays arguing that modern pastoral theology is a combination of psychology and counseling that often ignores the more traditional church experiences. Culbertson proposes, however, that contemporary Christians can benefit from selected reading of the Church fathers that supports the modern views of pastoral counseling, beginning with the Apostolitic Fathers and finishing with Gregory the Great. In a review of *The Pastor* for *Church History,* Joseph F. Kelly wrote, "The selections from *Verba Seniorium* include sayings of Syncletice, who, the editors explain, is 'unfortunately this book's only female author' . . . they deserve credit for attempting to broaden the all-male scope of the book. I would personally be surprised if many 'modern' seminary instructors took this book seriously in training their charges, but church historians will be grateful for this handy compendium of patristic readings on the notion and practice of pastoral work."

In *New Adam: The Future of Male Spirituality* and *Counseling Men,* Culbertson continues to explore the ways in which men can benefit from pastoral counseling. Howard Stone wrote in his foreword, "*Counseling Men* aims to help concerned men achieve a clearer identity in the whirlwind of change that is occurring in family and relationship structures. Philip Culbertson addresses the radical disparity between the stereotypes of how men are portrayed in our society and how they actually live their lives, between the media's macho, superhero, all-controlling, fantastic lovers and the fearful cogs in the wheel of today's impersonal business world, mortgaged to the hilt and worried about career and the responsibilities of providing for his family."

Caring for God's People continues to expand the ideal of Christian wholeness and maturity, e.g., a healthy interconnectedness of self-within-community. The heart of the book lies in its presentation of the three schools of counseling theory that Culbertson finds most helpful: family systems theory, narrative counseling theory, and object relations theory. Each of these is explained in detail, and then applied to such counseling situations as pre-marital counseling, marriage counseling, divorce counseling, counseling gay men and women, and grief counseling.

The Spirituality of Men: Sixteen Christians Write about Their Faith, which Culbertson both edited and contributed to, is a collection of writings that attempts to lay out what it means to be an adult male Christian. The essayists, who include men both deeply and scarcely religious, straight and gay, white and African American, Protestant and Catholic, and of various ages, move beyond old stereotypes of manliness and Christian identity to chart new identities, roles, and attitudes. As Culbertson notes of the book's contributors, "As pastoral theologians they are keen observers of and prophetic witnesses to the core issues, deepest wounds, and greatest potential for men—involving spirituality, relationships, sexuality, health and healing, violence and abuse, aging, and religious community. Together their reflections are a valuable next step for men in the church and offer promising glimpses of new, healthy, life-enhancing ways of being men of faith."

BIOGRAPHICAL AND CRITICAL SOURCES:

PERIODICALS

Choice, September, 1995, C.C. Newman, review of *A Word Fitly Spoken: Context, Transmission, and Adoption of the Parables of Jesus,* p. 144.

Church History, December, 1993, Joseph F. Kelly, review of *The Pastor: Readings from the Patristic Period,* p. 588.

Journal of Ecumenical Studies, summer, 1996, Zev Garber, review of *A Word Fitly Spoken,* p. 402.

National Catholic Reporter, November 9, 1990, William C. Graham, review of *The Pastor,* p. 32.*

*   *   *

CURTISS, Harriette Augusta 1856-1932
(Bachelor Girl)

PERSONAL: Born 1856, in Philadelphia, PA; died September 22, 1932, in Washington, DC; daughter of John Horace (an educator and organization executive) and Emma (Brightly) Brown; married Frank Homer Curtiss (a writer and foundation executive), 1907.

CAREER: Order of the Fifteen (renamed Order of Christian Mystics), cofounder and teacher of the occult, under the name Rahmea, 1907; Church of the Wisdom Religion, cofounder, during World War I, renamed Universal Religious Foundation, 1929. Clairvoyant.

WRITINGS:

WITH HUSBAND, F. HOMER CURTISS

Letters from the Teacher, by the Teachers of the Order of the 15, 1909, published in two volumes, Curtiss Philosophic (Hollywood, CA), 1918.

The Voice of Isis, by the Teacher of the Order of Christian Mystics, Curtiss Book Co. (Los Angeles, CA), 1912, reprinted, Curtiss Philosophic (Washington, DC), 1935.

The War Crisis, 1914.

The Philosophy of War, Curtiss Philosophic (Los Angeles, CA), 1914, third edition, Curtiss Philosophic (Washington, DC), 1939.

The Key to the Universe; or, A Spiritual Interpretation of Numbers and Symbols, Curtiss Book Co. (San Francisco, CA), 1915, sixth edition, Borgo Press (San Bernardino, CA), 1983.

Realms of the Living Dead: A Brief Description of Life after Death, Transmitted from the Teacher of the O.C.M., Curtiss Philosophic (San Francisco, CA), 1917, published as *Realms of the Living Dead: A Brief Description of Life after Death,* E. P. Dutton (New York, NY), 1919.

The Key of Destiny: A Sequel to The Key to the Universe, Dutton (New York, NY), 1919.

The Message of Aquaria: The Significance and Mission of the Aquarian Age, Curtiss Philosophic (San Francisco, CA), 1921.

The Divine Mother, Curtiss Philosophic (San Francisco, CA), 1921.

Coming World Changes, Curtiss Philosophic (Washington, DC), 1926.

The Truth about Evolution and the Bible, Curtiss Philosophic (Washington, DC), 1928.

The Love of Rabiacca, a Tragedy in Five Acts: A Tale of a Prehistoric Race Recovered Psychically, Curtiss Philosophic (Washington, DC), 1934.

The Mystic Life: An Introduction to Practical Christian Mysticism, compiled by Arthur Leslie Champion, Curtiss Philosophic (Washington, DC), 1934.

The Inner Radiance, Curtiss Philosophic (Washington, DC), 1935.

Also author of *The Soundless Sound, by the Teacher of the Order of the 15,* Curtiss Philosophic (Los Angeles, CA), 1911.

OTHER

Author of a column in the *Philadelphia Inquirer,* under the name Bachelor Girl.

BIOGRAPHICAL AND CRITICAL SOURCES:

BOOKS

Encyclopedia of Occultism and Parapsychology, fifth edition, Gale (Detroit, MI), 2001.

Religious Leaders of America, second edition, Gale (Detroit, MI), 1999.*

D

DAEN, Daniël
See ABMA, G(erben) Willem

* * *

D'AMICO, Jack (P.) 1939-

PERSONAL: Born July 30, 1939, in Buffalo, NY; son of Jack (a musician) and Carol (a homemaker; maiden name, Patti) D'Amico; married Susan Metzinger, 1993. *Ethnicity:* "Italian." *Education:* State University of New York—Buffalo, B.A., 1960, Ph.D., 1965. *Hobbies and other interests:* Music, playing the piano, swimming, cooking, travel.

ADDRESSES: Home—4755 Chestnut Ridge Rd., No. 2, Amherst, NY 14228. *Office*—Department of English, Canisius College, 2001 Main St., Buffalo, NY 14208. *E-mail*—jdamico@canisius.edu.

CAREER: University of California—Berkeley, assistant professor of English, 1965-70; American University of Beirut, Beirut, Lebanon, faculty member, 1971-72, 1973-76, visiting professor of English, 1999-2000; Dominican College of San Rafael, San Rafael, CA, assistant professor, 1972-73; Canisius College, Buffalo, NY, part-time faculty member, 1976-77, 1978-81, professor of English, 1981—, department chair, 1997-98, 2000-02, associate dean of arts and sciences, 1992-96, interim dean, 1998-99; Université Mohammed V, Rabat, Morocco, faculty member, 1977-78; Dalian Foreign Languages Institute, Dalian, China, foreign expert, 1981; D'Youville College, part-time faculty member, 1978-81.

MEMBER: Phi Beta Kappa, Delta Tau Kappa, Alpha Sigma Nu (life member).

AWARDS, HONORS: Fulbright grant for Istituto Universitario Orientale, Naples, Italy, 1963-64; National Endowment for the Humanities grant, 1981.

WRITINGS:

Knowledge and Power in the Renaissance, University Press of America (Washington, DC), 1977.
Petrarch in England: An Anthology of Parallel Texts from Wyatt to Milton, A. Longo (Ravenna, Italy), 1979.
The Moor in English Renaissance Drama, University of South Florida Press, 1991.
(Editor, with M. Verdicchio and Daim Trafton, and contributor) *The Legacy of Benedetto Croce,* University of Toronto Press (Toronto, Ontario, Canada), 1999.
Shakespeare and Italy: The City and the Stage, University Press of Florida (Gainesville, FL), 2001.

Contributor to academic journals, including *Italian Quarterly, Machiavelli Studies, Canadian Journal of Italian Studies, Modern Language Studies, Theatre Journal, Forum Italicum, Midwest Quarterly, Rivista di Studi Italiani, Comparative Drama,* and *Renaissance and Reformation.*

WORK IN PROGRESS: An essay on the figure of the "pregnant enemy" in the works of William Shakespeare; research on travel, translation, and the foundling in Shakespeare's *The Tempest.*

SIDELIGHTS: Jack P. D'Amico told *CA:* "My primary motivation for writing has typically been to pursue an idea that has arisen while teaching. I have been influenced by Anthony Caputi, professor emeritus of Cornell University, a scholar, writer of fiction, and one of the family; by Professor Salvatore Rosati, late of Rome and the Istituto Universitario Orientale; and by my dear friend and colleague at the American University of Beirut, the late Bernard Blackstone, student of life and the Romantic poets, particularly Byron. I think I was drawn to Shakespeare from an early age when my grandfather recounted tales of Principe Amleto, a hero—to him—at the level of Garibaldi and Dante. The pervasive atmosphere of music that was so much a part of my father's life inspired me to be creative in whatever way I could. My approach to writing has also been shaped in many indirect ways by the years I spent teaching abroad, in Italy, in Morocco, where I began to think about and to study the Moor and the relations between England and Morocco in the sixteenth century, at the Foreign Language Institute in Dalian, China, and in a long voyage to various theaters, ancient, Renaissance, and modern, in Italy, Greece, and Turkey, where I began to work on the idea of theatrical space."

* * *

DANIEL, John M. 1941-

PERSONAL: Born November 22, 1941, in Minneapolis, MN; son of Lewis (a doctor) and Hannah (a homemaker; maiden name, Mallon) Daniel; married Karen Mullenger, 1964 (divorced); married Susan Plumley (a publisher), July 9, 1987; children: Morgan Neil, Benjamin William Lewis. *Education:* Stanford University, A.B., 1964. *Politics:* Democrat. *Hobbies and other interests:* Music, graphic art.

ADDRESSES: Office—Daniel & Daniel, Publishers, Inc., P.O. Box 21922, Santa Barbara, CA 93121. *E-mail*—jmdaniel@danielpublishing.com.

CAREER: Stanford University Press, Stanford, CA, assistant editor, 1968-70; Kepler's Books, Menlo Park, CA, clerk and buyer, 1970-77; John Daniel Publication Services, Palo Alto, CA, editor and publisher, 1977-80; Capra Press, Santa Barbara, CA, editor and sales manager, 1983-85; Daniel & Daniel Publishers, Inc., Santa Barbara, CA, publisher and editor, 1985.

MEMBER: PEN Center USA West.

AWARDS, HONORS: Wallace Stegner fellowship in creative writing, Stanford University, 1967.

WRITINGS:

Play Melancholy Baby (fiction), Perseverance Press (Menlo Park, CA), 1986.
The Woman by the Bridge (fiction), Dolphin Moon Press (Baltimore, MD), 1991.
(Editor, with Steve Moss) *The World's Shortest Stories of Love and Death* (humor), Running Press (Philadelphia, PA), 1999.
(Editor, with Steve Moss) *QPB Presents the Best World's Shortest Stories of All Time* (humor), Quality Paperback Book Club, 2000.
Generous Helpings (fiction), Shoreline Press (Santa Barbara, CA), 2001.
(Editor) *Yellow Bricks and Ruby Slippers: An Anthology of Very Short Stories, Essays, and Poems,* Daniel & Daniel (Santa Barbara, CA), 2002.

Author of *One for the Book* (self-published memoir); and *Structure, Style & Truth* (book on writing short stories).

More than one hundred short stories and articles published in literary magazines. Also contributes crostic puzzles to *Tin House Magazine.*

SIDELIGHTS: John M. Daniel told *CA:* "I think the human condition is the only subject there is for fiction, but that allows for a lot of variety. Style is what makes writing fun to write and to read. I spend a lot of time in the persona of a fictional piano player named Casey, but I killed him off last year. I write for the fun of it. My favorite writer is (was) Richard Bissell."

* * *

DANIELS, Laura
See MYERS, Amy

* * *

DAOUD, Hassan

PERSONAL: Born in Lebanon.

ADDRESSES: Agent—c/o Author Mail, Granta Books, 1755 Broadway, 5th Floor, New York, NY 10019.

CAREER: Journalist and author. Worked for newspaper *Al Hayat.*

WRITINGS:

The House of Mathilde (novel), translated by Peter Theroux, Granta Books (New York, NY), 1999.

SIDELIGHTS: Hassan Daoud, a Lebanese journalist, used his experiences covering the civil war in Beirut as the basis for his debut novel, *The House of Mathilde.* Translated by Peter Theroux, the novel is considered one of the first works of fiction about the war to be published in the English language. Unlike many of his countrymen who fled to safer areas, Daoud, who was born in south Lebanon, stayed in Beirut for the duration of the sixteen-year war and reported on its events for *Al Hayat,* a Lebanese newspaper. Affected by the overall tragedy of the war, Daoud was inspired to write his novel. Rather than focus on the war as a whole, however, Daoud instead chose to use the events revolving around a fictional apartment complex to show how Beirut's social strings gradually come unraveled because of the war. In fact, the reader is not even aware that the building is in Beirut until later in the book.

Like pre-war Beirut itself, the apartment building is inhabited by families of many different ethnicities, religions, and economic statuses. Despite their differences, the residents have a strong community, as each neighbor looks out for the others. The main character, Mathilde, who is one of the older residents of the building, keeps an eye on the actions of all those who come and go, and is looked upon as a leader. The novel charts the lives of several of the building's families, as they experience births and deaths, and deal with the vents of their lives. The author gives detailed descriptions of each family's living quarters: what type of furniture they have, what can be seen from each balcony, and how some prefer Western-style bathrooms to more traditional Arab facilities. As some of the residents begin to abandon the building and city, Daoud finally lets the reader know that the building is located in Beirut, and the pressures that are causing the departures are war-related.

Eventually, bombs and fighting gain a larger presence in the book. The communal spirit of the building wanes as each successive family leaves, and strangers move in and squat in the abandoned apartments. The neighbors no longer greet one another, as they stay behind locked doors. As the fighting grows closer to the dwelling, the number of those who stay gradually dwindles, until only one woman remains. Even Mathilde is killed. A nameless man, who is the nephew of the last remaining woman, narrates the tale. His narration jumps back and forth through time, and the sentence, "My aunt was alone in the building" recurs throughout the book. Finally, the building takes a direct hit from a bomb, ripping it apart. Its remnants symbolize the fate of Beirut itself. Lucy Dallas, who reviewed *The House of Mathilde* for the *Times Literary Supplement,* was impressed by the uncomplicated, but profound nature of the book, and referred to it as a "simple, unnerving novel."

BIOGRAPHICAL AND CRITICAL SOURCES:

PERIODICALS

Times Literary Supplement, May 14, 1999, p. 33.*

*   *   *

DARWISH, Mustafa 1928-

PERSONAL: Born 1928, in Cairo, Egypt. *Education:* Cairo University, graduate in law, 1949, diploma in politics and economics, 1950, diploma in law, 1951. *Hobbies and other interests:* Swimming, cycling, cinema.

ADDRESSES: Home—13 al-Boustan St., Cairo, Egypt.

CAREER: Film critic and author. Censor of Arts, chief, 1962; administrative judge, 1969-82.

WRITINGS:

Dream Makers on the Nile: A Portrait of Egyptian Cinema, American University (Cairo, Egypt), 1997.

SIDELIGHTS: Egyptian film critic and author Mustafa Darwish published his debut work, *Dream Makers on the Nile: A Portrait of Egyptian Cinema,* in 1997, the year that marked the centenary of filmmaking in the author's native country. Darwish's book is devoted to the origins and evolution of Egyptian filmmaking, and particularly concentrates on the era between the 1930s and the early 1960s, which he considers the golden age of Egyptian film. Darwish explains that the advent of the "talkies," or films with sound dialogue, were wildly popular and had a tremendous impact on Egyptian audiences, largely because most of the people were illiterate and could not read the subtitles of the silent films that had come before. Since then, Egypt has produced far more films than any other Arab nation.

Darwish, who is considered by many to be the foremost Egyptian film critic, maintains that, in addition to loving musicals, Egyptian audiences have traditionally enjoyed melodramas, burlesques, and historical costume dramas. However, this trend began to change by the 1960s as Egyptian films were infused with themes of nationalism, which was spreading across the land because of the leadership of new president, Gamal Abdel Nasser. The author also describes to the reader some of the more important films in Egyptian history, including *Bab al-Hadid* ("Cairo Central Station," 1958) and *Al-Liss wa'l-Kilab* ("The Thief and the Dogs," 1962).

Darwish devotes much of the book to the industry's various film stars, some of whom became gigantic celebrities in Egypt. His study includes actors such as Muhammad 'Abd al-Wahhab, 'Abd al-Halim Hafiz, Layla Murad, Umm Kulthum, and Omar Sharif, who also became popular in American cinema. Kulthum, who often starred in various roles as a singing slave girl, was a particular favorite of Egyptian film audiences. In fact, more people came to her funeral in 1975 than attended Nasser's funeral in 1970. Upon the death of 'Abd al-Halim Hafiz in 1977, several fans took their own lives because of their grief. Darwish mined much of the information in the book from old gossip magazines such as *Akhbar al-Nujum* ("News of the Stars") and *Al-Kawakib* ("The Stars"), and he goes into the personal lives of the various film celebrities. For example, according to Darwish, Kulthum, who never allowed herself to be kissed in her films, led a chaste lifestyle. However, one of her great rivals of the screen, a woman named Asmahan, who was the star of "Romance and Revenge," allegedly had affairs with many men, including those of some prominence. Darwish recounts that when Asmahan was killed in a fiery car wreck in 1944, many people accused Kulthum of masterminding the crash, so she could eliminate her rival.

In the book, Darwish includes many photographs of the Egyptian film stars, including Kulthum, Naguib Rihani, and one of a youthful Omar Sharif. Some literary critics, such as *Times Literary Supplement* reviewer Robert Irwin, felt Darwish was more concerned about the celebrity-driven aspects of Egyptian film than he was about issues of content. "Darwish writes about film primarily as entertainment, and he is more interested in the industry's glamorous past than its earnest future," Irwin wrote.

BIOGRAPHICAL AND CRITICAL SOURCES:

PERIODICALS

Times Literary Supplement, May 14, 1999, p. 10.

OTHER

Al-Ahram Weekly, http://www.ahram.org/ (October 23, 2002).*

*   *   *

DAVIDSOHN, Hans 1887-1942
(Jakob van Hoddis)

PERSONAL: Born 1887; died in a Nazi concentration camp, 1942; son of Doris Davidsohn. *Nationality:* German.

CAREER: Poet. Contributor to magazine *Aktion.*

MEMBER: Neue Club (Berlin, Germany).

WRITINGS:

(Under pseudonym Jakob van Hoddis) *Weltende* (title means "End of the World"), Verlag der Wochenschrift die Aktion (Berlin, Germany), 1918, translation by G. P. Skratz published as *The End of the World,* G. P. Skratz (Norwich, CT), 1974.

(Under pseudonym Jakob van Hoddis) *Weltende: gesammelte Dichtungen,* edited by Paul Portner, Arche (Zurich, Switzerland), 1958.

SIDELIGHTS: German poet Hans Davidsohn, who wrote under the pseudonym Jakob van Hoddis, was an important participant in the expressionist cabarets and clubs in Berlin during the early 1900s. In fact, many academics and literary critics consider his most prominent and influential work, a poem titled "Weltende," as the first published example of German expressionism. The poem offers an apocalyptic view of the modern world, and includes scenes of destruction, particularly to the bourgeois elements of German society that Davidsohn appeared to despise. The *Oxford Companion to Germanic Literature* described Davidsohn as "capable of brilliant satire exposing the ugly face of city life to the point of the grotesque and absurd." Some of Davidsohn's other noted poems include "Tristitia ante" and "Aurora."

Born in 1887, Davidsohn wrote the majority of his poems between 1908 and 1914. Davidsohn suffered from schizophrenia, which first began to affect him in 1912, and which cut short his period of creativity. By late 1914, the affliction had greatly inhibited his ability to function normally, and he was considered mad. Davidsohn spent the remainder of his life moving from one home, hospital, or sanitarium to another. In April of 1942, with Germany caught up in World War II, the Nazis deported him from a hospital in Bendorf-Sayn to an unknown concentration camp where he was subsequently killed.

Written in 1910, "Weltende" was inspired by Halley's Comet, which made an appearance that year. Earlier in 1910 Davidsohn, along with Kurt Hiller, Erwin Loewenson, and some other writers, founded the Neue Club in Berlin and opened a cabaret where they read their poetry. It was there that Davidsohn first read versions of "Weltende" and some of his other early poems, many of which were being published in German periodicals such as *Der Sturm* and especially *Die Aktion.* Davidsohn used the poem as a warning against the destruction of war, which was symbolized by the coming of a comet-like force sweeping over the earth: "The hat flies away from the pointed head of the philistine./ Everywhere in the atmosphere there is a resounding as of screams./ Slaters fall from the roofs and break in two/ And on the coasts—one reads—the

waters are rising./ The storm is here, the unleashed seas are hopping/ On land in order to squash big dams./ Most people are having a cold in their head./ Railway trains are falling off the bridges." Despite warnings of the coming disaster, the bourgeois characters in the book ignore everything and continue on with life. In the periodical *Literaturwissenschaftliches Jahrbuch im Auftrage der Gorres Gesellschaft,* critic Richard Sheppard commented that, with the poem, Davidsohn created a scenario "where images of destructive irrationality are used to diagnose the situation of technological civilization and yet resisted through irony."

"Weltende" was very influential during the early part of the twentieth century, and continued to be discussed in college classrooms over four decades after its first appearance. "To print all essays devoted to Davidsohn's poem would fill volumes," literary critic Armin Arnold wrote in *Review of National Literatures.* In *Modern Language,* critic Michael Butler called the poem "the modernist breakthrough of Expressionism" and a "programmatic vision of the end of the world." Butler continued, "Davidsohn's vision is a sardonic and grotesque one which mocks any pretension to see causality as the mortar cementing the social fabric together."

In 1918 "Weltende" appeared in a collection of poems by the same name. It was the only collection of Davidsohn's poetry to be published during his lifetime. In more recent years, other collections of his work have appeared, including *Weltende: gesammelte Dichtungen,* edited by Paul Portner, and the English-language *The End of the World,* translated by G. P. Skratz. In addition to his published verse, Davidsohn left behind at least seventeen poems written later in his career that were never included in any collection. Among these are "Der Idealist," "Lebendes Bild," "En Ego," and "Herbst an den Zelten." Sheppard contended that these later poems are marked by "ragged disorder" and "characterized by a more pronounced note of irony." With the exception of one or two of these poems, Sheppard felt Davidsohn's work had become "ever more incoherent and nonsensical."

BIOGRAPHICAL AND CRITICAL SOURCES:

BOOKS

The Oxford Companion to Germanic Literature, 3rd edition, Oxford University (Oxford, England), 1997.

PERIODICALS

Literaturwissenschaftliches Jahrbuch im Auftrage der Gorres Gesellschaft, 1977, pp. 219-270.
Modern Languages, June, 1977, pp. 69-72.
Review of National Literatures, 1978, pp. 47-58.*

*   *   *

DEE, Catherine 1964-

PERSONAL: Born January 29, 1964, in Los Angeles, CA; daughter of Orson R. Dee (a cardiologist) and Frances Zeiner (a health care professional); married Jonathan Ganz (a technical publications consultant), September 29, 2001. *Education:* Pomona College, B.A., 1986. *Politics:* Democrat.

ADDRESSES: Home and office—P.O. Box 7035, Redwood City, CA 94063. *E-mail*—cate@deebest.com.

CAREER: Empowering Books for Girls, northern CA, author and public speaker. Also works as a technical and marketing writer and editor.

MEMBER: Society of Children's Book Writers and Illustrators.

AWARDS, HONORS: San Francisco Chronicle Best Bet, 1997, for *The Girls' Guide to Life: How to Take Charge of the Issues That Affect You;* Best Book Award, *Disney Adventures,* 1999; two American Library Association awards, both 2000, both for *The Girls' Book of Wisdom: Empowering, Inspirational Quotes from over 400 Fabulous Females.*

WRITINGS:

FOR YOUNG READERS

Kid Heroes of the Environment, illustrated by Michele Montez, Earth Works Press (Berkeley, CA), 1991.
The Girls' Guide to Life: How to Take Charge of the Issues That Affect You, illustrated by Cynthia Jabar, photographs by Carol Palmer, Little, Brown (New York, NY), 1997.

(Editor and author of introductions) *The Girls' Book of Wisdom: Empowering, Inspirational Quotes from over 400 Fabulous Females,* Little, Brown (New York, NY), 1999.
(Editor and author of introductions) *The Girls' Book of Friendship: Cool Quotes, True Stories, Secrets, and More,* illustrated by Ali Douglass, Little, Brown (New York, NY), 2001.
(Editor and author of introductions) *The Girls' Book of Love: Cool Quotes, Super Stories, Awesome Advice, and More,* Little, Brown (New York, NY), 2002.
(Editor and author of introductions) *The Girls' Book of Success: Winning Wisdom, Star Secrets, Tales of Triumph, and More,* Little, Brown (New York, NY), 2003.

OTHER

(Editor) *The Women's 1992 Voting Guide,* Earth Works Press (Berkeley, CA), 1992.
(Editor) *50/50 by 2000: The Woman's Guide to Political Power,* Earth Works Press (Berkeley, CA), 1993.

WORK IN PROGRESS: A new edition of *The Girls' Guide to Life.*

SIDELIGHTS: In *The Girls' Guide to Life* author Catherine Dee offers a feminist perspective on the political, cultural, social, and personal issues that face young women every day. As she told *CA,* she focuses in part on the stereotypes that help to perpetuate the age-old view that women are (or should be) passive, weak, or otherwise inferior to men. Dee explains the stereotypes and presents advice on how to counter them and how to help others to do the same, in what *Booklist* contributor Stephanie Zvirin called a "refreshingly nonstrident" way. Dee supports her advice with inspirational commentary from a diverse array of contributors in a variety of creative genres. Thus, whether the subject is political awareness, physical attractiveness, sexual harassment, or income disparity, a chapter might contain, in addition to historical facts and cultural background, a poem by Maya Angelou, a comic strip, a short story or nonfiction piece by an ordinary teenager, or a "self-study" quiz.

Dee's effort is not limited to offering inspirational support. Each chapter also includes a list of additional sources of information, ranging from relevant books or videos to addresses of organizations that can help. To *Horn Book* reviewer Marilyn Bousquin, one valuable component of each chapter is a "Things to Do" list that prompts the reader to become part of a solution, whether by improving her self-understanding or reaching out to others.

Dee explained, "Quotes were one component of *The Girls' Guide to Life* that girls especially liked, so my next project was a 'companion' book of empowering and inspirational quotes from women and girls, *The Girls' Book of Wisdom: Empowering, Inspirational Quotes from over 400 Fabulous Females*. This fun little book in turn launched a series that now includes *The Girls' Book of Friendship, The Girls' Book of Love,* and *The Girls' Book of Success*."

Like Dee's first book, *The Girls' Book of Wisdom* is divided into topical sections, nearly fifty of them, devoted to universal themes such as love, beauty, creativity, and leadership. She collected hundreds of inspirational quotations from women who achieved success in a wide range of careers, including pioneers, musicians and actors, politicians and activists for women's rights, and even famous mothers. Contributors range from Eleanor Roosevelt and writer Virginia Woolf to talk show host Rosie O'Donnell and athlete Jackie Joyner-Kersee.

The Girls' Book of Friendship is similar, with sections devoted to specific aspects of friendship, such as making new friends, nurturing relationships, and giving tokens of affection. Contributors come from the past, such as *Little Women* author Louisa May Alcott, and the present, including politician Hillary Rodham Clinton, television personality Oprah Winfrey, and typical teenagers with a message to share. In addition, *The Girls' Book of Friendship* offers tips on activities and projects that can help girls meet new people and strengthen the friendships they already enjoy.

Dee told *CA:* "After college and working as a copywriter in corporate America for a few years, I joined a small publisher, Earth Works Press, in Berkeley, California, and fell in love with the idea of writing books to help people and the planet. While editing a book called *The Women's 1992 Voting Guide* I realized that there were very few books available to help girls develop strong self-esteem and feel good about themselves. I certainly hadn't had a book like

that when I was growing up. So to fill this gap, I wrote *The Girls' Guide to Life: How to Take Charge of the Issues That Affect You.* I enjoyed every moment of the creation of this book, and I couldn't wait for it to come out so that girls could have access to the information. I'll never forget the way I felt when girls started showing up at my first book signing and began reading it.

"Inspiring and empowering girls through writing these books is the icing on the cake of my life. I feel very fortunate that Megan Tingley at Little, Brown believed in my first book proposal, and I look forward to continuing to provide helpful growing-up resources for girls!"

BIOGRAPHICAL AND CRITICAL SOURCES:

PERIODICALS

Booklist, July, 1997, Stephanie Zvirin, review of *The Girls' Guide to Life: How to Take Charge of the Issues That Affect You,* p. 1813.
Horn Book, July-August, 1997, Marilyn Bousquin, review of *The Girls' Guide to Life,* p. 473.
Plays, November, 2001, review of *The Girls' Book of Friendship: Cool Quotes, True Stories, Secrets, and More,* p. 70.
Publishers Weekly, September 20, 1999, review of *The Girls' Book of Wisdom: Empowering, Inspirational Quotes from over 400 Fabulous Females,* p. 90.
School Library Journal, December, 1999, Jennifer Ralston, review of *The Girls' Book of Wisdom,* p. 148; November, 2001, Elaine Baran Black, review of *The Girls' Book of Friendship,* p. 174.
Skipping Stones, September-October, 1997, review of *The Girls' Guide to Life,* p. 30.
Voice of Youth Advocates, December, 2001, Jennifer Hubert, review of *The Girls' Book of Friendship,* p. 380.

OTHER

Empowering Books for Girls, http://www.deebest.com (October 17, 2002).

*   *   *

de KRETSER, Michelle

PERSONAL: Born in Sri Lanka; immigrated to Australia at age fourteen and became a naturalized Australian citizen. *Education:* Studied French at Melbourne University, earned M.A. in Paris.

ADDRESSES: Home—Melbourne, Australia. *Agent*—c/o Author Mail, Random House, 201 East 50th St., New York, NY 10022.

CAREER: Freelance editor and writer. Taught for one year in Montpellier, France and worked for many years as an editor for a Melbourne publishing house.

WRITINGS:

(Editor) *Brief Encounters: Stories of Love, Sex, and Travel,* Lonely Planet (Oakland, CA), 1998.
The Rose Grower (historical novel), Random (New York, NY), 1999.

SIDELIGHTS: Michelle de Kretser is an Australia-based writer whose first book, *Brief Encounters: Stories of Love, Sex, and Travel,* features various writers' tales, all of which reveal the romantic, and sometimes erotic, nature of travel. De Kretser features a variety of writers—including Pico Iyer, Lisa St. Aubin de Teran, Mona Simpson, and Paul Theroux—and their stories evoke settings that range from a Mexican bathhouse to a Greek ferry. Anthony Sattin, in a London *Sunday Times* review, deemed *Brief Encounters* "a mixed bag," but added that the book contained "several excellent [previously unpublished] stories." Another reviewer, Helen Rumbelow, in the London *Times,* wrote that *Brief Encounters* acknowledged a "truism about travel: it is to have an anonymous but passionate fling while getting there," and described the book as "an absorbing read."

In de Kretser's novel, *The Rose Grower,* an American balloonist finds love and danger with a pair of sisters in Gascony, during the French Revolution. *Booklist* reviewer Margaret Flanagan called *The Rose Grower* "a mesmerizing debut novel" and added that it "builds quietly and elegantly toward an inevitably tragic climax." *Quadrant* critic Francesca Beddie, meanwhile, called this Australian novel about the French Revoluation "refreshing." Critic Thomas Wright, however, noted in the London *Daily Telegraph* that the novel "fails to evoke the flavour of the 1790s, offering the reader instead a kind of historical limbo which is neither wholly of the present nor of the past." Similarly, Rishi Dastidar, in the London *Times,* wrote that de Kretser proves "unable to create a satisfactory balance between the action and the horticulture." A

Publishers Weekly reviewer concluded that de Kretser's "characters never really come to life," but Joanne Harris, writing in the *New York Times Book Review,* called the novel "a lovely, meticulously researched first novel that evokes the beginnings of the Terror in crisp, elegant, compassionate prose." Margaret Gunning, in a *January* review, described de Kretser's writing as "heartbreakingly beautiful," and Ruth Gorb, in the London *Guardian,* wrote that *The Rose Garden* is "beautifully written, full of wit and pathos and evocative images." Although Gorb noted that the novel "lacks unity," she added that "there is a great deal to enjoy in the book" and concluded her review by acknowledging that "de Kretser's final pages are a triumph, quietly moving."

BIOGRAPHICAL AND CRITICAL SOURCES:

PERIODICALS

Booklist, June 1, 2000, Margaret Flanagan, review of *The Rose Grower,* p. 1852.
Guardian (London), November 6, 1999, Ruth Gorb, review of *The Rose Grower,* p. 10.
Library Journal, April 15, 2000, Andrea Lee Shuey, review of *The Rose Grower,* p. 122.
Daily Telegraph (London), November 13, 1999, Thomas Wright, review of *The Rose Grower.*
New York Times Book Review, August 27, 2000, Joanne Harris, "Pruning Season," p. 25.
Publishers Weekly, April 3, 2000, review of *The Rose Grower,* p. 60.
Quadrant, December, 1999, Francesca Beddie, review of *The Rose Grower,* p. 82.
Times (London, England), October 10, 1998, Helen Rumbelow, review of *Brief Encounters: Stories of Love, Sex, and Travel,* p. 22; October 30, 1999, Rishi Dastidar, review of *The Rose Grower,* p. 23.
Sunday Times (London), May 31, 1998, Anthony Sattin, review of *Brief Encounters: Stories of Love, Sex, and Travel,* p. 2.

OTHER

January, http://www.januarymagazine.com/ (December 2, 2001), Margaret Gunning, "Rose Focus."*

DENTON, James R. 1972-

PERSONAL: Born July 14, 1972, in Sault Ste. Marie, MI; son of Jim (a teacher) and Muriel (a teacher) Denton. *Ethnicity:* "White." *Education:* Evangel University, B.A., 1994. *Politics:* Republican. *Religion:* Assemblies of God.

ADDRESSES: Home and office—3877 South Cottage Ave., Springfield, MO 65807; fax: 417-883-5694. *E-mail*—jamesdenton@ureach.com.

CAREER: Writer.

WRITINGS:

The X $eries: The Money Guide with Gen X Appeal, J & R Associates, 2001.

WORK IN PROGRESS: Grow Up—Grow Rich.

SIDELIGHTS: James R. Denton told *CA:* "Essentially the writing [of *The X $eries: The Money Guide with Gen X Appeal,*] was the second step. The first was finding the answers for myself. Then I was moved to teach and share with my generation."

*   *   *

DERRY, Charles

PERSONAL: Born in Cleveland, OH; son of Charles Homer (a tool and die maker) and Rose (a factory worker; maiden name, Iacano) Derry; companion of Thomas Kohn. *Ethnicity:* "Italian/Irish." *Education:* Northwestern University, B.S., 1973, Ph.D., 1978; University of Southern California, M.A., 1975.

ADDRESSES: Home—1455 Cory Dr., Dayton, OH 45406. *Office*—Department of Theater Arts, Wright State University, Dayton, OH 45435. *E-mail*—charles.derry@wright.edu.

CAREER: Northwestern University, Evanston, IL, lecturer in film, 1975-77; Wright State University, Dayton, OH, assistant professor, 1978-83, associate professor, 1983-89, professor of theater arts, 1989—, coordinator of motion pictures program, 1979—. Frameline (annual festival and film distributor), member; Dayton Playhouse, past member of board of trustees; director of films and stage productions. Work represented in photography and multimedia exhibitions.

MEMBER: Society for Cinema Studies, Canyon Cinema Cooperative, Yellow Springs Writers Group.

AWARDS, HONORS: Multiple grants from Ohio Arts Council, beginning 1984; Bronze Awards, Houston International Film Festival, 1986, for *Cerebral Accident,* and 1987, for *Joan Crawford Died for Your Sins*; Culture Works prize, 1997, for a photographic exhibition titled "Snapshots: We Are Here"; award from Ohio Theater Alliance, for *God Bless Vivian Vance.*

WRITINGS:

Dark Dreams: A Psychological History of the Modern Horror Film, A. S. Barnes (Cranbury, NJ), 1977.

(With Jack Ellis and Sharon Kern) *The Film Book Bibliography, 1940-1975,* Scarecrow Press (Metuchen, NJ), 1979.

(And director, producer, and designer) *Cerebral Accident* (experimental film), Canyon Cinema (San Francisco, CA), 1986.

(With Patti Russo; and director, producer, and designer) *Joan Crawford Died for Your Sins* (short film), 1987.

The Suspense Thriller: Films in the Shadow of Alfred Hitchcock, McFarland and Co. (Jefferson, NC), 1988, new edition, 2001.

Marty's Fifteen Minutes (screenplay), 1988.

A Picture of Andy's Earth: The Last Resort (screenplay), 1991.

God Bless Vivian Vance (one-act play), produced in Columbus, OH, at Reality Theater, 1993.

(And director) "Ten Memories of My Mother, in the Order I Think of Them" (play), in *Art from Every Angle,* produced in Dayton, OH, at Boll Theater, University of Dayton, 1998.

(And director) *The Laramie Project* (play), 2002.

Contributor to books, including *American Television Genres,* edited by Stuart M. Kaminsky, Nelson Hall (Chicago, IL), 1985; *American Horrors,* edited by

Gregory A. Waller, University of Illinois Press (Urbana, IL), 1987; and *Reclaiming the Heartland: Lesbian and Gay Voices from the Midwest,* edited by Karen Lee Osborne and William J. Spurlin, University of Minnesota Press (Minneapolis, MN), 1996. Contributor of articles, interviews, short stories, and reviews to periodicals, including *Writers Forum, Chattahoochee Review, Chiron Review, Portland Literary Review, Cinefantastique, Journal of the University Film and Video Association,* and *Harvard Gay and Lesbian Review.* Member of editorial staff, *Film Reader,* 1976-77.

BIOGRAPHICAL AND CRITICAL SOURCES:

PERIODICALS

Book Report, March-April, 1989, Frances L. Cohen, review of *The Suspense Thriller: Films in the Shadow of Alfred Hitchcock,* p. 50.
Library Journal,, March 15, 2002, Michael Rogers, review of *The Suspense Thriller,* p. 113.

OTHER

Charles Derry, http://www.charlesderry.com/ (December 3, 2002).

*   *   *

DERRY, Margaret E. 1945-

PERSONAL: Born May 18, 1945, in Ottawa, Ontario, Canada. *Education:* University of Western Ontario, B.A., 1967; University of Toronto, M.A., 1970, Ph.D., 1997.

ADDRESSES: Home—Poplar Lane Farm, 20243 Heart Lake Rd., Caledon, Ontario, Canada L0N 1C0. *E-mail*—derry@poplarlaneholdings.com.

CAREER: Poplar Lane Farm, Caledon, Ontario, Canada, cattle breeder, 1988—. University of Guelph, adjunct professor of history; University of Toronto, associate scholar of Institute for the History and Philosophy of Science and Technology. Artist, with paintings in private and corporate collections; work also shown at exhibitions in Toronto. Guest on Canadian television and radio programs.

WRITINGS:

Ontario's Cattle Kingdom: Purebred Breeders and Their World, 1870-1920, University of Toronto Press (Toronto, Ontario, Canada), 2001.
Bred for Perfection: Shorthorn Cattle, Collies, and Arabian Horses since 1800, Johns Hopkins University Press (Baltimore, MD), 2003.

Contributor to books, including *Ontario since Confederation: A Reader,* edited by E. Montigny and L. Chambers, University of Toronto Press (Toronto, Ontario, Canada), 2000. Contributor of articles, art work, and reviews to periodicals, including *Ontario Living, Beaver, Canadian Historical Review,* and *Ontario History.*

WORK IN PROGRESS: Transformation: Cultural Patterns in Animal Improvement (tentative title); a monograph on art and science, history and memory.

SIDELIGHTS: Margaret E. Derry told *CA:* "I am a historian, an artist, and a breeder of purebred cattle. All of these activities are woven into my thrust as an author of books and articles on rural history and the development of ideas and initiatives for improvement of animals, from both a historical and a practical point of view. I am concerned with the cultural and technological themes of purebred animal breeding, evident over time.

"After graduating from the University of Toronto with a masters degree in American history, I embarked on a career of art and children. A painter in watercolors and oils, I was represented by a number of Toronto galleries in the 1980s and early 1990s. I held a number of solo exhibitions. My paintings are known for their development of themes around children and cattle in the Caledon countryside where I reside. Throughout that time and currently, I have had considerable success as a breeder of purebred Murray Grey cattle, winning many awards at fairs, including the grand champion bull, grand champion female, and best breeder's herd of cattle at the Royal Agricultural Winter Fair. I have also sold breeding stock all over North America.

"The 1990s brought me back to the academic world, and I completed my doctorate in history in 1997, with specialties in Canadian and modern British history as well as historical geography. I then embarked on a career of writing history. My first book, *Ontario's Cattle Kingdom: Purebred Breeders and Their World, 1870-1920,* explores the significance of beef cattle and livestock farming in Ontario. I concentrate much of my research on the herds themselves (purebred or otherwise), using them as cultural texts to explain patterns of innovation adoption and problems with strategies to control markets.

"My second book, *Bred for Perfection: Shorthorn Cattle, Collies, and Arabian Horses since 1800,* dwells on overarching themes in purebred breeding over the last two centuries, and focuses in particular on cultural, technical, and marketing implications of cattle, dog, and horse breeding. Again the emphasis is on the animals themselves, because they embody human vision.

"A third book is being developed: a philosophical journal dealing with the relationship of art to science and memory to history in knowledge. The story will also utilize my paintings. A fourth book with the working title *Transformation: Cultural Patterns in Animal Improvement* is underway as well. It will explore certain cultural patterns embedded in modern attempts to improve domestic animals. Gendered work in relation to livestock breeding, the cultural structure of pedigree keeping, and the role of fancy and utility in the breeding of animals for improvement serve as examples of issues that this monograph will deal with.

"As a professor and scholar my primary focus is on historical research of agricultural and animal-breeding themes in Britain and North America from the eighteenth century to the present, on publishing pertinent material generated by that work, and on giving guest lectures in my field of expertise."

BIOGRAPHICAL AND CRITICAL SOURCES:

PERIODICALS

Ontario Beef Farmer, fall, 2002, Catherine Brown, "Ontario's Cattle Kingdom: An Ontario Author and Professor Documents the Glory Days of Ontario's Beef Industry."

Ontario Dairy Farmer, October, 2002, Catherine Brown, "Ontario's Cattle Kingdom: An Author Explores the Evolution of Ontario's Breeders to Using Purebreds in the Early 1900s."
Ontario History, autumn, 2001, Terry Crowley, review of *Ontario's Cattle Kingdom: Purebred Breeders and Their World, 1870-1920.*

*   *   *

DICAIRE, David 1963-

PERSONAL: Born April 9, 1963, in Windsor, Ontario, Canada; son of Leon (a factory worker) and Juliette (a homemaker) Dicaire. *Ethnicity:* "French."

ADDRESSES: Home—Leamington, Ontario, Canada. *Agent*—c/o Author Mail, McFarland and Co., Inc., P.O. Box 611, Jefferson, NC 28640.

CAREER: Nonfiction author. Point Pelee National Park, Ontario, Canada, train driver.

WRITINGS:

Blues Singers: Biographies of Fifty Legendary Artists from the Early Twentieth Century, McFarland and Co. (Jefferson, NC), 1999.
More Blues Singers: Biographies of Fifty Artists from the Later Twentieth Century, McFarland and Co. (Jefferson, NC), 2001.

SIDELIGHTS: David Dicaire told *CA:* "My primary motivation for writing is that I am a lover of stories. I believe there is no greater magic in the entire world than the exact combination of words that can take readers away to some fantastic world that allows them the luxury of forgetting their troubles, if only for a few hours. The challenge in fitting the right words together is an endless motivation for me.

"There is a myriad of influences on my work. The list includes respected literary names such as William Faulkner, William Shakespeare, Eugene O'Neill, Mark Twain, and Charles Dickens as well as the romantic poets William Blake, Lord Byron, Percy Shelley, and John Keats. I also have a keen admiration for authors of popular fiction such as Stephen King, John Le Carre, and Kurt Vonnegut, among others. I also like rock biographies, in particular *No One Here Gets out Alive,* the biography of Jim Morrison, lead singer of the Doors. Other important influences are more obscure sources such as William Ashworth, who wrote *The Late, Great Lakes,* a book I have read several times. These are just some of the writers who have had a profound influence on my work.

"My writing process varies for each different project. For a nonfiction book I always work from an outline after I have done my research. For instance, both blues books I've had published had a clear blueprint. However, in writing fiction there are no guidelines. I let my intuition guide me.

"It is a common theory that people write what they know about. The first incarnation of my blues book was a biographical book on all of my favorite guitarists, since that was my prime passion. When I realized that most of the names I had written down were blues musicians, only then did it occur to me to write a blues book. I have always loved music and decided to venture down this avenue. I believe I will enjoy a very long journey down this particular musical highway that I have chosen."

BIOGRAPHICAL AND CRITICAL SOURCES:

PERIODICALS

Library Journal, May 1, 2002, Eric Hahn, review of *More Blues Singers: Biographies of Fifty Artists from the Later Twentieth Century,* p. 103.

*   *   *

DUNCAN, Julia K.
   See BENSON, Mildred (Augustine Wirt)

E

EAGLE, Kathleen 1947-

PERSONAL: Born November 8, 1947, in Fredericksburg, VA; daughter of Sidney Daniel (in the U.S. Air Force) and Mary Virginia (Garner) Pierson; married Clyde Spencer Eagle (a teacher), October 10, 1970; children: David Spencer, Elizabeth Marie, and Christopher Daniel. *Education:* Mount Holyoke College, B.A., 1970; North State College, Aberdeen, SD, M.S., 1982. *Religion:* Episcopalian.

ADDRESSES: Home—1437 Larch Lane N., Minneapolis, MN 55441-4774; fax: 612-541-9537. *E-mail*—KatEagle@aol.com.

CAREER: Romance novelist and educator. Fort Yates School District, ND, teacher, 1970-87; writer, 1984—; Minneapolis Star Tribune, reviewer.

MEMBER: North Dakota Council of Teachers of English (president, 1985-87), North Dakota Department of Education Curriculum Council (secretary, 1985-86), Romance Writers of America (national conference keynote speaker, 1993; adviser to board of directors, 1995-96), Novelists, Inc., Midwest Fiction Writers.

AWARDS, HONORS: Golden Heart Award, 1983; Golden Heart Award, Romance Writers of America (RWA), for *Someday Soon,* 1984; Lifetime Achievement Award, *Romantic Times Magazine,* 1989; RITA Award, RWA, for *This Time Forever,* 1993; RITA Award finalist, *Fire and Rain,* 1994; Midwest Fiction

Writer of the Year, RWA, 1995; RITA Award finalist, *Reason to Believe,* 1995; Write Touch Readers Award, for *Reason to Believe,* 1996; Janet Daily Award finalist, *Sunset Song,* 1996; Career Achievement Award for Contemporary Novel, *Romantic Times,* for *The Last True Cowboy,* 1998.

WRITINGS:

Someday Soon (Silhouette Special Edition), Silhouette (New York, NY), 1984.
A Class Act (Silhouette Special Edition), Silhouette (New York, NY), 1985.
Georgia Nights (Silhouette Special Edition), Silhouette (New York, NY), 1986.
For Old Times' Sake (Silhouette Intimate Moments), Silhouette (New York, NY), 1986.
Something Worth Keeping (Silhouette Special Edition), Silhouette (New York, NY), 1987.
Carved in Stone (Western Lovers), Silhouette (New York, NY), 1987.
Candles in the Night (Silhouette Special Edition), Silhouette (New York, NY), 1988.
More Than a Miracle (Silhouette Intimate Moments), Silhouette (New York, NY), 1988.
But That Was Yesterday (Silhouette Intimate Moments), Silhouette (New York, NY), 1988.
Private Treaty (Harlequin Historical), Harlequin (New York, NY), 1988.
Medicine Woman (Harlequin Historical), Harlequin (New York, NY), 1989.
Paintbox Morning, Harlequin (New York, NY), 1989.
Heat Lightning, Pageant Books (New York, NY), 1989.

Heaven and Earth (Harlequin Historical), Harlequin (New York, NY), 1990.

'Til There Was You (Silhouette Special Edition), Silhouette (New York, NY), 1990.

Bad Moon Rising (Silhouette Intimate Moments), Silhouette (New York, NY), 1991.

To Each His Own (Silhouette Intimate Moments), Silhouette (New York, NY), 1992.

Black Tree Moon: American Hero (Silhouette Intimate Moments), Silhouette (New York, NY), 1992.

This Time Forever, Avon (New York, NY), 1992.

Diamond Willow (Silhouette Intimate Moments), Silhouette (New York, NY), 1993.

Broomstick Cowboy (Silhouette Special Edition), Silhouette (New York, NY), 1993.

Defender (Silhouette Intimate Moments), Silhouette (New York, NY), 1994.

Fire and Rain, Avon (New York, NY), 1994.

Reason to Believe, Avon (New York, NY), 1995.

A Class Act: North Dakota (Men Made in America), Harlequin (New York, NY), 1995.

Surrender!, Harlequin (New York, NY), 1995.

(With Bronwyn Williams) *Dream Catchers (by Request),* Harlequin (New York, NY), 1996.

Sunrise Song, Avon (New York, NY), 1996.

The Night Remembers, Avon (New York, NY), 1997.

(With Kasey Michaels and Emilie Richards) *A Funny Thing Happened on the Way to the Delivery Room,* Harlequin (New York, NY), 1997.

(With Mary Lynn Baxter and Marie Ferrarella) *For the Baby's Sake,* Harlequin (New York, NY), 1997.

The Last True Cowboy, Avon (New York, NY), 1998.

What the Heart Knows, Avon (New York, NY), 1999.

The Last Good Man, Morrow (New York, NY), 2000.

You Never Can Tell, Morrow (New York, NY), 2001.

Once upon a Wedding, Morrow (New York, NY), 2002.

It Must Have Been Love, Morrow (New York, NY), 2002.

Contributor to anthologies, including *Silhouette Christmas Stories 1988, Silhouette Summer Sizzlers 1991,* and *Summer Sizzlers: Men of Summer 1996.* Also reviews popular fiction for the *Minneapolis Star Tribune.*

SIDELIGHTS: The writings of prolific American romance novelist Kathleen Eagle, who has written more than thirty-five books since publishing her debut work in 1984, have consistently appeared on regional and national best-seller lists. In fact, Eagle has won many of her genre's most important literary prizes, beginning with the Romance Writers of America's Golden Heart Award for her first novel, *Someday Soon.* The many other awards she has won include a Lifetime Achievement Award from *Romantic Times Magazine* and the Romantic Writers of America's prestigious RITA for her 1992 novel *This Time Forever.* Although many of her earlier novels were paperbacks published by Harlequin, most of her more recent efforts have been published in hardcover editions, including *The Night Remembers, The Last Good Man,* and *You Never Can Tell.*

Eagle spent most of her childhood moving around because her father, Sidney Pierson, was in the U.S. Air Force. After graduating from Mount Holyoke College in 1970, she began her professional career as a teacher on an Indian reservation in North Dakota. Around this time she met and married Clyde Spencer Eagle, a Native American of Lakota Sioux ancestry who was also a teacher. She began taking graduate courses at North State College in Aberdeen, South Dakota, graduating in 1982. As she explained in an interview with *Amazon. com,* it was around this time that she began to write her first book. "I was teaching high school English on Standing Rock Indian Reservation. I'd just finished getting my master's degree, and I decided to write a story for fun one summer," she said. "I didn't intend to become a novelist, but I'd dreamed of it when I was young enough to have such outlandish dreams."

Because of her relationship with her husband and her experiences while teaching on the reservation, Eagle understands the issues affecting Native Americans, both historically and in modern times. Many of her books use this firsthand knowledge and offer intimate glimpses of life on an Indian reservation. In fact, literary critics often point to her ability to portray these issues as strong points in her writing. For example, in her 1999 novel *What the Heart Knows,* Eagle examines the issue of gaming casinos on Indian reservations and the negative impact of legalized gambling on many Native American communities. Even when Eagle has written about something other than Native American life, she has still tackled serious issues, such as in *The Last True Cowboy,* in which she focuses on the greedy practices of corporate land development in the West. Critic Grace Lee, who reviewed the book for *Booklist,* called it "a compelling conflict between traditional love of the land and crass money-making."

Again drawing inspiration from her husband's Native-American heritage, *You Never Can Tell* follows the movements of Heather Reardon, an investigative journalist on the trail of an outlaw in hiding. The outlaw, Kole Kills Crow, reluctantly agrees to be the focus of her story. Lezlie Patterson, writing for *Knight Ridder/Tribune News Service* called it an "almost decent book, but Eagle took too much space to promote her cause, which left too little for romance."

Mix in three generations of women who reunite for a big wedding, an ex-husband or two, young people engrossed in lust, and you have the making of a sparkling romance in *Once upon a Wedding.* Patty Engelmann, of *Booklist,* called it a "sweet story about friendship, family, and the surprising changes weddings can put in motion." A *Publishers Weekly* reviewer added, "the wedding preparation details are frosting on the cake."

Despite the attention she gives to serious issues, Eagle is a romance writer at heart, and all her works center on romantic themes. In an *Amazon.com* interview, Eagle explained her primary concern when beginning a new book. "I always set out to write a book I'll enjoy reading myself. I write primarily to entertain." According to many critics, Eagle has succeeded in achieving this goal. Kristen Ramsdell, who has reviewed a number of Eagle's books for *Library Journal,* called her "a highly regarded writer of emotionally involving romances." With the success of her first work, Eagle gave up her job teaching at Standing Rock after seventeen years so that she could devote more time to writing. She lives in Minnesota with her husband and three children.

BIOGRAPHICAL AND CRITICAL SOURCES:

PERIODICALS

Booklist, June 1, 1997, Kathleen Hughes, review of *The Night Remembers,* p. 1655; April 1, 1998, Grace Lee, review of *The Last True Cowboy,* p. 1303; July, 1999, Alexandra Baker Shrake, review of *What the Heart Knows,* p. 1929; July, 2000, Patty Engelmann, review of *The Last Good Man,* p. 2015; July, 2001, Patty Engelmann, review of *You Never Can Tell,* p. 1990; June 1, 2002, Patty Engelmann, review of *Once upon a Wedding,* p. 1694.
Kirkus Reviews, May 1, 1997, review of *The Night Remembers,* p. 660.

Knight Ridder/Tribune News Service, February 6, 2002, Lezlie Patterson, review of *You Never Can Tell,* p. K1649.
Library Journal, February 15, 1996, review of *Sunrise Song,* p. 140; May 15, 1997, Kristin Ramsdell, review of *The Night Remembers,* p. 66; May 15, 1998, Kristin Ramsdell, review of *The Last True Cowboy,* p. 75; August, 1999, Kristin Ramsdell, review of *What the Heart Knows,* p. 68; August, 2000, Kristin Ramsdell, review of *The Last Good Man,* p. 82; May 15, 2001, Kristin Ramsdell, review of *You Never Can Tell,* p. 106.
Publishers Weekly, May 12, 1997, review of *The Night Remembers,* p. 60; May 4, 1998, review of *The Last True Cowboy,* p. 204; May 31, 1999, review of *What the Heart Knows,* p. 63; July 10, 2000, review of *The Last Good Man,* p. 44; July 30, 2001, review of *You Never Can Tell,* p. 60; April 15, 2002, review of *You Never Can Tell,* p. 47. July 8, 2002, review of *Once upon a Wedding,* p. 32.

OTHER

Amazon.com, http://www.amazon.com/ (March 16, 2002), "Amazon.com Talks to Kathleen Eagle."*

*   *   *

EGGER, Andrea (A.) 1967-

PERSONAL: Born December 7, 1967, in Elgin, IL; daughter of George W. and M. Marjorie (Boehm) Egger; children: Jeffrey A. Rider, Jr. (stepson). *Ethnicity:* "Caucasian." *Education:* University of Illinois—Urbana-Champaign, B.S. *Politics:* Democrat. *Religion:* Baptist.

ADDRESSES: Home—411 West Mesa Ave., Gallup, NM 87301. *Office*—Gallup Independent, 500 Ninth St., Gallup, NM 87301; fax: 505-722-5750. *Agent*—Danielle Chiotti, Lee Shore Agency, Philadelphia, PA. *E-mail*—katwmn@i4c.net.

CAREER: Gallup Independent, Gallup, NM, reporter, c. 1994—.

AWARDS, HONORS: Best in show award and first-place award, New Mexico Associated Press, for investigative reporting.

WRITINGS:

Grave Accusations (nonfiction), New Horizon Press (Far Hills, NJ), 2001.

WORK IN PROGRESS: Two "true-crime" books, *Ice upon My Soul* and *Trails and Tribulations,* with Thomas F. Mumford.

SIDELIGHTS: Andrea Egger told *CA:* "I have always been a writer, since I wrote short stories as a child. I didn't consider that as a career until I was in college and had to pick an undergraduate degree before going on to law school. However, once I took my first journalism course, I was hooked, and I never had the urge again to be a lawyer. (Well, OK, the money would be better.) I have worked at my current job on the crime beat for eight years, and I fell in love with the field. I would like to be the next Ann Rule and Edna Buchanan combined into one person. When I was inspired to write my first book, *Grave Accusations,* I found my true niche in writing—books, and true crime in general. Living in the small southwestern town of Gallup, New Mexico, I find this a very untapped area as far as true crime is concerned, and I see many more books coming out of this area. *Grave Accusations* was conceived after a trial I covered for the newspaper about a police officer in Farmington, New Mexico, two hours north, who was accused of shooting his wife to death in the abdomen with a shotgun.

"The issue of whether his wife could have killed herself seemed preposterous—or is it? The book investigates this and proves the killer's identity beyond almost *all* doubt. After this trial I kicked around the idea of a book, because it was such a bizarre occurrence and a serious injustice people needed to know about. After a few wasted years of 'You can't write a book; you're not that good' and other insecurities, I finished the book, found an agency, and they found New Horizon, my publisher. That's a lot easier-sounding than the process really was—lots of rejection letters before the agent and even more before the publisher. But I was inspired by a foreword in John Grisham's *A Time to Kill,* in which he described more rejection letters than I received for that book, his first book, and a first publication of an obscure 5,000 copies from a small publishing house until *The Firm* got him recognized and the movies began.

"Writing will always remain my passion in life, and although I am a terrible procrastinator, I will get my work published. I'm determined to do so."

*   *   *

EICK, Gretchen Cassel 1942-

PERSONAL: Born December 17, 1942, in Fairview Park, OH; daughter of Samuel H., Jr. (a minister) and Virginia (a government bureaucrat and writer; maiden name, Cunningham) Cassel; married Richard N. Eick (a teacher; divorced); married Michael J. Poage (a minister and poet), June 23, 1991; children: (first marriage) Alyson Joy Eick Shaw, Kendra Elizabeth; (second marriage) Joel, Sarah, Cora Elise. *Ethnicity:* "Anglo." *Education:* Attended Fourah Bay College in Sierra Leone; Kalamazoo College, B.A., 1964; Northwestern University, M.A., 1965; University of Kansas, Ph.D., 1997. *Religion:* United Church of Christ. *Hobbies and other interests:* Reading, sewing, crafts, teaching Sunday school.

ADDRESSES: Home—1705 North Holyoke, Wichita, KS 67208. *Office*—Department of History, Friends University, 2100 University Blvd., Wichita, KS 67213. *E-mail*—eick@friends.edu.

CAREER: Federal City College, Washington, DC, instructor, 1972-73; United Church of Christ, Office for Church in Society, Washington, DC, policy advocate, 1977-87; National IMPACT, Washington, DC, executive director, 1987-91; University of Kansas, Lawrence, project coordinator, 1992-93; Friends University, Wichita, KS, associate professor of history, 1993—. United Church of Christ, member of executive council and moderator of Potomac Association. Also worked as public school teacher in New Haven, CT, and junior high school teacher in Kensington, MD.

MEMBER: American Historical Association, Organization of American Historians, American Studies Association.

AWARDS, HONORS: Woodrow Wilson fellow; National Security Studies fellow, U.S. Army War College, 1986; Barbara Ward Award, Center for Theology and Public Policy, 1987; Fulbright fellow in Latvia, 2000.

WRITINGS:

Women: Economic Exile in the Promised Land, Disciples Press, 1993.

Dissent in Wichita: The Civil Rights Movement in the Midwest, 1954-72 University of Illinois Press (Urbana, IL), 2001.

WORK IN PROGRESS: A source book for a U.S. history survey course.

BIOGRAPHICAL AND CRITICAL SOURCES:

PERIODICALS

Washington Post, December 7, 1982, George C. Wilson, "Churches Lobbying the House against MX Missile," p. A16.

*   *   *

EISENBERG, Susan 1950-

PERSONAL: Born 1950.

ADDRESSES: Home—9 Rockview St., Jamaica Plain, MA 02130.

CAREER: Master electrician and poet. Teacher of writing and theatre. Creator of "Not on a Silver Platter," an interactive mixed media installation.

WRITINGS:

It's a Good Thing I'm Not Macho, Whetstone, 1984.

If I Had My Life to Live Over: Anthology, Papier-Mache (Watsonville, CA), 1992.

We'll Call You if We Need You: Experiences of Women Working Construction, Cornell University Press (Ithaca, NY), 1998.

Pioneering: Poems from the Construction Site, Cornell University Press (Ithaca, NY), 1998.

Eisenberg has published works in *Prairie Schooner, Willow Springs,* and *Mothering.*

SIDELIGHTS: When Susan Eisenberg decided to research the status of women in construction, she found positives as well as stories of difficulties—difficulties that she had already experienced. As a master electrician Eisenberg worked in the male-dominated construction field. To counter the poor female and minority representation in construction trades, the U.S. government had declared goals for increasing the percentages of women who worked in federally funded construction projects. But female representation in such trades only climbed to two percent in the early 1980s and remained at that level into the late 1990s. Many of the barriers faced by women who attempted to enter construction trades were brought about by threatened and bigoted men.

Eisenberg interviewed thirty women in her book *We'll Call You If We Need You: Experiences of Women Working Construction* and tells of the issues that these women faced as they attempted to forge new ground in their chosen fields. The author talked to tradeswomen including "carpenters, electricians, ironworkers, painters, and plumbers." Dealing with many obstacles, including threats to their lives, sexual harassment, isolation, little job security, barriers to joining trade unions, and on-the-job conflicts regarding whether they had the physical strength to do the job, these women also lacked an adequate support system of other women, since there are so few of them nationally to begin with. Gay and minority women are often exposed to extra, targeted discrimination.

In her book, Eisenberg covers each issue dealt with by these women. While *New York Times Book Review* critic Samuel C. Florman admitted that the format could have been "tedious," he concluded that the author has constructed events and interviews in a way that keeps the reader engaged.

Eisenberg was surprised by some of the positive reactions voiced by the women that she interviewed. While her book was undertaken originally as a type of protest against the situation, the author also found that many of the women gained self-confidence and pride from the skills that they learned and the completion of a tangible product, such as a building at which they could later look. The women even mentioned "exceptional men" who had assisted them during their struggles to forge roles as women construction workers. Eisenberg was amazed by women who were "consistently generous" as they related stories, some of them negative, and concluded that "At the most profound human level, I don't understand parts of this book."

Eisenberg published a companion volume to *We'll Call You If We Need You,* titled *Pioneering: Poems from the Construction Site.* According to Florman, the collection of poetry contains none of the optimism present in Eisenberg's first book. The author fully vents her anger about the status of women in construction in the lines of these poems, and uses imagery that includes male construction peers armed with knives, dismemberment, electrocuted animals, and falling human bodies. Florman commented that the poetry "made me wince" and hoped that in the future, the author would focus more strongly on some of the positive comments that women construction workers shared in their interviews.

BIOGRAPHICAL AND CRITICAL SOURCES:

BOOKS

A Directory of American Poets and Fiction Writers, 1997-1998 edition, Poets and Writers (New York, NY), 1997.

PERIODICALS

Journal of American History, June, 1999, Ileen A. de Vault, review of *We'll Call You If We Need You: Experiences of Women Working Construction,* p. 331.
Library Journal, June 1, 1998, Kay Meredith Dusheck, review of *We'll Call You If We Need You,* p. 135.
New York Times Book Review, April 26, 1998, p. 37.
Progressive, September, 1998, Leah Samuel, review of *We'll Call You If We Need You,* p. 40.
Women's Review of Books, November, 1998, Pat Cooper, review of *We'll Call You If We Need You,* p. 24.*

*   *   *

EMERSON, Alice B.
See BENSON, Mildred (Augustine Wirt)

EMMETT, Jonathan 1965-

PERSONAL: Born December 10, 1965, in Leicester, England; son of Robert (a rig fitter) and Joyce (a teacher; maiden name, Motley) Emmett; married Rachel Grover (an arts administrator), July 30, 1994; children: Max, Laura. *Education:* Nottingham University, B.A. (honors architecture), 1988, additional classwork, 1991-93. *Politics:* "Liberal Democrat." *Religion:* "Agnostic." *Hobbies and other interests:* "Walking, reading, furniture design, and tinkering with my Web site."

ADDRESSES: Agent—Caroline Walsh, David Hingham Associates, 5-8 Lower John Street, Golden Square, London W1F 9HA, England. *E-mail*—mail@scribblestreet.co.uk.

CAREER: Writer, illustrator, and paper engineer. Worked for several years as an architect, mid-1990s.

WRITINGS:

Doohickey and the Robot, Oxford University Press (Oxford, England), 1999.
Ten Little Monsters: A Counting Book, illustrated by Ant Parker, Kingfisher, (New York, NY), 2000, with finger puppet set, Houghton Mifflin (Boston, MA), 2002.
Fox's New Coat, illustrated by Penny Ives, Viking (London, England), 2000.
Bringing down the Moon, illustrated by Vanessa Cabban, Candlewick Press (Cambridge, MA), 2001.
Dinosaurs after Dark, illustrated by Curtis Jobling, Golden Books (New York, NY), 2001.
Cosmo for Captain, illustrated by Peter Rutherford, Oxford University Press (Oxford, England), 2002.
A Turtle in the Toilet, illustrated by Caroline Jayne Church, Tiger Tales Books (Wilton, CT), 2002.
A Mouse inside the Marmalade, illustrated by Caroline Jayne Church, Tiger Tales Books (Wilton, CT), 2002.
Terry Takes Off, illustrated by Peter Rutherford, Oxford University Press (Oxford, England), 2003.
Through the Heart of the Jungle, illustrated by Elena Gomez, Tiger Tales Books (Wilton, CT), 2003.
What Friends Do Best, HarperCollins (London, England), 2003.

Someone Bigger, illustrated by Nathan Reed, Oxford University Press (Oxford, England), 2003.

If We Had a Sailboat, illustrated by Adrian Reynolds, Oxford University Press (Oxford, England), forthcoming.

Once upon a Time, upon a Nest, illustrated by Rebecca Harry, Macmillan Children's Books (London, England), forthcoming.

Author's books have been translated into other languages, including French, German, Danish, Finish, Slovenian, Swedish, and Friesian.

"CONJUROR'S COOKBOOK" SERIES

Goblin Stew, illustrated by Colin Paine, Bloomsbury Children's Books (London, England), 2000.

Serpent Soup, illustrated by Colin Paine, Bloomsbury Children's Books (London, England), 2000.

Ghostly Goulash, illustrated by Colin Paine, Bloomsbury Children's Books (London, England), 2000.

Fairy Cake, Bloomsbury Children's Books (London, England), 2000.

WORK IN PROGRESS: No Place like Home and *A Diamond in the Snow,* both illustrated by Vanessa Cabban for Walker Books; *Brum-brum! Vroom-vroom!* a pop-up vehicles book, illustrated by Christyan Fox for Macmillan; *Creature Colours,* a self-illustrated pop-up book, and *Rabbit's Day Off,* both for Gullane Children's Books.

SIDELIGHTS: Wanting to write children's books, Jonathan Emmett itched to leave his job as an architect, but he didn't dare, even though his wife Rachel offered to support the family. "I couldn't face the possibility of giving up a steady job and then failing to get anything published," he told *CA.* Finally he got a push in 1995 when he was laid off. Within three months, he had found a literary agent and even sold a pop-up book called *Scraposaurus Wrecks,* which though never published, led to other opportunities, as he recalled: "Although this was a big disappointment, the fact that I had sold the story, and been commissioned to illustrate and paper-engineer it, gave me the confidence to continue working on children's books."

Emmett's interest in books dates from childhood, when as a young boy he made the spare bedroom into a library for his parents' books, arranging them by color and size. He told *CA,* "I can remember visiting our local library as a toddler. The books that we borrowed then, including *Where the Wild Things Are* by Maurice Sendak, *The Cat in the Hat* by Dr. Seuss, and *Harold and the Purple Crayon* by Crockett Johnson, have a great influence on the picture book stories that I now write. The first 'proper' book that I read for myself was *The Folk of the Faraway Tree* by Enid Blyton. I went on to read other popular children's authors like C. S. Lewis, but like many children of my generation, the author who made the biggest impression on my early childhood was Roald Dahl." While in grade school Emmett wrote a weekly serial instead of the assigned short stories.

"It wasn't until I was about fourteen years old that it occurred to me that I might write for a living." Emmett elaborately decorated his school notebook covers to look like the book jackets of novels, complete with publishers' blurbs. Yet he did not pursue a career in writing. Instead he studied architecture, beginning in 1984, but the urge to write simmered within him, as he recalled to *CA*: "It was while I was at college that I first started developing my skills as a writer and illustrator." When rehearsing with a band, one that never performed as it turned out, he started writing song lyrics. "I enjoyed this and kept on writing lyrics and poems long after the band had become no more than an embarrassing memory. Then one day, I decided to try and do an illustration to accompany the lyrics to one of the songs. I was pleased with the result, so I illustrated some of my poems, spending more and more time on each picture."

After graduating with his architecture degree in 1988, Emmett worked for an architecture firm on such projects as an art gallery, a theater, and an airport check-in building. Yet he yearned for more, and upon losing his job he finally gave himself the permission to reach for his dream. He did not achieve instant success, however. At his Web site, *Scribble Street,* Emmett remembered his early experiences: "My first three children's books (a chapter fiction, a novel and a pop-up book) got nowhere, but they whetted my appetite for creating children's books and my fourth book was accepted by a publisher in 1996." Since then he has published picture books, mostly illustrated by others, pop-up books, and early chapter books geared to children seven to nine years old. Although paper-engineering is now taught in technical schools in Great Britain, at the time Emmett had to teach himself the rudiments. "I learnt all of my paper-engineering by trial and error and by studying mechanisms from existing books and adapting them," he wrote at *Scribble Street.* To help others, at his Web site Emmett provides tips and refers future paper-engineers to some useful handbooks. He also answers the perennial question: Where do you get your ideas? "Anywhere and everywhere—books, television, cinema, real life. Working on one book will often throw out an idea for another. I jot the new idea down and come back to it later. Sometimes I can't get an idea to work well as a story the first time I look at it, but if I put it to one side and come back to it a few months (or even a few years) later, I'm often able to finish it off."

Among Emmett's titles are the "Conjuror's Cookbook" series of early chapter fiction with such titles as *Goblin Stew* and *Serpent Soup,* the pop-up book *Ten Little Monsters,* and the 2001 picture books *Dinosaurs after Dark* and *Bringing down the Moon. Bringing down the Moon,* about a mole who tries to touch the moon and fears he has broken it, and *Dinosaurs after Dark,* about a midnight jaunt along a dinosaur-filled street, earned modest praise. Although noting that the poetic meter is uneven in the Americanized printing of the book, a *Publishers Weekly* critic believed that the topic of dinosaurs and the illustrations would offset any flaws. As Carol L. MacKay wrote in *School Library Journal,* "Dino stories have huge appeal and Emmett's offering is no exception." On the other hand, enthusiasts of *Bringing down the Moon* highly praised its artwork, ambiance, and "unadorned gentle prose," to quote a *Publishers Weekly* writer. In *School Library Journal,* Anne Knickerbocker pointed out Emmett's use of onomatopoeia, which she found added to its attractiveness for reading out loud, and *Booklist*'s Connie Fletcher described the book as at once "comical" and "thought-provoking." Why thought-provoking? Because after Mole thinks he has broken the moon, not knowing it is only a reflection in the water, his other animal friends tell him the truth, explaining that some things should be enjoyed without being disturbed. It is a "sweet lesson in not getting what you want," summed up a *Kirkus Reviews* writer.

Though Mole in *Bringing down the Moon* did not get what he wanted, its author certainly has. Reflecting on his career for *CA,* Emmett said, "I am now a full-time author/paper-engineer with a growing number of books in print and I really love my new job. I just wish I'd had the courage to start doing it earlier!" At *Scribble Street* he gives would-be writers and illustrators some friendly advice: 1. "Get stuck in!" (meaning get going and "don't be disappointed if the first things you write are not as impressive as you'd hoped"); 2. "Think ahead!" (meaning make an outline); 3. "Always use the POINTY end of the pencil! You'll find it's much easier to write with."

BIOGRAPHICAL AND CRITICAL SOURCES:

PERIODICALS

Booklist, February 1, 2002, Connie Fletcher, review of *Bringing down the Moon,* p. 946.

Kirkus Reviews, September 15, 2001, review of *Bringing down the Moon,* p. 1357; January 1, 2002, review of *Dinosaurs after Dark,* p. 45.

Publishers Weekly, November 5, 2001, review of *Bringing down the Moon,* p. 66; December 24, 2001, review of *Dinosaurs after Dark,* p. 62.

School Library Journal, January, 2002, Anne Knickerbocker, review of *Bringing down the Moon,* p. 98; June, 2002, Carol L. MacKay, review of *Dinosaurs after Dark,* pp. 92-93.

OTHER

Scribble Street: The Web Site of Children's Author Jonathan Emmett, http://scribblestreet.co.uk (July 10, 2002).

*　　　*　　　*

EPSTEIN, Mark 1953-

PERSONAL: Born 1953, in United States. *Education:* Harvard University, M.D.

ADDRESSES: Office—c/o *Tricycle: The Buddhist Review,* 92 Vandam Street, New York, NY 10013.

CAREER: Psychiatrist and writer, Tricycle, consulting editor. New York University, clinical assistant professor.

WRITINGS:

Thoughts without a Thinker: Psychotherapy from a Buddhist Perspective, Basic Books (New York, NY), 1995.

Going to Pieces without Falling Apart: A Buddhist Perspective on Wholeness, Broadway Books (New York, NY), 1998.

Going on Being: Buddhism and the Way of Change; A Positive Psychology for the West, Broadway Books (New York, NY), 2001.

SIDELIGHTS: Mark Epstein is a New York psychiatrist and writer with a special interest in Buddhism. He first became interested in Buddhism as a college student, continued studying it while in medical school, and has imbued his medical practice with Buddhist principles. He has written about these principles and their influence on his approach to psychotherapy in three books.

Thoughts without a Thinker: Psychotherapy from a Buddhist Perspective shows how the practice of Buddhism can be complementary to modern psychotherapy. The first part presents basic Buddhist concepts; the second part discusses meditation and discusses its relationship to psychoanalysis, and the third part applies Buddhist concepts to the process of therapy. A *Publishers Weekly* reviewer called the book a "highly personal, thoughtful, illuminating synthesis" and wrote that readers "will find much spiritual nourishment." In *Bloomsbury Review,* Dixie Griffing commented that the book is "well-written, thoroughly researched" and that it "goes beyond popular psychotherapy."

Going to Pieces without Falling Apart: A Buddhist Perspective on Wholeness examines the concept of letting go, familiar in both psychotherapy and Buddhism. Using his own experiences and those of clients, Epstein gives examples of people learning to let go of the old self to discover their true selves. He also discusses the use of meditation to quiet anxious minds. The book is divided into four parts: "Looking," "Smiling," "Embracing," and "Orgasms," each based on Tibetan nicknames for various aspects of spiritual practice. According to a review in *Publishers Weekly,* Epstein shows "through sparkling prose and effervescent wit how spiritual practice can transform our everyday lives." In *Natural Health,* J. K. Tidmore praised Epstein's clear use of "everyday language," and noted that Epstein's strength is that "he is not only a Buddhist, he is a psychiatrist, and as such, he can talk in terms that people unfamiliar with Buddhism can very easily grasp."

Going on Being: Buddhism and the Way of Change; A Positive Psychology for the West is part memoir and part guide to therapy. It discusses Epstein's own experiences with Buddhist meditation, and advises that people would heal better from their emotional wounds if they let go of a traditionally Western concept about problems: that problems should be either explored fully, or completely let go of. Epstein, using Buddhist principles, says that one should let go of one's fears of being empty, not allow oneself to be distracted by problems, but not avoid them either, and that the practice of meditation can help one find this balance. June Sawyers wrote in *Booklist,* "Epstein tells wonderful stories, full of wisdom and flashes of inspiration." In *Library Journal,* Madeleine Nash wrote, "the book melds many Eastern and Western concepts in a clear and original manner." A *Publishers Weekly* reviewer commented, "Lucid writing and truly useful ideas abound."

In an interview in *Human Nature,* Epstein said, "What Buddhism teaches is that the connection, the ability to find intimacy or connection, is inherent within us, and that if we can just surrender back into that capacity for love, that is all of our birthrights—all babies are born with that; they instinctively love their caretakers. So if we can find that again, then our relationships will take care of themselves."

BIOGRAPHICAL AND CRITICAL SOURCES:

PERIODICALS

American Health for Women, June, 1998, Amy Gross, "Relaxing into Yourself," p. 34.

American Journal of Psychoanalysis, March, 1996, p. 121.

Bloomsbury Review, September, 1995, Dixie Griffin, review of *Thoughts without a Thinker,* p. 25.

Booklist, February 1, 1995, Alice Joyce, review of *Thoughts without a Thinker,* p. 982; June 1, 1998, Vanessa Bush, review of *Going to Pieces without Falling Apart,* p. 1678; March 15, 2001, June Sawyers, review of *Going on Being,* p. 1335.

Kirkus Reviews, February 15, 1995, review of *Thoughts without a Thinker,* p. 194.

Library Journal, February 15, 1995, p. 171; February 15, 2001, Madeleine Nash, review of *Going on Being,* p. 186.

Middle Way, February, 1997, p. 254.

Natural Health, July-August, 1996, Kurt Tidmore, review of *Thoughts without a Thinker,* p. 141; January, 1999, J. K. Tidmore, review of *Going to Pieces without Falling Apart,* p. 154.

New England Journal of Medicine, February 4, 1999, p. 396.

Publishers Weekly, February 27, 1995, review of *Thoughts without a Thinker,* p. 94; May 25, 1998, review of *Going to Pieces without Falling Apart,* p. 81; January 29, 2001, review of *Going on Being,* p. 84.

OTHER

Human Nature, http://www.human-nature.com/ (September 15, 2001), "Going to Pieces with Mark Epstein."*

F

FARMER, Rod(ney Bruce) 1947-

PERSONAL: Born June 9, 1947, in Carthage, MO; son of Alvin (a farmer) and Kathleen Farmer; married 1986; wife's name, Margaret. *Ethnicity:* "Anglo." *Education:* Central Missouri State University B.S., 1968, M.A., 1972; University of Missouri—Columbia, Ph. D., 1978; University of Maine, postdoctoral study, 1984-85.

ADDRESSES: Home—122 Anson St., Farmington, ME 04938. *Office*—Franklin Hall, University of Maine—Farmington, 252 Main St., Farmington, ME 04938. *E-mail*—farmer@maine.edu.

CAREER: Substitute schoolteacher in Kansas City, MO, 1968-69; high school teacher of history and social science, Lincoln, MO, 1973-76; University of Maine—Farmington, assistant professor, 1978-82, associate professor, 1982-87, professor of history and education, 1987—, chair, Department of Secondary Education, 1994-2001. Also worked as farm laborer, dump truck driver, and grocery store clerk. *Military service:* U.S. Army, 1969-70; served in Vietnam.

MEMBER: National Council for the Social Studies, National Council for History Education, New England History Teachers Association, Maine Council for the Social Studies (president, 1987-88; member of executive committee), Maine Writers and Publishers Alliance, Phi Kappa Phi, Kappa Delta Pi, Phi Delta Kappa, Phi Alpha Theta.

AWARDS, HONORS: Fulbright fellowships for India, 1980, Israel, 1982, and Pakistan, 1986; grant for Japan, Japan Institute for Social and Economic Affairs, 1981; grant for Taiwan, Republic of China, 1989; grant for Japan, Five College Center for East Asian Studies, 1991; Award for Excellence in Social Studies, Maine Council for the Social Studies, 1994.

WRITINGS:

American Government (study guide and workbook), University of Missouri Press (Columbia, MO), 1978.
Youth in Conflict (study guide and workbook), University of Missouri Press (Columbia, MO), 1979.
Universal Essence (poetry), Brunswick Publishing (Lawrenceville, VA), 1986.

Work represented in anthologies. Columnist for *Maine in Print,* 1997-99. Contributor of hundreds of poems and numerous articles, essays, and reviews to periodicals, including *Maine Historical Society Quarterly, Haight Ashbury Literary Journal, Green's, Rattle, Webster Review, New England Journal of History, Humanist, Mind Matters Review, Poet,* and *Art Times.*

SIDELIGHTS: Rod Farmer told *CA:* "My method of writing poetry is for me to write what I need to say and in the most attractive and comprehensible way I can write it. What I need to say determines, to a great extent, how I write. Often I do not know what I need to say until I have written the poem. I may come across a word, a phrase, or an image from reading or from daily life. That word, phrase, or image grabs me, pushes me to a yellow tablet, and places a pen in my hand. Then I write.

"I find the original writing of a poem, writing the first draft, somewhat similar to making love. Rather than analyze myself and my writing while I am writing, I just do it. Analysis comes later, after the composition and during the revisions. Watching myself write would lead to performance anxiety, a common cause of writer's block—and other problems. I want to enjoy the spiritual experience of creating my poem. I want the excitement; I employ the excitement in creating. Writing the first draft can be both a spiritual and a sensuous experience if I live inside of that creative moment, which is impossible if I play English teacher with myself while I am creating. I am the free and uninhibited lover while composing; I am the uptight English teacher while revising.

"I do lots of revising. I have revised poems after they have been published and even reprinted a time or two. Then I may revise again. I have had some poems reprinted several times, and each reprint usually was from a new revision. I am always revising because every poem is alive, capable of growth and refinement. As long as I am alive, my poems are alive and capable of change. As I grow and change, I see my earlier poems differently. Revision is, for me, a natural result of the poet growing over time.

"I write the poetry of Rod Farmer, not the poetry of some poetic school. Schools have walls and schedules. Writing poetry is my year-long spiritual summer vacation. The last thing I want to do is give up my independence by belonging to a poetic school or by joining some exclusive literary circle (box?). The poet's independent voice can select the subjects and fill the bodies of the poet's poems. I avoid writing formulas and stick with the spiritual experience of creating. According to Anaïs Nin, Freud said: 'Everywhere I go, I find a poet has been there before me.' In various areas of human life where Freud made discoveries, he later found that some poet had earlier traveled that same ground. These early explorer poets were, often, carried to distant shores by creative moments, not by writing formulas. So, my advice is, in a secular way, let the spirit move you when you write poetry."

BIOGRAPHICAL AND CRITICAL SOURCES:

PERIODICALS

Poetic Page, November/December, 1994, Rod Farmer, "How I Write," pp. 13-14.

FEISS, Hugh (Bernard) 1939-

PERSONAL: Born May 8, 1939, in Lakeview, OR; son of Sherman (a forester) and Margaret (a teacher; maiden name, Furlong) Feiss. *Education:* Mount Angel Seminary, B.A. (summa cum laude), 1962, M.A., M.Div., 1966; Catholic University of America, S.T.L., 1967, Ph.L., 1972; attended University of St. Thomas, Rome, Italy, 1974-75; Pontificum Athenaeum Anselmianum, Rome, S.T.D. (summa cum laude), 1976; University of Iowa, M.A., 1987. *Hobbies and other interests:* Ornithology.

ADDRESSES: Home—Monastery of the Ascension, 541 East 100 S., Jerome, ID 83338; fax: 208-324-2377. *E-mail*—hughf@idahomonks.org.

CAREER: Benedictine monk, 1960—; ordained Roman Catholic priest, 1966—; Mount Angel Seminary, St. Benedict, OR, began as instructor at Mount Angel Seminary College, became professor of philosophy, 1967-74, seminary professor of theology and humanities, 1976-96, director of Mount Angel Abbey Library, 1987-96; Monastery of the Ascension, Jerome, ID, member, 1996— , coordinator and instructor for monastery Elderhostels, 1997—. Yale University, fellow at Beinecke Rare Book and Manuscript Library, 1992. Sacred Heart Academy, Salem, OR, part-time chaplain, counselor, and instructor, 1977-83; Trappist Abbey of Our Lady of Guadalupe, lecturer, 1987-96; Benedictine Consortium for Distance Learning, coordinator and instructor, 1996—; instructor with adult Catholic education program in Boise, ID, 1997—; Mount Marty College, instructor in pastoral ministry, 2001—; speaker at other institutions, including St. Michael's College, Burlington, VT, and University of Calgary; leader of religious retreats. Also worked as part-time basketball and tennis coach for parochial secondary schools.

MEMBER: Medieval Academy, Catholic Theology Society of America, American Catholic Philosophical Association, Society of Biblical Literature, American Academy of Religion, American Benedictine Academy.

AWARDS, HONORS: Fellow of National Endowment for the Humanities, 1982, 1986, 1989, 1993.

WRITINGS:

(With Martin Pollard) *Mount of Communion: Mt. Angel Abbey, 1882-1982,* 1982, 2nd edition, 1985.

(Editor) *Glad for What He Has Made: A Guide to the Trees, Shrubs, Flowers, and Birds of Queen of Angels Monastery and Mount Angel Abbey,* 1982, 2nd edition, 1990.

(Editor and translator) Thomas de Cantimpré, *Supplement to The Life of Marie d'Oignies,* Peregrina Publishing (Saskatoon, Saskatchewan, Canada), 1987, 3rd edition, 1993.

(Editor and translator) Pierre de Celle, *Selected Works,* Cistercian Publications (Kalamazoo, MI), 1988.

(Editor and translator) Hildegard of Bingen, *Explanation of the Rule of St. Benedict,* Peregrina Press (Toronto, Ontario, Canada), 1990, 2nd edition, 1999.

(Translator and author of introduction) *The Life of the Saintly Hildegard,* Peregrina Press (Toronto, Ontario, Canada), 1996.

(Translator and author of introduction) *Hugh of St. Cher on the Prodigal Son,* Peregrina Press (Toronto, Ontario, Canada), 1996.

(Translator and author of notes, with Daniela Re and Marilyn Hall) Catherine of Bologna, *The Seven Spiritual Weapons,* Peregrina Press (Toronto, Ontario, Canada), 1998.

Essential Monastic Wisdom: Writings on the Contemplative Life, HarperSanFrancisco (San Francisco, CA), 1999.

(Translator and author of introduction, with Ronald Pepin and Catherine Hamaker) *Two Medieval Lives of Saint Winefride,* Peregrina Press (Toronto, Ontario, Canada), 2000.

(Editor, with Jan Emerson, and contributor) *Imagining Heaven in the Middle Ages,* Garland Publishing (New York, NY), 2000.

(Translator and author of introduction) *The Works of Archard of St. Victor,* Cistercian Publications (Kalamazoo, MI), 2001.

(With Ronald Pepin) *St. Mary of Egypt: Three Medieval Lives in Verse,* Cistercian Publications (Kalamazoo, MI), in press.

(Translator) Marbod of Rennes, *Life of Robert of Chaise-Dieu* (published with translation of *The Life of Stephen of Obazine* by Ronald Pepin), Cistercian Publications (Kalamazoo, MI), in press.

Contributor to books, including *Bernardus Magister,* edited by John R. Sommerfeldt, Cistercian Publications (Kalamazoo, MI), 1993; *The Joy of Learning and the Love of God: Studies in Honor of Jean Leclercq,* edited by E. Rozanne Elder, Cistercian Publications (Kalamazoo, MI), 1995; and *"And God Saw That It Was Good": Catholic Theology and the Environment,* edited by Drew Christiansen and Walter Grazer, USCC (Washington, DC), 1996. Contributor of articles; translations from Latin, French, German, Italian, and Spanish; and reviews to periodicals, including *Liturgy OCSO, Vox Benedictina, Cistercian Studies, Country Life, Studia Monastica,* and *Word and World.* Editor, *Desert Chronicle* and *Link,* both 1997—; associate editor, *American Benedictine Review.*

WORK IN PROGRESS: A reader in medieval monasticism; editions of *opuscula* of Hugh of St. Victor; a study of Richard of St. Victor.

SIDELIGHTS: Hugh Feiss told *CA:* "When I was in graduate school, Edward Duff, S.J., who had been editor of a magazine which promoted social justice, told me I should write. For the next fifteen years I was too busy teaching and continuing my education to give writing much thought. In 1982 I attended a National Endowment for the Humanities seminar with Daniel Sheerin and Ruth Steiner. I realized then that I wanted to spend more time doing scholarly research, which in turn gave me something to write about. When Father Chrysogonus Waddell accepted a study I had prepared during that seminar for publication in *Liturgy OCSO,* I was a published writer.

"Thereafter I began publishing scholarly articles and translations from Latin. I can do the latter without having access to a big library, which is important now that I live in a small monastery in Idaho. Most of what I write is of little interest except to a few monks and medievalists. One exception is *Essential Monastic Wisdom: Writings on the Contemplative Life.* Tom Grady, who was an editor for HarperCollins at the time, asked Kathleen Norris to write the book, but she recommended he ask me to do it, which I did. Tom helped me formulate the plan for the book and negotiate the contract.

"I write because I feel called to do so. Most of what I publish brings no royalties. I do both my research and my writing after my other tasks as monk and priest are finished. Sometimes I wonder whether anyone reads most of it. However, results and impact are secondary considerations.

"Lately a teenager has been sending me some of her poetry. She is a voracious reader. She may be called to be a writer. I gave her Mary Oliver's *Poetry Handbook* so she could learn more about the craft of poetry and also about what it is to be a writer and a poet. It is to have received a gift and a task."

*   *   *

FIELD, Tiffany (Martini) 1942-

PERSONAL: Born January 16, 1942; daughter of Harvey (an insurance company executive) and Betty (a special-education teacher) Martini; married Tom Willard (a boatbuilder); children: Tory. *Education:* University of Cincinnati, B.S., 1963; Tufts University, O.T.R., 1965, M.S., 1973; University of Massachusetts—Amherst, Ph.D., 1976. *Hobbies and other interests:* Boating, yoga, crafts.

ADDRESSES: Home—4218 North Surf Rd., Hollywood, FL 33019. *Office*—Touch Research Institutes, School of Medicine, University of Miami, P.O. Box 016820, Miami, FL 33101; fax: 305-243-6488. *E-mail*—tfield@med.miami.edu.

CAREER: Intern at Lemuel Shattuck Hospital, Boston, MA, Bellevue Hospital, New York, NY, and Illinois State Psychiatric Institute, Chicago, IL, between 1964 and 1965; Boston University Hospital, Boston, MA, acting director of occupational therapy, 1965-66; Psychiatric Institutes of America, Washington, DC, director of rehabilitation center, 1966-70; Marseille School for Retarded and Emotionally Disturbed Children, Marseille, France, lecturer, 1971-72; University of Massachusetts—Amherst, research associate, 1974-75, visiting assistant professor of psychology, 1976-77; University of Miami, Coral Gables, FL, assistant professor, 1977-78, associate professor of pediatrics, psychology, and psychiatry at Mailman Center for Child Development, 1979-83, director of Touch Research Institutes, Miami, 1984—. Psychiatric Institute Foundation, Washington, DC, faculty member of Group Psychotherapy Training Institute, 1966-70; Nova Southeastern University, dean of Family and School Center, 1997-2000. National Foundation/March of Dimes, chair of study section, 1993-96.

MEMBER: International Society on Infant Studies (president, 1992-94), International Society for the Study of Behavioral Development, International Society of Developmental Psychobiology, World Association of Infant Psychiatry and Allied Disciplines, American Psychological Association (fellow; divisional president, 2000), Society for Research in Child Development, American Psychological Society, American Occupational Therapy Association, Society for Perinatal Research, Society of Pediatric Psychology, American Massage Therapy Association, American Association for the Advancement of Science, Merrill-Palmer Society, Eastern Psychological Association, Southeastern Society for Research in Child Development, Sigma Xi, Phi Kappa Phi, Psi Chi.

AWARDS, HONORS: Boyd McCandless Distinguished Young Scientist Award, American Psychological Association, 1979; grants from National Institute of Mental Health, 1981-91, 1991-2002; Distinguished Alumna Awards, University of Cincinnati, 1986, 1989; additional grants from National Institutes of Health, Agency for International Development, National Foundation/March of Dimes, Society for Research in Child Development, National Institute of Drug Abuse, Johnson & Johnson, Gerber, National Institute of Child Health and Human Development, and Administration for Children, Youth, and Families.

WRITINGS:

Infancy, Harvard University Press (Cambridge, MA), 1990.
Touch in Early Development, Lawrence Erlbaum Associates (Hillsdale, NJ), 1995.
Touch Therapy, Churchill Livingston (New York, NY), 2001.
Touch, MIT Press (Cambridge, MA), 2001.

Contributor to more than 100 books, including *To Your Health: Psychology through the Life Span; Practice and Research Opportunities,* edited by R. J. Resnick and R. H. Rozensky, American Psychological Association (Washington, DC), 1996; *Essentials of Complementary and Alternative Medicine,* edited by W. Jonas and J. S. Levin, Lippincott, Williams & Wilkins (Baltimore, MD), 1999; *Stress, Coping, and Depression,* Lawrence Erlbaum and Associates (Mahwah, NJ), 2000; *Integrating Complementary Medicine into Health Systems,* edited by G. Lewith, N. Jones, and H. Wallach, Harcourt Health Sciences (Edinburgh, Scotland), 2001; and *Introduction to Infant Develop-*

ment, edited by A. Slater and M. Lewis, Oxford University Press (New York, NY), 2002. Contributor of articles and reviews to medical journals.

EDITOR

(With A. Sostek, S. Goldberg, and H. H. Shuman; and contributor) *Infants Born at Risk: Behavior and Development,* Spectrum Publications (New York, NY), 1979.

(With S. Goldberg, D. Stern, and A. Sostek; and contributor) *High-risk Infants and Children: Adult and Peer Interactions,* Academic Press (New York, NY), 1980.

(With K. Scott and E. Robertson; and contributor) *Teenage Parents and Their Offspring,* Grune & Stratton (New York, NY), 1981.

(With M. Sostek, P. Vietze, and A. H. Leiderman; and contributor) *Culture and Early Interactions,* Lawrence Erlbaum Associates (Hillsdale, NJ), 1981.

(With others; and contributor) *Review of Human Development,* Wiley (New York, NY), 1982.

(With A. Fogel; and contributor) *Emotion and Early Interaction,* Lawrence Erlbaum Associates (Hillsdale, NJ), 1982.

(With L. Lipsitt) *Infant Behavior and Development: Perinatal Risk and Newborn Behavior,* Ablex Publishing (Norwood, NJ), 1982.

(With A. Sostek; and contributor) *Infants Born-at-risk: Physiological, Perceptual, and Cognitive Processes,* Grune & Stratton (New York, NY), 1983.

(With J. Roopnarine and M. Segal; and contributor) *Friendships in Normal and Handicapped Children,* Ablex Publishing (Norwood, NJ), 1984.

(With N. Fox; and contributor) *Social Perception in Infants,* Ablex Publishing (Norwood, NJ), 1986.

(With P. McCabe and N. Schneiderman; and contributor) *Stress and Coping,* Lawrence Erlbaum Associates (Hillsdale, NJ), 1985.

(With M. Reite; and contributor) *Psychobiology of Attachment and Separation,* Academic Press (New York, NY), 1985.

(With E. Tronick) *Maternal Depression and Infant Disturbance,* Jossey-Bass (San Francisco, CA), 1986.

(With P. McCabe and N. Schneiderman; and contributor) *Stress and Coping across Development,* Lawrence Erlbaum Associates (Hillsdale, NJ), 1988.

(With T. B. Brazelton; and contributor) *Advances in Touch,* Johnson & Johnson (Skillman, NJ), 1990.

(With P. McCabe and N. Schneiderman; and contributor) *Stress and Coping during Infancy and Childhood,* Lawrence Erlbaum Associates (Hillsdale, NJ), 1991.

(With P. McCabe, N. Schneiderman, and J. Skyler) *Stress, Coping, and Illness,* Lawrence Erlbaum Associates (Hillsdale, NJ), 1992.

Infant Mental Health Journal, member of editorial board, 1981-82, associate editor, 1983-90; guest editor for special issues of *American Anthropologist, Autism and Developmental Disabilities, Developmental Psychology, Health Psychology, Human Development, Infancy, Interamerican Journal, Journal of Abnormal Child Psychology, Journal of Abnormal Psychology, Journal of Applied Developmental Psychology, Journal of Child Psychology and Psychiatry, Journal of Clinical Child Psychology, Journal of Consulting and Clinical Psychology, Journal of Experimental Child Psychology, Journal of Pediatric Psychology, Journal of Pediatrics, Journal of Social and Personal Relationships, Journal of Social Psychology, Life Science, Merrill-Palmer Quarterly, Monographs of the Society for Research in Child Development, New England Journal of Medicine, Pediatrics, Psychology Bulletin, Psychophysiology,* and *Science;* member of editorial board, *Child Development,* 1977-92, *Developmental Psychology,* 1979-92, *Infant Behavior and Development,* 1979-2000, *Topics in Early Childhood and Special Education,* 1981-92, *Development and Psychopathology,* 1992-95, *Better Ways to Health, Journal of Bodywork and Movement Therapies,* and *Alternative Therapies in Health and Medicine.*

SIDELIGHTS: Tiffany Field told *CA:* "My primary motivation for writing is to educate lay people regarding our research findings. The research data influences the work. I write on a dictaphone, and the tape is then transcribed for editing. It was my daughter's growth following being massaged as a 'preemie' that inspired our massage therapy research."

BIOGRAPHICAL AND CRITICAL SOURCES:

PERIODICALS

Adolescence, spring, 2000, review of *Touch in Early Development,* p. 222.

Booklist, October 15, 2001, Vanessa Bush, review of *Touch,* p. 357.

Economist, January 26, 2002, review of *Touch.*
Library Journal, October 1, 2001, Margaret Cardwell, review of *Touch,* p. 128.

* * *

FINLEY, Guy 1949-

PERSONAL: Born February 22, 1949, in Beverly Hills, CA; son of Larry (affiliated with late-night talk shows and the video industry) and Venise (a real estate entrepreneur) Finley; married Patricia Wangler, 1994. *Education:* Attended University of Southern California and University of California—Los Angeles.

ADDRESSES: Office—Life of Learning Foundation, P.O. Box 10, Merlin, OR 97532.

CAREER: Life of Learning Foundation, Merlin, OR, founder and principal. Composer and lyricist, 1969-79; public speaker on self-development and spiritual psychology; guest on more than 300 media programs, including *Larry King Live, Sally Jesse Raphael,* and *Entertainment Tonight.*

WRITINGS:

Herbal Pet Care, Sweetwater Books (Los Angeles, CA), 1974.
The Secret of Letting Go, Llewellyn Publications (St. Paul, MN), 1990.
The Secret Way of Wonder, Llewellyn Publications (St. Paul, MN), 1992.
Freedom from the Ties That Bind, Llewellyn Publications (St. Paul, MN), 1994.
Designing Your Own Destiny, Llewellyn Publications (St. Paul, MN), 1995, expanded edition published as *Design Your Destiny,* 1999.
(With Ellen Dickstein) *The Intimate Enemy,* Llewellyn Publications (St. Paul, MN), 1997.
The Lost Secrets of Prayer, Llewellyn Publications (St. Paul, MN), 1998.
Seeker's Guide to Self-Freedom, Llewellyn Publications (St. Paul, MN), 2002.

Author of audio tape albums, including *Only the Fearless Are Free, Waking up Together: Building Compassionate Relationships Founded in Higher Love, Seven Characteristics of Higher Consciousness, Secret Teachings of the Sacred Testaments, Living in the Light, Teachings of the Timeless Kindness, The Road to Good Fortune, Secrets of Cleansing Your Heart, Mind, and Soul, The Heart and Soul of Freedom,* and *The Kingdom of Heaven Is Like. . . .* Composer for recording artists, films, and television programs; also recorded his composition on albums of his own.

Finley's writings have been published in eleven languages.

SIDELIGHTS: Guy Finley told *CA:* "My career reached this point through a circuitous path. Born into a successful show business family, my childhood friends were the sons and daughters of major celebrities. As a young man I enjoyed success in a number of areas, including composing award-winning music for many popular recording artists, motion pictures, and episodic television. From 1970 through 1979 I wrote and recorded my own albums for the Motown and RCA record labels.

"Throughout my youth, I suspected there was more to life than the type of worldly success that led to the emptiness and frustration I saw among my own friends and colleagues. In 1979, after travels to India and parts of the Far East in search of truth and Higher Wisdom, I voluntarily retired from a flourishing career in order to simplify my life and continue my inner studies.

"My own path began at a very young age. Nothing made sense to me as a small child. The idea of happiness and contentment eluded me until I realized these were based in an invisible world. It was my good fortune in the late seventies to meet a wonderful, true, good human being—an enlightened individual by the name of Vernon Howard. I worked with him for many years. He said, 'Life is not a race to win, but a school for our Higher education.' [I believe that] life is not what it appears to be, but rather offers for those who are willing to use it properly a way to discover a life that is rooted in a completely different order of reality—whose basis is timeless as opposed to our present perception of things as rooted totally in the temporary—with all the torment that identification with the temporary brings.

"Today I write books and tape albums on self-liberation. My works have sold over a million copies and have been translated into eleven languages. I provide tools for uncovering secret self-sabotage, tapping into sources of new wisdom and self-assurance, and finding one's own way back home."

BIOGRAPHICAL AND CRITICAL SOURCES:

OTHER

Life of Learning Foundation, http://www.guyfinley. com/ (December 4, 2002).

*   *   *

FORTNEY, Steven D. 1937-

PERSONAL: Born January 2, 1937, in Minneapolis, MN; son of Albin (an army chaplain and Lutheran pastor) and Anita (a nurse; maiden name, Sodergren) Fortney; married Ruth Geyer (a teacher), February 19, 1960; children: Melissa, Minda, Alex, Sigrid. *Ethnicity:* "Norwegian-Swedish-American." *Education:* University of Wisconsin at Madison, B.S. (classics and philosophy), 1959, teacher certification, 1960-64, attended Luther Theological Seminary, St. Paul, MN, 1960-61. *Politics:* Democrat. *Religion:* Buddhist. *Hobbies and other interests:* Fishing, gardening, reading, family.

ADDRESSES: Home and office—501 West South St., Stoughton, WI 53589. *E-mail*—sfortney@facstaff.wisc. edu.

CAREER: Writer and teacher. Stoughton Schools, Stoughton, WI, teacher, department chairman, language arts, 1964-95. Labor negotiator and president of teachers' union; alderman, Third District, Stoughton, WI, 1977-98; management negotiator. *Military service:* U.S. Naval Reserve, 1953-55, became fireman apprentice.

MEMBER: Torske Klubben (Norwegian men's luncheon group).

WRITINGS:

Heg (novel), illustrated by Richard Fendrick, Badger Books (Oregon, WI), 1998.
The Thomas Jesus (novel), illustrated by Richard Fendrick, Badger Books (Oregon, WI), 2000.

Greatest Hits (chapbook), Puddinghouse Press (Johnstown, OH), 2001.
The Gazebo (novel), Badger Books (Oregon, WI), 2001.

Contributor to *This Sporting Life,* Milkweed Press, 1987, and *Poems That Thump in the Night,* New Spirit Press, 1993; also contributor to various periodicals, including *Milk Weed Chronicle, Yet Another Literary Magazine, Seems, Waterways: Poetry in the Mainstream, Pulpsmith, Cutting Edge Quarterly, Heaven Bone, Embers, Visions International, East West, Cape Cod Writers, Yahara Prairie Review,* and *North Coast Review.*

WORK IN PROGRESS: The Maitreya Novel: The Party.

SIDELIGHTS: Poet and novelist Steven D. Fortney told *CA:* "I was raised in the Lutheran Church by a chaplain and later pastor father, in a military family that traveled extensively all over the United States in army posts, including childhood residences in Germany and Austria." After completing his education, Fortney worked for a small newspaper for four years, doing everything from reporting to selling ads. Certified as a secondary teacher in 1964, he went on to teach high school for thirty-one years. He was active in the teachers' union during most of that time and also served as an alderman on the Stoughton City Council for twenty-one years.

Fortney explained to *CA* that he took early retirement in 1995 to devote himself full-time to writing. "I fish and hunt and garden and read like mad. As you see, I started my serious poetry career late. With four books published, three novels, and a book of poetry, I guess I can call myself—as the people of West Texas generally, and Lubbock specifically, called Molly Ivins after she published her first book—an 'arthur'"

Well aware that he is a late bloomer as a writer, Fortney feels that "I have cheated the American literary tradition by not being precocious, that is, having a spurt of high creativity when very young and then fading forever from the book-lists thereafter: American Literature, it is said, has no second acts. European literature and world art, however, are full of five-act lives. I firmly believe that I was spared precocity because probably I didn't have the strength of character to handle it well in any case. Therefore, it has been my delightful lot to have developed what talent I have carefully and slowly, so that at the age of sixty-four I feel close to the height of my powers and feel quite confident, health and vigor permitting, that I can finish the half a dozen or so unfinished and barely-begun books stored in my computer and the unwritten poems in my soul well into my seventh and eighth and even ninth decades."

Fortney's writing process is based on what he calls "Rereading and Dreams." "I've had several experiences with dreams," he told *CA*, "in both stories and poems, that have helped to continue or to finish the composition. For example, in one poem titled 'Pondering,' one of my final lines gave me trouble. The poem is about a fish, in this case a white koi, which was my metaphor for a mystic. The last lines of the first draft read as follows: 'I believe in / the wind because I've / felt it. I know wind / I feel it. I climb slopes / of water before the / What I leap into. God's / language is silence.' I was not satisfied with this version but didn't know what to do about it. It so happened I was in northern Wisconsin with my friends at our cabin in the deep woods there and was distracted for a couple of days with pleasurable hiking, fishing, and canoeing adventures. One night after a wonderfully relaxed night's sleep, I lapsed into my usual morning dream state. Then suddenly I dreamed the right word. I made a note in my dream not to forget the word and upon waking wrote out the new version, the lines of which went as follows: 'I believe in / the wind because I've / felt it. I know wind / I feel it. I scale slopes / of water before the / What I leap into. God's / language is silence.' This involved only one word-change but immeasurably improved the poem."

Both his awareness of his dream life and the rereading process he applies to his writing are informed by his Buddhist beliefs, which Fortney has practiced for more than twenty-five years. He explained to *CA* how this practice enters into the writing process: "The beginning is difficult. So I start anywhere. As I work, I begin the process of rereading. That is, I read the text I have written over and over again until it is firmly fixed at all levels of my mind. And then I reread some more to achieve surfeit. When I get stuck, I do one of two things. Simply wait until the deeper intentionalities of my nether consciousness indicate the next step. The second is more formal. I will sit at my puja table,

which is also my working desk (it is meet, right, and salutary that no distinction between work and worship be made) and do my freelance Buddhist ritual there and sit until I hear the next voice, see the next action of the characters and narrative I am working with. Sometimes this happens almost instantaneously. Sometimes it takes days or weeks. I literally hear voices. I see actual visions. It's all mental and internal. Given my positivist bias, the process is wholly natural but is so powerful that it feels like magic. The trick is to never lose faith that it will happen and the writing will proceed. So far this process has never failed.

"Using autogenic devices—principally, for me, the discipline of meditation—has done wonderful things in carving out the underbrush around the opening of consciousness at all levels to permit the right kind of synthesis in thinking, the wondrous fountains of narrative, character, and image to appear and flow. I see no reason that I can't continue until the day I drop, with the last poem or story (Copernicus and his treatise come to mind here) grasped in my chilling fingers on my deathbed just written for the teaching and delight of my family."

"Once the basic work has been composed," he continued, "rewriting happens. I love rewriting. It is a delightful combination of interweaving intuitive and rational processes in which, with my daylight consciousness, I can see where revision consistent with the original intention of the work can be made. That is pure thinking, but intuitively arrived at. Given the ease of using a computer word-processing program, I even look forward to it. Here one can layer both narrative and poem easily enough to achieve the density and resonance both works of art demand to be worthy of rereading on the part of the auditors of the work."

Fortnoy's first novel was *Heg,* about the real-life Hans Christian Heg, who emigrated from Norway to Wisconsin and became an antislavery activist and Civil War hero. His second novel, *The Thomas Jesus,* is a fictional account of the life of "Doubting" Thomas, a disciple of Jesus Christ. Based on the research of the Jesus Seminar, a group of scholars devoted to determining the historical accuracy of stories about Jesus, Fortney's Jesus, who "sounds more like a Buddhist than a savior," according to a *Wisconsin State Journal* writer, might have been hard for Fortney's Lutheran forebears to accept.

Also a prolific poet, Fortney was profiled in the Madison, Wisconsin *Capital Times.* His friend, neighbor, and illustrator, Richard Fendrick, quipped that if there is an afterlife, Fortney will spend it writing. As the author himself declared, "It's just so much fun for me."

BIOGRAPHICAL AND CRITICAL SOURCES:

PERIODICALS

Capital Times (Madison, WI), May 1, 2000, "Book Sold, Life Is Good for Author," p. 2A.
Library Journal, April 1, 2000, Melanie C. Duncan, review of *The Thomas Jesus,* p. 82.
Wisconsin State Journal (Madison, WI), April 16, 2000, "Stoughton Author Takes Novel Approach to Christ," p. 3F.

*   *   *

FOWELLS, Robert M. 1921-

PERSONAL: Born November 2, 1921; citizenship, U.S.; married, wife's name Frances B. *Education:* University of Oregon, B.S., 1947; New York University, M.A., 1953; University of Southern California, D.M.A., 1959. *Politics:* Democrat. *Religion:* Presbyterian.

ADDRESSES: Agent—c/o Author Mail, Paraclete Press, P.O. Box 1568, Orleans, MA 02653. *E-mail*—rmfowells@earthlink.net.

CAREER: Choral music teacher at a junior high school in Richmond, CA, 1951-63; California State University, Los Angeles, professor of music, 1963-88; Neighborhood Music School, member of board of directors, 1988—. *Military service:* U.S. Army Air Forces, 1942-43.

MEMBER: American Choral Directors Association, Music Educators National Conference, Early Music America, Southern California Early Music Society.

WRITINGS:

(Translator) *Gregorian Semiology,* Abbey of St. Pierre de Solesmes (France), 1982.
Chant Made Simple, Paraclete Press (Orleans, MA), 2000.

SIDELIGHTS: Robert M. Fowells told *CA:* "I have been interested in early music since doing my master's degree with Gustave Reese at New York University. In 1974 I was able to get Dom Jean Claire, chant master at the Abbey of St. Pierre de Solesmes in France, to teach for a month at California State University, Los Angeles. That started a hobby in teaching and writing about chant. Since 1979 I have sponsored an annual summer class in chant, alternating between the university in Los Angeles and the abbey in France.

"The Catholic church's concept of chant rhythm, which was used for sixty years after it was developed in the early 1900s by the monks of Solesmes, was revised in the 1970s by the discovery of another of their monks, Dom Eugene Cardine, that the very earliest of western notation which was devised by Charlemagne's monks in order to unify the church service in his empire gave distinct indications about movement and expression, even though it did not denote exact pitch. It is this new concept that is the basis of the book *Chant Made Simple.*"

*   *   *

FRIEDMAN, Laurie 1964-

PERSONAL: Born January 28, 1964, in Fayetteville, AR; daughter of Kenneth (a lawyer) and Annette (a business executive; maiden name, Applebaum) Baim; married David Friedman (a real estate developer), November 4, 1989; children: Becca, Adam. *Education:* Attended Sorbonne, University of Paris, 1984; Tulane University, B.A., 1986. *Religion:* Jewish.

ADDRESSES: Home—Miami, FL. *Agent*—Rosenstone/Wender, 38 East 29th St., 10th Floor, New York, NY 10016. *E-mail*—Lfriedman@aol.com.

CAREER: Grey Advertising, New York, NY, account executive, 1986-88; N. W. Ayer Advertising, Houston, TX, account executive, 1988-90; Ogilvy & Mather Advertising, Houston, TX, account executive, 1990-92; writer.

MEMBER: Society of Children's Book Writers and Illustrators, National Writer's Association.

AWARDS, HONORS: First-place award in children's division, writing competition of South Florida chapter, National Writer's Association, 1999, for *A Big Bed for Jed.*

WRITINGS:

A *Big Bed for Jed,* illustrated by Lisa Jahn-Clough, Dial Books for Young Readers (New York, NY), 2002.

WORK IN PROGRESS: Mallory on the Move, Back to School, Mallory, Happy Birthday, Mallory, and *Heart-to-Heart with Mallory,* chapter books in a continuing series, for Carolrhoda Books, expected beginning 2004; *A Style All Her Own* and *I'm Not Afraid of a Haunted House,* picture books, from Carolrhoda Books, expected 2005.

SIDELIGHTS: Laurie Friedman once told *CA:* "My first book, *A Big Bed for Jed,* is a rhyming picture book about a little boy who conquers his fears and makes 'the big switch' from his crib to a bed. For me, imagination and a bit of real-life frustration were the key to writing *A Big Bed for Jed.* My own son's reluctance to move from a crib to a bed inspired me to come up with a solution that, along with a little dash of reverse psychology, proved surprisingly effective and served as the basis for Jed's fun and quirky story line.

"I have written a series of chapter books that will be published beginning in 2004. The first book in the series, *Mallory on the Move,* is the story of an eight-year-old girl who has to move to a new city and make new friends. The sequel, *Back to School, Mallory,* takes place when Mallory starts third grade at a new school. Additional books are indevelopment.

"I like writing about change and transition, and the Mallory books are all about learning to accept change. Change is hard to deal with. I hope my books will give kids a fresh and funny way to look at having to make changes and help them realize that change doesn't have to be bad, just different.

"I live in Miami, Florida, where I enjoy spending time with my husband, David, and our two children, Becca and Adam. I start each day with a walk, thinking about what my characters might do or say, then I go home and put all those thoughts and ideas on paper. I love what I do, and I am hard at work on lots more books for kids of all ages."

FURBEE, Mary R.
    See FURBEE, Mary Rodd

*   *   *

FURBEE, Mary Rodd 1954-
    (Mary R. Furbee)

PERSONAL: Born November 1, 1954, in Hammond, IN; daughter of William Herron II and Elizabeth (Cartwright) Rodd; married Paul Michael Furbee, August 8, 1981; children: Jenny Louise. *Education:* West Virginia University, B.A. (liberal arts), 1984, M. Sc. (journalism), 1991. *Hobbies and other interests:* Reading, walking, swimming.

ADDRESSES: Home—1 Bryson St., Morgantown, WV 26505. *Office*—West Virginia School of Journalism, P.O. Box 6010, Morgantown, WV 26506. *E-mail*—mary-furbee@mail.wvu.edu; swpup@access.mountain. net.

CAREER: Writer, editor, and television producer. University of West Virginia, adjunct journalism instructor, 1994—.

MEMBER: Authors Guild, Society of Children's Book Writers and Illustrators, West Virginia Writers, Inc.

AWARDS, HONORS: Two West Virginia Writers, Inc. annual contest awards; second-place award, Wachtman Barbe essay-writing contest; Outstanding Service Learning Course award, West Virginia University, 2002.

WRITINGS:

ADULT NONFICTION

(As Mary R. Furbee) *The Complete Guide to West Virginia Inns,* South Wind Publishing, 1992.

JUVENILE

Women of the American Revolution, Lucent Books (San Diego, CA), 1999.
(With husband Mike Furbee) *The Importance of Mohandas Gandhi,* Lucent Books (San Diego, CA), 2000.

Shawnee Captive: The Story of Mary Draper Ingles, Morgan Reynolds (Greensboro, NC), 2001.

Outrageous Women of Colonial America, J. Wiley (New York, NY), 2001.

Outrageous Women of the American Frontier, J. Wiley (New York, NY), 2002.

Wild Rose: Nancy Ward and the Cherokee Nation, Morgan Reynolds (Greensboro, NC), 2002.

Anne Bailey: Frontier Scout, Morgan Reynolds (Greensboro, NC), 2002.

Contributor to periodicals, including the *Washington Post, Stars & Stripes, Cleveland Plain Dealer, Charleston Gazette, American Visions, Progressive, Goldenseal,* and *Now and Then.*

WORK IN PROGRESS: Outrageous Women of the Civil War Times, for J. Wiley.

SIDELIGHTS: Mary Ross Furbee once told *CA:* "I live in West Virginia—in Morgantown, which is a great place to live and work as an author.

"When I'm writing in my study—which overlooks my big, tree-filled backyard—I can look outside and see bluejays, woodpeckers, and hummingbirds. I've even seen wild turkeys, raccoons, and a very lost, young bear. If I need companionship or conversation, I can pop outside to visit with my neighbors as they work in their gardens. Or I can walk down the block to visit my mother. Her apartment is Grand Central Station for a clan that includes my six brothers and sisters and dozens of nieces and nephews, all of whom also live in West Virginia. I feel incredibly lucky to have work I enjoy and family, friends, and natural beauty all around me.

"People often ask me how I got started writing books for children. Well, a couple of things led me down this path, I think. Like most writers, I read a lot as a child. Also, I ask lots of questions and am not satisfied until I have answers. In fact, I began writing biographies of women in American history to answer a simple question.

"A few years back, I was writing for a newspaper and looking for a fresh idea for a Fourth of July feature article. That same week, my daughter brought home a biography of Thomas Jefferson. Together those things suddenly made me ask myself: 'I wonder what the colonial women were up to?'

"I had only ever heard of Betsy Ross and Molly Pitcher, but I knew they couldn't be the only interesting women of their time. So I went to the library and checked out some history books. In those books, I discovered there were dozens of fascinating women scouts, spies, soldiers, chiefs, planters, midwives and more. I also discovered that very few children's books tell their stories. So, I asked some publishers if they would be interested in such books. And, lucky for me, they said yes!

"Of course, when I was your age, I never dreamed I would someday write children's books. Not in a million years. That was the kind of thing I thought the smartest, coolest, most talented kids might someday do for a living—not ordinary, average old me. I was wrong, though, which proves something I believe with all my heart: Anything is possible if you work hard, have faith in yourself, and follow your heart.

"Take care and happy reading!"

BIOGRAPHICAL AND CRITICAL SOURCES:

PERIODICALS

Booklist, May 15, 2001, Anne O'Malley, review of *Shawnee Captive: The Story of Mary Draper Ingles,* p. 1747; May 15, 2001, Carolyn Phelan, review of *Outrageous Women of Colonial America,* p. 1747; December 1, 2001, Roger Leslie, review of *Anne Bailey: Frontier Scout,* p. 637.

School Library Journal, September, 1999, Debbie Feulner, review of *Women of the American Revolution,* p. 232; June, 2001, Linda Greengrass, review of *Shawnee Captive: The Story of Mary Draper Ingles,* p. 168; September 2001, Donna J. Helmet, review of *Wild Rose: Nancy Ward and the Cherokee Nation,* p. 242.

OTHER

Mary Rodd Furbee Web site, http://web.mountain.net/~swpub./bio.

G

GALLAGHER, Nora 1949-

PERSONAL: Born 1949; married Vincent Stanley (a novelist). *Education:* Graduate of St. John's College, Santa Fe, NM. *Religion:* Episcopalian.

ADDRESSES: Home—Santa Barbara, CA. *Agent*—Philippa Brophy, Sterling Lord Linguistic, Inc., 65 Bleecker St., New York, NY 10012.

CAREER: Author and journalist. *Time* magazine, West Coast bureau chief. Reads and lectures at colleges and churches.

AWARDS, HONORS: Has received fellowships from Wesleyan Writers Conference, 1992, Blue Mountain Center, 1995, 2000, MacDowell Colony, 1996, and the Mesa Refuge, 1999.

WRITINGS:

Parlor Games, illustrated by Annie Gusman, Addison-Wesley (Reading, MA), 1979.
Simple Pleasures: Wonderful and Wild Things to Do At Home, Addison-Wesley (Reading, MA), 1981.
How to Stop a Sentence, and Other Methods of Managing Words: A Basic Guide to Punctuation, Addison-Wesley (Reading, MA), 1982.
Things Seen and Unseen: A Year Lived in Faith, Knopf (New York, NY), 1998.
(Editor) *Patagonia: Notes from the Field,* Chronicle Books (San Francisco, CA), 1999.
Practicing Resurrection: A Memoir of Discernment, Random House (New York, NY), 2003.

Contributor to publications including: *New York Times Magazine, Los Angeles Times Magazine, DoubleTake, Village Voice, Mother Jones, Life, Washington Post, Detroit Free Press, Utne Reader,* and others.

SIDELIGHTS: Journalist and author Nora Gallagher has written books on a variety of subjects. Her first two books are guides to passing time. *Parlor Games,* published in 1979, describes fifty games that readers can use to while away the hours. *Simple Pleasures: Wonderful and Wild Things to Do At Home,* published in 1981, presents a number of ideas for family recreation ranging from simple things like sorting pictures, to the unusual, like trading houses. Reviewers noted that it is a particularly useful book on rainy or snowy days. *How to Stop a Sentence, and Other Methods of Managing Words: A Basic Guide to Punctuation,* published in 1982, is a book for children that explains to them a variety of ways to construct interesting sentences.

Things Seen and Unseen: A Year Lived in Faith, is an autobiographical tale about Gallagher's re-acquaintance with religion. Having grown up attending the Episcopalian church, she rejected it at the age of twenty. But over a decade later she found herself inclined to return and began to tentatively and secretly re-explore her spiritual side. Eventually Gallagher found a church where she wanted to become actively involved at a time when its membership was falling off sharply. At the Trinity Episcopal Church in Santa Barbara she helped to establish a soup kitchen, traveled with a group of women to Nicaragua, and became a member of the church vestry. These experiences gave her what she was searching for: a sense of community and purpose.

The process of reestablishing her faith, which Gallagher chronicles in *Things Seen and Unseen* takes about a year. The author structures her very personal tale by juxtaposing everyday events with church rituals and holidays. It begins with Advent and continues through Christmas, Epiphany and Lent, concluding with "Ordinary Time," a term borrowed from the Roman Catholic calendar. As Gallagher observes these holidays, she also deals with profound moments in her personal life, such as the death of a friend and learning that her brother has been diagnosed with cancer. Gallagher's narrative paints not only a portrait of her own experience but of the personality of her congregation as well. The money and member poor church suffers from its own obstacles, like the necessity of 'earthquake-proofing' their building and the touchy issue of their homosexual rector.

Several reviewers praised the author of *Things Seen and Unseen* for her unique and honest point of view and her sense of clarity and detail. Describing the work in *Christian Century*, Debra Bendis wrote, "*Things Seen and Unseen* is in some ways a '90s spiritual soup pot. Gallagher is a skeptical, irreverent and determined seeker. She sorts through experiences before investing in the Christian faith. . . . Nothing is taken for granted or simply accepted as tradition; everything must be reconsidered." On her quest for spirituality, Gallagher consults a number of interesting sources, from Margaret Drabble and M. Scott Peck, to Van Gogh, Theodore Roethke and Dorothy Day.

Gallagher's articles have appeared in a number of publications, including *Life* magazine, *New York Times Magazine, Los Angeles Times Magazine,* and *Utne Reader.* Among many other topics, she has written about the trail of Patricia Hearst.

BIOGRAPHICAL AND CRITICAL SOURCES:

PERIODICALS

Booklist, November 1, 1979, p. 434; January 1, 1982, p. 580.

Christian Century, March 17, 1999, Debra Bendis, review of *Things Seen and Unseen: A Year Lived in Faith,* p. 308.

Commonweal, March 12, 1999, p. 24.

New York Times Book Review, December 6, 1981, p. 91.

Reading Teacher, March 1984, pp. 642-646.

Sojourners, January, 2000, Jo Ann Heydron, review of *Things Seen and Unseen: A Year Lived in Faith,* p. 59.

Women's Review of Books, May 1999, pp. 20-21.

Yankee, January 1982, p. 169.*

*   *   *

GARBORG, Arne 1851-1924

PERSONAL: Born 1851, in Jaeren, Norway; died 1924; married Hulda Bergerson, December 3, 1887.

CAREER: Novelist, poet, playwright, and essayist. Worked as a teacher.

WRITINGS:

Henrik Ibsen's "Keiser og Galiliaeer," En kritisk studie af G, Aschehoug (Kristiania, Norway), 1873.

Den ny-norsk sprog, og nationalitetsbevaegelse, Cammermeyer (Kristiania, Norway), 1877.

Ein fritenkjar forteljing, Cammermeyer (Kristiania, Norway), 1881.

Forteljingar og sogur, O. Huseby & O. Olsen (Kristiania, Norway), 1884.

Bondestudentar. forteljing, Huseby & Co. (Kristiania, Norway), 1885.

Mannfolk: forteljing, Nygaards (Bergen, Norway), 1886.

Fri skilsmisse: indlaeg i diskussionen om kjaerlighed, M. Litleré (Bergen, Norway), 1888.

Norsk eller Dansk-norsk? Svar til Bjørnson, Mons Litleré (Bergen, Norway), 1888.

Fri forhandling. Ymse stykkje (på norsk og dansk) um tru tanke, Mons Litleré (Bergen, Norway), 1889.

Hjaa ho more, M. Litleré (Bergen, Norway), 1890.

Kolbrotnev og andre skildringar, Mons Litleré (Bergen, Norway), 1890.

Trætte mænd, Aschehoug (Kristiania, Norway), 1891.

Fred: forteljing, Mons Litleré (Bergen, Norway), 1892.

Jonas Lie: en udviklingshistorie, Aschehoug (Kristiania, Norway), 1893.

Fra det mørke fastland: reiseindtryk frå Stavanger og Jæderen, Olaf Norli (Kristiania, Norway), 1893.

Norges selvstændighedskamp fra 1814 til nu: en oversigt, J. Sørensen (Kristiania, Norway), 1894.

Mødre: drama i tre akter, Feilberg & Landmark (Kristiania, Norway), 1895.

Haugtusse: forteljing, Aschehoug (Kristiania, Norway), 1895.

Laeraren: eit spél i fem vendingar, Aschehoug (Kristiania, Norway), 1896.

Vor sprogudvikling: en redegjørelse, Maalkassa (Oslo, Norway), 1897.

Maalteater: eit fyredrag, Maalkassa (Oslo, Norway), 1898.

Den burtkomme faderen, Aschehoug (Kristiania, Norway), 1899.

Framlegg til skrivereglar for landsmaale i skularne, A. W. Brøggers (Kristiania, Norway), 1899.

Skriftir i samling, Aschehoug (Kristiania, Norway), 1900.

Fjell-luft og andre smaastykke, Aschehoug (Kristiania, Norway), 1903.

Knudahei-brev, Aschehoug (Kristiania, Norway), 1904.

Jesus Messias, Aschehoug (Kristiania, Norway), 1906.

Norske embættsmenner, Johanson & Nielsen (Oslo, Norway), 1906.

Den Burtkomne Messias: innlegg i ordskrifte um trui: (med eit tillegg um antikrist), Aschehoug (Kristiania, Norway), 1907.

Heinkomin son, Aschehoug (Kristiania, Norway), 1908.

På skuggesida: forteljingar, Norske samlaget (Oslo, Norway), 1908.

Ivar Aasen, Norigs Ungdomslag og Student-Maallaget (Oslo, Norway), 1909.

Kolbotn-brev, Aschehoug (Kristiania, Norway), 1911.

Vaknande spursmaal, Aschehoug (Kristiania, Norway), 1915.

Politik: blad-innlegg frå 1870-aari til riksretten, Aschehoug (Kristiania, Norway), 1919.

Odyssevskvædet, Aschehoug (Kristiania, Norway), 1919.

Straumdrag, literaere utgreidingar frå åtti-og nitti-aari, [Kristiania, Norway], 1920.

The Lost Father, Stratford Co. (Boston, MA), 1920.

Eventyr, [Oslo, Norway], 1921.

(With Hulda Garborg) *Dagbok 1905-1923,* Aschehoug (Kristiania, Norway), 1927.

Peace, Norton (New York, NY), 1929.

Tankar og utsyn: artiklar, Aschehoug (Kristiania, Norway), 1950.

Arne Garborg, 25/1/1851-25/1/1951, edited by Hans E. Hognestad, Jærprent (Bryne, Norway), 1951.

ADAPTATIONS: Garborg's long poem cycle about peasant life, *Haugtussa,* was set to music by composer Edvard Grieg.

SIDELIGHTS: Arne Garborg was the first Norwegian author to write using *landsmaal* or Norsk, the spoken language of ordinary Norwegians. He advocated social and linguistic reform, and was a noted leader in the movement to promote the use of Nynorsk, or "New Norse," as the new Norwegian literary language. In his later work, particularly *Fred* and *Den burtkomme federen,* Garborg is more obviously influenced by the Russian writer Leo Tolstoy, who was noted for his social and spiritual concerns.

Haugtussa, a collection of seventy poems later set to music by composer Edvard Grieg, is "one of a very small number of song cycles in Scandinavian art song literature," according to James Massengale in *Scandinavian Studies.* It is also the only Norwegian song cycle that continues to be consistently performed for modern audiences, despite the fact that it is written in Nynorsk. It is not often performed outside Scandinavia since, as Massengale pointed out, its translations have not received favorable critical attention.

The story of *Haugtussa* emphasizes the theme of the struggle between the individual's baser instincts, and higher forces, and focuses on a young girl who is a visionary. Garborg weaves together threads of mysticism, romance, sentimentality, and realism.

Garborg was pleased with Grieg's musical adaptation of the cycle; according to Massengale, he told Grieg that the composer had effectively conveyed that "subterranean music that I in my own way tried to sing into my words and verses, but that you (Grieg) have captured." Massengale summarized this quality as "a delicate balance between a folklike simplicity and an advanced harmonic sensibility."

It is perhaps surprising that *Haugtussa* was so well received, because Garborg wrote little poetry, and for the ten years before writing *Haugtussa* wrote no poetry at all. Massengale commented, "It is an anomaly both for its sheer size and poetic virtuosity and for its mastery of moods and attitudes." Reviewing the work, Lanae H. Isaacson wrote in *Scandinavica* that instead of relying on isolated sense impressions, Garborg creates "a unique medley of feelings, impressions, and connotations" by using his own experiences, dreams, daydreams, and memories to create an imaginary world and convey it to the reader. Isaacson noted that Garborg doesn't force his impressions on the reader, but instead "open[s] the door to a world of interwoven sights, sounds, and sensations . . . which the reader interprets, varies, and participates in at will."

BIOGRAPHICAL AND CRITICAL SOURCES:

BOOKS

Crystal, David, editor, *The Cambridge Biographical Encyclopedia,* Cambridge University Press (New York, NY), 1998.

Ingwersen, Faith, and Mary Kay Norsang, editors, *Fin(s) de Siècle in Scandinavian Perspective,* Camden House (Columbia, SC), 1993.

Murphy, Bruce, editor, *Benet's Reader's Encyclopedia,* 4th edition, HarperCollins (New York, NY), 1996.

Smith, Horatio, editor, *Columbia Dictionary of Modern European Literature,* Columbia University Press (New York, NY), 1980.

Zuck, Virpi, editor, *Dictionary of Scandinavian Literature,* Greenwood Press (Westport, CT), 1990.

PERIODICALS

Edda, 1978, Jan Sjåvik, "Intension og genre i Arne Garborgs *Bondenstudenter,*" pp. 333-339; Volume 1, 1982, Jan Sjåvik, "Arne Garborg," pp. 1-22; 1984, pp. 145-156; 1985, pp. 49-61; Volume 1, 1994, Gunnar Foss, "Fra Time til Itaka," pp. 27-41; Volume 3, 1996, Anne Amadou, "Arme Jorgen: Arne Garbog som oversetter av Molière," pp. 220-222.

Graphis, March-April, 1999, Chelsey Johnson, review of *Fred,* p. 15.

Scandinavica, May, 1984, Lanae H. Isaacson, "'Son et Lumière' in Arne Garborg's Poetry and Prose," pp. 39-50.

Scandinavian Studies, spring, 1981, James Massengale, "*Hugtussa:* From Garborg to Grieg," pp. 131-153; Volume 55, number 2, 1983, pp. 134-148; spring, 2000, Jan Sjavik, "Reading Arne Garborg's Irony," p. 63.

Selecta, Volume 1, 1980, Jan Sjåvik, "Form and Theme in Garborg's *Mannfolk* and *Hjaa ho Mor,*" pp. 87-90.*

GARCIA, Eric 1972-

PERSONAL: Born 1972, in Miami, FL; married; wife's name, Sabrina; children: Bailey (daughter). *Education:* Attended Cornell University and University of Southern California.

ADDRESSES: Home—Near Los Angeles, CA. *Agent*—c/o Author Mail, Random House, 299 Park Ave., New York, NY 10171-0002.

CAREER: Has worked variously as an instructor and screenwriter.

WRITINGS:

Anonymous Rex: A Detective Story, Random House (New York, NY), 2000.
Casual Rex, Villard (New York, NY), 2001.
Matchstick Men, Villard (New York, NY), 2002.

Writer of scripts for movies and television series, including *Babylon 5* and *Walker, Texas Ranger.*

ADAPTATIONS: Anonymous Rex was recorded as an audiobook by Publishing Mills Audio, and was optioned for a film adaptation.

WORK IN PROGRESS: Hot and Sweaty Rex, a sequel to *Anonymous Rex* and *Casual Rex.*

SIDELIGHTS: In 2000 Eric Garcia made a splash with his debut novel *Anonymous Rex: A Detective Story.* The main characters are miniature dinosaurs in latex human costumes. Readers follow the activities of Vincent Rubio, a tough velociraptor, as he investigates a case of arson. Why dinosaurs? Garcia recounted in an online interview at the *Anonymous Rex* Web site the genesis of Rubio. While flipping channels on his television, Garcia ran across a special on dinosaurs and the various theories for their disappearance. "It was amazing to me how few of these scientists—incredibly learned, intelligent, well-spoken men and women—could agree with one another, and showed not more than a little contempt for the others' viewpoints. So I decided I'd come up with a different theory altogether, since there were so many out there already." In Garcia's world, dinosaurs work in all walks of life, disguising themselves as humans to keep their existence secret. Rubio is the typical hard-boiled detective, who suffers from an addiction—in this case to the herb basil; he becomes romantically involved with a beautiful woman, and solves a knotty case.

Anonymous Rex caught the attention of reviewers, who particularly mentioned the work's humor. An *Entertainment Weekly* critic, who called the novel "awesomely funny" and at the same time a "good mystery," predicted that it could become a cult classic. "At odd moments the narrative veers into shtick, but while it's going on you're mostly going to be dazzled by Garcia's energy and chutzpah," declared a *Publishers Weekly* critic. Remarking on the "screw-ball details that make the story," *Booklist* reviewer Stephanie Zvirin judged the book a "hoot." "Apart from showing off a splendidly warped imagination, Garcia provides a solid mystery," praised Jennifer Wulff in *People*. "Dino-mite detective yarn," she punned. Writing in *Library Journal*, A. J. Anderson maintained that although the book would appeal to those people who enjoy anthropomorphic characters and absurd humor, it would probably "jar the sensibilities of hardcore detective fiction buffs who take their mysteries seriously."

Garcia followed *Anonymous Rex* with a prequel, *Casual Rex,* and a stand-alone novel, *Matchstick Men.*

BIOGRAPHICAL AND CRITICAL SOURCES:

PERIODICALS

Booklist, July, 1999, Stephanie Zvirin, review of *Anonymous Rex,* p. 1927.
Entertainment Weekly, September 10, 1999, p. 146.
Library Journal, July, 1999, A. J. Anderson, review of *Anonymous Rex,* p. 141.
New York Times Book Review, April 8, 2001, Scott Veale, review of *Anonymous Rex,* p. 28.
People, September 13, 1999, Jennifer Wulff, "Pages," p. 51.
Publishers Weekly, July 5, 1999, review of *Anonymous Rex,* p. 62.
Village Voice, September 28, 1999, David Bowman, "Eric Garcia's Jurassic Noir," p. 57.

OTHER

Anonymous Rex Web site, http://www.anonymousrex. com (December 10, 1999).
Casual Rex Web site, http://www.casualrex.com (November 4, 2002).
SF Site, http://www.sfsite.com/ (November 4, 2002).*

*   *   *

GARFIELD, Simon 1960-

PERSONAL: Born March 19, 1960; son of Herbert Sidney and Hella Helene (Meyer) Garfield; married, 1987; wife's name, Diana; children: two. *Education:* UCS Hampstead, B.Sc. *Hobbies and other interests:* Painting, poker, music, cricket.

ADDRESSES: Agent—c/o PFD, Drury House, 34-43 Russell St., London WC2B 5HA, England.

CAREER: Journalist. British Public Broadcasting (BBC), scriptwriter of radio documentaries, 1981-82; *Time Out* magazine, writer, 1982-88, editor, 1988-89; *Independent, London, England,* news feature writer, 1990-96; *Observer,* news feature writer, 2001-02.

WRITINGS:

Money for Nothing: Greed and Exploitation in the Music Industry, Faber and Faber (Boston, MA), 1986.
Expensive Habits: The Dark Side of the Music Industry, Faber and Faber (Boston, MA), 1986.
The End of Innocence: Britain in the Time of AIDS, Faber and Faber (Boston, MA), 1994.
The Wrestling, Faber and Faber (Boston, MA), 1996.
The Nation's Favourite: The True Adventures of Radio One, Faber and Faber (London, England), 1999.
Mauve: How One Man Invented a Colour That Changed the World, Faber & Faber (London, England), 2000.

SIDELIGHTS: British writer and social commentator Simon Garfield debuted with two consecutive books on the subject of music industry exploitation. Garfield's first book, *Money for Nothing,* according to *Booklist*'s Peter L. Robinson, is an "insider's account" of artist exploitation in the music industry and that it has "all the ingredients that produce a juicy public spectacle."

Garfield's next book, *Expensive Habits,* is an "excellent new book on the scabbier side of the music business" wrote Marcus Berkmann, in *Spectator.* Berkmann noted that the "industry always reasserts itself," perpetuating some of the internal difficulties. Dave Rimmer, reviewing the book for *Listener,* called the "dark side" of the music industry "the business side." He insisted this 'business' includes "greedy and uncertain" aspects. Rimmer stated that Garfield is "one of the few writers in Britain dealing regularly, intelligently and entertainingly with the business of music."

Garfield turned his attention to the effect of the AIDS epidemic on society in *The End of Innocence.* Peter Campbell, a reviewer in *London Review of Books,* considered the work to be "objective about difficult issues." He called it "broad enough in its account of the way institutions have responded to the epidemic to achieve his larger aim. That aim is to write a history of Britain" concerning a decade in which AIDS is "at its core."

Garfield investigated the world of the professional British wrestler in his book *The Wrestling.* Gordon Burn, a reviewer in the *Times Literary Supplement,* called the work "a kind of oral history . . . of a breed that is facing extinction." He noted that "some [people] blame the rising body-count for the fact that wrestling disappeared from [British] television." Garfield explores the "inside world" of wrestling 'personalities.'

Simon Garfield has also written a book regarding another 'inside view' of Britain's favorite popular music station titled *The Nation's Favourite: The True Adventures of Radio One.*

In 2000, Garfield published a book on the history of a color. *Mauve: How One Man Invented a Colour That Changed the World,* examines the creation of the color that is a cross between violet and blue. In 1856 William Perkins, using chemicals instead of the traditional plants that had always been used to make dye, created mauve. Marcia Bartusiak wrote in the *New York Times Book Review* that "By the turn of the 20th century,

because of Perkin's novel idea, dye makers had 2000 synthesized colors at their disposal. Today, the digital palette contains more than 16 million shades." Bartusiak continued, "Garfield's chronicle of Perkin's life and the ultimate fruits of his labors is straightforward and clear."

BIOGRAPHICAL AND CRITICAL SOURCES:

PERIODICALS

Book, July, 2001, review of *Mauve: How One Man Invented a Colour That Changed the World,* p. 13.
Booklist, September 1, 1986, p. 9; April 15, 2001, Donna Seaman, review of *Mauve,* p. 1518.
Choice, December, 2001, L. W. Fine, review of *Mauve,* p. 705.
Discover, June, 2001, Margaret Foley, review of *Mauve,* p. 85.
Library Journal, March 15, 2001, Wade M. Lee, review of *Mauve,* p. 103.
Listener, December 11, 1986, pp. 24-25.
London Review of Books, April 6, 1995, pp. 9-10.
New York Times Book Review, April 15, 2001, Marcia Bartusiak, review of *Mauve,* p. 17.
Spectator, December 6, 1986, pp. 49-50.
Times Higher Education Supplement, September 1, 2000, Jennifer Currie, review of *Mauve,* p. 21.
Times Literary Supplement, October 17, 1986, p. 1174; November 29, 1996, p. 36; November 27, 1998, Robert Edgely, review of *The Nation's Favourite: The True Adventures of Radio One,* p. 20; April 13, 2001, Alexander Masters, review of *Mauve,* p. 36.
U.S. News & World Report, April 30, 2001, Andrew Curry, review of *Mauve,* p. 54.*

*   *   *

GAY, William 1943(?)-

PERSONAL: Born c. 1943 (some sources say 1944), in Hohenwald, TN; son of a sharecropper; divorced; children: four.

ADDRESSES: Home—Hohenwald, TN. *Agent*—c/o Author Mail, Random House, 299 Park Ave., New York, NY 10171.

CAREER: Author. Worked variously as a television tube assembly-line worker, post-hole digger, roofer, painter, bricklayer, drywall hanger, and carpenter. *Military service:* Served in the U.S. Navy.

AWARDS, HONORS: William Peden Prize.

WRITINGS:

The Long Home, MacMurray & Beck (Denver, CO), 1999.
Provinces of Night, Doubleday (New York, NY), 2001.
I Hate to See That Evening Sun Go Down, Free Press (New York, NY), 2002.

Contributor of fiction to periodicals, including *Georgia Review, Oxford American,* and *Missouri Review.*

SIDELIGHTS: In 1999 Tennessee carpenter and dry-wall hanger William Gay surprised his friends, neighbors, and readers alike when he published his debut novel, the morality tale *The Long Home.* This story of love and retribution takes place in rural Georgia during the 1940s, though a prologue set in 1932 recounts how malicious Dallas Hardin murdered Nathan Winer, a tenant farmer, in a dispute over a whiskey still. The contemporary action revolves around Winer's son, who is also named Nathan, a carpenter unwittingly employed by Hardin to build a honky-tonk bar. By this time, through nefarious means Hardin has become the local tycoon and wields his power ruthlessly. To further complicate matters, Winer falls in love with Hardin's daughter, Amber Rose, before he discovers from local hermit William Tell Oliver the truth of Nathan's father's murder. For her part, Amber Rose sees Winer as her only chance to escape her dire situation.

The Long Home caught critics' attention, including that of Tony Earley, who remarked in the *New York Times Book Review,* "In the high tradition of the Southern novel, Gay is unafraid to tackle the biggest of the big themes, nor does he shy away from the grand gesture that makes those themes manifest." Earley noted similarities in style between Gay and Cormac McCarthy, such as the creation of new adjectives, a tendency toward melodrama, and a certain level of violence. Similarly, a *Kirkus Reviews* a critic noted the strong influence of William Faulkner on Gay, whom he called a "gifted author." Several critics praised Gay's characterizations. For instance, the *Kirkus Reviews* commentator applauded Gay for creating "several memorable scenes and striking characterizations" and asserted that at times the novel "tells a gripping and intermittently haunting story," and Earley called the characters "almost without exception, sharply observed, three-dimensional human beings." *Booklist* critic Grace Fill praised Gay's prose style as "unusual, with some startlingly beautiful, almost poetic, descriptive passages."

In his Raleigh, North Carolina *News & Observer* review, Michael Chitwood noted Gay's "real ear for mountain vernacular and for the delightful descriptive phrases mountaineers coin." Likewise, a *Publishers Weekly* a reviewer maintained that although Gay's "dialogue may sometimes be too twangy, Gay writes well-crafted prose that unfolds toward necessary (if occasionally unexpected) conclusions." "At his best," concluded Earley, "Gay writes with the wisdom and patience of a man who has witnessed hard times and learned that panic or hedging won't make better times come any sooner; he looks upon beauty and violence with equal measure and makes an accurate accounting of how much of each the human heart contains." Gay told a *Charlotte Observer* reporter, "I guess I learned to write by reading." He admitted, "I wasted years trying to write about stuff I didn't know anything about. . . . It only worked when I started writing about my own part of the country and the people I grew up with I could hear the dialogues exactly."

In 2002 Gay published *I Hate to See That Evening Sun Go Down,* a collection of short stories described by *Booklist*'s John Green as "gut-wrenching." All of the stories are set in rural Tennessee involve people who tend to make the wrong choice at a critical juncture in their lives. The results are murder, suicide, and arson. A *Kirkus Reviews* critic wrote, "These stories are loud—lots of guns, lots of death—but the plot-heaviness isn't a substitute for . . . plenty of dialogue that's as charming as it is wise." A *Publishers Weekly* reviewer commented that "this collection is a fine showcase for Gay's imaginative talent."

BIOGRAPHICAL AND CRITICAL SOURCES:

PERIODICALS

Booklist, October 15, 1999, Grace Fill, review of *The Long Home,* p. 418; November 15, 2000, John

Green, review of *Provinces of Night,* p. 609; September 1, 2002, John Green, review of *I Hate to See That Evening Sun Go Down,* p. 53.

Charlotte Observer (Charlotte, NC), March 5, 2000, "When Gay Wrote about What He Knew, It Worked," p. 8F.

Dallas Morning News, December 5, 1999, Gregory McNamee, "Vengeance Brews Slowly," p. 8J.

Kirkus Reviews, September 1, 1999, review of *The Long Home;* July 15, 2002, review of *I Hate to See That Evening Sun Go Down,* p. 977.

Library Journal, January 1, 2001, Shannon Haddock, review of *Provinces of Night,* p. 153; August, 2002, Christine DeZelar-Tiedman, review of *I Hate to See That Evening Sun Go Down,* p. 148.

New York Times Book Review, November 21, 1999, Tony Earley, "Mephisto Tennessee Waltz," p. 12; February 18, 2001, Art Winslow, review of *Provinces of Night,* p. 17.

News & Observer (Raleigh, NC), December 26, 1999, Michael Chitwood, "Murder, Moonshine, and Lyricism," p. G5.

Publishers Weekly, September 20, 1999, review of *The Long Home,* p. 72; November 13, 2000, review of *Provinces of Night,* p. 87; August 19, 2002, review of *I Hate to See That Evening Sun Go Down,* p. 66.

Times Literary Supplement, August 3, 2001, Benjamin Markovits, review of *Provinces of Night,* p. 20.*

*   *   *

GIFFORD, Paul 1944-

PERSONAL: Born 1944. *Education:* B.A.; M.Litt.

ADDRESSES: Agent—c/o Author Mail, Cambridge University Press, 40 West 20th St., New York, NY 10011.

CAREER: Writer.

WRITINGS:

The Religious Right in Southern Africa, Baobab Books/ University of Zimbabwe Publications (Harare, Zimbabwe), 1988.

Paul Valery: le dialogue des choses divines, Corti (Paris, France), 1989.

Christianity, Ecumenical Documentation and Information Centre of Eastern and Southern Africa (Hatfield, Harare, Zimbabwe), 1990.

The New Crusaders, Pluto (Concord, MA), 1991.

Christianity and Politics in Doe's Liberia, Cambridge University Press (New York, NY), 1993.

(Editor, with Brian Stimpson) *Paul Valery: Musique, Mystique, Mathematique,* Presses Universitaires de Lille (France), 1993.

Paul Valery: "Charmes", University of Glasgow French and German Publications (Glasgow, Scotland), 1995.

(Editor) *The Christian Churches and the Democratisation of Africa,* E. J. Brill (New York, NY), 1995.

African Christianity: Its Public Role, Indiana University Press (Bloomington, IN), 1998.

(Editor, with Brian Stimpson) *Reading Paul Valery: Universe in Mind,* Cambridge University Press (New York, NY), 1999.

(With others) *Two Thousand Years and Beyond: Faith, Identity, and the Common Era,* Routledge (New York, NY), 2002.

Contributor to *Exporting the American Gospel,* edited by Steve Brouwer, Routledge (New York, NY), 1996.

SIDELIGHTS: Paul Gifford has written and edited a number of works focused on Christianity in Africa. In *Christianity and Politics in Doe's Liberia,* according to *American Historical Review* contributor Geoffrey Johnston, Gifford "argues with hardly a pause. . . . [that] Christianity in Liberia during the 1980s was marked by the transfer of American fundamentalism to West Africa." "Because it was so other-worldly, fundamentalism provided significant support for Samuel Doe's corrupt and incompetent tyranny," continued Johnson's description of the book's thesis. "Far from being a positive force," related D. Elwood Dunn in *Journal of Church and State,* "this purported Christian growth is lamented as devoid of the substance of the gospel and social redemption."

In a *Times Literary Supplement* review of *Christianity and Politics in Doe's Liberia,* A. M. Daniels complained that Gifford's "hostility towards the kind of religion he describes means that the thousands of ordinary Liberians who have accepted it have no more than a walk-on part in the book, as mere creatures of circumstance." Daniels found further fault with Gifford's presentation and analysis of "politically quietist theology," as well as noting that "in ascribing the longevity of Doe's regime . . . he omits or underestimates internal factors." "Nevertheless," concluded Daniels, *Christianity and Politics in Doe's Liberia* "will be of interest to both Africans and sociologists of religion." Although Johnston was also unimpressed with some aspects of the book, he similarly found the "good book" to have value: "It is well written, clearly argued, and provides a very useful case study of African Christianity since the Pentecostal explosion." "It raises issues about the relationship between state and civil society that are sure to figure prominently in the aftermath of the civil war that has devastated [Liberia] over the past four years," complimented Dunn. Based solely on this view, continued Dunn, "the book is a welcome addition to the literature on Liberia."

Gifford's more recent works discussing Christianity in Africa include 1995's *The Christian Churches and the Democratisation of Africa*, which Gifford edited, and *African Christianity: Its Public Role*, a "fascinating survey," reported Christopher Fyfe in a *Times Literary Supplement* review. *The Christian Churches and the Democratisation of Africa* grew out of a 1993 conference at the University of Leeds. "This comparative volume" contains thirteen "extremely informative" chapters that underscore "the different ways in which the churches in Africa have responded to and, more particularly, *shaped,* the wider society," described Rosalind I. J. Hackett in *Journal of Church and State. The Christian Churches and the Democratisation of Africa* "should serve handsomely to counter any surviving political reductionist explanations that democracy is a purely Western or Protestant-derived phenomenon," praised Hackett. *African Christianity* is a "lucid, well-informed survey" in which "Gifford shows . . . the 'mainline' missionary Churches are more powerful than ever before, while the independent Churches are declining, eclipsed by the Pentecostal, 'born again', Churches which have swept over Africa from the United States in recent decades," summarized Fyfe. "[Gifford's] concern is with their public role," Fyfe added, "To put them in their public context, he has a masterly brief opening chapter outlining the successive, unusually contradictory, political theories expounded by Africanists over the years."

Among Gifford's other publication are several titles focused on Paul Valery; among them 1989's *Paul Valery: le dialogue des choses divines, Paul Valery: Musique, Mystique, Mathematique,* a 1993 volume he edited with Brian Stimpson, and *Paul Valery: "Charmes",* which was released in 1995.

BIOGRAPHICAL AND CRITICAL SOURCES:

PERIODICALS

Africa, summer, 2000, Donal B. Cruise O'Brien, review of *The Christian Churches and the Democratisation of Africa,* p. 520.

African Affairs, April, 1999, Kevin Ward, review of *African Christianity: Its Public Role,* p. 272.

American Historical Review, October, 1994, p. 1374.

Choice, June, 1999, D. Jacobsen, review of *African Christianity: Its Public Role,* p. 1805.

Church History, December, 1997, Joel A. Carpenter, review of *Exporting the American Gospel: Global Christian Fundamentalism,* p. 885.

French Studies, January, 2001, Peter Collier, review of *Reading Paul Valery: Universe in Mind,* p. 116.

International Bulletin of Missionary Research, January, 2000, Ogbu U. Kalu, review of *African Christianity: Its Public Role,* p. 36.

Journal of Asian and African Studies, August, 2001, Elias Bongmba, review of *African Christianity: Its Public Role,* p. 322.

Journal of Church and State, autumn, 1994, pp. 851-852; autumn, 1997, pp. 809-810; spring, 2000, Caleb O. Oladipo, review of *African Christianity: Its Public Role,* p. 374.

Journal of European Studies, December, 1999, Harry Guest, review of *Reading Paul Valery: Universe in Mind,* p. 446.

Journal of the Royal Anthropological Institute, September, 2001, Simon Coleman, review of *African Christianity: Its Public Role,* p. 576.

Modern Language Review, April, 1991, pp. 471-472; April, 1995, pp. 455-456; July, 1996, pp. 735-736.

Religion, April, 2000, Matthews A. Ojo, review of *The Christian Churches and the Democratisation of Africa,* p. 186; April, 2000, Matthews A. Ojo, review of *African Christianity: Its Public Role,* p. 187.

Times Literary Supplement, July 22, 1994, p. 29; December 25, 1998, p. 22.*

GILL, Christopher 1946-

PERSONAL: Born 1946.

ADDRESSES: Office—University of Exeter, Northcote House, The Queen's Drive, Exeter EX4 4QJ, England.

CAREER: University of Exeter, Exeter, England.

WRITINGS:

(Editor) *The Person and the Human Mind: Issues in Ancient and Modern Philosophy,* Oxford University Press (New York, NY), 1990.

(Editor, with T. P. Wiseman) *Lies and Fiction in the Ancient World,* University of Texas Press (Austin, TX), 1993.

(Editor) Epictetus, *The Discourses of Epictetus,* translation revised by Robin Hard, C.E. Tuttle (Rutland, VT), 1995.

Greek Thought, Oxford University Press (New York, NY), 1995.

Personality in Greek Epic, Tragedy, and Philosophy: The Self in Dialogue, Clarendon Press (New York, NY), 1995.

(Editor, with Mary Margaret McCabe) *Form and Argument in Late Plato,* Oxford University Press (New York, NY), 1996.

(Editor, with Susanna Morton Braund) *The Passions in Roman Thought and Literature,* Cambridge University Press (New York, NY), 1997.

(Editor, with Norman Postlethwaite and Richard Seaford) *Reciprocity in Ancient Greece,* Oxford University Press (New York, NY), 1998.

SIDELIGHTS: British scholar Christopher Gill has devoted much of his career to the study of human psychology as evidenced in the literature of classical Greece. Affiliated with the University of Exeter as an academic, he has written or edited a number of books on various topics in this field. He first edited the dozen essays in the 1990 Oxford University Press title *The Person and the Human Mind: Issues in Ancient and Modern Philosophy.* About half of the writings from other scholars or scientists explore the idea of the person in contrast to the human animal—what sets us apart as rational beings, and how did the ancient world

contemplate this? The other essays in the book examine the rational mind and the concept of personhood as it evolved through the centuries.

Gill also edited, with T. P. Wiseman, the 1993 work *Lies and Fiction in the Ancient World,* actually a collection of papers presented at a conference at the University of Exeter two years earlier. The poets, philosophers, and scholars of ancient Greece struggled with the border area between a lie and a statement of fiction—-if something is not true, is it meant to deceive? The essays here present the Greeks' alternate definition of truth, and the realization that an "untruth" can sometimes sound like the truth. His coeditor, Wiseman, wrote "Lying Historians: Seven Types of Mendacity," while Gill contributed the essay "Plato on Falsehood—Not Fiction." In it he posits that Plato recognized the difference between the two. "This book will profit and delight those scholars interested in poetry, philosophy, history, or the ancient novel," asserted Gareth Schmeling in a *Classical Outlook* review.

Gill's first authorship of a title came with the 1995 tome *Personality in Greek Epic, Tragedy, and Philosophy: The Self in Dialogue.* Here he investigates psychoanalytical concepts through the dramas of classical Greece's great literary era, the fifth century BCE. His text explores the idea of the "objective-participant" model of psychology: the Greeks considered themselves individuals, but also saw themselves as part of larger community. The concept of selfhood and its relationship to the heroic—defined as arduous efforts to serve a greater good than just mere self-aggrandizement—exploits chronicled in the *Iliad* and the *Odyssey* from this period are discussed, as are monologues from the plays of Homer, Euripides, and several writers of the Stoic era. The characters of Medea—who killed her children after murdering her spouse's lover—and Ajax, the courageous warrior who helped Odysseus, but committed suicide when his heroism went unacknowledged—are just two of the character studies that Gill explores in his text. Throughout the work, Gill interjects the concepts formulated during this same century by the philosophers of the time, including Plato and Aristotle.

Elsewhere in *Personality in Greek Epic,* Gill delves into other scholarly critiques of Greek drama—particularly in theories that evolved after the discipline of psychology emerged in the modern era—and rebuts some of the ideas about morality and the self that have become part of classical scholarship. He finds them far too reliant on a position that can be directly traced to the work of seventeenth-century philosopher Rene Descartes ("I think, therefore I am"), and his German counterpart, Emmanuel Kant, who formulated the notion of "rational agency." Gill argues that it is unwise to bring such interpretations to bear on the study of Greek drama and the idea of self, since they were so far removed from currents in Greek person-hood at the time. "In the end, what Gill sees is an objectivist, naturalist reading of ancient moral psychol-ogy that is socially rather than biologically based," stated Michael I. Morgan in a critique of the book in *Review of Metaphysics*. The reviewer, however argued that some of Gill's refutations were not wholly convincing and had a tendency to repeat themselves across the book, though its readership "will nonethe-less learn a good deal from his framing of the issues and clarification of the influences that shape recent readings of the Greeks."

In 1996 Gill edited, with Mary Margaret McCabe, another scholarly work: *Form and Argument in Late Plato*. Here, a collection of writings discuss the *Dia-logues*, written late in the philosopher's career, along with the work of Parmenides and Thaeaetetus, among other Greeks who wrote about virtue, the universe, a supreme deity, and just leadership. "In his 'Afterword,' Christopher Gill demonstrates how the late dialogues may be taken to illustrate an abiding Platonic commit-ment to the notion of philosophy as a dialectical search for truth," remarked Colm Luibheid in a *Classical Review* assessment.

Gill also served as coeditor for *Reciprocity in Ancient Greece*, a collaboration with Norman Postlethwaite and Richard Seaford. Here, fourteen writers explore the subject of reciprocity, or how individuals exchange favors among themselves and thereby establish a sense of community.

BIOGRAPHICAL AND CRITICAL SOURCES:

PERIODICALS

American Journal of Philology, spring, 1998, pp. 119-22.
Ancient Philosophy, spring, 2000, Robert J. Rabel, review of *The Passions in Roman Thought and Literature,* p. 259; fall, 2000.
Choice, October, 1996, p. 274.
Classical Review, no. 2, 1997, pp. 332-334.
Classical Outlook, summer, 1994, p. 142.
Classical Philology, October, 1999, David Wray, review of *The Passions in Roman Thought and Literature,* p. 481.
Classical World, May, 1997, p. 380.
Ethics, October, 1991, pp. 182-183.
Journal of the History of Philosophy, April, 1998, Francisco J. Gonzalez, review of *Form and Argu-ment in Late Plato,* p. 311.
Review of Metaphysics, March, 1998, pp. 686-688; September, 1998, pp. 150-152
Times Literary Supplement, December 31, 1993, p. 9; May 28, 1999, p. 9.*

*　　*　　*

GILL, Mary Louise G(lanville) 1950-

PERSONAL: Born July 31, 1950, in Alton, IL; daughter of John Glanville (a professor of philosophy) and Evalyn (a poet; maiden name, Pierpoint) Gill; married Paul Inman Coppock (a philosopher and writer), January 14, 1995. *Ethnicity:* "Caucasian." *Edu-cation:* Barnard College, B.A., 1972; Columbia University, M.A., 1974; Cambridge University, B.A., 1976, M.A., 1981, Ph.D., 1981.

ADDRESSES: Home—36 Bowen St., Providence, RI 02903. *Office*—Department of Philosophy, Brown University, Box 1918, Providence, RI 02912; fax: 401-273-2475. *E-mail*—Mary_Louise_Gill@brown.edu.

CAREER: University of Pittsburgh, Pittsburgh, PA, began as assistant professor, became professor of clas-sics, philosophy, and history and philosophy of sci-ence, 1979-2001; Brown University, Providence, RI, professor of philosophy and classics, 2001—. Dart-mouth College, visiting faculty member, 1985; Stan-ford University, Ethel Walter Kimball fellow and visit-ing faculty member, 1985-86; University of California—Los Angeles, visiting associate professor, 1994; University of California—Davis, visiting profes-sor, 1995; Harvard University, visiting professor, 1998-99; Institute for Advanced Study, Princeton, NJ, member, 1999-2000.

MEMBER: American Philosophical Association, American Philological Association.

WRITINGS:

Aristotle on Substance, Princeton University Press (Princeton, NJ), 1989.

(Editor, with James G. Lennox) *Self-Motion: From Aristotle to Newton,* Princeton University Press (Princeton, NJ), 1994.

(Editor, with Theodore Scaltsas and David Charles) *Unity, Identity, and Explanation in Aristotle's Metaphysics,* Oxford University Press (New York, NY), 1994.

(Translator, with Paul Ryan, and author of introduction) Plato, *Parmenides,* Hachett, 1996.

Series editor, Ashgate Publishers. Coeditor, *Ancient Philosophy.*

WORK IN PROGRESS: Translating, with James G. Lennox, and writing commentary for *Aristotle's Meteorology IV,* for Oxford University Press (New York, NY); editing, with Pierre Pellegrin, *The Blackwell Companion to Ancient Philosophy,* Blackwell Publishers.

*   *   *

GILLEY, Bruce 1966-

PERSONAL: Born 1966.

ADDRESSES: Agent—c/o Author Mail, University of California Press, 2120 Berkeley Way, Berkeley, CA 94720.

CAREER: Journalist, c. 1998—; *Far Eastern Economic Review,* Hong Kong correspondent.

WRITINGS:

Tiger on the Brink, University of California Press (Berkeley, CA), 1998.

Model Rebels: The Rise and Fall of China's Richest Village, University of California Press (Berkeley, CA), 2001.

China's New Rulers: The Secret Files, New York Review of Books (New York, NY), 2002.

SIDELIGHTS: Bruce Gilley is the Hong Kong correspondent for the *Far Eastern Economic Review. Tiger on the Brink* is the first book-length study of Jiang Zemin, who was appointed head of the Chinese Communist Party by Chinese leader Deng Xiaoping in 1989. Since that time, he has ruled China and is one of the few Asian leaders of a country with a relatively stable society and a healthy economy.

Gilley describes Jiang's early life and his rise to power. Jiang was an unexpected ruler, because he did not have any major role in the Chinese Revolution, and is not a charismatic leader; in fact, before joining the Communist Party, he took part in demonstrations against the nationalist government. He came from an educated family and studied electrical engineering in Shanghai. Despite his unspectacular origins, Gilley notes, Jiang was able to rise to power because of his skill at ingratiating himself with Communist Party leaders. Merle Goldman wrote in the *New York Times Book Review* that "Gilley's account is not spellbinding, yet it reveals much about a leader whose personal qualities may have been appropriate for the past nine years."

Chinese documents are still largely closed to foreign journalists, which caused Gilley some trouble in finding sources of information for his book. In *Foreign Affairs,* Seth Faison noted this difficulty, saying, "*Tiger on the Brink* is essentially a first-rate clip job. Gilley, facing the rigid limits of a culture of political secrecy, has had to rely overwhelmingly on secondary sources; as he relates in the preface, the closest he ever got to his subject was when he ran into the portly president in the men's room at the Great Hall of the People. And Jiang left the restroom before a surprised Gilley could think of a question to ask."

In *Model Rebels: The Rise and Fall of China's Richest Village,* Gilley documents the village of Daqiu, in China. A poor farming village, Daqiu was transformed into an industrial center with the reforms initiated by Chairman Deng Xiaoping in 1978. It became a wealthy town from its steel manufacturing, but also from the leadership of Yu Zuomin. Yu brought notoriety and prestige to the village by his endless self-promoting. However, Yu was also a tyrant, stepping on the rights of the people. This led to the murder of a worker and an armed standoff between the villagers and the police. Parks M. Coble, a reviewer for *Agricultural History,* wrote that the story "makes for riveting reading."

BIOGRAPHICAL AND CRITICAL SOURCES:

PERIODICALS

Agricultural History, winter, 2002, Parks M. Coble, review of *Model Rebels: The Rise and Fall of China's Richest Village,* p. 116.

Choice, July-August, 2001, C. A. Haulman, review of *Model Rebels,* p. 2004.

Foreign Affairs, January, 1999, p. 140.

History: Review of New Books, spring, 2001, John L. Rawlinson, review of *Model Rebels,* p. 130.

New York Times Book Review, September 14, 1998, p. 58; February 14, 1999.

Pacific Affairs, winter, 2001, Michelle Mood, review of *Model Rebels,* p. 592.

Publishers Weekly, September 14, 1998, p. 58.*

* * *

GILLHAM, Nicholas Wright 1932-

PERSONAL: Born May 14, 1932, in New York, NY; son of Robert Marty and Elizabeth (Enright) Gillham; married Carol Lenore Collins, June 2, 1956. *Education:* Harvard University, A.B., 1954, A.M., 1955, Ph. D., 1962.

ADDRESSES: Home—1183 Fearrington Post, Pittsboro, NC 27312. *Office*—Department of Biology, P.O. Box 91000, Durham, NC 27708-1000. *E-mail*—gillham@acpub.duke.edu.

CAREER: Geneticist, educator, and author. Harvard University, Cambridge, MA, began as instructor, became assistant professor, 1963-68; Duke University, Durham, NC, associate professor of zoology, 1968-72, professor, 1973-82, James B. Duke professor of zoology, 1982—, chairman, Department of Zoology, 1986-89. Member of President's Biomedical Research Panel on biochemistry, molecular genetics, and cell biology interdisciplinary cluster, 1975; member of study section in genetics, National Institute of Health, 1976-80. Board chairman of American Type Culture Collection, 1993-96. Member of editorial board, *Genetics,* 1975-78, *Journal of Cell Biology,* 1977-79, *International Review of Cytology,* 1987-97; *Plasmid,* senior editor, 1977-86. *Military service:* U.S. Air Force, 1st Lt., Medical Service Corps, 1955-58.

MEMBER: Genetics Society of America.

AWARDS, HONORS: Research Career Development Award grantee, 1972-77; Guggenheim fellow, 1984-85.

WRITINGS:

(With Joseph H. Coggin, Jr. and Robert G. Krueger) *Introduction to Microbiology,* Macmillan (New York, NY), 1973.

Organelle Heredity, Raven (New York, NY), 1978.

Organelle Genes and Genomes, Oxford University Press (New York, NY), 1994.

A Life of Sir Francis Galton: From African Exploration to the Birth of Eugenics, Oxford University Press (New York, NY), 2001.

SIDELIGHTS: American educator, geneticist and author Nicholas Wright Gillham has published several books detailing the academic research he has conducted while a professor at Duke University. Gillham began teaching at Duke in 1968, and has risen to the prestigious position of James B. Duke Professor of Biology Emeritus at the institution. Considered by some observers as a leader in the field of genetics, Gillham published his first book an introductory examination of micobiology, in the early 1970s. Since then he has published two books about the quick-growing field of organelle genetics, as well as a biography of Nintenth Century scientist Francis Galton, who is considered the father of a notorious field of eugenics.

In *Organelle Heredity,* Gillham examines the study of organelle genes. Gillham describes the basic structure, function, and behavior of these genes, including how they affect mitochondria and chloroplasts. In addition to numerous illustrations, graphs, and diagrams, the book includes helpful tables listing existing data about the organelle genes of many organisms. According to C. William Birky, Jr., the book is a good science contributor introductory look at the world of organelle genetics. "*Organelle Heredity* is a careful and thorough record of most of the main lines of progress in the field," Birky wrote in the periodical *Science*. "Questions of general interest for students of cell biology and genetics arise at every step."

Published in 2001, *A Life of Sir Francis Galton: From African Exploration to the Birth of Eugenics* was lauded by several literary critics and science writers, including *American Scientist* writer Daniel J. Kevles, who called the book a "highly readable biography." Born in 1822, Galton was a cousin of Charles Darwin. While his cousin is better known today, Galton, as Gillham points out in his book, also played a significant role in the scientific world of Victorian England. Galton's contributions to science include determining the latitudes and longitudes of part of Africa, which helped cartographers accurately map the area, and his participation in the discovery that each individual human has a unique set of fingerprints, which led British police officials to adopt the fingerprint identification system. Most importantly, however, Galton is considered the father of eugenics, which is the study of hereditary improvement of the human race through selective breeding. Gillham spends much of his book discussing Galton's link to eugenics, while also distancing him from the brutal eugenics policies practiced by the Nazis several decades after Galton's death. Gillham thinks many modern observers are mistaken to link Galton to the Nazi experiments during the World War II-era. Gillham writes in the book that Galton "would have been horrified had he known that little more than 20 years after his death forcible sterilization and murder would be carried out in the name of eugenics, for Galton was not a mean or vindictive man." While some of Galton's work might seem politically incorrect today, Gillham doesn't believe his work can be "properly appreciated by applying modern or revisionist standards to his career." Gillham admits in the book that he admires Galton's work, though he accepts some of his shortcomings. "Galton meant well in his efforts to improve mankind, but he viewed the world through the lens of class, privilege, and the predominant role played by men in virtually all affairs in Victorian England," he writes. Although there have been other biographies of Galton, some literary critics felt Gillham's work was especially good. "This may well prove to be the definitive biography," wrote a contributor for *Publishers Weekly*. David Reich of the *New York Times*, felt *A Life of Sir Francis Galton* was a "fascinating account" of Galton's life and work. "Gillham writes lucidly about Galton's science, and his contextualization of Galton's

work illuminates its considerable significance," Kevles similarly wrote in *American Scientist*.

BIOGRAPHICAL AND CRITICAL SOURCES:

BOOKS

A Life of Sir Francis Galton: From African Exploration to the Birth of Eugenics, Oxford University Press (New York, NY), 2001.

PERIODICALS

American Scientist, May, 2002, review of *A Life of Sir Francis Galton: From African Exploration to the Birth of Eugenics,* p. 270.
Booklist, October 1, 2001, review of *A Life of Sir Francis Galton,* p. 289.
National Review, January 28, 2002, review of *A Life of Sir Francis Galton,* p. 53.
New York Times Book Review, February 10, 2002, review of *A Life of Sir Francis Galton,* p. 16.
Publishers Weekly, October 15, 2001, review of *A Life of Sir Francis Galton,* p. 55.
Science, May 18, 1979, p. 761.

*   *   *

GIVENS, Kathleen 1950-

PERSONAL: Born 1950; married Stephan Leonard Lucas; children: two daughters.

ADDRESSES: Home and office—P.O. Box 1126, Laguna Beach, CA 92652. *E-mail*—kgivens@pacbell.net.

CAREER: Author. Accountant with engineering firm.

WRITINGS:

(With husband, Stephen Leonard Lucas) *Givens Family Chronicles,* self-published (Greenwood, IN), 1987.
Kilgannon, Dell (New York, NY), 1999.
The Wild Rose of Kilgannon, Dell (New York, NY), 1999.

The Legend, Warner (New York, NY), 2002.
The Destiny, Warner (New York, NY), 2003.

Contributor of short story to *My Scottish Summer,* edited by Connie Brockway, Warner (New York, NY), 2001.

WORK IN PROGRESS: Other novels in the "Kilgannon" series.

SIDELIGHTS: Kathleen Givens's historical romance novels, *Kilgannon* and *The Wild Rose of Kilgannon,* were originally written as one novel, but became two when purchased by Dell. Givens told Cathy Sova of *Romance Reader* online that she began her manuscript in 1996 and set a goal of five years to accomplish publication. She made it with time to spare. Givens had always had an interest in the history of the British Isles and drew on research she conducted while writing the novels.

Kilgannon is set in the early 1700s during Queen Anne's reign. The narrator, Mary Lowell, is an Englishwoman who is expected to wed a local lord but who becomes attracted to Scottish chieftain Alex MacGannon, Earl of Kilgannon, at a ball in London. The highlander is considered a barbarian by English society, and Alex's clan is not pleased with his relationship to Lowell as the likelihood of a Scottish rebellion increases. Patty Engelmann stated in *Booklist* that "the strong characters and involved plot keep the reader's attention," but felt that there is "no solid conclusion." A *Publishers Weekly* reviewer wrote that the book "subtly weaves a tale of personal and historical conflict."

The Wild Rose of Kilgannon finds Alex reluctantly leaving his bride Mary and two sons from a previous marriage to join James Stewart's fight against England. He is dismayed by the lack of leadership, and when Stewart escapes to France Alex stays on to help protect his men. Castle Kilgannon has been destroyed by fire, and Mary steadfastly protects her home and family, but when Alex is imprisoned in the Tower by the English, Mary travels to London with the hope of saving her husband, who is being tried as a traitor. Harriet Klausner wrote for *BookBrowser* online that the novel "is an exciting historical romance that brings to life the events and lead personalities of the Jacobite Rebellion."

Givens has also written two romance novels not part of the "Kilgannon" series titled *The Legend* and *The Destiny.*

BIOGRAPHICAL AND CRITICAL SOURCES:

PERIODICALS

Booklist, October 1, 1999, Patty Engelmann, review of *Kilgannon,* p. 346.
Publishers Weekly, August 23, 1999, review of *Kilgannon,* p. 54; June 17, 2002, review of *The Legend,* p. 49.

OTHER

BookBrowser, http://www.bookbrowser.com/ (October 31, 1999), Harriet Klausner, review of *The Wild Rose of Kilgannon.*
Romance Reader, http://www.theromancereader.com/ (October 11, 1999), Cathy Sova, "New Faces 50: Interviews."*

*   *   *

GLASSER, Ronald J. 1940(?)-

PERSONAL: Born c. 1940.

CAREER: Physician, nonfiction writer, and novelist. Pediatric nephrologist and rheumatologist in Minnesota, 1970—. *Military service:* Officer in U.S. Army Medical Corps1960s; stationed at U.S. Evacuation Hospital, Camp Zama, Japan. .

WRITINGS:

365 Days, G. Braziller (New York, NY), 1971.
Ward 402, G. Braziller (New York, NY), 1973.
The Body Is the Hero, Random House (New York, NY), 1976.
The Greatest Battle, Random House (New York, NY), 1976.

Another War, Another Place: A Novel, Summit Books, 1985.

The Light in the Skull: An Odyssey of Medical Discovery, Faber & Faber (Boston, MA), 1997.

ADAPTATIONS: 365 Days was adapted as *The Dramatization of 365 Days* by H. Wesley Balk and published by the University of Minnesota Press, 1972.

SIDELIGHTS: Ronald J. Glasser is one of the leading contemporary writers of medical-based novels. Using his own experiences as a physician, Glasser describes the intricate relationship between doctor and patient in each of his works. Glasser also examines several social and ethical problems that exist relating to the decisions doctors make in treating their patients as medicine advances in the age of technology. Harry Schwartz remarked in *Saturday Review,* "His ability to move readers emotionally while accurately describing the front lines, where doctors and very sick people come together, won him a large audience."

Glasser's first and best-known book, *365 Days,* is a collection of sketches about wounded and dying American soldiers fighting in the Vietnam War. He relates what it means to be a wounded young man fighting for his life in a foreign land and the freedom of humanity. "The war is the cause and excuse for the book, but the theme is the waste of war, the destruction of our American young," wrote Thomas Lask in the *New York Times.* The majority of the soldiers, who were eighteen to nineteen years old, came from the lower-middle and working classes and were compelled to serve their country for lack of any other alternative. Glasser writes of the courage of the soldiers, upheld even when they know their battle is lost. The last sketch, titled "The Burn Ward," was also published separately. In this story. Glasser tells the story of how David, with charred body and days numbered, first feels hope for life then becomes angry when reality sets in. The sketch ends with pleas from David to the doctor to accompany his coffin when he returns home.

In *Ward 402* Glasser deals with human concerns in relation to health care. The story centers on a young girl dying from leukemia who is brought by her parents to a well-known teaching and research hospital, not for treatment, but to die quickly and comfortably. Upon admission to the hospital, a pediatric resident and intern team up and begin a heroic effort to save the girl's life despite protests from her parents. After suffering major complications which invoke tremendous pain and suffering, the child dies within the month. The intern, who becomes emotionally attached to the girl, has second thoughts on the mode of treatment only after witnessing the outcome. The story describes the social and ethical implications regarding the mode of treatment chosen by the attending physician. Should a terminally ill patient be kept alive by heroic measures, even if it is against the wishes of patients or their families? Through this fictitious tale, Glasser stresses the need for greater communication between physicians and laymen.

Glasser's *The Greatest Battle* is a different kind of book, describing the basic facts of cancer. Glasser explains that most cases of cancer are self-inflicted and can be prevented if the people of today's society understood the consequences of their behavior. "We know the facts and we know the remedies, but the mixture of vested interests, fatalism, and indifference will no doubt ensure that this situation improves slowly, if at all," commented June Goodfield in the *Washington Post Book World.* Glasser presents evidence in each chapter to support the claim that the chemicals that are poisoning our atmosphere are equally playing havoc with our bodies.

BIOGRAPHICAL AND CRITICAL SOURCES:

BOOKS

Contemporary Literary Criticism, Volume 37, Gale (Detroit, MI) 1986.

PERIODICALS

Best Sellers, July, 1985, pp. 125-126.

Listener, June 1, 1972, pp. 735-736.

New Republic, August 18, 1973, p. 23.

New York Times, September 11, 1971, p. 25.; September 8, 1973, p. 29.

New York Times Book Review, April 21, 1985, p. 26.

Newsweek, September 13, 1971, pp. 101-102.

Publishers Weekly, February 15, 1985, p. 89.

Saturday Review, September 11, 1971, pp. 46-47; May 1, 1976, p. 36.

Washington Post Book World, January 9, 1977, pp. K3-5.*

*   *   *

GLIORI, Debi 1959-

PERSONAL: Surname pronounced "Lee-*oh*-ree"; born February 21, 1959, in Glasgow, Scotland; daughter of Lionel (a musical instrument maker) and Josephine (a tax inspector; maiden name, McEnhill) Gliori; married George Karl Carson, August 2, 1976 (divorced, February 14, 1978); married Jesse Earl Christman (a furniture maker), June 21, 1991 (divorced, 1999), companion of Michael Holton (a company secretary); children: (first marriage) Rowan Gliori; (second marriage) Benjamin, Patrick, Sophie, Katie Rose Christman. *Education:* Edinburgh College of Art, B.A. (with honors), 1984, postgraduate diploma in illustration. *Politics:* "Left of center."

ADDRESSES: Agent—Rosemary Sandberg, 6 Bayley St., London WC1B, England. *E-mail*—rosemary@sandberg.demon.co.uk.

CAREER: Author and illustrator. Debi Gliori Ltd., director.

AWARDS, HONORS: British Children's Book Award, 1997.

WRITINGS:

SELF-ILLUSTRATED

New Big Sister, Walker Books (London, England), 1990, Bradbury Press (New York, NY), 1991.

New Big House, Walker Books (London, England), 1991, Candlewick Press (Cambridge, MA), 1992.

My Little Brother, Candlewick Press (Cambridge, MA), 1992.

What a Noise, Creative Edge, 1992.

When I'm Big, Walker Books (London, England), 1992.

Mr. Bear Babysits, Artists & Writers Guild, 1994.

The Snowchild, Bradbury (New York, NY), 1994.

A Lion at Bedtime, Hippo (London, England), 1994.

Willie Bear and the Wish Fish, Macmillan Books for Young Readers (New York, NY), 1995, published as *Little Bear and the Wish-Fish,* Frances Lincoln (London, England), 1995.

Mr. Bear's Picnic, Golden Books (New York, NY), 1995.

The Snow Lambs, Scholastic (New York, NY), 1996.

The Princess and the Pirate King, Kingfisher (New York, NY), 1996.

Can I Have a Hug?, Orchard Books (New York, NY), 1998.

Tickly under There, Orchard Books (New York, NY), 1998.

Mr. Bear Says "Are You There, Baby Bear?," Orchard (New York, NY), 1999.

Mr. Bear's New Baby, Orchard Books (New York, NY), 1999.

No Matter What, Harcourt (San Diego, CA), 1999.

Mr. Bear to the Rescue, Orchard Books (New York, NY), 2000.

Mr. Bear's Vacation, Orchard Books (New York, NY), 2000.

Polar Bolero: A Bedtime Dance, Scholastic (London, England), 2000, Harcourt (San Diego, CA), 2001.

Flora's Blanket, Orchard Books (New York, NY), 2001.

Debi Gliori's Bedtime Stories: Bedtime Tales with a Twist, Dorling Kindersley (New York, NY), 2002.

Penguin Post, Harcourt (San Diego, CA), 2002.

Flora's Surprise, Orchard Books (New York, NY), 2003.

"MR. BEAR SAYS" SERIES

Mr. Bear Says I Love You, Little Simon (New York, NY), 1997.

Mr. Bear Says Good Night, Little Simon (New York, NY), 1997.

Mr. Bear Says Peek-a-Boo, Little Simon (New York, NY), 1997.

Mr. Bear Says a Spoonful for You, Little Simon (New York, NY), 1997.

ILLUSTRATOR

Roger McGough and Dee Reid, *Oxford Children's ABC Picture Dictionary,* Oxford University Press (Oxford, England), 1990.

Sue Stops, *Dulci Dando,* Deutsch (London, England), 1990, Holt (New York, NY), 1992.

Margaret Donaldson, *Margery Mo,* Deutsch (London, England), 1991.

Stephanie Baudet, *The Incredible Shrinking Hippo,* Hamish Hamilton (London, England), 1991.

Roger McGough, *Oxford 123 Book of Number Rhymes,* Oxford University Press (Oxford, England), 1992.

Sue Stops, *Dulcie Dando, Disco Dancer,* Scholastic (New York, NY), 1992.

Margaret Donaldson, *Margery Mo's Magic Island,* Scholastic (New York, NY), 1992.

Sue Stops, *Dulcie Dando, Soccer Star,* H. Holt (New York, NY), 1992.

Lisa Bruce, *Oliver's Alphabets,* Bradbury Press (New York, NY), 1993.

David Martin, *Lizzie and Her Puppy,* Candlewick Press (Cambridge, MA), 1993.

David Martin, *Lizzie and Her Dolly,* Candlewick Press (Cambridge, MA), 1993.

David Martin, *Lizzie and Her Kitty,* Candlewick Press (Cambridge, MA), 1993.

David Martin, *Lizzie and Her Friend,* Candlewick Press (Cambridge, MA), 1993.

Poems Go Clang!: A Collection of Noisy Verse, Candlewick Press (Cambridge, MA), 1997.

Joyce Dunbar, *Tell Me Something Happy before I Go to Sleep,* Harcourt (New York, NY), 1998.

Christina Rossetti, *Give Him My Heart,* Bloomsbury (London, England) 1998, published as *What Can I Give Him?,* Holiday House (New York, NY), 1998.

Joyce Dunbar, *The Very Small,* Harcourt (San Diego, CA), 2000.

The Dorling Kindersley Book of Nursery Rhymes, Dorling Kindersley (New York, NY), 2001.

Joyce Dunbar, *Tell Me What It's Like to Be Big,* Harcourt (San Diego, CA), 2001.

OTHER

A Present for Big Pig, illustrated by Kate Simpson, Candlewick Press (Cambridge, MA), 1995.

Pure Dead Magic, Alfred A. Knopf Books for Young Readers (New York, NY), 2001.

Pure Dead Wicked (sequel to *Pure Dead Magic,*) Alfred A. Knopf Books for Young Readers (New York, NY), 2002.

Pure Dead Brilliant (sequel to *Pure Dead Wicked*), Alfred A. Knopf Books for Young Readers (New York, NY), 2003.

Contributor of illustrations to *The Candlewick Book of Bedtime Stories,* Candlewick Press (Cambridge, MA), 1995; several of author's works have been translated into Spanish.

ADAPTATIONS: Pure Dead Magic and *Pure Dead Wicked* were adapted for audiocassette by Recorded Books (Frederick, MD), 2002.

SIDELIGHTS: Since 1990 Scottish author-illustrator Debi Gliori has made a name for herself on both sides of the Atlantic with colorful picture books on domestic themes and a trio of middle-grade novels dealing with magic. She has written and illustrated with black pen-and-ink and watercolor artwork more than a dozen titles of her own, as well as illustrating another dozen children's books by other writers. Her palette ranges in tone from pastels to brilliantly saturated color, and humor and attention to domestic details are hallmarks of her work. Gliori's portrayal of family life seems a given for her in more ways that one. She is mother to five children from two marriages, and working at home seemed to her the best option for quality family time. "I've never questioned my motivation for writing—it is as essential a part of my life as breathing and eating," Gliori told *CA.* "With five children, the option of working away from home was unthinkable. I want to be around my kids and to watch and marvel as they grow up. Writing for children is a natural extension of this process." Like many picture books for children, the majority of Gliori's books treat children's concerns, such as being afraid of the dark, accepting new siblings, outgrowing the family home, dealing with bullies, and making friends.

Gliori's first books feature human characters and portray changes in families. Adorned with "charming, humorous" illustrations, to quote *School Library Journal*'s Lucy Young Clem, *New Big Sister* describes the changes a pregnant mother undergoes and the arrival of twins from a young girl's viewpoint. A *Books for Keeps* reviewer called the title "refreshing," expressing similar praise for *New Big House,* which also treats the challenges of an expanding family. In *New Big House* a house-hunting family decides to add on to their existing home instead of move. *Booklist* contributor Hazel Rochman praised *New Big House* for its emotive illustrations, while *School Library Journal* reviewer Virginia E. Jeschelnig noted its verisimilitude. Another early title, *My Little Brother* recounts how an older sister tries to get rid of her exasperating toddler brother and concludes with what a *Books for Keeps* reviewer called a "delightful ending." Conversely, Gliori's *When I'm Big* describes in a "funny, jokey" manner, in the view of *School Librarian*'s Elizabeth J. King, how a young boy fantasizes about being older. Other titles by Gliori treat childhood fears. For example, the very real fear of monsters under the bed is the subject of the 1994 picture book *A Lion at Bedtime,* in which the fearless Ben shows his real stuff, dressing the lion from under the bed in his father's pajamas. While acknowledging the debt the book pays to Maurice Sendak, reviewer G. English praised the work for its "witty style" in a *Books for Your Children* review. London *Observer* reviewer Kate Kellaway also appreciated the work's style and what she called its "wonderful" illustrations. *The Snowchild* deals with another fear: bullies. Introverted Katie experiences the unkindness of her peers, then finally makes friends when other children join her in making small snow people. Reviewers gave the work qualified praise. While *Booklist*'s Julie Walton found the writing "uneven," she praised the "appealing" artwork. Janet Sims predicted in *School Librarian* that the book would be "useful" in discussions about self-esteem and bullies, and a *Books for Keeps* contributor found *The Showchild* thought-provoking.

Bears often get starring roles in children's books and Gliori's oeuvre is no exception. Some of her books feature them, including her "Mr. Bear Says" series of board books for toddlers as well as the picture books for children ages three to six that also feature Mr. Bear. In *Mr. Bear Babysits* he does just that, babysits the neighbor cubs, only he is not very good at it, and in *Mr. Bear's Picnic* he takes his own unappreciative cubs on an outing. *Mr. Bear's New Baby* recounts how the house is thrown into disarray with the new arrival, while *Mr. Bear to the Rescue* tells how papa bear rises to the occasion when disaster strikes. As with most of Gliori's work, reviewers commented on the humor and warmth of the illustrations. Writing about *Mr. Bear's Picnic* for *School Library Journal,* Lynn Crockett described the characters as "lovable." and apt for story time. Another bear character makes his debut in *Little Bear and the Wish Fish,* a cautionary tale of what can happen when we get what we supposedly want.

Other standards in children's literature are alphabet books and compilations of nursery rhymes and poems. In *Oliver's Alphabets* by Lisa Bruce, illustrator Gliori details a young boy's world, replete with "pleasing minutae" in the opinion of *School Library Journal*'s Mary Lou Budd. Gliori's *Poems Go Clang!: A Collection of Noisy Verse* contains fifty classic verses, making up what Jean Pollock deemed a "serviceable" collection in her *School Library Journal* review. Mother Goose gets a new look in Gliori's version of fifty rhymes and poems, with explanatory annotations. This combination of "beguiling artwork" and "fascinating tidbits of information" about the verse makes for a better-than-average work of its kind, remarked a *Kirkus Reviews* contributor.

Although Gliori first earned a reputation as a writer and illustrator of picture books, she has also tried her hand at writing novels for middle-school readers. Her trilogy, published in the early 2000s, includes *Pure Dead Magic, Pure Dead Wicked,* and *Pure Dead Brilliant.* About the eccentric Strega-Borgia family, these tales combine fantasy, high technology, action, and humor in what a *Kirkus Reviews* critic described as a "nonstop farce." In the debut novel, the three Strega-Borgia children are left to rescue their kidnaped father while their mother attends graduate school for witches. Eva Mitnick predicted in *School Library Journal* that *Pure Dead Magic* would appeal to fans of children's authors J. K. Rowling and Lemony Snicket, and she determined as well that "any plot deficiences" would be compensated for by the work's farcical tone. *Booklist*'s Ilene Cooper held a similar opinion, stating that although the plot is "occasionally tedious" *Pure Dead Magic* is "original" and provides "plenty of laughs." When the second novel of the trilogy appeared, reviewers judged it on the same basis. While calling the characters stereotypical, Lynn Evarts of *School Library Journal* applauded the humor. So too, in *Kirkus Reviews* a critic compared *Pure Dead Wicked* favorably to its predecessor as a "pedal-to-the-metal page turner." Perhaps with this trilogy Gliori has found a new niche because as she explained to *CA,* "Nothing in my working life has ever given me so much joy as these three books."

Gliori is diligent in her work habits, yet values her motherly role. She told *CA:* "I work in a little wooden shed in my garden, surrounded by fields and sky. The silence this provides is perfect for my needs. I start work at 9:15 a.m., after taking my youngest children (two girls) to school and nursery, stopping for coffee (11:00 a.m.) and lunch (1:00 p.m.) and coffee and cake with the children when they're home from school.

When the writing is going well, I find it very disorientating to stop and re-engage with the world, but two minutes in my daughters' company and I'm back on planet earth, no longer a writer but a full-on mummy!"

BIOGRAPHICAL AND CRITICAL SOURCES:

PERIODICALS

Booklist, May 15, 1992, Hazel Rochman, review of *New Big House,* p. 1687; December 1, 1992, Leone McDermott, review of *Dulcie Dando, Soccer Star,* pp. 677-678; December 15, 1994, Julie Walton, review of *The Snowchild,* p. 757; November 15, 1996, Karen Morgan, review of *The Snow Lambs,* p. 584; February 1, 1998, Hazel Rochman, review of *Mr. Bear Says Peek-a-Boo,* p. 922; September 1, 1998, Hazel Rochman, review of *What Can I Give Him?,* p. 132; February 1, 1991, Hazel Rochman, review of *Mr. Bear's New Baby,* p. 979; November 15, 1999, Tim Arnold, review of *No Matter What,* p. 635; May 15, 2000, Marta Segal, review of *Mr. Bear's Vacation,* pp. 1, 48; November 15, 2000, Marta Segal, review of *Mr. Bear to the Rescue,* p. 648; December 15, 2000, Lauren Peterson, review of *The Very Small,* p. 825; April 1, 2001, Hazel Rochman, review of *The Dorling Kindersley Book of Nursery Rhymes,* p. 1474; May 1, 2001, Shelle Rosenfeld, review of *Polar Bolero,* p. 1690; May 15, 2001, Ilene Cooper, review of *Flora's Blanket,* p. 1757; August, 2001, Ilene Cooper, review of *Pure Dead Magic,* p. 2118; June 1, 1998, Ilene Cooper, reviews of *Can I Have a Hug?* and *Tickly under There,* p. 1713.

Books for Keeps, November, 1994, reviews of *New Big House,* p. 10 and *My Little Brother,* pp. 11-12; March, 1995, review of *A Lion at Bedtime,* p. 9; November, 1995, review of *The Snow Child,* p. 9; May, 1996, review of *A Present for Big Pig,* p. 10; September, 1996, review of *Mr. Bear's Picnic,* p. 8; May, 1998, Elaine Moss, review of *Are You There, Baby Bear?,* p. 3; November, 1999, review of *Mr. Bear's New Baby,* p. 20.

Books for Your Children, spring, 1994, G. English, review of *A Lion at Bedtime,* p. 8.

Bulletin of the Center for Children's Books, May, 1994, Roger Sutton, review of *Mr. Bear Babysits,* p. 287; February, 1997, Lisa Mahoney, review of *The Snow Lambs,* pp. 204-205.

Children's Playmate, October-November, 1994, review of *Mr. Bear Babysits,* p. 19.

Horn Book Guide, fall, 1995, Sheila M. Geraty, review of *Willie Bear and the Wish Fish,* and review of *Mr. Bear's Picnic,* p. 95; spring, 1997, Martha Sibert, reviews of *The Princess and the Pirate King* and *The Snow Lambs,* p. 29; fall, 2001, Sheila M. Geraty, reviews of *Flora's Blanket, Mr. Bear to the Rescue,* and *Polar Bolero: A Bedtime Dance,* p. 231.

Junior Bookshelf, February, 1993, review of *When I'm Big,* p. 12; April, 1995, review of *A Present for Big Pig,* p. 66; August, 1995, review of *Little Bear and the Wish Fish,* p. 128.

Kirkus Reviews, June 1, 1994, review of *Mr. Bear Babysits,* pp. 774-775; November 1, 1999, review of *No Matter What,* p. 1741; January 15, 1999, review of *Mr. Bear's New Baby,* p. 144; February 1, 2001, review of *The Dorling Kindersley Book of Nursery Rhymes,* pp. 182-183; August 1, 2001, review of *Pure Dead Magic,* p. 1122; August 15, 2001, review of *Tell Me What It's Like to Be Big,* p. 1211; July 1, 2001, review of *Pure Dead Wicked,* p. 955.

Library Journal, August, 2001, Maria Otero-Boisvert, review of *No Matter What,* p. S60.

Magpies, November, 1998, Joan Zahnleiter, review of *Give Him My Heart,* p. 27.

Observer (London, England), November 28, 1993, Kate Kellaway, review of *A Lion at Bedtime,* p. 11.

Publishers Weekly, August 24, 1992, review of *My Little Brother,* p. 78; September 9, 1996, review of *The Princess and the Pirate King,* p. 82; May 2, 1994, review of *Mr. Bear Babysits* p. 306; June 5, 1995, review of *Mr. Bear's Picnic* p. 62; September 9, 1996, review of *The Princess and the Pirate King,* p. 82; October 28, 1996, review of *The Snow Lambs,* pp. 80-81; September 28, 1998, review of *What Can I Give Him?,* pp. 58-59, review of *Tell Me Something Happy before I Go to Sleep,* p. 101; February 15, 1999, review of *Mr. Bear's New Baby,* p. 106; November 8, 1999, review of *No Matter What,* p. 66; October 2, 2000, review of *The Very Small,* p. 80; March 12, 2001, review of *The Dorling Kindersley Book of Nursery Rhymes,* p. 93; April 9, 2001, review of *Flora's Blanket,* p. 73; May 7, 2001, review of *Polar Bolero,* p. 246; July 2, 2001, review of *Tell Me What It's Like to Be Big,* p. 74; August 27, 2001, review of *Pure Dead Magic,* p. 85.

School Librarian, February, 1993, Elizabeth J. King, review of *When I'm Big,* p. 15; November, 1994,

Janet Sims, review of *The Snowchild,* p. 146; August, 1995, Jane Doonan, review of *Little Bear and the Wish-Fish,* p. 103; February, 1997, Carloyn Boyd, review of *Mr. Bear to the Rescue,* and Chris Stephenson, review of *The Princess and the Pirate King,* p. 18.

School Library Journal, February, 1992, Lucy Young Clem, reviews of *New Big Sister,* p. 72; August, 1992, Virginia E. Jeschelnig, review of *New Big Sister,* p. 72 and *New Big House,* pp. 135-136; January, 1993, Virginia E. Jeschelnig, review of *My Little Brother,* p. 76; April, 1993, Lori A. Janick, review of *Dulcie Dando, Soccer Star,* pp. 102-103; December, 1993, Mary Lou Budd, review of *Oliver's Alphabets,* p. 80; August, 1994, Lauralyn Persson, review of *Mr. Bear Babysits,* p. 130; December, 1994, Margaret A. Chang, review of *The Snowchild,* pp. 74-75; July, 1995, Martha Gordon, review of *Willie Bear and the Wish Fish,* p. 61; August, 1995, Lynn Cockett, review of *Mr. Bear's Picnic,* p. 122; October, 1998, Anne Connor, review of *What Can I Give Him?,* p. 41; November 1, 1998, Judith Constantinides, review of *Tell Me Something Happy before I Go to Sleep,* pp. 83-84; March, 1998, Jean Pollock, review of *Poems Go Clang!,* pp. 200-201; March, 1999, Dawn Amsberry, review of *Mr. Bear's New Baby,* p. 175; November, 1999, Marlene Gawron, review of *No Matter What,* p. 116; January, 2000, Selene S. Vasquez, review of *Mr. Bear Says, Are You There, Baby Bear?,* p. 96; March, 2000, Faith Brautigam, review of *Mr. Bear's Vacation,* p. 197; November, 2000, Joy Fleishhacker, review of *The Very Small,* p. 119, and Jody McCoy, review of *Mr. Bear to the Rescue,* p. 120; June, 2001, Helen Foster James, review of *Polar Bolero,* p. 114; July, 2001, JoAnn Jonas, review of *The Dorling Kindersley Book of Nursery Rhymes,* p. 94, and Christina F. Renaud, review of *Flora's Blanket,* p. 81; September, 2001, review of *No Matter What,* p. S60, Alison Kastner, review of *Tell Me What It's Like to Be Big,* p. 188, and Eva Mitnick, review of *Pure Dead Magic,* p. 225; June, 2002, Teresa Bateman, review of *Pure Dead Magic,* pp. 70-71; August, 2002, Lynn Evarts, review of *Pure Dead Wicked,* p. 184.

Times Educational Supplement, June 28, 1996, Susan Young, "Bend Them, Shake Them, Any Way You Want Them"; October, 1996, Melissa Hudak, review of *The Snow Lambs,* p. 94; November 20, 1998, review of *Give Him My Heart.*

GOEMANS, Camille (Constant Ghislain) 1900-1960

PERSONAL: Born January 23, 1900, in Louvain, Belgium; died June 4, 1960, in Brussels, Belgium; married Lou Cosyn. *Education:* Attended University of Brussels.

CAREER: Photographer and writer. Founded periodical *Correspondences,* 1924, with Paul Nougé and Marcel Lecomte. *Military service:* Belgian army, 1940; attained rank of lieutenant.

WRITINGS:

Distances, D. Devillez (Brussels, Belgium), 1928, reprinted, 1994.

(Author of text) *Le sens propre* (exhibition catalogue for paintings by René Magritte), D. Devillez (Brussels, Belgium), 1929, reprinted, 1969.

Emile Mahy, Edition Apollo (Brussels, Belgium), 1942.

Poèmes pour la guerra, Les Lèvres Nues (Brussels, Belgium), 1968.

Grand comme une image: Avec un dessin de René Magritte, Les Lèvres Nues (Brussels, Belgium), 1968.

Arsène, Les Lèvres Nues (Brussels, Belgium), 1969.

Le bonheur des rois; ou, Quelques précisions pour un adolescent, Les Lèvres Nues (Brussels, Belgium), 1969.

Oeuvre, 1922-1957, Gilbert Meirsschaut à Kruishoutem (Brussels, Belgium), 1970.

René Magritte: Fondation de l'Hermitage, Lausanne, 19 juin-19 octobre 1987, Fondation de l'Hermitage (Lausanne, France), 1987.

Ecrits: anthologie, Labor (Brussels, Belgium), 1992.

SIDELIGHTS: In 1926 Camille Goemans was among several young Belgians, including the noted artist René Magritte, who founded the Belgian Surrealist art group. Goemans was a chronicler of Magritte's work in catalogs and books, such as, *Grand comme une image: Avec un dessin de René Magritte.*

BIOGRAPHICAL AND CRITICAL SOURCES:

PERIODICALS

Artnews, May, 1983, Emily Simson, "The Surrealist Spirit in Belgian Photography," p. 159.*

GOLDMAN, Jane 1970-

PERSONAL: Born 1970.

ADDRESSES: Home—London, England. *Agent*—c/o Author Mail, Simon & Schuster, 1230 Avenue of the Americas, New York, NY 10020.

CAREER: Journalist and author.

AWARDS, HONORS: Woman of Tomorrow award, *Cosmopolitan,* for achievement in journalism.

WRITINGS:

Thirteensomething: A Survivor's Guide, Puffin (London, England), 1993.
Sex: How? Why? What?: The Teenager's Guide, Piccadilly (London, England), c. 1994.
For Weddings, a Funeral and When You Can't Flush the Loo, Puffin (London, England), 1995.
Sussed and Streetwise, illustrated by S. Rugen, Piccadilly (London, England), 1995, reprinted as *Streetsmarts: A Teenager's Safety Guide,* Barron's Educational Series (Hauppauge, NY), 1996.
The X-Files Book of the Unexplained (two volumes), Simon & Schuster (London, England), 1995, HarperPrism (New York, NY), 1997.
Dreamworld (novel), Pocket/MTV (New York, NY), 2000.

SIDELIGHTS: London-based journalist Jane Goldman has written a number of books, among them several guides for teens. Joan Hamilton Jones, writing in *School Librarian,* noted the humor in *Thirteensomething: A Survivor's Guide,* and called Goldman's points "valuable." *Sex: How? Why? What?* is written for the older teen and discusses sexuality, attitudes, and physiological changes, all with emphasis on avoiding sexually transmitted diseases, particularly AIDS. *Times Literary Supplement* contributor Mary Gribbin found the guide to be "dull" but "worthy." *Books for Keeps* reviewer Val Randall described it as "extremely thorough." "A major strength of this book is its demolition of the sexual stereotypes purveyed by the mass media and insistence on the wonderful variety of human equipment and potential attractiveness of every human being," wrote Jane Inglis in *School Librarian.*

Etiquette is the focus of Goldman's *For Weddings, a Funeral and When You Can't Flush the Loo.* She covers all the awkward situations that can come up while dating, eating, socializing, partying, and communicating. *School Librarian* reviewer Valerie Caless called it "excellent," and thought Goldman's advice was "down to earth." *Sussed and Streetwise,* reprinted in the United States as *Streetsmarts: A Teenager's Safety Guide,* is a practical guide to threatening and unpleasant situations that can arise while traveling and dating and in environments that are usually thought of as safe, such as home or school. It is for boys as well as girls, and addresses the particular risks of alcohol and drugs. Goldman notes that so much emphasis has been put on the possibility of risk that pleasure and enjoyment are sometimes diminished. A *Junior Bookshelf* contributor called the guide a "useful book for teenagers." "It's not preachy but full of common sense," wrote Ann Treneman in the *Times Educational Supplement.*

Goldman's *The X-Files Book of the Unexplained* was published in two volumes in which she documents the themes and topics of the popular television show. *Skeptical Inquirer* contributor Gordon Stein noted that "journalists can rarely be jacks of all trades" and felt the book "is a piece of journalism that reads well, but seems incapable of properly evaluating the often conflicting evidence for or against the paranormal." Stein praised the layout and design, calling it "a superb piece of popular printing."

Goldman's first novel, *Dreamworld,* is set in an Orlando, Florida, theme park. Sylvia Avery is a security officer whose job includes maintaining the illusions presented by the park. Her job is made more difficult when two bodies are discovered and she is called on to help with the investigation. She finds that Dreamworld has been conducting research using experimental drugs, with the goal of creating the ideal entertainment experience. A *Publishers Weekly* reviewer wrote that Goldman presents the park as "a kind of *Twilight Zone* . . . where public relations supersedes justice. . . . Her tale guarantees that readers may henceforth regard theme parks with a dash of suspicion."

BIOGRAPHICAL AND CRITICAL SOURCES:

PERIODICALS

Books for Keeps, January, 1995, Val Randall, "Facts for the Teenage Life," p. 20.

Junior Bookshelf, October, 1995, review of *Sussed and Streetwise,* p. 1995.

Observer (London, England), December 15, 1996, Scott Bradfield, "X Terminate, X Terminate," p. 16.

Publishers Weekly, February 28, 2000, review of *Dreamworld,* p. 60.

School Librarian, May, 1994, Joan Hamilton Jones, review of *Thirteensomething,* p. 77; February, 1995, Anthony Hamilton Jones, review of *Sex: How? Why? What?,* p. 35; August, 1995, Valerie Caless, review of *For Weddings, a Funeral and When You Can't Flush the Loo,* p. 120.

Skeptical Inquirer, May-June, 1996, Gordon Stein, review of *The X-Files Book of the Unexplained,* p. 45.

Times Educational Supplement, March 10, 1995, Mary Gribbin, "Talking about Sex," p. R4; February 9, 1996, Ann Treneman, reviews of *Sussed and Streetwise* and *For Weddings, a Funeral and When You Can't Flush the Loo,* p. 13.*

*   *   *

GOODWIN, Jason 1964-

PERSONAL: Born 1964; children: two sons. *Education:* Attended Cambridge University.

ADDRESSES: Home—West Sussex, England. *Agent*—c/o Author Mail, Henry Holt and Company, 115 West 18th St., New York, NY 10011. *E-mail*—jcgood@hsc.usc.edu.

CAREER: Journalist, historian and travel writer; contributor to the *New York Times* and *Conde Nast Traveler.*

AWARDS, HONORS: John Llewellyn Rhys Prize for *On Foot to the Golden Horn.*

WRITINGS:

The Gunpowder Gardens: Travels through India and China in Search of Tea, Chatto & Windus (London, England), 1990, also published as *A Time for Tea: Travels through China and India in Search of Tea,* Knopf (New York, NY), 1991.

On Foot to the Golden Horn: A Walk to Istanbul, Chatto & Windus (London, England), 1993, Henry Holt (New York, NY), 1995.

Lords of the Horizons: A History of the Ottoman Empire, Henry Holt (New York, NY), 1999.

Otis: Giving Rise to the Modern City, Ivan R. Dee (Chicago, IL), 2001.

Greenback: How the Dollar Changed the World, Henry Holt (New York, NY), 2003.

SIDELIGHTS: English journalist, historian and travel writer Jason Goodwin has focused much of his writing on areas in which East meets West. From the history of the Ottoman Empire, to the history of tea in Asia and Europe, his travels and studies are interesting for their investigation of the two worlds' exchanges. A Cambridge graduate, Goodwin contributes regularly to the *New York Times* and *Conde Nast Traveler.* He lives with his wife and two sons in West Sussex, England.

Goodwin's first book, *The Gunpowder Gardens: Travels through India and China in Search of Tea,* is both history book and travelogue. Inspired by his grandmothers' teapots (which reside on his own mantle), he traveled through China and India to unravel the history of tea. He narrates tea's incarnations and culture in the East and throughout the West, especially in England: from the Chinese folk tale of its origins, to 1,000-year-old tea bushes, to the development of packaged tea bags by American millionaire Tommy Lipton, to the Mad Hatter's Tea party. Molly Mortimer, in *Contemporary Review,* noted that Goodwin does not include the tea histories of Japan, Tibet, or Africa: "Perhaps his lively imagination will find some interesting facets of British Colonials on the vast Brook Bond estates in Kenya." Graham Coster was unfavorable in his assessment in the *London Review of Books:* "Partly Goodwin's travels are a connoisseurial tea-tasting assignment, but his heart isn't really in it, and I'm not surprised, since the most highly-prized specimens he tries appear to have the furry consistency and heart-stopping strength of that last cup out of a well-stewed pot." But Christopher Lehmann-Haupt of the *New York Times Books Review* called the book "funny" and "evocative," writing, "Mr. Goodwin's imagination stays vibrant. It has summoned up all the tea in China and India. And made one thirst for a spicy cup of the brew."

The same year Goodwin's tea book was published in England, he embarked with two traveling companions on a walking tour of Eastern Europe. He describes his travels in his second book, *On Foot to the Golden Horn.* The early 1990s marked a time of transition for the former Soviet Block countries, and Goodwin notes this in his descriptions of the towns and people he encounters. The journey covers some two thousand miles, mostly through the countryside. Philip Glazebrook wrote in his review in *Spectator* that the book would have been better if Goodwin had established a purpose: "Goodwin's book, though it contains many an interesting page, and a good many remarks which show insight and intelligence . . . is really more of a ramble than a purposeful walk, a little too discursive and fragmented to hold the reader's attention." Jonathan Sunley, in the *Times Literary Supplement,* complained that there are numerous editorial mistakes, including misspelled place names. But he conceded, "Notwithstanding, Jason Goodwin is to be congratulated on producing one of the truest portraits of present-day Central Europe available." *On Foot to the Golden Horn* won the John Llewellyn Rhys Prize.

Lords of the Horizons: A History of the Ottoman Empire covers the history of the area, from the Byzantine empire's collapse in the fourteenth century to the Ottoman's own demise at the end of World War I. For 600 years the Ottoman Empire stretched from the border of Iran to the waters of the Danube. It encompassed over three dozen nations and hundreds of ethnic groups, including Spanish Jews, Albanian tribesmen, Venetian merchants, Orthodox Greeks, and Arab Bedouins. Under tolerant Sunni Muslim rule, Ottoman Turks created a culture that "was such a prodigy of pep, such a miracle of human ingenuity, that contemporaries felt it was helped into being by powers not quite human—diabolical or divine, depending on their point of view," as Goodwin writes. But the Turks neglected to keep up with the industrial revolution in Europe, and military, civilian, and royal turbulence weakened the once-mighty empire. Fouad Ajami praised Goodwin's style in his review in the *New York Times Book Review:* "He does it in a beguiling way, the pace of his narrative catching, at times, the speed and swiftness of those Ottoman horsemen of the frontier in their days of glory, and then the ponderous style of a decaying empire that answered the calls for reform with pretense and show and outright cruelty as well as with a frenzy of palace building that could not lift the gloom, as the unhappy sultans 'dragged the terrible burden of their line from one palace to the next.'" Ajami added, "He has . . . stripped that Ottoman past of its 'otherness,' the alienness that has been its lot in this age of unyielding nationalism."

In *Otis: Giving Rise to the Modern City,* Goodwin traces the history of the elevator company founded by Elisha Otis in the 1850s. According to Goodwin, Otis made the elevator a dependable part of life in the big cities. Due to the invention and refinement of the elevator, the building of skyscrapers was made possible. The book also touches on the less-than-ethical business practices within the elevator industry. A *Publishers Weekly* reviewer called *Otis: Giving Rise to the Modern City,* "a well-paced book, which weaves business, technological and social history into a seamless and entertaining narrative," and "a thumbnail history of American business, with its mistakes, sins and undeniable triumphs."

BIOGRAPHICAL AND CRITICAL SOURCES:

BOOKS

Goodwin, Jason, *Lords of the Horizons: A History of the Ottoman Empire,* Henry Holt (New York, NY), 1999.

PERIODICALS

Choice, February, 2002, F. Potter, review of *Otis: Giving Rise to the Modern City,* p. 1067.
Contemporary Review, September, 1990, pp. 167-168.
London Review of Books, July 26, 1990, pp. 18-19.
New York Times Book Review, September 9, 1991; May 2, 1999, p. 7.
Publishers Weekly, August 13, 2001, review of *Otis: Giving Rise to the Modern City,* p. 304.
Spectator, July 17, 1993, p. 27.
Technology and Culture, April, 2002, Robert M. Vogel, review of *Otis: Giving Rise to the Modern City,* p. 431.
Times Literary Supplement, August 6, 1993, p. 12.
Wall Street Journal, October 9, 2001, Daniel Akst, "Going Up," p. A20.*

*   *   *

GOODWIN, Joan W. 1926-

PERSONAL: Born December 2, 1926, in Dallas, TX. *Education:* Barnard College, graduated, 1947.

ADDRESSES: Home—Boston, MA. *Agent*—c/o Author Mail, Northeastern University Press, 360 Huntington Ave., 416 CP, Boston, MA 02115.

CAREER: Worked at the Unitarian Universalist Association, Boston, MA, 1973-87.

AWARDS, HONORS: Honorary doctorate of letters, Starr King School for the Ministry, 1984.

WRITINGS:

The Remarkable Mrs. Ripley: The Life of Sarah Alden Bradford Ripley, Northeastern University Press (Boston, MA), 1998.
(Editor, with Ann Fields) *We Believe: Learning and Living Our Unitarian Universalist Principles,* Unitarian Universalist Association (Boston, MA), 1998.

SIDELIGHTS: In *The Remarkable Mrs. Ripley,* Joan Goodwin has written a biography of Sarah Alden Bradford Ripley, who lived in New England during the first half of the nineteenth century. Her family connections brought her into contact with such notable contemporaries of the era as Ralph Waldo Emerson and his disciple, Henry David Thoreau, Nathaniel Hawthorne, and Bronson Alcott. "In this wonderful book . . . we witness the quivering excitement in the New England air and meet all the local sages," remarked Jane Langton in *Christian Science Monitor.* Ripley managed to exercise her remarkable intellect despite strict adherence to the "woman's sphere" demanded by her role as a Unitarian minster's wife, as well as the demands of birthing and carrying for numerous children. Reviewers particularly noted the strength of mind Ripley displays in the anecdote Goodwin relates of her subject rocking an infant with one foot, listening and correcting a student in Greek, while attending to a household chore held in her lap. Although she never wrote anything herself, Ripley is long believed to have exerted a strong influence over the circle around Emerson, as the circle's members themselves were the first to acknowledge.

Goodwin draws upon Ripley's letters and journals to reconstruct the conflicted inner world of a woman who longed to live the life of the mind but whom duty compelled to live the life of the flesh. "Without over-idealizing her subject, Goodwin shows Ripley wasting no time in self-pity but instead finding ways to remain intellectually engaged," observed Paula Friedman in the *New York Times Book Review.* Although Morris Hounion complained in *Library Journal* of the lack of sufficient genealogical detail to keep track of the numerous births, deaths, and weddings scattered throughout *The Remarkable Mrs. Ripley, Booklist* reviewer Danise Hoover highlighted no gaps in Goodwin's scholarship. Instead, Hoover remarked that Goodwin's research has created the first "complete picture of this extraordinary woman's life," a work which will have special appeal for historians and feminists.

BIOGRAPHICAL AND CRITICAL SOURCES:

PERIODICALS

Booklist, October 15, 1998, p. 391.
Choice, April, 1999, S. S. Arpad, review of *The Remarkable Mrs. Ripley: The Life of Sarah Alden Bradford Ripley,* p. 1517.
Christian Science Monitor, October 22, 1998, pp. B7, B10.
Kirkus Reviews, September 1, 1998, p. 1256.
Library Journal, November 1, 1998, p. 81.
New England Quarterly, December, 1999, Joel Myerson, review of *The Remarkable Mrs. Ripley,* p. 625.
New York Times Book Review, July 4, 1999, p. 14.
Publishers Weekly, September 28, 1998, p. 89.
William and Mary Quarterly, July, 2000, Catherine Kaplan, review of *The Remarkable Mrs. Ripley,* p. 719.

OTHER

Unitarian Universalist Association Web site, http://www.uua.org (November 7, 2002).*

*   *   *

GRACE, Tom

PERSONAL: Born in Detroit, MI; married; children: three daughters. *Education:* University of Michigan, B.A., M.A.

ADDRESSES: Home—MI. *Agent*—c/o Author Mail, Warner Books, 1271 Avenue of the Americas, New York, NY 10020.

CAREER: Architect and writer.

WRITINGS:

Spyder Web, Seanachaoi Press (Dexter, MI), 1997.
Quantum, Warner (New York, NY), 2000.

ADAPTATIONS: Spyder Web and *Quantum* have been released as audiobooks.

SIDELIGHTS: Michigan architect Tom Grace penned his first work of fiction in his free time between designing buildings for corporate clients. When it was finished in 1997, Grace self-published his novel, *Spyder Web,* and sold it out of his car. The book was chosen by a Traverse City, Michigan, bookstore as the "manager's pick of the summer," and sales there gained it the number-three spot behind the latest novel by John Grisham. With sales of a thousand copies under his belt, Grace eventually found agent Esther Margolis to represent him, and Warner Books released *Spyder Web* in 1998.

Spyder Web is set in Ann Arbor, Michigan, and features protagonist Nolan Kilkenny, a decorated former Navy SEAL working towards his doctorate in advanced computer science. Nolan is maintaining the super computers of the Michigan Applied Research Consortium (MARC), his father's research project. A prototype hacking program being developed for the Central Intelligence Agency (CIA) is stolen by former KGB agent Alex Roe and his accomplice, Ian Parnell. The program has been developed to gather information on the Peoples' Republic of China. The thieves test it on the MARC mainframe, and Nolan detects a signal he first perceives as a minor technical problem. Assisted by professor and love interest Kelsey Newton, Nolan cooperates with the CIA and applies both his SEAL and technology experience in tracking down the hackers. The trail leads him to a series of locales that ends at the London hideout of Roe and Parnell. Chinese intelligence operative Kang Fa makes several unsuccessful attempts to kill Nolan as he closes in on the thieves.

Reviews of Grace's novel were mixed. A *Publishers Weekly* reviewer wrote, "The sizzle of a good thriller is missing," and called the story's language "jargon-larded." While dubbing the novel's plot "promising," the reviewer maintained that "Grace's pacing impedes it." In a *Kirkus Reviews* evaluation, the critic noted that the finale "offers an exciting close to an otherwise all-too-predictable story," calling *Spyder Web* "a spirited if clunky technothriller. . . . A first effort that puts the right pieces in play, but moves them around without flair." *Library Journal* reviewer Rebecca House Stankowski countered with her opinion that *Spyder Web* offers "international intrigue, realistic characters, lots of technical wizardry, and a reasonably suspenseful story line." A *Booklist* reviewer called *Spyder Web* an "entertaining thriller" and "solid genre fare for the computer literate."

In an interview with *Publishers Weekly* contributor Charles Hix, Grace commented on his newly gained status as a novelist. "My job description has flipped over," he stated. "I used to be an architect first, a writer second. Now I'm a writer first who practices architecture." Grace had hopes that *Spyder Web* would be "the worst thing I'll ever write, and that everything else will be better."

Grace's second book featuring Nolan Kilkenny, *Quantum,* garnered postive critical reviews. In 1948, a German scientist working at the University of Michigan in Ann Arbor makes a staggering discovery, a "Theory of Everything," that will create an endless energy supply and make all other sources obsolete, but is shot dead just minutes later. Fifty years later, Kilkenny and his research group, MARC, comes across the research. They are soon attacked by Russian mercenaries hired by a rich businessman in Russia. A *Publishers Weekly* reviewer wrote, "A few explosive action scenes . . . enliven this nicely textured adventure," while *Booklist* reviewer Budd Arthur called *Quantum* a "classy, stylish thriller."

BIOGRAPHICAL AND CRITICAL SOURCES:

PERIODICALS

Booklist, September 1, 1998, review of *Spyder Web,* p. 70; July, 2000, Budd Arthur, review of *Quantum,* p. 2012.

Kirkus Reviews, November 1, 1998, review of *Spyder Web.*

Library Journal, October 15, 1998, Rebecca House Stankowski, review of *Spyder Web,* p. 97.

Publishers Weekly, September 15, 1997, Judy Quinn, "Margolis Gets Big Deal—From Another House," p. 12; August 3, 1998, Charels Hix, "Tom Grace," p. 52; November 9, 1998, review of *Spyder Web,* p. 56; July 24, 2000, review of *Quantum,* p. 69.

OTHER

Time Warner Web site, http://www.twbookmark.com/ (November 7, 2002), interview with Tom Grace.

*   *   *

GRAND, David 1968-

PERSONAL: Born 1968.

ADDRESSES: *Agent*—c/o Author Mail, Random House, 299 Park Ave., New York, NY 10171-0002.

CAREER: Writer.

AWARDS, HONORS: Creative writing fellowship for fiction from New York University.

WRITINGS:

Louse (novel), Arcade (New York, NY), 1998.
The Disappearing Body, Nan A. Talese (New York, NY), 2002.

SIDELIGHTS: David Grand's debut novel, *Louse,* is a "brave-new-world" story with a central character based on fact. *Library Journal* reviewer Margaret A. Smith wrote that the novel "has an aura of fantasy," while *Booklist* contributor Michele Leber added that Grand "takes readers on a surrealistic ride, and they're unlikely to get off before it's over."

In *Louse,* protagonist Herman Q. Louse is the valet of billionaire Herbert Horatio Blackwell, a man he has been told to call "Poppy." Poppy, like the late Howard Hughes, is a former aviator, film producer, investor, playboy, and the owner of a huge gambling operation in a state that might be Nevada. Poppy, also like Hughes, is deathly afraid of germs. Hughes and his caretakers lived on the floor of a hotel, sealed off from the outside world. Poppy has built a chrome and glass fortress called "G," where his drugged servants—gamblers who have become indebted to Poppy—have been relieved of their long-term memory and now comply with contracts dictating their duties and behavior. As gamblers lose money in the casino on the ground floor, they are inducted into the growing work force of thousands who serve Poppy as accountants, clerks, and kitchen workers, existing in a brainwashed stupor with no will to escape under the watchful eyes of surveillance cameras. They can never work off their debt as penalties are added for every disciplinary infraction.

The story is related through Louse and information revealed in public relations copy, staff memos, and other official papers. Louse, dressed in the required gray flannel suit, administers drugs to the dying Poppy, kills any bugs that find their way into Poppy's sanctuary, and has sex with women chosen for him. Meanwhile, the staff are kept motivated by the possibility of being among those who will be selected to inhabit a new building called Paradise that is under construction. The one rebel is Mortimer Blank, an executive who is being sought by Poppy's guards for diverting money. Louse begins to regain some of his senses, including an attraction to one of the women he works with. A man who says he is Poppy's son emerges and begins to plan an escape from G.

A *Publishers Weekly* reviewer wrote that Grand "methodically and convincingly constructs Louse's antiseptic, delusionary environment with . . . dark humor and vertiginous imagination." David Sacks wrote in the *New York Times Book Review* that *Louse* "mirrors the plight of real-life workers in an era of job insecurity, video surveillance, and shameless corporate euphemisms. Yet Grand has even larger aspirations: the novel's hallucinatory world suggests a religious allegory (apparently sincere) about God's will or presence in the universe. Although not every part of this ambitious agenda succeeds, *Louse* is often provocative and hilarious, occasionally stunning."

Comparing *Louse* to George Orwell's *1984* and Donald Antrim's *Elect Mr. Robinson for a Better World,* Sacks concluded that "The master, of course, is Franz Kafka.

Certainly the little people in Grand's fiction are caught in a Kafkaesque system of guilt and obligation, a kind of corporate purgatory." A *Kirkus Reviews* critic was less sure, questioning whether the novel is "a scathing satire of organizational mores, a chilling tour of a murky authoritarian world where reality is plastic, or simply a dizzying litany of comings and goings that challenges the readers to figure out what (if anything) is really going on." While Sacks ultimately considered the novel's symbolism and Louse's passivity to be flaws in the storyline, he concluded that "this *Louse* sticks to you, for its wit and imaginative vision."

In *The Disappearing Body,* Grand writes a dark thriller set in an unnamed American city in the 1930s. Victor Ribe is released from jail after years of imprisonment for a crime he didn't commit, but doesn't know who is responsible for his sudden freedom. Multiple storylines involve a friend of Ribe's who finds a dead body, only to have it disappear, drug trafficking, arms deals, and crooked politicians. *Booklist*'s Bill Ott wrote that Grand "manages admirably" to write "a twisted version of the noir mood." A *Publishers Weekly* reviewer called the book "a kind of postmodern thriller . . . [with] a satirical edge."

BIOGRAPHICAL AND CRITICAL SOURCES:

PERIODICALS

Booklist, September 1, 1998, Michele Leber, review of *Louse,* p. 65; February 15, 2002, Bill Ott, review of *The Disappearing Body,* p. 995.

Kirkus Reviews, September 1, 1998, review of *Louse.*

Library Journal, September 1, 1998, Margaret A. Smith, review of *Louse,* p. 213.

New York Times Book Review, January 24, 1999, David Sacks, review of *Louse,* p. 14.

Publishers Weekly, August 31, 1998, p. 44, review of *Louse;* February 4, 2002, review of *The Disappearing Body,* p. 49.

OTHER

Salon.com, http://www.salon.com/ (November 7, 2002), Amy Reiter, review of *The Disappearing Body.**

GRANICH, Reuben

PERSONAL: Male. *Education:* Attended Boston University, 1981-82; University of California, B.A. (cum laude), 1985; attended Alliance Française, 1986; Stanford Medical School, M.D., 1993; California Pacific Medical Center, residency in internal medicine, 1996. *Hobbies and other interests:* Amateur soccer (Atlanta Soccer League, U.C. San Diego soccer team, Issy-les-Molineaux-French 4th division); photography, with exhibits held at Standford University and in Uruapan, Michoacan, Mexico.

ADDRESSES: Office—California Department of Health Services, Division of Communicable Disease Control, Tuberculosis Control Branch, 2151 Berkeley Way, Room 608, Berkeley, CA 94704-1011; fax: 510-540-3535. *E-mail*—rgranich@dhs.ca.gov.

CAREER: Epidemiologist. Centers for Disease Control and Prevention, Epidemic Intelligence Service, 1996-98; California State Tuberculosis Control Branch, CDC/NCHSTP/FSB, medical epidemiologist for U.S. Public Health Service, 1999—. *Military service:* Commissioned Corps, lieutenant commander (0-4), 1999—.

Also involved in extensive research on tuberculosis, HIV/AIDS, pediatric infectious disease, and related health issues in the United States and internationally. Member of Palo Alto Stanford Medical Aid Committee for Central America, 1987-88; Stanford-East Palo Alto AIDS project co-founder, 1988-90; International and Cross-Cultural Medicine Association co-founder, 1988-92; Stanford Medical Schools ARS Medica co-chair, 1990-91; American Medical Student Association president, 1990-91; Stanford University AIDS Task Force member, 1990-91; Stanford Medical School's Office of Public Service Opportunities co-founder, 1990-91; Stanford University Hospitals AIDS Subcommittee student representative, 1992; Beijing 99 Collaborative Group, honorary secretary, 1999—.

AWARDS, HONORS: National Merit Finalist, Philip J. Grasso Memorial Scholarship; Boston University Scholarship; UCSD Center for U.S. Mexican Studies Grant; Stanford Medical School's Peter Emgee Traveling Scholars Award; Medical Scholar's Award; Halper Scholarship; MacKenzie Scholarship; Morrison Institute Study Grant; Hillel Scholarship; Santa Clara

County Health Auxiliary Scholarship; Albert Strickler Scholarship; Stanford Haas Center Summer Public Service Fellowship; Stanford Saturn Award; Stanford University James W. Lyons Award for Service; Stanford University School of Medicine Dean's Award for Outstanding Community Service; Diplomat of the American Board of Internal Medicine; USPHS Foreign Duty award and commendation.

WRITINGS:

(With J. Mermin), *HIV, Health, and Your Community: A Guide for Action,* Stanford University Press (Stanford, CA), 1999.

Contributor of numerous letters and articles to professional journals.

WORK IN PROGRESS: "Drug Resistant Tuberculosis in Foreign-born Persons from Mexico, the Philippines, and Vietnam—United States, 1993-1997" (with Marisa Moore and Nancy Binkin); *Guidelines for the Prevention of Tuberculosis among Health Care Workers in Resource-Limited Settings* (with N. Binkin and W. Jarvis), a joint CDC/WHO/IUATLD document; "Infection with Mycobacterium Leprae (Leprosy)" (with J. Mermin), in *Internal Medicine,* 5th Edition, Mosby-Yearbook, Inc.

*　　*　　*

GRANT, Mark N. 1952-

PERSONAL: Born July 3, 1952 in New York, New York; son of Bernard Grant and Joyce (maiden name Gordon), both professional doctors. *Education:* University of Rochester, NY, B.A., 1974.

ADDRESSES: Agent—c/o Author Mail, Northeastern University Press, 360 Huntington Ave., 416 CP, Boston, MA 02115.

CAREER: Composer and writer.

WRITINGS:

Maestros of the Pen: A History of Classical Music Criticism in America, Northeastern University Press (Boston, MA), 1998.

Author of introduction, *Remembering Franz Liszt* by Arthur Friedheim and Alexander Siloti, 1986.

WORK IN PROGRESS: The Rise and Fall of the Broadway Musical (tentative title), Northeastern University Press (Boston, MA), 2004.

SIDELIGHTS: Mark N. Grant is a composer and the author of *Maestros of the Pen: A History of Classical Music Criticism in America.* The history of music criticism began in the 1830s. It first took the form of notices of musical events and post-performance acknowledgments of who was in attendance. With the huge influx of European immigrants, music criticism expanded to meet the needs of a larger audience, offering opinions as to what was or was not good music and growing over the next two hundred years to become a lucrative industry.

Grant examines nearly fifty music journalists during what he calls the First and Second Empires. The first, the Gilded Age, lasted from Reconstruction until World War I. It was during this period that reviewers gained the status of professional critics. They were widely read in daily newspapers and rose to the height of their influence, particularly in New York City. The Old Guard included such notables as W. J. Henderson, H. T. Finch, H. E. Krehbiel, Richard Aldrich, and James Gibbons Huneker. These critics wrote from the 1880s until the 1920s. Krehbiel was often mistaken for his friend, President William Howard Taft, and was so popular that his name was placed in lights on Broadway by the *New York Tribune.* Once the most influential reviewer in the country, Huneker covered music, literature, the visual arts, and theater. He also wrote fiction.

Dana Gioia wrote in the *New York Times Book Review* that "fueled by a dozen or more daily bottles of Pilsner, Huneker published half a million words per year and still found time to chase divas, hold court at Luchow's, and practice Chopin. Helping move American arts from puritan provincialism to cosmopolitan sophistication, Huneker became the model for later culture czars like H. L. Mencken. For Grant, Huneker serves as a representative figure of a vanished intellectual authority, a magisterial critic and trained instrumentalist who understood music's importance to general culture." Grant's Second Empire began in 1940. Influential critics included B. H. Haggin, Henry Pleasants, Olin Downes, Alfred Frankenstein, and composer Virgil Thomson, whom Grant considers America's foremost music critic.

Grant speculates on the role of critics in music history and their influence on composition and performance. He notes that the Old Guard were Wagnerians and that their attention has ensured that Wagner's operas remain popular. Other composers were not treated as kindly. Krehbiel called Arnold Schoenberg's work "excreta," and upon hearing the first performance of Schoenberg's *Pierrot Lunaire* in Berlin in 1912, Huneker called it "the very ecstasy of the hideous." Huneker also thought Berg's *Lulu* suite to be "squalid and repulsive." Fifty years earlier he trashed Tchaikovsky's "First Piano Concerto," and in 1888 he wrote that Bruckner's *Fourth Symphony* "is without melodious themes of any kind." Other critics offered their views of Bruckner and his music. Deems Taylor said he "has the talent, but not the mind to control it," while Winthrop Sargeant called Bruckner "vastly superior to Brahms."

Mahler had the support of very few American critics. In writing Mahler's obituary, Krehbiel continued to fault his work, and forty years later Downes was still calling Mahler's *Seventh Symphony* "detestably bad" and his *Fifth Symphony* "vulgar music." Gioia pointed out that Mahler eventually developed a huge following, due, for the most part, to the efforts of conductors like Bruno Walter, Otto Klemperer, and Leonard Bernstein. In some cases, critics were key in providing exposure for composers. Olin Downes was an advocate of Sibelius, which brought the Finnish composer into the American limelight, and Paul Rosenfeld promoted the work of Charles Ives and Aaron Copeland. John Rockwell is an example of a critic who reviews rock as well as classical music.

By 2000, critics had become reviewers, and almost none were composers. Reviewing rock became much more lucrative than reviewing classical music, and so the latter was not only not widely reviewed, it was also not promoted. Gioia noted that although there are now fewer classical music critics, there are nonetheless more opera companies, orchestras, and music festivals, and there is an ever-widening range of classical music available through recordings and broadcasts. Gioia said that "perhaps all we need to reinvigorate criticism is a few books as good as this one."

Washington Times reviewer Rufus Hallmark wrote that, in *Maestros of the Pen*, Grant "declares at the outset that he will not include musicologists in his coverage, but he does make an exception for the late Columbia professor Paul Henry Lang, long a music critic for the *New York Herald Tribune* (successor to Virgil Thomson). Given this exception, one wonders how on the contemporary scene he could ignore Richard Taruskin of Berkeley, a brilliant, opinionated, and at times vitriolic 'think-piece' writer for the *New York Times*." Hallmark noted that some of Taruskin's writings fall into the category of concert previews within feature articles. Hallmark noted that Grant makes no mention of Andrew Porter, who wrote regularly about music for the *New Yorker* in the 1970s and 1980s. Hallmark wrote that "a simultaneous strength and weakness of the book is that while Mr. Grant's characterization of the critics makes one yearn to read the actual reviews and essays they penned, his book provides only tiny snippets, mere tastes that whet our appetites for more."

A *Publishers Weekly* reviewer called Grant's history "rich with cultural context." *Times Literary Supplement* reviewer Paul Griffiths wrote that the book "is a gallery of portraits, done in prose of robust American flavour and assembled to make a history that follows one of the great narrative forms. Music criticism in the United States is born, reaches maturity, and dies." Griffiths concluded that "perhaps . . . what changes musical life is not the solitary voice in print but the commercial opportunism of recording companies. . . . But so long as we believe that a mindless machine can be stayed by one new thought, the dream is worth holding on to."

BIOGRAPHICAL AND CRITICAL SOURCES:

PERIODICALS

American Record Guide, November-December, 1998, p. 346.
Choice, June, 1999, M. Meckna, review of *Maestros of the Pen: A History of Classical Music Criticism in America,* p. 1799.
New York Times Book Review, June 15, 1986, p. 34; January 24, 1999, p. 12.
Notes, March, 2000, Karen Alquist, review of *Maestros of the Pen,* p. 691.
Publishers Weekly, December 21, 1998, p. 49.
Times Literary Supplement, June 18, 1999, p. 21.
Washington Times, December 20, 1998, p. B8.*

GREEN, Alan 1950-

PERSONAL: Born 1950.

ADDRESSES: Agent—c/o Author Mail, Public Affairs, 250 West 57th St., New York, NY 10019.

CAREER: AlterNet, founding editor.

AWARDS, HONORS: Worth Bingham Prize.

WRITINGS:

The Directory of Athletic Scholarships, Putnam (New York, NY), 1981.

(With Bill Hogan) *Gavel to Gavel: A Guide to the Televised Proceedings of Congress,* Benton Foundation (Washington, DC), 1982.

(With Larry Kahaner) *The Phone Book: The Most Complete Guide to the Changing World of Telephones,* Penguin (New York, NY), 1983.

(Editor, with Joel Makower) *Instant Information,* Prentice Hall (New York, NY), 1987.

Justice for All: A Guide to the Supreme Court of the United States, Benton Foundation, 1987.

(With Andy Clark) *Athletic Scholarships: Thousands of Grants and over $400 Millions for College-bound Athletes,* Facts on File (New York, NY), 1994.

Animal Underworld: Inside America's Black Market for Rare and Exotic Species, Public Affairs (New York, NY), 1999.

SIDELIGHTS: Award-winning investigative reporter Alan Green, with the support of the Center for Public Integrity, a nonprofit center that studies ethics-related issues, investigated the trade in exotic animals in the United States. To fit together the pieces of this complex puzzle, Green conducted hundreds of interviews and studied trade documents from forty-eight states. He reported the results of his study in *Animal Underworld: Inside America's Black Market for Rare and Exotic Species.* According to Green, mainstream zoos and amusement parks—as well as research laboratories—dispose of surplus animals in unethical ways, hiding their activities with a trail of incomplete and confusing paperwork. Eventually many of these exotic animals end up at unlicensed petting zoos, at private hunting facilities, in the hands of private pet owners, and on grocery store shelves as exotic meat or health supplements such as aphrodisiacs. In many cases, these former zoo or laboratory animals suffer cruelly from neglect and abuse.

A *Kirkus Reviews* critic justified Green's "pull-no-punches style" because Green has "done the legwork" with his thorough research. In the view of *Booklist* reviewer Grace Fill, *Animal Underworld* is "a must for concerned animal lovers." Calling the work a "major feat of investigative reporting," a *Publishers Weekly* reviewer remarked, "Green's important eye-opening report could spark a national debate." "This shocking book is an eye-opener that belongs in every collection," wrote a *Library Journal* commentator.

BIOGRAPHICAL AND CRITICAL SOURCES:

PERIODICALS

Booklist, October 15, 1999, Grace Fill, review of *Animal Underworld: Inside America's Black Market for Rare and Exotic Species,* p. 398.

Kirkus Reviews, September 1, 1999, review of *Animal Underworld.*

Library Journal, October 15, 1999, Peggie Partello, review of *Animal Underworld,* p. 93.

Publishers Weekly, September 20, 1999, review of *Animal Underworld,* p. 58.*

*   *   *

GREENWOOD, Pippa

PERSONAL: Female. Education: Durham University, MSc.

ADDRESSES: Agent—c/o Author Mail, Dorling Kindersley, 95 Madison Ave., New York, NY 10016.

CAREER: Botanist and author. Host of BBC's *Gardener's World.*

MEMBER: Royal Horticultural Society.

WRITINGS:

Fruit and Vegetable Clinic, Ward Lock (London, England), 1993.

House Plant Clinic, Ward Lock (London, England), 1993.

The New Gardener: The Practical Guide to Gardening Basics, Dorling Kindersley (New York, NY), 1995.

Gardening Hints and Tips, Dorling Kindersley (New York, NY), 1996.

Basic Gardening, Dorling Kindersley (New York, NY), 1998.

The New Flower Gardener, Dorling Kindersley (New York, NY), 1998.

10,001 Hints and Tips for the Home, Dorling Kindersley (New York, NY), 1998.

AHS Pests and Diseases, Dorling Kindersley (New York, NY), 2000.

Gardener's Question Time: All Your Gardening Problems Solved, Orion (London, England), 2002.

A Garden for All Seasons: Create a Year-round Beautiful Garden, Headline (London, England), 2002.

AHS Garden Problem Solver, Dorling Kindersley (New York, NY), 2002.

Contributor to periodicals, including *Amateur Gardening* and *Mirror.*

SIDELIGHTS: Pippa Greenwood is a British botanist who shares her knowledge of plants as host of a British Broadcasting Corp. (BBC) television program and in a number of popular books. Her *Fruit and Vegetable Clinic* advises gardeners on the elimination of pests and diseases in the kitchen garden. In *House Plant Clinic* Greenwood discusses the diagnosis and treatment of plant diseases and general care of indoor plants, including pest control. She lists the common names of plants and suggests individual humidity, light, and temperature requirements.

The New Gardener: The Practical Guide to Gardening Basics is divided into eleven chapters which include advice on control of insects and weeds and care and culture. Greenwood discusses the planning of lawns, beds, borders, vegetables, and gardens, including container gardens and water gardens. She advises on the planning and maintenance of greenhouses and cold frames, planting and pruning of fruit trees, and the tools essential to successful gardening. Each chapter contains a project, and color photographs and line drawings accompany the text. Molly Newling wrote in *Library Journal* that Greenwood's gardens "are very much in the English style," but noted the absence of a hardiness zone map for the United States. "This delightful companion is highly recommended to all garden enthusiasts and plant lovers," wrote Brij M. Kapoor in *Science Books & Films. Booklist* reviewer Alice Joyce noted that *The New Gardener* "brings considerable freshness to standard, if fairly extensive, material."

Gardening Hints and Tips offers more than two thousand suggestions and hundreds of color photographs and illustrations. Mewling noted in another *Library Journal* review that the book "is like a video in print." Included are a seasonal diary gardeners can follow to perform necessary tasks and tips for saving money and time. Newling remarked that *Gardening Hints and Tips* is "most useful for gardeners just beyond the novice stage to browse for ideas."

Basic Gardening is one of the small books in Dorling Kindersley's "101 Essential Tips" series. The book's gardening tips cover selection, preparation, planting, watering, feeding, weeding, pruning, propagation, and protection. It also covers the care of container plants and lawns. Plant and weed varieties are identified, as well as types of fertilizer and disease.

The New Flower Gardener starts out with basic advice, such as the choosing of plants, feeding, watering, staking, and deadheading. It discusses beginning new plants with seed and by rooting and dividing. The book is filled with color photographs, which a *Publishers Weekly* reviewer called "traffic-stopping. . . . This hardworking book covers a lot of ground. . . . She sets an encouraging tone for those just getting their horticultural feet wet." Following the basics, Greenwood introduces her forty favorite flowers by shape. Categories include "Spikes & Spires" and "Trumpets & Bells." She profiles each plant, providing information on color, hardiness, mature size, time of flowering, site selection, watering, and soil type. The final section of the book lists flowers that attract butterflies and bees and those best for cutting. It suggests flowers and groundcovers most suitable to specific sites, such as shady areas. *Library Journal* reviewer Phillip Oliver observed that *The New Flower Gardener* "should motivate any novice gardener, and even advanced gardeners will love browsing through it." *Booklist* reviewer George Cohen called the book "engaging and helpful."

BIOGRAPHICAL AND CRITICAL SOURCES:

PERIODICALS

Booklist, October 15, 1993, p. 404; April 15, 1994, Alice Joyce, review of *The House Plant Clinic,* p. 1494; March 15, 1995, Alice Joyce, review of *The New Gardener,* p. 1297; October 15, 1996, George Cohen, review of *Gardening Hints and Tips,* p. 392; April 15, 1998, Mary Carroll, review of *Basic Gardening,* p. 1407; September 1, 1998, George Cohen, review of *The New Flower Gardener,* p. 46.

Books, March, 1993, p. 24.

Christian Science Monitor, March 23, 1995, p. 14.

Library Journal, April 1, 1995, Molly Newling, review of *The New Gardener,* p. 117; October 15, 1996, Molly Newling, review of *Gardening Tips and Hints,* p. 82; October 1, 1998, Philip Oliver, review of *The New Flower Gardener,* p. 125.

Publishers Weekly, July 20, 1998, review of *The New Flower Gardener,* p. 214.

Science Books & Films, April 1996, Brij M. Kapoor, review of *The New Gardener,* p. 76.*

*   *   *

GUR, Batya 1947-

PERSONAL: Born 1947, in Tel Aviv, Israel. *Education:* Hebrew University of Jerusalem, M.A.

ADDRESSES: Agent—c/o Author Mail, HarperCollins Publishers, 10 E. 53rd St., 7th Fl., New York, NY 10022.

CAREER: Writer and teacher.

WRITINGS:

MYSTERY NOVELS

Retsah beShabat baboker: roman balashi, Keter (Yerushalayim, Israel), 1988, translation by Dalya Bilu published as *The Saturday Morning Murder: A Psychoanalytic Case,* Aaron Asher (New York, NY), 1992.

Mavet bahug lesifrut: roman balashi, Keter (Yerushalayim, Israel), 1989, translation by Dalya Bilu published as *Literary Murder: A Critical Case,* HarperCollins (New York, NY), 1993.

Mikevish hara'av 'semolah: temunah kevutsatit 'im nashim, gevarim viyeladim be'ayarat pituah (title means "Next to Hunger Road"), Keter (Yerushalayim, Israel), 1990.

Linah meshutefet: retsah bakibuts: roman balashi, Keter (Yerushalayim, Israel), 1991, translation by Dalya Bilu published as *Murder on a Kibbutz: A Communal Case,* HarperCollins (New York, NY), 1994.

Lo kakh te 'arti li (title means "Afterbirth"), Keter (Yerushalayim, Israel), 1994.

haMerhak haNakhon: retsah musikali, Keter (Yerushalayim, Israel), 1996, translation published as *Murder Duet: A Musical Case,* HarperCollins (New York, NY), 1999.

Even tahat even (title means "Stone for a Stone"), Keter (Yerushalayim, Israel), 1998.

Meragel be-tokh ha-bayit (title means "Spy eithin the House"), Keter (Yerushalayim, Israel), 2000.

Retsah be-Derekh Bet Lehem (title means "Murder on Beth Lehem Road"), Keter (Yerushalayim, Israel), 2001.

SIDELIGHTS: Bestselling and critically lauded Israeli author Batya Gur is a literature teacher in Jerusalem. She is the author of what is considered the first mystery novel by an Israeli author to reach an American audience, *Saturday Morning Murder: A Psychoanalytic Case.* The novel introduces Gur's detective, Chief Inspector Michael Ohayon.

"With sly, affectionate humor and acute insight, this flawless mystery by an Israeli literature professor traces the parallel processes of police detection and psychoanalysis," wrote a *Publishers Weekly* critic. The novel revolves around the death of a senior analyst at the Jerusalem Psychoanalytic Institute. Marilyn Stasio, in the *New York Times Book Review,* called the work a "subtly provocative procedural mystery," arguing that "characters are examined in such depth and detail that the motive eventually uncovered for the murder makes perfect, if perfectly horrid, sense." A *Time* critic also lauded the work, and noted that Gur "sketches characters with deft, quick brushstrokes." A critic for *Publishers Weekly* concluded: "A complex, fully satisfying resolution wraps up this masterful American debut."

Gur's *Literary Murder: A Critical Case,* was similarly received by critics. The work follows now-Superintendent of Criminal Investigations Michael Ohayon as he investigates the deaths of two professors from the literature department of Hebrew University in Jerusalem who are both killed the same weekend. A *Publishers Weekly* critic described the work as a "complex mystery set in an unusual, well-developed milieu with a full cast of multidimensional characters" and called it "a literary pleasure." Susan Kenney offered a more mixed review of the novel in the *New York Times Book Review:* "Unfortunately for hardcore detective story readers, the answers . . . are all too obvious and the outcome predictable early on. However, for those who savor the scholarly questions and literary meditations that fill out the rest of this somewhat overlong narrative, it is well worth pressing on to the conclusion." Gail Pool in *Wilson Library Bulletin* called Ohayon "intelligent, cultured, handsome, tough but caring, and brilliant but modest. . . . [Batya] leads us capably through a thoroughly absorbing, exceptionally thought-provoking mystery."

Murder on a Kibbutz, originally published in Hebrew in 1991 and published in English translation in 1994, again features Ohayon, who now finds himself promoted to the head of the Serious Crimes Unit in Jerusalem. The novel explores the institution of the kibbutz after Ohayon becomes embroiled in a case involving the death of a beautiful kibbutz secretary named Osnat Harel. The work "yields a fascinating account of the ways in which this quintessential Israeli institution has changed, and in some ways failed to change," wrote a critic for *Publishers Weekly.* The critic faulted the work for an overabundance of subplots, but found that toward the end "the pace picks up nicely, and the resolution has a powerful inevitability." Ilene Cooper in *Booklist* called the work "a compelling mix of character study and social history," concluding: "A superb, multidimensional novel, the best in an outstanding series."

Gur's 1996 novel, published in English translation in 1999 as *Murder Duet: A Musical Case,* involves the possible discovery of a previously unknown Vivaldi requiem and the murder of cellist Nita van Gelden's father. Chief Superintendent Ohayon, now divorced, is torn between his affection for Nita and his duty to impartially investigate the murder. The novel explores in detail the lives of classical musicians and music history. A critic for *Publishers Weekly* wrote that, though "Gur constructs her plot carefully, the novel is most memorable for its abundant digressions on music history and musical life." Marilyn Stasio in the *New York Times Book Review* added that "for pure reading pleasure, nothing touches the smart discussions on music and art (which flow like dinner conversation in Dalya Bilu's translation from the Hebrew), along with the intimate scenes of musicians at serious work and at murderous play." Bill Ott in *Booklist* concluded: "From the foreboding opening notes of Brahms' First Symphony, which Ohayon plays in the novel's first scene, through Nita's brother's discussion of the classical style, the 'music-saturated air' informs the novel's substance as powerfully as it does its atmosphere. A virtuoso performance."

BIOGRAPHICAL AND CRITICAL SOURCES:

PERIODICALS

Booklist, November 15, 1994, Ilene Cooper, review of *Murder on a Kibbutz,* p. 581; September 15, 1999, Bill Ott, review of *Murder Duet,* p. 236.

New York Times Book Review, June 21, 1992, Marilyn Stasio, review of *The Saturday Morning Murder,* p. 21; December 26, 1993, Susan Kenney, "Death Comes to the Professor"; November 21, 1999, Marilyn Stasio, review of *Murder Duet,* p. 80.

Publishers Weekly, April 13, 1992, review of *The Saturday Morning Murder,* p. 45; October 11, 1993, review of *Literary Murder,* p. 72; October 17, 1994, review of *Murder on a Kibbutz,* p. 66; November 1, 1999, review of *Murder Duet,* p. 76.

Time, August 3, 1992, review of *The Saturday Morning Murder,* p. 75.

Wilson Library Bulletin, January, 1994, Gail Pool, review of *Literary Murder,* p. 107.*

H

HADFIELD, Vic(tor Edward) 1940-

PERSONAL: Born October 4, 1940, in Oakville, Ontario, Canada.

ADDRESSES: Office—c/o New York Rangers, Madison Square Garden, 4 Pennsylvania Plaza, New York, NY 10001.

CAREER: New York Rangers, New York, NY, professional hockey player, beginning 1961.

WRITINGS:

(With Tim Moriarty) *Vic Hadfield's Diary: From Moscow to the Play-Offs,* Doubleday (Garden City, NY), 1974.*

*   *   *

HADLICH, Roger L(ee) 1930-

PERSONAL: Born January 10, 1930, in St. Paul, MN. *Education:* Yale University, B.A., 1951 Middlebury College, M.A., 1957; University of Michigan, Ph.D., 1961.

ADDRESSES: Office—c/o Department of European Languages and Literature, University of Hawaii at Manoa, Honolulu, HI 96822.

CAREER: University of Hawaii at Manoa, Honolulu, faculty member, beginning 1965, professor of Spanish, beginning 1969. Also taught at University of Michigan, Cornell University, and University of Rome.

WRITINGS:

(With David L. Wolfe) *A Structural Course in Spanish,* Macmillan (New York, NY), 1963.
The Phonological History of Vegliote, University of North Carolina Press (Chapel Hill, NC), 1965.
(With James S. Holton and Matias Montes) *A Drillbook of Spanish Pronunciation,* Harper (New York, NY), 1968.
A Transformational Grammar of Spanish, Prentice-Hall (Englewood Cliffs, NJ), 1971.
(With James S. Holton and Norhma Gomez-Estrada) *A Spanish Review Grammar: Theory and Practice,* Prentice-Hall, 1977, 3rd edition published as *Spanish Grammar in Review: Theory and Practice,* 2001.
(Editor, with J. D. Ellsworth) *East Meets West: Homage to Edgar C. Knowlton, Jr.,* Department of European Languages and Literature, University of Hawaii at Manoa (Honolulu, HI), 1988.

BIOGRAPHICAL AND CRITICAL SOURCES:

PERIODICALS

Modern Language Journal, April, 1972.*

HAHNEL, Robin (Eric) 1946-

PERSONAL: Born March 25, 1946, in St. Louis, MO; son of Eugene and Jean Hahnel; married Ivy Leichman (divorced, 1996); children: Jesse, Ilana, Sara, Tanya, Dylan Feldpausch. *Ethnicity:* "White." *Education:* Harvard University, B.A., 1968; American University, Ph.D., 1979. *Politics:* "Radical." *Religion:* Atheist.

ADDRESSES: Home—8802 Manchester Rd., No. 7, Silver Spring, MD 20901. *Office*—Department of Economics, American University, Washington, DC 20016; fax: 202-885-3790. *E-mail*—rhahnel@american.edu.

CAREER: Catholic University of Panama, Panama City, instructor in mathematics, 1968-69; University of Maryland at College Park, instructor in economics, 1974-76; American University, Washington, DC, instructor, 1976-79, assistant professor, 1979-83, associate professor, 1983-90, professor of economics, 1991—. Pontificia Universidad Catolica, Lima, Peru, Fulbright senior lecturer, 1986; Universidad Ricardo Palma, Fulbright senior lecturer, 1986; Universidad de Habana, senior visiting economist, 1991; lecturer at colleges and universities, including University of California—Riverside, 1995 and 1999, Columbia University, 1996, University of Massachusetts at Amherst, 1997, and Howard University and Evergreen State University, both 1999. Econometric Research, Inc., senior economist, 1981-82; Banco Central de Reserva, Lima, senior visiting economist, 1986; Junta Central de Planificacion, Havana, Cuba, senior visiting economist, 1991; Institute for Economic Democracy, director.

MEMBER: Union of Radical Political Economics.

WRITINGS:

(With Michael Albert) *Unorthodox Marxism,* South End Press (Cambridge, MA), 1979.
(With Michael Albert) *Marxism and Socialist Theory,* South End Press (Cambridge, MA), 1981.
(With Michael Albert) *Socialism Today and Tomorrow,* South End Press (Cambridge, MA), 1981.

(With Michael Albert, Leslie Cagan, Noam Chomsky, and others) *Liberating Theory,* South End Press (Cambridge, MA), 1986.
(With Michael Albert) *Quiet Revolution in Welfare Economics,* Princeton University Press (Princeton, NJ), 1990.
(With Michael Albert) *The Political Economy of Participatory Economics,* Princeton University Press (Princeton, NJ), 1991.
(With Michael Albert) *Looking Forward: Participatory Economics for the Twenty-first Century,* South End Press (Cambridge, MA), 1991.
Panic Rules! Everything You Need to Know about the Global Economy, South End Press (Cambridge, MA), 1999.
The ABCs of Political Economy: A Modern Approach, Pluto Press (London, England), 2002.

Contributor to books, including *Between Labor and Capital,* South End Press (Cambridge, MA), 1979; *Socialist Visions,* South End Press (Cambridge, MA), 1983; *Human Well-Being and Economic Goals,* Island Press (Washington, DC), 1997; *Crossing the Mainstream: Ethical and Methodological Issues in Economics,* University of Notre Dame Press (Notre Dame, IN), 2000; *Essays in Political Economy,* Edward Elgar (Northampton, MA), 2000. Contributor of articles and reviews to periodicals, including *Socialist Review, Science and Society, Review of Radical Political Economics, Left Green Notes, Cambridge Journal of Economics,* and *Journal of Economic Issues.* The book *Looking Forward* was published in Turkish.

WORK IN PROGRESS: "Edward Bellamy and the Twenty-first Century," to be included in *Edward Bellamy: Yesterday, Today, Tomorrow,* edited by Toby Widdicombe, publication by Edwin Mellen (Lewiston, NY).

SIDELIGHTS: Robin Hahnel told *CA:* "I became convinced the United States war against Vietnam was wrong during my freshman year at Harvard in 1965. As a participant in the anti-war movement I came to understand over the course of the next few years that, as long as the United States economy operated on the basis of competition and greed, United States foreign and military policy would be prone to serve the interests of United States business abroad to the detriment of the majority of United States citizens—not to speak of the majority of citizens in countries where the United States intervened. Ever since then I have been studying, writing, and teaching about the unfortunate consequences of organizing our economic endeavors through a commercial system where businesses are driven to compete for profits even when that proves detrimental to human and environmental well-being, and about how we could better coordinate our economic activities through a system of equitable cooperation.

"The most recent reaction to the economics of competition and greed began as an international intellectual movement against neoliberalism, and it has recently blossomed into a popular movement opposed to corporate-sponsored globalization. What has been aptly dubbed 'the Washington consensus,' centered in the United States Treasury and the International Monetary Fund, began to lose credibility during the East Asian crisis of 1997 and 1998 and is now widely questioned even inside the United States in the aftermath of the 'Battle of Seattle.' My most recent book, *Panic Rules! Everything You Need to Know about the Global Economy* began as a series of articles for *Z* magazine in 1998, where I tried to explain to a concerned audience of non-economists the origins of the East Asian crisis in neoliberal 'reforms' and punish-the-victim policies of the International Monetary Fund. The book went on to evaluate various 'new international economic architecture' reforms and to discuss strategy for the growing international movement against corporate-sponsored globalization."

BIOGRAPHICAL AND CRITICAL SOURCES:

PERIODICALS

Choice, January, 2000, M. Veeth, review of *Panic Rules! Everything You Need to Know about the Global Economy,* p. 983.*

*   *   *

HALL, Florence (Marion) Howe 1845-1922

PERSONAL: Born August 25, 1845, in Boston, MA; died April 10, 1922, in High Bridge, NJ; daughter of Samuel Gridley (a philanthropist) and Julia Ward (an author who wrote "The Battle Hymn of the Republic") Howe; married David Prescott Hall (an attorney),

November 15, 1871 (died 1907); children: Samuel P., Caroline M., Henry M., John H. *Education:* Attended private schools in Boston, MA; studied music with Otto Dresel in Boston, MA.

CAREER: Writer and lecturer. Woman Suffrage Party, leader of 12th Assembly District, New York, NY, 1914-16. Lecturer.

MEMBER: Daughters of the American Revolution (regent of Continental Chapter, 1902-04, 1905-10; honorary vice president, 1914), General Federation of Women's Clubs (first chairman of correspondence for New Jersey), New Jersey State Federation of Women's Clubs (vice president, 1911-13), New Jersey Woman Suffrage Association (president, 1893-1900; honorary president), Plainfield Alliance of Unitarian Women (president, 1903-04, 1905-10), Monday Afternoon Club (president), Women's Republican Club (president of Newport County, RI, chapter).

AWARDS, HONORS: Pulitzer Prize (with sisters Laura E. Richards and Maude Howe Elliott), 1917, for *Julia Ward Howe, 1819-1910.*

WRITINGS:

Social Customs, Estes (Boston, MA), 1887.
The Correct Thing in Good Society, Estes (Boston, MA), 1888, revised edition, 1902.
Little Lads and Lassies: Stories in Prose and Verse about and for Them, Lothrop (Boston, MA), 1898.
(With sister, Maud Howe Elliott) *Laura Bridgman, Dr. Howe's Famous Pupil and What He Taught Her,* Little, Brown, 1903.
Flossy's Play-Days, Estes (Boston, MA), 1906.
Social Usages at Washington, Harper (New York, NY), 1906.
A Handbook of Hospitality for Town and Country, Estes (Boston, MA), 1909.
Boys, Girls, and Manners, Estes (Boston, MA), 1913.
(Editor and author of introduction) Laura E. Richards and Maude Howe Elliott, *Julia Ward Howe and the Woman Suffrage Movement: A Selection from Her Speeches and Essays,* Estes (Boston, MA), 1913, reprinted, Arno (New York, NY), 1969.
Good Form for All Occasions: A Manual of Manners, Dress, and Entertainment for Both Men and Women, Harper (New York, NY), 1914.

(With Laura E. Richards and Maude Howe Elliot) *Julia Ward Howe, 1819-1910,* Houghton (New York, NY), 1915, reprinted, Cherokee Publishing (Atlanta, GA), 1990.

ABC of Correct Speech and the Art of Conversation, Harper (New York, NY), 1916.

The Story of "The Battle Hymn of the Republic," Harper (New York, NY), 1916, reprinted, Books for Libraries Press (Freeport, NY), 1971.

Memories Grave and Gay (autobiography), Harper (New York, NY), 1918.

Manners for Boys and Girls, Page Company (Boston, MA), 1920.

SIDELIGHTS: As a child of a well-known philanthropist and a prominent author, Florence Howe Hall was greatly influenced by her parents' prestige. In addition to her success as a writer, she was also known for her work for the public good. She was active in many clubs and involved in the women's suffrage movement. Hall married in 1871, but when her husband's legal practice could not provide the family financial security, she decided to find work. She started lecturing and writing for magazines and gradually began writing books. Her career as a writer of children's stories was short lived, however, because her books failed to sell well. Having grown up surrounded by wealthy and prominent people, Hall decided to concentrate her writings in two genres with which she was familiar—etiquette books and memoirs of the famous people she knew, including her parents.

Using her expertise gained from growing up in high society, Hall wrote a series of popular etiquette books. To distinguish her work from other etiquette books, she took a different direction and covered a broad range of issues, taking a tongue-in-cheek approach by dispensing advice using humor and wit. Her success established her place in this genre. Hall continued to write a number of books about manners, including *The Correct Thing in Good Society, Boys, Girls, and Manners,* and *Good Form for All Occasions: A Manual of Manners, Dress, and Entertainment for Both Men and Women.* Despite the popularity of her etiquette books, her advice was only pertinent to those in the upper-middle class and sometimes impractical for ethnic groups or the working-class.

Hall also wrote numerous books about her family and their connections. For example, she edited a biography of her mother written by her sisters, Laura E. Richards

and Maude Howe Elliott. The result, *Julia Ward Howe, 1819-1910,* won a Pulitzer Prize in 1917. Another biography, which she wrote with her sister Maude, *Laura Bridgman, Howe's Most Famous Pupil and What He Taught He,* is about their father's blind, deaf, and mute pupil. Although Hall and her sisters provided some background information as well as personal anecdotes, for the most part, both biographies contain extensive quotes from family letters and diaries. Hall also produced a book on her mother's famous poem, *The Story of "The Battle Hymn of the Republic,"* and on the role her mother played in the suffrage movement, *Julia Ward Howe and the Woman Suffrage Movement: A Selection from Her Speeches and Essays.*

In 1918 Hall published her autobiography, *Memories Grave and Gay.* Unlike her biographical novels, Hall took a direct approach and avoided quoting letters and diaries in this popular book. As an essayist for *American Women Writers* commented, "Her simple, direct, and anecdotal style of writing, combined with glimpses into her own personal and professional life, explain the wide appeal of this book of reminiscences."

BIOGRAPHICAL AND CRITICAL SOURCES:

BOOKS

American Women Writers, Volume 2, Ungar, 1982, pp. 218-220.

PERIODICALS

Boston Transcript, November 15, 1916, review of *The Story of "The Battle Hymn of the Republic,"* p. 8; December 24, 1918, review of *Memories Grave and Gay,* p. 9.

New York Times, November 13, 1909; December 4, 1909; September 6, 1914.*

*   *   *

HALTERMAN, H. Lee 1935-

PERSONAL: Born 1935.

ADDRESSES: Home—San Francisco, CA. *Office*—1736 Franklin Street, Suite 500, Oakland, CA 94612. *Agent*—Akin & Randolph Agency, 156 West 56th St., New York, NY, 10019.

CAREER: Lawyer. House of Representatives, director of policy for Armed Services Committee; advisor to former Congressman Ronald V. Dellums.

WRITINGS:

(With Ronald V. Dellums and R. H. Miller) *Defense Sense: The Search for a Rational Military Policy,* Ballinger (Cambridge, MA), 1983.
(With Ronald V. Dellums) *Lying down with the Lions: Public Life from the Streets of Oakland to the Halls of Power,* Beacon (Boston, MA), 2000.

SIDELIGHTS: H. Lee Halterman is a lawyer who served as former Congressman Robert V. Dellums' political advisor. Halterman's first book, written with Dellums and R. H. Miller, focuses on the need for changing the focus of U.S. military spending. *Defense Sense: The Search for a Rational Military Policy* contains a collection of witnesses' testimony from Dellums' congressional hearings on the implications of the military budget. The authors question the motives behind commerce involving weapons, both domestically and globally, as well as the moral implications of changing military values. In a review for *Library Journal,* Robert L. Beckman called the book "a humane and searching analysis of the U.S. defense budget."

Halterman's second book, *Lying down with the Lions: Public Life from the Streets of Oakland to the Halls of Power,* is a memoir of Dellums' political career. The book, written with Dellums, details more than thirty years of his career in public service starting with his work in Oakland, California as a social worker. *Lying down with the Lions,* called "engaging and informative" by Karl Helicher of *Library Journal,* focuses on Dellums' congressional career and highlights his most prominent successes.

BIOGRAPHICAL AND CRITICAL SOURCES:

PERIODICALS

American Prospect, April 24, 2000, Alexander Nouyen, review of *Lying down with the Lions,* p. 54.
Booklist, December 15, 1999, Vernon Ford, review of *Lying down with the Lions,* p. 741.

Choice, July-August, 2000, M. J. Birkner, review of *Lying down with the Lions,* p. 2037.
Emerge, March, 2000, David Dante Troutt, review of *Lying down with the Lions,* p. 60.
Library Journal, January, 1984, review of *Defense Sense,* p. 97; November 1, 1999, Ann Burns and Emily Jones, review of *Lying down with the Lions,* p. 107; November 15, 1999, Karl Helicher, review of *Lying down with the Lions,* p. 83.
Publishers Weekly, January 17, 2000, review of *Lying down with the Lions,* p. 52.*

*   *   *

HAMILTON, Lyn

PERSONAL: Born in Toronto, Ontario, Canada. *Education:* Attended University of Toronto.

ADDRESSES: *Home*—Toronto, Ontario, Canada. *Agent*—c/o Author Mail, Penguin Putnam, 375 Hudson St., New York, NY 10014.

CAREER: Novelist. Canadian Opera Company, director of public affairs. Government of Ontario, director of arts and cultural industries programs.

WRITINGS:

The Xibalba Murders, Berkley (New York, NY), 1997.
The Maltese Goddess, Berkley (New York, NY), 1998.
The Moche Warrior: An Archaeological Mystery, Berkley Prime Crime (New York, NY), 1999.
The Celtic Riddle, Berkley Prime Crime (New York, NY), 2000.
The African Quest, Berkley Prime Crime (New York, NY), 2001.
The Etruscan Chimera, Berkley Prime Crime (New York, NY), 2002.
The Thai Amulet, Berkley Prime Crime (New York, NY), 2003.

SIDELIGHTS: Lyn Hamilton, director of public affairs for the Canadian Opera Company, writes archeological mysteries in her spare time. Her debut, *The Xibalba Murders,* was nominated for a best birst novel prize by the Crime Writers of Canada Association. Her 1998 follow-up, *The Maltese Goddess,* again features Toronto antiques dealer, Lara McClintoch. A decorating job for an architect client takes McClintoch to the Mediterranean isle of Malta, but it soon appears that her life is in peril; next, the arrival of the furniture brings with it an unpleasant surprise. "Several twists at the end add emotional depth," noted a *Publishers Weekly* reviewer, who also praised Hamilton's evocation of the island.

In *The Moche Warrior: An Archaeological Mystery,* McClintoch finds herself in trouble when she unwittingly acquires a box of priceless Moche figurines at auction, which had at first appeared to be Peruvian reproductions. She flees to Peru and attempts to solve the mystery by matching wits with a gang of graverobbers there. A *Maclean's* reviewer called it "a fun read," and praised Hamilton's heroine as "an amusing, likable creation." A *Booklist* critic commented favorably on Hamilton's ability to write convincingly about archeological matters, and "the richly woven descriptions of Lima make it obvious that the author has spent time there."

Hamilton is an avid traveler who draws upon her own experiences for her plots. Her next work, *The Celtic Riddle,* sends McClintoch off to remote coastal Ireland with her friend and co-worker Alex, one of several heirs summoned to participate in a treasure hunt for the bequest, whose value, the will hints, is enormous. The two are thwarted by the surviving family members who reveal themselves to be a dysfunctional but determined lot, apparently spurred on in the treasure hunt by clues from ancient Celtic mythology. Only cooperation between the guests can find the fortune, hidden somewhere in the county Kerry countryside. The sudden deaths of household servants complicate the plot further. A *Publishers Weekly* reviewer called *The Celtic Riddle* "a sparkling classical puzzle mystery" that "will please both puzzle enthusiasts and those who demand a logical but totally surprising solution to a crime." Wes Lukowsky, writing in *Booklist,* called the novel "funny, cleverly plotted, and rich in ancient Celtic lore."

In *The Etruscan Chimera,* Lara goes to Tuscany to find a 2,500-year-old sculpture, the Etruscan Chimera, for a billionaire. While in Tuscany, she contacts a local antique collector, who refuses to sell any of his pieces, the Chimera being one of them. The next day, the collector is found dead and the sculpture mysteriously appears in the trunk of Lara's car. *Booklist* reviewer Connie Fletcher called *The Etruscan Chimera* an "engaging, intelligent romp," while a *Publishers Weekly* reviewer wrote that "erudite mystery fans will enjoy the sophisticated wit."

BIOGRAPHICAL AND CRITICAL SOURCES:

PERIODICALS

Booklist, February 1, 1999, Jenny McLarin and Jack Helbig, review of *The Moche Warrior,* p. 964; January 1, 2000, Wes Lukowsky, review of *The Celtic Riddle,* p. 884; May 15, 2002, Connie Fletcher, review of *The Etruscan Chimera,* p. 1578.

Kirkus Reviews, April 1, 2002, review of *The Etruscan Chimera,* p. 457.

Library Journal, March 1, 1999, Rex E. Klett, review of *The Moche Warrior,* p. 113; February 1, 2000, Rex E. Klett, review of *The Celtic Riddle,* p. 120.

Maclean's, May 3, 1999, review of *The Moche Warrior,* p. 63.

New York Times Book Review, June 9, 2002, Marilyn Stasio, review of *The Etruscan Chimera,* p. 18.

Publishers Weekly, February 2, 1998, review of *The Maltese Goddess,* p. 87; January 24, 2000, review of *The Celtic Riddle,* p. 295; April 29, 2002, review of *The Etruscan Chimera,* p. 46.*

* * *

HAMMER, Joshua 1957-

PERSONAL: Born 1957. *Education:* Princeton University, B.A., 1979.

ADDRESSES: Office—c/o *Newsweek,* 251 West 57th St., New York, NY 10019.

CAREER: People magazine, staff writer; *Manhattan, Inc.,* contributing editor, 1985-86; *Newsweek,* general editor in New York, NY, 1988-93, bureau chief in Nairobi, Kenya, 1993-97, bureau chief in Buenos Aires, Argentina, January-November, 1997, bureau chief in Los Angeles, CA, 1997-99, bureau chief in Berlin, Germany, 1999-2000, bureau chief in Jerusalem, 2000—.

AWARDS, HONORS: Chosen by God was named a 1999 *Los Angeles Times* Book Award finalist.

WRITINGS:

(With Rosemary Breslin) *Gerry!: A Woman Making History* (biography of Geraldine Ferraro), Pinnacle Books (New York, NY), 1984.
Chosen by God: A Brother's Journey (memoir), Hyperion (New York, NY), 1999.

Contributor of articles to magazines including *Newsweek, Washington Monthly, Harper's, Seattle Times, New York Times Magazine, Esquire,* and others.

SIDELIGHTS: After his graduation from Princeton University in 1979 with a degree in English, Joshua Hammer traveled throughout southeast Asia, Africa, and South America, learning to speak Japanese, French, and Spanish. To help finance his travels and yearnings to experience cultures other than his own, Hammer honed his skills as a freelance writer, contributing stories to magazines such as *Esquire, Nation, GQ, Premiere, New York Times Magazine,* and *Los Angeles Times Magazine.* He also worked as an English teacher and film critic in Japan.

Eventually Hammer settled down in New York City and, following in his father's footsteps, became a correspondent for the *New York Times,* as well as taking a job as a staff writer for *People* magazine. In 1988, Hammer obtained his first post at *Newsweek* magazine, where he began as a general editor for the business section. Five years later, Hammer, now a foreign correspondent for *Newsweek,* was appointed bureau chief in Nairobi, Kenya, becoming one of the magazine's key correspondents.

Hammer was transferred to South America in 1997, where he became *Newsweek's* bureau chief in Buenos Aires. After a brief stint as the magazine's bureau chief in Los Angeles in 1998, Hammer was again transferred to Europe in 1999, this time as bureau chief in Berlin, Germany. The following year, Hammer covered the upheaval in Kosovo, and in the winter of 2000, he became *Newsweek's* bureau chief in Jerusalem, where he began reported on the conflict between Israel and the Palestinians.

In the midst of all his reportage from around the world, Hammer published a 1999 memoir, *Chosen by God: A Brother's Journey.* The book, a finalist for the *Los Angeles Times* Book Award, explores Hammer's relationship with his younger brother, Tony, from whom Hammer had been estranged. In an excerpt from the book which was published in *Newsweek,* Hammer explained that he had decided to return to the United States in late 1997 after several years overseas, with the idea of "re-establishing contact with [my brother]." The two had maintained only minimal contact over the past twenty years. The break came, wrote Hammer, "shortly after Tony turned 21, when my brother seemed to shed his personality like an old skin." It was at this time that Hammer's brother "decided to devote his life to God . . . identifying himself with the ultra-Orthodox fringe of Judaism." At this point the two brothers' lives became, in Hammer's words, "something like mirror opposites." His brother eventually married, had six children and "rarely strayed from his community." Hammer continued: "As I reported on bodies piled high in Rwandan churches, child-killers in Liberia, paramilitary death squads in Colombia, the very idea of God seemed like an indulgence." It was this wide disparity between the brothers' lives that eventually drew Hammer in, as he became "intrigued" by the thought of the search for "common psychological denominators that seemed to underpin our divergent lives."

A *Kirkus Reviews* critic described *Chosen by God* as "a deeply affecting family memoir about the author's brother, who, within a matter of months, changed from a kind of hippie lost soul in Jerusalem to a *baal teshuva* (literally, 'master of repentance')—a newly pious Jew." Gilbert Taylor in *Booklist* wrote, "A memoir with understated emotional impact, Hammer's story potently explores the universals of sibling rivalry and religious commitment." Paul M. Kaplan, writing for *Library Journal,* referred to *Chosen by God* as "an insightful look at modern orthodox Jewish life from the inside." And a reviewer for *Publishers Weekly* felt that "[Hammer's] journalistic experience is evidenced by a well-written, accessible account and easy-to-read prose."

BIOGRAPHICAL AND CRITICAL SOURCES:

PERIODICALS

Booklist, November 1, 1999, Gilbert Taylor, review of *Chosen by God,* p. 505.

Commentary, May, 2000, Wendy Shalit, review of *Chosen by God,* p. 62.

Kirkus Reviews, October 1, 1999, review of *Chosen by God,* p. 1544.

Library Journal, November 15, 1999, Paul M. Kaplan, review of *Chosen by God* p. 74.

Los Angeles Times, April 1, 2000, Jonathan Kirsch, review of *Chosen by God,* p. A18.

Newsweek, November 8, 1999, Joshua Hammer, "A Tale of Two Brothers."

Publishers Weekly, November 15, 1999, review of *Chosen by God,* p. 74.

OTHER

Newsweek Web site, http://www.newsweek.com/ (June 17, 2001), "Newsweek Reporter Detained by Palestinians."*

*   *   *

HARPER, T(imothy) N(orman) 1965-

PERSONAL: Born 1965. *Education:* M.A. and Ph.D.

ADDRESSES: Agent—c/o Author Mail, Cambridge University Press, 40 West 20th St., New York, NY 10011.

CAREER: Cambridge University, Cambridge, England, fellow of Magdalene College, beginning 1990, director of studies in history, 1993—. Institute of Southeast Asian Studies, Singapore, associate.

WRITINGS:

The End of Empire and the Making of Malaya, Cambridge University Press (New York, NY), 1998.

BIOGRAPHICAL AND CRITICAL SOURCES:

PERIODICALS

Asian Affairs, February, 2000, J. M. Gullick, review of *The End of Empire and the Making of Malaya,* p. 96.

Economic History Review, November, 2000, Ian Brown, review of *The End of Empire and the Making of Malaya,* p. 846.

English Historical Review, June, 2000, Matthew Jones, review of *The End of Empire and the Making of Malaya,* p. 775.

Ethnic and Racial Studies, March, 2001, Steve Fenton, review of *The End of Empire and the Making of Malaya,* p. 338.

Historical Journal, September, 2000, D. K. Field-house, review of *The End of Empire and the Making of Malaya,* p. 912.

International History Review, June, 2001, Albert Lau, review of *The End of Empire and the Making of Malaya,* p. 477.

Journal of Asian Studies, May, 2001, Loh Wei Leng, review of *The End of Empire and the Making of Malaya,* p. 610.

Journal of Southeast Asian Studies, June, 2001, Cheah Boon Kheng, review of *The End of Empire and the Making of Malaya,* p. 279.

Times Literary Supplement, October 29, 1999, John Gullick, review of *The End of Empire and the Making of Malaya.**

*   *   *

HARRIS, David A. 1957-

PERSONAL: Born 1957. *Education:* Northwestern University, B.A.; Yale University Law School, LL.B., 1983; Georgetown University, LL.M..

ADDRESSES: Office—College of Law, University of Toledo, Toledo, OH 43606. *E-mail*—dharris@uoft.utoledo.edu.

CAREER: Balk Professor of Law and Values, University of Toledo College of Law, Toledo, OH, 1990—.

MEMBER: Civil Liberties Advisory Board to the White House Commission on Aviation Safety and Security.

AWARDS, HONORS: Soros senior justice fellow.

WRITINGS:

Profiles in Injustice: Why Racial Profiling Cannot Work, New Press (New York, NY), 2002.

Contributor to numerous scholarly and legal journals, including *Journal of Constitutional Law, Michigan Journal of Race & Law, Minnesota Law Review, George Washington Law Review, Journal of Criminal Law & Criminology, Temple Law Review,* and *Indiana at Bloomington Law Journal.*

SIDELIGHTS: David A. Harris is a law professor at the University of Toledo and a Soros senior justice fellow who has written widely on racial profiling, stop and frisk, and other Fourth Amendment issues. In *Profiles in Injustice: Why Racial Profiling Cannot Work,* he describes what racial profiling is, what tactics are commonly used, and the costs of such profiling in dollars, casualties, relations with police, and wasted police time. As he shows, the impact is not just on African Americans ("driving while black"); Latinos are targeted as criminals and/or illegal immigrants, Asian-Americans as gang members, Arab-Americans as terrorists, and so on. Harris argues that statistical evidence shows profiling to be ineffective and recommends many useful alternatives, among them establishing appropriate policies in police departments, incentives, training, and collecting data to analyze trends.

Harris's early work on racial profiling became the basis for the Traffic Stops Statistics Act of 1997, the first legislative proposal at any level of government to take on the problem of racial profiling. Sponsored by Representative John Conyers of Michigan, the act quickly became the national model for antiprofiling legislation; thirteen other states have since passed laws based on the original Conyers bill. Hundreds of police departments around the country have begun efforts to collect data on traffic stops and set new policies. Harris also helped members of Congress draft the proposed federal End Racial Profiling Act of 2001.

In *Profiles in Injustice,* Harris cites statistics challenging the efficacy of racial profiling despite its widespread use. He examines the moral, ethical, and constitutional issues surrounding racial profiling and offers true accounts of minorities, including a black military officer and a Hispanic judge, who have been victimized. Finally, he examines the social costs of racial profiling and efforts by law enforcement agencies to eliminate the practice, even as profiling gained new notoriety in the wake of the terrorist attack on America of September 11, 2001, and increased scrutiny of people of Arab heritage.

"Not many people, of course, are willing to defend racial profiling as a stand-alone good," wrote a *Kirkus Reviews* contributor, "but the constant refrain from the practice's supporters, especially those in law enforcement, has been that it's necessary because racial minorities commit more crimes than other members of society. Harris convincingly explains what is known as the lamppost phenomenon: If law enforcement agencies look for violations amid a particular group, they are bound to find them at higher rates." A reviewer for *Publishers Weekly* praised the book as an important argument in safeguarding civil liberties, and noted, "He analyzes how each [type of police intervention], aside from often not passing basic legal or ethical standards, nearly always fails to discover criminals or deter crime. These conclusions are supplemented by his often surprising analysis of arrest statistics. . . . This book lays some of the groundwork for post-September 11 books on profiling that are sure to come, and is rock solid on specifics that remain disturbing."

BIOGRAPHICAL AND CRITICAL SOURCES:

PERIODICALS

Booklist, January 1, 2002, Vanessa Bush, review of *Profiles in Injustice: Why Racial Profiling Cannot Work,* p. 783.
Kirkus Reviews, December 15, 2001, review of *Profiles in Injustice,* p. 737.
Los Angeles Times, May 5, 2000, p. A18.
Publishers Weekly, November 26, 2001, review of *Profiles in Injustice,* p. 47.
St. John's Law Review, summer, 1998, Daniel C. Richman, "Terry v. Ohio in the Trenches" p. 911.*

*   *   *

HASKINS, Lola 1943-

PERSONAL: Born 1943. *Education:* Stanford University, B.A. (social thought; summa cum laude), 1965.

ADDRESSES: Office—P.O. Box 18, LaCrosse, FL 32658-0018. *E-mail*—lola@cise.ufl.edu

CAREER: University of Florida, lecturer in computer and information sciences, 1979—; North Shore Young Writers' Conference, member of faculty, 1993-96;

Florida Humanities Council, lecturer, 1994; Suncoast Writer's Conference, member of faculty faculty, 1997; Writer's Conference, Charleston, SC, member of faculty, 1998; writer-in-residence, The Writer's Voice, Tampa, FL, 2000. Annual Convention of Federation of State Poetry Societies, Melbourne, FL, featured speaker, 2001.

MEMBER: Poets and Writers (NY), Phi Beta Kappa, Creative Arts Committee, Poetry Society of America.

AWARDS, HONORS: Florida Division of Cultural Affairs, fellowships in literature, 1979, 1981, 1990; *Southern Poetry Review* prize for narrative poetry, 1981, for "Changing the Speed Limit,"; National Endowment for the Arts fellowship in literature, 1984; First Lectureship in Historical Poetry, Library Company of Philadelphia, 1986; *New York Quarterly,* Madeline Sadin Award, 1987, for "The Man Who Worked with Fellini,"; *New England Review,* prize in narrative poetry, 1989, for "Six Cairns for Mary,"; Edwin Ford Piper Award, 1992, and Iowa Poetry Prize, 1993, both for *Hunger,. Writer/*Emily Dickinson Award for poetry, 1995, for "Tuning,"; Teaching Improvement Program Award, 1997; MacDowell Colony, fellow, 1998.

WRITINGS:

Planting the Children, University Press of Florida (Orlando, FL), 1983.
Castings, Countryman Press (Woodstock, VT), 1984.
Across Her Broad Lap Something Wonderful, Betony Press (Woodstock, VT), 1989.
Forty-four Ambitions for the Piano, University Press of Florida (Orlando, FL), 1990.
Hunger, University of Iowa Press (Iowa City, IO), 1993.
(With Woody Walters) *Visions of Florida,* University Press of Florida (Orlando, FL), 1994.
Extranjera, Story Line Press (Brownsville, OR), 1998.
Desire Lines, New and Selected Poems, Story Line Press (Ashland, OR), 2001.
The Rim-Benders, Anhinga Press (Tallahassee, FL), 2001.

WORK IN PROGRESS: Working on a book of environmental essays, a children's story, and a book of advice for young poets.

SIDELIGHTS: Lola Haskins has published seven collections of poetry, and she has done most of this while employed as a professor of computer and information sciences. Many critics have proclaimed her a multi-faceted poet.

Although Haskins explained in an interview for the online *3rd Muse Poetry Journal,* that she has loved poetry all her life, she admitted that she didn't think about writing until she went to Greece when she was twenty-three years old. "When I saw the landscape, it swept over me. Now, I see, I thought. And I started writing."

Her publishing career began with the collection, *Planting the Children* (1983). The overall theme of the poems in this collection is change, such as the transitions that occur in marriage, in moving from one country to another, in giving birth to children and watching them grow, and in witnessing the death of loved ones. In his *Hudson Review* article about Haskin's first collection, James Finn Cotter wrote that in "her fine first volume of verse," Haskins reminds her readers that "our journeys take us no further than ourselves."

In 1990, Haskins produced another collection, *Forty-four Ambitions for the Piano,* reflecting her own interest, as well as that of one of her children, in music. Some of Haskins's poems play with specific musical terms as she uses metaphorical images to give her readers an almost cinematic explanation of how a musician might understand certain ways of playing musical passages. For instance, in one poem she describes the term *pianissimo,* which indicates that the music should be played softly. Haskins compares this to laying a shawl around the shoulders of an old woman.

Other poems in this collection use musical motifs to explore psychological insights. Like a musical virtuoso skillfully beginning a recital in very quite tones, Paul Cooper, writing for *American Music Teacher,* stated that "Haskins commands our immediate attention," while Pat Monaghan, writing for *Booklist,* declared, "More books like this would widen poetry's audience." Monaghan maintained that Haskins' collection should appeal not only to general reading audiences, but also especially to musicians.

Hunger: Poems (1993) is Haskins's fourth published collection, and critics have described it as having a feminist tone. Scott Ward, writing in the *Southern*

Humanities Review, referred to the feminist approach in Haskins's writing: "If they are feminist," Ward wrote, they "are so in the best sense of that term, because they do more than prescribe political territory. They engage in real exploration and do not rush to portray their characters as victims." In some of the poems, Haskins employs historical images to express the confinements that society often places on women. "It is in the section of historical poems that Haskins is her strongest," stated critic Robert Schultz in the *Hudson Review.* "When Haskins takes on the voices of historical speakers, image and conceit become more striking and original, while syntax becomes more varied and inventive."

In other poems, such as when Haskins uses Mexico as a backdrop, artists and their paintings work as mediums through which Haskins expresses emotional hungers that ties these poems together. *Hunger* won the Iowa Poetry prize and was a co-winner of the Edwin Ford Piper Poetry Award.

In a more recent publication, *Extranjera* (1998), Haskins again draws on the people and environment of Mexico. She focuses on the lives of locals and travelers who are passing through, offering colorful vignettes of Mexican culture to her readers in the process. Haskins's poems in this collection, as stated by Janet St. John in *Booklist,* showed "an acuteness of perception and a maturity of restraint that are refreshing."

Women are the main subject matter in Haskins's 2001 collection, *Desire Lines: New and Selected Poems,* which contains some poems previously published, and over twenty new ones. Spanning five historical periods, the female characters that color this collection are busy doing things that most women find themselves doing, such as housework, enjoying the arts, emotionally supporting a husband, bearing, and sometimes mourning the loss of children.

Haskins has also written an introduction to photographer Woody Walters's book, *Visions of Florida,* which explores the landscape of that southern state. When she's not busy teaching, she collaborates with the dance troupe Dance Alive!

BIOGRAPHICAL AND CRITICAL SOURCES:

PERIODICALS

American Book Review, September, 1995, Lynne Lawner, "Brushstrokes," p. 19.

American Music Teacher, April/May, 1991, Paul Cooper, review of *Forty-four Ambitions for the Piano,* p. 50.

Booklist, July 1983, review of *Planting the Children,* p. 1384; October 15, 1990, Pat Monaghan, review of *Forty-four Ambitions for the Piano,* p. 411; February 15, 1998, Janet St. John, review of *Extranjera,* p. 969.

Hudson Review, winter, 1983, James Finn Cotter, review of *Planting the Children,* p. 715; Autumn 1994, Robert Schultz, review of *Hunger,* p. 475.

Kirkus Review, March 1, 1998, review of *Extranjera,* p. 301.

Library Journal, January 1994, Jessica Grim, review of *Hunger,* p. 119.

Music Educators Journal, May, 1991, review of *Forty-four Ambitions for the Piano,* p. 63.

Publishers Weekly, February 23, 1998, "Strangers in Strange Lands," p. 71.

Southern Humanities Review, summer, 1995, Scott Ward, review of *Hunger,* pp. 303-08.

OTHER

3rd Muse Poetry Journal, http://www.3rdmuse.com/ (March 7, 2002), "Interview with Lola Haskins."*

*   *   *

HAYES, Elvin 1945-

PERSONAL: Born November 17, 1945, in Rayville, LA; married; wife's name, Erna; children: Elvin, Jr., Erna, Erica, Ethan. *Education:* Attended University of Houston, earned degrees (recreation and speech).

ADDRESSES: Office—Elvin Hayes Ford, P.O. Box 1547, Crosby, TX 77532.

CAREER: San Diego Rockets, San Diego, CA, professional basketball player, 1968-71; Houston Rockets, Houston, TX, basketball player, 1971-72, 1981-84; Baltimore Bullets, Baltimore, MD, basketball player, 1972-73; Capital Bullets, basketball player, 1973-74; Washington Bullets, basketball player, 1974-81; cattle rancher near Brenham, TX. Elvin Hayes Volkswagen, Houston, TX, owner of dealership; Elvin Hayes Ford, Crosby, TX, owner of dealership.

AWARDS, HONORS: Named college basketball player of the year, *Sporting News,* 1968; National Basketball Association, member of all-star teams, twelve times between 1969 and 1980, member of Fiftieth Anniversary All-Time Team, 1996; named all-American player while playing with Houston Rockets; inducted into Naismith Memorial Basketball Hall of Fame, 1990.

WRITINGS:

(With Bill Gilbert) *They Call Me "the Big E,"* Prentice-Hall (Englewood Cliffs, NJ), 1978.

BIOGRAPHICAL AND CRITICAL SOURCES:

BOOKS

Who's Who among Black Americans, 6th edition, Gale (Detroit, MI), 1990, p. 563.

PERIODICALS

Black Sports, August, 1976.
Ebony, March, 1968; July, 1975.
Library Journal, April 1, 1978, Milton Mitchell, review of *They Call Me "the Big E."*
School Library Journal, April, 1978, JoAnne Posch, review of *They Call Me "the Big E."*
Sports Illustrated, November 25, 1968; October 16, 1978.
Washington Post, June 9, 1978.

OTHER

National Basketball Association History, http://www.nba.com/ (March 2, 2000).*

*   *   *

HAYWARD, Joel S. A.

PERSONAL: Male.

ADDRESSES: Office—Coordinator of Defence and Strategic Studies, School of History, Philosophy, and Politics, Massey University, Private Bag 11-222, Palmerston North, New Zealand. *E-mail*—J.S.Hayward@massey.ac.nz.

CAREER: Historian. Massey University, Palmerston North, New Zealand, historian, and program coordinator for Defence and Strategic Studies program. Lecturer at New Zealand Army's Officer Cadet School and Royal New Zealand Air Force's Command and Staff College; research associate, U.S. Air Force Historical Research Agency.

WRITINGS:

Stopped at Stalingrad: The Luftwaffe and Hitler's Defeat in the East, 1942-1943, University of Kansas Press (Lawrence, KS), 1998.
Adolf Hitler and Joint Warfare, New Zealand Defence Force, 2000.
For God and Glory: Lord Nelson and His Way of War, Naval Institute Press (Annapolis, MD), 2003.

Contributor to academic journals, including *Journal of Strategic Studies, Airpower Journal, Air Power History, Journal of Slavic Military Studies,* and *New Zealand Army Journal.*

SIDELIGHTS: In *Stopped at Stalingrad: The Luftwaffe and Hitler's Defeat in the East, 1942-1943,* Joel S. A. Hayward, an historian at Massey University in New Zealand, has taken a new look at the role of the German Luftwaffe in Germany's disastrous defeat at Stalingrad during World War II. Growing out of a doctoral dissertation, Hayward's study, according to P. L. de Rosa in *Choice,* departs from the usual scholarly emphasis on the vicissitudes of the doomed German Sixth Army in that campaign. Hayward asserts that the role of the Luftwaffe IV, diverted from other campaigns to hold Stalingrad, was an important one despite the defeat. De Rosa called *Stopped at Stalingrad* "[a] solid study of the Luftwaffe in 1942 that establishes its role within the broader context of the Stalingrad campaign." A reviewer for the *Reference and Research Book News* wrote that the book "fills many of the gaps left by other studies of the eastern war"

The siege of Stalingrad was noteworthy for the mass slaughter of thousands of soldiers and civilians, a starving citizenry in freezing weather conditions, and needless sacrifices in the name of both Soviet and German ideologies. After Hitler's retreat from Stalingrad and his demise, Soviet dictator Josef Stalin was ultimately able to reassert his control over most of eastern Europe.

Hayward's book focuses on the generals in charge of the Luftwaffe. According to Omer Bartov in the *Times Literary Supplement,* Hayward is not concerned with the effects of the war on the average soldier, but rather dwells on what he sees as the positive contributions of the generals. Bartov stated that Hayward paints Field Marshall Wolfram Frieherr von Richthofen in particular as "positively heroic" and felt that the author occasionally sounds "downright apologetic" when describing the leadership of the Luftwaffe; according to Bartov, Hayward cites the "conventional wisdom" that Germany might have prevailed in the war if Hitler had not interfered in the war against the Soviet Union. Bartov thought that Hayward's book has some of the shortcomings of a dissertation, especially his "insistence on providing background for his major theme [which] clutters the text with long discussions on German and Soviet land forces and navies." The reviewer also felt that Hayward is too uncritical of German claims and German documents, remaining "under the spell of the German rhetoric of the period." In his zeal to outline the "organization of destruction," said Bartov, Hayward does not take into account that the goal of the German war leadership was "to bring about German world domination, whose result would have been ever more genocide and enslavement of millions." While criticizing Hayward's lack of attention to the possible moral consequences of a German victory, de Rosa called the book a "competent and heavily documented study" which mines material "previously neglected by many scholars."

BIOGRAPHICAL AND CRITICAL SOURCES:

PERIODICALS

Aerospace Power Journal, spring, 2002, Herman Reinhold, review of *Stopped at Stalingrad: The Luftwaffe and Hitler's Defeat in the East, 1942-1943,* p. 122.

Choice, October, 1997, p. 374.

German Studies Review, Larry L. Ping, review of *Stopped at Stalingrad,* p. 372.

History: Review of New Books, fall, 1998, Russell Lemmons, review of *Stopped at Stalingrad,* p. 27.

International History Review, March, 1999, Earl F. Ziemke, review of *Stopped at Stalingrad,* p. 219.

Journal of Military History, October, 1998, Richard R. Muller, review of *Stopped at Stalingrad,* p. 951.

Reference and Research Book News, May, 1998, p. 22.

Times Literary Supplement, October 23, 1998, Omer Bartov, review of *Stopped at Stalingrad,* p. 12.*

HAZAREESINGH, Sudhir

PERSONAL: Male. *Education:* M.Phil.; Oxford University, D.Phil.

ADDRESSES: Office—Balliol College, University of Oxford, Oxford OX1 3BJ, England. *E-mail*—sudhir. hazareesingh@balliol.ox.ac.uk.

CAREER: Fellow and tutor in politics, Balliol College, Oxford, England.

WRITINGS:

Intellectuals and the French Communist Party: Disillusion and Decline, Clarendon Press (Oxford, England), 1991.

Political Traditions in Modern France, Oxford University Press (Oxford, England), 1994.

From Subject to Citizen: The Second Empire and the Emergence of Modern French Democracy, Princeton University Press (Princeton, NJ), 1998.

Intellectual Founders of the Republic: Five Studies in Nineteenth-Century French Republican Political Thought, Oxford University Press (New York, NY), 2001.

(Editor) *The Jacobin Legacy in Modern France: Essays in Honour of Vincent Wright,* Oxford University Press (New York, NY), 2002.

SIDELIGHTS: A fellow and tutor in politics in the philosophy, politics, and economics program at Balliol College, Oxford, Sudhir Hazareesingh has produced several penetrating works on the political culture of France. His first, *Intellectuals and the French Communist Party,* published in 1991, outlines the decline of the French Communist Party (PCF), beginning in the mid-1970s. According to Hazareesingh, some of the reasons for the breakdown of the party include the increasing ineffectiveness of the party's organization, the difficulty of functioning within a liberal democracy, and the arrogance of French Communist intellectuals who could not live up to their self-proclaimed slogan of "workerism."

Jack Hayward in the *Times Literary Supplement,* said that Hazareesingh writes "stylishly and by means of penetrating example" about the persistently self-assured attitude of communist intellectuals even as their party went into "irreversible disintegration." Hayward noted that the French Catholic Church, the other "great authoritarian sub-culture" has also lost its hold on its followers, and wondered what would fill the "intellectual void" left by the decline of both Communism and Catholicism. According to Hayward, Hazareesingh is a "worthy obituarist" of the Communist cause and "has cleared the ground of the non-agenda."

Hazareesingh's second book, *Political Culture in Modern France,* is a more general study of French political history. Here the author asserts that "history exercised a vital influence in shaping the structure of political argument"; he spends a great deal of time describing the many instances of compromise and negotiation in France's political culture. Hazareesingh also notes that there are significant aspects of continuity between the various political regimes he outlines. According to James F. McMillan in the *Times Literary Supplement,* Hazareesingh assumes the conventional idea that ideology has been very important in French politics; McMillan felt, however, that Hazareesingh "does not always convey the powerful hatreds and antagonisms which characterized the political traditions in question."

McMillan complimented the author's handling of the history of the French Communist Party, which Hazareesingh contends in *Political Culture in Modern France* has become "a retirement home for old men and women." McMillan also found "useful" the chapters on socialism, the *Etatiste* tradition, and Gaullism. McMillan, however, found errors and omissions in Hazareesingh's chapters on clericalism and social Catholicism, and felt that the author should not have omitted mention of feminism and regionalism as significant political forces. Still, said McMillan, this book "should help to illuminate some of the specifics of French political culture and stimulate further interest."

In the *Journal of Modern History,* David L. Schalk commented that *Political Traditions in Modern France* could have benefited from a more astute editor. He felt, for example, that the second chapter, "The Political Role of Intellectuals," is out of place and that the repetition of "stock phrases as mnemonic devices" should have been omitted. Schalk also noted that the ordering of chapters does not seem logical and

wondered why Hazareesingh ends only with an account of the decline of French Communism and not with an overview of the subjects he has discussed in the book. Schalk did compliment Hazareesingh, however, on his handling of subjects like the Republican tradition, the National Front, and French fascism. Schalk called the book "richly detailed, lucidly and often wittily written, clearly argued, and superbly documented."

In 1998 Hazareesingh published *From Subject to Citizen: The Second Empire and the Emergence of Modern French Democracy.* This book offers a re-evaluation of the importance of the period of the Second Empire under Napoleon III that began following a coup d'etat against the radical republican government and resulted in the development of French democracy. An overview of the intellectual ferment that characterized this transitional period, *From Subject to Citizen* examines the written record of political debates among such groups as Bonapartists, republicans, liberals, Jacobins, and moderates. Hazareesingh argues that the various debates of this contentious era allowed Frenchmen to sort out what would finally emerge as the doctrines of individual liberty, democracy, and civic responsibility.

From Subject to Citizen is, on one level, an examination of the interchange between the central state and local politics. Eugen Weber, writing in the *Times Literary Supplement,* called the book a "useful corrective" to the common historical interpretation that the Second Empire was only an "unfortunate hiccup" between two revolutions. Weber, however, felt that Hazareesingh relies too heavily on the intellectual records, to the exclusion of other factors such as "mass awareness, perceptions, [and] participation." Weber also noted that Hazareesingh writes too much as if "France" were a single entity going "beyond geographical and formal definitions. . . . A word about local liberties would be wise to show some sensitivity to local context," the critic asserted. On the other hand, even if the author dwelled too much on the thoughts of intellectual elites, Weber added that "[Debates do] suggest, facilitate, legitimate and, as such, deserve to be remembered."

BIOGRAPHICAL AND CRITICAL SOURCES:

PERIODICALS

American Historical Review, October, 1999, James R. Lehning, review of *From Subject to Citizen: The*

Second Empire and the Emergence of Modern French Democracy, p. 1390.

Choice, February 1995, pp. 1000-1001.

English Historical Review, April, 1999, D. R. Watson, review of *From Subject to Citizen,* p. 475.

History: The Journal of the Historical Association, January, 2000, Roger Price, review of *From Subject to Citizen,* p. 180.

Journal of Modern History, June, 1996, pp. 470-471; June, 2000, Stephanie Gerson, review of *From Subject to Citizen,* p. 539.

Social History, October, 1999, Michael Hanagan, review of *From Subject to Citizen,* p. 325.

Times Literary Supplement, July 17, 1992, p. 27; June 26, 1995; March 19, 1999, p. 27; March 15, 2002, James F. McMillan, "The Empire the French fFrget: New Views of Napoleon III," p. 6.*

*　　*　　*

HEGEMAN, Susan 1964-

PERSONAL: Female. *Education:* Harvard University, A.B., 1986; Duke University, Ph.D., 1992.

ADDRESSES: Office—Department of English, University of Florida, P.O. Box 117310, Gainesville, FL 32611-7310; fax: 352-392-0860. *E-mail*—shegeman@english.ufl.edu.

CAREER: University of Florida, Gainesville, member of English faculty, 1995—. Taught at University of California—Berkeley. Vanderbilt University, Robert Penn Warren Center for the Humanities, William S. Vaughn visiting fellow, 1996.

WRITINGS:

Patterns for America: Modernism and the Concept of Culture, Princeton University Press (Princeton, NJ), 1999.

WORK IN PROGRESS: Working Girls.

BIOGRAPHICAL AND CRITICAL SOURCES:

PERIODICALS

American Literary History, summer, 2001, Richard Keller Simon, review of *Patterns for America: Modernism and the Concept of Culture,* p. 343.

American Literature, June, 2001, Jared Gardner, review of *Patterns for America,* p. 423.

Choice, November, 1999, J. J. Benardete, review of *Patterns for America,* p. 536.

Modern Fiction Studies, winter, 2000, Jean Gallagher, review of *Patterns for America,* p. 966.*

*　　*　　*

HEGGAN, Christiane

PERSONAL: Born in Nice, France; immigrated to United States; naturalized U.S. citizen; married; husband's name, Bob. *Hobbies and other interests:* Traveling.

ADDRESSES: Home—P.O. Box 251, Medford, NJ 08055.

CAREER: Writer.

AWARDS, HONORS: Reviewers Choice Award, *Romantic Times,* for *Gloss;* Award of Excellence for *Passions;* National Readers' Choice Award for *Silver Lining.*

WRITINGS:

ROMANTIC THRILLERS

Cannes, Onyx (New York, NY), 1990.

Gloss, Onyx (New York, NY), 1991.

Passions, Onyx (New York, NY), 1993.

Betrayals, Onyx (New York, NY), 1994.

Silver Lining, Onyx (New York, NY), 1995.

Never Say Never, Onyx (New York, NY), 1996.

Suspicion, Harlequin (New York, NY), 1997.

Deception, Mira (New York, NY), 1998.

Enemy Within, Mira (New York, NY), 2000.

Blind Faith, Mira (New York, NY), 2001.

Moment of Truth, Mira (New York, NY), 2002.

Deadly Intent, Mira (New York, NY), 2003.

SIDELIGHTS: Christiane Heggan is a prize-winning novelist who is known for her romantic thrillers.

Her 1997 offering, *Suspicion* is the story of defense attorney Kate Logan, who must defend her ex-husband, the primary suspect in the killing of a blackmailing prostitute. While trying to aid her former spouse, Logan also mounts a legal defense for a client wrongfully convicted of committing a murder. Logan, with the assistance of a police detective who becomes her lover, eventually learns that her two cases are related to a suspicious senator eager to maintain a career-threatening secret. A reviewer in *Publishers Weekly* noted that Heggan "creates believable characters and spins a pleasant romance."

Deception, which Heggan published in 1998, concerns young architect, Jill Bennett, who suspects that the death of her father, a fellow architect, was the result of mayhem. After she also finds herself marked for death, she reluctantly agrees to the protection of her ex-husband, Dan Santini, who had worked as a homicide investigator. While Jill attempts to stay alive and sustain the family's architecture business, she once again finds herself drawn to Dan. A *Publishers Weekly* reviewer noted that *Deception* contains "enough twists to keep readers guessing."

In *Blind Faith,* reporter Kelly Robolo is recuperating from a gunshot wound when a friend asks her to look into the disappearance of her husband, who she fears is dead. In a story that includes a police department that blames Kelly for one of its officers getting shot, a mysterious character with possible mob ties, and a female impersonator with important information, a *Publishers Weekly* reviewer called *Blind Faith* "an addictive read."

In an interview with *Writers Write,* Heggan gave some advice for aspiring mystery writers: "Write what you want and don't listen to those who say write only what you know. Look at Agatha Christie and Mary Higgins Clark, such proper ladies. They had no knowledge of criminology, or of the deviant mind. They just let their imagination soar and they did their research."

BIOGRAPHICAL AND CRITICAL SOURCES:

PERIODICALS

Publishers Weekly, November 24, 1997, review of *Suspicion,* p. 70; August 17, 1998, review of *Deception,* p. 69; January 10, 2000, review of *Enemy Within,* p. 49; December 11, 2000, review of *Blind Faith,* p. 68; November 26, 2001, review of *Moment of Truth,* p. 45.

OTHER

Christiane Heggan Home Page, http://www.eclectics. com/ (January 8, 1999).
Writers Write, http://www.writerswrite.com/ (November 15, 2002).*

* * *

HELBERG, Shirley Adelaide Holden 1919-

PERSONAL: Born March 19, 1919, in Solvay, NY; daughter of Edgar (a construction supervisor) and Gladys Tucker (a homemaker) Holden; married Burton E. Helberg (a research supervisor), February 14, 1942; children: Keir, Kristin, Kecia, Kandace, Kraig. *Education:* Attended Syracuse University, 1936-37; Syracuse City Normal Teachers School, graduated, 1937; Johns Hopkins University, B.S. (education), 1969; Maryland Institute of Arts, M.F.A., 1975. *Politics:* Republican. *Religion:* Methodist. *Hobbies and other interests:* Dancing, gourmet cooking, antiques.

ADDRESSES: Home—5433 Pigeon Hill Rd., Spring Grove, PA 17362; and 727 South Ann St., Baltimore, MD 21231.

CAREER: Artist and educator. Held various teaching posts in elementary schools in New York, Pennsylvania, and Maryland, 1965-84; Baltimore City Schools, Baltimore, MD, 1988-92. *Exhibitions:* One-woman shows at museums including Cayuga Museum of Art and History, 1974, Historic Society Museum, York, PA, 1977, and York College, 1984.

MEMBER: American Association of University Women, National League of American PEN Women (Pennsylvania chapter), member and national scholarship chair, 1974-98, D Union Veterans, Daughters of American Revolution.

AWARDS, HONORS: Distinguished Service awards, 1978, 1980, 1982, 1984, 1986, 1988, 1990, and 1992, and Distinguished Achievement awards, 1988, and

1994, from Pennsylvania State Education Association, International Platform Association, Harrisburg Art Association, York Art Association, Pennsylvania Watercolor Society, and Johns Hopkins University Club.

WRITINGS:

Chosen Few (poetry), 1995.
(Illustrator) *Kitty Cat Who Wanted to Fly,* Morris Publishing (Kearney, NE), 1999.
(Illustrator) Mark Twain, *The Jumping Frog of Calaveras County,* 1999.

Contributor to various periodicals, including *PEN Woman.*

WORK IN PROGRESS: A children's book on the Iroquois.

BIOGRAPHICAL AND CRITICAL SOURCES:

PERIODICALS

York Sunday News (York, PA), March 10, 1974.

* * *

HEYSE, Paul (Johann Ludwig von) 1830-1914

PERSONAL: Born March 15, 1830, in Berlin, Germany; died April 2, 1914, in Munich, Germany; buried in Munich, Germany; son of Karl Wilhelm Ludwig and Julie (Saaling) Heyse; married Margarethe Kugler, May 15, 1854 (died September 30, 1862); married Anna Schubard, 1867; children: (first marriage) two sons; (second marriage) one son, one daughter. *Education:* University of Bonn, Ph.D. (romance philology), 1852.

CAREER: Short story writer, novelist, editor, translator, and essayist. From 1854 to 1868 received a stipend from the King of Bavaria.

AWARDS, HONORS: Nobel Prize for literature, 1910.

WRITINGS:

Frühlingsanfang 1848, Schade (Berlin, Germany), 1848.
Der Jungbrunnen: Neue Märchen von einem fahrenden Schüler (includes "Das Märchen von der guten Seele," "Glückspilzchen," "Das Märchen von Musje Morgenroth und Jungfer Abendbrod," "Veilchenprinz," "Das Märchen von Blindekuh," "Fedelint und Funzifudelchen"), Duncker (Berlin, Germany), 1850, revised edition, Pätel (Berlin, Germany), 1878.
Francesca von Rimini: Tragödie in fünf Akten, Hertz (Berlin, Germany), 1850.
Die Brüder: Eine chinesische Geschichte in Versen, Hertz (Berlin, Germany), 1852.
Studia romanensia: Particula I. Dissertatio inauguralis, Schade (Berlin, Germany), 1852.
Urica: Novelle in Versen, Hertz (Berlin, Germany), 1852.
Hermen: Dichtungen (includes "Margherita Spoletina," "Urica," "Idyllen von Sorrent," "Die Furie," "Die Brüder," "Michel-Angelo Buonarotti," "Perseus: Eine Puppentragödie"), Hertz (Berlin, Germany), 1854.
Meleager: Eine Tragödie, Hertz (Berlin, Germany), 1854.
Novellen (includes "Die Blinden," "Marion," "L'Arrabbiata," "Am Tiberufer"), Hertz (Berlin, Germany), 1855.
Die Braut von Cypern: Novelle in Versen. Mit einem lyrischen Anhang, Cotta (Stuttgart & Augsburg, Germany), 1856.
Thekla: Ein Gedicht in neun Gesängen, Cotta (Stuttgart, Germany), 1858.
Neue Novellen: 2. Sammlung, (includes "Erkenne dich selbst"; "Das Mädchen von Treppi," translated by A.W. Hinton as *The Maiden of Treppi; or, Love's Victory,* Hinton [New York, NY], 1874; "Der Kreisrichter"; "Helene Morten"), Cotta (Stuttgart, Germany), 1858.
Vier neue Novellen: 3 Sammlung (includes "Die Einsamen," translated anonymously as "The Lonely Ones," in *Eugenie Marlitt, Magdalena; Paul Heyse, The Lonely Ones,* Lippincott [Philadelphia, PA], 1869; "Anfang und Ende"; "Maria Franziska"; "Das Bild der Mutter"), Hertz (Berlin, Germany), 1859.
Die Sabinerinnen: Tragödie in fünf Akten, Hertz (Berlin, Germany), 1859.
Die Grafen von der Esche: Schauspiel in fünf Akten, Deschler (Munich, Germany), 1861.

Neue Novellen: 4, Sammlung (includes "Annina"; "Im Grafenschlo"; "Andrea Delfin," translated as *Andrea Delfin,* Burnham [Boston, MA], 1864); "Aufder Alm"), Hertz (Berlin, Germany), 1862

Ludwig der Bayer: Schauspiel in fünf Akten, Hertz (Berlin, Germany), 1862.

Rafael: Eine Novelle in Versen, Kröner (Stuttgart, Germany), 1863.

Elisabeth Charlotte: Schauspiel in fünf Akten, Hertz (Berlin, Germany), 1864.

Andrea Delfin, Burnham (Boston, MA), 1864.

Gesammelte Novellen in Versen (includes "Die Braut von Cypern," "Die Brüder," "König und Magier," "Margherita Spoletina," "Urica," "Die Furie," "Rafael," "Michel-Angelo Buonarotti," "Die Hochzeitsreise an den Walchensee"), Hertz (Berlin, Germany), 1864, enlarged edition, (includes "Thekla," "Syritha," "Der Salamander," "Schlechte Gesellschaft," "Das Feenkind"), 1870

Meraner Novellen: 5. Sammlung (includes "Unheilbar," translated by Mrs. H. W. Eve as *Incurable Nutt* [London, England], 1890; "Der Kinder Sünde der Väter Fluch"; "Der Weinhüter") Hertz (Berlin, Germany), 1864.

Maria Moroni: Trauerspiel in fünf Akten, Hertz (Berlin, Germany), 1865.

Hadrian: Tragödie in fünf Akten, Hertz (Berlin, Germany), 1865.

Hans Lange: Schauspiel in fünf Akten, Hertz (Berlin, Germany), 1866.

Fünf neue Novellen: 6. Sammlung (includes "Franz Alzeyer," "Die Reise nach dem Glück," "Die kleine Mama," "Kleopatra," "Die Witwe von Pisa") Hertz (Berlin, Germany), 1866.

Die glücklichen Bettler: Morgenländisches Märchen in drei Akten, frei nach Carlo Gozzi, Hertz (Berlin, Germany), 1867.

Novellen und Terzinen: 7. Sammlung der Novellen (includes "Syritha: Novelle in Versen," "Mutter und Kind: Novelle," "Auferstanden: Novelle," "Der Salamander: Novelle in Versen," "Beatrice: Novelle"), Hertz (Berlin, Germany), 1867.

Colberg: Historisches Schauspiel in fünf Akten, Hertz (Berlin, Germany), 1868.

Der Rothmantel: Komische Oper in drei Aufzügen nach Musäus' Volksmärchen, Wolf (Munich, Germany), 1868.

Moralische Novellen: 8. Sammlung (includes "Die beiden Schwestern," "Lorenz und Lore," "Vetter Gabriel," "Amtoten See," "Der Thurm von Nonza"), Hertz (Berlin, Germany), 1869.

Die Göttin der Vernunft: Trauerspiel in fünf Akten, Hertz (Berlin, Germany), 1870.

Adam und Eva: Operette in lein Aufzuge, music by Robert von Hornstein, Straub (Munich, Germany), 1870.

Ein neues Novellenbuch: 9. Sammlung (includes "Barbarossa," "Die Stickerin von Treviso," "Lottka," "Der letzte Centaur," "Der verlorene Sohn," "Das schöne Käthchen," "Geoffroy und Garcinde," "Die Pfadfinderin"), Hertz (Berlin, Germany), 1871.

Die Franzosenbraut: Volksschauspiel in fünf Akten, Straub (Munich, Germany), 1871.

Der Friede: Ein Festspiel für das Münchener Hof- und National-Theater, music by Baron von Perfall, Oldenbourg (Munich, Germany), 1871.

Gesammelte Werke, Volumes 1-29 (Volume 9 includes *Die Pfaulzer in Irland: Trauerspiel in fünf Akten*), Hertz (Berlin, Germany), Volumes 30-38, Cotta (Stuttgart & Berlin, Germany), 1872-1914.

Kinder der Welt: Roman in sechs Büchern, three volumes, Hertz (Berlin, Germany), 1873, translated as *Children of the World: A Novel,* Chapman & Hall (London, England), 1882, Munro (New York, NY), 1883.

The Maiden of Treppi; or, Love's Victory, translated by A.W. Hinton, Hinton (New York, NY), 1874.

Neue Novellen: Der Novellen 10. Sammlung (includes "Er soll dein Herr sein," "Die ungarische Gräfin," "Ein Märtyrer der Phantasie," "Judith Stern," "Nerina"), Hertz (Berlin, Germany), 1875.

Ehre um Ehre: Schauspiel in fünf Akten, Hertz (Berlin, Germany), 1875.

Im Paradiese: Roman in sieben Büchern, three volumes, Hertz (Berlin, Germany), 1875, translated as *In Paradise,* two volumes, Appleton (New York, NY), 1878.

Skizzenbuch: Lieder und Bilder, Hertz (Berlin, Germany), 1877.

Graf Königsmark: Trauerspiel in fünf Akten, Hertz (Berlin, Germany), 1877.

Elfride: Trauerspiel in fünf Akten, Hertz (Berlin, Germany), 1877.

Neue moralische Novellen: 11. Sammlung der Novellen (includes "Jorinde," "Getreu bis in den Tod," "Die Kaiserin von Spinetta," "Das Seeweib," and "Die Frau Marchesa"), Hertz (Berlin, Germany), 1878.

Zwei Gefangene: Novelle, Reclam (Leipzig, Germany), 1878, translated as *Two Prisoners,* Simpkin (London, England), 1893.

Das Ding an sich und andere Novellen: 12. Sammlung der Novellen (includes "Das Ding an sich," "Zwei

Gefangene," "Die Tochter der Excellenz," "Beppe der Sternseher"), Hertz (Berlin, Germany), 1879.

Die Madonna im Ölwald: Novelle in Versen, Hertz (Berlin, Germany), 1879.

Verse aus Italien: Skizzen, Briefe und Tagebuchblätter, Hertz (Berlin, Germany), 1880.

Die Weiber von Schorndorf: Historisches Schauspiel in vier Akten, Hertz (Berlin, Germany), 1880.

Frau von F. und römische Novellen: 13. Sammlung der Novellen (includes "Frau von F."; "Die talentvolle Mutter"; "Romulusenkel"; "Die Hexe vom Korso"), translated by George W. Ingraham as *The Witch of the Corso* Munro (New York, NY), 1882.

Das Glück von Rothenburg: Novelle, Reichel (Augsburg, Germany), 1881, translated by C. L. Townsend as "The Spell of Rothenburg," in *The German Classics of the Nineteenth and Twentieth Centuries,* Volume 13, edited by Kuno Francke and William Guild Howard, German Publication Society (New York, NY), 1914.

Troubadour-Novellen: 14. Sammlung der Novellen (includes "Der lahme Engel," "Die Rache der Vizgräfin," "Die Dichterin von Carcassonne," "Der Mönch von Montaudon," "Ehre über alles," "Der verkaufte Gesang"), Hertz (Berlin, Germany), 1882, Munro (New York, NY), 1883.

Alkibiades: Tragödie in drei Akten, Hertz (Berlin, Germany), 1883.

Das Recht des Stärkeren: Schauspiel in drei Akten, Hertz (Berlin, Germany), 1883.

Don Juan's Ende: Trauerspiel in fünf Akten, Hertz (Berlin, Germany), 1883, translated as *The Last Days of Don Juan,* (London, England).

Unvergebare Worte und andere Novellen: 15. Sammlung der Novellen (includes "Unvergebare Worte," "Die Eselin," "Das Glück von Rothenburg," "Geteiltes Herz"). Hertz (Berlin, Germany), 1883.

Buch der Freundschaft: Novellen. 16. Sammlung der Novellen (includes "David und Jonathan," "Grenzen der Menschheit," "Nino und Maso," translated by Alfred Remy as "Nino and Maso: A Tale Drawn from a Sienese Chronicle," in *The German Classics of the Nineteenth and Twentieth Centuries,* volume 13, 1914), Hertz (Berlin, Germany), 1883.

Children of the World: A Novel, Chapman & Hall (London, England), 1882, Munro (New York, NY), 1883.

Siechentrost: Novelle, Reichel (Augsburg, Germany), 1883.

Buch der Freundschaft: Neue Folge. 17. Sammlung der Novellen (includes "Siechentrost," "Die

schwarze Jakobe," "Gute Kameraden," "Im Bunde der Dritte"), Hertz (Berlin, Germany), 1884.

Drei einaktige Trauerspiele und ein Lustspiel (includes *Ehrenschulden, Frau Lukrezia, Simson,* and *Unter Brüdern: Lustspiel in einem Akt*), Hertz (Berlin, Germany), 1884.

Spruchbüchlein Hertz (Berlin, Germany), 1885.

Gedichte, Hertz (Berlin, Germany), 1885, enlarged edition, 1889.

Himmlische und irdische Liebe—F.V.R.I.A.—auf Tod und Leben: Novellen. 18. Sammlung der Novellen, Munro (New York, NY), 1886.

Getrennte Welten: Schauspiel in vier Akten, Hertz (Berlin, Germany), 1886.

Die Hochzeit auf dem Aventin: Trauerspiel in fünf Akten, Hertz (Berlin, Germany), 1886.

Die Weisheit Salomo's: Schauspiel in fünf Akten, Hertz (Berlin, Germany), 1887.

Der Roman der Stiftsdame: Eine Lebensgeschichte, Hertz (Berlin, Germany), 1887, translated by J. M. Percival (pseudonym for Mary Joanna Safford) as *The Romance of the Canoness: A Life-History* Appleton (New York, NY), 1887.

Villa Falconieri und andere Novellen: 19. Sammlung der Novellen (includes "Villa Falconieri," "Doris Sengeberg," "Emerenz," "Die Märtyrerin der Phantasie"), Hertz (Berlin, Germany), 1888.

Gott schütze mich vor meinen Freunden: Lustspiel in drei Akten, Hertz (Berlin, Germany), 1888.

Prinzessin Sascha: Schauspiel in vier Akten, Hertz (Berlin, Germany), 1888.

Weltuntergang: Volksschauspiel in fünf Akten, Hertz (Berlin, Germany), 1889.

Kleine Dramen: Erste Folge (includes *Im Bunde der Dritte, Der Venusdurchgang, Nur keinen Eifer,* and *In sittlicher Entrüstung*), Hertz (Berlin, Germany), 1889.

Kleine Dramen: Zweite Folge (includes *Eineerste Liebe, Eine Dante-Lektüre, Zwischen Lipp und Bechersrand,* and *Die schwerste Pflicht*), Hertz (Berlin, Germany), 1889.

Liebeszauber: Orientalische Dichtung, Hanfstängl (Munich, Germany), 1889.

Novellen: Auswahl fürs Haus (includes "L'Arrabbiata," "Anfang und Ende," "Andrea Delfin," "Unheilbar," "Vetter Gabriel," "Die beiden Schwestern," "Er soll dein Herr sein," "Der verlorene Sohn," "Nerina," "Unvergebare Worte," "Die Dichterin von Arcassonne," "Das Glück von Rothenburg," "Siechentrost"), three volumes, Hertz (Berlin, Germany), 1890.

Ein überflüssiger Mensch: Schauspiel in vier Akten, Hertz (Berlin, Germany), 1890.

Die schlimmen Brüder: Schauspiel in vier Akten und einem Vorspiel, Hertz (Berlin, Germany), 1891.

Weihnachtsgeschichten (includes "Eine Weihnachtsbescherung," "Das Freifräulein," "Die Geschichte von Herrn Wilibald und dem Frosinchen," "Die Dryas"), Hertz (Berlin, Germany), 1891.

Merlin: Roman in sieben Büchern, three volumes Hertz (Berlin, Germany), 1892.

Marienkind, Engelhorn (Stuttgart, Germany), 1892.

Wahrheit?: Schauspiel in drei Akten, Hertz (Berlin, Germany), 1892.

Ein unbeschriebenes Blatt: Lustspiel in vier Akten, Hertz (Berlin, Germany), 1893.

Jungfer Justine: Schauspiel in vier Akten, Hertz (Berlin, Germany), 1893.

Aus den Vorbergen: Novellen (includes "Vroni," "Marienkind," "Xaverl," "Dorfromantik"), Hertz (Berlin, Germany), 1893.

In der Geisterstunde und andere Spukgeschichten (includes "In der Geisterstunde: Die schöne Abigail," translated by Frances A. Van Santford as *At the Ghost Hour: The Fair Abigail Dodd* [New York, NY], 1894, "In der Geisterstunde: Mittagszauber," translated by Van Santford as "Mid-Day Magic," in *At the Ghost Hour: Mid-Day Magic,* Mead, 1894, "In der Geisterstunde: 's Lisabethle," translated by Van Santford as "Little Lisbeth," in *At the Ghost Hour: Mid-Day Magic;* "In der Geisterstunde: Das Waldlachen," translated by Van Santford as *At the Ghost Hour: The Forest Laugh,* Dodd, Mead [New York, NY], 1894, "Martin der Streber"; "Das Haus 'Zum ungalubigen Thomas' oder des Spirits Rache," translated by Van Santford as *At the Ghost Hour: The House of the Unbelieving Thomas* Dodd, Mead [New York, NY], 1894), Hertz (Berlin, Germany), 1894.

Wolfram von Eschenbach: Ein Festspiel, Knorr & Hirth (Munich, Germany), 1894.

Melusine und andere Novellen (includes "Hochzeit auf Capri," translated anonymously as "The Wedding at Capri," in *Cosmopolitan,* [January, 1894]; "Fedja"; "Donna Lionarda"; "Die Rächerin"; "Melusine"), Hertz (Berlin, Germany), 1895.

Über allen Gipfeln: Roman, Hertz (Berlin, Germany), 1895.

Roland's Schildknappen; oder, Die Komödie vom Glück: Volksmärchen in drei Akten und einem Vorspiel, Hertz (Berlin, Germany), 1896.

Vanina Vanini: Trauerspiel in vier Akten, Hertz (Berlin, Germany), 1896.

Die Fornarina: Trauerspiel in fünf Akten, Naumann (Leipzig, Germany), 1896.

Das Göthe-Haus in Weimar, Hertz (Berlin, Germany), 1896.

Verrathenes Glück; Emerenz: Zwei Geschichten, Krabbe (Stuttgart, Germany), 1896.

Einer von Hunderten und Hochzeit auf Capri, Franckh (Stuttgart, Germany), 1896.

Abenteuer eines Blaustrümpfchens (translated as "Adventures of a Little Blue-Stocking" in *International,* 1896), Krabbe (Stuttgart, Germany), 1897.

Das Räthsel des Lebens und andere Charakterbilder (includes "Der Dichter und sein Kind," "Der Siebengescheite," "Ehrliche Leute," "Einer von Hunderten," "Ein Mädchenschicksal," "Das Steinchen im Schuh," "Das Räthsel des Lebens"), Hertz (Berlin, Germany), 1897.

Männertreu; Der Sohn seines Vaters: Zwei Novellen, Krabbe (Stuttgart, Germany), 1897.

Drei neue Einakter (includes *Der Stegreiftrunk: Drama in einem Akt, Schwester Lotte: Lustspiel in einem Akt,* and *Auf den Dächern: Dramatischer Scherz in einem Akt*), Hertz (Berlin, Germany), 1897.

Neue Gedichte und Jugendlieder, Hertz (Berlin, Germany), 1897.

Der Sohn seines Vaters und andere Novellen (includes "Der Sohn seines Vaters," "Verratenes Glück," "Medea," "Männertreu," "Abenteuer eines Blaustrümpfchens"), Hertz (Berlin, Germany), 1898.

Der Bucklige von Schiras: Komödie in vier Akten, Hertz (Berlin, Germany), 1898.

Martha's Briefe an Maria: Ein Beitrag zur Frauenbewegung, Cotta (Stuttgart), 1898.

Neue Märchen (includes "Holdrio, oder Das Märchen vom wohler zogenen Königssohn," "Das Märchen vom Herzblut," "Die vier Geschwister," "Der Jungbrunnen," "Lilith," "Die gute Frau," "Die Nixe," "Das Märchen von Niels mit der offenen Hand," "Johannisnacht," "Die Dryas"), Hertz (Berlin, Germany), 1899.

Das literarische München: 25 Porträtskizzen, Bruckmann (Munich, Germany), 1899.

Die Macht der Stunde; Vroni: Zwei Novellen, Krabbe (Stuttgart, Germany), 1899.

Maria von Magdala: Drama in fünf Akten, Hertz (Berlin, Germany), 1899, translated by A. I. Coleman as *Mary of Magdala,* Lederer (New York, NY), 1900.

Fräulein Johanne; Auf der Alm: Zwei Novellen, Krabbe (Stuttgart, Germany), 1900.

Der Schutzengel: Novelle, Keil (Leipzig, Germany), 1900.

Jugenderinnerungen und Bekenntnisse, Hertz (Berlin, Germany), 1900, revised and enlarged edition, two volumes, Cotta (Stuttgart, Germany), 1912.

Das verschleierte Bild zu Sais: Drama in drei Akten, Lederer (New York, NY), 1901.

Tantalus; Mutter und Kind: Zwei Novellen, Krabbe (Stuttgart, Germany), 1901.

Ninon und andere Novellen (includes "Ninon," "Zwei Seelen," "Der Blinde von Dausenau," "Fräulein Johanne," "Tantalus," "Ein Mutterschicksal"), Cotta (Stuttgart and Berlin, Germany), 1902.

Der Heilige: Trauerspiel in fünf Akten, Cotta (Berlin and Stuttgart, Germany), 1902.

Novellen vom Gardasee (includes "Gefangene Singvögel," "Die Macht der Stunde," "San Vigilio," "Entsagende Liebe," "Eine venezianische Nacht,""Antiquarische Briefe"), Cotta (Stuttgart and Berlin, Germany), 1902.

Romane und Novellen, forty-two volumes, Cotta (Stuttgart, Germany), 1902-1912.

Moralische Unmöglichkeiten und andere Novellen (includes "Moralische Unmöglichkeiten," "Er selbst," "Zwei Wittwen," "Ein Idealist"), Cotta (Stuttgart and Berlin, Germany), 1903.

Ein Wintertagebuch (Gardone 1901-1902), Cotta (Stuttgart, Germany), 1903.

Mythen und Mysterien (includes "Lilith: Ein Mysterium," "Kain: Ein Mysterium," "Perseus: Puppentragödie in vier Akten," "Am Thor der Unterwelt," "Der Waldpriester: Ein Satyrspiel," "Gespräche im Himmel"), Cotta (Stuttgart, Germany), 1904.

Crone Stäudlin: Roman, Cotta (Stuttgart, Germany), 1905.

Die theorichten Jungfrauen: Lustspiel in drei Akten, Cotta (Stuttgart and Berlin, Germany), 1905.

Ein Canadier: Drama in drei Akten, Cotta (Stuttgart and Berlin, Germany), 1905.

Sechs kleine Dramen (includes *Eine alte Geschichte: Familienszene in einem Akt, Die Zaubergeige: Drama in einem Akt, Zu treu: Genrebild in einem Akt, Horaz und Lydia, Der Stern von Mantua: Schauspiel in zwei Akten,* and *Die Tochter der Semiramis: Tragödie in einem Akt*), Cotta (Stuttgart and Berlin, Germany), 1905.

Victoria Regia und andere Novellen (includes "Victoria Regia," "Lucile," "Tante Lene," "Die Arztin," "Der Hausgeist," "Ein Ring"), Cotta (Stuttgart and Berlin, Germany), 1906.

Gegen den Strom: Eine weltliche Klostergeschichte, Cotta (Stuttgart, Germany), 1907.

Menschen und Schicksale: Charakterbilder (includes "Das Karussell," "Das Unglück, Verstand zu haben," "Lottchen Täppe," "Verfehlter Beruf," "Die gute Tochter," "Ein Luftschiffer," "Mei Bübche," "Fromme Lüge," "Florian," "Iwan Kalugin," "Ein Christuskopf," "Ein Menschenfeind," "Ein literarischer Vehmrichter"), Cotta (Stuttgart, Germany), 1908.

Helldunkles Leben: Novellen (includes "Unüberwindliche Mächte," "Rita," "Ein unpersönlicher Mensch," "Eine Collegin," and "Clelia"), Cotta (Stuttgart, Germany), 1909.

Die Geburt der Venus: Roman, Cotta (Stuttgart and Berlin, Germany), 1909.

König Saul: Biblische Historie in fünf Akten, Reclam (Leipzig, Germany), 1909.

Mutter und Tochter: Drama in fünf Akten, Reclam (Leipzig, Germany), 1909.

Das Ewigmenschliche: Erinnerungen aus einem Alltagsleben von ***; Ein Familienhaus: Novelle, Cotta (Stuttgart, Germany), 1910.

Plaudereien eines alten Freundespaares (includes "Faustrecht," "Das schwächere Geschlecht," "Altruismus," "Don Juan," "Erste Liebe," "Oliva von Planta," "Vendetta," and "Der Jubilar"), Cotta (Stuttgart, Germany), 1912.

Letzte Novellen (includes "Die bessere Welt," "Fanchette," and "Unwieder-bringlich"), Cotta (Stuttgart, Germany), 1914.

Ausgewählte Gedichte, edited by Erich Petzet Cotta (Stuttgart and Berlin, Germany), 1920.

Gesammelte Novellen, five volumes, edited by Petzet Cotta (Stuttgart and Berlin, Germany), 1921.

Italienische Novellen, two volumes, Cotta (Stuttgart, Germany), 1924.

Gesammelte Werke, fifteen volumes, Cotta (Stuttgart, Germany), 1924, Olms (New York, NY), 1984.

Die Reise nach dem Glück: Eine Auswahl aus dem Werk, selected by Gerhard Mauz, Cotta (Stuttgart, Germany), 1959.

Das Mädchen von Treppi: Italienische Liebesgeschichten, Morgen (Berlin, Germany), 1965.

Andrea Delfin und andere Novellen, Aufbau (Berlin and Weimar, Germany), 1966.

Die Hexe vom Corso und andere Novellen mit der Novellen-theorie, Goldmann (Munich, Germany), 1969.

L'Arrabbiata; Das Mädchen von Treppi, edited by Karl Pörnbacher, Reclam (Stuttgart, Germany), 1969.

Novellen, introduction by Manfred Schunicht (includes "L'Arrabbiata," "Andrea Delfin," "Kleopatra,"

"Beatrice," "Der letzte Zentaur," "Der lahme Engel," "Das Glück von Rothenburg," "Die Kaiserin von Spinetta," "Siechentrost," "Einleitung zu deutscher Novellenschatz," "Meine Novellistik"), Johnson Reprint (New York, NY), 1970.

Werke, mit einem Essay von Theodor Fontane, two volumes, edited by Bernhard Knick, Johanna Knick, and Hildegard Korth, Insel (Frankfurt am Main, Germany), 1980.

Novellen, Die Groß Erzähler-Bibliothek der Weltliteratur, Volume 54 (includes "L'Arrabbiata," "Helene Morten," "Andrea Delfin," "Der letzte Zentaur," "Judith Stern," "Victoria Regia."), Harenberg (Dortmund, Germany), 1986.

ENGLISH EDITIONS

Four Phases of Love (includes "Eye-Blindness and Soul-Blindness," "Marion," "La Rabbiata," and "By the Banks of the Tiber"), translated by G. H. Kingsley, Routledge (London, England), 1857.

L'Arrabiata and Other Tales (includes "Count Ernest's Home," "Blind," and "Walter's Little Mother"), translated by Mary Wilson, Leypoldt & Holt (New York, NY), 1867.

The Dead Lake and Other Tales (includes "A Fortnight at the Dead Lake," "Doomed," "Beatrice," "Beginning and End"), translated by Mary Wilson, Low, Marston, Searle & Rivington (New York, NY), 1870.

Barbarossa and Other Tales (includes "The Embroideress of Treviso," "Lottka," "The Lost Son," "The Fair Kate," and "Geoffroy and Garcinde"), translated by L. C. S., Low, Marston, Low & Searle (London, England), 1874.

Tales from the German of Paul Heyse (includes "Count Ernest's Home," "The Dead Lake," "The Fury [L'Arrabiata]," and "Judith Stern"), Appleton (New York, NY), 1879.

Selected Stories, from the German of Paul Heyse (contains "L'Arrabiata," "Beppe, the Star-Gazer," and "Maria Francisca"), Schick (Chicago, IL), 1886.

La Marchesa, a Tale of the Riviera and Other Tales, translated by John Philips (includes "La Marchesa," "Her Excellency's Daughter," and "A Divided Heart"), Stock (London, England), 1887.

Words Never to Be Forgotten and The Donkey: Two Novellettes from the German of Paul Heyse, translated by A. E. Fordyce, Hoff (Union Springs, NY), 1888.

A Divided Heart, and Other Stories, translated by Constance Stewart Copeland (includes "A Divided Heart," "Minka," and "Rothenburg on the Tauber"), Brentano's (New York, NY), 1894.

LETTERS

Der Briefwechsel von Jakob Burckhardt und Paul Heyse, edited by Erich Petzet, Lehmann (Munich, Germany), 1916.

Der Briefwechsel zwischen Paul Heyse und Theodor Storm, two volumes, edited by Plotke, Lehmann (Munich, Germany), 1917-1918.

Paul Heyse und Gottfried Keller im Briefwechsel, edited by Max Kalbeck, Westermann (Braunschweig, Germany), 1919.

Der Briefwechsel von Emanuel Geibel und Paul Heyse, edited by Eric Petzet, Lehmann (Munich, Germany), 1922.

Der Briefwechsel von Theodor Fontane und Paul Heyse, 1850-1897, edited by Eric Petzet, Weltgeist-Bücher Verlags-Gesellschaft (Berlin, Germany), 1929.

Briefwechsel zwischen Joseph Victor von Scheffel und Paul Heyse, edited by Conrad Höfer, Gräff (Karlsruhe, Germany), 1932.

Monika Walkhoff, *Der Briefwechsel zwischen Paul Heyse und Hermann Kurz in den Jahren 1869-1873 aus Anlass der Herausgabe des "Deutschen Novellenschatzes,"* Foto-Druck Frank (Munich, Germany), 1967.

Theodor Storm—Paul Heyse: Briefwechsel. Kritische Ausgabe, three volumes, edited by Clifford Albrecht Bernd, Schmidt (Berlin, Germany), 1969-1974.

Der Briefwechsel zwischen Theodor Fontane und Paul Heyse, edited by Gotthard Erler Aufbau (Berlin and Weimar, Germany), 1972.

"Du hast alles, was mir fehlt . . .": Gottfried Keller im Briefwechsel mit Paul Heyse, edited by Fridolin Stähli, Gut (Stafa), 1990.

OTHER

(Editor) *Romanische inedita auf Italiänischen Bibliotheken gesammelt,* Hertz (Berlin, Germany), 1856.

(Translator) Jose Caveda, *Geschichte der Baukunst in Spanien,* edited by Kugler, Ebner & Seubert (Stuttgart, Germany), 1858.

(Editor and translator) *Italienisches Liederbuch,* Hertz (Berlin, Germany), 1860.

(Translator) William Shakespeare, *Antonius und Kleopatra,* Brockhaus (Leipzig, Germany), 1867.

(Translator) William Shakespeare, *Timon von Athen,* Brockhaus (Leipzig, Germany), 1868.

(Editor) *Antologia dei moderni poeti italiani,* Hallberger (Stuttgart, Germany), 1869.

(Editor, with Hermann Kurz) *Deutscher Novellenschatz,* twenty-four volumes, Oldenbourg (Munich, Germany), 1871-1876.

(Editor, with Hermann Kurz) *Novellenschatz des Auslandes,* 14 volumes, Oldenbourg (Munich, Germany), 1872-1875.

(Editor) Hermann Kurz, *Gesammelte Werke: Mit einer Biographie des Dichters,* ten volumes, Kröner (Stuttgart, Germany), 1874.

(Editor and translator) Giuseppe Guisti, *Gedichte, Hofmann* (Berlin, Germany), 1875.

(Editor) *Italienische Novellisten,* six volumes, Grunow (Leipzig, Germany), 1877-1878.

(Translator) Giacomo Leopardi, *Werke,* Hertz (Berlin, Germany), 1878.

(Editor) Lodovico Ariosto, *Rasender Roland,* two volumes, translated by Hermann Kurz, Schottländer (Breslau, Germany), 1880-1881.

Neues Münchener Dichterbuch, Kröner (Stuttgart, Germany), 1882.

(Editor, with Ludwig Laistner) *Neuer deutscher Novellenschatz,* twenty-four volumes, Oldenbourg (Munich, Germany), 1884-1887.

(Translator) *Italienische Dichter seit der Mitte des 18. Fahrhunderts: Übersetzungen und Studien,* five volumes, Volumes 1-4, Hertz (Berlin, Germany), Volume 5, Cotta (Stuttgart and Berlin, Germany), 1889-1905.

(Editor) *Lodovico Ariostos Satiren,* translated by Otto Gildemeister, Behr (Berlin, Germany), 1904.

(Editor) Hermann Lingg, *Ausgewählte Gedichte,* Cotta (Stuttgart and Berlin, Germany), 1905.

(Translator) *Italienische Volksmärchen,* Lehmann (Munich, Germany), 1914.

(Translator) *Drei italienische Lustspiele aus der Zeit der Renaissance* (includes *Die Cassaria,* by Ariosto; *Die Aridosia,* by Lorenzino de' Medici; and *Mandragola,* by Niccolo Machiavelli), Diederichs (Jena), 1914.

Contributor to books, including *Fünfzehn neue deutsche Lieder zu alten Singweisen: Den deutschen Männern Ernst Moritz Arndt und Ludwig Uhland gewid-* *met,* edited by Franz Kugler, [Berlin, Germany], 1848; (with Emanuel Geibel) *Spanisches Liederbuch,* Hertz (Berlin, Germany), 1852; *Die Geschichte des Erstlingswerkes,* edited by Karl Emil Franzos, Titze (Leipzig), 1894; and *Die Lebens- und Weltanschauung der Freifrau Marie von Ebner-Eschenbach,* by Mechtild Alkemade, Volume 15: *Deutsche Quellen und Studien,* Wächter (Würzburg & Graz), 1935. Also contributor to periodicals, including *Süddeutsche Monatshefte* and *Euphorion.*

SIDELIGHTS: Paul Heyse was an enormously popular writer, best known for his "novellen," or short stories, a form he helped establish in Germany during the last half of the nineteenth century. His short stories most often feature exotic locales, fanciful, romantic plots, and beautiful, strong-willed heroines. Heyse also formulated a theory of short-story composition the so-called "falcon theory"—which stressed the need for unique points of plot and character above all else. Although he was respected highly enough to win the Nobel Prize for literature, his reputation fell into sharp decline soon after his death. The chief critical complaint against his work was a lack of depth. This, contention not unheard of even during his life, is well represented by an 1882 article in the English journal, *Spectator,* which read: "Heyse loves to skim the surface of life, he is afraid of its deeper emotions, and even when a serious note is touched in his writings, it is rarely elicited by a nobler feeling than that of sensuous passion."

Heyse was born in 1830, in Berlin, to an artistically talented and academically accomplished family. As a youth he excelled in language studies and helped his father, a philologist, proofread a dictionary he was compiling. He also wrote poetry, mostly romantic lyrics to a friend's sister. In 1847, Heyse enrolled at the University of Berlin to study classical philology. He continued writing poetry and frequented the cultured salons of Berlin. In 1849, he transferred to the University of Bonn and changed his major to Romance languages. Soon he had published a fairy-tale collection, *Der Fungbrunnen* ("The Fountain of Youth"), and a play,*Francesca von Rimini,* that was inspired by his love for a professor's young wife.

Two years later, Heyse returned to Berlin to deliver his dissertation on the poetry of the medieval troubadours. There he became a member of a literary circle made up of young, aspiring writers from the Prussian military and government. The following summer Heyse was awarded his doctorate, and that fall he received a grant from the Prussian Ministry of Culture to study unpublished Italian manuscripts. For much of 1852 and 1853, Heyse toured Rome, Naples, and Sorrento working and socializing, and in 1856, he would publish a volume of the manuscripts he translated there. But as Charles H. Helmetag wrote in the *Dictionary of Literary Biography*, "the main product of the trip was a series of poems and stories with Italian settings and passionate female characters, works that would be associated with Heyse in the mind of the German middle-class reading public for the rest of his life."

After his Italian sojourn, Heyse accepted an invitation from King Maximilian II of Bavaria to live in Munich. In exchange for a living stipend, Heyse was required only to write and participate in the court's literary salons. Heyse and his new bride, Margarethe Kugler, quickly settled in to Munich society, and later that year the most important of the works inspired by Heyse's Italian venture, "L'Arrabbiata," appeared.

The story concerns Antonio, a young fisherman, and Laurella, his neighbor, a beautiful, dark woman, just eighteen, and possessed of a wild and haughty manner. Antonio loves her, though he is also somewhat intimidated. He does not know that her boldness is actually an overcompensation for her fear of romantic involvement. Laurella's father mistreats her mother, and thus she is fearful of men, and wary of their attentions. Nevertheless, she accepts Antonio's invitation to accompany him one afternoon. Upon the spur of the moment, Antonio declares his love for her, and she rejects him. Despairing, he grabs her and leaps into the Bay of Sorrento, attempting to drown them both. Laurella bites his hand, drawing blood, and swims away. That night, Laurella brings Antonio herbs to help heal his hand, and reveals that she has been in love with him all along. Later, she confesses these events to her parish priest, and he is secretly overjoyed that her fears have been overcome by true love. Lawrence A. McLouth, wrote in a "Biographical Sketch" for an edition of Heyse's *Anfang und Ende*, that Heyse "never surpassed L'Arrabbiata, in which he at once struck the key-note of a successful story: supreme interest, a situation not a development, rapid action, beautiful, transparent language, only a few characters but all so well drawn that they fairly live and breathe."

In Munich, Heyse earned his stipend. He organized a literary circle to help further the careers of Munich writers, and also continued voluminous correspondence with other German writers, several books of which were published. Over the course of his career, he would write 120 short stories, forty plays, fifteen novels in verse, and seven novels, as well as numerous essays and poems. In short, he became a major figure in German letters celebrated by critics and extremely popular with the reading public. In 1867, Heyse and his second wife, Anna Schubard (his first wife having died in 1862), moved into a villa which became the center of Munich's cultural life. The following year, he gave up his stipend.

In 1871, Heyse coedited the twenty-four-volume *Deutscher Novellenschatz* ("Treasury of German Novellas"). In the introduction, he put forth a critical theory of the short story, which many consider his most lasting literary contribution. Heyse uses Giovanni Boccaccio's "Decameron"—in which an impoverished nobleman serves his prize falcon as a meal to please his lady—to illustrate his point that a successful story has a single "basic motif" that stands out in "strong silhouette" against the story's background and thus makes an indelible impression on the reader's mind. Each good story then, according to Heyse, has a "falcon": a marked element that distinguishes it immediately from every other story. Heyse's "falcon theory" became enormously popular among German critics, although some misinterpreted him as meaning that the central "falcon" of the story should be symbolic in nature, and others were overzealous in their application of the theory. But as Christiane Ullmann pointed out in the journal *Seminar*, Heyse "[did] not necessarily speak of a symbol . . . but of an occurrence which clearly and definitely impresses the reader as unique." And Donald LoCicero has cautioned in the journal *Modern Language Notes*, that Heyse did not intend his theory to be dogma, and "had no intention of precipitating the great falcon hunt which ensued."

In the mid-1870s, Heyse focused on writing novels as that form became more popular with the reading public. *Kinder der Welt*, translated as *Children of the World*, his first, was typical of his novels, in that it was long, complex, very popular, and received generally good reviews, although critics agreed that it was not on par with his short stories. *Children of the World* concerns a group of eight Berlin artists and academics, following their shifting allegiances and affairs of the heart from their college years through middle age. The novel aroused some controversy for its espousal of free love. Indeed, Helmetag has noted that Heyse was "considered by many a dangerously immoral writer, a reputation that contributed to his immense popularity."

By way of justifying his challenges to social convention, Heyse had proposed, in his introduction to *Moralische Novellen* that "Ausnahmemenschen" (exceptional individuals) should not be burdened by the same codes of conduct which guide the common people. Not all critics, however, have been convinced of his seriousness as a social theorist. E. K. Bennett, for instance, wrote in *A History of the German Novelle: From Goethe to Thomas Mann,* that Heyse "was merely a frondeur tilting at the social conventions of his generation."

Regardless of his purported threats to a moral society, Heyse was widely honored throughout his long life. In 1910, the year of his eightieth birthday, and four years before his death, he was elevated to the nobility, had a street in Munich named for him, and won the Nobel Prize for literature.

BIOGRAPHICAL AND CRITICAL SOURCES:

BOOKS

Bennett, E. K., *A History of the German Novelle,* revised and continued by H. M. Waidson, Cambridge University Press (Cambridge, England), 1961.

Berndin, Clifford Albrecht, *The Nobel Prize Winners: Literature,* edited by Frank N. Magill, Salem Press (Pasadena, CA), 1987.

Bianquis, Genevieve, *Nobel Prize Library: André Gide, Karl Gjellerup, Paul Heyse,* CRM Publishing (Del Mar), 1971.

Brandes, Georg, *Creative Spirits of the Nineteenth Century,* translated by Rasmus R. Anderson, Crowell (New York, NY), 1923.

Dictionary of Literary Biography, Volume 129: *Nineteenth-Century German Writers, 1841-1900,* Gale (Detroit, MI), 1993.

LoCicero, Donald, *The Practicality of the Theoretical,* Mouton (The Hague, Netherlands), 1970.

Maurer, Warren R., *The Naturalist Image of German Literature, Fink* (Munich, Germany), 1972.

McLouth, Lawrence A., *Anfang und Ende,* Holt (New York, NY), 1910.

Mitchell, Robert McBurney, *Heyse and His Predecessors in the Theory of the Novelle Baer* (Frankfurt am Main, Germany), 1915.

Swales, Martin, *The German Novelle,* Princeton University Press (Princeton, NJ), 1977.

PERIODICALS

Atlantic Monthly, March, 1893, pp. 410-415.

Germanic Review, May 1965.

Modern Language Notes, October 4, 1967, Donald LoCicero, "Paul Heyse's Falkentheorie: 'Bird Thou Never Wert,'" pp. 434-439.

Seminar, May 2, 1976, Christiane Ullman, "Form and Content of Paul Heyse's Novelle 'Andrea Delfin,'" pp. 109-120.

Spectator, December 9, 1882, "Books: 'Children of the World,'" pp. 1583-1584.*

*   *   *

HILL, Elizabeth Ann 1952-

PERSONAL: Born January 8, 1952, in London, England; daughter of William Strawbridge Phillips (an insurance broker) and Mavis Florence (a shop assistant; maiden name, Collins) Hill. *Ethnicity:* "Welsh/Cornish." *Education:* Attended secondary school in Falmouth, Cornwall, England. *Politics:* "Center." *Religion:* Church of England. *Hobbies and other interests:* Gardening.

ADDRESSES: Home—Cornwall, England. *Agent*—c/o Author Mail, Severn House Publishers, Inc., 595 Madison Ave., New York, NY 10022.

CAREER: Western Evening Herald, Plymouth, England, secretary, 1975-76; Stratton & Holborow (estate agents), Truro, England, secretary, 1980-84; Leon Robertson (antiques dealer), Penryn, England, bookkeeper, 1983-89; Cornwall Motor Auctions, Penryn, England, bookkeeper, 1990-96; freelance writer, 1996—.

MEMBER: Society of Authors, British Mensa.

WRITINGS:

NOVELS

The Hidden Spring, Souvenir Press (England), 1987, Ballantine (New York, NY), 1989.

Pebbles in the Tide, Souvenir Press (England), 1989.

Bad Pennies, Mandarin (London, England), 1993.

Fields of Clover, Mandarin (London, England), 1994.

The Driftwood Fire, Mandarin (London, England), 1996.

The Kendrick Girls, Severn House Publishers (New York, NY), 1997.

Remember Rachel, Severn House Publishers (New York, NY), 1997.

Genevra, Severn House Publishers (New York, NY), 2002.

WORK IN PROGRESS: Tinder Box (tentative title), a novel set in the 1920s; a second novel, "a psychological chiller."

SIDELIGHTS: Elizabeth Ann Hill told *CA:* "I write purely to entertain, for the sheer pleasure of playing with the language and, with any luck, to make some kind of a living. As I recall, it was the only school subject which greatly interested me as a child. As an adult, writing is the only work to which I've given serious commitment.

"I find it impossible to write while sitting at a keyboard. I need an easy chair, a scribble pad, and a felt-tip pen, and I generally work for about four hours of a morning. Only when I have about thirty sheets in longhand do I put it on the computer. A book takes four or five drafts to complete, beginning with a short, experimental one and gradually expanding. The plot remains flexible, subject to substantial changes, until about the third draft, when the whole thing finally 'gels.' After that, it's a matter of fine-tuning.

"I'm seldom short of ideas; the difficulty lies in choosing between them. A surprising number come from music, from song lyrics or even instrumental pieces. The first hazy notion of *Genevra* came into my head one evening while I was listening to Vaughan Williams's 'Fantasia on a Theme by Thomas Tallis,' which, of course, features in the story. Poetry also supplies images which I sometimes follow up; Tennyson's 'Mariana' poems were another source of the *Genevra* idea.

"As to author influences, there are many. H. E. Bates, Daphne du Maurier, Stella Gibbons, Ray Bradbury, Fay Weldon—the list is eclectic and very long. Theirs are the books I can open anywhere, read again and again, and still enjoy. That's the magic touch which I admire.

"I was twenty-seven when I started my first book, having won a prize in a short-story competition the previous summer. In a couple of years I turned out two short novels, *Remember Rachel* and *The Kendrick Girls.* They were apprentice work and I was learning the craft on them, but fortunately they had enough entertainment value to be published, and after that there was no going back. After *The Hidden Spring,* which was really a bit of black humor written for my own amusement, the next four books were all West Country sagas, one set in Victorian times, the others in the 1920s and 1930s. This brings me to *Genevra.* It was an idea which would not go away, a complete departure from the saga genre. I wanted to do it, enjoyed every minute, but my publishers at the time were none too keen on an excursion into the supernatural and turned it down. No matter, it had to be done. Anyway, it doesn't seem wise or realistic to tie oneself to a single genre.

"Character is always my fundamental interest, followed by colorful historical periods and settings. There are no messages, no axes I wish to grind. I simply know, from my own experience, the therapeutic value of a diverting story. I aim to provide those few hours' escape which everybody needs."

BIOGRAPHICAL AND CRITICAL SOURCES:

PERIODICALS

Booklist, April 15, 2002, Megan Kalan, review of *Genevra,* p. 1382.

* * *

HOAK, Dale 1941-

PERSONAL: Born December 12, 1941, in Springfield, OH; son of Eugene Q. (a university professor) and Thelma (Kohl) Hoak; married Berry Marshall (a museum administrator), April 9, 1968; children: Brady

Dale, Megan Elizabeth. *Ethnicity:* "White." *Education:* College of Wooster, B.A., 1963; University of Pittsburgh, M.A., 1964; Clare College, Ph.D., 1971. *Politics:* "Registered Democrat." *Religion:* "Protestant Episcopal." *Hobbies and other interests:* Sailing, gardening, cycling.

ADDRESSES: Home—209 Hemsptead Rd., Williamsburg, VA 23188. *Office*—Department of History, College of William & Mary, P.O. Box 8795, Williamsburg, VA 23187. *E-mail*—dehoak@wm.edu.

CAREER: Carnegie-Mellon University, Pittsburgh, PA, instructor, 1966-67; Florida Atlantic University, Boca Raton, FL, assistant professor of history, 1971-75; College of William & Mary, Williamsburg, VA, chancellor professor of history, 1975—.

MEMBER: North American Conference on British Studies, Renaissance Society of America, American Historical Association.

AWARDS, HONORS: Research grants, National Endowment for the Humanities, 1986 and 1989; Outstanding Faculty Award, Commonwealth of Virginia, 1997; fellow, Royal Historical Society; visiting fellow, Clare Hall, Cambridge.

WRITINGS:

The King's Council in the Reign of Edward VI, Cambridge University Press (New York, NY), 1976.
Images as History: From Earliest Times to 1715, Wadsworth Educational, 1994.
(Editor and contributor) *Tudor Political Culture,* Cambridge University Press (New York, NY), 1995.
(Co-editor and contributor) *The World of William and Mary: Anglo-Dutch Perspectives on the Revolution of 1688-89,* Stanford University Press (Stanford, CA), 1996.

Contributor to encyclopedias and other books, including *Tudor Rule and Revolution,* edited by J. McKenna and D. Guth, Cambridge University Press, 1982; *Encyclopedia of the Reformation,* edited by Hans Hillerbrand and others, Oxford University Press, 1996; and *Encyclopedia of the Renaissance,* edited by P. Grendler and others, Charles Scribner's Sons, 1999. Also contributor to periodicals, including *Journal of British Studies* and *Renaissance Quarterly.* Member, Board of editors, *Sixteenth-Century Journal;* advisor editor, *Eighteenth-Century Life.*

WORK IN PROGRESS: The Reign of Edward VI, for Longman; *Henry VIII,* for Macmillan; *Imperial Kingship from Henry V to Charles I,* for Macmillan; *War, Reformation, and Rebellion: Essays in Tudor Politics and Government,* for Cambridge University Press; research on Tudor coronations.

SIDELIGHTS: Dale Hoak told *CA:* "I began writing professional history, in this case the history of Tudor government, under the inspiration of my graduate supervisor at Cambridge, the late Sir Geoffrey Elton, whom I had first met in Pittsburgh in 1963.

"After teaching a course in the history of Northern Renaissance art, I became interested in the iconography of witchcraft in Europe in the sixteenth century. This interest led on to iconographical studies in Tudor political culture, especially the iconography of the Tudors' 'imperial' kingship. Concurrently I became interested in symbolic political rituals, especially royal coronations and funerals. An interest in art-as-history prompted me to write a series of fifty short essays on great European art from the Paleolithic era to 1715, a course packet used by instructors in over 400 American colleges and universities."

*   *   *

HOROWITZ, David 1903-2002

OBITUARY NOTICE—See index for *CA* sketch: Born April 9, 1903, in Malmo, Sweden; died October 27, 2002, in New York, NY. Journalist and author. Horowitz had a lengthy career reporting events in Israel and the Middle East for the United Nations. As a young man, he lived in Palestine from 1924 to 1934, learning about that region's people and politics before returning to the United States. After World War II he found work as a correspondent for the newly formed United Nations, and wrote the regular column "Behind the Scenes at the UN." He remained with the U.N. press corps for the rest of his career, reporting on events in

Israel from the perspective of a Zionist. In addition, Horowitz founded the United Israel World Union in 1943 and wrote for and edited its official journal, the *United Israel Bulletin;* he was also the founder, in 1954, of the World Union Press, a former president of the Foreign Press Association and the United Nations Correspondents Association, and a managing editor for the *American Examiner* (now the *Jewish Week*). Horowitz was the author of three books, *Thirty-three Candles* (1949), *An Answer to Tom Paine's Age of Reason* (1950), and *Pastor Charles Taze Russell: An Early American Christian Zionist* (1986); he also translated Moses Guibbory's *The Bible in the Hands of Its Creators* (1943) and was coeditor of *Public Broadcasting and the Public Trust* (1995).

OBITUARIES AND OTHER SOURCES:

BOOKS

Who's Who in World Jewry: A Biographical Dictionary of Outstanding Jews, Pitman (New York, NY), 1980.

PERIODICALS

New York Times, November 14, 2002, p. C18.

*   *   *

HOUSE, Adrian

PERSONAL: Born in England. *Education:* Attended New College, Oxford.

ADDRESSES: Office—c/o HiddenSpring/Paulist Press, 997 Macarthur Blvd., Mahwah, NJ 07430-2096.

CAREER: William Collins Publishers, London, England, managing director and publisher.

WRITINGS:

The Great Safari: The Lives of George and Joy Adamson, William Morrow (New York, NY), 1993.
Francis of Assisi: A Revolutionary Life, HiddenSpring (New York, NY), 2001.

SIDELIGHTS: In 1960, London publishing house William Collins released the book *Born Free,* the story of a couple who raised a lion cub and returned her to the wild. As the one-time managing director of the publishing firm, Adrian House had access to the story behind the story: the volatile relationship between Joy and George Adamson, the heroes of *Born Free,* Joy Adamson's multiple affairs, including one with William Collins himself, and the emotional turmoil documented in diaries, letters, and interviews. House, who also assisted George Adamson with his autobiography, eventually transformed this information into his own book, *The Great Safari: The Lives of George and Joy Adamson.*

The Great Safari is not a tell-all biography detailing numerous scandals—although the scandals are there—but a portrait of the early years of the wildlife conservation movement and two passionate, if sometimes violent, defenders of animal rights. House depicts Joy Adamson as a jealous neurotic whose sexual appetite was legendary, but softens that picture by discussing the influence of a difficult childhood and her ability to channel her passions into her writings and art. As an illustrator and photographer, Joy exposed African wildlife and people to a larger world. Robert S. O. Harding, who reviewed *The Great Safari* in the *New York Times Book Review,* wrote that Joy's "studies of East African flowers and paintings of Kenya's tribal peoples have had lasting scientific and ethnographic value," a point House strives to make clear in his own work. House also portrays George as a skilled rehabilitator, observing that the scientific community of the Adamsons's era failed to see the value in his work. The story of the Adamsons continues until their separate murders, Joy in 1980, George in 1989. But reviewers suggested that the value of *The Great Safari* is not in the tragic, sometimes incomprehensible marriage, but in the book's emphasis on ecological concerns. Harding, in the *New York Times Book Review,* said *The Great Safari* was "well worth reading for a picture of this formative time and place in wildlife conservation." Similarly, a reviewer for *Publishers Weekly* concluded, "This moving story is flecked with piercingly beautiful evocations of African flora and fauna that make it a resounding plea for preservation of the earth and its multiple species."

House's second book is also concerned with the early influences on environmentalism. After spending four years researching in Italy, Britain, Spain, Egypt, and the United States, House produced *Francis of Assisi: A Revolutionary Life,* a biography of the saint who was a friend to the poor, to women, and to animals. In the book, House writes he was motivated to write about St. Francis out of simple curiosity. Reviewers have suggested that although House's version of St. Francis's life is a relatively straightforward and respectful account, his attention to detail and his excellent writing made the book stand out among numerous earlier works as the definitive modern biography of the well-known saint.

House's time in Assisi, where he spent six months, also helps to distinguish his work. Living and working where Francis walked allowed House to put Francis's life in context. Writing for *Library Journal,* David Bourquin said that a major strength of the book is that House "effectively sets Francis's life within the social, economic, military, and religious forces of Italy" between the years 1182 and 1226. House also worked to write a book that would appeal to readers of any faith, focusing not only on Francis as a religious icon, but also as a man from a wealthy family and hedonistic background who developed modern ideas about morality. As John McMurtrie wrote in the *San Francisco Chronicle,* "The strength of House's book is in portraying Francis as a human being. Francis comes across as a man blessed with great humility, decency, and intellect, but he's also a showman with razor wit. On his bad days, he's a crank whose fondness for rules gets the better of him."

A special focus of House's biography is Francis's relationship with Clare di Favarone, who founded her own religious order according to Francis's tenets and was canonized herself in 1255. In writing for a diverse readership, however, House omits or discounts some of Francis's more supernatural experiences. Some readers questioned this decision. Ann Wroe, writing for the London *Daily Telegraph,* suggested that while House "clearly sympathises deeply with Francis . . . the miraculous stories embarrass him." His selectiveness, Wroe proposed, reflects that "House can find modern psychological explanations for some of these phenomena, but not for others." Reviewing the book for the London *Independent,* Peter Stanford found that House is "hopelessly caught between the religious symbolism of much of the material and the agnosticism of the majority of his desired audience."

In general, however, House's approach to his subject resonated with critics, who suggested that in his ef-forts to create a broad appeal he created a highly readable biography. A reviewer for *Publishers Weekly* remarked on House's skill as a storyteller and his ability to relate Francis's concerns to the modern world while avoiding anachronism: "Without casting Francis as a modern environmentalist or feminist, House nonetheless shows how the saint's great love for creation and regard for women captured the essence of these later movements." Catherine Pepinster, writing about the book for the London *Independent,* concluded that "the man who commits his life to identification with the urban poor, who believes in the need for man to develop a harmonious relationship with nature and is as concerned with the welfare of animals as with his fellow human beings, seems a cool hero for our own time."

BIOGRAPHICAL AND CRITICAL SOURCES:

PERIODICALS

Audobon, January-February, 1994, Graham Boynton, review of *The Great Safari: The Lives of George and Joy Adamson,* p. 104.

Booklist, September 15, 1993, review of *The Great Safari,* p. 139; March 15, 2001, Ilene Cooper, review of *Francis of Assisi: A Revolutionary Life,* p. 1335.

Daily Telegraph (London, England), April 22, 2000, Ann Wroe, "God's New Sort of Fool."

Economist, October 30, 1993, review of *The Great Safari,* p. 104.

History Today, November 2001, Anne Pointer, review of *Francis of Assisi,* p. 54.

Independent (London, England), April 21, 2000, Peter Stanford, "Francis of Assisi: The Do-Good Dr Dolittle of Hagiography," p. 5; May 7, 2000, Catherine Pepinster, review of *Francis of Assisi,* p. 49.

Kirkus Reviews, September 1, 1993, review of *The Great Safari,* p. 1119.

Library Journal, October 15, 1993, review of *The Great Safari,* p. 71; January 1, 2001, David Bourquin, review of *Francis of Assisi,* p. 114.

Los Angeles Times Book Review, review of *The Great Safari,* p. 6.

New York Times Book Review, October 10, 1993, Robert S. O. Harding, "Elsa's Mom Was Hard to Bear," p. 14; March 11, 2001, Geoffrey Moorhouse, "The Patron Saint of Greenies," p. 13.

Publishers Weekly, September 13, 1993, review of *The Great Safari,* p. 108; February 26, 2001, review of *Francis of Assisi,* p. 81.

San Francisco Chronicle, March 25, 2001, John Mc-Murtrie, "A Revolutionary Who Took Jesus at His Word," p. 6.

Soujourners, July 2001, Beth Isaacson, review of *Francis of Assisi,* p. 53.

Spectator, January 1, 1994, review of *The Great Safari,* p. 26; April 29, 2000, Christopher Howse, "The Case of the Camel That Passed through the Eye of a Needle," pp. 34-35.

Times Literary Supplement, January 28, 1994, Deborah L. Manzolillo, "Lionized Again," p. 27.

OTHER

Eclectica, http://www.eclectica.org/ (August 22, 2001), Ann Skea, review of *Francis of Assisi.**

*   *   *

HUDSON, Harriet
See MYERS, Amy

*   *   *

HURD, Barbara 1949-

PERSONAL: Born 1949, in Detroit, MI. *Education:* College of William and Mary, 1971; University of Maryland, 1984.

ADDRESSES: Office—Dunle Hall 132A, Frostburg State University, 101 Braddock Road, Frostburg, MD 21532. *Agent*—Beacon Press, 25 Beacon Street, Boston, MA 02108. *E-mail*—bhurd@frostburg.edu.

CAREER: Writer and educator. Frostburg State University, Frostburg, MD, 1985—, professor of creative writing, poetry, environmental literature and composition.

AWARDS, HONORS: Finalist, Annie Dillard Award for nonfiction, 2001.

WRITINGS:

Stirring the Mud: On Swamps, Bogs, and Human Imagination, Beacon Press (Boston, MA), 2001.
Entering the Stone: On Caves and Feeling through the Dark, Houghton Mifflin (New York, NY), 2003.

SIDELIGHTS: The Finzel and Cranesville swamps in Maryland provided Barbara Hurd with a rich departure point for journeys into mythology, literature, and spirituality in *Stirring the Mud: On Swamps, Bogs, and Human Imagination.* Hurd sees this often unexplored and misunderstood terrain as a place to feed the human spirit and imagination, a landscape that reminds us "what hungers in us is so large. What we feed it is so small."

Reviewers of *Stirring the Mud* have compared Hurd to the great American nature writers of the past and present. She "is a consummate naturalist, writing with the grace and precision of a Peter Matthiessen or an Annie Dillard," wrote a contributor to the *Los Angeles Times,* "but she is also remarkably curious about human nature, spinning her discussion to bring in Joseph Campbell, the I Ching and Thomas Edison." Knitting together such diverse subjects as Buddhist philosophy, mythology, and her own childhood, noted *Publishers Weekly,* "Hurd evokes the landscape through a series of unexpected and sometimes fascinating physical and mental wanderings."

Like Marjory Stoneman Douglas, author of the 1947 classic *The Rivers of Grass,* Hurd loves the stories of the eccentric characters who are drawn to swamps, and like Thoreau himself, has a flair for conveying her chosen patch of earth. Reflecting on the prevalence of animal-like plants in a swamp, for instance, Hurd infers that "there's a camaraderie here, a tolerance for hybrids and mongrels, a kinship among the patrons of an all-night, half-sunken bar for cross-dressers."

"It's such a sensual, gorgeous landscape," the author said in an interview with the online edition of the *Washington Post.* "I think a swamp is one of the most erotic landscapes because in order to enjoy it, you really have to pay attention. That's what a swamp asks—that you pay attention to it."

Maureen Delaney-Lehaman wrote in *Library Journal,* "Much of this short book is filled with Hurd's wanderings, both literally and figuratively, through the Finzel swamp in the Maryland Appalachians. She muses on the ambiguity of life in the swamp, a place where trees with needles shed them in autumn and plants eat insects. She speculates on what lurks beneath the mud and ponders the space between life and death. Hurd's prose is sprinkled with delightful images, such as skunk cabbages she imagines as tiny Yodas and Indian pipes as whimpled nuns in prayer."

A contributor to *Acorn Naturalist* online observed, "Hurd's new book steeps the reader in the strange beauty of swamps and bogs—a landscape where the hoods of skunk cabbages poke through the mud, where hundreds of amphibians perform nocturnal concerts while rare bog turtles forage about. A stirring account by a contemporary literary master, reminiscent of the exacting yet poetic style of Thoreau. A blend of nature, lore and poetic philosophy that replicates the feelings one gets when exploring these rich environments that bridge land and water."

BIOGRAPHICAL AND CRITICAL SOURCES:

PERIODICALS

Library Journal, November 15, 2000, Maureen J. Delaney-Lehman, review of *Stirring the Mud: On Swamps, Bogs, and Human Imagination,* p. 93.
Los Angeles Times, February, 2001.
Publishers Weekly, January 22, 2001, review of *Stirring the Mud,* p. 314.

OTHER

Acorn Naturalist, http://www.acornnaturalists.com/ (August 22, 2001), review of *Stirring the Mud: On Swamps, Bogs, and Human Imagination.*
Beacon Press Online, http://www.beacon.org/ (August 22, 2001).
Washington Post.com, http://www.washingtonpost.com/ (August 22, 2001), Peter Carlson, "Bogged up in Mud" (interview with Barbara Hurd).

J

JAFFE, Adam B. 1955-

PERSONAL: Born May 1, 1955, in Cleveland, OH; son of Harold L. (an engineer) and Patricia H. Jaffe; married Pamela J. Jorgensen (an artist), September 25, 1977. *Ethnicity:* "White."

ADDRESSES: Office—Department of Economics, Brandeis University, Waltham, MA 02454-9110. *E-mail*—ajaffe@brandeis.edu.

CAREER: Harvard University, Cambridge, MA, assistant professor, 1985-94; Brandeis University, Waltham, MA, professor of economics, 1994—, and department chair. President's Council of Economic Advisors, senior staff economist, 1990-91; National Bureau of Economic Research, member of program in productivity and technological change.

WRITINGS:

(Editor, with Josh Lerner and Scott Stern) *Innovation Policy and the Economy,* MIT Press (Cambridge, MA), Volume 1, 2000, Volume 2, 2001.
(With Manuel Trajtenberg) *Patents, Citations, and Innovations: A Window on the Knowledge Economy,* MIT Press (Cambridge, MA), 2002.

BIOGRAPHICAL AND CRITICAL SOURCES:

PERIODICALS

NBER Reporter, winter, 2000, review of *Innovation Policy and the Economy,* Volume 1, p. 44; winter, 2001, review of *Innovation Policy and the Economy,* Volume 2, p. 37.

JAKUBOWSKI, Maxim 1944-

PERSONAL: Born 1944, in Barnet, England; son of Marjaov and Brenda (Rothberg) Jakubowski; married Dolores Rotenberg; children: two. *Education:* Educated in France.

ADDRESSES: Home—95 Finchley Lane, London NW4 1BY England. *Office*—c/o Murder One, 71-73 Charing Cross Rd., London, England. *E-mail*—murder_london@compuserve.com.

CAREER: Author, editor, and publisher. Murder One (bookshop), London, England, co-owner; *Mystery Scene,* contributing editor; columnist for *Crime Time Time Out,* and *Guardian;* Literary director of Crime Scene Festival at National Film Theatre, London. Advisor to several international film festivals.

AWARDS, HONORS: Anthony Critical Award, 1992, for *100 Great Detectives;* Karel Award for contribution to European science fiction. Erotic Author of the Year, 2002, for *Kiss Me Sadly,*.

WRITINGS:

(With Ron Van der Meer) *The Great Movies—Live!: A Pop-up Book,* Simon & Schuster (New York, NY), 1987.
Life in the World of Women: A Collection of Vile, Dangerous, and Loving Stories, Do-Not Press (London, England), 1996.

It's You That I Want to Kiss (novel), Do-Not Press (London, England), 1996, published as *It's You That I Want to Kiss, and Other Erotic Thrillers,* Venus Book Club (New York, NY), 2001.

Because She Said She Loved Me (stories), Do-Not Press (London, England), 1997.

The State of Montana: A Novella of Erotica, Do-Not Press (London, England), 1998.

On Tenderness Express, Do-Not Press (London, England), 2000.

Kiss Me Sadly (novel), Do-Not Press (London, England), 2002.

The Erotic Novels, Do-Not Press (London, England), 2002.

EDITOR

(And translator with Beth Blish) *Travelling towards Epsilon: An Anthology of French Science Fiction,* New English Library (London, England), 1977.

Twenty Houses of the Zodiac: An Anthology of International Science Fiction, New English Library (London, England), 1979.

(With Malcolm Edwards) *The SF Book of Lists,* Berkley Books (New York, NY), 1983.

The Wit and Wisdom of Rock and Roll, Unwin (London, England), 1983.

Lands of Never: An Anthology of Modern Fantasy, Unwin (London, England), 1983.

MTV Music Television, Who's Who in Rock Video, Zomba Books (London, England), 1983, Morrow (New York, NY), 1984.

Beyond Lands of Never: A Further Anthology of Modern Fantasy, Unwin (London, England), 1984.

Rear Window and Other Stories, Simon & Schuster (New York, NY), 1988.

New Crimes (annual), Robinson (London, England), 1989-1991.

100 Great Detectives (directory), Carroll & Graf (New York, NY), 1991.

Constable New Crimes 1, Constable (London, England), 1992.

Constable New Crimes 2, Constable (London, England), 1993.

(With Edward James) *The Profession of Science Fiction: SF Writers on Their Craft and Ideas,* foreword by Arthur C. Clarke, St. Martin's Press (New York, NY), 1992.

Murders for the Fireside: The Best of Winter's Crimes, Pan Books (London, England), 1992.

More Murders for the Fireside, Pan Books (London, England), 1994.

Crime Yellow, Victor Gollancz (London, England), 1994.

The Mammoth Book of Erotica, Carroll & Graf (New York, NY), 1994.

London Noir, Serpent's Tail (London, England), 1994.

(With Dolores Jakubowski) *The Best of the Journal of Erotica,* Titan Books (London, England), 1995.

No Alibi: The Best New Crime Fiction, Ringpull (Manchester, England), 1995.

The Mammoth Book of International Erotica, Robinson, London, Carroll & Graf (New York, NY), 1996.

The Mammoth Book of Pulp Fiction, Robinson, London, Carroll & Graf (New York, NY), 1996.

(With Mike Ripley) *Fresh Blood,* Do Not Press (London, England), 1996.

(With Mike Ripley) *Fresh Blood 2,* Do Not Press (London, England), 1997.

Past Poisons: An Ellis Peters Memorial Anthology of Historical Crime, Headline (London, England), 1998.

The Mammoth Book of Historical Erotica, Robinson, London, Carroll & Graf (New York, NY), 1998.

The Mammoth Book of New Erotica, Robinson, London, Carroll & Graf (New York, NY), 1998.

(With Mike Ripley) *Fresh Blood 3,* Do Not Press (London, England), 1999.

(With Nathan Braund) *The Mammoth Book of Jack the Ripper,* Carroll & Graf (New York, NY), 1999.

Chronicles of Crime, Headline (London, England), 1999.

(With Michael Hemmingson) *The Mammoth Book of Short Erotic Novels,* Carroll & Graf (New York, NY), 2000.

New English Library Book of Internet Stories, New English Library (London, England), 2000.

Murder through the Ages, Headline (London, England), 2000.

Mammoth Book of Best New Erotica, Robinson, London, Carroll & Graf (New York, NY), 2001.

Mammoth Book of Pulp Action, Robinson, London, Carroll & Graf (New York, NY), 2001.

(With Marilyn Taye-Lewis) *Mammoth Book of Erotic Photography,* Robinson, London, Carroll & Graf (New York, NY), 2001.

(With M. Christian) *Mammoth Book of Tales From the Road,* Robinson, London, Carroll & Graf (New York, NY), 2003.

Mammoth Book of Best New Erotica, Volume 2: 2002, Robinson, London, Carroll & Graf (London, England), 2003.

TRANSLATOR

Michel Jeury, *Chronolysis,* Macmillan (New York, NY), 1980.

Columnist with *Time Out;* contributor to publications, including London *Observer, Daily Telegraph, Independent* and *Guardian.* Contributor to anthologies, including *Noirotica 1, Noirotica 2,* Masquerade Books, 1997, *Noirotica 3: Stolen Kisses,* edited by Thomas S. Roche, Black Books (San Francisco, CA), 2000, and many others.

WORK IN PROGRESS: History of Erotic Fiction.

SIDELIGHTS: Maxim Jakubowski is a British author, editor, and publisher in the genres of erotica, fantasy, science fiction, and crime and mystery fiction, as well as the owner of the popular Murder One bookshop in London. Jakubowski was born in England and raised in Paris, and as a young adult he became a voracious reader of science fiction, then crime novels. He edited a number of science fiction and fantasy anthologies in the 1970s and 1980s, including *Travelling Towards Epsilon: An Anthology of French Science Fiction,* to which he contributed and which he also translated with Beth Blish. In a *Times Literary Supplement* review, Eric Korn wrote that "too many stories are wrong-headed pastiches of Anglophone models: they are often literary in a literal way, which is to say they frequently mention other writers." *New Statesman* reviewer J. G. Ballard called it "one of the most interesting collections I have read." Included is the 1975 prize-winning story, "Thomas," by Dominique Douay, in which computer controls are used to treat the mentally ill.

Jakubowski and Malcolm Edwards collaborated on *The SF Book of Lists,* which *Los Angeles Times Book Review* contributor Dick Lochte felt contains "a number of treats for the science fiction fan and a few amusements for other readers." Some of the lists were first published in science fiction magazines or reference books. A useful list, "The Years of Futures Past," is a chronology of the editors' picks of the best science fiction novels and short stories over the years, including Hugo, Nebula, and other award winners or nominees. *The SF Book of Lists* names pseudonyms of science fiction authors, collaborators, and books that

have been adapted for film. There are other lists of stories influenced by chess, stories of sex between humans and aliens, and humans and robots, science fiction writers who have written gay science fiction or pornography, and Nobel literary prize-winners who have done the same. *Analog Science Fiction/Science Fact* writer Tom Easton wrote that because the book has neither a table of contents nor an index, it "is useless to anyone except the browser." However, a *Washington Post Book World* reviewer commented that a science fiction fan "will go into hyperdrive over this book."

Colin Greenland reviewed *The SF Book of Lists* and *Lands of Never: A Further Anthology of Modern Fantasy* for *British Books News.* He also felt the former to be incomplete due to its lack of index and contents, but did call it a "remarkable collection." Greenland noted that contributors to the latter include Angela Carter, Robert Silverberg, William Horwood, Christopher Evans, Steve Rasnic Tem, J. G. Ballard, and John Grant. Greenland noted that "the book as a whole is lightweight" and felt that only Carter and Evans "seem to have their customary presence, both refashioning the stuff of Germanic legend, both vivid and sombre."

Jakubowski and Ron Van der Meer produced *The Great Movies Live!: A Pop-up Book.* Chicago *Tribune Books* contributor Richard Christiansen called it "a slick variation on children's popup books that presents cutout scenes from five movies." Included are scenes from *King Kong, High Noon, Gone with the Wind, The Seven-Year Itch,* and *Casablanca,* which features a tiny music box that plays *As Time Goes By.*

Jakubowski's imprint, Black Box Thrillers, reissued books by popular American noir authors, such as David Goodis, Jim Thompson, Cornell Woolrich, W. R. Burnett, and Horace McCoy, as well as a small number of contemporary writers. He told Joyce Park in an interview for *MysteryGuide.com* online that sales did not start out strong. "But what I didn't realize myself is that a whole new generation of people were coming to crime writers, and now, fourteen or fifteen years later, what I would term the whole Fresh Blood generation . . . of British crime writers are people who started reading crime writing for real. I mean, a lot of them had probably read some of the Golden Age people, but they weren't hooked by crime writing until they started reading all these reissues, many of which I was involved in."

Jakubowski edited annual editions of *New Crimes,* beginning in 1989. In the 1990 edition, he includes nineteen stories, including several vintage pieces by Woolrich and Goodis. Additional stories in the collection come from Sara Paretsky, John le Carré, Robert Barnard, Peter Lovesey, Derek Raymond (also known as Robin Cook), James Crumley, Andrew Vachss, Peter Lovesey, and others. Also included is an interview with author Patricia Highsmith. A *Kirkus Reviews* contributor called it "a decidedly eccentric collection." *Publishers Weekly* contributor Sybil Steinberg reviewed *New Crimes 2* and wrote that "Jakubowski's veneration of American Jim Thompson . . . permeates this entire collection" and felt that the best reading was to be found in the stories of Reginald Hill, H. R. F. Keating, Ed McBain, Bill Pronzini, and Charles Willeford, writers who have long been on the scene. Steinberg also praised Paul Buck's "Twisting the Blade" and Susan Moody's "Freedom." *New Crimes 3* was reviewed by a *Publishers Weekly* reviewer who felt the standout stories are the previously unpublished "Surrogate," by Robert B. Parker and "Jukebox Jungle," by John D. MacDonald. The reviewer also praised "The Monk's Ale," by P. C. Doherty, "Star," by Molly Brown, "The Persian Apothecary," by Cay Van Ash, "Until I Do," by Robert Lopresti, and "Squeezer," by Steve Rasnic Tem. *Crime Yellow* features sixteen stories by contributors who include Mat Coward, Martin Edwards, Howard Douglas, Susan Kelly, Robert Richardson, Ed Gorman, Joe Bannister, Lesley Grant-Adamson, Russell James, Michael Z. Lewin, and Janwillem van de Wetering. A *Kirkus Reviews* writer observed that the best of the stories "are brief and acerbic." A *Publishers Weekly* reviewer wrote that "among the most appealing is Robert Richardson's 'The Woman of Goodwill,' a Holmesian pastiche that would have offended the Victorians' sense of propriety."

For *100 Great Detectives,* one hundred mystery writers penned essays on their favorite literary detectives, some of whom make frequent fictional appearances, while others appeared briefly, sometimes only once. "Among the most obscure inclusions are Charles Burns's comic-strip sleuth El Borbah and John Russell Fearn's 'Black Maria,'" wrote Jon L. Breen in *Armchair Detective.* Linda Semple writes about her favorite, V. I. Warshawski, while Anne Hart discusses Hercule Poirot. Julian Symons's piece is on Sam Spade, Paula Gosling's is about Rex Stout, and Loren D. Estleman writes about Philip Marlowe. *Booklist* reviewer Elliott Swanson found that the book "has the

potential to get fans of the genre moving in some new directions." A *Kirkus Reviews* contributor felt that readers who love mysteries "will enjoy these generous, generally upbeat homages—many written with appropriate stylistic flourish."

Jakubowski and Edward James collected sixteen of several dozen articles by American and British authors published in *Foundation: A Review of Science Fiction* and presented them in a book of the same name as the original series, *The Profession of Science Fiction.* The contributors explore their genre, why they began writing science fiction, and the relationship between science fiction and mainstream writing. Writer and astrophysicist David Brin writes in the essay: "We are the ones who toy with new myths, with the images and ideas our culture may need as it rushes headlong toward a future that may glow or may burn but in any event will certainly feature profound change." *Locus* reviewer Gary K. Wolfe said that Naomi Mitchison's account of her friendships with H. G. Wells and Olaf Stapledon "is certainly one of the high points of the collection. . . . Mitchison's essay also demonstrates one of this book's hidden strengths: namely, that its best parts are not necessarily to be found in the contributions of those authors we in the States view as 'celebrities.'" Wolfe noted "thoughtful and provocative pieces" by Michael Coney, Richard Cowper, M. John Harrison, Gwyneth Jones, and Richard Grant. Other writers include J. G. Ballard, Jack Williamson, Gene Wolfe, James Blish, Ursula Le Guin, Norman Spinrad, Garry Kilworth, and Pamela Sargent. *New Scientist* reviewer David Barrett called the book "fascinating." "Whimsical or deadly serious, each essay contributes significantly to the enjoyment and understanding of science fiction," wrote J. R. Cox in *Choice.*

The first of Jakubowski's "Mammoth" books is *The Mammoth Book of Erotica,* which a London *Observer* reviewer called "an uncompromising selection." *London Noir* is a collection British noir fiction, featuring writers who include Mark Timlin, John Harvey, Derek Raymond, Chaz Brenchley, and Molly Brown. A *Publishers Weekly* reviewer wrote that "the London of these fifteen effective, workmanlike stories is sleazy and brutal, not cozy or literary." The reviewer felt that as a collection, these stories "make up a good sampler of current British crime writing."

Jakubowski and Mike Ripley edited a series of three books of noir fiction, the first of which was reviewed by Marilyn Stasio in the *New York Times Book Review*. Stasio called *Fresh Blood* "a terrific introduction" to the new British authors being showcased by independent publisher Do-Not Press. A *Publishers Weekly* contributor who reviewed *Fresh Blood 2* noted that "it offers reason to imagine that some of the talent on display will soon crack crime fiction's top rank."

A *Kirkus Reviews* contributor observed that *Life in the World of Women: A Collection of Vile, Dangerous, and Loving Stories,* written by Jakubowski, is a collection "of nine erotic (and largely sadistic) fantasies in which males provide the agency and women the geography." Jakubowski's novel, *It's You That I Want to Kiss,* is a story of diamond smuggling and sex. Model and escort Anne Ryan carries gems for a group of smugglers but leaves the operation after she is assaulted by two of them. She teams up with Jacob Jones, both in bed and in staying alive, as they are chased from Miami to New Orleans to Seattle by her former cohorts. A *Kirkus Reviews* contributor noted the "copious interludes of rough sex" and added that by the time the couple reaches Seattle, "even the rawest appetites seem to have been burned as deeply from their story as from their bodies, and what's left is perversely tender." *Library Journal* reviewer Rex E. Klett called the novel "literate, sophisticated prose."

In *The Mammoth Book of Historical Erotica,* Jakubowski offers a fictional look at sexual depravity over time—in ancient Egypt, Renaissance Italy, and in Victorian public schools. Authors include Poppy Z. Brite, Julian Rathbone, and Thomas S. Roche. A *Books* reviewer called it "a raunchy collection." By the time Jakubowski's *The Mammoth Book of Short Erotic Fiction* was published, the previous four "Mammoth" books of erotica had sold nearly half a million copies. The new volume, which was edited with Michael Hemmingson, is comprised of eleven erotic novellas from authors who include Jakubowski, Michael Perkins, William Vollmann, Josephine Jarmaine, M. Christian, and Robert Coover. A *Kirkus Reviews* contributor called Perkins's "Night Moves" "an appealingly believable tale" and said that Jakubowski's contribution, "Hotel Room Fuck," is "a gooey tale juicy with exertions undertaken amid much body heat."

Victoria Esposito-Shea reviewed Jakubowski's novel, *On Tenderness Express* for *HandHeldCrime* online. As the book begins, protagonist Martin Jackson, a London

private investigator, says that he is a liar and an unreliable witness and offers the reader the choice of believing him, or not. Esposito-Shea wrote that "the absolute starkness of this opening absolutely took my breath away; I couldn't imagine that the rest of the book could possibly live up to it." The book is about Jackson's searches for a man's wife, a woman's sister, and a rare book, which take him from Europe to New Orleans, with stops along the way. The book is also about searching for human relationships and sex. Esposito-Shea wrote that as Jackson becomes more and more involved in the searches, the story becomes "by and large, astounding. Calling what happens plot twists is simply inadequate; it's more as though the reader's on an elevator which suddenly drops five floors. . . . And yes, it does live up to the promise of the book's beginning."

Jakubowski told *CA:* "I have always been both a fan and an appreciator of genre fiction. Early forays into writing were in the field of science fiction and fantasy and it's my interest for popular literature which, after some years in international business, prompted me to move into book publishing. Here, I was responsible for various crime and erotic imprints, but corporate politics finally got the best of me and I returned to writing, albeit buffered by my ownership of a major bookshop.

"I feel strongly that crime and erotic fiction are wonderful areas to work in, even more so in view of the fact that my own themes, obsessions, and preoccupations stand uncomfortably against the mainstream of most modern writing because of their highly charged sexual content and partly ironic post-modernist approach to narrative.

"I believe I am still at an early stage of my career, having arrived late to the realisation that I had no need to compromise my themes or realism and would just write what I wanted to write.

"Some commentators have described my work as 'romantic pornography,' a label which pleases me. One has to push the boundaries, but essentially I write about real people, of blood and flesh, struggling with the world of relationships and life. And people have feelings, and sex. The rest I leave to commentators."

BIOGRAPHICAL AND CRITICAL SOURCES:

PERIODICALS

Analog Science Fiction/Science Fact, July, 1984, pp. 165-171.

Armchair Detective, spring, 1992, Jon L. Breen, "What about Murder," p. 249.

Bloomsbury Review, January, 1997, Patricia J. Wagner, review of *The Mammoth Book of Pulp Fiction,* p. 17.

Booklist, April, 1990, Stuart Miller, review of *New Crimes,* p. 1611; August, 1991, Elliott Swanson, review of *100 Great Detectives,* p. 2092.

Books, summer, 1999, review of *The Mammoth Book of Historical Erotica,* p. 21.

British Book News, March, 1984, Colin Greenland, "Science Fiction," pp. 134-136.

Choice, February, 1993, J. R. Cox, review of *The Profession of Science Fiction,* p. 964.

Kirkus Reviews, April 1, 1990, review of *New Crimes,* pp. 468-469; August 15, 1991, review of *100 Great Detectives,* p. 1082; June 15, 1995, review of *Crime Yellow,* p. 819; March 15, 1997, review of *Life in the World of Women,* p. 422; July 15, 1997, review of *It's You That I Want to Kiss,* p. 1068; February 15, 2000, review of *The Mammoth Book of Short Erotic Novels,* p. 201.

Library Journal, August, 1997, Rex E. Klett, review if *It's You That I Want To Kiss,* p. 139.

Locus, February, 1993, Gary K. Wolfe, review of *The Profession of Science Fiction,* p. 93.

Los Angeles Times Book Review, January 1, 1984, p. 10.

New Scientist, March 20, 1993, David Barrett, review of *The Profession of Science Fiction,* p. 44.

New Statesman, April 15, 1977, J. G. Ballard, "Science Fiction: French Polish," p. 499.

New Statesman & Society, October 27, 1995, review of *No Alibi,* p. 46.

New York Times, November 30, 1987, p. C17.

New York Times Book Review, January 25, 1981, Gerald Jonas, "Science Fiction," p. 24; March 30, 1997, Marilyn Stasio, "Crime," p. 23.

Observer (London, England), October 9, 1994, Albert Manguel, review of *The Mammoth Book of Erotica,* p. 25.

Publishers Weekly, January 25, 1991, Sybil Steinberg, review of *New Crimes 2,* p. 50; November 22, 1991, review of *New Crimes 3,* p. 41; February 20, 1995, review of *London Noir,* p. 201; June 12, 1995, review of *Crime Yellow,* p. 51; February 16, 1998, review of *Fresh Blood 2,* p. 207; February 7, 2000, review of *The Mammoth Book of Short Erotic Novels,* p. 66.

Reference & Research Book News, December, 1991, review of *100 Great Detectives,* p. 29.

Times Literary Supplement, July 1, 1977, Eric Korn, "Ne vaut pas le détour," p. 795.

Tribune Books (Chicago, IL), December 6, 1987, Richard Christiansen, review of *The Great Movies Live!,* p. 3.

Wall Street Journal, December 9, 1996, Tom Nolan, review of *The Mammoth Book of Pulp Fiction,* p. A12.

Washington Post Book World, December 25, 1983, p. 12.

OTHER

HandHeldCrime, http://www.handheldcrime.com/ (March 23, 2001), Victoria Esposito-Shea, review of *On Tenderness Express.*

MysteryGuide.com, http://www.mysteryguide.com/ (May 10, 2001), Joyce Park, interview with Maxim Jakubowski.

*   *   *

JENSEN, Erik Frederick 1906-

PERSONAL: Born 1906, in England.

ADDRESSES: Agent—c/o Author Mail, Oxford University Press, 200 Madison Ave., New York, NY 10016.

CAREER: Writer.

WRITINGS:

The Iban and Their Religion, Clarendon Press (Oxford, England), 1974.

SIDELIGHTS: Erik Jensen wrote *The Iban and Their Religion,* an analysis of Iban culture as it has developed on the island of Borneo. The book also discusses Iban myths and legends, and it examines the relationship of agricultural concerns to the Iban conception of religion. "Jensen's study takes up the traditional view of myths as charters or explanations," affirmed D. A. Buchdahl in *American Anthropologist.* He added, however, that Jensen "also demonstrates how myths live fully within the community." According to Buchdahl, "For the Iban, the practical everyday world is filled with spirits, and they must, in order to survive, pay constant attention to them." A *Choice* reviewer deemed Jensen's book an "impressive study" and added that it "probably will remain the definitive account of the subjects discussed." Buchdahl, in his *American Anthropologist* appraisal, called *The Iban and Their Religion* "a wonderfully detailed study," and he declared that Jensen proves to be "thoroughly conversant with [Iban] history and idiom . . . and sensitive to the mood and style of [Iban culture]." In addition, Buchdahl noted that the book manages to "blend useful quantitative data with evocative descriptions of rites and worship," and he observed that it "provides a clear idea of . . . how religion enters significantly into the everyday life of individuals."

BIOGRAPHICAL AND CRITICAL SOURCES:

PERIODICALS

American Anthropologist, June, 1977, D. A. Buchdahl, review of *The Iban and Their Religion,* pp. 407-410.
Choice, October, 1975, review of *The Iban and Their Religion,* p. 1041.*

*   *   *

JOHNSON, Lionel (Pigot) 1867-1902

PERSONAL: Born March 15, 1867, in Broadstairs, Kent, England; died of a skull fracture, October 4, 1902, in London, England; son of William Victor (an army captain) and Catherine Delicia (Walters) Johnson. *Education:* Attended Winchester College; New College, Oxford, B.A., 1890. *Politics:* "Interested in Irish nationalistic politics." *Religion:* Catholic.

CAREER: Journalist for *Academy, National Observer, Spectator, Athenaeum,* and *Daily Chronicle,* c. early 1890s. Lecturer on Irish affairs, 1894.

MEMBER: Century Guild, Rhymers' Club.

WRITINGS:

The Art of Thomas Hardy, Dodd, Mead (New York, NY), 1894.
Poems, Copeland & Day (Boston, MA), 1895.

Ireland with Other Poems, Copeland & Day (Boston, MA), 1897.
Twenty-one Poems, selected by W. B. Yeats, Dun Imer Press (Dundrum, Ireland), 1904.
(With W. B. Yeats) *Poetry and Ireland: Essays by W. B. Yeats and Lionel Johnson,* Cuala Press (Churchtown, Dundrum, Ireland), 1908.
Post Liminium: Essays and Critical Papers, edited by Thomas Wittemore, Elkin Matthew's (London, England), 1911, Kennerley (New York, NY), 1912.
Some Poems of Lionel Johnson, edited by Louise Imogen Guiney, Elkin Matthews (London, England), 1912.
Poetical Works of Lionel Johnson, edited by Ezra Pound, Macmillan (New York, NY), 1915.
The Religious Poems of Lionel Johnson, Burns & Oates (London, England), 1916.
Some Winchester Letters of Lionel Johnson, edited by J. F. Russell, Macmillan (New York, NY), 1919.
Reviews and Critical Papers, edited by Robert Shafer, Dutton (New York, NY), 1921.
The Complete Poems of Lionel Johnson, edited by Iain Fletcher, Unicorn (London, England), 1953, published as *The Collected Poems of Lionel Johnson,* Garland (New York, NY), 1982.
Three Poets of the Rhymers' Club: Ernest Dowson, Lionel Johnson, John Davidson, selected and introduced by Derek Stanford, Carcanet Press (Cheadle), 1974.
(With Walter Burgess and Richard Le Gallienne) *Bits of Old Chelsea,* Garland (New York, NY), 1978.
Poetry and Fiction: Reflections on Three Nineteenth-Century Authors: Herbert P. Horne, Hubert Crackanthorpe, William Johnson Cory, Tragara Press (Edinburgh, Scotland), 1982.
Selected Letters of Lionel Johnson, edited by Murray Pittock, Tragara Press (Edinburgh, Scotland), 1988.
Three Decadent Poets: Ernest Dowson, John Gray, and Lionel Johnson, Garland (New York, NY), 1990.
Poems, Woodstock Books (Oxford, England), 1993.

Also contributor to *The Prose Writings of James Clarence Mangan,* AMS Press (New York, NY), 1978.

SIDELIGHTS: Like so many of his fellow writers of his era, Lionel Johnson was a tragic figure who produced works of poetry that showed brilliant promise, all the while cutting his life short with bouts of alcoholism and hard living. Johnson's homosexuality was in direct conflict with the structured and strict confines of the Catholic Church that he admired. This led to the production of what some critics call the best work of that generation and would indirectly also lead to his death.

Johnson was born on March 15, 1867, to William Victor Johnson, a captain in the light infantry and Catherine Delicia (Walters) Johnson. Born in Broadstairs in Kent, England, Johnson was the third son of a Protestant family of Welsh descent. However, a distant ancestor of the family was of Irish descent and fought in an uprising against the Catholics. This ancestor sparked Johnson's interest in Ireland and Irish politics, and later in life he would lecture on the subject. As a member of a military family, Johnson was subjected to a structured upbringing that he found unbearable. From an early age, he expressed an interest in converting to Catholicism, something his family strongly opposed.

Johnson was schooled at Winchester College, where he won numerous prizes for his poetry and where he was named editor of the *Wykehamist.* In 1885 he won a scholarship to New College Oxford. It was while at Oxford that he made the acquaintance of W. B. Yeats and other members of the Rhymers' Club. Called the "tragic generation" by Yeats, this group and other members of the literary community at the time were all marked by moments of great literary success and lives that contained mental illness, homosexuality, and sickness. It was also during this time that Johnson began to drink heavily and his friends noted that he was never without a bottle of whiskey in his hands. He also published several poems in two small volumes of work by the Rhymers' Club in 1892 and 1894. In 1890, Johnson graduated from Oxford with a degree in classical moderations and litterae humaniores.

After graduation, Johnson moved to London to pursue a literary career full time. He wrote critical essays for the *Daily Chronicle,* the *Academy,* and the *National Observer.* Johnson fulfilled his childhood ambition to convert to Catholicism in 1891, when he was admitted to the Roman Catholic Church. It was here that the structural restraints of the world that Johnson craved again came into direct conflict with his own lifestyle. After converting to Catholicism, Johnson renounced his homosexuality. It was also the catalyst for some of his best poetry. "The struggle between spiritual aspiration and the wayward flesh is the theme of Johnson's best poetry. For the most part it is a conflict which, in

spite of its melodramatic potential, he nonetheless handles with a curious kind of dignity, in much the same way as Johnson himself behaved, maintaining a courtly demeanor and striving always to face the world in clean linen, while stumbling around in an alcoholic haze," commented John Munro in the *Dictionary of Literary Biography.*

The Art of Thomas Hardy further secured Johnson's position as a serious literary critic. His other critical writings were collected and posthumously produced in *Post Liminum* and *Reviews and Critical Papers.* "From the day of its first publication in 1894 this book has had a very special place in the field of literary criticism; not so much, perhaps, for its restrained, clear-sighted estimate of Hardy's genius as from the fact that in its pages one is initiated into the very quintessence of the author's own refined and solitary temper," wrote Llewlyn Powys in *Freeman.*

In 1895 Johnson published *Poems* and two years later produced *Ireland with Other Poems.* Many critics believe that *Poems* contains some of his best works. Among the collection were the poems "The Dark Angel" and "Mystic and Cavalier." In the "Dark Angel," Johnson again shows the anguish between the temptation of his lifestyle and his attempt to abide by the codes of the Catholic Church. "Mystic and Cavalier" begins with Johnson's famous line, "Go from me: I am one of those, who fall." It is the poem of a man who believes he will fail at what he tries to attain. "The Destroyer of a Soul," written in 1892, is a poem addressed to Oscar Wilde and in it, Johnson denounces Wilde's lifestyle. Ironically, it was Johnson who had introduced Wilde to Lord Alfred Douglas, the man whose relationship with Wilde would lead to Wilde's trial and imprisonment.

Johnson also returned to his preoccupation with Ireland in his poems, in his book *Ireland with Other Poems.* He had visited Ireland for a year in 1893 and soon after began lecturing on Irish politics. For Johnson, his admiration of Ireland was another way for him to restore order in his chaotic personal life. During his time in London, he continued to drink heavily and found himself in debt, being evicted from his home on several occasions. "Lionel Johnson had two passions that controlled his life—his Catholic faith and his love for Ireland. In his short life he dreamed perpetually about these realizations of his spirit. They were the whitest dreams expressed in the poetry of his day," said W. S. Braithwaite in the *Boston Transcript* of Johnson's poetry.

In the latter part of the 1800s and into the early 1900s, Johnson continued his downward spiral into alcoholism and poverty. He became a paranoid recluse who suffered a series of strokes that left him partially paralyzed. On October 4, 1902, at the age of thirty-four, Johnson suffered a fatal stroke. His death took on a mythical quality when Ezra Pound reported that Johnson had actually died after falling off a stool in a local tavern. His tragic persona was further vilified by W. B. Yeats' portrayal of Johnson in his poem, "In Memory of Major Robert Gregory," in which he called Johnson a man "much falling," who "brooded on sanctity." This sort of portrayal caused Johnson's work to be rounded up with other "Decadent" artists. The Decadent movement was based on the mantra "art for art's sake."

However, technically, while Johnson's lifestyle was similar to those characteristics of what defines an artist from the Decadent movement, his technical prose sets him apart. While some of his works such as "Oxford," rely heavily on repetition of words that do not add much importance to his prose, other works showed successful structure of verse. "Generally speaking, however, Johnson's poetry is tightly controlled. It is as if he felt keenly the disorderliness of his life and recognized the necessity of constraining the tumultuous energies of his frustrated soul in carefully sculpted, marmoreal meters," stated Munro. Ironically, Johnson, a man seeking structure through Catholicism and Ireland for his chaotic life and bouts with alcoholism, was at his best when writing of the complexities and hardships of living with the conflicts of those two worlds.

BIOGRAPHICAL AND CRITICAL SOURCES:

BOOKS

Boyd, Ernest, *Ireland's Literary Renaissance,* revised edition, Knopf (New York, NY), 1922.
Charlesworth, Barbara, *Dark Passages: The Decadent Consciousness in Victorian Literature,* University of Wisconsin Press, 1965.
Dictionary of Literary Biography, Volume 19: *British Poets, 1880-1914,* Gale (Detroit, MI), 1983.

Halladay, Jean R., *Eight Late Victorian Poets Shaping the Artistic Sensibility of an Age: Alice Meynell, John Davidson, Francis Thompson, Mary Coleridge, Katherine Tynan, Arthur Symons, Ernest Dowson, Lionel Johnson,* E. Mellen Press, 1993.
Parekh, Pushpa Naidu, *Response to Failure: Poetry of Gerard Manley Hopkins, Francis Thompson, Lionel Johnson, and Dylan Thomas,* P. Lang, 1998.
Pound, Ezra, *Literary Essays of Ezra Pound,* edited by T. S. Eliot, New Directions, 1954.
Scott, Dixon, *Men of Letters,* Hodder & Stoughton, 1923.
Thornton, R. K. R., *The Decadent Dilemma,* Edward Arnold, 1983.
Twentieth Century Literary Criticism, Volume 19, Gale (Detroit, MI), 1986.

PERIODICALS

Academy, October 20, 1894, p. 297.
Antigonish Review, spring, 1973, pp. 95-109.
Bookman, June, 1895, pp. 343-344; February, 1898, pp. 155-156; October, 1912, pp. 179-185.
Boston Transcript, December 11, 1911, p. 3.
Dublin Review, Volume 142, number 283, 1907, pp. 327-344.
Freeman, November 23, 1921.
New York Times Review, September 1, 1912, pp. 469-470.
Poet Lore, summer, 1953, pp. 140-160.*

*   *   *

JOHNSTON, A(ndrew) J(ohn) B(ayly) 1949-

PERSONAL: Born November 7, 1949, in Truro, Nova Scotia, Canada; son of James Andrew Little (a technical representative for a photographic equipment and supplies company) and Clarissa Alice (a homemaker; maiden name, Bayly) Johnston; married Mary Margaret Topshee (a secretary), April 27, 1974; children: Jennifer Lyne, Colin Andrew, Michael James. *Education:* Dalhousie University, B.A. (with honors), 1972, M.A., 1977; Université Laval, Ph.D., 1998.

ADDRESSES: Agent—c/o Author Mail, McGill-Queen's University Press, 845 Sherbrooke St., West, Montreal, Quebec H3A 2T5, Canada. *E-mail*—jmjohnston@hfx.eastlink.ca.

CAREER: Fortress of Louisbourg National Historic Site, Louisbourg, Nova Scotia, Canada, historian, 1977-2000; Parks Canada, Atlantic Service Center, Halifax, Nova Scotia, Canada, historian, 2000—. Conference speaker throughout North America, Scotland, and Australia.

MEMBER: French Colonial Historical Society (president, 2001-03).

WRITINGS:

Defending Halifax: Ordnance, 1825-1906, Parks Canada (Ottawa, Ontario, Canada), 1981.

The Summer of 1744: A Portrait of Life in 18th-Century Louisbourg, Parks Canada (Ottawa, Ontario, Canada), 1983, revised edition, 1991.

Religion in Life at Louisbourg, 1713-1758, 1984, published as *Life and Religion at Louisbourg, 1713-1758,* McGill-Queen's University Press (Montreal, Quebec, Canada), 1996.

(Editor) *From the Hearth: Recipes from the World of 18th-Century Louisbourg,* recipes by Hope Dunton, University College of Cape Breton Press (Sydney, Nova Scotia, Canada), 1986.

(Editor and contributor) *Louisbourg: An 18th-Century Town,* Nimbus Publishing (Halifax, Nova Scotia, Canada), 1991.

Toward a New Past: Report on the Current Presentation of Aboriginal History by Parks Canada, Parks Canada (Ottawa, Ontario, Canada), 1995.

(Editor) Brian Campbell, *Tracks across the Landscape: A Commemorative History of the S&L Railway,* University College of Cape Breton Press (Sydney, Nova Scotia, Canada), 1995.

Louisbourg: The Phoenix Fortress, photographs by Chris Reardon, Nimbus Publishing (Halifax, Nova Scotia, Canada), 1997.

(Editor) *Essays in French Colonial History,* Michigan State University Press (East Lansing, MI), 1997.

Control and Order: The Evolution of French Colonial Louisbourg, 1713-1758, Michigan State University Press (East Lansing, MI), 2001.

Endgame: Louisbourg and the Siege of 1758: Promise, Glory, and Despair, McGill-Queen's University Press (Montreal, Quebec, Canada), in press.

Editor of conference proceedings. Contributor to periodicals, including *Reader's Digest, Gardening Life, Canadian House and Home, Beaver, Canadian Collec-*tor, *Dalhousie Review, Fortress: Castles and Fortifications Quarterly, French Colonial History, Island: New Perspectives on Cape Breton's History,* and *Material History Review.* Guest editor, *Nova Scotia Historical Review,* 1990.

WORK IN PROGRESS: Colonial Louisbourg: Seaport, Community, and Stronghold, for University of Florida Press.

SIDELIGHTS: A. J. B. Johnston told *CA:* "As far as I can see, at least for myself, writing is one of the ways humans try to do battle with their own mortality. I have been fortunate in that I have usually been able to follow my interests as they developed. It turns out that questions of control and order are often foremost, but I did not realize that for many years."

BIOGRAPHICAL AND CRITICAL SOURCES:

PERIODICALS

American Historical Review, December, 2001, Geoffrey Plank, review of *Control and Order: The Evolution of French Colonial Louisbourg, 1713-1758,* p. 1786.

Beaver, June-July, 1987, Douglas Cole, review of *From the Hearth: Recipes from the World of 18th-Century Louisbourg,* p. 61.

Canadian Historical Review, June, 1984, G. A. Rawlyk, review of *The Summer of 1744: A Portrait of Life in 18th-Century Louisbourg,* p. 302.

Historical Journal, September, 1999, Emily Clark, review of *Life and Religion at Louisbourg, 1713-1758,* p. 903.

History, October, 1999, Colin M. Coates, review of *Life and Religion at Louisbourg, 1713-1758,* p. 708.

Journal of Ecclesiastical History, July, 1998, Marguerite van Die, review of *Life and Religion at Louisbourg, 1713-1758,* p. 578.

*   *   *

JONES, Dennis 1945-

PERSONAL: Born 1945, in St. Thomas, Ontario, Canada; married; wife's name, Sandi. *Education:* Attended Queens University and York University.

ADDRESSES: Home—Ferguson Falls, Ontario, Canada. *Agent*—c/o Author Mail, HarperCollins, 10 East 53rd St., 7th Floor, New York, NY 10022.

CAREER: Former technical writer; full-time novelist, 1988—.

AWARDS, HONORS: Book of the year, Foundation for the Advancement of Canadian Letters, 1984, for *Rubicon One.*

WRITINGS:

NOVELS

Rubicon One (thriller), General (Toronto, Ontario), 1983.
Winter Palace (thriller), General (Toronto, Ontario), 1988.
Warsaw Concerto (thriller), General (Toronto, Ontario), 1989.
The Minstrel Boy (thriller), Random House Canada (Toronto, Ontario), 1990.
The Stone and the Maiden (fantasy), Avon Eos (New York, NY), 1999.
The Mask and the Sorceress (fantasy), Eos (New York, NY), 2001.

Also author of *Russian Spring* and several other novels.

SIDELIGHTS: Dennis Jones is a Canadian author who switched from penning cold war thrillers like *Rubicon One* and *Russian Spring* to fantasy fiction because by the 1980s, as he told Pieter van Hiel in online *Illusionary Minds Chat,* "the cold war seemed to be pretty much over, and it got pretty difficult to sell those books."

Jones's works include the first two entries of a proposed trilogy. *The Stone and the Maiden,* which begins the saga of the House of Pandagore, is a "promising fantasy debut," according to Jackie Cassada of *Library Journal.* This story introduces Mandine Descaris. An heiress to the royal throne, Mandine must first prove her worth by facing the Tathars, a horde of barbaric horsemen. She joins forces with a young soldier to save their kingdom. Meanwhile, Mandine's scheming half-sister, Theatana, has allied herself with the would-be usurper Lord Baras, further complicating the heroine's quest. While a *Publishers Weekly* reviewer faulted the novel as lacking in original and nuanced personalities, the critic ended on a positive note and added, "the author's persuasive plot should keep most fantasy readers engaged."

Princess Theatana also takes center stage in part two of the saga, *The Mask and the Sorceress.* Set twenty years after *The Stone and the Maiden,* the book presents the wicked Theatana exiled for her past misdealings. Driven insane by her punishment for her previous plots—she is forced to re-live the deaths of those she ordered executed—Theatana escapes from her island prison and discovers a form of black magic that can restore her to power while wreaking havoc on the kingdom, which Mandine rules in peace. Theatana's industrious nephew, Ilarion, learns of his aunt's scheme and embarks on a quest to avert warfare. In an online *BookBrowser* review, Harriet Klausner praised Jones for setting up a story that, though part of a series, "can stand alone (what a unique thought for the genre)." Indeed, Jones told van Hiel that he could well end the House of Pandagore series with the second book. "It was thought to be a trilogy originally," he said, "but I had never really committed myself to that."

BIOGRAPHICAL AND CRITICAL SOURCES:

PERIODICALS

Canadian Book Review Annual, 2000, review of *The Stone and the Maiden,* p. 172.
Kirkus Reviews, June 1, 1999, review of *The Stone and the Maiden,* p. 840; February 1, 2001, review of *The Mask and the Sorceress,* p. 149.
Library Journal, July, 1999, Jackie Cassada, review of *The Stone and the Maiden,* p. 143; April 15, 2001, Cassada, review of *The Mask and the Sorceress,* p. 137.
Locus, October, 1999, review of *The Stone and the Maiden,* p. 27.
Publishers Weekly, July 26, 1999, review of *The Stone and the Maiden,* p. 68; February 19, 2001, review of *The Mask and the Sorceress,* p. 73.
Quill & Quire, July, 1999, review of *The Stone and the Maiden,* p. 42.

School Library Journal, January, 2000, Susan Salpini, review of *The Stone and the Maiden,* p. 156; March, 2001, Salpini, review of *The Mask and the Sorceress,* p. 281.

OTHER

BookBrowser, http://www.bookbrowser.com/ (March 28, 2001), Harriet Klausner, review of *The Mask and the Sorceress.*

Illusionary Minds Chat, http://im-chat.com/ (July 7, 2001), Pieter van Hiel, "Tinker, Tailor, Sorcerer, Spy."

Made in Canada, http://www.geocities.com/canadian_sf/ (September 12, 2001).*

*　　*　　*

JUDD, Frances K.
　　See BENSON, Mildred (Augustine Wirt)

K

KAMM, Herbert 1917-2002

OBITUARY NOTICE—See index for *CA* sketch: Born April 1, 1917, in Long Branch, NJ; died September 25, 2002, in Avila Beach, CA. Journalist and author. Kamm was a prominent newspaper editor best known for his tenure as executive editor of the *New York World Journal Tribune* during the 1960s. He got his start as a sports writer for the *Asbury Park Press* in New Jersey in 1935, moving up to reporter and sports editor, as well as author of the column "Sports Angles." After a brief stint with the Associated Press, he joined the *New York World-Telegram & Sun* in New York City in 1943, rising to the post of managing editor during the mid-1960s. The newspaper merged with two other papers to become the *New York World Journal Tribune* in 1966, and Kamm was its executive editor from 1966 to 1967. During the late-1960s he worked as an editorial consultant for Scripps-Howard Newspapers before moving on to the *Cleveland Press* as an associate editor and editor of the editorial page in 1969. Kamm remained there until the paper folded in 1982, and stayed in Cleveland to become the editorial director of WJKW-TV until 1985. He also taught journalism at Case Western Reserve University during the 1970s and at California Polytechnic in San Luis Obispo in 1991. He was the author of the *Junior Illustrated Encyclopedia of Sports* (1960; fifth edition, 1975).

OBITUARIES AND OTHER SOURCES:

BOOKS

Who's Who in America, 56th edition, Marquis (New Providence, NJ), 2001.

PERIODICALS

New York Times, September 27, 2002, p. A27.

＊　　＊　　＊

KANG, Chol-Hwan 1968(?)-

PERSONAL: Born 1968(?).

ADDRESSES: Home—South Korea. *Agent*—c/o Publicity Director, Basic Books, 387 Park Ave. S, New York, NY 10016-8810.

CAREER: Journalist and author.

WRITINGS:

(With Pierre Rigoulot) *Les aquariums de Pyongyang: dix ans au goulag,* Laffont (Paris, France), 2000, English translation by Yair Reiner published as *The Aquariums of Pyongyang: Ten Years in a North Korean Gulag,* Basic Books (New York, NY), 2001.

SIDELIGHTS: Korean journalist Kang Chol-Hwan published a well-received book, cowritten with Pierre Rigoulot, about his experiences as a political prisoner, titled *The Aquariums of Pyongyang: Ten Years in a North Korean Gulag.* Many literary critics considered the book an important work because it has been one of the first to shed light on North Korea's policy of imprisoning many of its own citizens for political reasons in the years since North and South Korea became separate nations. "The important thing about this book is that it is the first detailed account of life in North Korea to reach the outside world," wrote Peter Walker, reviewing the book for the *Financial Times.*

Kang spent all of his teen years in a remote labor camp called Yodok, which is surrounded by several mountain chains. Kang, who now lives and works as a journalist in Seoul, South Korea, was sent to Yodok in 1977 with his entire family because his grandfather was accused of counterrevolutionary tendencies by North Korea's Communist government. His grandfather, like many other Yodok prisoners, had lived in Japan during the 1930s and amassed a fortune. When the Communist Party took over North Korea, many of the Koreans living in Japan returned home to help build the new nation. After taking the financial fortunes of these people, however, the government sent thousands of them to prison without even giving many of them a trial.

In *The Aquariums of Pyongyang: Ten Years in a North Korean Gulag,* Kang describes the deplorable conditions he endured at Yodok, where public executions, beatings. and rapes were common occurrences and the daily diet included rats and frogs. Kang, who testified about his Yodok experiences before the U.S. Senate Foreign Relations Committee in 1999, also describes in the book how the children at the camp were put through daily indoctrination lessons by Communist Party teachers, who often murdered students they did not like. Despite these daily lessons, Kang writes that during his imprisonment the only lesson he came away with was the one "pounded into me . . . about man's limitless capacity to be vicious." Kang and his family members were inexplicably released from the prison in 1987. Kang explains that when he learned that they were to be released, he felt a flood of happiness tempered by both guilt and some fear. "I was actually afraid of leaving the place, of no longer seeing those mountain ridges all around me. Deep down, I had come to love . . . the bars of my prison," Kang writes. Shortly after being freed, Kang escaped to South Korea.

Charles W. Hayford of *Library Journal* called the book an "affecting and directly written memoir" that is

"important to record and witness." Not all critics were impressed with Kang's writing ability, though they still noted the book's importance. "Kang's memoir is notable not for its literary qualities, but for the immediacy and drama of the personal testimony," wrote a contributor for *Publishers Weekly.*

BIOGRAPHICAL AND CRITICAL SOURCES:

PERIODICALS

Christianity Today, August 6, 2001, Jeff M. Sellers, "Forgotten Gulag," p. 62.
Financial Times, January 12, 2002, Peter Walker, "Documentary of a Dictatorship," p. 5.
Kirkus Reviews, July 1, 2001, review of *The Aquariums of Pyongyang: Ten Years in a North Korean Gulag.*
Library Journal, October 1, 2001, Charles W. Hayford, review of *The Aquariums of Pyongyang,* p. 126.
New American, February 11, 2002, Thomas R. Eddlem, review of *The Aquariums of Pyongyang,* p. 31.
Publishers Weekly, July 30, 2001, review of *The Aquariums of Pyongyang,* p. 72.
Reader's Digest, December, 1993, David Tracey, review of *The Aquariums of Pyongyang,* p. 149.*

*   *   *

KEENE, Carolyn
See BENSON, Mildred (Augustine Wirt)

*   *   *

KERLEY, Barbara 1960-

PERSONAL: Born June 26, 1960, in Washington, DC; daughter of Ernest (an attorney) and Betty (a librarian; maiden name, Klippel) Kerley; married Scott Kelly (an engineer); children: Anna. *Education:* University of Chicago, B.A. (English), 1981; University of Washington, M.A., 1987 (teaching English as a second language), 1988. *Hobbies and other interests:* "Hiking, biking, gardening, cooking, and reading—always reading!, walking the dog, waking up the cat, cruising bookstores, sweetening tea, embarrassing my daughter, asking directions, napping."

ADDRESSES: Agent—c/o Author Mail, Scholastic, Inc., 555 Broadway, New York, NY 10012-3999. *E-mail*—bkerley@humboldt1.com.

CAREER: Author. English teacher at various institutions, including U.S. Peace Corps, Nepal, 1981-83, University of Guam, 1988-90, College of the Redwoods, Eureka, CA, 1993-95; special education aide in McKinleyville, CA, 1998-2002. Co-founder, with Scott Kelly, of the Recycling Association of Guam, 1988-90; member of Dow's Prairie Elementary School Site Council, 1997-2001.

MEMBER: Society of Children's Book Writers and Illustrators, Friends of the McKinleyville Library (president, 2001—).

AWARDS, HONORS: Notable Book citation, American Library Association (ALA), and included in "100 Titles for Reading and Sharing" list, New York Public Library, both 1995, both for *Songs of Papa's Island;* Notable Book citation from ALA, Outstanding Science Trade Book from National Science Teachers Association, and Texas Bluebonnet Award master list, all 2001, all for the *Dinosaurs of Waterhouse Hawkins;* National Parenting Publications Silver Award, *Bulletin of the Center for Children's Books* Blue Ribbon, and named to the Indiana Young Hoosiers Award master list, all 2002, all for *A Cool Drink of Water.*

WRITINGS:

Songs of Papa's Island, illustrated by Katherine Tillotson, Houghton (New York, NY), 1995.
The Dinosaurs of Waterhouse Hawkins: An Illuminating History of Mr. Waterhouse Hawkins, Artist and Lecturer, illustrated by Brian Selznick, Scholastic (New York, NY), 2001.
A Cool Drink of Water, National Geographic Society (Washington, DC), 2002.

WORK IN PROGRESS: A nonfiction picture book about Walt Whitman during the U.S. Civil War years; a nonfiction picture book about parents and children around the world; a novel about man's exploration of space.

SIDELIGHTS: The author of several nonfiction books for children, Barbara Kerley has drawn much critical attention since her account of nineteenth-century British artist Waterhouse Hawkins as *The Dinosaurs of Waterhouse Hawkins: An Illuminating History of Mr. Waterhouse Hawkins, Artist and Lecturer* was published. Although much of Hawkins' work on dinosaurs has since proven to be inaccurate, Kerley tells a thrilling tale, noted *Booklist* critic GraceAnne A. DeCandido, in this "favorite dinosaur book for years to come." Commenting on the biographical focus of the work, *School Library Journal* contributor Patricia Manning was also appreciative of the painstaking research, writing, and illustrations that combine to create a "distinguished book in every way."

Kerley, writing to *CA,* offered this advice to readers who want to become writers: "Read. A lot. Experiment with different kinds of writing. Creepy alien stories. Funny food poems. High sea adventure. Cosy bedtime tales. Try them all and see what suits you. Stay open to trying new things. I never expected to SCUBA dive—until I moved to Guam and it soon became a favorite hobby. I never tried tofu when I was a kid, and now it's a favorite food. And how could I have known I'd love cross-country skiing until I tried it? New experiences will enrich your life and make you a better writer."

"Hang in there," Kerley continued. "Writing is not always easy, but it's rewarding, even if you never get published. Pay attention . . . to the things you see, the things you read about, the things you hear and the things you hear mentioned. Most importantly, pay attention to the things that move you. That's where the best stories are."

BIOGRAPHICAL AND CRITICAL SOURCES:

PERIODICALS

Booklist, September 1, 2001, GraceAnne A. DeCandido, review of *The Dinosaurs of Waterhouse Hawkins: An Illuminating History of Mr. Waterhouse Hawkins, Artist and Lecturer,* p. 109.
New York Times Book Review, November 18, 2001, Lawrence Downs, "Fossil Fueled," p. 40.
Publishers Weekly, September 10, 2001, review of *The Dinosaurs of Waterhouse Hawkins,* p. 92; October 22, 2001, Shannon Maughan, review of *The Dinosaurs of Waterhouse Hawkins,* p. 24.

School Library Journal, October, 1995, Maggie McEwan, review of Songs of Papa's Island, pp. 104-105; October, 2001, Patricia Manning, review of The Dinosaurs of Waterhouse Hawkins, p. 142; April, 2002, Pamela K. Bombay, review of A Cool Drink of Water, p. 134.

*   *   *

KING, Eleanor (Campbell) 1906-1991

PERSONAL: Born February 8, 1906, in Middletown, PA; died February 27, 1991, in Haddonfield, NJ; daughter of George Ilgenfritz and Emma Kate Campbell King. Education: Attended Clare Tree Major School of the Theatre, 1925, and Theatre Guild School, 1926; studied dance with Doris Humphrey and Charles Weidman, 1927-35; studied mime with Etienne Decroux, 1955; studied Noh and classical Korean dance.

CAREER: Dancer, choreographer, educator, and company director. Humphrey-Weidman Company, dancer, 1928-35; The Little Group, founder with José Limón, Ernestine Stodelle, and Charles Laskey, 1931; Theater Dance Company, founder with others, 1937; Eleanor King Dance Repertory Company and the Eleanor King Creative Dance Studio, Seattle, WA, founder, 1944. As teacher, Dalton School, New York, assistant to Doris Humphrey, 1930-31; New School for Social Research, New York, assistant to Doris Humphrey, 1932-33; Perry Mansfield Theatre Dance Camp, Steamboat Springs, CO, 1936, 1945, 1956; Brooklyn Museum of Art, 1937; Carleton College, Northfield, MN, dance instructor, 1942-43; Cornish School of Arts, Seattle, WA, 1943-44; Rotterdam Dansschool Academie, Rotterdam, Holland, 1952, 1954-55, 1961; Toynbee Hall, London, England, 1954-55; American Cultural Centers, Tokyo, Kyoto, and Osaka, Japan, 1958, 1960, 1961; University of Arkansas, teacher, 1952-71, professor emeritus, 1971-91; Rencontres Internationales de Danse Contemporaines, Paris, France, 1973; Goldsmith College, London University, 1978; College of Santa Fe, 1979.

AWARDS, HONORS: Jane Cowl Romeo and Juliet Essay Contest, gold medal, 1923; Bennington School of the Dance, fellowship, 1938; Fulbright research grants, 1967, 1976, 1977; American Association of Dance Companies, honoree, 1975; Vogelstein Foundation grant, 1976; Santa Fe Dance Umbrella, 1980; Santa Fe Living Treasure, 1986; New Mexico Governor's Award for Excellence in the Arts, 1987; NEA Fellowship, 1988.

WRITINGS:

The Way of Japanese Dance, 1970.
Transformations: The Humphrey-Weidman Era, Dance Horizons (Brooklyn, NY), 1978.

Also contributor to Dance Observer, Christian Science Monitor, Northwest Times Weekly, Japan Quarterly, Dance Magazine, Journal of Health, Physical Education, and Recreation, Focus on Dance, Dance Research Monograph, Korea Journal, Arirang, Quarterly Journal of Performing Arts, Korean Culture, Dance Research Annual, and Music and Dance in California and the West, 1947.

WORK IN PROGRESS: Began work on Transformations II: To The West.

SIDELIGHTS: Eleanor King began her career as a dancer and choreographer in New York City during the formative years of American modern dance. She left the dance mecca in 1942 to create her own company in Seattle and to explore a variety of cultural influences, including mime and Asian dance forms. She created the Theatre of the Imagination program at the University of Arkansas, where she taught for decades, and had visiting positions at numerous other schools. Fueled by seemingly endless curiosity and energy, she was professionally active until her death in 1991. King published two books, The Way of Japanese Dance and the memoir Transformations: The Humphrey-Weidman Era, and began a third, Transformations II: To The West.

King was studying dance with Doris Humphrey at the Denishawn School when she left to join her teacher in the newly created Humphrey-Weidman Company. She made her 1928 debut in Color Harmony, which has been called the first American abstract ballet. With fellow dancers Ernestine Stodelle, Letitia Ide, and José Limón, she began exploring her own creative impulses in the Little Group. In 1935 King struck out as an independent soloist and choreographer. This work introduced her to the founding members of the Theater Dance Company, which performed her first major work of choreography, *Icaro,* in 1938.

The year 1942 marked King's break with the New York dance establishment. After brief teaching assignments, she moved to Seattle, where she created the Eleanor King Dance Repertory Company and the Eleanor King Creative Dance Studio in 1945. During this period, several of her works showed American Indian and Western themes. King's longest association would be with the University of Arkansas, where she created the Theater of the Imagination. She served on the faculty from 1952 to 1971, and then was awarded professor emeritus status.

King always remained a student. In the late 1950s, she began studying Japanese Noh dances and in 1958 she gave her first performance in Tokyo. During extensive travel in Asia, King learned forms including classic Korean dance, which she began studying at age seventy. The impact of these pursuits was evident in her choreography, which is known for stylistic variety and an eclectic choice of musical scores. Reconstructions of King's work by Annabelle Gamson revived interest in the dancer-choreographer during the 1980s.

BIOGRAPHICAL AND CRITICAL SOURCES:

BOOKS

International Dictionary of Modern Dance, St. James Press (Detroit, MI), 1998.

OBITUARIES:

PERIODICALS

Village Voice, March 13, 1991, obituary by Deborah Jowitt.*

*　　*　　*

KISHKAN, Theresa 1955-

PERSONAL: Born January 6, 1955, in Victoria, British Columbia, Canada; married John Pass (a poet), October 20, 1979; children: Forrest, Brendan, Angelica. *Education:* University of Victoria, B.A. (with honors), 1978; University of British Columbia, graduate study. *Hobbies and other interests:* Natural and regional history, textiles, classical literature, gardening.

ADDRESSES: Home and office—R.R.1, Site 20 C11, Madeira Park, British Columbia, Canada V0N 2H0. *Agent*—Kathryn Mulders, Transatlantic Literary Agency, 185-911 Yates St., Victoria, British Columbia, Canada V8V 1R6. *E-mail*—tkishkan@uniserve.com.

CAREER: Writer. Teacher of writing classes and workshops; gives readings in Canada and the United States, including appearances in "Birth Project," staged in Vancouver, British Columbia, Canada, in 1985, and at University of Washington, Eastern Washington State University, and in Ireland and England; guest on media programs.

AWARDS, HONORS: Canada Council grants, 1978, 2000; Cultural Services Award, Province of British Columbia, 1991-92, 1996; Pushcart Prize nomination, 1999.

WRITINGS:

Arranging the Gallery, Fiddlehead Poetry Books, 1976.
Ikons of the Hunt (poetry), Sono Nis Press, 1978.
I Thought I Could See Africa, High Ground Press, 1991.
Morning Glory, Reference West, 1991.
Black Cup, Beach Holme/Press Porcepic, 1993.
Red Laredo Boots, New Star Books, 1996.
Inishbream: A Novella, Barbarian Press, 1999, published as *Inishbream,* Goose Lane Editions (Fredericton, New Brunswick, Canada), 2001.
Sisters of Grass, Goose Lane Editions (Fredericton, New Brunswick, Canada), 2000.

Author of broadsides, "A Shadow of Antlers," Barbarian Press, 1981; and "Ten Small Fingers," High Ground Press, 1985. Work represented in anthologies. Contributor to periodicals, including *Brick, Canadian Forum, Fiddlehead, Fine Madness, Grapevine Dublin, Malahat Review, Poetry Canada, Prism International, Quarry,* and *West Coast Review.*

ADAPTATIONS: A cycle of poems from *Ikons of the Hunt* was set to music by composer Steve Tittle, sung by Rosemarie Landrie as "Charms and Spells" at the Scotia Festival in 1987; it was recorded by CBC Stereo.

WORK IN PROGRESS: A Man in a Distant Field, a novel; *Phantom Limb,* an essay collection; research on utopian communities in British Columbia prior to World War I, with a novel expected to result.

SIDELIGHTS: Theresa Kishkan told *CA:* "I write to pursue threads, to understand their significance in the patterns of narrative and also their importance as a means of exploration (think of Theseus in the maze of King Minos). I am interested in history and landscape and how the two influence one another. Places which have witnessed significant history (whether it is human history or natural history) often shimmer with presences and shadows. I tend to imagine the stories associated with these places and try to give them voice."

Kishkan added: "I have lived on both coasts of Canada as well as in Greece, Ireland, and England. I make my home on the Sechelt Peninsula in British Columbia, Canada, with my husband and our three children. I have worked as a freelance writer for twenty years. My writing has appeared in many magazines, anthologies, and books. I have taught writing classes over the years, ranging from workshops for young children to writing courses for adults at the college level. As well as workshops, I have given many public readings of my work and participated in a number of literary festivals."

*   *   *

KNELL, Simon J. 1955-

PERSONAL: Born December 29, 1955, in Colden Common, Hampshire, England; son of Joseph (a greengrocer) and Marjorie (a greengrocer; maiden name, Halkes) Knell; married Margaret Mahony, May 9, 1976; children: Callum, Ciaran. *Education:* University of Leeds, B.Sc., 1978; University of Manchester, M.Sc., 1980; University of Leicester, graduate certificate in museum studies, 1984; University of Keele, Ph.D., 1996.

ADDRESSES: Office—Department of Museum Studies, University of Leicester, 105 Princess Rd. E., Leicester LE1 7LG, England. *E-mail*—sjk8@leicester.ac.uk.

CAREER: Leeds City Museum, Leeds, England, research assistant, 1980; Manchester Museum, Manchester, England, conservation assistant, 1981-82; Area Museums Council for South Eastern England, London, England, traveling geology curator, 1985-87; Scunthorpe Museum, Scunthorpe, England, keeper of natural science, 1987-92; University of Leicester, Leicester, England, member of museum studies faculty and department head, 1992—.

MEMBER: International Commission on the History of the Geological Sciences, Museums Association, Geological Curators Group, Biology Curators Group, History of Geology Group (committee member, 1997-2000).

WRITINGS:

(With Michael Taylor) *Geology and the Local Museum,* H.M.S.O., 1989.
(Editor) *Care of Collections,* Routledge (New York, NY), 1994.
(Editor) *A Bibliography of Museum Studies,* Scolar/Ashgate Publishing (Burlington, VT), 1994.
(Editor) *Museums and the Future of Collecting,* Ashgate Publishing (Burlington, VT), 1999.
The Culture of English Geology, 1815-1851: A Science Revealed through Its Collecting, Ashgate Publishing (Burlington, VT), 2000.
(Editor, with C. Lewis) *The Age of the Earth: From 4004 B.C. to A.D. 2002,* Geological Society (London, England), 2001.

Coauthor of a column in *Local Geologist;* contributor of articles and reviews to books; contributor to periodicals, including *Geological Curator.* Member of editorial board, *Geology Today,* 1990-2002.

WORK IN PROGRESS: A trans-European project examining the operation of communities of practice in natural history museums; research on material culture and collecting; historical research on Hugh Miller.

SIDELIGHTS: Simon J. Knell told *CA:* "I started writing the simple guide to geological curation while a student in the department in which I now teach. Soon afterwards I met Mike Taylor, who had similar thoughts and a similarly strange job, 'peripatetic curation,' and through collaboration that project grew to become *Geology and the Local Museum.* I am still writing with Mike today, and we continue to bounce ideas off each other via e-mail.

"In the 1970s and 1980s I became involved in a number of projects to rescue geological collections, partly inspired by Phil Doughty's report on the state and status of British geology collections. Phil's report gave me a sense of purpose which I have pursued ever since. I soon became active in the Geological Curators Group, and as a traveling geology curator in southeastern England I had a very privileged insight into the nature of these collections.

"Following much effort to get the situation improved and my return to Leicester to teach, I became increasingly interested in the intellectual, rather than the physical, restoration of these collections. I reacquainted myself with Hugh Torrens at Keele, one of the founders of the Geological Curators Group and a pioneer of histories of the little people of science, and asked him to supervise a doctoral degree aimed at understanding what these collections meant in the history of geology. I think Hugh thought I was being a little ambitious when he saw my huge list of research questions, but the doctorate was finished rapidly and the big book, *The Culture of English Geology, 1815-1851: A Science Revealed through Its Collecting,* followed. I soon took the method of that book and applied it to the late twentieth century. Since then these interests, and a move to teaching material culture, has led to my research diversifying and becoming increasingly focused on aspects of social practice which may make future literary productions slightly less geology-centered."

BIOGRAPHICAL AND CRITICAL SOURCES:

PERIODICALS

British Journal for the History of Science, December, 2001, Samuel J. M. M. Alberti, review of *The Culture of English Geology, 1815-1851: A Science Revealed through Its Collecting,* p. 471.
Isis, March, 2001, Dennis R. Dean, review of *The Culture of English Geology, 1815-1851,* p. 191.

Times Literary Supplement, May 4, 2001, Martin Rudwick, review of *The Culture of English Geology, 1815-1851,* p. 27.

*   *   *

KROPP, (Lars Olaf) Göran 1966-2002

OBITUARY NOTICE—See index for *CA* sketch: Born November 12, 1966 (one source says December 11), in Sweden; died in a fall September 30, 2002, in Vantage, WA. Adventurer, lecturer, and author. Kropp was renowned as an enthusiastic mountaineer who became famous for climbing Mt. Everest and K2 without the use of guides or bottled oxygen. He was introduced to climbing by his father, who first took him on expeditions in the mountains of Sweden when Kropp was only seven years old. Later, when he was a paratrooper with the Swedish Army in the 1980s, Kropp's interest in climbing was fanned into an roaring flame, and he determined to spend his life ascending new heights. In addition to climbing the world's tallest peaks, he also went on bicycle trips all across Europe, the Middle East, and Asia, and he attempted a lengthy ski trip across Siberia that failed because of extremely low temperatures and dangerous polar bears. Kropp shared his enthusiasm for his travels by giving entertaining lectures around the world that were famous for the speaker's wide-eyed sense of humor and natural storytelling gifts. He related some of his adventures in the book *Ultimate High: My Everest Odyssey* (1999) and produced the 1997 movie *I Made It: Göran Kropp's Incredible Journey to the Top of the World,* which won the Best Film award at the Banff Mountain Film Festival. He was also named "The Most Entertaining Adventurer on Earth" in 2002 by *National Geographic* magazine. Kropp died after falling seventy-five feet while climbing the Air Guitar route near Frenchmen Coulee.

OBITUARIES AND OTHER SOURCES:

PERIODICALS

Independent (London, England), October 3, 2002, p. 22.
Seattle Post-Intelligencer, October 2, 2002, p. A1.
Times (London, England), October 4, 2002.

L

LABAN, Rudolf von 1879-1958

PERSONAL: Born December 15, 1879, in Pozsony, Austria-Hungary (now Bratislava), Hungary; immigrated to England, 1938; died July 1, 1958. *Education:* Attended architecture school of École des Beaux Arts.

CAREER: Choreographer, company director, dance and movement theorist, and teacher. Formed a dance school in Zurich, Germany, 1910; founded Choreographic Institute at Zurich, 1915, and created branches in Italy, France, and central Europe; choreographer and director of movement at Berlin State Opera, 1930-34; director of movement under Nazi Ministry of propaganda, 1934-36; after 1938, studied industrial efficiency in England; with Lisa Ullmann, formed Art of Movement Studio at Manchester, 1946. Choreographed large "movement choirs"; created Labanotation system for recording human movement.

WRITINGS:

Die welt des tänzers; fünf gedankenreigen, W. Seifert (Stuttgart, Germany), 1920.

Choreographie, E. Diederichs (Jena, Germany), 1926.

Gymnastik und Tanz, G. Stalling (Oldenburg, Germany), 1926.

Des kindes gymnastik und tanz, G. Stalling (Oldenburg, Germany), 1926.

Schrifttanz, Universal-edition (Vienna, Austria), 1928.

(Editor) *Tanzfestspiele 1934,* [Dresden, Germany], 1934.

Ein Leben für den Tanz, [Dresden, Germany], 1935, translation by Lisa Ullman published as *A Life for Dance: Reminiscences,* Theatre Arts Books (New York, NY), 1975.

Die tänzerische situation unserer zeit, ein querschnitt, C. Reissner (Dresden, Germany), 1936.

(With F. C. Lawrence) *Laban/Lawrence Industrial Rhythm and Lilt in Labour,* [Manchester, England], 1942.

(With F. C. Lawrence) *Effort,* [London, England], 1947, second edition, Macdonald & Evans (London, England), 1974.

Modern Educational Dance, Macdonald and Evans (London, England), 1948.

Mastery of Movement on the Stage, Macdonald and Evans (London, England), 1950.

Principles of Dance and Movement Notation, Macdonald and Evans (London, England), 1956, published as *Laban's Principles of Dance and Movement Notation,* Plays, Inc. (Boston, MA), 1975.

Choreutics, edited by Lisa Ullmann, [London, England], 1966, published as *The Language of Movement: A Guidebook to Choreutics,* Plays, Inc. (Boston, MA), 1966.

A Vision of Dynamic Space, compiled by Lisa Ullmann, [London, England], 1984.

SIDELIGHTS: After first working as an illustrator and graphic artist, Rudolf von Laban decided to dedicate his life to creating a new kind of dance. Unimpressed by the theatrical dance that was common during the early twentieth century and concerned that dance was disappearing from the lives of ordinary people, his response helped to lay the foundations for European modern dance. He became a successful choreographer and artistic director, as well as an influential theoretician. He developed a form of movement notation called Labanotation with the hope that it would help elevate the intellectual status of dance. Labanotation and the later evolution of Laban Movement Analysis (LMA), has since impacted many other fields of study, including industrial efficiency, physical education, and psychology. Laban wrote numerous works on his theories about dance, movement, education, and choreography. The earliest of these books are written in German; after Laban moved to England in 1938, he published in English.

A Hungarian, Laban studied in Paris and traveled extensively before forming his first dance school in Germany in 1910. For a time he taught Mary Wigman, who would become the most prominent German modern dancer of the era. By 1920 he was deeply involved in experimental performances that included nudity, group improvisation, dance without music, and abstract choreography. He appeared in performances with his companies the Tanzbühne Laban and the Kammertanzbühne Laban until he was injured in 1926. Laban also created large-scale choric works which relied on his system of dance notation to share the choreography with amateur participants in other locations. In this way, he found a means of offering creative dance experiences to the average person. Working as an educator, Laban wrote books on dance philosophy, movement analysis, notation, and dance study for children and adults. He also created the Choreographic Institute, a then rare venue for advanced dance study.

These achievements made Laban a notable figure in Germany and helped him land the position of choreographer and director of movement at the Berlin State Opera in 1930. Four years later he found himself working for the Nazi Ministry of Propaganda, but when his choreography for a program at the 1936 Olympic games in Berlin failed to glorify National Socialism and instead championed individual expression, Laban was removed from the job. Under virtual house arrest, he struggled with extreme poverty and illness until he was able to go to Great Britain in 1938. There, he was helped by former students and given work by F. C. Lawrence. Laban applied his understanding of movement in the study of industrial efficiency. He found industrial work less stressful if slower movements improved efficiency over quick, awkward actions. He

also gave factory workers corrective exercises to improve their comfort and performance.

Laban went on to introduce creative dance as a recreational activity in Great Britain. He wrote several books during this period, including two with F. C. Lawrence, *Laban/Lawrence Industrial Rhythm and Lilt in Labour* and *Effort*. Two works published posthumously, *Choreutics* and *A Vision of Dynamic Space*, as well as the translation *A Life for Dance: Reminiscences* were made possible by the work of Lisa Ullmann, who co-founded the Art of Movement Studio at Manchester with Laban in 1946.

In the *Journal of Physical Education*, Ed Groff considered the continued importance of Laban's work, particularly in the use of Laban Movement Analysis in the United States. Groff commented, "Laban did not leave a legacy of choreographic masterpieces, nor a recognizable distinct dance vocabulary or technique, yet he is praised as having made a major contribution to dance and movement study in the twentieth century." The writer further asserted, "His ambition to give to the art of dance and movement study an intellectual identity, a theoretical system capable of articulating movement experience enabling it to be documented, preserved, and analyzed, has contributed to the rising status of dance as a primary art, and laid a foundation for a scientific examination of movement within a variety of disciplines."

BIOGRAPHICAL AND CRITICAL SOURCES:

BOOKS

International Dictionary of Modern Dance, St. James Press (Detroit, MI), 1998.

PERIODICALS

Journal of Physical Education, Recreation & Dance, February, 1995, Ed Groff "Laban Movement Analysis: Charting the Ineffable Domain of Human Movement," p. 27.*

*   *   *

LANGDO, Bryan 1973-

PERSONAL: Born January 7, 1973, in Denville, NJ; son of Steven (an engineer) and Barbara (a homemaker; maiden name, Kesselman) Langdo. *Ethnicity:* "Caucasian." *Education:* Attended Art Student's

League of New York, 1992-95; Rutgers University, B.A. (cum laude), 1998. *Hobbies and other interests:* Hiking, camping, reading, watching movies, museums.

ADDRESSES: Home—819 Bloomfield Ave., Apt. 4, Montclair, NJ 07042. *E-mail*—tasteesub@earthlink. net.

CAREER: Mount Olive Child Care and Learning Center, Flanders, NJ, head teacher, 1998-99, 2000-01; Children's Institute, Verona, NJ, teacher's assistant, 2001—; Tusk Entertainment, Califon, NJ, production assistant, 2001.

WRITINGS:

(And illustrator) *The Dog Who Loved the Good Life,* Holt (New York, NY), 2001.
(Illustrator) Marianne Mitchell, *Joe Cinders* (picture book), Holt (New York, NY), 2002.

SIDELIGHTS: Bryan Langdo's *The Dog Who Loved the Good Life* is about a dog named Jake who expects to be treated just like a pampered human being. He wants to eat at the dinner table, sit on the furniture, and use the television remote control. Jake's owner, Mr. Hibble, is not pleased with the situation, but does not know what to do to control his pet, so he tries to get rid of him, first by putting Jake on a bus and then sending him into outer space. But Jake keeps coming back, until Mr. Hibble finally comes up with the solution of giving the dog to his niece. Some critics were disturbed by Mr. Hibble's efforts to rid himself of the dog, while others felt that Langdo's illustrations conveyed that the situations should be taken tongue-in-cheek. Lucinda Synder Whitehurst commented in *School Library Journal* that the "narrative is supposed to be funny, but children who see themselves in Jake and animal-rights activists may be disturbed." On the other hand, a *Kirkus Reviews* contributor said that while the book "ought to give lawless kiddos a pause . . . [it] is softened considerably by Langdo's meltingly affectionate artwork."

Langdo told *CA:* "I have been drawing for as long as I can remember. It has always been the one area of my life where I have total focus. Growing up, I most often would draw from comic books and fantasy art. I also

loved Dr. Seuss as a young kid, just like everyone else. My favorite book was *The Sailor Dog,* though, by Margaret Wise Brown. I've always loved big adventures, and I think that book does a great job capturing the feel of a big adventure in a small book.

"I never considered doing picture books until I met Robert J. Blake, from whom I took lessons all through middle and high school. Watching his books develop and come to completion week by week firsthand was an invaluable experience alone, not to mention all he taught me about composition, drawing, and painting. After high school, I studied at the Art Student's League of New York, doing life drawing and life painting—very academic.

"How I got into writing was just the next logical step. In order to practice illustrating and to develop a personal style, I began making up scenarios and/or stories to make pictures about. I sent out stories and illustrations constantly for a year, hoping to get published. A big part of me assumed it would never happen, but I stuck with it anyway. The day I found out *The Dog Who Loved the Good Life* was going to be published was possibly the best day of my life. I remember it like it was yesterday, and I'm still having trouble believing it.

"I write sporadically at best. If and when an idea comes, I try to develop it and work when inspired. I draw every day and usually am working on an illustration, even if it's not for something being published. I just can't stop myself from working on art. My main goal in making a book is to entertain kids, make them laugh out loud if possible. Hopefully, their parents will laugh, too."

BIOGRAPHICAL AND CRITICAL SOURCES:

PERIODICALS

Booklist, December 1, 2001, Michael Cart, review of *The Dog Who Loved the Good Life,* p. 649.
Kirkus Reviews, October 1, 2001, review of *The Dog Who Loved the Good Life,* p. 1426.
Publishers Weekly, November 19, 2001, review of *The Dog Who Loved the Good Life,* p. 66.
School Library Journal, December, 2001, Lucinda Snyder Whitehurst, review of *The Dog Who Loved the Good Life,* p. 105.

OTHER

Bryan Langdo Web site, http://www.bryanlango.com/ (October 16, 2002).

*   *   *

LASTER, James H. 1934-

PERSONAL: Born April 19, 1934, in Philadelphia, PA; son of J. Hayden (a Presbyterian minister) and Willie Nell (a homemaker; maiden name, Harold) Laster; married Madlon Travis, June 21, 1959; children: J. Travis. *Ethnicity:* "Caucasian." *Education:* Maryville College, B.A., 1956; Vanderbilt University, M.A., 1963, Ph.D., 1973; Catholic University of America, M.S. in L.S., 1992. *Religion:* Episcopalian. *Hobbies and other interests:* Music composition, acting, travel.

ADDRESSES: Home—125 Garden Ct., Winchester, VA 22601. *E-mail*—jlaster@shentel.net.

CAREER: Elementary schoolteacher in Tehran, Iran, 1957-61; Grove City College, Grove City, PA, assistant professor of music, 1966-67; Beirut College for Women, Beirut, Lebanon, associate professor of music, 1967-73; Shenandoah University, Winchester, VA, professor of music at Shenandoah Conservatory, 1973-2000, professor emeritus, 2000—. Worked as an organist and choirmaster for twenty-five years.

MEMBER: American Choral Directors Association, American Guild of Organists, American Society of Composers, Authors, and Publishers, Actors' Equity Association, Screen Actors Guild.

WRITINGS:

Catalogue of Choral Music Arranged in Biblical Order, Scarecrow Press (Lanham, MD), 1983, supplement, 1996.
A Catalogue of Vocal Solos and Duets Arranged in Biblical Order, Scarecrow Press (Lanham, MD), 1984, 2nd edition, 2003.

A Discography of Treble-Voice Recordings, Scarecrow Press (Lanham, MD), 1985.
So You're the New Musical Director! An Introduction to Conducting a Broadway Musical, Scarecrow Press (Lanham, MD), 2001.
Annotated Bibliography of Music for Organ and Instruments, Scarecrow Press (Lanham, MD), in press.

Composer of choral works published by various music publishers, including Treble Clef Press. Contributor to "Research Memorandum" Series.

WORK IN PROGRESS: A History of the Women's Choral Ensemble at the Collegiate Level in the United States from 1880 to the Present.

SIDELIGHTS: James H. Laster told *CA:* "Even though I have a number of published musical compositions and many others in manuscript, I do not call myself a composer because I have never studied composition. I write music because I need something for my choirs to sing or because someone has been nice enough to commission me to write for him.

"This description also fits my published books. I jokingly say that my only book with complete sentences is *So You're the New Musical Director! An Introduction to Conducting a Broadway Musical,* because the other titles are only lists! The musical director book came about when a student asked, 'Dr. Laster, what does a musical director do?' And he was a music theater major! My reaction was, if he had to ask that question, there might be people who are actually attempting to conduct a production and could use some help. A few ideas were jotted down and presented to a class I was teaching. The little pamphlet was expanded because of students' questions and comments.

"Need was also the stimulus for the catalogs. The *Catalogue of Choral Music Arranged in Biblical Order* evolved when I was searching for treble-voice settings of the 'Magificat' and 'Nunc Dimittis' for a women's ensemble I conducted. The project evolved into my cataloging Shenandoah's choral library to see how much of the collection used biblical texts. After collecting 500 or more titles, I asked if such a catalogue would be of help to church musicians trying to coordinate anthems with sermons or scripture readings. And a book was born. While going through piles of music, I noticed vocal solos with biblical texts. The following year there was another catalog.

"Since I am neither an author nor a composer, yet have both music and book publications, I would say that I've been fortunate!"

BIOGRAPHICAL AND CRITICAL SOURCES:

PERIODICALS

Library Journal, June 15, 2001, Janet Brewer, review of *So You're the New Musical Director! An Introduction to Conducting a Broadway Musical,* p. 75.

*   *   *

LEMON, Ralph 1952-

PERSONAL: Born August 1, 1952, in Cincinnati, OH; married Mary Good; children: Chelsea. *Education:* University of Minnesota, B. A., 1975; also studied dance with Zvi Gotheiner, Cindi Green, Zena Rommet, Ping Chong, Meredith Monk, Viola Farber, and Nancy Hauser.

ADDRESSES: Home—New York, NY. *Office*—P.O. Box 143, New York, NY 10011.

CAREER: Mixed Blood Theatre Company, Minneapolis, MN, founding member; Nancy Hauser Dance Company, Minneapolis, dancer, 1977-79; Meredith Monk/The House, dancer, 1979-81; Ralph Lemon Dance Company, founder and artistic director, 1985-95; Cross Performance, artistic director, 1995—; Yale Repertory Theatre, New Haven, CT, associate artist. Produced first evening-length concert, 1981; also performed with Dana Reitz, Blondell Cummings, and Bebe Miller; conducts master classes, composition workshops, and participates in artistic residencies throughout the United States, Mexico, and Europe; collaborated on documentary video *Konbit* with Lionel Saint Pierre, Dan El Diaz, and Zao, and film *Three* with Isaac Julien and Bebe Miller. Major works include *Joy* (1990), *Folkdance/Sextet* (1991), *Phrases Almost Biblical* (1992), *Their Eyes Rolled Back in Ecstasy* (1993), *Killing Tulips* (1993-95), *Threestep (Shipwreck)* (1995), *Geography, Part 1: Africa* (1997), and *Geography, Part 2: Asia* (2000).

MEMBER: Danspace Project at St. Marks Church, board member; Dance/USA, 1989-91.

AWARDS, HONORS: National Endowment for the Arts choreographic fellowships, 1986-88, 1992-94, 1995-97; New York Foundation for the Arts fellowships, 1986, 1992, 1998; American Choreographers Award, 1987; Boston International Choreography Competition, gold medal, 1988; New York Dance and Performance (Bessie) award, 1987; Cal-Arts/Alpert Award, 1999; National Theatre Artist residency program grant, Theatre Communications Group, 1999.

WRITINGS:

(With photographer Philip Trager) *Persephone,* poems by Eavan Boland and Rita Dove, text by Andrew Szegedy-Masak, Wesleyan University Press (Middletown, CT), 1996.
Geography: art/race/exile, performance text by Tracie Morris, afterword by Ann Daly, Wesleyan University Press (Hanover, NH), 2000.

SIDELIGHTS: Ralph Lemon is a critically acclaimed American choreographer and dancer who has expanded his artistic vision to include other creative disciplines and cultural traditions. He discovered dance while studying literature and theater at the University of Minnesota and began working in New York City during the modern dance boom of the early 1980s. After running his own company for ten years, Lemon has chosen the less restrictive task of heading the Cross Performance organization in 1995. In this capacity, he has worked on film and video projects and the multimedia series *Geography,* a three-part collaboration with artists from Africa, Asia, and America. This project also resulted in the publication of the book *Geography: art/race/exile,* which documents Lemon's experiences in Africa using journal entries, photographs, drawings, and dance scores. Lemon previously worked with photographer Philip Trager on *Persephone,* a volume that includes poems by Eavan Boland and Rita Dove.

Early on, Lemon developed a reputation for creating philosophically motivated, introspective work. His studies with Wigman-based choreographer Nancy Hauser instilled a sense that artistic expression was more important than technical training. When Lemon came to New York City to dance with Meredith Monk's company, he began doing his own choreography with an informal group of dancers and in 1981 premiered his first dance pieces. In 1985 he formed his own company and was soon earning critical praise, awards, and NEA funding. In an article for *Dance,* analyst Christopher Reardon described Lemon's choreographic style from this period as being "smooth, organic, and enigmatic."

In 1995 Lemon disbanded his company to devote more time to other art forms, including writing and the visual arts. He contributed to the making of *Konbit,* a video documentary about the Haitian community in Miami, and the film *Three* with choreographer Bebe Miller and filmmaker Isaac Julien. The multi-faceted *Geography* trilogy was scheduled to fill a seven-year span. Combining live, evening-length performances with a book, gallery exhibits, and video, the project began in Africa, where Lemon collaborated with dancers and drummers on *Geography.* He sought to combine his own postmodern style with traditional forms in a production that examined racial and cultural identities. An interest in Zen Buddhism took Lemon to Asia for the second installment, titled *Tree,* which mingled modern dance and hip hop with traditional Indian, Chinese, and Japanese performances. The third segment was to explore Lemon's roots in the American south in a work called *Home.*

Reviews of the book *Geography* showed it to be an illuminating component in this enormous project. *Dance* critic K. C. Patrick judged that the book had growing relevance, with its reflections on African and African American existences. A *Publishers Weekly* writer called the book a "searching, brutally frank travelogue." The writer deemed that *Geography* was at its strongest "when Lemon hones in on the physical, spiritual, and cultural contradictions inherent in his attempts at placing the rhythm-based sensibilities of the African dancers into formal Western structures," valuing it as a cultural study as well as an examination of artistic endeavors. Lemon's prose, which reminded the critic of the work of poet Bill Luoma, was said to add to the book's appeal.

BIOGRAPHICAL AND CRITICAL SOURCES:

BOOKS

International Dictionary of Modern Dance, St. James Press (Detroit, MI), 1998.

PERIODICALS

Dance, September, 2000, Christopher Reardon, "Pilgrim's Progress," p. 64; December, 2001, K. C. Patrick, review of *Geography: art/race/exile,* p. 76.
Publishers Weekly, November 27, 2000, review of *Geography: art/race/exile,* p. 67.*

*   *   *

LIMÓN, José (Arcadio) 1908-1972

PERSONAL: Born January 12, 1908, in Mexico; naturalized U.S. citizen, 1946; died December 2, 1972, in Flemington, NJ; son of Florencio Limón (a military band leader) and Francisca Traslaviña; married Pauline Lawrence (a dancer, company manager, and costume designer), October 13, 1941. *Education:* Studied painting at University of California, Los Angeles, and Art Students League; studied dance at Humphrey-Weidman School, 1929-40; attended summer programs at Bennington School of Dance and Mills College. *Religion:* Catholic.

CAREER: Dancer, choreographer, and educator. Humphrey-Weidman Company, New York, NY, dancer, 1930-40; José Limón Dance Company, founder, 1946, artistic director, 1958-72; Juilliard School of Music, faculty member, 1953-72; American Dance Festival at Connecticut College, faculty member, summers 1948-72; American Dance Theatre at Lincoln Center, artistic director, 1964-65. Also formed The Little Group with Ernestine Henoch and Eleanor King, 1930; performances on Broadway included *Lysistrata* (1930), *Americana* (1932), and *As Thousands Cheered* (1933); choreographed Jerome Kern's *Roberta,* 1933; created touring company with May O'Donnell and Ray Green, 1940; guest choreographer, Instituto Nacional de Bellas Artes, Mexico City, 1951. *Military service:* U.S. Armed Forces, 1943, member of the Special Services.

AWARDS, HONORS: Bennington College, choreography fellow, 1937; *Dance* awards, 1950, 1957; Capezio Award, 1964; National Endowment for the Arts grants, beginning 1966; Samuel S. Scripps Award from American Dance Festival, 1989; inducted into National Museum of Dance Hall of Fame, 1997; several honorary doctorate degrees.

WRITINGS:

Limón: A Catalogue of Dances, Limón Institute, c. 1994.

José Limón: An Unfinished Memoir, edited by Lynn Garafola, University Press of New England (Hanover, NH), 1998.

Contributor of articles to journals, including *Juilliard Review, Impulse, Dance Observer,* and *Dance Scope.*

SIDELIGHTS: José Limón was a passionate advocate of modern dance. As a dancer and choreographer, he strengthened the role of male dancers and developed a bold, masculine style of movement. Following a long affiliation with the Humphrey-Weidman Company, he went on to create the José Limón Company in 1946. He most often made dances based on literary and biblical stories, but also used cultural themes from his native country of Mexico. Limón taught dance at several schools and was a faculty member at the Juilliard School of Music. His influence continues to be felt in the Limón Dance Company, which became the first organization of its kind to survive its founder. When he died in 1972, Limón left an autobiographical manuscript that discussed his childhood and the first part of his career. More than twenty-five years later, it was published as *José Limón: An Unfinished Memoir.*

Born in Culiacán, Mexico, Limón came to the United States when his family escaped the dangers of the Mexican Revolution by moving to Tucson, Arizona. At age eighteen he was devastated by the death of his mother in childbirth, a tragedy he blamed on his father and the Catholic Church. He started studying painting at University of California, Los Angeles and at the Art Students League in New York City, but was unsatisfied with this experience. By chance he attended a modern dance program by German Expressionists Harald Kreutzberg and Yvonne Georgi that immediately convinced him that dancing was his calling. He enrolled at the Humphrey-Weidman School and, after fairly little training, became a member of the company and was performing on Broadway. Limón also began doing his own choreographic work for duets and small groups.

Limón broke away from the Humphrey-Weidman Company because of personal conflicts, but he later returned to New York to collaborate with Doris Humphrey. She became the artistic director of the company he formed in 1946, a role that he took over after her death in 1958. Among his most famous works are *The Moor's Pavane* (1949), based on the story of Othello, *There is a Time* (1956), and *Missa Brevis* (1957). Limón created several dances for all-male ensembles that danced bare chested. Toward the end of his career, he experimented with pieces incorporating silence.

In his unfinished memoir, Limón shows himself to be a skilled, careful writer. Editor Lynn Garafola turned the document into a book that sheds light on his early family life and career prior to 1942. Critics were eager to discover what insights would be found in his detailed descriptions of the premieres of his most prominent contemporaries as well as of his own performances. In *Library Journal,* Carolyn M. Mulac said the book is comprised of "elegant, often formal prose" and provides a "serious consideration" of the early days of modern dance. Mulac explained that the limited scope of Limón's commentary is augmented by an introduction by Deborah Jowitt and remarks by Norton Owen and Carla Maxwell. She deemed it a "fascinating look at a legendary performer." A *Publishers Weekly* writer noted that there are indeed "significant gaps in his writing," including only the barest mention of Limón's wife. The writer suggested that the stories, including those about Martha Graham, would be appreciated by "dance aficionados."

BIOGRAPHICAL AND CRITICAL SOURCES:

BOOKS

Dictionary of Hispanic Biography, Gale (Detroit, MI), 1996.

International Dictionary of Modern Dance, St. James Press (Detroit, MI), 1998.

PERIODICALS

Library Journal, March 15, 1999, Carolyn M. Mulac, review of *José Limón: An Unfinished Memoir,* p. 82.

Publishers Weekly, January 11, 1999, review of *José Limón: An Unfinished Memoir,* p. 62.*

LIPSYTE, Sam 1968-

PERSONAL: Born 1968, in New York, NY; son of Robert (a writer) and Marjorie (a novelist) Lipsyte; married Ceridwen Morris. *Education:* Brown University, 1990.

ADDRESSES: Agent—Donadio and Olson, 127 West 27th St., Ste. 704, New York, NY 10001.

CAREER: Feed, coeditor-in-chief and writer, 1995-2001. Former front man for the noise rock band, Dungbeetle.

WRITINGS:

Venus Drive (short stories), Open City Books (New York, NY), 2000.
The Subject Steve, Broadway Books (New York, NY), 2001.
The Meat Dreamer (play), produced in Los Angeles, 2003.

WORK IN PROGRESS: Home Land, to be published in England in 2004.

SIDELIGHTS: Sam Lipsyte was coeditor-in-chief of the now dissolved online site *Feed.* In an interview with Katharine Mieszkowski for *Salon.com* Lipsyte stated, "I think it is sad. Six years after there really is not a lot of smart writing on the Web." Although he is no longer writing for *Feed,* he continues his writing with his books *Venus Drive* and *The Subject Steve.* It is clear in both works that Lipsyte likes to play with language. The rhythm of the prose sends him into a hypnotic state which produces a rush of material that is "fresh, funky and almost completely meaningless," according to Bruno Maddox with the *New York Times.*

In Lipsyte's collection of short stories, *Venus Drive,* "he deftly weaves themes of drug abuse . . . [with] the misery of office life, and the decay of urban youth," in the opinion of a critic for *Salon.com.* The critic noted that he writes of this minutia of life "with a powerful emotional current that carries though each of the stories." A critic for *Open City Books* expressed that, "Sam Lipsyte's stories comprise a chorus of gallows humor and good will gone bad." A writer for *Kirkus Reviews* conveyed that Lipsyte "shows off the prose equivalent of three chords on a one-string guitar. . . . he has no qualms about hanging the reader up on a sentence whose sense has gone south." Many critics were in awe of Lipsyte's use of language, but at the same time were amused and disturbed by the antics of the unscrupulous characters that pervade each story. A reviewer for *Seminary Co-Op Bookstore* explained the backdrop of these stories as a "beaten-down, shabby atmosphere." The reviewer continued, "innocence mixes uneasily with cruelty and indifference. . . . Lipsyte definitely nails down a certain mental atmosphere in his stories."

Lipsyte's first novel, *The Subject Steve,* unravels a tale of a man who is supposedly dying of a disease concocted by his doctors (one is actually a dentist) to bring them fame and notoriety. The plan backfires when they are discovered to be frauds, however, this does not keep "Steve" from searching for the cure to this now-trendy disease. His pursuit of a cure ultimately leads to his untimely death. As in Lipsyte's previous work, he uses his stylized language to engross the reader. Bruno Maddox in the *New York Times* observed that *The Subject Steve* "distinguishes itself is on the verbal level. . . . intended as an attack on language itself." Bruno believes that "the message falls victim to the medium: the impenetrable barrier Lipsyte has chosen to erect between the reader and the action of the novel." A reviewer for *Entertainment Weekly* stated that "the book jacket promises a novel, but what Lipsyte delivers is more a fusillade of language . . . that doesn't let up until the last line." In an interview with the author, Ron Hogan of *Beatrice* surmised, "some readers might see in the novel a bleakness that hints at the world in which the disaster became possible." In that same interview Lipsyte himself stated, "the thing that destroys Steve isn't the illness, but the hunt for the so-called cure." The reviewer for *Seminary Co-Op Bookstore* concluded that Lipsyte is "a versatile, very funny, and engaging writer unafraid to delve into ambiguity."

Lipsyte told *CA:* "I've been fairly pleased with the level of criticism my books have engendered. But the truth is I've tried to seperate my writing life from my publishing life. They really don't mesh well. Publishing is a market-driven enterprise, and more and more, especially in America, the idea of putting out books just because they're good is in danger of extinction in mainstream publishing. It used to be the bad stuff paid for the good stuff. Now the bad stuff pays for more bad stuff. I've been at work on a new novel, *Home Land,* and I've also taken a stab at playwriting."

BIOGRAPHICAL AND CRITICAL SOURCES:

PERIODICALS

Booklist, August, 2001, Kristine Huntley, review of *The Subject Steve,* p. 2087.

Entertainment Weekly, September 21, 2001, review of *The Subject Steve,* p.78.

Kirkus Reviews, May 1, 2000, review of *Venus Drive,* p. 593; August 1, 2001, review of *The Subject Steve,* p. 1054.

New York Times Book Review, May 28, 2000, Christine Muhlke, "Human Resumés," p. 19; October 18, 2001, "A Curious Case," p. 19.

Publishers Weekly, April 10, 2000, review of *Venus Drive,* p. 76; August 13, 2001, review of *The Subject Steve,* p. 284.

OTHER

Beatrice Interview, http://www.beatrice.com/ (July 1, 2001), Ron Hogan, interview with Sam Lipsyte.

Open City Books, http://www.opencity.org/ (April 16, 2002).

Salon.com, http://www.salon.com/ (April 16, 2002); (July 1, 2002).

Seminary Co-Op Bookstore Web site, http://www. semcoop.com/ (April 16, 2002).

*   *   *

LITTLEWOOD, Joan (Maud) 1914-2002

OBITUARY NOTICE—See index for *CA* sketch: October 6, 1914, in London, England; died September 20, 2002, in London, England. Stage director, producer, and author. Littlewood was renowned, especially in her native England, for heading the Theater Workshop in London, where she put on plays by and about working-class people and was considered by some to be the "mother of modern theater." She developed a love for the theater as a child, and as a teenager won a scholarship to attend the Royal Academy of Dramatic Art. However, coming from a working-class family, she was put off by the more elitist attitudes of the students and teachers there, so she dropped out. Rejecting the trappings of popular theater that appealed to middle- and upperclass playgoers, Littlewood wanted to strip play production down to the essential bones. She began her mission in the 1930s by founding the Theater of Action in Manchester, which was followed by her creation of the traveling company Theater Union, which often did improvisational work. After World War II she founded the Theater Workshop, which started as a touring company and in 1953 settled down at the dilapidated Royal Theater in London. She and her company of actors worked on a shoestring budget, sleeping in hammocks and running and maintaining the theater. Under these tough conditions, however, Littlewood became famous for producing thought-provoking plays that were largely about the struggles of working-class people. She also was responsible for discovering and adapting the works of talented playwrights such as Irish writer Brendan Behan, whose plays *The Quare Fella* and *The Hostage* she directed; Shelagh Delaney, whose first play, *A Taste of Honey,* Littlewood directed when the playwright was only eighteen years old; and ex-convict Frank Norman's *Fings Ain't Wot They Used T'Be;* she is, furthermore, often credited with discovering the actor Richard Harris. The most successful play produced by the Theater Workshop was perhaps the improvisational *Oh What a Lovely War,* an anti-war farce about World War I that won a Tony Award in 1965. Littlewood disbanded the Theater Workshop in 1964 to work at a cultural center in Tunisia and then at Image India in Calcutta during the late 1960s. Returning to England in the early 1970s, she reformed her acting company; but after her long relationship with theater manager Gerry Raffles ended with his death in 1975, she moved to Vienne, France, and retired from the theater scene. Littlewood's influence on modern theater, especially during the 1950s and 1960s, is undeniable, and she wrote about her experiences in her 1994 autobiography, *Joan's Book: Joan Littlewood's Peculiar History as She Tells It.* She was also the author of *Baron Philippe: The Very Candid Autobiography of Baron Philippe de Rothschild* (1985), about the man with whom she became friends in France after Raffles' death.

OBITUARIES AND OTHER SOURCES:

BOOKS

Frick, John W., and Stephen M. Vallillo, *Theatrical Directors: A Biographical Dictionary,* Greenwood Press (Westport, CT), 1994.
International Dictionary of Theatre, Volume 3: *Actors, Directors, and Designers,* St. James Press (Detroit, MI), 1996.
Oxford Companion to English Literature, sixth edition, Oxford University Press (Oxford, England), 2000.
Partnow, Elaine T., and Lesley Anne Hyatt, *The Female Dramatist: Profiles of Women Playwrights from the Middle Ages to Contemporary Times,* Fact on File (New York, NY), 1998.

PERIODICALS

Chicago Tribune, September 23, 2002, Section 2, p. 6.
Los Angeles Times, September 25, 2002, p. B11.
New York Times, September 24, 2002, p. A29.
Times (London, England), September 23, 2002, p. 10.

*   *   *

LLOYD, Roseann 1944-

PERSONAL: Born 1944, in Springfield, MO. *Ethnicity:* "Welsh, Scottish, Irish, Spanish, English." *Education:* University of Minnesota, B.S., M.A; studied with Richard Hugo, Madeline DeFrees, and Tess Gallagher at University of Montana. *Hobbies and other interests:* Walking.

ADDRESSES: Home—Minneapolis, MN. *Office*—University of St. Thomas, English Department, JRC 333, 2115 Summit Avenue, St. Paul, MN 55105 *E-mail*—roseannlloyd@Hotmail.com/, lloyd009@tc.umn.edu/.

CAREER: Poet, author, editor, and educator. Currently visiting professor at University of St. Thomas, St. Paul; adjunct professor in Hamline graduate program in St. Paul. Taught in the writers-in-the-schools program and community programs; leads annual poetry writing workshop in Antigua, Guatemala.

MEMBER: The Loft, S.A.S.E.; the Write Place, Lyndale UCC Church, Mineapolis, MN.

AWARDS, HONORS: Loft-McKnight Award of Distinction in Poetry, 1991; American Book Award, Before Columbus Foundation, 1991, for *Looking for Home: Women Writing about Exile;* Minnesota Book Award for Poetry, 1997, for "War Baby Express"; Minnesota State Arts Board fellowship, 1998; Jerome travel grant, 1998; Bush Foundation fellowship, 1999.

WRITINGS:

Tap Dancing for Big Mom (poetry), illustrated by Arne Nyen, New Rivers Press (St. Paul, MN), 1986.
(With Richard Solly) *Journeynotes: Writing For Recovery and Spiritual Growth,* Harper & Row (San Francisco, CA), 1989.
(Editor with Deborah Keenan) *Looking for Home: Women Writing about Exile* (anthology), illustrated by R. W. Scholes, Milkweed Editions (Minneapolis, MN), 1990.
(With Merle Fossum) *True Selves: Twelve-Step Recovery from Codependency,* photographs by Tony Nelson and Terry Gydesen, Hazelden (Center City, MN), HarperCollins (New York, NY), 1991.
(Translator with Allen Simpson) *Herbjörg Wassmo, The House with the Blind Glass Windows,* Seal Press, 1995.
War Baby Express (poetry), Holy Cow! Press (Minneapolis, MN), 1996.

WORK IN PROGRESS: Because of the Light (poetry), 2002, to be published by Holy Cow! Press (Minneapolis, MN).

SIDELIGHTS: Roseann Lloyd was born in Springfield, Missouri and educated in Missoula, Montana and her current home of Minneapolis, Minnesota. She teaches at the college level and is involved in community projects that use poetry as a healing tool. Some of her programs are tailored for adolescents or adults recovering from addiction and victims of sexual assault. *Journeynotes: Writing for Recovery and Spiritual Growth,* which Lloyd co-wrote with Richard Solly, is a guide to keeping a journal for reflection and self-discovery. It includes excerpts from the diaries of famous writers in recovery that demonstrate the effectiveness of writing about issues that are difficult to discuss. The authors use the word "recovery" in the broadest sense, since they believe everyone has recovery work that needs to be accomplished.

Lloyd's *War Baby Express* is a poetry collection in which she writes of wars ranging from the Vietnam War to the war waged against battered and abused women. Nick DiSpoldo wrote in *Small Press Review* that "although Lloyd writes with all the urgency of a 911 call, she is careful and thoughtful, dissecting domestic discord to reveal the social cancer that is domestic violence." In several poems, Lloyd writes of her brother's early death from narcotics. In "Angles of Vision" the narrator speaks about the connections between militarism, family dynamics, and physical/sexual abuse. Alison Townsend wrote in *Women's Review of Books* that in this poem Lloyd "uses repetition, mid-line caesuras, and lack of punctuation to capture the halting, gliding movement of memory and mind on the page." Townsend said that in the narrative poems, including "Cloud of Witnesses, All Saint's Day" and "County Mental Health Clinic, 1976," Lloyd "employs a longer, almost Whitmanesque, iambic line and mostly endstopped couplets that underscore the pain and solemnity of wife abuse." Townsend concluded by saying: "Long one of my favorite poets for the courage of her art, in this collection, Lloyd is both stylistically original and emotionally whole, transforming the landscape of loss into one of possession."

Lloyd and Deborah Keenan edited the anthology *Looking for Home: Women Writing about Exile. Booklist* reviewer Pat Monaghan noted that "the subtitle only hints at the breadth of work within this exemplary collection." The forms of exile addressed in the 125 poems written by American women, many of whom were born abroad, go beyond geographical movement to exclusion as exile, forced by racial and economic oppression, abuse, poverty, chemical dependency, sexual nonconformity, and sickness. Monaghan described as "piercing" Mitsuye Yamada's "I Learned to Sew," about her mail order bride grandmother who was rejected for being homely. *Publishers Weekly* reviewer Penny Kaganoff called the entry "a stunning narrative of immigration and social hierarchy." The

poems reflect the difficulty of women entering the United States, particularly in adapting to market-driven, male-defined values. *New York Times Book Review* contributor Devon Jersild wrote that the collection "richly communicates both the singularity and the universality of women's deepest concerns. . . . In most of them one hears language freighted with experience, the real voices of real women." The nature of exile may be cultural, but is also spatial, temporal, and psychological, observed Marie Noëlle Ng in *Canadian Literature.* "One is immediately struck by the overwhelming sadness in these poems: to travel is not to have an adventure, to explore. Instead, to travel is to be displaced, to escape, sometimes without destination."

Lloyd and Allen Simpson were the first to translate the work of Norwegian writer Herbjörg Wassmo. *The House with the Blind Glass Windows* is the first volume of a trilogy that had previously been published in Scandinavia. A *Publishers Weekly* reviewer called the novel a "heartbreaking tale." The title refers to the house in which young Tora and her mother, Ingrid, live. Tora's natural father was a Nazi deserter who was killed before he and Ingrid could escape. Ingrid is now married to Henrik, who sexually abuses the eleven-year-old child while her indifferent mother works the night shift in a fish-packing plant. Tora, the only German in her village, is picked on by the other children, causing her to retreat into a world of fantasy. Only when Tora is helped by an aunt and uncle and begins to form relationships with others outside the family, including a deaf and mute boy and a Jewish peddler, is she able to trust again. "Ms. Wassmo has written a deeply moving novel, compassionate but not sentimental, whose earthy language is able to express the complex feelings of a complicated time," wrote Kaj Schueler in the *New York Times Book Review.* Schueler called this a "fine English translation." In terms of its impact on young people, the book has been compared to *Catcher in the Rye.*

Lloyd told CA: "In the process of writing *Because of the Light,* I've been working with the Ghazal, the prose poem and persona poem, as well as other free verse forms, to explore aspects of our contemporary world. I'm interested in integrating many voices into my poems and these forms have given me a wide range of voices, tonal variation and complexity. My first two collections of poetry emerged from my personal history. This new book comes from a wider community of people and cultures. For many years, I've joked seriously that anyone who survives junior high school has a lifetime of material for writing. However, in the last few years, traveling has also become a rich source for my poems and so I've had to give up that junior high motto, although it is still true. About my process: I write/revise my poems by saying them out loud. I grew up in the Ozarks around people who told long stories and I seem to have picked up that habit myself. My poems start with phrases and rhythms more often than images. The corollary to that is that I love giving readings—that is, giving my poems to the world. I also send new poems on email to friend for quick feedback, so I experience a strange mix of real-time and cyber-time in my current working process. Off and on, I post new poems on my Web Site as well, which is located at www.roseannlloyd.com."

Poet Jim Moore has written the following comment for the cover of my book *Because of the Light*: "I have followed Roseann Lloyd's work with pleasure and admiration for many years now. Each book has given me a new way not just to look at and be in the world, but new worlds at which to look: Guatemala, Norway and Wales. Whatever a 'global soul' might come to resemble in this post-September 11th world, Lloyd's poems will surely help Americans understand its textures and contours, its rewards and challenges." The book's last two lines are: "I had come around/the long way home. Home to the heart? Yes, that. But also to the larger world in which the heart must find its way."

BIOGRAPHICAL AND CRITICAL SOURCES:

PERIODICALS

Booklist, September 15, 1990, Pat Monaghan, review of *Looking for Home,* p. 135.

Canadian Literature, spring, 1994, Maria Noëlle Ng, "Travelling Women," pp. 92-94.

Et cetera, winter, 1989, Jeremy Klein, review of *Journey Notes,* pp. 384-85.

Hungry Mind Review, fall, 1996, review of *War Baby Express,* p. 30.

New York Times Book Review, January 17, 1988, p. 24; November 25, 1990, Devon Jersild, "Women and Other Foreigners," p. 18.

Publishers Weekly, September 11, 1987, review of *The House with the Blind Glass Windows,* p. 83; August 17, 1990, Penny Kaganoff, review of *Looking for Home,* p. 63.

Small Press Review, April, 1997, Nick DiSpoldo, review of *War Baby Express,* p. 11.

Women's Review of Books, March, 1997, Alison Townsend, "No Pain, no Gain," p. 12.

OTHER

Roseann Lloyd Web Site, http://www.Roseannlloyd.com (April 29, 2003).

*   *   *

LORD, Tom
See BRAUN, Matt

M

MAC, Bernie 1957-

PERSONAL: Born Bernard Jeffrey McCullough, 1957, in Chicago, IL; married; wife's name Rhonda; children: J'Neice. *Ethnicity:* "African American."

ADDRESSES: *Office*—c/o Def Comedy Jam, HBO, 1100 Avenue of the Americas, New York, New York, United States 10036.

CAREER: Stand-up comic and actor. Film debut, *Mo' Money*, 1992; appeared in over a dozen films. Creator and star, *Midnight Mac*, HBO, 1995; founding member, *The Original Kings of Comedy*, 1997-00; concert film, *The Original Kings of Comedy*, 2000; star, *The Bernie Mac Show* (television series), 2001—.

WRITINGS:

(With Darrell Dawsey) *I Ain't Scared of You!*, MTV Books (New York, NY), 2001.
(With Pablo F. Fenjves) *Maybe You Never Cry Again*, Regan Books (New York, NY), 2003.

SIDELIGHTS: Although actor and comedien Bernie Mac, born Bernard Jeffery McCullough, has lived the proverbial Hollywood success story, it took decades to achieve. The "Original Kings of Comedy," a hit concert tour featuring Steve Harvey, D. L. Hughley, and Cedric the Entertainer that was turned into a hit film by Spike Lee, brought Mac crossover fame. He began performing comedy in 1977 and it led him off the streets of Chicago. Bernie's first real standup routine was when he was eight years old. At church, he did a routine about his grandparents sitting at the kitchen table. As a result, Mac's grandmother came up and smacked him, took him outside, and proceeded to "whip" him. It was then that Mac realized the joke was more important than discipline.

In Mac's autobiographical *I Ain't Scared of You!*, he takes on professional athletes, sex, religion, marriage, child rearing, and his South-side Chicago childhood. A *Publishers Weekly* reviewer noted that the book "skillfully captures the rhythm and color of street vernacular. . . . Mac shows on more than one occasion that he can reach deep in the pockets of human distress and bring forth a smile."

BIOGRAPHICAL AND CRITICAL SOURCES:

BOOKS

Contemporary Black Biography, Volume 29, Gale (Detroit, MI), 2001.

PERIODICALS

Black Issues Book Review, January-February 2002, Michelle Gipson, "Bernie Mac on How Life Is: *I Ain't Scared of You*," p. 69.
Daily Variety, June 3, 2002, Michael Fleming, "Mac Stacks up Pic Roles," p. 1.

Electronic Media, November 26, 2001, Michael Freeman, review of *The Bernie Mac Show,* p. 1A.

Entertainment Weekly, August 11, 2000, Noah Robischon, movie review of the Kings of Comedy Tour, p. 42; December 1, 2000, p. 90; November 16, 2001, Ken Tucker, review of *The Bernie Mac Show,* p. 155; December 21, 2001, Ken Tucker, "9 Bernie Mac," p. 42.

Esquire, November, 2001, review of *The Bernie Mac Show,* p. 42.

Essence, October, 2001.

Hollywood Reporter, November 14, 2001, Barry Garron, review of *The Bernie Mac Show,* p. 6.

Interview, August, 2000, Susan Johnson, review of The Kings of Comedy Tour, p. 57.

Jet, September 30, 2002, Aldore Collier, "The Bernie Mac Show Back for Second Season," p. 61; December 3, 2001, "Bernie Mac Brings Tough Love and Comedy to *The Bernie Mac Show,*" p. 56.

Knight-Ridder/Tribune News Service, March 28, 1994, Nick Charles, review of *The Bernie Mac Show,* p. K4373; November 13, 2001, Ken Parish Perkins, review of *The Bernie Mac Show,* p. K4; November 13, 2001, Manuel Mendoza, review of *The Bernie Mac Show,* p. K4374; November 13, 2001, Mike Duffy, review of *The Bernie Mac Show,* p. K4374.

Los Angeles Times, November 4, 2001, Greg Braxton, review of *The Bernie Mac Show,* p. F5.

New York Times, August 18, 2000, Elvis Mitchell, review of *The Kings of Comedy Tour,* p. E12; March 2, 2001, review of Kings of Comedy Tour (video recording), p. E31; November 14, 2001, Neil Genzlinger, review of *The Bernie Mac Show,* p. 103; December 5, 2001, Bernard Weintraub, review of Kings of Comedy Tour, p. E1.

New York Times Magazine, May 12, 2002, Chris Norris, "Bernie Mac Smacks a Nerve," p. 30.

Publishers Weekly, October 1, 2001, review of *I Ain't Scared of You,* p. 50; October 15, 2001, review of *I Ain't Scared of You,* p. 60; November 6, 2001, John F. Baker, review of *I Ain't Scared of You,* p. 18.

Rolling Stone, December 26, 2002, Mark Binelli, "Bernie Mac's Hostile Takeover," p. 39.

Savoy, May 2002, Jay A. Fernandez, "Papa Don't Take No Mess," p. 53.

Sight and Sound, October, 1998, review of *The Players Club,* p. 49.

Time, November 5, 2001, James Poniewozik, review of *The Bernie Mac Show,* p. 103.

TV Guide, February 2, 2002, David Hochman, "Make Room for Bernie Mac," p. 14.

Variety, April 13, 1998, Joe Leyden, movie review of *The Players Club,* p. 28; April 12, 1999, review of *Life,* p. 63; November 19, 2001, Michael Speier, review of *The Bernie Mac Show,* p. 46; January 28, 2002, "Bernie Mac Cooks," p. 21.

OTHER

NetNoir.com, http:www.netnoir.com/ (February 2, 2001).

SimonSays.com, http://www.simonsays.com/ (January 8, 2002), review of *I Ain't Scared of You.* *

*   *   *

MacDONALD, Andrew
See PIERCE, William L(uther)

*   *   *

MADDOX, John (Royden) 1925-

PERSONAL: Born November 27, 1925, in England; son of Arthur John and Mary Elizabeth (Davies) Maddox; married Nancy Fanning, November 11, 1960. *Education:* Oxford University, B.A., 1947, M.A., 1952.

ADDRESSES: Office—c/o *Nature,* 4 Little Essex St., London WC2R 3LF, England. *E-mail*—j.maddox@ nature.com.

CAREER: University of Manchester, Manchester, England, assistant lecturer, 1949-55; *Manchester Guardian,* Manchester, science correspondent, 1955-64; Nuffield Foundation, assistant director, 1964-66, director, 1975-80; *Nature,* London, England, editor, 1966-73, 1980-95; Maddox Editorial Ltd., chairman, 1973-75; writer.

AWARDS, HONORS: Edward Rhein Cultural Award, 1997; knighted for his contribution to science; honorary degrees from University of Surrey, 1988, University of East Anglia, 1993; University of Liverpool, 1995; Nottingham Trent University, 1996; and University of Glamorgan, Wales, 1997.

WRITINGS:

(With Leonard Beaton) *The Spread of Nuclear Weapons,* 1962.
Revolution in Biology, Macmillan (New York, NY), 1964.
The Doomsday Syndrome, McGraw (New York, NY), 1972.
Beyond the Energy Crisis, McGraw, 1975.
Prospects for Nuclear Proliferation, International Institute for Strategic Studies (London, England), 1975.
What Remains to Be Discovered: Mapping the Secrets of the Universe, the Origins of Life, and the Future of the Human Race, Martin Kessler (New York, NY), 1998.

Contributor to periodicals, including *World Press Review.*

SIDELIGHTS: Long-time *Nature* editor John Maddox is a theoretical physicist and writer who is known for his general expertise in the various sciences. He is a compelling advocate of greater scientific awareness for political leaders, government officials, and the general public. "I . . . hope that far more politicians and civil servants will understand what science is about," Maddox told a *World Press Review* interviewer, adding: "People who do not understand [science] should not regulate public affairs. The sooner we can integrate science into the general culture again the better off we will be." In that same interview, Maddox also expressed a desire for greater communication between scientific figures and the remaining civilian population. "I wish," he added, "that more member of the scientific community were able to talk about the larger problems as convincingly to the public as they seem to do among themselves."

Maddox has published books on subjects ranging from the proliferation of nuclear weaponry to the consumption of natural resources. In *What Remains to Be Discovered: Mapping the Secrets of the Universe, the Origins of Life, and the Future of the Human Race,* he writes on the nature of science throughout history, ad-

dressing such subjects as quantum mechanics, genetics, and cosmology. He renews his advocacy of greater scientific understanding between scientists and political figures. *New Yorker* reviewer Jim Holt notes that the book provides "a careful working out . . . of the near-term discoveries about matter and life which were augured by a couple of decades' worth of *Nature* articles." And Paul Raeburn, writing in *New York Times Book Review,* affirms that *What Remains to Be Discovered* "attempts to set an agenda for the coming decades, even centuries." Raeburn adds that Maddox "discusses what scientists need to find out, and where they might look." A *Publishers Weekly* reviewer describes *What Remains to Be Discovered* as "admirable if sometimes difficult," while an *Economist* critic adds "that there are few crannies of science he does not command." The *Economist* critic also noted that the book "offers a detailed catalogue of existing discoveries, especially during this century, and then draws particular attention to the points where this edifice displays gaps or tensions."

BIOGRAPHICAL AND CRITICAL SOURCES:

PERIODICALS

Booklist, October 1, 1998, Gilbert Taylor, review of *What Remains to Be Discovered: Mapping the Secrets of the Universe, the Origins of Life, and the Future of the Human Race,* p. 298.
Economist, October 17, 1998, "Scientific Sense," pp. 12-13.
Information Services and Use, October, 1998, Tony Cawkell, review of *What Remains to Be Discovered,* p. 282.
New Statesman, November 27, 1999, Will Self, review of *What Remains to Be Discovered,* p. 64.
New Yorker, October 26, 1998, Jim Holt, "What's Left to Learn?," pp. 240-45.
New York Times Book Review, January 10, 1999, Paul Raeburn, review of *What Remains to Be Discovered.*
Physics Today, August 1999, Joel Primack, review of *What Remains to Be Discovered,* p. 64.
Publishers Weekly, August 17, 1998, review of *What Remains to Be Discovered,* p. 54.
Science, October 30, David L. Goodstein, review of *What Remains to Be Discovered,* p. 886.
Sciences, January 1999, Joseph Traub, review of *What Remains to Be Discovered,* p. 39.
World Press Review, July, 1983, pp. 31-33.

OTHER

Third Culture Web site, http://digerati.edge.org/ (January 8, 1999).*

*   *   *

MANLEY, Rachel 1947-

PERSONAL: Born July 3, 1947, in Cornwall, England; daughter of Michael (a trade unionist, politician, and prime minister of Jamaica) and Jacqueline (a librarian; maiden name, Gill) Manley; married Paul Ennevor (a builder; marriage ended); married Israel Cinman (a journalist); children: Drummond Druh, Luke Ennevor. *Ethnicity:* "Jamaican." *Education:* University of the West Indies, B.A. (with honors); also attended Radcliffe College, Harvard University. *Politics:* Democratic Socialist. *Religion:* Methodist.

ADDRESSES: Agent—c/o Author Mail, Random House Canada, 33 Yonge St., Toronto, Ontario, Canada.

CAREER: Worked as a teacher at a secondary school in Jamaica in the 1970s; Caribbean Broadcasting, deputy director of advertising in Barbados, 1980-82, director of advertising, 1982-86; writer. Member of Edna Manley Foundation.

AWARDS, HONORS: Century Medal for poetry, Institute of Jamaica, 1979; Canadian Governor General's Award for nonfiction, 1997, for *Drumblair: Memories of a Jamaican Childhood;* Bunting fellow, 1999; Rockefeller Foundation fellow, 2000; Guggenheim fellow in Bellagio, Italy, 2001-02.

WRITINGS:

(Editor) *Edna Manley: The Diaries,* Andre Deutsch (London, England), 1989.
A Light Left On (poetry), People Tree Press (Yorkshire, England), 1992.
Drumblair: Memories of a Jamaican Childhood, Knopf (Toronto, Ontario, Canada), 1996.
Slipstream: A Daughter Remembers, Knopf (Toronto, Ontario, Canada), 2000.

Author of additional poetry collections.

WORK IN PROGRESS: A novel.

SIDELIGHTS: Rachel Manley told *CA:* "I simply cannot help writing. It is my voice. My work is influenced by my late grandparents, Norman and Edna Manley, and the national and cultural movements of Jamaica. My subjects chose me; they were out of the ordinary, and I had the extraordinary good fortune to be placed as a bystander to their unfolding."

BIOGRAPHICAL AND CRITICAL SOURCES:

PERIODICALS

Canadian Literature, spring, 2000, Anthony Boxhill, review of *Drumblair: Memories of a Jamaican Childhood,* p. 162.
Maclean's, October 21, 1996, Donna Nurse, review of *Drumblair,* p. 84; October 23, 2000, "A Father Lost, Loved, and Longed For," p. 61.

*   *   *

MANN-BORGESE, Elisabeth
See BORGESE, Elisabeth Mann

*   *   *

MANNINO, Mary Ann Vigilante 1943-

PERSONAL: Born August 3, 1943, in Philadelphia, PA; daughter of Pasqualle and Marion (Mercaldo) Vigilante; married Edward Mannino, July 17, 1965 (marriage ended, 1991); children: Robert, Jennifer. *Ethnicity:* "Italian/American." *Education:* University of Pennsylvania, B.A., 1965; Temple University, M.A., 1986, Ph.D., 1995. *Hobbies and other interests:* Folk songs, dancing.

ADDRESSES: Office—Department of English, Temple University, Philadelphia, PA 19122. *E-mail*—mmannino@astro.temple.edu.

CAREER: Germantown Friends School, Philadelphia, PA, teacher of creative writing, 1990; Temple University, Philadelphia, instructor in English and women's studies, 1989-95, visiting assistant professor of English, 1995—. Speaker at Passaic County Community College, State University of New York, and New York University, and other venues; gives readings from her works; guest on public television programs.

MEMBER: Modern Language Association of America, American Italian Historical Association, Society for the Study of Multi-Ethnic Literature of the United States, Philadelphia Folksong Society.

WRITINGS:

Revisionary Identities: Strategies of Empowerment in the Writing of Italian American Women, Peter Lang Publishing (New York, NY), 2000.

Contributor to books, including *Shades of Black and White: Conflict and Collaboration between Two Communities,* edited by Dan Ashyk, American Italian Historical Association (Staten Island, NY), 1999; *Selected Essays from the Thomas Wolfe Newsletter/Review,* edited by Deborah Borland and John Idol, Thomas Wolfe Society (Rocky Mount, NC), 1999; and *Unsettling America.* Contributor of short stories, poems, articles, and reviews to periodicals, including *Il Café, Villager, Aldebaran, Painted Bride Quarterly, Proof Rock, Thomas Wolfe Review, Turn-of-the-Century Women, Voices in Italian Americana, Creative Woman,* and *Sons of Italy Times.*

WORK IN PROGRESS: Editing an anthology of essays by Italian-American creative writers and literary critics, with Justin Vitiello; *Hershey Kiss Stars,* a collection of short fiction.

BIOGRAPHICAL AND CRITICAL SOURCES:

PERIODICALS

Painted Bride Quarterly, November, 1989.

*   *   *

MANSEL, Philip 1943-

PERSONAL: Born March 3, 1943, in Carmarthen, Wales; son of John Philip Ferdinand and Anne Rees Harrison Mansel; married Margaret Docker, August 24, 1968; children: Nicol, John, Richard. *Education:*

Attended Grosvenor College, Carlisle. *Religion:* Conservative Church of England. *Hobbies and other interests:* Golf, skiing, shooting.

ADDRESSES: Home—2 Deyncourt Close, Darris Hall, Ponteland, Northumberland, NE20 9RP, England. *E-mail*—manselphilip@hotmail.com.

CAREER: Historian. Eden-Vale Engineering Company, Ltd., former chairman.

MEMBER: Washington Rotary Club (youth exchange officer, 1995).

WRITINGS:

Lily and the Lion, HBJ Press, 1980.
Louis XVIII, Blond and Briggs (London, England), c. 1981.
Pillars of Monarchy: An Outline of the Political and Social History of the Royal Guards, 1400-1984, Quartet Books (New York, NY), 1984.
The Eagle in Splendour: Napoleon I and His Court, George Philip (London, England), 1987.
The Court of France: 1789-1830, Cambridge University Press (New York, NY), 1988.
Sultans in Splendour: The Last Years of the Ottoman World, Vendome (New York, NY), 1989.
Constantinople: City of the World's Desire, 1453-1924, St. Martin's (New York, NY), 1995.
(Co-editor with Kirsty Carpenter), *The French Emigrés in Europe and the Struggle against Revolution: 1789-1814,* St. Martin's Press (New York, NY), 1999.
Paris between Empires, 1814-1852, John Murray (London, England), 2001.

SIDELIGHTS: Philip Mansel is a leading historian and author of many books detailing revolutionary and post-revolutionary France, the rise and fall of the Ottoman Empire, and other phases in world history.

Louis XVIII is a biography about the decadent French king best known in textbooks for tactlessness and indulgence. Aiming for a more extensive portrait, Mansel writes about Louis XVIII's exile, his decision to switch his exile locale from Russia to England, and his complicated return to the throne by the indecisive

Allies of post-revolutionary France in 1814. Mansel plumbs the day-to-day details of Louis' life, tracking mood swings, broken promises, smart and poor choices, and manipulations.

Mansel surveys the impact resulting from Louis's stepping down from the throne—he aimed to preserve royal rule by rejecting the revolution—as well as the mood in France in the days after his return. According to Irene Collins in *Times Literary Supplement,* Louis XVIII was considered to be out of touch with post-revolutionary, post-Napoleonic France, an overeater too lazy for analysis or pro-action who embraced religion late in life simply because his married mistress told him to do so. Collins said, "Philip Mansel's Louis is a more credible figure, however, than this historical caricature. . . . His realism and adaptability were too easily construed as cynicism and cowardice." She added, however, "The scholarly nature of Mr. Mansel's book is to some extent belied by the phrases he often uses, reminiscent of a children's story."

Collins, on the other hand, commended Mansel for sharing engaging tidbits throughout: for instance, Louis was not allowed to learn English because his mother deemed it immoral, did not receive a first name until age six, and collected furniture obsessively, purchasing 574 beds over five years.

Douglas Johnson wrote in *Spectator,* "One of Philip Mansel's more telling phrases is to describe Louis as 'tenacious rather than tough' and one of his convincing arguments is to point out that people often began by serving other masters, but they usually ended up by serving Louis; governments sometimes began by telling Louis that he could not do certain things, but sooner or later we find that Louis is doing what he wanted to do."

Roger Bullen, in *British Book News,* praised Mansel's book as a "fresh and lively portrait" that excavates information to paint a realistic picture of the seldom-studied ruler. He wrote, "[Mansel] argues that [Louis'] ten-year reign was in fact a triumph of accommodation and moderation, with a record of consistent success in many fields."

Pillars of Monarchy: An Outline of the Political and Social History of the Royal Guards, 1400-1984 traces the tradition of royal security troops and personal bodyguards to the fifteenth century. For hundreds of years, monarchs in Europe and the Middle East have depended upon guards to protect them and enhance their public image. Mansel outlines the guards' function and practices during the Middle Ages, Enlightenment years, and modern times. Roger Mettam wrote in *History Today,* "Mansel errs towards modesty in calling his book 'an outline'. It . . . includes nearly every Christian and Islamic monarchy, is easy to read, well illustrated, and contains many entertaining details."

A king could staff his guard by choosing among his aristocracy or enlisting foreign men with no real ties to the throne. Some aristocrats expected appointments as guardsmen, saw it as their inalienable right, and kings granted them positions. In other cases, Albanians, Arabs, and others traveled to distant lands to protect unfamiliar rulers. These elite guardsmen, according to Mansel, were well rewarded. In some cases, however, their elevated status went to their heads.

Tom Hartman suggested in *Spectator* that Mansel performed more research—he consulted 720 texts—and touched upon more information than may ever have been matched in a book less than 200 pages. "It is not in the least surprising that the result is sometimes hard to digest when so many facts have to be crammed into so little space. . . . Nevertheless, on the whole the author has risen splendidly to the challenge he has set himself and the book is a mine of fascinating information."

In the illustrated *The Eagle in Splendour: Napoleon I and His Court,* Mansel examines the post-revolutionary French court, the dynamics of Napoleon and his family, the role of courtiers, the organization of the court, Napoleon's mistakes, triumphs, and legacy, and other details. Mansel portrays French courtiers, for example, as self-serving and often deceitful.

James K. Kieswetter, in *American Historical Review,* bemoaned the lack of information about Napoleon's considerable effect on music, and on the subject of his possible murder. "Although this work contains little that is highly original, it makes a useful contribution to Napoleonic studies. But it must be used with care for it suffers from occasional overgeneralizations and from various omissions."

Writing for *History Today,* Nigel Nicolson said of *The Eagle in Splendour,* "The book is of the cut-down coffee-table type, with many reproductions of grandiloquent paintings, some double-spread, some in colour, and accompanied by a text which is clear, well-researched, always interesting, and ultimately, by intention, stupefying."

The Court of France, 1789-1830 is a follow-up of sorts. Mansel, emphasizing the political and administrative details of the courts of Louis XVI, Napoleon I, Louis XVIII, Charles X, and that of the July Monarchy, also touches upon social and personal affairs. Readers learn the court's significance in establishing a monarch's power and esteem. Mansel also delineates between courts' organizations. For example, Napoleon's court was quite different from that of the Bourbons, with acceptance depending upon one's official position rather than inherited nobility. Conversely, Louis XVIII's post-revolutionary regime separated the court from "officialdom." After 1820, in what Mansel terms "the golden age," the court regularized hierarchy. It was then decided that official position and financial status should determine court membership.

Switching to a survey of rulers in the Middle East, Mansel published *Sultans in Splendour: The Last Years of the Ottoman World*. It analyzes the final period of the Ottoman Empire and features 200 previously unpublished photographs of the chronicled autocrats. Sheila Allen said in *School Librarian*, "The book begins with the opening of the Suez Canal in 1869 and ends with the departure of King Farouk from Egypt in 1952. . . . the history must be superficial but this is an ideal book for extra or background reading." Mansel describes, among other things, the lives of self-possessed harem women, the Khedive with his solid-gold toilet and other eccentricities, and the European overtaking of the Muslim empire. Rana Kabbani remarked in *Observer,* "It makes poignant reading, jerking the reader's feelings in different directions."

In *Constantinople: City of the World's Desire, 1453-1924* Mansel traces the trials and tribulations of the Ottoman Empire's capital city, Constantinople. Michael Moorcock wrote in the *Times Literary Supplement,* "The Ottoman Centuries brought fresh wealth, magnificent public art and one of the world's greatest cuisines. Mansel describes the gorgeous emergence from the medieval world . . . to the modern, to which they were sublimely unsuited, of the House of Osman, which gradually relinquished the power of life and death over its subjects . . . then quietly vanished . . . in 1924."

Mansel explains that Constantinople was larger than Paris or London at the start of the eighteenth-century, but lacking modern industry, began to lose ground in the nineteenth-century. Readers also learn that Ottoman Constantinople was half-Muslim, and for some time functioned as a diverse community of Muslims, Christians, and Jews. Cyril Mango, covering *Constantinople* for *Spectator,* remarked on the wide-ranging material, "The accumulation is sometimes excessive, but does succeed in producing a richly evocative panorama."

Edited with Kirsty Carpenter, *The French Emigrés in Europe and the Struggle against Revolution: 1789-1814* is a collection of essays depicting the French emigration at the end of the eighteenth century. Taking samples from journals, personal letters, and archival sources, the book analyzes the movement's long-term effects on European and American history.

Readers learn that the first emigrés left France because they disagreed with the Revolution's stance, but most emigrés, in fact, departed post-1792, after the start of the French civil war. Many of them were poverty-stricken men and women.

Giulia Pacini remarked in *French Forum,* "Countering legendary representations of the emigré as a nostalgic and decadent aristocrat doggedly attached to ancien regime life, this book is at its best when it illustrates the fundamental heterogeneity of the French emigrés."

Paris between Empires, 1814-1852 maps the history of Paris between the fall of Napoleon I and the proclamation of Napoleon III, a period during which the affairs of society were of central political importance. Gillian Tindal, in her *Times Literary Supplement* review, criticized Mansel's consistent emphasis on affluence and nobility. "The sources on which the author has drawn are admirably copious, yet the overall impression is of a Paris populated exclusively by the nobility, varied only by the super-rich. . . . More common stock tend to be represented by the actresses, singers and *demi-mondaines* . . . not exactly a comprehensive view of Paris at the period." The book was nominated for England's Samuel Johnson Prize for nonfiction.

Philip Hensher, however, wrote in *Spectator,* "Philip Mansel has written an excellent, entertaining history. It benefits from his having slogged through the life of

Louis XVIII before, and he has an eye for the good story and the telling detail." In *Times Higher Education Supplement*, reviewer Shusha Guppy commended, "Mansel's deep scholarship, elegant prose, narrative pace and cohesion dazzle."

BIOGRAPHICAL AND CRITICAL SOURCES:

PERIODICALS

American Historical Review, October 1988, James K. Kieswetter, review of *The Eagle in Splendour: Napoleon I and His Court,* pp. 1064-1065; December 1990, James K. Kieswetter, review of *The Court of France: 1789-1830,* pp. 1552-1553.

Asian Affairs, October 1996, Geoffrey Lewis, review of *Constantinople: City of the World's Desire, 1453-1924,* pp. 340-341.

Booklist, September 15, 1985, Brad Hooper, review of *Pillars of Monarchy: An Outline of the Political and Social History of the Royal Guards, 1400-1984,* p. 96; October 1, 1996, Sandy Whiteley, review of *Constantinople,* p. 319.

British Book News, May 1981, review of *Louis XVIII,* p. 318.

Canadian Journal of History, April 1990, Michael Grenon, review of *The Court of France,* pp. 131-132.

Choice, 1989, B. Rothaus, review of *The Court of France,* p. 371.

Contemporary Review, January 2002, review of *Paris Between Empires, 1814-1852,* p. 59.

Economist, July 14, 2001, article, "Fun and Games; 19th Century French History," p. 7; July 14, 2001, review of *Paris Between Empires: 1814-1852,* pp. 100-101.

French Forum, Spring 2001, Giulia Pacini, review of *The French Emigres in Europe and the Struggle Against Revolution: 1789-1814,* pp. 113-115.

French Review, April 2001, Tom Conner, review of *The French Emigres in Europe and the Struggle Against Revolution,* pp. 1028-1029.

History: The Journal of the Historical Association, June 1989, John Mackrell, review of *The Eagle in Splendour,* p. 329; February 1991, Geoffrey Cubitt, review of *The Court of France,* pp. 146-147.

History Today, June 1985, Roger Mettam, review of *Pillars of Monarchy,* p. 57; February 1988, Nigel Nicolson, review of *The Eagle in Splendour,* pp.

51-52; December 1992, Richard Vinen, review of *The Court of France,* p. 57; April 2002, Pamela Pilbeam, review of *Paris Between Empires, 1814-1852,* p. 62.

International History Review, December 2000, William S. Cormack, review of *The French Emigres in Europe and the Struggle Against Revolution,* pp. 910-911.

Library Journal, September 15, 1996, Robert J. Andrews, review of *Constantinople,* p. 80.

Los Angeles Times Book Review, January 12, 1992, Charles Solomon, review of *The Courts of France,* p. 10.

New York Times Book Review, December 26, 1996, Robin Cormack, review of *Constantinople,* p. 9.

Observer (London), 1989, Rana Kabbani, review of *Sultans in Splendour: The Last Years of the Ottoman World,* p. 43.

School Librarian, May 1989, Sheila Allen, review of *Sultans in Splendour,* p. 82.

Spectator, January 31, 1981, Douglas Johnson, review of *Louis XVIII,* pp. 18-19; February 16, 1985, Tom Hartman, review of *Pillars of Monarchy,* p. 29; August 22, 1987, Peter Quennell, review of *The Eagle in Splendour,* pp. 25-26; July 22, 1989, Richard Cobb, review of *The Court of France,* pp. 28-29; November 11, 1995, Cyril Mango, review of *Constantinople,* p. 44; June 9, 2001, Philip Hensher, review of *Paris Between Empires,* p. 32.

Times Higher Education Supplement, September 20, 1996, Averil Cameron, review of *Constantinople,* pp. 21-22; August 24, 2001, Shusha Guppy, review of *Paris Between Empires,* p. 25.

Times Literary Supplement, May 1, 1981, Irene Collins, review of *Louis XVIII,* p. 494; November 17, 1995, Michael Moorcock, review of *Constantinople,* p. 10; September 21, 2001, Gillian Tindall, review of *Paris Between Empires,* p. 26.

Washington Post Book World, February 2, 1997, John Ash, review of *Constantinople,* p. 7.*

*   *   *

MATTHEWS, Andrew 1948-

PERSONAL: Born November 17, 1948, in Barry, Wales; son of Richard Charles (a grocery manager) and Edith May Josephine (a homemaker; maiden name, Glanvil) Matthews; married Sheena Green (a management consultant), November 10, 1970. *Ethnic-*

ity: "Welsh." *Education:* Reading University, B.A. (English and history; with honors), 1970.

ADDRESSES: Home—27, The Drive, Earley Reading, Berkshire, RG6 1EG, England. *Agent*—Rosemary Canter, Peters, Fraser and Dunlop, Drury House, 34-43 Russell St., London WC2B 5HA, England. *E-mail*—and@matthews1.demon.co.uk.

CAREER: Writer. Yateley Comprehensive School, Hampshire, England, English teacher, 1971-94.

AWARDS, HONORS: Consell Català del Llibre per a Infants i Joves second prize, for *À de la llumde la lluna* (translation of *Seeing in Moonlight*); *Moonsoon Taggert's Amazing Finishing Academy* was shortlisted for a Smarties Award, as was *Cat Song,* 1994.

WRITINGS:

Wolf Pie, Methuen (London, England), 1987.
Dixie's Demon, Methuen (London, England), 1987.
The Quiet Pirate, Methuen (London, England), 1988.
A Summer Witching, Blackie (London, England), 1989.
S. Claus—The Truth! Magnet (London, England), 1989.
Monsoon Taggert's Amazing Finishing Academy, Methuen (London, England), 1989.
Monster Hullaballoo, Methuen (London, England), 1990.
The Jar of the Sun, Hutchinson (London, England), 1990.
Mallory Cox and His Magic Socks, Dent (London, England), 1990, Dent (New York, NY), 1993.
The Great Sandwich Racket and Other Stories, Blackie (London, England), 1990.
Wickedoz, Methuen (London, England), 1990.
Mistress Moonwater, Mammoth (London, England), 1990.
Loads of Trouble, Methuen (London, England), 1990.
Mallory Cox and the Viking Box, Dent (London, England), 1991.
Monster Nursery School, Methuen (London, England), 1991.
Wickedoz and the Dragons of Stonewade, Methuen (London, England), 1991.
Jar of the Sun, Hutchinson (London, England), 1991.
The Great Granny Dust-up, Hamish Hamilton (London, England), 1992.

Denzil the Dog Polisher, Methuen (London, England), 1993.
(Reteller) *Stories from Hans Christian Andersen,* illustrated by Alan Snow, Orchard (New York, NY), 1993.
Mallory Cox and His Interstellar Socks, Dent (London, England), 1993.
Cat Song, Hutchinson (London, England), 1993.
Writing in Martian, Methuen (London, England), 1993.
Crackling Brat, illustrated by Tomek Bogacki, Holt (New York, NY), 1993.
The Orion Book of Silly Stories, Orion Children's Books (London, England), 1994.
The Check-out Princess, Mammoth (London, England), 1994.
The Story of Theseus, Ginn (London, England), 1994.
The Story of King Arthur, Orchard (New York, NY), 1995.
Tod and the Clock Angel, illustrated by Christian Birmingham, Frances Lincoln (New York, NY), 1995.
A Bunch of Baddies, Orchard (New York, NY), 1995.
Seeing in Moonlight, Mammoth (London, England), 1995.
The Beasts of Boggart Hollow, Orion Children's Books (London, England), 1995.
The Spooks of Biddlecombe Manor, Hodder (London, England), 1995.
Treasury of Funny Stories, Kingfisher (New York, NY), 1995.
Spooks to the Rescue, Hodder (London, England), 1995.
A Winter Night's Dream, Mammoth (London, England), 1996.
How the World Began, MacDonald (London, England), 1996.
The Mouse Flute, illustrated by Vanessa Julian-Ottie, Dell (New York, NY), 1997.
Marduk the Mighty and Other Stories of Creation, illustrated by Sheila Moxley, Millbrook Press (Brookfield, CT), 1997.
Darker, Point Horror Unleashed, 1998.
Monster Surprise, Mammoth (London, England), 1998.
Monster Mayhem, Mammoth (London, England), 1989.
Stiks and Stoans, Mammoth (London, England), 1999.
Family Stuff, Mammoth (London, England), 2000.
Dissolvers, Scholastic (New York, NY), 2000.
Freckles, Pearson ESL, 2000.
Love Street, Red Fox (London, England), 2000.
Crawlers, Scholastic (New York, NY), 2001.

Gsoh Red Fox, 2001.

Wolf Summer, Orchard (New York, NY), 2001.

(Reteller) *The Orchard Book of Stories from Shakespeare,* Orchard (New York, NY), 2001.

From above, with Love, Red Fox, 2002.

Moonchildren, Scholastic (New York, NY), 2002.

(Reteller) *Book of Shakespeare Stories,* Random House (New York, NY), 2003.

Flip Side, Delacorte (New York, NY), 2003.

Contributor of poems and stories to collections, including *Your're Late Dad,* Methuen (London, England), 1989; *A Brontosaurus Chorus,* Methuen (London, England), 1991; *A Moon, a Star, a Story,* Blackie (London, England), 1990; *An Armful of Bears,* Mammoth, 1993; *Prickly Poems,* Hutchinson (London, England), 1993; *Magic Carpet,* Ginn (London, England), 1995; *Paws and Claws,* Hutchinson (London, England), 1995; and *Heart to Heart,* edited by Miriam Hodgson, Mammoth (London, England), 1996.

Matthews's books have been translated into other languages, including French, Swedish, Dutch, Spanish, German, Danish, Italian, and Catalan.

ADAPTATIONS: Monsoon Taggert's Amazing Finishing Academy, was adapted for audio cassette, read by Jennifer Saunders, Chivers Audio Books, 1992; *Monster: Hullabaloo* and *Monster Nursery School* were recorded on audio cassette, read by Brian Glover, Chivers Audio Books, 1993; and *Wolf Pie,* and *Stories from Hans Christian Andersen,* read by Willy Rushton, were adapted for audio cassette, Chivers Audio Books, 1996.

WORK IN PROGRESS: "The Whilight Witch" trilogy, expected 2003.

SIDELIGHTS: Andrew Matthews has enjoyed several rewarding careers. After teaching English for twenty-three years, he began his second career as a writer of children's books and reteller of classic tales. Although he had begun writing at age seven while recovering from an illness, Matthews did not truly pursue that interest until he was in middle age. As he told *CA,* "My first book was published when I was forty, so it only took me thirty-three years to get it right." Believing that "children's literature is currently better than it

has ever been, and far superior to adult fiction, which seems to have forgotten that writers are meant to tell stories," Matthews's main aim is "to entertain my readers, and to tell the best stories I can tell as well as I can."

Over a fifteen-year period, the prolific Matthews has penned several dozen books, including adventures, fantasies, monster stories, and realistic fiction. Among his retellings number the tales of Hans Christian Andersen and plays of Shakespeare, the King Arthur Legends, and creation stories. "When I was first approached about the *Orchard Book of Shakespeare Stories,* I was very intimidated," he recalled. "The idea of tinkering with the work of one of history's greatest literary geniuses was frankly terrifying. Then I remembered that Shakespeare had taken almost all of the plots of his plays from other sources. My job was to turn the plays back into stories—to borrow back the stories that Shakespeare had borrowed. It was the hardest work I had ever done and contains some of my best writing (I hope)."

Book reviewers have focused their attention on Matthews's story collections, which are grouped by author or theme. The *Stories of Hans Christian Andersen* contains eleven familiar tales, which Matthews simplifies in the retelling. In a *School Library Journal* review, critic Karen James considered these tales to be a "serviceable" introduction to Andersen's work, though she felt they lack the depth of the originals. Matthews also used a liberal hand when retelling the twenty-four creation myths in *Marduk the Mighty and Other Stories of Creation.* Because teachers often use thematic collections of stories, requiring students to compare and contrast similar stories among cultures, *Booklist* reviewer Julie Corsaro, predicted that the work would likely interest teachers.

Matthews believes that he is, in his words, "a really lucky person because I love what I do. I'm one of the few people I know who wakes up looking forward to going to work." He both described his work habits and urged budding writers to persevere: "I work Monday to Friday, from 10 a.m. until 5:25 p.m. I write in longhand first. When my wife comes home from work, I read what I've written out loud to her. This helps me to hear what the story sounds like, and my wife tells me what parts of the writing don't work. I value her opinion because she's always right." Noting that there are "more great writers writing for children now than at any other time," Matthews advised aspiring authors: "Don't Give Up. If you start collecting rejection slips, it means that the world isn't ready for you yet."

BIOGRAPHICAL AND CRITICAL SOURCES:

PERIODICALS

Booklist, June 1, 1997, Julie Corsaro, review of *Marduk the Mighty and Other Stories of Creation,* pp. 1693-1694.

Publishers Weekly, August 2, 1993, review of *Stories from Hans Christian Andersen,* p. 81.

School Library Journal, December, 1993, Karen James, review of *Stories from Hans Christian Andersen,* p. 78; June, 1994, Suzanne Hawley, review of *Crackling Brat,* p. 111; July, 1997, Kathleen Odean, review of *Marduk the Mighty,* p. 86.

*   *   *

McBRIDE, Regina 1956-

PERSONAL: Born 1956, in NM; children: one daughter.

ADDRESSES: Home—929 West End Ave., No. 7A, New York, NY 10025. *Office*—c/o Scribner, 1230 Avenue of the Americas, New York, NY 10020.

CAREER: Poet and novelist. Instructor, Hunter College, New York, NY; Writer's Voice, instructor.

AWARDS, HONORS: American Book Series award, for *Yarrow Field;* National Endowment for the Arts fellowship; New York Endowment for the Arts fellowship.

WRITINGS:

Yarrow Field, San Diego Poets Press (La Jolla, CA), 1990.

The Nature of Water and Air: A Novel, Scribner Paperback Fiction (New York, NY), 2001.

Also contributor of poems to journals, including *Ironwood, High Plains Literary Review, Antioch Review,* and *Denver Quarterly.*

ADAPTATIONS: Gabriel Byrne acquired the film rights to *The Nature of Water and Air.*

SIDELIGHTS: Poet and writing teacher Regina McBride had already achieved modest success with her first novel, *The Nature of Water and Air: A Novel* when Irish actor Gabriel Byrne discovered the book. Byrne contacted McBride to see if film rights had been sold, and when he found out they had not, he bought them himself and began work with McBride on a screenplay.

Published a decade before *The Nature of Water and Air,* McBride's first publication was a small book of poetry, *Yarrow Field,* for which she won the American Book Series award. Kay Murphy, a critic for the *American Book Review,* compared McBride's poems about incest, parental suicide, and shame to the work of poets Anne Sexton and Sharon Olds. Murphy suggested that McBride's first collection of poetry is too melodramatic, adding that "the poet is controlled by the subject matter rather than the other way around." Nonetheless, Murphy wrote that the imagery of *Yarrow Field* is "viscerally powerful."

McBride's first novel tells of a mother's suicide. *The Nature of Water and Air* is narrated by Clodagh Sheehy who, at the age of thirteen, watches her mother Agatha, who bore Clodagh and her twin sister when she was a teenager herself, walk into the sea to end her life. The novel traces Clodagh's coming of age, including her talent for the piano, her relationship with the tinker Angus Kilheen, and her gradual discovery of tragic family secrets. McBride merges this domestic drama with Irish myth, connecting Agatha's wildness to the half-human, half-seal selkies.

Critics of *The Nature of Water and Air* responded to McBride's impressionistic style and the book's melancholic tone, which evokes an almost gothic atmosphere. Emily White, for the *New York Times Book Review,* said, "Regina McBride writes in a shimmering and often hypnotic prose style, one that's full of incantatory repetition. The story builds like a fugue." A critic for *Publishers Weekly* wrote that while

McBride sometimes "veers into portentous sentimentality," overall the novel is "finely wrought and deeply felt . . . a work of supercharged imagination." J. Uschuk, in *Tucson Weekly,* called *The Nature of Water and Air* a "spectacular writing debut."

BIOGRAPHICAL AND CRITICAL SOURCES:

PERIODICALS

Albuquerque Journal, June 1, 2001, Marika Brussel, "Poet's Prose Is Rich, Evocative," p. 5.

American Book Review, October, 1991, Kay Murphy, "Richly Allusive," p. 28.

Library Journal, March 1, 2001, Beth Gibbs, review of *The Nature of Water and Air,* p. 132.

New York Times Book Review, June 17, 2001, Emily White, review of *The Nature of Water and Air,* p. 22.

People Weekly, October 15, 2001, Christina Cheakalos, review of *The Nature of Water and Air,* p. 55.

Publishers Weekly, April 23, 2001, review of *The Nature of Water and Air,* p. 49; July 30, 2001, John F. Baker, "A Browser's Movie Buy," p. 12.

OTHER

Tucson Weekly, http://www.tucsonweekly.com/ (September 27-October 3, 2001), J. Uschuk, "Evil Battles Good in Regina McBride's Debut Novel."*

* * *

McCAIN, Becky Ray 1954-

PERSONAL: Born May 8, 1954, in Brooksville, FL; daughter of Carl Ray (a Presbyterian minister) and Jackie (an artist and legal assistant; maiden name, Lowman) McCain; married James Russell MacKoy, April 11, 1981 (divorced April 16, 1993); children: Kimberly Allyne, James Richard, Emma Ray. *Education:* Tarkio College, B.A. (psychology, special education, elementary education). *Politics:* "Rational." *Religion:* "Simple." *Hobbies and other interests:* Sketching, roller skating, biking, operating heavy equipment, singing, making jewelry, reading.

ADDRESSES: Home—10871 West Dartmouth Ave., Lakewood, CO 80227. *E-mail*—mcmac@uswest.net.

CAREER: Cherry Creek Schools, special education teacher, 1998—. Colorado Center for the Book, member, 2002-03.

MEMBER: National Organization for Year-Round Education.

WRITINGS:

(With Stephen B. McCarney) *Behavior Dimensions Intervention Manual,* Hawthorne Educational Services (Columbia, MO), 1995.

The Hide-out Lizard, Hawthorne Educational Services (Columbia, MO), 1995.

Grandmother's Dreamcatcher, illustrated by Stacey Schuett, A. Whitman (Morton Grove, IL), 1998.

Nobody Knew What to Do: A Story about Bullying, illustrated by Todd Leonardo, A. Whitman (Morton Grove, IL), 2001.

WORK IN PROGRESS: A novel; research on Native American stories and traditions; research on current topics in education and psychology.

SIDELIGHTS: Becky Ray McCain is both an author and a teacher. Her books reflect her concern for children. In *Nobody Knew What to Do: A Story about Bullying* it is not the children in the story who resolve the problem when bullies begin to pick on a boy named Ray, but rather it is the adults who end the situation. However, the bullying is reported by a concerned fellow student who becomes uncomfortable about what is going on in his school. Critics praised *Nobody Knew What to Do* as a more realistic tale about bullying than others having a taunted boy or girl vanquish bullies using unusual wit or skill. The book also includes a section for adults called "Bully Prevention" to aid in class discussions. Overall, critics thought the book would be helpful to students and teachers alike. For example, Carolyn Phelan, who called McCain's book "sobering," wrote in *Booklist* that "as our society grapples with the relationship between bullying and school violence, teachers will be looking for picture books [like this] to spark discussion." "McCain successfully presents a problem without sentimentalizing or sensationalizing it," concluded *School Library Journal* reviewer Teri Markson.

McCain told *CA:* "Two conceptually accurate (yet paraphrased) thoughts have been pivotal to me: the first, that a society is judged by how well it (we) cares for the weakest among us; and the concept or perception of our youth as our future. With a preacher for a dad, I was (likely) genetically and environmentally programmed to care about educational and mental health issues. My dad definitely influenced me to be as sensitive to the needs of others as I can be. This references a style of living that defies class structure and 'thinking in the box.' I don't think I even own a box, much less a proverbial one!

"My father and my other heroes teach me still about what it means to be alive. It means, simply, to care too much about our children, and the children of parents in other cultures, to ignore their basic needs, which include needs for nurturing, for education. It's the only *real* savings account we have toward a happy future."

BIOGRAPHICAL AND CRITICAL SOURCES:

PERIODICALS

Booklist, October 1, 1998, Carolyn Phelan, review of *Grandmother's Dreamcatcher,* p. 336; May 15, 2001, Carolyn Phelan, review of *Nobody Knew What to Do: A Story about Bullying,* p. 1760.
Publishers Weekly, October 5, 1998, review of *Grandmother's Dreamcatcher,* p. 89; April 16, 2001, review of *Grandmother's Dreamcatcher,* p. 67.
School Library Journal, May, 2001, Teri Markson, review of *Nobody Knew What to Do,* p. 128.

* * *

McCOWN, Clint 1952-

PERSONAL: Born March 7, 1952, in Fayetteville, TN; son of James E. (a secret service agent) and Mary Jane (Wallace) McCown; married, September 2, 1982; wife's name, Cynthia P. (a professor); children: Caitlin Ann, Mary Alison. *Ethnicity:* "Caucasian." *Education:* Attended Circle-in-the-Square Theatre School, 1973-74; Wake Forest University, B.A., 1974, M.A., 1978; attended University of Alabama, 1980-81; Indiana University, M.F.A., 1985. *Politics:* Democrat. *Religion:* Presbyterian.

ADDRESSES: Home—1826 Sherwood, Beloit, WI 53511. *Office*—Box 23, Beloit College, 700 College St., Beloit, WI 53511. *Agent*—Curtis Brown Ltd., 10 Astor Place, New York, NY 10003. *E-mail*—mccownc@beloit.edu.

CAREER: National Shakespeare Company, actor, 1974-75; North Carolina Visiting Artist Program, poet-in-residence, 1976-78; Alabama Information Network (Alanet), investigative reporter, 1978; James Sprunt Technical College, instructor, 1979; Beloit College, Beloit, WI, professor of creative writing, 1984—, director of Creative Writing, 1988—, chair of Department of English, 1991-94, 1999—; University of Glasgow, visiting professor, 1988; Associated Writing Programs, member, 1988—; Antioch Writers Workshops, board of directors member, 1999—; faculty member at several writers' conferences and workshops; judge for numerous writing contents; gives public readings and guest lectures.

MEMBER: Writers Guild of America (East).

AWARDS, HONORS: American Fiction Prize, 1991 and 1993; Society of Midland Authors Award for Best Fiction, 1995; Pulitzer prize nominations, 1995 and 2000.

WRITINGS:

Love Poem (play), produced on Broadway by the Circle-in-the-Square Theatre, 1974.
A Christmas Carol (play; adapted from the book by Charles Dickens), produced at the Neuse Theatre, Smithfield, NC, 1976.
Sidetracks (poetry), Jackpine (Winston-Salem, NC), 1977.
Elections in Alabama: Exercise in Futility (documentary), broadcast 1978.
Wind over Water (poetry), Northwoods (Thomaston, ME), 1985.

The Member-Guest (novel), Doubleday (New York, NY), 1995.

Exclusions in the Policy (play), produced at Wake Forest University, 1997.

War Memorials (novel), Graywolf (St. Paul, MN), 2000.

Also author of *Public Affairs* (thirty half-hour radio documentaries), Alanet, 1978; and eight hundred five-minute news broadcasts for Alanet, 1978. Editor, *Indiana Review*, 1982-83, and *Beloit Fiction Journal*, 1985—. Contributing editor, *Colorado Review*, 1997—; and *Hayden's Ferry Review*, *Puerto del Sol*, *Mid-American Review*, *Quarterly West*, *Bellingham Review*, *Cimmaron Review*, *Willow Springs*, and *Fourth Genre*, all 1999—. More than thirty-five contributions to anthologies and periodicals, including *Clackamas Review*, *Colorado Review*, *Golf Digest*, *Hawai'i Review*, *Writers' Forum*, *Mid-American Review*, *American Fiction*, *Sewanee Review*, *Denver Quarterly*, *American Fiction*, and *Gettysburg Review*.

WORK IN PROGRESS: The Member-Guest (screenplay), for River One Films; *The Rave Mocker* (screenplay), for Warner Bros.

SIDELIGHTS: Clint McCown told *CA*: "I suppose I write to try to get at a better understanding of things.

"Besides my own life, I'd say my strongest literary influences are Flannery O'Connor and Raymond Carver.

"I have to work slowly. I'm not one who tends to gush out a draft; instead I tend to focus on the craft in minute detail.

"Perhaps the greatest shaping force was the fact that my family had moved seven times by the time I entered eighth grade. Throughout my formative years I was cast continually in the role of the outsider. As a consequence, a major theme in my work seems to be the examining of artificial cultural barriers that dictate behavior. I like exploring the ways in which people do—or don't—struggle to fit into society."

*   *   *

MEALLET, Sandro 1965-

PERSONAL: Born 1965, in San Pedro, CA; married; wife's name Melissa; children: Alonzo. *Education:* University of California, Santa Cruz; New School for Social Research, M.F.A.; Johns Hopkins University, M.F.A.

ADDRESSES: Home—Sonoma, CA. *Office*—c/o Doubleday Publicity, 1540 Broadway, New York, NY 10036.

CAREER: Novelist.

WRITINGS:

Edgewater Angels, Doubleday Publishing (New York, NY), 2001.

SIDELIGHTS: Edgewater Angels is Sandro Meallet's first book, a story about surviving the slums of San Pedro, California, where Meallet himself grew up. *Edgewater Angels* portrays a group of young boys living in a world of long-absent fathers, murders, stray bullets, and gangs. At the same time, the boys go fishing and crabbing, oversee a swimming contest, and eventually engage in auto theft. Their story is told by Sonny Toomer, one of the few boys who grows up and escapes the fate awaiting most of his friends: drug addiction, prison, and death. Toomer watches his uncles beat and maim a hitchhiker, but he visits the library to indulge his secret interest in reading and classical music. He and his friends go on a long crime spree, a series of GTA's (grand theft auto), but they also give a homeless man they have never known a funeral and help deliver the baby of an injured woman. The unexpected kindness of such acts is the source of the book's title. The dying homeless man tells them, "How wonderful you've become . . . like angels."

Meallet's combination of love for his protagonists and ghetto realism won over several critics. *Washington Post* contributor Carolyn See found *Edgewater Angels* to be "in a class by itself." Katherine Dieckmann, writing for the *New York Times Book Review,* said that the book "forgoes easy sociological posturing and pity-inducing story lines, presenting instead an exuberantly absurdist look at growing up poor and shrouded by violence." Thomas Curwen of the online *Calendar Live,* remarked that Meallet's young heroes give a human, sympathetic face to the parade of juvenile criminals in Southern California. Ianthe Brautigan, writing for *Metroactive,* similarly noted Meallet's ability to "write about poverty in a way that doesn't make the reader feel like a voyeur." Brautigan concluded, "Meallet imbues all his characters with a dignity that helps us avoid the pity or the sense of the exotic that can infect a middle-class person reading about different cultures or classes."

BIOGRAPHICAL AND CRITICAL SOURCES:

PERIODICALS

Booklist, June 1, 2001, John Green, review of *Edgewater Angels,* p. 1847.
Library Journal, July, 2001, Andrea Caron Kempf, review of *Edgewater Angels,* p. 125.
New York Times, August 9, 2001, Richard Eder, review of *Edgewater Angels,* p. B8.
New York Times Book Review, August 26, 2001, Katherine Dieckmann, review of *Edgewater Angels,* p. 20.
Progressive, October 2001, Dennis Bernstein, review of *Edgewater Angels,* p. 44.
Publishers Weekly, July 16, 2001, review of *Edgewater Angels,* p. 159.
Washington Post, July 20, 2001, Carolyn See, "Life Between the Fusillades," p. C4.

OTHER

Calendar Live, http://www.calendarlive.com/ (August 19, 2001), Thomas Curwen, "Angel Dust."
Metroactive, http://www.metroactive.com/ (October 7, 2001), Ianthe Brautigan, "Heaven Sent: Sandro Meallet Dazzles Readers With 'Edgewater Angels.'"*

*   *   *

MITCHELL, James 1926-2002
(James Munro)

*OBITUARY NOTICE—*See index for *CA* sketch: Born March 12, 1926, in South Shields, County Durham, England; died of cancer September 15, 2002, in Newcastle, England. Author. Mitchell was a well-known writer of British television series and spy novels. Receiving his master's degree from Saint Edmund Hall, Oxford, in 1949 and a diploma in education from the University of Durham, Mitchell started his career as an actor, travel agent, and civil service employee before being hired to the faculty of Shields Technical College in 1950. Also doing some secondary school teaching, he remained at Shields through the 1950s. However, Mitchell did not find teaching a satisfying occupation, so at the age of twenty-eight he began to write novels. He soon found success with his first book, *Here's a Villain!* (1957), which was published in the United States as *The Lady Is Waiting.* Mitchell also discovered he had a talent for script writing and, except for a brief period as a lecturer at the Sunderland College of Art in 1963, he became a full-time script writer in 1959. As a writer for television, Mitchell completed over one hundred scripts. He was most well known for the popular spy series *Callan,* which ran from 1967 to 1972 and was adapted as two movies in 1974 and 1981, and for the Depression-era drama *When the Boat Comes In,* which was broadcast in 1976 to 1977, with more episodes being produced in 1981. Other series by Mitchell include *Goodbye Darling* and *Justice.* As an author of novels, Mitchell wrote over two dozen books, some under the pseudonym James Munro, that were mostly in the espionage genre. For his 1959 novel *A Way Back,* he won the British Crime Writers' Association Award; more recent books include *So Far from Home* (1995) and *Dancing for Joy* (1997).

OBITUARIES AND OTHER SOURCES:

BOOKS

Who's Who, 153rd Year of Issue, Palgrave (New York, NY), 2001.

PERIODICALS

Los Angeles Times, September 26, 2002, p. B12.
New York Times, September 23, 2002, p. A25.
Times (London, England), September 26, 2002.

*   *   *

MITCHISON, Rosalind (Mary) 1919-2002

*OBITUARY NOTICE—*See index for *CA* sketch: Born April 11, 1919, in Manchester, England; died following a stroke September 20, 2002, in Edinburgh, Scotland. Historian, educator, and author. Mitchison was a respected social historian who was particularly interested in the history of Scotland. She was educated at Lady Margaret Hall, Oxford, where she earned her master's degree in 1942. Mitchison found work as an assistant lecturer at Manchester University during World War II, and after the war was briefly a tutor in modern history at her alma mater. Married in 1947, she did not work again until after the family moved to Edinburgh, and it was here that Mitchison became interested in Scottish history. She was hired as an assistant in history at the University of Edinburgh in 1954, taught for a few years at the University of Glasgow during the 1960s, and returned to Edinburgh to become a lecturer and, in 1976, reader in economic history; she was professor emeritus of social history from 1981 to 1986. Mitchison's many books on Scottish history are credited with helping to popularize the subject. Among these works are *A History of Scotland* (1970), *The Making of the Scottish Poor Law* (1974), *Lordship to Patronage: Scotland, 1603-1745* (1983), *Life in Scotland* (1987), and the coauthored book *Sexuality and Social Control: Scotland 1660-1780* (1989), which was revised in 1998 as *Girls in Trouble: Sexuality and Social Control in Rural Scotland 1660-1780* and under the titillating title *Sin in the City*. For her distinguished work, Mitchison received honorary doctorates from the Open University and St. Andrews University; she was also a fellow of the Royal Society of Edinburgh and former president of the Scottish Historical Society.

OBITUARIES AND OTHER SOURCES:

BOOKS

Writers Directory, 17th edition, Gale (Detroit, MI), 2002.

PERIODICALS

Daily Telegraph (London, England), September 24, 2002.
Guardian, October 4, 2002, p. 20.
Herald (Glasgow, Scotland), September 28, 2002, p. 16.
Independent (London, England), September 21, 2002, p. 20.
Scotsman, September 26, 2002, p. 16.
Times (London, England), September 27, 2002, p. 34.

*   *   *

MÜELLER, Melissa 1967-

PERSONAL: Born 1967, in Vienna, Austria.

ADDRESSES: Office—c/o Henry Holt and Company, Inc., 115 West 18th Street, New York, NY 10011.

CAREER: Journalist and author.

WRITINGS:

Anne Frank: The Biography, translated by Rita and Robert Kimber, Metropolitan Books (New York, NY), 1998.

ADAPTATIONS: Anne Frank: The Biography was adapted for film by ABC-TV and broadcast as *Anne Frank,* 2001, and adapted for documentary in the Home Vision Entertainment Collection as *Anne Frank: The Missing Chapter.*

SIDELIGHTS: Melissa Müller, an Austrian-born journalist living in Germany, decided to write a biography of one of the Holocaust's best-known victims, Anne Frank, after re-reading as an adult the tragic diary of this teenage girl. In *Anne Frank: The Biography,* Müller addresses the context in which Frank wrote of the two years she and her family spent in Holland hiding from Nazi persecution.

Müller's background research included Frank's two original versions of her diary (what Anne first wrote in her notebook she later edited on loose sheets of paper), family correspondence, Nazi documents and personal interviews. Müller sought out and recorded the memories of several of Frank's childhood friends as well as those of Miep Gies, Otto Frank's secretary who aided the family when they were in hiding and rescued the diary after the police had arrested the Franks.

Müller also uncovered five pages of Anne's diary that Otto Frank omitted from the published version because they include candid remarks about his relationship with Anne's mother, Edith. These pages, in the hands of Cor Suijk at the Anne Frank Center in New York, reveal some insights into Edith Frank's character. Müller, however, could only paraphrase this material in her biography since legally she could not quote from them directly.

Müller's biography begins with Anne's death from typhus in a concentration camp at Bergen-Belsen, near Hannover, Germany, and then flashes back to her birth and early childhood in Frankfurt. She follows the family through Otto Frank's decision to take his family to Amsterdam in 1942, where they hid out in the back of one of his office buildings. Anne herself best chronicles those two years, but Müller attempts to answer such questions as the reasons behind Anne's difficult relationship with her mother, and who finally betrayed the family's secret whereabouts to the Nazis.

Müller does not end her story with Anne's final journal entry on August 1, 1944. Instead she recounts what happened to each member of the Frank family following their arrest three days after Anne wrote her last words. Though records are sketchy, Müller details what she learned about the separation of the family, the death of each—except for Otto who survived Auschwitz and lived until 1980—and even the numbers tattooed on the Franks' arms.

R. Z. Sheppard wrote in *Time* magazine, "Müller pays respect to the legend, but she also does something long overdue. She saves Anne Frank from idolatry and impersonal symbolism by restoring her physical presence: an extraordinary woman-not-to-be with greenish eyes, a trick shoulder and an overbite that kept her from whistling."

BIOGRAPHICAL AND CRITICAL SOURCES:

PERIODICALS

National Review, December 7, 1998, Julie Crane, review of *Anne Frank: The Biography,* p. 73.
New York Times Book Review, November 1, 1998, Jonathan Rosen, review of *Anne Frank,* p. 18.
Newsweek, September 21, 1998, Laura Shapiro, "Anne Frank Out of Hiding," p. 96.
School Library Journal, April 1999, Frances Reiher, review of *Anne Frank,* p. 165.
Time, September 28, 1998, R. Z. Sheppard, review of *Anne Frank,* p. 88.
Women's Review of Books, Volume XVI, number 8, Nina Auerbach, May 1999, p. 8.

OTHER

Denver Post Wire Service, http://www.denverpost.com/ (July 1, 1999), review of *Anne Frank.*
Page One Radio, http://www.wiesenthal.org/ (July 1, 1999), Jane Lueders, review of *Anne Frank.**

MUNRO, James
See MITCHELL, James

*   *   *

MURA, David (Alan) 1952-

PERSONAL: Born June 17, 1952, in Great Lakes, IL; son of Tom K. and Teruko Mura; married Susan Sencer (a pediatric oncologist), June 18, 1983; children: Samantha Lyn, Nikko, Tomo. *Education:* Grinnell College, B.A. (with honors), 1974; graduate study at University of Minnesota—Twin Cities, 1974-79; Vermont College, M.F.A., 1991.

ADDRESSES: Home—1920 East River Terr., Minneapolis, MN 55414. *Agent*—Margaret Troupe, Sandra Dijkstra Literary Agency, PMB 515, 1155 Camino del Mar, Del Mar, CA 92014-2605. *E-mail*—DAVSUS@ aol.com.

CAREER: COMPAS Writers-and-Artists-in-the-Schools, creative writing instructor, 1979-85, associate director of literature program, 1982-84; The Loft, Minneapolis, MN, core faculty member and instructor in poetry and creative nonfiction, beginning 1984, member of board of directors and head of long range planning committee, 1982-84, president of board of directors, 1987-88, vice president of board, 1988-89, Asian-American Inroads instructor, 1993, 1994, 1998. St. Olaf College, instructor, 1990-91; University of Oregon, visiting professor, 1991; University of Minnesota—Twin Cities, instructor, summers, 1993-94, Edelstein-Keller Visiting Professor of Creative Writing, 1995; Hamline University, visiting professor, 2001—. Center for Arts Criticism, member of board of directors, 1990-92, president, 1991-92, vice president, 1992—; Jerome Foundation, member of board of directors, 1991-2000, program officer, 1999; Asian-American Renaissance Conference, member of board of directors and development and volunteer artistic director, 1991—; Pangea World Theater, volunteer artistic associate, 1997. Gives readings from his works and speaks on race and diversity at colleges and universities and at public gatherings.

MEMBER: Phi Beta Kappa.

AWARDS, HONORS: Fanny Fay Wood Memorial Prize, American Academy of Poets, 1977; U.S.-Japan creative artist fellow, Japan-U.S. Friendship Commis-

David Mura

sion, 1984; literature fellow, National Endowment for the Arts, 1985 and 1995; creative nonfiction prizes, from *Milkweed,* 1985, and The Loft, 1987; "Discovery"/*Nation* Award, 1987; winner of National Poetry Series contest, 1989, for *After We Lost Our Way*; Pushcart Prize, 1990; Minnesota State Arts Board grant and fellowship, 1991; grant from Rockefeller Foundation Bellagio Center, 1993; Martha Scott Trimble Poetry Award, *Colorado Review,* 1991; Josephine Miles Book Award, Oakland chapter, International PEN, 1991, for *Turning Japanese,* which was also cited as a notable book of the year, *New York Times;* Loft McKnight Award of Distinction for poetry, 1992, award for prose, 1998; PEW/Playwrights' Center Exchange, 1993, for *Painted Bride;* McKnight grant, Playwrights' Center, 1993; fellow, Salzburg Seminar, 1994; travel grant, Center for Arts Criticism, 1994; Carl Sandburg Literary Award, 1995, for *The Colors of Desire;* Lila Wallace-*Reader's Digest* Writers' Award, 1995; D.H.L., Grinnell College, 1997.

WRITINGS:

A Male Grief: Notes on Pornography and Addiction, Milkweed Editions (Minneapolis, MN), 1987.

After We Lost Our Way (poetry), Dutton (New York, NY), 1989.

Relocations: Images from a Japanese American (multimedia performance piece), first performed at Intermedia Arts Gallery, 1990.

Turning Japanese: Memoirs of a Sansei, Atlantic Monthly Press (New York, NY), 1991.

(With Tom Rose, Kim Hines, and Maria Cheng; also performer) *Silence and Desire* (play), first performed at Red Eye Theater, 1994.

(With Alexs Pate; also performer) *The Colors of Desire* (performance piece; also known as *Secret Colors*), first produced at Southern Theater, Walker Art Center, 1994.

(With Alexs Pate; also performer) *Slowly This* (documentary film), Alive TV, 1995.

The Colors of Desire (poetry), Anchor/Doubleday (New York, NY), 1996.

Where the Body Meets Memory: An Odyssey of Race, Sexuality, and Identity (memoir), Anchor/Doubleday (New York, NY), 1996.

After Hours (theater piece), first performed at Intermedia Arts, 1996.

(With Esther Suzuki) *Internment Voices* (theater piece), first performed at Theater Mu at Intermedia Arts, 1997.

(Adaptor) *The Winged Seed* (theater piece; adaptation of memoir by Li-Young Lee), first performed by Pangea World Theater, at Guthrie Laboratory Theater, 1997.

(With Meena Natarajan) *Silent Children* (theater piece), 1997.

Song for Uncle Tom, Tonto, and Mr. Moto: Poetry and Identity, University of Michigan Press (Ann Arbor, MI), 2002.

Author of *Listening* (poetry chapbook), Minnesota Center for Book Arts. Work represented in anthologies, including *The Language of Life: A Festival of Poets,* edited by Bill Moyers and James Haba, Doubleday (New York, NY); *Poets of the New Century,* David R. Godine; *Men and Intimacy: Personal Accounts Exploring the Dilemmas of Modern Male Sexuality,* Crossing Press; *Breaking Silence: An Anthology of Contemporary Asian-American Poets,* Greenfield Review Press; and *The Open Boat: Poems from Asian America,* Anchor/Doubleday (New York, NY). Contributor of poems and articles to periodicals, including *Nation, New Republic, River Styx, New England Review, Quarry,* and *American Poetry Review.* Some of Mura's works have been published in Japan and the Netherlands.

WORK IN PROGRESS: Two novels, *Harry Ohara* and *The Warlord's Daughter;* a poetry collection, *Angels for the Burning,* for Boa Editions (Brockport, NY), 2004.

SIDELIGHTS: Poet and memoirist David Mura creates his work from the perspective of a Sansei—a third-generation Japanese-American. In both his poetry and his nonfiction, Mura deals with themes such as racism, sexuality, and what it means to be Japanese American.

Mura's first memoir, *Turning Japanese: Memoirs of a Sansei,* Mura writes of the year he spent in Japan on a writing fellowship. His account of the year abroad, which brought him to a greater understanding of his own identity as a Japanese American, was warmly received by critics. In an article for *Canadian Literature,* Guy Beauregard wrote, "Make no mistake about it: Mura's narrative is not a naive search for lost 'roots' or an essential 'Japanese-ness.' Instead, Mura works through the more difficult task of rethinking what precisely 'home,' 'nation,' and 'culture' can mean to a Japanese American who would rather have gone to Paris than Tokyo to spend a year writing." A reviewer for *Washington Post Book World* praised, "Mura's nonfiction is a potent antidote to one-dimensional portrayals of the Japanese." In the *New Yorker,* a contributor commended, "There is brilliant writing in this book, observations of Japanese humanity and culture that are subtly different from and more penetrating than what we usually get from Westerners." R. Bruce Schauble of *Kirkus Reviews* called *Turning Japanese* "noteworthy for its seriousness of purpose and for its unusual intelligence, sophistication, and honesty," and Donna Seaman of *Booklist* described the book as "an eloquent account of a catharsis that illuminates both personal and societal aspects."

Mura continues to discuss the themes of racial and sexual identity in *Where the Body Meets Memory.* The book delves into not only how his racial identity was shaped by the fact that his parents were both sent to internment camps during World War II, but how his racial identity impacted his sexuality. Jonathan Rauch of *Washington Post Book World* wrote that in *Where the Body Meets Memory,* Mura writes "with a novelist's humane eye and a poet's taut economy. His prose is diamond-pure, and he uses it to tell two stories in counterpoint, one of his parents' flight from their eth-nicity and their past, the other of his own recovery of both." A writer for *Transpacific* lauded Mura's use of humor in the text, calling the book "seriously hilarious," and Donna Seaman of *Booklist* praised the writing as "unique, invaluable, and skillfully conveyed." Though the book hinges on Mura's sense of what it means to be Asian American, Rauch was struck "not by the ethnic uniqueness of Mura's experience, but by its universality. . . . . [T]he story has rarely been so movingly told."

In Mura's poetry, many of the same themes appear. Zhou Xiaojing, in an essay on Mura's poetry for *ME-LUS,* cited an interview with the author in 1989, in which he stated that "everything I write, except for certain pieces of criticism, reflects an outlook which is conditioned by my being Japanese American." Xiaojing goes on to write, "In confronting his ethnic identity and the Japanese-American experience, Mura opens up new areas of inquiry and new artistic challenges and possibilities for his poetry." Tim Brady, writing in *MPLS-St. Paul* noted that Mura's heritage as a Sansei is "a fact that informs a good chunk of his writing." Brady continued that because Mura's poetry tells history from the side not of the victors, but of the colonized, "A lot of readers are cupping their ears to hear more."

After We Lost Our Way, Mura's first book of poetry and the winner of the 1989 National Poetry Series contest, uses the technique of the monologue to explore several points of view, allowing Mura to critique racial discrimination from several angles. Though the content explores Asian-American identity, critics have noted that his poetry in this collection has a more European than American feel to it. Edward Butscher of *American Book Review* wrote that *After We Lost Our Way* "flares up in passion and ambition against traditional walls, blazes a lushness of metaphor that is constantly seeking political and social associations."

In *The Colors of Desire* Mura focuses on the interplay between race and eroticism. Though continuing to explore the Japanese-American identity, Mura also discusses sexual desire and addiction, infidelity, and the difference between memory and truth. In *Booklist,* Elizabeth Gunderson praises his "powerful" poems for their combination of brutality and sweetness, writing, "Mura bares his soul and amazes his readers with the beauty and darkness in his work."

Though best known for his award-winning nonfiction, Mura has also been active in creating performance and theater pieces, and he has made himself a presence in the Minneapolis arts community through his work in founding the Asian-American Renaissance, an Asian-American arts organization, where he served as artistic director. As a contributor to newspapers and magazines, Mura has spoken out against the inherent racism and orientalism present in such lauded works as *Miss Saigon.*

AUTOBIOGRAPHICAL ESSAY:

David Mura contributed the following autobiographical essay to *CA*:

The Facts & Fictions of Autobiography

I was born in 1952 at the Great Lakes Naval Training Center in northern Illinois. My birth took place there because my father was in the U.S. Army, stationed in Germany. This was the nearest military facility that my mother, who was living on the south side of Chicago then, could make use of. When my father returned six months later, we lived for a while on the south side, then moved to the near north side, about a mile from Wrigley Field.

David (left), age one, with cousin Steve

Perhaps because of this, I grew up as both a White Sox and a Cubs fan, loving Nellie Fox and Ernie Banks. In the summer after my third grade, we moved to a near north suburb, Morton Grove, which bordered a Jewish suburb, Skokie. In part my father moved there because of the good schools, which he associated with Jewish people. He worked at the AMA, then at Blue Shield, moving up eventually to a position as vice-president. He wanted me to go even further.

In high school, I studied long hours, played baritone in the band, played on the football and basketball team, and was often desperately unhappy. I went out a couple times with a couple of girls, but my dating was thwarted in part because the parents of the Jewish girls I dated found out I wasn't Jewish, and of course, they couldn't pass me off as a Jew, as they could some of my *goyim* classmates. The only people of color at my high school were a few Japanese and Chinese Americans, whom I generally tried to disassociate myself from. I thought of the Japanese and Chinese

American guys in my classes as nerds. Yes, I got good grades like them, but I was athletic. I at least sat with the cool kids in the lunch room, but I always sensed I was merely tolerated because, though a third stringer, I lettered on the basketball team.

Autobiographical facts. Many of them are like any typical American childhood of the fifties and sixties. And yes, I was in many ways typical. A smart and lonely teenager who felt his parents didn't understand him and his peers didn't appreciate him. Who couldn't get a date and would only begin to find success with girls in college, at a school—Grinnell—where it was cool to be smart and where most of the student body considered themselves freaks or hippies. For the first three years there I thought I wanted to get my J.D. and practice civil rights or poverty law.

While in college I met the girl who was to become my wife. She grew up in Atlanta, the daughter of northerners, her father a doctor and the director of the

Center for Disease Control. Through three of her grandparents, she had relatives all the way back to the *Mayflower*. The fourth, her paternal grandfather, had origins we only found out years later: He was a Jew, of a family that originally came from Austria-Hungary. (At this news, my immediate reaction was, "I always knew I was going to marry a Jew.") At the time we met, I was mainly conscious of the fact that she was pretty and smart. We'd both chosen the same wacky leftist high-pressured academic school; we'd both grown up in suburban middle class neighborhoods. Race? That wasn't something we discussed in terms of our relationship. I was obviously an American just like her, and if we were different, it was because she had grown up in the South and I in the North.

When I speak at universities these days, I sometimes tell the white students that I am more like them than they would probably guess. And, at the same time, more different. It took me years to discover what that difference was. It took me years to see how race affected my sense of sexuality and my relationship with my wife. It took two books of poetry, two memoirs, and countless essays to investigate an identity I was taught—by my parents, by the educational system, by the culture and society around me—to deny.

In retrospect, this denial is hardly surprising. Asian Americans are usually offered the choice of two identities. The first is as a perpetual alien, a foreigner, someone who just came here yesterday and isn't familiar and doesn't quite belong—and this may be true even if you're a seventh generation Chinese American or your family first came to America, as mine did, a century ago. The second identity is as a honorary white person, someone I very much wanted to be growing up.

A third identity, which my writing and those of other Asian-American authors are now exploring, is still being articulated. It involves the obvious permutations and combinations of cultural identity that we Asian Americans grapple with, the tensions and interminglings we make between the American culture we live in and the ethnic culture of a country in Asia where we were born or our parents or our grandparents were born. But, less obviously, this third identity involves understanding what it means to look racially Asian and live in America; how this situation affects the way others look at you and the way you look at yourself.

I tell people that I wrote my books, especially my memoirs, because when I looked up at my book-shelves, I never saw a book about someone like me, someone who grew up not just where I did and when I did, but who was a Sansei—a third-generation Japanese American—and who experienced that appellation not simply as a name but as a question of identity. For a long time I deferred that question; then I confronted and wrote about it, and in doing so, reexamined and reimagined my life and the lives of those around me.

*

Though I always got good grades in school, English was my weakest subject (math was my best). Freshman year in high school, I was in the honors track for all of my classes except English, and I asked my English teacher if I could transfer into honors English. She decided I was uppity. After that, every time I made a mistake in class, she'd raise her eyebrows and say disdainfully before the whole class, "Honors?"

She made me read Henry James' *Portrait of a Lady* for extra credit, implying it was a hurdle I needed to get over if I was going to have any chance of switching classes. I got through what I thought was the whole book only to find I had read only the first of two volumes. I had absolutely no desire to pick up the second volume. In retrospect, I can't imagine what I made of the opening paean to English tea time or the differences James invoked between the sophisticated, refined British and the brash, naive and unsuspecting Americans, embodied in his Bostonian heroine, Isabelle Archer. It must have all tumbled over my head.

I might have been considered brash and boorish. I talked too much in class, didn't respect my teacher. Or so she thought. Though I was getting an A in the class, she sent home a failing notice because of my behavior. Not surprisingly, I never made it into the honors English class that year.

In my junior year, I wrote a few poems for a contest. The only one I recall was about a young black boy in the ghetto. I associated him with a young Puerto Rican boy who lived in my cousin's uptown neighborhood in Chicago and would stare down at the street from his third story window. In the poem, the young black boy is gazing down at the street, taking in the shabbiness of his neighborhood.

Age four, with paternal grandfather Jinosuke Uyemura

When my father read the poem, he told me I should write what I knew.

In a way, I see now that I *was* writing about what I knew, only I didn't know that. My father's remarks implied that I had nothing in common with this young black boy. We didn't live in a ghetto section of Chicago, we weren't black.

My father made his living writing; he worked in the communications division at the American Medical Association. Even after I eventually made it into honors English, he would correct my English compositions, marking mistake after mistake, muttering about where in the world did I learn how to write (my math, on the other hand, was far beyond him).

In college, I suddenly started getting *A*'s in English, and I sometimes surmise now that this was in part because my father was no longer going over my compositions. I was writing songs then, and I took a course on major British poets, in part because I thought it might help with my lyrics. One assignment was to write imitations of Spenser and Pope. I not only got an *A*, but my professor read my version to the class as a model example. I said to myself, "Well, that wasn't too hard. Maybe I can do some more."

I didn't know then that I had just chosen my life's vocation. I thought of poetry as something that might

interest girls, though perhaps not as much as writing songs like Neil Young or James Taylor. But I was a freshman, and the freshman coeds were interested in upper classmen. I took to taking long walks beyond the campus on weekends, or spending weekend nights in the dark listening to the moody, jazz influenced ballads of Laura Nyro. Songs about empty streets in Manhattan after midnight, about loneliness and heart-searing relationships, lovers pining for the one who'd left them.

As the young tend to do, I thought of such brooding behavior as poetic. But if you told me that eventually I would write poems about something other than my loneliness and sad love life, I wouldn't have believed you. Nor would I have had the slightest idea what that something else might be.

After the major British poets course, I continued to take English and writing courses, and wrote poetry. But that was for fun; I was planning to go to law school. Then, while working in an insurance office between my junior and senior year, I found myself hiding poetry books in my desk. I realized if I became a lawyer I would have to do this the rest of my life. I decided to pursue a path where I could keep the books on top of my desk.

Looking back, I feel it's both unlikely and inevitable that I became a writer. Of course, one can say that about many or even most writers. Who would expect that the best-known poet writing in English in the twentieth century would be born and raised in St. Louis? Or that the greatest poet in English would come not from London but from some out-of-the-way small town called Stratford. Still, though both T. S. Eliot and Shakespeare appear to have arrived, in certain ways, out of left field, on closer inspection there's a revealing difference. Eliot came from a family with prominent Boston connections; growing up he knew he was headed for Harvard. In the end, he rejected his family's ambitions for him and never returned to graduate school there. He was an insider who felt like, or wanted to be, an outsider. Shakespeare possessed no such connections; he was a commoner who eventually purchased his family a coat of arms. In other words, he was an outsider who wanted to be an insider.

The distinction I'm making here comes from the poet Richard Hugo, who saw himself as an outsider who wanted to be an insider. I too see myself in this group.

For me, my outsider status comes from my race and ethnicity. When I was growing up in the 1950s I never read a book with any characters remotely resembling me or my family. Nor did I see any such characters on television or the movies. Instead, I learned to read from the Dick and Jane books, with brown-haired Dick and fair-haired Jane and their blonde little sister, Sally. I watched TV shows like *Donna Reed* and *Father Knows Best* and *Leave It to Beaver,* white suburban middle class families who always seemed chipper and healthy and good humored. If there was an "oriental," it would be someone like Peter the cranky houseboy in *Bachelor Father* or the cook, Hop Sing, in the cowboy show *Bonanza,* or the Chinese messenger in *Have Gun Will Travel.*

This last show featured a hired gunslinger named Paladin, who was one of my childhood heroes. In the childhood photographs of many American boys of the fifties, whatever their race or ethnicity, there will often be a five or six year old with a cowboy hat and six-guns tied at his side. So, in certain ways, it's not surprising that my cowboy dreams would appear in a poem of mine. Here's a section from the title poem of my second book, *The Colors of Desire*:

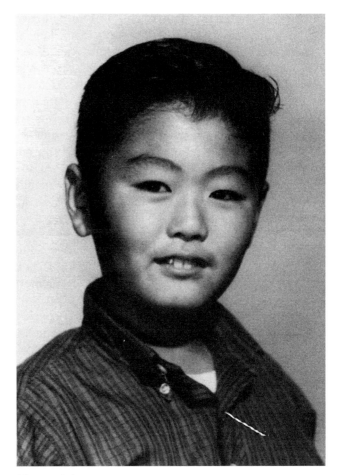

Mura, age nine

Cut to Chicago, June. A boy of six.
Next year my hero will be Mickey Mantle,
but this noon, as father eases the Bel-Air past
  Wilson,
with cowboy hat black, cocked at an angle,
my skin dark from the sun, I'm Paladin,
and my six guns point at cars whizzing past,
blast after blast ricocheting the glass.
Like all boys in such moments, my face
attempts a look of what—toughness? bravado?
  ease?—
until, impatient, my father's arm wails
across the seat, and I sit back, silent at last.

Later, as we step from IGA with our sacks,
a man in a serge suit—stained with ink?—
steps forward, shouts, "Hey, you a Jap?"
"You from Tokyo? You a Jap? A Chink?"
I stop, look up, I don't know him,
my arm yanks forward, and suddenly,
the sidewalk's rolling, buckling, like lava melting,
and I know father will explode,
shouts, fists, I know his temper.

And then,
I'm in that dream where nothing happens—
The ignition grinds, the man's face presses
the windshield, and father stares ahead,
fingers rigid on the wheel...

That night in my bedroom, moths,
like fingertips, peck the screen;
from the living room, the muffled t.v.
As I imagine Shane stepping into the dusty
  street,
in the next bed, my younger brother starts
to taunt—*you can't hurt me, you can't hurt
me...*—
Who can explain where this chant began?
Or why, when father throws the door open,
shouts stalking chaos erupted in his house,
he swoops on his son with the same swift motion
that the son, like an animal, like a scared and
  angry little boy,
fell on his brother, beating him in the dark?

I refer to this poem often when I talk to audiences about race and ethnicity. I tell them that when my friend, the Japanese-Canadian playwright Rick Shiomi read this poem, he asked me if I remembered what happened at the beginning of *Have Gun Will Travel*. I replied that Richard Boone as Paladin would come walking down these stairs, dressed in black, his six-guns at his side: the epitomé of cowboy cool. But Rick told me that wasn't the whole opening. Just before Paladin appears, a Chinese messenger, in a little cap and with pig-tail flapping, comes running through the hotel lobby, shouting, "Terragram for Mr. Paladin, Terragram for Mr. Paladin!"

But even after Rick told me this, I could not recall the Chinese messenger, whose name, Rick informed me, was "Hey Boy." I've wiped him from my memory. And what I believe happened, way back when I was five or six, was that I looked at this opening scene and knew who I wanted to be and look like: I wanted to be the gunslinger, the hero, the white guy. The Chinese messenger? He was a figure of ridicule, a lowly servant, a peon. I must have sensed people—and here I mean white people—would associate him with me, and I wanted no part of that association. It was easier to distance myself from him if I simply forgot he ever existed.

So the background of this poem and the opening stanza brings up the question of memory in autobiographical writing. I don't know if the poem would have been different if I had remembered "Hey Boy," the Chinese messenger. Perhaps I would have tried to bring him in, perhaps not. But his absence from my memory speaks volumes about my development: I grew up wanting to be white.

*

If this poem brings up the limitations and distortions of memory, there's another way the poem points to the unreliability of autobiographical writing. The poem focuses on a confrontation with racism, and my father's reaction to that confrontation. In part the poem implies that the anger my father represses, and my own emotions that arise out of this incident, both culminate in what happens that night: the fight between me and my brother; my father hitting me and punishing me for fighting.

But in actuality, this confrontation with the man in the serge suit never occurred. Or rather, it happened to

As a high-school football player, age seventeen

someone else I know, another Sansei, whose father reacted as my father reacts in the poem: frozen, numbed, paralyzed. Now my father did hit me one night for fighting with a sibling, and my sibling did taunt, "you can't hurt me, you can't hurt me." But that sibling was my sister, who was two years younger than me, and not my brother, who was six years younger.

Poets, said T. S. Eliot, are "constantly amalgamating disparate experience." In other words, poets will often bring together in their poems various different and seemingly unconnected experiences, and weld them together in a new and unexpected whole. To the ordinary person, said Eliot, there's little connection between a rose, the smell of steaks in a passageway, the sound of typing, falling in love, and reading Spinoza. But for the poet, in the act of writing a poem, these experiences can be fused together.

In my poem above, I've brought together various experiences—riding with my father in the car, wanting to be and pretending to be a cowboy at age six, a story a friend told me about an incident with his father, a fight between my sister and me and my father's reaction to that fight. The poem also connects to larger more generalized experiences—television icons, American heroes and the cultural milieu of the fifties, and, in a more subtle yet powerful way, the internment camps.

In 1942 the U.S. government rounded up 110,000 Japanese Americans living on the West Coast, herded them into assembly centers, and sent them to prisons in desolate areas inland—the deserts of California and Arizona, the swamps of Arkansas, the high mountain plains of Idaho and Montana. My parents and their families were among those "interned." (Several decades later, the government apologized to the Japanese Americans and admitted that the camps were not a military necessity or protection against "fifth column" activities, but were instead caused by racism, war-time hysteria, and a failure of leadership.)

My parents were in their teens when they were ripped from their homes and put into these camps. They never spoke about this experience to us children. Sometimes, when the name of a Japanese American came up in their conversation with relatives, someone would ask, "What camp were they in?" But no one told me or any of the other children what the camps were for, much less what my parents experienced there, or how they felt being taken from their homes and put behind barbed wire fences with rifle towers and armed guards.

Later, when I was much older and asked them about it, my parents downplayed the effect of the camps. My father told me that when he was in Los Angeles before the war, he had to mow lawns for his father's nursery. When he got to the camps, after school, he could just go outside and play baseball. My mother claimed she was too young to remember the camps.

So, as a child, I never thought about the internment camps. They meant nothing to me. And even as a young adult I believed what my parents told me.

It was only as I began to write about the camps and my parents and my own life that I came to understand that the real truth was much more complicated and contradictory—that what my parents had told me about their past was only partly the truth; or perhaps, even a lie.

*

In the poem "The Colors of Desire," I incorporated the story of a friend into a seemingly autobiographical poem. When I was a young poet I came upon an essay where Richard Hugo argued that the poet should not tie himself to the literal truth but the aesthetic truth of the poem. If you need to alter the facts because the poem seems to demand it, Hugo maintained that the poet should do so. Sometimes that change might involve a word choice, such as making the color of a car "blue" instead of "tan"; sometimes it could involve larger divagations from fact.

But I didn't need Hugo to learn this. I could see from any number of poems ways in which poets had altered or distorted autobiographical facts for the sake of the poem. I had read poems where I had at first believed the facts to be autobiographically true to the poet, only to learn later in an interview or article that this was not the case.

Hugo spoke not just of changing the facts, but also of an adherence to an aesthetic truth. In my poem, what happens to the father and boy outside the grocery store is not a literal truth from my life. Yet the incident and the father's reaction does seem true to how my father would have acted had such an incident happened to us.

Even more importantly, the incident for me reads as an allegory to the experience of my father and many other Japanese Americans who were in the camps. The camps were an attack on them racially. In face of this massive attack by the government, there was little or nothing they could do. They felt helpless, paralyzed. I would argue that this feeling of helplessness, paralysis, and amnesia affected them after the war, and thus affected their children. The incidents in the poem helped me embody this aesthetic truth.

With future wife, Susan Sencer, 1972

It's an intricate and contradictory business writing poems. But then so is our experience of history.

*

I wrote "The Colors of Desire" after I had completed my first memoir, *Turning Japanese: Memoirs of a Sansei*. In the process of writing that book, I had a major epiphany about my father's life and his relationship to the internment camps, without which I could not have written this poem in the way I did.

Turning Japanese recounts the events of a year I spent in Japan, and at one point in my stay there, my wife and I went to Hiroshima. I wrote about the experience of going to the memorial museum in Hiroshima, of seeing a child's charred lunch box and the shadow of

a man's hand burned into a brick. Later, this experience and writing about it made me wonder about where my father was at the end of World War II. By that time, he had been released from the internment camps and was enrolled at Western Michigan University in Kalamazoo, living there in the house of a white professor.

As I wrote, I pictured in my mind what it would have been like for my father on the day they held the V-J celebrations in town:

It is the year the war has ended, the summer between his freshman and sophomore year. August, a few days after Hiroshima and Nagasaki. A holiday has been declared, men sweep women up in their arms in the middle of streets and kiss them, and the women, abandoned for a moment, respond; firecrackers, streamers, confetti, all the trappings of a carnival, whirl through intersections and squares throughout the country. People sport the smiles and laughter of peace, as if the muscles, clenched like a fist for so long, have moved on to another task, all brightness, promise and plenty.

On August 11, 1945, my father is sitting on the steps of a house in Kalamazoo, Michigan. He hears the swooping sirens of the fire trucks from the center of town, the high school band blaring "Stars and Stripes Forever," the tooting of horns, loudspeakers filling with speeches. He sees in his mind the street filled with banners and flags, the men with faces bright and beet-red from joy and drink, the women yanking their children at the wrist, dabbing their eyes with handkerchiefs. A squirrel comes chattering across the lawn, rears up on its haunches, begging as usual for a handout. My father picks up a stone from the dirt, pulls back his arm, and then drops the stone to his feet. A voice rises inside him, insistent and restless, a twitch in his muscles, an urge to move, go somewhere, do something. "It won't always be like this," he remembers his teacher in the camps saying. "After the war you will be free again and back in American society. But for your own sakes try and be not one, but two hundred per cent American. . . ."

I am American he says to himself. I am glad we won. The light through the leaves is bright, blinding. The heat immense, oppressive. The sounds all over town joyous. He repeats his mantra over and over. He learns to believe it.

My father had always told me that when he got out of the internment camps, his return to American society was uneventful and went smoothly. Writing this passage, I realized that he had not told the whole truth to me. His experience of American society and his racial identity and the legacy of the internment camps were far more complicated than he had let on.

And yet, this passage which led me to this truth, a truth which I now believe absolutely, this passage describes events which I never witnessed and which may or may not have occurred. The whole passage in a way is an act of fiction: It is a passage of fiction in an autobiography or memoir; a lie which tells me, and hopefully the reader, an important truth about my life and my father's life.

On the other hand, there is also another sense in which the passage is actually true: It is a true picture of a sansei or third generation Japanese American trying to imagine what life was like for his Nisei—second generation—father after he left the internment camps.

*

I began writing as a poet and have written two books of poetry, but I may be better known as a memoirist. As I've implied above, poets, when they falsify or distort their biographies, seem to have precedence and to function within certain literary traditions. Memoirists, one might think, are another matter.

And yet, as a memoirist, I know one obvious facet of the genre is this: A memoir could not or should not be used in a court as evidence.

Unfortunately sophomore readers and sometimes their seniors don't know or want to believe this. Some readers, for instance, pick up memoirs believing such works contain the unvarnished and real goods, or at least the eye-witness version of the goods. This desire has been heightened by the popularity of talk-show confessions and the *Oprah-Jerry Springer* atmosphere of the age; many claim such an atmosphere has helped spawn the recent wave (or glut) of memoirs. To certain media critics the memoir becomes then another unwholesome and narcissistic journey into psychobabble, filled with unpolished self-pity, woundings and complaints—from eating disorders to incest with one's father, from coming out of the closet sexually to coming out of the closet racially (to use my own case).

There is a certain "truth" to this characterization and criticism of the genre of memoir. But such a critique ignores other truths about the nature and construction of autobiography and the ways we read such works. The "whole truth" here is a lot more complicated.

David and Susan on their wedding day, 1983

To highlight the fictitious nature of autobiography, I often talk of how one could write accounts of one's childhood at the ages of twenty-five, thirty-five, forty-five, and so on until death, and each account would differ. Which then would be the "true" account?

My question points to the subjectivity of autobiography. In general we feel we're more likely to receive an objective account of a person's life from their biographer than from the person themselves (though the biographer can possess her own biases). One current criticism of the recent wave of memoirs cites instances of egregious self-justification and/or the incessant vilification of various oppressive others—from one's parents to media projections, from homophobia to racism. Implicit in such criticism is the charge that the memoirist is not able to put his life in a proper perspective: If he has not distorted the actual events in his life, he certainly errs in his description of motives, tenor, and outcome.

And yet it is the very subjectivity of autobiography that draws us towards these works. More sophisticated readers realize that the autobiography is not going to be an accurate, neutral, or objective accounting, such

as we might expect from a news reporter or presumably from a biographer. We go to an autobiography because we receive the words of the person without the mediation of a third party; in the process we hope to gain access not to the truth of their life but to their subjectivity.

But subjectivity is a tricky thing. As post-modern theory has reminded us, all writing is in a sense a fiction and at the same time a revelation of subjectivity.

Beyond this there's the question of who is permitted to possess subjectivity, and thus, whose life can be a legitimate subject for memoir.

*

In *Turning Japanese,* my memoir about a year I spent in Japan, one reason I paid so much attention to my own personal story and the personal nature of my take on Japan was instructional: I wanted to point out the falseness of the objective and commanding tone many Western authors evince when writing about Japan. I felt it was truer to be up front with my own biases and to explore their nature and etiology than to pretend I could attain a scientifically neutral viewpoint. I wanted readers to see when I was confused and uncertain, to sense the limitations of my knowledge and position. I had read contemporary cultural theory and was aware of the issues of ethnocentrism and Orientalism explored by such writers as Edward Said; I also saw how those issues had been ignored by so-called experts on Japan such as James Fallows. As Said points out, there has been this tradition of white Western authors writing about the "orient" as if their observations were the objective and unvarnished truth.

In light of all this, *Turning Japanese* constantly points to the fact that the account of my encounter with Japan is intensely personal and not objective. At various points in the narrative, events in Japan cause me to reflect on my identity. There are periodic flashbacks concerning my own life, the life of my parents and grandparents, and the history of Japanese-Americans in general. I focus on the way the internment of Japanese-Americans was occluded both in my schooling and in my family. I explore how the process of assimilation in a racist culture exacts a terrific price, one many Americans, including my own family, do not

Family photo on David's wedding day, 1983: (from left) brother John, sister Linda, David, mother Teruko, father Tom, sister Susan

want to examine. That price is self-hatred and self-neglect, an inability to acknowledge crucial parts of one's experience and psyche.

Whenever I describe the book to people, I stress how it centers on my going to Japan not just as an American, but as a Japanese-American. Yet it has been enlightening for me to see how some people wanted to ignore how my book as a memoir of a Sansei is intimately tied to my vision of Japan. Certain white reviewers, for example, focused almost entirely on the book as a travelogue and generally ignored the sections on my Japanese-American identity. A couple critics found the sections on identity self-conscious, and intimated that this self-consciousness intruded on the book's picture of Japan.

In a generally favorable review for *Conde Nast Traveler,* Simon Winchester wrote that my book presented an "illuminating essay" on the bewildering complexities of contemporary Japanese society. He also noted that I had written honestly about my understandable confusions concerning my Japanese American identity, but this element of the book seemed to him definitely of secondary importance: "While it would be impolite to indicate a lack of real interest in Mura and his trials . . . it is his notes on the society that temporarily surrounds . . . and prevents him from really 'turning Japanese' that are the more valuable." (I should note that Mr. Winchester's belief that I felt Japan rejected me is more his own interpretation than what's in my book.)

I received a similar response in a letter about my book from someone who appears to have lived in Japan for some time: "I read it not as a 'Sansei's memoirs' but as a 'gaijin's encounter' with Japan. Because—Japanese ancestry aside—your encounter is in many ways like all first-time coming-to-grips-with Japan type experiences. And therein lies its universal appeal." In this letter writer's mind, there's an implicit assumption that a "sansei's memoirs" cannot be as important as a book about encountering Japan.

Beyond this, the letter writer assumes that universality can only be achieved by ignoring questions of identity which a white American does not feel is substantial. If I write as a generic American, that's okay, but if I write as a third generation Japanese-American, that's being self-conscious; that's less than universal.

Revealingly, this is an assumption which no Asian-American critic of my book has made. All of them have chosen to use the focus of identity as their prime starting point. The Asian-American reviewers understood that in writing *Turning Japanese,* in order to be more truthful or more accurate, I had tried to acknowledge openly the subjective nature of the writing. As a result, their reading of my work strikes me as more complex and comprehensive than a reviewer like Simon Winchester or this letter writer above.

For a critic like Winchester to understand fully the nature of my enterprise he would have to question his own identity and subjectivity and compare them with mine. This would alter significantly his view of himself and the world, particularly his position in the world. He would have to exchange his illusion of centrality and objectivity for an encounter between two subjectivities.

*

But subjectivity is a confusing and contradictory area of inquiry. With my memoirs, I sensed both Asian-American and readers in general tended to view the revelations about my personal life as an act of truth telling. In other words, their reading saw the work as a truthful account of my own subjectivity.

In certain ways this is how I wished them to read the work. In both memoirs, I explore the intimate details of my family life and various aspects of my sexuality. My own struggles to access areas of my experience that were unflattering and shameful was something I had worked hard on. I spent draft after draft going over and over those experiences, trying to move the writing deeper and at the same time shaping it aesthetically. As a writer I can sense those times or places where I know I'm crossing some boundary, both in my own psyche and in the greater culture, that I'm not supposed to cross. At such points, I push myself further because I know this is where my most powerful writing often comes from.

Still, the view of my memoirs as "truth telling" brought up for me certain questions about the nature of autobiography and the ways readers receive the form. Sometimes this "confessional" lens made readers look more favorably on my work, and they praised my boldness and candor. At other times, especially from less sophisticated readers, their dislike of the subjective David Mura in the work seemed to anchor their dislike of the work as a whole.

Of course a similar response sometimes occurs with novels; some readers dislike the main character and so dislike the book. But with a work of fiction, even autobiographical fiction, there's always the caveat that the main character is not the author and a certain aesthetic distance is achieved in the act of judging the book. With novels, we make a division between the main character and the book as a whole; we separate the main character's view of himself from how the author wants us to judge that character.

Obviously, the division between the subject of an autobiography and the author is not so clearly marked. Yet there is a distinction between these two. The fact is that the protagonist of an autobiography and his subjectivity is constructed, a fiction in its own right, and this is true not just for my work but in any autobiography. On one level this protagonist and his subjectivity can be seen as a convention which entails the manipulations of tone, style, and content. As such, there is no one Platonic and true formulation of identity, only the choices made by a particular author at a particular time (and which could very well be different the next time the author takes up the subject of himself). Certainly, in literature, the strategies for constructing one's subjectivity differs greatly from author to author.

Many readers, though, are not aware of just how widely these practices vary. Just as importantly, we have not yet devised an adequate critical vocabulary

With Japanese poet Kazuko Shiraishi, Japan, 1986

for these practices and therefore an adequate method of aesthetically judging this form.

*

In *A Poetics of Women's Autobiography*, Sidonie Smith writes of the impossibility of the autobiographer ever recapturing the entirety of her subjectivity or her experience. She argues then that the "I" of the narrative "becomes a fictive persona":

> Involved in a kind of masquerade the autobiographer creates an iconic representation of continuous identity that stands for, or rather before, her subjectivity as she tells of this "I" rather than of that "I." She may even create several, sometimes competing, stories or versions of herself as her subjectivity is displaced by one or multiple textual representations (Indiana University Press, 1987, p. 47).

Even if one admits the "fictive" nature of autobiography, the question remains about how the autobiographer on a practical level addresses the problem of this form. I'm talking here about the sorts of strategies and questions that might anchor a discussion in a writers' workshop or the mind of the writer rather than an academic analyses.

In my own case, I began to write *Turning Japanese* with the skills of a poet and an essayist, someone familiar with the writerly tools of description and analysis but not those of a fiction writer. My first draft of the book used as its raw material notes, letters, diary entries, and cultural analyses I had made during my year in Japan. The result was a series of personal though fairly detached and intellectual essays on Japanese culture and society, a postmodern take influenced by various structuralists and post-structuralists including Claude Levi-Strauss, Roland Barthes, and Michel Foucault; Marxists such as Walter Benjamin, Theodor Adorno, and Fredric Jameson; and the revolutionary writings of Frantz Fanon on race.

When I brought the first draft of *Turning Japanese* to my writing group, their response was simple and straightforward: "More narrative, more you." I rewrote the book and came back to them and the response was the same: "More narrative, more you." I rewrote it a third time—the same response. Then I obtained an agent and my agent sold the book and my editor said, "More narrative, more you." In all, I did five major drafts of the book with this imperative in mind.

From the very start this imperative of "More narrative, more you" required new and different skills and involved at times two distinctly different tasks. I will start with the simpler and more defined problem—how to bring the qualities of story and fiction to writing that had begun in the mode of intellectual analyses. I read various books on fiction writing; I learned about constructing scenes, about character development, about organizing dialogue. At a certain point I could only tackle scenes involving myself and one other person, but gradually I felt more comfortable doing scenes with several individuals. My models for this work came from both fiction and non-fiction, from favorite books to works that seemed to echo something of the situation or scenes I was describing. A partial listing would include fictional works by James Salter, Hemingway, Garcia Marquez, Saul Bellow, Philip Roth, Marguerite Duras, Fumiko Enchi, Yukio Mishima, Kawabata, Joyce, Proust, and Kafka. I also searched for models in creative nonfiction, reportage, and memoirs: Jon Berger, Tracy Kidder, James Fenton, Maxine Hong Kingston, James Baldwin, Michelle Cliff, Czeslaw Milosz, Paul Auster, Bruce Chatwin, and various authors in *Granta* (a literary journal that often publishes travelogues).

In terms of narrative technique, *Writing for Story* by Jon Franklin was particularly useful. In his book, Fran-

klin demonstrates how he used certain narrative strategies to organize non-fiction material and achieve the readerly pull such stories elicit. To create story, Franklin argued that the protagonist must face a properly articulated problem. Then, through a series of actions or events, the protagonist must solve that problem. In a longer narrative, the process of solving or addressing one problem should create or bring up another complication, which will lead to another problem. Through solving or addressing a series of problems, the narrative takes the protagonist and reader on a journey from which the protagonist emerges changed in some significant way.

In adapting these fictional and narrative structures to my experiences in Japan, I had to address certain basic questions: How much was I willing to fictionalize in order to achieve narrative structure? Could I alter events? Could I rearrange the sequence of events? Could I alter the cast and persona of the characters I encountered in Japan? Could I alter the picture I was creating of myself? My wife? What were the ethical and aesthetic issues involved in answering these questions?

And then, just as importantly, what was accuracy? Sometimes I was working from notes written almost immediately after the events. But with other events, I had no notes or more significantly was dealing with events from my childhood or even from my parents' and grandparents' lives before I was born. What did it mean to be accurate to my memories or to events I had not even witnessed?

Over the course of the writing I constructed my own answers to these questions. For example, with dialogue I wrote what felt was accurate according to my memory or sense of the people I knew. Or at least I started the dialogues in such a fashion. When the conversations relied on notes I generally kept to these. And yet I also let the dialogues move in ways which didn't absolutely reflect my memory or which I had not planned if somehow the scene demanded this. My sense of these demands sometimes had to do with practical questions, such as transition, logic, and progression of the conversation or placement of the people, but I also allowed for heightening tension and dramatic interest or even to make some ideological or intellectual point.

In this way, I was invoking the principle I had learned from writing poetry: If the aesthetic truth of the writing seems to ask for fictionalizing, I would do so. Yet

With novelist and friend Alexs Pate

I was writing a memoir, not a novel. So where did the line between the two exist for me?

*

In the end, I came up with a set of rules for the memoir which allowed a certain amount of what might be called fictionalizing, but still kept the writing for me in the realm of memoir.

In terms of the overall narrative, I decided I could not alter major events. This proved particularly tricky when dealing with my encounter with Gisela, the German woman with whom I have a brief flirtation (the name, of course, is not her real name). Though nothing overtly sexual occurs—there is no physical contact between us—the fact that I did not immediately inform her I was married constituted a breach of marital trust, and I wanted to make this clear to the reader. I realized that the whole question of betrayal would have been more dramatic and easily rendered if I were writing fiction. There the obvious solution would have

been for the protagonist to have sex with Gisela or at least for them to physically touch. To choose the more accurate rendering required a subtlety and complications that were more difficult to convey.

I did decide that I could alter minor events on a more drastic level, particularly rearranging the sequence of events in order to heighten the narrative flow. For example, take the fire festival that ends the first half of the book and comes immediately after the argument between me and my wife over my flirtation with Gisela. In actuality, the fire festival did not take place at this time, nor did I go there alone, as I do in the book, but instead I went with my wife. But placing me in isolation at the fire festival increased the uncertainty and consequences of the argument and my actions; such tension seemed to me worth the dramatic license. In a similar fashion, the trip to my grandparents' home town did not come at the end of my stay in Japan, as it does in the book. But I wanted to use the trip as the ultimate goal, which keeps being deferred and which could act as a culmination of my time there.

Another way I altered actual events occurs later in the book when I take a trip to Osore-san, where I engage in a seance with one of the famous blind women shamans there. In real life I took this trip with friends who do not appear in the book. But to introduce a whole new set of friends near the end of the book would have bogged down the narrative momentum and also been diluting and confusing, providing the reader with too many characters to digest. My solution was to have friends who had already been introduced accompany me on the trip; in writing about the trip, I used dialogue reconstructed from actual conversations we had had at other times and in other places.

But it was easy to change the sequence of events in my trip to Japan and accept that as a legitimate aesthetic device. A more knotty problem was how to portray myself and those around me. Obviously, the portrayal and analysis of oneself and others involves subjective judgments. But beyond this, as I began to rearrange and construct a narrative throughline, as I began to work to dramatize rather than describe or analyze, the nature of the book and its characters began to change. In some ways this change enlivened me both creatively and intellectually. For instance, in a dialogue I could occupy both or even several sides of an issue, whereas the essay format tended to force me into a univocal and unitary response. In other words, the dramatic and fictional form allowed for a more dialogic voice (to use the term of the Russian critic Bakhtin). I felt such a portrayal was actually more accurate and complex than the intellectual pronouncements of the earlier, more essay-like drafts.

At the same time, as I set various characters, including myself, in opposition, it became apparent that if I exaggerated slightly certain personality traits or tendencies in myself and others, I could create more tension and interest. Again, I gave myself permission to make use of these fictional techniques.

Then too I developed in the writing my own sense of how I would portray my relationship with my wife and our marriage. I wanted to be as open about our conflicts and tensions as I could. My wife and I, after some discussion, reached an agreement about this (the issue of how memoir writing interacts with the author's personal relationships is the subject of anoter essay). But I also felt that because I was the one telling the tale, if anyone was going to look worse in the relationship, it would be me. This decision to tilt things against myself was also reinforced by my sense that it made the book more interesting and highlighted certain issues in ways that were more revealing.

Self-assessment is difficult, as is evaluating one's own writing. But it's my belief that the person portrayed in *Turning Japanese* is a bit more naive, a bit more self-righteous, a bit more irritable and opinionated, a bit more insecure, and a bit more self-centered than I am in real life. For instance one alteration of my personality occurs at the very start of *Turning Japanese*. There I deliberately exaggerated my reticence about going to Japan and learning about Japanese culture and deliberately heightened my Francophone—as opposed to Japanophile—leanings and my general fear of travel. Such exaggeration provided the protagonist with a much further distance to travel, as he acclimated himself to Japan and learned to love the culture there. It also provided opportunities for humor and drama that wouldn't otherwise be available.

On a more general level, perhaps it's almost inevitable that the consciousness that creates the book, almost by necessity, must be more complex and knowing than the character "I" portrayed in the book. In writing the memoir, I am creating or at least recording voices contrary to the views and consciousness of the "I" who experiences the events of the memoir. Moreover, I am conscious of how these voices play off against the words of that "I." In other words I must be more aware of the gaps, insecurities, and contradictions in his statements than he is himself. Part of this comes from the retrospective nature of the memoir—the older wiser self looking at a younger less wise self. But part of it derives from the dialectics of constructing a narrative and the limitations of convention and language in the portrayal of consciousness. Again, this points to the similarities between a work of autobiographical fiction and memoir. As Borges has implied, there is a never ending labyrinth of consciousness that can be portrayed in the telling of any tale.

Or at least this seems to be the case with my experience with memoir. I can imagine a writer of memoir coming to these questions with less self-consciousness than I did, and I cannot say whether such self-consciousness improves or detracts from the work. What I do know is that other writers have voiced similar questions and come up with their own answers, sometimes echoing my own, sometimes not.

*

Of course fiction writers have used these techniques over and over again, and the uncertainties such exaggerations bring up have plagued writers of autobiographical fiction. For instance I have been guided in my thinking and influenced in my writing by Philip Roth. As Roth frequently notes, readers often mistake Roth the author for his protagonists. In actuality, maintains Roth, he is constantly distorting and changing real life to accord with the demands of fiction; autobiography and fiction, he insists, are not the same. In an interview with the *Paris Review,* Roth is asked whether his character Zuckerman's rage at Milton Appel, a critic who accuses Zuckerman of being a self-hating anti-Semitic Jew, reflects "the expression of a kind of guilt on your part?" Here is Roth's answer:

> Guilt? Not at all. As a matter of fact, in an earlier draft of the book, Zuckerman and his young girlfriend Diana took exactly opposition positions in their argument about Appel. She, with all her feisty inexperience, said to Zuckerman, "Why do you let him push you

around, why do you take this shit shitting down?" and Zuckerman, the older man, said to her, "Don't be ridiculous, Dear, calm down, he doesn't matter." There was the real autobiographical scene, and it had no life at all. I had to absorb the rage into the main character even if my own rage on this topic had long since subsided. By being true to life I was actually ducking the issue. So I reversed their positions, and had the twenty-year-old college girl telling Zuckerman to grow up, and gave Zuckerman the tantrum. Much more fun. I wasn't going to get anywhere with a Zuckerman as eminently reasonable as myself. (George J. Searles, ed., *Conversations with Philip Roth*, University Press of Mississippi, 1992, pp. 181-82).

One way of stating this is that issues of accuracy in fiction are not as important as issues of aesthetic interest. But such a tension also applies to autobiography. There were countless times in Japan when my wife and I got along amicably, when we sat spooning together in bed reading or watching television. But I myself get bored with the idea of writing about such incidents, so I'm certainly not going to inflict them on the reader. No, what was more revealing and energizing and interesting during our stay in Japan were our arguments. But by highlighting these and even at times exaggerating them slightly, I did not give a full or accurate portrayal of our marriage. I did expect readers to intuit our more congruent periods and to see our arguments within the dynamics of any intimate relationship. But it's clear to me that the response from some readers is bewilderment at our marriage and my wife's tolerance of my presence.

Admittedly, this perception is perhaps one I helped create, but it brings up a critical question: How do such alterations and exaggerations of the protagonist affect our readings of autobiography? When Clark Blaise and Bharati Mukherjee wrote a book about their travels together in India, they decided that the book would be improved if they demonized slightly Clark's character and his position as a white male. Not only was the book made more interesting but certain other truths were revealed. But a reader expecting an accurate portrayal of their marriage might wonder how the two even wrote the book together. Would a more satisfactory way of reading be to take the portrayal of

The Mura family, 2001: (clockwise, from left) daughter Samantha, David, Susan, son Tomo, son Nikko

their relationship as a version of the truth, rather than the whole truth? But isn't this what we do with autobiographical fiction?

In my memoirs I've tried to avail myself of some of the techniques of fiction and even mythology and dream life, and still maintain a level of fidelity to the facts that would not transform the work into fiction. This has meant allowing for a the inadmissible, the shameful, the unregenerate, or at least some larger section of this portion of my life than is generally considered permissible in polite society or certain literary circles. This, for many, is one of the blasphemies of contemporary memoir. Conversely, it is also one of the difficulties one experiences in writing a memoir: if you're too careful and circumspect, the book may lack a strong raison d'etre or may fail to interest the reader.

At the same time, certain details in a memoir will be more charged than in a work of fiction and compel the reader in ways fiction cannot. Characters in novels have adulterous affairs all the time; it's quite another thing to reveal such an affair in a memoir. If the protagonist in a novel announces she has a fatal disease, we may be moved, but not in the same way as when an autobiographer writes about his struggles with AIDS.

So, in certain areas, it does seem to me that there is a line between autobiography and fiction. After all, if readers found out I wasn't Japanese-American or that my parents hadn't been in the internment camps, the work could not be considered a legitimate memoir or work of nonfiction.

Yet once we stray from these larger areas, things become more gray. In the eyes of many readers, Bruce Chatwin, for instance, has written two travelogues—*In Patagonia* and *Songlines*—the second a book about his investigation of the ways Aborigines in Australia map the landscape through songs. Yet after I finished *Songlines,* I read an interview with Chatwin where he pronounced the book a work of fiction. There's nothing to indicate that on the book cover and, in fact, the narrator of the book calls himself Bruce Chatwin. But Chatwin declared it a work of fiction in part because he made up a major character, the Russian émigré who serves as his travel guide and intermediary with the Aborigines. In the interview Chatwin is asked about the division between fiction and nonfiction; he replies:

> I don't think there is one. There definitely should be, but I don't know where it is. I've always written very close to the line. I've tried applying fiction techniques to actual bits of travel. I once made the experiment of counting up the lies in the book I wrote about Patagonia. It wasn't in fact, too bad: there weren't too many. But with *Songlines,* if I had to tote up the inventions, there would be no question in my mind that the whole thing added up to a fictional work. (*Granta 21: The Story-Teller,* 1987, p. 24)

According to Chatwin then, there is a line but the line isn't clear cut.

Part of what Chatwin implies here is that once you let in the imagination, your unconscious, it's the work itself and not your conscious mind which tells you where you'll stop.

*

Beyond the facts and events of one's life, it's clear to me that if you are writing a memoir and your memoir involves your relationship with your parents, your imagination must inevitably enter the writing. How else can you picture the lives of your parents before you were born or who they might have been beyond their interactions with you as a child? And beyond that, what about your grandparents or even your great-grandparents?

In Japan, for instance, I realized that as my knowledge of Japanese culture and history grew, as I felt more and more comfortable living in Japan, I could create in my mind a more complete picture of who my grandparents were. This in turn affected my understanding of my parents, because I realized that until I visited Japan, I had really only known the side of my parents that grew up in America, in American culture. I could not picture what it was like for them to go from the household of their Japanese immigrant parents to the streets of America, because I had not known much about Japan or the Japanese.

So, as I proceeded in the drafts of *Turning Japanese,* I began to imagine moments in the lives of my grandparents and parents, particularly my grandfather and my father. But even though I now knew something about Japan and Japanese culture, I was then faced with another void: Neither of my parents had talked to me much about their parents or about their lives as children, just as they had not said anything to me about the internment camps. For them the past was better kept in the past; silent and forgotten.

In *China Men,* which is about the men in her family, Maxine Hong Kingston encountered a similar dilemma. While her mother was quite voluble about her past, Kingston's father was not; she was faced then with the problem of how she would write his story. In the book, Kingston says finally to her father, "I'll tell what I suppose from your silences and few words, and you can tell me that I'm mistaken. You'll just have to speak up with the real stories if I've got you wrong" (Ballantine Books, 1980, p. 10).

With Kingston's words in my head, I decided I would simply recreate the past as best I could. What I discovered, even early on in *Turning Japanese,* was that this represented a different task from writing about my own life. At one point, looking at an early draft, my editor remarked that it seemed some of my writing about my father was more vivid than anything in the book. I thought about this and realized that when I was dealing with my own life I was only putting down what I could remember. If I could not remember what a person was wearing or what the weather was like that day, I wouldn't place these elements in the scene. When I was writing about my father's life, all of it was imaginative recreation; I had the freedom one enjoys in fiction to provide all the details and to use whatever details my imagination came up with.

In a way, this marked a crucial turning point in my writing of the memoir. I realized then that I should avail myself of the same freedom when I was writing about my own memories. As a result the scenes involving my life became both more fictional and more vivid, more compelling as writing, and this seemed more important than any rigid distinctions between genres. The line between memoir and fiction still did not seem clear. But the line between dull and interesting writing? That was a line I wanted to cross.

*

In *Pedagogy of the Oppressed,* the great educator Paulo Freire argues that for the oppressed to become liberated, they need two basic languages. The first language must express or convey the experiences of their lives, their thoughts and feelings about the immediate world around them, what they encounter day by day. The second language must enable them to connect their own individual life with the workings of the society around them, to place and connect themselves to the great world. Without these languages, Freire argues, the oppressed cannot discover the limits of their lives and thus, cannot begin to devise strategies for overcoming those limits.

I know that my memoirs were involved with my own discovery and creation of these two languages. I also felt that such a discovery could not take place in fiction. In one sense, I felt the encounter with the hard facts of my life and the construction of my own identity needed to take place before I could even embark upon a work of fiction. Certainly the writing of *Turning Japanese* unlocked for me an aspect of my poetic voice I could not have found otherwise. Previous to the writing of that work most of my poems had been written in the voice of others or about the lives of others. With *Turning Japanese,* I discovered a language for writing about myself, my consciousness, and identity. At the same time, I discovered a way of writing about my family and the history of our com-

munity and the larger issues of race that I blocked out and ignored as a child growing up in the heart of America.

And yet, somewhat to my chagrin, I feel that even after writing two memoirs I still have not understood, much less described adequately, my subjectivity. My identity still remains a mystery to me. When I read over my writings, my formulations seem to me both useful and true on one hand, and inadequate and fictitious on the other, too pat, too armed with the shield of completion. At the same time, this duality reflects the position from which I speak, in this culture, at this historical moment.

Still my two memoirs have, in another sense, given me an island upon which I can exist, a place to stand on to make my forays into the consciousness of others. It's no mistake that I am finally writing a work of fiction and feel I could not be doing so at this time without having written my memoirs. I needed to write them in order to move further along the arc of my own writing; they were steps I could not avoid if I wanted to grow and flourish as a writer. In this I feel they bear the stamp of both a personal and historical imperative and are not simply reflective of a confessional narcissistic age. In a way, growing up as a child of color who wanted to be white, I did not understand how to read the details of my own life, nor did the culture provide me with that reading. I had to perform and articulate that reading myself.

BIOGRAPHICAL AND CRITICAL SOURCES:

PERIODICALS

American Book Review, June, 1991, Edward Butscher, "Angst, American and Otherwise," p. 28; February, 1996, Frank Steward, "The Color of Shame," p. 22.

Booklist, February 1, 1991, Donna Seaman, review of *Turning Japanese: Memoirs of a Sansei,* p. 1110; December 15, 1994, Elizabeth Gunderson, review of *The Colors of Desire,* p. 732; May 1, 1996, Donna Seaman, review of *Where the Body Meets Memory: An Odyssey of Race, Sexuality, and Identity,* p. 1476.

Canadian Literature, August, 1997, review of *Turning Japanese,* p. 162.

Condé Nast Traveller, April, 1991, p. 80.

KLIATT, November, 1992, R. Bruce Schauble, review of *Turning Japanese,* pp. 41-42.

Los Angeles Times Book Review, April 28, 1991, Karl Taro Greenfeld, review of *Turning Japanese,* p. 10.

MELUS, fall, 1998, Zhou Xiaojing, "David Mura's Poetics of Identity," p. 145; fall-winter, 2000, Mary Slowik, "Beyond Lot's Wife: The Immigration Poems of Marilyn Chin, Garrett Hongo, Li-Young Lee, and David Mura," p. 221.

MPLS-St. Paul, January 1990, Tim Brady, "Poet of the Not-so-Pretty," p. 17.

New Yorker, April 15, 1991, review of *Turning Japanese,* p. 104.

New York Times Book Review, March 31, 1991, p. 10.

Onthebus, summer-fall, 1990.

Publishers Weekly, January 18, 1991, Genevieve Stuttaford, review of *Turning Japanese,* p. 51; March 11, 1996, review of *Where the Body Meets Memory,* p. 49.

Transpacific, May, 1997, review of *Where the Body Meets Memory,* p. 20.

Washington Post Book World, April 21, 1991, Kunio Francis Tanabe, review of *Turning Japanese,* p. 6; May 31, 1992, review of *Turning Japanese,* p. 12; July 28, 1996, Jonathan Rauch, "Discovering His True Colors," p. 11.

*   *   *

MUSSIO, Laurence B. 1964-

PERSONAL: Born December 15, 1964, in Sarnia, Ontario, Canada; son of Egidio (a maintenance supervisor at a petrochemical refinery) and Vittorina (Pighin) Mussio; married Flavia Gonsalves (a communications strategist), October 25, 1997. *Ethnicity:* "Italian-Friulano." *Education:* University of Western Ontario, B.A. (with honors), 1987; McMaster University, M.A., 1988; York University, Ph.D., 1995. *Religion:* Roman Catholic. *Hobbies and other interests:* International travel, enology, languages, jogging.

ADDRESSES: Office—Executive Research and Communications, 275 Coleridge Ave., Toronto, Ontario, Canada M4C 4J2. *E-mail*—laurence.mussio@ sympatico.ca.

CAREER: Self-employed historian, Toronto, Ontario, Canada, 1994-98; Executive Research and Com-

munications, Toronto, Ontario, Canada, principal and senior communications and strategic consultant, 1999—. McMaster University, lecturer, 2001—.

AWARDS, HONORS: Fellow in Italy, Regione Autonoma, Friuli Venezia-Giulia, 1986.

WRITINGS:

Telecom Nation: Telecommunications, Computers, and Governments in Canada, McGill-Queen's University Press (Montreal, Quebec, Canada), 2001.

Sun Ascendant: A History of Sun Life of Canada, McGill-Queen's University Press (Montreal, Quebec, Canada), 2002.

Contributor to books, including *Perspectives on the New Economics and Regulation of Telecommunications,* edited by W. T. Stanbury, Institute for Research on Public Policy (Montreal, Quebec, Canada), 1996. Contributor to periodicals, including *Canadian Journal of Communication.*

WORK IN PROGRESS: Research on the struggle over international standards, specifically the politics, regulation, and emergence of a global communications infrastructure; research on twentieth-century Canadian business in the global economy; "The Digital and the Divine," a research project on religion in culture in the contemporary West.

BIOGRAPHICAL AND CRITICAL SOURCES:

PERIODICALS

Business History Review, winter, 2001, Hudson Janisch, review of *Telecom Nation: Telecommunications, Computers, and Governments in Canada,* p. 869.

Technology and Culture, July, 2002, Vincent Mosco, review of *Telecom Nation,* p. 627.

*   *   *

MYERS, Amy 1938-
(Alice Carr, Laura Daniels, Harriet Hudson)

PERSONAL: Born August 3, 1938, in Kent, England; daughter of Albert Edward (an electrical contractor) and Grace Violet (Hudson) Howlett; married James K. Myers, 1976. *Ethnicity:* "English/Caucasian." *Educa-*

tion: University of Reading, B.A., 1959. *Politics:* "Variable." *Religion:* Church of England. *Hobbies and other interests:* Country walking, theater history, "thinking up new plots."

ADDRESSES: *Agent*—Dorian Literary Agency, Upper Thornhill, 27 Church Rd., St. Marychurch, Torquay, South Devon TQ1 4QY, England.

CAREER: William Kimber and Co. Ltd. (publisher), London, England, director, 1960-88; novelist, 1988—.

MEMBER: European Association of Planned Giving, Crime Writers Association, Romantic Novelists Association, Society for Theatre Research.

WRITINGS:

CRIME NOVELS

Murder in Pug's Parlour, Malvern Publishing (Worcestershire, England), 1986, revised edition, Headline (London, England), 1989, Avon (New York, NY), 1992.

Murder in the Limelight, Malvern Publishing (Worcestershire, England), 1986, Avon (New York, NY), 1992.

Murder at Plum's, Headline (London, England), 1990, Avon (New York, NY), 1993.

Murder at the Masque, Headline (London, England), 1991, Avon (New York, NY), 1993.

Murder Makes an Entree, Headline (London, England), 1992, St. Martin's Press (New York, NY), 1996.

Murder under the Kissing Bough, Headline (London, England), 1993.

Murder in the Smokehouse, Headline (London, England), 1994, St. Martin's Press (New York, NY), 1997.

Murder in the Music Hall, Headline (London, England), 1995.

Murder in the Motor Stable, Headline (London, England), 1996.

Murder with Majesty, Severn House Publishers (Sutton, Surrey, England), 1999.

Murder in the Queen's Boudoir, Severn House Publishers (Sutton, Surrey, England), 2000.

Myers's crime novels have also been published in Germany.

NOVELS; UNDER PSEUDONYM HARRIET HUDSON

Look for Me by Moonlight, Headline (London, England), 1989.

When Nightingales Sang, Headline (London, England), 1990.

The Sun in Glory, Headline (London, England), 1991.

The Wooing of Katie May, Headline (London, England), 1992.

The Girl from Gadsby's, Headline (London, England), 1996.

Into the Sunlight, Severn House Publishers (New York, NY), 1996.

Not in Our Stars, Severn House Publishers (New York, NY), 1998.

Winter Roses, Severn House Publishers (New York, NY), 1999.

The Songs of Spring, Severn House Publishers (New York, NY), 2000.

To My Own Desire, Severn House Publishers (New York, NY), 2000.

Quinn, Severn House Publishers (New York, NY), 2001.

Here Comes the Sun (novel), Severn House Publishers (New York, NY), 2003.

Other titles as Hudson include *Tomorrow's Garden,* Severn House (New York, NY).

OTHER

(Editor) *Ghost Stories,* Volumes 1-4, William Kimber (England), 1995-98, Volume 5, Robert Hale (England), 1991.

(With Jean Cockett) *Lenham and Boughton Malherbe in Old Photographs,* Meresborough Books (England), 1991, revised edition, privately printed, 1998.

(Under pseudonym Laura Daniels) *Pleasant Vices* (novel), Headline (London, England), 1994.

(Under pseudonym Laura Daniels) *The Lakenham Folly* (novel), Headline (London, England), 1995.

(Under pseudonym Alice Carr) *The Last Summer* (novel), Orion (London, England), 1996.

(Under pseudonym Alice Carr) *Dark Harvest* (novel), Orion (London, England), 1997.

(Under pseudonym Harriet Hudson) *Murder Most 'Orrible* (short stories), Crippen & Landru (New York, NY), 2003.

Work represented in anthologies. Contributor of short stories to periodicals, including *Ellery Queen.*

WORK IN PROGRESS: Murder by Moonlight: A Parson Pennywick Mystery (tentative title); research on the history and prehistory of Kent, England.

SIDELIGHTS: Amy Myers told *CA:* "I started out with the intention of changing the world, but have found that what I'm best at is telling stories. So that's what I do—and as the world will always need stories, that satisfies me and I enjoy it.

"The first influence on my writing was working my way as a child through my parents' bookshelves, including the forbidden territory. The second was the 'Golden Age' crime writers, an influence that remains with me, though I adapt it to our modern age.

"My writing process is, in one word, tortuous. I usually begin a novel in longhand, put it into the computer, rewrite it in longhand, put it into the computer again, and then revise, revise, revise. I plot, say, sixty percent of the novel before I begin, including the beginning and the end, and the remaining part works itself out as I go along.

"My early married life in Paris gave me the idea of using a French master cook as a detective, and my love of history gave me the Victorian/Edwardian setting for my crime novels. My love of history, together with editing historical nonfiction and fiction in my publishing career, led to my women's fiction novels. In particular, a present of two Victorian photographs from an author whose theatrical memoirs I edited led to a great interest in theater history."

BIOGRAPHICAL AND CRITICAL SOURCES:

PERIODICALS

Publishers Weekly, July 22, 1996, review of *Murder Makes an Entree,* p. 230.

*   *   *

MYOMU, Zentatsu
    See BAKER ROSHI, Richard

N-P

NOVENTA, Giacomo
See CA'ZORCI, Giacomo

*   *   *

NYSTROM, David P. 1959-

PERSONAL: Born April 27, 1959, in San Mateo, CA; married, August 28, 1982; wife's name, Kristina; children: Annika. *Education:* University of California, B.A., 1981, Ph.D., 1992; Fuller Theological Seminary, M.Div., 1986.

ADDRESSES: Office—North Park University, 3225 West Foster Ave., Chicago, IL 60625. *E-mail*—dnystrom@northpark.edu.

CAREER: North Park University, Chicago, IL, professor, 1992—. Also taught at University of California—Davis.

MEMBER: Society for the Promotion of Roman Studies, Society of Biblical Literature, Institute for Biblical Research (fellow), Phi Beta Kappa.

AWARDS, HONORS: Teaching excellence awards from University of California—Davis, and North Park University.

WRITINGS:

James, Zondervan (Grand Rapids, MI), 1997.

Contributor to periodicals devoted to Roman social history, the New Testament, and first-century Judaism.

*   *   *

OWENS, Suzanne (R.)

PERSONAL: Born in Canada; daughter of E. Cullen (a surgeon) and Evelyn (a nurse) Bryant; married M. Snow (marriage ended); married E. Owens, October 17, 1970; children: (second marriage) Evangeline, Cullen. *Ethnicity:* "White." *Education:* University of Western Ontario, B.A., 1967; American Musical and Dramatic Academy, graduated, 1968; Emerson College, M.F.A., 1990; trained for the stage at Guildhall School of Music and Drama, London, England. *Religion:* Protestant. *Hobbies and other interests:* Art, theater.

ADDRESSES: Home—12 Paula Beth St., Littleton, MA 01460. *E-mail*—sowens@net1plus.com.

CAREER: Poet. University of Massachusetts—Lowell, teacher of writing and literature, 1990-93; Fitchburg State College, teacher of acting and writing, 1993-2000; also taught classes at Emerson College, 1988, Anna Maria College, 1990, 1991, Endicott College, 1991-93, Salem State College, 1992, 1993, Mount Wachusetts State College, 1992, 1997, 1998, and Worcester State College, 1995; teacher of creative-writing workshop at Lancaster Prison, 1992. Professional actress; appeared with First National Company in the play *The Star- spangled Girl;* stage manager of musical *Stage Struck,* produced in Long Island, NY; also appeared in plays *The Crucible, Arms and the Man, A Winter's Tale, Lord Halewyn, A View from the Bridge, Caesar and Cleopatra, The Lark, The Rivals, Teach Me How to Cry, Murder in the Cathedral, The Late Christopher Bean, Gigi, The Rainmaker, The Cave Dwellers, Fiorello!, Bye Bye Birdie, In Half an Hour,* and *Hello out There;* appeared in film *The Honest Truth,* released by National Film Board of Canada; appeared in the Canadian television series *Scarlet Hill* and in *Christ in the Concrete City,* Canadian Broadcasting Corp.; created and managed a weekly radio program in Waterloo, Ontario, Canada; also appeared in television commercials.

MEMBER: Screen Actors Guild, Actors' Equity Association, Actors' Equity Association of Canada, Wedgewood Hunting and Fishing Club (Quebec), Friends of Concord Library.

AWARDS, HONORS: Beatrice Albert fellow, Millay Colony for the Arts, 1993; Chapbook Award, Frank Cat Press, 1996, for *Theater Poems;* Phyllis Smart Young Prize, 1998, for the poem "God Is a Cowboy Who Rides a Lame Horse."

WRITINGS:

Theater Poems (poetry chapbook), Frank Cat Press (Boulder, CO), 1996.
The Daughters of Discordia (poetry), BOA Editions (Rochester, NY), 2000.

Author of play, *The Black Shawl.* Work represented in anthologies, including *Emily Dickinson Award Anthology,* [Flagstaff, AZ], 1998. Contributor of poetry to periodicals, including *Salmagundi, Earth's Daughters, Mississippi Review, Ploughshares, Spoon River Poetry Review, Seneca Review, Queen's Quarterly, Calliope, Lullwater Review,* and *Fiddlehead.* Poetry editor, *Beacon,* 1990.

WORK IN PROGRESS: A book on "theater poems and play theater."

BIOGRAPHICAL AND CRITICAL SOURCES:

PERIODICALS

Kirkus Reviews, June 15, 2000, review of *The Daughters of Discordia.*

PALMER, Don
    See BENSON, Mildred (Augustine Wirt)

*   *   *

PIERCE, William L(uther) 1933-2002
    (Andrew MacDonald)

OBITUARY NOTICE—See index for *CA* sketch: Born September 11, 1933, in Atlanta, GA; died of renal failure July 23, 2002, in Mill Point, WV. Activist, publisher, broadcaster, educator, physicist, and author. Pierce gained his greatest notoriety as the author of the novel *The Turner Diaries,* first published under the pseudonym Andrew MacDonald in 1978. The novel was denounced by the Federal Bureau of Investigation as one of the most dangerous books in America, and Pierce was later vilified as the inspiration for the bombing of the Oklahoma City federal building by Timothy McVeigh in 1995. Pierce had worked in the 1960s as a physics teacher at Oregon State University and as a scientist at a jet propulsion laboratory; his novel has been described as a textbook for making and detonating explosives. Pierce spread a radical message of white supremacy via his neo-Nazi organization, the National Alliance. *The Turner Diaries* was originally published as a serial in Pierce's newspaper, *Attack,* through which he promoted his vision of America as a white homeland devoid of African Americans, Jews, and other minorities. He also presented a weekly short-wave radio program, *American Dissident Voices,* owned a publishing company called National Vanguard Books, and operated Resistance Records, which some have called one of the world's biggest distributors of hate-based music. Pierce's supporters insisted that his message was not one of violence and hatred for minorities, but rather a statement of his passionate love for white American culture; others found little distinction between the two. For many years, the bulk of Pierce's writing was nonfiction, but the success of *The Turner Diaries* convinced him, he once told *CA,* that he could reach a wider audience through fiction. He published his second novel, *Hunter,* in 1990.

OBITUARIES AND OTHER SOURCES:

PERIODICALS

Chicago Tribune, July 24, 2002, section 2, p. 8.

Los Angeles Times, July 24, 2002, obituary by Jeffrey Gettleman, p. B10.

New York Times, July 24, 2002, obituary by David Cay Johnston, p. A16.

Times (London, England), August 16, 2002.

Washington Post, July 24, 2002, p. 35.

*   *   *

PLESHAKOV, Constantine 1959-

PERSONAL: Born September 18, 1959, in Yalta, Crimea, USSR. (now Russia); permanent resident of the United States; son of Elza Bilenko (an editor); children: Anton and Anna (twins). *Ethnicity:* "Russian." *Education:* Attended Moscow State University, 1982; Soviet Academy of Sciences, Ph.D., 1986 and 1994.

ADDRESSES: Office—Department of History, Mount Holyoke College, South Hadley, MA 01075. *E-mail*—cpleshak@mtholyoke.edu.

CAREER: Institute for United States and Canada Studies, Moscow, USSR, affiliate, including director of Geopolitics and Pacific Studies Center, 1982-96; freelance researcher and writer, 1996-98; Mount Holyoke College, South Hadley, MA, visiting professor, 1998—.

AWARDS, HONORS: Lionel Gelber Prize (with Vladislav Zubok), 1996, for *Inside the Kremlin's Cold War: From Stalin to Khrushchev.*

WRITINGS:

(With Vladislav Zubok) *Inside the Kremlin's Cold War: From Stalin to Khrushchev,* Harvard University Press (Cambridge, MA), 1996.

(With John Curtis Perry) *The Flight of the Romanovs: A Family Saga,* Basic Books (New York, NY), 1999.

The Tsar's Last Armada: The Epic Voyage to the Battle of Tsushima, Basic Books (New York, NY), 2002.

Author of seven novels and one short-story collection, all published in Moscow, Russia, 1992—.

WORK IN PROGRESS: Research for *From Russia with Love.*

SIDELIGHTS: Constantine Pleshakov told *CA*: "Growing up in a totalitarian society is in itself an excellent motivation for an author. You can't speak up, but you can write. You can't read what you want, but you can write. Also, the environment teaches you to take nothing for granted."

BIOGRAPHICAL AND CRITICAL SOURCES:

PERIODICALS

Booklist, April 15, 1996, Gilbert Taylor, review of *Inside the Kremlin's Cold War: From Stalin to Khrushchev,* p. 1417; October 1, 1999, Joe Collins, review of *The Flight of the Romanovs: A Family Saga,* p. 341; March 1, 2002, Gilbert Taylor, review of *The Tsar's Last Armada: The Epic Voyage to the Battle of Tsushima,* p. 1080.

Contemporary Review, September, 2002, review of *The Tsar's Last Armada,* p. 183.

Foreign Affairs, July-August, 1996, Robert Levgold, review of *Inside the Kremlin's Cold War,* p. 153.

History, spring, 1998, Richard W. Shyrock, review of *Inside the Kremlin's Cold War,* p. 162; fall, 1999, Victor Rosenberg, review of *The Flight of the Romanovs,* p. 30.

Kirkus Reviews, January 15, 2002, review of *The Tsar's Last Armada,* p. 91.

Library Journal, July, 1999, Robert H. Johnston, review of *The Flight of the Romanovs,* p. 111; February 15, 2002, Mark Ellis, review of *The Tsar's Last Armada,* p. 160.

National Interest, winter, 1997, Robert Jervis, review of *Inside the Kremlin's Cold War,* p. 82.

New Leader, August 12, 1996, Robert V. Daniels, review of *Inside the Kremlin's Cold War,* p. 19.

Political Science Quarterly, summer, 1997, Marshall D. Shulman, review of *Inside the Kremlin's Cold War,* p. 311.

Publishers Weekly, June 7, 1999, review of *The Flight of the Romanovs,* p. 64; April 1, 2002, review of *The Tsar's Last Armada,* p. 66.

*   *   *

PORTER, Roy S. 1946-2002

OBITUARY NOTICE—See index for *CA* sketch: Born December 31, 1948, in Hitchin, England; died of a heart attack March 3, 2002, in St. Leonards-on-the-Sea, England. Historian, educator, and author. Porter was a prolific author of popular yet erudite history books. He attended Christ College, Cambridge where he earned his bachelor's degree in 1968 and a Ph.D. in 1974. After graduating, Porter stayed at Cambridge, joining Christ's College in 1970 as a research fellow and becoming director of studies in history at Churchill College in 1972 and dean in 1977. He left that institution in 1979 to go to the Wellcome Institute for the History of Medicine at the University of London, where he was a senior lecturer from 1979 to 1991, a reader from 1991 to 1993, and a professor of the social history of medicine until his early retirement in 2001. Porter was remarkable in his ability to write on a wide range of topics, including social history, medical history, geology, psychology, and the Enlightenment. His book *London: A Social History* was very popular and won the *Los Angeles Times* Book Award for History in 1998; and his *Enlightenment: Britain and the Creation of the Modern World* (2000), was awarded the Wolfson Prize for history and was adapted for British television. Porter's interest in medicine and psychology led to such books as *A Social History of Madness: Stories of the Insane, Health for Sale: Quakery in England, 1660-1850,* and *The Greatest Benefit to Mankind: A Medical History of Humanity.* In addition to his authored books, Porter also edited and coedited over fifty other works, including *The Cambridge History of Science* (2001).

OBITUARIES AND OTHER SOURCES:

BOOKS

Who's Who 2000, St. Martin's Press (New York, NY), 2000.

PERIODICALS

Guardian (London, England), March 5, 2002, p. 18.
Independent (London, England), March 6, 2002, p. 6.
Los Angeles Times, March 9, 2002, p. B17.
New York Times, March 13, 2002, p. A24.
Times (London, England), March 6, 2002, p. 37.
Washington Post, March 17, 2002, p. C6.

*   *   *

PRINGLE, Eric

PERSONAL: Born in Morpeth, Northumberland, England; son of Ernest (a farmer) and Hannah Pringle; married Pat Baker; children: David, Susannah. *Education:* University of Nottingham, B.A. (English and American literature; with honors). *Religion:* Protestant. *Hobbies and other interests:* Walking, music, traveling, reader, theater, history.

ADDRESSES: Agent—Cecily Ware Literary Agents, 19C John Spencer Sq. Cannonbury, London N1 2LZ, England. *E-mail*—childrenspublicity@bloomsbury. com.

CAREER: Freelance author and playwright. Previously worked in various occupations, including insurance sales, farming, and teaching.

AWARDS, HONORS: Sony "Gold" Radio Academy Award, for *Hymns Paradisi.*

WRITINGS:

Dr. Who, The Awakening (based on the BBC television serial by Pringle), W. H. Allen (London, England), 1985.
Big George (for children), illustrated by Collin Paine, Annick Press (Toronto, Ontario, Canada), 2001.
Big George and the Seventh Knight (for children), illustrated by Collin Paine, Bloomsbury (London, England), 2002.

Creator and writer of the *Dr. Who* series televised by BBC; author of numerous television and radio plays.

SIDELIGHTS: Eric Pringle related to *CA* that his "love for history has been behind quite a few of my plays, and now *Big George.* To me, history is real and not just an academic subject—we too, will one day be history—and I love to imagine myself in other times and places with real people. Hence, the medieval background of *Big George.* And in one way the character of the alien, George, looking at this savage world and trying to make sense of it, is me."

BIOGRAPHICAL AND CRITICAL SOURCES:

PERIODICALS

Kirkus Reviews, October 15, 2001, review of *Big George,* p. 1490.
School Librarian, autumn, 2001, Teresa Scragg, review of *Big George,* p. 146.

R

RAYNER, Richard 1955-

PERSONAL: Born 1955, in Bradford, England; married; wife's name Paivi; children: Harry, Charlie. *Education:* Graduated from Cambridge University, 1977.

ADDRESSES: Home—Venice, CA. *Agent*—Jeff Posternak, The Wylie Agency Inc., 250 West 57th Street, New York, NY 10107.

CAREER: Writer.

WRITINGS:

The Elephant, Turtle Bay Books (New York, NY), 1992.
The Blue Suit: A Memoir of a Crime, Houghton Mifflin (Boston, MA), 1995.
Murder Book, Houghton Mifflin (Boston, MA), 1997.
Los Angeles without a Map, Houghton Mifflin (Boston, MA), 1997.
The Cloud Sketcher, HarperCollins (New York, NY), 2001.
Drake's Fortune: The Fabulous Story of the World's Greatest Confidence Artist, Doubleday (New York, NY), 2002.

WORK IN PROGRESS: A novel tentatively titled *The Devil's Wind,* set in 1950s California, about the House Un-American Activities Committee, be-bop, and European émigrés.

SIDELIGHTS: Richard Rayner, in an interview with Penelope Rowlands for *Publishers Weekly,* made it very clear that all of his writing is autobiographical. "The story of my childhood is very much the story" in his 1995 memoir *The Blue Suit: A Memoir of a Crime.* As described in that book, his car-salesman father really did sell £100,000 worth of cars, then absconded with the money rather than reimbursing the manufacturer. Rayner's father faked his own death, vanishing abroad for a decade, only to reappear when the author was an undergraduate. "Obviously he was a mythic figure for me," Rayner says of his father, who died—for real this time—in 1991.

After graduating from Cambridge University in 1977, Rayner worked for *Time Out* magazine in London, "a sex and drugs and rock and roll sort of place," he said, where he eventually became an editor. "One was able to invent spurious reasons to do a story," he recalls. "I kept finding reasons to come to L.A." He eventually wrote about that city in his 1988 book *Los Angeles without a Map,* in which, accompanied by his new *Playboy* Bunny-girlfriend Barbara, he meets a wide variety of eccentric Californians. Romance and Hollywood become one long reel of disillusionment. "I thought how few genuinely fat people I'd seen in California," he writes. "Where did they go? Perhaps there was a state ordinance against obesity. Perhaps sleek, surf-Nazi police would arrive in the middle of the night, herd the fatties in to cattle trucks, and dump them in Oregon. Or Nevada." One of the Californians he meets, a James Dean memorabilia collector, owns a script of *Rebel without a Cause* bound in human skin. Jess Cagel commented in *People Weekly,* "One is never sure how much of this book is fiction and how much is based on fact, and Rayner, a British journalist, isn't saying. He does, however, draw a reader in by picking up on some telling details and characters, making L.A. sound like somewhere nobody would want to live or visit."

Although Rayner's first novel, *The Elephant,* received critical praise, the author remembers the work as being plagued by first-novel mistakes. "It was autobiographical and kind of undisciplined," he told *Publishers Weekly.* Rayner's real life father-son reconciliation is told through the character of Jack Hamer, a ladies' man who works as an undertaker in Bradford, England. He embezzles a sizable amount of money in empty coffins, fakes his own death, and sixteen years later returns home, much to the astonishment of his adult son, a journalist who is also a talented liar. Together again, the two compete against each other in seducing women, but by the end of the novel the son has broken free of his father and is ready to forge his own life. A reviewer for *Publishers Weekly* noted, "Rayner manages to transform this self-conscious, protean narrator into an ordinary man who tells a moving truth."

Rayner's next book, *The Blue Suit: A Memoir of a Crime,* was written as memoir and recounts how the college-aged author began shoplifting first editions of his favorite books, then forging checks and, eventually, breaking into houses. Donna Steffens commented in *Entertainment Weekly,* "Rayner's conversational, comic writing is reminiscent of a youthful Martin Amis, and you can't help but admire how this stone-hearted criminal carves out his own path of savage humor and fierce irony. Rayner's just a smart, funny bloke, telling you his life story over a pint of Guinness at the corner pub, and making you laugh your head off."

Rayner considers himself fortunate to have avoided jail (he was arrested only once, while shoplifting a book). "More clinical than apologetic in his flashbacks, Rayner fleshes out his horrors, adding a sometimes vicious mother to his psychohistory. He proceeded as an apprentice journalist and failed novelist in London; he consorted—even in crime—with a high-born woman married to a junkie," wrote a reviewer for *Publishers Weekly,* "It was good fortune in life, not any moral epiphany, that eased him out of crime. Now in L.A. and a new relationship, he has liberated his family secrets and personal demons."

Despite his personal background as a thief, Rayner worked the police beat for a time, covering the 1992 L.A. riots for *Granta* magazine and later writing a *New York Times Magazine* cover story about the Los Angeles Police Department. Some of the experiences he had during this time entered into the writing of his crime novel *Murder Book,* in which the main character is Billy McGrath, an LAPD homicide detective with a philosophical bent. Although McGrath is the top homicide detective in the city, his marriage has collapsed and he is desperately short of money. After the mother of a major drug dealer is murdered, the dealer, Ricky Lee Richards, promises McGrath half a million dollars if he will bring him the murderer. A heretofore honest cop, McGrath agrees, but raises the price of the delivery to one million dollars. A reviewer for *Publishers Weekly* commented, "While Rayner's prose is occasionally too hardboiled, as if it's parodying pulp detective novels, these missteps are rare. Mostly the novel has just the right punch, and its' portraits of the contemporary American city gone bad are oddly moving."

Based on the success of *Murder Book,* Rayner signed a contract for his next novel, *The Cloud Sketcher,* and started writing. The project changed one night when Rayner's wife Paivi told him about the business deal that went with future bestseller *The Horse Whisperer.* She came back one night and said "there's 200 pages of this novel and they're getting $1 million for it." He decided to "write big" and aim for a blockbuster. Rayner threw himself into researching *The Cloud Sketcher,* reading numerous books, touring famous skyscrapers and poring over other material as well as the history of his wife's native Finland.

Set in Finland around the time of the Russian Revolution, and later in 1920s New York, *The Cloud Sketcher* is equal parts history of an era, thriller, and crime novel. The protagonist, Esko, is a Finnish man born during the Russian Civil War whose passion for architecture turns into a desire to build skyscrapers. The book was partly inspired by works of architecture, including Finnish architect Eero Saarinen's Art Nouveau-style train station in Helsinki. "I'd always been struck by that building," Rayner says. He was also impressed by the Finnish architect himself, who, already world famous and in his 50s, headed off to the United States to start a new life. Rayner acknowledges debts to two favorite novels: Ayn Rand's *The Fountainhead* and Boris Pasternak's *Doctor Zhivago,* which he loves for its "gorgeous romanticism."

In *Drake's Fortune: The Fabulous True Story of the World's Greatest Confidence Artist,* Rayner chronicles the true story of Oscar Hartzell, a failed Illinois farmer who managed to convince thousands of credulous Midwesterners that they would be given a share of Sir Frances Drake's fortune if they donated to a legal fund set up on behalf of the famous explorer's American heirs. Of course, Hartzell claimed that even very small donations would yield enormous returns. At the height of the scam, he was receiving tens of thousands of dollars a day at the American Exchange office in London, where he claimed to be in negotiations with genealogical experts and government officials. He lived the high life in London for years, until Scotland Yard built enough of a case against him to have him deported back to Sioux City to stand trial for fraud. Despite his speedy conviction, the majority of those he'd fleeced remained convinced he was going to deliver their shares of Drake's fortune, and, amazingly, continued to send him money. A contributor to *Publishers Weekly* noted that Rayner's "account of Hartzell's life and times is brisk and breezy, a terrifically entertaining read, and the author's obvious fascination with his subject is infectious. But this is more than just a gripping tale: Rayner also laces his narrative with savvy commentary—including insights into the psyches of swindler and victim alike—that helps explain why cons like Hartzell occupy such a place in American history."

BIOGRAPHICAL AND CRITICAL SOURCES:

PERIODICALS

Booklist, June, 1988, review of *Los Angeles without a Map,* p. 20; September 15, 1995, review of *The Blue Suit: A Memoir of a Crime,* p. 148; November 15, 2000, Brian Kenney, review of *The Cloud Sketcher,* p. 588.
Books, July, 1992, review of *The Elephant,* p. 17.
Cosmopolitan, January, 1989, Louise Bernikow, review of *Los Angeles without a Map,* p. 22.
Entertainment Weekly, January 12, 1996, Daneet Steffens, review of *The Blue Suit,* p. 52; August 1, 1997, review of *The Blue Suit,* p. 67.
Guardian, July 27, 1995, Peter Lennon, article on Richard Raynor, p. S4.
Guardian Weekly, June 4, 1989, review of *Los Angeles without a Map,* p. 29.

Hungry Minds Review, Winter, 1997, review of *Los Angeles without a Map,* p. 41.
Kirkus Reviews, October 15, 1988, review of *Los Angeles without a Map,* p. 1490; December 15, 1991, review of *The Elephant,* p. 1554; August 1, 1995, review of *The Blue Suit,* p. 1089; September 1, 1997, review of *Murder Book,* p. 1335.
Library Journal, January, 1989, Timothy L. Zindel, review of *Los Angeles without a Map,* p. 103; February 15, 1992, Brian Kenney, review of *The Elephant,* p. 197; August, 1995, Jim Burns, review of *The Blue Suit,* p. 84.
Listener, June 16, 1988, review of *Los Angeles without a Map,* p. 32.
London Review of Books, June 27, 1991, review of *The Elephant,* p. 18; October 19, 1995, review of *The Blue Suit,* p. 39.
Los Angeles Times Book Review, November 12, 1995, review of *The Blue Suit,* p. 1; October 19, 1997, review of *Murder Book,* p. 12.
Nation, December 4, 1995, review of *The Blue Suit,* p. 84.
People Weekly, May 22, 1989, Jess Cagle, review of *Los Angeles without a Map,* p. 29; December 4, 1995, Louisa Ermelino, review of *The Blue Suit,* p. 30; November 3, 1997, Pam Lambert, review of *Murder Book,* p. 40.
Publishers Weekly, October 21, 1988, Sybil Steinberg, review of *Los Angeles without a Map,* p. 49; December 15, 1989, review of *Los Angeles without a Map,* p. 62; January 6, 1992, review of *The Elephant,* p. 48; August 7, 1995, review of *The Blue Suit,* p. 449; November 27, 2000, John F. Baker, article on Richard Rayner.
Times Literary Supplement, July 29, 1988, review of *Los Angeles without a Map,* p. 827; May 24, 1991, David Montrose, review of *The Elephant,* p. 21; July 14, 1995, Phil Baker, review of *The Blue Suit,* p. 7.

OTHER

January Magazine, http://januarymagazine.com/ (March 28, 2002), Margaret Gunning, review of *The Cloud Sketcher,* p. C02.
Mystery Reader.com, http://www.mysteryreader.com/ (March 28, 2002), Jeri Wright, review of *The Cloud Sketcher,* p. C02.*

REISER, Lynn (Whisnant) 1944-

PERSONAL: Born July 28, 1944, in Charlotte, NC; daughter of Ward William (a businessman) and Susan Richardson (a college professor; maiden name, Carpenter) Whisnant; married Morton F. Reiser (a physician, professor, psychoanalyst, and author), December 19, 1976. *Education:* Duke University, B.S., 1966; Yale Medical School, M.D., 1970, psychiatric residency, 1970-75; Western New England Institute for Psychoanalysis, psychoanalytic training, 1976-85. *Hobbies and other interests:* Watercolor painting, gardening, cats and dogs, nature.

ADDRESSES: Home—99 Blake Rd., Hamden, CT 06517. *Office*—Department of Psychiatry, Yale Medical School, 25 Park St., New Haven, CT 06511.

CAREER: Yale University School of Medicine, New Haven, CT, assistant clinical professor, 1975-84, associate clinical professor, 1984-94, clinical professor, 1994—, director of undergraduate education in psychiatry, 1985—. Private practice in psychiatry and psychoanalysis, 1975—; author and illustrator of children's books, 1991—. Research fellow under Dr. Myrna Weissman, Yale University School of Epidemiology and Public Health, 1976-77; member of clinic committee, 1988—, faculty, 1991—, and board of trustees, 1993—, Western New England Psychoanalytic Institute; member, Center for Advanced Psychoanalytic Studies at Aspen, 1992—, and at Princeton, 1993—. Member, Muriel Gardiner Program in Psychoanalysis and the Humanities, and fellow, Davenport College, both Yale University.

MEMBER: International Psychoanalytic Association, American Psychiatric Association (fellow, 1986), American Psychoanalytic Association, American College of Psychoanalysts (fellow, 1990; board of regents, 1992—), Association of Academic Psychiatry, American Board of Psychiatry and Neurology (examiner, 1980—), Western New England Psychoanalytic Society (treasurer, 1989-91), Sigma Xi.

AWARDS, HONORS: Peter Parker Research fellowship, 1968; Connecticut Heart Association Research Award, 1968; Falk Fellowship, American Psychiatric Association, 1972-74; Lustman Research Prize, Yale University Department of Psychiatry, 1974; *Dog and Cat* was selected for the Child Study Children's Book Committee List of Children's Books of the Year, 1991; *Any Kind of Dog* was selected as Picture Book Honor Book, Parent's Choice Award, 1992; Nancy C. A. Roeske, M.D., Certificate of Recognition for Excellence in Medical Student Education, American Psychiatric Association, 1992.

WRITINGS:

PICTURE BOOKS; SELF-ILLUSTRATED, EXCEPT AS NOTED

Dog and Cat, Greenwillow (New York, NY), 1991.
Bedtime Cat, Greenwillow (New York, NY), 1991.
Any Kind of Dog, Greenwillow (New York, NY), 1992.
Christmas Counting, Greenwillow (New York, NY), 1992.
Tomorrow on Rocky Pond, Greenwillow (New York, NY), 1993.
Margaret and Margarita/Margarita y Margaret, Greenwillow (New York, NY), 1993.
The Surprise Family, Greenwillow (New York, NY), 1994.
Two Mice in Three Fables, Greenwillow (New York, NY), 1995.
Night Thunder and the Queen of the Wild Horses, Greenwillow (New York, NY), 1995.
Beach Feet, Greenwillow (New York, NY), 1996.
Best Friends Think Alike, Greenwillow (New York, NY), 1997.
Cherry Pies and Lullabies, Greenwillow (New York, NY), 1998.
(With translator Rebecca Hart) *Tortillas and Lullabies/ Tortillas y Cancioncitas,* illustrated by Corazones Valientes, Greenwillow (New York, NY), 1998.
Little Clam, Greenwillow (New York, NY), 1998.
Earthdance, Greenwillow (New York, NY), 1999.
My Dog Truffle, Greenwillow (New York, NY), 2000.
My Cat Tuna: A Book about the Five Senses, Greenwillow (New York, NY), 2000.
(With M. J. Infante) *The Lost Ball/La Pelota Perdida,* Greenwillow (New York, NY), 2002.
Ten Puppies, Greenwillow (New York, NY), 2003.

OTHER

Also contributor of "Two Mice," to *First Grade Reading Program,* D. C. Heath, 1994. Illustrator of *Making Yourself at Home in Charlotte, North Carolina,* by

Susan Whisnant, published yearly since 1972. Author, as Lynn Whisnant Reiser, of medical and professional articles on psychiatry, psychoanalysis, and medical education.

ADAPTATIONS: Margaret and Margarita/Margarita y Margaret was adapted for audio cassette, read by Chloë Patellis, with music by Jeff Wasman, Scholastic, 1993, and *Any Kind of Dog* was adapted for audio cassette, Live Oak Media, 1996.

SIDELIGHTS: A respected psychiatrist and educator, Lynn Reiser is also a prolific author and illustrator of children's picture books, averaging two books a year for over a decade. As one might expect of a person in her medical line of work, among her titles are books that treat relationships among family and friends, but she has also published animal tales and celebrations of nature. Her illustrations, varying in complexity from simple line drawings to watercolor paintings and photograph-painting hybrids, reflect the maturity of her intended audience, which ranges from toddlers to grade-school students.

In her first published effort, *Dog and Cat,* Reiser portrays the meeting of a restless dog and his neighbor, a drowsy cat. The dog gets more than he bargained for when he heeds his instinct and chases the cat. The cat jumps on him, and with a trick teaches the dog a scary lesson he's unlikely to forget. Reiser "deftly presents this bustling confrontation in a cheerful style," to quote a *Publishers Weekly* reviewer. Among other enthusiasts of Reiser's debut were *Horn Book* reviewer Mary M. Burns, who noted the emphasis on "shape and movement" in the illustrations, which, the reviewer added, are sure to "attract the attention" of young readers. *School Library Journal* contributor Joan McGrath found the story "enlivened by wild and woolly artwork" that reflects the cat-dog synergy.

Reiser followed *Dog and Cat* with a number of other animals stories, including *Bedtime Cat,* about a young girl and her cat's nightly routine, and *Any Kind of Dog,* about that frequently desired pet. All goes well in *Dog and Cat* until bedtime, when the cat, who sleeps with a girl, disappears. While the anxiety builds, the girl and her parents search for the cat without success. The girl returns to her bed, only to find the cat under a blanket, right where it has been all along. Reviewers noted the work's child appeal in its text

and pen-and-ink and watercolor illustrations: "The simple, childlike pictures and text are just right for this small but universal drama," remarked Carolyn K. Jenks in *Horn Book,* and a *Kirkus Reviews* writer credited the book with "real sensitivity to the child's world," and remarked on the sense of security it evoked in its recitation of the girl's routine. Similarly, Liza Bliss commended the book's simplified artwork, calling it "just right" in her *School Library Journal* review.

In *Any Kind of Dog* Richard begs his mother for a dog. She refuses but instead presents Richard with a series of substitute pets, which do not satisfy the boy, reminding him instead of different dog breeds. When each of these other pets (both real and imaginary) causes its own brand of trouble, Richard's mother gives in, and he gets his dog. Again, reviewers found the illustrations apt; yet they noted the book's humor as well. According to a *Kirkus Reviews* critic, the art is "unpretentious but amusingly expressive." The "boldly colored pictures filled with funny details embellish the text nicely," to quote Anna Biagioni Hart in *School Library Journal.* Both *School Library Journal* reviewer Fritz Mitnick and a *Publishers Weekly* reviewer pointed out that the repetitive text has toddler appeal. Other dog-cat books for the pre-reader include Reiser's lift-the-flap books *My Cat Tuna: A Book about the Five Senses* and *My Dog Truffle,* both of which treat the same topic, and *Ten Puppies.*

Relationship books form an important part of Reiser's oeuvre. In *The Surprise Family* Reiser tells how when a chick that has been raised by a boy grows up, she in turn raises a clutch of ducklings. Although the plot could appeal particularly to adoptive families, the theme is universal: Love transcends boundaries and labels. *School Library Journal* reviewer Beth Tegart praised the work as a "delightful story," and *Booklist* critic Mary Harris Veeder dubbed it a "graceful fable" that is "well served by" Reiser's signature illustrations. Reiser further simplified her artwork in *Best Friends Think Alike.* She drew line drawings in red and blue marker, each color representing the thoughts of one friend, a technique that Susan Dove Lempke described in *Booklist* as "ingenious." While the thoughts of Ruby are pictured in red, her best friend Beryl's thoughts are pictured in blue; unfortunately at their upcoming play date, they both want to be the horse in their game of horse and rider. A negotiation and resolution follow that preschoolers, according to Roger Sutton in *Horn*

Book, "should appreciate." Even boundaries of language can be overcome for the sake of friendship, according to Reiser's *Margaret and Margarita/ Margarita y Margaret.* About two young girls who visit the park with their mothers, the tale is told in mirror images. On each left page the text is in English in red ink, while on the right it is in Spanish in blue ink. By the end of the story, however, the girls have become friends and the text merges over the double-page spread. Such a work could be judged on its merits as a story and as a means of teaching Spanish.

The author continues to explore expressions of affection, including traditions passed down from generation to generation, in her more recent books. In 1998 she published *Cherry Pies and Lullabies* and its Spanish-English analog, *Tortillas and Lullabies.* In each, generations of women show their affection for each other by making the food item of the title and doing other necessary tasks. Readers see that, over time, some details of life change, but not the love behind the efforts, and the simple and repetitive text reflects the unchanging nature of love. Reiser illustrated *Cherry Pies and Lullabies* with her own cartoon-like, pen-and-watercolor illustrations. Although *Horn Book* reviewer Roger Sutton believed the illustrations "resist emotional resonance," Mirta Ojito praised them in the *New York Times Book Review,* describing them as "gorgeous pictures" and "exquisitely detailed full-page illustrations." However, after seeing a Peace Corps exhibit of work by "Valiant Hearts (Corazones Valientes)," a Costa Rican cooperative, Reiser opted to have this group illustrate *Tortillas and Lullabies* with colorful paintings stylized in a Hispanic fashion. In this version, Reiser shows different activities being passed down from generation to generation, activities that reflect life in rural Central or South America rather than that of Caucasians or Hispanics in the United States. Because of this, Ojito suggested that Reiser was supporting the erroneous stereotype that modern Hispanic mothers fulfill more traditional women's roles than do American women of other ethnicities.

In a number of books, Reiser gives readers the opportunity to enjoy nature vicariously. In *Tomorrow on Rocky Pond* she explores a young girl's anticipation on the eve of a family vacation, when the family will fish at Rocky Pond. This ritual includes a special breakfast, clothes, the journey to the pond, and finally the fishing. Text and artwork work well together, several reviewers noted. The text "aptly portrays the

eagerness of the girl," wrote *Booklist* reviewer Christie Sylvester, while in *School Library Journal* Susan Hepler remarked, "Reiser's precise watercolor and black line illustrations clarify details and evoke emotions." With *Beach Feet,* which is about various sea creatures with different kinds of feet, and *Little Clam,* which concerns the clam' self-defense mechanisms, Reiser brings the ocean home.

Reiser continues her celebration of nature in a larger context with *Earthdance,* a lyrical introduction to the solar system. In verse and illustrations that combine drawings and photographs of earth as seen from outer space, she tells of how a girl named Terra dances the lead role in the school production of "Earthdance," while her astronaut mother takes to the skies. Reviewers pointed out the work's strong and weak points. Although *Booklist*'s Susan Dove Lempke and a *Kirkus Reviews* critic noted errors in the scientific content, the latter critic called the picture book "charming." Finding the work successful over all, Tina Hudak praised Reiser's "imaginative approach" in *School Library Journal.*

BIOGRAPHICAL AND CRITICAL SOURCES:

PERIODICALS

Booklist, May 1, 1992, Denia Hester, review of *Any Kind of Dog,* pp. 1609-1610; August, 1993, Christie Sylvester, review of *Tomorrow on Rocky Pond,* p. 2071; September 15, 1993, Janice Del Negro, review of *Margarita y Margaret/Margaret and Margarita,* p. 160; June 1, 1994, Mary Harris Veeder, review of *The Surprise Family,* p. 1844; March 1, 1995; Lauren Peterson, review of *Two Mice in Three Fables,* p. 1249; October 15, 1995, Kay Weisman, review of *Night Thunder and the Queen of the Wild Horses,* p. 90; June 1, 1997, Susan Dove Lempke, review of *Best Friends Think Alike,* p. 1721; March 1, 1998, Shelley Townsend-Hudson, review of *Cherry Pies and Lullabies,* p. 1141; April, 1998, Susan Dove Lempke, review of *Tortillas and Lullabies/Tortillas y Cancioncitas,* p. 1333; August, 1998, John Peters, review of *Little Clam,* p. 2016; December 1, 1999, Susan Dove Lempke, review of *Earthdance,* p. 713.

Horn Book, May-June, 1991, Carolyn K. Jenks, review of *Bedtime Cat,* p. 321, Mary M. Burns, review of *Dog and Cat,* p. 321; September-October, 1993;

March-April, 1997, Roger Sutton, review of *Best Friends Think Alike*, pp. 194-195; May, 1998, Roger Sutton, review of *Cherry Pies and Lullabies*, pp. 335-336; September-October, 1998, Susan P. Bloom, review of *Little Clam*, pp. 599-600; March, 2001, J.R.L., reviews of *My Dog Truffle* and *My Cat Tuna*, p. 201.

Horn Book Guide, fall, 1996, Suzy Schmidt, review of *Beach Feet*, p. 272; fall, 2001, Joanna Rudge Long, reviews of *My Cat Tuna* and *My Dog Truffle*, p. 239.

Kirkus Reviews, February 1, 1992, review of *Any Kind of Dog*; February 15, 1992, review of *Bedtime Cat*, p. 251; June 1, 1994; April 1, 1998, review of *Cherry Pies and Lullabies*, p. 500, and review of *Tortillas and Lullabies/Tortillas y Cancioncitas*, p. 501; July 15, 1999, review of *Earthdance*, p. 1138.

Language Arts, November, 1996, Miriam Martinez and Marcia Nash, review of *Beach Feet*, p. 522.

New York Times Book Review, September 20, 1998, Mirta Ojito, reviews of *Cherry Pies and Lullabies* and *Tortillas and Lullabies*, p. 32.

Publishers Weekly, January 18, 1991, review of *Dog and Cat*, p. 57; March 9, 1992, review of *Any Kind of Dog*, p. 56; September 7, 1992, Elizabeth Devereaux, review of *Christmas Counting*, p. 67; May 31, 1993, review of *Tomorrow on Rocky Pond*, p. 53; September 25, 1995, review of *Night Thunder and the Queen of the Wild Horses*, p. 56; February 2, 1998, review of *Cherry Pies and Lullabies*, p. 90; September 14, 1998, review of *Little Clam*, p. 68; January 22, 2001, "Experience the Seasons," p. 326.

School Library Journal, May, 1991, Liza Bliss, review of *Bedtime Cat*, p. 82; June, 1991, Joan McGrath, review of *Dog and Cat*, pp. 88-89; June, 1992, Anna Biagioni Hart, review of *Any Kind of Dog*, p. 102; October, 1992; September, 1993, Susan Hepler, review of *Tomorrow on Rocky Pond*, p. 218; July, 1994, Beth Tegart, review of *The Surprise Family*, pp. 87-88; August, 1994, Rose Zertuche Trevino, review of *Margarita y Margaret*, p. 182; April, 1995, Jane Marino, review of *Two Mice in Three Fables*, pp. 114, 116; December, 1995, Meg Stackpole, review of *Night Thunder and the Queen of the Wild Horses*, p. 90; February, 1997, Fritz Mitnick, review of *Any Kind of Dog* (audio version), p. 70; May, 1997, Marianne Saccardi, review of *Best Friends Think Alike*, pp. 111-112; April, 1998, Denise E. Agosto, review of *Tortillas and Lullabies*, p. 108; September, 1998,

Lisa S. Murphy, review of *Cherry Pies and Lullabies*, p. 180; November 1, 1998, Shelley Woods, review of *Little Clam*, p. 92; October, 1999, Tina Hudak, review of *Earthdance*, p. 123; March, 2001, DeAnn Tabuchi, reviews of *My Cat Tuna* and *My Dog Truffle*, p. 219.

Science Books and Films, December, 1996, Frank M. Truesdale, review of *Beach Feet*, p. 275.

Teaching Children Mathematics, David J. Whitin, review of *Beach Feet*, p. 294.*

*   *   *

REISS, Bob
(Ethan Black)

PERSONAL: Male. *Education:* Northwestern University, B.A. (journalism); University of Oregon, M.F.A.

ADDRESSES: Home—New York, NY. *Agent*—c/o Hyperion Editorial Department, 77 West 66th Street, 11th Floor, New York, NY 10023.

CAREER: Journalist, novelist, and nonfiction author. *Chicago Tribune,* Chicago, IL, reporter; Bread Loaf Conference, Middlebury College, Middlebury, VT, creative writing instructor, eight summers between 1983-95; University of North Carolina, Wilmington, writer-in-residence, 1996, conducted master of fine arts workshop, 1998.

WRITINGS:

NOVELS

Summer Fires: A Novel, Simon & Schuster (New York, NY), 1980.

The Casco Deception, Little, Brown (Boston, MA), 1983.

Divine Assassin, Little, Brown (Boston, MA), 1985.

Saltmaker, Viking (New York, NY), 1988.

Flamingo: A Novel, St. Martin's Press (New York, NY), 1990.

The Last Spy, Simon & Schuster (New York, NY), 1993.

Purgatory Road, Simon & Schuster (New York, NY), 1996.

AS ETHAN BLACK

The Broken Hearts Club, Ballantine Publishing (New York, NY), 1999.

Irresistible, Ballantine Publishing (New York, NY), 2000.

All the Dead Were Strangers, Ballantine Publishing (New York, NY), 2001.

Dead for Life, Ballantine Simon & Schuster (New York, NY), 2003.

NONFICTION

(With Gary Wohl) *Franco Harris* (biography), Tempo Books (New York, NY), 1977.

The Road to Extrema, Summit Books (New York, NY), 1992.

Frequent Flier: One Plane, One Passenger, and the Spectacular Feat of Commercial Flight, Simon & Schuster (New York, NY), 1994.

The Coming Storm: Extreme Weather and Our Terrifying Future, Hyperion (New York, NY), 2001.

Contributor to periodicals, including the *Washington Post, Rolling Stone, Smithsonian, GQ, Mirabella, Parade, Outside,* and *Glamour.* Contributor to books, including *Out of the Noosphere: Adventure, Sports, Travel, and the Environment,* compiled by *Outside* magazine, 1998.

ADAPTATIONS: Film rights for two of his books have been optioned, *The Last Spy* to Paramount and *Purgatory Road* to CinemaLine; a number of Reiss's fiction works have been recorded on audio cassette.

SIDELIGHTS: Bob Reiss is a world traveler, often using his travels to gather information for his articles and books. He has honed his writing skills over the years and now passes on some of the lessons he has learned by teaching writing workshops at various colleges and writers conferences. While primarily known for his novels and nonfiction books, he also publishes thrillers under a pseudonym, Ethan Black. He told a *Campus Communique* reporter that he uses the pseudonym for these thrillers, "since these books are somewhat of a departure from my other books."

Reiss's first book, *Franco Harris,* is a biography for children that he coauthored with Gary Wohl. Harris was a former National Football League running back who played for the Pittsburgh Steelers. The book was part of a series featuring "well-written biographies" emphasizing recent events in the subjects' lives, observed Judith Goldberger in *Booklist.*

From biography, Reiss jumped to fiction, with a murder mystery, *Summer Fires: A Novel,* praised by critics for a first attempt in this genre. The main character is Miles Bradshaw, a man who accidentally set his bed afire, killing his wife and daughter. Prior to this tragedy, Bradshaw was a well-to-do lawyer, but after the fire, he chooses to take on legal cases that help economically deprived people. He ultimately becomes embroiled in a murder mystery when he witnesses a fire that kills a child. A *Publishers Weekly* reviewer called the book an "entertaining and for the most part exciting first novel." William Bradley Hooper, writing in *Booklist,* also enjoyed *Summer Fires* despite "some contrivances" he found to be "glaring." Newgate Callendar stated in the *New York Times Book Review* that *Summer Fires* is "a smashing first novel."

Reiss has also written a suspense novel set in World War II. *The Casco Deception* takes place on Captain's Island, Maine, a site chosen as a hideout by a group of Nazi spies hoping to avoid detection. American-born German-sympathizer John Ryker tries to commandeer a battery of long-range guns but is thwarted by Lt. Tom Heiden, a U.S. soldier stationed at this outpost because he was deemed unfit to serve anywhere else. "The action rises to a fever pitch," wrote a reviewer for *Publishers Weekly,* calling the book "a marvelously suspenseful tale." Rex E. Klett, for *Library Journal,* praised this "strong, intensely absorbing novel" for its "good characterization and plot."

Divine Assassin is allegedly based on real events and real people, namely U.S. hostages held in Iran in the 1980s and Libyan political leader Muammar al-Qaddafi. The story is filled with a lot of "bloody violence and mercilessly detailed tortures," wrote a reviewer for *Publishers Weekly,* but despite this, "the story is timely and it fixes attention on the frustratingly ineffective means of dealing with international terrorists." The protagonist, Tim Currie, seeks revenge for his own hostage experience and for the murder of his girlfriend. He blames Qaddafi for both events and sets out to kill him. A writer for *Booklist* described the plot as "exciting" but "improbable," concluding that the book is a "mind-jarring thriller."

Saltmaker "tackles the ethics of the Bomb," wrote a reviewer for *Kirkus.* In this story, the president of the

United States refuses to retaliate when he learns that the Soviet Union has launched a strike against America, in essence surrendering to the Soviet government. Moments later, U.S. military leaders discover that no attack had been launched. Rather, the Pentagon received false signals as a result of a computer glitch. The president resigns after this event when people begin calling him a traitor for not standing up to the Soviets. Brian Alley for *Library Journal*, like many other critics, found the story somewhat unbelievable. To enjoy this book, readers must "accept that an American President would surrender," Alley wrote, adding that "no strong character or plot emerges" in the book.

Reiss has received mixed reviews for his other novels. The most praised is *The Last Spy*, which a writer for *Kirkus Reviews* called "Reiss's best [thriller] by far." Burke Wilkinson in the *Christian Science Monitor* said *The Last Spy* is "impressive," noted that Reiss "shows a firm grasp of the techniques of international espionage." "A very readable thriller," wrote Albert Wilhelm in *Library Journal*. Reiss "perfectly captures the undercover agent's sense of paranoia," noted a *Publishers Weekly* reviewer.

Reiss's investigative reporting, however, has garnered the most positive overall attention by reviewers of all his writing. *The Road to Extrema* explains how the ongoing destruction of the Amazon rain forest may cause "catastrophic changes in the earth's climate," observed Steve Weingartner in *Booklist*. "Brazil's highway BR-364," noted a writer for *Kirkus Reviews*, "has been called the 'most controversial road in Latin America.'" The road has provided a way for migrant workers to gain access to the jungle and to raise crops there. However, as the *Kirkus Reviews* writer remarked, this road has been "reviled in the States as 'a straw sucking up the Amazon.'" Reiss traveled between the United States and Brazil in his search to find out how ten years of development has affected the Amazon. The *Kirkus Reviews* writer called the account of these travels "captivating and original."

In *Frequent Flier: One Plane, One Passenger, and the Spectacular Feat of Commercial Flight*, Reiss "probes the history, the science, the business, and the human component of the airline industry," wrote David Greising in *Business Week*. In order to find out what keeps a large plane airborne, Reiss took a seventy-two-hour flight with Delta Airlines that transported him from

Atlanta to Salt Lake City to Los Angeles, Honolulu, Dallas, and back home. Reiss really wanted to find out what it was like to fly the plane, so he sat in the cockpit and talked to the pilots, crew, people in the control tower, and in between flights, to the ground crews. "*Frequent Flyer* will entertain anyone who wonders how airlines keep their planes running," said Greising. "Not a book to make nervous fliers any calmer," wrote Denise Perry Donavin in *Booklist*, concluding that the book was "fascinating." A *Kirkus Reviews* writer called the book "an enjoyable history both of commercial aviation and a leading U.S. airline." "Anyone who loves to fly—or anyone who has to fly," said a *Publishers Weekly* reviewer, "should read this comprehensive book."

The Coming Storm: Extreme Weather and Our Terrifying Future is a "carefully documented, intelligently reasoned account," according to David Pitt in *Booklist*. *The Coming Storm* "examines the scientific and political conflict that's been raging since signs of the greenhouse effect appeared in the late 1980s," observed Suzy Hansen in a *Salon.com* interview with Reiss. In 1988 scientist Jim Hansen testified to the U.S. Senate that the so-called greenhouse effect could cause disastrous weather, and it is with Hansen's testimony that Reiss begins his book. Reiss's book includes stories about weather calamities such as the 1993 Mississippi River flood, the 1991 fire that devastated parts of Oakland, California, and the 1995 Chicago heat wave, along with testimony from climatologists. A reviewer for *Publishers Weekly* stated that "Reiss writes in the urgent yet reasoned voice of a person sounding an alarm while there is still time to act."

BIOGRAPHICAL AND CRITICAL SOURCES:

PERIODICALS

Armchair Detective, summer, 1996, S. M. Tyson, review of *Purgatory Road*, p. 377.

Booklist, October 15, 1977, Judith Goldberger, review of *Franco Harris*, p. 318; February 1, 1980, William Bradley Hooper, review of *Summer Fires: A Novel*, p. 757; May 15, 1985, review of *Divine Assassin*, p. 1296; January 15, 1990, Denise Perry Donavin, review of *Flamingo*, p. 976; March 1, 1992, Steve Weingartner, review of *The Road to Extrema*, p. 1184; January 1, 1994, Denise Perry Donavin, review of *Frequent Flyer: One Plane,*

One Passenger, and the Spectacular Feat of Commercial Flight, p. 794; February 1, 1996, George Needham, review of *Purgatory Road,* p. 920; August, 2001, David Pitt, review of *The Coming Storm,* p. 2066.

Business Week, April 11, 1994, David Greising, review of *Frequent Flyer,* p. 17.

Christian Science Monitor, October 7, 1983, Randy Shipp, review of *The Casco Deception,* p. B8; June 7, 1993, Burke Wilkinson, "Heroines, Spies, and Lies," p. 13.

Kirkus Reviews, November 1, 1979, review of *Summer Fires,* p. 1286; May 1, 1985, review of *Divine Assassin,* p. 390; March 1, 1988, review of *Saltmaker,* p. 317; November 1, 1989, review of *Flamingo,* pp. 1557-1558; February 1, 1992, review of *The Road to Extrema,* pp. 168-169; November 1, 1992, review of *The Last Spy,* p. 1331; December 1, 1993, review of *Frequent Flyer,* p. 1509; December 1, 1995, review of *Purgatory Road,* pp. 1662-1663.

Library Journal, May 15, 1983, Rex E. Klett, review of *The Casco Deception,* p. 1018; June 1, 1985, Barbara Conaty, review of *Divine Assassin,* p. 146; May 1, 1988, Brian Alley, review of *Saltmaker,* p. 91; November 15, 1992, Robert H. Donahugh, review of *The Last Spy,* p. 102; August, 2001, Jeffrey Beall, review of *The Coming Storm,* p. 154.

New York Observer, December 3, 2001, Bill McKibbon, review of *Summer Fires,,* p. 18.

New York Times Book Review, January 6, 1980, Newgate Callendar, review of *Summer Fires,* p. 14.

Publishers Weekly, November 26, 1979, review of *Summer Fires,* p. 41; April 1, 1983, review of *The Casco Deception,* p. 51; April 19, 1985, review of *Divine Assassin,* p. 71; November 24, 1989, review of *Flamingo,* p. 62; February 3, 1992, review of *The Road to Extrema,* pp. 73-74; October 19, 1992, review of *The Last Spy,* p. 57; January 17, 1994, review of *Frequent Flyer,* p. 396; January 8, 1996, review of *Purgatory Road,* pp. 58-59; July 23, 2001, review of *The Coming Storm,* p. 61.

Quill & Quire, April, 1990, Paul Stuewe, review of *Flamingo,* p. 29.

Smithsonian, October, 1992, Dee McRae, review of *The Road to Extrema,* p. 170.

Voice of Youth Advocates, February, 1989, Dorothy M. Broderick, review of *Saltmaker,* p. 204.

OTHER

Campus Communique, http://www.uncwil.edu/ (October 7, 1999), "King's Road Writer Series Hosts Reading by Author Bob Reiss."

Salon.com, http://www.salon.com/ (October 23, 2001), Suzy Hansen, "Stormy Weather."*

* * *

RINGER, Alexander L(othar) 1921-2002

OBITUARY NOTICE—See index for *CA* sketch: Born February 3, 1921, in Berlin, Germany; died May 3, 2002, in Lansing, MI. Educator and author. Ringer was a professor of music and an expert on such areas as nineteenth-century music. He studied music in Europe, receiving a bachelor's degree from the University of Amsterdam in 1947, before coming to the United States, where he earned his master's degree in 1949 from the New School for Social Research and a Ph.D. from Columbia University in 1955. He then embarked on a long academic career. During the 1950s he taught music at the City College of the City University of New York, the University of California at Berkeley, and the University of Oklahoma. In 1958 he joined the University of Illinois, where he remained for the rest of his career, becoming emeritus professor in 1991. Always encouraging to his students, Ringer was a well regarded teacher who was also an expert on such composers as Arnold Schoenberg, Harrison Kerr, and George Rochberg, as well as on the music of Hebrew, Middle Eastern, and Dutch cultures. He was the author of several titles, including *Arnold Schoenberg and the Prophetic Image in Music* (1979), *Arnold Schoenberg: The Composer as Jew* (1990), and *Beethoven: Interpretationen seiner Werke* (1994).

OBITUARIES AND OTHER SOURCES:

PERIODICALS

Chicago Tribune, May 11, 2002, section 1, p. 24.

* * *

RIVARD, Adjutor 1868-1945

PERSONAL: Born January 22, 1868, in Saint-Grégoire de Nicolet, Québec, Canada; died July 17, 1945; son of Louis and Pamela (Harper) Rivard; married Joséphine Hamel, 1896; children: Antoine. *Education:* Université Laval, law degree, 1891.

CAREER: Author, lawyer, and linguist. Professor, faculty of arts, Université Laval; founder, with Stanislas A. Lortie, Société du Parler Français au Canada and *Bulletin du Parler Français au Canada;* judge, Québec Court of Appeal, 1921-1941. Batonnier of the provincial bar in 1918.

MEMBER: Royal Society, beginning 1908.

AWARDS, HONORS: Knight of the Order of St. St. Gregory, 1914; Prix Davaine, French Academy, 1920, for fiction writing; Lorne Pierce medal, 1931.

WRITINGS:

Monseigneur de Laval, Roy (Levis, Québec, Canada), 1891.

L'Art de dire: Traité de lecture et de récitation (title means "The Art of Speaking: A Treatise on Reading and Reciting"), Chasse (Québec City, Québec, Canada) 1898.

Manuel de la parole, Garneau (Québec City, Québec, Canada), 1901.

(With Stanislas A. Lortie) *L'Origine et le parler des Canadiens français,* Champion (Paris, France), 1903.

(With James Geddes) *Bibliographie du parler français au Canada,* Marcotte (Québec City, Québec, Canada), 1906.

Etudes sur les parlers de France au Canada, Garneau (Québec City, Québec, Canada), 1914.

Chez nous, L'Action Sociale Catholique, 1914, translation by W.H. Blake published as *Our Old Québec Home,* Doran (New York, NY), 1924.

Chez nos gens (title means "Home of Our People"), L'Action Sociale Catholique (Québec City, Québec, Canada), 1918.

De la liberté de la presse, Garneau (Québec City, Québec, Canada), 1923.

(Editor with Louis-Phillipe Geoffrion) *Glossaire du parler français au Canada,* L'Action Sociale (Québec City, Québec, Canada), 1930.

Manuel de la cour d'appel, Editions Varietes (Montréal, Québec, Canada), 1941.

Contes et propos divers (title means "Stories and Various Remarks"), Garneau (Québec City, Québec, Canada), 1944.

Contributor to publications, including *Bulletin du Parler Français au Canada* and *Proceedings of the Royal Society of Canada.*

SIDELIGHTS: Adjutor Rivard, an award-winning linguist, fiction writer, social critic, and lawyer, was influential in Canada's Québec province early in the twentieth century. "His scientific studies of the French-Canadian language, together with his fictional evocation of traditional French-Canadian values, helped foster pride in Quebec's distinctive culture," Margot Northey wrote in *Dictionary of Literary Biography.* Rivard's best-known fictional works, *Chez Nous* and *Chez nos gens,* were popular among young French-Canadian writers. They contain short sketches and stories about provincial life.

Rivard's parents relocated from Saint-Grégoire de Nicolet to Québec City during his youth. In Québec, he received his primary and secondary education, then his law degree at the Université Laval. During Rivard's early years practicing law in Chicoutimi, Québec, the author was inspired to study language as well, and to teach elocution at a nearby seminary. In 1896, when Rivard married Joséphine Hamel, he began teaching full-time on the faculty of arts at Université Laval. Thus began a career dedicated to his culture, language, and values.

L'Art de dire: Traite de lecture et de recitation includes Rivard's thorough explanation of the basic principles of elocution. Northey, a scholar at the University of Western Ontario, wrote, "[*L'Art de dire*] reveals his characteristic, well-organized approach to language, as does his next work, *Manuel de la parole* (1901), a textbook on phonetics."

In 1902, Rivard and the Right Reverend Stanislas A. Lortie, a genealogist at Séminaire de Québec, founded the Société du Parler Français au Canada and its signature publication, *Bulletin du Parler Français au Canada.* Rivard served as general secretary of the organization, contributing articles, reviews and short stories to its bulletin. He and Lortie also collaborated to write *L'Origine et le parler des Canadiens français,* which outlined the linguistic connections between French-Canadian speech patterns and the regional dialects of France, which early settlers brought to Canada. Northey explained, "Fighting the widespread attitude that the Québec dialect was an inferior form of French, he endorsed many old words and forms of expression that had disappeared in France but survived in Québec."

In 1907, Rivard, who remained a lawyer and social critic throughout his career, founded, with Lortie and

Msgr. Paul-Eugene Roy, L'Action Sociale Catholique, an intellectual forum for social and political issues.

In 1914, Rivard again analyzed the French-Canadian language through its grammar rules, history, and literature. Through meticulous scientific research, he demonstrated how the French-Canadian language had evolved. He applauded change to some extent, suggesting that the language was thriving and vital, but disproved of increasing anglicisms. His goal was to support the language he loved, through from a purist's perspective.

Rivard was influential early in the twentieth century, with a new school of literature devoted to le terroir ("native soil") becoming more popular. His linguistic interests, and his love of French-Canadian history and culture, inspired his fiction during this era. Because of *Chez Nous* and *Chez nos gens,* Rivard was popular among young French-Canadian writers. Both books, Northey said, emphasize rural values and a devotion to the land at a time of increasing urbanization.

Rivard published a legal study, *De la liberte de la presse,* and co-edited *Glossaire du parler français au Canada,* a linguistic text, with Louis-Phillipe Geoffrion. Inspired by his experience as a judge in the Québec court of appeal, he wrote *Manuel de la cour d'appel* in 1941. As he continued to study law, linguistics, and history, more short fiction would follow.

BIOGRAPHICAL AND CRITICAL SOURCES:

BOOKS

Northey, Margot, *Dictionary of Literary Biography, Volume 92: Canadian Writers, 1890-1920,* Gale (Detroit, MI), 1990, pp. 298-300.

PERIODICALS

Canada Français, September, 1945, Arthur Maheux, "Un grand Canadien: Adjutor Rivard," pp. 39-42.
Enseignement Secondaire au Canada, January, 1927, Emile Chartier, "Hommage au parler des aïeux," pp. 505-521.

Journal de L'Instruction Publique, January, 1959, Maurice Lebel, "Adjutor Rivard (1868-1945)," pp. 441-445.

OTHER

Site for Language Management in Canada, http://www.salic-slmc.ca/langues/ (March 7, 2002).
Université Laval Web site, http://www.bibl.ulaval.ca/ (August 7, 2002) "Archives Nationales du Québec à Québec."*

*　　*　　*

RIZZOLO, S(uzanne) K(aye) 1962-

PERSONAL: Born February 10, 1962, in Aspen, CO; daughter of Charles Farmer and Yolanda Jean (Potestio) Pitts; married Michael J. Rizzolo (a television sound producer), June 28, 1992; children: Miranda. *Ethnicity:* "White." *Education:* California State University—Fullerton, B.A.; California State University—Northridge, M.A. *Hobbies and other interests:* Travel, collecting antiques.

ADDRESSES: Home—CA. *Agent*—c/o Author Mail, Poisoned Pen, 6962 East First Ave., Suite 103, Scottsdale, AZ 85251. *E-mail*—rizzolo@earthlink.net.

CAREER: Buckley School, Los Angeles, CA, teacher of British literature, 1990-2002.

MEMBER: Sisters in Crime, Historical Mystery Appreciation Society.

WRITINGS:

The Rose in the Wheel (mystery novel), Poisoned Pen (Scottsdale, AZ), 2000.
Blood for Blood (mystery novel), Poisoned Pen (Scottsdale, AZ), 2003.

SIDELIGHTS: S. K. Rizzolo told *CA:* "There's a sentence in *The Rose in the Wheel,* 'At dusk in Temple Gardens, the barrier between past and present turned fluid and ghosts walked.' I think that historical novelists attempt to make ghosts walk, resurrect the faint voices of the past. The echoes are there, but we have to listen carefully. That's one reason why London continues to be such an inspiring setting for me—all those layers of history.

"Set in 1811 London, my novel, the first in a series, explores the murder of an eccentric lady philanthropist and introduces a large cast of characters from all walks of life. So, unlike many Regency novels, this is not a book about the polished, restrained gentry, a segment of society that in actuality represents only a narrow slice out of the range of experiences at that time. That's why I made my heroine Penelope Wolfe the daughter of an expatriate radical philosopher and the wife of an artist. Her background helps me to get away with some rather unconventional behavior on her part!"

BIOGRAPHICAL AND CRITICAL SOURCES:

PERIODICALS

Publishers Weekly, December 24, 2001, review of *The Rose in the Wheel,* p. 46.

OTHER

S. K. Rizzolo Web site, http://www.skrizzolo.com/ (December 22, 2002).

* * *

ROBERTS, Patricia L(ee) 1936-

PERSONAL: Born 1936, in Coffeyville, KS; daughter of Philip Lee and Lois Ethel (Wortham) Brighton; married James E. Roberts, October 5, 1953; children: James Michael, Jill Frances. *Education:* California State University, Fresno, B.A., 1953, M.A., 1964; University of the Pacific, Ed.D., 1975.

ADDRESSES: Agent—c/o Author Mail, Scarecrow Press, Inc., 4720 Boston Way, Suite A, Lanham, MD 20706.

CAREER: California State University, Sacramento, professor of education, 1969—.

MEMBER: International Reading Association, National Council for Research on English.

AWARDS, HONORS: Cited among distinguished alumnae of the year, University of the Pacific, 1975-76.

WRITINGS:

Counting Books Are More than Numbers: An Annotated Action Bibliography, Library Professional Publications (Hamden, CT), 1990.

Alphabet: A Handbook of ABC Books and Book Extensions for the Elementary Classroom, 2nd edition, Scarecrow Press (Lanham, MD), 1994.

Developing Multicultural Awareness through Children's Literature: A Guide for Teachers and Librarians, McFarland (Jefferson, NC), 1994.

Integrating Language Arts and Social Studies for Kindergarten and Primary Children, Merrill (Englewood Cliffs, NJ), 1996.

Taking Humor Seriously in Children's Literature: Literature-based Mini-Units and Humorous Books for Children Ages 5-12, Scarecrow Press (Lanham, MD), 1997.

Multicultural Friendship Stories and Activities for Children Ages 5-14, Scarecrow Press (Lanham, MD), 1997.

Literature-based History Activities for Children, Grades 4-8, Allyn & Bacon (Boston, MA), 1997.

Literature-based History Activities for Children, Grades 1-3, Allyn & Bacon (Boston, MA), 1998.

Language Arts and Environmental Awareness: 100 Integrated Books and Activities for Children, Shoe String (North Haven, CT), 1998.

A Guide for Developing an Interdisciplinary Thematic Unit, 2nd edition, 1999, 3rd edition, Merrill (Upper Saddle River, NJ), 2002.

Family Values through Children's Literature, Grades K-3, Scarecrow Press (Lanham, MD), 1999.

A Resource Guide for Elementary School Teaching, 5th edition, Merrill (Upper Saddle River, NJ), 2000.

Family Values through Children's Literature, Grades 4-6, Scarecrow Press (Lanham, MD), 2002.

WORK IN PROGRESS: Research on best teaching practices for the elementary grades.

SIDELIGHTS: Patricia L. Roberts told *CA:* "What torques me up for writing? Well, it is the dynamics of what is going on in our world that affects teaching in the elementary classroom. What influences me? The needs of the teachers in the classroom. What inspires me? When there's a teaching need that interests me and that could be supported by a written teaching resource—then I'm into it. An interest in whale language launched the alphabet book on presenting language patterns; an interest in best practices for teaching launched *A Resource Guide for Elementary School Teaching;* the reports of poor student performance in history knowledge launched the two literature-based history activities books; an interest in integrated curriculum was the springboard for the thematic unit guide; and my current focus is on values and family."

BIOGRAPHICAL AND CRITICAL SOURCES:

PERIODICALS

Arithmetic Teacher, February, 1991, George Nattrass, review of *Counting Books Are More than Numbers: An Annotated Action Bibliography,* p. 48.
Booklist, August, 1998, Hazel Rochman, review of *Language Arts and Environmental Awareness: 100 Integrated Books and Activities for Children,* p. 2020.
Choice, February, 1995, S. R. Johnson, review of *Alphabet: A Handbook of ABC Books and Book Extensions for the Elementary Classroom,* 2nd edition, p. 919.
School Library Journal, May, 1990, Phyllis Matill, review of *Counting Books Are More than Numbers,* p. 48; May, 1994, Naomi Caldwell-Wood, review of *Developing Multicultural Awareness through Children's Literature: A Guide for Teachers and Librarians,* p. 36; May, 1998, Penny Peck, review of *Taking Humor Seriously in Children's Literature: Literature-based Mini-Units and Humorous Books for Children Ages 5-12,* p. 55; October, 1998, Kathleen Isaacs, review of *Multicultural Friendship Stories and Activities for Children Ages 5-14,* p. 51; March, 1999, Marcia Brightman, "Nurturing with Nature," p. 125.
Wilson Library Bulletin, May, 1990, James Rettig, review of *Counting Books Are More than Numbers,* p. 124.

*   *   *

ROBINSON, Matt(hew Thomas, Jr.) 1937-2002

OBITUARY NOTICE—See index for *CA* sketch: Born January 1, 1937, in Philadelphia, PA; died of complications from Parkinson's disease August 5, 2002, in Los Angeles, CA. Actor, producer, television writer, playwright, screenwriter, and author. To children in the United States and around the world, Robinson was known as Gordon and the voice of the Muppet Roosevelt Franklin on the public television series *Sesame Street,* roles he performed from 1969 to 1971. This role was only one facet of Robinson's career; he also produced the series for the Public Broadcasting Service. After leaving *Sesame Street,* Robinson wrote and produced films, including *Amazing Grace,* before returning to television as a writer for the comedy series *Sanford and Son* and *Eight Is Enough.* He worked as both writer and coproducer for comedian Bill Cosby's television series for several years in the 1980s. Robinson wrote a solo stage play, *The Confessions of Stepin Fetchit,* based on the career of one of the first African-American film stars, Lincoln Perry. He also wrote children's books, including *The Six-Button Dragon* and the *Gordon of Sesame Street Story Book.*

OBITUARIES AND OTHER SOURCES:

PERIODICALS

Chicago Tribune, August 9, 2002, section 2, p. 9.
Los Angeles Times, August 8, 2002, p. B13.
New York Times, August 8, 2002, p. C13.
Washington Post, August 10, 2002, p. B6.

*   *   *

RODMAN, Maia
See WOJCIECHOWSKA, Maia (Teresa)

ROSE, Reginald 1920-2002

OBITUARY NOTICE—See index for *CA* sketch: Born December 10, 1920, in New York, NY; died April 19, 2002, in Norwich, CT. Screenwriter. Rose wrote numerous television scripts that were well received over the years, but is most famous for one of his earliest: *Twelve Angry Men*. The story became a movie starring Henry Fonda and garnered Rose an Academy Award nomination for best screenplay based on material from another medium. What became an illustrious career began in New York City, with Rose attending what is now City University of New York for one year during the 1930s. He did a four-year stint in the U.S. Army, becoming a first lieutenant, then returned to writing and tried to get into advertising while completing short stories on the side. His first script, *The Bus to Nowhere* for the *Out There* series on CBS, was sold in 1951. He wrote several scripts for the *Studio One* series, also on CBS, including *Dino* and *The Death and Life of Larry Benson*. Then, in 1954, inspired by his own experience on a jury, Rose wrote *Twelve Angry Men*. The film recounts the story of eleven jurors convinced of the guilt of a man accused of killing his father, but who are eventually persuaded by Juror Number Eight—after a hot day of shouting and cajoling—that the evidence doesn't add up and the man is innocent. The story was a hit on television and netted Rose an Emmy for best-written drama and a Writer's Guild of America Award, went to the stage in London, and made it to Hollywood as a film whose script was written by Rose. Co-produced by Rose and Fonda and directed by Sidney Lumet, the film also was nominated for best picture Oscar. Rose's successful run of television scripts later included the pilot (and subsequent episodes) for *The Defender, A Quiet Game of Cards,* and the *Studs Lonigan* miniseries. He received four additional Emmy nominations during his career. His screenplays include *Somebody Killed Her Husband, The Wild Geese* (based on a novel by Daniel Carney), and *Whose Life Is It Anyway,* starring Richard Dreyfuss.

OBITUARIES AND OTHER SOURCES:

PERIODICALS

Los Angeles Times, April 23, 2002, p. B10.
New York Times, April 21, 2002, p. A33.
Times (London, England), May 11, 2002.
Washington Post, April 23, 2002, p. B6.

*   *   *

ROSENTHAL, Norman (Leon) 1944-

PERSONAL: Born November 8, 1944, in England; son of Paul and Kate (Zucker) Rosenthal; married Manuela Beatriz Mena Marques, 1989. *Education:* University of Leicester, B.A. (history, with honors). *Hobbies and other interests:* Music, especially opera.

ADDRESSES: Office—Royal Academy of Arts, Burlington House, Piccadilly, London W1J 0BD England.

CAREER: Cornwall Leicester Museum and Art Gallery, art exhibitions organizer, 1965; Thomas Agnew and Sons, librarian, 1966-68; Brighton Museum and Art Gallery, Brighton, England, exhibitions officer, 1970-71. Writer and editor. Royal Opera House, London, England, board member, 1995-99; Palazzo Grassi, Venice, Italy, board member, 1995—.

MEMBER: Palazzo Grassi Venice; Opera Board Royal Opera House Covent Garden.

AWARDS, HONORS: Royal College of Art, London, England, honorary fellow, 1987; Chevalier l'Ordre des Art et des Lettres, France, 1987; Cavaliere Ufficiale, Order of Merit, Italy, 1992; Cross, Order of Merit, Germany, 1993.

WRITINGS:

(Editor, with Margravine of Bayreuth Wilhelmina) *Misfortunate Margravine,* Macmillan (London, England), 1970.
(With Christos M. Joachimides and Wieland Schmied) *German Art in the Twentieth Century,* Prestel Publishing Ltd. (London, England), 1985.
(Editor, with Mike Weaver and Daniel Wolf) *The Art of Photography 1839-1989,* Yale University Press (New Haven, CT), 1989.
(Editor, with Susan P. Compton), *British Art in the Twentieth Century: The Modern Movement,* Prestel Publishing Ltd. (London, England), 1989.

(Editor, with Emily Braun) *Italian Art in the Twentieth Century: Painting and Sculpture, 1900-1988,* Te Neues Publishing Company (New York, NY), 1989.

Recent Paintings of Georg Baselitz, edited by Judy Adam, Anthony d'Offay Gallery (London, England), 1990.

(Designer, with Georg Baselitz), *Georg Baselitz: Recent Paintings,* Distributed Art Pub., 1991.

(Editor, with Christos M. Joachimides) *Metropolis: International Art Exhibit, Berlin, 1991,* Rizzoli (New York, NY), 1991.

(Editor, with Christos M. Joachimides) *The Age of Modernism: Art in the Twentieth Century,* Hatje Verlag (Stuttgart, Germany), 1993.

(Editor, with Christos M. Joachimides and David Anfam) *American Art in the Twentieth Century: Painting and Sculpture, 1913-1993,* Prestel Publishing Ltd. (London, England), 1993.

Allen Jones: Prints, edited by Richard Lloyd and Marco Livingstone, Prestel Publishing Ltd. (London, England), 1995.

(Editor, with Henry Brooks Adams), Christos M. Joachimides, *The Age of Modernism: Art in the Twentieth Century,* Verlag Gerd Hatje (Stuttgart, Germany), 1997.

(With Danilo Eccher) *Julian Schnabel,* Distributed Art Pub. 1997.

(With Heiner Bastian) *Joseph Beuys,* Royal Academy of Arts (London, England), 1999.

(With Richard Shone, Lisa Jardine, and others) *Sensation: Young British Artists from the Saatchi Collection,* Thames & Hudson (New York, NY), 1999.

Gary Wragg: The Quiet Paintings, Flowers East/ Momentum, 2000.

(Editor, with Max Wigram) *Sex and the British: Slap and Tickle: A Perspective on the Sexual Content of British Art since the 1960s,* Galerie Thaddaeus Ropac (Paris, France), 2000.

(With Louise Neri and Francesco Clemente) *Alighiero e Boetti,* Gagosian Gallery (New York, NY), 2001.

(With Catherine Lampert and Isabel Carlisle) *Frank Auerbach: Paintings and Drawings, 1954-2001,* Royal Academy of Arts (London, England), 2001.

(With Isabel Carlisle) *Joe Tilson (1950-2002),* Thames and Hudson (New York, NY), 2002.

SIDELIGHTS: Norman Rosenthal is the exhibitions secretary for the Royal Academy of Arts in London. He has organized and curated numerous art exhibitions and written text for many museum catalogues.

Credited with a "dramatic financial recovery" at the Royal Academy of Arts, according to a *Studio International* correspondent, Rosenthal appears to attract controversy. Flachra Gibbons described him as a "flamboyant impresario" for *Guardian Unlimited.* In an *Observer* article on the *Guardian Unlimited* Web site, Euan Ferguson commented, "Rosenthal does not come across as a man totally at ease with the outside world," while praising Rosenthal's great intellect and "splendidly learned" catalogue notes.

Rosenthal teamed with Christos M. Joachimides to edit *Metropolis: International Art Exhibit, Berlin, 1991,* which catalogues an exhibition featuring works from more than seventy artists. The volume includes biographical accounts of the various artists, but it also presents a series of essays on what Eric Bryant, writing in *Library Journal,* called "the meaning of art in the Nineties." Bryant acknowledged *Metropolis* as "surely *the* decontexualizing catalog of the year."

Rosenthal and Joachimides again collaborated in editing *The Age of Modernism: Art in the Twentieth Century* and *American Art in the Twentieth Century: Painting and Sculpture, 1913-1993.* Eric Bryant, in a *Library Journal* assessment, called *The Age of Modernism* "inarguably an important study," and he noted that it includes "compelling arguments for the continuing vitality of Modernism." *American Art in the Twentieth Century,* meanwhile, received recognition from Paula Frosch, another *Library Journal* reviewer, as a "very thorough view of a complex and fascinating period." A *Publishers Weekly* critic deemed *American Art in the Twentieth Century* "a fresh, vibrant, major reassessment of modern American art." Two other critics, Kent Anderson and David Baker, wrote in *School Arts* that *American Art in the Twentieth Century* constitutes "a unique view." *Choice* reviewer R. J. Merrill noted the accompanying essays are "a refreshing selection of methodologies." Further recognition came from John Golding, who summarized *American Art in the Twentieth Century* in the *Times Literary Supplement* as an "enormous catalogue."

Frank Auerbach: Paintings and Drawings, 1954-2001 is a museum catalogue that Rosenthal produced with Catherine Lampert and Isabel Carlisle. In a *Times Literary Supplement* appraisal, Michael Podro observed that "Auerbach's work has a constant self-revising dynamic which never allows the subject to disengage from the distinctive properties of the painter's medium, nor does it allow the relation between medium and subject to be taken for granted." He added, "In his fine catalogue essay for this exhibition, Norman Rosenthal shows Auerbach to be central to the tradition of twentieth-century figurative expressionism."

Rosenthal united with other writers, including Richard Shone and Lisa Jardine, to publish *Sensation: Young British Artists from the Saatchi Collection.* "It doesn't matter whether Norman Rosenthal was thinking about box-office when he launched *Sensation* on the Royal Academy," declared Peter Wollen in *London Review of Books.* Wollen also commented: "His show is significant because it has provided us with a chance to take stock of the complex context in which art is made today. [*Sensation*] exposes a cross-section . . . enabling us to look into the contemporary London art world from new angles and meditate on its past and its future."

"First [Rosenthal] brought the world *Sensation,* the most controversial art show of the last decade," observed Gibbons in her *Guardian* article, "Now [he] . . . may have surpassed himself with a new exhibition called *Apocalypse,* featuring 'the extremes of horror and beauty.'" *Apocalypse: Beauty and Horror in Contemporary Art* caused quite a stir when it opened at the Royal Academy of Art, and the exhibition catalogue followed suit. Peter Plagens, writing in *Newsweek International,* described it as a "festival of shock value." Plagens noted Maurizio Cattelan's "The Ninth Hour," an artwork depicting Pope John Paul II's encounter with a meteorite. Plagens hailed "The Ninth Hour" as "the best piece in the exhibition," and he described it as "slapstick blasphemy." "What we really hope," Rosenthal told Jonathan Jones for *Guardian Unlimited,* "is that the whole thing will be a cathartic experience for people who come and engage with the work rather than those who come to gawp and be shocked. It's like going to the theatre or reading a book or seeing a great film that contains elements of horror in it and beauty. It's about catharsis."

On the future of the Royal Academy of Art and its "rivalry" with the Tate Gallery in London, Rosenthal told Louisa Buck in an interview for *The Art Newspaper.com:* "I think that the Royal Academy is going to position itself not as a rival to the Tate, but as another important theatre of art. . . . we are going to do more contemporary exhibitions as well as the great

historic shows that we try to do. I am hoping that we are soon going to be in a position of doing big one-person shows of major artists who would enjoy the Royal Academy."

BIOGRAPHICAL AND CRITICAL SOURCES:

PERIODICALS

Burlington Magazine, December, 1997, "Exhibition Reviews," p. 886.
Choice, May, 1994, R. J. Merrill, review of *American Art in the Twentieth Century,* p. 1424.
Independent, October 7, 1997, David Lister, "What Norman Really Means to the RA," p. 18.
Interview, April, 1991, Eric Bryant, "How Two Cowboy Curators Traveled the World," p. 96.
Library Journal, August, 1991, Eric Bryant, review of *Metropolis,* p. 96; September 15, 1993, Paula Frosch, review of *American Art in the Twentieth Century,* p. 71; September 15, 1997, Eric Bryant, review of *The Age of Modernism,* p. 66.
London Review of Books, October 30, 1997, Peter Wollen, "Thatcher's Artists," pp. 7-9.
Newsweek International, October 2, 2000, Peter Plagens, "Apocalypse Now," p. 110.
New York Review of Books, December 16, 1999, James Fenton, "Giving Offense," pp. 18-22.
New York Times Book Review, December 5, 1971, review of *The Misfortunate Margravine,* p. 80.
Observer, September 24, 2000, Euan Ferguson, "A Hell of His Own Making," p. 15.
Publishers Weekly, September 20, 1993, review of *American Art in the Twentieth Century,* p. 57.
School Arts, April, 1994, Kent Anderson and David Baker, review of *American Art in the Twentieth Century,* p. 49.
Times Literary Supplement, October 1, 1993, John Golding, "Innocence and Invention," pp. 16-17; September 21, 2001, Michael Pedro, "At the Edge of Awareness," pp. 18-19.
Wall Street Journal, Lesley Downer, "Artists See Visions of Apocalypse Now," p. A24.

OTHER

Art Newspaper.com, http://www.allemadi.com/TAN/ (May 31, 2002), Louisa Buck, "Apocalypse Now: A Global Sensation."

Guardian Unlimited, http://www.guardian.co.uk/ (May 3, 2000), Flachra Gibbons, "Sensation's Over, Now It's Apacalypse"; September 7, 2000), Jonathan Jones, "Shock Treatment"; (September 24, 2000), Euan Ferguson, "A Hell of His Own Making."

Royal Academy of Arts, http://www.royalacademy.org.uk/ (May 31, 2002), "Curators."

Studio International, http://www.studio-internation.co.uk/ (May 31, 2002), "Apocalypse: Beauty and Horror in Contemporary Art."*

*   *   *

ROTENBERG, David

PERSONAL: Male. *Education:* University of Toronto, B.A.; Yale University, M.F.A.

ADDRESSES: *Home*—Toronto, Canada. *Office*—York University, 4700 Keele St., Toronto, Ontario, Canada M3J 1P3. *E-mail*—davidr@yorku.ca.

CAREER: York University, Toronto, Ontario, Canada, acting and directing teacher, 1987—.

WRITINGS:

The Shanghai Murders: A Mystery of Love and Ivory, St. Martin's Press (New York, NY), 1998.

The Lake Ching Murders: a Mystery of Fire and Ice, St. Martin's Press (New York, NY), 2002.

SIDELIGHTS: An acting and directing teacher in Toronto, David Rotenberg earned critical success with his first novel, *The Shanghai Murders.* The book, set in contemporary Shanghai, is both a murder mystery and an exploration of cultural differences and rapid social change. It begins when the mutilated corpse of a New Orleans cop is found in a city alley—an event reported in the *Shanghai Daily News* before police even arrive on the scene. Zhong Fong, head of the city's Special Investigation Unit, suspects from the start that the case could turn into a political scandal of international dimensions. As Fong tracks the case's many puzzling clues, including shards of ivory in the corpse's lungs, he is confronted with painful memories of the death of his adulterous actress wife, Fu Tsong, four years earlier. Rotenberg used his professional familiarity with the stage to develop a subplot about Geoffrey Hyland, a Canadian theatre director and Fu Tsong's former lover, who has returned to Shanghai to direct a Chinese production of Shakespeare's *Twelfth Night.* Also adding to the novel's complexity are the appearance of ritual killer Loa Wei Fen, the prime suspect in the murder, and the victim's widow Amanda Pitman, who comes to Shanghai to retrieve his body.

Many critics gave *The Shanghai Murders* superlative reviews. A reviewer for *Publishers Weekly* deemed it "irresistibly exotic," while *Library Journal* critic Rex E. Klett hailed it as an "awesome" achievement with "a wonderfully nefarious plot." Wes Lukowsky, in *Booklist,* praised Rotenberg's literary debut with an "extraordinarily accomplished" thriller and especially admired the book's surprising conclusion. Though a critic for *Kirkus Reviews* felt that Fong did not emerge as a sufficiently interesting character, the writer noted that Rotenberg "scores points for [his] vivid Shanghai sets."

In *The Lake Ching Murders* Zhong Fong is again featured. After spending two years in a Chinese prison, Fong hopes to salvage his career by discovering who killed seventeen people aboard a yacht. The people were not only killed, but were tortured in a hideous way. As many of the dead were not Chinese, it has the potential to develop into an international political situation. *Booklist*'s Wes Lukowsky called it an "enlightening glimpse into the inner workings of justice in rural China." A *Publishers Weekly* reviewer noted the twisted plot and called *The Lake Ching Murders* "sheer entertainment."

BIOGRAPHICAL AND CRITICAL SOURCES:

PERIODICALS

Booklist, July 1998, p. 1866; April 1, 2002, Wes Lukowsky, review of *The Lake Ching Murders,* p. 1310.

Kirkus Reviews, June 1, 1998, p. 782.

Library Journal, June 1, 1998, p. 165; March 1, 2002, Rex E. Klett, review of *The Lake Ching Murders,* p. 144.

Publishers Weekly, May 18, 1998, p. 72; January 21, 2002, review of *The Lake Ching Murders,* p. 67.*

RUCKA, Greg

PERSONAL: Born in San Francisco, CA; married; children: one. *Education:* Attended Vassar College; University of Southern California, M.A.

ADDRESSES: Home—Portland, OR. *Agent*—c/o Author Mail, Random House, 1540 Broadway, New York, NY 10036.

CAREER: Writer. Formerly worked as a house painter, waiter, EMT, security guard, technical writer, beta tester, and fight choreographer.

AWARDS, HONORS: Eisner Award, Best Limited Series, 2000, for *Whiteout.*

WRITINGS:

NOVELS

Keeper, Bantam (New York, NY), 1996.
Finder, Bantam (New York, NY), 1997.
Shooting at Midnight, Bantam (New York, NY), 1999.
Smoker, Bantam (New York, NY), 1998.
Critical Space, Bantam (New York, NY), 2001.
Fistful of Rain, Bantam (New York, NY), 2003.

GRAPHIC NOVELS

Whiteout, Oni Press (Portland, OR), 1999.
Batman: No Man's Land, DC Comics (New York, NY), Volume 2, 1999, Volume 5, 2001.
Grendel: Past Prime, Dark Horse (Milwaukie, OR), 2000.
Batman: Evolution, DC Comics (New York, NY), 2001.
Wonder Woman: The Hiketeia, DC Comics (New York, NY), 2002.
Queen & Country: Operation Broken Ground, Oni Press (Portland, OR), 2002.

SIDELIGHTS: Greg Rucka is a novelist and a writer of comic books and graphic novels. Most of his novels feature the protagonist Atticus Kodiak, a tough, smart bodyguard who follows his heart rather than his pocketbook when it comes to taking on assignments.

Keeper takes up the abortion controversy in all its violence and pathos. Early on in the novel, Kodiak accompanies his pregnant girlfriend to a Manhattan abortion clinic that is being targeted by a militant right-to-life group, Sword of the Silent. That difficult and frightening experience causes him to sympathize with the clinic's director, Felice Romero, who is herself a target of violent threats from the group and its fanatical leader, Jonathan Crowell. As the battle between the pro-life and pro-choice contingents heats up and threatens to become increasingly violent, some concerned parties initiate a forum called "Common Ground" to try to help clear the air. When Romero makes her intention to attend Common Ground known, she receives letters from Sword of the Silent that threaten not only her life but that of her Down's Syndrome-afflicted daughter. Kodiak takes on the arduous task of keeping both safe from their would-be assassins.

Critics were impressed by a number of the novel's elements, from its even handling of the abortion controversy to how the author orchestrates the scenes of violence. A *Publishers Weekly* critic stated that the "pros and cons of abortion are intelligently presented." The reviewer also admired Rucka's storytelling for its fast, smooth pace, interesting characters, and "clean and visual" prose. Dawn L. Anderson, writing in the *Library Journal,* called *Keeper* a "story as timely as today's headlines" and a "tense and exciting novel." And *Booklist* contributor Thomas Gaughan appreciated its "characterizations of people twisted enough to murder to protect life."

Finder follows *Keeper* by only a year. The novel finds Atticus Kodiak not far from where *Keeper* left him—still in New York but now working as a bouncer for a swank "bondage-and-discipline" club. The book presents the tale of Erika Wyatt, a fifteen-year-old on the run, whose father, Colonel Wyatt, is a promiscuous military intelligence agent for whom Kodiak used to work, and whose mother, when still the colonel's wife, was briefly Kodiak's lover. When Erika shows up at the sex club and is threatened at knife-point, Kodiak helps her escape, little knowing that she is the target of not just one menacing male but a whole crew of British S.A.S. officers (a group that operates with the same menace and stealth as the U.S. Navy SEALS). Unfortunately, the intensity of Erika's dislike at being protected is only equaled by the S.A.S.'s fervor for kidnapping her. Heavy suspense and regular eruptions of violence are the result.

A *Publishers Weekly* critic was guarded in responding to *Finder,* saying that "if Rucka . . . ever finds a subject big enough for his tough-guy talents, he'll be a writer to watch." Robert C. Moore said in his *Library Journal* review that if the reader can deal with the violence "*Finder* pulls you to a satisfying conclusion." And a *Kirkus Reviews* contributor appreciated the book's "fine cliff-hangers, well-executed violence, and skillfully sketched characters"; the reviewer ultimately deemed it "flawed, but still superior to most lone-wolf genre tales."

In *Smoker,* Kodiak is hired to protect a biomedical research scientist who is going to testify against the tobacco industry, accusing them of putting additives in their cigarettes to make them more addicting. *Booklist*'s Wes Lukowsky called *Smoker* an "exciting action adventure."

Critical Space finds Kodiak protecting a woman who is, in fact, a professional killer. Kodiak finds himself up against the FBI, his own best friends, and possibly the woman herself. *Booklist*'s David Pitt called *Critical Space* "a first-rate thriller."

Rucker is also the author of numerous graphic novels, including *Whiteout,* which won the Eisner Award for Best Limited Series in 2000, and *Queen & Country: Operation Broken Ground,* which was nominated for an Eisner Award.

BIOGRAPHICAL AND CRITICAL SOURCES:

PERIODICALS

Booklist, May 1, 1996, p. 1491; October 1, 1998, Wes Lukowsky, review of *Smoker,* p. 312; September 1, 1999, George Needham, review of *Shooting at Midnight,* p. 73; December 15, 1999, Roland Green, review of *Batman: No Man's Land,* p. 761; August, 2001, David Pitt, review of *Critical Space,* p. 2099.

Kirkus Reviews, May 15, 1997, p. 750.

Library Journal, May 1, 1996, p. 134; June 1, 1997, p. 150; November 1, 1998, Dawn L. Anderson, review of *Smoker,* p. 126; January, 2000, Jackie Cassada, review of *Batman: No Man's Land,* p. 168; September 15, 2001, Ronnie H. Terpening, review of *Critical Space,* p. 114.

Publishers Weekly, April 29, 1996, p. 53; May 26, 1997, p. 66; September 21, 1998, review of *Smoker,* p. 72; September 27, 1999, review of *Shooting at Midnight,* p. 75; December 13, 1999, review of *Batman: No Man's Land,* p. 64; July 30, 2001, review of *Critical Space,* p. 55; June 3, 2002, review of *Queen & Country: Operation Broken Ground,* p. 66.

OTHER

The Bear Cave: The Official Greg Rucka Web Page, http://www.gregrucka.com (November 27, 2002).*

*　　　　*　　　　*

RYAN, Patrick 1957-

PERSONAL: Born March 10, 1957, in Springfield, IL; son of Richard Joseph (a medic) and Frances Conner Dougherty (a speech therapist) Ryan. *Education:* University of Illinois—Urbana, B.F.A., 1978; University of Chicago, M.S., 1981; University of Glamorgan, doctoral study, 2000—. *Politics:* Democrat. *Religion:* Roman Catholic. *Hobbies and other interests:* Hill walking, football, soccer, rugby, travel, theater, reading, swimming.

ADDRESSES: Home and office—72A Huxley Rd., London E10 5QU, England. *E-mail*—patryan@telltale. dir.co.uk.

CAREER: Part-time storyteller, 1978-89; primary school teacher in Chicago, IL, 1981-84, and in London, England, 1984-89; professional storyteller in Britain and Ireland, with additional tours, residence, and projects in the United States, Italy, Germany, Hong Kong, and Australia. Founding member, Northlands Storytelling Network, Upper Midwest, 1980-84; founding member, Society for Storytelling, England and Wales, 1992, member of board, 1992, 1995, chair, 1994-95; consultant to Ragdoll Productions for *The Teletubbies.*

MEMBER: International Board on Books for Young People (British branch), Society for Storytelling, American Folklore Society, Equiry, English Folk Dance and Song Society.

WRITINGS:

The Bigwidemouthed Toad Frog, illustrated by Mary Medlicott, Kingfisher (London, England), 1990.

Storytelling in Ireland: A Re-Awakening, Verbal Arts Centre (Londonderry, England), 1995.

Words in Action, Verbal Arts Centre (Londonderry, England), 1997.

Listen Up! (video), Verbal Arts Centre (Londonderry, England), 2000.

(Re-teller) *Shakespeare's Storybook: Folktales That Inspired the Bard,* illustrated by James Mayhew, Barefoot Books (New York, NY), 2001.

Has written various scripts for BBC Radio; contributor to periodicals.

WORK IN PROGRESS: Doctoral thesis; a book on Irish storytellers.

SIDELIGHTS: A professional storyteller, Patrick Ryan presents the sources behind Shakespeare's seven greatest works in his book titled *Shakespeare's Storybook: Folktales That Inspired the Bard.* In addition to providing some biographical and historical background to Shakespeare's writing, Ryan also includes an introduction in the book that recounts the transformation of storytelling, from early oral traditions to the written word. The book was well received by critics, many of whom praised Ryan's adaptations as being entertaining even if they had no connection to Shakespeare. And John Peters, writing in *Booklist,* added that "children who have already been exposed to the Bard will find plenty of new insight here."

BIOGRAPHICAL AND CRITICAL SOURCES:

PERIODICALS

Booklist, November 15, 2001, John Peters, review of *Shakespeare's Storybook: Folktales That Inspired the Bard,* p. 569.

Kirkus Reviews, September 1, 2001, review of *Shakespeare's Storybook,* p. 1300.

Publishers Weekly, August 20, 2001, review of *Shakespeare's Storybook,* p. 83.

School Library Journal, January, 2002, Margaret Bush, review of *Shakespeare's Storybook,* p. 166.

*   *   *

RYUFU, Zenshin
  See WHALEN, Philip (Glenn)

S

SARPI, Emilio
   See CA'ZORCI, Giacomo

*   *   *

SCHANZER, Ros
   See SCHANZER, Rosalyn (Good)

*   *   *

SCHANZER, Rosalyn (Good) 1942-
   (Ros Schanzer, Roz Schanzer)

PERSONAL: Born November 26, 1942, in Knoxville, TN; daughter of Sam Good (an architectural engineer) and Bess (Mark) Hazelwood (a homemaker); married Steven Terry Schanzer (a business manager), July 24, 1966; children: Adam, Kimberly. *Education:* University of Cincinnati, B.F.A. and B.S., 1964. *Religion:* Jewish. *Hobbies and other interests:* "Swimming (nationally ranked Masters swimmer), worldwide adventure travel, photography."

ADDRESSES: Home and office—11630 Havenner Rd., Fairfax Station, VA 22039. *E-mail*—schanze@attglobal.net.

CAREER: Author and illustrator of trade books for children, 1993—. Hallmark Cards, Kansas City, MO, designer, 1964-71; freelance illustrator of books, magazines, posters, and filmstrips, 1971-96. George Washington University, assistant professorial lecturer in art, 1982-88.

MEMBER: Society of Children's Book Writers and Illustrators, Children's Book Guild of Washington.

AWARDS, HONORS: The Golden Happy Birthday Book was listed as one of the twenty-five best picture books of the year by *Saturday Review of Books,* 1976; Best in Show and Dukane Gold Camera Award, International Film Festival, 1980, for *Comparing Sizes* (filmstrip); *All about Hanukkah* was voted one of the three best Jewish picture books of the year by the Jewish Book Council, 1989; Notable Children's Book of Jewish Content, Association of Jewish Libraries, 2000, and a Sydney Taylor Notable Book, both for *Escaping to America: A True Story;* American Library Association (ALA) "Books for Youth" Editor's Choice, 2001, Oppenheim Toy Portfolio-Platinum, 2002, and Children's Choice Award, International Reading Association/Childern's Book Council, 2002, all for *Davy Crockett Saves the World;* Silver Award in Folklore, Poetry, and Song, National Parenting Publications Association, 2001, for *The Old Chisholm Trail: A Cowboy Song;* Notable Children's Trade Book in the Field of Social Studies, National Council of Social Studies/Children's Book Council, for *How We Crossed the West: The Adventures of Lewis and Clark.*

WRITINGS:

SELF-ILLUSTRATED

The Beggar's Treasure, Holt (New York, NY), 1973.
(Under name Roz Schanzer) *My First Jewish Word Book,* Kar-Ben (Rockville, MD), 1992.

Ezra in Pursuit: The Great Maze Chase, Doubleday (New York, NY), 1993.

Ezra's Quest: Follow That Dog, Doubleday (New York, NY), 1994.

How We Crossed the West: The Adventures of Lewis and Clark, National Geographic Society (Washington, DC), 1997.

Gold Fever: Tales from the California Gold Rush, National Geographic Society (Washington, DC), 1999.

Escaping to America: A True Story, HarperCollins (New York, NY), 2000.

Davy Crockett Saves the World, HarperCollins (New York, NY), 2001.

The Old Chisholm Trail: A Cowboy Song, National Geographic Society (Washington, DC), 2001.

How Ben Franklin Stole the Lightning, HarperCollins (New York, NY), 2003.

ILLUSTRATOR

Dean Walley, *Puck's Peculiar Pet Shop: A Tongue Twister Story,* Hallmark (Kansas City, MO), 1970.

Gail Mahan Peterson, *A Day on the Farm,* Hallmark (Kansas City, MO), 1970.

Dean Walley, *The Zany Zoo,* Hallmark (Kansas City, MO), 1970.

Barbara Bartocci, *Jungle Jumble,* Hallmark (Kansas City, MO), 1971.

Peter S. Seymour, compiler, *The Pop-Goes-the-Joke Book: A Hallmark Pop-up Book,* Hallmark (Kansas City, MO), 1971.

Peter S. Seymour, *Mr. Backer's Amazing Marching Band,* Hallmark Children's Editions (Kansas City, MO), 1971.

Barbara Shook Hazen, *The Golden Happy Birthday Book,* Western Golden Press (New York, NY), 1976.

Barbara Kunz Loots, *The Lost-and-Found Town: A Picture Story with Hidden Objects to Find on Every Page,* Hallmark (Kansas City, MO), 1978.

Ranger's Rick's Surprise Book, National Wildlife Federation (Washington, DC), 1979.

Animal Architects, National Geographic Society Books for Young Readers (Washington, DC), 1987.

Wendy Lewison, *When an Elephant Goes Shopping,* Marvel Monkey Tales, 1988.

Harriet K. Feder, *It Happened in Shushan,* Kar-Ben (Rockville, MD), 1988.

Jean Waricha, *Ben's Three Wishes,* Marvel Monkey Tales, 1988.

Judyth Groner and Madeline Wikler, *All about Hanukkah,* Kar-Ben (Rockville, MD), 1988.

Ann Eisenberg, *I Can Celebrate,* Kar-Ben (Rockville, MD), 1988.

Lawrence Balter, *Sue Lee's New Neighborhood,* Barron's (New York, NY), 1989.

Lawrence Balter, *What's the Matter with A. J.?: Understanding Jealousy,* Barron's (New York, NY), 1989.

Lawrence Balter, *The Wedding: Adjusting to a Parent's Remarriage,* Barron's (New York, NY), 1989.

Lawrence Balter, *Linda Saves the Day: Understanding Fear,* Barron's (New York, NY), 1989.

Judyth Saypol Groner and Madeline Wikler, *Where Is the Afikomen?,* Kar-Ben (Rockville, MD), 1989.

Judy Nayer, *The Happy Little Engine,* McClanahan Books (New York, NY), 1990.

Ann Eisenberg, *Bible Heroes I Can Be,* Kar-Ben (Rockville, MD), 1990.

Lawrence Balter, *Alfred Goes to the Hospital: Understanding a Medical Emergency,* Barron's (New York, NY), 1990.

Lawrence Balter, *A. J.'s Mom Gets a New Job: Adjusting to a Two-Career Family,* Barron's (New York, NY), 1990.

Arlene Block, *Phonics, Consonants,* McClanahan Books (New York, NY), 1991.

Lawrence Balter, *A Funeral for Whiskers: Understanding Death,* Barron's (New York, NY), 1991.

Lawrence Balter, *Sue Lee Starts School: Adjusting to School,* Barron's (New York, NY), 1991.

Susan Remick Topek, *Ten Good Rules,* Kar-Ben (Rockville, MD), 1991.

Madeline Wikler and Judyth Saypol Groner, *In the Synagogue,* Kar-Ben (Rockville, MD), 1991.

Judy Nayer, compiler, *My First Picture Dictionary,* McClanahan Book Co. (New York, NY), 1992.

Deborah Shine, *Where's the Puppy?,* Newbridge Communications (New York, NY), 1993.

Muff Singer, *Puppy Says 1, 2, 3,* Joshua Morris (Westport, CT), 1993.

Muff Singer, *Hello Piglet,* Reader's Digest Association (Pleasantville, NY), 1993.

Muff Singer, *Little Lost Lamb,* Reader's Digest Association (Pleasantville, NY), 1993.

Muff Singer, *What Does Kitty See?,* Reader's Digest Association (Pleasantville, NY), 1993.

Muff Singer, *Bunny's Hungry,* Reader's Digest Association (Pleasantville, NY), 1994.

Muff Singer, *Little Duck's Friends,* Reader's Digest Association (Pleasantville, NY), 1994.

Muff Singer, *All Year round with Little Frog,* Reader's Digest Association (Pleasantville, NY), 1995.

Judy Nayer, *Little Fish, Little Fish,* Willowisp Press (St. Petersburg, FL), 1995.

Alice Cary, *Panda Band,* Open Court (Chicago, IL), 1995.

Patricia Lauber, *The True-or-False Book of Cats,* HarperCollins (New York, NY), 1998.

Cheri Holland, *Maccabee Jamboree: A Hanukkah Countdown,* Kar-Ben (Rockville, MD), 1998.

Patricia Lauber, *The True-or-False Book of Horses,* HarperCollins (New York, NY), 2000.

Patricia Lauber, *The True-or-False Book of Dogs,* HarperCollins (New York, NY), 2003.

Also illustrator, sometimes under name Roz Schanzer, of several hundred books, posters, magazine articles, games, and filmstrips for children, including the filmstrip *Comparing Sizes,* Harcourt, 1980, and a series of eight books by Dr. Lawrence Balter, "Dr. Balter's Stepping Stone Stories," Barron's, 1989 and 1990.

SIDELIGHTS: Rosalyn Schanzer is a prolific author and illustrator of children's books. Beginning her career as an illustrator of books and greeting cards for Hallmark Cards, Schanzer has branched off into writing and illustrating her own books for children, as well as creating the pictures for scores of books written by others. In *Gold Fever,* a self-illustrated work, she provides a detailed account of the California gold rush, complete with original materials from the period, including journal entries, letters, and other documents, providing a "uniquely exciting introduction to a fascinating period," according to Steven Engelfried in *School Library Journal.* Similar to *Gold Fever* is Schanzer's *How We Crossed the West: The Adventures of Lewis and Clark.* As the title indicates, the book recounts the adventures of explorers Lewis and Clark as they set out across the United States in their famous journey. Once again, Schanzer combines her illustrations with anecdotes, original documents, and journal entries to create an "exuberant picture book," enthused a reviewer for *Publishers Weekly.*

In *Escaping to America: A True Story,* Schanzer presents an account of her own father's escape from war-torn Poland in 1921, and his exciting journey to the United States. Although based on a personal ac-count, critics have noted that Schanzer's subject matter is relevant to the immigrant experience even today, making this work a "timeless" contribution to the genre, said *School Library Journal* contributor Diane S. Marton. In *Davy Crockett Saves the World* Schanzer returns to her retelling of American history in a "thundering good choice for reading aloud," wrote Carolyn Phelan in her *Booklist* assessment. Told in the tradition of the tall tale, the book recreates the legend of this American folk hero in a work that "frame[s] this zesty slice of Americana admirably," noted a reviewer for *Publishers Weekly.*

Schanzer told *CA,* "I made my debut on Thanksgiving Day, 1942, with a paintbrush in one fist and a Crayola in the other, and I have been coloring ever since. So far, I have colored hundreds of books for kids and an untold number of magazine illustrations, filmstrips, posters, and other items too numerous and sundry to mention.

"Here are some interesting things I have done when I was not chained to my desk watching words and pictures fall out of my fingers: I have helped sail a very famous sailboat over eight hundred miles from Bermuda to Boston with five men. I have had my dislocated ankle repaired in the jungles of Ecuador by an illiterate peasant who wielded a five-foot machete and told me not to dance for a week. I have flown in a tiny plane through a storm over the ruins of Tikal in Guatemala, swum with sharks in the reefs of Belize, explored ancient Incan ruins in Peru, and kayaked with whales in Alaska. I have been married to my husband, Steve, since 1966, and we have two adult children, Adam and Kim. We also have a dog named Jones.

"For years I illustrated literally hundreds of books, magazine articles, posters, and games for children. Finally, I decided that if I wanted to do books my own way, I would have to write them myself. So in 1993 I began writing and illustrating books about adventurers I would like to have met and exotic places I would like to have visited. The first two of these books, *Ezra in Pursuit* and *Ezra's Quest,* represent a real break-through for me. They introduced me to writing stories in a historical context for the first time. The idea was to tell about the past in an exciting, unusual way that would appeal strongly to a young audience. The complex picture mazes in those two books virtually allowed readers to step directly into the landscapes and adventures depicted on each page, sort of like Alice in *Through the Looking Glass.* The text and art are funny, historically accurate, and full of outrageous characters, authentic detail, and surprising twists and turns.

"Ever since that time, I have tried to think up as many new ways as possible to shake the cobwebs out of history and to make the characters from our past spring to life. I have written entire books using quotes from history's real heroes. I've used an authentic cowboy song to tell the story of a cattle drive, have written some stories entirely in rhyme, and have practically drowned in a sea of research material in order to insure that everything I write and paint is absolutely accurate down to the last tiny detail. What a hoot, and besides, history is never boring. By writing and illustrating these books, I've learned about some of the greatest adventures of all time."

BIOGRAPHICAL AND CRITICAL SOURCES:

PERIODICALS

Booklist, September 5, 1997, Carolyn Phelan, review of *How We Crossed the West: The Adventures of Lewis and Clark,* p. 233; November 15, 2001, Carolyn Phelan, review of *Davy Crockett Saves the World,* p. 573.

Bulletin of the Center for Children's Books, November, 1997, Elizabeth Bush, review of *How We Crossed the West,* p. 100.

Kirkus Reviews, March 15, 1999, review of *Gold Fever: Tales from the California Gold Rush,* p. 456.

Publishers Weekly, September 29, 1997, review of *How We Crossed the West,* p. 89; July 31, 2000, review of *Escaping to America: A True Story,* p. 95; July 23, 2001, review of *Davy Crockett Saves the World,* p. 77.

School Library Journal, April, 1999, Steven Engelfried, review of *Gold Fever: Tales from the California Gold Rush,* p. 123; September, 2000, Diane S. Marton, review of *Escaping to America: A True Story,* p. 222; August, 2001, Barbara Buckley, review of *Davy Crockett Saves the World,* p. 161.

OTHER

Children's Book Guild Web site, http://www.childrensbookguild.org/ (May 7, 2003).

SCHANZER, Roz
    See SCHANZER, Rosalyn (Good)

*   *   *

SCHILDGEN, Brenda Deen 1942-

PERSONAL: Born December 17, 1942, in London, England; daughter of Nasir Din (in business) and Anna (Friedman) Deen; married Robert D. Schildgen (an editor), July 11, 1964; children: Jacob, Anna Schildgen Rodas, Matthew. *Ethnicity:* "Indian; South Asian." *Education:* Attended University of Wisconsin—Madison, 1965; Indiana University—Bloomington, M.A., 1969; University of San Francisco, Ph.D., 1972, M.A., 1989. *Politics:* "Leftist." *Religion:* Roman Catholic. *Hobbies and other interests:* Gardening, nature, art history, architecture, landscape, Indian culture.

ADDRESSES: Home—2418 Spaulding Ave., Berkeley, CA 94703. *Office*—Department of English, 811 Sproul Hall, University of California— Davis, Davis, CA 95616. *E-mail*—bdschildgen@ucdavis.edu.

CAREER: University of San Francisco, San Francisco, CA, director and associate dean of writing programs, 1980-88; University of California—Davis, faculty member, 1988-2001, professor of comparative literature and English, 2002—.

MEMBER: Modern Language Association of America, American Association of Italian Studies, New Chaucer Society, Medieval Association of the Pacific.

AWARDS, HONORS: Selection for "best academic book," *Choice,* 1999, for *Power and Prejudice: The Reception of the Gospel of Mark.*

WRITINGS:

The Rhetoric Canon, Wayne State University Press (Detroit, MI), 1997.

Crisis and Continuity: Time in the Gospel of Mark, Sheffield Academic Press (Sheffield, England), 1998.

Power and Prejudice: The Reception of the Gospel of Mark, Wayne State University Press (Detroit, MI), 1999.

(Editor, with Leonard Michael Koff, and contributor) *The "Decameron" and the "Canterbury Tales": New Essays on an Old Question,* Fairleigh Dickinson University Press (Madison, NJ), 2000.

Pagans, Tartars, Jews, and Moslems in Chaucer's "Canterbury Tales," University Press of Florida (Gainesville, FL), 2001.

Dante and the Orient, University of Illinois Press (Champaign, IL), 2002.

WORK IN PROGRESS: City of Gods, for Johns Hopkins University Press (Baltimore, MD), completion expected in 2004; research on "the vernacular Bible in the Middle Ages."

SIDELIGHTS: Brenda Schildgen told *CA:* "My motivation is the search for knowledge and for an understanding of history, culture, meaning, and myself. My work is influenced by disciplinary training and formation by dedicated teachers from the beginning of school until the present. My models are the scholars who share their time and support the work of others. My writing process involves research, thought, writing, more research, more thinking, rewriting. Ideas are not spontaneous but the product of reading, thinking, and probing subjects outside my area of expertise. My primary inspiration is a passionate interest in the subjects, due to intellectual and personal quests for understanding."

BIOGRAPHICAL AND CRITICAL SOURCES:

PERIODICALS

Catholic Biblical Quarterly, February, 2002, Kevin Madigan, review of *Power and Prejudice: The Reception of the Gospel of Mark,* p. 762.

Choice, June, 1998, R. B. Shuman, review of *The Rhetoric Canon,* p. 1701; November, 1999, D. Bourquin, review of *Power and Prejudice,* p. 558; February, 2002, D. Pesta, review of *Pagans, Tartars, Jews, and Moslems in Chaucer's "Canterbury Tales,"* p. 1051.

Journal of Theological Studies, April, 2000, W. R. Telford, review of *Power and Prejudice,* p. 250.

Medium Aevum, spring, 2002, Jill Mann, review of *The "Decameron" and the "Canterbury Tales": New Essays on an Old Question,* p. 144.

*   *   *

SCHIMMEL, Betty 1929(?)-

PERSONAL: Born c. 1929, in Czechoslovakia; immigrated to United States, 1949; daughter of Jacob and Ethel Markowitz; married Otto Schimmel, 1948; children: three.

ADDRESSES: Agent—c/o Author Mail, Penguin Putnam, 375 Hudson St., New York, NY 10014.

CAREER: Writer.

WRITINGS:

(With Joyce Gabriel) *To See You Again: A True Story of Love in a Time of War,* Dutton (New York, NY), 1999.

ADAPTATIONS: To See You Again was produced as an audiobook.

SIDELIGHTS: Holocaust survivor Betty Schimmel, with the help of Joyce Gabriel, wrote a memoir of her experiences, *To See You Again.* In it Schimmel describes her childhood years in rural Czechoslovakia, where she enjoyed a large extended family. After Adolf Hitler annexed the Sudentenland, Schimmel's family escaped to Hungary, settling in Budapest where twelve-year-old Betty fell in love with rich and handsome Richie Kovacs. After Betty's father, who was working for the underground in North Africa, disappeared, her mother held the family together. Schimmel recounts in *To See You Again* how, despite the best efforts of courageous individuals, the Jews of Budapest were sent on a wintertime death march to the Mauthausen concentration camp on the Austrian border. Through sheer force of will, Betty, her mother, and two siblings survived the march and a year at the camp. After they were liberated, Schimmel searched for Kovacs, but eventually she gave him up for dead.

Later she married Otto Schimmel, also a Holocaust survivor, and the family immigrated to the United States, where they raised three children.

In 1975 Schimmel's world was turned upside down when she and her daughter met Kovacs in a hotel dining room while visiting Budapest. Though it was a dream come true to see her long-lost love again, Schimmel remained with her husband. Upon its publication in 1999, *To See You Again* attracted the attention of reviewers. A *Kirkus Reviews* critic praised Schimmel for "effectively" using "evocative description throughout," while in *Library Journal* Kim Baxter judged the work to be a "gripping memoir." "*To See You Again* is at its best a wonderful evocation of life in Central Europe before the Second World War," Caroline Moorehead commented in the *Times Literary Supplement*.

BIOGRAPHICAL AND CRITICAL SOURCES:

PERIODICALS

Entertainment Weekly, December 10, 1999, Gay Daly, review of *To See You Again,* p. 104.

Jewish News of Greater Phoenix, October 29, 1999, "Finding Lost Romance Closes Chapter in Woman's Life."

Kirkus Reviews, August 15, 1999, review of *To See You Again,* p. 1292.

Library Journal, October 1, 1999, Kim Baxter, review of *To See You Again,* p. 104.

Publishers Weekly, August 16, 1999, review of *To See You Again,* p. 68.

Times Literary Supplement, December 24, 1999, Caroline Moorehead, "Among the Ruins," p. 25.*

*   *   *

SCHISSLER, Hanna 1946-

PERSONAL: Born May 3, 1946, in Bad Kreuznach, Germany. *Ethnicity:* "Caucasian." *Education:* University of Bielefeld, D.Phil., 1978; attended University of Hannover, 1994.

ADDRESSES: Home—Cranachstrasse 1, 12157 Berlin, Germany. *Office*—Georg-Eckert-Institut für internationale Schulbuchforschung in Braunschweig, Cellestrasse 3, 38114 Braunschweig, Germany; fax: 44-531-590- 9999. *E-mail*—schissler@gei.de.

CAREER: Georg-Eckert-Institut für internationale Schulbuchforschung in Braunschweig, Braunschweig, Germany, senior research fellow, 1981—. German Historical Institute, Washington, DC, senior research fellow, 1988-92; University of Minnesota, associate professor of history, 1992-97; New York University, Max Weber Professor of German Studies, 1999-2000.

MEMBER: American Historical Association, German Studies Association, Verband des Historikerinnen und Historikes in Deutschland.

WRITINGS:

Preußische Agrargesellschaft im Wandel: Wirtschaftliche, gesellschaftliche und politische Transformationsprozesse von 1763 bis 1847, Vandenhoek & Ruprecht (Göttingen, Germany), 1978.

(With others) *Deutschlandstudien,* Volume 1, edited by Robert Picht, [Bonn, Germany], 1978.

(Editor, with Karl-Ernst Jeismann) *Englische und deutsche Geschichte in den Schulbüchern beider LänderL Wahrnehmungsmuster und Urteilsstrukturen in Darstellungen zur Neueren Geschichte,* [Braunschweig, Germany], 1982.

(With others) *Die Bundesrepublik Deutschland und die Vereinigten Staaten von Amerika: Empfehlungen zue Behandlung ihrer Geschichte nach dem Zweiten Weltkrieg,* edited by Karl-Ernst Jeismann, [Braunschweig, Germany], 1983.

(Editor, with Hans-Ulrich Wehler, and author of introduction) *Preußische Finanzpolitik 1806-1810: Quellen zur Verwaltung der Ministerien Stein und Altenstein,* Vandenhoek & Ruprecht (Göttingen, Germany), 1984.

(Editor and contributor) *Schulbuchverbesserung durch internationale Schulbuchforschung? Probleme der Vermittlung zwischen Schulbuchkritik und Geschichtsbuch am Beispiel englischer Geschichte,* [Braunschweig, Germany], 1985.

(Editor, with Volker R. Berghahn) *National Identity and Perceptions of the Past: International Textbook Research in Britain, the United States, and West Germany,* Berg Publishers (Oxford, England), 1987.

(Editor, with Jürgen C. Heß) *Nachbarn zwischen Nähe und Distanz: Deutschland und die Niederlande,* Diesterweg (Frankfurt, Germany) 1988.

(Editor and contributor) *Geschlechterverhältnisse im historischen Wandel,* Campus (Frankfurt, Germany), 1993.

(Editor and contributor) *The Miracle Years: West German Society from 1949 to 1968; A Cultural History,* Princeton University Press (Princeton, NJ), 2001.

(Editor, with Yasemin Soysal) *The Nation, Europe, the World: Textbooks in Transition,* Berghahn Publishers (Providence, RI), 2003.

Contributor to books, including *An Interrupted Past: German-Speaking Refugee Historians in the United States after 1933,* edited by Hartmut Lehmann and James J. Sheehan, Cambridge University Press (Cambridge, England), 1991; *Landownership and Power in Europe,* edited by Martin Blinckhorn and Ralph Gibson, HarperCollins (London, England), 1991; *From Bundesrepublik to Deutschland: German Politics after Unification,* edited by Michael Huelshoff, Andrei S. Markovits, and Simon Reich, University of Michigan Press (Ann Arbor, MI), 1993; *Between Reform and Revolution: Studies in the History of German Socialism and Communism from 1840 to 1990,* edited by David E. Barclay and Eric D. Weitz, Berghahn Publishers (Providence, RI), 1998; and *Germany and the United States in the Era of the Cold War, 1945-1990,* edited by Detlev Junker, Cambridge University Press (Cambridge, England), 2001. Contributor of articles and reviews to academic journals, including *International Journal of Social Education, German Studies Review, Central European History,* and *German Politics and Society.* Coeditor, *Internationale Schulbuchforschung,* 1981-88, 1997—.

SIDELIGHTS: Hanna Schissler told *CA:* "I am fascinated by the different ways in which people approach and make sense of the world. To look at the world through the historical lens has always appealed to me. I have come a long way from structural approaches in history writing (very un- personal, very 'objectified') to what today, rather vaguely, is called cultural history. In my first book on agrarian society I attempted a secularized explanation of broad developments, basically of the transition from traditional to 'modern' society in Germany. In my book *The Miracle Years: West German Society from 1949 to 1968; A Cultural History,* I pondered the idea of what it means to write about one's own time. Writing about one's own time is a particular challenge, since there is so much memory, transference, legitimation, et cetera— all issues which historians tend to overlook, but which I find increasingly fascinating. Writing is hard work. I have always regretted that I cannot write for the broader public. It is my dream to write a novel which captures the *Zeitgeist* and entertains people more than dry scholarly prose."

*   *   *

SCHURZ, Carl 1829-1906

PERSONAL: Born March 2, 1829, in Liblar, Prussia; died May 14, 1906, New York, NY; son of Christian Schurz (a schoolmaster), and Marianne Jussen Schurz; married Margarethe Meyer (a kindergarten teacher), July 6, 1852 (died 1876); children: Agathe, Marianne, Emma, Carl Lincoln, Herbert. *Education:* Attended Jesuit Gymnasium, Cologne, Germany; University of Bonn, Ph.D., 1847. *Religion:* Catholic.

CAREER: Journalist, soldier, speech writer, and editor. *Watertown Anzeiger,* Watertown, WI, editor, 1859; *Deutsche Volkszeitung,* Watertown, WI, founder and editor, 1859; U.S. minister to Spain, 1861-62; brigadier general of volunteers, 1862; engaged at Second Bull Run, Chancellorsville, Gettysburg; U.S. senator, 1869-75; founded Liberal Republican Party, 1872; named secretary of the interior under President Rutherford B. Hayes, 1877-81. *New York Tribune,* Washington correspondent; *Detroit Post,* editor; *St. Louis Westliche Post,* co-owner and editor, beginning 1867; *New York Evening Post,* editor, 1881-83; *Harper's Weekly,* editorial writer, 1892-98. *Military service:* U.S. Army, major general, 1863.

MEMBER: National Civil Service Reform League (president, 1892-1901), Civil Service Reform Association of New York (president, 1893-1906).

WRITINGS:

Court of Inquiry on Major General Hooker's Report of the Night Engagement of Wauhatchie, [Washington, DC], 1864.

Speeches of Carl Schurz, Collected and Revised by the Author, Lippincott (Philadelphia, PA), 1865.

The Condition of the South, [Washington, DC], 1866.

Eulogy on Charles Sumner, Lee, Shepard, and Dillingham (New York, NY), 1874.

The Spoils System, an Address to the Civil Service Reform League, Washington, DC, December 12, 1895, H. Altemus (Philadelphia, PA), 1896.

American Imperialism, the Convocation Address Delivered on the 27th Convocation of the University of Chicago, [Chicago, IL], 1899.

For Truth, Justice, and Liberty, Anti-Imperialist League of New York (New York, NY), 1900.

The Reminiscences of Carl Schurz, three volumes, McClure (New York, NY), 1907-1908.

Bancroft, Frederic, editor, *Speeches, Correspondence and Political Papers of Carl Schurz,* six volumes, Putnam, (New York, NY), 1913.

Intimate Letters of Carl Schurz, 1841-1869, edited and translated by Joseph Schafer, State Historical Society of Wisconsin (Madison, WI), 1928.

SIDELIGHTS: Soldier and statesman, linguist and historian, orator and journalist, Carl Schurz was the first German-born member of the United States Senate. He also was an antislavery leader and served as minister to Spain under President Abraham Lincoln and secretary of the interior under President Rutherford B. Hayes.

Schurz was born in Liblar, a small village on the Rhine, near Cologne, Prussia. His schoolmaster father and devoted mother worked hard to help their son fulfill his dreams of becoming a history scholar, possibly a professor. In the evenings, his grandfather shared colorful tales of the Napoleonic Wars.

As young Schurz's interest in history, literature, and languages flourished, his interest in organized religion declined. Turned off by what he considered church intolerance, Schurz could not reconcile the limiting principals of strict denominational faith with his emerging liberal world view.

After entering the University of Bonn as a doctoral candidate in history in 1847, Schurz helped lead a student revolutionary movement. Oswald Garrison Villard wrote in *Dictionary of American Biography,* "His rare gift of oratory he discovered when he suddenly addressed, to great applause, a meeting in the university hall at Bonn, to which he came without the slightest intention of speaking."

In 1850, after serving as lieutenant in the revolutionary army and facing defeat at the hands of the Prussians, Schurz took a huge risk and rescued his imprisoned professor friend, Gottfried Kinkel. Soon after, Schurz contributed articles to revolutionary presses in Germany and throughout Europe. He and his wife, Margarethe Meyer of Hamburg, relocated to America a couple of years later, as did many other German revolutionaries. Upon their arrival in New York, Schurz, twenty-four at the time, was already internationally known. The Schurzes lived in Philadelphia upon arrival.

Once settled, Schurz mastered English, opposed slavery, campaigned for Abraham Lincoln, fought against the Confederacy in the civil war, helped plan civil reform strategy and opposed American imperialism in the Spanish-American war.

In 1856, he and his wife settled in Wisconsin and helped form the Republican party. Villard remarked, "Having espoused the antislavery cause with all the ardor and enthusiasm he gave to the revolution of 1849, Schurz was immediately drawn into Republican politics."

Schurz ran for lieutenant governor in 1858. "His forceful support of antislavery forces brought him instant attention nationally, but he was defeated in the general election by 107 votes," wrote John M. Butler, also in *Dictionary of Literary Biography.*

In the presidential election that year, Schurz wrote and delivered speeches for John C. Fremont, and for Abraham Lincoln against Stephen Douglas in the Illinois campaign for the U.S. Senate. During this period, he also acquired a law degree and penned one of his most famous speeches, "True Americanism," for Senator Henry Wilson of Massachusetts, which went far in defeating a proposal to deny foreign-born voters the ballot until two years after naturalization.

After serving as minister to Spain from 1860-1862, Schurz returned to help organize a Union offensive. Promoted to major general of volunteers in 1863, he served at Chancellorsville, Gettysburg, and Nashville. Butler said, "Schurz took his military duties seriously and soon won the respect of his officers and men." Schurz, however, left the following year to work on Lincoln's re-election campaign.

In 1865, working as a journalist for President Andrew Johnson and for a major Boston paper, he proclaimed that Southern whites were determined to oppress black people. Though the president would not acknowledge Schurz's findings, congressional Republicans made sure his report was published and circulated. According to an essayist in the *Encyclopedia of World Biography,* "This document was of great influence in molding a radical Reconstruction policy based on Negro suffrage."

Schurz served as Washington correspondent for the *New York Tribune,* editor of the *Detroit Post,* and co-owner and editor of the *St. Louis Westliche Post,* a German-language publication, in 1867.

On March 4, 1869, his fortieth birthday, amid a bitter showdown between Radicals and Liberals within his party, he joined the U.S. Senate. Butler wrote, "Schurz was also a distinguished linguist, amazing his fellow senators on one occasion by translating at sight lengthy passages . . . into four different languages. It has been said that 'he was the only statesman of his generation who could make an eloquent speech either in English or German without revealing which was his native tongue."

According to Villard, Schurz quickly joined the group of anti-Grant senators, opposing Grant's plan to annex Santo Domingo, among other points of his agenda, and added, "He was at his best in his incessant attacks upon political corruption. The news that he would speak at a given hour usually crowded the public galleries. But the high rank he took and held in the Senate, and his national reputation as an orator and a leader, did not assure him reelection in 1875, for, because of the Republican split, the Democrats had gained control of the Missouri legislature. He was again compelled to turn to journalism and the lecture platform for support."

On March 4, 1877, Schurz became President Rutherford B. Hayes' secretary of the interior. While in charge, he adopted a more enlightened policy toward Indians, installed a merit system in his department, and helped preserve the public domain and develop national parks.

Schurz was editor of the *New York Evening Post* and of the *Nation* for several years beginning in 1881. Later, he freelanced for *Harper's Weekly.* There, his controversial identity was briefly kept anonymous, as it had been at the *Nation.*

In 1884, Schurz supported the "Mugwumps" or reform Republicans in their campaign against nominee James G. Blaine, in favor of replacing Grover Cleveland. Schurz campaigned long and hard against the Spanish-American War of 1898, and against annexing the Philippines. His outspoken opposition of U.S. involvement in this war effectively ended his relationship with *Harper's.*

Three of Schurz's more celebrated works remain his biography, *Life of Henry Clay;* his pamphlet, *The New South;* and his autobiography, *The Reminiscences of Carl Schurz.*

BIOGRAPHICAL AND CRITICAL SOURCES:

BOOKS

Almanac of Famous People, sixth edition, Gale (Detroit, MI), 1998.

Ashley, Perry J., editor, *Dictionary of Literary Biography,* Volume 23: *American Newspaper Journalists, 1873-1900,* Gale (Detroit, MI), pp. 313-322.

Bancroft, Frederic, editor, *Speeches, Correspondence and Political Papers of Carl Schurz,* six volumes, Putnam (New York, NY), 1913.

Dictionary of American Biography, American Council of Learned Societies, 1928-1936, reprinted, Gale (Detroit, MI), 2002.

Easum, C.V., *The Americanization of Carl Schurz,* University of Chicago Press (Chicago, IL), 1929.

Encyclopedia of World Biography, second edition, 17 volumes, Gale (Detroit, MI), 1998.

Fuess, C. M., *Carl Schurz, Reformer,* Dodd, Mead (New York, NY), 1932.

O'Brien, Marjorie, *Carl Schurz: Patriot Illustrated,* State Historical Society of Wisconsin (Madison, WI), 1960.

Schafer, Joseph, *Carl Schurz, Militant Liberal,* Center Press (Evansville, WI), 1930.

Schafer, Joseph, editor, *Intimate Letters of Carl Schurz, 1841-1869,* State Historical Society of Wisconsin (Madison, WI), 1928.

Slone, William M., *In Memoriam: A Book of Record,* The American Academy of Arts and Letters, 1922.

Trefousse, Hans L., *Carl Schurz: A Biography,* University of Tennessee Press (Knoxville, TN), 1982.

Tutt, Carol Little, *Carl Schurz, Patriot,* State Historical Society of Wisconsin (Madison, WI), 1960.

OTHER

Balch Institute for Ethnic Studies Web site, http://www.balchinstitute.org/manuscript_guide/html/schurz.html/ (July, 1990), Ernest K. Giese and Monique Bourque, "Register of the Papers of Carl Schurz."*

* * *

SCRIBNER, Keith 1962(?)-

PERSONAL: Born c. 1962. *Education:* Vassar College, graduated, 1984; University of Montana, M.F.A.

ADDRESSES: Home—Menlo Park, CA. *Agent*—c/o Author Mail, Penguin Putnam, 375 Hudson St., New York, NY 10014.

CAREER: Stanford University, Stanford, CA, Wallace Stegner fellow and Jones Lecturer in creative writing, 1999-2000.

WRITINGS:

The Goodlife (novel), Riverhead Books (New York, NY), 1999.

Contributor of stories to periodicals, including *North Atlantic Review* and *American Short Fiction.*

WORK IN PROGRESS: A novel.

BIOGRAPHICAL AND CRITICAL SOURCES:

PERIODICALS

Entertainment Weekly, November 12, 1999, review of *The Goodlife,* p. 74.
Library Journal, October 15, 1999, Patrick Sullivan, review of *The Goodlife,* p. 108.
Publishers Weekly, August 30, 1999, review of *The Goodlife,* p. 46.

OTHER

Keith Scribner Web site, http://www.keithscribner.com/ (November 25, 2002).*

* * *

SEAL, Jeremy 1962-

PERSONAL: Born 1962; married; children: one daughter.

ADDRESSES: Home—Bath, England. *Agent*—c/o Author Mail, Harcourt, 15 East 26th St., New York, NY 10003-4793.

CAREER: Writer and teacher.

WRITINGS:

A Fez of the Heart: Travels around Turkey in Search of a Hat, Picador (London, England), 1995, Harcourt Brace (San Diego, CA), 1996.
The Snakebite Survivors' Club: Travels among Serpents, Harcourt Brace (San Diego, CA), 2000.
Treachery at Sharpnose Point: Unraveling the Mystery of the Caledonia's Final Voyage, Harcourt (New York, NY), 2001.

SIDELIGHTS: Jeremy Seal is a British writer who taught English in Turkey for several years. Seal's book *A Fez of the Heart: Travels around Turkey in Search of a Hat* documents his visits to Turkish towns to learn more about the headgear that was banned by Mustafa Kermal Ataturk in 1925 in a move to make his country more up-to-date. A similar ban on the turban had been instituted in 1826 by Mahmud II. An inferior facsimile of the fez is sometimes worn by tourists, but Turks continue to face arrest for this infraction. Seal's trip during winter weather took him to the cities of Istanbul, Ankara, Cappadocia, and the Moroccan city of Fez, as well as many small towns seldom visited by tourists. Phoebe-Lou Adams noted in *Atlantic Monthly* that since Seal is familiar with Turkey, his complaints about his weather-related problems with snow, cold, and winds "arouse more impatience than pity." Adams called *A Fez of the Heart* "intelligent travel writing about a trip that does not arouse any impulse toward emulation."

William Grimes wrote in the *New York Times Book Review* that although Seal "is poor at describing scenery, he has the British gift for seizing upon absurdities, awkward situations, and the miseries of travel." A *Publishers Weekly* reviewer said Seal offers "both an engaging, often very funny travelogue, and real insights into Turkey's troubled balancing act between modernity and tradition." *New Statesman & Society* reviewer Robert Carver called Seal "a writer to watch."

In researching *Treachery at Sharpnose Point: Unraveling the Mystery of the Caledonia's Final Voyage,* Seal discovered that many of the recorded facts about the ship—wrecked and sunk in 1842—were wrong. Using narrative and fiction to recount the last days of the Caledonia, Seal tries to uncover the mysteries and inaccuracies surrounding the ship's demise. *Booklist*'s Gilbert Taylor wrote that "Seal's riveting story will be a certain winner." A *Publishers Weekly* reviewer felt that Seal doesn't really recreate the history of the Caledonia, but rather "recounts the unearthing process," which he called "less engaging." *Library Journal*'s Elizabeth Coates, however, found the book "lively" and "well-paced."

BIOGRAPHICAL AND CRITICAL SOURCES:

PERIODICALS

Atlantic Monthly, May, 1996, p. 120.
Bloom Review, November, 1996, p. 25.
Booklist, March 15, 1996, p. 1237; October 15, 2001, Gilbert Taylor, review of *Treachery at Sharpnose Point: Unraveling the Mystery of the Caledonia's Final Voyage,* p. 376.
BookWatch, April 14, 1996, p. 12.
Kirkus Reviews, January 15, 1996, p. 122.
Library Journal, April 1, 1996, p. 106; October 15, 2001, Isabel Coates, review of *Treachery at Sharpnose Point,* p. 93.
Publishers Weekly, January 29, 1996, p. 96; November 4, 1996, p. 46; October 8, 2001, review of *Treachery at Sharpnose Point,* p. 55.
Spectator, February 4, 1995, p. 29.
New Statesman, March 19, 1995, pp. 38-39.
New York Times Book Review, June 16, 1996, p. 13.
Times Educational Supplement, August 16, 1996, p. 17.
Times Literary Supplement, July 28, 1995, p. 10; March 12, 1999, Annette Kobak, review of *The Snakebite Survivors' Club: Travels among Serpents,* p. 10.
Wall Street Journal, March 27, 1996, p. A20; March 3, 2000, Andrew Horton, *The Snakebite Survivors' Club,* p. W10.*

*   *   *

SERIN, Judith Ann 1949-

PERSONAL: Born May 16, 1949, in Perth Amboy, NJ; daughter of Bernard (a physicist) and Bernice (a biologist) Serin; married Herbert Yeung Yee, May 17, 1986. *Education:* Bennington College, B.A., 1971; San Francisco State University, M.A., 1974. *Hobbies and other interests:* Gardening, walking, reading.

ADDRESSES: Home—259 Staples Ave., San Francisco, CA 94112-1836. *Office*—California College of Arts and Crafts, 5212 Broadway, Oakland, CA 94618-1426.

CAREER: Poet. California College of Arts and Crafts, professor of English, 1990—.

AWARDS, HONORS: Honorable mention, Academy of American Poets, 1974.

WRITINGS:

Hiding in the World, Eidolon Editions (San Francisco, CA), 1998.

Work represented in anthologies, including *What's a Nice Girl like You Doing in a Relationship like This?,* Crossing Press, 1992, and *Bridge: Poems about Marriage,* Grayson Books, 2003.

*   *   *

SEROUSSI, Karyn 1965-

PERSONAL: Born 1965; married a chemist; children: Miles.

ADDRESSES: Office—ANDI, P.O. Box 17711, Rochester, NY 14617-0711.

CAREER: Small-business owner; cofounder of Autism Network for Dietary Intervention (ANDI) and publisher of *ANDI News* (newsletter).

WRITINGS:

Unraveling the Mystery of Autism and Pervasive Developmental Disorder: A Mother's Story of Research and Recovery (memoir), Simon & Schuster (New York, NY), 2000.

SIDELIGHTS: Karyn Seroussi's book, *Unraveling the Mystery of Autism and Pervasive Developmental Disorder: A Mother's Story of Research and Recovery,* documents her successful struggle to help her son, Miles, who was diagnosed with autism at the age of eighteen months. Miles developed normally until he was fifteen months old and then stopped communicating normally. He began to act in a manner associated with autism: repeating actions, crying, and refusing to be held. He also developed chronic diarrhea and ear infections. Seroussi noted in an article in *Parents Magazine* that "autism—or autistic spectrum disorder, as doctors now call it—is not a mental illness. It is a developmental disability thought to be caused by an anomaly in the brain. The National Institute of Health estimates that as many as one in 500 children are affected. But according to several recent studies, the incidence is rapidly rising: In Florida, for example, the number of autistic children has increased nearly 600 percent in the last ten years." Seroussi and her husband, a chemist, were told that Miles would grow up severely impaired.

When Seroussi began researching autism she discovered references to a link between the condition and milk allergy. She realized that her son's ear infections had begun when she switched him from soy to cow's milk. She then eliminated all dairy from his diet. His condition improved, and when Seroussi took him to see Susan Hyman, a developmental psychologist, she described these improvements, but Hyman, after testing the child, confirmed a diagnosis of autism. Improvement continued, and to test their theory, Seroussi and her husband gave Miles two glasses of milk and watched his behavior temporarily deteriorate.

Seroussi sent a videotape to Dr. Hyman, who was amazed by Miles's improvement. Seroussi bought a modem for her computer and found an autism support group on the internet. What she discovered was that preliminary evidence on the milk link had already been verified by researchers in England and Norway. She found that in journal articles "it was theorized that a subtype of children with autism break down milk protein (casein) into peptides that affect the brain in the same way that hallucinogenic drugs do. A handful of scientists, some of whom were parents of kids with autism, had discovered compounds containing opiates—a class of substances including opium and heroin—in the urine of autistic children. The researchers theorized that, either these children were missing an enzyme that normally breaks down the peptides into a digestible form, or the peptides were somehow leaking into the bloodstream before they could be digested." Seroussi realized that this was the reason Miles had craved milk; opiates are highly addictive.

The Seroussis also found that gluten found in wheat, rye, oats, and barley, which are added to thousands of packaged foods, can break down into a toxic form. Within two days of being gluten-free, Miles, now twenty-two months old, had his first solid stool, and his coordination and balance improved. A month later he began to speak again. Seroussi's theories received no support from her doctors, including Miles's pediatrician, geneticist, and neurologist, who dismissed any connection between autism and diet. The parents attended conferences, e-mailed European researchers, and organized a local support group. Although Seroussi acknowledges that not all autistic children are helped by dietary modifications, fifty families who made the dietary changes did see improvement in their children. Seroussi finally found local professional support with a new pediatrician, and by Miles's third birthday, he was declared cured. At age six he was reading at a fourth-grade level and living a normal happy life.

Seroussi established the Autism Network for Dietary Intervention (ANDI) with Lisa Lewis, author of *Special Diets for Special Kids.* They maintain a Web site, publish a newsletter, and communicate by e-mail with parents around the world. Seroussi continued her research, which indicated that autism is related to the immune system. She discovered that nearly all the children in her group had at least one immune-related problem, but she was still looking for the factor that triggered the disease. Some parents felt their children's behavior changed after they received the MMR (measles, mumps, rubella) vaccine. Seroussi realized that following Miles's MMR, she had taken him to the emergency room with febrile seizures and a temperature of 106 degrees. Seroussi noted that British researcher Andrew Wakefield had published a study linking the measles portion of MMR to small intestine damage, "which might help explain the mechanism by which the hallucinogenic peptides leak into the bloodstream." Seroussi said that if this is the case, it should be determined if some children are at higher risk, and whether they should receive the vaccine at a later age or not at all. Seroussi's husband is one of a group of researchers who study the abnormal presence of peptides in the urine of autistic children. Seroussi writes that her hope "is that eventually a routine diagnostic test will be developed to identify children with autism at a young age and that when some types of autism are recognized as a metabolic disorder, the gluten and dairy-free diet will move from the realm of alternative medicine into the mainstream."

Booklist contributor William Beatty noted that in the book, Seroussi "gives practical advice to others facing similar child-development problems and points them to helping organizations." "Seroussi has written a book that will give hope to many families," wrote a *Publishers Weekly* reviewer.

BIOGRAPHICAL AND CRITICAL SOURCES:

BOOKS

Seroussi, Karyn, *Unraveling the Mystery of Autism and Pervasive Developmental Disorder: A Mother's Story of Research and Recovery,* Simon & Schuster (New York, NY), 2000.

PERIODICALS

Booklist, January 1, 2000, William Beatty, review of *Unraveling the Mystery of Autism and Pervasive Developmental Disorder,* p. 848.
Parents Magazine, February, 2000, Karyn Seroussi, "We Cured Our Son's Autism."
Publishers Weekly, December 13, 1999, review of *Unraveling the Mystery of Autism and Pervasive Developmental Disorder,* p. 71.

OTHER

Autism Network for Dietary Intervention, http://www.members.aol.com/autismndi/PAGES/ (April 25, 2000).*

*   *   *

SHABER, Sarah R. 1951-

PERSONAL: Born December 4, 1951; in Washington, DC; daughter of Frank and Frances Rock; married Steve Shaber (an attorney); children: Sam, Katie. *Education:* Graduate of Duke University, 1973.

ADDRESSES: Home—Raleigh, NC. *Agent*—c/o Vicky Bijur Literary Agency, 333 West End Ave., New York, NY 10023.

CAREER: Author.

AWARDS, HONORS: Malice Domestic Award for best first traditional mystery, 1996, for *Simon Said.*

WRITINGS:

Simon Said, St. Martin's (New York, NY), 1997.
Snipe Hunt, Thomas Dunne (New York, NY), 2000.
The Fugitive King, Thomas Dunne (New York, NY), 2002.

SIDELIGHTS: Sarah R. Shaber's first novel, *Simon Said,* is a mystery set at Kenan College in Raleigh, North Carolina. *Library Journal* contributor Rex E. Klett deemed that the "setting and historic elements should please most readers." A mansion once belonging to the Bloodworth family has been deeded to the college which then leased it to the preservation society. During an archaeological dig on the grounds, the skeletal remains of a woman with a bullet hole through her skull are found, and Simon Shaw, a young Pulitzer Prize-winning history professor who wrote a history of the mansion, is called in. Simon identifies the woman as Anne Bloodworth, heiress to the estate, who disappeared in 1926. As the investigation progresses, Simon meets with several accidents, and it soon becomes obvious that someone wants to prevent him from learning more. A *Publishers Weekly* reviewer felt that Simon, police counsel Julia McGloughlan, and Sergeant Gates "are realistically portrayed." In reviewing *Simon Said* for *Booklist,* Gail Pool called it a "personable book, with a likable, vulnerable protagonist [and] an abundance of wry humor."

Simon returns in *Snipe Hunt,* set on Pearlie Beach, an island off the North Carolina coast. He is joined for the Thanksgiving holiday by his friend Julia, archeologist David Morgan, and his colleague Marcus Cleggs, who arrives with his wife and three daughters. Simon is thrust into another mystery from the past when a body in a World War II diving suit containing Confederate gold coins is dredged up offshore. A *Publishers Weekly* reviewer called the mystery an "appealing cozy, which pleasingly mixes regional history and lore, a bit of romance, and a soupcon of suspense." Klett felt the "beach scenes, folksy locals, and mild humor" would be especially appealing to regional audiences.

In *The Fugitive King,* Simon is accosted at gunpoint by an escaped convict, Roy Freedman, who needs Simon's help to prove his claim that he is innocent of a murder he was convicted of many years earlier. Simon agrees to help and begins interviewing people in the town in which the murder took place. In the process, Simon begins to think that Freedman is indeed innocent, as he runs up against a lying sheriff, an amazing lack of evidence tying Freedman to the crime, and the question of why Freedman pleaded guilty if he was in fact, innocent. *Booklist*'s Sue O'Brien called *The Fugitive King* "an engaging mystery in a too-little-known series."

BIOGRAPHICAL AND CRITICAL SOURCES:

PERIODICALS

Booklist, April 15, 1997, Gail Pool, review of *Simon Said,* p. 1414; September 1, 2002, Sue O'Brien, review of *The Fugitive King,* p. 64.

Kirkus Reviews, July 15, 2002, review of *The Fugitive King,* p. 998.

Library Journal, April 1, 1997, Rex. E. Klett, review of *Simon Said,* p. 133; February 1, 2000, Rex E. Klett, review of *Snipe Hunt,* p. 121.

Publishers Weekly, February 10, 1997, review of *Simon Said,* p. 70; February 28, 2000, review of *Snipe Hunt,* p. 66; September 2, 2002, review of *The Fugitive King,* p. 58.*

*   *   *

SHAFFER, Brian W. 1960-

PERSONAL: Born 1960. *Education:* Washington University, A.B., 1983; University of Iowa, Ph.D., 1989.

ADDRESSES: Office—Department of English, Rhodes College, 2000 North Parkway, Memphis, TN 38112-1624. *E-mail*—shaffer@rhodes.edu.

CAREER: Rhodes College, Memphis, TN, associate professor of English, 1996—02, Associate Dean of Academic Affairs, 2000—, professor of English, 2002—.

MEMBER: Phi Beta Kappa, 1983.

AWARDS, HONORS: Fellow, University of Iowa, 1984-88; Frederick P. W. McDowell Graduate Scholar Award, University of Iowa, 1986-87 and 1989-90; National Endowment for the Humanities fellow, University of North Carolina, 1989-90, and University of California, 1993; Clarence Day Dean's Award, 1995 and 2000.

WRITINGS:

The Blinding Torch: Modern British Fiction and the Discourse of Civilization, University of Massachusetts Press (Amherst, MA), 1993.

Understanding Kazuo Ishiguro, University of South Carolina Press (Columbia, SC), 1998.

(Editor, with Hunt Hawkins) *Approaches to Teaching Conrad's "Heart of Darkness" and "The Secret Sharer,"* Modern Language Association of America, 2002.

SIDELIGHTS: Brian W. Shaffer, an associate professor of English at Rhodes College in Memphis, Tennessee, attracted academic notice for his first book of literary criticism, *The Blinding Torch: Modern British Fiction and the Discourse of Civilization.* Critics found this work—which considers the fiction of Joseph Conrad, D. H. Lawrence, James Joyce, Virginia Woolf, and Malcolm Lowry, and the theories of Mikhail Bakhtin, Terry Eagleton, and Clifford Gertz—to be highly specialized. In his analysis, Shaffer identifies the centrality, during the period between 1897 and 1947, of cultural debates in literature around the concept of "civilization." These, he shows, were often structured around conflicts or oppositions: between Western and non-Western, materialistic and organic, Anglo-Saxon and Celtic, male privilege and female marginality.

Nicola Bradbury noted in *Review of English Studies* that Shaffer's thesis is strongly supported, cogently argued, and informed by "fresh thinking," though sometimes "not merely packed but sometimes pickled with scholarship." *Modern Language Review* critic Macdonald Dalyalso appreciated the originality of Shaffer's thesis, but the critic also found several flaws in the author's theoretical analysis, particularly in the argument that the literary texts "absorb the discourse of civilization even as they assault it," a conclusion Daly dismissed a "a dusty old tune played on a shiny new instrument." *Choice* reviewer A. R. Nourie found *The Blinding Torch* to be lucidly written but likely to be of importance primarily to graduate students and faculty.

BIOGRAPHICAL AND CRITICAL SOURCES:

PERIODICALS

Choice, November, 1993, p. 456; September, 1999, J. Tharp, review of *Understanding Kazuo Ishiguro,* p. 147.
College Literature, June, 1994, p. 191.
Modern Language Review, January, 1995, pp. 166-167.
Review of English Studies, January, 1995, pp. 111-112.*

*   *   *

SHAFIK, Viola 1961-

PERSONAL: Born 1961. *Education:* University of Hamburg, Ph.D.

ADDRESSES: Office—c/o Author Mail, American University in Cairo Press, 113 Sharia Kasr el Ainy, Cairo, Egypt.

CAREER: Filmmaker, researcher, and author. American University in Cairo, Cairo, Egypt, professor of film.

AWARDS, HONORS: FIMA Prize, Paris, for best Arab short film, 1993, for *Shadjarat al-Laymun;* Rockefeller fellow, 1996-97.

WRITINGS:

Arab Cinema: History and Cultural Identity, American University in Cairo Press (Cairo, Egypt), 1999.

SIDELIGHTS: Viola Shafik is a professor of film at the American University in Cairo and the author of the first English-language book to discuss both the content and form of Arabic film. Shafik researched her subject in the Arab world and in Germany in writing *Arab Cinema: History and Cultural Identity.* Shafik addresses the artistic, political, historical, and economic considerations that impact film in the Arab world. An *Egypt Today* reviewer called the book "a rich, multi-layered (albeit academic) study" and felt that "the inclusion of films from all over the Arab world is perhaps the book's greatest accomplishment, with large sections covering the often marginalized films of Algeria, Tunisia, and Morocco." Shafik examines the beginnings of film in Arab countries and points to independence from colonialism as an important factor in its development. She focuses on political films and art films which were produced after Farouk's fall in Egypt, the French departure from Algeria, and the strengthening of the Palestinian conflict. Egypt is the only country to have developed a national cinema prior to independence, and its films were modeled after Hollywood productions. Shafik discusses the economics of the Arab industry—how films were first produced by foreign companies, then by Arab entrepreneurs, and then by government-run companies. She discusses how films are now often co-produced with Western companies and evaluated and defined on a more international level.

The *Egypt Today* reviewer noted that Shafik "outlines the process of 'cultural repackaging' that turned cinema from an imported medium to an 'Arab' cinema, and explains how Arab-Islamic culture accommodated cinema, in spite of the fact that Islam prohibits visual representation of human beings." This explains why music and dialogue are so important in creating a "word-centered" rather than an "image-centered" medium. Shafik says that with socialism came a need for realism, especially since those who had been colonized had not been allowed to have an image.

In a *Times Literary Supplement* review, Robert Irwin cited some of the films that have been produced since the 1960s. Shadi 'Abd al-Sallam's *Al-Mumia* (1968) was shown in Great Britain as *The Night of Counting the Years.* Irwin said this film about a young Egyptian who chooses not to rob tombs, a practice that had been carried on for generations, "serves as a vehicle for a meditation on Egypt's national identity and on its relationship to its past." Irwin noted that although most Arab films are made in local vernaculars, in this film, "the protagonists conduct their fierce debates in a stately classical Arabic." Nacer Khemir's *Tawq al-Hamama al-Maqfud* ("The Lost Ring of the Dove," 1999), a "'picture-book' of a film, has also attracted much praise and attention," wrote Irwin. Irwin described Yusuf Chahine's *Wada'a Bonaparte* ("Adieu Bonaparte," 1985) as "visually ravishing." It is the story of the friendship between a French doctor and two Arab boys during Bonaparte's occupation. Irwin said Shafik criticized this film as being historically inaccurate and because it did not include important Egyptian characters. Irwin felt that Shafik "takes some films too seriously." He cited Chahine's *Al-Nasir Salah al-Din* ("Saladin," 1963), a historical drama Shafik praises for its costumes and sets.

Irwin agreed with Shafik's observations of the obstacles faced by the Arab film industry. There are too few movie houses to sustain the productions, and many films are adapted to Western audiences. In the process, Arab audiences are easily alienated, and still the films do not garner international praise. It is very difficult for aspiring Arab filmmakers to find the training they require. Irwin pointed out that even Egypt, which had been able to export most of its films to the Gulf, is now faced with increasing competition from satellite television and videos. The upside is that there is renewed interest in some of the classic films as they are being shown on television.

Arab filmmakers have been pressured to adapt their films to propaganda and have been targeted by fundamentalist criticism. In 1952, a pan-Islamic conference in Karachi proposed a ban on all film. Irwin said that Hassan al-Imam's *Khalli balak min Zou-Zou* ("Watch out for Zou-Zou," 1972), about a student who belly-dances to pay for college, and Chahine's *Al-Massir* are two of the few films "to engage directly with fundamentalist bigotry."

Shafik writes of the Egyptian censorship law of 1976 that dictates that the "heavenly" religions of Islam, Christianity, and Judaism are not to be criticized. There should be no positive portrayals of magic, vices, and immoral acts (which must be punished). Nakedness and emphasis on erotic body parts, sexually arousing scenes, scenes involving drug or alcohol use, excessive violence and horror, and obscenity, are not allowed. Respect must be shown to families, marriage and parents. It is also forbidden "to represent social problems as hopeless, to upset the mind, or divide religions, classes, and the national unity." Irwin noted that a 1949 censorship law "equated realism with social subversion." Irwin concluded by asking and answering the question: "What does this leave space for? Some wonderful films."

BIOGRAPHICAL AND CRITICAL SOURCES:

PERIODICALS

Egypt Today, December 4, 1998.
Times Literary Supplement, May 14, 1999, p. 10.*

*   *   *

SHAKOOR, Jordana Y. 1956-

PERSONAL: Born 1956.

ADDRESSES: Agent—c/o Author Mail, University Press of Mississippi, 3825 Ridgewood Rd., Jackson, MS 39211-6492.

CAREER: Freelance writer. JYS Consultants, founder and director.

WRITINGS:

Civil Rights Childhood, University Press of Mississippi (Jackson, MS), 1999.

SIDELIGHTS: Jordana Y. Shakoor combined her own memories with reminiscences from her father's journals to create *Civil Rights Childhood,* which she describes as a tribute to her father, Cleveland Jordan. Jordan grew up in a sharecropping family near Greenwood, Mississippi, where he picked cotton and was regularly cheated of his pay and deprived of his pride. Despite the rigors of farming, Jordan excelled at school and made a better life for himself, serving in the army and getting a college teaching degree. During the 1960s Jordan was active in the civil rights movement, Shakoor recounts. She also describes the harshness of the Jim Crow laws and the shameful activities of the Ku Klux Klan, including the lynching of Emmitt Till. In 1963, when Jordan and his wife attempted to register to vote, Jordan was fired from his teaching job. This setback prompted him to move his family to Toledo, Ohio, where Jordana grew up. *Civil Rights Childhood* garnered praise from critics. In *Publishers Weekly* a reviewer remarked that Shakoor avoids overwrought prose and declared the work "engrossing and vital." Although Shakoor noted in an interview for *Online in Worthington* that although improved race relations exist in the United States, she reminded readers, "We still have work to do to eradicate racism in our society. Racial hatred destroys lives and it destroys families."

BIOGRAPHICAL AND CRITICAL SOURCES:

PERIODICALS

Booklist, September 15, 1999, Mary Carroll, review of *Civil Rights Childhood,* p. 228.
Publishers Weekly, August 2, 1999, review of *Civil Rights Childhood,* p. 61.

OTHER

Online in Worthington, http://thisweeknews.com/ (June 1, 2000).*

*   *   *

SHAW, Marion

PERSONAL: Female. *Education:* T.Cert., B.A., Ph.D., R.S.A.

ADDRESSES: Office—c/o Loughborough University, Loughborough, Leicestershire LE11 3TU, England.

CAREER: Loughborough University, Loughborough, England, professor of English and head of department, 1993-98, part-time teacher, 1998—; Quality Assurance Agency, review chair, 1999—. Member of English panel for Research Assessment Exercise, 1996, 2001; former member of executive committee and organizer of conferences for the Council for College and University English.

MEMBER: Tennyson Society (chair).

AWARDS, HONORS: National lottery grant, 1999.

WRITINGS:

NONFICTION

Alfred Lord Tennyson (criticism), Humanities Press International (Atlantic Highlands, NJ), 1988.
(With Clifton U. Snaith) *An Annotated Critical Bibliography of Alfred, Lord Tennyson,* Harvester Wheatsheaf (London, England), 1989.
(With Sabine Vanacker) *Reflecting on Miss Marple* (criticism), Routledge (London), 1991.
(Editor) *Man Does, Woman Is: An Anthology of Work and Gender,* Faber and Faber (London, England), 1995.
(Editor) *An Introduction to Women's Writing: From the Middle Ages to the Present Day,* Prentice Hall (New York, NY), 1998.
The Clear Stream: A Life of Winifred Holtby (biography), Virago (London, England), 1999.

OTHER

(Editor, with Susan Shatto) Alfred Lord Tennyson, *In Memoriam* (poetry), Clarendon Press (Oxford, England), 1982.
(Editor, with Paul Berry) Winifred Holtby, *Remember! Remember!* (short stories), Virago Press (London, England), 1997.

Contributor to *Festschrift for John Lucas: Critical Survey Special Issue,* 1999. Founding editor, *Journal of Gender Studies;* former editor, *Tennyson Research Bulletin.*

SIDELIGHTS: Marion Shaw was a professor at Loughborough University until she retired from full-time teaching in 1998. Her works typically focus on nineteenth-century poetry, in particular, the works of Alfred Lord Tennyson, and on women's literature.

After coediting Tennyson's *In Memoriam* in 1982, Shaw published two works on the renowned poet. The first, simply titled *Alfred Lord Tennyson,* was published in 1988 and was part of Humanities Press International's "Feminist Readings" series. Critical reaction to the book was mixed. Though L. M. Tenbusche in *Choice* found that the book could "give readers a sufficient slice of feminist criticism," the critic felt it could be "tiresomely one-sided." On the other hand, Laurel Brake in *Victorian Studies* called the work "provocative," concluding: "This is a book which offers a number of fresh readings, and rather than viewing Tennyson as a misogynist, Shaw provides a view of the male author reproducing and creating structures of a particular male culture."

Shaw's second work was *An Annotated Critical Bibliography of Alfred, Lord Tennyson,* a bibliography of works on Tennyson and his poetry. The work lists just over 400 major works on Tennyson and is aimed primarily at the upper-level university or graduate student. Joseph Sendry in *Victorian Poetry* praised both the comprehensiveness of Shaw's annotations and the organization of the volume as a whole. R. Hanson in *Choice* wrote: "[The bibliography] puts a good deal of information within easy reach, and its annotations are especially well informed on biographical and bibliographical entries."

In addition to works on Tennyson, Shaw has also written a literary analysis of Agatha Christie's Miss Marple, *Reflecting on Miss Marple,* two volumes of women's literature history, *Man Does, Woman Is: An Anthology of Work and Gender* and *An Introduction to Women's Writing: From the Middle Ages to the Present Day,* and a biography of activist and author Winifred Holtby, *The Clear Stream: A Life of Winifred Holtby.* Critics were largely positive in their assessments of Shaw's other works as well. L. Babener in *Choice* called *Reflecting on Miss Marple,* co-written with Sabine Vanacker, "a major contribution to popular culture and feminist scholarship." Pamela Norris in the *Times Literary Supplement* lauded Shaw's biography of Holtby. Norris, referencing Sarah Burton, a character from Holtby's 1936 novel *South Riding,* concluded:

"Burton . . . mirrors the Winifred Holtby portrayed in Shaw's scrupulously even-handed biography, whose attitude to life may be summarized by Sarah's final advice to her girls: 'Question everything . . . and see that you get sensible answers to your questions.'"

BIOGRAPHICAL AND CRITICAL SOURCES:

PERIODICALS

Choice, March, 1989, L. M. Tencusch, review of *Alfred Lord Tennyson,* p. 1162; February, 1990, R. Hanson, review of *An Annotated Critical Bibliography of Alfred, Lord Tennyson,* p. 937; February, 1992, L. Babener, review of *Reflecting on Miss Marple,* p. 898.
Contemporary Review, May, 2000, Catherine Wade, review of *A Life of Winifred Holtby,* p. 271.
Times Educational Supplement, July 14, 1995, Julia Neuberger, review of *Man Does, Woman Is,* p. 14.
Times Literary Supplement, September 3, 1999, Pamela Norris, review of *The Clear Stream,* p. 28.
Victorian Poetry, summer, 1990, Joseph Sendry, review of *An Annotated Critical Bibliography of Alfred, Lord Tennyson,* pp. 229-241.
Victorian Studies, winter, 1991, Laurel Brake, review of *Alfred Lord Tennyson,* pp. 280-281.*

* * *

SIEGEL, Sheldon

PERSONAL: Born July 14, 1958; married; wife's name, Linda; children: Alan, Stephen. *Ethnicity:* "Caucasian." *Education:* University of Illinois, Champaign, BS Accounting, 1980; Boalt Hall School of Law, University of California—Berkeley, J.D., 1983. *Religion:* "Jewish." *Hobbies and other interests:* "Sports, reading."

ADDRESSES: Home—Marin County, CA. *Agent*—Margret McBride, Margaret McBride Literary Agency, 7744 Fay Avenue, Suite 201, La Jolla, CA 92037. *E-mail*—sheldon@sheldonsiegel.com.

CAREER: Attorney and novelist.

WRITINGS:

Special Circumstances, Bantam (New York, NY), 2000.
Incriminating Evidence, Bantam (New York, NY), 2001.
Criminal Intent, Putnam (New York, NY), 2002.
Final Verdict, Putnam (New York, NY), 2003.

WORK IN PROGRESS: Reasonable Doubt, a novel.

SIDELIGHTS: Sheldon Siegel is an attorney who began his first novel, *Special Circumstances,* during his commute by ferry from Marin County, California, to his San Francisco office. He dedicated the novel to his colleagues who were killed by a former client who gunned them down on July 1, 1993. He began the book in 1995, took creative writing courses in 1997, and found an agent and a publisher in 1998. Siegel is a corporate lawyer, but his protagonist and narrator, Mike Daley, is a criminal lawyer, a former priest, and a public defender. A *Publishers Weekly* contributor called Daley "flawed, often-desperate . . . Siegel humanizes his hero by depicting Daley's charged, still-sexual relationship with his ex-wife, a tough lawyer who retains custody of their six-year-old daughter."

Daley leaves Simpson & Gates, a large San Francisco law firm, and sets up his own neighborhood practice. His first client is his friend and former colleague, Joel, the son of a rabbi, who is accused of killing two slimy Simpson & Gates attorneys. He is opposed in court by Prentice Marshall "Skipper" Gates III, who left the firm to become district attorney. *People Weekly* contributor Ralph Novak felt Siegel "borrows far too heavily from the O. J. Simpson trial." *Library Journal* reviewer Jeff Ayers, however, judged that the novel is "filled with sparkling court scenes that are a rarity in legal thrillers today." "It shouldn't take Siegel long to join the best-selling firm of Turow and Grisham," wrote Jenny McLarin in *Booklist.*

In *Incriminating Evidence,* District Attorney Skipper Gates wakes up in a hotel with a dead male prostitute in his bed. Despite his personal dislike for Gates, Daley believes that he might be innocent, and takes on his case. *Library Journal*'s Jeff Ayers noted that the "courtroom scenes ring true," while *Booklist*'s Joanne Wilkinson called *Incriminating Evidence* "a solid . . . legal thriller."

Criminal Intent again features Daley and his law partner—and ex-wife—Rosie Fernandez. Rosie's actress niece, Angel, is accused of murdering her husband, a movie director many years older than Angel. He was directing his "comeback" film, which starred Angel. Mike and Rosie have to defend Angel, while also dealing with other extended family issues, including Rosie's brother's dealings with the mob, and Mike's secret affair with a judge. *Booklist*'s Mary Frances Wilkins noted that "a surprise ending will keep readers yearning for more."

BIOGRAPHICAL AND CRITICAL SOURCES:

PERIODICALS

Booklist, December 1, 1999, Jenny McLarin, review of *Special Circumstances,* p. 661; May 1, 2001, Joanne Wilkinson, review of *Incriminating Evidence,* p. 1641; August, 2002, Mary Frances Wilkens, review of *Criminal Intent,* p. 1888.
Kirkus Reviews, June 15, 2002, review of *Criminal Intent,* p. 836.
Library Journal, December, 1999, Jeff Ayers, review of *Special Circumstances,* p. 189; June 15, 2001, Jeff Ayers, review of *Incriminating Evidence,* p. 105; July, 2002, Jill M. Tempest, review of *Criminal Intent,* p. 122.
People Weekly, March 13, 2000, Ralph Novak, review of *Special Circumstances,* p. 55.
Publishers Weekly, December 13, 1999, review of *Special Circumstances,* p. 63; February 28, 2000, Judy Quinn, "A New Grisham?" p. 21; July 23, 2001, review of *Incriminating Evidence,* p. 48; July 8, 2002, review of *Criminal Intent,* p. 30.

OTHER

Official Sheldon Siegel Web site, http://www.sheldon siegel.com (May 14, 2001).*

*   *   *

SKINNER, Constance Lindsay 1877-1939

PERSONAL: Original name, Constance Annie Skinner, born December 7, 1877 in Quesnel, British Columbia, Canada; died of influenza, March 27, 1939, in New York, NY; daughter of Robert (a Hudson's Bay factor), and Annie Lindsay.

CAREER: Poet, novelist, playwright, essayist, and historian.

AWARDS, HONORS: Prizes from *Poetry, Bookman,* and *Lyric West* for poems from *Songs of the Coast Dwellers,* 1930.

WRITINGS:

Good Morning, Rosamund!, Doubleday (Garden City, NY), 1917.

(Contributor) *The Path on the Rainbow: An Anthology of Songs and Chants from the Indians of North America* edited by George W. Cronyn, Boni and Liveright (New York, NY), 1918.

Pioneers of the Old Southwest: A Chronicle of the Dark and Bloody Ground, Yale University Press (New Haven, CT), 1921.

Adventures of Oregon: A Chronicle of the Fur Trade, Yale University Press (New Haven, CT), 1921.

(With Clark Wissler and William Wood) *Adventures in the Wilderness,* Yale University Press (New Haven, CT), 1925.

Silent Scot, Frontier Scout, Macmillan (New York, NY), 1925.

Becky Landers: Frontier Warrior, Macmillan (New York), 1926.

The White Leader, Macmillan (New York, NY).

Roselle of the North, Macmillan (New York), 1927.

The Tiger Who Walks Alone, Macmillan (New York, NY), 1927.

Andy Breaks Trail, Macmillan (New York, NY), 1928.

The Ranch of the Golden Flowers, Macmillan (New York, NY), 1928.

The Search Relentless, Coward-McCann (New York, NY), 1928.

Red Willows, Coward-McCann (New York, NY), 1929.

Red Man's Luck, Coward-McCann (New York, NY), 1930.

Songs of the Coast Dwellers, Coward-McCann (New York, NY), 1930.

Debby Barnes, Trader, McMillan (New York, NY), 1932.

Beaver, Kings and Cabins, Macmillan (New York, NY), 1933.

Rob Roy: The Frontier Twins, MacMillan (New York, NY), 1934.

(Editor) *The Rivers of America,* six volumes, Farrar and Rhinehart (New York, NY), 1937-1939.

(Contributor) *The Book of Canadian Poetry,* edited by A.J.M. Smith, University of Chicago Press (Chicago, IL), 1943.

OTHER

David (play), produced at the Forest Theatre, Carmel, CA, July, 1910.

The plays *The Lady of Gray Gables* (1911-1912) and *Birthright* were performed in several U.S. cities.

Contributor to numerous publications, including *Poetry Review, North American Review,* and *Poetry.* Skinner's works have been translated into German.

SIDELIGHTS: Constance Lindsay Skinner was a Canadian poet, novelist, playwright, essayist, journalist, and historian. She is recognized primarily for adapting Indian songs. But, as Diana M. A. Relke explained in *Dictionary of Literary Biography,* Skinner was also a significant creative writer whose best-remembered West Coast Indian song adaptations involve original free-verse and imagistic poetry.

By age five Skinner had completed her first story; by age eleven an entire novel. She wrote *In Gelderland,* a musical sketch for children. Her father encouraged her interest in literature, while her surroundings fueled her creativity. Relke wrote, "Among Skinner's literary forefathers were the major eighteenth and nineteenth-century writers whose work she read as a child in her father's well-stocked library. In addition, she was personally acquainted with several Indian bards of the tribes with whom her father did business."

At sixteen, Skinner moved to California to stay long-term with an aunt, but her Canadian childhood experiences and her knowledge of Canadian history continued to appear in her creative work. She published a couple of short stories, also at age sixteen, and also contributed freelance to the *Los Angeles Times,* the *San Francisco Examiner,* and other periodicals.

Later, she relocated to New York City and continued to work professionally, publishing fourteen novels, twenty-eight short stories, three plays, sixty poems, almost two hundred book reviews, four histories of

American pioneer life, and a few history-related pieces. Her novels feature historical settings and detail pioneer circumstances, Indian culture, and the North American fur trade. She wrote several novels for young audiences, including *Roselle of the North,* which tells of a white girl the Cree Indians adopted. *Red Willows,* a novel for adults, takes place in British Columbia during the gold rush and dramatizes the relationship between a white man and an Indian.

Many American high schools used one of Skinner's histories, *Adventures of Oregon: A Chronicle of the Fur Trade,* their required reading lists in 1934. *Songs of the Coast Dwellers* is set in the Squamish Indian settlement on the north shore of Burrard Inlet in British Columbia.

Skinner won three writing prizes for *Songs of the Coast Dwellers,* from *Poetry,* where several pieces ran prior to book publication, *Bookman,* and *Lyric West.*

Several of her unpublished plays were performed: *David,* a three-act adaptation of the Biblical reign of King Saul; *The Lady of Gray Gables,* a romantic comedy; and *Birthright,* a tragedy set in British Columbia. In 1943, A. J. M. Smith's *Book of Canadian Poetry* featured several of Skinner's poems and, in a literary sense, returned her to Canadian readers. She had died five years earlier in New York City.

BIOGRAPHICAL AND CRITICAL SOURCES:

BOOKS

New, W.H., editor, *Dictionary of Literary Biography,* Volume 92: *Canadian Writers, 1890-1920,* Gale (Detroit, MI), 1990, pp. 366-369.

OTHER

New York Public Library Web site, http://www.nypl. org/research/chss/spe/rbk/faids/skinner.html/ (January, 1999), "Guide to the Constance Lindsay Skinner Papers, 1873-1939."*

*　　*　　*

SLOBODKINA, Esphyr 1908-2002

OBITUARY NOTICE—See index for *CA* sketch: Born September 22, 1908, in Cheliabinsk, Siberia; died July 21, 2002, in Glen Head, NY. Abstract artist, author, and illustrator. Born in a small town in rural Siberia,

Slobodkina immigrated to the United States in 1928 with her family. She was an abstract artist who worked in paintings and sculptures, and her work was eventually acquired for permanent collections at noted museums, including the Whitney Museum of American Art and the Philadelphia Museum of Art. A founding member of the American Abstract Artists, Slobodkina started writing and illustrating children's books during the Great Depression of the 1930s to make extra money for her family, and was helped in publishing her books by a friendship with noted children's author Margaret Wise Brown. Her most well-known book, *Caps for Sale,* was first published in 1938 and continues to sell steadily. *Caps for Sale* tells the story of a cap salesman who is pestered by a group of playful monkeys who take the street peddler's caps high up into the trees. Slobodkina wrote and illustrated a number of children's books for other authors, Brown among them, including *The Wonderful Feast* (1955), *The Long Island Ducklings* (1961), and *Circus Elephant* (published as *Circus Caps for Sale* in 2002).

OBITUARIES AND OTHER SOURCES:

PERIODICALS

Los Angleles Times, July 29, 2002, p. B8.
New York Times, July 27, 2002, p. A24.
Publishers Weekly, August 12, 2002, p. 151.
Washington Post, July 28, 2002, p. C1.

*　　*　　*

SMITH, Henry Holmes 1909-1986

PERSONAL: Born October 23, 1909 in Bloomington, IL; died March 24, 1986, in Marin County, CA; married Wanda Lee Phares, in 1947; children: Christopher, Theodore. *Education:* Attended State Normal College, Bloomington, 1927-29 and 1930-31; School of the Art Institute of Chicago, 1929-30; Ohio State University, Columbus, B.S., 1933.

CAREER: Independent photographer; New Bauhaus School, instructor of photography, Chicago, IL, 1937-38; *Minicam Photography,* associate editor, Cincinnati, OH, 1940-42; Indiana University, instructor, Bloomington, 1947-65, professor, 1965-67; *College Art Jour-*

nal, associate editor, Bloomington, 1955-64; Maryland Institute College of Art, visiting professor, Baltimore, MD, 1967; *Exhibitions:* Works included in permanent collections at Indiana University, Bloomington, IN; Museum of Modern Art, New York, NY; International Museum of Photography and Film, Rochester, NY; George Eastman House, Rochester, NY; Library of Congress, Washington, DC; New Orleans Museum of Art, New Orleans, LA; Museum of Fine Arts, St. Petersburg, FL; Center for Creative Photography, University of Arizona, Tucson; University Art Museum, University of New Mexico, Albuquerque; Oakland Art Museum, Oakland, CA; San Francisco Museum of Modern Art, San Francisco, CA; Museum of the Art Institute of Chicago, Chicago, IL; Museum of Fine Arts, Houston, TX; Cincinnati Art Museum, Cincinnati, OH; Kalamazoo Art Institute, Kalamazoo, MI; Crocker Art Museum, Sacramento, CA; Metropolitan Museum of Art, New York, NY; Sheldon Memorial Art Gallery, University of Nebraska, Lincoln; Princeton University Museum, Princeton, NJ; Bibliothèque Nationale, Paris, France; Victoria and Albert Museum, London, England; Bauhaus Archive, Berlin, Germany; National Gallery of Canada, Ottawa; and National Museum of Modern Art, Kyoto, Japan. Solo exhibitions include Illinois Wesleyan University, Bloomington, IL, 1946; Indiana University, Bloomington, 1947; University of North Dakota, Grand Forks, 1956; State University of New York at New Paltz, 1958; Indiana Art Directors Association, Indianapolis, 1959; Akron Art Institute, Akron, OH, 1960; Merchants Bank Building, Indianapolis, IN, 1960; Institute of Design, Illinois Institute of Technology, Chicago, 1962; San Francisco State University, San Francisco, CA, 1964; Skidmore College, Saratoga Springs, NY, 1971; Polaroid Corporation, Cambridge, MA, 1971; University of California, Berkeley, 1971; Phos/Graphos Gallery, San Francisco, CA, 1972; Center for Photographic Studies, Louisville, KY, 1972; New Orleans Museum of Art, New Orleans, LA, 1972; *Henry Holmes Smith's Art: Fifty Years in Retrospect,* Indiana University, Bloomington, 1973; Friends of Photography, Carmel, CA, 1974; J.B. Speed Museum (with Ralph Eugene Meatyard), Louisville, KY, 1974; Indiana National Bank, Indianapolis, 1974; Addison Gallery, Andover, MA, 1975; Fort Wayne Art Institute, Fort Wayne, IN, 1975; University of Oregon, Eugene, 1978; Indiana University, 1982; Philadelphia College of Art, Philadelphia, PA, 1983; Silver Image Gallery, Seattle, WA, 1984; Robert Klein Gallery, Boston, MA, 1984; Focus Gallery, San Francisco, CA, 1985; *Works 1974-84,* California State University, Fresno, 1985; and *Photographs 1931-86: A Retrospective,* Howard Greenberg Gallery, New York, NY. Group exhibitions include *Abstract Photography,* Museum of Modern Art, New York, NY, 1951; *Photographer's Choice,* Indiana University, Bloomington, 1959; *Sense of Abstraction,* Museum of Modern Art, New York, NY, 1960; *Photography in the Twentieth Century,* National Gallery of Canada, Ottawa (toured Canada and the United States, 1967-73), 1967; *Contemporary American Photographs,* University of California, Los Angeles, 1975; *Photographer's Choice,* Witkin Gallery, New York, NY, 1976; *Photography in the Fifties,* Center for Creative Photography, University of Arizona, Tucson, 1980; *American Images 1945-80,* Barbican Art Gallery, London, England, 1985; *Photography and Art 1946-86,* Los Angeles County Museum of Art, Los Angeles, 1987; *50 Jahre New Bauhaus,* Bauhaus-Archiv, Berlin, Germany, 1987; *Extending the Boundaries of Photography,* University of Arizona, Center for Creative Photography, Tucson, 1987; *Modern Photography and Beyond,* National Museum of Modern Art, Kyoto, Japan, 1987; *Photographic Legacy: The Influence of Henry Holmes Smith at Indiana University,* Indiana University Fine Arts Museum, Bloomington, 1988; *Decade by Decade: Twentieth Century American Photography,* Center for Creative Photography, Tucson, AZ, 1989; *Personal Engagements: Abstract Photography of the Sixties,* The University of Rochester and the International Museum of Photography at George Eastman House, Rochester, NY, 1990; and *Patterns of Influence,* Center for Creative Photography. *Military service:* U.S. Army, Gilbert Islands and Iwo Jima, 1942-45.

MEMBER: Society for Photographic Education (board of directors; founding member, 1963, vice-chairman, 1963-67), Friends of Photography (trustee, 1975-83).

AWARDS, HONORS: Herman Frederick Lieber Distinguished Teaching Award, Indiana University, 1968; D.F.A., Maryland Institute College of Art, 1968, Indiana University, 1982, and Philadelphia College of Art, 1983.

WRITINGS:

(With Thomas B. Hess) *Aaron Siskind, Photographer,* edited by Nathan Lyons, George Eastman House (Rochester, NY), 1965.

Henry Holmes Smith, Center for Photographic Studies (Louisville, KY), 1973.

Henry Holmes Smith: Selected Critical Writings, edited by Terence R. Pitts, Center for Creative Photography (Tucson, AZ), 1977.

Henry Holmes Smith Papers, compiled by Charles Lamb and Mary Ellen McGoldrick, Center for Creative Photography (Tucson, AZ), 1983.

Henry Holmes Smith: Collected Writings 1935-85, edited by James L. Enyeart and Nancy Solomon, Center for Creative Photography (Tucson, AZ), 1986.

Contributor to anthology *Photographers on Photography,* edited by Nathan Lyons, [New York, NY], 1966.

Contributor to periodicals, including *Aperture, Photography, Contemporary Photographer, Exposure,* and *Afterimage.*

SIDELIGHTS: Photographer, critical writer, and art teacher Henry Holmes Smith began taking photographs as a teenager using a primitive box camera. As an adult, he devised a method for making abstract photographs using light and liquid without needing a traditional camera.

Inspired by the work of photographers Edward Weston, Francis Bruguière, and Edward Steichen, Smith studied photography at the School of the Art Institute of Chicago and Ohio State University. László Moholy-Nagy's book on experimental photography, *The New Vision,* heavily influenced Smith. "The photogram is a realization of spatial tension in black-white-gray," Moholy-Nagy wrote.

In 1937, Smith was experimenting with color, making color-separation negatives and dye-transfer prints, when he met Moholy-Nagy and forged a longtime professional friendship. Their concepts on image-making were congruent.

Also that year, Smith accepted Moholy-Nagy's invitation to teach at the prestigious New Bauhaus School in Chicago, although World War II interrupted his first teaching assignment, during which he worked alongside Moholy-Nagy and the artist Gyorgy Kepes.

In 1946, Smith's central goal was to abandon the constraints of the traditional camera while still using light to make pictures. Preparing to teach a class on the light principles of refraction and reflection at Indiana University, where he would work for about twenty years, he attempted a new process. The technique involved pouring syrup on glass, possibly throwing water on it, and printing it. Smith discovered that light would cast crisp shadows he could manipulate and print onto his photographer's paper. This experimenting lead to a major phase in his career and the creation of his celebrated "refraction prints."

Among the images Smith's artwork frequently presents are mythological figures such as the phoenix, Castor, and Pollux.

BIOGRAPHICAL AND CRITICAL SOURCES:

BOOKS

Bossen, Howard, *Henry Holmes Smith: Man of Light,* UMI Research Press (Ann Arbor, MI), 1982.

Decade by Decade, Twentieth-Century American Photography, Bulfinch (Boston, MA), 1988.

Gauss, Kathleen McCarthy, and Andy Grundberg, *American Images 1945-1986* (exhibition catalogue), Los Angeles County Museum of Art (Los Angeles, CA), 1987.

Lyons, Nathan, *Photography in the Twentieth Century,* Horizon Press (New York, NY), 1967.

Henry Holmes Smith's Art: Fifty Years in Retrospect (exhibition catalogue) [Bloomington, IN], 1973.

Henry Holmes Smith: Non-Camera Photographer (exhibition catalogue), [Bloomington, IN], 1982.

Photographers' Choice (exhibition catalogue), [Bloomington, Indiana], 1959.

PERIODICALS

Art Forum International, January, 2000, David Levi Strauss, p. 116.

Art Forum International, summer, 1999, Carol Squiers, "Photographs, Drawings, and Collages by Frederick Sommer," p. 148.*

*   *   *

SMITH, Justin Harvey 1857-1930

PERSONAL: Born January 13, 1857, in Boscawen, NH; died March 21, 1930; son of Ambrose (a minister) and Cynthia Maria (Egerton) Smith. *Education:* Dartmouth College, A.B., 1877, A.M., 1881, Litt.D., 1920; attended Union Theological Seminary, 1879-81.

CAREER: Union Theological Seminary, New York, NY, private secretary, 1879-81; worked in publishing, 1881-90; Ginn & Co., head of editorial department, 1890-98; Dartmouth College, professor of modern history, 1899-1908; writer. Member of visiting committee on Romance philology at Harvard University, 1896-1906.

MEMBER: American Historical Association.

AWARDS, HONORS: Pulitzer Prize for best book on American history, 1920 and First Loubat Prize for Best Book in English, 1923, both for *The War with Mexico.*

WRITINGS:

Troubadours at Home: Their Lives and Personalities, Their Songs and Their World, two volumes, 1899.

Arnold's March from Cambridge to Quebec: A Critical Study: Together with a Reprint of Arnold's Journal, 1903.

A Tale of Two World and Five Centuries, 1903.

(Editor) *The Historie Booke,* 1903.

Our Struggle for the Fourteenth Colony: Canada and the American Revolution, two volumes, Putnam (New York, NY), 1907.

The Annexation of Texas, P. Smith (Glouchester, MA), 1911, reprinted, AMS Press (New York, NY), 1971.

(Editor) *Letters of Santa Anna,* 1919.

The War with Mexico, two volumes, Macmillan (New York, NY), 1919, reprinted, P. Smith (Glouchester, MA), 1963.

Also contributor to periodicals.

SIDELIGHTS: Justin Harvey Smith was an historian whose passions and dedication for his topics resulted in intensive research efforts that helped him produce his award-winning history books, including the Pulitzer Prize-winning *The War with Mexico.* Smith taught modern history at Dartmouth College before resigning to devote himself full time to traveling and writing. His travels to Provence, Italy, and his study of Provencal poets of the tenth and early eleventh century resulted in his first publication, *Troubadours at Home: Their Lives and Personalities, Their Songs and Their*

World. Smith's goal for this work was to introduce the world to the writings of the troubadours and categorize their literature in the sequence in which it first appeared.

Smith also authored two books on the American Revolution: *Arnold's March from Cambridge to Quebec: A Critical Study,* an in-depth study of Benedict Arnold, and *Our Struggle for the Fourteenth Colony: Canada and the American Revolution,* in which he examines the tumultuous times of the thirteen colonies in America and their declaration of independence from England's dominance. In the latter work, Smith focuses on the colonies efforts to force Lower Canada into declaring independence. Considered a definitive work on the subject, *Our Struggle for the Fourteenth Colony* was praised by an *Outlook* reviewer who wrote that the book "is so fresh, so original, and so informing that it deserves the heartiest of welcomes."

For his next project, Smith examines another tumultuous time in American history, this time focusing on the annexation of Texas. As a reviewer said in *Choice,* "Few works on this climatic period of Texas history are more valuable than *The Annexation of Texas.*" Another reviewer, writing in the *Annual of the American Academy,* praised Smith's in-depth research: "The great value of Dr. Smith's book is that it represents original research, wide and deep. What others have done by parts he has done as a whole."

In 1919 Smith released his critically praised *The War with Mexico,* a two-volume set about the war between the United States and Mexico. Only after an intensive effort was Smith able to provide the vivid details surrounding the war. The first volume deals with the turmoil in Mexico, giving details about the social, political, and economic situation there prior to its declaration of independence from Spain, while the second volume focuses on the actual war between Mexico and the United States. A *Boston Transcript* critic said, "This book must be regarded as the definitive work on this important episode in the history of the expansion of our country." Smith also received praise from a *Springfield Republican* reviewer, who wrote, "The public is deeply indebted to Professor Smith, who after years of patient delving in the vaults of historical societies, in local archives in private collections, etc., has produced a scholarly and well thought-out history." Not only did *The War with*

Mexico win the Pulitzer Prize for best book in American history in 1920, but it proved to be a timeless reference tool that was still consulted almost a century later.

BIOGRAPHICAL AND CRITICAL SOURCES:

PERIODICALS

American History Review, April, 1912, review of *The Annexation of Texas;* July, 1920, review of *The War with Mexico.*
Annual of the American Academy, November, 1912, review of *The Annexation of Texas.*
Boston Transcript, February 4, 1920, review of *The War with Mexico,* p. 6.
Choice, July/August, 1972, review of *The Annexation of Texas,* p. 713.
Dial, May, 1920, review of *The War with Mexico.*
English Historical Review, July, 1912, review of *The Annexation of Texas.*
New York Times, September 7, 1907, review of *Our Struggle for the Fourteenth Colony: Canada and the American Revolution.*
Outlook, October 12, 1912, review of *Our Struggle for the Fourteenth Colony;* June 2, 1920, review of *The War with Mexico.*
Political Science Quarterly, June, 1912, review of *The Annexation of Texas.*
Spectator, September 7, 1907, *Our Struggle for the Fourteenth Colony.*
Springfield Republican, March 8, 1920, review of *The War with Mexico,* p. 5.*

* * *

SNEAD, Sam(uel Jackson) 1912-2002

OBITUARY NOTICE—See index for *CA* sketch: Born May 27, 1912, in Hot Springs, VA; died May 23, 2002, in Hot Springs, VA. Professional golfer and author. Snead was one of the best golfers of his generation, earning eighty-one tour victories (135 counting non-PGA tournaments), including three Masters tournaments, the British Open, three PGA championships, five World Senior Professional championships, and a Legends of Golf championship. An excellent athlete since high school, Snead originally tried his hand as a

boxer, but only fought in one match. Taking a job in a restaurant, he quit in 1935 to become an assistant pro at the Greenbriar resort in White Sulphur Springs, West Virginia. By the next year he was making news when he shot a 61 in the West Virginia pro tournament. After that, Snead was a major player well into the 1960s, becoming famous for his picture-perfect golf swing and earning the nickname "Slammin' Sammy." He went into semi-retirement in 1979, but continued to play the Senior PGA tour, which he cofounded, until 1987; he did exhibition tours well into the 1990s. Snead also wrote several books about golf, including *Golf Lessons from Sam Snead* (1964), *Sam Snead Teaches You His Simple "Key" Approach to Golf* (1975), and *Golf Begins at Forty* (1978).

OBITUARIES AND OTHER SOURCES:

BOOKS

Crystal, David, editor, *The Cambridge Biographical Encyclopedia,* second edition, Cambridge University Press, 1998.
The International Who's Who, 63rd edition, Europa Publications (London, England), 2000.
Legends in Their Own Time, Prentice Hall (New York, NY), 1994.
Who's Who in America, 52nd edition, Marquis (New Providence, NJ), 1997.

PERIODICALS

Los Angeles Times, May 24, 2002, pp. A1, A26.
New York Times, May 24, 2002, p. C11.
Washington Post, May 24, 2002, pp. D1, D2.

* * *

SNOW, Michael (James Aleck) 1929-

PERSONAL: Born December 10, 1929 in Toronto, Ontario, Canada; married Joyce Wieland (an artist and filmmaker), 1959 (died June 27, 1998); *Education:* Upper Canada College, Toronto, 1946-51; Ontario College of Art, Toronto, 1951-55.

ADDRESSES: *Office*—c/o The Isaacs Gallery, 832 Yonge Street, Toronto, Ontario M4W 2H1, Canada.

CAREER: Independent artist, musician, filmmaker, and photographer, beginning 1955. Yale University, New Haven, CT, professor of advanced film, 1970; Nova Scotia College of Art and Design, Halifax, visiting artist, 1970, 1974; Ontario College of Art, Toronto, instructor, 1973, 1974, 1976. *Exhibitions:* Works included in permanent exhibitions at National Gallery of Canada, Ottawa; Canada Council Art Bank, Ottawa; Art Gallery of Ontario, Toronto; Museum of Modern Art, New York; Philadelphia Museum of Art; and Musée d'Art Contemporain, Montreal. Solo exhibitions include Hart House, University of Toronto, 1956; Isaacs Gallery, Toronto, 1957 and 1958; Art Gallery of Ontario, Toronto, 1960 and 1962; Gallery XII, Montreal Museum of Fine Arts, 1963; Hart House, 1963; Isaacs Gallery, 1964; Poindexter Gallery, New York, 1964, 1965 and 1968; 20/20 Gallery, London, Ontario, 1966; Isaacs Gallery, 1966; *Retrospective '63-'66;* Vancouver Art Gallery, 1967; Isaacs Gallery, 1969; *Michael Snow: A Survey,* Art Gallery of Ontario, Toronto, 1970; Canadian Pavilion, *Biennale,* Venice, 1970; Bykert Gallery, New York, 1970; Center for Inter-American Relations, New York, 1972; Bykert Gallery, 1972; *Camera Works by Michael Snow,* University of Manitoba, Winnipeg, 1973; *Projected Images,* Walker Art Center, Minneapolis, 1974; Isaacs Gallery, 1974; Museum of Modern Art, New York, 1976; 7 *Films et Plus Tard,* Centre Georges Pompidou, Paris (toured France 1977-79), 1977; *Michael Snow,* Centre Georges Pompidou (traveled to the Kunstmuseum, Lucerne, Switzerland); Rheinisches Landesmuseum, Bonn; Stadtische Galerie im Lenbachhaus, Munich; Musée des Beaux-Arts, Montreal; and Vancouver Art Gallery, 1978-80), 1978; Isaacs Gallery, 1979; Museum Boymans-van Beuningen, Rotterdam, 1979; Isaacs Gallery, 1982; *Snow in England,* Canada House, London, Ontario, 1983; University of California, Los Angeles, 1983; *Walking Woman Works 1961-67;* Agnes Etherington Art Centre, Kingston, Ontario (traveled to Ithaca, New York; Halifax, Nova Scotia, London, Ontario; Victoria, British Columbia; and Toronto); Isaacs Gallery, 1984, *Still Living,* Vu Centre de la Photographie, Quebec City, 1984; and Isaacs Gallery, 1986. Group exhibitions include *The Satirical in Art,* York University, Toronto, 1966; *Anti-Illusion: Procedures and Materials,* Whitney Museum, New York, 1969; *Festival International du Film,* Cannes, France, 1970; *Prospect '71,* Kunsthalle, Düsseldorf, 1971; *Options and Alternatives,* Yale University, 1973; *Another Di-* mension, National Gallery of Canada, Ottawa (toured Canada 1977-78), 1977; *Re-Visions,* Whitney Museum, 1979; *Photoalchemy,* Robert Freidus Gallery, New York, 1982; *Seeing People/Seeing Space,* The Photographers' Gallery, London, 1984; and *Aurora Borealis,* Centre d'Art Contemporain, Montreal, 1985.

MEMBER: Canadian Centre for Marine Communications.

AWARDS, HONORS: Purchase Award, Winnipeg Exhibition, 1958; Canada Council of Arts grant, 1959; senior arts grant, 1966, 1973, 1980; Henry Street Settlement Exhibition Award, 1964; First Prize, Knokke-le-Zoute Film Festival (Belgium), 1967; Guggenheim fellowship, 1972; LL.D., Brock University, St. Catharines, Ontario, 1975; Order of Canada, 1981; Best Independent Experimental Film Award, Los Angeles Film Critics Association, 1983; honorary doctorate, Yale University.

WRITINGS:

(Illustrator) *Place of Meeting,* text by Raymond Souster, Gallery Editions (Toronto, Ontario, Canada), 1962.

Michael Snow: A Survey, text by P. Adams Sitney, Art Gallery of Ontario (Toronto, Ontario, Canada), 1970.

Cover to Cover, New York University Press (New York, NY), 1975.

High School, [Toronto, Ontario, Canada], 1980.

Collected Writings of Michael Snow, Wilfrid Laurier University Press (Waterloo, Ontario, Canada), 1994.

Screen Writings: Scripts and Texts by Independent Filmmakers, edited by Scott MacDonald, University of California Press (Berkeley, CA), 1995.

FILMS

A to Z, 1956.

New York Eye and Ear Control (A Walking Woman Work), 1964.

Short Shave, 1965.

Wavelength, 1967.

Standard Time, 1967.

Back and Forth, 1969.

One Second in Montreal, 1969.
Dripping Water, 1969.
Side Seat Paintings Slides Sound Films, 1970.
La Region Centrale, 1970-71.
Table Top Dolly, 1972.
Rameau's Nephew by Diderot (Thanks to Dennis Young) by Wilma Schoen, 1974.
Presents, 1980.
So Is This, 1982.

SOUND RECORDINGS:

The Artists Jazz Band, 1974.
CCMC, 5 vols., 1974-80.
Michael Snow: Music for Whistling, Piano, Microphone, and Tape Recorder, 1975.
The Artists Jazz Band: Live at the Edge, 1977.

Contributor to various publications including *Film Culture, Artforum,* and *Cinemanews.*

SIDELIGHTS: Toronto native Michael Snow is an independent artist, musician, and photographer best known for his filmmaking and his "Walking Woman" series, which he introduced in 1961. It involves a cutout figure portrayed in a series of media and in various styles.

The "Walking Woman" series inspired several other pieces, including "Four to Five," Snow's first serious photographic experiment, a year later. A montage of the "Walking Woman" cut-out, consisting of twelve rectangular photos arranged in three horizontal lines, "Four to Five" features a fourth line containing two photos hung vertically, with one horizontal photograph positioned on either side.

Much of Snow's photography and film work examines themes of representation: placement versus perception. His 1969 photographic project, "Tap," combines elements of sound, image, text, object, and line. The work emphasizes the connection between images, as well as their distinctive values.

"In several works I have created both the subject and its representation," Snow once commented.

Snow, in his celluloid work, emphasizes through art the camera's function, the relationship of image to light, the intensity of focus, and the relationship among sight, sound, and memory. One of his earliest films, *New York Eye and Ear Control (A Walking Woman Work),* features a jazz soundtrack and serves as an extension, through new media, of the "Walking Woman" concept.

Wavelength, perhaps his best-known film, explores the illusionary properties of the zoom lens. Describing Snow's artwork in *Contemporary Artists,* one writer remarked, "Snow's film *Wavelength*—an obsessive 45-minutes zoom across a loft space to a photograph of the sea—defined the artist's commitment to a 'new cinema of structure.'"

Another writer said of *Wavelength* in *International Dictionary of Films and Filmmakers,* "That set the program for his most ambitious cinematic works, several of which examine the range of possibilities inherent in a given technique."

Snow links his filmmaking and photography to his experience as a painter. His film *Authorization,* for example, experiments with composition, form, size, scale, and embraces abstraction.

Rameau's Nephew by Diderot (Thanks to Dennis Young) by Wilma Schoen, continues Snow's investigation of topics related to image and sound. According to the writer for the *International Dictionary of Films and Filmmakers,* "For 285 minutes, in . . . 24 distinct sections, the film explores the human body as a source of sound. . . . *Rameau's Nephew* was the turning point in Snow's career. . . . [It] was also a transition insofar as Snow shifted his attention from baroque examinations of camera movement to another dimension of cinema." According to the writer, Snow's subsequent films, shot mostly in Canada, reflect older types of movie-making made popular in the 1960s and '70s.

In the film *Presents,* an artificial-feeling apartment set rolls back and forth on camera, complicating life for residents aiming to touch an object in the moving room. Describing the film in *Art in America,* Ken Johnson said, "The subject is the rickety, old-fashioned construction of 'reality.' At a certain point, the picture plane attacks the set: the camera is mounted on an invisible machine . . . which moves onto the set and begins crushing everything in its path. Thus the modernist picture plane flattens illusionism."

Another highly involved exercise, Snow's heavily abstract film, *Corpus Callosum,* is a five-hour-long movie, five years in the making. Nancy Princethal wrote in *Art in America,* "Eventually, the whole scene gets cataclysmically wobbly: the woman, in close-up, is shown crying big, plainly artificial tears that slowly work their way down her gradually broadening features and seem to contribute to the progressive distortion of her face, which . . . melts and runs down the screen."

In honor of *Expo '86,* the World's Fair in Vancouver, British Columbia, Snow was commissioned to create *Spectral Image,* holography depicting images tied to transportation, communication, and industry. The abstract work stands 929 feet tall.

Snow, who has received many awards, has published sound recordings and several books of photography, including the multi-volume *Michael Snow Project.* Dana Polan wrote of these books in *Film Quarterly,* "From these first three volumes, one can extract reiterations of many of the themes that Snow criticism has concentrated on: the conceptuality of an art that focuses on its own processes of fabrication . . . the interactions of calculated control and randomness and improvisation in modern art production . . . the responsiveness (or not) of avant-gardism to popular culture, everyday life, and the public sphere."

In 1993 the Art Gallery of Toronto presented a retrospective exhibition of Snow's multi-media work and published *The Michael Snow Project.* Reviewing the show for *Art in America,* Ken Johnson wrote, "The strategic willfulness apparent in the Walking Woman works is here directed full force at the viewer, and one understands why audiences sometimes erupted into riotous protest during early showings of Snow's films. But that ruthless quality is also the strength of the film. . . . Each film follows its own predetermined logic and, in the best of them, there is an awesome grandeur about the implacability with which it fulfills itself."

Snow's wife, the late Joyce Wieland, was also an accomplished artist and filmmaker.

BIOGRAPHICAL AND CRITICAL SOURCES:

BOOKS

Contemporary Artists, fourth edition, St. James Press (Detroit, MI), 1996.

Cornwell, Regina, *Snow Seen,* PMA Books (Toronto, Ontario, Canada), 1979.

Dewdney, Christopher, and Pierre Théberge, *Michael Snow: Selected Photographic Works* (exhibition catalogue), Frederick S. Wight Gallery, University of California, Los Angeles (Los Angeles, CA), 1983.

Dompierre, Louise, Philip Monk, and Dennis Reid, *The Michael Snow Project: Visual Art 1951-1993,* [Toronto, Ontario, Canada], 1995.

Dompierre, Louise, *Walking Woman Works: Michael Snow 1961-67* (exhibition catalogue), [Kingston, Ontario, Canada], 1983.

Gidal, Peter, *Structural Film Anthology,* British Film Institute (London, England), 1976.

Hanhardt, John, and others, *A History of the American Avant-Garde,* [New York, NY], 1976.

Honnef, Klaus, and Evelyn Weiss, *Documenta 6/Band 2* (exhibition catalogue), [Cologne, Germany], 1977.

International Dictionary of Films and Filmmakers, Volume Two: *Directors,* St. James Press (Detroit, MI), 1996.

Kubelka, Peter, and others, *Une Histoire du cinéma,* Centre national d'art et de culture Georges-Pompidou, Musée national d'art moderne (Paris, France), 1976.

The Michael Snow Project: Music/Sound: 1948-1993, Knopf (Toronto, Ontario, Canada), 1995.

Shedden, Jim, editor, *Presence and Absence: The Films of Michael Snow 1956-1991,* Knopf (Toronto, Ontario, Canada), 1995.

PERIODICALS

Art in America, July, 1994, Ken Johnson, review of Michael Snow at the Art Gallery of Ontario, pp. 70-78; May, 2001, Nancy Princenthal, "Michael Snow at White Box," p. 173.

Film Quarterly, spring, 1996, Dana Polan, review of *The Critical Writings of Michael Snow,* pp. 55-57.

Independent, November 6, 2001, Phil Johnson, review of Michael Snow at Arnolfini Gallery Bristol, p. 12.

Maclean's, March 21, 1994, Pamela Young, "Snow Storm: A Sprawling Retrospective Spotlights a Prolific Creator," pp. 56-57; July 1, 2001, p. 40.

Times, September 22, 2001, Amber Cowan, "The Best Shows Nationwide: Art," p. 24.

OTHER

Moore Gallery Web site, http://www.mooregallery. com/ (April 28, 2003), biography of Snow.*

SOMMER, Frederick 1905-1999

PERSONAL: Born September 7, 1905, in Angri, Italy; died January 23, 1999, in Prescott, AZ; son of Carlos Sommer (a city planner); married, wife's name Frances.

CAREER: Photographer. *Exhibitions:* Works included in permanent collections at Museum of Modern Art, New York, NY; International Museum of Photography, George Eastman House, Rochester, NY; Princeton University, Princeton, NJ; Fogg Art Museum, Harvard University, Cambridge, MA; Art Institute of Chicago, University of Illinois, Champaign-Urbana; Dayton Art Institute, Dayton, OH; University of New Mexico, Albuquerque; Center for Creative Photography, University of Arizona, Tucson; Norton Simon Museum of Art, Pasadena, CA. Solo exhibitions include Increase Robinson Gallery, Chicago, IL, 1934; Howard Putzel Gallery, Hollywood, CA, 1937; Santa Barbara Museum of Art, CA, 1946; Egan Gallery, New York, NY, 1949; Institute of Design; Illinois Institute of Technology, Chicago, 1957; Wittenborn Gallery, New York, NY, 1959; Art Institute of Chicago, 1963; Washington Gallery of Modern Art, Washington, DC, 1965 (traveled to the Pasadena Art Museum, CA); Museum of Northern Arizona, Flagstaff, 1967; San Fernando State College (with Wynn Bullock and Edmund Teske), Northridge, CA, 1967; Philadelphia College of Art, 1968; Light Gallery, New York, NY, 1972; Center for Contemporary Photography, Chicago, IL, 1973; Light Gallery (with Michael Bishop and Carl Toth), 1977; Arizona Bank Gallery (with Ansel Adams), Phoenix, 1977; Princeton Art Museum, New Jersey Light Gallery, 1979; *Frederick Sommer at 75,* California State University at Long Beach (retrospective; toured United States, 1980-81, traveled to London, 1981); *Venus, Jupiter and Mars: The Photographs of Frederick Sommer,* Delaware Art Museum, Newark, 1980; Serpentine Gallery, London, 1981; High Museum of Art, Atlanta, GA, 1985; *Frederick Sommer: Photographs and Drawings,* Pace/MacGill Gallery, New York, 1986; *Frederick Sommer: Horizonless Landscapes,* Pace/MacGill Gallery, 1992; and *Recent Collages,* Pace/MacGill Gallery, 1994.

Group exhibitions include *Realism in Photography,* Museum of Modern Art, 1949; *Photography at Mid-Century,* International Museum of Photography, George Eastman House, 1950; *Abstraction in Photog-* *raphy,* Museum of Modern Art, 1951; *Contemporary Photography: Japan and America,* National Museum of Modern Art, Tokyo, Japan, 1953; *Photography in America 1850-1965,* Yale University, New Haven, CT, 1965; *Photography in the Twentieth Century,* National Gallery of Canada, Ottawa (toured Canada and the United States, 1967-74), 1967; *Photographic Surrealism,* New Gallery of Contemporary Art, Cleveland (traveled to Dayton Art Institute, Ohio, and Brooklyn Museum, New York), 1979; *Photography in the '50s,* International Center of Photography, New York (traveled to the University of Arizona, Tucson, Minneapolis Institute of Art, California State University at Long Beach, and the Delaware Art Museum, Wilmington); *American Images 1945-80,* Barbican Art Gallery, London, 1985; *Photography and Art 1946-86,* Los Angeles County Museum of Art, 1987; and Pace/MacGill Gallery, 1990 and 1992.

AWARDS, HONORS: Arizona Governor's Arts Award, 1987.

WRITINGS:

(With John Weiss) *Venus, Jupiter, and Mars: The Photographs of Frederick Sommer,* Delaware Art Museum (Wilmington, DE), 1980.
The Mistress of This World Has No Name, with essay by Stephen Aldrich, Denver Art Museum (Denver, CO), 1987.

SIDELIGHTS: Sidetracked from a landscape-architect career because of tuberculosis, Frederick Sommer opted for a life in the arts and succeeded as a photographer. Margarett Loke, in a *New York Times* obituary, said Sommer's "distinctive images of surrealist collages, horizonless landscapes, blurry nudes and cameraless abstractions influenced generations of photographers."

Loke quoted Sommer as saying, "Life is the most durable fiction that matter has yet to come up with, and art is the structure of matter as life's most durable fiction."

Sommer, the son of a city planner, studied architecture in Brazil as a youth and received a scholarship to attend Cornell University's graduate program before completing his undergraduate education, and before he could even speak English fluently.

After he contracted tuberculosis in 1930, he taught painting and drawing privately. Several years later, he moved to Prescott, Arizona, to recuperate. He lived there the rest of his life, photographing the town's landscapes and sights regularly. The beauty and decay of the desert influenced much of his work. He continued to paint, draw, and make abstract photographs—including camera-less shots and others employing montage—and write music and treatises on aesthetics until his death.

Sommer's trademark photography depicts the likes of peeling walls, sculpture, portraits of trash, chicken parts, and other found-object abstractions. Inspired by his correspondence with photographer Alfred Stieglitz and by the work of Edward Weston, Sommer began to concentrate on photography in the mid-1930s. Based on Stieglitz's advice, Sommer started to reinvent himself as an artist. Weston inspired him to adopt a much larger camera, and his meeting with painter Max Ernst at a party in California in 1941 marked the start of his lifelong experimentation with surrealist images.

Loke suggested that Sommer was photography's "best-kept secret" until his final years, when some top critics were finally acknowledging him and large collections, such as the Getty Museum, began acquiring his works. She wrote, "His obscurity stemmed in part from the 1950s, when many of the important shapers of the public's view of photography, who clearly favored documentary essays and aesthetically pleasing landscapes, dismissed Sommer's work as unphotographic." Loke held up Sommer's 1939 untitled photographs of an amputated leg and foot as two of his most critically controversial early pieces.

In 1999, less than two months after his death, the Baltimore Museum of Art presented *Photographs, Drawings, and Collages by Frederick Sommer,* featuring "Arizona Landscape" (1943) and "Untitled" (the amputated foot photo) from 1939. Carol Squiers wrote in *Artforum International,* "you do have to overcome a certain amount of fear to look closely at this photo: A hobo's foot marked by a gaping wound is not intrinsically enticing. Once the squeamishness is put aside, though, the foot—and especially its wound—takes on a decided fascination."

Leah Ollman, in the *Los Angeles Times,* described a 2000 exhibit at the Norton Simon Museum, "He photographed animal carcasses and placenta with unapologetic frankness and combined old engravings to make complex photographic montages."

"Many of the images evoke horror, but usually the physical precision of the surfaces is such that they seem 'beautiful' at the same time, and thus hang, dialectically poised, between these two extremes," said a *Contemporary Photographers* writer. The writer cited Sommer's 1948 photograph "Livia," the portrait of a young child juxtaposed against an old weathered wall, and "Medallion," in which a doll's head replaces the image of the child, intensifying the feeling of decay. The writer identified characteristic Sommer elements in each work: a sense of field and a textured gray background that extends beyond the frame.

The same writer described a phase of romantic tone in Sommer's career, falling in the late 1940s, during which the artist completed "Venus, Jupiter and Mars," a work depicting two men and a woman drinking tea. The figures inhabit an old advertising poster, yet are repositioned. "In a gentler, more romantic mode, Sommer's photographs of old posters, usually containing human figures, repeat the theme of dissolution," the writer said. Describing "Venus, Jupiter and Mars," he wrote, "The poster is ripped, and peels away to reveal the wall beneath. At the same time the peeling process partially obliterates the features of the three figures. The image suggests the transience of human passion and beauty."

Reviewing the artist's 2000 show for *Artforum International,* David Levi Strauss wrote, "One might not expect paintings and drawings of organic abstraction in a show drawn from the photographer's estate, but there they were, provocatively on display among four of the more familiar gelatin-silver prints: four drawings in ink on charcoal paper and four paintings in tempera on stretched canvas." Strauss deemed the show "risky and delightful."

Sommer in the 1960s painted sheets of cellophane or coated them with grease or smoke, and manipulated the images with a stylus, ultimately making photographic prints. "The images," Ollman said, "are abstract, vaguely organic, biomorphic—one evokes a slippery tangle of kelp, another a twisting human torso—and sumptuous in their range of tones against an inky background."

BIOGRAPHICAL AND CRITICAL SOURCES:

BOOKS

Ades, Dawn, *Dada and Surrealism Reviewed* (exhibition catalogue), Arts Council of Great Britain (London, England), 1978.

All Children are Ambassadors, Nazraeli Press (Tucson, AZ), 1992.

Almanac of Famous People, sixth edition, Gale (Detroit, MI), 1998.

Amerikanische Landschafts-photographie 1860-1978 (exhibition catalogue), introduction by Klaus-Jürgen Sembach (Munich, Germany), 1978.

Bledsoe, Jane K. and Constance W. Glenn, *Frederick Sommer at Seventy-Five: A Retrospective,* Long Beach: Art Museum and Galleries, California State University (Long Beach, CA), 1980.

Browne, Turner and Elaine Partnow, *Macmillan Biographical Encyclopedia of Photographic Artists and Innovators,* Macmillan (New York, NY), 1983.

Conkelton, Sheryl, *Frederick Sommer,* G. K. Hall (New York, NY), 1995.

Frederick Sommer: An Exhibition of Photographs (exhibition catalogue), text by Gerald Nordland, [Philadelphia, PA], 1968.

Frederick Sommer: Photographs, Drawings and Musical Scores (exhibition catalogue), [London, England], 1981.

Gauss, Kathleen McCarthy, and Andy Grundberg, *Photography and Art 1946-86* (exhibition catalogue), [Los Angeles, CA], 1987.

Hall-Duncan, Nancy, *Photographic Surrealism,* exhibition catalogue, The Gallery (Cleveland, OH), 1979.

Photographic Process as Medium (exhibition catalogue), text by Rosanne T. Livingston, Rutgers University Art Gallery (New Brunswick, NJ), 1975.

Weiss, John, editor, *Venus, Jupiter and Mars: The Photographs of Frederick Sommer* (exhibition catalogue), Delaware Art Museum (Newark, DE), 1980.

PERIODICALS

Art in America, July 1995, Michael Duncan, "Frederick Sommer at the Getty Museum," pp. 92-93.

Art Forum International, summer 1999, Carol Squiers, "Photographs, Drawings, and Collages by Frederick Sommer," p. 148; January, 2000, p. 116.

Los Angeles Times, January 9, 1997, Susan Kandel, "A Mix of the Irrational and Elegance in Sommer Works," p. 6; January 6, 2000, Leah Ollman, "Sommer's Photos Capture Complex, Mystical Worlds," p. F-27.

OTHER

Profotos, http://www.profotos.com/ (August 3, 2002).

OBITUARIES:

PERIODICALS

Fresno Bee, February 1, 1999, p. C-13.

Independent, February 5, 1999, Edward Helmore, p. 7.

New York Times, February 1, 1999, Margarett Loke, "Frederick Sommer, 93, Maker of Inventive, Surreal Images."*

*   *   *

SPENCE, Jo 1934-1992

PERSONAL: Born June 15, 1934, in South Woodford, Essex, England; died of cancer June 24, 1992, in England.

CAREER: Photographer. *Exhibitions:* Solo exhibitions include *Silent Health,* Camera Work Gallery, London, England, 1991; *Missing Persons/Damaged Lives,* Leeds City Art Gallery, Leeds, England, 1991; and *Jo Spence: Matters of Concern Collaborative Images 1982-1992,* Festival Hall, London, England and Impressions Gallery, York, England, 1994.

Group exhibitions include *Beyond the Family Album,* Cockpit Gallery, London, England, 1979; *The Picture of Health,* Photography Workshop, London, England, 1985; and *Exploring the Unknown Self,* Tokyo Metropolitan Museum of Photography, Tokyo, Japan, 1991.

WRITINGS:

(Editor with Patricia Holland and Simon Watney) *Photography/Politics,* Boyars (New York, NY), 1986.

Putting Myself in the Picture, Camden (London, England), 1986.

(Editor with Patricia Holland) *Family Snaps: The Meaning of Domestic Photography,* Virago (London, England), 1991.

(With Joan Solomon) *What Can a Woman Do with a Camera?: A Handbook of Photography for Women,* Open Letters (London, England), 1993.

Cultural Sniping: The Art of Transgression, Routledge (New York, NY), 1995.

TELEVISION PROGRAMS

Opening up the Family Album, produced Channel 4, 1988.

Tip of the Iceberg, 1989.

Video Diary, British Broadcasting Corporation, 1991.

SIDELIGHTS: Remembered internationally for photographic studies documenting her decade-long battle with breast cancer, Jo Spence intended her so-called "camera-therapy" photos to record her experience, and invite viewers to confront death-and-disease-related issues. Spence died in 1992—her mother also had died of breast cancer years earlier. In the preface to the artist's exhibition "Jo Spence: The Healing Camera," Hagiwara Hiroko wrote, "The photos urge us to see highly social issues, how this society deals with a woman's body, cultural implications . . . and medical professionalism and authoritarianism. Spence's insightful social criticism and search for survival as a dignified person provide us with power."

Already known for her honest, often humorous, approach to art, Spence, upon her diagnosis, began diligently reviewing her life. She had been born into a working-class home and was grateful for her strong education. She launched her career as a studio photographer in Hampstead, England. She felt thankful, in some ways, for middle-class boyfriends even if they dumped her in the end, because they elevated her quality of life. Still, her battle with asthma and numerous other personal hardships had taken their toll.

Contributing a paper on Spence's camera-therapy to the magazine *Afterimage,* Spence's partner and longtime collaborator, Terry Dennett, broke down the photographer's complex "final-decade" process for readers. According to Dennett, Spence was inspired, in building her camera-therapy project, by a 1979 book by Augusto Boal, *The Theatre of the Oppressed,* which details the experimental Workers Theatre, Film, and Photo Movements. At the same time, Dennett explained, Spence took interest in alternative medicine, and was frustrated by her limited access in England to certain procedures.

Dennett wrote, "With no professional rules to guide her, Spence had to 'hand-make' her cancer survival and camera-therapy program. Unable to gain easy access to medical libraries she was also forced to gather most of her survival materials from outside of conventional medicine."

In the early 1970s, Spence and Dennett established a grass-roots teaching organization, Photography Workshop Ltd., to provide artists a forum for discussing socially relevant photography and photographic history. Spence looked to this group for inspiration. According to Dennett, a quote by Czech Republic President Vaclav Havel sums up one of the basic tenets of the group: "The intellectual should constantly disturb, should bear witness to the misery of the world, should be provocative by being independent, should rebel against all hidden and open pressure and manipulations, should be the chief doubter of systems, of power and its incantations, should be a witness to their mendacity."

In 1986, as part of her camera therapy, Spence published the book, *Putting Myself in the Picture: A Political, Personal, and Photographic Autobiography,* detailing her hospitalization and lumpectomy operation. "In that work," Dennett observed, "she explained that none of her previous projects on self-image and body politics prepared her for the problems of life-threatening illness."

According to Dennett, Spence's photos from this phase can be described as autobiographic portrayal, done with a "dramatological" approach. One example, "Framing My Breast," shows Spence's nude breast the night before the hospital visit.

In 1994 a posthumous exhibition, "Jo Spence: Matters of Concern, Collaborative Images 1982-1992" was presented at Festival Hall in London, and at the Impressions Gallery in New York. Val Williams wrote in *New Statesman and Society,* "Spence clowned her way through photography, appearing as a dowdy fairy, a screaming bride, a disconsolate baby sucking on a dummy. She posed naked in a motorcycle helmet, displaying a recent breast operation, and pinned a placard to her fairy's costume advertising herself as a photographer 'available for divorces, funerals, illnesses, social injustice, scenes of domestic violence, explorations of sexuality, and any joyful events."

Spence was featured in several television programs including, *Putting Ourselves in the Picture—the Work of Jo Spence,* produced by the British Broadcasting Corporation. She co-edited *Family Snaps: The Meaning of Domestic Photography,* with Patricia Holland. *What Can a Woman Do with a Camera?: A Handbook of Photography for Women,* is a book of open letters. Reviewing *Cultural Sniping: The Art of Transgression* for *Signs,* Elspeth Probyn remarked, "If much of Spence's work tended to be quite brutal, but also lyrical, in its immediacy, these collected essays remind us of the sophisticated intellectual work that went on in the elaboration of Spence's photographs. Against the facile dismissal of the early period of feminist cultural analysis of the 'images of women'. . . it is salutary to remember that the interventions of Spence and others served to reconceptualize the links between class and the psychic and social construction of femininity that fueled the deconstructive work that 'images of women' compelled."

Spence's work has been exhibited in many spaces, including Leeds City Art Gallery, Gallery d'Art Santa Monica, Barcelona, and Tokyo's Metropolitan Museum of Photography.

Established in 1992, the Jo Spence Memorial Archive serves as a source of print information and photography for students completing projects, theses, or research related to Spence or to experimental photography.

BIOGRAPHICAL AND CRITICAL SOURCES:

PERIODICALS

Afterimage, November-December, 2001, Terry Dennett, "The Wounded Photographer: The Genesis of Jo Spence's Camera Therapy," pp. 26-27.
New Statesman, September 16, 1994, Val Williams, "My Bleeding Heart." pp. 31-32.

Signs, summer, 1997, Elspeth Probyn, review of *Cultural Sniping: The Art of Transgression,* pp. 1046-1047.

OTHER

Putting Ourselves in The Picture: the Work of Jo Spence, Arena (television special), British Broadcasting Corporation, March 1987.*

*   *   *

SPLÌCHAL, Jan 1929-

PERSONAL: Born December 17, 1929; in Sloupnice, Czechoslovakia; married Libuse Struplova, in 1953; children: Daniel, Vera. *Education:* School of Decorative Arts, Jablonec nad Nisou, 1945-49.

ADDRESSES: Home—Ladova Street, 7, CZ-12800 Prague, 2-Nove Mesto, Czech Republic.

CAREER: Photographer and printer. Polygrafia, Prague, Czech Republic, graphic artist. *Exhibitions:* Works included in permanent collections at Moravian Gallery, Brno, Czech Republic; Municipal Gallery, Hodonin, Czech Republic; and Town Hall, Bielefeld, Germany. Solo exhibitions include Club of the Arts, Cheb, Czechoslovakia, 1964; Gallery Dromedaris, Enkhuizen, Netherlands, 1967; Bunker Ulmenwall, Bielefeld, West Germany, 1968; Gallery of the Castle, Duchcov, Czechoslovakia, 1968; Gallery Dromedaris, Enkhuizen, Netherlands, 1969; University of Purmerend, Netherlands, 1969; Municipal Gallery, Wieringerwerg, Netherlands, 1969; Gallery Fronta, Prague, 1970; Municipal Gallery, Hodonin, Czechoslovakia, 1975; Zentrum ZIF, Bielefeld, West Germany, 1979; Jaromir Funke Studio, Brno, Czechoslovakia, 1980; Fotogalerie Lindemann, Stuttgart, West Germany, 1983; Gallery of Rumanian Creative Artists, Bucharest, Romania, 1984; Gallery Fotochema, Prague, Czechoslovakia, 1984; Galerie Bünde, Dammhaus, West Germany, 1986; Galerie Fotoforum, Frankfurt am Main, West Germany, 1986; Municipal Museum, Horice, Czechoslovakia, 1987; Czech Cultural Centre, Havana, Cuba, 1988; Bödelschwinggemeinde, Bielefeld, Germany, 1988; Goethe Institut, Cordoba, Argentina, 1989; Municipal Museum, Freiburg,

Germany, 1990; Gallera Genesis, Prague, Czech Republic, 1991; Fotogalerie Lindemanns, Stuttgart, Germany, 1992; Gallery Genesis, Prague, Czech Republic, 1992; Ravensberger Spinerei, Bielefeld, Germany, 1993; European Parliament, Strasbourg, France, 1993; Land Parliament, Düsseldorf, Germany, 1993, Rathauspavillon, Brackwede, Germany, 1993; Prague House of Photography, Prague, Czech Republic, 1994; Goethe Institut, Santiago de Chile, Chile, 1994. Group exhibitions include *Creative Photography,* House of Exhibition Services, Prague, Czechoslovakia, 1958; *Fotosalon,* Municipal Gallery, Prague, Czechoslovakia, 1965; *Czechoslovak Photography,* Pala Kultury i Nauky, Warsaw, Poland, 1965; *Surrealism and Photography,* Museum Folkwang, Essen, Germany, 1966; *Promena Artists Group,* Capek's Gallery, Prague, Czechoslovakia, 1973; *Lyrismo de Fotografia Cecoslovacci,* at *SICOF,* Milan, Italy (traveled to Fotokabinett Jaromir Funke, Brno, Czechoslovakia, and Stadisches Museum, Freiburg, West Germany), 1973; *Contemporary Photography,* Fragner's Gallery, Prague, Czechoslovakia, 1977; *Tschechoslowakische Photographie 1918-1978,* Fotoforum, Kassel, West Germany, 1979; *Aktualni Fotografie,* Moravian Gallery, Brno, Czechoslovakia, 1982; *Czechoslovak Creative Photography,* Gallery of Czechoslovak Writers, Prague, Czechoslovakia, 1984; and *Tschechoslowakische Photografie der Gegenwart,* Cologne, Erlangen, Metz, Freiburg, Odense, Barcelona, Luxembourg, Texas, Kansas, 1990, and Festival of Photography at Zdár, Czech Republic, 1991.

MEMBER: Union of Czechoslovak Artists.

WRITINGS:

The Sculptor Frantisek Bilek, [Prague, Czechoslovakia], 1966.
V tvarné projevy surrealismu, Odeon (Prague, Czechoslovakia), 1969.
Jan Splìchal: Photographs, [Prague, Czechoslovakia], 1971.
Tau und Regen zu sein, Evang (Berlin, Germany).
Barockzeichnung: Meisterwerke d. böhm, Dausien (Hanau, Germany), 1979.
Praha nasich snu, Vysehrad (Prague, Czechoslovakia), 1980.
Naúpatí hory, Kalich, 1984.
Jan Splìchal: Photography, Foto Mida (Ceské Budejovie), 1993.

Published article, "On Photomontage," with Karel Dvorak, in *Fotografie '73,* 1973.

SIDELIGHTS: Czech photographer and painter Jan Splìchal's signature work is the photomontage. "Photomontage means for me multiplied expression of a creative character . . . that could not be mediated by means of pure photography," he said.

Splìchal, who lives in his favorite city, Prague, studied at the Fine Arts Academy in Jablonci and the Academy of Applied Arts in Prague before beginning a wide-ranging career incorporating print-work, photography, and stage design. He worked in a print shop beside Josef Sudek, a renowned photographer who would later publish much of Splichal's artwork. Splìchal was once entrusted with the negatives of master Czech photographers Jaromir Funke and Frantisek Drtikol.

As Splìchal began to work in photomontage, he experimented by combining images from various negatives to create unified artwork. He would start with ideas at the beginning, but do the major portion of his work in the dark room, combining the images to create a montage.

As Splìchal continued to grow artistically and technically, he began to concentrate less on formality and more on theme. He portrayed painters and sculptors pictured in dialogue with their artwork. Other Splìchal montage series feature towers of Prague, cathedrals, and landscapes, organic and inorganic, that underline the effects of industrial pollution on vegetation. Two audiovisual presentations, titled *Creation and Landscapes,* produced in the early 1980s, incorporate music and photomontage. His series on Prague serves as an homage to author Franz Kafka, depicting a dreamlike city, pasting together portraits of Kafka, ancient archways and staircases, and other long-vanished images.

Marc Archuleta, in *nearbycafe.com,* noted that Splìchal's photography generally does not generally emphasize formal. Archuleta said, "He searches out varied intricacies of light and dark subjects that are not always tangible but reveal beauty intuitively through the heart."

His exhibitions have shown in the Czech Republic, Germany, Chile, and elsewhere.

BIOGRAPHICAL AND CRITICAL SOURCES:

BOOKS

Dufek, Antonín, *Aktuálni Fotografie* (exhibition catalogue), [Brno, Czechoslovakia], 1982.

Dufek, Antonín, *Soucasna Ceskoslovenska Fotografie* (exhibition catalogue), [Brno, Czechoslovakia], 1969.

Hofstätter, H., and Petr Tausk, *100 Temi di Fotografia* [Milan, Italy], 1977.

Photographers' Encyclopedia International 1839 to the Present, Edition Camera Obscura, 1985.

Tausk, Petr, *Contemporary Photographers,* Macmillan (New York, NY), 1982.

Tausk, Petr and others, *Encyclopedia of Practical Photography,* [Prague, Czechoslovakia], 1972.

Tausk, Petr, *History of Photography in the Twentieth Century,* DuMont (Cologne, Germany), 1977.

OTHER

Nearby Café, http://www.nearbycafe.com/ (April, 1966), Marc Archuleta, "The Approach of Jan Splìchal."*

*   *   *

SPRING, Michelle
See STANWORTH, Michelle

*   *   *

SPURIS, Egons 1931-1990

PERSONAL: Born October 5, 1931, in Riga, Latvia; died May 20, 1990, in Riga, Latvia; married Lia Kimene, 1953; children: Egils. *Education:* Riga Polytechnical Institute, B.A., 1962.

CAREER: Photographer; VEF electro-technical factory, locksmith, laboratory assistant, radio technician and engineer-designer, Riga, 1947-62; Rigas Radioizotopu Aparatu Buves Zinatniski Petnieciskais Institut, design leader, Riga, 1960-72; Specialais Maksli-Nieciskas Konstru Esanas un Technologisko Projektu

Biro JS, Riga, chief designer of projects, 1972-76, chief artist/photographer, 1976-78; Riga Polytechnical Institute, lecturer, 1962-64; People's Photo Studio, Riga, art director, 1975—. *Exhibitions:* Works included in permanent collections at Museum of Photography, Siauliai, Lithuania; Bibliothèque Nationale, Paris, France; and International Museum of Photography, George Eastman House, Rochester, NY.

Solo exhibitions include City Museum, Tallinn, Estonia, 1973; People's Photo Studio Exhibition Gallery, Riga, Latvia, 1974; City Museum, Valmiera, Latvia, 1974; City Museum, Cesis, Latvia, 1974; Town Museum, Dikli, Latvia, 1974; Museum of Photography, Lithuanian Society of Art Photographers, Vilnius, 1975; USSR Palace of Culture, Prague, Czechoslovakia, 1976; USSR Palace of Culture, Helsinki, Finland, 1978; Gunar Binde/Egons Spuris/Peeter Tooming, Dum Panu z Kunstatu, Brno, Czechoslovakia, 1979 (traveled to the Museum of Olomouc, Czechoslovakia, 1979, and Kiek in de Kok, Tallinn, Estonia, 1980); Bremen, Germany, 1981; Ogre, Latvia, 1981; Kaunas, Lithuania, 1983; Bremen, Germany, 1985; Tallin, Estonia, 1986; Latvian Photography Museum, Riga, 1993.

Group exhibitions include *Fourth Exhibition of Latvian Photographers,* Kaunas, Lithuania, 1968; *Vision and Expression,* International Museum of Photography, George Eastman House, Rochester, NY (toured United States and Canada, 1969-71), 1969; *12 Top Photographers,* Ghent, Belgium, 1971; City Museum, Liepaja, Latvia, 1973; *Photographers Dialogue,* Bielefeld, Germany, 1989; Moscow, Russia, 1989; *Three Days of Awakening,* Museum of Pharmacy, Riga, 1989; *L'Année de l'Est,* Musée d'Elysée, Lausanne, Switzerland, 1990; Galerie Van der Berlage, Amsterdam, 1990; *Photographs from Latvia and Other Soviet Republics,* Santa Barbara, CA, 1991; *Parmijas—Contemporary Art from Riga,* City Exhibition Hall, Munster, Germany, 1992; *Baltisk Fotografi,* Museum of Photographic Art, Odense, Denmark, 1992, and *The Memory of Images—Baltic Photo Art Today,* Kiel and Rostock, Germany and Riga, Latvia, 1993.

MEMBER: People's Photo Studio (Riga, Latvia), Ogre Photo Club (leader, 1975-90), Latvian Designers Society, Natron (Maglaj, Bosnia-Herzegovina; honorary member).

AWARDS, HONORS: Gold Medal, *Premio Michelangelo,* Petrasanta, Italy, 1970; Prix de la Ville de Monaco, 1970; Grand Prize, *Dzintarzeme* (Amber

Land), Siauliai, Lithuania, 1970, Riga, 1979; Gold Medal, Norwegian Photo Federation, 1971; Gold Medal, Photographic Society of America, 1971; Charles Kingsley Memorial Award, Toronto, Ontario, Canada, 1971; Medal, *12 Top Photographers,* Ghent, 1971; Artist Award, Federation Internationale de l'Art Photographique, 1975; Grand Prize, Latvia '75, Riga, and Latvia '77, Riga; honorary artist, Art-Photo Society of Ceylon (ANPAS).

WRITINGS:

The Woman I Left, [Riga, Latvia, USSR], 1971.
Sacred is Your Land (Armenian poetry), [Riga, Latvia, USSR], 1971.
(Photo-illustrator) *Dance around a Steam Engine,* text by Mats Traat, [Riga, Latvia, USSR], 1972.
(Photo-illustrator) *Empress Ficke,* text by Ivanov, [Riga, Latvia, USSR], 1972.

Also author of article, "Photography in Design," in *Maksla,* October, 1973.

SIDELIGHTS: Egons Spuris, whose photography expressed Latvian sentiment during much of the twentieth century, considered himself an artist for art's sake. He is considered important to Soviet Baltic Photography, which consists of Latvian, Lithuanian, and Estonian work. Spuris supported himself by working variously as a locksmith, lab assistant, radio technician and engineer-designer at the VEF electrotechnical factory in Riga, as a lecturer in radio engineering at his alma mater, Riga Polytechnical Institute, and as art director of the People's Photo Studio in Riga. His work, which features wide-angle landscape photography, portraiture, and city scenes, heavily relies on black-and-white images, sharp contrast, and minimalist devices.

Spuris once said of his work, "Usually there is no action in my photographs. Compositions are mainly stable, even static. I try to see and reflect the character (not characteristic) of things or environment, the fascinating mood, inner dynamism, or stillness." Spuris' work was not known for reproducing reality, but instead for communicating his ideas about reality. Before 1970 Spuris shot mostly landscape photography, often with wide-angle lenses. He captured the haunting quality of empty seacoasts, sand, jagged rocks, wind-swept grass, the black curtain of the Baltic Sea. His earlier work celebrated the natural beauty of his region and, through portraits and fishing boats, its working man.

Spuris used the technique of photomontage during the late 1960s. He had learned color photography techniques but after 1976 ceased using them because he decided they made his process and public reception too smooth and easy. Instead, he worked almost exclusively in black and white and employed basic techniques of masking and bleaching to achieve desired tonal quality and intensity.

After the mid-1970s Spuris shifted his emphasis from themes of cultural celebration and observation to problems of urban life and expansion. New topics of interest included architectural structures, old and new, and urban surroundings, roofs, cement-paved roads, and wall surfaces. His later works contrasted ancient and modern Riga.

Spuris also liked to portray the arrangement of physical space, of subject versus background, and his attraction to ordinary objects, people, and sights. He published several books and received numerous awards. His work has toured Latvia, Germany, Lithuania, and Estonia.

BIOGRAPHICAL AND CRITICAL SOURCES:

BOOKS

Mangolds, Boris, *Stepping out of Line* (exhibition catalogue), 1992.
Parmijas (exhibition catalogue), Munster, 1992.
Skalbergs, Atis, *Masters of Latvian Art Photography* (Riga, USSR), 1981.
Zeile, Peteris, *The History of Latvian Art Photography,* (Riga, USSR), 1981.*

*   *   *

STANWORTH, Michelle
(Michelle Spring)

PERSONAL: Born in Victoria, British Columbia, Canada; married a political theorist; children: two.

ADDRESSES: Home—England. *Agent*—c/o Author Mail, Ballantine Publishing Group, 1540 Broadway, New York, NY 10036.

CAREER: Author. Cambridge University, Cambridge, England, sociology professor.

AWARDS, HONORS: Arthur Ellis award for best mystery or crime novel, 2002, for *In the Midnight Hour.*

WRITINGS:

Gender and Schooling: A Study of Sexual Divisions in the Classroom, Women's Research and Resources Centre (London, England), 1981.

AS MICHELLE SPRING

Every Breath You Take: Introducing Laura Principal, Pocket Books (New York, NY), 1994, reprinted as *Every Breath You Take,* Ballantine (New York, NY), 1999.
Running for Shelter: A Laura Principal Mystery, Pocket Books (New York, NY), 1996.
Standing in the Shadows, Ballantine (New York, NY), 1998.
Nights in White Satin, Ballantine (New York, NY), 1999.
In the Midnight Hour, Ballantine (New York, NY), 2001.

Contributor to periodicals, including London *Times, Observer, Independent,* and *Sunday Telegraph.*

SIDELIGHTS: Michelle Stanworth is a Cambridge University sociology professor who writes under the pseudonym Michelle Spring. Her mysteries feature Laura Principal, a private investigator who formerly worked in an academic setting similar to Stanworth's. Principal plays the saxophone and has an on-and-off-the-job partner, Sonny Mendlowitz. She is introduced in *Every Breath You Take,* where she and her friend Helen decide to add a third housemate, Monica, to share the expenses of their cottage. Before the arrangements are finalized, Laura finds Monica in her

Cambridge flat, tied to a chair, beaten, stabbed, and dead. A *Publishers Weekly* reviewer wrote that the debut novel has "a few plot holes . . . but a smart pace."

In *Running for Shelter* Laura has been retained to find out who has been stealing from the cast and crew during the rehearsals of Thomas Butler's West End production. When Laura visits his London townhouse, she meets Maria Flores, a Filipina domestic who asks for Laura's help in collecting wages owed by a former employer. Laura later returns to find Maria missing, and the producer disclaims any knowledge of her. In her attempt to find Maria, Laura learns about the world of undocumented workers serving in near-slavery conditions in the homes of the London rich. A *Publishers Weekly* reviewer wrote that "Spring's offering is carefully plotted, but Principal's meditations on friendship and on the gap between rich and poor are way too easy."

Standing in the Shadows finds Laura working for Howard Platt, whose brother is in prison for committing murder. Daryll had been abused by his family, and he was placed in foster care with sixty-three-year-old Geraldine King. He was eleven when he confessed to her murder after she was found with her skull bashed in. Howard feels guilt because he had gone to Australia, rather than stay and look after Daryll, and wants Laura to find out why his brother committed the crime. As Laura begins to delve into the circumstances, she finds that all the people involved are not who or what they seem and may have hidden motives. They include Daryll's mother, another brother, and a social worker. Geraldine had withdrawn money from her bank account just before her death, and it is now missing. It appears that Daryll may not have committed the crime.

Alice DiNizo observed in *Library Journal* that Laura "is not a fully developed character with whom readers will bond," and called Sonny "a detraction from the main action." "There's not a great deal of action," wrote a *Publishers Weekly* reviewer, "but what there is turns out to be as honestly and respectably crafted as everything else in the book." A *Kirkus Reviews* writer noted the "highly competent parboiled British detective work, even if a crucial few of the dramatis personae remain muffled." *Washington Post Book World* reviewer Bill Kent wrote that the novel "achieves a powerful emotional intensity through the gradual understanding of the kind of evil that would corrupt a child for its own purposes."

Laura and Sonny provide security for the May Ball at St. John's College, Cambridge in *Nights in White Satin.* *Booklist* reviewer Jenny McLarin said the tale "convincingly weaves the city's geography and history into its well-crafted plot." Laura is retained when a frightened student, Katie Arkwright, disappears from the dance in her silvery gown. Senior tutor Stephen Fox turns up dead, with his faced smashed by a cricket bat, after he tells Laura that Katie may have been involved in prostitution. Laura is given a history of prostitution by an historian who makes romantic overtures to Laura while Sonny is out of town. As Laura digs for the truth, she finds that the young women of Cambridge are being victimized. A *Publishers Weekly* reviewer said that "if Dr. Principal aspires to become Cambridge's female answer to Oxford's Inspector Morse, she will have to give up puns and develop a deeper understanding of academia's dark side." Marilyn Stasio observed in the *New York Times Book Review* that the author "uses the setting with a sharp sense of irony about the power of beautiful things to distract from their ugly interiors."

In the Midnight Hour, Spring's next entry in the series, won the Arthur Ellis award for best mystery or crime novel. Olivia and Jack Cable, a famous couple, hire Laura to investigate whether a scruffy street musician is really their son, who disappeared from a beach when he was four years old. Laura becomes entangled in a maze of family relationships and problems in her quest to decide whether the young man is, in fact, their son, or if he is out to con the couple. While a *Publishers Weekly* reviewer found the book "strained and formulaic," *Booklist*'s Connie Fletcher wrote that with *In the Midnight Hour,* Spring succeeds in creating an "English cozy with a hard edge."

BIOGRAPHICAL AND CRITICAL SOURCES:

PERIODICALS

Booklist, June 1, 1999, Jenny McLarin, review of *Nights in White Satin,* p. 1801; February 1, 2001, Connie Fletcher, review of *In the Midnight Hour,* p. 65.
Kirkus Reviews, March 1, 1998, p. 305.

Library Journal, March 1, 1994, p. 123; April 15, 1998, Alice DiNizo, review of *Standing in the Shadows,* p. 116; July, 2000, Susan Connell, review of *Nights in White Satin,* p. 172.
New York Times Book Review, July 11, 1999, Marilyn Stasio, review of *Nights in White Satin,* p. 29.
Publishers Weekly, March 14, 1994, p. 66; July 22, 1996, review of *Running for Shelter,* p. 229; March 2, 1998, review of *Standing in the Shadows,* p. 62; May 3, 1999, review of *Nights in White Satin,* p. 69; February 5, 2001, review of *In the Midnight Hour,* p. 65.
Times Literary Supplement, July 16, 1999, Mary Beard, review of *Nights in White Satin,* p. 23.
Washington Post Book World, August 9, 1998, p. 4.
Wilson Library Bulletin, May, 1994, Gail Pool, review of *Every Breath You Take,* p. 86.*

*   *   *

STEARN, Jess 1915(?)-2002

OBITUARY NOTICE—See index for CA sketch: Born c. 1915; died of congestive heart failure March 27, 2002, in Malibu, CA. Journalist and author. Stearn became well known for his many books on reincarnation and the occult. Having attended Syracuse University, he began his career as a reporter for the *New York Daily News,* where he was a journalist for seventeen years before joining *Newsweek* briefly as an associate editor. His early books, such as *Sisters of the Night: The Startling Story of Prostitution in New York Today* and *The Sixth Man,* were straight reportage on prostitution and homosexuality respectively. But Stearn then became interested in the occult, writing books like *The Door to the Future* and *Yoga, Youth, and Reincarnation* before publishing his best-known books, the biographies *The Sleeping Prophet: The Life and Work of Edgar Cayce* and *A Prophet in His Own Country: The Story of the Young Edgar Cayce.* Through his interviews with psychic healer Cayce, Stearn became convinced that such things as reincarnation were possible. He continued to pursue this interest as a freelancer, writing many other books on the paranormal and the occult, including *A Matter of Immortality: Dramatic Evidence of Survival, The Truth about Elvis, In Search of Taylor Caldwell, Elvis: His Spiritual Journey,* and *Soulmates.*

OBITUARIES AND OTHER SOURCES:

PERIODICALS

Los Angeles Times, April 1, 2002, p. B9.
New York Times, April 2, 2002, p. A21.
Washington Post, April 2, 2002, p. B7.

*   *   *

STECHA, Pavel 1944-

PERSONAL: Born December 20, 1944; in Prague, Czechoslovakia; married Alice Bubníková, 1969; children: Martina. *Education:* FAMU (Film & TV Faculty of Academy of Performing Arts), Prague, 1967-71; Fulbright scholar, 1990.

ADDRESSES: Home—V Horce 189, Cz-25228 Cernosice, Czech Republic.

CAREER: Photographer; FAMU, Prague, assistant lecturer, 1975-78, senior lecturer, 1978-90; Department of Photography, Prague University of Arts, Design, and Architecture, founder, 1994. *Exhibitions:* Works included in permanent collections at Museum of Decorative Arts, Prague; Moravian Gallery, Brno, Czechoslovakia; San Francisco Museum of Modern Art; International Center of Photography, New York; and National Gallery, Prague. Solo exhibitions include *Weekend Houses,* Cinoherni Klub Theatre, Prague, Czechoslovakia, 1978; *Traffic,* Cinoherni Klub Theatre, Prague, Czechoslovakia, 1980; Hippolyte Gallery, Helsinki, Finland, 1982; Istanbul, Turkey, 1989; Jerusalem Theatre, Israel, 1990; Fronta, Prague, 1992; Dortmund, Germany, 1993; and Berlin, Germany, 1993. Group exhibitions include *Youth Photography Exhibition,* at *Photokina,* Cologne, West Germany, 1968; *The Rest Home at St. Thomas,* Roudnice Art Gallery, Czechoslovakia, 1971 (traveled to the Fotokabinett Jaromir Funke, Brno, Czechoslovakia, 1972); *Fotoforum 73,* Ruzomberok, Czechoslovakia, 1973; *Tschechoslowakische Fotografie 1918-78,* Fotoforum der Gesamthochschule, Kassel, West Germany, 1979; *9+9,* Plasy, Czechoslovakia, 1981; *Topical Photography,* Moravian Gallery, Brno, Czechoslovakia, 1982; *Czechoslovakian Photography,* San Francisco Museum of Modern Art, San Francisco, CA, 1984; *27 Contem-* *porary Czechoslovakian Photographers,* The Photographers' Gallery, London, England, 1985; *37 Photographers,* 1989; and *Choice,* Houston Fotofest, Houston, TX, 1990. *Military service:* Czech Army, 1963-65.

AWARDS, HONORS: Youth Photography International Prize, Photokina, 1968; World Press Photo award, 1992.

WRITINGS:

Heart of Europe, Artia.
(Photo-illustrator) *Prag im Herzen Europas,* text by Bohumir Mráz, Dausien (Hanau, Germany), 1986.
(Photo-illustrator) *Domovní znamení staré Prahy* (title means "House Signs in Old Prague"), text by Lydia Petránová, Panorama (Prague, Czechoslovakia), 1988.
Listopad '89, Odeon.
(With Jiri Matejka) *Dobe navzdory,* Orbis Pictus (Prague, Czechoslovakia), 1990.
(With Arno Parik) *The Jewish Town of Prague,* Oswald (Prague, Czechoslovakia), 1992.
Prague—Hidden Splendours, Flammarion (Paris, France), 1993.
Prague Passages et Galleries (title means "Prague Passages and Galleries"), [Norma, France], 1993.

Contributor to publications, including *Revue Fotografie* and *Fotografie.*

SIDELIGHTS: Czech photographer Pavel Stecha's work, much of which examines man's habitation within his dwelling and town, has been done in conjunction with social scientists. Stecha, who studied under photographers Anna Fárová and Ján Smok and attended the FAMU Arts Academy, has explored old houses on the verge of being torn down and has featured, in a gallery of portraits, the men and women inside them. At other times, he has turned to new Czech neighborhoods and their bright-eyed inhabitants.

One Stecha study features portraits of log-cabin owners standing outside their weekend cottages. This early series inspired a follow-up project fifteen years later. The more recent photographs document the effects of time: homeowners have aged but, in many cases, their houses appear renewed. For the updated study, Stecha invited dwellers to hold up his portraits of themselves and their weekend houses taken fifteen years earlier. The dated works were enlarged to emphasize the before-and-after intensity. Critics have suggested that in the neighborhood project, Stecha aims to address sociological questions and have noted that he could reveal an entire environment through one situation. Stecha's study of the new neighborhoods, the writer said, was equally successful.

Another favorite Stecha subject is municipal transportation: traffic, people, buses, cars, and the subway system. He examines the growing distance between modern districts and city centers. The photographer said of his own work, "I believe in the power and narrative potential of thematic photography, as opposed to the single, all-encompassing picture."

Stecha's photographs have been the subject of several books. While he photographs mostly in Prague and neighboring regions, his assignments and experiments have also taken him to the industrial center of Ostrava.

BIOGRAPHICAL AND CRITICAL SOURCES:

BOOKS

Dufek, Antonin, *Aktualni Fotografie* (exhibition catalogue), [Brno, Czechoslovakia], 1982.*

* * *

STEEL, Duncan (I.) 1955-

PERSONAL: Born 1955, in Midsomer Norton, England. Immigrated to Australia. *Education:* Queen Elizabeth College, London, BSc., 1977; Imperial College, London, MSc., DIC, 1979; University of Canterbury (New Zealand), Ph.D., 1984.

ADDRESSES: Agent—Curtis Brown Group, 28-29 Haymarket, London SW1Y 4SP, England. *E-mail*—d.i. steel@salford.ac.uk

CAREER: Teacher and researcher. The Spaceguard Foundation, vice-president.

MEMBER: Royal Astronomical Society (fellow); International Astronomical Union.

WRITINGS:

Rogue Asteroids and Doomsday Comets: The Search for the Million-Megaton Menace That Threatens Life on Earth, John Wiley (New York, NY), 1995.
Marking Time: The Epic Quest to Invent the Perfect Calendar, John Wiley (New York, NY), 2000.
Target Earth, Reader's Digest (Pleasantville, NY), 2000.
Eclipse: The Celestial Phenomenon That Changed the Course of History, Joseph Henry Press (Washington, DC), 2001.

Contributor to periodicals, including *Sky and Space, Astronomy Now,* and *Guardian.*

SIDELIGHTS: Considered the leading Near-Earth-Objects (NEO) researcher in the southern hemisphere, research astronomer Duncan Steel is the director of Spaceguard Australia, is affiliated with the Anglo-Australian Observatory, and is a research fellow at the University of Adelaide, Australia. He has also served on the U.S. National Aeronautics and Space Administration's detection and intercept committees, which were created to assess asteroid threats and to develop technologies to avert damaging collisions. Steel provoked critical controversy with his first book, *Rogue Asteroids and Doomsday Comets: The Search for the Million-Megaton Menace That Threatens Life on Earth.* Steel theorizes that a devastating asteroid could be expected to collide with Earth about once every one hundred thousand years and recommends the creation of an international search program to find and intercept potentially dangerous asteroids and comets. He also speculates that asteroids were responsible for the mass extinction of dinosaurs and other species.

Lucy McFadden, writing in *Sky and Telescope,* also judged *Rogue Asteroids* to be both important and flawed. She appreciated the book's value in bringing attention to the subject of asteroid danger, but observed that its statistics were questionable and its logic difficult to follow. Though McFadden commented that Steel's "highly unusual" hypothesis should be taken "as fiction, not even science fiction," she concluded that its message "is important and could well be the most significant scientific result coming from the space programs of all the world's governments in the latter years of this millennium." Offering a more laudatory view, *Astronomy* reviewer John Shibley found *Rogue Asteroids* "intriguing" and informative, considering its "quirkiness" a significant merit. He deemed the book highly readable, as did a reviewer for *Publishers Weekly,* who hailed it as a "gripping report."

Marking Time: The Epic Quest to Invent the Perfect Calendar received less attention than Steel's earlier book. A *Publishers Weekly* reviewer considered it an excellent study of calendar systems through history but observed that the book suffers from a surfeit of unrelated facts. *Booklist* reviewer Bryce Christensen, however, admired Steel's ability to untangle the cultural intrigues behind the development of the calendar. "No book," Christensen concluded, "could serve as a better guide to the cumulative invention that defines the imaginary threshold to the new millennium."

In *Eclipse: The Celestial Phenomenon That Changed the Course of History* Steel examines the scientific discoveries and superstitions related to eclipses throughout history. Included in these scientific discoveries is the 1919 eclipse that helped Einstein develop his theory of relativity. Christopher Columbus used his knowledge of an impending eclipse to convince Jamaican chieftains to supply his ships with food, or be punished by the gods. *Booklist*'s Gilbert Taylor wrote, "Generously illustrated, Steel's informative discourse also promises staying power by ending with a guide to the next two decades of solar eclipses." *Library Journal*'s Jeffrey Beall recommended *Eclipse* "for all astronomy collections."

BIOGRAPHICAL AND CRITICAL SOURCES:

PERIODICALS

Astronomy, September, 1995, p. 96.
Booklist, May 15, 1995, p. 1619; October 15, 1999, p. 402; October 15, 2001, Gilbert Taylor, review of *Eclipse: The Celestial Phenomenon That Changed the Course of History,* p. 364.
Choice, April, 2000, V. V. Raman, review of *Marking Time: The Epic Quest to Invent the Perfect Calendar,* p. 1490; April, 2002, M. K. Hemenway, review of *Eclipse,* p. 1444.

Library Journal, November 1, 2001, Jeffrey Beall, review of *Eclipse,* p. 130.
Nation, October 28, 1996, p. 38.
Nature, November 2, 1995, p. 106.
New Scientist, August 19, 1995, p. 48.
Physics Today, February 1997, p. 65.
Publishers Weekly, April 17, 1995, p. 47; October 25, 1999, p. 62.
Science News, June 1, 2002, review of *Eclipse,* p. 351.
Sky & Telescope, January 1996, p. 54; March, 2000, review of *Marking Time,* p. 84.
Washington Post Book World, July 30, 1995, p. 13.

* * *

STEHR, Hermann 1864-1940

PERSONAL: Born February 16, 1864, in Habelschwerdt, Poland; died September 14, 1940, in Oberschreiberhau, Silesia; son of Robert (an upholsterer) and Theresa Farber Stehr; married Hedwig Nentwig, 1894.

CAREER: Novelist, writer of narratives, and poet. Schoolteacher in Poland.

AWARDS, HONORS: Bauernfeld prize, 1907; Fastenrath prize, Real Academia Española, 1911; Schiller prize, 1913; Rathenau prize, 1930; Goethe prize, 1933.

WRITINGS:

Auf Leben und Tod: Zwei Erzählungen (title means "On Lives and Death"), Fischer (Berlin, Germany), 1898.
Der Schindelmacher: Novelle (title means "The Schindelmacher"), Fischer (Berlin, Germany), 1899.
Leonore Griebel: Roman (title means "Leonore Griebel"), Fischer (Berlin, Germany), 1900.
Das lezte Kind (title means "The Last Child"), Fischer (Berlin, Germany), 1903.
Meta Konegen: Drama, Fischer (Berlin, Germany), 1904.
Der begrabene Gott: Roman (title means "The Buried God"), Fischer (Berlin, Germany), 1905.
Drei Nächte: Roman (title means, "Three Nights"), Fischer (Berlin, Germany), 1909.

Geschichten aus dem Mandelhause (title means "Stories from the Almond House"), Fischer (Berlin, Germany), 1913, enlarged edition published as *Das Mandelhaus: Roman,* List (Munich, Germany), 1953.

Das Abendrot: Novellen (title means "Evening Bread"), Fischer (Berlin, Germany), 1916.

Der Heiligenhof: Roman (title means "The Farm of the Saintly"), two volumes, Fischer (Berlin, Germany), 1918.

Meicke, der Teufel: Erzählung (title means "Meicke the Devil"), Hillger (Berlin, Germany), 1919.

Das Lebensbuch: Gedichte aus zwei Jahrzehnten, Fischer (Berlin, Germany), 1920.

Die Krähen (title means, "The Crows"), Fischer (Berlin, Germany), 1921.

Das entlaufene Herz (title means "The Runaway Heart"), Lintz (Trier, Germany), 1923.

Wendelin Heinelt: Ein Marchen, Lintz (Trier, Germany), 1923.

Peter Brineisener: Roman (title means "Peter Breineisner"), Lintz (Trier, Germany), 1924.

Gesammelte Werke (title means "Collected Works"), nine volumes, Lintz (Trier, Germany), 1924.

Der Schatten: Novelle (title means "The Shade"), Gesellschaft der Bücherfreunde (Chemnitz, Germany), 1924.

Wanderer zur Höhe: Erzahung (title means "Wanderer to the Height"), Osterreichischer Bundesverlag (Vienna, Austria), 1925.

Der Geigenmacher: Eine Geschichte, (title means "The Violin Maker"), Horen (Leipzig, Germany), 1926, edited by Walter A. Reichart, Oxford University Press (New York, NY), 1934.

Das Märchen vom deutschen Herzen: Dret Geschichten (title means "The Fairy Tale of the German Heart"), List (Leipzig, Germany), 1926.

Gesammelte Werke (title means "Collected Works"), twelve volumes, List (Leipzig, Germany), 1927-36.

Mythen und Mären, Horen (Berlin, Germany), 1929.

Nathanael Maechler: Roman, Horen (Berlin, Germany), 1929, republished in *Droben Gnade, drunten Recht* (title means "Grace on High, On Earth Justice"; volume one of "Das Geschlecht der Maechler: Roman einer deutschen Familie"), List (Leipzig, Germany), 1944.

Uber aussere, unde inneres Leben, Horen (Berlin, Germany), 1931.

Meister Cajetan: Novelle (title means "Master Cajetan"), List (Leipzig, Germany), 1931.

An der Tür des Jenseits: Zwei Novellen (title means "At the Door of the Other Life"), Langen-Müller (Munich, Germany), 1932.

Die Nachkommen: Roman (title means, "The Posterity"; volume two of "Das Geschlecht der Maechler: Roman einer deutschen Familie"), List (Leipzig, Germany), 1933, republished in *Droben Gnade drunten Recht,* List (Leipzig, Germany), 1944.

Gudnatz: Eine Novelle (title means "Gudnatz"), Insel (Leipzig, Germany), 1934.

Mein Leben (title means "My Life"), Junker und Dünnhaupt (Berlin, Germany), 1934.

Der Mittelgarten: Frühe und neue Gedichte (title means "The Central Garden: Early and New Poems"), List (Leipzig, Germany), 1936.

Das Stundenglas: Reden, Schriften, Tagebücher (title means "The Hourglass: Speeches, Writings, Diaries"), List (Leipzig, Germany), 1936.

Im Zwischenreich (Title means "In the Intermediate Realm"), Oehmigke (Breslau, Germany), 1937.

Der Himmelsschlüssel: Eine Geschichte zwischen Himmel und Erde, List (Leipzig, Germany), 1939.

Von Mensch und Gott: Worte des Dichters (title means "Of Humans and God"), List (Leipzig, Germany), 1939.

Hermann Stehr und das junge Deutschland: Bekenntnis zum fünfundsiebzigster Geburtstag des Dichters (title means "Hermann Stahr and Young Germany"), edited by F. Hammer, Roth (Eisenach, Germany), 1939.

Damian oder Das große Schermesser (volume three of "Das Geschlecht der Maechler: Roman einer deutschen Familie"), edited by Wilhelm Meridies, List (Leipzig, Germany), 1944.

Contributed introduction to *Schlesien: Ein Bildband,* Velhagen and Klasing (Bielefeld, Germany), 1937.

Stehr's papers are housed at the Hermann Stehr Archive in Wangen, Bavaria.

SIDELIGHTS: Hermann Stehr completed nine novels, thirty-one narratives, and hundreds of poems during his long career. Stehr's writing deals with human complexities, and religious and philosophical questions, and helped provide solace for an author afflicted with serious depression. His work has been translated into French, Czech, Norwegian, Celtic, English, and Japanese.

Erich P. Hofacker, writing in *Dictionary of Literary Biography,* said Stehr was esteemed in the early twentieth century, although his work has since gone out of print. Hofacker quoted from Hugo von Hofmannsthal's review of Stehr's *Der begrabene Gott:* "One word I must use in describing it is grandeur. And another is reverence, and awe."

Stehr rebelled against his parents' strict Catholic dogma. He trained to be an elementary school teacher but upset authorities with his dark, seemingly atheistic viewpoint. Between 1885 and 1889 Stehr lived hand to mouth, substitute-teaching in the remote Silesian mountains. Upon accepting his first permanent job, he felt persecuted by authority figures, became lonely and alienated, and battled with persistent insomnia. Hofacker wrote, "He developed a marked persecution complex which is reflected in the literary works of the period." Townspepople considered him a blasphemer.

In 1898 a reader at the S. Fischer publishing house, Moritz Hermann, took an interest in Stehr's work, publishing two of his novellas in a book titled *Auf Leben und Tod.* Commenting upon one of the novellas, Hofacker wrote, "In 'Der Graveur' (The Engraver) concrete images reflect the spiritual and psychological abuse the author felt at the hands of his fellow men." "Der Graveur" tells of pious Joseph Schramm, a hardworking engraver, who becomes mute and delusional after his drunken brother punches him in the face. Hungry for revenge, Joseph murders an innocent man.

In the second novella published in *Auf Leben und Tod,* "Meicke der Teufel," the protagonist Marx brings his off-putting devil-dog Meicke wherever he goes. "Though Marx claims to wish to . . . put an end to misery, the bad company, and the liquor, his drunkenness is only replaced by licentiousness," Hofacker noted. In this novella, as well as in "Der Graveur," Stehr's protagonist commits suicide.

In the novel *Leonore Griebel* the central conflict of marital incompatibility is introduced; this theme would reappear in all Stehr's later fiction. (Hofacker insists this may not reflect Stehr's life, since he claimed to greatly enjoy his long marriage). In the story, Leonore Griebel marries before she is mature enough to understand herself. After giving birth to one child, she feels alienated from the baby and eventually loses interest in caring for it. Later, she has an affair. Hofacker suggested, "After a bitter inner struggle she renounces her extramarital relationship; her spirit slowly ebbs away until she finds release in death. For

Stehr, perfect love comes naturally from a heart that is in harmony with itself and with God. It is not a purely spiritual love. . . . Perfect love combines elements of both, but in Stehr's works such a relationship proves difficult."

According to Hofacker, the novel *Der begrabene Gott* is so dark that contemporary reviewers claimed they had to take breaks from reading it to collect themselves. The plot involves Marie, a woman who takes the Bible verse, Matthew 16:24, too much to heart—"If any man will come after me, let him deny himself and take up his cross and follow me"—but also misunderstands it. She marries an abusive, crippled man who constantly torments her. Her faith in God enables her to stay in the marriage, but when she gives birth to a horribly deformed baby she can stand no more suffering, revolts against God, and murders the child. "It transports us to depths we have never before experienced," Hofmannsthal wrote.

In 1900, thanks to the approval of the regional ministry of culture in Breslau, Stehr earned a transfer to Dittersbach. Dark bitterness no longer dominated his writing, according to Hofacker. For instance, the novel *Drei Nächte,* which follows young schoolteacher Franz Faber, is written in a confessional style, with Faber describing his life before relocating to a new town. The book is considered lighter than *Der begrabene Gott.* Hofacker observed, "Confession brings freedom from old psychological and spiritual bonds and permits one to turn inward to seek the dwelling place of the soul and of God. . . . *Der Nächte* marked the end of Stehr's years of despair; his next works were stories in a generally lighter vein."

Der Heiligenhof is one of Stehr's top-selling novels, though its readership was less than half a million. "Indeed," Hofacker wrote, "Stehr feared that his works would be misinterpreted if they were read by the masses."

The story, reminiscent of *Romeo and Juliet,* introduces two feuding families on two farms, one silent and forsaken, the other brimming with festivity and life. Eventually, the families put aside their differences, thanks to the love affair between a representative son and daughter. As the story unfolds, young, blind daughter Helene from the more optimistic farming family plays with unruly neighbor boy Peter Brindeisener, from the pessimistic clan. As the two fall in love, Helene's father, Sintlinger, starts to feel alienated and depressed. As if summoned, Franz Faber of *Drei Nächte* visits the farm with some words of wisdom, his central message conveying the importance of universal laws, which prevent even God from committing arbitrary gesture.

Peter has actually changed little—he is still unruly, undisciplined, and a poor match for Helene."The problem of the balance between spiritual and sensual love so frequently present in Stehr's works remains unresolved," Hofacker remarked. In a characteristic Stehr plot-twist, Helene drowns herself in desperation. "At this point, Franz Faber reappears to aid . . . Sintlinger in reaching his final goal: only when he has learned understanding . . . and love for his fellow man will he be ready for life," Hofacker wrote.

Peter Brindeisener retells the *Der Heiligenhof* saga from the mind of Brindeisener, now a solitary old man. As his life ends he seems to believe he was predestined to make immoral choices and walk a shady path. Furthermore, he decides that only by confessing his sins and mystically returning to the *Seelengrund*— "the ground of his soul"—can he redeem himself. After his confessional journey, he also drowns himself.

Stehr published several stories in *Die Krähen* and *Der Geigenmacher*, the story in the latter portraying the challenges of artistic creation. The main character is a violin maker working toward perfection in a secluded forest. He falls in love with a young girl, but their passion is not to be. Instead, the violin maker crafts a one-of-a-kind instrument expressing the beauty and mystery of the young woman.

Published in 1934, *Mein Leben* is an autobiographical work. Hofacker quoted one relevant passage: "The more pitilessly the blows of life beat down upon me, the more fervently did I devote myself to the visions within me. All the world's accusations, all disquietude, all my disappointments I offered for resolution to that other-worldly court presided over by poetry, the goddess whom I served."

BIOGRAPHICAL AND CRITICAL SOURCES:

BOOKS

Hardin, James, editor, *Dictionary of Literary Biography*, Volume 66: *German Fiction Writers, 1885-1913*, Gale (Detroit, MI), 1988, pp. 450-458.

OTHER

Biographisch-Bibliographisches Kirchenlexikon, http://www.bautz.de/ (February 7, 1999).*

* * *

STEWART, Jon 1962-

PERSONAL: Born Jonathan Stewart Leibowitz, November 28, 1962, in Lawrence, NJ; son of an RCA physicist and a teacher of gifted students; married Tracy McShane. *Education:* College of William and Mary, B.S., 1984.

ADDRESSES: Office—c/o *The Daily Show,* Comedy Central, Viewer Services, 1775 Broadway, 10th Floor, New York, NY 10019.

CAREER: Stand-up comic and writer. Host of *The Jon Stewart Show,* MTV, 1993-94; host of *The Daily Show,* Comedy Central, 1999—. Appeared in films, including *Mixed Nuts,* 1994, *First Wives' Club,* 1996, *Wishful Thinking,* 1997, *Playing by Heart,* 1998, *Half Baked,* 1998, *Since You've Been Gone,* 1998, *Big Daddy,* 1999, and *Committed,* 2000.

WRITINGS:

Naked Pictures of Famous People, Rob Weisbach Books/Morrow (New York, NY), 1998.

SIDELIGHTS: Bruce Fretts, writing for *Entertainment Weekly,* called comedian and actor Jon Stewart's *Naked Pictures of Famous People* "brutally witty." American pop culture got a glimpse of Stewart's irreverent brand of humor from his late-night MTV talk show, *The Jon Stewart Show,* which a *People* reviewer characterized by asserting: "what makes Stewart unique is his complete lack of pretense. He seems like Letterman's younger, hipper brother, taking the *Late Show* star's laid back approach one step further." For example, Stewart has been known to feature a ten-year-old harmonica player or a piano-playing grandma instead of a band. Or, instead of the expected celebrity interview, Stewart had a Foosball match with Kelsey

Grammar one night, and, on another night's show, he demonstrated a basic life-saving technique—mouth-to-mouth resuscitation—on Pamela Anderson of *Baywatch* fame.

By the time Stewart wrote *Naked Pictures of Famous People,* America was primed and ready. Fretts wrote, "A funny thing happened when stand-up comic Jon Stewart sat down to write a book: He actually wrote a funny one. Rather than merely transcribe his monologues (like Jerry Seinfeld did) or pen a confessional tell-all (like Roseanne did—twice), Stewart's *Naked Pictures of Famous People* consists of 18 original humor pieces on a par with Woody Allen's *Without Feathers* and Steve Martin's *Cruel Shoes.*" One piece is titled "Martha Stewart's Vagina." Another piece, "Pen Pals," features the correspondence between Princess Di and Mother Teresa. Other pieces include Larry King's interview with Hitler (plugging Hitler's new book, *Mein Comfortable Shoes*), and a visit to a room where the Kennedys keep their unsuccessful children. As Fretts concluded in his review, *Naked Pictures* "reveals a basic truth that's too often forgotten by the shock-for shock's-sake satirists of the South Park era: You've got to be smart to be a smart-ass."

BIOGRAPHICAL AND CRITICAL SOURCES:

PERIODICALS

Entertainment Weekly, October 2, 1998, p. 66.
People, October 31, 1994, p 13.
Publishers Weekly, September 28, 1998, review of *Naked Pictures of Famous People,* p. 73.*

* * *

STOFFEL, Albert Law 1909-2002

OBITUARY NOTICE—See index for *CA* sketch: Born May 20, 1909, in Racine, WI; died May 6, 2002, in Santa Monica, CA. Journalist, cartoonist, editor, and author. Stoffel will be best remembered as the cartoonist of the "Bugs Bunny" strip that was syndicated nationally from 1946 until the 1970s. After earning his B.A. at the University of Kentucky in 1931, Stoffel was a reporter for the *Wisconsin News* during the early 1930s. From 1938 to 1939, he was a news and features

writer in Italy before World War II started, and from 1940 to 1942 he was on staff at the *Richmond News-Leader.* During the war, Stoffel was an aircraft carrier communications officer. When he returned to civilian life, he joined Western Publishing in Los Angeles as an editor and manager. It was here that he began to produce the "Bugs Bunny" comic strip, which lasted until his retirement in 1975. He also wrote books for children, including *How to Care for Your Dog.*

OBITUARIES AND OTHER SOURCES:

PERIODICALS

Los Angeles Times, May 13, 2002, p. B9.

* * *

STOLPER, Wolfgang F(riedrich) 1912-2002

OBITUARY NOTICE—See index for *CA* sketch: Born May 13, 1912, in Vienna, Austria; died from complications due to heart disease April 1, 2002, in Ann Arbor, MI. Economist, educator, and author. Stolper is best known as the coauthor, along with economist Paul Samuelson, of the important Stolper-Samuelson economic theory. After studying at the universities of Berlin, Bonn, and Zurich in the early 1930s, Stolper and his family came to the United States, where he completed his education at Harvard University, earning a Ph.D. in 1938. His teaching career also began at Harvard, where he was an instructor and tutor from 1936 to 1941 before moving on to Swarthmore College as an assistant and then associate professor of economics during the 1940s. After joining the University of Michigan in Ann Arbor in 1949, Stolper remained at that university for the rest of his career, becoming a professor of economics in 1954 until his retirement in 1983. Stolper devised his famous theory early in his career; it asserts that while international trade can have positive economic benefits for nations overall, it can also cause wages for many workers to go down. In addition to this still-widely accepted theory, Stolper was also interested in the economies of Germany and developing nations such as Nigeria and Tunisia, and he was the author of such books as *Structure of the East Germany Economy, Germany between East and West,* and *Planning without Facts.* Besides his work as an economist, Stolper was also an accomplished pianist.

OBITUARIES AND OTHER SOURCES:

PERIODICALS

Detroit Free Press, April 4, 2002.
Los Angeles Times, April 6, 2002, p. B17.
New York Times, April 4, 2002, p. A21.
Washington Post, April 6, 2002, p. B7.

*   *   *

STONEMAN, Elvyn Arthur 1919-2002

OBITUARY NOTICE—See index for *CA* sketch: Born November 5, 1919, in Lincoln, NE; died of complications from diabetes February 19, 2002, in Rockville, MD. Geographer, educator, foreign service officer, and author. For a few years after the end of World War II, Stoneman taught geography at Indiana University in Bloomington. He then worked as a geographer, first for the U.S. Department of Defense from 1951 to 1960, then for the Department of State, beginning in 1960. His foreign service assignments took him to South Africa for a brief period, but the bulk of his career was spent in Washington, D.C., where he retired in 1979. Stoneman was a coauthor of the books *The Changing Map of Africa* and *A Handbook of New Nations.*

OBITUARIES AND OTHER SOURCES:

PERIODICALS

Washington Post, February 23, 2002, p. B5.

*   *   *

STOTT, (Charlotte) Mary 1907-2002

OBITUARY NOTICE—See index for *CA* sketch: Born July 18, 1907, in Leicester, England; died September 16, 2002, in London, England. Journalist, activist, and author. As the editor of the Manchester *Guardian*'s women's section from 1957 to 1972, Stott was an influential liberal voice in the British media. She first began working in the newspaper business at the age of seventeen, when her mother got her a job with the *Leicester Mail.* There, against her desires, she was assigned to writing for the women's page from 1927 to 1931. She moved to the *Bolton Evening News* in 1931, followed in 1933 by a position with the Co-operative Press, where she wrote about women's issues. With the onset of World War II and the subsequent shortage of men writers and editors, Stott was allowed the opportunity to be a sub-editor for the *Manchester Evening News* from 1945 to 1950. In 1957, after focusing her time on being a wife and mother for several years, she joined the staff at the *Guardian.* Although editing the women's page was supposed to be an assignment involving nothing more important than stories on fashion, cooking, sewing, and gossip, Stott transformed it into another type of animal altogether. She boldly included stories that were truly important to women, including articles on child care, depression, and domestic violence. Retiring from the *Guardian* in 1972, Stott continued to contribute articles for some time thereafter. However, she slso became more politically active, joining several women's groups, among them Women in Media, the National Association of Widows, where she was president from 1993 to 1995, and the Fawcett Society, for which she served as chairperson from 1980 to 1982. In 1981 she also joined the Social Democratic Party. Stott's work as a journalist helped pave the way for other women in the profession, and her courage in addressing important issues for women was instrumental in seeding a growing awareness of feminism at a time when women were still largely ignored by the media. Stott, who also loved to sing, paint, and play the piano, was the author of several books, including *Ageing for Beginners* (1981) and the memoirs *Forgetting's No Excuse* (1973) and *Before I Go* (1985). For her work as a journalist, she was made an officer in the Order of the British Empire in 1975 and was awarded an honorary D.Litt. from De Montfort University in 1996.

OBITUARIES AND OTHER SOURCES:

BOOKS

Writers Directory, 16th edition, St. James (Detroit, MI), 2001.

PERIODICALS

Daily Post (Liverpool, England), September 20, 2002, p. 14.

Daily Telegraph (London, England), September 19, 2002.

Guardian (London, England), September 18, 2002, p. 20.

Independent (London, England), October 1, 2002, p. 20.

Scotsman, September 27, 2002, p. 18.

Times (London, England), September 19, 2002, p. 36.

*   *   *

STRAUSZ-HUPÉ, Robert 1903-2002

OBITUARY NOTICE—See index for *CA* sketch: Born March 25, 1903, in Vienna, Austria; died of a stroke and cardiovascular disease February 24, 2002, in Newtown Square, PA. Diplomat, political scientist, educator, and author. During the years of the cold war, Strausz-Hupé was a strong critic of Soviet communism and a firm believer that the United States should support European efforts to unite against Soviet encroachments into Eastern Europe. From that perspective, he served as a foreign policy advisor to Republican presidential candidates in the 1960s. Strausz-Hupé also believed in the power of diplomacy; he was appointed U.S. ambassador to Ceylon (now Sri Lanka) and the Maldives in 1970; assignments to Belgium, Sweden, the North Atlantic Treaty Organization, and Turkey followed until his retirement in the late 1980s. Despite his hard line against communism, he was described as an effective representative of American attempts at compromise and conciliation. Strausz-Hupé had begun teaching political science at the University of Pennsylvania in 1940; he founded and directed the Foreign Policy Research Institute there from 1955 to 1969 and was a member of the Council on Foreign Relations. In 1992 he was named a distinguished fellow of the United States Institute for Peace. Strausz-Hupé shared his conservative political views in several books, including *Geopolitics: The Struggle for Space and Power,* published in 1942 and one of the first volumes to treat the new concept of "geopolitics". Other books include *Power and Community, The Estrangement of Western Man,* and *The Zone of Indifference,* all published in the 1950s, as well as a memoir, *In My Time,* published in 1965, and *Democracy and American Foreign Policy: Reflections on the Legacy of Alexis de Tocqueville,* published in 1995.

OBITUARIES AND OTHER SOURCES:

BOOKS

Strausz-Hupé, Robert, *In My Time,* Norton (New York, NY), 1965.

PERIODICALS

Los Angeles Times, February 26, 2002, p. B11.

New York Times, February 26, 2002, obituary by Paul Lewis, p. A25.

Times (London, England), March 13, 2002.

Washington Post, February 25, 2002, obituary by Louie Estrada, p. B6.

*   *   *

STREIT, Jindrich 1946-

PERSONAL: Born September 5, 1946, in Vsetin, Czechoslovakia; married, April 20, 1971; wife's name Agnes; children: Monika. *Education:* Palack University, degree in art education, teacher training department, 1967; studied at Institute of Creative Photography, 1974-77.

ADDRESSES: Home—Sovinec 6, Autoposta Bruntál, cz79201, Czech Republic.

CAREER: Photographer, gallery owner, and teacher. Primary school teacher, Rymarov in 1967; headmaster of village school in Sovinec and Jiríkov. Directed gallery specializing in avante-garde artists, Sovinec, from 1973; photographer of village life during communist rule in Sovinec; arrested and imprisoned for ten months in 1982, forbidden from photographic activity or teaching; external lecturer in photography, Film and TV Academy of Prague and Institute of Creative Photography of the Theatre of Music, Silesian University in Opava, 1990—; freelance photographer throughout France, 1991-92. *Exhibitions:* Individual exhibits include *Tension,* University Club, Olomouc, Czechoslovakia, 1967; *The Man,* Theatre of Music, Olomouc, Czechoslovakia, 1974; *Gypsies without Romanticism,* Gallery V Podloubí, Olomouc, Czechoslovakia, 1975; *The Theatre of Life,* Gallery V Podloubí,

Olomouc, Czechoslovakia, 1978; *Photographs from Journies,* Factory Club, Unicov, Czechoslovakia, 1979; Bruntál, Czechoslovakia, 1980; Theatre, Cinoherní Klub, Prague, Czechoslovakia, 1981; J. Chloupka Gallery, Brno, Czechoslovakia, 1988; House of the Lords of Kunstát, Brno, Czechoslovakia, 1989; Side Gallery, Newcastle upon Tyne, England, 1990; Mai de la Photo, Reims, France, 1991; Prague House of Photography, Prague, Czechoslovakia, 1992; and Spála Gallery, Prague, Czech Republic, 1993. Group exhibitions include *Twenty-seven Contemporary Czechoslovak Photographers,* Photographers Gallery, London, England, 1985; *Personalities of Czechoslovak Social Documentary Photography,* Gallery F. Banská, Brno, Czechoslovakia, 1986; *On the Art of Fixing a Shadow,* Smithsonian Institution, Washington, DC, 1989; *Choice,* Houston Fotogrest, Houston, TX, 1990; *Contemporary Czechoslovak Photographers,* Shwayder Gallery, Denver, University, CO, 1991; *More than One Photograph,* Museum of Modern Art, New York, NY, 1992; *Czech and Slovak Photography from Between the Wars to the Present,* Fitchburg Art Museum, Fitchburg, MA, 1993; and *Another Continent,* Tokyo Metropolitan Museum of Photography, Tokyo, Japan, 1994. Works are in several collections, including Moravian Gallery, Brno, Czech Republic; Sztuki Museum, Lodz, Poland; Ludwig Museum, Cologne, Germany; Museum of Fine Arts, Houston, TX; Art Institute of Chicago; Museum of Modern Art, New York, NY; Districe de Saint-Quentin, France, Stanford University Museum of Art, Stanford, CA; Harvard University of Art, Cambridge, MA; Victoria and Albert Museum, London, England; National Gallery of Art, Washington, DC; and Musée de l'Elysée, Lausanne, Switzerland.

WRITINGS:

14 Regards sur le District de Saint-Quentin, [Saint-Quentin, France], 1992, English version with Antonín Dufek published as *Saint-Quentin: 14 Views of the Region,* [Brno, Czech Republic], 1993.
(Photographer) Antonín Dufek, *The Village Is a Global World,* [Prague, Czech Republic], 1993.
(Photographer) Patrick Bernier, *La Quai de Rohan—Nouvelle Ville,* [Lorient, France], 1994.
Myslenky do kapsy, Olomouc, (Czech Republic), 1994.
Zabavené fotografie (title means "The Confiscated Photographs"), Sedlácek (Brno, Czech Republic), 1999.

SIDELIGHTS: Jindrich Streit is a Czech photographer who achieved worldwide acclaim beginning in the late 1980s. His photos of village life in Czechoslovakia—now the Czech Republic—and his organizing of exhibitions and performances for dissident artists earned him the wrath of Communist officials. Streit was imprisoned briefly in 1982, authorities having accused him of slandering the president.

Stret's photos, according to a *Photographer's International* writer, "are never short of the author's deep knowledge of life, his sympathetic understanding of life's light and dark aspects and, at the risk of sounding too pompous, his unpretending love and respect for love, whatever he may be and wherever he may live."

Essentially shooting Czech village subjects much of his career, Streit has exhibited as far away as Japan, where he was invited for three months after a Toyko exhibition. And, in Budapest, Hungary in November, 2000, Streit's exhibits showed the conflicts of the computer revolution and globalization. "His photographs show a disappearing world with people unable to adapt to new technologies," said a writer for the Web site *Artcult.*

After graduating from college Streit and his wife taught at Sovinec, a village where he compiled portraits of residents under the title *Man.* In his next collection, *Gypsies without Romanticism,* he sought to contrast the dramatic potrayal of gypsies completed by his predecessor, Josef Koudelka, and instead focused on human characteristics with a more universal application.

After finishing his studies at the Institute of Creative Photography, according to the writer, he photographed actors in dressing rooms as well as on stage. Then, the *Contemporary Photographers* writer added, "Streit captured cracked, muddy paths, dilapidated yards, and the cheerless stereotype of new prefabricated houses. He also photographed boring meetings and formal celebrations of various communist festivals and the sincere relationships of people in a convivial rural community where everyone knows everyone else."

Streit's raw photos of Czech village life contrast with the idyllic pictures appearing in government newspapers and magazines. This put Streit in conflict with the communist leader Gustáv Husák, and Streit was arrested in the spring of 1982. At the time of his arrest, he received a suspended sentence of ten months, but was forced to give up teaching and become a packer at the state farm in Ryzoviste. But this did not stop him from organizing cultural events or continuing on with his photography.

After the fall of communism in 1989, Streit taught at the Faculty of Film and Television in Prague and the Institute of Creative Photography of the Silesian University in Opava. He also undertook to care for the reconstruction of the medieval castle at Sovinec and additionally to continue organizing various cultural events.

BIOGRAPHICAL AND CRITICAL SOURCES:

OTHER

Artcult, http://www.artcult.com/ (November, 2000), "Exhibitions in Budapest."*

*   *   *

SUKENICK, Ronald 1932-

PERSONAL: Born July 14, 1932, in Brooklyn NY; son of Louis (a dentist) and Ceceile (Frey) Sukenick; married Lynn Luria, March 19, 1961 (divorced, 1984); married Julia Frey (a writer), 1992. *Education:* Cornell University, B.A., 1955; Brandeis University, M.A., 1957, Ph.D., 1962.

ADDRESSES: Home—200 Rector Pl., Apt. 26B, New York, NY 10280.

CAREER: Brandeis University, Waltham, MA, instructor, 1956-60; Hofstra University, instructor, 1961-62; toured Europe, wrote, and taught in various schools, 1962-66; City College of the City University of New York, assistant professor of English, 1966-67; Sarah Lawrence College, Bronxville, NY, assistant professor of English and writing, 1968-69; writer-in-residence, Cornell University, Ithaca, NY, 1969, and University of California, Irvine, 1970-72; University of Colorado, Boulder, professor of English, 1975—, director of creative writing, 1975-77, director of Publications

Ronald Sukenick

Center, 1986—, founder of exchange program and first exchange professor to l'Université Paul Valéry, Montpellier, France, 1979. Lecturer, Brandeis University, 1956-60, Hofstra University, 1961-62. Butler Chair, State University of New York, Buffalo, spring, 1981. Publisher, *American Book Review,* 1977, and *Black Ice,* 1989—. Member of *Publication of the Modern Language Association (PLMA)* advisory committee, 1987-90.

MEMBER: PEN, Authors Guild, Authors League of America, National Book Critics Circle, Coordinating Council of Literary Magazines (chairman of board of directors, 1975-77), Fiction Collective (founding member).

AWARDS, HONORS: Fulbright fellowships, 1958 and 1984; Guggenheim Foundation fellowship, 1977; National Endowment for the Arts fellowships, 1980 and 1989; CCLM Award for Editorial Excellence, 1985; Western Book Award for publishing, 1985; American Book Award, Before Columbus Foundation, 1988, for *Down and In,* and 1999, for literature; Zabel Award, American Academy of Arts and Letters, 2003, for innovative fiction.

WRITINGS:

Wallace Stevens: Musing the Obscure, New York University Press (New York, NY), 1967.

Up (novel), Dial (New York, NY), 1968, reprinted, Fiction Collective Two (Normal, IL), 1998.

The Death of the Novel, and Other Stories, Dial (New York, NY), 1969.

Out (novel), Swallow Press (Chicago, IL), 1973.

(Contributor) Ray Federman, editor, *Surfiction,* Swallow Press (Chicago, IL), 1974.

98.6 (novel), Fiction Collective (New York, NY), 1975.

Long Talking Bad Conditions Blues, Fiction Collective (New York, NY), 1979.

In Form, Digressions on the Act of Fiction, Southern Illinois University Press (Carbondale, IL), 1985.

The Endless Short Story, Fiction Collective (New York, NY), 1986.

Blown Away (novel), Sun & Moon (Los Angeles, CA), 1987.

Down and In: Life in the Underground (nonfiction narrative), Beech Tree Books (New York, NY), 1987.

(Editor) *Witness Magazine: Experimental Fiction,* Witness Publishers, Inc., 1989.

Doggy Bag, Black Ice Books/Fiction Collective Two (Normal, IL), 1994.

(Editor with Mark Amerika) *Degenerative Prose,* Black Ice/Fiction Collective Two (Normal, IL), 1995.

(Editor with Curtis White) *In the Slipstream: An FC2 Reader,* Fiction Collective Two (Normal, IL), 1999.

Mosaic Man, Fiction Collective Two (Normal, IL), 1999.

Narralogues: Truth in Fiction, State University Press of New York (Albany, NY), 2000.

Cows (e-book), altX Press, 2001.

Contributing editor, *The Pushcart Prize Anthology,* Pushcart/Avon. Fiction appears in several anthologies published in the United States and Poland. Contributor of fiction to *Epoch, California Quarterly, New American Review, Fiction, TriQuarterly, Iowa Review, Paris Review, Partisan Review, Ploughshares,* and other periodicals.

Contributor of reviews to periodicals, including *New York Times Book Review, Partisan Review, Nation,* and *Village Voice.* Contributing editor, *Fiction International,* 1970-84; guest editor, *Witness,* 1989.

ADAPTATIONS: Out was filmed in 1982, produced and directed by Eli Hollander.

SIDELIGHTS: Writer and theorist Ronald Sukenick was one of the leaders in the meta-fiction trend of the 1960s. "Ronald Sukenick has been prominent among writers of innovative fiction in America," stated Julian Cowley in the *Dictionary of Literary Biography.* "In addition to producing his own novels and collections of short stories, he has acted as theorist, publisher, and catalyst for new writing. His fiction is notable for its improvisatory energy and its focus on the processes of writing and reading, which take precedence over the conventional concerns of characterization and plot. Against the flow of those processes, he often counterpoints bold structural arrangements, which make his books visually striking and distinctive. Far from being innovative for the sake of innovation, Sukenick aims through his art to intensify and expand his readers' experience of their own lives."

Like other avant garde novelists during the mid-twentieth century, Sukenick recognized that conventional literary tradition—a standardized way of looking at an art form—had become one of fiction's strongest enemies. "There are all these talented people around trying to write in this form which doesn't suit them at all, so that instead of releasing their energies it blocks them out," Sukenick told interviewer Joe David Bellamy in 1970 for *The New Fiction: Interviews with Innovative American Writers.* Sukenick posited that a new tradition could be built to replace the old without rejecting the works upon which the old was built. "It must already be there awaiting only one final element—that we say it exists," Sukenick wrote in "The New Tradition in Fiction," an essay collected in Ray Federman's *Surfiction.* Sukenick elaborated: "It's not modern. . . . The modern behaved as if a new age were due tomorrow, and as if it were it, the final goal of progress. Here in tomorrowland we have a more tragic sense of things. We know there's no such thing as progress, that a new age may be a worse one, and that since the future brings no redemption, we better look to the present. In consequence the new tradition makes itself felt as a presence rather than a development. Instead of a linear sequence of historical influences it seems a network of interconnections revealed to our particular point of view. Like Eliot's view of tradition, it would resemble a reservoir rather than a highway project, a reservoir that is ahistorical, international, and multilingual." Sukenick's criticism and fiction supported the establishment of this new tradition. His first book, *Wallace Stevens: Musing the Obscure,* studies a poet who was concerned with the complex relation between language, imagination, and reality. Sukenick looks at forty poems separately, taking them as "chapters in the life of the poet's mind," according to Denis Donoghue in the *New York Review of Books.* Condemned for being unconventional by some reviewers, the book was hailed by others as the first study to offer an accurate approach to Stevens's work. *Wallace Stevens* became the first installment of a body of criticism that was esteemed for its clarity and well-defended iconoclasm.

Sukenick's novels have been noted for the attempt "to define a distinct voice while expanding the genre's potential," according to Frederick R. Karl in *American Fictions, 1940-1980: A Comprehensive History and Critical Evaluation.* "They show that there is some territory novelists have yet to explore." In addition, noted Jerome Klinkowitz in *Literary Subversions: New American Fiction and the Practice of Criticism,* they present some of "the strongest American innovations" in fiction and fiction theory. Sukenick's innovations are best understood in the context of his thinking about the relation between fiction and reality at this crucial point in the history of the genre.

In the 1970s many writers turned away from writing realistic fiction. "Realistic fiction presupposed chronological time as the medium of a plotted narrative, an irreducible individual psyche as the subject of its characterization, and, above all, the ultimate, concrete reality of things as the object and rationale of its description. In the world of post-realism, however, all of these absolutes have become absolutely problematic," Sukenick explained in *The Death of the Novel, and Other Stories.* "The contemporary writer—the writer who is acutely in touch with the life of which he is a part—is forced to start from scratch: Reality doesn't exist, time doesn't exist, personality doesn't exist." Sukenick told Bellamy: "People are surrounded by all sorts of information coming in to them through all sorts of media now, and the novel, on that level, doesn't have anything to say to them." However,

Sukenick argued, with readers going to other media to experience "reality," writers were presented with a challenge to create new forms and techniques for handling new types of content. "One model for a work of fiction is the jigsaw puzzle," Sukenick explained in "The New Tradition in Fiction." The picture "is filled out but there is no sense of development involved. . . . Situations come about through a cloudburst of fragmented events that fall as they fall and finally can be seen to have assumed some kind of pattern. . . . A novel is both a concrete structure and an imaginative structure—pages, print, binding containing a record of the movements of a mind."

In some of Sukenick's novels, instead of progressing through time, the narrative expands only through space; the sequential order follows the author's sense of what is to be revealed at any point in the continuum. In *Out,* the pages count down from Section Nine to Section Zero; the spaces between lines of type increase so that the reader turns pages faster when approaching the end; in Section Zero, words disappear into white space on a blank page. *Out* "is a spatial fiction, the idea being to conquer space so as to convey the sense of moving on, fragmentation, things breaking up and never cohering," noted Karl in *American Fictions, 1940-1980,* who further suggested: "Sukenick wanted some way to convey the spaced out dimensions of the sixties: spaced out in terms of those who move counterculturally as a consequence of drugs or radical politics; spaced out in the alternative sense of those who move continually. . . . [His] characters belong to a loose organization that blows things up; they carry explosives and move across the country according to certain plans which develop at the last moment. The point is that at any given time, they do not know what they are supposed to do, who their cohorts are, or where their next move will come from. They are lost in space, spaced out, and yet they must move in it." In *Dictionary of Literary Biography,* Cowley commented that *Out* "challenges the dominance of analytical intelligence; in its place it offers synthesis, attained through intuitive and extrarational means."

The novel *Long Talking Bad Conditions Blues* is one long sentence broken into paragraphs. Its style conveys the workings of the narrator's consciousness to connect disparate worlds of "individual and culture," to build bridges of contact between a personal inner world and an alien environment, according to Karl. "At every level," he continued, "Sukenick's inhabitants are exiled: men from women, each from the other, as individuals or as people seeking, however tentatively, a community. Sukenick tries to wrap these meditations in stylistic equivalents: mainly interior monologue, paragraphs that occupy only a fraction of the page, endlessly run-together sentences which become coils and wraparounds, phrases and sentences interrupted by white space, removal of punctuation so as to approximate consciousness."

98.6 is a record of the search for community as it plays itself out in three different spatial contexts. The landscape of the first section, "Frankenstein," is America, a patchwork of dispossessed remnants. "The land of the living dead," Frankenstein "is a territory the Aztecs would have recognized, death-oriented," observed Karl. The nightmarish lives of "Frankenstein's Children," troubled by experimentation with drugs, group sex, and violent altercations with people from outside their commune, comprise the second section. "Palestine," the third section in which members of a kibbutz achieve the sought-after communal life, seems utopian by contrast. Parallel to the search for new forms of social organization in the novel is Sukenick's quest for a new kind of fiction. "For the unities of realistic fiction—plot, character and causation—Sukenick substitutes the 'discipline of inclusion,' an unceasing energy, and a belief in the primacy of language," Thomas LeClair noted in the *New York Times Book Review*. LeClair credited the novel's success to Sukenick's approach: "Because he sees life as continual invention, he can get at the imaginative bases of the alternative culture with sympathy and humor, without trapping himself in hip cliches." E. M. Potoker, writing in a *Nation* review, commented that Sukenick's work holds together better than the shattered culture he writes about: "Out of broad humor and a sense of structural irony . . . Sukenick manages to balance the sentimental, the emotional, and the pathetic with the obscene, the trivial and the absurd."

Because personality as it was traditionally perceived also "no longer exists," characters in Sukenick's novels do not conform to traditional expectations. The narrator may give a character contradictory traits at different times in the story. He may describe another character first as short, then as tall, then confess he doesn't know what the other looks like. Some characters are Sukenick's actual acquaintances and others merely borrow their names. His fictional people are

amorphous, he told Bellamy, because contemporary people are multi-faceted, and because readers engage in the act of imagining who people are apart from their reality at all times. "You're always making people up, in effect. . . . There you are, and I don't know much about you, but, in a way, I'm making you up. I'm filling up the gaps in my mind, and I create the Joe Bellamy that happens to be there. And probably there's a great gap between my version, which is imaginative, and the real Joe Bellamy. . . . Maybe there isn't a real Joe Bellamy. Maybe there aren't real characters. That's the important thing. Maybe people are much more fluid and amorphous than the realistic novel would have us believe." In *The Life of Fiction*, Klinkowitz commented: "His characters are not so real that they 'walk off the pages.' Instead they stay right there, on the pages, as figures remain on the canvas, so it might be appreciated as art and not life. What the reader reads is an honest account of the artist's work, and what the artist presents is a piece of genuine fabrication and craftsmanship, his *imaginative* response to a world we share. Not the shabby lie that this is the world itself."

Such fiction does not represent reality, it represents itself. However it highlights the role of the imagination in order to make readers more, not less, sensitive to reality. Sukenick told Bellamy, "I don't want to present people with illusions, and I don't want to let them off cheaply by releasing their fantasies in an easy way. . . . What that does is allow people to escape, obviously, from reality, and I want to bang them with it." He explained that in *Out* and *98.6*, he employed different techniques to deconstruct standard form in fiction in order to reach beyond literary artifice to actual experience, though conscious of the inherent contradictions. He commented that the same paradox is at the heart of post-modern literature; behind new fiction is the urge "to get at the truth of experience beyond our fossilizing formulas of discourse, to get at a new and more inclusive 'reality,' if you will. This is a reality that includes what the conventional novel tends to exclude and that encompasses the vagaries of unofficial experience, the cryptic trivia of the quotidian that help shape our fate, and the tabooed details of life—class, ethnic, sexual—beyond sanctioned descriptions of life." The actual business of writing, he said later, "is to tell it like, to use a cliche, it is. That's not as easy as it looks and you get it only in the greatest, yes, literature."

In the Bellamy interview, Sukenick commented, "I think that writing styles are very personal things, and it's a mistake to make theories of writing, really. My theories of writing are for two things: mainly, they're to release me into my writing, but also, I suppose, there is a propaganda side. I want people to get off one kind of book and get onto another kind of book which seems to me more appropriate for what's going on now—to get people unstuck from a formulated kind of response and open them up to another thing." Connected to this, Sukenick continued, is his belief that fiction is "a normal, if I may use the word, epistemological procedure; that is, [fiction] is at the very center of everybody all the time at any period, and you don't have to search for psychological reasons [behind it], although they may be there too. But I think the epistemological ones are far more important and anterior. It's a way of making up the world and making sense of it."

The practice of fiction persists also because it is an exercise of freedom against all that tries to regulate experience, as Sukenick said in the journal *Lillabulero*: "writers . . . are not thinking of Poetry or The Great Novel or Humanism or even of Experimental Writing or of anything more ponderous than stringing words together in ways that give pleasure and allow one to survive one's particular experience. And in so doing meet the only serious obligations of art in a world that constantly pushes in the direction of the impersonal and systematic and that is to be completely personal and unsystematic thereby saving experience from history from ideology and even from art."

Down and In: Life in the Underground is an autobiographical tour through the New York counterculture of the eighties by way of Manhattan's bars. Included are "the confidences of friends, high times" and "4:00 A.M. despair," Stuart Klawans noted in the *Nation*. "The final ingredient, of course, is an argument, which should flare up periodically and be left unsettled when day finally breaks . . . : a debate on the nature of adversary culture, moderated by Sukenick with rare intelligence." The work also affords the author a retrospective glance at his electronic novel—an earlier work in which a tape recorder was used as a technique of writing. It was never published because it proved too complex for transcription. In the *Dictionary of Literary Biography*, Cowley maintained that in *Down and In*, "Sukenick's skills as a collagist stand him in good stead as he weaves fragments of report and recollection into a vivid and highly informative evocation of a place and its people."

In 1994 Black Ice Books/Fiction Collective Two released *Doggy Bag*, Sukenick's "sometimes painful, sometimes funny, occasionally graphic but always intriguing" view of a world "littered with the flotsam and jetsam of American, European and Egyptian culture," to quote a *Publishers Weekly* reviewer. The novel displays Sukenick's sociopolitical dimension, which is also evident in his earlier works. "The main aim of *Doggy Bag* is to analyze a polarized cultural situation in which mass media implement behavioral programming in the guise of entertainment, while the European tradition of high culture constitutes no real alternative for those who would live fully in contemporary conditions," declared Cowley. In *Contemporary Novelists*, Klinkowitz observed of *Doggy Bag*: "Here scenes from the global culture of European travel and international terrorism are played out within a cleverly comic language in which imaginatively dead citizens are not only called 'Zombies' but are said to suffer from an unstoppable mind control plague called Zombie Immune Tolerance Syndrome, or 'ZITS.' Thus life becomes atomized, everyone mounting his or her own private revolution in isolation from others, a condition the author calls 'the privatization of revolution.'" Klinkowitz added: "Though clearly recognizable as a satire of contemporary life, Sukenick's writing moves a step further by creating its own typologies, taxonomies, grammars, and eventually a language itself in which to comment on present conditions."

Mosaic Man is a fiction that explores Jewish identity through wordplay and innovative text design. In *Booklist*, James O'Laughlin commented: "The perennial postmodern epistemological concern with truth/fiction is wrung out again here . . . with sometimes comic results." Section titles allude to the Hebrew Bible, with titles such as "Genes," "Ex/Ode," "Umbilicus," "Autonomy," and "Profits." In the *New York Times Book Review*, William Ferguson called *Mosaic Man* "an expertly fictionalized journal," in which the narrator, Ron, muses about his family, his experiences as a writer in Paris, and his journey to Jerusalem, where he experiences "a fountain of epiphanies," to quote Ferguson. The critic further cited the work for its "carefully managed disorder, [which] this book reminds us, may be closer to human truth than even the cleverest artifice."

The impact of Sukenick's technical innovations and his call for a new tradition in literature have been considered radical and far-reaching. Considering

Sukenick's contribution to the establishment of a new tradition for fiction, Malcolm Bradbury concluded in *The Modern American Novel:* "the transformation from older realism into new systems of creative notation has been of the largest importance, and has had the deepest implications for the novel internationally, because it has questioned the act of imaginative writing at its heart." In *Contemporary Novelists,* Klinkowitz deemed Sukenick "the most representative example of the innovative writers who contributed to the transformation of both American fiction and its supporting culture. . . . Sukenick has undertaken a revolution himself, leading developments that have reformed the culture in and of which Americans write."

AUTOBIOGRAPHICAL ESSAY:

Ronald Sukenick contributed the following autobiographical essay to *CA:*

AUTOGYRO: MY LIFE IN FICTION

Unfortunately my life is not very interesting, even to me. However, what is even less interesting is certain accounts of my life and work that are sloppy or inaccurate if not downright false. It is the impulse to correct such accounts that is the chief motive in this exercise.

My first novel, *Up,* to begin at the beginning of the confusion, was a way of relating my Brooklyn past to my underground present. In order to do it I invented a new genre, which I call pseudo-autobiography. Novelists have always used their own lives, more or less disguised, as the main source of data for their fictions. Why not do away with the subterfuge and frankly use one's own identity? On the other hand, fiction does not aspire to the factuality of history. Fiction is *recreation*—in both senses. The distinction between Ronald Sukenick and "Ronald Sukenick," one of the "real" characters who appear in many of my works, has confounded some naïve critics, though I've never had any complaints from common readers, who seem to assume, correctly, that fiction is an extension of fact. This mode derived basically from Henry Miller, but there was a lot of iconoclastic Laurence Sterne influence in *Up* that challenged the by-then overly literary artifice of the dominant realistic novel. From the beginning my major effort was entirely in the mainstream

"In Pasadena, 1952, after breaking an ankle falling off of a cliff at Bryce Canyon, Utah"

of the novel in its effort to pierce the veil of conventional artifice that has become so familiar we don't even realize that it's artifice anymore, don't realize that it's not real or even interestingly "real"—to break through the artificial to the actualities of experience.

Ironically, the label for this effort bestowed by some reviewers and book marketeers interested in maintaining a standard literary product was "experimental."

If you call me an experimental writer, you assume that I disdain the wider audience for writing. You can call me anything you want but let me set the record straight. The question of audience is always a painful question for American writers in a way that it is not for writers in other countries. In other countries you either have an educated class for whom you write, or you have a popular tradition of respect for and interest in the well-written word, as in Eastern Europe. In either case, you know for whom—and for what taste—you are writing. In this country the case is much more complicated. We have a large and half-educated audience that prefers cheap, simplistic writing, or the electronic media, but, not to underestimate it, will on capricious occasion take to its heart in large numbers some of the best writing around. So, for the American writer, the problem is always to find that elusive formula for communication that will satisfy his sense of quality as well as the audience's mysterious imaginative needs. Needless to say, you avoid the debased formulas favored and encouraged by the merchandising system. If you're actually getting rich, you're probably doing something wrong. Though you, no doubt, will be the exception.

This is essentially a rhetorical problem, though I have always contended that no real distinction can be made between what is said and how it is said. Of course, in the equation expressing the relation between author and reader, the author is the more important term. He has to be. People ask me whether I write for myself, as if, in a democratic country, that were some sort of sin. Of course I write for myself. What do you think I'm in it for? I could make more bucks in any number of other professions, not to mention businesses. But since I'm in it for the kicks, the kicks I get out of the writing itself, if you deny me that then I'm left with nothing.

And yet, besides that, there's nothing I'd like better than to reach the large, general audience. Not merely the professionals of the book—the critics, editors, and academics—but, much more important to me, the common reader and especially those on the fringe of the reading public. In fact, it's always been certain of the book pros who've given me most trouble, probably because those who pretend to know what good writing is are often precisely those who are stuck with an idea of good writing they learned about in their sophomore English classes from professors who are themselves often forty years behind what's going on in contemporary writing. Or they are class-bound, Ivy League white males with corresponding attitudes and a usually nonconscious reflex to defend their turf. Or they belong to the ex-socialist elite, loosely defined as intellectuals, who used to wear jackets and ties to demonstrations and still wear them when reading fiction. So that in many ways I prefer an audience that is innocent, open, and unspoiled by preconceived notions. If I can reach it through the distribution monopoly the book pros exercise.

To illustrate the problem let me tell you a story. A true story, since this is autobiography. Once upon a time, when I was a young writer, a well-known editor agreed to publish a section of my soon-to-appear first novel, *Up,* in a well-known magazine he was starting. This editor was widely known as one of the quality saints in the publishing establishment. By quality saint I mean those editors known to favor quality at all costs as against the tide of shlock that always threatens to overwhelm the industry, editors known for their willingness to make a stand for integrity, editors who are willing to take risks and go out on a limb for literature by, say, giving Philip Roth a million-dollar advance on a new novel. Such editors are few and far between and when you meet one you can sometimes actually see a halo hovering over his head in dim light.

Anyway, this editor called me in to talk about my piece before finally agreeing to print it. Turned out he wanted me to change the punctuation. It's true my punctuation in that book is quirky, though not as quirky as in some of my books. I was using punctuation as a kind of scoring, as in music, rather than as an adjunct to grammar. The editor was bugged by this, and I couldn't quite figure out why. I guess it was too experimental. Despite the fact that I was terribly intimidated by my first meeting with a big-time editor, I had no intention of changing my punctuation. But we went back and forth for a while and finally the reason for his wanting the change came out. It was the first issue of the magazine and this editor was afraid the readers would think he didn't know correct grammar. Smart, smart. He chose the one argument that would bring me over to his way of seeing things. My piece was threatening his literary integrity. Of course, I agreed to change the punctuation.

I left his office, nevertheless, feeling that I had sold my soul. After lying awake all night, I called him in the morning and told him I was sorry, but I'd changed my mind about the punctuation. Much to my amazement he published the damn thing anyway, but I'm sure that to this day there are people out there in the reading public who are convinced this guy doesn't know a comma from a coma.

I have to say that I think it's preferable to write for people who have no attitudes about the placement of commas and colons than for people with the knee-jerk

At Grand Army Plaza, New York City, at the time of publication of his first book, Up, *1968*

conventionality that shores up Proper English Usage. If nothing else, punctuation illiterates are at least likely to know their colons from their elbows.

*

Which brings me to my childhood. And this is the point. Which is that, though I eventually blundered onto Ivy League turf, I grew up outside the great middle class. Proper English Usage we didn't know from. We were too experimental. And when as a college-bound adolescent I finally found myself in the middle of the great middle class I didn't think it was so great. In fact, I thought it was absolutely loony. The only thing that made sense to me about the great middle class was that it liked to make a great deal of money. Okay, that's what it was supposed to do. But that everything else should be so geared to that seemed to me a little, frankly, sick. This made me even more experimental.

If you've read Malamud's *Assistant* then you know where I grew up. And if you know where I grew up you begin to understand why I ain't got no. Satisfaction. I ain't got, I ain't got, I ain't got, I ain't got. I ain't got no. Not in the great middle class. And why whatever it was that I did I did it—my way. I did it my way. I did it my w-a-a-a-y.

They used to make me go to Malamud's depressing delicatessen, my parents, down the block and around the corner under the El. I hated going there because it was such a down, empty shelves and a herring or two in the refrigerator case, the glum old guy behind the counter always looking like he was about to go out of business. This was the deli of *The Assistant,* a moralistic, if not Pollyannish, book I'm not crazy about, but interesting to me because my father used to give me the lowdown on who was who in what seemed in fact to be a neighborhood *roman à clef.* My parents made me go there because, number one, the Malamuds were poor, number two, my father was their dentist, and number three, they were among the few other Jews in the neighborhood. My father used to fix their teeth at very cut rates, even after Bernie started making money on teaching and his books—I remember that in later days he even had to urge my father to charge more to make false teeth for Bernie's brother, who was, according to my father, not "quite right." My father was very experimental with money. When I told Malamud that my father had died he reacted with the kind of regret you have over the death of a good man. This should be said, so I say it.

I wrote bluntly about this Malamudian scene in *Up.* When my father sent Malamud the book, he wrote back a note saying it was "an interesting experiment that doesn't quite come off."

My playing fields were the streets, East Second Street between Avenues I and J in Brooklyn, to be specific, my companions were kids who probably found it easier to imagine going to jail than to college, and my discipline was stickball and stoopball. Not that life was all that rosy. I was a Christ killer among the Christians, a clumsy kid among energetic athletes, and my family was New Deal liberal while the neighbors literally ran through the streets cheering the day the news spread that FDR had died. These kids had no ambitions. They never thought about their "future." Instead they were very experimental. They improvised a present. They played hard at sports because they enjoyed it. The kid next door raised chickens and rabbits with his father in their backyard. They plodded through school, learning little, because education was minimally relevant to their concerns. They didn't have to know a hell of a lot to be cops, postmen, factory workers.

We lived halfway between Ebbets Field and Coney Island, where we used to play hookey. The big thing for all of us, for the whole community, the thing that even created community, was the Dodgers. The most exciting thing in my life was going to Ebbets Field. On the radio, Red Barber's anomalously soothing southern voice serenaded the neighborhood with the play-by-play. If a game was on you could hear it in the streets, out the windows, in the shops. Little kids who pronounced oil like erl and Earl like oil, including me, would talk about eatin' high on the hog and sittin' in the catbird seat. Probably because we were experimental. None of us had ever seen a hog, and I used to imagine a catbird as something like an alley cat with furry wings. Instead of saying, Hello, you said, What's the score? Malamud's best novel (if you subtract the mythy modernist *Golden Bough* bullshit), *The Natural,* is about the old Dodgers.

The other big community amusements were betting on the horses and the numbers, small-time rackets run by the local Mafia types, though the neighborhood Mafia wasn't all that local. The brick house where all the Murder Incorporated killings were planned under the supervision of Louis "Lepke" Buchalter was a few blocks away. But nobody talked about this stuff. Mysterious gestures were exchanged, small wads of paper were passed in the local barbershop.

It was a vestigially bucolic world in some ways. People grew grapes and a few other things in their yards, raked and burned their leaves in the autumn. We played in the numerous empty lots and in the tall grass and bushes of the Long Island railroad "cut" a block away. There also we hopped freights when the frequent steam locomotives chuffed ferociously through. As a result of which a thumb would be mangled here, a leg amputated there, sometimes an entire child sent to the netherworld either by the steel wheels or the high-tension electric wires they put up when they modernized the locomotives. Death was literally all around us in the form of the giant cemeteries that bordered the neighborhood on two sides and my grammar school, P.S. 121, on three. The main drag was called Gravesend Avenue, though it was later renamed McDonald. The vegetable man, the milkman, the coal and ice man would come around on horse-drawn carts. Later the milkman and the baker got these little trucks, but I still remember the sparrows pecking at the horse shit in the streets, and there was a stable across the avenue and halfway down the block. I've written about this scene, particularly in my novel *Out.* It was, of course, experimental.

Not so many people had cars early on. My uncle Benny was one of the first in our family—we never got one—and his was a beauty, a bright red coupe with a glorious rumble seat that everyone in the neighborhood loved to ride in. He kept it for years. It was probably from him that I developed my respect for durable old cars, like the '37 Ford I used to crisscross the country in during the early fifties and which may have been, I figured out later, the same '37 Ford immortalized in Kerouac's *On the Road* (see my book *Down and In).* Or the Deux Chevaux I travelled all over Europe in. Or the '68 Dodge Dart my ex-wife still drives. Or the '66 Volvo P 1800 I've driven for the last fifteen years. By the way, if anyone knows where I can get a piece of side trim for a '66 Volvo P1800, please let me know.

Anyway, my uncle Benny, an exceedingly humble mechanic who in some ways resembled Dostoyevsky's idiot, had a romantic streak which expressed itself in gestures like suddenly showing up with a spectacular red coupe or, later, dropping out and living in Mexico for some years. He was a role model. While almost everybody else in the family was out grubbing money his attitude seemed to be why not do something magnificent?—though he would never, in his timidity, have put it that way. I have to say that my father never cared much about money either, much to the aggravation of my mother. He was something like a playboy jock without the bucks. Benny and my father were both very experimental.

Benny was my first literary influence, having more or less taught me how to read with comic books and the Sunday funnies. I think a lot of kids in my generation would still be illiterate if it weren't for comic books. And I suspect that comic books are still the most experimental influence on my style, an influence that separates me unbridgeably from the classics. While I'm at it, let me say that, contrary to a lot of well-meaning commentary on my work, Wallace Stevens was not a major influence on my writing, though I did write the first, and some say still best, extensive explication of his poetry. (Published by New York University Press in 1967, it's still available from Small Press Distribution in Berkeley.) Rather, the case is that I chose to work on Stevens because I felt he was close to my already formed, if not totally crystallized, literary posture. The really crucial influences, the ones that got me going finally, were Laurence Sterne and Henry Miller. Some smart critic could probably trace my whole evolution on the basis of those two. Sterne, Miller, and the experimental rhythm of the Gravesend Local rumbling over the nearby El when I was a kid going to sleep at night. Clickety-clack, take me back, clickety-clack, take me back.

Arthur Miller partially catches the quality of the family life I grew up in, especially in *Death of a Salesman*. In fact, Miller is in a vague, in-law way related to my mother's family through the Mendelwitz family, in some complicated manner that only my mother and Sadie Mendelwitz can figure out. One of my mother's most radiant memories is of going to the funeral of Miller's father and exchanging a few words with Marilyn Monroe. ("Excuse me," said Marilyn as she passed my mother. "Of course," answered my mother. Just so the immortal conversation doesn't go unrecorded.) Miller and Monroe had already been divorced. "He wouldn't even look at her," says my mother. "And she was so timid." But the Brooklyn tone that Miller gets is one of pathos—the pathos of uprooted first and second immigrant generations with no values but money—or, rather, nothing to measure their innate values by except money. In this, Miller is quite experimental.

"Probably the orangutan cage of the San Diego Zoo," early seventies

*

In my mid-teens my life took a new turn because my sister married a guy who was taking a doctorate at Columbia. This guy, who had a European background, was openly contemptuous of Brooklyn culture. One day he showed up at the door with dollar bills sticking out of his ears, nose, and mouth. He never missed an issue of the *New Yorker*. He papered his walls with old *New Yorker* covers. I mean, sophisticated. I'd never even heard of the *New Yorker*. But there were kids in Brooklyn who had never seen the ocean. Certainly a lot of them had never been to Manhattan, except maybe to go to Times Square to see a movie. Anyway, my brother-in-law opened up new vistas. The snide *New Yorker* comments on snippets from the media were a revelation. I discovered the possibility of irony.

When the time came for me to go to college there was trouble. My parents didn't know from college—my father had gone to dental school before it was necessary to go to undergraduate school first—though they understood it was important to go if you were a boy. I had already in effect dropped out of the mad grade grind in middle-class Midwood High (see *Down and In*) and my grades were no match for the median 99.8 average of most of my classmates. I was hardly considered precocious, or even interested, and students and teachers alike were always surprised that someone who did not want to go to Harvard Medical School or Yale Law School would show occasional signs of intelligence. My main claim to fame in the community was in writing a sports column for a local paper.

I didn't even know where to apply to college, and my school advisers told me the application limit was three. Actually, nobody could stop you from applying to as many schools as you wanted to, and kids who knew the ropes applied to as many as ten colleges, I discovered too late. My only criterion was that the school not be in Brooklyn, and I applied to some unlikely places, one of which I got into. Then I won a New York State scholarship as the result of an exam, but it could only be used in-state and the school I got into was not. This vexed my father, who was very—shall we say—thrifty. So he asked a lawyer friend who sent his kid to prep school and on to the Ivy League how to do such things. The answer—as I discovered years later—was bribe somebody. As naive as this may seem, it worked. The quid pro quo was a gift certificate for a suit to an admissions dean at Colgate.

So there I was at Colgate, mid-America, 1950. There were three Jews there, including me, all with complicated, unpronounceable names, and all three were the smartest kids in the school. There was one "Negro." His name was Laff. He did. All the time. Or else. There were no girls. Everyone had to belong to a fraternity, and you were beaten out into the snow to learn the football songs. The school elite were the guys on the cheerleading squad. Turned out they were all secretly gay and would seduce freshmen in their frat rooms. I left after a term.

I got a scholarship to a crazy place in L.A. called Pasadena Branch of the Telluride Association. Nothing could have been more different from Colgate. Though Telluride is nationally a conservative and boring organization that pretends to turn out "leaders"—it actually turns out boring and conservative liberals—Pasadena Branch was run by a radical Quaker pacifist and was full of dissident New York intellectuals and West Coast kids in the Wobbly tradition. My roommate, Norman Rush, was taken off by the FBI for refusing to register for the draft during the Korean War. Recently he's published an acclaimed collection of stories about his experiences in the Peace Corps in Africa.

Pasadena Branch was in some ways a mini Black Mountain, chaotic but challenging. I remember meeting there Richard Feynman, the famous physicist, the one who torpedoed NASA by dipping a piece of O-ring into a glass of ice water at the congressional hearings on the Challenger disaster. When he came over to Pasadena Branch, he started talking about how he drove the authorities crazy at Los Alamos during the A-bomb project by cracking safes and leaving notes inside for the security people, about bongo-drum rhythms—he was about to go down to the Amazon to study drum rhythms—and I don't remember what else, all very funny, nonstop, very fast, and in a glorious Brooklyn accent (Far Rockaway branch). It was the speed and complexity of connection that fascinated me. No plod. This was the opposite of the kind of education that had been pushed on me since P.S. 121. His discourse was a perfect model for good writing, though I didn't know it at the time, nor did I know that I was observing one of the major geniuses of his generation.

Not to make a whole short story out of it, what was going on with me at this period was the discovery of thinking. The best way I can describe what that felt like is through an erotic analogy. I remember, long ago, making love to a virgin (I say long ago not because I'm so old but because I have the impression that there are no longer any virgins—or I should say virgins as a distinct class—as there were then). At first it was like trying to make love to something inert, self-contained, and impossible—like trying to kiss a statue. Then at a certain point there was a sudden awakening, I could feel it in her body, an opening, a flowing, a coming to life, desire, and possibility. This is what I began to feel in myself—the possibility of and the desire for the worlds within worlds, and worlds within words, that thinking opens up. The discovery of thinking was for me like the discovery of the fifth dimension—oh, this is what it's all about.

The discovery of sex, never mind analogies, was another dimension evolving in my life at the time. My own experience persuades me that evolution in the sexual dimension is connected with evolution in the intellectual dimension, especially during times of rapid development (and I'm not speaking only of youth). Any suppression of the sex glands suppresses the intellectual glands. The mind is part of the body and is part of its economy. But just as an unbalanced mind can repress sexuality, so can an unbalanced sexuality repress the mind. Like the *Playboy* mentality. However in the fifties the imbalance was tipped way over toward the mind. Forget sex, anything to do with the body was taboo. I was almost kicked out of Cornell for using the word "birdshit" in a story (see *Down and In*). Girls at the time were American as apple pie—frozen apple pie. Luckily for me there was a community of European women on campus, emigrés or children of emigrés, very sophisticated in the academic context, and these were the women I hung out with. Thanks, ladies.

It was at Cornell that I first stumbled across the swine factor in American life. I had met rich people before, I had met ambitious people before, I had met unprincipled people before. But this was a genteel set that you ran across in the wealthier fraternities that combined these charming traits with an element of supercilious callousness that they seemed to consider the key to success. And you have to think that maybe they were right when you look at the Reagan administration. I have a heavy streak of Jewish moral-

Ronald with Lynn Luria-Sukenick at their home in Ben Lomond, California, in the mid-seventies

ism and I find the domestic swine offensive. Foreign swine are usually more up front—the American equivalent would be somebody like Roy Cohn or maybe Jimmy Hoffa, but these types ultimately enrage the domestic swine. The essential trait of the American Swine is a certain nasty smugness. Plus all of the above. Add a dash of hypocrisy where necessary. The Ivy League schools are full of this type, some are even famous for it. Despite William Buckley's title, I doubt that you can find either God *or* Man at Yale. Or Cornell or you name it. But you can find a lot of *Swinus americanus.* And these people end up controlling most of our institutions, the swine factor going off the scale in corporate and bureaucratic circles. These are the people I don't write for. I wouldn't be caught dead writing anything they could understand or, worse, like.

*

California, to get back to California, was also the opening of a new life: the discovery of the possibility of life beyond New York. Some of my novels show the impact of California on me, especially *Out, 98.6,* and *Blown Away.* Again there was an opening out, a relaxation, a discovery of new possibilities. California, where I have lived on and off for a considerable time, was a place that immediately felt both strange and familiar. Strange compared to Brooklyn but, yes, this

was the way one should live, in a supportive harmony with one's physical environment, as opposed to the mean puritan attitude of life as struggle and survival. My new California attitudes brought me into some comic conflicts with people back east. I remember flying in from California and arriving at the door of a New York friend in my comfortable Mexican shirt. He opened the door, blinked, and said, "Why are you wearing your nightgown?" There is still a big difference between the East and the West in the U.S., despite the same fast-food restaurants, and the two cultures still have a lot of trouble understanding one another. There aren't too many fiction writers around who can take in both without animosity, contempt, or paranoia. I guess it's appropriate that I now spend most of my time in Colorado (when I'm not in New York or Paris), practically on top of the Continental Divide, so I can look both ways.

I owe my academic career to the U.S. Army. I created my own GI Bill of Rights—the right not to be drafted. Every time I was about to drop out of college the swine started some new war to stay out of. That's how I got a Ph.D. at Brandeis. There I studied with J. V. Cunningham, the poet, and Irving Howe, the critic, and it was a study in contrasts. Howe is one of the more respectable New York Jewish Intellectuals and Cunningham was basically a cowboy from Montana. I didn't agree with either of them about anything. But, much more important to me, they were both very smart. They both provided me with effective new thought weapons to use against them. I think that's the best thing a teacher can do for a student.

Somewhere during that period I went to France on a Fulbright, thanks to Howe. The fellowship was about to be cancelled at the last minute because the French-language reference had come in and it was apparently devastating. I had requested it from an old French teacher of mine who also, it happened, had been a lover. How was I supposed to know she was mad at me, mad enough to be vindictive? But she was older, and French, and her rules were different from the ones I was so far familiar with. Of course she was right, my spoken French was lousy, but why did that skin her teeth? I figured after a year in France it would be a lot better, and it was. Anyway, Howe persuaded poet Claude Vigée, then head of the French Department, to right the injustice, and so began my long and ambivalent relation with French culture. That was my first chance to see French culture on the hoof. I loved it.

And I hated it. I still do. Not only that, I had the chance to do the Grand Tour, which gave me my first inkling that Pound, Eliot, and that bunch were basically culture tourists creating an intellectual Baedeker for the deprived American intelligentsia.

Many years later, in Paris, I invited Vigée over to my apartment. At that time I was renting an apartment on Place St.-Michel, spectacular in its way, black walls, mirrors, I think it must have been decorated by a hooker. I had published several books, one of them translated into French, I had been the subject of articles in French journals, I had participated in Paris symposia, and I spoke fluent French. A grey-haired Vigée walked in, looked at me in disbelief, and said, I quote: "This is little Ronnie?"

When I finally left the shelter of graduate school for good I thought I was home free because the army wasn't supposed to be drafting anyone over twenty-five. But I hadn't counted on the antiwar movement. I had been protesting. I had been photographed at the famous Justice Department-Pentagon demonstrations of *The Armies of the Night.* I had signed petitions. I had contributed money. Suddenly, at the age of thirty-four and a half, I got a draft notice. The legal cutoff was thirty-five. Anyone who thinks the government doesn't keep secret lists for illegal purposes, baloney. I investigated every possibility, physical and mental, but none of my recorded maladies would get me a 4-F. I went to my physical with a sense of doom, but for once being from Brooklyn turned out to be helpful. The physical was at an army base in Brooklyn. At the very end of the physical, last stop, there was this very Brooklyn sergeant who was supposed to gather all the papers and give you your final rating. Here was a guy I knew how to talk to. He looked at me, he looked at the papers, he looked back at me.

"You're thirty-four and a half?" he asked.

"Yeah."

"And they're drafting you?"

"Yeah." I shrugged. "So what can I do?"

He looked back through my papers.

Finally he said, "You had a collapsed lung once."

"Yeah," I said. "But I already checked it out. It was too long ago. And besides, it doesn't keep you out."

He looked at me. He didn't say it but I knew what he was thinking: *Shmuck.* "So you use it for an appeal," he added.

"What good does that do?"

"They have to process it," he says, exasperated.

"So?"

"So it takes six months and by that time you're thirty-five."

Wherever you are, buddy, here's to you. I would have fought in World War II. I would have enlisted. If it's true as they say that FDR manipulated us into it, he was right. But the wars since then have been bullshit, basically swine wars tragic for those fooled or flogged into them. That's the truth and you know it. Ask a Viet vet.

*

By this time I had pretty much dropped out of academe. I was living on New York's lower east side in an apartment that cost thirty-three dollars a month. For the next fifteen years I would live basically on academic odd jobs and free-lance writing. A lot of people couldn't figure out why I lit out for the underground at this point, but the answer is simple: freedom. In America, freedom for an artist means freedom from money, and there are only two ways of getting it—having money, or not needing it, i.e., low overhead. So I retired to the lower east side to begin my campaign against Literature with my first novel, *Up.*

Literature is both the friend and the enemy of the novelist. The novel is a way of salvaging experience from the flux of time and the impositions of official history and the media. It is inherently experimental. By the point some form has become certified as

Literature it has become a formula useable in prefabricated repetitions. But experience is never prefab. It is immediate, metamorphic, and unpredictable. Writing that tries to package experience can only falsify it. Literature is packaged experience. You can and must learn a lot from the best Literature but you don't learn anything new from it, unless it happens to be new to you. So half the fight when you're writing is to avoid Literature. The other half is to find forms that accommodate, discover, and even create your particular experience.

When I started writing there had already been some breakthroughs. Burroughs was a good model, though his collage technique was still the tail end of the exhausted Modern tradition. Beckett had utterly broken down the convention of verisimilitude, and Genet had shown how fiction could be used to invent rather than imitate reality. Borges I always thought of as a secondary figure, Kafka without anguish. The best of the modern Latin American tradition comes from Faulkner, whom I had long since absorbed. Of the best contemporary examples Barth was inventive but bookish, in his attempt to exhaust the literary tradition of its treasures exhausting to read; Brautigan was brilliant at transferring techniques of poetry to fiction, but a little facile; Gass knew how to use the medium as medium but was a little too heavy with ideas to be useful to me; Hawkes was splendid but had been doing the same thing for years; Barthelme wrote wonderful sentences and used language as language, broken away from reference to create new reference, but seemed to have no sense of longer form. Besides, his style was too much of the world he was out to subvert, the consumer world, which may be why he had such a successful relation with the *New Yorker.* Coover was lively, but just getting started.

While I'm at it, let me spike a cliché that went around for years, that Barthelme was America's most imitated writer. Nobody, but nobody ever imitated Barthelme. First of all he's inimitable. His particular stylistic fingerprint is so characteristic anyone trying to imitate him would immediately be run out of town as a copycat. I was teaching hundreds of creative-writing students all over the country during those years and I never ran across one who was imitating Barthelme. There was some character actually writing Barthelme stories and getting them published under Barthelme's name, but that's a different story. Though maybe that's what they meant—that Barthelme was America's most *completely* imitated writer, by this particular counterfeiter.

What I did, following the success of *Up,* was I started working with the tape recorder. My idea was, all right, you want to get an accurate description of reality into fiction, let's find out what reality really sounds like. Hey, very experimental. It was in a way a challenge both to "realistic" fiction and the formalist tradition out of Modernism and especially Joyce and Gertrude Stein. The result was the stories in *The Death of the Novel and Other Stories.* Immediately, of course, the intellocrats, confronting a kind of writing beyond their narrow ideological categories, labeled me an experimentalist, a formalist, and even worse, an elitist. Masturbatory, academic, pretentious, and art-for-art's-sake were also pulled out of the old epithet bag. What, me, a kid from Brooklyn, an experimentalist? a formalist? I was almost flattered.

Some of the New York Intelligentsia got absolutely hysterical in their criticism of the work I and friends like Steve Katz and Raymond Federman were doing. Whether I liked it or not, I became part of a movement, but it was better than being part of a stasis. I suppose it is no accident, as they say, that many of these same critics turned out to be among the worst Reaganite neoconservatives. Since there's no arguing with people of hardened understanding, there was nothing to do but bait them, which I did in a *Partisan Review* essay called "The New Tradition," in which I made light of every literary term I could think of in the social(ist) realism that these people held up as the one valid model for fiction. I suppose it's partly my fault, then, that the label "experimentalist" stuck, just as later the label "postmodernist" stuck. I wonder what the next one will be. But of course movements are often labeled by their enemies, derisively in intention, though the derisive label often turns into a term with the cachet of prestige. The label "surfiction," invented by Raymond Federman, would have been a much more accurate one to apply to those of us who published with the early Fiction Collective, the writer-controlled publishing house, writers such as Clarence Major, Russell Banks, Jonathan Baumbach, or to others like Walter Abish, Rudolfo Anaya, Steve Dixon, Harry Mathews, and Ishmael Reed.

But though there were critics who were hostile, there were also those who were friendly. One who never gets the credit he deserves, and is practically boycotted by the old-boy academic establishment, is Jerome Klinkowitz. Klinkowitz's voluminous commentary on writers like myself and Clarence Major has been of

"With The Captain, model for a character in Blown Away," *late seventies*

great importance in bringing us into the public eye. His criticism is sometimes put down as naive and inadequately bedded in contemporary theory. But those critics interested in contemporary theory are usually not interested in contemporary writing, unless it illustrates their theory, so there's a sort of catch-22 operative here. I think the crude fact of it is that Klinkowitz, out there in Iowa, just isn't part of the Ivy League old-boy network. Klinkowitz is what I would call an advocacy critic. He actually reads contemporary fiction, he actually tries to explicate it and so create a bridge to the general reading public, and he actually takes the writers seriously enough to ask them what it is they're trying to do. This, I believe, is an old and honorable and critical critical role, one only recently surrendered by theory-oriented academics. Okay, Jerry?

As to the neocon intelligentsia, let's not pretend they're not influential. They're more influential than I would like to believe. They grasp the connection between culture and politics in a country where that connection is beyond the civic imagination of most people. What? police dramas on TV? what has that got to do with

politics? Social realism? what has that got to do with distributing a standardized commodity to the maximum number of people? what has that got to do with using your imagination only in prescribed ways that don't conjure up any visions of any oppositional flies in any establishment ointments? The ointments of the establishment, its facilities, its networks, and its rewards to dispose, thus flow oleaginously into the neocon troughs, where the swine lap gratefully and become strong. I won't even bother to go into the effect of similar influences on the grunt reviewer out in the journalistic trenches. Do you think it was purely coincidental, amigo, that cultural conservatism began to establish its hold the year, the very year, after Nixon was elected? that certain films were discouraged by the studios (I was writing one of them) and others soft-pedaled in distribution? that music with lyrics about social issues began to disappear? that some writers, especially those from Eastern Europe with certified anti-red attitudes were promoted, while domestic "experimentalists" were tabooed as elitists?—even as their foreign experimentalist clones, writing of course about strictly elsewhere, were welcomed? Ay, ay, ay, amigo! We live in the real world, where we are nothing but cucarachas on the levers of power. La cucaracha, la cucaracha. Allan Bloom is culture czar. La cucaracha, La cucaracha. Irving Howe is commissar.

And now I have a startling announcement to make. I am actually Tom Pynchon, and it's me who's written all his books. If Jerzy Kosinski could do it why can't Pynchon? All right, just kidding. Just trying to get your attention for the next episode, which is titled— The Resistance.

*

Besides cultural conservatism, by the early seventies the economics of the publishing industry, which were changing, made it doubly hard for the kind of writing that needs a certain amount of economic support because it takes time to be absorbed by the culture.

The first step in the direction of an organized resistance to the difficult cultural situation had been the establishment of the Coordinating Council of Literary Magazines (CCLM), which had wrested money from federal and state governments to subsidize the country's literary magazines—an important development since just about all such magazines run at a permanent deficit.

CCLM was started by William Phillips of *Partisan Review,* and editors of some other, similar magazines. These magazines were mostly East Coast, intellectually oriented, and had substantial budgets, but as the organization grew into a genuinely national one, the membership tipped in the direction of small-budget West Coast poetry journals with distinctly different tastes. This created an organizational strain that eventually helped to tear CCLM apart. I was brought onto the board of CCLM, I believe, to mediate between the East and West Coast contingents, since I was one of the few who had allegiances to both.

At my first meeting in San Francisco, organized to conciliate the two groups, the strains were symbolized by Phillips's misguided attempts to extend friendly hospitality to the Frisco underground poetry scene. He made the mistake of holding the meeting in a well-appointed hotel room instead of somebody's pad, and served whisky instead of jug wine. This confirmed all of the poets' worst suspicions about the New York Establishment.

When Phillips retired as chairman of CCLM, he was replaced by Michael Anania, and then by myself. I had to deal with the political situation created by the minorities moving into CCLM, trying to mediate among different interest groups. Middlemen in such situations always get caught in the middle, and I was no exception, almost losing some good minority friends like Ishmael Reed (who succeeded me as chairman) and Rudy Anaya, as well as friends from Phillips's East Coast faction and Anania's Midwest bunch. In fact, probably the greatest benefit of CCLM was in the network of underground literary people it generated, a network I would draw on in future organizational projects. However, the grants function of CCLM should not be underestimated: during my time as chairman, its budget reached the one-million-dollar mark, and its grant support changed the underground literary scene enormously, some say for the better, some say for the worse. Both are right, but those who opt for the better are righter, in that it represented a first significant step by writers (and editors) to take their economic fate into their own hands.

I helped start the Fiction Collective during my CCLM days, aiding the main movers, Peter Spielberg and Jon Baumbach, from the West Coast, where I was living, while B. H. Friedman also provided considerable help.

The Collective was a very visible success, and perhaps for that very reason aroused animosity in certain quarters of the publishing industry. The attitude of many editors, as expressed in a *Partisan Review* symposium I participated in, was basically that, yes, it's a shame we can't publish more good fiction, but don't worry, if anything good comes along, we'll publish it. Speaking of logic. The resentment lingered. Many years later, critics Larry McCaffery and Tom LeClair presented a manuscript of interviews with eminent contemporary novelists to Knopf. The manuscript was accepted on the condition that it contain no Fiction Collective writers. Since the book contained three Collective authors out of fifteen, and the editors refused to take them out, McCaffery and LeClair took the book to the University of Illinois Press, which published it under the title *Anything Can Happen.* There are other stories of this sort. For example, Knopf later published Tom Glynn's second novel as his first, ignoring the one published by the Collective.

The next link in the chain was *American Book Review.* Actually, a review magazine that would give a fair shake to non-publishing-industry presses was first suggested to me by Ishmael Reed in a cab to the airport from a CCLM meeting in Louisville, Kentucky, only he wanted me to do it and I wanted him to do it. Both of us were already doing too many things. Still are. Somehow I ended up doing it, largely because one year I had a big income-tax refund, and someone pointed out that if I spent it that would be that, but that if I used it to start a book-review magazine, I might end up with something important and durable. So we plunged in, Clarence Major, Suzanne Zavrian, and Charles Russell—the original editors—and myself, with some help from the University of Colorado (where by then I was organizing and directing the creative-writing program), and some other writers. As I write this, *ABR,* under myself and editors Rochelle Ratner and John Tytell, has just put out its tenth-anniversary issue.

Meanwhile I was still writing steadily. *Out,* which later became a movie starring Peter Coyote, was a novel about the hope generated by the era called the sixties, despite all its conflict and insanity, and *98.6* was about the failure of the sixties. In both books I used techniques—very different in each—to break down standard form in fiction in order to reach beyond literary artifice to actual experience (don't think I'm not aware of the contradictions involved). In general, I think this is the misunderstood thrust of the "Postmodern" in fiction: an attempt to get at the truth of experience beyond our fossilizing formulas of discourse, to get at a new and more inclusive "reality," if you will. This is a reality that includes what the conventional novel tends to exclude and that encompasses the vagaries of unofficial experience, the cryptic trivia of the quotidian that help shape our fate, and the tabooed details of life—class, ethnic, sexual—beyond sanctioned descriptions of life. It is an orientation that is distinctly democratic in tendency, which may explain some of the hostility it meets. What is currently called "Minimalism" seems to be a subgenre of this mode that does some of the same things. Maybe that's why some critics are down on it lately.

In *Long Talking Bad Conditions Blues* I pushed the narrative form as far in the direction of poetry as I could, using the symmetries of poetic form, albeit idiosyncratic, within which to improvise the rhythms that most accurately express the unpredictable flow of experience. *Blown Away* explores my idea of the novel as related to suppressed traditions of magic, shamanism, prophecy, and the functions of the holy book, all this based on an interpretation of Prospero, our tradition's most eminent literary wizard. My idea is that narrative is or can be a mediumistic form, rather than the empirical form that positivism has delineated for it. The interconnected pieces in *The Endless Short Story* represent a variety of formal improvisations, reflecting my conviction that improvisation is at the heart of art in the American mode.

Down and In, though nonfiction, goes back to my interest in the use of tape recorder as technique for writing, and presents the same narrative considerations as any of my fictions. It looks back to a little-known electronic novel I did for the Berkeley Pacifica station, using recorded voices, which I consider unsuccessful because it got so complicated sonically that it became impossible to reproduce it on the page. Warning! Technique as such is baloney. Lately I've seen any number of techniques out of James Joyce, Laurence Sterne, or Nabokov used to produce slick, tricky novels that are the fictive equivalent of fast food. Give me Theodore Dreiser. In a way, *Down and In* is continuous with *Up* in its interest in autobiography. There is one major difference, however, in that it is not pseudo-autobiography. "My wife, Lynn," for example, in *Up* is not Lynn, my ex-wife, but a

In the Colorado mountains, 1986

character in a novel, just as "Ronald Sukenick" in that book, or in any of my fictions, is not Ronald Sukenick.

But of course, as soon as a real-life character is inscribed on the page, even the page of history, s/he becomes a construct of words. And that includes this page. And, curiously, the character "Ronald Sukenick," initially unleashed in the pages of my own fiction, has since become a persona in a number of novels by other writers—Steve Katz, E. L. Doctorow, Raymond Federman, to name some. He has also become a character in a plenitude of critical works, one who has attained an independent existence to the point where he is sometimes unrecognizable, at least to me. But what the hell, we continually make one another up, we make ourselves up, we make our lives up, do we not? That's not experimental, that's experiential. All I'm trying to do is keep fiction as close as possible to the available data, despite the often profitable make-believe of that Romantic concept Coleridge and Walt Disney call Imagination. What can you say about Imagination? Imagination is . . . funny. It makes a cloudy day sunny. It gave us the Easter Bunny. It brings in a lot of money. But aside from that it's irrelevant to the real business of writing, which is to tell it like, to use a cliche, it is. That's not as easy as it looks and you get it only in the greatest, yes, Literature.

POSTSCRIPT

Ronald Sukenick contributed the following update to *CA* in 2003:

To continue: My book on underground culture, *Down and In,* was a success d'estime; e.g., reviewed, among elsewhere, by famous boho painter and member of the scene, Larry Rivers, in the *New York Times Book Review.* Rivers gave the book an elaborately favorable review, but while the *Book Review*'s policy is to call everyone Mr.—for example, Mr. Hitler—he referred to me throughout as "Ronnie." When I met the editor at the book party I told him he could have at least changed it to Mr. Ronnie.

Looking back at this stage of my life I see that I must have been heavily committed to trying to have an impact on public taste. I was involved, often simultaneously, with Fiction Collective Two (FC 2), the writer-controlled publishing house; *American Book Review,* the oppositional book review; as well as the super-establishment *Publication of the Modern Language Association,* the National Book Critics Circle, and the PEN Freedom to Write committee; plus *Black Ice* magazine, dedicated to extreme fiction, Black Ice Books, an offshoot of the magazine under the auspices of FC 2, and *Black Ice* online; an anthology of innovative fiction called *In the Slipstream* (with Curtis White), *Degenerative Prose,* an anthology of extreme fiction (with Mark Amerika), Altx Press (e-books and print on demand), and a literary prize, the Nilon Award for excellence in minority fiction. Add to these my position as director of the English department publications center at University of Colorado, Boulder, and first director of the English department's creative writing program, plus my earlier long association with the Coordinating Council of Literary Magazines (CCLM), which funded all the literary magazines in the country, and two years as its chairman. It all adds up in retrospect to a sustained effort to do something about the literary scene other than complain about it. And I have to confess that above all, needling the establishment was fun.

All of the above were continuous with the ideas implicit in *Down and In,* which is basically a critique of the recent history of oppositional art in the United States. In the publishing world, the crunch came down to the fact that the underground writing scene had been co-opted at the same time that the publishing industry was imploding into five or six largely foreign-owned conglomerates with supercommercial publishing criteria. At a symposium held by the National Books Critics Circle I made fun of this trend in a mordant satire that did little to endear me to the publishing establishment present, for whom my name was mud anyway so I had little to lose. (I was probably named Mud from my similar participation in a symposium held by *Partisan Review* some fifteen years earlier.)

Speaking of losing, around this time I lost another agent—the last in a whole string of lost agents—over the quality of the novel I was working on, which would later become *Mosaic Man* (this was the agent who said of *Down and In* that the last draft was the best and the least likely to sell). My next agent was so slow in handling the manuscript I gave him that I had to give it finally to another agent, who quickly came out of the closet, moved to Fire Island, became a painter, and stopped agenting. These are just the last phases of a long history of agent catastrophes involving missed opportunities, mistiming, and just plain mistakes.

But somehow the books kept getting written. This is especially astonishing given that my life was usually divided among several geographic locations remote from one another. For example, when I was running the CCLM, I was living in Santa Cruz, CA, and running a six-person office in Greenwich Village to which I would fly in one week per month. I stayed in New York at the staid Algonquin Hotel, where the English maitre d' would never let me into the dining room in my leather vest. I would claim that the vest was my national costume of the American West, and he would retort that in his country a vest was an undershirt. I finally gave in and bought a suit, not for the anglophile Algonquin but for lobbying Congress for the literary arts. Later, my life was divided among New York, Paris, and Boulder, Colorado, where I held down a full-time teaching job. I had bought apartments in New York and Paris with my second wife, and we have been triangulating ever since approximately 1983.

Add to these activities eight or ten readings per year accompanied by travel to and fro, drinking, partying, and attendant groupies. What? I could have skipped

With companion Julia Frey, Colorado, 1987

the partying you say? And watched television for hours, insomniac in a lonely motel, as opposed to a lovely and admiring fan, chatting at the bar or bouncing on a mattress? Which would you choose?

I don't know where I got the energy to do all this stuff.

I think it comes from my philosophy of fertile disorder. Time is a one-way ticket to a single destination in a predetermined age-related order. You've got to mix it up, jam circuits, introduce a little disorder by taking things as they come rather than imposing your own agenda. If it's confusing, life is confusing, and my life could serve as a model for my writing. Expect the unexpected is my motto. Disorganization can lead to deeper organization. And you gain all the energy you would use trying to impose an alien order.

Of course all this implies that you're going to recognize and be receptive to new kinds of order, which in itself implies that you are at some level an

order freak rather than a nihilist. It's very hard to maintain disorder, disorganization, and nonsense, for there is a bedrock tendency hardwired into our biological being that pushes toward order. It takes a whole screwed up society to create long-term disorder—while individuals, sometimes madmen, discover new levels of order in the midst of disorder. Paradoxically, it's consistency, logic, and linearity that you have to beware of as an order freak.

My life has been both unpredictable and perfectly imaginable from the start. When I was eighteen I imagined that I would have just the kind of life I have had, and yet when I was in the midst of it it seemed that everything would turn out quite differently. Fame, eclipse, rediscovery by a younger generation—it has all been as I imagined when I was eighteen. Illogical but true.

Who could have predicted that I would be looking out my window at the World Trade Center two blocks away when the airplanes hit? But that is precisely what I was writing about the very week before. Writing at a certain level reveals the subterranean structure of experience through which one can extrapolate the spectrum of event. But such speculation aside, what a breath of fresh air it is to come across writing touched by the randomness and illogic of experience. Henry Miller is the master of the mode, and I follow him in writing what I would call fictive nonfiction. The more my fiction is taken as nonfiction the more successful it is, even at the expense of giving me a bad character rep. The convincingness of my fiction, it seems, is in inverse proportion to the virtue of my character. But who cares? Novelists don't have to win elections. Politicians, on the other hand, do, and sometimes the two modes clash. There is a story in my collection *Doggy Bag* called "The Burial of Count Orgasm," which is what you might call pseudo pornographic. It's like, "she opened her blank, and he reached in blank while she caressed blank." This raised the ire of certain politicians in the Midwest, where the publisher was located, despite the fact that the porn was wholly the product of the reader's imagination. My writing has frequently been labeled "graphic" or "explicit," and it has in fact lately been moving in the direction of the graphic thanks to the resources of the computer. But I digress. The World Trade Center attacks. I was there, I had a narrow escape, I'm in some sense a victim and in some sense also the beneficiary, guilty of exploiting the event in the sense that, having written about it before the fact, I simply continued writing about it after. But before I pursue this train of thought, let me add that digression is a method I believe in, a trope as true to life as any in the rhetorical toolbox. If you want examples, take my last book, *Cows,* which proceeds on the basis of action by digression, or my next to last, *Narralogues,* which proceeds on the basis of digressive ideas.

Yes, in reality as opposed to fiction you never know what's going to happen next.

One day I was sitting at my desk and my assistant came in with the mail, including a letter from the American Academy of Arts and Letters. Well, the only mail I ever get from such organizations is asking for money, so I almost threw it away. My hand was halfway to the wastebasket when I thought, I have so little mail today I might as well open it. And guess what? It was notification that I had been awarded a sizable cash prize for innovative fiction, the Zabel Award.

Boulder, Colorado, 1988

But to continue, the World Trade Center. So there I was, stark naked, having just gotten out of bed, watching the World Trade Center go up in flames. Two blocks away. I got out of there fast, just taking the time to throw some clothes on. Just time enough to get to the river when the first tower jiggled a bit and imploded sending a dense black cloud careening toward us and enveloping us in a blinding element, neither solid nor quite gaseous, and for incalculable minutes inside it we didn't know whether we were going to live or die. Weeks later, on getting back to my apartment, when I saw that I had already broached the subject in my work in progress, I had the uncanny feeling that I had foreseen all this, and the rest of the novel became a meditation of sorts on the World Trade Center disaster and the process of digging out of the wreckage.

You might well wonder what I was doing living in New York. In the year 2000 I quit teaching and left Boulder for good. I was almost always a part-time resident anyway, spending parts of each year in New York and Paris. So I came back to the place where I grew up twice: once in Brooklyn, and once in the lower east side where I spent ten years of my life, from 1960 to 1970, living in an apartment for $33 a month while writing my first three books, including the manuscript of my first novel, *Up,* handwritten in ten or twenty spiral notebooks. Which now reside in the Ransom Humanities Center in Austin, TX. Where one day my wife, Toulouse Lautrec biographer, Julia Frey, was perusing the archival collections and came across scores of letters I had sent to a friendly critic. Whereupon she suggested they might be interested in purchasing my entire archive. This insight eventually grew into purchase not only of my archives but of those of Fiction Collective, *American Book Review,* some of her (Julia's) papers, and the complete posthumous collection of my ex-wife, Lynn Luria Sukenick.

If the impact of New York on my writing is evident, that of Paris is not so obvious. New York was the fabric out of which the story emerges in my first novel, *Up,* and it is the explicit subject of *Down and In. Out-* explodes out of New York, giving it the momentum that drives it all the way to the West Coast. *Mosaic Man* starts in Paris but ends in New York City, stretches out all over the map but is predominantly a New York book. *Long Talking Bed Conditions Blues* perhaps gives the truest geographic spectrum of my writing. The combination is of New York, the West Coast, and Paris, with perhaps an exile's Paris striking the strongest note. But my Paris is not that of American intellectuals or expatriates. For example, at the end of the '70s the editor of *Partisan Review,* knowing I was about to spend the year in Paris, asked me to write an article about what was going on in France. After interviewing a lot of people in Paris I concluded that nothing was going on in France. The editor reassigned the article to a New York intellectual, one of the usual suspects, who wrote an article about new developments in critical theory. That was my idea of nothing going on.

My Paris was the eleventh arrondissement, a working-class international melting pot, where when I first moved in there were so few tourists that the banks wouldn't even cash travelers checks, where the politics were workers left-wing, and where the bread and croissants were better than those in middle- and upper-class snob bakeries. There I knew the local storekeepers and a lot of people living in the building. Some of them were crazies, but by and large they were a friendly, level-headed community of workers and artisans, with a few artists and actors just beginning to move in because of cheap rent. It was like living in the beginning of the lower east side as the "East Village" all over again. Finally, after fifteen years of on-off residency, I had to move to a rich neighborhood where the buildings had elevators. Besides, the eleventh had acquired a kind of bohemian chic, and the population that went with it had robbed it of its distinctive character.

I first went to the West Coast when I was nineteen. Pasadena. There was only one short freeway and the word smog had just entered the vocabulary. Palm trees and orange groves. From Los Angeles, where I soon moved, I could see snowcapped mountains. This is the Los Angeles of my novel *Blown Away.* And northern California, where I lived in a later phase, in Santa Cruz especially, is the scene for *98.6* and the end of *Out.*

Not to mention a stint of three years in Laguna Beach. And don't forget I spent twenty-five years in Boulder. My recent novel, *Cows,* released as an e-book, is my valedictory to the Rocky Mountains. So with this geographical itinerary I suppose I can lay claim to being one of America's most representative writers.

*

Change gears:

American Book Review is now twenty-five years old. Fiction Collective is twenty-eight. These are astronomical ages in the small press universe, unexpected longevity for these institutions I helped found. Almost as unexpected as my seventieth birthday this year. As unexpected as my pace of publication since *Down and In* when we let the story lapse: *Doggie Bag*, stories; *Mosaic Man,* a novel; *Narralogues,* essays; *Cows,* a novel. A couple of anthologies edited. Three books about me in various stages of preparation and another already out—a pastiche of my novel *98.6* called *1998.6,* which uses the plot, the characters, and the style of the original novel. They say that parody is the deepest compliment.

And Gale's *Contemporary Authors* series just asked me to write an update.

BIOGRAPHICAL AND CRITICAL SOURCES:

BOOKS

Bellamy, Joe David, editor, *The New Fiction: Interviews with Innovative American Writers,* University of Illinois Press (Champaign, IL), 1974.

Bradbury, Malcolm, *The Modern American Novel,* Oxford University Press (New York, NY), 1984.

Carlisle, Janice and Daniel R. Schwarz, editors, *Narrative and Culture,* University of Georgia Press (Athens, GA), 1994, pp. 216-37.

Contemporary Literary Criticism, Gale (Detroit, MI), Volume 3, 1975, Volume 4, 1975, Volume 6, 1976, Volume 48, 1988.

Contemporary Novelists, sixth edition, St. James (Detroit, MI), 1996, pp. 962-64.

Dictionary of Literary Biography, Gale, Volume 173: *American Novelists since World War II, Fifth Series,* Gale (Detroit, MI), 1997.

Dictionary of Literary Biography Yearbook: 1981, Gale (Detroit, MI), 1982.

Federman, Ray, editor, *Surfiction,* Swallow Press (Athens, OH), 1974.

Hassan, Ihab, *Liberations,* Wesleyan University Press (Middletown, CT), 1971.

Karl, Frederick R., *American Fictions, 1940-1980: A Comprehensive History and Critical Evaluation,* Harper (New York, NY), 1983.

Kiernan, Robert F., *American Writing since 1945: A Critical Survey,* Ungar (New York, NY), 1983.

Klinkowitz, Jerome, *Innovative Fiction,* Dell (New York, NY), 1972.

Klinkowitz, Jerome, *Literary Disruptions: The Making of a Post-Contemporary Fiction,* University of Illinois Press (Champaign, IL), 1975.

Klinkowitz, Jerome, *The Life of Fiction,* University of Illinois Press (Champaign, IL), 1977.

Klinkowitz, Jerome, *Literary Subversions: New American Fiction and the Practice of Criticism,* Southern Illinois University Press (Carbondale, IL), 1985.

Kutnik, Jerzy, *Fiction as Performance: The Fiction of Ronald Sukenick and Raymond Federman,* Southern Illinois University Press (Carbondale, IL), 1986.

LeClair, Thomas, and Larry McCaffery, editors, *Anything Can Happen: Interviews with Contemporary American Novelists,* University of Illinois Press (Champaign, IL), 1983.

McHale, Brian, *Postmodernist Fiction,* Methuen (New York, NY), 1987.

Pearce, Richard, *The Novel in Motion,* Ohio State University Press (Columbus, OH), 1983.

Sukenick, Ronald, *Wallace Stevens: Musing the Obscure,* New York University Press (New York, NY), 1967.

Sukenick, Ronald, *The Death of the Novel, and Other Stories,* Dial (New York, NY), 1969.

Sukenick, Ronald, *In Form, Digressions on the Act of Fiction,* Southern Illinois University Press (Carbondale, IL), 1985.

PERIODICALS

Best Sellers, July, 1973.

Booklist, February 15, 1999, p. 1042.

Chicago Review, winter, 1972, pp. 73-82.

Christian Science Monitor, October 9, 1969.

Contemporary Literature, spring, 1982, pp. 129-44.

Critique, Volume 20, number 9, 1978, pp. 27-39; winter, 1987, pp. 88-99.

Esquire, December, 1972.

Fiction International, fall, 1973.

Georgia Review, winter, 1983.

Harpers, May, 1968.

Hudson Review, summer, 1968.

Lillabulero, number 12, 1973.

Los Angeles Times, February 9, 1987.

Los Angeles Times Book Review, October 18, 1987.

Modern Fiction Studies, winter, 1985.

Nation, July 22, 1968; September 27, 1975; September 19, 1987.

New York Review of Books, February 1, 1968; February 27, 1969.

New York Times, June 22, 1968; September 25, 1969; September 29, 1969.

New York Times Book Review, July 14, 1968; October 21, 1973; May 18, 1975; September 22, 1985; November 16, 1986; March 15, 1987; November 1, 1987; July 11, 1999, p. 22.

North American Review, summer, 1973.

Partisan Review, winter, 1974.

Publishers Weekly, March 7, 1924, p. 66; January 18, 1999, p. 327; August 16, 1999, p. 65.

Saturday Review, July 6, 1968.

Tribune Books (Chicago, IL), August 30, 1987.

Washington Post Book World, July 21, 1968.

OTHER

Fiction Collective Two, http://fc2.org/ (April 2, 2003).

SUMMERS, Marc

PERSONAL: Born in Indianapolis, IN; married; children: two.

ADDRESSES: Agent—c/o Author Mail, Penguin Putnam, 375 Hudson St., New York, NY 10014.

CAREER: Comedian, magician, producer, and director. Nickelodeon (television studio), programming consultant. National spokesman, Obsessive-Compulsive Foundation. Former host of children's television game shows *Double Dare* and *Family Double Dare,* Nickelodeon; former host of *Home Show,* ABC-TV, and *Our Home,* Lifetime; host of television talk show, *Great Day America,* PAX-TV. Has appeared in children's educational programs, including *It's OK to Say No to Drugs,* True North Entertainment, 1988, *Kids Have Rights Too,* True North Entertainment, 1989, and *Tuning in to Media,* Continental Cablevision, 1994. Has appeared on television talk shows, including *Oprah, Today,* and *The Tonight Show with Jay Leno.*

MEMBER: Obsessive-Compulsive Foundation.

WRITINGS:

(With Eric Hollander) *Everything in Its Place: My Trials and Triumphs with Obsessive Compulsive Disorder,* J. P. Tarcher/Putnam (New York, NY), 1999.

SIDELIGHTS: Marc Summers became known in children's education circles while hosting television shows, including *Double Dare* and *Great Day America.* After learning about Obsessive-Compulsive Disorder (OCD) while hosting a talk show in 1994, Summers was treated with drug and behavior therapies for the condition by noted authority Eric Hollander. Summers has since become the national spokesperson for the Obsessive-Compulsive Foundation.

Summers wrote of his struggle with OCD in his 1999 memoir *Everything in Its Place: My Trials and Triumphs with Obsessive Compulsive Disorder,* co-written with Hollander. Though OCD affects an estimated six million people in America, the disorder still has a stigma associated with it; Summers chronicles the "fear and shame he felt about his compulsions, [and] the toll they took on his family," noted a critic for *Publishers Weekly.* The critic praised the work for it's upbeat tone, and summarized it as both a memoir and a guide. The work was also praised by some critics for disseminating information on OCD in a positive light, encouraging sufferers to seek treatment.

BIOGRAPHICAL AND CRITICAL SOURCES:

PERIODICALS

Booklist, January 1, 1995, p. 834; October 1, 1999, review of *Everything in Its Place: My Trials and Triumphs with Obsessive Compulsive Disorder,* p. 332.
Library Journal, October 1, 1999, Lisa S. Wise, review of *Everything in Its Place,* p. 118.
Publishers Weekly, August 23, 1999, review of *Everything in Its Place,* p. 33.
School Library Journal, March, 1990, Debra Kornegay, review of *Kids Have Rights Too,* p. 170; April, 1990, p. 58.*

*   *   *

SUTHERLAND, Zena Bailey 1915-2002

OBITUARY NOTICE—See index for *CA* sketch: Born September 17, 1915, in Winthrop, MA; died of cancer June 12, 2002, in Chicago, IL. Educator, critic, editor, and author. Sutherland may have possessed a more comprehensive knowledge of children's literature than any living person without ever having been a children's author herself. For nearly thirty years as an editor and reviewer for the *Bulletin of the Center for Children's Books* at the University of Chicago, beginning in 1958, she is credited with reading and reviewing tens of thousands of children's books. Sutherland's reviews differed from the standard fare of her day. She treated her subjects as she would treat adult literature, providing substantive descriptive information and adding her own critical interpretations. Sutherland was also a children's literature columnist for the *Saturday Review* in the 1960s and a children's book editor and columnist for the *Chicago Tribune* in the 1970s and 1980s. Upon the death of May Hill Arbuthnot in 1969, Sutherland succeeded her as the author of the classic textbook *Children and Books,* continuing as editor through its ninth edition in 1996. She also wrote *History in Children's Books, The Best in Children's Books,* and *Children and Libraries,* and edited a handful of anthologies. Sutherland taught librarianship at the University of Chicago from 1972 to 1986; the Zena Sutherland lecture series of the University of Chicago and the Chicago Public Library was established in her honor. She also served on the International Board on Books for Young People and judged prestigious literary awards, including the Newbery Award, the Caldecott Award, and the National Book Award.

OBITUARIES AND OTHER SOURCES:

PERIODICALS

Los Angeles Times, June 16, 2002, p. B19.
New York Times, June 15, 2002, obituary by Eden Ross Lipson, p. A27.
Washington Post, June 16, 2002, obituary by Richard Pearson, p. C8.

*   *   *

SUZUKI, David T(akayoshi) 1936-

PERSONAL: Born March 24, 1936, in Vancouver, British Columbia, Canada; son of Kaoru Carr (owner of a dry-cleaning store) and Setsu Sue (Nakamura) Suzuki; married Joane Sunahara, 1958 (divorced, 1965); married Tara Elizabeth Cullis, 1972; children: (first marriage) Tamiko Lynda, Troy Takashi, Laura Miye; (second marriage) Severn Setsu Elizabeth, Sarika Freda. *Education:* Amherst College, B.S. (biology; cum laude), 1958; University of Chicago, Ph.D. (zoology), 1961. *Hobbies and other interests:* Skiing, fishing, camping, snorkeling, hiking, canoeing.

ADDRESSES: Home—2477 Pt. Grey Rd., Vancouver, British Columbia, Canada V6K 1A1. *Office*—219-2211 West 4th St., Vancouver, British Columbia, Canada V6K 4S2.

CAREER: Geneticist, university professor, broadcast journalist, environmentalist, writer, and educator. Amherst College, Amherst, MA, teaching assistant, 1957;

University of Chicago, Chicago, IL, research assistant, 1958, teaching assistant in zoology, 1959; Oak Ridge National Laboratory, Oak Ridge, TN, research associate in biology division, 1961; University of Alberta, Edmonton, Alberta, Canada, assistant professor of genetics, 1962; University of British Columbia, Vancouver, British Columbia, Canada, assistant professor, 1963, associate professor, 1965, professor of zoology, 1969; Sustainable Development Research Institute, senior associate. Host of Canadian Broadcasting Corporation (CBC) television series *Suzuki on Science,* 1971-72, *Science Magazine,* 1974-79, *Nature of Things,* 1979—, and *A Planet for the Taking,* 1985; host of CBC radio programs *Quirks and Quarks,* 1974-79, *It's a Matter of Survival,* 1989, and *From Naked Ape to Super Species,* 1999. Founder with wife, Dr. Tara E. Cullis, of David Suzuki Foundation, 1990—. Member, Science Council of Canada, 1978-84. International speaker and lecturer.

MEMBER: Royal Society of Canada, Canadian Society of Cell Biology (president, 1969-70), Canadian Civil Liberties Association (director, 1982-87), American Association for the Advancement of Science (fellow), Genetics Society of America (secretary, 1980-82).

AWARDS, HONORS: Seacie Memorial fellowship, 1969-72; officer, Order of Canada, 1976; Bell-Northern Award for radio, 1976, 1978, and 1979, and for television, 1983; Cybil Award, Canadian Broadcasters League, 1977; Sanford Fleming Medal, 1982; Canadian Medical Association Medal of Honour, 1984; Quill Award, 1985; United Nations Environmental Progress Medal, 1985, and Progress Global 500, 1989; Governor General's Award for Conservation, 1985; ACTRA Award for Television, 1985; Gemini Award for Television, 1986, 1992; UNESCO Kalinga Prize, 1986; Gold Medal Award, Biology Society of Canada, 1986; Information Book Award, 1987, for *Looking at Insects;* Author of the Year, Canadian Booksellers Association, 1990. Has received honorary degrees from University of Prince Edward Island, 1974, Acadia University, 1979, University of Windsor, 1979, Trent University, 1981, Lakehead University, 1986, University of Calgary, 1986, Governor's State University, 1986, Queen's University, 1987, McMaster University, 1987, Carleton University, 1987, and Amherst College, 1989; recipient of honorary doctoral degrees in Canada, the U. S., and Australia; adopted by two First Nations and conferred seven names from aboriginal people in Canada and Australia.

WRITINGS:

(With Anthony J. F. Griffiths and Richard C. Lewontin) *An Introduction to Genetic Analysis,* W. H. Freeman (San Francisco, CA), 1981.

Metamorphosis: Stages in a Life (memoir), Stoddart (Toronto, Ontario, Canada), 1987.

(With Peter Knudtson) *Genethics: The Ethics of Engineering Life,* Harvard University Press (Cambridge, MA), 1989.

Inventing the Future, Allen & Unwin (Boston MA), 1990.

(With Anita Gordon) *It's a Matter of Survival,* Harvard University Press (Cambridge, MA), 1991.

(With Peter Knudtson) *Wisdom of the Elders: Honoring Sacred Native Visions of Nature,* Bantam Books (New York, NY), 1992.

(With Joseph Levine) *The Secret of Life: Redesigning the Living World,* WGBH Boston (Boston, MA), 1993.

Time to Change: Essays, Stoddart (Toronto, Ontario, Canada), 1994.

(With Keibo Oiwa) *The Japan We Never Knew: A Journey of Discovery,* Allen & Unwin (Sydney, New South Wales, Australia), 1996.

(With Amanda McConnell) *The Sacred Balance: Rediscovering Our Place in Nature,* Greystone Books (Vancouver, British Columbia, Canada), 1997, Prometheus Books (Amherst, NY), 1998.

Earth Time: Essays, Stoddart (Toronto, Ontario, Canada), 1998.

(With Holly Dressel) *From Naked Ape to Superspecies: A Personal Perspective on Humanity and the Global Eco-Crisis,* Stoddart (Buffalo, NY), 1999.

(With Holly Dressel) *Good News for a Change,* Stoddart (Toronto, Ontario, Canada), 2002.

FOR CHILDREN

(With Barbara Hehner) *Looking at Plants,* illustrated by Debbie Drew-Brooke, Stoddart (Toronto, Ontario, Canada), 1985, Wiley (New York, NY), 1992.

(With Barbara Hehner) *Looking at the Body,* illustrated by Lou Reynolds, Stoddart (Toronto, Ontario, Canada), 1986, Wiley (New York, NY), 1991.

(With Barbara Hehner) *Looking at Insects,* Stoddart (Toronto, Ontario, Canada), 1986, Wiley (New York, NY), 1992.

(With Barbara Hehner) *Looking at Senses,* Stoddart (Toronto, Ontario, Canada), 1986.

(With Eileen Thalenberg and Peter Knudtson) *David Suzuki Talks about AIDS,* General Paperbacks (Toronto, Ontario, Canada), 1989.

(With Barbara Hehner) *Looking at the Environment,* Stoddart (Toronto, Ontario, Canada), 1989.

(With Barbara Hehner) *Looking at Weather,* Wiley (New York, NY), 1991.

Nature in the Home, illustrated by Eugenie Fernandes, Stoddart (Toronto, Ontario, Canada), 1993.

If We Could See the Air, illustrated by Eugenie Fernandes, Stoddart (Toronto, Ontario, Canada), 1994.

The Backyard Time Detectives, illustrated by Eugenie Fernandes, Stoddart (Buffalo, NY), 1995.

(With Kathy Vanderlinden) *You Are the Earth: From Dinosaur Breath to Pizza,* Greystone Books (Vancouver, British Columbia, Canada), 2001.

(With Kathy Vanderlinden) *Eco-Fun: Great Experiments, Projects, and Games for A Greener Earth,* Greystone Books (Vancouver, British Columbia, Canada), 2001.

SIDELIGHTS: "Canada's best teacher is . . . geneticist David Takayoshi Suzuki, whose lectures and broadcasts have turned science from being boring to being fun," wrote Peter C. Newman in *Maclean's.* Suzuki, a trained and award-winning zoologist and geneticist, has become a major voice in Canada and across North America in popularizing science and in the battle to protect the environment. Moderator and host of several popular television and radio shows for the Canadian Broadcasting Corporation, Suzuki has become know internationally for his popular show *The Nature of Things,* which airs in over fifty countries.

In addition to his academic duties and broadcast ventures, Suzuki also writes books for both children and adults. Teaming up with Barbara Hehner, he has published six books in the "Looking At" series, books which introduce young readers to biological topics from the life of plants to the environment and the human body. Additionally, Suzuki has taken a look at science for preschoolers with his books about Megan and Jamie in the "Nature All Around" series. Working with Kathy Vanderlinden, Suzuki has also written a pair of books, *Your Are the Earth* and *Eco-Fun,* which blend environmental awareness with practical experiments and projects for budding scientists. Suzuki's writings for adults include *Genethics: The Ethics of*

Engineering Life, Wisdom of the Elders, Secrets of Life, and *The Sacred Balance,* books that look at mankind's role in nature and how we can reestablish the lost ecological balance plaguing our contemporary world. His *Introduction to Genetic Analysis* is the most widely used genetics textbook in the world, and is in its eighth edition.

Born in 1936 in Vancouver, British Columbia, Suzuki is a third-generation Japanese Canadian and the only boy in a family of four children. His parents ran a dry-cleaning business and encouraged their precocious son to speak only English and to identify more with Canadians of European descent rather than looking to his Japanese roots. With the bombing of Pearl Harbor in December, 1941, the lives of the Suzuki family and thousands of other Japanese Canadians were altered forever. Relocated from the west coast of Canada, these citizens of Japanese descent lost their homes, businesses, and savings. The Suzukis ended up in Slocan City, an old mining town in the Rocky Mountains, living in a one-room apartment in a run-down building with the mother barely making enough to support the family as a secretary. After a year of working on the Trans-Canada Highway, the father was also sent to Slocan City, where he found employment in a store.

In 1943 Suzuki was finally able to attend a school opened by several young, untrained teachers. Attending with other Japanese-Canadian children, he made rapid progress because of his understanding of English, but as a result he did not fit in well with the other students, who were largely Japanese speakers. The family made the best of these bad circumstances and encouraged their son to do as well as he could in his studies. Suzuki's father questioned him each night about what he had learned that day at school, as Suzuki recalled in his memoir, *Metamorphosis: Stages in a Life,* and listened closely to what his son told him: "It gave me a sense that what I was reciting was important and I loved dredging up the details." Their lives as outsiders in Canada also influenced Suzuki to study and work hard so he could prove his worth. Another important influence from his father was a love of nature and the natural world. From the time when he was a small child Suzuki would accompany his father on fishing expeditions or camping and hiking trips in the woods, experiences that helped to shape him into the biologist he later became.

The discrimination the family faced during the war did not end with the war's conclusion, for the govern-

ment of British Columbia declared that no Japanese or Japanese Americans were to be allowed to live in the province. So the family moved east to Leamington, Ontario, where Suzuki's father found work at a dry-cleaning business. Here Suzuki began demonstrating a keen interest in the natural world, collecting all manner of flora and fauna. As a young high school student he won several awards in speech and oratory, and with the family's move to London, Ontario, he entered London Central Collegiate High School. There, as a senior, he became student body president despite the fact that he was among only a handful of non-white students.

Earning a scholarship, Suzuki attended Amherst College in Massachusetts, where he finally began to accept his racial identity and stopped longing to be more European looking. Here he was particularly drawn to classes in embryology and genetics, and a senior project in the genetics of fruit fly propagation convinced him that he had the unique ability to relate technical facts in a highly digestible format. Graduating cum laude in biology in 1958, he later earned his Ph.D. in zoology at the University of Chicago, where he worked further on the genetics of the fruit fly and their so-called chromosomal cross-overs. This early research in genetic mutation won him a reputation—at the age of only twenty-five—as a "brash, dynamic young research scientist," according to B. K. Adams in a *Books in Canada* review of Suzuki's *Metamorphosis.* After a year as a postdoctoral researcher in the United States, however, and with offers from three top-notch American universities in hand, he abruptly returned to Canada, profoundly affected by the racism he experienced in America. Eventually he found a home at the University of British Columbia in Vancouver, where he became a full professor in 1969.

Increasingly, though, Suzuki was drawn to the field of broadcasting and the popularization of science. Working with the Canadian Broadcasting Corporation, he hosted and moderated numerous radio and television programs that brought science to the layperson. After the 1970s, his energies became funneled more into such projects and away from genetic research. Suzuki also became an outspoken advocate for environmentalism and for minority rights, championing the causes of indigenous peoples in Canada and in other countries.

Suzuki's career in writing for young readers began in 1985 with publication of the first title in the "Looking At" series, *Looking at Plants,* "an enjoyable, stimulating way to introduce children to the wide connection our lives have with plants," according to Bob Marquis in *Quill and Quire*. Divided into two parts, "Plants All around You" and "Plants up Close," the book presents botany for young readers in a "non-threatening way," as Marquis noted. Donn Kushner, writing in *Canadian Children's Literature*, felt that Suzuki "presents clearly written and well-illustrated accounts" of all the functional parts of plants in *Looking at Plants*. Full of amazing facts and activities, the book was a "real delight," according to Marquis, and set the tone for the remaining five titles in the series.

Reviewing *Looking at Insects* in *Quill and Quire*, Emily Hearn felt that the book, "with its lucid, lively prose and many explicit activities, is a boon." The human body gets the Suzuki treatment in *Looking at the Body*, in which the functions of the major organs are explained. Eve Williams, writing in *Canadian Materials*, felt the book lived up to the standards set by previous volumes in the series, and further praised the "cheerful style and clear explanations," as well as the tone, which she found "encouraging." Williams also noted that the entire series presents science in a "non-patronizing" manner. In *Looking at the Senses* Suzuki examines the mechanics of sight, hearing, touch, smell, and taste, while "injecting learning with a sense of fun," as Pamela Young wrote in *Maclean's*.

While *Canadian Children's Literature* critic Ronald Melzack took issue with some of the activities and with the organization of both *Looking at the Body* and *Looking at the Senses*, he also applauded Suzuki's "characteristic enthusiasm, curiosity and delight in knowledge," and praised the text in both books for being "straightforward, pitched at young people, and enjoyable." Other books in the series include *Looking at Weather* and *Looking at the Environment*. Fred Leicester, writing in *Canadian Materials*, felt that Suzuki dealt with most of the major environmental issues—from acid rain to endangered species—"in a way that makes these serious issues relevant to children." Leicester also praised Suzuki for putting forward scientific facts "accurately and in an engaging fashion." In a combined review of *Looking at Plants*, *Looking at Insects*, and *Looking at the Environment*, Lyle E. Craker remarked in *Science Books and Films* that the books "offer an exciting adventure in the world of science." And reviewing *Looking at the Body*, *Looking at Senses*, and *Looking at Weather* in *School Library Journal*, Elaine Fort Weischedel commended

Suzuki's "chatty, lucid explanations [which] should keep [youngsters] reading."

Suzuki has penned another science series, "Nature All Around," teaming up with illustrator Eugenie Fernandes and targeting preschool audiences. Using the two children Jamey and Megan, he assembles interesting and intriguing introductions to basic scientific principles. With *Nature in the Home* the duo has to take their usual nature walk indoors because of the rain. With their father, they discover all sorts of natural products inside the house, from the mahogany in the picture frames to rubber in the tires of a bike. Though Mary Beaty, writing in *Quill and Quire*, found Suzuki's premise of blurring the line between nature out there and within us "admirable," she also felt that the "format is so slight that the information it contains is misleading." Beaty felt that the true "natural" products in most homes consist of spiders and dust mites. Janet McNaughton, writing in *Books in Canada*, was more positive about the title, calling it a "painless way" to get children to understand how nature plays such an important role in our lives.

Suzuki followed this book with two more in the same series, *If We Could See the Air* and *The Backyard Time Detectives*. In the former book, Megan goes for a walk with her mother, who comments on how the air supports birds and airplanes and gives people oxygen while providing the plant world with carbon dioxide. Theo Hersh, reviewing the picture book in *Quill and Quire*, called it a "helpful introduction to a difficult and important topic." Jamey and Megan team up again in *The Backyard Time Detectives* in which they learn about the eternal rule of change in nature from their parents. They see how plants come from seeds and how the entire structure of their garden is the result of long-ago glaciers. *Quill and Quire* contributor Fred Boer felt this was a book that "young children will enjoy," and also one that "teachers will find useful."

Suzuki serves up more nature activities in *You Are the Earth: From Dinosaur Breath to Pizza* and *Eco-Fun: Great Projects, Experiments, and Games for a Greener Earth*, both written with Kathy Vanderlinden. *You Are the Earth* presents a "reminder that we are part of a greater whole," according to John Peters in *School Library Journal*. Suzuki provides a chapter each for the essentials of life: water, soil, energy, air, love, and a sense of "spiritual connection" with a larger universe, as Peters noted. Included with these chapters are review questions and ten activities middle grade children can do to enhance their eco-awareness. With *Eco-Fun* the authors gather together forty-eight different types of ecological activities "with a holistic view," as *Booklist* reviewer Gillian Engberg noted. These activities range from making environment-friendly cleaning agents to constructing a worm bin and a solar water heater. Patricia Ann Owens, writing in *School Library Journal*, felt that these projects were designed "to stimulate understanding, knowledge, and appreciation of our ecosystem."

In his long and prolific career Suzuki has managed to overcome personal setbacks to create a unique voice in the world of science and environmental awareness. In his children's books, just as in his adult nonfiction works and his broadcasting work, he has provided a lively and impassioned introduction to a world of scientific knowledge that many would otherwise find daunting.

BIOGRAPHICAL AND CRITICAL SOURCES:

BOOKS

Children's Literature Review, Volume 74, Gale (Detroit, MI), 2001.

Suzuki, David T., *Metamorphosis: Stages in a Life,* Stoddart (Toronto, Ontario, Canada), 1987.

PERIODICALS

American Biology Teacher, March, 2001, Jim Wandersee, review of *You Are the Earth,* p. 221.

Booklist, November 15, 1987, p. 577; February 15, 1990, p. 1175; June 1, 2001, Gillian Engberg, review of *Eco-Fun: Great Experiments, Projects, and Games for a Greener Earth,* p. 1876.

Books in Canada, December, 1987, B. K. Adams, review of *Metamorphosis: Stages in a Life,* p. 35; November, 1993, Janet McNaughton, review of *Nature in the Home,* p. 58.

Canadian Materials, January, 1988, Kenneth Elliott, review of *David Suzuki Talks about AIDS,* p. 21, Eve Williams, review of *Looking at the Body,* p. 25; May, 1988, Ronald Jobe, review of *David Suzuki Talks about AIDS,* p. 76; September, 1989, Fred Leicester, review of *Looking at the Environment,* p. 215.

Canadian Children's Literature, Volume 46, 1987, p. 110; Volume 47, 1987, Donn Kushner, review of *Looking at Plants* and *Looking at Insects,* pp. 61-62; Volume 50, 1988, Ronald Melzack, review of *Looking at Senses* and *Looking at the Body;* Volume 62, 1991, Donn Kushner, review of *Looking at Insects,* p. 105.

Maclean's, July 13, 1987, Pamela Young, review of *Looking at Senses* and *Looking at the Body,* pp. 50-51; April 3, 1995, Peter C. Newman, "Welcome to the World of Suzuki Economics," p. 42.

Quill and Quire, December, 1985, Bob Marquis, review of *Looking at Plants,* p. 25; June, 1986, Emily Hearn, review of *Looking at Insects,* p. 30; October, 1993, Mary Beaty, review of *Nature in the Home,* pp. 42-43; January, 1995, Theo Hersh, review of *If We Could See the Air,* p. 42; November, 1995, Fred Boer, review of *The Backyard Time Detectives,* p. 46.

School Library Journal, May, 1992, Elaine Fort Weischedel, review of *Looking at the Body, Looking at Senses,* and *Looking at Weather,* pp. 128-129; April, 2000, John Peters, review of *You Are the Earth,* p. 155; August, 2001, Patricia Ann Owens, review of *Eco-Fun,* p. 205.

Science Books and Films, August, 1992, Lyle E. Craker, review of *Looking at Plants, Looking at Insects,* and *Looking at the Environment,* p. 178.*

*   *   *

SWEENEY, John Thomas 1958-

PERSONAL: Born 1958.

ADDRESSES: Agent—c/o Author Mail, Bloomsbury Publishing, 38 Soho Square, London W1V 5DF, England.

CAREER: Journalist.

WRITINGS:

The Life and Evil Times of Nicolae Ceausescu, Hutchinson (London, England), 1991.

Purple Homicide: Fear and Loathing on Knutsford Heath, Bloomsbury (London, England), 1997.

SIDELIGHTS: In his nonfiction books, journalist John Thomas Sweeney chronicles the events contributing to both the rise and fall of Romanian dictator Nicolae Ceausescu and the British Parliamentary election race between Neil Hamilton and Martin Bell. Sweeney adopts "gonzo" journalism techniques that include writing in first-person narrative, minimal attempt at objectivity, and a personalized political agenda. In a review of *Purple Homicide*, Edward Pearce wrote in the *Times Literary Supplement*, "John Sweeney is a trying fellow. His prose, wearingly hectic and chippily demotic, comes out in a tumble, and he is partisan in the way of a headbutter reaching for another man's lapels." On the other hand, *Observer* critic Anthony Burgess, reviewing Sweeney's *The Life and Evil Times of Nicolae Ceausescu*, complimented the author's "admirable journalism. Sweeney's line is the personal and immediate."

Times Literary Supplement critic Mircea Iorgulescu found Sweeney "unable in *The Life and Evil Times of Nicolae Ceausescu* to rid himself of the tyranny of journalistic cliché. He does not even try." Iorgulescu faulted Sweeney's efforts to reveal the rotten core of the Ceausescu regime as "a very salesworthy, gruesome story, based on the repetition of stereotypes and on a long string of piquant, excessively emphasized details." Marek Kohn, writing in *New Statesman & Society*, similarly said, "Sweeney has a weakness for garish images as a substitute for explanation, writing at one point of a Romania held in the 'decadent, perfumed palm' of the Ottoman Empire." Kohn described Sweeney's work: "The start of Sweeney's tale finds the author right there, in the first person, surrounded by putrefying corpses; and strafed, shortly thereafterwards, by Kalashnikov bullets. His version of Romania's past comes with buckets of blood, Vlad the Impaler, and a digression on vampirism." Kohn also noted that in "the course of his research, Sweeney devoted considerable mischievous energy to soliciting recollections from figures in British public life who had paid court to the dictator."

Sweeney borrows his subtitle for *Purple Homicide: Fear and Loathing on Knutsford Heath,* from the gonzo socio-political writings of American writer Hunter S. Thompson. Of this work, Pearce wrote, "All the Sweeney qualities are present in *Purple Homicide,* a book both irksome and essential." Although Pearce applauded Sweeney's research into the private remarks made by the political rivals whose opposing campaigns are the center of the book, he remarked that "for all the work done and the indignation Hamilton inspires in him, Sweeney writes too noisily for the book as a whole to be effective." Reviewing the book in the *Observer,* William Leith stated, "This is a story about how politics is sometimes very little to do with technical stuff, and a lot to do with things such as personal style, and not being hideously deformed." Leith continued, "The book is written with the spirit of a reporter who is drunk on the events he is reporting." He concluded that "Sweeney is not a model of impartiality. He is a model of obsessive, contemptuous ranting, and a tireless trawler for detail."

BIOGRAPHICAL AND CRITICAL SOURCES:

PERIODICALS

New Statesman, March 29, 1991, pp. 36-37.
Observer, April 14, 1991, p. 62; October 17, 1997, p. 18.
Publishers Weekly, August 17, 1998.
Sunday Times Books, August 9, 1998, p. 10.
Times Literary Supplement, May 24, 1991, p. 13; January 2, 1998, p. 26.*

T

TAYLOR, Yuval 1963-

PERSONAL: Born February 27, 1963, in CA; son of Milton William (a professor) and Miriam (a weaver; maiden name, Reifer) Taylor; married Kathryn A. Duys (a professor), May 11, 1997; children: Thalia, Jacob. *Ethnicity:* "Jewish." *Education:* Princeton University, A.B., 1985; University of Iowa, M.A., 1988. *Politics:* "Left wing." *Religion:* Jewish. *Hobbies and other interests:* Music, nature.

ADDRESSES: Home—5801 South Harper Ave., Chicago, IL 60637. *Office*—Chicago Review Press, 814 North Franklin St., Chicago, IL 60610. *E-mail*—yuval@ipgbook.com.

CAREER: Da Capo Press, New York, NY, editor, 1989-97; Chicago Review Press, Chicago, IL, editor of Lawrence Hill Books and A Cappella Books, 1998— .

WRITINGS:

(Editor, with Charles Johnson) *I Was Born a Slave: An Anthology of Classic Slave Narratives,* Volume 1: *1770-1849,* Volume 2: *1849-1866,* Lawrence Hill Books (Chicago, IL), 1999.
(Editor) *The Future of Jazz,* A Cappella Books (Chicago, IL), 2002.
The Cartoon Music Book, A Cappella Books (Chicago, IL), 2002.

BIOGRAPHICAL AND CRITICAL SOURCES:

PERIODICALS

Independent Sunday (London, England), July 11, 1999, Kevin Le Gendre, review of *I Was Born a Slave: An Anthology of Classic Slave Narratives,* p. 12.

Library Journal, May 15, 1999, Thomas J. Davis, review of *I Was Born a Slave,* p. 108; April 15, 2002, Ronald S. Russ, review of *The Future of Jazz,* p. 87.
Observer (London, England), May 16, 1999, Sukhdev Sandhu, review of *I Was Born a Slave,* p. 12.

*　　*　　*

TESKE, Edmund (Rudolph) 1911-1996

PERSONAL: Born March 7, 1911, in Chicago, IL; died, 1996. *Education:* Attended Chicago public schools, 1916-28; self-taught in photography.

CAREER: Hull House, Theatre Department, Chicago, IL, designer, actor, make-up artist, photographer, 1933-34; A. George Muller's Photography, Inc., Chicago, assistant photographer, 1934-36; Frank Lloyd Wright's Taliesin, Spring Green, WI, honorary fellow, 1936-37; New Bauhaus Institute of Design, Chicago, instructor, 1937-38; Katharine Kuh Gallery, Chicago, assistant, 1937-38; Federal Arts Project, Chicago, instructor, 1939-40; Berenice Abbott (photographer), New York, NY, assistant, 1940-41; United State Engineers, Rock Island Arsenal, IL, various jobs, 1941-43; Paramount Pictures, Hollywood, CA, worked in photographic department, 1944; appeared in film *Lust for Life,* 1956; Chouinard Art Institute, Los Angeles, CA, instructor, 1962-64; University of California—Los Angeles, visiting professor, 1965-70; Immaculate Heart College, Los Angeles, CA, visiting instructor, 1974; California State University of Los Angeles, visiting professor, 1979.

AWARDS, HONORS: Certificate of Recognition, Photographic Society of America, 1969.

WRITINGS:

Untitled 22: Images from Within—The Photographs of Edmund Teske, Friends of Photography (Carmel, CA), 1980.

SIDELIGHTS: Renowned as a master of photography, particularly in the use of montage and a solarization process he called "duo-toning," Edmund Teske produced works of lyric mysticism and dreamy sensuality. While often relegated to the fringe because of his homoerotic images and his unconventional techniques, Teske earned the admiration of some of the giants of twentieth-century art, including photographers Alfred Stieglitz and Man Ray, radical filmmaker Kenneth Anger, and architect Frank Lloyd Wright.

"An eccentric, self-trained artist of the vanishing romantic school," wrote Mark Alice Durant in *Art in America,* Teske's images are notable for a sense of timelessness, connecting past memories with current realities. Durant wrote that "for Teske there are no fissures or breaks in history. As writer Aron Golberg has said of Teske, 'Memory and present are one to him.'" One method Teske used to convey this was through a kind of photomontage he called "composite printing," creating a singular effect out of disconnected moments. "His particular method yields a seamless image, harmonizing the newly united elements rather than producing the jarring dislocations commonly associated with montage," noted Durant.

When asked how he approached montages, Teske told an interviewer for *Petersen's Photographic,* "I don't approach it; it approaches me. The image material of my life experiences is like a vocabulary within me. It floats around. The images come." This dreamy quality, open to internal psychic dynamics, also marks Teske's work. As a *Los Angeles Times* reviewer put it, "In a sense, Teske's photographs are the visual equivalent of daydreams. In these works the texture and nuance of memories do not fade with the passing of time but grow more poignant, haunting the moment with ghostly presence."

In addition to montage, Teske conveyed this feeling through his use of a technique called the Sabattier Effect in the 1930s, but perfected by him as duotone solarization. By re-exposing negatives and manipulating darkroom chemistry, this solarization produced uniquely mysterious prints. As Durant wrote, "His prints are one-of-a-kind, gemlike objects whose opacity and mystery conjure up the image of Teske as a sort of darkroom alchemist."

While his technique set him apart, Teske was also noteworthy for his choice of subject matter. In the face of bigotry and McCarthyite attacks, he continued to produce homoerotic images and remained unapologetic in his own homosexuality. As Durant wrote in his summation in *Art in America,* Teske "developed an esthetic of the male body, showing unabashed joy in the expression of homoeroticism. An archivist and appropriator of his own work, Teske reuses his own images from past decades . . . unearthing photographic traces of male sensuality, re-imaging and re-imagining his longing."

After a prolific career spanning more than sixty years, Teske died in 1996, at the age of eighty-five. In an obituary for the *Los Angeles Times,* Weston Naef summarized the appeal of Teske's work: "Through his manipulations of both negatives and prints, Teske succeeded in turning back the mental clock, as though they were arrested dreams. Teske traveled in the realm of the imagination and persistently avoided linear thinking in favor of the poetic irrational."

BIOGRAPHICAL AND CRITICAL SOURCES:

PERIODICALS

Art in America, November 1993, Mark Alice Durant, "Darkroom Alchemist," p. 54.
Los Angeles Times, October 6, 2000, David Pagel, "Art Reviews: Daydreaming with the Surreal Photographs of Edmund Teske," p. F30.
Petersen's Photographic, July 1985, Franklin Cameron, "Edmund Teske," p. 12.

OBITUARIES:

PERIODICALS

Los Angeles Times, December 2, 1996, Weston Naef, "Remembering Edmund Teske, a Poet-Pioneer of Photography," p. 6.*

THOMSON, James C(laude), Jr. 1931-2002

OBITUARY NOTICE—See index for CA sketch: Born September 14, 1931, in Princeton, NJ; died of a heart attack August 11, 2002, in Cambridge, MA. Political advisor, educator, and author. Thomson was a highly regarded expert on Asian politics who served as an advisor to presidents Kennedy and Johnson and was later curator of the Nieman Foundation for Journalism. Although he was born in New Jersey, his mother's missionary work took the family to China and Japan. He spent much of his childhood in China and attended the University of Nanking from 1948 to 1949 until the Communist revolution forced the family to return to America. Thomson earned B.A. degrees from Harvard University in 1953 and Clare College, Cambridge, in 1955. His master's degree, earned in 1959, was also from Cambridge, and he received his doctorate from Harvard in 1961. Thomson's involvement in politics began with his work for the Adlai Stevenson presidential campaign. Work as a staff member for Congressman Chester Bowles led to his post as a foreign policy advisor to Kennedy in 1960 and then for the National Security Council under President Johnson from 1964 to 1966. However, Thomson became critical of U.S. foreign policy in Asia, especially Vietnam, and left government to teach history at Harvard in 1966. While there, he was an associate at the Institute of Politics and the Fairbanks Center for East Asia Research. In 1972 he was named curator of the Nieman Foundation for Journalism, and during his tenure strove to increase the enrollment of female, minority, and foreign students, as well as broadening the program to include photographers and editorial cartoonists. Leaving the foundation in 1984, Thomson joined Boston University, where he continued to teach history until his retirement in 1997. During his career, Thomson wrote extensively about foreign policy and Asia, receiving an Overseas Press Club Award for foreign affairs journalism for an article he wrote on Vietnam, and publishing such books as *While China Faced West: American Reformers in Nationalist China, 1928-1937* (1969) and the coauthored work *Sentimental Imperialists: The American Experience in East Asia* (1981).

OBITUARIES AND OTHER SOURCES:

BOOKS

Who's Who in American Politics, 17th edition, Marquis (New Providence, NJ), 1999.

PERIODICALS

Chicago Tribune, August 18, 2002, section 4, p. 9.
Los Angeles Times, August 15, 2002, p. B12.
New York Times, August 15, 2002, p. A21.

*   *   *

THORNDYKE, Helen Louise
See BENSON, Mildred (Augustine Wirt)

*   *   *

THYRET, Isolde R. 1955-

PERSONAL: Born February 11, 1955, in Stuttgart, Germany; naturalized U.S. citizen; daughter of Egon (in sales) and Berta (in sales) Thyret. *Education:* Attended University of Würzburg, 1975-77, and Eastern Washington University, 1978-79; University of Washington, Seattle, B.A., M.A., Ph.D., 1992. *Hobbies and other interests:* Music, gardening, museums.

ADDRESSES: Office—Department of History, Kent State University, Kent, OH 44242. *E-mail*—ithyret@ kent.edu.

CAREER: Kent State University, Kent, OH, professor of history.

MEMBER: American Historical Association, American Association for the Advancement of Slavic Studies, Early Slavic Studies Association (treasurer, 1995-2002).

AWARDS, HONORS: Fellow of Joint Committee on the Soviet Union and Its Successor State, American Council of Learned Societies and Social Sciences Research Council, 1993.

WRITINGS:

Between God and Tsar: Religious Symbolism and the Royal Women of Muscovite Russia, Northern Illinois University Press (DeKalb, IL), 2001.

Contributor to books, including *Religion and Culture in Early Modern Russia and Ukraine,* edited by Samuel H. Baron and Nancy Shields Kollmann, Northern Illinois University Press, 1997. Contributor to periodicals, including *North Dakota Quarterly* and *Russian Review.*

WORK IN PROGRESS: The Role of Relics in Medieval Russia; research on popular piety in medieval Russia.

SIDELIGHTS: Isolde R. Thyret told *CA:* "I have always had a lively interest in women's and gender history. Originally trained as a Western medievalist, during my graduate career I became increasingly interested in Eastern Europe and Russia. Methodologically I was broadly trained, developing an expertise in religious studies, art history, and literary analysis. This training influenced my approach to the royal women of medieval Russia in my book *Between God and Tsar: Religious Symbolism and the Royal Women of Muscovite Russia.*"

BIOGRAPHICAL AND CRITICAL SOURCES:

PERIODICALS

Canadian Slavonic Papers, December, 2001, T. Allan Smith, review of *Between God and Tsar: Religious Symbolism and the Royal Women of Muscovite Russia,* p. 594.

*   *   *

TRAGER, Philip 1935-

PERSONAL: Born February 27, 1935, in Bridgeport, CT; married Ina Shulkin, 1957; children: Julie, Michael. *Education:* Wesleyan University, B.A., 1956; Columbia University School of Law, J.D., 1960; self-taught in photography.

ADDRESSES: Home—20 Rolling Ridge Road, Fairfield, CT 06430.

CAREER: Trager and Trager counselors-at-law, Fairfield, CT, attorney, 1960—; independent photographer, Fairfield, CT, 1966—.

AWARDS, HONORS: Book of the Year Award, American Institute of Graphic Arts, 1977; Twenty-five Best Books Award, Association of American University Presses, 1977; Recommended Book of the Year citation, *New York Times,* 1977, 1980; Distinguished Alumnus Award, Wesleyan University, 1981; Lay Person Award, Connecticut Society of Architects, 1981.

WRITINGS:

Echoes of Silence, Scroll Press (Danbury, CT), 1972.
Photographs of Architecture, Wesleyan University Press (Middletown, CT), 1977.
Philip Trager: New York, Wesleyan University Press (Middletown, CT), 1980.
Wesleyan: Photographs, text by Vincent Scully, Wesleyan University Press (Middletown, CT), 1982.
The Villas of Palladio, text by Vincent Scully, Little, Brown (Boston, MA), 1986.
Dancers, essays by Joan Acocella and David Freedberg, Little, Brown (Boston, MA), 1992.
Persephone, text by Ralph Lemon and Andrew Szegedy-Maszak, poems by Eavan Boland and Rita Dove, Wesleyan University Press (Middletown, CT), 1996.
Changing Paris: A Tour along the Seine, commentary by Thomas Mellins, Arena Editions (Santa Fe, NM), 2000.

SIDELIGHTS: Philip Trager is a renowned photographer of architecture, capturing the aesthetic essence behind New York City brownstones, Italian villas, and Parisian monuments, both old and new. From the anonymous, modern buildings of Manhattan, crowded together and forming a whole, Trager turned to the monumental works of a famed Italian Renaissance architect in *The Villas of Palladio.* "If buildings could be, so to speak, unclothed, then what Trager has done is analogous to rendering Palladio's architecture nude. He has taken some of the most familiar buildings of the Renaissance and jarred that familiarity by creating at once an atmosphere of intimacy and detachment," wrote a reviewer for *Progressive Architecture.* For this reviewer, "the forms seem to contain the memory of many human experiences, whose presence is felt in the sounds of former life that hang hauntingly in the air."

Trager brings history and modernism together in *Changing Paris: A Tour along the Seine.* In recommending the book in *Library Journal,* Thomas Fry wrote, "Trager moves through the city following the Seine in an attempt to show the . . . particularly effective juxtaposition of varying architectural styles."

BIOGRAPHICAL AND CRITICAL SOURCES:

PERIODICALS

Library Journal, April 1, 2000, Thomas K. Fry, review of *Changing Paris: A Tour along the Seine,* p. 120.
Progressive Architecture, August, 1987, John DiGregorio, review of *The Villas of Palladio,* p. 115.*

*   *   *

TUMANOV, Vladimir A. 1961-

PERSONAL: Born December 29, 1961, in Moscow, USSR (now Russia); married Larissa Klein Tumanov (a teacher of French); children: Alexander, Vanessa. *Education:* University of Alberta, Ph.D., 1993.

ADDRESSES: Home—50 Rexway Rd., London, Ontario, Canada N6G 3C3. *E-mail*—vtumanov@uwo.ca.

CAREER: University of Western Ontario, London, Ontario, Canada, assistant professor, 1991-96, associate professor, 1996—.

MEMBER: Canadian Society of Children's Authors, Illustrators, and Performers.

WRITINGS:

Listening to Okudzhava: Twenty-three Aural Comprehension Exercises in Russian, Focus Publishing (Newburyport, MA), 1996.
Mind Reading: Unframed Direct Interior Monologue in European Fiction, Rodopi (Amsterdam, Netherlands), 1997.
Jayden's Rescue (for children), Scholastic Canada (Markham, Ontario, Canada), 2002.

Contributor to books, including *Ecce Bellum: Garshin's "Four Days,"* edited by Peter Henry, Northgate Press, 2000. Contributor to journals, including

Neophilologus, Romantic Review, Orbis Litterarum, Yiddish, Russian Literature, Russian Language Journal, Canadian Literature, and *Scando-Slavica.*

WORK IN PROGRESS: A sequel to *Jayden's Rescue* titled *Old Scroll;* a new novel for children titled *Greggie-Boy the Bug.*

SIDELIGHTS: Vladimir A. Tumanov told *CA,* "Before coming to write for children, I published academic books and articles on topics related to comparative literature and second- language acquisition. My first children's novel is *Jayden's Rescue.* This book—intended for children in grades four to six—is an adventure story complete with sorcery, narrow escapes, and suspense. However, this fantasy comes with a twist: The entire plot revolves around mathematical puzzles presented in verse. The protagonists must solve the puzzles (with the reader's help) in order to save an imprisoned queen and extricate themselves from a very dangerous predicament. The ultimate aim of *Jayden's Rescue* is to present math for what it really is: an adventure, a quest, and a true thrill for the mind."

"I wrote this book to inspire my son to enjoy math. I knew that he loved fantasy fiction. The novel began as a simple concept: getting out of a prison by solving math puzzles. It evolved into an adventure story with my son and daughter as protagonists. Several teachers have pointed out to me how useful they have found *Jayden's Rescue* for motivating children to view math in a positive light." A reviewer for *Canadian Living* called *Jayden's Rescue* a book "that will intrigue young readers and have them pulling out a pencil to solve the puzzles."

BIOGRAPHICAL AND CRITICAL SOURCES:

PERIODICALS

Canadian Living, July, 2002, review of *Jayden's Rescue,* p. 127.

OTHER

Vladimir Tumanov Web site, http://www.canscaip.org/bios/tumanovv.html/ (January 29, 2003).

TURNER, Thomas B(ourne) 1902-2002

OBITUARY NOTICE—See index for *CA* sketch: Born January 28, 1902, in Prince Frederick, MD; died September 22, 2002, in Baltimore, MD. Physician, administrator, and author. Turner, who spent much of his career studying infectious diseases, was a microbiologist and former dean of the Medical School at Johns Hopkins University. He earned his bachelor's degree in 1921 from St. John's College in Annapolis and his medical degree from the University of Maryland in 1925. From early on he was interested in the study of infectious diseases, and he spent several years in the Caribbean doing research. When he returned to America, he continued this work at the Rockefeller Foundation's International Health Division during the 1930s. In 1939 Turner joined the faculty at Johns Hopkins as a professor of microbiology. His university work was interrupted by World War II, during which he spearheaded the U.S. Army's efforts to control the spread of syphilis and championed the use of prophylaxis to prevent transmittal of sexual diseases among the troops. Returning to Johns Hopkins after the war, Turner served as dean from 1957 to 1968, when he became the first person to work as the medical archivist there. He retired as professor and dean emeritus in 1971, but he continued his work as archivist until 1981, and during the 1980s was the director of the Alcoholic Beverage Medical Research Foundation. A prolific author of scholarly papers, Turner also wrote or edited several books, including *Fundamentals of Medical Education* (1963), *Heritage of Excellence: The Johns Hopkins Medical Institutions, 1914-1947* (1974), the 1981 autobiography *Art of Medicine, Art of Me: Musings of a Johns Hopkins Dean,* and his last book, written with V. L. Bennett, *Forward Together: Industry and Academia* (1993). For his contributions to science, Turner received an honorary L.H.D. from Johns Hopkins in 1991, among other awards.

OBITUARIES AND OTHER SOURCES:

BOOKS

Who's Who in Science and Engineering, sixth edition, Marquis (New Providence, NJ), 2001.

PERIODICALS

Los Angeles Times, September 26, 2002, p. B12.
New York Times, October 2, 2002, p. A27.
Washington Post, September 25, 2002, p. B6.

TURRINI, Peter 1944-

PERSONAL: Born September 26, 1944, in St. Margarethen/Carinthia, Austria.

ADDRESSES: Agent—c/o Lucherhand Publishing House, Widenmayerstrasse 5, D-80538 Munich, Germany.

CAREER: Playwright and novelist. Also worked as a steelworker and woodworker, hotel manager, and advertising copywriter.

AWARDS, HONORS: Gerhardt Haputmann prize, Freie Volksbühne, 1981.

WRITINGS:

Rozznjogd (play; title means "Rat Hunt", produced in Vienna, Austria at Volkstheater, 1971), translation published as *Chasing down Rats,* Sessler (Vienna, Austria), 1979.
Zero Zero: Ein Kunst-Stuck (play), produced in Vienna, Austria at Theater an der Wien, 1971.
Erlebnisse in der Mundhöhle (novel), Rowohlt (Reinbeck, Germany), 1972.
Sauschlachten (play; title means "Slaughter of the Sow"; produced in Munich, Germany, 1972), Lentz (Vienna, Austria), 1974.
Der tollste Tag: Frei nach Beaumarchais (play; title means "The Craziest Day"), produced in Darmstadt, Germany at Landestheater, 1972.
Kindsmord (play), produced in Klagenfurt, Germany at Stadttheater, 1973.
Die Wirtin: Frei nach Goldoni (play; title means "The Innkeeper's Wife"; produced in Nuremberg, Germany at Schauspielhaus, 1973), Sessler (Vienna, Austria), 1978.
Phonoptical: Terror (play), produced in Villach, Germany at Studiobüne, 1974.
(With Wilhelm Pevny) *Der Dorfschullehrer,* Sessler (Vienna, Austria), 1975.
Turrini Lesebuch: Stücke, Pamphlete, Filme, Reaktionen etc., Europaverlag (Vienna, Austria), 1978, 2nd edition published as *Turrini Lesebuch: Zwei Stücke, Film, Gedichte, Reaktionen, etc.,* Europaverlag (Vienna, Austria), 1983.
Josef und Maria (play; produced in Vienna, Austria at Volkstheater, 1980), Frisfleisch und Löwenmaul (Vienna, Austria), 1980.

(With Wilhelm Pevny) *Alpensaga: Eine sechsteilige Fernsehserie aus dem bäuerlichen Leben* (three volumes; title means "The Saga of the Alps"; based on *Die Alpensaga* television series), Residenz (Salzburg, Germany), 1980.

Ein paar Schritte zurück: Gedichte (poetry), Autorenedition (Munich, Germany), 1980.

(With others) *Bruno Kreisky,* Nicolai (Berlin, Germany), 1981.

Die Bürger (play; title means "The Citizens"; produced in Vienna, Austria at Volkstheater, 1982), Sessler (Vienna, Austria), 1982.

Campiello: Frei nach Goldoni (play; produced in Vienna, Austria at Volkstheater, 1982), Sessler (Vienna, Austria), 1982.

(With Käthe Kratz) *Jugend: Buch zum film "Atemnot,"* Europaverlag (Vienna, Austria), 1984.

Es ist ein gutes Land: Text zu Anlässen, Europaverlag (Vienna, Austria), 1986.

Faust III: Eine Komödie, teils teils (play), produced in Vienna, Austria at Theater Nero im Theater im Künstelerhaus, 1987.

Die Minderleister (play; title means "The Underachievers"; produced in Vienna, Austria, at Akademietheater, 1988), Europaverlag (Vienna, Austira), 1988.

(With Rudi Palla) *Die Verlockung,* Europaverlag (Vienna, Austria), 1988.

Mein Österrich: Reden, Polemiken, Aufsätze, Luchterhand (Darmstadt, Germany), 1988.

(With Rudi Palla) *Müllomania: Ein Drehbuch,* Europaverlag (Vienna, Austria), 1988.

(With Rudi Palla) *Das Plakat: Ein Drehbuch,* Europaverlag (Vienna, Austria), 1990.

Tod und Teufel (play), Luchterhand (Frankfurt, Germany), 1990.

Peter Turrini: Texte, Daten, Bilder, Luchterhand (Hamburg, Germany), 1991.

Alpenglühen: ein Stück, Luchterhand (Hamburg, Germany), 1992, translation published as *Alpine Glow,* Aridne Press (Riverside, CA), 1994.

In Namen der Liebe (poetry), Luchterhand (Hamburg, Germany), 1993.

Grillparzer im Pornoladen (play), produced in Berlin, Germany at Berliner Ensemble, 1993.

Die Schlacht um Wien: Schauspiel in dri Akten, Luchterhand (Hamburg, Germany), 1995.

(With others) *Liebe Mörder!: von der Gegenwart, dem Theater und vom lieben Gott,* Luchterhand (Hamburg, Germany), 1996.

(With Walter Baco) *Literatalk: Worte über Wort,* Albatros (Vienna, Austria), 1996.

(With others) *Aufbruch aus der Dunkelheit: Hilfe in der Depression: eine Dokumentation,* Ibera & Molden (Vienna, Austria), 1997.

Endlich Schluß: Ein Monolog (monologue), produced in Vienna, Austria at Akademietheater, 1998.

Die Liebe in Madagaskar: Theaterstück, Luchterhand (Hamburg, Germany), 1998.

Die Verhaftung des Johann Nepomuk Nestroy: Eine Novelle, Luchterhand (Hamburg, Germany), 1998.

(With others) *Lesebuch 1: Ein irrer Traum,* Luchterhand (Hamburg, Germany), 1999.

Lesebuch 2: Das Gegenteil ist wahr, Luchterhand (Hamburg, Germany), 1999.

Lesebuch 3: Zu Hause bin ich nur hier: am Theater, Luchterhand (Hamburg, Germany), 1999.

Kasino, ein Tanzspiel (play), produced in Vienna, Austria at Kasino am Schwarzenbergplatz, 2000.

Die Eröffnung (play), produced in Bochum, Germany at Schauspielhaus, 2000.

Ich liebe dieses land. Stück und Materialien, Suhrkamp (Frankfurt, Germany), 2001.

Contributor to *Spectaculum 51: sechs moderne Theaterstücke,* Suhrkamp (Frankfurt, Germany), 1991. Works have been translated in *The Slackers and Other Plays,* translated by Richard Dixon, Ariadne Press, 1992, and *Shooting Rats, Other Plays and Poems,* translated by Richard Dixon, Ariadne Press (Riverside, CA), 1996. Author's works have been translated into twenty languages.

SIDELIGHTS: A sedate night out at the theater is not part of Peter Turrini's plan for his audiences. Instead, the playwright/poet/novelist specializes in "shock tactics," as Jutta Landa put it in *Modern Austrian Literature.* Landa described Turrini's stageworks as fashioned using both explicit and implicit shock strategies. Among the explicit are "crude dialect or slang replete with four-letter words and a hyperrealism focusing on murder, rape, promiscuity, and even cannibalism. Implicit strategies are aimed at the destruction of the dramatic code and the subversion of the audience's theatrical expectations."

Born in rural Austria during World War II, Turrini, whose roots are Italian and Syrian, felt an outsider among the more traditional residents. He escaped into the world of literature, but made his initial living in the blue-collar trades like woodworking and steelworking, "occupations that figure prominently in his plays," as Bernd Fischer pointed out in a *Dictionary of Literary Biography* essay. A freelance writer in his youth, Turrini realized virtually overnight success with his first major play production, *Rozznjogd.* This drama set the stage for the author's confrontational style: The plot has a young couple on their first date stopping at a junkyard where the man shows his girlfriend his talent for shooting rats. "In an attempt to overcome their feelings of alienation and falsehood the two slowly remove all the trappings of civilization—false eyelashes, false teeth, hairpieces, cosmetics, money, and finally clothes," as Fischer noted. As they make love, passersby mistake their movement for that of vermin—and shoot the lovers dead. "These snipers then turn toward the [audience] and start firing shots at this 'pack of rats,'" according to Landa.

Turrini's take on bigotry, *Sauschlachten* "is a parody of the tradition of affirmative and uncritical German folk plays," said Fischer. When the son of a farmer refuses to speak and communicates only in pig grunts, his family joins the villagers in treating him like a pig: setting him in a sty, feeding him suet and, finally, slaughtering him for a feast.

While critical of the rural mindset that can tolerate such cruelty, Turrini is no less gentle with city folk who engage in "functional barbarism," as he described the behavior in Gabrielle Robinson's *Theatre Journal* piece. In Turrini's view, Robinson added, both city and country types "not only lead meaningless lives but persecute the more sensitive protagonists. The social functionaries for the most part are presented in grotesque distortion," singling out the "mother who gives only the most conventional admonishments as her family tortures her son to death" in *Sauschlachten*. To Robinson, Turrini's protagonists "are stereotypes of abuse, hunted animals in a world of butchers. Even in view of the succession of the absurdist anti-heroes of modern drama, Turrini's mute or screaming victims embody an ultimate transformation of the romantic rebel-hero."

After the commercial and critical failure of some of his later plays, Turrini became disenchanted with the stage, according to Fischer, "and denounced it as outmoded bourgeois entertainment." He turned to television for his dramas, and collaborated on a nine-hour dramatic depiction of a mountain village from the turn of the twentieth century to the post-World War II years. The series was hailed as one of the best ever produced for German-language television, and its neo-realist style provided the basis for another Turrini drama, *Josef und Maria*, a story of two lonely people who find each other in a closed department store. *Die Bürger*, a drama revolving around greed, bourgeois values, and suicidal tendencies, remarked Fischer, "attacks Turrini's generation, which controls the levers of power in society but lacks backbone or goals and—more important—has nothing to say."

With *Die Minderleister*, the playwright examines the effect of joblessness, homelessness, and hopelessness on a steelworker and his wife. The husband, Hans, invariably loses out to a system designed to keep him weak: "the director of personnel dismisses him in a scene which slips momentarily into a parodic horror film; the tv game show host slaps Hans down when he refuses to eradicate his competitors, including his wife," as Robinson wrote. In this play as well, suicide is the final solution.

Turrini's portraits "of a cruel and dehumanized country life have given way to more realistic—although sometimes highly stylized—analyses of the decay of the traditional class struggle," Fischer concluded. "Nevertheless, the basic topic of [his] dramas and television plays has remained the same: his homeland and the injustices, cruelties, and suffering of its people."

BIOGRAPHICAL AND CRITICAL SOURCES:

BOOKS

Centre Stage: Contemporary Drama in Austria, Rodopi, 1999.
Dictionary of Literary Biography, Volume 124: *Twentieth-Century German Dramatists, 1919-1992,* Gale (Detroit, MI), 1992.

PERIODICALS

Modern Austrian Literature, Volume 24, numbers 3-4, 1991, Jutta Landa, "Minderleister": Problems of Audience Address in Peter Turrini's Plays," pp. 161-172.
Theatre Journal, May, 1991, Gabrielle Robinson, "Slaughter and Language Slaughter in the Plays of Peter Turrini," pp. 195-208.
World Literature Today, autumn, 1991, Franz Haberl, review of *Tod und Teufel,* p. 700.

V-W

van HODDIS, Jakob
    See DAVIDSOHN, Hans

*   *   *

VIVIAN, Robert 1967-

PERSONAL: Born June 30, 1967, in Englewood, CO; son of David and Mary Amy Vivian. Ethnicity: "Scottish and Hungarian." Education: University of Nebraska, Ph.D., 2001. Politics: Socialist. Religion: Roman Catholic.

ADDRESSES: Agent—c/o Author Mail, University of Nebraska Press, 312 North 14th St., P.O. Box 880484, Lincoln, NE 68588-0484.

CAREER: Writer.

WRITINGS:

Cold Snap as Yearning (creative nonfiction), University of Nebraska Press (Lincoln, NE), 2001.

WORK IN PROGRESS: Mover of Bones, a novel.

SIDELIGHTS: Robert Vivian told CA: "I write out of a sense of personal necessity and awe: these are both essential and inexplicable to me. Influences abound—music, drama, scientific reading, geography. I think of writing (when it is going well) as a privileged and wide-awake kind of sleepwalking—such times are like extended prayers. I am desperate to find beauty in the least thing—and find it nearly everywhere, in blowing newspapers, scrap heaps, certain slants of light. Notice this moment and pay it homage—that is the refrain sounding in my heart and mind."

*   *   *

WAHLBECK, Östen 1965-

PERSONAL: Born September 2, 1965, in Lappfjärd, Finland; son of Kaj and Litti (Kylander) Wahlbeck. Education: Åbo Akademi University, M.A., 1992; University of Warwick, Ph.D., 1998.

ADDRESSES: Office—Department of Sociology, Åbo Akademi University, FIN-20500 Åbo, Finland; fax: 358-2-2154808. E-mail—osten.wahlbeck@abo.fi.

CAREER: Åbo Akademi University, Åbo, Finland, acting professor and head of Sociology Department, 1998-99, senior lecturer, 1999—.

AWARDS, HONORS: Award for best sociology master's thesis written in Finland in 1992, Finnish Sociological Association/Westermarck-Society, 1993; Overseas Research Student Award, Committee of Vice-Chancellors and Principals of the Universities of the United Kingdom, 1994.

WRITINGS:

Qualitative Social Research and Refugee Reception (in Swedish), Åbo Akademi (Vasa, Finland), 1992.

Kurdish Diasporas: A Comparative Study of Kurdish Refugee Communities, St. Martin's Press (New York, NY), 1999.

BIOGRAPHICAL AND CRITICAL SOURCES:

PERIODICALS

Choice, November, 1999, K. Tölölyan, review of *Kurdish Diasporas,* p. 9.
European Societies, Volume 4, issue 4, 2000, Ellie Vasta, review of *Kurdish Diasporas,* pp. 558-560.

*   *   *

WALKER, (Harold) Todd 1917-1998

PERSONAL: Born September 25, 1917, in Salt Lake City, UT; died of cancer, September 13, 1998, in Tucson, AZ; married Betty Mae McNutt, 1944; children: Kathleen, Melanie. *Education:* Glendale Junior College, Glendale, CA, 1939-40; Art Center School, Los Angeles, CA, 1939-41.

CAREER: RKO Film Studios, Scenic Department, Hollywood, CA, painter, 1935-41; Tradefilms, Inc. (educational films), Hollywood, photographer, 1941-43; freelance advertising, industrial, and magazine photographer, Los Angeles, CA, 1946-51, and Beverly Hills, CA, 1951-70; independent photographer, Gainesville, FL, 1970-77, and Tucson, AZ, 1977-98. Art Center College of Design, Los Angeles, instructor in photography, 1966-70; University of California Extension—Los Angeles, instructor in photography, 1969-70; California State College, Northridge, CA, associate professor of photography, 1970; University of Florida, Gainesville, associate professor of art, printmaking, and photography, 1970-77; University of Arizona, Tucson, professor of art, 1977-85, professor emeritus, 1985-98. *Military service:* U.S. Army Corps, 1943-45; air cadet, then flying instructor, Second Lieutenant.

AWARDS, HONORS: National Foundation for the Arts grant, 1971; Florida Council on the Arts fellowship, 1976.

WRITINGS:

Pacific Oaks Friends School, General Printing Corporation (Los Angeles, CA), 1955.
The Story of an Abandoned Shack in the Desert, Thumbprint Press (Los Angeles, CA), 1966.
(Editor) *A Few Poems by John Donne and Photographs by Todd Walker,* The Thumbprint Press (Los Angeles, CA), 1966.
How Would It Feel to be Able to Dance like This?, Thumbprint Press (Los Angeles, CA), 1967.
(Editor) *The Causes of Love-Melancholy* (excerpt from *The Anatomy of Melancholy* by Robert Burton, 1621), The Thumbprint Press (Los Angeles, CA), 1968.
Twenty-seven Photographs, Thumbprint Press (Los Angeles, CA), 1974.
For Nothing Changes . . . (excerpts from *The Anatomy of Melancholy* and excerpts from local news), Thumbprint Press (Los Angeles, CA), 1976.
A Few Notes (selected from Lesson A of *Wilson's Photographics,* 1881), Thumbprint Press (Los Angeles, CA), 1976.
Three Soliloquies, Thumbprint Press (Los Angeles, CA), 1977.
(With Becky Gaver) *A Rudimentary Guide to the Little-known Art of Photo-Silkscreen,* Thumbprint Press (Gainesville, FL), 1977.
'58 Chevrolet Revisited!, Chicago Books at the Chicago Art Institute (Chicago, IL) 1977.
The Edge of the Shadow, Thumbprint Press (Los Angeles, CA), 1977.
See, Thumbprint Press (Los Angeles, CA), 1978.

SELF-PUBLISHED

Harold T. Walker, 1939.
Aloyisius in Abstractionland, 1941.
Good Humor, 1941.
Tradefilms, 1943.
Harold Todd Walker, 1946.
Harold Todd Walker, 1950.
Eight of William Shakespeare's Sonnets & Eight of Todd Walker's Photographs, 1966.*

*   *   *

WAMBA, Philippe 1971-2002

OBITUARY NOTICE—See index for *CA* sketch: Born June 3, 1971, in Pomona, CA; died in an automobile accident September 11, 2002, in Kenya. Journalist and author. Though young when he died, Wamba had already begun to build a reputation for his insightful writings about the people of Africa. The son of an African who moved to the United States to work as a professor and then became the leader of a group of rebels in the Congo, Wamba consequently led a peripatetic life. He attended several universities before graduating from Harvard University with an A.B. in 1993 and Columbia University with a master's degree in 1994, and he spent his early life living in cities in both the United States and Africa. During the mid-1990s he worked as a researcher and writer for the W. E. B. du Bois Institute in Cambridge, Massachusetts and then as an editor for Macmillan Publishing. In 1999 he took a job as the online editor-in-chief of Africana.com. He captured his personal feelings about being torn between two worlds in his memoir *Kinship: A Family's Journey in Africa and America* (1999), and he was researching a new book when he died. Wamba was also a contributor to journals in the United States and Europe, and was especially concerned about the plight of young people in Africa.

OBITUARIES AND OTHER SOURCES:

PERIODICALS

Chicago Tribune, September 19, 2002, section 2, p. 9.
New York Times, September 14, 2002, p. A26.
Los Angeles Times, September 16, 2002, p. B9.
Washington Post, September 15, 2002, p. C8.

*   *   *

WEISS, Paul 1901-2002

OBITUARY NOTICE—See index for *CA* sketch: Born May 19, 1901, in New York, NY; died July 5, 2002, in Washington, DC. Philosopher, educator, author, and editor. Weiss taught philosophy at some of America's most prestigious institutions for more than sixty years. Toward the end of his career he repeatedly fought age discrimination in academia, sometimes without success, but when he finally retired in his nineties, it was on his own terms. Weiss was affiliated with Yale University from 1946 until his forced retirement as Sterling Professor of Philosophy in 1969. He was appointed Heffer Visiting Professor of Philosophy at the Catholic University of America on an annual basis

from 1969 through 1992, when his contract was not renewed. Weiss sued the university for age discrimination, won his suit, and taught for at least two more years before his final retirement. Weiss was a founding member of the Metaphysical Society of America from 1947 and the editor of the *Review of Metaphysics* from 1947 through 1964. He was also an energetic writer with many published books and a handful in progress at the time of his death. Weiss's writings include *Beyond All Appearances, You, I, and the Others, Being and Other Realities, Emphatics,* published in 2000, and *Surrogates,* published in 2002.

OBITUARIES AND OTHER SOURCES:

BOOKS

Hahn, Lewis Edwin, editor, *The Philosophy of Paul Weiss,* Open Court (Chicago, IL), 1995.

PERIODICALS

Los Angeles Times, July 27, 2002, p. B19.
New York Times, July 24, 2002, obituary by Ari L. Goldman, p. A16.
Washington Post, July 7, 2002, obituary by Richard Pearson, p. C8.

*   *   *

WELSBY, Paul A(ntony) 1920-2002

OBITUARY NOTICE—See index for *CA* sketch: Born August 18, 1920, in Alcester, Warwickshire, England; died March 1, 2002. Anglican minister and author. Welsby was an important leader of the Church of England in the 1970s and 1980s. Educated at the University of Durham, where he earned an M.A. in 1945, and the University of Sheffield, where he received his Ph.D. in 1944, Welsby was ordained a minister of the Church of England in 1944. During the 1940s and 1950s he held several positions as a curate, rector, and rural dean before becoming a canon residentiary at Rochester Cathedral, where he was made vice dean in 1974. Welsby became a national figure when he joined the Church Assembly—later the General Synod—in 1964 and rose to the position of chairman of House of Clergy and prolocutor of Convocation at Canterbury from 1974 to 1980. He was also a member of the Bishops' Council at that time. In addition, Welsby was a noted author of eight books, including *A History of the Church of England, 1945-1980* and *How the Church of England Works.*

OBITUARIES AND OTHER SOURCES:

BOOKS

Who's Who 2000, St. Martin's Press (New York, NY), 2000.

PERIODICALS

Times (London, England), March 8, 2002, p. 35.

*　　*　　*

WEST, Dorothy
　　See BENSON, Mildred (Augustine Wirt)

*　　*　　*

WERKEMA, Mark A. 1965-

PERSONAL: Born August 9, 1965, in Orange City, IA; son of Gordon R. and Jacklyn N. (Brumels) Werkema; married Christine Molree, December 22, 1990; children: Ashley, Chloe. *Education:* Malone College, B.A., 1987. *Religion:* Presbyterian. *Hobbies and other interests:* Travel, flying, reading, skeet and sporting clay shooting, running, college football.

ADDRESSES: Home—P.O. Box 37, Granger, IN 46530-0037. *Agent*—Catlin Hale, Cat Design Talent Division, 11915 River Dr., Michawaka, IN 46565. *E-mail*—jetbooks@flightline.com.

CAREER: Delta Air Lines, Atlanta, GA, airline pilot and first officer, 1997—. *Military service:* Michigan Air National Guard, navigator with 171st Fighter Interceptor Squadron, 1986-90.

WRITINGS:

On Fulcrum's Wings (novel), iUniverse/Writer's Club Press, 2000.

Contributor to magazines and newspapers.

WORK IN PROGRESS: Aviation and sports fiction.

SIDELIGHTS: Mark A. Werkema told *CA:* "My primary motivation for writing is personal expression, the challenge of producing 'good writing' and relating the experiences of flying to the reader. I want to provide insightful, realistic views through the power of a well-told story. My inspiration comes from personal experiences in my aviation career and from an affection for aviation history, flying subjects, and aeronautical topics."

*　　*　　*

WESTCOTT, Rich

PERSONAL: Male. *Education:* Drexel University, B.S.; Johns Hopkins University, M.A.

ADDRESSES: Home—119 Summit Rd., Springfield, PA 19064.

CAREER: Writer, editor, and publisher, c. 1960—. College journalism teacher.

WRITINGS:

Diamond Greats: Profiles and Interviews with SIxty-five of Baseball's History Makers, Meckler Books (Westport, CT), 1988.
(With Frank Bilovsky) *The Phillies Encyclopedia,* Leisure Press (New York, NY), revised edition published as *The New Phillies Encyclopedia,* Temple University Press (Philadelphia, PA), 1993.
Phillies '93: An Incredible Season, photographs by Alan Kravetz, Temple University Press (Philadelphia, PA), 1994.
Masters of the Diamond: Interviews with Players Who Began Their Careers More than Fifty Years Ago, McFarland and Co. (Jefferson, NC), 1994.
Mike Schmidt, Chelsea House Publishers (New York, NY), 1995.
(With Allen Lewis) *Philadelphia's Old Ballparks,* Temple University Press (Philadelphia, PA), 1996.
Splendor on the Diamond: Interviews with Thirty-five Stars of Baseball's Past, University Press of Florida (Gainesville, FL), 2000.

(With Allen Lewis) *No-Hitters: The 225 Games, 1893-1999,* McFarland and Co. (Jefferson, NC), 2000.

Great Home Runs of the Twentieth Century, Temple University Press (Philadelphia, PA), 2001.

(With Edward G. Rendell) *A Century of Philadelphia Sports,* Temple University Press (Philadelphia, PA), 2001.

Winningest Pitchers: Baseball's 300-Game Winners, Temple University Press (Philadelphia, PA), 2002.

Also author of *A Century of Phillies Baseball,* Philadelphia Phillies (Philadelphia, PA). Contributor to magazines and newspapers.

*   *   *

WHALEN, Philip (Glenn) 1923-2002
(Zenshin Ryufu)

OBITUARY NOTICE—See index for *CA* sketch: Born October 20, 1923, in Portland, OR; died June 26, 2002, in San Francisco, CA. Monk, poet, and author. Whalen earned a lasting place among the poets of the Beat generation whose work kindled a historic poetry renaissance in San Francisco in the 1950s. A compatriot of and sometimes mentor to the likes of Allen Ginsburg, Gary Snyder, Gregory Corso, and Jack Kerouac, Whalen created a voice that critics lauded as uniquely his own. Admirers cited in particular Whalen's ability to blend the principles of eastern spirituality with the earthly pleasures of everyday life and to express himself with a freedom that belied the discipline with which he approached his muse. He was described as a modest man who eschewed the celebrity of an academic poet in favor of a life of contemplation; he wrote, not for the critics, but for his own fulfillment. After spending several years in Japan, during which he produced the bulk of his published work, Whalen was ordained a Zen Buddhist priest in 1973. Taking the name Zenshin Ryufu, he served as a monk in the San Francisco area, including a term as abbot of the Hartford Street Zen Center. Whalen wrote nearly two dozen books, including a few novels, but it is for his poetry that he will be remembered. Selected titles include *Memoirs of an Interglacial Age, Like I Say, On Bear's Head, The Kindness of Strangers: Poems, 1969-1974, Canoeing up Cabarga Creek: Buddhist Poems, 1955-1986,* and *Overtime: Selected Poems.* For the originality and experimental nature of his

work, Whalen received the Morton Dauwen Zabel Award of the American Academy and Institute of Arts and Letters in 1985.

OBITUARIES AND OTHER SOURCES:

PERIODICALS

Independent (London, England), July 2, 2002, obituary by Tom Raworth, p. 16.

Los Angeles Times, June 28, 2002, obituary by Tony Perry, p. B13.

New York Times, July 2, 2002, p. C18.

San Francisco Chronicle, June 27, 2002, obituary by Heidi Benson, p. A19.

Washington Post, June 29, 2002, p. B6.

*   *   *

WIESNER, David 1956-

PERSONAL: Surname is pronounced "*weez*-ner"; born February 5, 1956, in Bridgewater, NJ; son of George (a research manager at a chemical plant) and Julia (a homemaker; maiden name, Collins) Wiesner; married Kim Kahng (a surgeon), May 21, 1983; children: Kevin, Jaime. *Education:* Rhode Island School of Design, B.F.A., 1978.

ADDRESSES: Home—Milwaukee, WI. *Agent*—c/o Clarion Books, 215 Park Ave., S., New York, NY 10003.

CAREER: Author and illustrator of children's books. Has appeared as a guest on the *Today* show, NBC-TV, 1992. *Exhibitions:* Wiesner's paintings have been displayed in the Metropolitan Museum of Art, New York, NY, 1982, as well as in various galleries, including Master Eagle Gallery, New York, NY, 1980-89, Academy of Natural Sciences, Philadelphia, PA, 1986—(permanent exhibit), Museum of Art at Rhode Island School of Design, Providence, RI, 1989, Brooklyn Public Library, Brooklyn, NY, 1990, Muscarele Museum of Art, College of William and Mary, Williamsburg, VA, 1990, Society of Illustrators, New York, NY, 1991 and 1992, and Greenwich Public Library, Greenwich, CT.

AWARDS, HONORS: Children's Picturebook Award, *Redbook* magazine, 1987, for *The Loathsome Dragon;* Caldecott Honor Book citation, American Library Association (ALA), 1989, for *Free Fall;* Pick of the Lists citation, American Booksellers Association, 1990, for *Hurricane;* Notable Children's Book citation, ALA, Reviewer's Choice citation, *Sesame Street Parents' Guide,* "Ten Best Books of 1991" citation, *Parenting* Magazine, and Pick of the Lists citation, American Booksellers Association, all 1991, and Caldecott Medal, ALA, 1992, all for *Tuesday;* Parent's Choice citation, 1992, for *June 29, 1999;* Caldecott Medal, ALA, 2002, for *The Three Pigs.*

WRITINGS:

SELF-ILLUSTRATED PICTURE BOOKS

(Reteller, with wife, Kim Kahng) *The Loathsome Dragon,* Putnam (New York, NY), 1987.
Free Fall, Lothrop (New York, NY), 1988.
Hurricane, Clarion Books (New York, NY), 1990.
Tuesday, Clarion Books (New York, NY), 1991.
June 29, 1999, Clarion Books (New York, NY), 1992.
Sector 7, Clarion Books (New York, NY), 1999.
The Three Pigs, Clarion Books (New York, NY), 2001.

ILLUSTRATOR

Gloria Skurzynski, *Honest Andrew,* Harcourt (New York, NY), 1980.
Avi, *Man from the Sky,* Knopf (New York, NY), 1980.
Nancy Luenn, *The Ugly Princess,* Little, Brown (Boston, MA), 1981.
David R. Collins, *The One Bad Thing about Birthdays,* Harcourt (New York, NY), 1981.
Jane Yolen, *The Boy Who Spoke Chimp,* Knopf (New York, NY), 1981.
Jane Yolen, *Neptune Rising: Songs and Tales of the Undersea Folk,* Philomel (New York, NY), 1982.
Mike Thaler, *Owly,* Harper (New York, NY), 1982.
Vera Chapman, *Miranty and the Alchemist,* Avon (New York, NY), 1983.
Allan W. Eckert, *The Dark Green Tunnel,* Little, Brown (Boston, MA), 1984.
William Kotzwinkle, *E. T.: The Storybook of the Green Planet* (based on a story by Steven Spielberg), Putnam (New York, NY), 1985.

Allan W. Eckert, *The Wand: The Return to Mesmeria,* Little, Brown (Boston, MA), 1985.
Dennis Haseley, *Kite Flier,* Four Winds Press (New York, NY), 1986.
Nancy Willard, *Firebrat,* Knopf (New York, NY), 1988.
Marianna Mayer, reteller, *The Sorcerer's Apprentice: A Greek Fable,* Bantam (New York, NY), 1989.
Laurence Yep, *The Rainbow People,* HarperCollins (New York, NY), 1989.
Laurence Yep, reteller, *Tongues of Jade* (Chinese American folk tales), HarperCollins (New York, NY), 1991.
Eve Bunting, *Night of the Gargoyles,* Houghton (Boston, MA), 1994.

ADAPTATIONS: Free Fall has been adapted into a videocassette with teacher's guide, distributed by American School Publications, 1990; *Tuesday* has also been adapted into a videocassette, distributed by American School Publications, 1992.

SIDELIGHTS: "I create books I think I would have liked to have seen when I was a kid," David Wiesner once told *CA.* "I loved being able to get lost in paintings and to get involved in all the details." Winner of the 1992 Caldecott Medal for his picture book *Tuesday* and the 2002 Caldecott Medal for *The Three Pigs,* Wiesner combines his imaginative powers with his talent for illustration, producing award-winning works like *Free Fall, Hurricane,* and *The Loathsome Dragon.* He was born into a creatively inclined family—art and music number among his sibling's interests—and grew up in an environment that encouraged his own flair for drawing. "I never had the sense that I had to rebel at home so my parents would let me be an artist," he recalled in his interview. "They made my love of drawing seem like something natural—I thought it was the norm." Eventually, his love of drawing fused with his fascination for storytelling, and he found his niche in children's literature, particularly in picture books. He works primarily in watercolors, and expresses his passion for creativity in humorous and inventive tales. "What I really find interesting is that opportunity to take a normal, everyday situation and somehow turn it on its end, or slightly shift it. I love to introduce a 'what if?,' or juxtapose things that aren't normally together. Those just happen to be the kind of ideas I generate."

Born in 1956 to George and Julia Wiesner, David found the diverse landscape of his Bridgewater, New

Jersey, hometown well-suited to his active imagination. Making use of the local cemetery, the river that bordered it (which neighborhood kids called a swamp), the nearby woods, and the town dump, Wiesner and his friends concocted all sorts of games, among which "army" was a particular favorite. "We had very specific rules when we played army," Wiesner once recalled, "that said if you were chasing someone and came to a road in the cemetery (which was to us a river), you had to shuffle your feet and hold your hands over your head to keep your gun dry (which was usually a stick). As soon as you got to the other side you could run again because you'd be on dry land." Ordinary objects were also transformed by the young Wiesner's creativity: wire hangers and plastic bags formed homemade hot-air balloons for a pastime called UFO, and a tree and some sticks made wonderful tree forts. "There was that constant ability to transform the everyday world into the pretend. We continually reinvented the world around us when we played."

Even though neighborhood companions in Bridgewater were in abundance, Wiesner enjoyed spending long stretches of time by himself, so much so, he laughingly admitted, that "there were times my parents were probably worried that, somehow, I didn't have any friends." During these periods of solitude, Wiesner often found himself drawing. "Art has always been a part of my life. I can't pinpoint the exact time when I began drawing; it was something I was always doing, and it became part of how I was perceived. It also defined my personality to a certain extent: clearly when relatives were aware of my interest in art, I would get various art supplies on Christmas and birthdays, and a lot of hand-me-downs—boxes of pastels, watercolors—from Carol, my oldest sister, and George, my brother, who are both pretty artistically inclined. I loved to watch them draw things."

Wiesner's penchant for drawing was fueled further by a television show he watched when he was about six or seven years old. Hosted by artist Jon Gnagy and originally aired in the late 1940s, *You Are an Artist* marked one of TV's first forays into instructional programming. Wiesner, who caught the telecast in reruns, was fascinated with Gnagy's work, particularly with the artist's attention to perspective, light, and scale. The youngster bought Gnagy's instruction books and earnestly practiced drawing all the pictures first in charcoal, then in color. "The books and program probably provided my first formal exposure to techniques

and ideas about drawing," Wiesner recalled for *CA*. "Gnagy could stand there and in fifteen or twenty minutes turn out these drawings. I thought it was just miraculous. I still keep a framed picture of him on my wall."

By junior high school Wiesner had discovered the Renaissance and Surrealism, two creative movements that helped shape his artistic style. The Renaissance artists of the late fifteenth and early sixteenth centuries appealed to the youngster because of their sensitivity to space and perspective. He found himself particularly enchanted by the works of Michelangelo, Leonardo da Vinci, Albrecht Duerer, and Pieter Brueghel the Elder—"the real draftsmen," he declared in an interview for *Clarion News*. "I could sit and look at those paintings for hours. There was so much happening in them, from the foreground back to the very, very far distance. You could follow things back to deep space." Surrealism, a twentieth-century art movement committed to the distorted portrayal of reality, also captured Wiesner's attention. "When I finally came across the surrealists," he once observed, "it was like all hell broke loose—not only because they were painting with a similar quality that I saw in the Renaissance painters, but because the subject matter was just unbelievable. I really responded to it. Conceptually, I was really taken with the imagery, the bizarreness, that other-worldliness, that weirdness—it was really very appealing."

That love of the fantastic found its way into Wiesner's creative outlets throughout his teenage years. Horror movies and sci-fi films provided favorite forms of entertainment, and one film in particular, Stanley Kubrick's *2001: A Space Odyssey,* even helped inspire his enthusiasm for wordless storytelling. "I remember going to see *2001* in 1968," Wiesner recalled in *Clarion News.* "I don't want to be too dramatic, but I remember coming out of the theater a changed person. It was unlike anything I'd ever seen. It's almost a silent film; there's very little dialogue. It's all pictures, which tell a remarkably complex story and set of ideas, up there for the viewer to decipher."

Drawing continued to engage Wiesner's interest throughout high school, and he especially enjoyed sketching "sort of odd subjects," he once recalled. "I would conjure up images that usually got some very strange responses. It was really a direct response to the surrealist work that I saw—lots of weird, creepy, floating and flying things which have always been part of the work I do." His own anti-hero super-hero creation, Slop the Wonderpig, grew out of his love of comic books, and his own film, *The Saga of Butchula,* about a milquetoast-turned-vampire who avenges an attack by young thugs, grew out of his desire to experiment with the storytelling process. "Showing *Butchula* at the senior talent show at Bridgewater Raritan East was one of the high points of high school," Wiesner exclaimed, "because the audience reacted at all the right points. I experienced this incredible feeling. It was great!"

High school provided Wiesner with one other strong creative influence: his art teacher Robert Bernabe. "In Mr. Bernabe I finally found someone I could talk to about art," Wiesner told *CA*. "He essentially encouraged me to follow whatever inclinations I had and was willing to do what he could to facilitate that. This was the first time something like that had happened. He became a sort of confidant for me—I think that to a large degree art is this very personal thing, and Mr. Bernabe was someone with whom I could share my work. He didn't so much influence the projects I was pursuing as he provided me with a sense of encouragement."

However strong his interest in art, Wiesner scarcely entertained the idea of turning his craft into a career until a student from the Rhode Island School of Design (RISD; pronounced "*riz*-dee") visited his art class. "He gave this presentation to the class," Wiesner said, "and brought along these eight millimeter films of some of the projects he had completed at RISD—interactive sorts of things that were set up in the middle of school. He brought some little contraptions he had made as well as a commercial he had developed for one of his classes. I was just amazed at all the wonderfully creative stuff. I thought, 'Here's a place where everybody is doing art all the time, as opposed to once a week,' and it finally dawned on me that I could actually keep doing this and go to school and study it and make this my living. I kept expecting someone to say, 'okay, now you have to figure out what you want to do before you go to college for four years.' It finally became clear that I could in fact be an artist."

With encouragement from his parents, Wiesner applied to five art schools in 1973, including New York's Pratt Institute, the Philadelphia College of Art, the Cleveland Institute of Art, and RISD. Accepted by all five, there was no question as to which one he would attend: "I was totally ready for RISD and ready to immerse myself in what the school had to offer," Wiesner said. The aspiring artist was greeted with a "pretty intense first year"—one in which he had unlearn many old habits and absorb new ideas and ways of thinking about art. "I remember going to my life-drawing class and noticing that while the teacher didn't really respond to my work, he would look at another student's work and say, 'this is really terrific,' or something like that. I would look at the same work and wonder, 'why is he saying that? He doesn't understand.' Yet by the end of the year I was able to look at that same work and realize 'that's great stuff.' RISD helped me reorient myself and helped me get rid of some of my preconceived notions."

In short, though Wiesner's experience at RISD was an active one, it was hardly a painful one. In fact, when asked to describe just one highlight he recalls from the school, he was at a loss for words; there were too many, he explained. However, one project does stand out in his memory with particular fondness. The assignment was simply the word "metamorphosis"—a vague suggestion that Wiesner finds challenging; a ten-foot-long, forty-inch-tall painting was the result. "I had this big piece of paper I'd been waiting to use," Wiesner once explained, "and I started to play around with these images that began to change and metamorphosize. I suppose it also relates to Dutch artist M. C. Escher (whose work I admire), who tended to focus on flat, graphic objects that shift and change from one to the other. I began the painting with images of oranges, then drew the orange sections falling away and turning into sailing ships. The ground then turned into water, and the ships changed and mutated into giant fish swimming out in the ocean. When I finished I knew I was on to something—the response in class was really good and I just kept thinking about it. Clearly there was more I could do with this."

The thought of expanding the painting into a narrative—either with words or without—fascinated Wiesner, and his assignments at RISD began to reflect this interest. At first he directed his talent toward adult-fantasy, short, wordless sequences done in oils. As he gained experience, he began developing his own style, primarily using watercolors, and experimenting with characters, settings, and story lines of a lengthier nature. By his senior year he completed a forty-page wordless picture book for adults based on the short story "Gonna Roll the Bones" by science fiction author Fritz Leiber. "The idea of wordless storytelling was really appealing to me," Wiesner once commented. "I was learning how to compress information as well as how to convey that information visually."

As graduation loomed, Wiesner tossed around the idea of working as an illustrator in some kind of published format, possibly for adult fantasy magazines. Pursuing a career in children's literature hardly crossed his mind. "If you looked at the work I was doing, though," he admitted to *CA,* "it was obvious I should be going into children's books." Evidently Lester Abrams, one of his instructors at RISD, thought the same thing, for he encouraged his pupil to show his work to noted children's author and illustrator (and later Caldecott Medalist) Trina Schart Hyman, who happened to be speaking at RISD. Hyman, who in 1978 was the art director for *Cricket,* a children's magazine recognized for its exceptional illustrations, took one look at Wiesner's work and promptly offered the young artist a magazine cover. Wiesner was both surprised and pleased to discover an audience for his work in children's literature. "I realized," he once said, "that there really is this remarkable range in children's literature open to very different personal visions of books. Not all illustrations are fuzzy bunnies and little cute things."

In children's literature Wiesner found his artistic niche. After graduating with his bachelor of fine arts in illustration in the spring of that same year, he procured work illustrating textbooks, which allowed him to compile a professional portfolio and compelled him to work under a variety of constraints involving size, medium, and content. "It's funny," he once noted. "One of the harder things to resolve coming out of school was moving from a situation in which I wasn't working with too many restrictions into an environment where someone would say, 'Okay, down here in these couple inches along the bottom and maybe partly up the side we want to see Robin Hood, his band of men, the archery contest, the bleachers in the back, the king, and the sheriff of Nottingham.' It's a very difficult thing to adapt to without losing some of your spontaneity. It took me a while to reconcile these different ways of working. Early on, it was somewhat intimidating."

Intimidating or not, Wiesner persevered, and in 1980 secured contracts (with the help of agent Dilys Evans) to illustrate two children's books: Gloria Skurzynski's

Honest Andrew and Avi's *Man from the Sky.* By this time he had moved to New York City with Kim Kahng, who would later become his wife, and during the next few years he kept busy illustrating a variety of children's books. He also used the time to experiment with and fine-tune his own technique and form. At first, as he candidly admitted, his work appeared a bit unpolished—due in part to his inexperience in the field and in part to having to work with preseparated art, in which color is added only at the printing stage. However, with experience came the development of his own distinctive style as well as the ever-increasing desire to pursue his own book ideas. (The idea for *Free Fall,* inspired by the ten-foot long painting he had completed at RISD, was already forming in his mind.) However, in 1983 his career was unexpectedly put on hold. The apartment building housing himself and his wife, Kahng, burned to the ground, destroying everything the newly married couple owned.

By the time the Wiesners rebuilt their lives, David faced pressing deadlines for illustrations that had been contracted for a year or two years down the road. Consequently, he was compelled to work on *Free Fall* only in pieces—he would complete a picture or two for the book, then be forced to stop and work on other titles. The pattern continued throughout the 1980s, during which time he illustrated such works as William Kotzwinkle's *E. T.: The Storybook of the Green Planet,* Allan W. Eckert's *Wand: The Return to Mesmeria,* and Dennis Haseley's *Kite Flier.* In 1987 he tackled another self-illustrated project—*The Loathsome Dragon,* retold with Kahng and based on the English fairy tale *The Laidly Worm of Spindleston Huegh.* The narrative relates the story of the beautiful Princess Margaret, who becomes trapped inside the body of an enormous dragon through the sorcery of her evil, jealous stepmother. Only three kisses from Margaret's brother, Childe Wynd, who is traveling in a far-off land, will free the princess from the spell. Wiesner captured *The Loathsome Dragon's* medieval setting with double-page watercolor paintings, which portray detailed landscapes and seascapes, sprawling castles, elaborate robes, jewelry, and armor, and the frightful, yet gentle dragon. Reviewers applauded Wiesner's carefully crafted and attractive scenes as well as his regard for historical accuracy. Wiesner's artwork is "delicate, misty, and enchanting, extending and harmonizing with the traditional motifs of this fairy tale," noted *School Library Journal* contributor Constance A. Mellon. Perhaps the most flattering remarks came from 1991 Caldecott Medalist and RISD department head David Macaulay, who wrote in *Horn Book:* "Take a look at the watercolor landscapes [*The Loathsome Dragon*] contains and tell me you don't see a little Da Vinci in there."

By the time *The Loathsome Dragon* was completed, Wiesner was at the point of finishing *Free Fall.* "It had taken me longer than I had hoped to get to the point of completing *Free Fall,*" he once observed, "and the breaks in working on it were hard. But it was better than rushing it. Throughout that time I was focusing on the RISD assignment about metamorphosis—the continuous picture that tells a story. It was when I came up with the idea of the dream, using sleeping and then waking as a framework, that *Free Fall* really began to come together and make sense. The structure of the dream afforded me the opportunity to have the book be less a strict narrative and more a sort of free floating imagery—more impressionistic than a straight storyline."

Released in 1988, *Free Fall* is an imaginative, wordless picture book that follows a young boy through the fantastic journey he experiences during one of his dreams. Featuring images that continually transform into other images, the narrative opens as the youngster falls asleep while studying a book of maps. Reality fades as his bedspread metamorphosizes into a landscape, and he is transported along with exotic companions onto a chessboard with live pieces, to a medieval castle housing knights and a dragon, to rocky cliffs that merge into a city skyline, and to a larger-than-life breakfast table. Finally he floats among swans, fishes, and leaves back to his starting place. Especially characteristic of Wiesner's creative ingenuity are the many events and characters the young boy encounters during his dream; most of them correspond to objects in the youngster's bedroom—from the goldfish next to his bed, to the chess pieces stashed in his nightstand, to the pigeons hovering near his window, to the leaves sketched on his wallpaper.

"When I finished *Free Fall,*" Wiesner emphasized, "I realized that this was the type of work I really wanted to do. A lot of the sample pieces I had shown to publishers were geared toward typical fairy tale/folk tale kind of works, but there were also these other illustrations in the back of my portfolio that were just weird—editors would usually look at them and go 'oh, this is very interesting. . . .' I would ask if they had any manuscripts to fit the drawings, and they'd invari-

ably say 'no.' So I knew that ultimately I would have to invent my own ideas for books. *Free Fall* was the first true expression of the kind of work that I wanted to be doing."

Critical reaction to *Free Fall* was decidedly mixed. On one hand, reviewers admired the author's technical skill, his attention to architectural detail and form, and his visual creativity. The book is "an excellent replication of a dream," decided one *Bulletin of the Center for Children's Books* critic. On the other hand, some commentators found the book too complex to be readily understood by a young audience, and they criticized what they perceived as a murky narrative sequence. "The nameless protagonist's . . . adventures are confusing, complicated, and illogical," assessed Julie Corsaro in *School Library Journal.* Instead of being upset by the critical response to his first book, Wiesner was amused: "I sort of enjoyed the fact that some reviewers got it," he once confessed. "Some of the reviews were absolutely right on and connecting with everything, and others seemed not at all there. It was actually kind of interesting to get that very mixed reaction."

The mixed reaction did not extend to the committee selecting the Caldecott Honor Books in that year, for "the phone rang one Monday morning," Wiesner once related, "and the chair of the committee said they had chosen *Free Fall* as an honor book. I experienced the classic reaction: I was left speechless—I just hung up the phone." After some time passed, Wiesner was able to verbalize his reaction: "Having *Free Fall* named a Caldecott Honor Book was a wonderful confirmation that 'yes, this does seem to be the way to go.' It felt really, really satisfying because all along I had the feeling I had been going in the right direction with the pieces I had done and conceived on my own. It was really encouraging that they [the committee] chose a work that isn't in the strict mold of the usual picture book—one that was even perceived by a lot of reviewers as difficult and something that kids wouldn't even relate to."

Wiesner's next book was based on a real incident from his childhood, when a storm toppled over a tree in his neighborhood. *Hurricane* opens with the artist's "detailed, exquisitely rendered paintings [which] draw the reader into his story of a hurricane's progress," as a *Publishers Weekly* reviewer described it. After the storm, two young boys (named David and George, just like Wiesner and his brother) create exotic imaginative landscapes using a tree that was downed by the hurricane. Each adventure is anticipated by the wallpaper pattern in the brothers' bedroom—details that Wiesner drew from his own childhood memories— and each painting also features the cat that was a childhood pet. "The child-focused, low perspective gives even ordinary scenes an extra measure of drama," Patricia Dooley observed in *School Library Journal,* "and the fantasy spreads are detailed delights."

The same year *Free Fall* was named an honor book, Wiesner was asked by *Cricket* to design an cover (ironically, ten years from the time he illustrated his first *Cricket* cover). Given the artistic freedom to draw whatever he wished—the folks at *Cricket* told him only that the March issue would feature articles on St. Patrick's Day, frogs, and the like—Wiesner responded enthusiastically. "St. Patrick's Day didn't strike a chord—but frogs, they had potential," he said in his Caldecott acceptance speech, as reprinted in *Horn Book.* "I got out my sketchbook and some old *National Geographic*s for reference. Frogs were great fun to draw—soft, round, lumpy, and really goofy-looking. But what could I do with them?" The rhetorical question was no sooner asked by Wiesner, than it was answered. As he once recalled: "I envisioned a frog on a lily pad, which reminded me of a flying saucer in a 1950s B movie. As soon as I saw that frog on the lily pad fly, the cover was pretty much right there—this whole bunch of frogs flying out of the swamp."

But a simple cover didn't satisfy the storyteller in Wiesner, who was already envisioning a narrative featuring the frogs. "I was sitting in an airplane, looking through my sketchbook," he continued in his Caldecott acceptance speech, "and I thought, Okay, if I were a frog, and I had discovered I could fly, where would I go? What would I do? Images quickly began to appear to me, and for fear of losing them I hastily scribbled barely legible shapes onto the page: a startled man at a kitchen table; a terrified dog under attack; a roomful of frogs bathed in the glow of a television. A chronology began to take shape, and within an hour I had worked out a complete layout, which remained essentially unchanged through to the finished book. Everything was there: the story, the use of the panels, the times of day, and the title." *Tuesday,* Wiesner's almost wordless 1991 picture book, was created.

Winner of the 1992 Caldecott Medal, *Tuesday* is a whimsical tale about a night when a crowd of frogs

ascend to the sky on lily pads and soar over the surrounding neighborhood. Zooming past startled birds and an incredulous resident indulging in a late-night snack, the frogs speed through a clothesline (causing some minor entanglements), and spook Rusty, a sizable dog. They even sneak into a living room housing a sleepy elderly lady and watch some television (one member of the assemblage operates the remote control with his spindly tongue). "I really felt good when I finished *Tuesday,*" Wiesner told *CA,* "and the response was immediate from everyone who saw it."

Critics not only hailed the creativity and composition of Wiesner's paintings, but their humor as well. A *Publishers Weekly* critic termed the illustrations "stunning . . . and executed with a seeming flawless command of palette and perspective." "What saves this book from simply being a gorgeous gallery of paintings," Roger Sutton explained in *Bulletin of the Center for Children's Books,* "is its warmth and humor: these frogs are having a lot of fun." Carolyn Phelan likewise noted the humor of the illustrations, writing in *Booklist* that "the narrative artwork tells a simple, pleasant story with a consistency and authenticity that make the fantasy convincing." *School Library Journal* contributor Patricia Dooley also praised Wiesner's use of color and perspective, and predicted that "kids will love its lighthearted, meticulously imagined, fun-without-a-moral fantasy."

Despite critical acclaim, winning the Caldecott Medal was something Wiesner hardly imagined. As he once described his reaction: "I couldn't quite really believe it had happened . . . My reaction is hard to explain . . . The Children's Book Council puts out little bookmarks that list all the Caldecott winners back to 1938, and each year they just add the new winner. Looking at that list and seeing my name at the end of it as part of that tradition . . . whatever else happens, that's there forever. It really felt good to be included in that."

Wiesner followed up *Tuesday* with an off-beat tale, 1992's *June 29, 1999.* This amusing, innovative picture book revolves around young Holly Evans, who sends an assortment of vegetable seedlings into the atmosphere as part of a science experiment for school. A little more than a month later, on June 29, 1999—a Tuesday, of course—gigantic rutabagas, avocados, lima beans, artichokes, cucumbers, peas, and all sorts of vegetables begin falling to the earth. Amazement, anxiety, and confusion overcome citizens. In addition, rumors spread ("4000 lb. Radish Has Face of ELVIS!" screams one tabloid headline); business opportunities in real estate flourish ("Gourd Estates" quickly sprouts in North Carolina); and at least one Iowa farmer is ecstatic ("At last, the blue ribbon at the state fair is mine!" he announces upon finding a gargantuan head of cabbage on his property). Critics observed that with this book, Wiesner managed to create a text that matched the wit of his artwork. A *Kirkus Reviews* critic called the "brief tongue-in-cheek text . . . a plus for story time," while Linda Perkins commented in the *New York Times Book Review* that "the succinct story . . . provides just enough background with perfect deadpan wit and even a few alliterative flourishes, and packs a final punch of its own."

While the text earned much praise, it was again Wiesner's artwork that garnered the most glowing comments. "The exquisite watercolors are truly out of this world," Luann Toth remarked in *School Library Journal,* pointing out the artist's use of "unusual perspective" and "clever detail." As Perkins explained, "Wiesner's real strength is vivid, innovative illustration," and his "sly details" add greatly to the book's humor. "Wiesner's dry humor, irony and artistic wizardry have been masterfully marshaled into a visual and literary feast," a *Publishers Weekly* reviewer similarly noted, concluding: "Spectacular to look at, great fun to read—it is, in sum, executed with consummate skill."

Odd metamorphoses are again evident in *Sector 7,* a wordless book that follows an imaginative young boy from a visit to the Empire State Building to a tour of the celestial cloud factory known as Sector 7. "The illustrations . . .," wrote a *Horn Book* reviewer, "are startlingly and powerfully conceived, the fanciful cloud-shapes both funny and elegant." A *Publishers Weekly* contributor lauded the book as a glimpse into "an ingenious world of nearly unlimited possibilities," adding that Wiesner's paintings "contain such a wealth of details that they reveal new discoveries even after repeated examinations."

In *The Three Pigs,* Wiesner brings such visual inventiveness to the classic tale that *Booklist* critic Gillian Engberg described it as a "post-modern fantasy" that "deliciously reinvents the pigs' tale [and] invites readers to step beyond the boundaries of story and picture book altogether." Instead of adhering to the traditional narrative in which the wolf blows down the pig's straw house, for example, Wiesner makes his wolf blow the pig right out of the picture; soon the other pigs escape as well, capering through flying pages of text and discovering story-book "planets." Finally, they put the pages of their own story back together, returning to a world in which they outwit the still-waiting wolf. "Wiesner has created a funny, wildly imagined tale that encourages kids to leap beyond the familiar," wrote Engberg, "to think critically about conventional stories and illustration, and perhaps to flex their imaginations and create wonderfully subversive versions of their own stories."

In early 2002, Wiesner received another call from the Caldecott Medal committee, this time informing him that with *The Three Pigs,* he again won the highest honor for children's picture books in the United States. He admitted in his 2002 acceptance speech published in *Horn Book* that when he first received word that *Tuesday* was a Caldecott Medalist, he was alone in his studio, and "after a flurry of phone calls I . . . went to work." However, with two young children in the family, news of the second award found a more receptive audience. According to Wiesner, his wife and children celebrated the honor, "chanting 'Daddy won the Caldecott! Daddy won the Caldecott!' Being able to share that moment with my family has been the best part of this experience."

Wiesner continued to collaborate with writers during the 1990s as well, earning favorable notice for his illustrations for Eve Bunting's story *Night of the Gargoyles.* This oddly macabre tale of stone gargoyles at play while the city sleeps is interpreted by Wiesner with a surreal sense of whimsy. The illustrator's charcoal pictures "capture the huge heaviness of the stone figures and their gloomy malevolence," wrote reviewer Hazel Rochman in *Booklist.* Claiming "if anyone could bring gargoyles to life pictorially, it's Wiesner," *School Library Journal* contributor Julie Cummins applauded the artist's work, saying the illustrations combine to create "a deliciously eerie, spooky scenario."

If there is one common thread running through Wiesner's works, it is that his books are entertaining. "I'm hoping kids have fun when they read my books," he expressed to *CA.* Wiesner has fun creating them—the abundance of innovative, imaginative, and fantastic events and characters in his works attest to that—yet he also enjoys the challenge of expressing his ideas in a visual format. "I have found that wordless picture books are as enriching and as involving as a book with words in it. In a wordless book, each reader really completes the story; there is no author's voice narrating the story. In books like *Free Fall* or *Tuesday,* there is a lot going on there, and you really need to *read* the picture. A reader can't just flip through the book; all the details add up to more fully tell the story. It's exciting to me to develop that visual literacy."

BIOGRAPHICAL AND CRITICAL SOURCES:

BOOKS

Authors of Books for Young People, edited by Martha E. Ward, third edition, Scarecrow Press (Metuchen, NJ), 1990.

Children's Book Illustration and Design, edited by Julie Cummins, Library of Applied Design, PBC International (New York, NY), 1992.

Children's Books and Their Creators, edited by Anita Silvey, Houghton Mifflin (Boston, MA), 1995, pp. 679-680.

Children's Literature Review, Volume 43, Gale (Detroit, MI), 1997, pp. 196-217.

St. James Guide to Children's Writers, 5th edition, St. James Press (Detroit, MI), 1999, pp. 1118-1119.

Wiesner, David, *June 29, 1999,* Clarion Books (New York, NY), 1992.

PERIODICALS

Booklist, May 1, 1991, Carolyn Phelan, review of *Tuesday,* p. 1723; October 1, 1994, Hazel Rochman, review of *Night of the Gargoyles,* p. 331; September 15, 1999, Stephanie Zvirin, review of *Sector 7,* p. 270; May 15, 2001, Gillian Engberg, review of *The Three Pigs,* p. 1761.

Bulletin of the Center for Children's Books, May, 1988, review of *Free Fall,* p. 193; November, 1990, p. 74; May, 1991, Roger Sutton, review of *Tuesday,* p. 231; November, 1992, pp. 93-94.

Horn Book, January-February, 1991, pp. 61-62; January-February, 1992, p. 84; July-August, 1992, David Macaulay, "David Wiesner," pp. 423-428; July-August, 1992, David Wiesner, "Caldecott Acceptance Speech," pp. 416-422; September, 1999, review of *Sector 7,* p. 603; May, 2001, review of *The Three Pigs,* p. 341; July-August, 2002, David Wiesner, "Caldecott Medal Acceptance," p. 393; July-August, 2002, Anita Silvey, "David Wiesner," p. 401.

Instructor, September, 2001, Judy Freeman, review of *The Three Pigs,* p. 26.

Kirkus Reviews, October 1, 1992, review of *June 29, 1999,* p. 1262.

Mosaic (Winnipeg, Manitoba, Canada), June, 2001, Perry Nodelman, "Private Places on Public View: David Wiesner's Picture Books," p. 1.

New York Times Book Review, August, 1988, p. 99; September 25, 1988, p. 51; November 8, 1992, Linda Perkins, "Hocus-Pocus in Ho-Ho-Kus," p. 31; November 21, 1999, Andrew Leonard, review of *Sector 7,* p. 36; May 20, 2001, Sean Kelly, review of *The Three Pigs,* p. 20.

Publishers Weekly, July 25, 1986, pp. 187-188; October 30, 1987, review of *The Loathsome Dragon,* p. 70; May 12, 1989, p. 294; August 31, 1990, review of *Hurricane,* p. 66; March 1, 1991, review of *Tuesday,* p. 73; September 20, 1991, p. 134; October 26, 1992, review of *June 29, 1999,* p. 69; August 8, 1994, p. 436; August 31, 1999, review of *Sector 7,* p. 83; November 1, 1999, review of *Sector 7,* p. 57; November 22, 1999, Cindi Di Marzo, interview with David Wiesner, p. 22; February 26, 2001, review of *The Three Pigs,* p. 86.

School Library Journal, January, 1986, p. 66; November, 1986, p. 78; March, 1988, Constance A. Mellon, review of *The Loathsome Dragon,* p. 178; June-July, 1988, Julie Corsaro, review of *Free Fall,* p. 95; August, 1988, p. 99; May, 1990, pp. 107-108; October, 1990, Patricia Dooley, review of *Hurricane,* p. 104; December, 1990, p. 25; January, 1991, p. 56; May, 1991, Patricia Dooley, review of *Tuesday,* p. 86; December, 1991, p. 132; November, 1992, Luann Toth, review of *June 29, 1999,* p. 81; October, 1994, Julie Cummins, review of *Night of the Gargoyles,* p. 86; September, 1999, Julie Cummins, review of *Sector 7,* p. 209; April, 2001, Wendy Lukehart, review of *The Three Pigs,* p. 26.

OTHER

Clarionews, spring, 1992, "An Interview with David Wiesner."

David Wiesner Web Site, http://www.houghtonmifflin books.com/ (March 22, 2003).

WISNEWSKI, David 1953-2002

OBITUARY NOTICE—See index for *CA* sketch: Born March 21, 1953, at South Ruislip Air Force Base, Middlesex, England; died September 11, 2002, in Alexandria, VA. Illustrator, puppeteer, clown, and author. Wisnewski won acclaim as an illustrator of children's books using a cut-paper technique. After briefly attending the University of Maryland at College Park, he gave in to his love for the theatrical by enrolling in the Ringling Brothers and Barnum & Bailey Clown College. He worked as a clown for several years before finding a job as a puppeteer with the Maryland National Capital Park Planning Commission. With his wife, Wisnewski founded the Clarion Shadow Theatre in Laurel, Maryland, in 1980, and in 1987 he became vice president of Clarion Graphics. Wisnewski began illustrating children's books in the late-1980s, and his first published work was *The Warrior and the Wise Man* (1989). At first, his illustrations were completely comprised of black cut-outs that were similar to the shadow puppets he and his wife had used, but in later works he added more colors and details to his art. He won awards for his books *Elfwyn's Saga* (1990) and *The Wave of the Sea-Wolf* (1994), culminating in a Caldecott Medal for *Golem* (1996). His more recent works, including *The Secret Knowledge of Grown-Ups* (1998) and *Tough Cookie* (1999), were more light-hearted than his early books, which were often based on old epic tales and myths. Wisnewski was also the author of *Worlds of Shadow: Teaching with Shadow Puppetry* (1997).

OBITUARIES AND OTHER SOURCES:

BOOKS

St. James Guide to Children's Writers, fifth edition, St. James (Detroit, MI), 1999.
Who's Who in America, 56th edition, Marquis (New Providence, NJ), 2000.

PERIODICALS

New York Times, September 21, 2002, p. A16.

* * *

WITKIN, Joel-Peter 1939-

PERSONAL: Born September 13, 1939, in Brooklyn, NY. *Education:* Cooper Union, B.F.A., 1974; University of New Mexico, M.A., 1976, M.F.A., 1986.

ADDRESSES: Agent—Pace/MacGill, 32 East 57th Street, New York, NY 10022.

CAREER: Independent photographer, 1956—; worked as color photo printer, New York, NY, 1958-61; owner of an artwork photography business, New York, NY, 1964-70; University of New Mexico, Albuquerque, instructor in photography, 1976-81. Visiting lecturer in photography at numerous universities and institutes throughout U.S. beginning 1981. *Military service:* U.S. Army, 1961-64, served as a combat photographer in Texas and Europe.

AWARDS, HONORS: Grants from Creative Artists, 1974, Ford Foundation, 1977, National Endowment for the Arts, 1981, 1986, 1992, American Institute of Graphic Arts, 1986; First Prize, Art/Quest National Photography Competition, 1986; Art Matters Photography Grant, 1986; Chevalier Des Arts et de Lettres, 1990.

WRITINGS:

Joel-Peter Witkin: Forty Photographs (exhibition catalog), San Francisco Museum of Modern Art (San Francisco, CA), 1985.
Gods of Earth and Heaven, Twelvetrees Press (Pasadena, CA), 1989.
Witkin (exhibition catalog), Galerie Baudoin Lebon (Paris, France), 1991.
(Editor) *Harm's Way: Lust & Madness, Murder & Mayhem,* Twin Palms Publishers (Santa Fe, NM), 1994.
(Photographer) *The Bone House,* text by Eugenia Parry, Twin Palms Publishers (Santa Fe, NM), 1998.

Contributor to periodicals, including *Infinity* and *Aura.*

SIDELIGHTS: Joel-Peter Witkin's images of death and mutilation have been called macabre, exploitive, and outrageous. According to one London *Times* critic, reviewing a Witkin exhibit, "It's possible that Witkin's photos are right up your street, but only if your street has been the scene of a multiple pile-up and is littered with legless accident victims and deformed corpses." But that is clearly not the whole story. As an *Times* critic wrote, "The strange case of Joel-Peter Witkin would not be so controversial if his tableaux remained crudely repellent. As it is, the best of them can attain a stillness that is sublime as well as troublesome, as though their function is, through long exposure, to draw the sting of the very nightmares which they have conjured."

Witkin's subjects have included transvestism, bestiality, and necrophilia, often combined with religious iconography and mythological symbolism, an unusual synthesis of shocking images and subtle symbolism. Reviewing *The Bone House* in *Library Journal,* Eric Bryant wrote, "Witkin explains . . . that 'I consider myself a portraitist; not of people, but conditions of being.'" *Harm's Way: Lust & Madness, Murder & Mayhem,* an anthology edited by Witkin, brings together images of murder, pornography, and insanity, ranging from old police photos to newer tabloid images. According to a reviewer in *Afterimage,* "The selection principles go unstated, but they're evident enough, since the pictures have the unmistakable stamp of Witkin's aesthetic. Many of these subjects would surely have found their way into Witkin's photographs, if only they hadn't had the misfortune to die long ago."

Witkin himself has commented on his photos, "I make this work in the hope that we, or some other form, will see this work as part of the history of a diverse and desperate time."

BIOGRAPHICAL AND CRITICAL SOURCES:

PERIODICALS

Afterimage, summer, 1996, David L. Jacobs, review of *Harm's Way,* p. 8.
Library Journal, April 1, 1999, Eric Bryant, review of *The Bone House,* p. 93.
Times (London, England), March 14, 1998, Alan Franks, "Freakshow: Interview," p. 34; March 24, 1998, Joe Joseph, "Snapshots of an Altogether Different World," p. 51.*

*　　*　　*

WOJCIECHOWSKA, Maia (Teresa) 1927-2002 (Maia Rodman)

OBITUARY NOTICE—See index for *CA* sketch: Born August 7, 1927, in Warsaw, Poland; died after a stroke June 13, 2002, in Long Beach, NJ. Author of books

for young adults. Wojciechowska wrote nineteen books, including *The Hollywood Kid, Tuned Out,* and *Shadow of a Bull,* the last which was translated into eighteen languages and was in its 68th printing by 2000. The necessity of finding one's own identity was a recurring theme in her books, though they also dealt with contemporary teen problems like divorce, suicide, and drug abuse. At age twelve Wojciechowska and her family fled Nazi-occupied Poland for France, then moving to the United States where she and her brothers had difficulty adjusting. After graduating from high school, she attended Immaculate Heart college for a year before leaving in 1946. After her first novel was rejected by more than thirty publishers, she tried her hand at various careers, at one point holding more than seventy jobs during one year. Finally, as an accompaniment to the artwork of Wilson Bigaud, her *Market Day for Ti Andre* was published in 1952 under the name Maia Rodman, launching Wojciechowska's writing career. *Shadow of a Bull,* her next major work, was awarded the Newberry Medal in 1965. The story about a young man torn between fulfilling his village's expectations as a bullfighter or following his own dreams received critical praise. Wojciechowska herself had received training as a bullfighter, and had killed a bull in the ring. Of her subsequent works, *Tuned Out* (1968) was adapted for film and released as *Stoned: An Anti-Drug Film* by Learning Corp. of America in 1981 and her *A Single Light* (1968) was adapted and released by the same company five years later.

OBITUARIES AND OTHER SOURCES:

PERIODICALS

Chicago Tribune, July 4, 2002, section 2, p. 8.
Los Angeles Times, July 1, 2002, p. B9.
New York Times, June 21, 2002, p. A23; June 21, 2002, p. C13.
Record (Bergen County, NJ), June 15, 2002, p. A15.
St. Petersburg Times (St. Petersburg, FL), July 12, 2002, p. 6A.
Washington Post, June 23, 2003, p. C8.

*　　*　　*

WOJDOWSKI, Bogdan 1930-1994

PERSONAL: Born November 16, 1930, in Warsaw, Poland; committed suicide, 1994. *Education:* Clandestine secondary school in Warsaw during Nazi occupation; Secondary Agricultural School, Lubartów;

Electromechanical School in Lublin and school in Karpacz; completed secondary school at Warsaw University, 1954.

CAREER: Novelist and essayist. Reporter, *Wieś* weekly, 1951-54; reporter, columnist, and literary critic for *Przegląd Kulturalny* weekly, 1954-56; primary school teacher in Olsztyn, 1957-58; staff writer and head of theater and film section, *Wspólczesność* biweekly, Warsaw, 1960-65.

MEMBER: Polish Writers Union (ZLP).

AWARDS, HONORS: Kościelski Foundation prize, Geneva, 1964.

WRITINGS:

Chleb rzucony umarlym, Panstwowy Instytut Wydawniczy (Warsaw, Poland), 1978, translation by Madeline G. Levine published as *Bread for the Departed,* Northwestern University Press (Evanston, IL), 1997.
Siedem opowiadań, (Title means "Seven Stories") Panstwowy Instytut Wydawniczy (Warsaw, Poland), 1978.
Wybor opowiadan, Panstwowy Instytut Wydawniczy (Warsaw, Poland), 1981.
Konotop, Czytelnik (Warsaw, Poland), 1982.
Tamta strona, Dolnoslaskie (Wroclaw, Poland: Wydawn), 1997.

SIDELIGHTS: Bogdan Wojdowski, a Polish novelist with a background in journalism and teaching, wrote several books in his native language, publishing his first literary work in 1956. He is known to English-speaking readers for his fictional memoir of life in the Warsaw ghetto during World War II, *Chleb rzucony umarlym,* published in the United States in 1997 as "Bread for the Departed." The bread for which ghetto inhabitants fight daily is the central metaphor. Wojdowski, himself a ghetto survivor, writes a chilling story of how Jews fought for survival there, mostly to no avail. Some critics believe the horrendous ghetto life contributed to Wojdowski's 1994 suicide.

What a *Kirkus Reviews* writer called "this shapeless yet powerful documentary novel" begins when the ghetto is established in 1940 and ends when nearly the entire population of 350,000 is shipped to the Treblinka death camp in 1942. The book is written in ungrammatical Polish (in translation), probably taken directly from the Yiddish that ghetto residents spoke. Abraham Brumberg, in the *New York Times Book Review,* noted Wojdowski's "absence of moral judgment" in his matter-of-fact accounts. In what Brumberg calls Wojdowski's "[playwright Bertolt] Brechtian" mode, many of the young characters have names linking them with a characteristic: Egg Yolk, Five-Fingers Mundek and Chaim the Orphan, for example. Haunting images pervade the novel—a teenager snatching bread from an elderly woman who waited for it all day, children digging up the dead to retrieve gold from their dental work and starving people slicing up a dead horse or finding lice in their watery soup.

As the story ended, the Jews are rounded up and taken to a deportation point. Brumberg wrote, "There is talk about resistance, about acquiring weapons, about reaching the woods near Warsaw and joining partisan groups. Yet true to reality, and true to the spirit of the book, the deportation goes on." Many try to escape, but even their Jewish guards can't avoid the death camp. The German troops discover the young protagonist David and others, sending them to their doom.

Brumberg wrote that Wojdowski won only second prize in a Polish national literary contest when the book first appeared in Polish in 1971, citing its uncompromising portrayal of rampant anti-Semitism. According to Brumberg, Wojdowski paints some characters positively, such as David and his parents, and Dr. Obuchowski, who continues treating those he knew would die. Yet he "depicts his characters' behavior with the detachment of a surgeon performing a disagreeable operation." The *Kirkus Reviews* writer found the novel "deeply flawed" but nevertheless impressed by its "raw, emotional impressionistic scenes." Molly Abramowitz in *Library Journal* said the descriptions in the book were "excruciating," but that they "[add] immeasurably to the canon of Holocaust literature."

BIOGRAPHICAL AND CRITICAL SOURCES:

BOOKS

Juliusz Stroynowski, editor, *Who's Who in the Socialist Countries of Europe,* K.G Saur Publishing, Munich, Germany, 1989.

PERIODICALS

Kirkus Reviews, November 15, 1997, p. 1670.
Library Journal, December, 1997, p. 157.
New York Times Book Review, September 20, 1998, p. 36.*

*   *   *

WOLFF, Maritta M(artin) 1918-2002

OBITUARY NOTICE—See index for CA sketch: Born December 25, 1918, in Grass Lake, MI; died of lung cancer July 1, 2002, in West Los Angeles, CA. Author. Wolff was a best-selling novelist who was highly regarded for her realistic portrayals of the American underclass. A University of Michigan graduate who earned her bachelor's degree in 1940, Wolff wrote her first novel as a college senior. Earning the university's Hopwood Award for Fiction, it was published in 1941 as *Whistle Stop* and praised by Sinclair Lewis as the most important novel of the year. It was later adapted as a 1946 movie starring George Raft and Ava Gardner. Wolff's second novel, *Night Shift* (1942), was also highly praised and became the 1946 film *The Man I Love,* starring Ida Lupino. Although not a prolific author, Wolff was consistently praised for her ability to capture true-to-life, working-class dialogue in stories that sometimes touched on controversial subjects such as incest. She wrote seven novels altogether, including *About Lyddy Thomas* (1947), *Back of Town* (1952), *The Big Nickelodeon* (1956), *Buttonwood* (1962), and one unpublished work. Wolff disappointed her many fans when she stopped writing after arguments with her publisher about edits and her refusal to help promote her fiction.

OBITUARIES AND OTHER SOURCES:

PERIODICALS

Chicago Tribune, July 17, 2002, section 2, p. 8.
Los Angeles Times, July 16, 2002, p. B11.
New York Times, July 14, 2002, p. A27.
Times (London, England), August 7, 2002.
Washington Post, July 17, 2002, p. B6.

WOLK, Lauren 1956-

PERSONAL: Born 1956.

ADDRESSES: Agent—c/o Author Mail, Random House, 299 Park Ave., New York, NY 10171-0002.

CAREER: Nelson Canada, Toronto, Ontario, senior editor.

WRITINGS:

Those Who Favor Fire: A Novel, Random House (New York, NY), 1998.

Contributing editor for children's magazine *Owl.*

SIDELIGHTS: Lauren Wolk impressed critics with her debut novel, a romantic drama called *Those Who Favor Fire.* The book's title is taken from a Robert Frost poem and its setting, with the fictional name Belle Haven, is based on a real Pennsylvania town where uncontrollable, unpredictable fires in underlying coal mining shafts have forced most of the residents to leave the area. Wolk peoples her story with individuals who refuse to flee in the face of this peculiar danger and she imagines what life would be like in such a place.

The novel occurs more than ten years after the fires began. A few residents remain, including Rachel Hearn who has only recently returned to Belle Haven because of the deaths of both her parents in a car accident. Rachel is also leaving college before graduation, fleeing the memory of an abusive encounter with a fraternity member. In her hometown she meets a young man who is simply known as "Joe." He is also trying to escape an unhappy past, namely his wealthy family. Joe has learned that his father has long abused his twin sister. After finding a safe haven for her, Joe adopts a new identity and home in Belle Haven. The two characters are drawn to each and fall in love.

Rachel becomes something of a leader among the locals when a government agent tries to buy out the remaining homeowners. Guilt and grief have tightened the young woman's grasp on the security she finds in her home, even when Joe's trailer is burned and his dog is cruelly killed. Joe builds a nearby community for his neighbors and tries desperately to convince Rachel to leave Belle Haven.

Reviews of *Those Who Favor Fire* found many merits and a few flaws in the debut novel. In *Library Journal*, Starr E. Smith commented that despite some slow intervals the book's combination of romance, danger, and developing friendships "keep the often preposterous but entertaining plot moving along to a satisfying conclusion." *Christian Science Monitor* writer Merle Rubin also praised the author: "Wolk writes clean, well-crafted prose, and she paints an appealing picture of life in a small, close-knit community." However, Rubin found fault in two areas: first, that Wolk sometimes fails to flesh out details such as explaining Joe's father's behavior, and secondly, that Rachel's "pig-headedness becomes downright infuriating."

Booklist's GraceAnne A. DeCandido enjoyed Wolk's picture of small-town life and the relationships between characters, especially Joe and Rachel. "Wolk has made a ravishing love story in this lyrical novel," DeCandido wrote. "The fire scenes are horrific, the eroticism etched in honey and heat, all of the language supple and creamy." A *Publishers Weekly* reviewer commended the book's "engrossing plot" and "appealing characters," and likened Wolk's work to that of Shirley Jackson: "folk elements and environmental caveats combine with a subtle yet unrelenting sense of horror."

BIOGRAPHICAL AND CRITICAL SOURCES:

PERIODICALS

Booklist, January 1, 1999, p. 834.
Christian Science Monitor, February 4, 1999, p. 20.
Library Journal, May 1, 1998, p. 141.
Publishers Weekly, November 2, 1998, p. 70.*

*   *   *

WOODTOR, Dee
See WOODTOR, Delores Parmer

*   *   *

WOODTOR, Dee Parmer
See WOODTOR, Delores Parmer

WOODTOR, Delores Parmer 1945(?)- 2002
(Dee Parmer Woodtor, Dee Woodtor)

OBITUARY NOTICE—See index for *CA* sketch: Born c. 1945, in Greenville, AL; died of stomach cancer, August 6, 2002, in Evanston, IL. Gallery owner, educator, genealogist, and author. In 1982 Woodtor became the co-owner of a gallery called Window to Africa, a name that could be used to describe Woodtor herself. Her original training was in political science, but after earning a doctorate in 1986, Woodtor began teaching at the School of New Learning at De Paul University and at the Newberry Library in Chicago. She devoted much of her remaining time to promoting African culture in America, as a cofounder and program director of the African Festival of the Arts and through her affiliation with the Africa International House. One of the ways in which Woodtor encouraged African Americans to explore their origins was to write genealogy resource materials, such as *Case Studies in Afro-American Genealogy,* which she wrote as "Dee" Woodtor, with David T. Thackery, and *A Place Called Down Home: An African-American Guide to Genealogy and Historical Identity,* which she wrote as "Dee" Parmer Woodtor, and for which she received a book award from the Black Caucus of the American Library Association in 2000. Woodtor also wrote a children's book, *Big Meeting,* which emphasizes the importance of family and identity.

OBITUARIES AND OTHER SOURCES:

PERIODICALS

Chicago Tribune, August 14, 2002, obituary by H. Gregory Meyer, section 2, p. 9.

*   *   *

WOOLDRIDGE, Frosty 1947-

PERSONAL: Born January 26, 1947. *Education:* Michigan State University, 1970. *Politics:* Independent. *Religion:* Religious Science. *Hobbies and other interests:* Bicycling, photography, mountain climbing.

ADDRESSES: Home—1458 Ford Pl., Louisville, CO 80027. *E-mail*—frostyw@juno.com.

CAREER: Author. Worked variously as a college guidance counselor, math and science teacher, truck driver, bartender, dance teacher, ski instructor for the handicapped, cardiac catheterization technician, freelance writer, public speaker, personal trainer, and lifestyle coach. *Military service:* U.S. Army, Medical Service Corps officer during the Vietnam War.

WRITINGS:

The Handbook for Touring Bicyclists (for adults), Chockstone Press (Evergreen, CO), 1996.
Strike Three! Take Your Base (for young adults), illustrated by Pietri Freeman, Brookfield Reader (Sterling, VA), 2001.

Contributor of articles to periodicals; creator of *Alcohol, Drugs, and Unique Alternatives,* drug and alcohol prevention program, and *Closing Fast—A Global Environmental Crisis,* an environmental program.

WORK IN PROGRESS: An Extreme Encounter: Antarctica; Zero Visibility: A Blind Man's Quest for the Summit of Everest; When Your Father Left Too Soon.

SIDELIGHTS: With the varied activities of adventurer, teacher, and writer, Frosty Wooldridge seems to have lived many lifetimes. After serving in the U.S. Army Medical Corps during the Vietnam War, he worked as a college guidance counselor and high school math and science teacher. Over a quarter century, he has bicycled around the world, pedaling some 100,000 miles on six continents. In addition to creating such educational programs as *Alcohol, Drugs, and Unique Alternatives* and *Closing Fast—A Global Environmental Crisis,* Wooldridge has written regularly for newspapers and magazines, such as the *Christian Science Monitor* and *Rocky Mountain News.* He has also published several books in the print media, including the *Handbook for Touring Bicyclists* and *Strike Three! Take Your Base,* for young adult readers.

Wooldridge's first book geared specifically to young readers is the baseball book *Strike Three! Take Your Base.* In this "carefully crafted narrative," to quote Janice C. Hayes of *School Library Journal,* he tells the story of two teenage brothers, Bob and Rex, who

deal very differently with their father's sudden death. According to *Boulder Daily Camera* books editor Clay Evans, the novel is "entertaining," "full of truths," and sends "an especially important message" about the different ways members of the same family grieve.

BIOGRAPHICAL AND CRITICAL SOURCES:

PERIODICALS

School Library Journal, March, 2002, Janice C. Hayes, review of *Strike Three! Take Your Base,* p. 240.

ONLINE

The Daily Camera, http://www.cfapps.bouldernews. com (January 16, 2003), Clay Evans, "Louisville Author's YA Novel Centers on Grief."
Pedaling Adventures, http://www.pedalingadventures. com (November 20, 2002).

*   *   *

WOOLEY, Peter 1934-

PERSONAL: Born December 26, 1934, in East Liverpool, OH; son of Marvin and June (a secretary) Wooley; married October 13, 1956; wife's name, Linda (a singer); children: Stephanie Wooley Angelini, Christopher. *Education:* Kent State University, A.B., 1959. *Politics:* Democrat. *Religion:* Protestant.

*ADDRESSES: Home—*5131 Penfield Ave., Woodland Hills, CA 91364; fax: 818-340-8985. *E-mail—*petergo@earthlink.net.

CAREER: Art director and production designer. Production designer for films, including *Under the Rainbow, Going Home, Second-Hand Hearts, Sounder, Cleopatra Jones, Oh God, You Devil, High Anxiety, Fatso,* and *Blazing Saddles;* production designer for television movies and miniseries, including *The Day After, Blind Rage, Zoya, Murder between Friends, Hart to Hart, Hidden in Silence, Death Pays the Sitter, Her Last Change,* and *Bed of Roses;* art director for television series, including *Missing Persons, Baby Huey's*

Adventures, My World and Welcome to It, and *The Streets of San Francisco;* also worked as television director. University of California—Los Angeles, guest lecturer at film school extension. *Military service:* U.S. Army, 1952-55.

MEMBER: International Art Directors Guild (past member of executive board), Academy of Motion Picture Arts and Sciences, Academy of Television Arts and Sciences.

AWARDS, HONORS: Emmy Award nomination, Academy of Television Arts and Sciences, for *The Day After.*

WRITINGS:

What! And Give up Show Business? A View from the Hollywood Trenches (autobiography), Fithian Press (Santa Barbara, CA), 2001.

Also writer and director of *The Very Last Ride* (documentary film), British Broadcasting Corp.

SIDELIGHTS: Motion picture production designer Peter Wooley admitted to *CA:* "I write out of fear and loathing."

* * *

WOUTERS, Liliane 1930-

PERSONAL: Born February 5, 1930, in Brussels, Belgium. *Education:* Graduated from Gysegen teacher training school, Alost, Belgium.

ADDRESSES: Agent—c/o Editions les Éperonniers, Box 7, rue Picard, B-1000, Brussels, Belgium.

CAREER: Poet and playwright, c. 1954—; teacher.

MEMBER: Académie royale de langue et de littérature françaises de Belgique, Académie européenne de poésie.

AWARDS, HONORS: Nuit de la Poésie jury prize, 1955, for *La marche forcée;* Prix Triennal de Poésie, 1962; Grand Prix de Poésie de la Maison de Poésie, 1989; Prix du Conseil de la Communauté française de Belgique pour théâtre, 1990; Prix Triennal de traduction de la Communauté Flamande, 1992; Prix Montaigne, Fondation Frédéric von Schiller, 1995, for body of work; Prix Quinquénal de la Communauté française, 2000, and Bourse Goncourt de la Poésie, 2001, both for *Le billet de Pascal.*

WRITINGS:

POETRY

La marche forcée (title means "Forced March"), Éditions des Artistes (Brussels, Belgium), 1954.
Le bois sec (title means "Dry Wood"), Gallimard (Paris, France), 1960.
Le Gel (title means "The Thaw"), P. Seghers (Paris, France), 1966.
Chansons et enluminures, Éditions J. Antoine (Brussels, Belgium), 1980.
L'alöes (title means "The Aloe"), Luneau Ascot (Paris, France), 1983.
Parenthèse, Atelier d'Art, Saint Laurent du Pont (Isere, Belgium), 1984.
Journal de scribe, Les Éperonniers (Brussels, Belgium), 1990.
La salle des profs: piece en douze sequences, Éditions Labor (Brussels, Belgium), 1994.
Tous les chemins conduisent à la mer: poèmes, Les Éperonniers (Brussels, Belgium), 1997.
La saveur du pain, Les Éperonniers (Brussels, Belgium), 1998.
Le billet de Pascal, Éditons Phi (Echternach, Luxembourg), 2000.
Les sept portiques du chemin de Paques, Taillis Pre (Chatelineau, Belgium), 2000.

TRANSLATIONS

Belles heures de Flandre, P. Seghers (Paris, France), 1961.
Guido Gezelle, P. Seghers (Paris, France), 1965.
Bréviaire des Pays-Bas: anthologie de la littérature neerlandaise du XIIIe au Xve siècle, Éditions Universitaires (Brussels, Belgium), 1973.

Reynart le Goupil, Renaissane du Livre (Brussels, Belgium), 1973.

Un compagnon pour toutes les saisons, Guido Gezelle, Autres Temps (Marseille, France), 1999.

PLAYS

Oscarine ou les tournesols (title means "Oscarine, or The Sunflowers"), produced in Brussels, Belgium, at Rideau de Bruxelles, 1964.

La porte (title means "The Door"), produced in Liege, Belgium, at Théâtre de la Communaute, 1967.

Vies et morts de Mademoiselle Shakespeare (title means "Life and Death of Miss Shakespeare"), produced in Brussels, Belgium, at Théâtre de l'Esprit Frappeur, 1979.

Celéstine, based on the play by Fernando de Rojas, produced in Brussels, Belgium, at Théâtre Royal du Parc, 1981.

La salle des profs: pièce en douze sequences (produced at Théâtre de l'Esprit Frappeur, 1983), Les Eperonniers (Brussels, Belgium), 1983.

L'équateur (sequel to *Vies et morts de Mademoiselle Shakespeare,)* Les Éperonniers (Brussels, Belgium), 1984, produced at Théâtre de l'Esprit Frappeur, 1986.

Charlotte ou la nuit Mexicaine: pièce en douze sequences (produced at Théâtre de l'Ancre, 1989), Les Éperonniers (Brussels, Belgium), 1989.

Le jour du narval (produced at Théâtre du Grand Midi, 1991), Les Éperonniers (Brussels, Belgium), 1991.

OTHER

(Editor with Alain Bosquet, and contributor) *La Poésie francophone de Belgique: 1903-1926,* Académie Royale de Langue et de Littérature Françaises (Brussels, Belgium), 1992.

(Editor with Alain Bosquet, and contributor) *La Poésie francophone de Belles heures de Flandre: anthologie de la poésie flamande du XIIeme au XVIeme siècle,* Les Éperonniers (Brussels, Belgium), 1997.

Also compiler of *Feux* by Marguerite Yourcenar, Les Éperonniers (Brussels, Belgium).

Poetry represented in anthologies, including *Panorama de la poésie française de Belgique,* Éditions J. Antoine (Brussels, Belgium), 1976; *Terre d'écarts: ecrivains*

français de Belgique, Éditions Universitaires (Brussels, Belgium), 1980; *La poésie francophone de Belgique: 1804-1884,* Éditions Traces (Brussels, Belgium), 1985; *Ça rime et ça rame: anthologie thematique des poétes francophones de Belgique,* Éditions Labor (Brussels, Belgium), 1985; *La Poésie francophone de Belgique: 1885-1900,* Éditions Traces (Brussels, Belgium), 1987; *Belgique: 1928-1962,* Académie Royale de Langue et de Littérature Françaises (Brussels, Belgium), 1992; *Le siècle des femmes: Poésie francophone en Belgique et au Grand-Duche de Luxembourg, XXe siècle,* Les Éperonniers (Brussels, Belgium), 2000.

SIDELIGHTS: Liliane Wouters is an acclaimed poet, playwright, editor, and translator. Her translations of Flemish Medieval and Renaissance literature are noted for their attention to the complexities and subtleties of the original works. Wouters's own poetry also shows the influence of the "mysticism and sensuality of older Flemish literature," according to Donald Friedman in *Encyclopedia of Continental Women Writers.* Her first volume of poetry, *La marche forcée,* includes imagery of quest and pilgrimage. *Le bois sec* contains spatial metaphors, while *L'alöes* has a more sensual atmosphere. "The tensions, dichotomies and melding of spiritual and physical experience," wrote Friedman, "is the dominant thematic of her four expansive volumes of poetry."

Among Wouters's best-known plays is *Vie et mort de Mademoiselle Shakespeare,* which is noted for its skillful blend of irony, humor, and feeling. Her *La salle des profs* is considered a milestone in contemporary Belgian theater.

BIOGRAPHICAL AND CRITICAL SOURCES:

BOOKS

Encyclopedia of Continental Women Writers, Garland Publishing (New York, NY), 1991, p. 1357.

OTHER

La Communauté française de Belgique, http://www.cfwb.be/ (February 21, 2001), "Prix litteraire de la Communaute francaise 2000: Liliane Wouters."*

Y-Z

YOVKOV, Yordan 1880-1937

PERSONAL: Born November 9, 1880, in Zheravna, Bulgaria; died October 15, 1937, in Plovdiv, Bulgaria; son of Stefan Yovkov (a sheep farmer) and Pena Boychova; married Despina Koleva, 1918; children: Elka. *Education:* University of Sofia, law degree program, unfinished.

CAREER: Teacher in Dobrudzha, Bulgaria; Bulgarian Legation, Bucharest, Hungary, translator and press attaché, 1920-27; *La Bulgarie,* Sofia, Bulgaria, editorial board, 1927-29; Sofia press department, 1936-37; Ministry of Foreign Affairs, Sofia, Bulgaria.

AWARDS, HONORS: Kiril and Metodiy Prize for literature (upon recommendation by the Bulgarian Academy of Sciences), 1929.

WRITINGS:

Razkazi (Title means "Short Stories"), 2 volumes, Kniga (Sofia, Bulgaria), 1917.

Zhetvaryat Povest (Title means "The Harvester"), Obrazovanie (Sofia, Bulgaria), 1920, revised edition, Khemus (Sofia, Bulgaria), 1930.

Posledna radost Razkazi (Title means "Last Joy"), Khemus (Sofia, Bulgaria), 1926, republished as *Pesenta na koleletata,* Khemus (Sofia, Bulgaria), 1933.

Staroplaninski legendi (Title means "Legends of Stara Planina"), Khemus (Sofia, Bulgaria), 1927.

Vecheri v Antimovskiya khan (Title means "Evenings at the Antomovo Inn") Zh. Marinov (Sofia, Bulgaria), 1928.

Razkazi (Title means "Short Stories"), 3 volumes, Khemus (Sofia, Bulgaria), 1928, 1929, 1932.

Albena Drama, Khemus (Sofia, Bulgaria), 1930.

Milionerut Komediya (Title means "The Millionaire"), Khemus (Sofia, Bulgaria), 1930.

Boryana Drama, Khemus (Sofia, Bulgaria), 1932.

Chiflikut kray granitsata Roman (Title means "The Farmland at the Frontier"), Khemus (Sofia, Bulgaria), 1934.

Zhensko surtse Razkazi, (Title means "A Woman's Heart") Khemus (Sofia, Bulgaria), 1935.

Ako mozhekha da govoryat Razkazi (Title means "If They Could Speak"), Khemus (Sofia, Bulgaria), 1936.

Obiknoven chovek Drama, (Title means "An Ordinary Man"), Khemus (Sofia, Bulgaria), 1936.

Priklyucheniyata na Gorolomov Roman (Title means "Gorolomov's Adventures") Khemus (Sofia, Bulgaria), 1938.

Subrani suchineniya, 7 volumes, edited by Angel Karaliychev and others, Bulgarski pisatel (Sofia, Bulgaria), 1956.

Subrani suchineniya, 6 volumes, edited by Simeon Sultanov, Bulgarski pisatel (Sofia, Bulgaria), 1970-1973.

EDITIONS IN ENGLISH

The White Swallow and Other Short Stories, translated by Milla Cholakova and Marko Minkov, Ministry of Information and Arts (Sofia, Bulgaria), 1947.

Short Stories, edited by Mercia MacDermott, translated by Minkov and Marguerite Alexieva, Vanous (New York, NY), 1965.

The Inn at Antimovo, and, Legends of Stara Planina, translated by John Burnip, Slavica (Columbus, OH), 1990.

SIDELIGHTS: Yordan Yovkov, an early twentieth-century Bulgarian writer, is known, along with Elin Pelin, as the most important interwar prose writer in Bulgaria. Yovkov rose to the country's literary elite through his stories about the Balkan Wars (1912-13). Over a career that spanned twenty years, Yovkov published seventeen volumes, three posthumously. Charles A. Moser, in the *Encyclopedia of World Literature,* wrote, "In a literature that has always been strongest in the shorter genres, [Yovkov] stands as the supreme master of the short story."

Yovkov, raised in Bulgaria's Sliven district, was the fifth child in his family. He finished high school in Sofia in 1900, and then started teaching in Dolen Izvor, but was drafted and then attended a school for reserve officers in Knyazhevo. In these two years, 1902 to 1904, Yovkov began writing poetry. He was first published in the journal *Suznanie,* in which his 1902 poem "Pod tezhkiya krust" (Under the Heavy Cross), appeared. After leaving the military, he started a degree study in law at the University of Sofia, but financial hardship forced his withdrawal.

Yovkov resumed teaching in 1904, working for a school in village near Dobruja, where he published some short stories. Only one of these, "Ovcharova zhalba" (A Shepherd's Grief) appeared in a later collection of his work, entitled *Staroplaninski legendi.*

Yovkov was drafted for the first Balkan War in 1912, serving as an officer in Eastern Thrace and Macedonia. His stories about the Balkan wars, particularly "Balkan," earned Yovkov national recognition. In 1915, he was again called to duty, for World War I, serving until July of the following year, when he received an appointment to the editorial staff of *Voenni izvestiya* (Military News) in Sofia. In the capital, he joined a group of young writers that included Konstantin Konstantinov, Nikolay Liliev, and Georgi Raychev. He stayed on the front lines, but only as an observer, and wrote war stories. Lyubomira Parpulova-Gribble, writing in *Dictionary of Literary Biography,* said these war stories "exhibit most of the main features of Yovkov's literary work. One is the tendency to view the individual works as parts of thematically and emotionally bound units or, as Bulgarian scholars call them, the first cycles of stories." She added, "This early work also has the typical Yovkovian structure of the plot that is not organized around a single main episode but unfolds as a series of relatively minor events." Other stories with this cyclical structure include "Beli rozi" (White Roses), "Kray Mesta" (Near the River Mesta), and "Zemlyatsi" (Countrymen). These tales appeared in *Voenni izvestiya* as well as several other periodicals, including *Demokraticheski pregled* (Democratic Review), *Narod i armiya* (People and Army), *Otechestvo* (Fatherland), *Suvremenna misul* (Contemporary Thought), *Zlatorog* (Golden Horn), and *Zora* (Dawn).

Parpulova-Gribble noted that "Balkan" contains "several of the major themes and ideological concerns of his writings, including the themes of Dobruja, the border, and the unity between humanity and nature." The Romanian takeover of Dobruja after the second Balkan war deeply affected Yovkov. Consequently, "Balkan" contains nationalistic elements, but, Parpulova-Gribble wrote, it also "explores the psychological impact of ethnic and political frontiers by juxtaposing the animal world and the world of people." Yovkov continued to examine animal psychology in his short story collection entitled *Ako mozhekha da govoryat.*

In 1918, Yovkov married Despina Koleva, a University of Sofia student. That year, Yovkov decided to limit his life to literature and his wife and daughter, Elka. He continued to work, however, serving as a translator and press attaché to the Bulgarian Legation in Bucharest beginning in 1920. After seven years there, he joined the editorial board at *La Bulgarie,* a Sofia newspaper, where he stayed until 1929. In 1936, he worked for a year in the Sofia press department.

While Yovkov gained popularity writing about the wars, he also wrote much about the world and myths surrounding Bulgarian peasant life. He chronicles these village activities not only in *Staroplaninski legendi,* but also in his other major short story collections, *Vecheri v Antimovskiya khan* and *Zhensko surtse.* In his novelette *Zhetvaryat: Povest,* Yovkov depicted the life of the village Lyulyakovo during peacetime. Parpulova-Gribble found that the "main idea of the work is that the attitude of the peasants toward their land and work is the foundation of their moral and spiritual values." Moser wrote that Yovkov "is never blind to the cruelties of life, but he is always persuaded that even its apparent catastrophes in the end work for the good. Among his most characteristic protagonists is the good-hearted dreamer entranced by beauty who does not quite fit into a world not made by dreamers."

In *Staroplaninski legendi,* Yovkov writes about nineteenth-century Balkan life in ten stories. Parpulova-Gribble asserted that these stories concern "extraordinary love, bravery, treachery, and suffering. Each piece has an epigram taken from a folk song, legend, or chronicle that sets the stage for the main conflict." These tales, she argued, do not embellish or simulate past writing styles. She maintained that "Yovkov is independent in both style of the narrative and the development of the plot. The texts unfold in a manner that seems natural and effortless . . . masterfully painted landscapes and portraits lend depth to the events." In "Shibil," the title character, a fugitive gypsy, falls in love with Rada, the beautiful daughter of the richest man of the town Zheruna. In "Prez chumavoto," the most powerful man of Zheruna plans a wedding for his daughter amid rumors of a plague.

Chilikut kray granitsata is the first and most important of his novels. Set in 1923, it investigates the violence and politics surrounding a domestic insurrection, and describes the progressive dissolution of the antiquated patriarchy and rural estate system. In the 1930s, Yovkov was already enjoying his status. In 1927, he received the Kiril and Metodiy Prize for literature, and was contributing to the esteemed periodicals *Zlatorog* and *Bulgarska misul* (Bulgarian Thought). Then, he turned his attention to theater and penned his first play, *Albena.* In this dramatic piece, taken from a short story by that name that appeared in *Vecheri v Antomovskiya khan,* Yovkov tells of the beautiful Albena who falls in love with another man and together they kill her husband. Moser wrote that in this work, "he described the destructive potential of that very beauty and harmony which he himself had consistently been devoted." Yovkov died in 1937, from a malignant tumor that stemmed from ongoing stomach ailments.

BIOGRAPHICAL AND CRITICAL SOURCES:

BOOKS

Dictionary of Literary Biography, Volume 147: *South Slavic Writers Before World War II,* Gale (Detroit, MI), 1995.

Encyclopedia of World Literature in the 20th Century, Third edition, St. James Press (Detroit, MI), 1999.

Mozejko, Edward, *Yordan Yovkov,* Slavica (Columbus, OH), 1983.*

* * *

ZIEM, Jochen 1932-1994

PERSONAL: Born 1932, in Magdeburg, Germany; died, 1994; immigrated to West Germany (now Germany), 1955. *Education:* Studied German literature at Hälle and Leipzig universities.

CAREER: Novelist, short-story writer, and scriptwriter. Worked as a laborer, a reporter, and editor of a magazine. Full-time freelance writer, beginning late 1960s.

WRITINGS:

Die Einladung: Schauspiel in drei Akten (play; originally published in *Theater Heute,* July, 1967), Suhrkamp (Frankfurt am Main, Germany), 1967.

Nacrichten aus der Provinz (play), produced in West Berlin, Germany, 1967.

Zahltage (short stories), Suhrkamp (Frankfurt am Main, Germany), 1968.

Die Versöhnung (play; sequel to *Die Einladung;* originally published in *Theater Heute,* June, 1971), Theater Heute (Velbert, Germany), 1971.

Die Klassefrau (short stories), Luchterhand (Darmstadt, Germany), 1974.

Der Junge: eine Engtwicklung in sieben Bildern, Fischer Taschenbuch (Frankfurt am Main, Germany), 1980.

Uprising in East Germany and Other Stories, translated by Jorn K. Bramann and Jeanette Axelrod, Adler (Rochester, NY), 1985.

Boris, Kreuzberg, 12 Jahre (novel), Erika Klopp (Berlin, Germany), 1988.

Author of television scripts; contributor to periodicals, including *Theater Heute.*

SIDELIGHTS: Jochen Ziem grew up during the Nazi era and witnessed the defeat of Germany at the conclusion of World War II. While living in East Germany,

Ziem studied German literature at Hälle and Leipzig universities. After moving to West Germany in 1955, he worked as a laborer, a reporter, and as an editor of a magazine. He became a full-time freelance writer by the late 1960s.

Prior to his death in 1994, Ziem penned a number of novels and short-story collections as well as plays and television scripts. He gained a reputation in Germany as a scriptwriter of "high social conscience." Ulrike S. Rettig, a reviewer in *Library Journal,* described the ten stories by Ziem that were translated and published as *Uprising in East Germany and Other Stories* as "realistic portrayals of everyday life" in post-World War II Germany. A reviewer in *Publishers Weekly* stated that taken "together," the stories "produce a haunting image of emptiness and despair." Martin Tucker, reviewing *Uprising in East Germany and Other Stories* for the *New York Times Book Review,* claimed that Ziem "speaks in the voice of the exile pleading for a return to wholeness while knowing he can do little to alter the course of history."

BIOGRAPHICAL AND CRITICAL SOURCES:

BOOKS

Literary Exiles in the Twentieth Century, Greenwood Press (New York, NY), 1991.

PERIODICALS

Library Journal, March 15, 1985, Ulrike S. Rettig, review of *Uprising in East Germany and Other Stories,* p. 74.
New York Times Book Review, September 15, 1985, Martin Tucker, review of *Uprising in East Germany and Other Stories,* p. 24.
Publishers Weekly, March 22, 1985, review of *Uprising in East Germany and Other Stories,* p. 56.*

*   *   *

ZIMMETT, Debbie
See BECKER, Deborah Zimmett

*   *   *

ZINOVIEVA-ANNIBAL, Lydia 1866-1907

PERSONAL: Born 1866, in Russia; died in 1907.

CAREER: Russian novelist.

WRITINGS:

The Tragic Menagerie, translated from the Russian and with an introduction by Jane Costlow, Northwestern University Press (Evanston, IL), 1999.

SIDELIGHTS: Lydia Zinovieva-Annibal was born in Russia in 1866. Her book of short stories, *The Tragic Menagerie,* was originally published in Russia in 1907, the year she died. Jane Costlow translated it into English and published it in 1999. Vera, the main character in this fictionalized autobiography, is a mischievous girl in pre-Revolutionary Russia who lives with her wealthy family in St. Petersburg and at their summer country estate. Throughout the book she contends with the death of her pet donkey, her mother's illness, wolves, bear cubs and a red spider. As it turns out, the animals at the country estate entertain Vera better than the people do and she becomes spoiled. Vera, with a bit of a mean streak, plays cruel tricks on her family, schoolmates and servants. "I love to lie," she says without guilt or shame. As her mother's nurturing diminishes, she becomes uncontrollable. Vera, however, is also highly sensitive. In the main story, "The Devil," the reader sees the teen-age girl through the eyes of the other townspeople as she is thrown out of local schools and develops crushes on her boarding schoolmates. Her family finally takes the intractable Vera to Italy, where she defiantly faces a four-eyed, red spider in a grotto. Towards the end of this story Vera declares, "Everything that is clenched tight, completely contemptuous, deft and courageous, strong against pain and pity and shame—that is me! That is me!"

William Ferguson writes in the *New York Times Review,* "Zinovieva-Annibal's book invites comparison with Turgenev's 'Sportsman's Notebook,' in which an aristocratic hunter is repeatedly distracted by visions of the brutal, unprotected life of serfs and peasants who share the land with their masters; Turgenev's volume is said to have moved Czar Alexander II to free the serfs in 1861. Vera's social epiphanies are far more muted, if they can be said to occur at all." Despite the book's seeming lack of social redemption, Ferguson pronounces *The Tragic Menagerie* "a marvelous evocation of life among the aristocracy before the Bolshevik Revolution." According to Joe Collins, in *Booklist,* "the tales are some of the most emotional you will ever read. . . . the all-or-nothing prose of the author only heightens the drama." He describes Vera as "weird," but adds, "like many people who can be described that way, she holds our interest." Harold Augenbraum in *Library Journal* recommends the book for literary and feminist collections. He describes "The Devil" as "extraordinary, powerful, and very current," and concludes, "Though readers might find the early stories too childlike, those who stay the course will be rewarded."

BIOGRAPHICAL AND CRITICAL SOURCES:

PERIODICALS

Booklist, February 1, 1999, Joe Collins, review of *The Tragic Menagerie*.
Library Journal, January, 1999, Harold Augenbraum, review of *The Tragic Menagerie*.
New York Times Book Review, May 16, 1999, William Ferguson, review of *The Tragic Menagerie*.

*   *   *

ZUGGER, Christopher Lawrence 1954-

PERSONAL: Born November 22, 1954, in Buffalo, NY; son of Henry (a police officer) and Margaret (Watkins) Zugger. *Education:* St. Bonaventure University, B.A., 1977; Washington Theological Union, M.Div., 1981. *Politics:* "Moderate." *Religion:* Byzantine Catholic. *Hobbies and other interests:* History of Eastern Europe, railroads.

ADDRESSES: Home and office—1840 Palomas NE, Albuquerque, NM 87110. *E-mail*—user14681@msn. com.

CAREER: Byzantine Catholic priest; youth minister at Byzantine Catholic church in Beltsville, MD, 1977-81; assistant pastor of Byzantine Catholic church in Rahway, NJ, 1981-82; founding pastor of Byzantine Catholic church in Gilbert, AZ, 1982-85; Our Lady of Perpetual Help, Albuquerque, NM, pastor, 1985—. Assistant at Byzantine Catholic church in Phoenix, AZ, 1982-85; teacher for OASIS.

MEMBER: American Historical Society of Germans from Russia, Germans-from-Russia Heritage Society, Association for the Study of Nationalities, Mission Society of the Mother of God (chaplain, 1998-2002).

AWARDS, HONORS: Friends Award, 2002, for "living well in medical adversity."

WRITINGS:

The Forgotten: Catholics of the Soviet Empire from Lenin through Stalin, Syracuse University Press (Syracuse, NY), 2001.

Editor of diocesan newspaper.

WORK IN PROGRESS: A second book on the Catholic church in the USSR, 1953-91; research on the Greek-Catholic church underground in communist-era Central Europe.